# List of Minicases

**Chapter 2**
Cash Flows at Warf Computers Ltd., 48–49

**Chapter 3**
Ratios and Financial Planning at East Coast
    Yachts, 81–82

**Chapter 5**
The MBA Decision, 145

**Chapter 6**
Stock Valuation at Ragan Engines, 178

**Chapter 7**
Bullock Gold Mining, 222

**Chapter 8**
Beaver Mining Company, Goodweek
    Tires Inc., 253–254

**Chapter 9**
Bunyan Lumber, LLC, 285

**Chapter 10**
A Job at Deck Out My Yacht Corporation, 307–308

**Chapter 11**
A Job at Deck Out My Yacht, Part 2, 349

**Chapter 12**
The Fama-French Multifactor Model and Mutual Fund
    Returns, 371

**Chapter 13**
The Cost of Capital for Goff
    Communications Inc., 406

**Chapter 14**
Your Retirement Plan at Deck Out My Yacht, 446–447

**Chapter 16**
Stephenson Real Estate Recapitalization, 495

**Chapter 17**
McKenzie Restaurants Capital Budgeting, 532

**Chapter 18**
The Leveraged Buyout of Cheek Products Ltd., 553

**Chapter 19**
Electronic Timing Ltd., 591

**Chapter 20**
East Coast Yachts Goes Public, 617

**Chapter 21**
Financing the Expansion of East Coast Yachts with
    a Bond Issue, 642

**Chapter 22**
The Decision to Lease or Buy at Warf
    Computers Ltd., 668

**Chapter 23**
Clissold Industries Options, 708

**Chapter 24**
Exotic Cuisines Employee Stock Options, 732

**Chapter 25**
S&S Air's Convertible Bond, 753

**Chapter 26**
Williamson Mortgage Inc., 789

**Chapter 27**
Keafer Manufacturing Working
    Capital Management, 817

**Chapter 28**
Cash Management at Richmond Ltd., 836

**Chapter 29**
Credit Policy at Braam Industries, 856

**Chapter 30**
The Birdie Golf-Hybrid Golf Merger, 894

**Chapter 32**
East Coast Yachts Goes International, 935

SEVENTH CANADIAN EDITION

# CORPORATE
# FINANCE

Stephen A. Ross

Sloan School of Management, Massachusetts Institute of Technology

Randolph W. Westerfield

Marshall School of Business, University of Southern California

Jeffrey F. Jaffe

Wharton School of Business, University of Pennsylvania

Gordon S. Roberts

Schulich School of Business, York University

McGraw-Hill Ryerson

## McGraw-Hill Ryerson

**Corporate Finance**
**Seventh Canadian edition**

Copyright © 2015, 2011, 2008, 2005, 2003, 1999, 1995 by McGraw-Hill Ryerson Limited. All rights reserved. No part of this publication may be reproduced or transmitted in any form or by any means, or stored in a database or retrieval system, without the prior written permission of McGraw-Hill Ryerson Limited, or in the case of photocopying or other reprographic copying, a licence from The Canadian Copyright Licensing Agency (Access Copyright). For an Access Copyright licence, visit www.accesscopyright.ca or call toll free to 1-800-893-5777.

The Internet addresses listed in the text were accurate at the time of publication. The inclusion of a website does not indicate an endorsement by the authors or McGraw-Hill Ryerson, and McGraw-Hill Ryerson does not guarantee the accuracy of information presented at these sites.

ISBN-13: 978-0-07-133957-5
ISBN-10: 0-07-133957-4

3 4 5 6 7 8 9 MQ 1 9 8 7 6

Printed and bound in Canada.

Care has been taken to trace ownership of copyright material contained in this text; however, the publisher will welcome any information that enables it to rectify any reference or credit for subsequent editions.

Director of Product Management: Rhondda McNabb
Senior Product Manager: Kimberley Veevers
Senior Marketing Manager: Joy Armitage Taylor
Product Developer: Erin Catto
Photo/Permissions Research: Alison Lloyd Baker
Senior Product Team Associate: Marina Seguin
Supervising Editor: Joanne Limebeer
Copy Editor: Julia Cochrane
Production Coordinator: Scott Morrison
Manufacturing Production Coordinator: Emily Hickey
Cover Design: Peter Papayanakis
Cover Image: Ivan Mikhaylov/Alamy
Interior Design: Peter Papayanakis
Page Layout: First Folio Resource Group, Inc.
Printer: Marquis

**Library and Archives Canada Cataloguing in Publication**

Ross, Stephen A., author
    Corporate finance/Stephen A. Ross (Sloan School of Management, Massachusetts Institute of Technology), Randolph W. Westerfield (Marshall School of Business, University of Southern California), JeffreY F. Jaffe (Wharton School of Business, University of Pennsylvania), Gordon S. Roberts (Schulich School of Business, York University). — Seventh Canadian edition.

Revision of: Corporate finance/Stephen A. Ross ... [et al.]. — 6th Canadian ed. — Toronto: McGraw-Hill Ryerson, (c)2011. Includes bibliographical references and index. ISBN 978-0-07-133957-5 (bound)

    1. Corporations—Finance—Textbooks. 2. Corporations—Canada— Finance—Textbooks. I. Westerfield, Randolph, author II. Jaffe, Jeffrey F., 1946-, author III. Roberts, Gordon S. (Gordon Sam), 1945-, author IV. Title.

HG4026.R64 2014           658.15           C2014-905417-3

# ABOUT THE AUTHORS

STEPHEN A. ROSS *Sloan School of Management, Massachusetts Institute of Technology* Stephen Ross is the Franco Modigliani Professor of Financial Economics at the Sloan School of Management, Massachusetts Institute of Technology. One of the most widely published authors in finance and economics, Professor Ross is recognized for his work in developing the arbitrage pricing theory, as well as for having made substantial contributions to the discipline through his research in signalling, agency theory, option pricing, and the theory of the term structure of interest rates, among other topics. A past president of the American Finance Association, he currently serves as an associate editor of several academic and practitioner journals. He is a trustee of CalTech and a director of the College Retirement Equity Fund (CREF), Freddie Mac, and Algorithmics Inc. He is also the co-chairman of Roll and Ross Asset Management Corporation.

RANDOLPH W. WESTERFIELD *Marshall School of Business, University of Southern California* Randolph W. Westerfield is Dean of the University of Southern California's Marshall School of Business and holder of the Robert R. Dockson Dean's Chair of Business Administration.

He came to USC from the Wharton School, University of Pennsylvania, where he was the chairman of the finance department and a member of the finance faculty for 20 years. He is a member of several public company boards of directors, including Health Management Associates Inc., William Lyon Homes, and the Nicholas Applegate growth fund. His areas of expertise include corporate financial policy, investment management, and stock market price behaviour.

JEFFREY F. JAFFE *Wharton School of Business, University of Pennsylvania* Jeffrey F. Jaffe has been a frequent contributor to finance and economic literature in such journals as the *Quarterly Economic Journal, The Journal of Finance, The Journal of Financial and Quantitative Analysis, The Journal of Financial Economics,* and *The Financial Analysts Journal.* His best-known work concerns insider trading, where he showed both that corporate insiders earn abnormal profits from their trades and that regulation has little effect on these profits. He has also made contributions concerning initial public offerings, regulation of utilities, the behaviour of marketmakers, the fluctuation of gold prices, the theoretical effect of inflation on the interest rate, the empirical effect of inflation on capital asset prices, the relationship between small capitalization stocks and the January effect, and the capital structure decision.

GORDON S. ROBERTS *Schulich School of Business, York University* Gordon Roberts is Canadian Imperial Bank of Commerce Professor of Financial Services at the Schulich School of Business, York University. A winner of numerous teaching awards, his extensive experience includes finance classes for undergraduate and MBA students, executives, and bankers in Canada and internationally. Professor Roberts conducts research in corporate finance and banking. He has served on the editorial boards of several Canadian and international academic journals. Professor Roberts has been a consultant to a number of regulatory bodies responsible for the oversight of financial institutions and utilities.

# BRIEF CONTENTS

## PART 1

Overview    1

**1** Introduction to Corporate Finance    1
    Appendix 1A Taxes    28
    Appendix 1B Finance Professional Careers    Connect
**2** Accounting Statements and Cash Flow    33
    Appendix 2A Financial Statement Analysis    49
    Appendix 2B Statement of Cash Flows    60
**3** Financial Planning and Growth    65

## PART 2

Value and Capital Budgeting    83

**4** Financial Markets and Net Present Value: First Principles of Finance    83
**5** The Time Value of Money    104
    Appendix 5A Using Financial Calculators    Connect
**6** How to Value Bonds and Stocks    146
    Appendix 6A The Term Structure of Interest Rates    179
**7** Net Present Value and Other Investment Rules    191
**8** Net Present Value and Capital Budgeting    223
    Appendix 8A Capital Cost Allowance    255
    Appendix 8B Derivation of the Present Value of the Capital Cost Allowance Tax Shield Formula    259
**9** Risk Analysis, Real Options, and Capital Budgeting    261

## PART 3

Risk    286

**10** Risk and Return: Lessons from Market History    286
    Appendix 10A The U.S. Equity Risk Premium: Historical and International Perspectives    Connect
**11** Risk and Return: The Capital Asset Pricing Model    309
    Appendix 11A Is Beta Dead?    Connect
**12** An Alternative View of Risk and Return: The Arbitrage Pricing Theory    350
**13** Risk, Return, and Capital Budgeting    372
    Appendix 13A Economic Value Added and the Measurement of Financial Performance    407

## PART 4

Capital Structure and Dividend Policy    412

**14** Corporate Financing Decisions and Efficient Capital Markets    412
**15** Long-Term Financing: An Introduction    448

**16** Capital Structure: Basic Concepts    465
**17** Capital Structure: Limits to the Use of Debt    496
    Appendix 17A Some Useful Formulas of Financial Structure    Connect
    Appendix 17B The Miller Model and the Graduated Income Tax    Connect
**18** Valuation and Capital Budgeting for the Levered Firm    533
    Appendix 18A The Adjusted Present Value Approach to Valuing Leveraged Buyouts    Connect
**19** Dividends and Other Payouts    555

## PART 5

Long-Term Financing    592

**20** Issuing Equity Securities to the Public    592
**21** Long-Term Debt    618
**22** Leasing    643
    Appendix 22A Adjusted Present Value Approach to Leasing    Connect

## PART 6

Options, Futures, and Corporate Finance    669

**23** Options and Corporate Finance: Basic Concepts    669
**24** Options and Corporate Finance: Extensions and Applications    709
**25** Warrants and Convertibles    733
**26** Derivatives and Hedging Risk    754

## PART 7

Financial Planning and Short-Term Finance    790

**27** Short-Term Finance and Planning    790
**28** Cash Management    818
**29** Credit Management    837
    Appendix 29A Inventory Management    Connect

## PART 8

Special Topics    857

**30** Mergers and Acquisitions    857
**31** Financial Distress    896
    Appendix 31A Predicting Corporate Bankruptcy: The Z-Score Model    Connect
**32** International Corporate Finance    910
**Appendix A: Mathematical Tables**    Connect
**Appendix B: Answers to Selected End-of-Chapter Problems**    Connect

# CONTENTS

Preface

## PART 1
Overview .......................................................... 1

### CHAPTER 1

**Introduction to Corporate Finance** 1

**Executive Summary** 1
1.1 **What Is Corporate Finance?** 2
  The Balance-Sheet Model of the Firm 2
  Capital Structure 3
  The Financial Manager 4
  Identification of Cash Flows 6
  Timing of Cash Flows 6
  Risk of Cash Flows 7
    *Concept Questions* 7
1.2 **Corporate Securities as Contingent Claims on Total Firm Value** 8
    *Concept Questions* 9
1.3 **The Corporate Firm** 9
  The Sole Proprietorship 9
  The Partnership 10
  The Corporation 11
  The Income Trust 12
    *Concept Questions* 12
1.4 **Goals of the Corporate Firm** 12
  Agency Costs and the Set-of-Contracts Perspective 13
  Managerial Goals 13
  Separation of Ownership and Control 14
  *In Their Own Words:* B. Espen Eckbo on corporate governance 16
    *Concept Questions* 18
1.5 **Financial Institutions, Financial Markets, and the Corporation** 18
  Financial Institutions 18
  Money Versus Capital Markets 20
  Primary Versus Secondary Markets 20
  Listing 21
  Foreign Exchange Market 22
    *Concept Questions* 23
1.6 **Trends in Financial Markets and Management** 23
  *In Their Own Words:* Maria Strömqvist on hedge funds and the financial crisis of 2008 24
    *Concept Question* 26

1.7 **Outline of the Text** 26
1.8 **Summary and Conclusions** 27
  Appendix 1A Taxes 28
  Appendix 1B Finance Professional Careers Connect

### CHAPTER 2

**Accounting Statements and Cash Flow** 33

**Executive Summary** 33
2.1 **The Statement of Financial Position** 33
  Liquidity 34
  Debt versus Equity 34
  Value versus Cost 35
    *Concept Questions* 36
2.2 **Statement of Comprehensive Income** 36
  International Financial Reporting Standards 36
  Non-cash Items 37
  Time and Costs 37
    *Concept Questions* 38
2.3 **Net Working Capital** 38
    *Concept Questions* 38
2.4 **Financial Cash Flow** 39
    *Concept Questions* 41
2.5 **Summary and Conclusions** 42
  *Minicase:* Cash Flows at Warf Computers Ltd. 48
  Appendix 2A Financial Statement Analysis 49
  Appendix 2B Statement of Cash Flows 60

### CHAPTER 3

**Financial Planning and Growth** 65

**Executive Summary** 65
3.1 **What Is Financial Planning?** 65
    *Concept Questions* 66
3.2 **A Financial Planning Model: The Ingredients** 66
3.3 **The Percentage of Sales Method** 67
  The Statement of Comprehensive Income 69
  The Statement of Financial Position 70
  *In Their Own Words:* Robert C. Higgins on sustainable growth 72
3.4 **What Determines Growth?** 73
    *Concept Questions* 76
  Some Caveats on Financial Planning Models 76

**3.5  Summary and Conclusions**                    **77**
*Minicase:* Ratios and Financial Planning
at East Coast Yachts                                 81

# PART 2

Value and Capital Budgeting                          83

## CHAPTER 4

**Financial Markets and Net Present Value:**
**First Principles of Finance**                      **83**

**Executive Summary**                               **83**
**4.1  The Financial Market Economy**               **84**
The Anonymous Market                                85
Market Clearing                                     85
*Concept Questions*                                 *86*
**4.2  Making Consumption Choices over Time**       **86**
*Concept Questions*                                 *88*
**4.3  The Competitive Market**                     **89**
How Many Interest Rates Are There in a
Competitive Market?                                 89
*Concept Questions*                                 *90*
**4.4  The Basic Principle**                        **90**
*Concept Question*                                  *90*
**4.5  Practising the Principle**                   **90**
A Lending Example                                   91
A Borrowing Example                                 92
*Concept Questions*                                 *93*
**4.6  Illustrating the Investment Decision**       **94**
*Concept Questions*                                 *97*
**4.7  Corporate Investment Decision Making**       **97**
*Concept Question*                                  *99*
**4.8  Summary and Conclusions**                    **100**

## CHAPTER 5

**The Time Value of Money**                         **104**

**Executive Summary**                               **104**
**5.1  The One-Period Case**                        **104**
*Concept Questions*                                 *107*
**5.2  The Multiperiod Case**                       **107**
Future Value and Compounding                        107
The Power of Compounding: A Digression              111
Present Value and Discounting                       112
Finding the Number of Periods                       115
The Algebraic Formula                               116
*Concept Questions*                                 *116*
**5.3  Compounding Periods**                        **116**
Compounding over Many Years                         118
*Concept Questions*                                 *119*
Continuous Compounding (Advanced)                   119

**5.4  Simplifications**                            **121**
Perpetuity                                          121
Growing Perpetuity                                  122
Annuity                                             124
Mortgages                                           126
Using Annuity Formulas                              127
Growing Annuity                                     130
*Concept Questions*                                 *131*
**5.5  What Is a Firm Worth?**                      **131**
**5.6  Summary and Conclusions**                    **133**
*Minicase:* The MBA Decision                        145
Appendix 5A  Using Financial Calculators            Connect

## CHAPTER 6

**How to Value Bonds and Stocks**                   **146**

**Executive Summary**                               **146**
**6.1  Definition and Example of a Bond**           **146**
**6.2  How to Value Bonds**                         **146**
Pure Discount Bonds                                 146
Level-Coupon Bonds                                  147
A Note on Bond Price Quotes                         149
Consols                                             150
*Concept Questions*                                 *150*
**6.3  Bond Concepts**                              **150**
Interest Rates and Bond Prices                      150
Yield to Maturity                                   151
The Present Value Formulas for Bonds                152
Holding-Period Return                               152
*Concept Questions*                                 *152*
**6.4  The Present Value of Common Stocks**         **152**
Dividends versus Capital Gains                      152
Valuation of Different Types of Stocks              153
**6.5  Estimates of Parameters in the**
**Dividend Discount Model**                         **157**
Where Does $g$ Come From?                           157
Where Does $r$ Come From?                           158
A Healthy Sense of Skepticism                       158
**6.6  Growth Opportunities**                       **159**
NPVGOs of Real Companies                            160
Growth in Earnings and Dividends versus
Growth Opportunities                                162
Dividends or Earnings: Which to Discount?           162
The No-Dividend Firm                                163
**6.7  The Dividend Growth Model and**
**the NPVGO Model (Advanced)**                      **163**
The Dividend Growth Model                           164
The NPVGO Model                                     164
Summary                                             165
**6.8  Comparables**                                **165**
Price–Earnings Ratio                                166
*Concept Questions*                                 *167*

| | | |
|---|---|---|
| 6.9 | **Valuing the Entire Firm** | **168** |
| 6.10 | **Stock Market Reporting** | **169** |
| 6.11 | **Summary and Conclusions** | **170** |
| | *Minicase:* Stock Valuation at Ragan Engines | 178 |
| Appendix 6A | The Term Structure of Interest Rates | 179 |

## CHAPTER 7

### Net Present Value and Other Investment Rules 191

| | | |
|---|---|---|
| **Executive Summary** | | **191** |
| 7.1 | **Why Use Net Present Value?** | **191** |
| | *Concept Questions* | *193* |
| 7.2 | **The Payback Period Rule** | **193** |
| | Defining the Rule | 193 |
| | Problems with the Payback Method | 194 |
| | Managerial Perspective | 195 |
| | Summary of Payback | 195 |
| | *Concept Questions* | *195* |
| 7.3 | **The Discounted Payback Period Rule** | **196** |
| 7.4 | **The Average Accounting Return** | **196** |
| | Defining the Rule | 196 |
| | Analyzing the Average Accounting Return Method | 198 |
| | *Concept Questions* | *198* |
| 7.5 | **The Internal Rate of Return** | **199** |
| | *Concept Question* | *201* |
| 7.6 | **Problems with the Internal Rate of Return Approach** | **201** |
| | Definition of Independent and Mutually Exclusive Projects | 201 |
| | Two General Problems Affecting Both Independent and Mutually Exclusive Projects | 202 |
| | Problems Specific to Mutually Exclusive Projects | 206 |
| | Redeeming Qualities of the Internal Rate of Return | 211 |
| | A Test | 211 |
| | *Concept Questions* | *211* |
| 7.7 | **The Profitability Index** | **211** |
| | *Concept Questions* | *213* |
| 7.8 | **The Practice of Capital Budgeting** | **213** |
| 7.9 | **Summary and Conclusions** | **215** |
| | *Minicase:* Bullock Gold Mining | 222 |

## CHAPTER 8

### Net Present Value and Capital Budgeting 223

| | | |
|---|---|---|
| **Executive Summary** | | **223** |
| 8.1 | **Incremental Cash Flows** | **223** |
| | Cash Flows—Not Accounting Income | 223 |

| | | |
|---|---|---|
| | Sunk Costs | 224 |
| | Opportunity Costs | 224 |
| | Side Effects | 225 |
| | Allocated Costs | 225 |
| | *Concept Questions* | *225* |
| 8.2 | **The Majestic Mulch and Compost Company: An Example** | **226** |
| | An Analysis of the Project | 228 |
| | Which Set of Books? | 229 |
| | A Note on Net Working Capital | 230 |
| | Interest Expense | 231 |
| | *Concept Questions* | *231* |
| 8.3 | **Inflation and Capital Budgeting** | **231** |
| | Interest Rates and Inflation | 231 |
| | Cash Flow and Inflation | 232 |
| | Discounting: Nominal or Real? | 233 |
| | *Concept Questions* | *235* |
| 8.4 | **Alternative Definitions of Operating Cash Flow** | **236** |
| | The Bottom-Up Approach | 236 |
| | The Top-Down Approach | 237 |
| | The Tax Shield Approach | 237 |
| | Conclusion | 237 |
| 8.5 | **Applying the Tax Shield Approach to the Majestic Mulch and Compost Company Project** | **237** |
| | Present Value of the Tax Shield on Capital Cost Allowance | 239 |
| | Total Project Cash Flow versus Tax Shield Approach | 240 |
| | *Concept Questions* | *240* |
| 8.6 | **Investments of Unequal Lives: The Equivalent Annual Cost Method** | **240** |
| | The General Decision to Replace (Advanced) | 242 |
| | *Concept Question* | *246* |
| 8.7 | **Summary and Conclusions** | **246** |
| | *Minicase:* Beaver Mining Company | 253 |
| | *Minicase:* Goodweek Tires Inc. | 254 |
| Appendix 8A | Capital Cost Allowance | 255 |
| Appendix 8B | Derivation of the Present Value of Capital Cost Allowance Tax Shield Formula | 259 |

## CHAPTER 9

### Risk Analysis, Real Options, and Capital Budgeting 261

| | | |
|---|---|---|
| **Executive Summary** | | **261** |
| 9.1 | **Decision Trees** | **261** |
| | *Concept Questions* | *263* |
| 9.2 | **Sensitivity Analysis, Scenario Analysis, and Break-Even Analysis** | **263** |
| | Sensitivity Analysis and Scenario Analysis | 263 |

Break-Even Analysis                          266
    Concept Questions                        269
Break-Even Analysis, Equivalent Annual
Cost, and Capital Cost Allowance            269
9.3    Monte Carlo Simulation               270
Step 1: Specify the Basic Model             271
Step 2: Specify a Distribution for Each
Variable in the Model                       271
Step 3: The Computer Draws One Outcome      273
Step 4: Repeat the Procedure                273
Step 5: Calculate Net Present Value         274
9.4    Real Options                         275
The Option to Expand                        275
The Option to Abandon                       276
Timing Options                              277
Real Options in the Real World              278
    Concept Questions                       279
9.5    Summary and Conclusions              279
Minicase: Bunyan Lumber, LLC                285

PART 3

Risk                                        286

CHAPTER 10

Risk and Return: Lessons from
Market History                              286

Executive Summary                           286
10.1   Returns                              287
Dollar Earnings                             287
Percentage Returns or Rate of Return        288
    Concept Questions                       290
10.2   Holding-Period Returns               290
    Concept Questions                       293
10.3   Return Statistics                    294
    Concept Question                        294
10.4   Average Stock Returns and Risk-Free
Returns                                     295
    Concept Questions                       297
10.5   Risk Statistics                      297
Variance and Standard Deviation             298
Normal Distribution and Its Implications
for Standard Deviation                      298
Value at Risk                               299
Further Perspective on Returns and Risk     300
    Concept Questions                       301
10.6   More on Average Returns              301
Arithmetic versus Geometric Averages        301
Calculating Geometric Average Returns       301
Arithmetic Average Return or Geometric
Average Return?                             303

10.7   2008: A Year of Financial Crisis     303
10.8   Summary and Conclusions              304
Minicase: A Job at Deck Out My
Yacht Corporation                           307
Appendix 10A  The U.S. Equity Risk Premium:
Historical and International Perspectives   Connect

CHAPTER 11

Risk and Return: The Capital Asset
Pricing Model                               309

Executive Summary                           309
11.1   Individual Securities                309
11.2   Expected Return, Variance, and
Covariance                                  310
Expected Return and Variance                310
Covariance and Correlation                  312
11.3   The Risk and Return for Portfolios   315
The Example of Supertech and Slowpoke       316
The Expected Return on a Portfolio          316
Variance and Standard Deviation of a
Portfolio                                   317
    Concept Questions                       320
11.4   The Efficient Set for Two Assets     320
Application to International Diversification 323
    Concept Question                        324
11.5   The Efficient Set for Many Securities 324
Variance and Standard Deviation in a
Portfolio of Many Assets                    325
    Concept Questions                       327
11.6   Diversification: An Example          327
Risk and the Sensible Investor              329
    Concept Questions                       330
11.7   Risk-Free Borrowing and Lending      330
The Optimal Portfolio                       332
    Concept Questions                       334
11.8   Market Equilibrium                   334
Definition of the Market Equilibrium Portfolio 334
Definition of Risk When Investors Hold
the Market Portfolio                        335
The Formula for Beta                        337
A Test                                      337
    Concept Questions                       338
11.9   Relationship between Risk and Expected
Return (Capital Asset Pricing Model)        338
Expected Return on Market                   338
Expected Return on Individual Security      339
    Concept Questions                       342
11.10  Summary and Conclusions              342
Minicase: A Job at Deck Out My Yacht,
Part 2                                      349
Appendix 11A  Is Beta Dead?                 Connect

## CHAPTER 12

**An Alternative View of Risk and Return:**
**The Arbitrage Pricing Theory** 350

**Executive Summary** 350
**12.1 Factor Models: Announcements,**
**Surprises, and Expected Returns** 351
*Concept Questions* 352
**12.2 Risk: Systematic and Unsystematic** 352
*Concept Questions* 353
**12.3 Systematic Risk and Betas** 353
*Concept Questions* 356
**12.4 Portfolios and Factor Models** 356
Portfolios and Diversification 358
*Concept Questions* 360
**12.5 Betas and Expected Returns** 360
The Linear Relationship 360
The Market Portfolio and the Single Factor 361
*Concept Question* 362
**12.6 The Capital Asset Pricing Model and**
**the Arbitrage Pricing Theory** 362
Differences in Pedagogy 362
Differences in Application 363
*Concept Questions* 364
**12.7 Parametric Approaches to Asset Pricing** 364
Empirical Models 364
Style Portfolios 366
*Concept Questions* 366
**12.8 Summary and Conclusions** 367
*Minicase:* The Fama–French Multifactor
Model and Mutual Fund Returns 371

## CHAPTER 13

**Risk, Return, and Capital Budgeting** 372

**Executive Summary** 372
**13.1 The Cost of Equity Capital** 373
*Concept Questions* 375
**13.2 Estimation of Beta** 375
*Concept Questions* 377
Beta Estimation in Practice 377
Stability of Beta 378
Using an Industry Beta 379
*Concept Questions* 380
**13.3 Determinants of Beta** 380
Cyclicality of Revenues 380
Operating Leverage 380
Financial Leverage and Beta 382
*Concept Questions* 383
**13.4 Extensions of the Basic Model** 383
The Firm versus the Project:
*Vive la différence* 383

The Cost of Debt 384
The Cost of Preferred Stock 385
The Weighted Average Cost of Capital 385
The Capital Structure Weights 386
Taxes and the Weighted Average Cost
of Capital 386
*Concept Questions* 388
**13.5 Estimating the Cost of Capital for**
**Suncor Energy** 391
*Concept Question* 393
**13.6 Flotation Costs and the Weighted**
**Average Cost of Capital** 393
The Basic Approach 393
Flotation Costs and Net Present Value 395
Internal Equity and Flotation Costs 395
**13.7 Reducing the Cost of Capital** 396
What Is Liquidity? 396
Liquidity, Expected Returns, and the
Cost of Capital 397
Liquidity and Adverse Selection 397
What the Corporation Can Do 398
*Concept Questions* 398
**13.8 Summary and Conclusions** 399
*Minicase:* The Cost of Capital for Goff
Communications Inc. 406
Appendix 13A Economic Value Added and
the Measurement of Financial Performance 407

## PART 4

**Capital Structure and Dividend Policy** 412

## CHAPTER 14

**Corporate Financing Decisions and**
**Efficient Capital Markets** 412

**Executive Summary** 412
**14.1 Can Financing Decisions Create Value?** 412
*Concept Question* 414
**14.2 A Description of Efficient Capital Markets** 414
Foundations of Market Efficiency 416
*Concept Question* 418
**14.3 The Different Types of Efficiency** 418
The Weak Form 418
The Semistrong and Strong Forms 419
Some Common Misconceptions About
the Efficient Market Hypothesis 421
*Concept Questions* 422
**14.4 The Evidence** 422
The Weak Form 422
The Semistrong Form 424
The Strong Form 427
*Concept Questions* 428

**14.5 The Behavioural Challenge to Market Efficiency** — 428

**14.6 Empirical Challenges to Market Efficiency** — 430

**14.7 Reviewing the Differences** — 434

*In Their Own Words:* A random talk with Burton Malkiel — 436

**14.8 Implications for Corporate Finance** — 437

Accounting and Efficient Markets — 437

The Timing Decision — 438

Speculation and Efficient Markets — 439

Information in Market Prices — 441

*Concept Question* — 443

**14.9 Summary and Conclusions** — 443

*Minicase:* Your Retirement Plan at Deck Out My Yacht — 446

## CHAPTER 15

**Long-Term Financing: An Introduction** — 448

**Executive Summary** — 448

**15.1 Common Stock** — 448

Authorized versus Issued Common Stock — 449

Retained Earnings — 449

Market Value, Book Value, and Replacement Value — 450

Shareholders' Rights — 450

Dividends — 452

Classes of Shares — 452

*Concept Questions* — 453

*In Their Own Words:* Shares climb as Stronach to give up voting control — 454

**15.2 Corporate Long-Term Debt: The Basics** — 455

Interest versus Dividends — 455

Is It Debt or Equity? — 455

Basic Features of Long-Term Debt — 456

Different Types of Debt — 456

Repayment — 456

Seniority — 457

Security — 457

Indenture — 457

*Concept Questions* — 458

**15.3 Preferred Shares** — 458

Stated Value — 458

Cumulative and Non-cumulative Dividends — 458

Are Preferred Shares Really Debt? — 459

Preferred Shares and Taxes — 459

Beyond Taxes — 460

*Concept Questions* — 460

**15.4 Income Trusts** — 461

Income Trust Income and Taxation — 461

**15.5 Patterns of Long-Term Financing** — 461

*Concept Questions* — 462

**15.6 Summary and Conclusions** — 463

## CHAPTER 16

**Capital Structure: Basic Concepts** — 465

**Executive Summary** — 465

**16.1 The Capital Structure Question and the Pie Theory** — 465

*Concept Question* — 466

**16.2 Maximizing Firm Value versus Maximizing Shareholder Interests** — 466

*Concept Question* — 467

**16.3 Financial Leverage and Firm Value: An Example** — 468

Leverage and Returns to Shareholders — 468

The Choice between Debt and Equity — 469

A Key Assumption — 472

*Concept Questions* — 473

**16.4 Modigliani and Miller: Proposition II (No Taxes)** — 473

Risk to Equityholders Rises with Leverage — 473

Proposition II: Required Return to Equityholders Rises with Leverage — 473

Modigliani and Miller: An Interpretation — 479

*In Their Own Words:* In Professor Miller's words ... — 480

*Concept Questions* — 481

**16.5 Taxes** — 481

The Basic Insight — 481

Present Value of the Tax Shield — 483

Value of the Levered Firm — 483

Expected Return and Leverage under Corporate Taxes — 485

The Weighted Average Cost of Capital and Corporate Taxes — 486

Stock Price and Leverage under Corporate Taxes — 487

*Concept Questions* — 489

**16.6 Summary and Conclusions** — 489

*Minicase:* Stephenson Real Estate Recapitalization — 495

## CHAPTER 17

**Capital Structure: Limits to the Use of Debt** — 496

**Executive Summary** — 496

**17.1 Costs of Financial Distress** — 496

Bankruptcy Risk or Bankruptcy Cost? — 496

*Concept Questions* — 498

**17.2 Description of Costs** — 499

Direct Costs of Financial Distress: Legal and Administrative Costs of Liquidation or Reorganization — 499

Indirect Costs of Financial Distress — 500

Agency Costs — 500

|  | *Concept Questions* | *503* |
|---|---|---|
| **17.3** | **Can Costs of Debt Be Reduced?** | **503** |
|  | Protective Covenants | 503 |
|  | Consolidation of Debt | 505 |
|  | *Concept Question* | *505* |
| **17.4** | **Integration of Tax Effects and Financial Distress Costs** | **505** |
|  | Pie Again | 507 |
|  | *Concept Questions* | *508* |
| **17.5** | **Signalling** | **508** |
|  | *Concept Questions* | *510* |
| **17.6** | **Shirking, Perquisites, and Bad Investments: A Note on Agency Cost of Equity** | **510** |
|  | Effect of Agency Costs of Equity on Debt-to-Equity Financing | 512 |
|  | Free Cash Flow | 512 |
|  | *Concept Questions* | *513* |
| **17.7** | **The Pecking-Order Theory** | **513** |
|  | Rules of the Pecking Order | 514 |
|  | Implications | 515 |
|  | *Concept Questions* | *516* |
| **17.8** | **Growth and the Debt-to-Equity Ratio** | **516** |
|  | No Growth | 516 |
|  | Growth | 517 |
|  | *Concept Question* | *518* |
| **17.9** | **Personal Taxes** | **518** |
|  | The Miller Model | 520 |
|  | *Concept Question* | *523* |
| **17.10** | **How Firms Establish Capital Structure** | **523** |
|  | *Case Study:* The Decision to Use More Debt: The Case of Campeau Corporation's Acquisition of Federated | 526 |
|  | *Concept Questions* | *527* |
| **17.11** | **Summary and Conclusions** | **528** |
|  | *Minicase:* McKenzie Restaurants Capital Budgeting | 532 |
| Appendix 17A | Some Useful Formulas of Financial Structure | Connect |
| Appendix 17B | The Miller Model and the Graduated Income Tax | Connect |

## CHAPTER 18

**Valuation and Capital Budgeting for the Levered Firm** — 533

| **Executive Summary** |  | **533** |
|---|---|---|
| **18.1** | **Adjusted Present Value Approach** | **533** |
|  | *Concept Questions* | *535* |
| **18.2** | **Flow to Equity Approach** | **535** |
|  | Step 1: Calculating Levered Cash Flow | 535 |
|  | Step 2: Calculating $r_s$ | 536 |
|  | Step 3: Valuation | 536 |
|  | *Concept Questions* | *536* |
| **18.3** | **Weighted Average Cost of Capital Method** | **536** |
|  | *Concept Question* | *537* |
| **18.4** | **A Comparison of the Adjusted Present Value, Flow to Equity, and Weighted Average Cost of Capital Approaches** | **537** |
|  | Caveat: Adjusted Present Value, Flow to Equity, and Weighted Average Cost of Capital Do Not Always Yield the Same Results | 538 |
|  | A Guideline | 539 |
|  | *Concept Questions* | *541* |
| **18.5** | **Adjusted Present Value Example** | **541** |
|  | *Concept Question* | *543* |
| **18.6** | **Capital Budgeting When the Discount Rate Must Be Estimated** | **543** |
|  | *Concept Question* | *545* |
| **18.7** | **Beta and Leverage** | **545** |
|  | The Project Is Not Scale Enhancing | 547 |
|  | *Concept Question* | *548* |
| **18.8** | **Summary and Conclusions** | **548** |
|  | *Minicase:* The Leveraged Buyout of Cheek Products Ltd. | 553 |
| Appendix 18A | The Adjusted Present Value Approach to Valuing Leveraged Buyouts | Connect |

## CHAPTER 19

**Dividends and Other Payouts** — 555

| **Executive Summary** |  | **555** |
|---|---|---|
| **19.1** | **Different Types of Dividends** | **555** |
| **19.2** | **Standard Method of Cash Dividend Payment** | **556** |
|  | *Concept Questions* | *558* |
| **19.3** | **The Benchmark Case: An Illustration of the Irrelevance of Dividend Policy** | **558** |
|  | Current Policy: Dividends Set Equal to Cash Flow | 558 |
|  | Alternative Policy: Initial Dividend Is Greater Than Cash Flow | 559 |
|  | The Indifference Proposition | 559 |
|  | Homemade Dividends | 561 |
|  | A Test | 562 |
|  | Dividends and Investment Policy | 563 |
|  | *Concept Questions* | *563* |
| **19.4** | **Repurchase of Stock** | **563** |
|  | Dividend versus Repurchase: Conceptual Example | 565 |
|  | Dividends versus Repurchases: Real-World Considerations | 566 |
|  | *Concept Questions* | *567* |

**19.5  Personal Taxes, Issuance Costs, and Dividends**                                **567**
Firms without Sufficient Cash to Pay a Dividend                                         567
Firms with Sufficient Cash to Pay a Dividend    568
Summary of Personal Taxes                        570
*Concept Questions*                              *570*

**19.6  Real-World Factors Favouring a High-Dividend Policy**                           **570**
Desire for Current Income                        570
Behavioural Finance                              571
Agency Costs                                     572
Information Content of Dividends and Dividend Signalling                                573
*Concept Question*                               *575*

**19.7  The Clientele Effect: A Resolution of Real-World Factors?**                     **575**
*Concept Questions*                              *576*
*In Their Own Words:* Why Amazon.Com Inc. pays no dividend, Why Rogers Communications pays dividends                        577

**19.8  What We Know and Do Not Know about Dividend Policy**                            **578**
Corporate Dividends Are Substantial              578
Fewer Companies Pay Dividends                    578
Corporations Smooth Dividends                    579
Some Survey Evidence on Dividends                580

**19.9  Putting It All Together**                **581**

**19.10 Stock Dividends and Stock Splits**       **582**
Some Details on Stock Splits and Stock Dividends                                        583
Value of Stock Splits and Stock Dividends        584
Reverse Splits                                   584
*Concept Questions*                              *585*

**19.11 Summary and Conclusions**                **585**
*Minicase:* Electronic Timing Ltd.               591

# PART 5

Long-Term Financing                              592

# CHAPTER 20

Issuing Equity Securities to the Public          592

**Executive Summary**                            **592**
**20.1  The Public Issue**                       **592**
**20.2  The Basic Procedure for a New Issue**    **593**
The Prompt Offering Prospectus System            594
Alternative Issue Methods                        595
*Concept Questions*                              *595*
**20.3  The Cash Offer**                         **595**
Types of Underwriting                            596
The Selling Period                               596
The Overallotment Option                         596

Investment Banks                                 596
The Offering Price and Underpricing              597
The Decision to Go Public                         598
Pricing Initial Public Offerings                 598
Underpricing: A Possible Explanation             599
*In Their Own Words:* Jay Ritter on initial public offering underpricing around the world                                     600
*Concept Questions*                              *601*

**20.4  The Announcement of New Equity and the Value of the Firm**                      **601**

**20.5  The Cost of Issuing Securities**         **602**
The Costs of Going Public: A Case Study          604
*Concept Questions*                              *604*

**20.6  Rights**                                 **604**
The Mechanics of a Rights Offering               605
Subscription Price                               605
Number of Rights Needed to Purchase a Share                                            606
The Value of a Right                             606
Ex-Rights                                        608
Value of Rights after Ex-Rights Date             609
The Underwriting Arrangements                    609
Effects on Shareholders                          610
Cost of Rights Offerings                         610
*Concept Questions*                              *611*

**20.7  The Private Equity Market**              **611**
Private Placement                                611
The Private Equity Firm                          611
Venture Capital                                  611
Suppliers of Venture Capital                     612
Stages of Financing                              613
Some Venture Capital Realities                   614
*Concept Questions*                              *614*

**20.8  Summary and Conclusions**                **614**
Minicase: East Coast Yachts Goes Public          617

# CHAPTER 21

Long-Term Debt                                   618

**Executive Summary**                            **618**
**21.1  Long-Term Debt: A Review**               **618**
**21.2  The Public Issue of Bonds**              **619**
The Basic Terms                                  620
Security                                         621
Seniority                                        622
Protective Covenants                             622
The Sinking Fund                                 622
The Call Provision                               623
*Concept Questions*                              *623*
**21.3  Bond Refunding**                         **624**
Should Firms Issue Callable Bonds?               624

Calling Bonds: When Does It Make Sense? 627
*Concept Questions* 629

**21.4 Bond Ratings** **630**
Junk Bonds 631
*Concept Questions* 634

**21.5 Some Different Types of Bonds** **634**
Zero-Coupon Bonds 634
Floating-Rate Bonds 635
Financial Engineering and Bonds 636
*Concept Questions* 637

**21.6 Direct Placement Compared to Public Issues** **637**
*Concept Questions* 637

**21.7 Long-Term Syndicated Bank Loans** **638**
*Concept Question* 638

**21.8 Summary and Conclusions** **639**
*Minicase:* Financing the Expansion of East Coast Yachts with a Bond Issue 642

**CHAPTER 22**

**Leasing** 643

**Executive Summary** **643**
**22.1 Types of Leases** **643**
The Basics 643
Operating Leases 644
Financial Leases 645
*Concept Questions* 645

**22.2 Accounting and Leasing** **646**
*Concept Questions* 648

**22.3 Taxes and Leases** **648**
*Concept Questions* 648

**22.4 The Cash Flows of Financial Leasing** **648**
The Incremental Cash Flows 649
*Concept Questions* 650

**22.5 A Detour on Discounting and Debt Capacity with Corporate Taxes** **651**
Present Value of Risk-Free Cash Flows 651
Optimal Debt Level and Risk-Free Cash Flows (Advanced) 652
*Concept Question* 652

**22.6 Net Present Value Analysis of the Lease-versus-Buy Decision** **652**
The Discount Rate 653
Asset Pool and Salvage Value 653

**22.7 Debt Displacement and Lease Valuation** **654**
The Basic Concept of Debt Displacement (Advanced) 654
Optimal Debt Level in the TransCanada Taxis Example (Advanced) 655

**22.8 Does Leasing Ever Pay? The Base Case** **658**

**22.9 Reasons for Leasing** **659**
Good Reasons for Leasing 659

Bad Reasons for Leasing 662
Leasing Decisions in Practice 663
*Concept Question* 663

**22.10 Some Unanswered Questions** **663**
Are the Uses of Leases and of Debt Complementary? 663
Why Are Leases Offered by Both Manufacturers and Third-Party Lessors? 664
Why Are Some Assets Leased More Commonly Than Others? 664

**22.11 Summary and Conclusions** **664**
*Minicase:* The Decision to Lease or Buy at Warf Computers Ltd. 668

Appendix 22A Adjusted Present Value Approach to Leasing Connect

**PART 6**

Options, Futures, and Corporate Finance 669

**CHAPTER 23**

**Options and Corporate Finance: Basic Concepts** 669

**Executive Summary** **669**
**23.1 Options** **669**
**23.2 Call Options** **670**
The Value of a Call Option at Expiration 670
*Concept Questions* 671

**23.3 Put Options** **672**
The Value of a Put Option at Expiration 672
*Concept Questions* 672

**23.4 Selling Options** **673**
**23.5 Stock Option Quotations** **674**
Long-Term Equity Anticipation Securities 677

**23.6 Combinations of Options** **677**
*Concept Question* 679

**23.7 Valuing Options** **679**
Bounding the Value of an American Call 680
The Factors Determining Call Option Values 681
A Quick Discussion of Factors Determining Put Option Values 683
*Concept Questions* 684

**23.8 An Option Pricing Formula** **684**
A Two-State Option Model 685
The Black–Scholes Model 687
*Concept Questions* 691

**23.9 Stocks and Bonds as Options** **692**
The Firm Expressed in Terms of Call Options 692
The Firm Expressed in Terms of Put Options 694
A Resolution of the Two Views 695

A Note on Loan Guarantees                696
  *Concept Questions*                     697
23.10 **Investment in Real Projects and Options 697**
  *Concept Question*                      699
23.11 **Contingent Value Rights, Mergers, and
      Corporate Decisions**              **699**
  *Concept Question*                      700
23.12 **Summary and Conclusions**        **700**
  *Minicase:* Clissold Industries Options 708

## CHAPTER 24

**Options and Corporate Finance: Extensions
and Applications**                       **709**

**Executive Summary**                    **709**
24.1 **Executive Stock Options**         **709**
  Why Options?                            709
  Executive Compensation: Where Are
  We Now?                                 710
  *In Their Own Words:* Jim Middlemiss on
  options backdating                      711
  Valuing Executive Compensation         712
  *Concept Question*                      714
24.2 **Valuing a Start-Up**              **715**
  *Concept Questions*                     718
24.3 **More about the Binomial Model**   **718**
  Heating Oil                             718
24.4 **Shutdown and Reopening Decisions** **724**
  Valuing a Gold Mine                     724
  The Abandonment and Opening Decisions  725
  Valuing the Simple Gold Mine           726
24.5 **Summary and Conclusions**         **730**
  *Minicase:* Exotic Cuisines Employee Stock
  Options                                 732

## CHAPTER 25

**Warrants and Convertibles**            **733**

**Executive Summary**                    **733**
25.1 **Warrants**                        **733**
  *Concept Question*                      735
25.2 **The Difference between Warrants and
      Call Options**                     **735**
  How the Firm Can Hurt Warrant Holders  738
  *Concept Questions*                     738
25.3 **Warrant Pricing and the Black–Scholes
      Model (Advanced)**                 **738**
  *Concept Question*                      739
25.4 **Convertible Bonds**               **739**
  *Concept Question*                      740
25.5 **The Value of Convertible Bonds**  **740**
  Straight Bond Value                     740

Conversion Value                         741
Option Value                             742
  *Concept Questions*                     743
25.6 **Reasons for Issuing Warrants and
      Convertibles**                     **743**
  Convertible Debt versus Straight Debt  743
  Convertible Debt versus Common Stock   744
  The "Free Lunch" Story                  745
  The "Expensive Lunch" Story             745
  A Reconciliation                        746
  *Concept Questions*                     746
25.7 **Why Are Warrants and Convertibles
      Issued?**                          **746**
  Matching Cash Flows                     746
  Risk Synergy                            747
  Agency Costs                            747
  Backdoor Equity                         748
  *Concept Question*                      748
25.8 **Conversion Policy**               **748**
  *Concept Questions*                     749
25.9 **Summary and Conclusions**         **749**
  *Minicase:* S&S Air's Convertible Bond 753

## CHAPTER 26

**Derivatives and Hedging Risk**         **754**

**Executive Summary**                    **754**
  Derivatives, Hedging, and Risk         754
  The Impact of Financial Risk: The Credit
  Crisis of 2007–2009                     755
26.1 **Forward Contracts**               **755**
  *Concept Questions*                     756
26.2 **Futures Contracts**               **756**
  *Concept Questions*                     761
26.3 **Hedging**                         **761**
  Hedging with Futures versus Hedging with
  Options                                 763
  *Concept Questions*                     763
26.4 **Interest Rate Futures Contracts** **763**
  Pricing of Government of Canada Bonds   763
  Pricing of Forward Contracts           764
  Futures Contracts                       765
  Hedging in Interest Rate Futures       766
  *Concept Questions*                     770
26.5 **Duration Hedging**                **770**
  The Case of Zero-Coupon Bonds          770
  The Case of Two Bonds with the Same
  Maturity but with Different Coupons     771
  Duration                                772
  Matching Liabilities with Assets       774
  Duration in Practice                    776
  *Concept Questions*                     776

**26.6 Swap Contracts** 777
Interest Rate Swaps 777
Currency Swaps 778
*Concept Question* 779
Credit Default Swaps 779
Exotics 780
Movement toward Exchange Trading for Swaps 781
**26.7 Actual Use of Derivatives** 781
*In Their Own Words:* Robert A. Jarrow on an expensive education 782
**26.8 Summary and Conclusions** 786
*Minicase:* Williamson Mortgage Inc. 789

**PART 7**

Financial Planning and Short Term Finance 790

**CHAPTER 27**

**Short-Term Finance and Planning** 790

**Executive Summary** 790
**27.1 Tracing Cash and Net Working Capital** 790
**27.2 Defining Cash in Terms of Other Elements** 791
The Sources and Uses of Cash Statement 793
*Concept Questions* 794
**27.3 The Operating Cycle and the Cash Cycle** 794
Interpreting the Cash Cycle 796
*Concept Questions* 797
**27.4 Some Aspects of Short-Term Financial Policy** 797
The Size of the Firm's Investment in Current Assets 797
Alternative Financing Policies for Current Assets 800
Current Assets and Liabilities in Practice 802
*Concept Questions* 803
**27.5 Cash Budgeting** 803
Cash Outflow 804
The Cash Balance 804
*Concept Questions* 805
**27.6 The Short-Term Financial Plan** 805
Short-Term Planning and Risk 805
Short-Term Borrowing 805
*Concept Questions* 808
In the Absence of Short-Term Borrowing 808
**27.7 Summary and Conclusions** 809
*Minicase:* Keafer Manufacturing Working Capital Management 816

**CHAPTER 28**

**Cash Management** 818

**Executive Summary** 818
**28.1 Reasons for Holding Cash** 818
The Speculative and Precautionary Motives 818
The Transaction Motive 819
Costs of Holding Cash 819
Cash Management versus Liquidity Management 819
*Concept Questions* 820
**28.2 Managing the Collection and Disbursement of Cash** 820
Electronic Data Interchange: The End of Float? 823
Accelerating Collections 823
Controlling Disbursements 827
Ethical and Legal Questions 827
*Concept Questions* 828
**28.3 Investing Idle Cash** 828
Seasonal or Cyclical Activities 829
Planned Expenditures 829
Characteristics of Short-Term Securities 829
Some Different Types of Money Market Securities 831
*In Their Own Words:* Credit crisis made in Canada 832
*Concept Questions* 833
**28.4 Summary and Conclusions** 834
*Minicase:* Cash Management at Richmond Ltd. 836

**CHAPTER 29**

**Credit Management** 837

**Executive Summary** 837
**29.1 Terms of the Sale** 838
Why Trade Credit Exists 838
The Basic Form 839
Credit Period 839
Cash Discounts 840
Credit Instruments 842
*Concept Questions* 843
**29.2 The Decision to Grant Credit: Risk and Information** 843
The Value of New Information about Credit Risk 844
Future Sales 845
*Concept Question* 845
**29.3 Optimal Credit Policy** 846
Credit Insurance 848
*Concept Question* 848

29.4  **Credit Analysis**                          **848**
      Credit Information                         848
      Credit Evaluation and Scoring              848
      *Concept Questions*                        *849*
29.5  **Collection Policy**                         **849**
      Average Collection Period                  849
      Aging Schedule                             850
      Collection Effort                          850
      *Concept Question*                         *851*
29.6  **Other Aspects of Credit Policy**            **851**
      Factoring                                  851
      How to Finance Trade Credit                851
      *Concept Question*                         *852*
29.7  **Summary and Conclusions**                   **853**
      *Minicase:* Credit Policy at Braam Industries  856
Appendix 29A  Inventory Management          Connect


# PART 8

## Special Topics                                   857


# CHAPTER 30

## Mergers and Acquisitions                        857

**Executive Summary**                              **857**
30.1  **The Basic Forms of Acquisitions**          **857**
      Merger or Consolidation                    857
      Acquisition of Stock                       858
      Acquisition of Assets                      859
      A Classification Scheme                    859
      A Note on Takeovers                        859
      *Concept Questions*                        *861*
30.2  **The Tax Forms of Acquisitions**            **861**
      Determinants of Tax Status                 861
      Taxable versus Tax-Free Acquisitions       861
      *Concept Questions*                        *862*
30.3  **Accounting for Acquisitions**              **862**
      The Acquisition Method                     862
      *Concept Question*                         *863*
30.4  **Determining the Synergy from an
      Acquisition**                                **863**
30.5  **Sources of Synergy from Acquisitions**     **864**
      Revenue Enhancement                        864
      Cost Reduction                             865
      Tax Gains                                  867
      The Cost of Capital                        868
      *Concept Question*                         *868*
30.6  **Calculating the Value of the Firm after
      an Acquisition**                             **868**
      Avoiding Mistakes                          869

30.7  **A Cost to Shareholders from Reduction
      in Risk**                                    **870**
      The Base Case                              870
      The Case Where One Firm Has Debt           871
      How Can Shareholders Reduce Their
      Losses from the Coinsurance Effect?        872
      *Concept Question*                         *872*
30.8  **Two "Bad" Reasons for Mergers**            **872**
      Earnings Growth                            872
      Diversification                            873
      *Concept Questions*                        *874*
30.9  **The Net Present Value of a Merger**        **874**
      Cash                                       874
      Common Stock                               875
      Cash versus Common Stock                   876
      *Concept Question*                         *877*
      Defensive Tactics                          877
      Divestitures                               877
      The Control Block and the Corporate
      Charter                                    879
      Standstill Agreements                      880
      Exclusionary Offers and Non-voting Stock   881
      Going Private and Leveraged Buyouts        881
      Other Defensive Devices                    882
      *Concept Question*                         *883*
30.10 **Some Evidence on Acquisitions**            **883**
      Do Acquisitions Benefit Shareholders?      883
      The Managers versus the Shareholders       886
      Real Productivity                          888
      *Concept Question*                         *888*
30.11 **Summary and Conclusions**                  **888**
      *Minicase:* The Birdie Golf–Hybrid Golf Merger  894


# CHAPTER 31

## Financial Distress                              896

**Executive Summary**                              **896**
31.1  **What Is Financial Distress?**              **896**
      *Concept Questions*                        *899*
31.2  **What Happens in Financial Distress?**      **899**
      *Concept Questions*                        *901*
31.3  **Bankruptcy Liquidation and
      Reorganization**                             **901**
      Bankruptcy Liquidation                     901
      Bankruptcy Reorganization                  903
      Agreements to Avoid Bankruptcy             904
      *Concept Questions*                        *904*
31.4  **Current Issues in Financial Distress**     **904**
      Private Workout or Bankruptcy: Which
      Is Better?                                 904
      Holdouts                                   905
      Complexity                                 905
      Lack of Information                        905

          Prepackaged Bankruptcy                906
             *Concept Questions*                906
31.5  **The Decision to Seek Court Protection: The
      Case of Canwest Global Communications
      Corporation**                            **906**
             *Concept Questions*                907
31.6  **Summary and Conclusions**             **908**
Appendix 31A  Predicting Corporate Bankruptcy:
The Z-Score Model                             Connect


CHAPTER 32

**International Corporate Finance**            **910**

**Executive Summary**                          **910**
32.1  **Terminology**                          **910**
             *Concept Question*                 911
32.2  **Foreign Exchange Markets and Exchange
      Rates**                                  **912**
      Exchange Rates                            912
      Types of Transactions                     914
             *Concept Question*                 915
32.3  **The Law of One Price and Purchasing
      Power Parity**                           **915**
             *Concept Questions*                917
32.4  **Interest Rates and Exchange Rates**    **917**
      The Dollar Investment                     918
      The Euro Investment                       918

      The Forward Discount and Expected
      Spot Rates                                919
      Exchange Rate Risk                        919
      More Advanced Short-Term Hedges           920
      The Hedging Decision in Practice          921
             *Concept Questions*                921
32.5  **International Capital Budgeting**       **922**
      Foreign Exchange Conversion               922
      Unremitted Cash Flows                     923
      The Cost of Capital for International Firms  923
             *Concept Questions*                925
32.6  **International Financing Decisions**     **926**
      Short-Term and Medium-Term Financing      926
      International Bond Markets                 927
      *In Their Own Words:* Merkel: Europe faces
      historic test in euro crisis              928
             *Concept Questions*                930
32.7  **Reporting Foreign Operations**         **930**
             *Concept Question*                 931
32.8  **Political Risk**                        **931**
32.9  **Summary and Conclusions**             **932**
      *Minicase:* East Coast Yachts Goes
      International                              935
Appendix A  Mathematical Tables               Connect
Appendix B  Answers to Selected End-of-Chapter
Problems                                       Connect
**Glossary**                                   **GL-1**
**Index**                                      **IN-1**

# PREFACE

The teaching and practice of corporate finance in Canada are more challenging and exciting than ever before. The last decade has seen fundamental changes in financial markets and financial instruments. In the early years of the twenty-first century, we still see announcements in the financial press about such matters as takeovers, junk bonds, financial restructuring, initial public offerings, bankruptcy, and derivatives. In addition, there is the new recognition of "real" options (Chapter 9), private equity and venture capital (Chapter 20), and the reappearing dividend (Chapter 19). The world's financial markets are more integrated than ever before. Both the theory and practice of corporate finance have been moving ahead with uncommon speed, and our teaching must keep pace.

These developments place new burdens on the teaching of corporate finance. On one hand, the changing world of finance makes it more difficult to keep materials up to date. On the other hand, the teacher must distinguish the permanent from the temporary and avoid the temptation to follow fads. Our solution to this problem is to emphasize the modern fundamentals of the theory of finance and make the theory come to life with contemporary examples. All too often, the beginning student views corporate finance as a collection of unrelated topics that are unified largely because they are bound together between the covers of one book. As in the previous editions, our aim is to present corporate finance as the working of a small number of integrated and powerful institutions.

This book has been written for the introductory courses in corporate finance at the MBA level and for the intermediate courses in many undergraduate programs. Some instructors will find our text appropriate for the introductory course at the undergraduate level as well.

We assume that most students either will have taken, or will be concurrently enrolled in, courses in accounting, statistics, and economics. This exposure will help students understand some of the more difficult material. However, the book is self-contained, and a prior knowledge of these areas is not essential. The only mathematics prerequisite is basic algebra.

## New to the Seventh Canadian Edition

- Discussions of the 2007–2009 credit crisis and its impact on the world of business have been added where appropriate throughout the text.
- Minicases have been reviewed and replaced to ensure that each has a business decision focus.
- Numerical examples and problems have been added that integrate capital cost allowance tax shields with the equivalent annual net present value.
- Tables, figures, and examples have been updated throughout the text.
- Recent Canadian examples have been added.
- Financial statements and text discussions (tax, leases, and business combinations, among others) have been updated to comply with the newly adopted IFRS accounting standards.
- End-of-chapter material has been substantially updated and refreshed.
- The discussion of corporate social responsibility, taxation of income trusts, and *Sarbanes-Oxley* in Chapter 1 has been updated.
- New discussion on firm valuation has been added in Chapter 6.
- Capital market data has been updated through 2013 in Chapter 10.
- The discussion on behavioural finance has been expanded in Chapter 14.

- A new discussion of research results on initial public offerings has been added in Chapter 20.
- A new discussion of contingent value rights has been added in Chapter 23.
- The discussion of executive compensation since the onset of the financial crisis has been updated in Chapter 24.
- A new discussion on the movement to exchange-traded swaps has been added in Chapter 26.

## Pedagogy

Keeping the theory and concepts current is only one phase of developing our corporate finance text. To be an effective teaching tool, the text must present the theory and concepts in a coherent way that can be easily learned. With this in mind, we have included several study features.

### Executive Summary

Each chapter begins with a roadmap that describes the objectives of the chapter and how it connects with concepts already learned in previous chapters. Real company examples that will be discussed are highlighted in this section.

> **EXECUTIVE SUMMARY**
>
> We now examine one of the most important concepts in all of corporate finance: the relationship between $1 today and $1 in the future. Consider the following example. A firm is contemplating investing $1 million in a project that is expected to pay out $200,000 per year for nine years. Should the firm accept the project? One might say yes at first glance, since the total inflows of $1.8 million (= $200,000 × 9) are greater than the $1 million outflow. However, the $1 million is paid out *immediately*, whereas the $200,000 per year is received in the future. Also, the immediate payment is known with certainty, whereas the later inflows can only be estimated. Thus, we need to know the relationship between a dollar today and a (possibly uncertain) dollar in the future before deciding on the project.
>
> This relationship is called the *time value of money* concept. It is important in such areas as capital budgeting, lease-versus-buy decisions, accounts receivable analysis, financing arrangements, mergers, and pension funding.
>
> The basics are presented in this chapter. We begin by discussing two fundamental concepts: future value and present value. Next, we treat simplifying formulas such as perpetuities and annuities.

### In Their Own Words Boxes

Located throughout the chapters, this unique series consists of articles written by distinguished scholars or practitioners on key topics.

## IN THEIR OWN WORDS

### Robert C. Higgins on Sustainable Growth

Most financial officers know intuitively that it takes money to make money. Rapid sales growth requires increased assets in the form of accounts receivable, inventory, and fixed plant, which, in turn, require money to pay for assets. They also know that if their company does not have the money when needed, it can literally "grow broke." The sustainable growth equation states these intuitive truths explicitly.

Sustainable growth is often used by bankers and other external analysts to assess a company's creditworthiness. They are aided in this exercise by several sophisticated computer software packages that provide detailed analyses of the company's past financial performance, including its annual sustainable growth rate.

Bankers use this information in several ways. Quick comparison of a company's actual growth rate to its sustainable rate tells the banker what issues will be

management's problem will be what to do with all the cash that keeps piling up in the till.

Bankers also find the sustainable growth equation useful for explaining to financially inexperienced small business owners and overly optimistic entrepreneurs that, for the long-run viability of their business, it is necessary to keep growth and profitability in proper balance.

Finally, comparison of actual to sustainable growth rates helps a banker understand why a loan applicant needs money and for how long the need might continue. In one instance, a loan applicant requested $100,000 to pay off several insistent suppliers and promised to repay in a few months when he collected some accounts receivable that were coming due. A sustainable growth analysis revealed that the firm had been growing at four to six times its sus-

## Concept Questions

Included after each major section in a chapter, Concept Questions point to essential material and allow students to test their recall and comprehension before moving forward.

## Figures and Tables

This text makes extensive use of real data and presents them in various figures and tables. Explanations in the narrative, examples, and end-of-chapter problems will refer to many of these exhibits.

## Examples

Separate called-out examples are integrated throughout the chapters. Each example illustrates an intuitive or mathematical application in a step-by-step format. There is enough detail in the explanations that students don't have to look elsewhere for additional information.

---

EXAMPLE **3.1**

The Computerfield Corporation's 2015 financial statements are as follows:

**Statement of Comprehensive Income 2015**

| Sales | $1,000 |
|---|---|
| Costs | 800 |
| Net income | $ 200 |

**Statement of Financial Position Year-End 2015**

| Assets | $500 | Debt | $250 |
|---|---|---|---|
| | | Equity | 250 |
| Total | $500 | Total | $500 |

In 2015, Computerfield's profit margin is 20 percent, and it has never paid a dividend. Its debt-to-equity ratio is 1. This is also the firm's *target* debt-to-equity ratio. Unless otherwise stated, the financial planners at Computerfield assume that all variables are tied directly to sales and that current relationships are optimal.

---

## Equations

Key equations are numbered and highlighted for easy reference.

## Highlighted Concepts

Throughout the text, important ideas are pulled out and presented in a box—signalling to students that this material is particularly relevant and critical to their understanding.

**A Comparison of Partnerships and Corporations**

| | Corporation | Partnership |
|---|---|---|
| Liquidity and marketability | Common stock can be listed on a stock exchange. | Units are subject to substantial restrictions on transferability. There is no established trading market for partnership units. |
| Voting rights | Usually each share of common stock entitles each holder to one vote per share on matters requiring a vote and on the election of the directors. Directors determine top management. | Limited partners have some voting rights. However, general partners have exclusive control and management of operations. |
| Taxation | Corporate income is taxable. Dividends to shareholders are also taxable with partial integration through use of the dividend tax credit. | Partnership income is taxable. |
| Reinvestment and | Corporations have broad latitude on dividend | Partnerships are generally prohibited from |

## End-of-Chapter Material

The end-of-chapter material reflects and builds upon the concepts learned in the chapter.

### Summary and Conclusions

The numbered summary provides a quick review of key concepts in the chapter.

---

**3.5**

### SUMMARY AND CONCLUSIONS

Financial planning forces the firm to think about and forecast the future. It involves the following:

1. Building a corporate financial model.
2. Describing different scenarios of future development from worst to best cases.
3. Using the models to construct pro forma financial statements.
4. Running the model under different scenarios (conducting sensitivity analysis).
5. Examining the financial implications of ultimate strategic plans.

Corporate financial planning should not become a purely mechanical activity. If it does, it will probably focus on the wrong things. In particular, plans are formulated all too often in terms of a growth target with an explicit linkage to creation of value. We talk about a particular financial planning model called sustainable growth and provide a useful summary of formulas used in this chapter in Table 3.6. Although the financial planning model presented is simple, needless to say, it is an important concept to grasp.

---

### List of Key Terms

A list of the boldfaced key terms in the text with page numbers is included for easy reference.

### Questions and Problems

Because solving problems is so critical to a student's learning, new questions and problems have been added and existing questions and problems have been revised. All problems have also been thoroughly reviewed and checked for accuracy. Problems have been grouped according to the concepts they test, with the concept headings listed at the beginning of each group.

Additionally, we have tried to make the problems in the critical "concept" chapters, such as those on value, risk, and capital structure, especially challenging and interesting. We provide answers to selected problems in Appendix B, available on Connect.

### Microsoft Excel Problems

Indicated by the Microsoft Excel icon in the margin, these Microsoft Excel problems can be found at the end of almost all chapters. Located on Connect, Microsoft Excel templates have been created for each of these problems, where students can use the data in the problem to work out the solution using Microsoft Excel skills.

### Minicase

These Minicases, located in most chapters, apply what is learned in a number of chapters to a real-world scenario. After presenting the facts, the case gives students guidance in rationalizing a sound business decision.

# Online Technology

**connect**

McGraw-Hill Connect™ is a web-based assignment and assessment platform that gives students the means to better connect with their coursework, with their instructors, and with the important concepts that they will need to know for success now and in the future.

With **Connect**, instructors can deliver assignments, quizzes, and tests online. Nearly all the questions from the text are presented in an autogradeable format and tied to the text's learning objectives. Instructors can edit existing questions and author entirely new problems, track individual student performance—by question or assignment or in relation to the class overall—with detailed grade reports, and integrate grade reports easily with Learning Management Systems (LMS). **Connect** houses all the instructor support materials for instructors, including the following:

- **Solutions Manual.** Prepared by **Pan Zhang**, from NAIT, and **Larbi Hammami**, from McGill University. Includes complete solutions for all end-of-chapter problems and appendix problems, calculator solutions, and suggested solutions for all Minicase and case material.

- **Instructor's Manual.** Prepared by **Larbi Hammami**, from McGill University. Part I of the Instructor's Manual contains, by chapter, a brief chapter outline, an introduction, and an annotated outline. This outline provides additional explanations, examples, and teaching tips. Part II consists of answers to all Concept Questions. Part III consists of solutions for all end-of-chapter problems and has been thoroughly reviewed for accuracy.

- **Microsoft PowerPoint Presentations.** Prepared by **Ingrid McLeod-Dick**, from York University. These slides contain useful outlines, summaries, and exhibits from the text.

- **Computerized Test Bank.** Prepared by **Sujata Madan**, from McGill University. The Test Bank contains multiple-choice questions, problems, and essay questions. The computerized test bank is available through EZ Test Online, a flexible and easy-to-use electronic testing program that allows instructors to create tests from book-specific items. EZ Test accommodates a wide range of question types and allows instructors to add their own questions. Test items are also available in Microsoft Word (rich text) format. For secure online testing, exams created in EZ Test can be exported to WebCT and Blackboard. EZ Test Online is supported at http://www. mhhe.com/eztest, where users can download a Quick Start Guide, access FAQs, or log a ticket for help with specific issues.

- **Microsoft Excel Templates (with solutions).** Prepared by **Ian Rakita**, from Concordia University. Microsoft Excel templates and solutions are included for the end-of-chapter problems with a Microsoft Excel icon in the margin.

By choosing **Connect**, instructors are providing their students with a powerful tool for improving academic performance and truly mastering course material. **Connect** allows students to practise important skills at their own pace and on their own schedule. Importantly, students' assessment results and instructors' feedback are all saved online—so students can review their progress and plot their course to success.

**Connect** also provides 24/7 online access to an eBook—an online edition of the text—to aid students in successfully completing their work, wherever and whenever they choose.

**LEARNSMART**

No two students are alike. Why should their learning paths be? LearnSmart uses revolutionary adaptive technology to build a learning experience unique to each student's needs. It starts by identifying the topics a student knows and does not know. As the student progresses, LearnSmart adapts and adjusts the content based on the student's individual strengths, weaknesses, and confidence, ensuring that every minute spent studying with LearnSmart is the most efficient and productive study time possible.

**█ISMARTBOOK**  As the first and only adaptive reading experience, SmartBook is changing the way students read and learn. SmartBook creates a personalized reading experience by highlighting the most important concepts a student needs to learn at that moment. As a student engages with SmartBook, the reading experience adapts by highlighting content based on what the student knows and doesn't know. This ensures that he or she is focused on the content needed to close specific knowledge gaps, while it simultaneously promotes long-term learning.

## SUPERIOR LEARNING SOLUTIONS AND SUPPORT

The McGraw-Hill Ryerson team is ready to help you assess and integrate any of our products, technology, and services into your course for optimal teaching and learning performance. Whether it's helping your students improve their grades, or putting your entire course online, the McGraw-Hill Ryerson team is here to help you do it. Contact your Learning Solutions Consultant today to learn how to maximize all of McGraw-Hill Ryerson's resources!

For more information on the latest technology and Learning Solutions offered by McGraw-Hill Ryerson and its partners, please visit us online: mcgrawhill.ca/he/solutions.

# Acknowledgments

Many people have contributed their time and expertise to the development and writing of this text. We extend our thanks once again for their assistance and countless insights.

A special thank you must be given to the tech checkers at AnsrSource for their vigilant efforts as the technical reviewers for the text and solutions. Their keen eyes and attention to detail have contributed greatly to the quality of the final product.

Kenneth Liu, recent Schulich BBA graduate, deserves special mention for his role in producing the Seventh Canadian Edition. He capably researched updates, drafted revisions, and responded to editorial queries; his excellent input was essential to this edition.

Much credit must go to a first-class group of people at McGraw-Hill Ryerson who worked on the Seventh Canadian Edition. Leading the team were Kimberley Veevers, Senior Product Manager, and Erin Catto, Product Developer. Copy editing and proofreading of the manuscript were handled ably by Julia Cochrane, with the in-house supervision of Joanne Limebeer.

Through the development of this edition, we have taken great care to discover and eliminate errors. Our goal is to provide the best Canadian textbook available on this subject. Please write and tell us how to make this a better text. Forward your comments to:

Professor Gordon S. Roberts
Schulich School of Business
4700 Keele Street
York University
North York, Ontario
M3J 1P3
Or, e-mail your comments to *groberts@schulich.yorku.ca*.

| | |
|---|---|
| **Stephen A. Ross** | **Jeffrey F. Jaffe** |
| **Randolph W. Westerfield** | **Gordon S. Roberts** |

## PART 1

# CHAPTER 1

# Introduction to Corporate Finance

## EXECUTIVE SUMMARY

Barrick Gold Corporation has long been known as the largest gold mining company in the world. With the recent recession, gold prices and Barrick's share price increased as investors sought a safe investment. However, in 2013 Barrick's shares plunged in value by 54 percent to a 20-year low. While the accompanying fall in the value of gold was beyond the company's control, the poor performance was attributed primarily to the failure of key projects, misallocation of capital resources, and the legal mess associated with the Pascua Lama mine in Chile. Accompanying this poor performance, the company's proxy circular revealed that six executives were to be compensated for a combined $47.4 million and board chair Peter Munk was to receive $4.3 million. In addition, the company awarded a US$11.9-million signing bonus to John Thornton for joining the company as co-chair.[1] Consequently, several major shareholders of Barrick Gold Corporation invoked a "say on pay" vote, which rejected the pay packages and led to the appointment of new independent directors and Mr. Munk stepping down as board chair. Recent events at Barrick Gold Corporation illustrate both the importance of governance issues and the need for management to make key corporate finance decisions relating to the following questions:

1. What long-term investment strategy should a company take on?
2. How can cash be raised?
3. How much short-term cash flow does a company need to pay its bills?

These are not the only questions of corporate finance. For example, another important question covered in this text is: how should a company divide earnings between payouts to shareholders (dividends) and reinvestment? The three questions on our list are, however, among the most important and, taken in order, they provide a rough outline of our book.

One way that companies raise cash to finance their investment activities is by selling or issuing securities. The securities, sometimes called *financial instruments* or *claims*, may be roughly classified as *equity* or *debt*, loosely called *stocks* or *bonds*. The difference between equity and debt is a basic distinction in the modern theory of finance. All securities of a firm are claims that depend on or are contingent on the value of the firm.[2] In Section 1.2 we show how debt and equity securities depend on the firm's value, and we describe them as different contingent claims.

In Section 1.3 we discuss different organizational forms and the pros and cons of the decision to become a corporation.

In Section 1.4 we take a close look at the goals of the corporation and discuss why maximizing shareholder wealth is likely to be its primary goal. Throughout the rest of the book, we assume that the firm's performance depends on the value it creates for its shareholders. Shareholders are made better off when the value of their shares is increased by the firm's decisions.

---

[1] Howard Green, "Barrick's governance issues may not be over," Business News Network, December 19, 2013.

[2] We tend to use the words *firm, company,* and *business* interchangeably. However, there is a difference between these and a corporation. We discuss this difference in Section 1.3.

A company raises cash by issuing securities in the financial markets. In Section 1.5 we describe some of the basic features of the financial markets. Roughly speaking, there are two types of financial markets: money markets and capital markets.

Section 1.6 covers trends in financial markets and management, and the last section of this chapter (Section 1.7) outlines the rest of the book.

# 1.1 WHAT IS CORPORATE FINANCE?

Suppose you decide to start a firm to make tennis balls. To do this, you hire managers to buy raw materials, and you assemble a workforce that will produce and sell finished tennis balls. In the language of finance, you make an investment in assets, such as inventory, machinery, land, and labour. The amount of cash you invest in assets must be matched by an equal amount of cash raised by financing. When you begin to sell tennis balls, your firm will generate cash. This is the basis of value creation. The purpose of the firm is to create value for you, the owner (shareholder). In other words, the goal of the firm and its managers should be to maximize the value of the shareholders' wealth. The value is reflected in the framework of the simple balance-sheet model of the firm.

## The Balance-Sheet Model of the Firm

Suppose we take a financial snapshot of the firm and its activities at a single point in time. Figure 1.1, a graphic conceptualization of the balance sheet, will help introduce you to corporate finance.

The assets of the firm are on the left side of the balance sheet. These assets can be thought of as current and fixed. *Fixed assets* are those that will last a long time, such as a building. Some fixed assets are tangible, such as machinery and equipment. Other fixed assets are intangible, such as patents, trademarks, and the quality of management. The other category of assets, *current assets*, comprises those that have short lives, such as inventory. The tennis balls that your firm has made but not yet sold are part of its inventory. Unless you have overproduced, they will leave the firm shortly.

**FIGURE 1.1**

**The Balance-Sheet Model of the Firm**

Left side: total value of assets. Right side: total value of the firm to investors, which determines how the value is distributed.

Before a company can invest in an asset, it must obtain financing, which means that it must raise the money to pay for the investment. The forms of financing are represented on the right side of the balance sheet. A firm will issue (sell) pieces of paper called *debt* (loan agreements) or *equity shares* (share certificates). Just as assets are classified as long lived or short lived, so too are liabilities. A short-term debt is called a *current liability.* Short-term debt represents loans and other obligations that must be repaid within one year. Long-term debt is debt that does not have to be repaid within one year. Shareholders' equity represents the difference between the value of the assets and the debt of the firm. In this sense, it is a residual claim on the firm's assets.

From the balance-sheet model of the firm, it is easy to see why finance can be thought of as the study of the following three questions:

1. In what long-lived assets should the firm invest? This question concerns the left side of the balance sheet. Of course, the type and proportions of assets the firm needs tend to be set by the nature of the business. We use the terms **capital budgeting** and *capital expenditure* to describe the process of making and managing expenditures on long-lived assets.

2. How can the firm raise cash for required capital expenditures? This question concerns the right side of the balance sheet. The answer involves the firm's **capital structure**, which represents the proportions of the firm's financing from current and long-term debt and equity.

3. How should short-term operating cash flows be managed? This question concerns the upper portion of the balance sheet. There is a mismatch between the timing of cash inflows and cash outflows during operating activities. Furthermore, the amount and timing of operating cash flows are not known with certainty. Financial managers must attempt to manage the gaps in cash flow. From an accounting perspective, short-term management of cash flow is associated with a firm's **net working capital**. Net working capital is defined as current assets minus current liabilities. From a financial perspective, the short-term cash flow problem comes from the mismatching of cash inflows and outflows. It is the subject of short-term finance.

## Capital Structure

Financing arrangements determine how the value of the firm is sliced up like a pie. The persons or institutions that buy debt from the firm are called *creditors*.[3] The holders of equity shares are called *shareholders*.

Thinking of the firm as a pie, initially, the size of the pie will depend on how well the firm has made its investment decisions. After the firm has made its investment decisions, financial markets determine the value of its assets (e.g., its buildings, land, and inventories).

The firm can then determine its capital structure. It might initially have raised the cash to invest in its assets by issuing more debt than equity; now it can consider changing that mix by issuing more equity and using the proceeds to buy back some of its debt. Financing decisions like this can be made independently of the original investment decisions. The decisions to issue debt and equity affect how the pie is sliced.

The pie we are thinking of is depicted in Figure 1.2. The size of the pie is the value of the firm in the financial markets. We can write the value of the firm, *V*, as

$$V = B + S$$

where *B* is the value of the debt (bonds) and *S* is the value of the equity (shares). The pie diagram considers two ways of slicing the pie: 50 percent debt and 50 percent equity, and 25 percent debt and 75 percent equity. The way the pie is sliced could affect its value. If so, the goal of the financial manager is to choose the ratio of debt to equity that makes the value of the pie—that is, the value of the firm, *V*—as large as it can be.

---

[3] We tend to use the words *creditors, debtholders,* and *bondholders* interchangeably. In later chapters we examine the differences among the kinds of creditors.

FIGURE 1.2

**Two Pie Models of the Firm**

**Capital structure 1**          **Capital structure 2**

## The Financial Manager

In large firms the finance activity is usually associated with a senior officer of the firm (such as a vice-president of finance) and some lesser officers. Figure 1.3 depicts one example of a general organizational structure emphasizing the finance activity within the firm. Reporting to the vice-president of finance are the treasurer and the controller. The treasurer is responsible for handling cash flows, analyzing capital expenditures, and making financing plans. The controller handles the accounting function, which includes taxes, cost and financial accounting, and information systems. Our discussion of corporate finance is much more relevant to the treasurer's function.

FIGURE 1.3

**Hypothetical Organization Chart**

As Figure 1.3 shows, there are four general position categories under the treasurer. Corporations usually hire BA or MBA graduates with a finance background for these positions. In contrast, the positions under the controller are geared more toward graduates with accounting majors or professional designations, such as CGA, CMA, or CA.

We think that a financial manager's most important job is to create value from the firm's capital budgeting, financing, and liquidity activities. How do financial managers create value?

1. The firm should try to buy assets that generate more cash than they cost.
2. The firm should sell bonds, shares, and other financial instruments that raise more cash than they cost.

Thus, the firm must create more cash flow than it uses. The cash flow paid to bondholders and shareholders of the firm should be higher than the cash flows put into the firm by the bondholders and shareholders. To see how this is done, we can trace the cash flows from the firm to the financial markets and back again.

The interplay of the firm's finance with the financial markets is illustrated in Figure 1.4. To finance its planned investment, the firm sells debt and equity shares to participants in the financial markets. The result is cash flows from the financial markets to the firm ($A$). This cash is invested in the investment activities of the firm ($B$) by the firm's management. The cash generated by the firm ($C$) is paid to shareholders and bondholders ($F$). Shareholders receive cash from the firm in the form of dividends or as share repurchases; bondholders who lent funds to the firm receive interest and, when the initial loan is repaid, principal. Not all of the firm's cash is paid out to shareholders and bondholders. Some is retained ($D$), and some is paid to governments as taxes ($E$).

Over time, if the cash paid to shareholders and bondholders ($F$) is greater than the cash raised in the financial markets ($A$), value will be created.

**FIGURE 1.4**

**Cash Flows between the Firm and the Financial Markets**

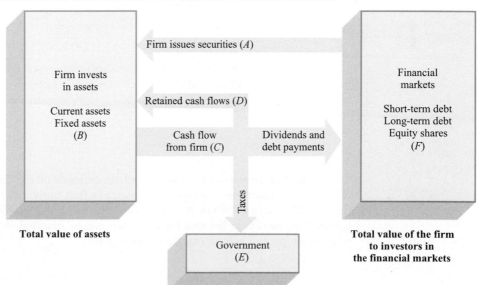

(*A*) Firm issues securities to raise cash (the financing decision).
(*B*) Firm invests in assets (capital budgeting).
(*C*) Firm's operations generate cash flows.
(*D*) Retained cash flows are reinvested in firm.
(*E*) Cash is paid to government as taxes.
(*F*) Cash is paid out to investors in the form of interest and dividends.

## Identification of Cash Flows

Unfortunately, it is not all that easy to observe cash flows directly. Much of the information we obtain is in the form of accounting statements, and much of the work of financial analysis is to extract cash flow information from accounting statements. Example 1.1 illustrates how this is done.

---

**EXAMPLE 1.1**

The Midland Company refines and trades gold. At the end of the year it sold some gold for $1 million. The company had acquired the gold for $900,000 at the beginning of the year. The company paid cash for the gold when it was purchased. Unfortunately, it has yet to collect from the customer to whom the gold was sold.

The following is a standard accounting of Midland's financial circumstances at year-end:

**THE MIDLAND COMPANY**
**Accounting View**
**Income Statement**
**Year Ended December 31**

| | |
|---|---|
| Sales | $1,000,000 |
| Costs | −900,000 |
| Profit | $ 100,000 |

By International Financial Reporting Standards (IFRS), the sale is recorded even though the customer has yet to pay. It is assumed that the customer will pay soon. From the accounting perspective, Midland seems to be profitable. The perspective of corporate finance is different. It focuses on cash flows:

**THE MIDLAND COMPANY**
**Corporate Finance View**
**Income Statement**
**Year Ended December 31**

| | |
|---|---|
| Cash inflow | 0 |
| Cash outflow | −$900,000 |
| | −$900,000 |

The perspective of corporate finance examines whether cash flows are being created by the gold-trading operations of Midland. Value creation depends on cash flows. For Midland, value creation depends on whether and when it actually receives the $1 million.

## Timing of Cash Flows

The value of an investment made by the firm depends on the timing of cash flows. One of the most important principles of finance is that individuals prefer to receive cash flows earlier rather than later. One dollar received today is worth more than one dollar received next year because today's dollar can be invested to earn interest. This time preference plays a role in stock and bond prices.

EXAMPLE **1.2**

The Midland Company is attempting to choose between two proposals for new products. Both proposals will provide cash flows over a four-year period and will initially cost $10,000. The cash flows from the proposals are as follows:

| Year | New Product A | New Product B |
|------|---------------|---------------|
| 1 | 0 | $ 4,000 |
| 2 | 0 | 4,000 |
| 3 | 0 | 4,000 |
| 4 | $20,000 | 4,000 |
| Total | $20,000 | $16,000 |

At first it appears that new product A is better. However, the cash flows from proposal B come earlier than those of A. Without more information, we cannot decide which set of cash flows would create greater value. It depends on whether the value of getting cash from B upfront outweighs the extra total cash from A. Bond and stock prices reflect this preference for earlier cash, and we will see how to use them to decide between A and B.

## Risk of Cash Flows

**The firm must consider risk. The amount and timing of cash flows are not usually known with certainty. Most investors have an aversion to risk.**

EXAMPLE **1.3**

The Midland Company is considering expanding operations overseas. It is evaluating Europe and Japan as possible sites. Europe is considered to be relatively safe, whereas Japan is seen as very risky. In both cases the company would close down operations after one year.

After doing a complete financial analysis, Midland has come up with the following cash flows of the alternative plans for expansion under three equally likely scenarios: pessimistic, most likely, and optimistic.

|  | Pessimistic | Most Likely | Optimistic |
|--------|-------------|-------------|------------|
| Europe | $75,000 | $100,000 | $125,000 |
| Japan | 0 | 150,000 | 200,000 |

If we ignore the pessimistic scenario, perhaps Japan is the better alternative. When we take the pessimistic scenario into account, the choice is unclear. Japan appears to be riskier, but it may also offer a higher expected level of cash flow. What is risk and how can it be defined? We must try to answer this important question. Corporate finance cannot avoid coping with risky alternatives, and much of our book is devoted to developing methods for evaluating risky opportunities.

***CONCEPT***
***QUESTIONS***
- What are three basic questions of corporate finance?
- Describe capital structure.
- List three reasons why value creation is difficult.

## 1.2 CORPORATE SECURITIES AS CONTINGENT CLAIMS ON TOTAL FIRM VALUE

What is the essential difference between debt and equity? The answer can be found by thinking about what happens to the payoffs to debt and equity when the value of the firm changes.

The basic feature of debt is that it is a promise by the borrowing firm to repay a fixed dollar amount by a certain date.

**EXAMPLE 1.4**

The Canadian Corporation promises to pay $100 to the True North Insurance Company at the end of one year. This is a debt of the Canadian Corporation. Holders of the Canadian Corporation's debt will receive $100 if the value of the Canadian Corporation's assets equals $100 or more at the end of the year.

Formally, the debtholders have been promised an amount, $F$, at the end of the year. If the value of the firm, $X$, is equal to or greater than $F$ at year-end, debtholders will get $F$. Of course, if the firm does not have enough to pay off the promised amount, the firm will be broke. It may be forced to liquidate its assets for whatever they are worth, and bondholders will receive $X$. Mathematically, this means that the debtholders have a claim to $X$ or $F$, whichever is smaller. Figure 1.5 illustrates the general nature of the payoff structure to debtholders.

### FIGURE 1.5

**Debt and Equity as Contingent Claims**

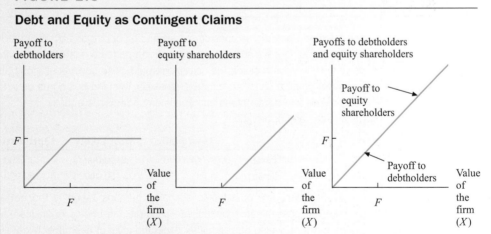

$F$ is the promised payoff to debtholders. $X - F$ is the payoff to equity shareholders if $X - F > 0$. Otherwise the payoff is 0.

Suppose at year-end the Canadian Corporation's value is $100. The firm has promised to pay the True North Insurance Company $100, so the debtholders will get $100.

Now suppose the Canadian Corporation's value is $200 at year-end and the debtholders are promised $100. How much will the debtholders receive? It should be clear that they will receive the same amount as when the Canadian Corporation was worth $100.

Suppose the firm's value is $75 at year-end and debtholders are promised $100. How much will the debtholders receive? In this case the debtholders will get $75.

The shareholders' claim on firm value at the end of the period is the amount that remains after the debtholders are paid. Of course, shareholders get nothing if the firm's value is equal to or less than the amount promised to the debtholders.

The Canadian Corporation will sell its assets for $200 at year-end. The firm has promised to pay the insurance company $100 at that time. The shareholders will get the residual value of $100.

Algebraically, the shareholders' claim is $X - F$ if $X > F$ and zero if $X \leq F$. This is depicted in Figure 1.5. The sum of the debtholders' claim and the shareholders' claim is always the value of the firm at the end of the period.

The debt and equity securities issued by a firm derive their value from the total value of the firm. In the words of finance theory, debt and equity securities are **contingent claims** on the total firm value.

When the value of the firm exceeds the amount promised to debtholders, the shareholders obtain the residual of the firm's value over the amount promised the debtholders, and the debtholders obtain the amount promised. When the value of the firm is less than the amount promised to the bondholders, the shareholders receive nothing and the debtholders get the value of the firm.

***CONCEPT QUESTIONS***
- What is a contingent claim?
- Describe equity and debt as contingent claims.

## 1.3    THE CORPORATE FIRM

The firm is a way of organizing the economic activity of many individuals. There are many reasons why so much economic activity is carried out by firms and not by individuals. The theory of firms, however, does not tell us much about why most large firms are corporations rather than any of the other legal forms that firms can assume.

A basic problem of the firm is how to raise cash. The corporate form of business (that is, organizing the firm as a corporation) is the standard method for solving problems encountered in raising large amounts of cash. However, business can take other forms. In this section we consider the three basic legal forms of organizing firms (sole proprietorship, partnership, and corporation), and we see how firms raise large amounts of money under each form. We also introduce the income trust, a noncorporate form of business organization.

### The Sole Proprietorship

A **sole proprietorship** is a business owned by one person. Suppose you decide to start a business to produce mousetraps. Going into business is simple: Announce to all who will listen, "Today I am going to build a better mousetrap."

Most large cities require that you obtain a business licence. Afterward, you can try to hire as many people as you need and borrow whatever money you need. At year-end all the profits and the losses will be yours.

Here are some important factors in considering a sole proprietorship:

1. The sole proprietorship is the cheapest type of business to form. No formal charter is required, and few government regulations must be satisfied.

2. A sole proprietorship pays no corporate income taxes. All profits of the business are taxed as individual income.

3. The sole proprietorship has unlimited liability for business debts and obligations. No distinction is made between personal and business assets.

4. The life of the sole proprietorship is limited by the life of the sole proprietor.

5. Because the only money invested in the firm is the proprietor's, the equity money that can be raised by the sole proprietor is limited to the proprietor's personal wealth.

## The Partnership

Any two or more people can get together and form a **partnership**. Partnerships fall into two categories: general partnerships and limited partnerships.

In a *general partnership* all partners agree to provide some fraction of the work and cash and to share the profits and losses. Each partner is liable for the debts of the partnership. A partnership agreement specifies the nature of the arrangement. The partnership agreement may be an oral agreement or a formal document setting forth the understanding.

*Limited partnerships* permit the liability of some of the partners to be limited to the amount of cash each has contributed to the partnership. Limited partnerships usually require that (1) at least one partner be a general partner and (2) the limited partners do not participate in managing the business.

Here are some points that are important when considering a partnership:

1. Partnerships are usually inexpensive and easy to form. In complicated arrangements, including general and limited partnerships, written documents are required. Business licences and filing fees may be necessary.

2. General partners have unlimited liability for all debts. The liability of limited partners is usually limited to the contribution each has made to the partnership. If one general partner is unable to meet his or her commitment, the shortfall must be made up by the other general partners.

3. The general partnership is terminated when a general partner dies or withdraws (but this is not so for a limited partner). It is difficult for a partnership to transfer ownership without dissolving. Usually, all general partners must agree. However, limited partners may sell their interest in a business.

4. It is difficult for a partnership to raise large amounts of cash. Equity contributions are limited to a partner's ability and desire to contribute to the partnership. Sometimes the partners have no choice about contributing. For example, in 2001, a major global management consulting firm, McKinsey & Company, called on its partners to contribute up to $300,000 each to finance growing accounts receivable. Many companies start life as a proprietorship or partnership, but at some point they need to convert to corporate form. For example, Tim Hortons Inc., which was founded in 1964, went public in March 2006.

5. Income from a partnership is taxed as personal income to the partners.

6. Management control resides with the general partners. Usually a majority vote is required on important matters, such as the amount of profit to be retained in the business.

It is very difficult for large business organizations to exist as sole proprietorships or partnerships. The main advantage is the cost of getting started. Afterward, the disadvantages, which may become severe, are (1) unlimited liability, (2) limited life of the enterprise, and (3) difficulty of transferring ownership. These three disadvantages lead to (4) the difficulty of raising cash.

## The Corporation

Of the many forms of business enterprise, the **corporation** is by far the most important. Most large Canadian firms, such as Bank of Montreal and Bombardier, are organized as corporations. As a distinct legal entity, a corporation can have a name and enjoy many of the legal powers of natural persons. For example, corporations can acquire and exchange property. Corporations may enter into contracts and may sue and be sued. For jurisdictional purposes, the corporation is a citizen of its province of incorporation. (It cannot vote, however.)

Starting a corporation is more complicated than starting a proprietorship or partnership. The incorporators must prepare articles of incorporation and a set of bylaws. The articles of incorporation must include

1. Name of the corporation.
2. Business purpose.
3. Number of shares that the corporation is authorized to issue, with a statement of limitations and rights of different classes of shares.
4. Nature of the rights granted to shareholders.
5. Number of members of the initial board of directors.

### A Comparison of Partnerships and Corporations

|  | Corporation | Partnership |
|---|---|---|
| Liquidity and marketability | Common stock can be listed on a stock exchange. | Units are subject to substantial restrictions on transferability. There is no established trading market for partnership units. |
| Voting rights | Usually each share of common stock entitles each holder to one vote per share on matters requiring a vote and on the election of the directors. Directors determine top management. | Limited partners have some voting rights. However, general partners have exclusive control and management of operations. |
| Taxation | Corporate income is taxable. Dividends to shareholders are also taxable with partial integration through use of the dividend tax credit. | Partnership income is taxable. |
| Reinvestment and dividend payout | Corporations have broad latitude on dividend payout decisions. | Partnerships are generally prohibited from reinvesting partnership cash flow. All net cash flow is distributed to partners. |
| Liability | Shareholders are not personally liable for obligations of the corporation. | Limited partners are not liable for obligations of partnerships. General partners may have unlimited liability. |
| Continuity of existence | Corporations have perpetual life. | Partnerships have a limited life. |

The bylaws (the rules to be used by the corporation to regulate its own existence) concern its shareholders, directors, and officers. Bylaws for the corporation's management range from the briefest possible statement of rules to hundreds of pages of text.

In its simplest form, the corporation comprises three sets of distinct interests: the shareholders (the owners), the directors, and the corporation officers (the top management). Traditionally, the shareholders control the corporation's direction, policies, and activities. The shareholders elect a board of directors, who in turn select top management who serve as corporate officers.

The separation of ownership from management gives the corporation several advantages over proprietorships and partnerships:

1. Because ownership in a corporation is represented by shares, ownership can be readily transferred to new owners. Because the corporation exists independently of those who own its shares, there is no limit to the transferability of shares, as there is in partnerships.

2. The corporation has unlimited life. Because the corporation is separate from its owners, the death or withdrawal of an owner does not affect its existence. The corporation can continue on after the original owners have withdrawn.

3. The shareholders' liability is limited to the amount invested in the ownership shares. For example, if a shareholder purchased $1,000 in shares of a corporation, the potential loss would be $1,000. In a partnership, a general partner with a $1,000 contribution could lose the $1,000 plus any other indebtedness of the partnership.

Limited liability, ease of ownership transfer, and perpetual succession are the major advantages of the corporate form of business organization. These give the corporation an enhanced ability to raise cash.

There is, however, one great disadvantage to incorporation. Federal and provincial governments tax corporate income. Corporate dividends received by shareholders are also taxable. The dividend tax credit for individual shareholders and a corporate dividend exclusion provide a degree of tax integration for Canadian corporations. These tax provisions are discussed in Appendix 1A.

### The Income Trust

The income trust, a non-corporate form of business organization, grew in importance in Canada after 2001. Within this sector, the fastest-growing component of this form of business organization was business income trusts, especially in real estate and oil and gas. Businesses—such as telephone listings, container ports, and restaurant chains—usually organized as corporations were also included in this component. In response to the growing importance of this sector, provincial legislation extended limited liability protection—previously limited to corporate shareholders—to trust unitholders. Along the same lines, at the end of 2005, the TSX began to include trusts in its benchmark S&P/TSX composite index.

Business income trusts (also called income funds) hold the debt and equity of an underlying business and distribute the income generated to unitholders. Because income trusts are not corporations, they are not subject to corporate income tax and their income is typically taxed only in the hands of unitholders. As a result, investors saw trusts as tax efficient and were generally willing to pay more for a company after it converted from a corporation to a trust. This tax advantage largely disappeared in 2006 when the government announced plans to tax income trusts as corporations, prompting Bell Canada Enterprises (BCE) to reverse its mid-October 2006 announced plan to convert to an income trust. As of mid-2014, most income trusts had converted to corporations, with only 67 income trusts listed on the TSX and the TSX Venture Exchange, with a quoted market value of $65.5 billion.[4]

**CONCEPT QUESTIONS**

- Define a proprietorship, a partnership, a corporation, and an income trust.
- What are the advantages of the corporate form of business organization?

## 1.4    GOALS OF THE CORPORATE FIRM

What is the primary goal of the corporation? The traditional answer is that managers in a corporation make decisions for the shareholders because the shareholders own

---

[4] http://www.tmxmoney.com/en/sector_profiles/income_trusts/.

and control the corporation. If so, the goal of the corporation is to add value for the shareholders. This goal is a little vague and so we will try to come up with a precise formulation. It is also impossible to give a definitive answer to this important question because the corporation is an artificial being, not a natural person. It exists in the "contemplation of the law."[5]

It is necessary to identify precisely who controls the corporation. We shall consider the **set-of-contracts viewpoint**. This viewpoint suggests that the corporate firm will attempt to maximize the shareholders' wealth by taking actions that increase the current value per share of existing stock of the firm.

## Agency Costs and the Set-of-Contracts Viewpoint

The set-of-contracts viewpoint of the firm states that the firm can be viewed as nothing more than a set of contracts.[6] One of the contract claims is a residual claim (equity) on the firm's assets and cash flows. The equity contract can be defined as a principal-agent relationship. The members of the management team are the agents hired to act on behalf of the equity investors (shareholders), who are the principals. This discussion focuses on conflict between shareholders and managers. It is assumed that each of the two groups, left alone, will attempt to act in its own self-interest. We also assume that shareholders are unanimous in defining their self-interest. (We explain how perfect markets make this happen in Chapter 4).

The shareholders, however, can discourage the managers from diverging from the shareholders' interests by devising appropriate incentives for managers and then monitoring their behaviour. Doing so, unfortunately, is complicated and costly. The costs of resolving the conflicts of interest between managers and shareholders are special types of costs called **agency costs**. These costs include the monitoring costs of the shareholders and the incentive fee paid to the managers. It can be expected that contracts will be devised that will provide the managers with appropriate incentives to maximize the shareholders' wealth. Thus, agency problems do not mean that the corporate firm will not act in the best interests of shareholders, only that it is costly to make it do so. However, agency problems can never be perfectly solved, and managers may not always act in the best interests of shareholders. *Residual losses* are the lost wealth of the shareholders due to divergent behaviour of the managers.

## Managerial Goals

Managerial goals are different from those of shareholders. What will managers maximize if they are left to pursue their own goals rather than shareholders' goals?

Williamson proposes the notion of *expense preference*.[7] He argues that managers obtain value from certain kinds of expenses. In particular, company cars, office furniture, office location, and funds for discretionary investment have value to managers beyond that which comes from their productivity.

Donaldson conducted a series of interviews with chief executives of several large companies.[8] He concluded that managers are influenced by three underlying motivations in defining the corporate mission:

---

[5] These are the words of U.S. Chief Justice John Marshall from *The Trustees of Dartmouth College v. Woodward*, 4, Wheaton 636 (1819).

[6] M. C. Jensen and W. Meckling, "Theory of the Firm: Managerial Behavior, Agency Costs and Ownership Structure," *Journal of Financial Economics* 3 (1976).

[7] O. Williamson, "Managerial Discretion and Business Behavior," *American Economic Review* 53 (1963).

[8] G. Donaldson, *Managing Corporate Wealth: The Operations of a Comprehensive Financial Goals System* (New York: Praeger, 1984).

1. *Survival.* Organizational survival means that management must always command sufficient resources to support the firm's activities.
2. *Independence.* This is the freedom to make decisions and take action without encountering external parties or depending on outside financial markets.
3. *Self-sufficiency.* Managers do not want to depend on external parties.

These motivations lead to what Donaldson concludes is the basic financial objective of managers: the maximization of corporate wealth. Corporate wealth is that wealth over which management has effective control; it is closely associated with corporate growth and corporate size. Corporate wealth is not necessarily shareholder wealth. Corporate wealth tends to lead to increased growth by providing funds for growth and limiting the extent to which equity is raised. Increased growth and size are not necessarily the same thing as increased shareholder wealth.

## Separation of Ownership and Control

Some people argue that shareholders do not control the corporation. They argue that shareholder ownership is too diffuse and fragmented for effective control of management. A striking feature of the modern large corporation is the diffusion of ownership among thousands of investors. For example, Table 1.1 shows that the largest corporations in Canada are widely held, with no shareholder owning 10 percent or more of the shares. While this argument is certainly worth considering, it is less true in Canada than in the United States. Over 70 percent of U.S. corporations were widely held compared to only around 15 percent in Canada. Many domestically owned Canadian corporations have controlling shareholders.[9] Further, restricted voting shares, which facilitate narrow control, are more popular in Canada.[10] Still, controlling agency costs through re-examining the rules of corporate governance is of considerable interest in corporate Canada.

**TABLE 1.1**

### The Five Largest Canadian Corporations, Company 2013 Year-End*

|  | Revenue (in $ millions)* | Market value (in $ millions)** | Ownership |
|---|---|---|---|
| Suncor Energy Inc. | 42,439 | 62,002 | Widely held |
| Magna International | 35,049 | 23,475 | Widely held |
| Royal Bank of Canada | 35,982 | 105,653 | Widely held |
| Alimentation Couche-Tard | 35,569 | 17,175 | Widely held |
| George Weston Ltd. | 32,873 | 10,374 | Widely held |

*Year-end for Suncor, Magna, and George Weston is December. For Royal Bank of Canada and Alimentation Couche-Tard, year-ends are October and April, respectively.

**May 2014.

Source: "Canada's 100 Biggest Companies by Revenue," and "Canada's 100 Biggest Companies by Market Cap," *Globe and Mail Report on Business Magazine,* June 2014.

As we discussed earlier, one of the most important advantages of the corporate form of business organization is that it allows ownership of shares to be transferred. The resulting diffuse ownership, however, brings with it the separation of ownership and control of the large corporation. The possible separation of ownership and control raises an important question: Who controls the firm?

---

[9] Important exceptions are chartered banks. The *Bank Act* prohibits any one interest from owning more than 20 percent of the shares.

[10] V. Jog, P. C. Zhu, and S. Dutta, "Impact of Restricted Voting Share Structure on Firm Value and Performance," *Corporate Governance: An International Review* 18:5 (2010), 415–437.

**Do Shareholders Control Managerial Behaviour?**   The claim that managers can ignore the interests of shareholders is deduced from the fact that ownership in large corporations is widely dispersed. As a consequence, it is often claimed that individual shareholders cannot control management. There is some merit in this argument, but it is too simplistic.

The extent to which shareholders can control managers depends on (1) the costs of monitoring management, (2) the costs of implementing the control devices, and (3) the benefits of control.

When a conflict of interest exists between management and shareholders, who wins? Do managers or shareholders control the firm? Ownership in large corporations is diffuse compared to that in closely held corporations. However, shareholders have several control devices (some more effective than others) to bond management to the self-interest of shareholders:

1.  Shareholders determine the membership of the board of directors by voting. Thus, shareholders control the directors, who in turn select the management team.
2.  Contracts with management and arrangements for compensation, such as stock option plans, can be made so that management has an incentive to pursue shareholders' goals. Similarly, management may be given loans to buy the firm's shares.
3.  If the price of a firm's stock drops too low because of poor management, the firm may be acquired by a group of shareholders, another firm, or an individual. This is called a takeover. In a takeover, top management of the acquired firm may find itself out of a job. For example, the CEO of Chapters Inc. lost his job when the bookseller was taken over by Indigo in 2001. This pressures management to make decisions in the shareholders' interests. Fear of a takeover gives managers an incentive to take actions that will maximize stock prices.
4.  Competition in the managerial labour market may force managers to perform in the best interest of shareholders; otherwise, they will be replaced. Firms willing to pay the most will lure good managers. These are likely to be firms that compensate managers based on the value they create for shareholders. Compensation design is far from perfect, however, and many firms have come under intense criticism for having high rates of executive compensation. Further, there is some evidence that such compensation schemes encouraged bank executives to take on greater risk: banks with performance-based executive pay did worse during the financial crisis.[11]

The available evidence and theory are consistent with the idea of shareholder control. However, there can be no doubt that at times, corporations pursue managerial goals at the expense of shareholders. In addition to the issue of excessive executive compensation already discussed, management may change the firm's corporate governance rules by removing independent directors who might challenge management. Major pension funds, such as the Alberta Teachers' Retirement Fund Board and the Ontario Teachers' Pension Plan Board, have joined with professional money managers to form the Canadian Coalition for Good Governance. The Coalition has set up detailed governance guidelines backed by action in voting its shares at annual meetings.[12]

**Stakeholders**   In addition to shareholders and management, employees, customers, suppliers, and the public all have a financial interest in the firm and its decisions. This enlarged stakeholder group may introduce alternative goals such as preserving the environment or avoiding alcohol, tobacco, gambling, nuclear power, and military

---

[11] R. Fahlenbrach and Rene Stulz, "Bank CEO Incentives and the Credit Crisis," *Journal of Financial Economics* 99:1 (2011), 11–26.

[12] http://www.ccgg.ca.

# IN THEIR OWN WORDS

## B. Espen Eckbo on corporate governance

Voluntary shareholder absenteeism and a powerful culture of "corporate insiders" have led to a crisis in corporate governance. Without a fundamental shift in the balance of power, the problems will only worsen. Recent corporate scandals have resurrected public suspicion that there is plenty of potential for mischief inside large public companies.

In countries with highly developed financial systems, much of the governance debate focuses on the balance of power between shareholders, boards, and top executives in widely held public companies. This balance is the result of three main influences, which differ substantially across countries: legal precedent (case law), the cost of shareholder activism, and the political strength of employee unions. When a company is founded, this balance of power is hardly an issue. However, as the company grows and prospers, attitudes start to change. With growth comes the need for additional capital. Naturally, with limited wealth, the founding shareholders relinquish control, preferring instead to diversify personal holdings. New investors are brought in and the shareholder base becomes dispersed. Corporate insiders increasingly view shareholders as a remote constituency and as largely irrelevant for the company on a daily basis. By choosing to diversify, shareholders for their part agree to play a diminished role in the company's affairs. The cost of actively monitoring the performance of management swamps investment returns, so they no longer show up to annual meetings and either vote with management or throw the proxy in the wastebasket. The combination of voluntary shareholder absenteeism and strong corporate insiders creates a problem that lies at the heart of today's governance crisis. The important historical lesson is that the absentee shareholder system breeds arrogance on the part of corporate insiders. A vigorous corporate governance system is thus required to prevent shareholder rights being expropriated by insiders.

A major task of the board is to hire and fire top managers and to set their compensation. Therefore, corporate insiders come with an inherent conflict of interest when they sit on boards. Nevertheless, corporate insiders sit on boards in all major developed countries. In the United States, it is common for the chief executive officer (CEO) to also occupy the post of board chair. For the first time, the governance debate is openly questioning this tradition. Institutional shareholders and other governance activists recommend separation of the roles. In Europe, the tradition has been not to place the CEO in the chair, in some countries by statute. However, while nonexecutive members make up a clear majority of directors in the United States, there is a tradition in Europe for placing a greater portion of employees on boards. The typical defence of having insiders on boards is one of efficiency: the board requires CEO and other management input to make proper decisions. What is not explained, however, is why the CEO needs a vote on the board—let alone the chair—in order to supply the board with his or her input. It takes strong-willed character to resist the will of the CEO-chair, even for directors that meet technical criteria for independence. In today's system, the vast majority of directors sit on boards because the CEO recommended their appointment, so a certain loyalty can be expected.

weapons. Stakeholder concerns are attaining additional clout through the growth of interest in ethical or **socially responsible investing**. Such investors and ethical investment mutual funds screen and select securities based on social or environmental criteria and may utilize the services of Sustainalytics, which provides social responsibility ratings for Canadian firms based on over 200 indicators covering stakeholder issues involving community and society, customers, corporate governance, employees, environment, and human rights. Interest in socially responsible investing is growing, and assets invested according to such guidelines in Canada have increased to $600.9 billion from $503.61 billion over the 2006 through 2012 period.[13] This raises the question of the performance of socially responsible investing, and the results to date are mixed. Most studies find that socially responsible investment practices do

---

[13] Drawn from the Social Investment Organization report "Canadian Socially Responsible Investment Review 2012," http://riacanada.ca/wp-content/uploads/CSRIR-2012-English.pdf.

Research shows more generally that countries with a French civil law tradition—as opposed to British common law—rely primarily on banks to finance corporate growth. With poorly developed stock markets, and with creditors and employees having a major influence on boards, risk-taking is muted. In addition to France, civil law countries with historically small stock markets but broad-based banking systems include Germany, the countries of Scandinavia, Italy, Spain, Japan, South Korea, and China. These economies are also characterized by insider-controlled companies, corporate cross-holdings of voting stock, and pyramidal ownership structures allowing founding families to maintain control.

In contrast, countries with a common law tradition, such as the United Kingdom, the United States, English Canada, Australia, and India, have developed a greater reliance on external equity markets, resulting in a more pronounced dispersion of share ownership and a more specialized role for banks. Ultimately, international trade and the global competition for capital force a Darwinian convergence of both civil law and common law countries toward a system of corporate governance and finance that promotes maximum economic efficiency. Countries with small stock markets today must prepare these markets for the influx of future pension savings. In western countries, pension funds increasingly prefer to use broadly diversified, international stock and bond portfolios.

In his best-selling book *Economics*, Nobel laureate Paul Samuelson explains that "Takeovers, like bankruptcy, represent one of Nature's methods of eliminating deadwood." In the case of a hostile takeover bid designed to replace inefficient executives (presumably one form of "deadwood"), those very same executives sit on a board vested with powers to thwart the takeover. Are they likely to put the interests of shareholders ahead of their own? Insiders have largely succeeded in blocking the right of small shareholders to even sell their shares to someone who wants to accumulate a controlling block of stock.

A particularly effective defence is the so-called poison pill. This is typically triggered if an investor accumulates a 15 percent shareholding in the target company. When this happens, all shareholders except the 15 percent blockholder get to purchase new shares for, say, half their market value. It is equivalent to asking the blockholder to pay a dividend to all the other shareholders, financed out of the blockholder's private wealth. Boards can issue such pills without consulting shareholders, even right after receiving a hostile bid (a so-called morning-after pill).

The poison pill has proven extremely effective. Hostile takeovers, which in the period 1975 through 1985 resulted in numerous restructurings of inefficiently run companies, have come to a virtual standstill in the United States. The poison pill stands as a symbol of state-sanctioned expropriation of the fundamental shareholder right to sell shares to the highest bid. Today, no takeover can go ahead unless corporate insiders agree to remove the pill. Some boards refuse to remove the pill because it means they will lose their positions in the company. It is no accident that this legal precedent has precipitated an era of governance decline in corporate America.

B. Espen Eckbo is the Tuck Centennial Professor of Finance and founding director of the Center for Corporate Governance at the Tuck School of Business at Dartmouth College. b.espen.eckbo@dartmouth.edu. This material is excerpted with permission from B. Espen Eckbo.

not consistently affect portfolio returns and risk. While this finding raises doubts over whether corporate social responsibility translates into a financial advantage, it is at least consistent with the view that such practices do no harm: "investing for the soul may not hurt the bottom line."[14] Given the mixed evidence, major Canadian institutional investors, such as the Ontario Teachers' Pension Plan and the Ontario Municipal Employees' Retirement System, pay careful attention to corporate social responsibility in selecting investments but place financial considerations first.

---

[14] A Canadian study supporting the view that socially responsible investing does not harm returns is P. Amundson and S. R. Foerster, "Socially Responsible Investing: Better for Your Soul or Your Bottom Line?" *Canadian Investment Review* (Winter 2001), pp. 26–34. A U.S. meta-study surveying 25 published papers reached a similar conclusion: S. Rathner, "The Influence of Primary Study Characteristics on the Performance Differential between Socially Responsible and Conventional Investment Funds: A Meta-Analysis," *Journal of Business Ethics* 118 (2013), 349–363.

**CONCEPT QUESTIONS**

- What are two types of agency costs?
- How are managers bonded to shareholders?
- Can you recall some managerial goals?
- What is the set-of-contracts viewpoint?
- What is socially responsible investing?

## 1.5 FINANCIAL INSTITUTIONS, FINANCIAL MARKETS, AND THE CORPORATION

We have seen that the primary advantages of the corporate form of organization are that (1) ownership can be transferred more quickly and easily than with other forms and (2) money can be raised more readily. Both advantages are significantly enhanced by the existence of financial institutions and markets. Financial markets play an extremely important role in corporate finance.

### Financial Institutions

Financial institutions act as intermediaries between investors (funds suppliers) and firms raising funds. (Federal and provincial governments and individuals also raise funds in financial markets, but our examples will focus on firms.) Financial institutions justify their existence by providing a variety of services that promote efficient allocation of funds. Canadian financial institutions include chartered banks and other depository institutions (trust companies and credit unions) as well as non-depository institutions (investment dealers, insurance companies, pension funds, and mutual funds).[15]

Table 1.2 ranks Canada's top 10 financial institutions by total assets. They include the "Big Six" domestically owned chartered banks, one credit union (Mouvement des caisses Desjardins), two financial holding companies (Power Financial, Fairfax Financial Holdings), and one mortgage company (Canada Mortgage and Housing Corp.).

Because they are allowed to diversify by operating in all provinces, Canada's chartered banks are good sized on an international scale. Table 1.2 shows that the chartered banks also held the top slots domestically in 2013. Over time, financial holding companies offering one-stop financial shopping are gaining on the banks.

**TABLE 1.2**

### The Largest Financial Institutions in Canada, Q2–Q3 2013

|  | Rank by total assets | Assets (in $ millions) |
|---|---|---|
| Royal Bank of Canada | 1 | 851,304 |
| Toronto-Dominion Bank | 2 | 835,100 |
| Bank of Nova Scotia | 3 | 742,625 |
| Bank of Montreal | 4 | 549,331 |
| Canadian Imperial Bank of Commerce* | 5 | 397,547 |
| Canada Mortgage and Housing Corp. | 6 | 289,766 |
| Power Financial Corp.* | 7 | 264,158 |
| Mouvement des caisses Desjardins* | 8 | 204,751 |
| National Bank of Canada | 9 | 187,719 |
| Fairfax Financial Holdings Ltd.* | 10 | 36,122 |

All asset figures taken from company Q3 2013 reports, except * denotes figures taken from Q2 2013.

---

[15] Our discussion of Canadian financial institutions builds on and updates the framework in L. Kryzanowski and G. S. Roberts, "Bank Structure in Canada," in *Banking Structure in Major Countries*, ed. G. G. Kaufman (Boston: Kluwer, 1992).

FIGURE 1.6

**Two Types of Finance**

| Funds suppliers | → Deposits → | Financial intermediaries | → Loans → | Funds demanders | **Indirect finance** |

| Funds suppliers | Financial intermediaries | Funds demanders | **Direct finance** |

Chartered banks operate under federal regulation, accepting deposits from suppliers of funds and making commercial loans to mid-sized businesses, corporate loans to large companies, and personal loans and mortgages to individuals. Banks make the majority of their income from the spread between the interest paid on deposits and the higher rate earned on loans. This process is called indirect finance because banks receive funds in the form of deposits and engage in a separate lending contract with funds demanders. The top panel of Figure 1.6 illustrates indirect finance.

Chartered banks also provide other services that generate fees instead of spread income. For example, a large corporate customer seeking short-term debt funding can borrow directly from another large corporation with funds to supply through a banker's acceptance. This is an interest-bearing IOU that is stamped by a bank guaranteeing the borrower's credit. Instead of spread income, the bank receives a stamping fee. Banker's acceptances are an example of direct finance, as illustrated in the lower panel of Figure 1.6. Notice that in this case, funds do not pass through the bank's balance sheet in the form of a deposit and loan. This is often called securitization because a security (the banker's acceptance) is created.

Trust companies also accept deposits and make loans. In addition, trust companies engage in fiduciary activities—managing assets for estates, registered retirement savings plans, and so on. Banks own all the major trust companies. Like trust companies, credit unions also accept deposits and make loans.

Investment dealers are non-depository institutions that assist firms in issuing new securities in exchange for fee income. Investment dealers also aid investors in buying and selling securities. Chartered banks own majority stakes in Canada's top investment dealers.

Insurance companies include property and casualty insurance as well as health and life insurance companies. Life insurance companies make loans and accept funds in a form similar to deposits.

Pension funds invest contributions from employers and employees in securities offered by financial markets. Mutual funds pool individual investments to purchase a diversified portfolio of securities.

We base this survey of the principal activities of financial institutions on their main activities today. Recent deregulation now allows chartered banks, insurance companies, and investment dealers to engage in most activities of the others with one exception: chartered banks are not allowed to sell life insurance through their branch networks. Currently, banks sell insurance through their subsidiaries, which use a variety of permitted channels, such as the Internet. In August 2009, the Bank of Nova Scotia established a separate subsidiary, Scotia Life Financial, which then set up an office next to one of the bank branches in order to sell insurance products. The federal government intends, however, to stop banks from using the Internet to promote and sell insurance products on their websites. Although not every institution plans to become a one-stop financial supermarket, the different types of institutions will likely continue to become more alike.

Like financial institutions, financial markets differ. Principal differences concern the types of securities that are traded, how trading is conducted, and who the buyers and sellers are. Some of these differences are discussed next.

## Money versus Capital Markets

Financial markets can be classified as either money markets or capital markets. Short-term debt securities of many varieties are bought and sold in **money markets**. These short-term debt securities are often called money-market instruments. For example, a banker's acceptance represents short-term borrowing by large corporations and is a money-market instrument. Treasury bills are promissory notes of the Government of Canada. **Capital markets** are the markets for long-term debt and shares of stock, so the Toronto Stock Exchange, for example, is a capital market.

The money market is a dealer market. Generally speaking, dealers buy and sell something for themselves at their own risk. A car dealer, for example, buys and sells automobiles. In contrast, brokers and agents match buyers and sellers, but they do not actually own the commodity. A real estate agent or broker, for example, does not normally buy and sell houses.

The largest money-market dealers are chartered banks and investment dealers. Their trading facilities, along with other market participants, are connected electronically via telephone and computer so the money market has no actual physical location.

## Primary versus Secondary Markets

Financial markets function as both primary and secondary markets for debt and equity securities. The term *primary market* refers to the original sale of securities by governments and corporations. The *secondary markets* are those where these securities are bought and sold after the original sale. Equities are, of course, issued solely by corporations. Debt securities are issued by both governments and corporations. The following discussion focuses on corporate securities only.

**Primary Markets**  In a primary market transaction, the corporation is the seller and raises money through the transaction. For example, in 1999 and early 2000, many untested dot-com companies issued public shares for the first time in initial public offerings (IPOs). Corporations engage in two types of primary market transactions: public offerings and private placements. A public offering, as the name suggests, involves selling securities to the general public, while a private placement is a negotiated sale involving a specific buyer. These topics are detailed in Chapters 20 and 21, so we only introduce the bare essentials here.

Most publicly offered debt and equity securities are underwritten. In Canada, underwriting is conducted by investment dealers specializing in marketing securities. Three of Canada's largest underwriters are RBC Dominion, CIBC World Markets, and TD Securities Inc.

When a public offering is underwritten, an investment dealer or a group of investment dealers (called a *syndicate*) typically purchases the securities from the firm and markets them to the public. The underwriters hope to profit by reselling the securities to investors at a higher price than they paid the firm for them.

By law, public offerings of debt and equity must be registered with provincial authorities, the most important being the Ontario Securities Commission (OSC). Registration requires the firm to disclose a great deal of information before selling any securities. The accounting, legal, and underwriting costs of public offerings can be considerable.

Partly to avoid the various regulatory requirements and the expense of public offerings, debt and equity are often sold privately to large financial institutions such as life insurance companies and pension funds. Such private placements do not have to be registered with the OSC and do not require the involvement of underwriters.

**Secondary Markets**    A secondary market transaction involves one owner or creditor selling to another. It is therefore the secondary markets that provide the means for transferring ownership of corporate securities. There are two kinds of secondary markets: auction markets and dealer markets.

Dealer markets in stocks and long-term debt are called over-the-counter (OTC) markets. Today, like the money market, a significant fraction of the market for stocks and all of the market for long-term debt has no central location; the many dealers are connected electronically. NASDAQ in the United States is a well-known OTC market. As Table 1.3 shows, it is the second-largest stock market in the world. The name comes from the National Association of Securities Dealers (NASD), which sets up the automated quotation (AQ) system. Many smaller technology stocks are listed on NASDAQ, and the NASDAQ 100 index reflects the rise and fall of tech stocks.

**TABLE 1.3**

**The Largest Stock Markets in the World by Market Capitalization, as of June 2014**

|  | Market value (in US$ millions) | Rank in 2014 |
|---|---|---|
| NYSE | 19,178,094.2 | 1 |
| NASDAQ OMX | 6,671,959.8 | 2 |
| Japan Exchange Group—Tokyo | 4,624,443.6 | 3 |
| Euronext | 3,818,240.7 | 4 |
| Hong Kong Exchanges | 3,089,438.2 | 5 |
| Shanghai SE | 2,408,078.7 | 6 |
| TMX Group | 2,333,976.1 | 7 |
| Deutsche Börse | 1,936,332.9 | 8 |
| SIX Swiss Exchange | 1,606,591.8 | 9 |
| Shenzhen SE | 1,526,323.7 | 10 |

Source: *World Federation of Exchanges.* June 2014. http://www.world-exchanges.org/statistics/monthly-reports.

The equity shares of most large firms in Canada trade in organized auction and dealer markets. The largest stock market in Canada is the Toronto Stock Exchange (TSX). Table 1.3 shows the top 10 stock exchanges in the world in 2014. The TMX, which owns and operates the TSX, ranked seventh. Smaller exchanges in Canada include the Montreal Exchange and the TSX Venture, which consists primarily of small oil and gas, mining, IT, and biotechnology companies that do not have the market capitalization to list on the TSX.

Auction markets differ from dealer markets in two ways. First, an auction market or exchange, unlike a dealer market, has a physical location (like Bay Street or Wall Street). Second, in a dealer market, most buying and selling is done by the dealer. The primary purpose of an auction market, on the other hand, is to match those who wish to sell with those who wish to buy. Dealers play a limited role. For example, the TSX has computerized its floor trading, replacing the trading floor with a wide-area computer network. This technological shift makes the TSX a hybrid of auction and dealer markets.

## Listing

Stocks that trade on an organized exchange are said to be *listed* on that exchange. Companies seek exchange listing in order to enhance the liquidity of their shares, making them more attractive to investors by facilitating raising equity.[16] To enhance

---

[16] Two relevant studies of Canadian companies listing in the United States are S. R. Foerster and G. A. Karolyi, "The Effects of Market Segmentation and Investor Recognition on Asset Prices: Evidence from Foreign Listings in the U.S.," *Journal of Finance* 54 (June 1999), 981–1013, and U. R. Mittoo, "The Winners and Losers of Listings in the U.S.," *Canadian Investment Review* (Fall 1998), 13–17.

liquidity benefits, companies can engage in cross-listing—the act of listing on domestic and foreign exchanges—which generally provides for higher security valuations. This effect is most notably seen with foreign firms that cross-list in the United States.[17] To be listed, firms must meet certain minimum criteria concerning, for example, the number of shares and shareholders and the market value. These criteria differ for different exchanges. To be listed on the TSX, a company must have at least 1 million shares trading, at least 300 public shareholders, and a market value of $4 million. Smaller companies may list on the TSX Venture Exchange, which has less stringent requirements while offering access to the benefits of exchange listing.

Listed companies face significant disclosure requirements. Particularly relevant for Canadian companies listing in the United States is the *Sarbanes-Oxley Act* of 2002. The act, better known as "Sarbox" or "SOX," is intended to protect investors from corporate abuses. For example, one section of Sarbox prohibits personal loans from a company to its officers, such as the ones that were received by WorldCom CEO Bernie Ebbers.

Section 404 of Sarbox requires, among other things, that each company's annual report have an assessment of the company's internal control structure and financial reporting. The auditor must then evaluate and attest to management's assessment of these issues.

Sarbox contains other key requirements. For example, the officers of the corporation must review and sign the annual reports. They must explicitly declare that the annual report does not contain any false statements or material omissions, that the financial statements fairly represent the financial results, and that they are responsible for all internal controls. Finally, the annual report must list any deficiencies in internal controls. In essence, Sarbox makes company management responsible for the accuracy of the company's financial statements.

Of course, as with any law, there are compliance costs, and Sarbox has increased the cost of corporate audits, sometimes dramatically. In 2004, the average compliance cost for large firms was $4.51 million. By 2007, the average compliance cost had fallen to $1.7 million, so the burden seems to be dropping, but it is still not trivial, particularly for a smaller firm.

In Canada, governance follows a comply-or-explain regime, which requires good governance and disclosure, but does not mandate compliance with the recommendations. In June 2005, Canada introduced National Policy 58-201 and National Instrument 58-101, which enhance disclosure requirements and require firms to outline areas in which they do not comply and to explain how they plan to reach the objectives of the recommendation. Similar to the effects of Sarbox, the policies of 2005 have improved the corporate governance practices of Canadian firms and increased uniformity of compliance.[18]

In 2011, Canada moved to the IFRS accounting standards used by public enterprises in other parts of the world. This makes company financial information provided to regulators and shareholders more comparable and transparent. As a result, Canadian companies should have easier access to international capital, funding, and investment opportunities.

## Foreign Exchange Market

The **foreign exchange market** is undoubtedly the world's largest financial market. It is the market where one country's currency is traded for another's. Most of the trading

---

[17] Michael R. King and Dan Segal, "The Long-Term Effects of Cross-Listing, Investor Recognition, and Ownership Structure on Valuation," *Review of Financial Studies* 22 (2009), 2393–2421.

[18] Additional readings: K. MacAulay, S. Dutta, M. Oxner, and T. Hynes, "The Impact of a Change in Corporate Governance Regulations on Firms in Canada," *Quarterly Journal of Finance and Accounting* 48:4 (2009), 29–52.

takes place in a few currencies: the U.S. dollar ($), the euro (€), the British pound sterling (£), the Japanese yen (¥), and the Swiss franc (SF).

The foreign exchange market is an OTC market. There is no single location where traders get together. Instead, traders are located in the major commercial and investment banks around the world. They communicate using computer terminals, telephones, and other telecommunication devices. One element in the communications network for foreign transactions is the Society for Worldwide Interbank Financial Telecommunications (SWIFT), a Belgian not-for-profit cooperative. A bank in Toronto can send messages to a bank in London via SWIFT's regional processing centres. The connections are through data-transmission lines.

The many different types of participants in the foreign exchange market include the following:

1. Importers converting their domestic currency to foreign currency to pay for goods from foreign countries.
2. Exporters receiving foreign currency and wanting to convert to the domestic currency.
3. Portfolio managers buying and selling foreign stocks and bonds.
4. Foreign exchange brokers matching buy and sell orders.
5. Traders making the market in foreign exchange.

*CONCEPT*
*QUESTIONS*
- Distinguish between money markets and capital markets.
- What is listing?
- What is the difference between a primary market and a secondary market?
- What are the principal types of financial institutions in Canada? What is the principal role of each?
- What are direct and indirect finance? How do they differ?
- What is a dealer market? How do dealer and auction markets differ?
- What is the largest auction market in Canada?

## 1.6   TRENDS IN FINANCIAL MARKETS AND MANAGEMENT

Like all markets, financial markets are experiencing rapid globalization. At the same time, interest rates, foreign exchange rates, and other macroeconomic variables have become more volatile. The toolkit of available financial management techniques has expanded rapidly in response to a need to control increased risk from volatility and to track complexities arising from dealings in many countries. Improved computer technology makes new financial engineering applications practical.

When financial managers or investment dealers design new securities or financial processes, their efforts are referred to as financial engineering. Successful financial engineering reduces and controls risk and minimizes taxes. Financial engineering creates a variety of debt securities and reinforces the trend toward securitization of credit introduced earlier. In addition, options and option-like securities are becoming important in risk management.

Financial engineering also seeks to reduce financing costs of issuing securities as well as the costs of complying with rules laid down by regulatory authorities. An example is the Short Form Prospectus Distribution (SFPD) system, which allows firms that frequently issue new equity to bypass repetitive OSC registration requirements.

In addition to financial engineering, advances in computer technology also create opportunities to combine different types of financial institutions to take advantage of economies of scale and scope. Large institutions operate in all provinces and

# IN THEIR OWN WORDS

## Maria Strömqvist on hedge funds and the financial crisis of 2008*

"Hedge fund" is a collective term for different types of investment funds. A common feature of these funds is the absolute earnings target; that is, targets for earnings are set irrespective of developments on, for example, the stock exchange. Hedge funds are primarily intended for institutional investors and financially strong private individuals. Many hedge funds protect their investments against losses (so-called hedging), although this does not apply to all funds. Instead, hedge funds use a wide range of investment strategies that are more dynamic, when compared to strategies used by traditional funds. This is possible because hedge funds are governed by a more liberal regulatory framework that permits both long and short positions and the use of derivatives. Hedge funds can also have a high level of leverage, which can provide a higher return on the capital invested.

Over the last ten years, the hedge fund market has grown dramatically. In 1996, the roughly 2,000 hedge funds around the world managed a total of approximately US$135 billion. By the end of 2007, a total of 10,000 hedge funds managed US$2,000 billion.

### Hedge funds in the current financial crisis
Since the emergence and growth of hedge funds, there has been recurring discussion of the role they play in financial crises. Even though the course of events in the crises of the 1990s and 2000s were very different, criticisms of hedge funds have tended to be the same: that a highly leveraged hedge fund or group of hedge funds could have a strong impact on prices on the financial markets by launching speculative attacks on certain companies, sectors, or currencies. This effect may be reinforced if the speculation of the funds generates herd behaviour among investors. The

hedge funds have also been accused of manipulating asset prices and contributing to the development of financial bubbles.

The discussion about hedge funds and financial crises has, nevertheless, arisen once again during the current period of turbulence on the financial markets. The question is, what has the role of the hedge funds been in the current crisis so far? While hedge funds have generally coped well in times of financial crisis, we could, simplifying somewhat, say that the hedge funds have been more affected by the present financial crisis than they have affected it. The main argument for this is that hedge funds have experienced more problems in handling this financial crisis than they have previous ones.

### Broad decline for hedge funds
Between October 2007 and June 2008, the hedge funds had more stable and thus better development than did share prices. Thereafter, both the hedge fund index and the share index declined, although the fall was greater for the share index.

The negative development of the hedge funds during the latter part of 2008 cannot be related to a particular investment strategy. In this respect, the current course of events on the hedge fund market differs from the situation during the Asian crisis when it was mainly funds focusing on developing markets that suffered. According to the Barclay's database on hedge funds, as many as 89 percent of the hedge funds had a negative return in September 2008.

### Changes to the regulations
A unique feature of the current crisis was the decision to prohibit short selling made by the authorities

internationally, enjoying more lax regulations in some jurisdictions than in others. Financial institutions pressure authorities to deregulate in a push-pull process called the regulatory dialectic.

Another trend underlying the global financial crisis that began in 2007 was excessive financial leverage. Following the technology bubble and the attacks of September 11, 2001, the United States Federal Reserve looked to aggressively lower interest rates in order to restore confidence in the economy. In the United States, individuals with poor credit ratings, known as subprime borrowers, obtained money to purchase houses during this period of historically low interest rates. At the same time, investors reacted to these low rates by seeking higher returns. The financial industry responded by manufacturing subprime mortgages and asset-backed securities. Once housing prices began to cool and interest rates to rise, subprime borrowers began defaulting on their loans and the collapse of the subprime market ensued. With mortgages serving in several countries (including the United States and the United Kingdom) and implemented in September of 2008. The decision to prohibit short selling (primarily of shares in financial companies) affected different investment strategies to different degrees. There was a major negative impact on those in which short selling was a natural strategy component, or where there was a high level of exposure to the financial sector. The ban affected hedge funds more than mutual funds, because hedge funds use short selling to a greater extent.

A ban on short selling in a falling market makes it more difficult to use strategies that reinforce negative market movements, as was the aim of the ban. However, in the autumn of 2008, the ban on short selling also made it more difficult to protect long positions through short positions and to use certain arbitrage strategies.

**Broad decline in asset values**
Under normal circumstances, hedge funds receive premiums for assuming credit risk, duration risk, and liquidity risk. These risk premiums normally constitute a large part of the hedge funds' profits. In the current financial crisis, however, higher risk-taking has not led to higher profits for the hedge funds, but rather the opposite. The downturn in the autumn of 2008 that hit many different types of assets and many markets at once meant that all these premium profits disappeared at the same time. The increased risk premiums could simply not compensate for the losses of the hedge funds.

Many hedge funds generated considerable profits in the period 2001–03 by diversifying their portfolios

to include property or commodities. In the current financial crisis, however, investors have been less willing to take risks and have reduced the degree of leverage in their portfolios by selling assets. This has pushed down the prices of almost all types of asset, including commodities and property, which has weakened the positive effects of diversification in the hedge funds' portfolios.

It appears that the hedge funds have found it difficult to predict the current downturn in asset values. Unlike, for example, the IT bubble in 2000, when there were historically high values for a certain type of asset, this time it is not a question of the price correction of a single market. Many funds were taken by surprise by the dramatic fall in share prices.

The current crisis is also characterized by an extreme volatility in the prices of both shares and commodities. This has made it more difficult to predict future movements in asset values. For example, many hedge funds that had invested in a negative stock market trend and high commodity prices experienced problems in July 2008 when the trend suddenly reversed, with a considerable increase in share prices and a considerable fall in commodity prices.

In addition, unlike previous crises, the present financial crisis is rooted in a bank crisis. The banks' problems have had a direct impact on the hedge funds in the form of more restrictive lending, higher borrowing costs, and assets tied up in connection with bankruptcies (e.g., Lehman Brothers). The funds have, therefore, been forced to sell off assets in a falling market, and this has had a negative effect on their earnings.

\* All instances of "the current crisis" and the like in Maria Strömqvist's comments refer to the 2007–09 financial crisis.

Maria Strömqvist works in the Financial Stability Department of Sveriges Riksbank. Her comments are excerpted from the bank's Economic Commentaries, NO. 3, 2009 with permission.

© Sveriges Riksbank

as the underlying asset supporting much of the financial instruments that investment banks, institutions, and retail buyers had acquired, these assets lost most of their value, and hundreds of billions of dollars of write-downs and bank bailouts followed.

Canada faced much the same external environment in the lead-up to the crisis as did the United States. But despite the financial and economic integration of the two countries, Canada did not experience a single bank failure or bailout. The difference was that a highly stable branch banking system dominated by six large institutions forms the heart of Canada's financial system. Banks dominate lending and credit creation nationally and account for over 60 percent of total financial assets in Canada.[19]

---

[19] D. J. S. Brean, L. Kryzanowski, and G. S. Roberts, "Canada and the United States: Different Roots, Different Routes to Financial Sector Regulation," *Business History*, 53:2 (2011), 249–269.

The results of the financial crisis were the worst global economic recession since the Great Depression of the 1930s and the European sovereign debt crisis, in which many countries in the European Union were hard put to service their debt. To combat the recession, the U.S. Federal Reserve (Fed) practised quantitative easing—the practice of buying bonds to expand the money supply to keep liquidity plentiful in the U.S. economy and interest rates artificially low. The Bank of Canada and other central banks followed similar policies. Low interest rates resulted in higher bond prices, and stock prices were also higher as funds moved out of bonds into higher-earning stocks. At the time of writing in early 2014, the Fed was planning to start tapering off quantitative easing as the U.S. economy recovered.[20]

These trends have made financial management a much more complex and technical activity. For this reason, many business students find introductory finance one of their most challenging subjects. The trends we reviewed have also increased the stakes. In the face of increased competition globally, the payoff for good financial management is great. The finance function is also becoming important in corporate strategic planning. The good news is that career opportunities (and compensation) in financial positions are highly competitive.

 **CONCEPT QUESTION**
- How do key trends in financial markets affect Canadian financial institutions?

# 1.7    OUTLINE OF THE TEXT

Now that we have taken a quick tour through all of corporate finance, we can take a closer look at this book. The book is divided into eight parts. The long-term investment decision is covered first. Financing decisions and working capital are covered next. Finally, a series of special topics is covered. Here are the eight parts:

| | |
|---|---|
| Part I: | Overview |
| Part II: | Value and Capital Budgeting |
| Part III: | Risk |
| Part IV: | Capital Structure and Dividend Policy |
| Part V: | Long-Term Financing |
| Part VI: | Options, Futures, and Corporate Finance |
| Part VII: | Financial Planning and Short-Term Finance |
| Part VIII: | Special Topics |

Part II describes how investment opportunities are valued in financial markets. This part contains the basic theory. Because finance is a subject that builds understanding from the ground up, this material is very important. The most important concept in Part II is net present value (NPV). We develop the NPV rule into a tool for valuing investment alternatives. We discuss general formulas and apply them to a variety of financial instruments.

Part III introduces basic measures of risk. The capital asset pricing model (CAPM) and the arbitrage pricing theory (APT) are used to devise methods for incorporating risk in valuation. As part of this discussion, we describe the famous beta coefficient. Finally, we use the preceding pricing models to handle capital budgeting under risk.

---

[20] Additional readings: A. R. Sorkin, *Too Big to Fail: The Inside Story of How Wall Street and Washington Fought to Save the Financial System—and Themselves* (New York: Viking Press, 2009); G. Soros, *The New Paradigm for Financial Markets: The Credit Crisis of 2008 and What It Means* (New York: Public Affairs, 2008); P. Krugman, *The Return of Depression Economics and the Crisis of 2008* (New York: W.W. Norton & Company, 2009).

Part IV examines two interrelated topics: capital structure and dividend policy. Capital structure is the extent to which the firm relies on debt. It cannot be separated from the amount of cash dividends the firm decides to pay out to its equity shareholders.

Part V concerns long-term financing. We describe the securities that corporations issue to raise cash, as well as the mechanics of offering securities for public sale. Here we discuss call provisions and leasing.

Part VI covers options and futures and their use in risk management. We introduce these derivatives and show how understanding the underlying concepts opens up new insights into corporate finance. Next, we focus on warrants and convertibles—two important kinds of corporate securities with options embedded in them. In the final chapter in this section, we introduce the important topic of risk management.

Part VII is devoted to short-term finance. We focus on managing the firm's current assets and current liabilities. We describe aspects of the firm's short-term financial management. Separate chapters on cash management and credit management are included.

Part VIII covers three important special topics: mergers, financial distress, and international corporate finance.

## 1.8

# SUMMARY AND CONCLUSIONS

Besides introducing you to the basic ideas of corporate finance, the chapter covers several important topics:

1. The effect of financing decisions, such as the issuance of debt and equity, on the value of the firm.
2. The ways in which financial managers can create value for the firm.
3. The different types of firms, such as sole proprietorships, partnerships, income trusts, and corporations.
4. The role of financial markets in corporate finance.
5. The classification of financial markets as either money markets or capital markets.
6. The latest trends in the financial markets.

**KEY TERMS**

| | | |
|---|---|---|
| Agency costs   13 | Corporation   11 | Set-of-contracts |
| Capital budgeting   3 | Foreign exchange |   viewpoint   13 |
| Capital gains   31 |   market   22 | Socially responsible |
| Capital markets   20 | Money markets   20 |   investing   16 |
| Capital structure   3 | Net working capital   3 | Sole proprietorship   9 |
| Contingent claims   9 | Partnership   10 | |

**QUESTIONS & PROBLEMS**

1.1   Can our goal of maximizing the value of the shareholders' wealth conflict with other goals, such as avoiding unethical or illegal behaviour? In particular, do you think that topics such as customer and employee safety, the environment, and the general good of society fit into this framework? Think of some specific scenarios to illustrate your answer.

1.2 Who owns a corporation? Describe the process whereby the owners control the firm's management. What is the main reason that an agency relationship exists in the corporate form of organization? In this context, what kinds of problems can arise?

1.3 Corporate ownership varies around the world. Historically, individuals have owned the majority of shares in public corporations in the United States. In Canada this is also the case, but ownership is more often concentrated in the hands of a majority shareholder. In Germany and Japan, banks, other financial institutions, and large companies own most of the shares in public corporations. How do you think these ownership differences affect the severity of agency costs in different countries?

1.4 What are the major types of financial institutions and financial markets in Canada?

1.5 What are some major trends in Canadian financial markets? Explain how these trends affect the practice of financial management in Canada.

---

# Taxes

Taxes are very important, since cash flows are measured after taxes. In this section, we examine corporate and personal tax rates and how taxes are calculated. We apply this knowledge to see how different types of income are taxed in the hands of individuals and corporations.

The size of the tax bill is determined through tax laws and regulations in the annual budgets of the federal government (administered by the Canada Revenue Agency) and provincial governments. If the various rules of taxation seem a little bizarre or convoluted to you, keep in mind that tax law is the result of political as well as economic forces. The tax law is continuously evolving, so our discussion cannot make you a tax expert. Rather, it will give you an understanding of the tax principles important for financial management, along with the ability to ask the right questions when consulting a tax expert.

## Individual Tax Rates

Individual tax rates in effect for federal taxes and provincial and territorial taxes for 2014 are shown in Table 1A.1. These rates apply to income from employment (wages and salary) and from unincorporated businesses. Investment income is also taxable. Interest income is taxed at the same rates as employment income, but special provisions reduce the taxes payable on dividends and capital gains. We discuss these in detail later in the appendix.

In making financial decisions, it is frequently important to distinguish between average and marginal tax rates. The percentage rates shown in Table 1A.1 are all marginal rates.

To illustrate, suppose you live in British Columbia and have a taxable income of $120,000. Your tax on the next dollar is[21]

$$40.7\% = \text{Federal tax rate} + \text{Provincial tax rate} = 26\% + 14.7\%$$

Tax rates vary somewhat across provinces. For example, in Quebec the same taxable income faces tax on the next dollar at 51.75 percent.

With the exception of Quebec residents, taxpayers file one tax return. In computing your tax in Quebec, you first find the federal tax and then calculate the provincial tax as a percentage of the federal tax.

---

[21] Actual rates for 2014 are somewhat higher as we ignore surtaxes that apply in higher brackets.

**TABLE 1A.1**

## Individual Income Tax Rates, 2014

| | Tax Rate | Tax Bracket | Surtax Rate | Surtax Threshold | | Tax Rate | Tax Bracket | Surtax Rate | Surtax Threshold |
|---|---|---|---|---|---|---|---|---|---|
| Federal[1] | 15.00% | Up to $43,953 | | | New Brunswick[4] | 9.68% | Up to $39,305 | | |
| | 22.00 | 43,954–87,907 | | | | 14.82% | 39,306–78,609 | | |
| | 26.00 | 87,908–136,270 | | | | 16.52% | 78,610–127,802 | | |
| | 29.00 | 136,271 and over | | | | 17.84% | 127,803 and over | | |
| British Columbia[2,3] | 5.06% | Up to $37,606 | | | Nova Scotia[5] | 8.79% | Up to $29,590 | | |
| | 7.70 | 37,607–75,213 | | | | 14.95 | 29,591–59,180 | | |
| | 10.50 | 75,214–86,354 | | | | 16.67 | 59,181–93,000 | | |
| | 12.29 | 86,355–104,858 | | | | 17.50 | 93,001–150,000 | | |
| | 14.70 | 104,859–150,000 | | | | 21.00 | 150,001 and over | | |
| | 16.80 | 150,001 and over | | | Prince Edward Island[5] | 9.80% | Up to $31,984 | | |
| Alberta | 10.00% | All income | | | | 13.80 | 31,985–63,969 | | |
| Saskatchewan[4] | 11.00% | Up to $43,292 | | | | 16.70 | 63,970 and over | 10% | $12,500 |
| | 13.00 | 43,293–123,692 | | | Newfoundland and Labrador[9] | 7.70% | Up to $34,254 | | |
| | 15.00 | 123,693 and over | | | | 12.50 | 34,255–68,508 | | |
| Manitoba[5] | 10.80% | Up to $31,000 | | | | 13.30 | 68,509 and over | | |
| | 12.75 | 31,001–67,000 | | | Yukon[4] | 7.04% | Up to $43,953 | | |
| | 17.40 | 67,001 and over | | | | 9.68 | 43,954–87,907 | | |
| Ontario[6] | 5.05% | Up to $40,120 | | | | 11.44 | 87,908–136,270 | | |
| | 9.15 | 40,121–80,242 | 20% | $4,331 | | 12.76 | 136,271 and over | 5% | $6,000 |
| | 11.16 | 80,243–150,000 | 36 | 5,543 | Northwest Territories[4] | 5.90% | Up to $39,808 | | |
| | 12.16 | 150,001–220,000 | | | | 8.60 | 39,809–79,618 | | |
| | 13.16 | 220,001 and over | | | | 12.20 | 79,619–129,441 | | |
| Quebec[7] | 16.00% | Up to $41,495 | | | | 14.05 | 129,442 and over | | |
| | 20.00 | 41,496–82,985 | | | Nunavut[4] | 4.00% | Up to $41,909 | | |
| | 24.00 | 82,986–100,970 | | | | 7.00 | 41,910–83,818 | | |
| | 25.75 | 100,971 and over | | | | 9.00 | 83,819–136,270 | | |
| | | | | | | 11.50 | 136,271 and over | | |

Source: © 2014 KPMG LLP, a Canadian limited liability partnership and a member firm of the KPMG network of independent member firms affiliated with KPMG International Cooperative ("KPMG International"), a Swiss entity. All rights reserved.

**Notes:**

(1) The federal tax brackets are indexed each year by a calculated inflation factor, which is based on the change in the average federal inflation rate over the 12-month period ending September 30 of the previous year compared to the change in the rate for the same period of the year prior to that. The federal inflation factor is 0.9% for 2014.

(2) British Columbia indexes its tax brackets using the same formula as that used federally, but uses the provincial inflation rate rather than the federal rate in the calculation. The province's inflation factor is 0.1% for 2014. Residents of British Columbia are also required to make monthly payments under the province's Medical Services Plan.

(3) British Columbia introduced a new temporary sixth bracket effective January 1, 2014, for individuals earning more than $150,000 in a taxation year. The new bracket has a tax rate of 16.80%. This two-year temporary measure will expire December 31, 2015.

(4) Saskatchewan, New Brunswick, and the territories (Northwest Territories, Nunavut, and Yukon) index their tax brackets using the same formula as that used federally. The inflation factor is 0.9% for 2014.

(5) Manitoba, Nova Scotia, and Prince Edward Island do not index their tax brackets or surtax thresholds.

(6) Ontario indexes its tax brackets and surtax thresholds using the same formula as that used federally but uses the provincial inflation rate rather than the federal rate in the calculation. The province's inflation factor is 1.0% for 2014. Ontario resident individuals with taxable income over $20,000 are also required to pay a Health Premium each year.

(7) The 2014 Ontario budget proposed to create a new personal income tax bracket effective January 1, 2014, for taxable income between $150,000 and $220,000. This new bracket would have a tax rate of 12.16%. The budget also proposed to lower the taxable income threshold for the 13.16% tax rate from $514,090 to $220,000 effective January 1, 2014. The new income thresholds would not be indexed each year.

(8) Quebec indexes its tax brackets using the same formula as that used federally but uses the provincial inflation rate, excluding changes in liquor and tobacco taxes, rather than the federal rate in the calculation. The province's inflation factor is 0.97% for 2014. Residents of Quebec are required to pay a health contribution and to make payments to the province's Health Services Fund.

(9) Newfoundland and Labrador indexes its tax brackets using the same formula as that used federally, but uses the applicable provincial inflation rate rather than the federal rate in the calculation. Newfoundland and Labrador's inflation factor is 1.5% for 2014.

## Taxes on Investment Income

A dividend tax credit provides a degree of integration between corporate and individual taxation. This credit applies only to dividends paid by Canadian corporations. The result is to encourage Canadian investors to invest in Canadian companies as opposed to foreign ones.[22]

To see how dividends are taxed, we start with common shares held by individual investors. Table 1A.2 shows how the dividend tax credit reduces the effective tax rate on dividends for investors in the top federal tax bracket. The steps follow the instructions on federal tax returns. Actual dividends are grossed up by 38 percent, and federal tax is calculated on the grossed-up figure. A dividend tax credit of 15.0198 percent of the actual dividend is subtracted from the federal tax to get the federal tax payable. The provincial tax (for Ontario in this example) is calculated and added. Note that each province has its own dividend tax credit.

**TABLE 1A.2**

### Investment Income Tax Treatment for Ontario Residents in Top Bracket (over $220,001) for 2014

| | |
|---|---|
| **Interest Tax Treatment** | |
| Interest | $1,000.00 |
| Federal tax at 29% | 290.00 |
| Provincial tax at 13.16% | 131.60 |
| Total tax | $ 421.60 |
| **Capital Gains Tax Treatment** | |
| Capital gains | $1,000.00 |
| Taxable capital gains (50% × $1,000) | 500.00 |
| Federal tax at 29% | 145.00 |
| Provincial tax at 13.16% | 65.80 |
| Total tax | $ 210.80 |
| **Dividend Tax Treatment (Eligible Dividends)** | |
| Dividends | $1,000.00 |
| Gross up at 38% | 380.00 |
| Grossed-up dividend | 1380.00 |
| Federal tax at 29% | 400.20 |
| Less dividend tax credit (15.0198% × $1,380)* | 207.27 |
| Federal tax payable | $ 192.93 |
| Provincial tax at 13.16% (13.16% × $1,380) | $ 181.61 |
| Less dividend tax credit (6.4% × $1,380)* | 88.32 |
| Provincial tax payable | $ 93.29 |
| Total tax | $ 286.22 |

*The federal and provincial dividend tax credit calculations are based on 2013 credit rates. We refrain from using 2014 dividend tax credit rates because these rates are still subject to legislative approval.

Source: Adapted from 2013–2014 KPMG Tax Rate Publication and CRA and Government of Ontario websites.

*Ontario Ministry of Finance.* July 2014. http://www.fin.gov.on.ca/en/credit/dtc/.

*Canada Revenue Agency.* March 2013. http://www.cra-arc.gc.ca/gncy/bdgt/2013/qa04-eng.html.

---

[22] Evidence that the dividend tax credit causes investors to favour Canadian stocks is provided in L. Booth, "The Dividend Tax Credit and Canadian Ownership Objectives," *Canadian Journal of Economics* 20 (May 1987).

Individual Canadian investors also benefit from a tax reduction for **capital gains**. Capital gains arise when an investment increases in value above its purchase price. Only half of capital gains are taxable.

Additionally, capital gains are lightly taxed since individuals only pay taxes on realized capital gains when shares are sold. Since many individuals hold shares for a long time (have unrealized capital gains), the time value of money dramatically reduces the effective tax rate on capital gains.

## Corporate Taxes

Canadian corporations are subject to corporate taxes levied by the federal and provincial governments. Table 1A.3 shows corporate tax rates using Ontario as an example. You can see from the table that small corporations (income under $500,000) and, to a lesser degree, manufacturing and processing companies pay tax at lower rates.

**TABLE 1A.3**

**Corporate Tax Rates in Percentages, 2014**

|  | Federal | Ontario | Combined |
|---|---|---|---|
| Basic corporations | 15% | 11.50% | 26.5% |
| All small corporations with a taxable income less than $500,000 | 11% | 4.50% | 15.5% |

Source: Adapted from Canada Revenue Agency, "Corporation Tax Rates," March 2014. Available at http://www.cra-arc.gc.ca/tx/bsnss/tpcs/crprtns/rts-eng.html.

Comparing the rates in Table 1A.3 with the personal tax rates in Table 1A.1 appears to reveal a tax advantage for small businesses and professionals in forming a corporation. The tax rate on corporate income of, say, $150,000 is less than the personal tax rate assessed on income of unincorporated businesses. But this is oversimplified because dividends paid to the owners are also taxed, as we saw earlier.

## Taxable Income

Interest and dividends are treated differently in calculating corporate tax. Interest paid is deducted from EBIT (earnings before interest and taxes) in calculating taxable income, but dividends paid are not. Because interest is a tax-deductible expense, debt financing has a tax advantage over financing with common stock.

The tables are turned when we contrast interest and dividends earned by the firm. Interest earned is fully taxable, just like any other form of ordinary income. Dividends on common and preferred shares received from other Canadian corporations qualify for a 100 percent exemption and are received tax free.[23]

## Capital Gain, Carryforward, and Carryback

If a firm disposes of an asset for more than it paid originally, the difference is a capital gain. As with individuals, firms' capital gains are taxed at 50 percent of the tax rate.

When calculating capital gains for tax purposes, a firm nets out all capital losses in the same year. If capital losses exceed capital gains, the net capital loss may be carried back to reduce taxable income in the three prior years. Any capital losses remaining may be carried forward indefinitely. Under the carryback feature, a firm files a revised tax return and receives a refund of prior years' taxes.

A similar carryback and carryforward provision applies to operating losses. In this case, the carryback period is three years and carryforward is allowed for up to twenty years.

---

[23] We ignore refundable taxes on dividends here and discuss them in Chapter 19.

Investment Tax Credits

An investment tax credit applies in certain regions of the country—currently Atlantic Canada but applied more broadly in past years. An investment tax credit allows a qualified firm to subtract a set percentage of an investment directly from taxes payable.

QUESTIONS & PROBLEMS

1A.1    Distinguish between an average tax rate and a marginal tax rate.

1A.2    How does tax treatment of investment income differ among interest, dividends, and capital gains?

1A.3    Explain how carryback/carryforward provisions and investment tax credits reduce corporate taxes.

**Marginal versus Average Tax Rates**

1A.4    (Refer to Table 1A.3.) Corporation X has $100,000 in taxable income, and Corporation Y, a manufacturer, has $1 million in taxable income.
    *a.* What is the tax bill for each firm in Ontario?
    *b.* Suppose both firms have identified a new project that will increase taxable income by $10,000. How much in additional taxes will each firm pay? Why aren't these amounts the same?

**Taxes on Investment Income**

1A.5    Mary Song, a Toronto investor, receives $10,000 in dividends from B.C. Forest Products shares, $10,000 in interest from a deposit in a chartered bank, and a $10,000 capital gain from selling Central B.C. Mines shares. Use the information in Table 1A.2 to calculate the after-tax cash flow from each investment.

APPENDIX **1B**

# Finance Professional Careers

To access Appendix 1B, go to Connect.

# CHAPTER

# Accounting Statements and Cash Flow

EXECUTIVE SUMMARY

Chapter 2 describes the basic accounting statements used for reporting corporate activity. It focuses on practical details of cash flow. It will become clear in the next several chapters that knowing how to determine cash flow helps the financial manager make better decisions. The increasing number of corporate accounting scandals involving companies such as Hollinger, Tyco, and Adelphia has highlighted the importance of accurate financial reporting. Students who have taken accounting courses will not find the material new and can think of it as a review with an emphasis on finance. We discuss cash flow in more detail in later chapters.

## 2.1 THE STATEMENT OF FINANCIAL POSITION

The **statement of financial position** is an accountant's snapshot of the firm's accounting value on a particular date, as though the firm momentarily stood still.[1] The statement of financial position has two sides: on the left are the *assets* and on the right the *liabilities* and *shareholders' equity*. The statement of financial position states what the firm owns and how it is financed. The following accounting definition underlies the statement and describes the balance as

$$\text{Assets} \equiv \text{Liabilities} + \text{Shareholders' equity}$$

We have put a three-line equality in the equation to indicate that it must always hold, by definition. In fact, the shareholders' equity is defined to be the difference between the assets and the liabilities of the firm. In principle, equity is what the shareholders would have remaining after the firm discharged its obligations.

Table 2.1 gives the 2014 and 2015 statement of financial position for the fictitious Canadian Composite Corporation. The assets are listed in order by the length of time it normally takes a going concern to convert them to cash. The asset side depends on the nature of the business and how management chooses to conduct it. Management must make decisions about cash versus marketable securities, credit versus cash sales, whether to make or buy commodities, whether to lease or purchase items, the types of business in which to engage, and so on. The liabilities and the shareholders' equity are listed in the order in which they must be paid.

The liabilities and shareholders' equity side reflects the types and proportions of financing, which depend on management's choice of capital structure, as between debt and equity and between current debt and long-term debt.

When analyzing the statement of financial position, the financial manager should be aware of three accounting measures: liquidity, debt versus equity, and value versus cost.

---

[1] For all purposes, the statement of financial position and the balance sheet are one and the same. The terminology shifted from "balance sheet" to "statement of financial position" with the adoption of IFRS. Accordingly, we use the terms interchangeably throughout the chapter.

TABLE 2.1

### Statement of Financial Position of the Canadian Composite Corporation

CANADIAN COMPOSITE CORPORATION
Statement of Financial Position
2014 and 2015
(in $ millions)

| Assets | 2015 | 2014 | Liabilities (debt) and shareholders' equity | 2015 | 2014 |
|---|---|---|---|---|---|
| Current assets: | | | Current liabilities: | | |
| Cash and equivalents | $ 140 | $ 107 | Accounts payable | $ 213 | $ 197 |
| Accounts receivable | 294 | 270 | Notes payable | 50 | 53 |
| Inventories | 269 | 280 | Accrued expenses | 223 | 205 |
| Other | 58 | 50 | Total current liabilities | 486 | 455 |
| Total current assets | 761 | 707 | | | |
| | | | Long-term liabilities: | | |
| | | | Deferred taxes | 117 | 104 |
| Long-term assets: | | | Long-term debt | 471 | 458 |
| Property, plant, and equipment | 1,423 | 1,274 | Total long-term liabilities | 588 | 562 |
| Less accumulated depreciation | −550 | −460 | | | |
| Net property, plant, and equipment | 873 | 814 | Shareholders' equity: | | |
| Intangible assets and others | 245 | 221 | Preferred shares | 39 | 39 |
| | | | Common shares | 376 | 339 |
| Total long-term assets | 1,118 | 1,035 | Accumulated retained earnings | 390 | 347 |
| | | | Total equity | 805 | 725 |
| Total assets | $1,879 | $1,742 | Total liabilities and shareholders' equity | $1,879 | $1,742 |

## Liquidity

Liquidity refers to the ease and speed with which assets can be converted to cash. Current assets are the most liquid and include cash and those assets that can reasonably be expected to be turned into cash within a year from the date of the balance sheet. Accounts receivable are the amounts not yet collected from customers for goods or services sold to them (after adjustment for potential bad debts). Inventory is composed of raw materials to be used in production, work in process, and finished goods. Long-term assets are the least liquid kind of asset. Tangible long-term assets include property, plant, and equipment. These assets do not convert to cash from normal business activity, and they are not usually used to pay expenses, such as payroll.

Some long-term assets are not tangible. Intangible assets have no physical existence but can be very valuable. Examples of intangible assets are the value of a trademark, the value of a patent, and the value of customer recognition. The more liquid a firm's assets, the less likely the firm is to experience problems meeting short-term obligations. Thus, the probability that a firm will avoid financial distress can be linked to its liquidity. Unfortunately, liquid assets frequently have lower rates of return than long-term assets; for example, cash generates no investment income. To the extent a firm invests in liquid assets, it sacrifices an opportunity to invest in more profitable investment vehicles. In the credit crisis of 2008–09, liquidity diminished significantly, aggravating the collapse of the market.

## Debt versus Equity

*Liabilities* are obligations of the firm that require a payout of cash within a stipulated time period. Many liabilities involve contractual obligations to repay a stated amount with interest over a period. Thus, liabilities are debts and are frequently associated with nominally fixed cash burdens, called *debt service*, that put the firm in default of a contract if they are not paid. *Shareholders' equity* is a claim against the firm's assets that is residual and not fixed. In general terms, when the firm borrows, it gives the bond-holders first claim on the firm's cash flow.[2] Bondholders can sue if the firm defaults on its bond contracts. This may lead the firm to declare itself bankrupt. Shareholders' equity is the residual difference between assets and liabilities:

$$\text{Assets} - \text{Liabilities} = \text{Shareholders' equity}$$

This is the shareholders' share in the firm stated in accounting terms. The accounting value of shareholders' equity increases when retained earnings are added. This occurs when the firm retains part of its earnings instead of paying them out as dividends.

## Value versus Cost

The accounting value of a firm's assets is frequently referred to as the *carrying value* or the *book value* of the assets.[3] In 2011, publicly traded firms in Canada switched to **International Financial Reporting Standards (IFRS)**. Like GAAP, IFRS allows companies to use the historical cost method; it also allows use of the revaluation (fair value) method. When a company adopts the revaluation method, all items in a class of assets should be revalued simultaneously, and the revaluation should be performed with enough regularity to ensure that at the balance-sheet date, the carrying amount is not materially different from the fair value amount. Thus, a class of property, plant, and equipment with significant unpredictable changes in fair value will require more frequent revaluations (every one or two years) than will another class of asset that has insignificant changes in fair value (e.g., a building may only require revaluation every three to five years).

*Market value* is the price at which willing buyers and sellers trade the assets. Management's job is to create a value for the firm that is higher than its cost. When market values are considerably below book values, it is customary accounting practice to write down assets. For example, in February 2009, CTVglobemedia Inc., a multimedia company, took a massive $1.7 billion write-down as a result of a plunge in advertising revenues from Canadian subsidiaries of foreign multinationals and the fact that other large clients were on the verge of bankruptcy.[4] Sometimes, huge write-offs are also indicative of overstated profits in previous years, as assets were not depreciated properly.

There are many users of a firm's statement of financial position, and each may seek different information from it. A banker may look at the statement for evidence of liquidity and working capital. A supplier may also note the size of accounts payable, which reflects the general promptness of payments. Many users of financial statements, including managers and investors, want to know the value of the firm, not its cost. This is not found on the statement of financial position. In fact, many of a firm's true resources (good management, proprietary assets, and so on) do not appear on it. Henceforth, whenever we speak of the value of an asset or the value of the firm, we will normally mean its market value. So, for example, when we say the goal of the financial manager is to increase the value of the share, we mean the market value of the share.

---

[2] Bondholders are investors in the firm's debt. They are creditors of the firm. In this discussion, the term *bondholder* means the same thing as *creditor*.

[3] Confusion often arises because many financial accounting terms have the same meaning. This presents a problem with jargon for the reader of financial statements. For example, the following terms usually refer to the same thing: *assets minus liabilities*, *net worth*, *shareholders' equity*, *owner's equity*, and *equity capitalization*.

[4] G. Surridge, "CTVglobemedia takes $1.7B write-down on TV properties," *Canwest News Services*, February 28, 2009, http://www2.canada.com/saskatoonstarphoenix/news/story.html?id=b6b38987-8fb0-4a4c-ad5b-c308bfc9eca0.

**CONCEPT QUESTIONS**
• What is the statement of financial position (balance-sheet) equation?
• What three things should be kept in mind when looking at a statement of financial position?

## 2.2 STATEMENT OF COMPREHENSIVE INCOME

The **statement of comprehensive income** measures performance over a specific period of time (say, a year). Income has the following accounting definition:

$$\text{Revenue} - \text{Expenses} = \text{Income}$$

If the statement of financial position is like a snapshot, the statement of comprehensive income is like a video recording of what happened between two snapshots. Table 2.2 gives the statement of comprehensive income for the Canadian Composite Corporation for 2015.

**TABLE 2.2**

**Statement of Comprehensive Income for the Canadian Composite Corporation**

| CANADIAN COMPOSITE CORPORATION Statement of Comprehensive Income 2015 (in $ millions) | | |
|---|---|---|
| Total operating revenues | | $2,262 |
| Cost of goods sold | | (1,655) |
| Selling, general, and administrative expenses | | (327) |
| Depreciation | | (90) |
| Operating income | | 190 |
| Other income | | 29 |
| Earnings before interest and taxes | | 219 |
| Interest expense | | (49) |
| Pre-tax income | | 170 |
| Taxes | | (84) |
|    Current: | $71 | |
|    Deferred: | $13 | |
| Net income | | $ 86 |
|    Retained earnings: | $43 | |
|    Dividends: | $43 | |

The statement of comprehensive income usually includes several sections. The operations section reports the firm's revenues and expenses from principal operations. Among other things, the non-operating section includes all financing costs, such as interest expense. Usually a second section reports as a separate item the amount of taxes levied on income. The last item on the statement of comprehensive income is the bottom line, or net income. Net income is frequently expressed per share of common stock, that is, as earnings per share.

When analyzing this statement, the financial manager should keep in mind IFRS, non-cash items, time, and costs.

### International Financial Reporting Standards

As pointed out earlier, the focus in financial decisions is on market value, which depends on cash flow. However, like the statement of financial position, the statement of comprehensive income has many different users. The accounting profession has developed IFRS to provide information for a broad audience not necessarily concerned with cash flow. For this reason, it is necessary to make adjustments to information on the statement of comprehensive income to obtain cash flow.

For example, revenue is recognized on the statement of comprehensive income when the earnings process is virtually completed and an exchange of goods or services has occurred. In some cases under IFRS, fair market value may be used to value assets, in which case unrealized gains and losses are recognized in income as they occur. In other cases, based on accounting policies selected, increases in market value of assets are not recognized until the asset is sold. This provides a device for smoothing income by selling appreciated property at convenient times. Accounting principles require that revenues be matched with expenses incurred to generate the revenue. Thus, income is reported when it is earned or accrued, even though no cash flow has necessarily occurred. (For example, when goods are sold on credit, sales and profits are reported.)

## Non-cash Items

The economic value of assets is intimately connected to their future incremental cash flows. However, cash flow does not appear on the statement of comprehensive income. Several **non-cash items** are expenses against revenues but do not affect cash flow directly.[5] The most important of these are *depreciation* and *amortization*. Depreciation reflects the accountant's estimate of the cost of equipment used up in the production process.[6] For example, suppose an asset with a five-year life and no resale value is purchased for $1,000. According to accountants, the $1,000 cost must be expensed over the useful life of the asset. If straight-line depreciation is used, there will be five equal instalments, and $200 of depreciation expense will be incurred each year. From a finance perspective, the cost of the asset is the actual negative cash flow incurred when the asset is acquired (that is, $1,000, not the accountant's smoothed $200-per-year depreciation expense). Amortization is used to reflect the cost of an intangible asset over its useful life.

Another non-cash expense is *deferred taxes*. Deferred taxes result from differences between accounting income and true taxable income.[7] Notice that the accounting tax shown on the statement of comprehensive income for the Canadian Composite Corporation is $84 million. It can be broken down as current taxes and deferred taxes. The current tax portion is actually sent to the tax authorities (for example, Canada Revenue Agency). The deferred tax portion is not. However, the theory is that if taxable income is less than accounting income in the current year, it will be more than accounting income later. Consequently, taxes that are not paid today will have to be paid in the future, and they represent a liability of the firm. It shows up on the statement of financial position as a deferred tax liability. From the cash flow perspective, though, deferred tax is not a cash outflow.

## Time and Costs

It is often useful to think of the future as having two distinct parts: the *short run* and the *long run*. The short run is that period in which certain equipment, resources, and commitments of the firm are fixed, but it is long enough for the firm to vary its output by using more labour and raw materials. The short run is an imprecise period of time that may differ among industries. However, all firms making decisions in the short run have some fixed costs, that is, costs that will not change because of the fixed

---

[5] Although it is a non-cash expense, depreciation has tax implications (discussed later) that affect cash flow.

[6] Depreciation is the form of amortization that applies to capital assets.

[7] One situation in which taxable income may be lower than accounting income is when the firm uses capital cost allowance (CCA) depreciation expense procedures for calculating taxes but uses straight-line procedures allowed by IFRS for reporting purposes. We discuss CCA in Chapter 8. Accountants refer to deferred taxes as a future income tax liability.

commitments. In real business activity, examples of fixed costs are bond interest, overhead, and property taxes. Costs that are not fixed are variable. Variable costs change as the output of the firm changes; some examples are raw materials and wages for production line workers. In the long run, all costs are variable.[8]

Financial accountants do not distinguish between variable costs and fixed costs. Instead, accounting costs usually fit into a classification that distinguishes product costs from period costs. Product costs are the total production costs (raw materials, direct labour, and manufacturing overhead) incurred during a period and are reported on the statement of comprehensive income as the cost of goods sold. Both variable and fixed costs are included in product costs. Period costs are costs that are allocated to a time period; they are included in *selling, general, and administrative expenses*. An example of a period cost is the company president's salary.

**CONCEPT QUESTIONS**

- What is the statement of comprehensive income equation?
- What are three things to keep in mind when looking at the statement of comprehensive income?
- What are non-cash expenses?

## 2.3  NET WORKING CAPITAL

Net working capital is current assets minus current liabilities. Net working capital is positive when current assets are greater than current liabilities, that is, when the cash that will become available over the next 12 months is greater than the cash that must be paid out. The net working capital of the Canadian Composite Corporation is $275 million in 2015 and $252 million in 2014:

|  | Current assets (in $ millions) | − | Current liabilities (in $ millions) | = | Net working capital (in $ millions) |
|---|---|---|---|---|---|
| 2015 | $761 | − | $486 | = | $275 |
| 2014 | $707 | − | $455 | = | $252 |

In addition to investing in fixed assets (capital spending), a firm can invest in net working capital—called the *change in net working capital*. The **change in net working capital** in 2015 is the difference between the net working capital in 2015 and 2014, that is, $275 million − $252 million = $23 million. The change in net working capital is usually positive in a growing firm because higher levels of net working capital are necessary for increased sales.

Investment in net working capital occurs when raw materials and other inventory are purchased and stored. Keeping all raw material and other inventory purchases constant, the investment in net working capital will decrease when the raw materials are consumed for the manufacture of finished goods. Working capital also increases when cash is kept in a particular project as a buffer against unexpected expenditures or when credit sales are made, increasing accounts receivable instead of cash. Positive increases in current assets lead to greater investment in net working capital. However, investments in net working capital can be offset by any purchases made by the company on credit. Net working capital will be discussed in more depth in Chapter 8, where it will be applied in forecasting for capital budgeting and calculating the net present value.

**CONCEPT QUESTIONS**

- What is net working capital?
- What is the change in net working capital?

---

[8] When one famous economist was asked about the difference between the long run and the short run, he said, "In the long run we are all dead."

## 2.4    FINANCIAL CASH FLOW

Perhaps the most important item that can be extracted from financial statements is the actual **cash flow**. The accounting statement called the *statement of cash flows* helps to explain the change in accounting cash and equivalents, which for Canadian Composite is $33 million in 2015 (see Appendix 2B). Notice in Table 2.1 that cash and equivalents increases from $107 million in 2014 to $140 million in 2015. However, we will look at cash flow from a different perspective: the perspective of finance. In finance, the value of the firm depends on its ability to generate financial cash flow. (We will talk more about financial cash flow in Chapter 8.)

The first point we should mention is that cash flow is not the same as net working capital. For example, increasing inventory requires using cash. Because inventories and cash are both current assets, this does not affect net working capital. In this case, an increase in a particular net working capital account, such as inventory, is associated with decreasing cash flow.

Just as we established that the value of a firm's assets is always equal to the value of the liabilities plus the value of the equity, the cash flows from the firm's assets, CF(*A*), must equal the cash flows to the firm's creditors, CF(*B*), and equity investors, CF(*S*):

$$CF(A) = CF(B) + CF(S)$$

The first step in determining a firm's cash flows is to figure out the *cash flow from operations*. Table 2.3 shows that operating cash flow is the cash flow generated by business activities, including sales of goods and services. Operating cash flow reflects tax payments, but not financing, capital spending, or changes in net working capital:

|  | (in $ millions) |
|---|---|
| Earnings before interest and taxes | $219 |
| Depreciation[9] | 90 |
| Current taxes | (71) |
| Operating cash flow | $238 |

**TABLE 2.3**

**Statement of Cash Flows for the Canadian Composite Corporation**

| CANADIAN COMPOSITE CORPORATION<br>Statement of Cash Flows 2015<br>(in $ millions) | |
|---|---|
| **Cash flow of the firm** | |
| Operating cash flow<br>(Earnings before interest and taxes plus depreciation minus taxes) | $ 238 |
| Capital spending<br>(Acquisitions of long-term assets minus sales of long-term assets) | (173) |
| Additions to net working capital | (23) |
| Total | $  42 |
| **Cash flow to investors in the firm** | |
| Debt<br>(Interest plus retirement of debt minus new long-term debt financing) | $  36 |
| Equity<br>(Dividends plus repurchase of equity minus new equity financing) | 6 |
| Total | $  42 |

---

[9] Under IFRS, the term "amortization" is used with respect to allocating the cost of an intangible asset over its useful life. Under accounting standards for private enterprises, the term "amortization" is used for both tangible and intangible assets. Since "depreciation" is widely used in finance, we use the term to represent both amortization and depreciation expenses.

Another important component of cash flow involves *changes in long-term assets.* For example, when Canadian Composite sold its power systems subsidiary in 2015, it generated $25 million in cash flow. The net change in long-term assets equals sales of long-term assets minus the acquisition of long-term assets. The result is the cash flow used for capital spending:

| | |
|---|---|
| Acquisition of long-term assets | $198 |
| Sales of fixed assets | (25) |
| Capital spending | $173 |

We can arrive at the same number by adding the increase in property, plant, and equipment ($149) to the increase in intangible assets ($24).

Cash flows are also used for making investments in net working capital. For Canadian Composite Corporation in 2015, *additions to net working capital* are

| | |
|---|---|
| Additions to net working capital | $23 |

Total cash flows generated by the firm's assets are the sum of

| | |
|---|---|
| Operating cash flow | $238 |
| Capital spending | (173) |
| Additions to net working capital | (23) |
| Total cash flow of the firm | $ 42 |

The total outgoing cash flow of the firm can be separated into cash flows paid to creditors and cash flows paid to shareholders. The cash flow paid to creditors represents a regrouping of the data in Table 2.3 and an explicit recording of interest expense from Table 2.2. An important source of cash flow comes from issuing new debt. Thus, an increase in long-term debt is the net effect of new borrowing and repayment of maturing obligations plus interest expense:

**Cash Flow Paid to Creditors**
**(in $ millions)**

| | |
|---|---|
| Interest | $ 49 |
| Net proceeds from long-term debt sales | (13) |
| Total | $ 36 |

Cash flow of the firm is also paid to the shareholders. It is the sum of dividends plus net new equity from repurchasing outstanding shares and issuing new shares:

**Cash Flow to Shareholders**
**(in $ millions)**

| | |
|---|---|
| Dividends | $ 43 |
| Net new equity | (37) |
| Total | $ 6 |

In general, cash flow to shareholders can be determined as follows:

Cash flow to shareholders = Dividends paid − Net new equity raised
= Dividends paid − (Shares sold − Shares repurchased)

To determine shares sold, notice that the common stock and capital surplus accounts went up by a combined $23 + $20 = $43, which implies that the company sold $43 million worth of stock. Second, treasury stock went up by $6, indicating that the company bought back $6 million worth of stock. Net new equity is thus $43 − $6 = $37. Dividends paid were $43 million, so the cash flow to shareholders was

$$\text{Cash flow to shareholders} = \$43 − (\$43 − \$6) = \$6$$

which is what we previously calculated.

Some important observations can be drawn from our discussion of cash flow:

1.  Several types of cash flow are relevant to understanding the financial situation of the firm. **Cash flow from operations**, defined as earnings before interest and depreciation minus taxes, measures the cash generated from operations, not counting capital spending or working capital requirements. It should usually be positive; a firm is in trouble if operating cash flow is negative for a long time because the firm is not generating enough cash to pay operating costs.

    **Total cash flow of the firm** includes adjustments for capital spending and additions to net working capital. It will frequently be negative. When a firm is growing at a rapid rate, spending on inventory and fixed assets can be higher than cash flow from sales. On the other hand, positive total cash flow is not always a sign of financial health. An unprofitable firm with negative cash flow from operations could show positive total cash flow temporarily by selling assets. This was a common occurrence in the airline industry in the early 1990s.

2.  Net income is not cash flow. Net income is calculated based on accounting principles that allow accruals and deferrals and focus on matching revenues to expenses. Therefore, it is generally preferred to look at cash flows over net income, which can be subject to greater manipulation (Appendix 2B provides a discussion on this issue). The net income of the Canadian Composite Corporation in 2015 was $86 million, whereas cash flow was $42 million. The two numbers are not usually the same. In determining the economic and financial condition of a firm, cash flow is more revealing.

3.  Cash flow from assets sometimes goes by a different name: **free cash flow**. Free cash flow is an important measure with many uses in the world of finance. For instance, free cash flow provides insight into a company's financial flexibility and its ability to take advantage of investment opportunities, and it can even be used in the valuation of companies. The term refers to cash that the firm is free to distribute to creditors and shareholders and is calculated as cash flow from operations less capital expenditures (CAPEX) and increase in net working capital. It represents the amount of cash on hand after expenditures have been made to maintain or expand the current asset base. (We return to free cash flow in Chapter 17.)

**CONCEPT QUESTIONS**

- How is cash flow different from changes in net working capital?
- What is the difference between the operating cash flow and the total cash flow of the firm?
- What is free cash flow?

## 2.5

# SUMMARY AND CONCLUSIONS

Besides introducing you to corporate accounting, the purpose of this chapter was to teach you how to determine cash flow from the accounting statements of a typical company.

1. Cash flow is generated by the firm and paid to creditors and shareholders. It can be classified as
   a. Cash flow from operations.
   b. Cash flow from changes in long-term assets.
   c. Cash flow from changes in working capital.

2. There is a cash flow identity that says that cash flow from assets equals cash flow to bondholders and shareholders.

3. Calculations of cash flow are not difficult, but they require care and particular attention to detail in properly accounting for non-cash expenses such as depreciation and deferred taxes. It is especially important that you do not confuse cash flow with changes in net working capital and net income.

**KEY TERMS**

Cash flow   39
Cash flow from
   operations   41
Change in net working
   capital   38

Free cash flow   41
International Financial
   Reporting Standards
   (IFRS)   35
Non-cash items   37

Statement of comprehensive
   income   36
Statement of financial
   position   33
Total cash flow of the
   firm   41

**QUESTIONS &
PROBLEMS**

### Building a Statement of Financial Position

2.1   Culligan Inc. has current assets of $5,300, net fixed assets of $26,000, current liabilities of $3,900, and long-term debt of $14,200. What is the value of the shareholders' equity account for this firm? How much is net working capital?

### Building a Statement of Comprehensive Income

2.2   Ragsdale Inc. has sales of $493,000, costs of $210,000, depreciation expense of $35,000, interest expense of $19,000, and a tax rate of 35 percent. What is the net income for the firm? Suppose the company paid out $50,000 in cash dividends. What is the addition to retained earnings?

### Market Values and Book Values

2.3   Klingon Cruisers Inc. purchased new cloaking machinery three years ago for $9.5 million. The machinery can be sold to the Romulans today for $6.3 million. Klingon's current balance sheet shows net fixed assets of $5 million, current liabilities of $2.1 million, and net working capital of $800,000. If all the current assets were liquidated today, the company would receive $2.8 million cash. What is the book value of Klingon's assets today? What is the market value?

### Calculating Operating Cash Flow

2.4   Ranney Inc. has sales of $18,700, costs of $10,300, depreciation expense of $1,900, and interest expense of $1,250. If the tax rate is 40 percent, what is the operating cash flow?

### Calculating Net Capital Spending

2.5   Gordon Driving School's 2014 balance sheet showed net fixed assets of $1.65 million, and the 2015 balance sheet showed net fixed assets of $1.73 million. The company's 2015 statement of comprehensive income showed a depreciation expense of $284,000. What was Gordon's net capital spending for 2015?

### Building a Statement of Financial Position

2.6   The following table presents the long-term liabilities and shareholders' equity of Information Control Corp. one year ago:

|  |  |
| --- | --- |
| Long-term debt | $65,000,000 |
| Preferred shares | 4,000,000 |
| Common shares ($1 par value) | 15,000,000 |
| Accumulated retained earnings | 135,000,000 |
| Capital surplus | 45,000,000 |

During the past year, Information Control issued 10 million new shares at a total price of $58 million, and issued $35 million in new long-term debt. The company generated $9 million in net income and paid $2 million in dividends. Construct the current statement of financial position reflecting the changes that occurred at Information Control Corp. during the year.

### Cash Flow to Creditors

2.7   The 2014 statement of financial position of Anna's Tennis Shop Inc. showed long-term debt of $1.45 million, and the 2015 statement of financial position showed long-term debt of $1.52 million. The 2015 statement of comprehensive income showed an interest expense of $127,000. What was the firm's cash flow to creditors during 2015?

### Cash Flow to Shareholders

2.8   The 2014 statement of financial position of Anna's Tennis Shop Inc. showed $490,000 in the common shares account and $3.4 million in the additional paid-in surplus account. The 2015 statement of financial position showed $525,000 and $3.7 million in the same two accounts, respectively. If the company paid out $275,000 in cash dividends during 2015, what was the cash flow to shareholders for the year?

### Calculating Cash Flows

2.9   Given the information for Anna's Tennis Shop Inc. in the previous two problems, suppose you also know that the firm's net capital spending for 2015 was $945,000 and that the firm reduced its net working capital investment by $87,000. What was the firm's 2015 operating cash flow?

### Cash Flows

2.10 Ritter Corporation's accountants prepared the following financial statements for year-end 2015:

**RITTER CORPORATION**
**Statement of Comprehensive Income**
**2015**

| | |
|---|---:|
| Revenue | $750 |
| Expenses | 565 |
| Depreciation | 90 |
| Net income | $ 95 |
| Dividends | $ 75 |

**RITTER CORPORATION**
**Statement of Financial Position**
**December 31**

| | 2015 | 2014 |
|---|---:|---:|
| **Assets** | | |
| Cash | $ 65 | $ 55 |
| Other current assets | 170 | 165 |
| Net fixed assets | 390 | 370 |
| Total assets | $625 | $590 |
| **Liabilities and equity** | | |
| Accounts payable | $125 | $115 |
| Long-term debt | 145 | 140 |
| Shareholders' equity | 355 | 335 |
| Total liabilities and equity | $625 | $590 |

a. Explain the change in cash during 2015.
b. Determine the change in net working capital in 2015.
c. Determine the cash flow generated by the firm's assets during 2015.

### Financial Cash Flows

2.11 The Stancil Corporation provided the following current information:

| | |
|---|---:|
| Proceeds from long-term borrowing | $17,000 |
| Proceeds from the sale of common shares | 4,000 |
| Purchases of long-term assets | 21,000 |
| Purchases of inventories | 1,900 |
| Payment of dividends | 14,500 |

Determine the cash flows from the firm and the cash flows to investors of the firm.

### Building a Statement of Comprehensive Income

2.12 During the year, the Senbet Discount Tire Company had gross sales of $1.2 million. The firm's cost of goods sold and selling expenses were $450,000 and $225,000, respectively. Senbet also had notes payable of $900,000. These notes carried an interest rate of 9 percent. Depreciation was $110,000. Senbet's tax rate was 35 percent.
a. What was Senbet's net income?
b. What was Senbet's operating cash flow?

### Calculating Total Cash Flows

2.13 Schwert Corp. shows the following information on its 2015 statement of comprehensive income: sales = $167,000; costs = $91,000; other expenses = $5,400; depreciation expense = $8,000; interest expense = $11,000; taxes = $18,060; dividends = $9,500.

In addition, you're told that the firm issued $7,250 in new equity during 2015 and
redeemed $7,100 in outstanding long-term debt.

   *a.* What is the 2015 operating cash flow?

   *b.* What is the 2015 cash flow to creditors?

   *c.* What is the 2015 cash flow to shareholders?

   *d.* If net fixed assets increased by $22,400 during the year, what was the addition to
net working capital?

### Using Statements of Comprehensive Income

2.14 Given the following information for O'Hara Marine Co., calculate the depreciation
expense: sales = $41,000; costs = $26,400; addition to retained earnings = $4,900;
dividends paid = $1,570; interest expense = $1,840; tax rate = 35 percent.

### Preparing a Statement of Financial Position

2.15 Prepare a 2015 statement of financial position for Jarrow Corp. based on the following information: cash = $274,500; patents and copyrights = $860,000; accounts
payable = $697,500; accounts receivable = $207,000; tangible net fixed assets =
$4,393,000; inventory = $445,500; notes payable = $217,500; accumulated retained
earnings = $2,940,000; long-term debt = $2,325,000.

### Residual Claims

2.16 Huang Inc. must pay its creditors $10,900 very soon.

   *a.* What is the market value of the shareholders' equity if assets have a market
value of $12,400?

   *b.* What if assets equal $9,600?

### Net Income and Operating Cash Flow

2.17 During 2015, Raines Umbrella Corp. had sales of $630,000. Cost of goods sold,
administrative and selling expenses, and depreciation expenses were $470,000,
$95,000, and $140,000, respectively. In addition, the company had an interest expense
of $70,000 and a tax rate of 35 percent. (Ignore any tax loss carryback or carryfor-
ward provisions.)

   *a.* What is Raines's net income for 2015?

   *b.* What is its operating cash flow?

   *c.* Explain your results in (a) and (b).

### Accounting Values versus Cash Flows

2.18 In Problem 2.17, suppose Raines Umbrella Corp. paid out $34,000 in cash dividends.
Is this possible? If spending on net fixed assets and net working capital was zero, and
if no new shares were issued during the year, what was the change in the firm's long-
term debt account?

### Calculating Cash Flows

2.19 Cusic Industries had the following operating results for 2015: sales = $19,900; cost
of goods sold = $14,200; depreciation expense = $2,700; interest expense = $670;
dividends paid = $650. At the beginning of the year, net fixed assets were $15,340,
current assets were $4,420, and current liabilities were $2,470. At the end of the year,
net fixed assets were $16,770, current assets were $5,135, and current liabilities were
$2,535. The tax rate for 2015 was 40 percent.

   *a.* What is the net income for 2015?

   *b.* What is the operating cash flow for 2015?

   *c.* What is the cash flow from assets for 2015? Is this possible? Explain.

   *d.* If no new debt was issued during the year, what is the cash flow to creditors?
What is the cash flow to shareholders? Explain and interpret the positive and
negative signs of your answers in (a) through (d).

2.20 Consider the following abbreviated financial statements for Weston Enterprises:

**WESTON ENTERPRISES**
**2014 and 2015 Partial Statement of Financial Position**

| Assets | | | Liabilities and shareholders' equity | | |
|---|---|---|---|---|---|
| | **2014** | **2015** | | **2014** | **2015** |
| Current assets | $ 936 | $1,015 | Current liabilities | $ 382 | $ 416 |
| Net fixed assets | 4,176 | 4,896 | Long-term debt | 2,160 | 2,477 |

**WESTON ENTERPRISES**
**2015 Statement of**
**Comprehensive Income**

| | |
|---|---|
| Sales | $12,380 |
| Costs | 5,776 |
| Depreciation | 1,150 |
| Interest paid | 314 |

a. What is the shareholders' equity for 2014 and 2015?
b. What is the change in net working capital for 2015?
c. In 2015, Weston Enterprises purchased $2,160 in new fixed assets. How much in fixed assets did Weston Enterprises sell? What is the cash flow from assets for the year? (The tax rate is 40 percent.)
d. During 2015, Weston Enterprises raised $432 in new long-term debt. How much long-term debt must Weston Enterprises have paid off during the year? What is the cash flow to creditors?

Use the following information for Ingersoll Inc. for Problems 2.21 and 2.22 (assume the tax rate is 34 percent):

| | 2014 | 2015 |
|---|---|---|
| Sales | $ 7,835 | $ 8,409 |
| Depreciation | 1,125 | 1,126 |
| Cost of goods sold | 2,696 | 3,060 |
| Other expenses | 639 | 534 |
| Interest | 525 | 603 |
| Cash | 4,109 | 5,203 |
| Accounts receivable | 5,439 | 6,127 |
| Short-term notes payable | 794 | 746 |
| Long-term debt | 13,460 | 16,050 |
| Net fixed assets | 34,455 | 35,277 |
| Accounts payable | 4,316 | 4,185 |
| Inventory | 9,670 | 9,938 |
| Dividends | 956 | 1,051 |

**Financial Statements**

2.21 Draw up a statement of comprehensive income and a statement of financial position for Ingersoll for 2014 and 2015.

### Calculating Cash Flow

2.22 For 2015, calculate the cash flow from assets, cash flow to creditors, and cash flow to shareholders for Ingersoll.

### Cash Flows

2.23 You are researching Time Manufacturing and have found the following accounting statement of cash flows for the most recent year. You also know that the company paid $98 million in current taxes and had an interest expense of $48 million. Use the accounting statement of cash flows to construct the financial statement of cash flows.

TIME MANUFACTURING
Statement of Cash Flows
(in $ millions)

| Operations | |
|---|---|
| Net income | $173 |
| Depreciation | 94 |
| Deferred taxes | 19 |
| **Changes in assets and liabilities** | |
| Accounts receivable | (18) |
| Inventories | 22 |
| Accounts payable | 17 |
| Accrued expenses | (9) |
| Other | 3 |
| **Total cash flow from operations** | **$301** |
| **Investing activities** | |
| Acquisition of fixed assets | $(215) |
| Sale of fixed assets | 23 |
| **Total cash flow from investing activities** | **$(192)** |
| **Financing activities** | |
| Retirement of long-term debt | $(162) |
| Proceeds from long-term debt sales | 116 |
| Change in notes payable | 6 |
| Dividends | (86) |
| Repurchase of shares | (13) |
| Proceeds from new share issue | 44 |
| **Total cash flow from financing activities** | **$ (95)** |
| **Change in cash (on balance sheet)** | **$ 14** |

### Net Fixed Assets and Depreciation

2.24 On the statement of financial position, the net fixed assets (NFA) account is equal to the gross fixed assets (FA) account, which records the acquisition cost of fixed assets, minus the accumulated depreciation (AD) account, which records the total depreciation taken by the firm against its fixed assets. Using the fact that NFA = FA − AD, show that the expression given in the chapter for net capital spending, $NFA_{end} - NFA_{beg} + D$ (where D is the depreciation expense during the year), is equivalent to $FA_{end} - FA_{beg}$.

# CASH FLOWS AT WARF COMPUTERS LTD.

Warf Computers Ltd. was founded 15 years ago by Nick Warf, a computer programmer. The small initial investment to start the company was made by Nick and his friends. Over the years, this same group has supplied the limited additional investment needed by the company in the form of both equity and short- and long-term debt. Recently, the company has developed a virtual keyboard (VK). The VK uses sophisticated artificial intelligence algorithms that allow the user to speak naturally and have the computer input the text, correct spelling and grammatical errors, and format the document according to preset user guidelines. The VK even suggests alternative phrasing and sentence structure, and it provides detailed stylistic diagnostics. Based on a proprietary, very advanced software/hardware hybrid technology, the system is a full generation beyond what is currently on the market.

To introduce the VK, the company will require significant outside investment.

Nick has decided to seek this outside financing in the form of new equity investments and bank loans. Naturally, new investors and the banks will require a detailed financial analysis. Your employer, Angus Jones & Partners, LLC, has asked you to examine the financial statements provided by Nick. Below are the statements of financial position for the two most recent years and the most recent statement of comprehensive income.

Nick has also provided the following information: During the year the company raised $175,000 in new long-term debt and retired $151,000 in long-term debt. The company also sold $12,000 in new stock and repurchased $48,000 in stock. The company purchased $1,140,000 in fixed assets and sold $330,000 in fixed assets.

**WARF COMPUTERS**
**Statement of Financial Position**
**(in $ thousands)**

| | 2015 | 2014 | | 2015 | 2014 |
|---|---|---|---|---|---|
| **Current assets** | | | **Current liabilities** | | |
| Cash and equivalents | $ 348 | $ 301 | Accounts payable | $ 314 | $ 294 |
| Accounts receivable | 551 | 514 | Notes payable | 85 | 79 |
| Inventories | 493 | 510 | Accrued expenses | 190 | 308 |
| Other | 71 | 60 | Total current liabilities | $ 589 | $ 681 |
| Total current assets | $1,463 | $1,385 | **Long-term liabilities** | | |
| **Fixed assets** | | | Deferred taxes | $ 254 | $ 124 |
| Property, plant, and equipment | $3,191 | $2,446 | Long-term debt | 907 | 883 |
| Less accumulated depreciation | 1,031 | 840 | Total long-term liabilities | $1,161 | $1,007 |
| Net property, plant, and equipment | $2,160 | $1,606 | **Shareholders' equity** | | |
| Intangible assets and others | 610 | 545 | Preferred stock | $ 16 | $ 16 |
| Total fixed assets | $2,770 | $2,151 | Common stock | 97 | 97 |
| | | | Capital surplus | 611 | 599 |
| | | | Accumulated retained earnings | 1,904 | 1,233 |
| | | | Less treasury stock | 145 | 97 |
| | | | Total equity | $2,483 | $1,848 |
| Total assets | $4,233 | $3,536 | Total liabilities and shareholders' equity | $4,233 | $3,536 |

**WARF COMPUTERS**
**Statement of Comprehensive Income**
**(in $ thousands)**

| | |
|---|---:|
| Sales | $5,813 |
| Cost of goods sold | 3,430 |
| Selling, general, and administrative expense | 652 |
| Depreciation | 191 |
| Operating income | $1,540 |
| Other income | 58 |
| Earnings before interest and taxes (EBIT) | $1,598 |
| Interest expense | 105 |
| Pre-tax income | $1,493 |
| Taxes | 597 |
|    Current: $467 | |
|    Deferred: 130 | |
| Net income | $  896 |
| Addition to retained earnings | $  225 |
| Dividends | $  671 |

Angus has asked you to prepare the financial statement of cash flows and the accounting statement of cash flows. He has also asked you to answer the following questions:

1. How would you describe Warf Computers' cash flows?

2. Which cash flow statement more accurately describes the cash flows at the company?

3. In light of your previous answers, comment on Nick's expansion plans.

APPENDIX **2A**

# Financial Statement Analysis

This appendix shows how to rearrange data from financial statements into financial ratios that provide information about five areas of financial performance:

1. *Short-term solvency*—the firm's ability to meet its short-run obligations.
2. *Activity*—the firm's ability to control its investment in assets.
3. *Financial leverage*—the extent to which a firm relies on debt financing.
4. *Profitability*—the extent to which a firm is profitable.
5. *Value*—the value of the firm.

This appendix also discusses the interpretation, uses, and shortcomings of financial ratios.

Our discussion covers a representative sampling of ratios chosen to be consistent with the practice of experienced financial analysts and the output of commercially available financial analysis software.

For each of the ratios discussed, several questions are important:

1. How is the ratio calculated?
2. What is it intended to measure, and why might we be interested?
3. What might a high or low value be telling us? How might such values be misleading?
4. How could this measure be improved?

We consider each question in turn. The Canadian Composite Corporation financial statements in Tables 2.1, 2.2, and 2.3 provide inputs for the examples that follow. (Monetary values are given in millions of dollars.)

## Short-Term Solvency

Ratios of short-term solvency measure the firm's ability to meet recurring financial obligations (that is, to pay its bills). To the extent that a firm has sufficient cash flow, it can avoid defaulting on its financial obligations and thus avoid financial distress. Liquidity measures short-term solvency and is often associated with net working capital, the difference between current assets and current liabilities. Recall that current liabilities are debts due within one year from the date of the balance sheet. One source from which to pay these debts is current assets.

The most widely used measures of liquidity are the current ratio and the quick ratio.

**Current Ratio**    To find the current ratio, divide current assets by current liabilities. For the Canadian Composite Corporation, the figure for 2015 is

$$\text{Current ratio} = \frac{\text{Total current assets}}{\text{Total current liabilities}} = \frac{761}{486} = 1.57$$

If a firm is having financial difficulty, it may not be able to pay its bills (accounts payable) on time or it may need to extend its bank credit (notes payable). As a consequence, current liabilities may rise faster than current assets and the current ratio may fall. This could be the first sign of financial trouble. Of course, a firm's current ratio should be calculated over several years for historical perspective, and it should be compared to the current ratios of other firms with similar operating activities.

While a higher current ratio generally indicates greater liquidity, it is possible for the current ratio to be too high. A current ratio far above the industry average could indicate excessive inventory or difficulty in collecting accounts receivable.

**Quick Ratio**    The quick ratio is computed by subtracting inventories from current assets and dividing the difference (called *quick assets*) by current liabilities:

$$\text{Quick ratio} = \frac{\text{Quick assets}}{\text{Total current liabilities}} = \frac{492}{486} = 1.01$$

Quick assets are those current assets that are quickly convertible into cash. Inventories are the least liquid current assets. Many financial analysts believe it is important to determine a firm's ability to pay off current liabilities without relying on the sale of inventories. Comparing the quick ratio to the industry average may help to detect cases in which a high current ratio reflects excessive inventory.

**Cash Ratio**    The cash ratio provides a very short term look at solvency and a company's ability to repay current obligations:

$$\text{Cash ratio} = \frac{\text{Cash}}{\text{Total current liabilities}} = \frac{140}{486} = 0.29$$

## Activity

Activity ratios are constructed to measure how effectively the firm's assets are being managed. The level of a firm's investment in assets depends on many factors. For example, The Bay might have a large stock of toys at the peak of the Christmas season, yet that same inventory in January would be undesirable. How can the appropriate level of investment in assets be measured? One logical starting point is to compare assets with sales for the year to arrive at turnover. The idea is to find out how quickly assets are used to generate sales. We come back to these ideas in Chapter 27.

**Total Asset Turnover**    The total asset turnover ratio is determined by dividing total operating revenues for the accounting period by the average of total assets. The total asset turnover ratio for the Canadian Composite Corporation for 2015 is

$$\text{Total asset turnover} = \frac{\text{Total operating revenues}}{\text{Average total assets}} = \frac{2{,}262}{1{,}810.5} = 1.25$$

$$\text{Average total assets} = \frac{1{,}879 + 1{,}742}{2} = 1{,}810.5$$

This ratio is intended to indicate how effectively a firm is using its assets. If the total asset turnover ratio is high, the firm is presumably using its assets effectively in generating sales. If the ratio is low, the firm is not using its assets up to their capacity and must either increase sales or dispose of some of the assets. Total asset turnover ratio differs across industries. Firms with relatively small investments in fixed assets, such as retail and wholesale trade firms, tend to have high ratios of total asset turnover when compared with firms that require a large investment in fixed assets, such as manufacturing firms. One problem in interpreting this ratio is that it is maximized by using older assets because their accounting value is lower than newer assets.

**Receivables Turnover**    The receivables turnover ratio is calculated by dividing sales by average receivables during the accounting period. If the number of days in the year (365) is divided by the receivables turnover ratio, the average collection period can be determined. Net receivables are used for these calculations.[10] The average receivables, receivables turnover ratio, and average collection period for the Canadian Composite Corporation are

$$\text{Average receivables} = \frac{294 + 270}{2} = 282$$

$$\text{Receivables turnover} = \frac{\text{Total operating revenues}}{\text{Average receivables}} = \frac{2{,}262}{282} = 8.02$$

$$\text{Average collection period} = \frac{\text{Days in period}}{\text{Receivables turnover}} = \frac{365}{8.02} = 45.5 \text{ days}$$

The receivables turnover and the average collection period provide some information on the success of the firm in managing its investment in accounts receivable. The actual values of these ratios reflect the firm's credit policy. If a firm has a liberal credit policy, the amount of its receivables will be higher than under a restrictive credit policy. One common rule of thumb that financial analysts use is that the average collection period of a firm should not exceed the time allowed for payment in the credit terms by more than 10 days.

**Inventory Turnover**    The ratio of inventory turnover is calculated by dividing the cost of goods sold by average inventory. Because inventory is always stated in terms of historical cost, it must be divided by cost of goods sold instead of sales. (Sales include a margin for profit and are not commensurate with inventory.) The number of days in the year divided by the inventory turnover ratio yields the *days in inventory ratio* (the number of days it takes to get goods produced and sold). It is called *shelf life* for retail and wholesale trade firms. The inventory ratios for the Canadian Composite Corporation are

$$\text{Average inventory} = \frac{269 + 280}{2} = 274.5$$

$$\text{Inventory turnover} = \frac{\text{Cost of goods sold}}{\text{Average inventory}} = \frac{1{,}655}{274.5} = 6.03$$

$$\text{Days in inventory} = \frac{\text{Days in period}}{\text{Inventory turnover}} = \frac{365}{6.03} = 60.5 \text{ days}$$

---

[10] Net receivables are determined after an allowance for potential bad debts.

The inventory ratios measure how quickly inventory is produced and sold. They are significantly affected by the production technology of goods being manufactured. It takes longer to produce a gas turbine engine than a loaf of bread. The ratios are also affected by the perishability of the finished goods. A large increase in the ratio of days in inventory could suggest either an ominously high inventory of unsold finished goods or a change in the firm's product mix to goods with longer production periods.

The method of inventory valuation can materially affect the computed inventory ratios. Thus, financial analysts should be aware of the different inventory valuation methods and how they might affect the ratios.

## Financial Leverage

Financial leverage measures the extent to which a firm relies on debt financing rather than equity. Measures of financial leverage are tools in determining the probability that the firm will default on its debt contracts. The more debt a firm has, the more likely it is that the firm will become unable to fulfill its contractual obligations. In other words, too much debt can lead to a higher probability of insolvency and financial distress.

On the positive side, debt is an important form of financing and provides a significant tax advantage because interest payments are tax deductible. If a firm uses debt, creditors and equity investors may have conflicts of interest. Creditors may want the firm to invest in less risky ventures than those the equity investors prefer.

We discuss the advantages and disadvantages of debt in depth in Chapters 16 and 17.

**Debt Ratio**   The debt ratio is calculated by dividing total debt by total assets. We can also express the extent to which a firm uses debt in several other ways, such as the debt-to-equity ratio and the equity multiplier (that is, total assets divided by equity). The debt ratios for the Canadian Composite Corporation for 2015 are

$$\text{Debt ratio} = \frac{\text{Total debt}}{\text{Total assets}} = \frac{1{,}074}{1{,}879} = 0.57$$

$$\text{Debt-to-equity ratio} = \frac{\text{Total debt}}{\text{Total equity}} = \frac{1{,}074}{805} = 1.33$$

$$\text{Equity multiplier} = \frac{\text{Total assets}}{\text{Total equity}} = \frac{1{,}879}{805} = 2.33$$

Debt ratios provide information about protection of creditors from insolvency and the ability of firms to obtain additional financing for potentially attractive investment opportunities. However, debt is carried on the statement of financial position simply as the unpaid balance. Consequently, no adjustment is made for the current level of interest rates (which may be higher or lower than when the debt was originally issued) or risk. Thus, the accounting value of debt may differ substantially from its market value. Some forms of debt, such as pension liabilities and lease obligations, may not appear on the statement of financial position at all.

**Interest Coverage**   The interest coverage ratio is calculated by dividing earnings (before interest and taxes) by interest. This ratio emphasizes the ability of the firm to generate enough income to cover interest expense. For the Canadian Composite Corporation, this ratio is

$$\text{Interest coverage} = \frac{\text{Earnings before interest and taxes}}{\text{Interest expense}} = \frac{219}{49} = 4.5$$

Interest expense is an obstacle that a firm must surmount if it is to avoid default. The interest coverage ratio is directly connected to the firm's ability to pay interest. However, since interest is paid in cash, it would probably make sense to add back depreciation (a non-cash expense) to income in computing this ratio and to include other financing expenses paid in cash, such as payments of principal and lease payments.

A large debt burden is a problem only if the firm's cash flow is insufficient to make the required debt service payments. This is related to the uncertainty of future cash flows. Firms with predictable cash flows are frequently said to have more *debt capacity* than firms with highly uncertain cash flows. Therefore, it makes sense to compute the variability of the firm's cash flows. One possible way to do this is to calculate the standard deviation of cash flows relative to the average cash flow.

**Cash Coverage** As mentioned above, a problem with the interest coverage ratio is that it is not really a measure of the cash available to pay interest. Non-cash items like depreciation and amortization have been deducted. Accordingly, depreciation and amortization are added back to arrive at EBITDA (earnings before interest, tax, depreciation, and amortization). The cash coverage ratio resolves this problem and is calculated as follows:

$$\text{Cash coverage} = \frac{\text{EBIT} + (\text{Depreciation} + \text{Amortization})}{\text{Interest expense}} = \frac{219 + 90}{49} = 6.3$$

**Payable Turnover** This ratio looks at how long, on average, it takes the company to repay its bills. Although delaying payables is a good way to free up short-term cash flows, an excessively low payable turnover could signal liquidity and payment problems. Payable turnover is calculated by dividing total credit purchases by the average accounts payable:

$$\text{Average accounts payable} = \frac{213 + 197}{2} = 205$$

$$\text{Payable turnover} = \frac{\text{COGS (assuming all inventory was purchased on credit)}}{\text{Average accounts payable}}$$

$$= \frac{1,655}{205} = 8.07$$

$$\text{Average payment period} = \frac{\text{Days in period}}{\text{Payable turnover}} = \frac{365}{8.07} = 45.2 \text{ days}$$

## Profitability

One of the most difficult attributes of a firm to conceptualize and to measure is profitability. In a general sense, accounting profits are the difference between revenues and costs. Unfortunately, there is no completely unambiguous way to know when a firm is profitable. At best, a financial analyst can measure current or past accounting profitability. Many business opportunities, however, involve sacrificing current profits for future profits. For example, all new products require large start-up costs and, as a consequence, produce low initial profits. Thus, current profits can be a poor reflection of true future profitability.

Different industries employ different amounts of capital and differ in risk. For this reason, benchmark measures of profitability differ among industries.

**Profit Margin** Profit margins are computed by dividing profits by total operating revenue. Thus, they express profits as a percentage of total operating revenue. The most important margin is the net profit margin. The net profit margin for the Canadian Composite Corporation is

$$\text{Net profit margin} = \frac{\text{Net income}}{\text{Total operating revenue}} = \frac{86}{2,262} = 0.038 \ (3.8\%)$$

In general, profit margins reflect the firm's ability to produce a product or service at a low cost or to sell it at a high price. Profit margins are not direct measures of profitability because they are based on total operating revenue, not on the investment made in assets by the firm or the equity investors. Trade firms tend to have low margins and service firms tend to have high margins.

**EBITDA Margin**   Since EBITDA adds back interest, taxes, and non-cash items (depreciation and amortization), it looks more directly at operating cash flows than net income does. Instead of using net income as profit margin uses, the EBITDA margin uses EBITDA divided by total operating revenues as follows:

$$\text{EBITDA margin} = \frac{\text{EBITDA}}{\text{Total operating revenue}} = \frac{219 + 90}{2,262} = 0.137 \ (13.7\%)$$

Similar to profit margin, a higher EBITDA margin is desirable. As mentioned previously, higher margins reflect the company's ability to control costs more effectively and to sell more or at a higher price. Careful attention should be given to the relationship between price and sales volume. An increase in price may not necessarily increase EBITDA or profitability margins, as a price increase is usually met with a decline in sales.

**Return on Assets**   One common measure of managerial performance is the ratio of income to average total assets, both before tax and after tax. These ratios for the Canadian Composite Corporation for 2015 are

$$\text{Net return on assets} = \frac{\text{Net income}}{\text{Average total assets}} = \frac{86}{1,810.5} = 0.0475 \ (4.75\%)$$

$$\text{Gross return on assets} = \frac{\text{Earnings before interest and taxes}}{\text{Average total assets}}$$
$$= \frac{219}{1,801.5} = 0.121 \ (12.1\%)$$

One of the most interesting aspects of return on assets (ROA) is how some financial ratios can be linked to compute ROA in the *DuPont system of financial control*. This system expresses ROA in terms of the profit margin and asset turnover. The basic components of the system are as follows:

| ROA = | Profit margin | × | Asset turnover |
|---|---|---|---|
| ROA = | $\dfrac{\text{Net income}}{\text{Total operating revenue}}$ | × | $\dfrac{\text{Total operating revenue}}{\text{Average total assets}}$ |
| 0.0475 = | 0.038 | × | 1.25 |
| ROA (gross) = | $\dfrac{\text{Earnings before interest and taxes}}{\text{Total operating revenue}}$ | × | $\dfrac{\text{Total operating revenue}}{\text{Average total assets}}$ |
| 0.121 = | 0.097 | × | 1.25 |

Firms can increase ROA by increasing profit margins or asset turnover. Of course, competition limits their ability to do so simultaneously. Thus, firms tend to face a trade-off between turnover and margin. In retail trade, for example, mail-order companies have low margins and high turnover, whereas high-quality jewellery stores have high margins and low turnover.

It is often useful to describe financial strategies in terms of margins and turnover. Suppose a firm selling pneumatic equipment is thinking about providing customers with more liberal credit terms. This will probably decrease asset turnover (because receivables would increase more than sales). Thus, the margins will have to go up to keep ROA from falling.

**Return on Equity**   The return on equity (ROE) ratio is defined as net income after interest and taxes divided by average common shareholders' equity, which for the Canadian Composite Corporation is

$$\text{ROE} = \frac{\text{Net income}}{\text{Average shareholders' equity}} = \frac{86}{765} = 0.112 \ (11.2\%)$$

$$\text{Average shareholders' equity} = \frac{805 + 725}{2} = 765$$

The difference between ROA and ROE is due to financial leverage. To see this, consider the following breakdown of ROE expanding the DuPont equation:

$$\text{ROE} = \text{Profit margin} \times \text{Asset turnover} \times \text{Equity multiplier}$$

$$= \frac{\text{Net income}}{\text{Total operating revenue}} \times \frac{\text{Total operating revenue}}{\text{Average total assets}} \times \frac{\text{Average total assets}}{\text{Average shareholders' equity}}$$

$$0.112 = 0.038 \times 1.25 \times 2.36$$

From the preceding numbers, it would appear that financial leverage always magnifies ROE. Actually, this occurs only when ROA (gross) is greater than the interest rate on debt.

**Payout Ratio**    The *payout ratio* is the proportion of net income paid out in cash dividends. For the Canadian Composite Corporation,

$$\text{Payout ratio} = \frac{\text{Cash dividends}}{\text{Net income}} = \frac{43}{86} = 0.5$$

The *retention ratio* is the proportion of net income added to annual retained earnings. For the Canadian Composite Corporation, this ratio is

$$\text{Retention ratio} = \frac{\text{Annual retained earnings}}{\text{Net income}} = \frac{43}{86} = 0.5$$

$$\text{Retained earnings} = \text{Net income} - \text{Dividends}$$

## The Sustainable Growth Rate

One ratio that is very helpful in financial analysis is called the sustainable growth rate. It is the maximum rate of growth a firm can sustain with no external financing while maintaining a constant debt-to-equity ratio. The precise value of sustainable growth can be calculated as

$$\text{Sustainable growth rate} = \text{ROE} \times \text{Retention ratio}$$

For the Canadian Composite Corporation, ROE is 11.2 percent. The retention ratio is 1/2, so we can calculate the sustainable growth rate as

$$\text{Sustainable growth rate} = 11.2\% \times (1/2) = 5.6\%$$

The Canadian Composite Corporation can expand at a maximum rate of 5.6 percent per year with no external equity financing or without increasing financial leverage. (We discuss sustainable growth in Chapters 3 and 6.)

## Market Value Ratios

We can learn many things from a close examination of the statement of financial position and statement of comprehensive income. However, one very important characteristic of a firm that cannot be found on an accounting statement is its market value.

**Market Price**    The market price of a share of one common share is the price that buyers and sellers establish when they trade the share. The market value of the common equity of a firm is the market price of a common share multiplied by the number of shares outstanding.

Sometimes the term *fair market value* is used to describe market prices. Fair market value is the price at which common shares would change hands between a willing buyer and a willing seller, both having knowledge of the relevant facts. Thus, market prices guess the true worth of the assets of a firm. In an efficient stock market, market prices reflect all relevant facts about firms, thus revealing the true value of the firm's underlying assets.

The market value of Suncor Energy is many times greater than that of Celestica Inc. This may suggest nothing more than the fact that Suncor Energy is a bigger firm than Celestica (hardly a surprising revelation). Financial analysts construct ratios to extract information that is independent of a firm's size.

**Enterprise Value**   Enterprise value provides a closer measure of a company's true market value. Instead of appraising the market value of a firm solely by the market capitalization, enterprise value takes into consideration the market value of interest-bearing debt as well. When the market value of debt is unknown, the common practice is to take the book value of debt instead. Enterprise value can be calculated as

$$\text{Enterprise value} = \text{Market capitalization} + \text{Market value of interest-bearing debt} - \text{Cash}$$

This measure indicates how much it would cost to purchase all the outstanding shares of a firm and pay off its debt obligations. As a result, this measures the market value of an entire business rather than just the market value of its equity. The adjustment for cash is to recognize that if we were a buyer the cash would be used immediately to buy back debt or pay a dividend.

**Enterprise Value Multiple**   The enterprise value multiple measures the entire business and is a useful ratio for comparison with other companies since it is not affected by differences in capital structure, taxes, or capital spending. The enterprise value multiple is calculated as

$$\text{Enterprise value multiple} = \frac{\text{Enterprise value}}{\text{EBITDA}}$$

**Price–Earnings Ratio**   The price–earnings (P/E) ratio is the ratio of market price for a share to its current annual earnings per share. The following table shows average P/Es for three selected companies on the TSX on January 30, 2014:

|  | Price–earnings ratio | Dividend yield |
|---|---|---|
| Bombardier Inc. | 13.96 | 2.5 |
| Royal Bank of Canada | 12.53 | 3.9 |
| Pure Technologies Ltd. | 67.98 | 0.00 |

The P/E ratio shows how much investors are willing to pay for \$1 of earnings per share. Looking at our example, Pure Technologies had a greater P/E ratio than Bombardier and Royal Bank.

The P/E ratio reflects investors' views of the growth potential of different sectors. The reason an investor would pay \$67.98 for a dollar of earnings in a technology stock like Pure Technologies is that the investor expects large earnings growth. If this expectation is realized, higher P/E stocks will have higher returns. If earnings do not grow to meet expectations, these stocks will be very risky. We return to P/E ratios in Chapter 6.

**Dividend Yield**   The dividend yield is calculated by annualizing the last observed dividend payment of a firm and dividing by the current market price:

$$\text{Dividend yield} = \frac{\text{Dividend per share}}{\text{Market price per share}}$$

The table above shows dividend yields for selected indexes. Like P/E ratios, dividend yields are related to the market's perception of growth prospects for firms. Firms with high growth prospects will generally have lower dividend yields.

**Market-to-Book Ratio**   The market-to-book (M/B) ratio is calculated by dividing the market price per share by the book value per share. Since book value per share is an accounting number, it reflects historical costs. In a loose sense, the M/B ratio therefore compares the market value of the firm's assets to their cost. A value less than 1 could mean that the firm has not been successful overall in creating value for its shareholders.

## Using Financial Ratios

Financial ratios have a variety of uses within a firm. Among the most important is performance evaluation. For example, managers are frequently evaluated and compensated on the basis of accounting measures of performance such as profit margin and return on equity. Also, firms with multiple divisions frequently compare their performance using financial statement information. Another important internal use is planning for the future. Historical financial statement information is very useful for generating projections about the future and for checking the realism of assumptions made in those projections.

Financial statements are useful to parties outside the firm, including short-term and long-term creditors and potential investors. For example, such information is quite useful in deciding whether or not to grant credit to a new customer.[11] When firms borrow from chartered banks, loan agreements almost always require that financial statements be submitted periodically. Most bankers use computer software to prepare common-size statements expressing statement of comprehensive income items as percentages of sales and balance-sheet items as percentages of total assets. They also calculate ratios for their accounts. More advanced software uses expert system technology to generate a preliminary diagnosis of the borrower by comparing the company's ratios against benchmark parameters selected by the banker. Table 2A.1 shows such a table prepared for the financial statement ratios for our example, the Canadian Composite Corporation.

**TABLE 2A.1**

### Selected Ratios for Canadian Composite Corporation

|  | 2015 | Industry | Rating |
|---|---|---|---|
| **Short-term solvency** | | | |
| Current ratio | 1.57 | 1.52 | OK |
| Quick ratio | 1.01 | 1.10 | OK |
| **Activity** | | | |
| Total asset turnover | 1.25 | 1.31 | OK |
| Receivables turnover | 8.02 | 7.80 | OK |
| Average collection period (days) | 45.5 | 46.79 | OK |
| Inventory turnover | 6.03 | 7.12 | − |
| Days in inventory | 60.5 | 51.26 | − |
| **Financial leverage** | | | |
| Debt ratio | 0.57 | 0.60 | OK |
| Debt-to-equity ratio | 1.33 | 1.33 | OK |
| Equity multiplier | 2.33 | 2.33 | OK |
| Interest coverage | 4.5 | 4.0 | OK |
| **Profitability** | | | |
| Profit margin | 3.8% | 2.3% | + |
| Net return on assets | 4.75% | 3.0% | + |
| Return on equity | 11.2% | 7.0% | + |
| Payout ratio | 0.5 | 0.3 | |
| Retention ratio | 0.5 | 0.7 | |
| Sustainable growth rate | 5.6% | 4.9% | + |

---

[11] Chapter 31 shows how statistical models based on ratios are used to predict insolvency.

## Choosing a Benchmark

The firm's historical ratios are standard benchmarks for financial ratio analysis. Historical benchmarks are used to establish a trend. Another means of establishing a benchmark is to identify firms that are similar in the sense that they compete in the same markets, have similar assets, and operate in similar ways. In practice, establishing such a peer group involves judgment on the part of the analyst, since no two companies are identical.

Various benchmarks are available.[12] Statistics Canada publications include typical statements of financial position, statements of comprehensive income, and selected ratios for firms in around 180 industries. Statistics Canada also provides *Financial Performance Indicators*, which is a data file containing key financial ratios by industry, some of which include net profit margin, pre-tax profit margin, return on equity, and liabilities to assets. In addition to Statistics Canada publications, SEDAR is the official website for documents filed with securities regulators in Canada and provides a searchable database for public securities documents, profiles, and information on public companies and investment funds. These documents include, but are not limited to, annual reports, codes of conduct, and executive compensation.[13] *Dun & Bradstreet Industry Norms and Key Business Ratios* provides key business ratios for Canadian companies. Other sources of financial data are *Financial Post Advisor*, *Bloomberg*, and *Standard & Poor's Industry Surveys*.[14] Several financial institutions gather their own financial ratio databases by compiling information on their loan customers. In this way, they seek to obtain more current, industry-specific information than is available from services like Statistics Canada and Dun & Bradstreet.

Obtaining current information is not the only challenge facing the financial analyst. Most large Canadian corporations do business in several industries, so the analyst often compares the company against several industry averages. Further, it is necessary to recognize that the industry average is not necessarily optimal. For example, agricultural analysts know that farmers are suffering with painfully low average profitability coupled with excessive debt. Despite these shortcomings, the industry average is a useful benchmark for ratio analysis.

For a list of all the financial ratios and their equations, see Table 2A.2.

**TABLE 2A.2**

**Summary of Formulas**

| | |
|---|---|
| **Short-term solvency** | |
| Current ratio | $\dfrac{\text{Total current assets}}{\text{Total current liabilities}}$ |
| Quick ratio | $\dfrac{\text{Quick assets}}{\text{Total current liabilities}}$ |
| Cash ratio | $\dfrac{\text{Cash}}{\text{Total current liabilities}}$ |
| **Activity** | |
| Total asset turnover | $\dfrac{\text{Total operating revenues}}{\text{Average total assets}}$ |
| Receivables turnover | $\dfrac{\text{Total operating revenues}}{\text{Average receivables}}$ |

---

[12] This discussion draws on L. Kryzanowski, M. To, and R. Seguin, *Business Solvency Risk Analysis* (Institute of Canadian Bankers, 1990), Chapter 3.

[13] The website is http://www.sedar.com.

[14] Analysts examining U.S. companies will find comparable information available from Robert Morris Associates, *Bloomberg*, *EDGAR*, and *Marketline*.

| Activity | |
|---|---|
| Average collection period | $\dfrac{\text{Days in period}}{\text{Receivables turnover}}$ |
| Inventory turnover | $\dfrac{\text{Cost of goods sold}}{\text{Average inventory}}$ |
| **Financial leverage** | |
| Debt ratio | $\dfrac{\text{Total debt}}{\text{Total assets}}$ |
| Debt-to-equity ratio | $\dfrac{\text{Total debt}}{\text{Total equity}}$ |
| Equity multiplier | $\dfrac{\text{Total assets}}{\text{Total equity}}$ |
| Interest coverage | $\dfrac{\text{Earnings before interest and taxes (EBIT)}}{\text{Interest expense}}$ |
| Cash coverage | $\dfrac{\text{EBIT} + (\text{Depreciation} + \text{Amortization})}{\text{Interest expense}}$ |
| Payable turnover | $\dfrac{\text{COGS for total sales on credit}}{\text{Average accounts payable}}$ |
| Average payment period | $\dfrac{\text{Days in period}}{\text{Payable turnover}}$ |
| **Profitability** | |
| Net profit margin | $\dfrac{\text{Net income}}{\text{Total operating revenue}}$ |
| EBITDA margin | $\dfrac{\text{EBITDA}}{\text{Total operating revenue}}$ |
| Net return on assets | $\dfrac{\text{Net income}}{\text{Average total assets}}$ |
| Return on assets (ROA) | Profit margin $\times$ Asset turnover |
| Gross return on assets | $\dfrac{\text{Earnings before interest and taxes (EBIT)}}{\text{Average total assets}}$ |
| Return on equity (ROE) | $\dfrac{\text{Net income}}{\text{Average shareholders' equity}}$ |
| Payout ratio | $\dfrac{\text{Cash dividends}}{\text{Net income}}$ |
| Retention ratio | $\dfrac{\text{Annual retained earnings}}{\text{Net income}}$ |
| **Sustainable growth rate** | |
| Sustainable growth rate | ROE $\times$ Retention ratio |
| **Market value** | |
| Enterprise value | Market capitalization + Market value of interest-bearing debt − Cash |
| Enterprise value multiple | $\dfrac{\text{Enterprise value}}{\text{EBITDA}}$ |
| Price–earnings (P/E) ratio | $\dfrac{\text{Market price per share}}{\text{Current annual earnings per share}}$ |
| Dividend yield | $\dfrac{\text{Dividend per share}}{\text{Market price per share}}$ |
| Market-to-book (M/B) value | $\dfrac{\text{Market price per share}}{\text{Book value per share}}$ |

## Potential Pitfalls of Financial Ratio Analysis

Financial ratio analysis is not based on any underlying theory that helps identify which quantities to examine or guides the establishment of benchmarks. For this reason, individual judgment guided by experience plays an important role. Recognizing this, chartered banks are investing in expert system technology to pool the experience of many individual lenders and to standardize judgment.

Several other general problems frequently crop up. Different firms end their fiscal years at different times. For firms in seasonal businesses (such as a retailer with a large Christmas season), this can lead to difficulties in comparing balance sheets because of fluctuations in accounts during the year. For any particular firm, unusual or transient events, such as a one-time profit from an asset sale, may affect financial performance. In comparing firms, such events can give misleading signals.

---

**APPENDIX 2A**

# SUMMARY AND CONCLUSIONS

Much research indicates that accounting statements provide important information about the value of the firm. Financial analysts and managers learn how to rearrange financial statements to squeeze out the maximum amount of information. In particular, analysts and managers use financial ratios to summarize the firm's liquidity, activity, financial leverage, and profitability. When possible, they also use market values. This appendix describes the most popular financial ratios. The following points should be kept in mind when trying to interpret financial statements:

1. Measures of profitability such as return on equity (ROE) suffer from several potential deficiencies as indicators of performance. They do not take into account the risk or timing of cash flows.

2. Financial ratios are linked to one another. For example, ROE is determined from the profit margins, the asset turnover ratio, and the financial leverage.

3. Financial ratio analysis seldom looks at ratios in isolation. As we have illustrated, financial analysts compare a firm's present ratios against historical ratios and industry averages.

4. Because ratio analysis is based on experience rather than on theory, special care must be taken to achieve consistent interpretations. Since financial ratios are based on accounting numbers, ratios may be misleading if management engages in accounting window dressing to improve reported performance. The hardest performance measures for management to manipulate are those based on market values because the market can usually see through attempts to manipulate accounting numbers.

---

**APPENDIX 2B**

# Statement of Cash Flows

There is an official accounting statement called the statement of cash flows. This statement helps explain the change in accounting cash, which for Canadian Composite is $33 million in 2015. It is very useful in understanding financial cash flow. Notice in Table 2.1 that cash increases from $107 million in 2014 to $140 million in 2015.

The first step in determining the change in cash is to figure out cash flow from operating activities. This is the cash flow that results from the firm's normal activities producing and selling goods and services. The second step is to make an adjustment for cash flow from investing activities. The final step is to make an adjustment for cash flow from financing activities. Financing activities are the net payments to creditors and owners (excluding interest expense) made during the year.

The three components of the statement of cash flows are determined below.

## Cash Flow from Operating Activities

To calculate cash flow from operating activities we start with net income. Net income can be found on the statement of comprehensive income and is equal to $86. We now need to add back non-cash expenses and adjust for changes in current assets and liabilities (other than cash). The result is cash flow from operating activities:

**CANADIAN COMPOSITE CORPORATION**
**Cash Flow from Operating Activities**
**2015**
**(in $ millions)**

| | |
|---|---:|
| Net income | $ 86 |
| Depreciation | 90 |
| Deferred taxes | 13 |
| **Change in assets and liabilities** | |
| Accounts receivable | (24) |
| Inventories | 11 |
| Accounts payable | 16 |
| Accrued expense | 18 |
| Notes payable | (3) |
| Other | (8) |
| **Cash flow from operating activities** | **$199** |

## Cash Flow from Investing Activities

Cash flow from investing activities involves changes in capital assets: acquisition of fixed assets and sales of fixed assets (i.e., net capital expenditures). The result for Canadian Composite follows:

**CANADIAN COMPOSITE CORPORATION**
**Cash Flow from Investing Activities**
**2015**
**(in $ millions)**

| | |
|---|---:|
| Acquisition of fixed assets | $(198) |
| Sales of fixed assets | 25 |
| **Cash flow from investing activities** | **$(173)** |

## Cash Flow from Financing Activities

Cash flows to and from creditors and owners include changes in equity and debt:

**CANADIAN COMPOSITE CORPORATION**
**Cash Flow from Financing Activities**
**2015**
**(in $ millions)**

| | |
|---|---:|
| Retirement of debt (includes notes) | $ (73) |
| Proceeds from long-term debt sales | 86 |
| Dividends | (43) |
| Repurchase of shares | (6) |
| Proceeds from new share issue | 43 |
| **Cash flow from financing activities** | **$ 7** |

The statement of cash flows is the addition of cash flows from operations, cash flows from investing activities, and cash flows from financing activities, and is produced in Table 2B.1.

**Statement of Consolidated Cash Flows of the Canadian Composite Corporation**

| | |
|---|---|
| CANADIAN COMPOSITE CORPORATION<br>Statement of Cash Flows<br>2015<br>(in $ millions) | |
| **Operations** | |
| Net income | $ 86 |
| Depreciation | 90 |
| Deferred taxes | 13 |
| **Changes in assets and liabilities** | |
| Accounts receivable | (24) |
| Inventories | 11 |
| Accounts payable | 16 |
| Accrued expenses | 18 |
| Notes payable | (3) |
| Other | (8) |
| **Total cash flow from operations** | $ 199 |
| **Investing activities** | |
| Acquisition of fixed assets | $(198) |
| Sales of fixed assets | 25 |
| **Total cash flow from investing activities** | $(173) |
| **Financing activities** | |
| Retirement of debt (including notes) | $ (73) |
| Proceeds of long-term debt | 86 |
| Dividends | (43) |
| Repurchase of shares | (6) |
| Proceeds from new share issues | 43 |
| **Total cash flow from financing activities** | $ 7 |
| **Change in cash** (on the balance sheet) | $ 33 |

## Cash Flow Management

Cash flow analysis is popular because it is difficult to manipulate, or spin, cash flows. Accounting principles allow for significant subjective decisions to be made regarding many key areas. The use of cash flow as a metric to evaluate a company comes from the idea that there is less subjectivity involved, and, therefore, it is harder to spin the numbers. But several recent examples have shown that companies can still find ways to do it.

Tyco used several ploys to alter cash flows. For example, the company purchased more than $800 million of customer security alarm accounts from dealers. The cash flows from these transactions were reported in the financing activity section of the accounting statement of cash flows. When Tyco received payments from customers, the cash inflows were reported as operating cash flows. Another method used by Tyco was to make acquired companies prepay operating expenses. In other words, the company acquired by Tyco would pay vendors for items not yet received. In one case, the payments totalled more than $50 million. When the acquired company was consolidated with Tyco, the prepayments reduced Tyco's cash outflows, thus increasing the operating cash flows.

Nortel, the now bankrupt technology giant, enhanced its reported cash flow from operations through sales of assets from discontinued operations. The company originally reported cash flow from operations for 2000 as US$40 million, but in the following year, this cash flow was restated as US$824 million due to the addition of cash flow from discontinued operations.[15]

In both of these examples, the companies were trying to boost operating cash flows by shifting cash flows to a different heading. The important thing to notice is that these movements don't affect the total cash flow of the firm, which is why we recommend focusing on this number, not just operating cash flow.

**QUESTIONS & PROBLEMS**

2A.1   What effect would the following actions have on a firm's current ratio? Assume that net working capital is positive.
a. Inventory is purchased for cash.
b. A supplier is paid.
c. A bank loan is repaid.
d. A long-term debt matures and is paid.
e. A customer pays off an account.
f. Inventory is sold.

2A.2   If a company reports a 7 percent profit margin, a total asset turnover of 1.8, and a total debt ratio of 0.72, what are its ROA and ROE?

2A.3   Consider the following information for the PVI Corporation:

| | |
|---|---|
| Credit sales | $17,465 |
| Cost of goods sold | 12,216 |
| Accounts receivable | 3,210 |
| Accounts payable | 2,230 |

How long does it take PVI to collect on its sales? How long does PVI take to pay its suppliers?

Use the following financial statement information for Stowe Enterprises to solve Problems 2A.4 through 2A.7:

**STOWE ENTERPRISES**
**2015 Statement of Comprehensive Income**

| | |
|---|---|
| Sales | $4,500 |
| Cost of goods sold | 2,400 |
| Depreciation | 500 |
| Earnings before interest and taxes | $1,600 |
| Interest paid | 480 |
| Taxable income | $1,120 |
| Taxes | 380 |
| Net income | $ 740 |
| Addition to retained earnings | $ 186 |
| Dividends | $ 554 |

---

[15] F. Taylor, "Investors, beware cash flow wizardry," http://www.globeadvisor.com/printpage.html?/servlet/GIS.Servlets.WireFeedRedirect?cf=sglobeadvisor/config_blank&vg=BigAdVariableGenerator&date=20020619&archive=gam&slug=RVOXX, June 19, 2002.

### STOWE ENTERPRISES
#### Abbreviated Statement of Financial Position, 2014–2015

| Assets | 2014 | 2015 | Liabilities and shareholders' equity | 2014 | 2015 |
|---|---|---|---|---|---|
| **Current assets** | | | **Current liabilities** | | |
| Cash | $ 800 | $ 1,800 | Accounts payable | 1,550 | 1,630 |
| Accounts receivable | 1,950 | 2,040 | Notes payable | 1,629 | 1,380 |
| Inventory | 3,135 | 2,300 | Other | 746 | 625 |
| **Fixed assets** | | | Long-term debt | 3,487 | 3,780 |
| Net plant and equipment | 4,620 | 5,130 | **Shareholders' equity** common shares | 570 | 1,146 |
| | | | Accumulated retained earnings | 2,523 | 2,709 |
| Total assets | $10,505 | $11,270 | **Total liabilities and shareholders' equity** | $10,505 | $11,270 |

2A.4   Compute the following ratios for Stowe Enterprises for 2014 and 2015:

| Short-Term Solvency Ratios | Asset Management Ratios | Long-Term Solvency Ratios | Profitability Ratios |
|---|---|---|---|
| Current ratio | Total asset turnover | Debt ratio | Profit margin |
| Quick ratio | Inventory turnover | Debt-to-equity ratio | Return on assets |
| Cash ratio | Receivables turnover | Equity multiplier | Return on equity |
| | | Interest coverage | |
| | | Cash coverage ratio | |

2A.5   Prepare a statement of cash flows for Stowe.

2A.6   For how many days in 2015 could Stowe continue to operate if its production were suspended?

2A.7   Stowe has 80 shares outstanding in 2015. The price per share is $45. What are the P/E ratio and the M/B ratio?

2A.8   Select an industry featured in recent financial news. Then obtain annual reports on two companies in that industry and conduct a ratio analysis for the most recent two years. Make the relevant comparisons between the companies and against industry norms. Based on your ratio analysis, how do the two companies differ? Compare your comments against recent newspaper articles on the industry. (*Note:* This question is much easier to answer using ratio analysis software.)

# Financial Planning and Growth

EXECUTIVE SUMMARY

Corporate financial planning establishes guidelines for change in the firm. These guidelines should include (1) an identification of the firm's financial goals, (2) an analysis of the differences between these goals and the current financial status of the firm, and (3) a statement of the actions needed for the firm to achieve its financial goals. In other words, as one member of General Motors' board was heard to say, "Planning is a process that at best helps the firm avoid stumbling into the future backwards."

The basic elements of financial planning are (1) the investment opportunities the firm elects to take advantage of, (2) the amount of debt the firm chooses to employ, and (3) the amount of cash the firm thinks is necessary and appropriate to pay shareholders. These are the financial policies that the firm must decide upon for its growth, profitability, and shareholder value. For example, at Procter & Gamble, capital budgeting analysts screen project proposals submitted by division managers promoting new product ideas. Each proposal must contain a detailed financial plan for the suggested product showing how it will impact cash flow.

Almost all firms identify a companywide growth rate as a major component of their financial planning.[1] In one famous case, International Business Machines' stated growth goal was simple but typical: to match the growth of the computer industry, which was projected to be 15 percent per year through the end of the 1990s. Though we may have had some doubts about IBM's ability to sustain a 15 percent growth rate, we are certain there are important financial implications of the strategies that IBM adopted to achieve that rate. There are direct connections between the growth that a company can achieve and its financial policy. One purpose of this chapter is to look at the financial aspects of how fast a firm can grow.

The chapter first describes what is usually meant by financial planning. This enables us to make an important point: investment and financing decisions frequently interact. The different interactions of investment and financing decisions can be analyzed in the financial statements. We show how financial statements can be used to better understand how growth is achieved.

## 3.1 WHAT IS FINANCIAL PLANNING?

Financial planning formulates the method by which financial goals are to be achieved. It has two dimensions: a time frame and a level of aggregation.

A financial plan is a statement of what is to be done in a future time. The GM board member was right on target when he explained the virtues of financial planning. Most decisions have long lead times, which means they take a long time to implement. In an uncertain world, this requires that decisions be made far in advance of their implementation. If a firm wants to build a factory in 2016, it may need to line up contractors in 2015. It is sometimes useful to think of the future as having a short run

---

[1] We think that a firm's growth should be a consequence of its trying to achieve maximum shareholder value.

and a long run. The short run, in practice, is usually the coming 12 months. We focus our attention on financial planning over the long run, which is usually taken to be a two- to five-year period.

Financial plans are compiled from the capital budgeting analyses of each of a firm's projects. In effect, the smaller investment proposals of each operational unit are added up and treated as a big project. This process is called **aggregation**.

Financial plans always entail alternative sets of assumptions. For example, suppose a company has two separate divisions: one for consumer products and one for gas turbine engines. The financial planning process might require each division to prepare three alternative business plans for the next three years.

1. *A worst case.* This plan requires making the worst possible assumptions about the company's products and the state of the economy. It could mean divestiture and liquidation.

2. *A normal case.* This plan requires making the most likely assumptions about the company and the economy.

3. *A best case.* Each division works out a case based on the most optimistic assumptions. It could involve new products and expansion.

Because the company is likely to spend a lot of time preparing proposals on different scenarios that will become the basis for the company's financial plan, it seems reasonable to ask what the planning process will accomplish.

1. *Interactions.* The financial plan must make explicit the linkages between investment proposals for the different operating activities of the firm and the financing choices available to the firm. IBM's 15 percent growth target goes hand in hand with its financing program.

2. *Options.* The financial plan provides the opportunity for the firm to work through various investment and financing options. The firm addresses questions of what financing arrangements are optimal and evaluates options of closing plants or marketing new products.

3. *Feasibility.* The different plans must fit into the overall corporate objective of maximizing shareholder wealth.

4. *Avoiding surprises.* Financial planning should identify what may happen in the future if certain events take place. Thus, one of the purposes of financial planning is to avoid surprises.

**CONCEPT QUESTIONS**
• What are the two dimensions of the financial planning process?
• Why should firms draw up financial plans?

## 3.2    A FINANCIAL PLANNING MODEL: THE INGREDIENTS

Just as companies differ in size and products, financial plans are not the same for all companies. However, there are some common elements:

1. **Sales forecast.** All financial plans require a sales forecast. Perfectly accurate sales forecasts are not possible, because sales depend on the uncertain future state of the economy. Firms can get help from businesses specializing in macroeconomic and industry projections. A good sales forecast should be the consequence of having identified all valuable investment opportunities.

2. **Pro forma statements.** The financial plan will have a forecast balance sheet, a statement of comprehensive income, and a statement of cash flows. These are called *pro forma statements*, or *pro formas*.[2]

3. **Asset requirements.** The plan will describe projected capital spending. In addition, it will discuss the proposed uses of net working capital.

4. **Financial requirements.** The plan will include a section on financing arrangements. This part of the plan should discuss dividend policy and debt policy. Sometimes firms will expect to raise equity by selling new shares of stock. In this case the plan must consider what kinds of securities must be sold and what methods of issuance are most appropriate.

5. **Plug.** Suppose a financial planner assumes that sales, costs, and net income will rise at a particular rate, $g_1$. Further suppose that the planner wants assets and liabilities to grow at a different rate, $g_2$. These two different growth rates may be incompatible unless a third variable is also adjusted. For example, compatibility may only be reached if outstanding stock grows at a different rate, $g_3$. In this example, we treat the growth in outstanding stock as the *plug* variable. That is, the growth rate in outstanding stock is chosen to make the growth rate in statement of comprehensive income items consistent with the growth rate in balance sheet items. Surprisingly, even if the statement of comprehensive income items grow at the *same* rate as the balance sheet items, consistency might be achieved only if outstanding stock grows at a different rate.

   Of course, the growth rate in outstanding stock need not be the plug variable. One could have statement of comprehensive income items grow at $g_1$, and assets, long-term debt, and outstanding stock grow at $g_2$. In this case, compatibility between $g_1$ and $g_2$ might be achieved by letting short-term debt grow at a rate of $g_3$.

6. **Economic assumptions.** The plan must explicitly state the economic environment in which the firm expects to reside over the life of the plan. Among the economic assumptions that must be made is the level of interest rates.

## 3.3    THE PERCENTAGE OF SALES METHOD

In the previous section, we described a simple planning model in which every item increased at the same rate as sales. This may be a reasonable assumption for some elements. For others, such as long-term borrowing, it is probably not reasonable, because the amount of long-term borrowing is something set by management, and it does not necessarily relate directly to the level of sales. We return to the nuances of long-term borrowing in detail in Chapters 16 and 17.

In this section, we describe an extended version of our simple model. The basic idea is to separate the statement of comprehensive income and balance sheet accounts into two groups: those that do vary directly with sales, and those that do not. Given a sales forecast, we will then be able to calculate how much financing the firm will need to support the predicted sales level.

---

[2] Microsoft Excel is one of the most widely used software programs in the business world when it comes to financial modelling and pro forma forecasts. The program is sophisticated and provides the ability to do tasks much quicker than by hand. For more information on the use of Microsoft Excel as a tool for modelling, see Simon Benninga, *Principles of Finance with Excel*, Oxford, 2006.

EXAMPLE **3.1**

The Computerfield Corporation's 2015 financial statements are as follows:

### Statement of Comprehensive Income 2015

| | |
|---|---|
| Sales | $1,000 |
| Costs | 800 |
| Net income | $ 200 |

### Statement of Financial Position Year-End 2015

| Assets | $500 | Debt | $250 |
|---|---|---|---|
| | | Equity | 250 |
| Total | $500 | Total | $500 |

In 2015, Computerfield's profit margin is 20 percent, and it has never paid a dividend. Its debt-to-equity ratio is 1. This is also the firm's *target* debt-to-equity ratio. Unless otherwise stated, the financial planners at Computerfield assume that all variables are tied directly to sales and that current relationships are optimal.

Suppose that sales increase by 20 percent from 2015 to 2016. Because the planners would then also forecast a 20 percent increase in costs, the pro forma statement of comprehensive income would be as follows:

### Statement of Comprehensive Income 2016

| | |
|---|---|
| Sales | $1,200 |
| Costs | 960 |
| Net income | $ 240 |

The assumption that all variables will grow by 20 percent will enable us to construct the pro forma statement of financial position as well:

### Statement of Financial Position Year-End 2016

| Assets | $600 | Debt | $300 |
|---|---|---|---|
| | | Equity | 300 |
| Total | $600 | Total | $600 |

Now we must reconcile these two pro formas. How, for example, can net income be equal to $240 and equity increase by only $50? The answer is that Computerfield must have paid a dividend or repurchased stock equal to $190. In this case dividends are the plug variable.

Suppose Computerfield does not pay a dividend and does not repurchase its own stock. With these assumptions, Computerfield's equity will grow to $490, and debt must be retired to keep total assets equal to $600. In this case the debt-to-equity ratio is the plug variable; with $600 in total assets and $490 in equity, debt will have to be $600 − $490, or $110. Since we started with $250 in debt, Computerfield will have to retire $250 − $110, or $140 of debt. The resulting statement of financial position would look like this:

### Statement of Financial Position Year-End 2016

| Assets | $600 | Debt | $110 |
|---|---|---|---|
| | | Equity | 490 |
| Total | $600 | Total | $600 |

The thing to notice in our simple example is the way the change in liabilities and equity depends on the firm's financing policy and the firm's dividend policy. The firm ensures growth in assets by having a plan in place to finance such growth.

This example shows the interaction of sales growth and financial policy. The next section focuses on the need for external funds. It identifies a six-step procedure for constructing the pro forma statement of financial position, also known as the balance sheet.

The financial planning model we describe next is based on the percentage of sales approach. Our goal here is to develop a quick and practical way of generating pro forma statements. We defer discussion of some possible extensions to a later section.

## The Statement of Comprehensive Income

We start out with the most recent statement of comprehensive income for the Rosengarten Corporation, as shown in Table 3.1. Notice that we continue to simplify things by including costs, depreciation, and interest in a single cost figure. We separate these out in a later section.

**TABLE 3.1**

### Rosengarten Corporation Statement of Comprehensive Income

| ROSENGARTEN CORPORATION<br>Statement of Comprehensive Income<br>($ in thousands) | | |
|---|---:|---:|
| Sales | | $20,000.00 |
| Costs | | 16,969.70 |
| Taxable income | | $ 3,030.30 |
| Taxes (34%) | | 1,030.30 |
| Net income | | $ 2,000.00 |
| Dividends | $1,000.00 | |
| Addition to retained earnings | 1,000.00 | |

Rosengarten has projected a 10 percent increase in sales for the coming year, so we are anticipating sales of $20 million × 1.1 = $22 million. To generate a pro forma statement of comprehensive income, we assume that total costs will continue to run at $16.9697 million/$20 million = 84.85% of sales. With this assumption, Rosengarten's pro forma statement of comprehensive income is as shown in Table 3.2. The effect here of assuming that costs are a constant percentage of sales is to assume that the profit margin is constant. To check this, notice that the profit margin was $2 million/$20 million = 10%. In our pro forma, the profit margin is $2.2 million/$22 million = 10%, so it is unchanged.

**TABLE 3.2**

### Rosengarten Corporation Pro Forma Statement of Comprehensive Income

| ROSENGARTEN CORPORATION<br>Pro Forma Statement of Comprehensive Income<br>($ in thousands) | |
|---|---:|
| Sales (projected) | $22,000.00 |
| Costs (84.85% of sales) | 18,666.00 |
| Taxable income | $ 3,334.00 |
| Taxes (34%) | 1,134.00 |
| Net income | $ 2,200.00 |

Next, we need to project the dividend payment. This amount is up to Rosengarten's management. We will assume Rosengarten has a policy of paying out a constant fraction of net income in the form of a cash dividend. For the most recent year, the **dividend payout ratio** was

$$\text{Dividend payout ratio} = \frac{\text{Cash dividends}}{\text{Net income}}$$

$$= \frac{\$1 \text{ million}}{\$2 \text{ million}} = 50\% \qquad (3.1)$$

We can also calculate the ratio of the addition to retained earnings to net income as

$$\frac{\text{Addition to retained earnings}}{\text{Net income}} = \frac{\$1 \text{ million}}{\$2 \text{ million}}$$

This ratio is called the **retention ratio** or **plowback ratio**, and it is equal to 1 minus the dividend payout ratio because everything not paid out is retained. Assuming that the dividend payout ratio is constant, the projected dividends and addition to retained earnings will be (\$ in thousands)

$$\text{Projected dividends paid to shareholders} = \$2,200 \times \tfrac{1}{2} = \$1,100$$

$$\text{Projected addition to retained earnings} = \$2,200 \times \tfrac{1}{2} = \underline{1,100}$$
$$\underline{\underline{\$2,200}}$$

## The Statement of Financial Position

To generate a pro forma statement of financial position, we start with the most recent statement, as shown in the table below:

| Current Statement of Financial Position (\$ in thousands) | | Pro Forma Statement of Financial Position (\$ in thousands) | |
|---|---|---|---|
| | | | Explanation |
| Current assets | \$ 6,000 | \$ 6,600 | 30% of sales |
| Fixed assets | \$24,000 | \$26,400 | 120% of sales |
| Total assets | \$30,000 | \$33,000 | 150% of sales |
| Short-term debt | \$10,000 | \$11,000 | 50% of sales |
| Long-term debt | 6,000 | 6,600 | 30% of sales |
| Common stock | 4,000 | 4,000 | Constant |
| Retained earnings | 10,000 | 11,100 | Net income |
| Total financing | \$30,000 | \$32,700 | |
| | | \$    300 | Funds needed (the difference between total assets and total financing) |

On our statement of financial position, we assume that most of the items vary directly with sales. Only common stock does not. For those items that do vary with sales, we express each as a percentage of sales for the year just completed. When an item does not vary directly with sales, we write "constant."

For example, on the asset side, fixed assets are equal to 120 percent of sales (\$24 million/\$20 million) for the year just ended. We assume this percentage applies to the coming year, so for each \$1 increase in sales, fixed assets will rise by \$1.20.

From this information we can determine the pro forma statement of financial position, which is on the right-hand side. The change in retained earnings will be

Net income      −      Dividends      = Change in retained earnings

(0.10 × \$22 million) − (0.5 × 0.10 × \$22 million) =      \$1.1 million

In this example the plug variable is new shares of stock. The company must issue \$300,000 of new stock. The equation that can be used to determine if external funds are needed is

**External Funds Needed (EFN):**

$$\left(\frac{\text{Assets}}{\text{Sales}}\right) \times \Delta\text{Sales} - \frac{\text{Debt}}{\text{Sales}} \times \Delta\text{Sales} - (p \times \text{Projected sales}) \times (1 - d)$$

$$= (1.5 \times \$2 \text{ million}) - (0.80 \times \$2 \text{ million}) - (0.10 \times \$22 \text{ million} \times 0.5)$$
$$= \$1.4 \text{ million} - \$1.1 \text{ million}$$
$$= \$0.3 \text{ million}$$

where

$$\frac{\text{Assets}}{\text{Sales}} = 1.5 \qquad \frac{\text{Debt}}{\text{Sales}} = 0.8$$

$p$ = Net profit margin = 0.10

$d$ = Dividend payout ratio = 0.5

$\Delta$Sales = Projected change in sales

The steps in the estimation of the pro forma statement of financial position for the Rosengarten Corporation and the external funds needed (EFN) are as follows:

1. Express statement of financial position items that vary with sales as a percentage of sales.

2. Multiply the percentages determined in step 1 by projected sales to obtain the amount for the future period.

3. Where no percentage applies, simply insert the previous statement of financial position figure in the future period.

4. Compute projected retained earnings as follows:

> Projected retained earnings = Present retained earnings
> + Projected net income
> − Cash dividends

5. Add the asset accounts to determine projected assets. Next, add the liabilities and equity accounts to determine the total financing; any difference is the *shortfall*. This equals EFN.

6. Use the plug to fill EFN. In this example, new shares are the plug but debt could also be used. The choice depends on the firm's optimal capital structure, as we discuss in Chapters 16 and 17.

The same calculations can be done in a Microsoft Excel spreadsheet using pro formas.

Table 3.3 computes EFN for several different growth rates. For low growth rates, Rosengarten will run a surplus, and for high growth rates, it will run a deficit. The "break-even" growth rate is 7.7 percent. Figure 3.1 illustrates the relation between projected sales growth and EFN. As can be seen, the need for new assets from projected sales growth grows much faster than the additions to retained earnings plus new debt. Eventually, a deficit is created and a need for external funds becomes evident.

**TABLE 3.3**

**Projected Sales Growth and External Funds Needed for the Rosengarten Corporation**

| Projected Sales Growth | Increase in Assets Required | Addition to Retained Earnings | External Funds Needed |
|---|---|---|---|
| 0  % | $        0 | $1,000,000 | −$1,000,000 |
| 5 | 1,500,000 | 1,050,000 | −350,000 |
| 7.7 | 2,310,000 | 1,077,000 | — |
| 10 | 3,000,000 | 1,100,000 | 300,000 |
| 20 | 6,000,000 | 1,200,000 | 1,600,000 |

FIGURE 3.1

**Growth and External Funds Needed for the Rosengarten Corporation**

# IN THEIR OWN WORDS

## Robert C. Higgins on sustainable growth

Most financial officers know intuitively that it takes money to make money. Rapid sales growth requires increased assets in the form of accounts receivable, inventory, and fixed plant, which, in turn, require money to pay for assets. They also know that if their company does not have the money when needed, it can literally "grow broke." The sustainable growth equation states these intuitive truths explicitly.

Sustainable growth is often used by bankers and other external analysts to assess a company's creditworthiness. They are aided in this exercise by several sophisticated computer software packages that provide detailed analyses of the company's past financial performance, including its annual sustainable growth rate.

Bankers use this information in several ways. Quick comparison of a company's actual growth rate to its sustainable rate tells the banker what issues will be at the top of management's financial agenda. If actual growth consistently exceeds sustainable growth, management's problem will be where to get the cash to finance growth. The banker thus can anticipate interest in loan products. Conversely, if sustainable growth consistently exceeds actual, the banker had best be prepared to talk about investment products, because

management's problem will be what to do with all the cash that keeps piling up in the till.

Bankers also find the sustainable growth equation useful for explaining to financially inexperienced small business owners and overly optimistic entrepreneurs that, for the long-run viability of their business, it is necessary to keep growth and profitability in proper balance.

Finally, comparison of actual to sustainable growth rates helps a banker understand why a loan applicant needs money and for how long the need might continue. In one instance, a loan applicant requested $100,000 to pay off several insistent suppliers and promised to repay in a few months when he collected some accounts receivable that were coming due. A sustainable growth analysis revealed that the firm had been growing at four to six times its sustainable growth rate and that this pattern was likely to continue in the foreseeable future. This alerted the banker that impatient suppliers were only a symptom of the much more fundamental disease of overly rapid growth, and that a $100,000 loan would likely prove to be only the down payment on a much larger, multiyear commitment.

Robert C. Higgins is Professor of Finance at the University of Washington. He pioneered the use of sustainable growth as a tool for financial analysis.

# 3.4    WHAT DETERMINES GROWTH?

This section furthers our discussion of a firm's growth and its accounting statements. It is obvious that the need for external funds and growth are related. All other factors remaining equal, the higher the rate of growth in sales or assets, the greater will be the need for external funds. This text strongly emphasizes and focuses on growth, not because growth is an appropriate goal, but because growth is simply a convenient means of examining the interactions between investment and financing decisions.

Firms frequently make growth forecasts an explicit part of financial planning. Donaldson reports on the pervasiveness of stating corporate goals in terms of growth rates.[3] This may seem puzzling in the light of our previous emphasis on maximizing the shareholders' value as the central goal of management. One way to reconcile the difference is to think of growth as an intermediate goal that leads to higher value. Rappaport correctly points out that in applying the shareholder value approach, growth should not be a goal but must be a consequence of decisions that maximize shareholder value.[4] In fact, if the firm is willing to accept any project just to grow in size, growth will probably make the shareholders worse off.

Donaldson also concludes that most major industrial companies are very reluctant to use external equity as a regular part of their financial planning. To illustrate the linkages between the ability of a firm to grow and its accounting statements when the firm does not issue equity, we can make some planning assumptions:

1. The firm's assets will grow in proportion to its sales.
2. Net income is a constant proportion of its sales.
3. The firm has a given dividend payout policy and a given debt-to-equity ratio.
4. The firm will not change the number of outstanding shares of stock.

There is only one growth rate that is consistent with the preceding assumptions. In effect, with these assumptions, growth has been made a plug variable. To see this, recall that a change in assets must always be equal to a change in debt plus a change in equity:

Now we can write the conditions that ensure this equality and solve for the growth rate that will give it to us.

The variables used in this demonstration are as follows:

$T$ = The ratio of total assets to sales
$p$ = The net profit margin on sales
$d$ = The dividend payout ratio
$L$ = The debt-to-equity ratio
$S_0$ = Sales this year
$\Delta S$ = The change in sales ($S_1 - S_0 = \Delta S$)
$S_1$ = Next year's projected sales
RE = Retained earnings = Net income × Retention ratio = $S_1 \times p \times (1 - d)$
NI = Net income = $S_1 \times p$

[3] G. Donaldson, *Managing Corporation Wealth: The Operations of a Comprehensive Financial Goals System* (New York: Praeger, 1984).

[4] A. Rappaport, *Creating Shareholder Value: The New Standard for Business Performance* (New York: Free Press, 1986).

If the firm is to increase sales by $\Delta S$ during the year, it must increase assets by $T\Delta S$. The firm is assumed not to be able to change the number of shares of stock outstanding, so the equity financing must come from retained earnings. Retained earnings will depend on next year's sales, the dividend payout ratio, and the profit margin. The amount of borrowing will depend on the amount of retained earnings and the debt-to-equity ratio:

New equity:       $S_1 \times p \times (1 - d)$
plus
Borrowing:       $[S_1 \times p \times (1 - d)] \times L$
equals
Capital spending: $T\Delta S$

Moving things around a little gives the following:

$$T\Delta S = [S_1 \times p \times (1 - d)] + [S_1 \times p \times (1 - d) \times L]$$

and

$$\frac{\Delta S}{S_0} = \frac{p \times (1 - d) \times (1 + L)}{T - [p \times (1 - d) \times (1 + L)]} = \text{Growth rate in sales} \qquad (3.2)$$

This is the growth-rate equation. Given the profit margin ($p$), the dividend payout ratio ($d$), the debt-to-equity ratio ($L$), and the asset requirement ratio ($T$), the growth rate can be determined. It is the only growth possible with the preset values for the four variables. Higgins has referred to this growth rate as the firm's **sustainable growth rate**.[5]

---

EXAMPLE 3.2

Table 3.4 shows the current statement of comprehensive income, the sources-and-uses-of-cash statement, and the statement of financial position for the Hoffman Corporation. Net income for the corporation was 16.5 percent ($1,650/$10,000) of sales revenue. The company paid out 72.4 percent ($1,195/$1,650) of its net income in dividends. The interest rate on debt was 10 percent, and the long-term debt was 50 percent ($5,000/$10,000) of assets. (Notice that for simplicity we use the single term *net working capital* in Table 3.4 instead of separating current assets from current liabilities.) Hoffman's assets grew at a rate of 10 percent ($910/$9,090). In addition, sales grew at 10 percent, though this increase is not shown in Table 3.4.

The cash flow generated by Hoffman was enough not only to pay a dividend but also to increase net working capital and fixed assets by $455 each. The company did not issue any shares of stock during the year. Its debt-to-equity ratio and dividend payout ratio remained constant throughout the year.

The sustainable growth rate for the Hoffman Corporation is 10 percent, or[6]

$$\frac{0.165 \times 0.276 \times 2}{1 - (0.165 \times 0.276 \times 2)} = 0.1$$

However, suppose its desired growth rate was to be 20 percent. It is possible for Hoffman's desired growth to exceed its sustainable growth because Hoffman is able to issue new shares of stock. A firm can do several things to increase its sustainable growth rate, as seen from the Hoffman example:

1.   Sell new shares of stock.

---

[5] R. C. Higgins, "Sustainable Growth Under Inflation," *Financial Management* (Autumn 1981). The definition of sustainable growth was popularized by the Boston Consulting Group and others.

[6] This expression is exactly equal to the rate of return on equity (ROE) multiplied by the retention rate (RR)—ROE × RR—if by ROE we mean net income this year divided by equity *last year*, i.e., $1,650/$4,545 = 36.3%. In this case ROE × RR = 36.3% × 27.6% = 10% = sustainable growth in sales. On the other hand, if by ROE we mean net income this year divided by equity *this year*, i.e., $1,650/$5,000 = 33%, the sustainable growth rate in sales = ROE × RR/(1 − ROE × RR).

2.  Increase its reliance on debt.

3.  Reduce its dividend payout ratio.

4.  Increase profit margins.

5.  Decrease its asset requirement ratio.

Now we can see the use of a financial planning model to test the feasibility of the planned growth rate. If sales are to grow at a rate higher than the sustainable growth rate, the firm must improve operating performance, increase financial leverage, decrease dividends, or sell new shares. Unless these changes are sufficient to increase the sustainable growth rate to the targeted rate of 20 percent, Hoffman will experience a liquidity shortage and, ultimately, insolvency.

## TABLE 3.4

### Current Financial Statements: The Hoffman Corporation

| THE HOFFMAN CORPORATION Statement of Comprehensive Income ($ in thousands) | |
|---|---|
| | **This Year** |
| Net sales ($S$) | $10,000 |
| Cost of sales | 7,000 |
| Earnings before taxes and interest | 3,000 |
| Interest expense | 500 |
| Earnings before taxes | 2,500 |
| Taxes | 850 |
| Net income (NI) | $ 1,650 |

| Sources and Uses of Cash | |
|---|---|
| | **This Year** |
| **Sources:** | |
| Net income (NI) | $ 1,650 |
| Depreciation | 500 |
| Operating cash flow | 2,150 |
| Borrowing | 455 |
| New stock issue | 0 |
| Total sources | $ 2,605 |
| **Uses:** | |
| Increase in net working capital | 455 |
| Capital spending | 955 |
| Dividends | 1,195 |
| Total uses | $ 2,605 |

| Statement of Financial Position | | | |
|---|---|---|---|
| | **This Year** | **Last Year** | **Change** |
| **Assets** | | | |
| Net working capital | $ 5,000 | $4,545 | $455 |
| Fixed assets | 5,000 | 4,545 | 455 |
| Total assets | $10,000 | $9,090 | $910 |
| **Liabilities and shareholders' equity** | | | |
| Debt | $ 5,000 | $4,545 | $455 |
| Equity | 5,000 | 4,545 | 455 |
| Total liabilities and shareholders' equity | $10,000 | $9,090 | $910 |

EXAMPLE 3.3

At the other extreme, suppose the firm is losing money (has a negative profit margin) or is paying out more than 100 percent of earnings in dividends so that the retention rate $(1 - d)$ is negative. In each of these cases, the negative sustainable growth rate signals the rate at which sales and assets must shrink. Firms can achieve negative growth by selling off assets and laying off employees. The example of Nortel shows that bankruptcy can be the ultimate consequence of not paying attention to sustainable growth rates (see Table 3.5).

**TABLE 3.5**

| Nortel 2000 Annual Statement Excerpts (in $ millions)* | |
|---|---:|
| Cash dividends | $ 223 |
| Net income/loss | −3,470 |
| Total revenue | 30,275 |
| Total debt | 13,071 |
| Total equity | 29,109 |
| Total assets (2000) | 42,180 |
| Total assets (1999) | 24,007 |

*All figures taken from Nortel's 2000 annual report.

Table 3.5 shows that in 2000 net income for Nortel was −11.46 percent (−$3,470/$30,275) of total revenues. Nortel paid out −6.43% ($223/−$3,470) in dividends. The company had a debt-to-equity ratio of 44.9 percent ($13,071/$29,109) and total assets to sales of 1.39 ($42,180/$30,275). Now we have all the components necessary to calculate Nortel's sustainable growth rate for the year ended 2000 as follows:

$$\frac{-0.1146 \times [1 - (-0.0643)] \times (1 + 0.449)}{1.39 - \{-0.1146 \times [1 - (-0.0643)] \times (1 + 0.449)\}} = \frac{-0.1767}{1.5667}$$
$$= -0.1128 \text{ or } -11.28\%$$

As discussed previously, negative sustainable growth represents the rate at which a company's sales or assets must shrink. However, for the year ended 2000, instead of downsizing, Nortel reported asset growth of 75.7 percent [($42,180 − $24,007)/$24,007]. In hindsight, coming out of the dot-com bubble, Nortel continued to expand at a rate inconsistent with what was sustainable. Instead of downsizing as it should have, the company continued to grow, hiding losses through accounting misstatements. By the time this came to light in 2003, the company was long overdue for a drastic downsizing, shocking markets and investors, and leading to Nortel's bankruptcy protection filing in 2009.[7]

**CONCEPT QUESTIONS**

- When might the goals of growth and value maximization be in conflict, and when would they be aligned?
- What are the determinants of growth?

## Some Caveats on Financial Planning Models

Financial planning models such as sustainable growth suffer from a great deal of criticism. We present two commonly voiced attacks below.

---

[7] "Key Dates in Nortel Networks' History," CBC news business, January 14, 2013.

First, financial planning models do not indicate which financial policies are the best. For example, our model could not tell us whether Hoffman's decision to issue new equity to achieve a higher growth rate raises the shareholder value of the firm.

Second, financial planning models are too simple. In reality, costs are not always proportional to sales, assets need not be a fixed percentage of sales, and capital budgeting involves a sequence of decisions over time. These assumptions are generally not incorporated into financial plans.

Financial planning models are necessary to assist in planning the investment and financial decisions of the firm. Without some sort of long-term financial plan, the firm may find itself adrift in a sea of change without a rudder for guidance. But, because of the assumptions and the abstractions from reality necessary in the construction of the financial plan, we also think that they should carry the label: Let the user beware!

## 3.5

# SUMMARY AND CONCLUSIONS

Financial planning forces the firm to think about and forecast the future. It involves the following:

1. Building a corporate financial model.
2. Describing different scenarios of future development from worst to best cases.
3. Using the model to construct pro forma financial statements.
4. Running the model under different scenarios (conducting sensitivity analysis).
5. Examining the financial implications of ultimate strategic plans.

Corporate financial planning should not become a purely mechanical activity. If it does, it will probably focus on the wrong things. In particular, plans are formulated all too often in terms of a growth target with an explicit linkage to creation of value. We talk about a particular financial planning model called sustainable growth. We provide a useful summary of formulas used in this chapter in Table 3.6. Although the financial planning model presented is simple, needless to say, it is an important concept to grasp.

### TABLE 3.6

**Summary of Formulas**

Dividend payout ratio
$$\frac{\text{Cash dividends}}{\text{Net income}}$$

Retention ratio or plowback ratio
$$\frac{\text{Addition to retained earnings}}{\text{Net income}}$$

Retained earnings
$$\text{Net income} \times \text{Retention ratio}$$

External funds needed (EFN)
$$\left(\frac{\text{Assets}}{\text{Sales}}\right) \times \Delta\text{Sales} - \left(\frac{\text{Debt}}{\text{Sales}}\right) \times \Delta\text{Sales}$$
$$- (p \times \text{Projected sales}) \times (1 - d)$$
where $p$ = Net profit margin
$d$ = Dividend payout ratio
$\Delta\text{Sales}$ = Projected change in sales

Sustainable growth rate
$$\frac{p \times (1 - d) \times (1 + L)}{T - (p \times (1 - d)) \times (1 + L)}$$
where $L$ = Debt-to-equity ratio
$T$ = Asset retirement ratio

**KEY TERMS**    Aggregation  66               Financial requirements   67    Retention ratio (plowback
                 Asset requirements   67       Plug   67                           ratio)  70
                 Dividend payout ratio   69    Pro forma statements   67       Sales forecast  66
                 Economic assumptions   67                                     Sustainable growth rate   74

**QUESTIONS &** **External Funds Needed**
**PROBLEMS**

**3.1**  The most recent financial statements for Martin Inc. are shown here:

|  Statement of Comprehensive Income | | | Statement of Financial Position | | |
| --- | --- | --- | --- | --- | --- |
| Sales | $37,300 | Assets | $127,000 | Debt | $ 30,500 |
| Costs | 25,800 | | | Equity | 96,500 |
| Taxable income | $11,500 | Total | $127,000 | Total | $127,000 |
| Taxes (34%) | 3,910 | | | | |
| Net income | $ 7,590 | | | | |

Assets and costs are proportional to sales. Debt and equity are not. A dividend of $2,500 was paid, and Martin wishes to maintain a constant dividend payout ratio. Next year's sales are projected to be $42,300. What external funds are needed?

**Sales and Growth**

**3.2**  The most recent financial statements for Fontenot Co. are shown here:

|  Statement of Comprehensive Income | | | Statement of Financial Position | | |
| --- | --- | --- | --- | --- | --- |
| Sales | $67,000 | Current assets | $ 31,000 | Long-term debt | $ 68,000 |
| Costs | 43,800 | Fixed assets | 118,000 | Equity | 81,000 |
| Taxable income | $23,200 | Total | $149,000 | Total | $149,000 |
| Taxes (34%) | 7,888 | | | | |
| Net income | $15,312 | | | | |

Assets and costs are proportional to sales. The company maintains a constant 30 percent dividend payout ratio and a constant debt-to-equity ratio. What is the maximum increase in sales that can be sustained assuming no new equity is issued?

**Sustainable Growth**

**3.3**  If the Layla Corp. has a 15 percent return on equity and a 10 percent dividend payout ratio, what is its sustainable growth rate?

**3.4**  Assuming the following ratios are constant, what is the sustainable growth rate?

Total asset turnover = 1.90

Profit margin = 8.1%

Equity multiplier = 1.25

Dividend payout ratio = 30%

**Calculating External Funds Needed**

**3.5**  The most recent financial statements for Bradley Inc. are shown here (assuming no income taxes):

|  Statement of Comprehensive Income | | | Statement of Financial Position | | |
| --- | --- | --- | --- | --- | --- |
| Sales | $5,700 | Assets | $14,100 | Debt | $ 6,300 |
| Costs | 3,820 | | | Equity | 7,800 |
| Net income | $1,880 | Total | $14,100 | Total | $14,100 |

Assets and costs are proportional to sales. Debt and equity are not. No dividends are paid. Next year's sales are projected to be $6,669. What is the EFN?

**External Funds Needed**

3.6   Cheryl Colby, CFO of Charming Florist Ltd., has created the firm's pro forma state-
      ment of financial position for the next fiscal year. Sales are projected to grow by
      10 percent to $420 million. Current assets, fixed assets, and short-term debt are
      20 percent, 75 percent, and 15 percent of sales, respectively. Charming Florist pays
      out 30 percent of its net income in dividends. The company currently has $120 mil-
      lion of long-term debt and $48 million in common stock par value. The profit margin
      is 9 percent.
      a. Construct the current balance sheet for the firm using the projected sales figure.
      b. Based on Cheryl's sales growth forecast, how much does Charming Florist need
         in external funds for the upcoming fiscal year?
      c. Construct the firm's pro forma statement of financial position for the next fiscal
         year, and confirm the EFN that you calculated in (b).

**Sustainable Growth Rate**

3.7   The Steiben Company has a return on equity of 13.1 percent and a dividend payout
      ratio of 40 percent.
      a. What is the company's sustainable growth rate?
      b. Can the company's actual growth rate be different from its sustainable growth
         rate? Why or why not?
      c. How can the company increase its sustainable growth rate?

**External Funds Needed**

3.8   The Optical Scan Company has forecast a 20 percent sales growth rate for next year.
      The current financial statements are shown here:

<table>
<tr><td colspan="2" align="center">Statement of Comprehensive Income</td></tr>
<tr><td>Sales</td><td align="right">$30,400,000</td></tr>
<tr><td>Costs</td><td align="right">26,720,000</td></tr>
<tr><td>Taxable income</td><td align="right">$ 3,680,000</td></tr>
<tr><td>Taxes</td><td align="right">1,288,000</td></tr>
<tr><td>Net income</td><td align="right">$ 2,392,000</td></tr>
<tr><td>    Dividends</td><td align="right">$ 956,800</td></tr>
<tr><td>    Addition to retained earnings</td><td align="right">1,435,200</td></tr>
</table>

| Statement of Financial Position | | | |
|---|---|---|---|
| **Assets** | | **Liabilities and shareholder's equity** | |
| Current assets | $ 7,200,000 | Short-term debt | $ 6,400,000 |
| Fixed assets | 17,600,000 | Long-term debt | 4,800,000 |
| | | Common stock | $ 3,200,000 |
| | | Accumulated retained earnings | 10,400,000 |
| | | Total equity | $13,600,000 |
| Total assets | $24,800,000 | Total liabilities and shareholders' equity | $24,800,000 |

      a. Using the equation from the chapter, calculate the EFN for next year.
      b. Construct the firm's pro forma statement of financial position for next year and
         confirm the EFN that you calculated in (a).
      c. Calculate the sustainable growth rate for the company.
      d. Can Optical Scan eliminate the need for external funds by changing its dividend
         policy? What other options are available to the company to meet its growth
         objectives?

### Calculating External Funds Needed

3.9 The most recent financial statements for Moose Tours Inc. appear below. Sales for 2016 are projected to grow by 20 percent. Interest expense will remain constant; the tax rate and the dividend payout ratio will also remain constant. Costs, other expenses, current assets, fixed assets, and accounts payable increase proportionally with sales. If the firm is operating at full capacity and no new debt or equity is issued, what external funds are needed to support the 20 percent growth rate in sales?

**MOOSE TOURS INC.**
**2015 Statement of Comprehensive Income**

| | | |
|---|---|---|
| Sales | | $929,000 |
| Costs | | 723,000 |
| Other expenses | | 19,000 |
| Earnings before interest and taxes | | $187,000 |
| Interest expense | | 14,000 |
| Taxable income | | $173,000 |
| Taxes | | 60,550 |
| Net income | | $112,450 |
| Dividends | $33,735 | |
| Addition to retained earnings | 78,715 | |

**MOOSE TOURS INC.**
**Statement of Financial Position as of December 31, 2015**

| Assets | | | Liabilities and shareholders' equity | |
|---|---|---|---|---|
| Current assets | | | Current liabilities | |
| Cash | $ 25,300 | | Accounts payable | $ 68,000 |
| Accounts receivable | 40,700 | | Notes payable | 17,000 |
| Inventory | 86,900 | | Total | $ 85,000 |
| Total | $152,900 | | Long-term debt | $158,000 |
| Fixed assets | | | Shareholders' equity | |
| Net plant and equipment | $413,000 | | Common stock and paid-in surplus | $140,000 |
| | | | Retained earnings | 182,900 |
| | | | Total | $322,900 |
| Total assets | $565,900 | | Total liabilities and shareholders' equity | $565,900 |

3.10 In Problem 3.9, suppose the firm wishes to keep its debt-to-equity ratio constant. What is EFN now?

### External Funds Needed and Sustainable Growth

3.11 Redo Problem 3.10 using sales growth rates of 30 percent and 35 percent in addition to 20 percent. Illustrate graphically the relationship between EFN and the growth rate, and use this graph to determine the relationship between them.

### Constraints on Growth

3.12 Bulla Recording Inc. wishes to maintain a growth rate of 12 percent per year and a debt-to-equity ratio of 0.40. Profit margin is 5.3 percent, and the ratio of total assets to sales is constant at 0.75. Is this growth rate possible? To answer, determine what the dividend payout ratio must be. How do you interpret the result?

**External Funds Needed**

3.13  Using the definitions below, show that EFN can be written as

$$EFN = -PM(S)b + [A - PM(S)b] \times g$$

*Hint:* Asset needs will equal $A \times g$. The addition to retained earnings will equal $PM(S)b \times (1 + g)$.

$$S = \text{Previous year's sales}$$
$$A = \text{Total assets}$$
$$D = \text{Total debt}$$
$$E = \text{Total equity}$$
$$g = \text{Projected growth in sales}$$
$$PM = \text{Profit margin}$$
$$b = \text{Retention (plowback) ratio}$$

MINICASE

# Ratios and Financial Planning at East Coast Yachts

Dan Ervin was recently hired by East Coast Yachts to assist the company with its short-term financial planning and also to evaluate the company's financial performance. Dan graduated from university five years ago with a finance degree, and he has been employed in the treasury department of a Fortune 500 company since then.

East Coast Yachts was founded 10 years ago by Larissa Warren. The company's operations are located near Lunenburg, Nova Scotia, and the company is structured as an LLC (limited liability company). The company has manufactured midsize custom high-performance yachts for clients over this period, and its products have received excellent reviews for safety and reliability. The company's yachts have also recently received the highest award for customer satisfaction. The yachts are primarily purchased by wealthy individuals for pleasure use. Occasionally, a yacht is manufactured for purchase by a company for business purposes.

The custom yacht industry is fragmented, with a number of manufacturers. As with any industry, there are market leaders, but the diverse nature of the industry ensures that no manufacturer dominates the market. The competition in the market, as well as the product cost, ensures that attention to detail is a necessity. For instance, East Coast Yachts will spend 80 to 100 hours on hand buffing the stainless steel stem-iron, which is the metal cap on the yacht's bow that conceivably could collide with a dock or another boat.

To get Dan started with his analysis, Larissa has provided the following financial statements. Dan has gathered the industry ratios for the yacht manufacturing industry:

**East Coast Yachts 2015**
**Statement of Comprehensive Income**

| | | |
|---|---:|---:|
| Sales | | $234,300,000 |
| Cost of goods sold | | 165,074,000 |
| Other expenses | | 27,991,000 |
| Depreciation | | 7,644,000 |
| Earnings before interest and taxes | | $ 33,591,000 |
| Interest | | 4,212,600 |
| Taxable income | | $ 29,378,400 |
| Taxes (40%) | | 11,751,360 |
| Net income | | $ 17,627,040 |
| Dividends | $ 5,288,112 | |
| Addition to retained earnings | 12,338,928 | |

## East Coast Yachts
### Statement of Financial Position as of December 31, 2015

| Assets | | Liabilities and shareholders' equity | |
|---|---|---|---|
| Current assets | | Current liabilities | |
|   Cash | $ 3,650,700 |   Accounts payable | $ 7,753,000 |
|   Accounts receivable | 6,567,600 |   Notes payable | 15,936,300 |
|   Inventory | 7,363,700 |   Total | $ 23,689,300 |
|   Total | $ 17,582,000 | Long-term debt | $ 40,480,000 |
| Fixed assets | | Shareholders' equity | |
|   Net plant and equipment | $112,756,900 |   Common stock | $ 6,200,000 |
| | |   Retained earnings | 59,969,600 |
| | | Total equity | $ 66,169,600 |
|   Total assets | $130,338,900 | Total liabilities and equity | $130,338,900 |

### Yacht Industry Ratios

| | Lower quartile | Median | Upper quartile |
|---|---|---|---|
| Current ratio | 0.50 | 1.43 | 1.89 |
| Quick ratio | 0.21 | 0.38 | 0.62 |
| Total asset turnover | 0.68 | 0.85 | 1.38 |
| Inventory turnover | 6.85 | 9.15 | 16.13 |
| Receivables turnover | 6.27 | 11.81 | 21.45 |
| Debt ratio | 0.44 | 0.52 | 0.61 |
| Debt-to-equity ratio | 0.79 | 1.08 | 1.56 |
| Equity multiplier | 1.79 | 2.08 | 2.56 |
| Interest coverage | 5.18 | 8.06 | 9.83 |
| Profit margin | 4.05% | 6.98% | 9.87% |
| Return on assets | 6.05% | 10.53% | 15.83% |
| Return on equity | 9.93% | 16.54% | 28.14% |

1. Calculate all the ratios listed in the industry table for East Coast Yachts.

2. Compare the performance of East Coast Yachts to the industry as a whole. For each ratio, comment on why it might be viewed as positive or negative relative to the industry. Suppose you create an inventory ratio calculated as inventory divided by current liabilities. How do you interpret this ratio? How does East Coast Yachts compare to the industry average?

3. Calculate the sustainable growth rate of East Coast Yachts. Calculate EFN and prepare pro forma statements of comprehensive income and statements of financial position assuming growth at precisely this rate. Recalculate the ratios in the previous question. What do you observe?

4. As a practical matter, East Coast Yachts is unlikely to be willing to raise external equity capital, in part because the owners don't want to dilute their existing ownership and control positions. However, East Coast Yachts is planning for a growth rate of 20 percent next year. What are your conclusions and recommendations about the feasibility of East Coast's expansion plans?

5. Most assets can be increased as a percentage of sales. For instance, cash can be increased by any amount. However, fixed assets must often be increased in specific amounts because it is impossible, as a practical matter, to buy part of a new plant or machine. In this case a company has a "staircase" or "lumpy" fixed cost structure. Assume that East Coast Yachts is currently producing at 100 percent of capacity. As a result, to expand production, the company must set up an entirely new line at a cost of $30 million. Calculate the new EFN with this assumption. What does this imply about capacity utilization for East Coast Yachts next year?

## PART 2

**CHAPTER**

4

# Financial Markets and Net Present Value: First Principles of Finance

**EXECUTIVE SUMMARY**

Finance refers to the process by which special markets deal with cash flows over time. These markets are called *financial markets.* Making investment and financing decisions requires an understanding of the basic economic principles of financial markets. This introductory chapter describes a financial market as one that makes it possible for individuals and corporations to borrow and lend. As a consequence, financial markets can be used by individuals to adjust their patterns of consumption over time and by corporations to adjust their patterns of investment spending over time. The main point of this chapter is that individuals and corporations can use the financial markets to help them make investment decisions. We introduce one of the most important ideas in finance: net present value (NPV).

By far the most important economic decisions are those that involve investments in real assets. We don't mean savings decisions, which are decisions not to consume some of this year's income, but decisions regarding actual investments: building a machine or a whole factory or a Tim Hortons, for example. These decisions determine the economic future for a society. Economists use the word *capital* to describe the total stock of machines and equipment that a society possesses and uses to produce goods and services. Investment decisions are decisions about whether or not to increase this stock of capital.

The investment decisions made today determine how much additional capital society will add to its current stock of capital. That capital can then be used in the future to produce goods and services for the society. Some of the forms that capital takes are obvious, like steel mills and computers. But many kinds of capital are things that you probably never would have considered as part of a country's capital stock. Public roads, for example, are a form of capital, and the decisions to build them are investment decisions. Perhaps most important, the decision you are making to invest in an education is no different in principle from these other investment decisions. Your decision to invest in education is a decision to build your human capital, just as a company's decision to build a new factory is a decision to invest in physical capital.[1] The total of all the capital possessed by a society is a measure of its wealth. The purpose of this chapter is to develop the basic principles that guide rational investment decision making. We show that a particular investment decision should be made if it is superior to available alternatives in the financial markets.

---

[1] If you have any doubt about the importance of human capital as part of a country's wealth, think about the conditions of Germany and Japan at the end of World War II. The physical capital of these countries had been destroyed, and even the basic social capital, such as roads, sewer systems, and factories, was in rubble. Even though these countries might have appeared to be economically crippled beyond repair, a look below the surface would have revealed a different picture. A huge part of the wealth of these countries consisted of the human capital inherent in their literate and skilled populations. Building on this substantial base of capital by a long-term policy of investment has brought Germany and Japan to a very high standard of living.

# 4.1   THE FINANCIAL MARKET ECONOMY

Financial markets develop to facilitate borrowing and lending between individuals. Here we talk about how this happens. Suppose we describe the economic circumstances of two people: Frank and Leslie. Both Frank and Leslie have current income of $100,000. Frank is a very patient person, and some people call him a miser. He wants to consume only $50,000 of current income and save the rest. Leslie is a very impatient person, and some people call her extravagant. She wants to consume $150,000 this year. Frank and Leslie have different **intertemporal consumption** preferences.

Such preferences are personal matters and have more to do with psychology than with finance. However, it seems that Frank and Leslie could strike a deal: Frank could give up some of his income this year in exchange for future income that Leslie can promise to give him. Frank can *lend* $50,000 to Leslie, and Leslie can *borrow* $50,000 from Frank. This deal illustrates the useful role of financial markets in allowing borrowing and lending.

Suppose that they do strike this deal, with Frank giving up $50,000 this year in exchange for $55,000 next year. This is illustrated in Figure 4.1 with the basic cash flow time chart, a representation of the timing and amount of the cash flows. The cash flows that are received are represented by an arrow pointing up from the point on the time line at which the cash flow occurs. The cash flows paid out are represented by an arrow pointing down. In other words, for each dollar Frank trades away or lends, he gets a commitment to get it back as well as to receive 10 percent more.

**FIGURE 4.1**

**Frank's and Leslie's Cash Flows**

In the language of finance, 10 percent is the annual rate of interest on the loan. When a dollar is lent out, the repayment of $1.10 can be thought of as being made up of two parts. First, the lender gets the dollar back; that is the *principal repayment*. Second, the lender receives an *interest payment*, which is $0.10 in this example.

Now, not only have Frank and Leslie struck a deal, but as a by-product of their bargain they have created a financial instrument, the IOU. This piece of paper entitles whoever receives it to present it to Leslie next year and redeem it for $55,000. Financial instruments that entitle whoever possesses them to receive payment are called *bearer instruments* because whoever bears them can use them. Presumably there could be more such IOUs in the economy written by many different lenders and borrowers like Frank and Leslie.

## The Anonymous Market

If the borrower does not care whom she has to pay back, and if the lender does not care whose IOUs he is holding, we could just as well drop Frank's and Leslie's names from their contract. All we need is a record book, in which we could record the fact that Frank has lent $50,000 and Leslie has borrowed $50,000 and that the terms of the loan, the interest rate, are 10 percent. Perhaps another person could keep the records for borrowers and lenders—for a fee, of course. In fact—and this is one of the virtues of such an arrangement—Frank and Leslie wouldn't even need to meet. Instead of needing to find and trade with each other, they could each trade with the recordkeeper. The recordkeeper could deal with thousands of such borrowers and lenders, none of whom would need to meet the other.

Institutions that perform this sort of market function, matching borrowers and lenders or traders, are called **financial intermediaries**. Chartered banks, like TD-Bank Financial Group and RBC, are modern examples of financial intermediaries. A bank's depositors lend the bank money, and the bank makes loans from the funds it has on deposit. In essence, the bank is an intermediary between the depositors and the ultimate borrowers. To make the market work, we must be certain that the market clears. By *market clearing* we mean that the total amount that people like Frank wish to lend to the market, say $11 million, equals the total amount that people like Leslie wish to borrow.

## Market Clearing

If the lenders wish to lend more than the borrowers want to borrow, then presumably the interest rate is too high. Because there would not be enough borrowing for all of the lenders at, say, 15 percent, there are really only two ways that the market could be made to clear. One is to ration the lenders. For example, if the lenders wish to lend $20 million when interest rates are at 15 percent and the borrowers wish to borrow only $8 million, the market could take, say, 8/20 of each dollar, or $0.40, from each of the lenders and distribute it to the borrowers. This is one possible scheme for making the market clear, but it is not one that would be sustainable in a free and competitive marketplace. Why not?

To answer this important question, we return to our lender, Frank. Frank sees that interest rates are 15 percent and, not surprisingly, rather than simply lending the $50,000 that he was willing to lend when rates were 10 percent, Frank decides that at the higher rates he would like to lend more, say, $80,000. But since the lenders want to lend more money than the borrowers want to borrow, the recordkeepers tell Frank that they won't be able to take all of his $80,000; rather, they will take only 40 percent of it, or $32,000. With the interest rate at 15 percent, people are not willing to borrow enough to match up with all of the loans that are available at that rate.

Frank is not very pleased with that state of affairs, but he can do something to improve his situation. Suppose that he knows that Leslie is borrowing $20,000 in the market at the 15 percent interest rate. That means that Leslie must repay $20,000 on her loan next year plus the interest of 15 percent of $20,000, or $0.15 \times $20,000 = $3,000. Suppose that Frank goes to Leslie and offers to lend her the $20,000 for 14 percent. Leslie is happy because she will save 1 percent on the deal and will need to pay back only $2,800 in interest next year. This is $200 less than if she had borrowed from the recordkeepers. Frank is happy, too, because he has found a way to lend some of the money that the recordkeepers would not take. The net result of this transaction is that the recordkeepers have lost Leslie as a customer. Why should she borrow from them when Frank will lend her the money at a lower interest rate?

Frank and Leslie are not the only ones cutting side deals in the marketplace, and it is clear that the recordkeepers will not be able to maintain the 15 percent rate. The interest rate must fall if they are to stay in business.

Suppose, then, that the market clears at the rate of 10 percent. At this rate the amount of money that the lenders wish to lend, $11 million, is exactly equal to the amount that the borrowers desire. We refer to the interest rate that clears the market, 10 percent in our example, as the **equilibrium rate of interest**.

In this section we have shown that in the market for loans, bonds or IOUs are traded. These are *financial instruments*. The interest rate on these loans is such that the total demand for such loans by borrowers equals the total supply of loans by lenders. At a higher interest rate, lenders wish to supply more loans than are demanded, and if the interest rate is lower than this equilibrium level, borrowers demand more loans than lenders are willing to supply.

*CONCEPT*
*QUESTIONS*

- What is an interest rate?
- What do we mean when we say a market clears?
- What is an equilibrium rate of interest?

## 4.2   MAKING CONSUMPTION CHOICES OVER TIME

Figure 4.2 illustrates the situation faced by an individual in the financial market. This person is assumed to have an income of $50,000 this year and an income of $60,000 next year. The market allows him not only to consume $50,000 worth of goods this year and $60,000 next year, but also to borrow and lend at the equilibrium interest rate. The line *AB* in Figure 4.2 shows all of the consumption possibilities open to the person through borrowing or lending, and the shaded area contains all of the feasible choices. Notice that the lender chooses to consume less than $50,000 and the borrower more than this amount.

FIGURE 4.2

**Intertemporal Consumption Opportunities**

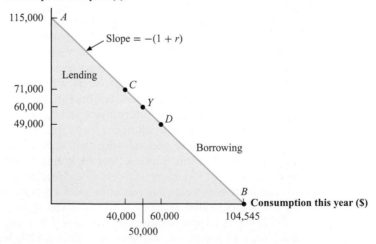

We will use the letter *r* to denote the interest rate—the equilibrium rate—in this market. The rate is risk free because we assume that no default can take place. Look at point *A* on the vertical axis of Figure 4.2. Point *A* represents consumption next year (on the vertical axis) of

$$A = \$60{,}000 + \$50{,}000 \times (1 + r)$$

For example, if the rate of interest is 10 percent, then point $A$ is

$$A = \$60{,}000 + \$50{,}000 \times (1 + 0.1)$$
$$= \$60{,}000 + \$55{,}000$$
$$= \$115{,}000$$

Point $A$ is the maximum amount of wealth that this person can spend in the second year. He gets to point $A$ by lending the full income that is available this year, $50,000, and consuming none of it. In the second year, then, he will have the second year's income of $60,000 plus the proceeds from the loan that he made in the first year, $55,000, for a total of $115,000.

Following the same logic, point $B$ is a distance of

$$B = \$50{,}000 + \$60{,}000/(1 + r)$$

along the horizontal axis. If the interest rate is 10 percent, point $B$ will be

$$B = \$50{,}000 + \$60{,}000/(1 + 0.1)$$
$$= \$50{,}000 + \$54{,}545$$
$$= \$104{,}545 \text{ (rounded off to the nearest dollar)}$$

Why do we divide next year's income of $60,000 by $(1 + r)$ or 1.1 in the preceding computation? Point $B$ represents the maximum amount available for this person to consume this year. To achieve that maximum he would borrow as much as possible and repay the loan from the income, $60,000, that he was going to receive next year. Because $60,000 will be available to repay the loan next year, we are asking how much he could borrow this year at an interest rate of $r$ and still be able to repay the loan. The answer is

$$\$60{,}000/(1 + r)$$

because if he borrows this amount, he must repay it next year with interest. Thus, next year he must repay

$$[\$60{,}000/(1 + r)] \times (1 + r) = \$60{,}000$$

no matter what the interest rate, $r$, is. In our example we found that he could borrow $54,545 and, sure enough,

$$\$54{,}545 \times 1.1 = \$60{,}000$$

(after rounding off to the nearest dollar).

Furthermore, by borrowing and lending different amounts, the person can achieve any point on the line $AB$. For example, at point $C$ he has chosen to lend $10,000 of today's income. This means that at point $C$ he will have

$$\text{Consumption this year at point } C = \$50{,}000 - \$10{,}000 = \$40{,}000$$

and

$$\text{Consumption next year at point } C = \$60{,}000 + \$10{,}000 \times (1 + r) = \$71{,}000$$

when the interest rate is 10 percent.

Similarly, at point $D$, the individual has decided to borrow $10,000 and repay the loan next year. At point $D$, then,

$$\text{Consumption this year at point } D = \$50{,}000 + \$10{,}000 = \$60{,}000$$

and

$$\text{Consumption next year at point } D = \$60{,}000 - \$10{,}000 \times (1 + r) = \$49{,}000$$

at an interest rate of 10 percent.

In fact, this person can consume at any point on the line *AB*. This line has a slope of $-(1 + r)$, which means that for each dollar that is added to the *x*-coordinate along the line, $(1 + r)$ dollars are subtracted from the *y*-coordinate. Moving along the line from point *A*, the initial point of $50,000 this year and $60,000 next year, toward point *B* gives the person more consumption today and less next year. In other words, moving toward point *B* is borrowing. Similarly, moving up toward point *A*, he is consuming less today and more next year and he is lending. The line is a straight line because the individual has no effect on the interest rate. This is one of the assumptions of perfectly competitive financial markets.

Where in Figure 4.2 will the person actually be? The answer to that question depends on the individual's tastes and personal situation, just as it did before there was a market. If the person is impatient, he might wish to borrow money at a point such as *D*, and if he is patient, he might wish to lend some of this year's income and enjoy more consumption next year at, for example, a point such as *C*.

Notice that whether we think of someone as patient or impatient depends on the interest rate he or she faces in the market. Suppose that our individual was impatient and chose to borrow $10,000 and move to point *D*. Now suppose that we raise the interest rate to 20 percent or even 50 percent. Suddenly our impatient person may become very patient and might prefer to lend some of this year's income to take advantage of the very high interest rate. The general result is depicted in Figure 4.3. We can see that lending at point *C'* yields much greater future income and consumption possibilities than before.[2]

FIGURE 4.3

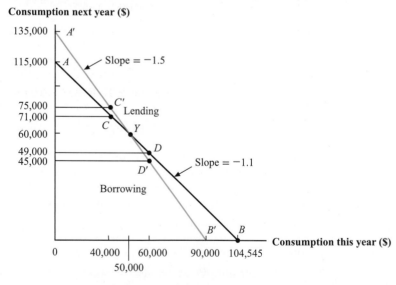

**The Effect of Different Interest Rates on Consumption Opportunities**

 **CONCEPT QUESTIONS**

- How does an individual change consumption across periods through borrowing and lending?
- How do interest rate changes affect one's degree of impatience?

_____

[2] Those familiar with consumer theory might be aware of the surprising case where raising the interest rate actually makes people borrow more or lowering the rate makes them lend more. The latter case might occur, for example, if the decline in the interest rate made the lenders have so little consumption next year that they have no choice but to lend out even more than they did before, just to subsist. Nothing we do depends on excluding such cases, but it is much easier to ignore them, and the resulting analysis fits the real markets much more closely.

# 4.3    THE COMPETITIVE MARKET

In the previous analysis we assumed the individual moves freely along the line *AB*, and we ignored—and assumed that the individual ignores—any effect his borrowing or lending decisions might have on the equilibrium interest rate itself. What would happen, though, if the total amount of loans outstanding in the market when the person was doing no borrowing or lending was $10 million, and if our person then decided to lend, say, $5 million? His lending would be half as much as the rest of the market put together, and it would not be unreasonable to think that the equilibrium interest rate would fall to induce more borrowers into the market to take his additional loans. In such a situation, the person has some power in the market to influence the equilibrium rate significantly, and he would take this power into consideration in making his decisions.

In modern financial markets, however, the total amount of borrowing and lending is not $10 million; rather, as we say in Chapter 1, it is far higher. In such a huge market no one investor or even any single company can have a significant effect (although a government might). We assume, then, in all of our subsequent discussions and analysis that the financial market is perfectly competitive. By that we mean no individuals or firms think they have any effect whatsoever on the interest rates that they face, no matter how much borrowing, lending, or investing they do. In the language of economics, individuals who respond to rates and prices by acting as though they have no influence on them are called *price takers*, and this assumption is sometimes called the *price-taking assumption*. It is the condition of **perfectly competitive financial markets** (or, more simply, *perfect markets*). The following conditions characterize perfect financial markets:

1. Trading is costless. Access to the financial markets is free.

2. Information about borrowing and lending opportunities is readily available.

3. There are many traders, and no single trader can have a significant impact on market prices.

In Chapter 14 we introduce the concept of efficient markets—the belief that current market prices reflect all available public information so that it is impossible to outperform the market consistently. Although efficient markets are less than perfectly competitive, available evidence suggests that most of the time, the three conditions above are a good approximation for financial markets.

## How Many Interest Rates Are There in a Competitive Market?

An important point about this one-year market where no defaults can take place is that only one interest rate can be quoted in the market at any one time. Suppose that some competing recordkeepers decide to set up a rival market. To attract customers, their business plan is to offer lower interest rates, say, 9 percent, to attract borrowers away from the first market and soon have all of the business.

Their business plan will work, but it will do so beyond their wildest expectations. They will indeed attract the borrowers, all $11 million worth of them! But the matter doesn't stop there. By offering to borrow and lend at 9 percent when another market is offering 10 percent, they have created the proverbial money machine.

The world of finance is populated by sharp-eyed inhabitants who would not let this opportunity slip by them. Any one of these, whether a borrower or a lender, would go to the new market and borrow everything she could at the 9 percent rate. At the same time she was borrowing in the new market, she would also be striking a deal to lend in the old market at the 10 percent rate. If she could borrow $100 million at 9 percent and lend it at 10 percent, she could net 1 percent, or $1 million, next year. She would repay the $109 million she owed to the new market from the $110 million she would receive when the 10 percent loan she had made in the original market was repaid, pocketing $1 million.

This process of striking a deal in one market and an offsetting deal in another simultaneously and at more favourable terms is called *arbitrage*; the individuals who do it are called *arbitrageurs*. Of course, someone must be paying for all of this free money, and it must be the recordkeepers because the borrowers and the lenders are all making money. Our intrepid, entrepreneurial recordkeepers will lose their proverbial shirts and go out of business. The moral of this is clear: as soon as different interest rates are offered for essentially the same risk-free loans, arbitrageurs will take advantage of the situation by borrowing at the low rate and lending at the high rate. The gap between the two rates will be closed quickly, and, for all practical purposes, there will be only one rate available in the market.

**CONCEPT**
**QUESTIONS**

- What is the most important feature of a competitive financial market?
- What conditions are likely to lead to this?
- What is arbitrage, and why does it result in one rate for risk-free loans?

# 4.4   THE BASIC PRINCIPLE

We have already shown how people use the financial markets to adjust their patterns of consumption over time to fit their particular preferences. By borrowing and lending, they can greatly expand their range of choices. They need only have access to a market with an interest rate at which they can borrow and lend.

In the previous section, we saw how these savings and consumption decisions depend on the interest rate. The financial markets also provide a benchmark against which proposed investments can be compared, and the interest rate is the basis for a test that any proposed investment must pass. The financial markets give the individual, the corporation, or even the government a standard of comparison for economic decisions. This benchmark is critical when investment decisions are being made.

The way we use the financial markets to aid us in making investment decisions is a direct consequence of our basic assumption that individuals can never be made worse off by increasing the range of choices open to them. People can always make use of the financial markets to adjust their savings and consumption by borrowing or lending. An investment project is worth undertaking only if it increases the range of choices in the financial markets. To do this, the project must be at least as desirable as what is available in the financial markets.[3] If it were not as desirable as what the financial markets had to offer, people could simply use the financial markets instead of undertaking the investment. This point will govern us in all of our investment decisions. It is the *first principle of investment decision making*, and it is the foundation on which all of our rules are built.

**CONCEPT**
**QUESTION**

- Describe the basic financial principle of investment decision making.

# 4.5   PRACTISING THE PRINCIPLE

Let us apply the basic principle of investment decision making to some concrete situations.

---

[3] You might wonder what to do if an investment is exactly as desirable as an alternative in the financial markets. In principle, if there is a tie, it doesn't matter whether or not we take on the investment. In practice, we've never seen an exact tie.

## A Lending Example

Consider a person who is concerned only about this year and next. He has an income of $100,000 this year and expects to make the same amount next year. The interest rate is 10 percent. This individual is thinking about investing in a piece of land that costs $70,000. He is certain that next year the land will be worth $75,000, a sure $5,000 gain. Should he undertake the investment? This situation is described in Figure 4.4 with the cash flow time chart.

**FIGURE 4.4**

**Cash Flows for Investment in Land**

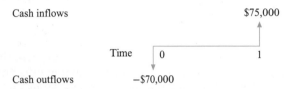

A moment's thought should be all it takes to convince him that this is not an attractive business deal. By investing $70,000 in the land, he will have $75,000 available next year. Suppose, instead, that he puts the same $70,000 into a loan in the financial market. At the 10 percent rate of interest, this $70,000 would grow to

$$(1 + 0.1) \times \$70,000 = \$77,000$$

next year.

It would be foolish to buy the land when the same $70,000 investment in the financial market would beat it by $2,000 (that is, $77,000 from the loan minus $75,000 from the land investment).

Figure 4.5 illustrates this situation. Notice that the $70,000 loan gives no less income today and $2,000 more next year. This example illustrates some amazing features of the financial markets. It is remarkable to consider all of the information that we did *not* use when arriving at the decision not to invest in the land. We did not need to know how much income the person has this year or next year. We also did not need to know whether the person preferred more income this year or next.

**FIGURE 4.5**

**Consumption Opportunities with Borrowing and Lending**

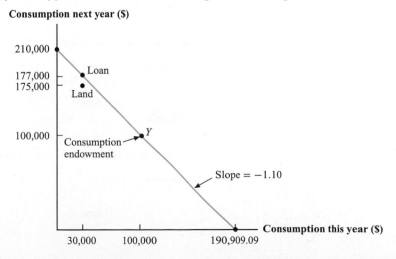

We did not need to know any of these other facts, and, more important, the person making the decision did not need to know them either. He only needed to be able to compare the investment with a relevant alternative available in the financial market. When the proposed investment fell short of that standard—by $2,000 in the previous example—regardless of what the individual wanted to do, he knew that he should not buy the land.

## A Borrowing Example

Let us sweeten the deal a bit. Suppose that instead of being worth $75,000 next year, the land will be worth $80,000. What should our investor do now? This case is a bit more difficult. After all, even if the land seems like a good deal, this person's income this year is $100,000. Does he really want to make a $70,000 investment this year? Won't that leave only $30,000 for consumption?

The answers to these questions are yes, the individual should buy the land; yes, he does want to make a $70,000 investment this year; and, most surprising of all, even though his income is $100,000, making the $70,000 investment will not leave him with $30,000 to consume this year! Now let us see how finance lets us get around the basic laws of arithmetic.

The financial markets are the key to solving our problem. First, the financial markets can be used as a standard of comparison against which any investment project must measure up. Second, they can be used as a tool to help the individual actually undertake investments. These twin features of the financial markets enable us to make the right investment decision.

Suppose that the person borrows the $70,000 initial investment that is needed to purchase the land. Next year he must repay this loan. Because the interest rate is 10 percent, he will owe the financial market $77,000 next year. This is depicted in Figure 4.6. Because the land will be worth $80,000 next year, he will be able to sell it, pay off his debt of $77,000, and have $3,000 extra cash.

**FIGURE 4.6**

**Cash Flows of Borrowing to Purchase the Land**

If he wishes, this person can now consume an extra $3,000 worth of goods and services next year. This possibility is illustrated in Figure 4.7. In fact, even if he wants to do all of his consuming this year, he is still better off taking the investment. All he must do is take out a loan this year and repay it from the proceeds of the land next year and profit by $3,000.

FIGURE 4.7

**Consumption Opportunities with Investment Opportunity and Borrowing and Lending**

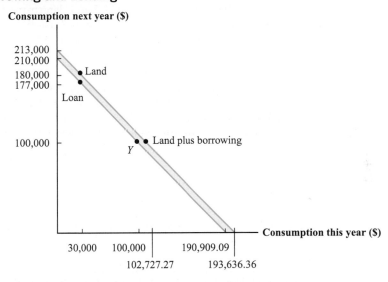

Furthermore, instead of borrowing just the $70,000 that he needed to purchase the land, he could have borrowed $72,727.27. He could have used $70,000 to buy the land and consumed the remaining $2,727.27. We will call $2,727.27 the NPV of the transaction. Notice that it is equal to $3,000 × 1/1.1. How did we figure out that this was the exact amount that he could borrow? It was easy; if $72,727.27 is the amount that he borrows, then, because the interest rate is 10 percent, he must repay

$$\$72,727.27 \times (1 + 0.1) = \$80,000$$

next year, and that is exactly what the land will be worth. The line through the investment position in Figure 4.7 illustrates this borrowing possibility.

The amazing thing about both of these cases, one where the land is worth $75,000 next year and the other where it is worth $80,000 next year, is that we needed only to compare the investment with the financial markets to decide whether it was worth undertaking or not. This is one of the most important points in all of finance. It is true regardless of the consumption preferences of the individual. This is one of a number of *separation theorems* in finance. It states that the value of an investment to an individual does not depend on consumption preferences. In our examples we showed that the person's decision to invest in land was not affected by consumption preferences. However, these preferences dictated whether the person borrowed or lent.

**CONCEPT QUESTIONS**
- Describe how the financial markets can be used to evaluate investment alternatives.
- What is the separation theorem? Why is it important?

# 4.6   ILLUSTRATING THE INVESTMENT DECISION

Figure 4.2, discussed earlier, describes the possibilities open to a person who has an income of $50,000 this year and $60,000 next year and faces a financial market in which the interest rate is 10 percent. But at that moment, the person has no investment possibilities beyond the 10 percent borrowing and lending that is available in the financial market.

Suppose that we give this person the chance to undertake an investment project that will require a $30,000 outlay of cash this year and that will return $40,000 to the investor next year. Refer to Figure 4.2 and determine how you could include this new possibility in that figure and how you could use the figure to help you decide whether the person should undertake the investment.

Now look at Figure 4.8. In Figure 4.8 we have labelled the original point with $50,000 this year and $60,000 next year as point A. We have also added a new point B, with $20,000 available for consumption this year and $100,000 next year. The difference between point A and point B is that at point A the person is just where we started him off, and at point B the person has also decided to undertake the investment project. As a result of this decision, the person at point B has

$$\$50,000 - \$30,000 = \$20,000$$

left for consumption this year, and

$$\$60,000 + \$40,000 = \$100,000$$

available next year. These are the coordinates of point B.

**FIGURE 4.8**

**Consumption Choices with Investment Opportunities but No Financial Markets**

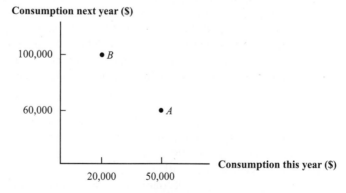

We must use our knowledge of the individual's borrowing and lending opportunities to decide whether to accept or reject the investment. This is illustrated in Figure 4.9. Figure 4.9 is similar to Figure 4.8, but in it we have drawn a line through point A that shows the possibilities open to the person if he stays at point A and does not take the investment. This line is exactly the same as the one in Figure 4.2. We have also drawn a parallel line through point B that shows the new possibilities that are available to the person if he undertakes the investment. The two lines are parallel because the slope of each is determined by the same interest rate, 10 percent. It does not matter whether the person takes the investment and goes to point B or does not and stays at point A; in the financial market, each dollar of lending is a dollar less available for consumption this year and moves him to the left by a dollar along the x-axis. Because the interest rate is 10 percent, the $1 loan repays $1.10 and it moves him up by $1.10 along the y-axis.

FIGURE 4.9

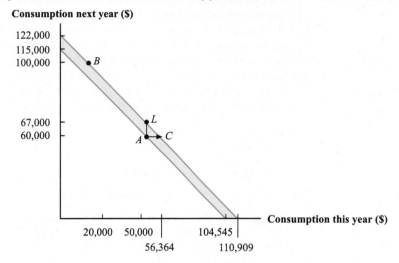

**Consumption Choices with Investment Opportunities and Financial Markets**

It is easy to see from Figure 4.9 that the investment has made the person better off. The line through point *B* is higher than the line through point *A*. Thus, no matter what pattern of consumption this person wanted this year and next, he could have more in each year if he undertook the investment.

For example, suppose that our individual wanted to consume everything this year. If he did not take the investment, the point where the line through point *A* intersected the *x*-axis would give the maximum amount of consumption he could enjoy this year: $104,545. To recall how we found this figure, review the analysis of Figure 4.2. But in Figure 4.9 the line that goes through point *B* intersects the *x*-axis at a higher point than the line that goes through point *A*. Along this line the person can have the $20,000 that is left after investing $30,000, plus all that he can borrow and repay with both next year's income and the proceeds from the investment. The total amount available to consume today is therefore

$$\$50,000 - \$30,000 + (\$60,000 + \$40,000)/(1 + 0.1) = \$20,000 + \$100,000/(1.1)$$
$$= \$110,909$$

The additional consumption available this year from undertaking the investment and using the financial market is the difference on the *x*-axis between the points where these two lines intersect:

$$\$110,909 - \$104,545 = \$6,364$$

This difference is an important measure of what the investment is worth to the person. It answers a variety of questions. For example, it is the answer to the question, how much money would we need to give the investor this year to make him just as well off as he is with the investment?

Because the line through point *B* is parallel to the line through point *A* but has been moved over by $6,364, we know that if we were to add this amount to the investor's current income this year at point *A* and take away the investment, he would wind up on the line through point *B* and with the same possibilities. If we do this, the person will have $56,364 this year and $60,000 next year, which is the situation of the point on the line through point *B* that lies to the right of point *A* in Figure 4.9. This is point *C*.

We could also ask a different question: how much money would we need to give the investor next year to make him just as well off as he is with the investment?

This is the same as asking how much higher the line through point *B* is than the line through point *A*. In other words, what is the difference in Figure 4.9 between the point where the line through *A* intersects the *y*-axis and the point where the line through *B* intersects the *y*-axis?

The point where the line through *A* intersects the *y*-axis shows the maximum amount the person could consume next year if all of his current income were lent out and the proceeds of the loan were consumed along with next year's income.

As we showed in our analysis of Figure 4.2, this amount is $115,000. How does this compare with what the person can have next year if he takes the investment? By taking the investment we saw that the person would be at point *B*, where he has $20,000 left this year and would have $100,000 next year. By lending the $20,000 that is left this year and adding the proceeds of this loan to the $100,000, we find the line through *B* intersects the *y*-axis at

$$\$20{,}000 \times (1.1) + \$100{,}000 = \$122{,}000$$

The difference between this amount and $115,000 is

$$\$122{,}000 - \$115{,}000 = \$7{,}000.$$

which is the answer to the question of how much we would need to give the person next year to make him as well off as he is with the investment.

There is a simple relationship between these two numbers. If we multiply $6,364 by 1.1 we get $7,000! Consider why this must be so. The $6,364 is the amount of extra cash we must give the person this year to substitute for having the investment. In a financial market with a 10 percent rate of interest, however, $1 this year is worth exactly the same as $1.10 next year. Thus, $6,364 this year is the same as $6,364 × 1.1 next year. In other words, the person does not care whether he has the investment, $6,364, this year or $6,364 × 1.1 next year. But we already showed that the investor is equally willing to have the investment and to have $7,000 next year. This must mean that

$$\$6{,}364 \times 1.1 = \$7{,}000$$

You can also verify the relationship between these two variables by using Figure 4.9. Because the lines through *A* and *B* have the same slope of −1.1, the difference of $7,000 between where they intersect on the *y*-axis and $6,364 between where they intersect on the *x*-axis must be in the ratio of 1.1 to 1.

Now we can show you how to evaluate the investment opportunity on a stand-alone basis. Here are the relevant facts: the individual must give up $30,000 this year to get $40,000 next year. These cash flows are illustrated in Figure 4.10.

FIGURE 4.10

**Cash Flows for the Investment Project**

The investment rule that follows from the previous analysis is the NPV rule. Here we convert all consumption values to the present and add them up:

$$\begin{aligned} NPV &= -\$30{,}000 + \$40{,}000 \times (1/1.1) \\ &= -\$30{,}000 + \$36{,}364 \\ &= \$6{,}364 \end{aligned}$$

The future amount, $40,000, is called the *future value (FV)*.

The NPV of an investment is a simple criterion for deciding whether or not to undertake it. NPV answers the question of how much cash an investor would need to have today as a substitute for making the investment. If the net present value is positive, the investment is worth taking on because doing so is essentially the same as receiving a cash payment equal to the NPV. If the NPV is negative, taking on the investment today is equivalent to giving up some cash today, and the investment should be rejected.

We use the term *net present value* to emphasize that we are already including the current cost of the investment in determining its value and not simply measuring what it will return. For example, if the interest rate is 10 percent and an investment of $30,000 today will produce a total cash return of $40,000 in one year, the *present value* of the $40,000 by itself is

$$\$40,000/1.1 = \$36,364$$

but the *NPV* of the investment is $36,364 minus the original investment:

$$\text{NPV} = \$36,364 - \$30,000 = \$6,364$$

The present value of a future cash flow is the value of that cash flow after considering the appropriate market interest rate. The NPV of an investment is the present value of the investment's future cash flows, minus the initial cost of the investment. We have just decided that our investment is a good opportunity. It has a positive NPV because it is worth more than it costs.

In general, the above can be stated in terms of the **net present value rule**:

> An investment is worth making if it has a positive NPV. If an investment's NPV is negative, it should be rejected.

*CONCEPT QUESTIONS*

- Give the definitions of NPV, future value, and present value.
- What information does a person need to compute an investment's NPV?

# 4.7  CORPORATE INVESTMENT DECISION MAKING

Until now, everything we have done has been from the perspective of the individual investor. How do corporations and firms make investment decisions? Are their decisions governed by a much more complicated set of rules and principles than the simple NPV rule that we have developed for individuals?

We discussed corporate decision making, corporate governance, and stakeholder issues in Chapter 1 and will return to these issues later in the book. But we can say here that it is remarkable how well our central ideas and the NPV rule hold up even when applied to corporations.

We may view firms as means by which many investors can pool their resources to make large-scale business decisions. Suppose, for example, that you own 1 percent of some firm. Now suppose further that this firm is considering whether or not to undertake some investment. If that investment passes the NPV rule, that is, if it has a positive NPV, then 1 percent of the NPV belongs to you. If the firm takes on this investment, the value of the whole firm will rise by the NPV and your investment in the firm will rise by 1 percent of the NPV of the investment. Similarly, the other shareholders in the firm will profit by having the firm take on the positive NPV project because the value of their shares in the firm will also increase. This means that the shareholders in the firm will be unanimous in wanting the firm to increase its value by taking on the positive NPV project. If you follow this line of reasoning, you will also be able to see why the shareholders would oppose the firm's taking on any project with a negative NPV, because this would lower the value of their shares.

One difference between the firm and the individual is that the firm has no consumption endowment. In terms of our one-period consumption diagram, the firm starts at the origin. Figure 4.11 illustrates the situation of a firm with investment opportunity *B*. *B* is an investment that has a future value of $33,000 and will cost $25,000 now. If the interest rate is 10 percent, the NPV of *B* can be determined using the NPV rule. This is marked as point *C* in Figure 4.11. The cash flows of this investment are depicted in Figure 4.12.

**FIGURE 4.11**

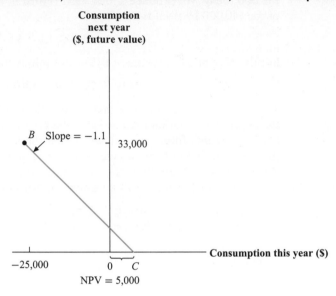

**Consumption Choices, the Net Present Value Rule, and the Corporation**

**FIGURE 4.12**

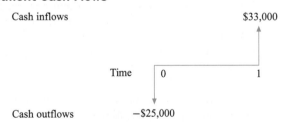

**Corporate Investment Cash Flows**

One common objection to this line of reasoning is that people differ in their tastes and they won't necessarily agree to take on or reject investments by the NPV rule. For instance, suppose that you and we each own some shares in a company. Further suppose that we are older than you and might be anxious to spend our money. Being younger, you might be more patient than we are and more willing to wait for a good long-term investment to pay off.

Because of the financial markets, we all agree that the company should take on investments with positive NPVs and reject those with negative NPVs. If there were no financial markets, then, being impatient, we might want the company to do little or no investing so that we could have as much money as possible to consume now, and, being patient, you might prefer the company to make some investments. With financial markets, we are both satisfied by having the company follow the NPV rule.

To see why this is so, suppose that the company takes on a positive NPV investment. Let us assume that this investment has a net payoff of $1 million next year. That means that the value of the company will increase by $1 million next year; consequently, if you own 1 percent of the company's shares, the value of your shares will increase by 1 percent of $1 million, or $10,000, next year. Because you are patient, you might be prepared to wait for your $10,000 until next year. Being impatient, we do not want to wait—and with financial markets, we do not need to wait. We can simply borrow against the extra $10,000 we will have tomorrow and use the loan to consume more today.

In fact, if there is also a market for the firm's shares, we do not even need to borrow. After the company takes on a positive NPV investment, our shares in the company increase in value today. This is because owning the shares today entitles investors to their portion of the extra $1 million the company will have next year. This means that the shares would rise in value today by the present value of $1 million. Because you want to delay your consumption, you could wait until next year and sell your shares then to have extra consumption next year. Being impatient, we might sell our shares now and use the money to consume more today. If we owned 1 percent of the company's shares, we could sell our shares for an extra amount equal to the present value of $10,000.

In reality, shareholders in big companies do not vote on every investment decision, and their managers must have rules to follow. We have seen that all shareholders in a company will be made better off, no matter what their levels of patience or impatience, if managers follow the NPV rule. This is a marvellous result because it makes it possible for many different owners to delegate decision-making powers to the managers. They need only tell the managers to follow the NPV rule, and if the managers do so, they will be doing exactly what the shareholders want them to do. Sometimes this form of the NPV rule is stated as having the managers maximize the value of the company. As we argued, the current value of the shares of the company will increase by the NPV of any investments that the company undertakes. This means that the managers of the company can make the shareholders as well off as possible by taking on all positive NPV projects and rejecting projects with negative NPVs.

For example, in December 2013, Air Canada announced the purchase of 61 new Boeing 737 MAX aircraft at an estimated cost of US$6.5 billion. The new planes will modernize the airline's fleet with expected savings of 20 percent on maintenance and fuel costs. Delivery of the new planes is planned to begin in 2017 and continue through 2021.[4] Before making such a major investment, Air Canada's financial analysts and executives undoubtedly conducted detailed NPV analysis.

Separating investment decision making from the shareholders is a basic requirement of the modern large firm. An important **separation theorem** in financial markets says that all investors will want to accept or reject the same investment projects by using the NPV rule, regardless of their personal preferences. Investors can delegate the operations of the firm and require that managers use the NPV rule. Of course, much remains for us to discuss about this topic. For example, what ensures that managers will actually do what is best for their shareholders?

We discussed this interesting topic in Chapter 1, and we take it up again later in the book. For now, though, we will no longer consider our perspective to be that of the lone investor. Instead, thanks to the separation theorem, we will use the NPV rule for companies as well as for investors. Our justification of the NPV rule depends on the conditions necessary to derive the separation theorem. These conditions are the ones that result in competitive financial markets. The analysis we have presented has been restricted to risk-free cash flows in one time period. However, the separation theorem can also be derived for risky cash flows that extend beyond one period.

**CONCEPT QUESTION**

• In terms of the NPV rule, what is the essential difference between the individual and the corporation?

[4] S. Deveau, "Air Canada Plans to Purchase 61 Boeing Narrow Body Aircraft in US$6.5 Billion Deal," *National Post*, December 11, 2013.

## 4.8

# SUMMARY AND CONCLUSIONS

Finance is a subject that builds understanding from the ground up. Whenever you encounter a new problem or issue in finance, you can always return to the basic principles of this chapter for guidance.

1. Financial markets exist because people want to adjust their consumption over time. They do so by borrowing and lending.

2. Financial markets provide the key test for investment decision making. Whether a particular investment decision should or should not be made depends only on this test: if there is a superior alternative in the financial markets, the investment should be rejected; if not, the investment is worth taking. The most important thing about this principle is that the investor need not use his or her preferences to decide whether the investment should be taken. Regardless of the individual's preference for consumption this year versus next, regardless of how patient or impatient the individual is, making the proper investment decision depends only on comparing it with the alternatives in the financial markets.

3. The net present value (NPV) of an investment helps us compare the investment and the financial market. If the NPV is positive, our rule tells us to undertake the investment. This illustrates the second major feature of the financial markets and investment. Not only does the NPV rule tell us which investments to accept and which to reject, but the financial markets also provide us with the tools for acquiring the funds to make the investments. In short, we use the financial markets to decide both what to do and how to do it.

4. The NPV rule can be applied to corporations as well as to individuals. The separation theorem developed in this chapter says that all of the shareholders of the firm would agree that the firm should use the NPV rule even though each might differ in personal tastes for consumption and savings.

In the next chapter we learn more about the NPV rule by using it to examine a wide array of problems in finance.

KEY TERMS

| | | |
|---|---|---|
| Equilibrium rate of interest   86 | Intertemporal consumption   84 | Perfectly competitive financial market   89 |
| Financial intermediaries   85 | Net present value rule   97 | Separation theorem   99 |

QUESTIONS & PROBLEMS

### Making Consumption Choices

4.1 Currently, Jack Morris makes $85,000 per annum. Next year his income will be $108,000. Jack is a big spender and he wants to consume $135,000 a year. The equilibrium interest rate is 7 percent. What will be Jack's consumption potential next year if he consumes $135,000 this year?

4.2 Rachel Pettit is a miser. Her current income is $55,000; next year she will earn $38,000. She plans to consume only $20,000 this year. The current interest rate is 9 percent. What will Rachel's consumption potential be next year?

4.3  Ben earns $4,000 this year and zero income the next year. Ben also has an investment opportunity in which he can invest $2,000 and receive $3,000 next year. Suppose Ben consumes $1,000 this year, invests in the project, and consumes $4,150 next year.

   a.  What is the market rate?
   b.  Suppose the interest rate increases. What will happen to Ben's consumption for this year? Is Ben better or worse off than before the interest rate rise?

### The Competitive Market

4.4  What is the basic reason that financial markets develop?

4.5  Suppose that the equilibrium interest rate is 5.3 percent. What would happen in the market if a group of financial intermediaries attempted to control interest rates at 4 percent?

### Illustrating the Investment Decision

4.6  The following figure depicts the financial situation of Jane Fawn. In period 0, her labour income and current consumption are $50; later, in period 1, her labour income and consumption will be $44. She has an opportunity to make the investment represented by point $D$. By borrowing and lending, she will be able to reach any point along the line $FDE$.

   a.  What is the market rate of interest? (*Hint:* The new market interest rate line $EF$ is parallel to $AH$.)
   b.  What is the NPV of point $D$?
   c.  If Jane wishes to consume the same quantity in each period, how much should she consume in period 0?

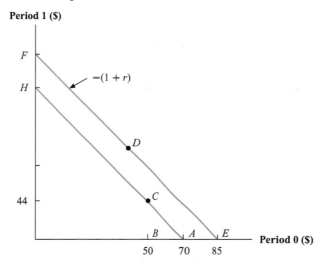

4.7  Enrique Rodrigues has $54,300 this year, as represented by point $A$. He has the opportunity to make an investment in productive assets represented by point $B$ in the following figure. He wants to consume $25,000 this year and $60,000 next year. This pattern of consumption is represented by point $F$. By borrowing or lending, he will be able to reach any point along the line $DBC$.

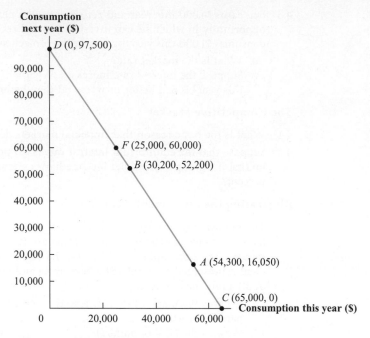

a. What is the market interest rate?
b. How much must Enrique invest in financial assets and productive assets today if he follows an optimum strategy?
c. What is the stand-alone NPV of the investment at point *B*?

4.8  To answer this question, refer to the figure below. The Badvest Corporation is an all-equity firm with *BD* in cash on hand. It has an investment opportunity at point *C*, and it plans to invest *AD* in real assets today. Thus, the firm will need to raise *AB* by a new issue of equity.

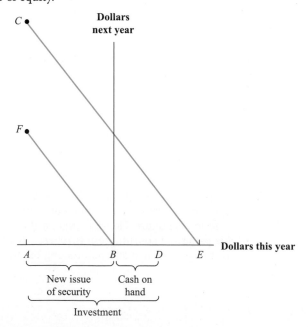

a. What is the NPV of the investment?
b. What is the rate of return on the old equity? Measure this rate of return from before the investment plans are announced to afterwards.
c. What is the rate of return on the new equity?

4.9  Assume that capital markets do not exist. Ryan has $70,000 today ($t = 0$) and will receive $90,000 in exactly one year ($t = 1$). The graph below illustrates point $Y$: having $70,000 now and receiving $90,000 next year. Here, if no capital or financial market exists, then Ryan must consume $70,000 now and $90,000 next year. Next consider this case when borrowing and lending at $r = 10\%$ are available in the financial markets; Ryan now has a real investment opportunity, or business project. If Ryan decides to accept this opportunity, it will cost $20,000 now ($t = 0$) and will offer a *risk-free* payoff of $25,000 next year. Now, revisit the point $Y$ where Ryan has $70,000 now and will receive $90,000 next year, but this time the real asset project exists. Assume that he still wants to consume $70,000 now ($t = 0$), and answer the following.

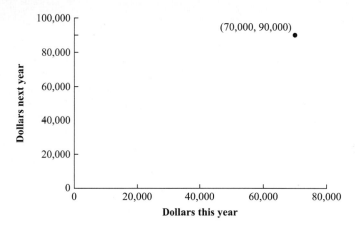

*a.* How much more can Ryan consume next year, with the investment opportunity, compared to when there was no borrowing or lending opportunity?

*b.* Calculate the NPV of the project.

# The Time Value of Money

**EXECUTIVE SUMMARY**

We now examine one of the most important concepts in all of corporate finance: the relationship between $1 today and $1 in the future. Consider the following example. A firm is contemplating investing $1 million in a project that is expected to pay out $200,000 per year for nine years. Should the firm accept the project? One might say yes at first glance, since the total inflows of $1.8 million (= $200,000 × 9) are greater than the $1 million outflow. However, the $1 million is paid out *immediately*, whereas the $200,000 per year is received in the future. Also, the immediate payment is known with certainty, whereas the later inflows can only be estimated. Thus, we need to know the relationship between a dollar today and a (possibly uncertain) dollar in the future before deciding on the project.

This relationship is called the *time value of money* concept. It is important in such areas as capital budgeting, lease-versus-buy decisions, accounts receivable analysis, financing arrangements, mergers, and pension funding.

The basics are presented in this chapter. We begin by discussing two fundamental concepts: future value and present value. Next, we treat simplifying formulas such as perpetuities and annuities.

## 5.1 THE ONE-PERIOD CASE

**EXAMPLE 5.1**

Antony Robart is trying to sell a piece of land in Saskatchewan. Yesterday, he was offered $10,000 for the property. He was ready to accept the offer when another individual offered him $11,424. However, the second offer was to be paid a year from now. Antony has satisfied himself that both buyers are honest, so he has no fear that the offer he selects will fall through. These two offers are pictured as cash flows in Figure 5.1. Which offer should Antony choose?

**FIGURE 5.1**

**Cash Flow for Antony's Sale**

Cynthia Titos, Antony's financial adviser, points out that if Antony takes the first offer, he could invest the $10,000 in the bank at 12 percent. At the end of one year, he would have

$$\underset{\text{Return of principal}}{\$10,000} + \underset{\text{Interest}}{(0.12 \times \$10,000)} = \$10,000 \times 1.12 = \$11,200$$

Because this is less than the $11,424 Antony could receive from the second offer, Cynthia recommends that he take the latter. This analysis uses the concept of **future value** or **compound value**, which is the value of a sum after investing over one or more periods. Here the compound or future value of $10,000 is $11,200.

An alternative method employs the concept of **present value (PV)**. One can determine PV by asking the following question: How much money must Antony put in the bank today so that he will have $11,424 next year? We can write this algebraically as

$$PV \times 1.12 = \$11{,}424 \tag{5.1}$$

We want to solve for present value (PV), the amount of money that yields $11,424 if invested at 12 percent today. Solving for PV, we have

$$PV = \frac{\$11{,}424}{1.12} = \$10{,}200$$

The formula for PV can be written as

**Present Value of Investment:**

$$PV = \frac{C_1}{1 + r}$$

where $C_1$ is cash flow at date 1 and $r$ is the interest rate.

*PV analysis* tells us that a payment of $11,424 to be received next year has a PV of $10,200 today. In other words, at a 12 percent interest rate, Antony should be indifferent to whether you give him $10,200 today or $11,424 next year. If you give him $10,200 today, he can put it in the bank and receive $11,424 next year.

Because the second offer has a PV of $10,200, whereas the first offer is for only $10,000, PV analysis also indicates that Antony should take the second offer. In other words, both future value analysis and PV analysis lead to the same decision. As it turns out, PV analysis and future value analysis must always lead to the same decision.

As simple as this example is, it contains the basic principles that we will be working with over the next few chapters. We now use Example 5.2 to develop the concept of net present value (NPV).

Geneviève Gagnon is thinking about investing in a piece of land that costs $85,000. She is certain that next year the land will be worth $91,000, a sure $6,000 gain. Given that the interest rate at the bank is 10 percent, should she undertake the investment in land? Geneviève's choice is described in Figure 5.2 with the cash flow time chart.

**FIGURE 5.2**

**Cash Flows for Land Investment**

A moment's thought should be all it takes to convince her that this is not an attractive business deal. By investing $85,000 in the land, she will have $91,000 available next year. Suppose, instead, that she puts the same $85,000 in the bank. At the interest rate of 10 percent, this $85,000 would grow to

$$(1 + 0.10) \times \$85,000 = \$93,500$$

next year.

It would be foolish to buy the land when investing the same $85,000 in the financial market would produce an extra $2,500 (that is, $93,500 from the bank minus $91,000 from the land investment). This is a future value calculation. Alternatively, she could calculate the PV of the sale price next year as

$$PV = \frac{\$91,000}{1.10} = \$82,727.27$$

Since the PV of next year's sale price is less than this year's purchase price of $85,000, PV analysis also indicates that she should not purchase the property.

Frequently, business people want to determine the exact *cost* or *benefit* of a decision. The decision to buy this year and sell next year can be evaluated as

**Net Present Value of Investment:**

$$-\$2,273 = \underset{\substack{\text{Cost of} \\ \text{land today}}}{-\$85,000} + \underset{\substack{\text{Present value of} \\ \text{next year's sales price}}}{\frac{\$91,000}{1.10}} \tag{5.2}$$

Equation (5.2) says that the value of the investment is −$2,273, after stating all the benefits and all the costs as of date 0. We say that −$2,273 is the **net present value (NPV)** of the investment. That is, NPV is the PV of future cash flows minus the PV of the cost of the investment. Because the NPV is negative, Geneviève should not purchase the land.

Both the Robart and the Gagnon examples deal with perfect certainty. That is, Antony Robart knows with perfect certainty that he could sell his land for $11,424 next year. Similarly, Geneviève Gagnon knows with perfect certainty that she could receive $91,000 for selling her land. Unfortunately, business people frequently do not know future cash flows. This uncertainty is treated in Example 5.3.

Atkinson Art Inc. is a firm that speculates in modern paintings. The manager is thinking of buying an original Picasso for $400,000 with the intention of selling it at the end of one year. The manager *expects* that the painting will be worth $480,000 in one year. The relevant cash flows are depicted in Figure 5.3.

**FIGURE 5.3**

**Cash Flows for Investment in Painting**

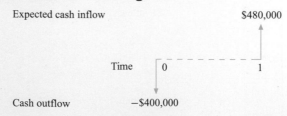

Of course, this is only an expectation—the painting could be worth more or less than $480,000. Suppose the interest rate granted by banks is 10 percent. Should the firm purchase the piece of art?

Our first thought might be to discount at the interest rate, yielding

$$\frac{\$480,000}{1.10} = \$436,364$$

Because $436,364 is greater than $400,000, it looks at first glance as if the painting should be purchased. However, 10 percent is the return one can earn on a risk-free investment. Because the painting is quite risky, a higher *discount rate* is called for. The manager chooses a rate of 25 percent to reflect this risk. In other words, he argues that a 25 percent expected return is fair compensation for an investment as risky as this painting.

The PV of the painting becomes

$$\frac{\$480,000}{1.25} = \$384,000$$

Thus, the manager believes that the painting is currently overpriced at $400,000 and does not make the purchase.

The above analysis is typical of decision making in today's corporations, though real-world examples are, of course, much more complex. Unfortunately, any example with risk poses a problem not faced by a risk-free example. In an example with risk-free cash flows, the appropriate interest rate can be determined by simply checking with a few banks.[1] The selection of the discount rate for a risky investment is quite a difficult task. We simply do not know at this point whether the discount rate on the painting should be 11 percent, 25 percent, 52 percent, or some other percentage.

Because the choice of a discount rate is so difficult, we merely wanted to broach the subject here. The rest of the chapter will revert back to examples under perfect certainty. We must wait until the specific material on risk and return is covered in later chapters before a risk-adjusted analysis can be presented.

**CONCEPT QUESTIONS**
- Define future value and PV.
- How does one use NPV when making an investment decision?

# 5.2    THE MULTIPERIOD CASE

The previous section presented the calculation of future value and PV for one period only. We will now perform the calculations for the multiperiod case.

## Future Value and Compounding

Suppose an individual were to make a loan of $1. At the end of the first year, the borrower would owe the lender the principal amount of $1 plus the interest on the loan at the interest rate of $r$. For the specific case where the interest rate is, say, 9 percent, the borrower owes the lender

$$\$1 \times (1 + r) = \$1 \times 1.09 = \$1.09$$

At the end of the year, though, the lender has two choices. He or she can either take the $1.09—or, more generally, $(1 + r)$—out of the capital market, or leave it in and lend it again for a second year, as shown in Figure 5.4. The process of leaving the money in the capital market and lending it for another year is called **compounding**.

---

[1] In Chapters 10 and 11, we discuss estimation of the risk-free rate in more detail.

Suppose that the lender decides to compound the loan for another year by taking the proceeds from the first one-year loan, $1.09, and lending this amount for the next year. At the end of next year, then, the borrower will owe

$$\$1 \times (1 + r) \times (1 + r) = \$1 \times (1 + r)^2 = 1 + 2r + r^2$$
$$\$1 \times (1.09) \times (1.09) = \$1 + \$0.18 + \$0.0081 = \$1.1881$$

This is the total the lender will receive two years from now by compounding the loan.

In other words, by providing a ready opportunity for lending, the capital market enables the investor to transform $1 today into $1.1881 at the end of two years. At the end of three years, the cash will be $1 \times (1.09)^3 = \$1.2950$. The dark shaded area indicates the difference between compound and simple interest. The difference is substantial over a period of many years or decades, as shown in Figure 5.4.

**FIGURE 5.4**

**Simple and Compound Interest**

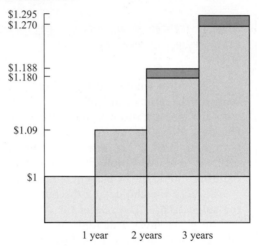

The dark-shaded area indicates the difference between compound and simple interest. The difference is substantial over a period of many years or decades.

The most important point to notice is that the total amount that the lender receives is not just the $1 lent out plus two years' worth of interest on $1:

$$2 \times r = 2 \times \$0.09 = \$0.18$$

The lender also gets back an amount $r^2$, which is the interest in the second year on the interest that was earned in the first year. The term $2 \times r$ represents **simple interest** over the two years, and the term $r^2$ is referred to as the *interest on interest*. In our example this latter amount is exactly

$$r^2 = (\$0.09)^2 = \$0.0081$$

When cash is invested at **compound interest**, each interest payment is reinvested. With simple interest, the interest is not reinvested. Benjamin Franklin's statement, "Money makes money and the money that money makes makes more money," is a colourful way of explaining compound interest. The difference between compound interest and simple interest is also illustrated in Figure 5.4. In this example, the difference does not amount to much because the loan is for $1. If the loan were for $1 million, the lender would receive $1,188,100 in two years. Of this amount, $8,100 is interest on interest. The lesson is that those small numbers beyond the decimal point can add up to significant dollar amounts when the transactions are for large amounts. In addition, the longer lasting the loan, the more important interest on interest becomes.

The general formula for an investment over many periods can be written as

**Future Value of an Investment:**

$$\text{FV} = C_0 \times (1 + r)^T$$

where $C_0$ is the cash to be invested at date 0, $r$ is the interest rate, and $T$ is the number of periods over which the cash is invested.

Irene Lau has put $500 in a savings account at the Home Bank of Canada. The account earns 7 percent, compounded annually. How much will Irene have at the end of three years?

$$\$500 \times 1.07 \times 1.07 \times 1.07 = \$500 \times (1.07)^3 = \$612.52$$

Figure 5.5 illustrates the growth of Irene's account.

**FIGURE 5.5**

**Irene's Savings Account**

Heather Courtney invested $1,000 in the stock of the BMH Company. The company pays a current dividend of $2 per share, which is expected to grow by 20 percent per year for the next two years. What will the dividend of the BMH Company be after two years?

$$\$2 \times (1.20)^2 = \$2.88$$

Figure 5.6 illustrates the increasing value of BMH's dividends.

**FIGURE 5.6**

**The Growth of Dividends**

Examples 5.4 and 5.5 can be calculated in any one of three ways: by hand, by calculator, or with the help of a table.[2] The appropriate table is Table A.3, which appears in Appendix A, available online at Connect. This table presents *future values of $1 at the end of T periods*. The table is used by locating the appropriate interest rate on the horizontal and the appropriate number of periods on the vertical.

For example, Irene Lau would look at the following portion of Table A.3:

| | | Interest rate | |
| Period | 6% | 7% | 8% |
| --- | --- | --- | --- |
| 1 | 1.0600 | 1.0700 | 1.0800 |
| 2 | 1.1236 | 1.1449 | 1.1664 |
| 3 | 1.1910 | 1.2250 | 1.2597 |
| 4 | 1.2625 | 1.3108 | 1.3605 |

She could calculate the future value of her $500 as

$$\underset{\substack{\text{Initial}\\\text{investment}}}{\$500} \times \underset{\substack{\text{Future value}\\\text{of }\$1}}{1.2250} = \$612.50$$

In Example 5.4 concerning Irene Lau, we gave you both the initial investment and the interest rate and then asked you to calculate the future value. Alternatively, the interest rate could have been unknown, as shown in Example 5.6.

EXAMPLE **5.6**

Raghu Venugopal, who recently won $10,000 in a lottery, wants to buy a car in five years. Raghu estimates that the car will cost $16,105 at that time. His cash flows are displayed in Figure 5.7.

### FIGURE 5.7

**Cash Flows for Future Purchase of a Car**

What interest rate must he earn to be able to afford the car? The ratio of purchase price to initial cash is

$$\frac{\$16,105}{\$10,000} = 1.6105$$

---

[2] To solve this problem on the BA II Plus financial calculator (see Appendix 5A on Connect),
1. Make sure to clear the calculator.
2. Enter the number of periods as 2 and press *N*.
3. Enter the interest rate of 20 percent as 20 (not 0.20) and press *I/Y*.
4. Enter the present value of −2.00 and press *PV*.
5. Calculate the future value by pressing the compute button (*CPT*) and then pressing *FV*.

Thus, he must earn an interest rate that allows $1 to become $1.6105 in five years. Table A.3 tells us that an interest rate of 10 percent will allow him to purchase the car. We can express the problem algebraically as

$$\$10,000 \times (1 + r)^5 = \$16,105$$

where $r$ is the interest rate needed to purchase the car. Because $\$16,105/\$10,000 = 1.6105$, we have

$$(1 + r)^5 = 1.6105$$

Either the table or any sophisticated hand calculator[3] solves for $r = 10\%$.

## The Power of Compounding: A Digression

Most people who have had any experience with compounding are impressed with its power over long periods of time. Take the stock market, for example. In Chapter 10, we use historical data to calculate that the average Canadian common stock averaged a 9.12 percent geometric average rate of return per year for the 57 years from 1957 through 2013. A return of this magnitude may not appear to be anything special over, say, a one-year period. However, $1 placed in these stocks at the beginning of 1957 would have been worth $144.89 at the end of 2013. Figure 10.4 shows the return of $1 from 1957 to 2013.

The example illustrates the great difference between compound and simple interest. At 9.12 percent, simple interest on $1 is 9.12 cents a year. Simple interest over 57 years is $5.20 (57 × 0.0912). That is, an individual withdrawing 9.12 cents every year would have withdrawn $5.20 over 57 years. This is quite a bit below the $144.89 that was obtained by reinvestment of all principal and interest.

The results are more impressive over even longer periods of time. A person with no experience in compounding might think that the value of $1 at the end of 114 years would be twice the value of $1 at the end of 57 years, if the yearly rate of return stayed the same. Actually the value of $1 at the end of 114 years would be the *square* of the value of $1 at the end of 57 years. That is, if the annual rate of return remained the same, a $1 investment in common stocks should be worth $20,993.11 (or $144.89 × 144.89).

A few years ago, an archaeologist unearthed a relic stating that Julius Caesar lent the Roman equivalent of one penny to someone. Since there was no record of the penny ever being repaid, the archaeologist wondered what the interest and principal would be if a descendant of Caesar tried to collect from a descendant of the borrower in the twentieth century. The archaeologist felt that a rate of 6 percent might be appropriate. To his surprise, the principal and interest due after more than 2,000 years was far greater than the entire wealth on Earth.

The power of compounding can explain one reason why the parents of well-to-do families frequently bequeath wealth to their grandchildren rather than to their children. That is, they skip a generation. The parents would rather make the grandchildren very rich than make the children moderately rich. We have found that in these families the grandchildren have a more positive view of the power of compounding than do the children.

---

[3] Conceptually, we are taking the fifth root of both sides of the equation. That is,
$$r = \sqrt[5]{1.6105} - 1$$
To solve this problem on the BA II Plus financial calculator,
1. Clear the calculator.
2. Enter the number of periods as 5 and press *N*.
3. Enter the present value of −10,000 and press *PV.*
4. Enter the future value of $16,105 and press *FV.*
5. Ask the calculator for the interest rate by pressing the compute button (CPT) and then pressing *I.*

## Present Value and Discounting

We now know that an annual interest rate of 9 percent enables the investor to transform $1 today into $1.1881 two years from now. In addition, we would like to know the following:

- How much would an investor need to lend today to make it possible to receive $1 two years from today?

Algebraically, we can write this as

$$PV \times (1.09)^2 = \$1 \tag{5.3}$$

In (5.3), PV is the amount of money we must lend today in order to receive $1 in two years. Solving for PV in (5.3), we have

$$PV = \frac{\$1}{1.1881} = \$0.84$$

This process of calculating the PV of a future cash flow is called **discounting**.[4] It is the opposite of compounding. The difference between compounding and discounting is illustrated in Figure 5.8.

**FIGURE 5.8**

**Compounding and Discounting**

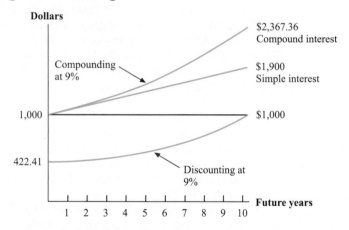

The top line shows the growth of $1,000 at compound interest with the funds invested at 9 percent: $1,000 × $(1.09)^{10}$ = $2,367.36. Simple interest is shown on the next line. It is $1,000 + 10 × ($1,000 × 0.09) = $1,900. The bottom line shows the discounted value of $1,000 if the interest rate is 9 percent.

To be certain that $0.84 is in fact the PV of $1 to be received in two years, we must check whether or not, if we lent out $0.84 and rolled the loan over for two years, we would get exactly $1 back. If this were the case, the capital markets would be saying that $1 received in two years is equivalent to having $0.84 today. Checking with the exact numbers, we get

$$\$0.84168 \times 1.09 \times 1.09 = \$1$$

In other words, when we have capital markets with a sure interest rate of 9 percent, we are indifferent between receiving $0.84 today and $1 in two years. We have no reason to treat these two choices differently from each other, because if we had $0.84 today and lent it out for two years, it would return $1 to us at the end of that time. The value 0.84[$1/(1.09)^2$] is called the **present value factor**. It is the factor used to calculate the PV of a future cash flow.

---

[4] The discount rate, $r$, is defined as the rate used to calculate the PV of future cash flows.

Pat Song will receive $10,000 three years from now. Pat can earn 8 percent on his investments. What is the PV of his future cash flow?

$$PV = \$10{,}000 \times (1/1.08)^3$$
$$= \$10{,}000 \times 0.7938$$
$$= \$7{,}938$$

Figure 5.9 illustrates the application of the PV factor to Pat's investment.

### FIGURE 5.9

**Discounting Pat's Opportunity**

When his investments grow at an 8 percent rate of interest, Pat is equally inclined toward receiving $7,938 now or receiving $10,000 in three years. After all, he could convert the $7,938 he receives today into $10,000 in three years by lending it at an interest rate of 8 percent.

Pat could have reached his PV calculation in one of three ways. He could have done the computation by hand, by calculator, or with the help of Table A.1 in Appendix A on Connect. This table presents *PV of $1 to be received after T periods.* The table is used by locating the appropriate interest rate on the horizontal and the appropriate number of periods on the vertical. For example, Pat would look at the following portion of Table A.1:

| | | Interest Rate | |
| Period | 7% | 8% | 9% |
| --- | --- | --- | --- |
| 1 | 0.9346 | 0.9259 | 0.9174 |
| 2 | 0.8734 | 0.8573 | 0.8417 |
| 3 | 0.8163 | 0.7938 | 0.7722 |
| 4 | 0.7629 | 0.7350 | 0.7084 |

The appropriate PV factor is 0.7938.

In Example 5.7, we gave both the interest rate and the future cash flow. Alternatively, the interest rate could have been unknown.

EXAMPLE 5.8

A customer of the Cristall Corp. wants to buy a tugboat today. Rather than paying immediately, he will pay $50,000 in three years. It will cost the Cristall Corp. $38,610 to build the tugboat immediately. The relevant cash flows to Cristall Corp. are displayed in Figure 5.10. By charging what interest rate would the Cristall Corp. neither gain nor lose on the sale?

FIGURE 5.10

**Cash Flows for Tugboat**

The ratio of construction cost to sale price is

$$\frac{\$38,610}{\$50,000} = 0.7722$$

We must determine the interest rate that allows $1 to be received in three years to have a PV of $0.7722. Table A.1 tells us that 9 percent is that interest rate.[5]

Frequently, an investor or a business will receive more than one cash flow. The PV of the set of cash flows is simply the sum of the PVs of the individual cash flows. This is illustrated in Example 5.9.

EXAMPLE 5.9

While on vacation in the United States, Terence Chiu won a lottery and will receive the following set of cash flows over the next two years:

| Year | Cash flow |
|------|-----------|
| 1    | $2,000    |
| 2    | $5,000    |

Terence can currently earn 6 percent in his savings account. The PV of the cash flows is

| Year | Cash flow × PV factor = PV | | |
|------|----------------------------|---------|--------|
| 1    | $2,000 × 1/1.06            | (= 0.943) = | $1,887 |
| 2    | $5,000 × 1/(1.06)²        | (= 0.890) = | $4,450 |
|      |                            | Total   | $6,337 |

In other words, Terence is equally inclined toward receiving $6,337 today and receiving $2,000 and $5,000 over the next two years.

---

[5] Algebraically, we are solving for $r$ in the equation

$$\frac{\$50,000}{(1 + r)^3} = \$38,610$$

or, equivalently,

$$\frac{\$1}{(1 + r)^3} = \$0.7722$$

EXAMPLE 5.10

Finance.com has an opportunity to invest in a new high-speed computer that costs $50,000. The computer will generate cash flows (from cost savings) of $25,000 one year from now, $20,000 two years from now, and $15,000 three years from now. The computer will be worthless after three years, and no additional cash flows will occur. Finance.com has determined that the appropriate discount rate is 7 percent for this investment. Should Finance.com make this investment in a new high-speed computer? What is the PV of the investment?

The cash flows and PV factors of the proposed computer are as follows:

| Year | Cash flow | Present value factor |
|------|-----------|----------------------|
| 0 | −$50,000 | $1 = 1$ |
| 1 | $25,000 | $\frac{1}{1.07} = 0.9346$ |
| 2 | $20,000 | $\left(\frac{1}{1.07}\right)^2 = 0.8734$ |
| 3 | $15,000 | $\left(\frac{1}{1.07}\right)^3 = 0.8163$ |

The PVs of the cash flows are

| Year | Cash flow × PV factor | = | PV |
|------|-----------------------|---|-----|
| 0 | −$50,000 × 1 | = | −$50,000 |
| 1 | $25,000 × 0.9346 | = | $23,365 |
| 2 | $20,000 × 0.8734 | = | $17,468 |
| 3 | $15,000 × 0.8163 | = | $12,244.5 |
| | | Total: | $ 3,077.5 |

Finance.com should invest in a new high-speed computer because the PV of its future cash flows is greater than its cost. The NPV is $3,077.5.

## Finding the Number of Periods

Suppose we are interested in purchasing an asset that costs $50,000. We currently have $25,000. If we can earn 12 percent on this $25,000, how long will it be until we have the $50,000? Finding the answer involves solving for the last variable in the basic PV equation, the number of periods. You may already know how to get an approximate answer to this particular problem. Notice that we need to double our money. From the Rule of 72 (see Problem 5.75 at the end of the chapter), this will take about 72/12 = 6 years at 12 percent.

To come up with the exact answer, we can again manipulate the basic PV equation. The PV is $25,000, and the future value is $50,000. With a 12 percent discount rate, the basic equation takes one of the following forms:

$$\$25,000 = \$50,000/1.12^t$$
$$\$50,000/\$25,000 = 1.12^t = 2$$

We thus have a future value factor of 2 for a 12 percent rate. We now need to solve for $t$. If you look down the column in Table A.3 that corresponds to 12 percent, you will see that a future value factor of 1.9738 occurs at six periods. It will thus take about six years, as we calculated. To get the exact answer, we have to explicitly solve for $t$ (by using logarithms, a financial calculator, or a spreadsheet). If you do this, you will see that the answer is 6.1163 years, so our approximation was quite close in this case.

You've been saving up to buy the Godot Company. The total cost will be $10 million. You currently have about $2.3 million. If you can earn 5 percent on your money, how long will you have to wait? At 16 percent, how long must you wait?

At 5 percent, you'll have to wait a long time. From the basic PV equation,

$$\$2.3 \text{ million} = \$10 \text{ million}/1.05^t$$
$$1.05^t = 4.35$$
$$t = 30 \text{ years}$$

At 16 percent, things are a little better. Verify for yourself that it will take about 10 years.

## The Algebraic Formula

To derive an algebraic formula for the NPV of a cash flow, recall that the PV of receiving a cash flow one year from now is

$$PV = C_1/(1 + r)$$

and the PV of receiving a cash flow two years from now is

$$PV = C_2/(1 + r)^2$$

We can write the NPV of a $T$-period project as

$$NPV = -C_0 + \frac{C_1}{1 + r} + \frac{C_2}{(1 + r)^2} + \cdots + \frac{C_T}{(1 + r)^T}$$
$$= -C_0 + \sum_{t=1}^{T} \frac{C_t}{(1 + r)^t}$$

The initial flow, $-C_0$, is assumed to be negative because it represents an investment. The symbol $\sum$ is shorthand for the sum of the series.[6]

**CONCEPT QUESTIONS**

- What is the difference between simple interest and compound interest?
- What is the formula for the NPV of a project?

## 5.3  COMPOUNDING PERIODS

So far we have assumed that compounding and discounting occur yearly. Sometimes compounding may occur more frequently than just once a year. For example, imagine that a bank pays a 10 percent interest rate compounded semiannually. This means that a $1,000 deposit in the bank would be worth $1,000 \times 1.05 = \$1,050$ after six months, and $1,050 \times 1.05 = \$1,102.50$ at the end of the year. The end-of-the-year wealth can be written as[7]

$$\$1,000(1 + 0.10/2)^2 = \$1,000 \times (1.05)^2$$
$$= \$1,102.50$$

---

[6] In Chapter 6 we apply the NPV formula to investments that have a cash inflow in year 0 and outflows in later years. For these investments, the term $-C_0$ is replaced by $-PV$ (outflows).

[7] In addition to using a calculator, one can still use Table A.3 when the compounding period is less than a year. Here, one sets the interest rate at 5 percent and the number of periods at 2.

Of course, a $1,000 deposit would be worth $1,100 (or $1,000 × 1.10) with yearly compounding. Note that the future value at the end of one year is greater with semiannual compounding than with yearly compounding. With yearly compounding, the original $1,000 remains the investment base for the full year. The original $1,000 is the investment base only for the first six months with semiannual compounding. The base over the second six months is $1,050. Hence, one gets *interest on interest* with semiannual compounding.

Because $1,000 × 1.1025 = $1,102.50, 10 percent compounded semiannually is the same as 10.25 percent compounded annually. In other words, a rational investor will be indifferent between a rate of 10 percent compounded semiannually and a rate of 10.25 percent compounded annually.

Quarterly compounding at 10 percent yields wealth at the end of one year of

$$\$1,000(1 + 0.10/4)^4 = \$1,103.81$$

More generally, compounding an investment $m$ times a year provides end-of-year wealth of

$$C_0(1 + r/m)^m \tag{5.4}$$

where $C_0$ is the initial investment and $r$ is the **stated annual interest rate**. The stated annual interest rate is the annual interest rate without consideration of compounding. Banks and other financial institutions may use other names for the stated annual interest rate. **Annual percentage rate** (APR) is perhaps the most common synonym.

EXAMPLE **5.12**

What is the end-of-year wealth if Julie Andrew receives a 24 percent rate of interest compounded monthly on a $1 investment? Using (5.4), her wealth is

$$\$1(1 + 0.24/12)^{12} = \$1 \times (1.02)^{12}$$
$$= \$1.2682$$

The annual rate of return is 26.82 percent.[8] This annual rate of return is called the **effective annual interest rate (EAR)**. Due to compounding, the EAR is greater than the stated annual interest rate of 24 percent. Algebraically, we can rewrite the EAR as

**Effective Annual Interest Rate:**

$$EAR = (1 + r/m)^m - 1 \tag{5.5}$$

Students are often bothered by the subtraction of 1 in (5.5). Note that end-of-year wealth is composed of both the interest earned over the year and the original principal. We remove the original principal by subtracting 1 in (5.5).

_____
[8] To solve this problem on the BA II Plus financial calculator,
1. 2nd | ICONV          (to access the worksheet)
2. 2nd | CLR Work  (to clear contents if any)
3. 24 | Enter            (to enter the nominal interest rate)
4. ↓ ↓                       (two down arrows)
5. 12 | Enter            (to change compounding periods per year to 12)
6. ↑                          (one up arrow to get to EFF)
7. CPT                     (the compute button produces the correct solution 26.824179 as a percentage)

EXAMPLE **5.13**

If the stated annual rate of interest, 8 percent, is compounded quarterly, what is the EAR? Using (5.5), we have

$$(1 + r/m)^m - 1 = (1 + 0.08/4)^4 - 1$$
$$= 0.0824$$
$$= 8.24\%$$

Referring back to our original example where $C_0 = \$1,000$ and $r = 10\%$, we can generate the following table:

| $C_0$ | Compounding frequency ($m$) | $C_1$ | Effective annual interest rate $= (1 + r/m)^m - 1$ |
|---|---|---|---|
| $1,000 | Yearly ($m = 1$) | $1,100.00 | 0.10 |
| 1,000 | Semiannually ($m = 2$) | 1,102.50 | 0.1025 |
| 1,000 | Quarterly ($m = 4$) | 1,103.81 | 0.10381 |
| 1,000 | Daily ($m = 365$) | 1,105.16 | 0.10516 |

As Example 5.13 shows, the formula converts any stated annual rate into an EAR.

## Compounding over Many Years

Equation (5.4) applies for an investment over one year. For an investment over one or more ($T$) years, the formula becomes

**Future Value with Compounding:**

$$\text{FV} = C_0(1 + r/m)^{mT} \tag{5.6}$$

EXAMPLE **5.14**

Margaret Cortes is investing $5,000 at 4 percent per year, compounded quarterly for five years. What is her wealth at the end of five years? Using (5.6), her wealth is

$$\$5,000 \times (1 + 0.04/4)^{4 \times 5} = \$5,000 \times (1.01)^{20}$$
$$= \$5,000 \times 1.2202 = \$6,101.00$$

Cost of Borrowing Disclosure regulations (part of the *Bank Act*) in Canada require that lenders disclose an APR on virtually all consumer loans. This rate must be displayed on a loan document in a prominent and unambiguous way. Unfortunately, this does not tell the borrower the EAR on the loan.

EXAMPLE **5.15**

Suppose that a credit card agreement quotes an APR of 18 percent. Monthly payments are required. Based on our discussion, an APR of 18 percent with monthly payments is really $0.18/12 = 0.015$ or 1.5 percent per month. The EAR is thus

$$\text{EAR} = [1 + 0.18/12]^{12} - 1$$
$$= 1.015^{12} - 1$$
$$= 1.1956 - 1$$
$$= 19.56\%$$

The difference between an APR and an EAR probably will not be great, but it is somewhat ironic that Cost of Borrowing Disclosure regulations sometimes require lenders to be a little misleading about the actual rate on a loan.

The distinction between the APR and the EAR is frequently troubling to students. We can reduce the confusion by noting that the APR becomes meaningful only if the compounding interval is given. For example, for an APR of 10 percent, the future value at the end of one year with semiannual compounding is $[1 + (0.10/2)]^2 = 1.1025$. The future value with quarterly compounding is $[1 + (0.10/4)]^4 = 1.1038$. If the APR is 10 percent but no compounding interval is given, we cannot calculate future value. In other words, we do not know whether to compound semiannually, quarterly, or over some other interval.

By contrast, the EAR is meaningful *without* a compounding interval. For example, an EAR of 10.25 percent means that a \$1 investment will be worth \$1.1025 in one year. We can think of this as an APR of 10 percent with semiannual compounding, or an APR of 10.25 percent with annual compounding, or some other possibility.

ATB Financial offers one-year Guaranteed Investment Certificates (GICs) at 4 percent per year compounded semiannually. TD Canada Trust offers one-year GICs at 4.25 percent compounded annually. Which would you prefer?

The EAR at TD Canada Trust is 4.25 percent since the compounding is annual. To find the EAR offered by ATB Financial, use equation (5.5):

$$EAR = (1 + r/m)^m - 1$$
$$= (1 + 0.04/2)^2 - 1 = 4.04\%$$

You would prefer the TD Canada Trust GIC since it offers a higher EAR.

**CONCEPT**
**QUESTIONS**

- What is a stated annual interest rate?
- What is an effective annual interest rate?
- What is the relationship between the stated annual interest rate and the EAR?

## Continuous Compounding (Advanced)

The previous discussion shows that one can compound much more frequently than once a year. One can compound semiannually, quarterly, monthly, daily, hourly, each minute, or even more often. The limiting case is to compound every infinitesimal instant, which is commonly called **continuous compounding**.

Though the idea of compounding this rapidly may boggle the mind, a simple formula is involved.[9] With continuous compounding, the value at the end of $T$ years is expressed as

$$C_0 \times e^{rT} \tag{5.7}$$

where $C_0$ is the initial investment, $r$ is the stated annual interest rate, and $T$ is the number of years over which the investment runs. The number $e$ is a constant and is approximately equal to 2.718. It is not an unknown like $C_0$, $r$, and $T$.

---

[9] Readers familiar with introductory calculus will recognize the expression

$$\lim_{m \to \infty} (1 + r/m)^m = e^r$$

**EXAMPLE 5.17**

John MacDonald invested $1,000 at a continuously compounded rate of 10 percent for one year. What is the value of his wealth at the end of one year?

From equation (5.7) we have

$$\$1,000 \times e^{0.10} = \$1,000 \times 1.1052 = \$1,105.20$$

This number can easily be read from Table A.5 in Appendix A on Connect. One merely sets $r$, the value on the horizontal, to 10 percent and $T$, the value on the vertical, to 1. For this problem, the relevant portion of the table is

| Period | Continuously compounded rate ($r$) 9% | 10% | 11% |
|--------|------|------|------|
| 1 | 1.0942 | 1.1052 | 1.1163 |
| 2 | 1.1972 | 1.2214 | 1.2461 |
| 3 | 1.3100 | 1.3499 | 1.3910 |

Note that a continuously compounded rate of 10 percent is equivalent to an annually compounded rate of 10.52 percent. In other words, John would not care whether his bank quoted a continuously compounded rate of 10 percent or a 10.52 percent rate compounded annually.

**EXAMPLE 5.18**

John MacDonald's brother, Robert, invested $1,000 at a continuously compounded rate of 10 percent for two years.

The appropriate formula here is

$$\$1,000 \times e^{0.10 \times 2} = \$1,000 \times e^{0.20} = \$1,221.40$$

Using the portion of the table of continuously compounded rates reproduced above, we find the value to be 1.2214.

Figure 5.11 illustrates the relationship among annual, semiannual, and continuous compounding. Semiannual compounding gives rise to both a smoother curve and a higher ending value than does annual compounding. Continuous compounding has both the smoothest curve and the highest ending value of all.

**FIGURE 5.11**

**Annual, Semiannual, and Continuous Compounding**

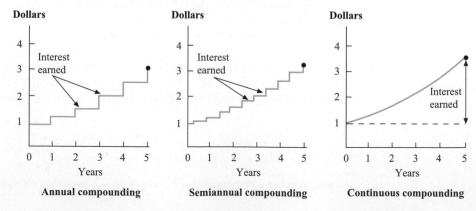

Annual compounding    Semiannual compounding    Continuous compounding

EXAMPLE **5.19**

An investment will pay you $1,000 at the end of four years. If the annual continuously compounded rate of interest is 8 percent, what is the PV of this payment?

$$\$1{,}000 \times \frac{1}{e^{0.08 \times 4}} = \$1{,}000 \times \frac{1}{1.3771}$$
$$= \$726.16$$

## 5.4    SIMPLIFICATIONS

The first part of this chapter examined the concepts of future value and PV. Although these concepts allow one to answer a host of problems concerning the time value of money, the human effort involved can frequently be excessive. For example, consider a bank calculating the PV on a 20-year mortgage with monthly payments. Because this mortgage has 240 (or 20 × 12) payments, a lot of time is needed to perform a conceptually simple task.

Because many basic finance problems are potentially so time-consuming, we search out simplifications in this section. We provide simplifying formulas for four classes of cash flow streams:

- Perpetuity
- Growing perpetuity
- Annuity
- Growing annuity

### Perpetuity

A **perpetuity** is a constant stream of cash flows without end. If you are thinking that perpetuities have no relevance to reality, it will surprise you that there is a well-known case of an unending cash flow stream: the British bonds called *consols*. An investor purchasing a consol is entitled to receive yearly interest from the British government forever.

How can the price of a consol be determined? Consider a consol that pays a coupon of $C$ dollars each year and will do so forever. Simply applying the PV formula gives us

$$\text{PV} = \frac{C}{1 + r} + \frac{C}{(1 + r)^2} + \frac{C}{(1 + r)^3} + \cdots$$

where the dots at the end of the formula stand for the infinite string of terms that continues the formula. Series like the preceding one are called *geometric series*. It is well known that even though they have an infinite number of terms, the whole series has a finite sum because each term is only a fraction of the preceding term. Before turning to a calculus book, though, it is worth going back to our original principles to see if a bit of financial intuition can help us find the PV.

The PV of the consol is the PV of all of its future coupons. In other words, it is an amount of money that if an investor had it today, would make it possible to achieve the same pattern of expenditures that the consol and its coupons would. Suppose that an investor wanted to spend exactly $C$ dollars each year. If our investor owned the consol, this spending pattern would be possible. How much money must the investor have today to spend the same amount? Clearly the amount needed is exactly enough so that the interest on the money would be $C$ dollars per year. If the investor had any more, spending could be more than $C$ dollars each year. If the amount were any less, the investor would eventually run out of money spending $C$ dollars per year.

The amount that will give the investor $C$ dollars each year, and therefore the PV of the consol, is simply

$$PV = \frac{C}{r} \tag{5.8}$$

To confirm that this is the right answer, notice that if we lend the amount $C/r$, the interest it earns each year will be

$$\text{Interest} = \frac{C}{r} \times r = C$$

which is exactly the consol payment.[10] To sum up, we have shown that for a consol

**Formula for the Present Value of a Perpetuity:**

$$PV = \frac{C}{1 + r} + \frac{C}{(1 + r)^2} + \frac{C}{(1 + r)^3} + \cdots$$
$$= C/r$$

It is comforting to know how easily we can use a bit of financial intuition to solve this mathematical problem.

EXAMPLE 5.20

Consider a perpetuity paying $100 a year. If the interest rate is 8 percent, what is the value of the consol? Using (5.8), we have

$$PV = \frac{\$100}{0.08} = \$1,250$$

Now suppose that the interest rate falls to 6 percent. Using (5.8), the value of the perpetuity is

$$PV = \frac{\$100}{0.06} = \$1,666.67$$

Note that the value of the perpetuity rises with a drop in the interest rate. Conversely, the value of the perpetuity falls with a rise in the interest rate.

## Growing Perpetuity

Imagine an apartment building where cash flows to the landlord after expenses will be $100,000 next year. These cash flows are expected to rise at 5 percent per year. If one assumes that this rise will continue indefinitely, the cash flow stream is termed a **growing perpetuity**. Positing an 11 percent discount rate, the PV of the cash flows can be represented as

$$PV = \frac{\$100,000}{1.11} + \frac{\$100,000(1.05)}{(1.11)^2} + \frac{\$100,000(1.05)^2}{(1.11)^3} + \cdots + \frac{\$100,000(1.05)^{N-1}}{(1.11)^N} + \cdots$$

Algebraically, we can write the formula as

$$PV = \frac{C}{1 + r} + \frac{C \times (1 + g)}{(1 + r)^2} + \frac{C \times (1 + g)^2}{(1 + r)^3} + \cdots + \frac{C \times (1 + g)^{N-1}}{(1 + r)^N} + \cdots \tag{5.9}$$

where $C$ is the cash flow to be received one period hence; $g$ is the rate of growth per period, expressed as a percentage; and $r$ is the interest rate.

---

[10] We can prove this by looking at the PVequation:
Let $C/(1 + r) = a$ and $1/(1 + r) = x$. We now have

$$PV = a(1 + x + x^2 + \cdots) \tag{a}$$

Next we can multiply by $x$:

$$xPV = ax + ax^2 + \cdots \tag{b}$$

Subtracting (2) from (1) gives

$$PV(1 - x) = a$$

Now we substitute for $a$ and $x$ and rearrange:

$$PV = C/r$$

Fortunately, (5.9) reduces to the following simplification:[11]

**Formula for the Present Value of a Growing Perpetuity:**

$$PV = \frac{C}{r - g} \qquad (5.10)$$

From (5.10), the PV of the cash flows from the apartment building is

$$\frac{\$100{,}000}{0.11 - 0.05} = \$1{,}666{,}667$$

There are three important points concerning the growing perpetuity formula:

1. *The numerator.* The numerator in (5.10) is the cash flow one period hence, not at date 0. Consider Example 5.21.

---

**EXAMPLE 5.21**

---

Hoffstein Corporation paid a dividend of $3.00 per share last year. Investors anticipate that the annual dividend will rise by 6 percent per year forever. The applicable interest rate is 11 percent. What is the price of the stock today?

The numerator in equation (5.10) is the cash flow to be received next period. Since the growth rate is 6 percent, the dividend next year is $3.18 (or $3.00 × 1.06). The price of the stock today is

$$\$63.60 = \frac{\$3.18}{0.11 - 0.06}$$
Present value of all dividends
beginning a year from now

The price of $63.60 represents the PV of all dividends beginning a year from now. Equation (5.10) only makes it possible to calculate the PV of all dividends beginning a year from now. Be sure you understand this example; test questions on this subject always seem to trip up a few of our students.

---

2. *The interest rate and the growth rate.* The interest rate, $r$, must be greater than the growth rate, $g$, for the growing perpetuity formula to work. Consider the case in which the growth rate approaches the interest rate in magnitude. Then the denominator in the growing perpetuity formula gets infinitesimally small and the PV grows infinitely large. The PV is in fact undefined when $r$ is less than $g$.

3. *The timing assumption.* Cash generally flows into and out of real-world firms both randomly and nearly continuously. However, equation (5.10) assumes that cash flows are received and disbursed at regular and discrete points in time. In the example of the apartment, we assumed that the net cash flows of $100,000 only occurred once a year. In reality, rent cheques are commonly received every month. Payments for maintenance and other expenses may occur any time within the year.

The growing perpetuity formula of (5.10) can be applied only by assuming a regular and discrete pattern of cash flow. Although this assumption is sensible because the formula saves so much time, the user should never forget that it is an assumption. This point will be mentioned again in the chapters ahead.

---

[11] PV is the sum of an infinite geometric series:

$$PV = a(1 + x + x^2 + \cdots)$$

where $a = C/(1 + r)$ and $x = (1 + g)/(1 + r)$. Previously we showed that the sum of an infinite geometric series is $a/(1 - x)$. Using this result and substituting for $a$ and $x$, we find

$$PV = C/(r - g)$$

Note that this geometric series converges to a finite sum only when $x$ is less than 1. This implies that the growth rate, $g$, must be less than the interest rate, $r$.

A few words should be said about terminology. Authors of financial textbooks generally use one of two conventions to refer to time. A minority of financial writers treat cash flows as being received on exact *dates*, for example date 0, date 1, and so forth. Under this convention, date 0 represents the present time. However, because a year is an interval, not a specific moment in time, the great majority of authors refer to cash flows that occur at the end of a year (or, alternatively, at the end of a period). Under this *end-of-the-year* convention, the end of year 0 is the present, the end of year 1 occurs one period hence, and so on.[12] (The beginning of year 0 has already passed and is not generally referred to.)

The interchangeability of the two conventions can be seen from the following chart:

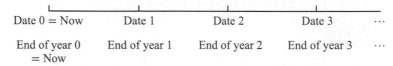

| Date 0 = Now | Date 1 | Date 2 | Date 3 | ... |

| End of year 0<br>= Now | End of year 1 | End of year 2 | End of year 3 | ... |

We strongly believe that the *dates convention* reduces ambiguity. However, we use both conventions because you are likely to see the *end-of-year convention* in later courses. In fact, both conventions may appear in the same example for the sake of practice.

## Annuity

An **annuity** is a level stream of regular payments that lasts for a fixed number of periods. Not surprisingly, annuities are among the most common kinds of financial instruments. The pensions that people receive when they retire are often in the form of an annuity. Leases, mortgages, and pension plans are also annuities.

To figure out the PV of an annuity, we need to evaluate the following equation:

$$\frac{C}{1+r} + \frac{C}{(1+r)^2} + \frac{C}{(1+r)^3} + \cdots + \frac{C}{(1+r)^T}$$

The PV of receiving only the coupons for $T$ periods must be less than the PV of a consol, but how much less? To answer this we have to look at consols a bit more closely. Consider the following time chart:

| Date (or end of year) | Now<br>0 | 1 | 2 | 3 | $T$ | | $(T+1)$ | $(T+2)$ |
|---|---|---|---|---|---|---|---|---|
| Consol 1 | | $C$ | $C$ | $C\ldots$ | $C$ | | $C$ | $C\ldots$ |
| Consol 2 | | | | | | | $C$ | $C\ldots$ |
| Annuity | | $C$ | $C$ | $C\ldots$ | $C$ | | | |

Consol 1 is a normal consol with its first payment at date 1. The first payment of consol 2 occurs at date $T + 1$.

The PV of having a cash flow of $C$ at each of $T$ dates is equal to the PV of consol 1 minus the PV of consol 2. The PV of consol 1 is given by

$$\text{PV} = \frac{C}{r} \qquad (5.11)$$

Consol 2 is just a consol with its first payment at date $T + 1$. From the perpetuity formula, this consol will be worth $C/r$ at date $T$.[13] However, we do not want the value at date $T$. We want the value now (in other words, the PV at date 0). We must discount $C/r$ back by $T$ periods. Therefore, the PV of consol 2 is

---

[12] Sometimes financial writers merely speak of a cash flow in *year x*. Although this terminology is ambiguous, such writers generally mean the *end of year x*.

[13] Students frequently think that $C/r$ is the present value at date $T + 1$ because the consol's first payment is at date $T + 1$. However, the formula values the annuity as of one period prior to the first payment.

$$PV = C/r \times 1/(1 + r)^T \tag{5.12}$$

The PV of having cash flows for $T$ years is the PV of a consol with its first payment at date 1 minus the PV of a consol with its first payment at date $T + 1$. Thus, the PV of an annuity is equation (5.11) minus equation (5.12). This can be written as

$$C/r - C/r[1/(1 + r)^T]$$

This simplifies to

**Formula for the Present Value of an Annuity:**[14,15]

$$PV = C\left[\frac{1}{r} - \frac{1}{r(1 + r)^T}\right] \tag{5.13}$$

**EXAMPLE 5.22**

Andrea Mullings has just won a lottery in the United States, paying $50,000 a year for 20 years. She is to receive her first payment a year from now. The lottery advertisements bill this as the Million Dollar Lottery because $1,000,000 = $50,000 × 20. If the interest rate is 8 percent, what is the true value of the prize?

Equation (5.13) yields

PV of Million Dollar Lottery = $50,000 × [1/0.08 − 1/0.08(1.08)$^{20}$]
　　　　　　　　　　　Periodic payment　　　Annuity factor
　　　　　　　　　　= $50,000 × 9.8181
　　　　　　　　　　= $490,905

Rather than being overjoyed at winning, Andrea sues the lottery authorities for misrepresentation and fraud. Her legal brief states that she was promised $1 million but received only $490,905.[16]

The term we use to compute the value of the stream of level payments, $C$, for $T$ years is called an **annuity factor**. The annuity factor in the current example is 9.8181. Because the annuity factor is used so often in PV calculations, we have included it in Table A.2 in Appendix A. The table gives the values of these factors for a range of interest rates, $r$, and maturity dates, $T$.

The annuity factor as expressed in the brackets of (5.13) is a complex formula. For simplification, we may from time to time refer to the annuity factor as

$$A_r^T \tag{5.14}$$

that is, expression (5.14) stands for the PV of $1 per year for $T$ years at an interest rate of $r$.

---

[14] This can also be written as $C[1 - 1/(1 + r)^T]/r$

[15] We can also provide a formula for the future value of an annuity:
$FV = C[(1 + r)T/r - 1/r]$

[16] To solve this problem using the BA II Plus, you should do the following:
1. Make sure $FV$ is set to zero.
2. Enter the payment 50,000 and press $PMT$.
3. Enter the interest rate 8 and press $I/Y$.
4. Enter the number of periods 20 and press $N$.
5. Finally, solve for $PV$.
Notice that your answer is $490,907.370372. The calculator uses 12 digits for the annuity factor and the answer, whereas the example uses only four digits in the annuity factor and rounds the final answer to the nearest dollar. That is why the answer in the text example differs from the one using the calculator. In practice, the answer using the calculator is better because it is more precise.

## Mortgages

Mortgages are a common example of an annuity with monthly payments. To understand mortgage calculations, you need to keep in mind two institutional arrangements. First, although payments are monthly, Canadian financial institutions typically quote mortgage rates with semiannual compounding. Further, payments on conventional mortgages are calculated to maturity (usually after 25 years), although rate adjustments after the initial locked-in period will cause payments to change subsequently.

---

**EXAMPLE 5.23**

A financial institution is offering a $100,000 mortgage at a stated rate of 6 percent. To find the payments, we first need to find the effective *monthly* rate. To do this, we convert the stated semiannual rate to an EAR:[17]

$$\text{EAR} = [1 + r/m]^m - 1$$
$$= [1 + 0.06/2]^2 - 1$$
$$= 1.0609 - 1$$
$$= 6.09\%$$

Then we find the effective monthly rate used to calculate the payments:

$$\text{Effective monthly rate} = (\text{EAR} + 1)^{1/m} - 1$$
$$= (1.0609)^{1/12} - 1$$
$$= 1.0049 - 1 = 0.49\%$$

The effective monthly rate is 0.49 percent and there are $12 \times 25 = 300$ payments, so we need to find $A_{0.0049}^{300}$. Since this in not in Table A.2, we use (5.13) as rearranged in footnote 14 to solve for $C$, the monthly payment:

$$\text{PV} = \$100,000 = C \times (1 - \text{PV factor})/r$$
$$\$100,000 = C \times (1 - 1/1.0049^{300})/0.0049$$
$$C = \$636.99$$

The monthly mortgage payments will be $636.99.

---

**EXAMPLE 5.24**

Earlier, we pointed out that while mortgages are amortized over 300 months (25 years), the rate is fixed for a shorter period, usually no longer than five years. Suppose the rate of 6 percent in the previous example is fixed for five years and you are wondering whether to lock in this rate or take a lower rate of 5 percent fixed for only one year. If you choose the one-year rate, how much lower will your payments be for the first year?

The payments at 5 percent are $579.94, a reduction of $57.05 per month. If you choose to take the shorter-term mortgage with lower payments, you are betting that rates will not take a big jump over the next year, leaving you with a new rate after one year much higher than 6 percent. While the mortgage formula cannot make this decision for you (it depends on risk and return, discussed in Chapter 10), it does give you the risk you are facing in terms of higher monthly payments. In 1981, mortgage rates were around 20 percent!

---

[17] Chartered banks use 10 decimal places for all calculations. This may result in some rounding error in using this formula to check the payments on an outstanding mortgage.

## Using Annuity Formulas

Our experience is that annuity formulas are not hard but can be tricky for the beginning student. Here we present four tricks.

**Trick 1: A Delayed Annuity**    One of the tricks in working with annuities or perpetuities is getting the timing exactly right. This is particularly useful when an annuity or perpetuity begins at a date many periods in the future. Consider Example 5.25.

**EXAMPLE 5.25**

Fauzia Mohammed will receive a four-year annuity of $500 per year beginning at date 6. If the interest rate is 10 percent, what is the PV of her annuity?

This situation can be graphed as

The analysis involves two steps:

1.    Calculate the PV of the annuity using (5.13). This is

**Present Value of Annuity at Date 5:**

$$\$500 \left[ \frac{1}{0.10} - \frac{1}{0.10(1.10)^4} \right] = \$500 \times A^4_{0.10}$$
$$= \$500 \times 3.1699$$
$$= \$1,584.95$$

Note that $1,584.95 represents the PV at date 5.

Students frequently think that $1,584.95 is the PV at date 6, because the annuity begins at date 6. However, our formula values the annuity as of one period prior to the first payment. This can be seen in the most typical case where the first payment occurs at date 1. The formula values the annuity as of date 5 here.

2.    Discount the PV of the annuity back to date 0. That is

**Present Value at Date 0:**

$$\frac{\$1,584.95}{(1.10)^5} = \$984.13$$

Again, it is worthwhile mentioning that because the annuity formula brings Fauzia's annuity back to date 5, the second calculation must discount over the remaining five periods. The two-step procedure is graphed in Figure 5.12.

### FIGURE 5.12

**Discounting Fauzia's Annuity**

Step 1: Discount the four payments back to date 5 by using the annuity formula.
Step 2: Discount the PV at date 5 ($1,584.95) back to the PV at date 0.

**Trick 2: Annuity in Advance (Annuity Due)** The annuity formula of (5.12) assumes that the first annuity payment begins a full period hence. This type of annuity is frequently called an *annuity in arrears*. What happens if the annuity begins today, in other words, at date 0?

EXAMPLE 5.26

In Example 5.22, Andrea Mullings received $50,000 a year for 20 years as a prize in a U.S. lottery. In that example, she was to receive the first payment a year from the winning date. Let us now assume that the first payment occurs immediately. The total number of payments remains 20. Under this new assumption, we have a 19-date annuity with the first payment occurring at date 1—plus an extra payment at date 0. The PV is

$$\$50,000 \qquad + \$50,000 \times A_{0.08}^{19}$$
$$\text{Payment at date 0} \qquad \text{19-year annuity}$$
$$= \$50,000 + \$50,000 \times 9.6036$$
$$= \$530,180$$

The PV in this example is greater than $490,905, the PV in the earlier lottery example. This is to be expected because the annuity of the current example begins earlier. An annuity with an immediate initial payment is called an *annuity in advance*. Always remember that both equation (5.13) and Table A.2 refer to an *annuity in arrears*.[18]

A second way to find the PV of our annuity in advance is to compute the PV of a 20-year annuity in arrears and compound the result for one period. This gives the same PV (except for a small rounding error):

$$\$50,000 \times A_{0.08}^{20} = \$50,000 \times 9.8181 = \$490,905$$
$$\$490,905(1.08) = \$530,177$$

**Trick 3: The Infrequent Annuity** Example 5.27 deals with an annuity with payments occurring less frequently than once a year.

EXAMPLE 5.27

Alex Bourne receives an annuity of $450 payable once every two years. The annuity stretches out over 20 years. The first payment occurs at date 2, that is, two years from today. The annual interest rate is 6 percent.

The trick is to determine the interest rate over a two-year period. The interest rate over two years is

$$1.06 \times 1.06 - 1 = 12.36\%$$

That is, $100 invested over two years will yield $112.36.

What we want is the PV of a $450 annuity over 10 periods, with an interest rate of 12.36 percent per period. This is

$$\$450\left[\frac{1}{0.1236} - \frac{1}{0.1236 \times (1.1236)^{10}}\right] = \$450 \times A_{0.1236}^{10} = \$2,505.57$$

---

[18] To solve this problem on the BA II Plus financial calculator,
1. Clear the calculator.
2. Set the calculator for an annuity in advance.
3. Enter the number of periods as 19 and press *N*.
4. Enter the payment as 50,000 and press *PMT*.
5. Enter the interest rate of 8 percent and press *I/Y*.
6. Ask the calculator for the present value by pressing the compute button and *PV*.

**Trick 4: Equating the Present Value of Two Annuities**    Example 5.28 equates the PV of inflows with the PV of outflows.

EXAMPLE **5.28**

Jon Rabinowitz and Gila Messeri are saving for the university education of their newborn daughter, Gabrielle. They estimate that expenses will run $30,000 per year when their daughter enters university in 18 years. The annual return on their university investment account over the next few decades will be 14 percent. How much money must they deposit in the bank each year so that their daughter will be completely supported through four years of university?

To simplify the calculations, we assume that Gabrielle is born today. Her parents will make the first of her four annual tuition payments on her 18th birthday. They will make equal deposits on each of her first 17 birthdays, but no deposit at date 0. This is illustrated as

| Date | 0 | 1 | 2 | ... | 17 | 18 | 19 | 20 | 21 |
|------|---|---|---|-----|----|----|----|----|----|
| | Gabrielle's birth | Parents' 1st deposit | Parents' 2nd deposit | | Parents' 17th and last deposit | Tuition payment 1 | Tuition payment 2 | Tuition payment 3 | Tuition payment 4 |

Jon and Gila will be making deposits over the next 17 years. They will be withdrawing $30,000 per year over the following four years. We can be sure they will be able to withdraw fully $30,000 per year if the PV of the deposits equals the PV of the four $30,000 withdrawals.

This calculation requires three steps. The first two determine the PV of the withdrawals. The final step determines yearly deposits that will have a PV equal to that of the withdrawals.

1.  We calculate the PV of the four years at university using the annuity formula:

$$\$30,000 \times \left[ \frac{1}{0.14} - \frac{1}{0.14 \times (1.14)^4} \right] = \$30,000 \times A_{0.14}^4$$

$$= \$30,000 \times 2.9137$$

$$= \$87,411$$

We assume that Gabrielle enters university on her 18th birthday.

Given our discussion in trick 1 above, $87,411 represents the PV at date 17.

2.  We calculate the PV of a university education at date 0 as

$$\frac{\$87,411}{(1.14)^{17}} = \$9,422.91$$

3. Assuming that Gila and Jon make deposits to the bank at the end of each of the 17 years, we calculate the annual deposit that will yield a PV of all deposits of $9,422.91 as

$$C \times A^{17}_{0.14} = \$9,422.91$$

Since

$$A^{17}_{0.14} = 6.3729$$

we find that

$$C = \frac{\$9,422.91}{6.3729} = \$1,478.59$$

Thus, deposits of $1,478.59 made at the end of each of the first 17 years and invested at 14 percent will provide enough money to make tuition payments of $30,000 over the following four years.

An alternative method would be to (1) calculate the PV of the tuition payments at Gabrielle's 18th birthday and (2) calculate annual deposits such that the future value of the deposits at her 18th birthday equals the PV of the tuition payments at that date. Although this technique can also provide the right answer, we have found that it is more likely to lead to errors. Therefore, we only equate PVs in our presentation.

## Growing Annuity

Cash flows in business are very likely to grow over time, due either to real growth or to inflation. The growing perpetuity, which assumes an infinite number of cash flows, provides one formula to handle this growth. We now consider a **growing annuity**, which is a *finite* number of growing cash flows. Because perpetuities of any kind are rare, a formula for a growing annuity is useful. The formula is[19]

**Formula for the Present Value of a Growing Annuity:**

$$\text{PV} = C\left[\frac{1}{r-g} - \frac{1}{r-g} \times \left(\frac{1+g}{1+r}\right)^T\right] \tag{5.15}$$

where, as before, $C$ is the payment to occur at the end of the first period; $r$ is the interest rate; $g$ is the rate of growth per period, expressed as a percentage; and $T$ is the number of periods for the annuity. It should be noted that for equation (5.15) the growth rate cannot equal the interest rate. If these two are equal, then $r - g$ is 0 and equation (5.15) becomes mathematically undefined.

---

[19] This can be proven as follows. A growing annuity can be viewed as the difference between two growing perpetuities. Consider a growing perpetuity $A$, where the first payment of $C$ occurs at date 1. Next, consider growing perpetuity $B$, where the first payment of $C(1 + g)^T$ is made at date $T + 1$. Both perpetuities grow at rate $g$. The growing annuity over $T$ periods is the difference between annuity $A$ and annuity $B$. This can be represented as follows:

| Date | 0 | 1 | 2 | 3 | ... | T | T + 1 | T + 2 | T + 3 |
|---|---|---|---|---|---|---|---|---|---|
| Perpetuity A | C | $C\times(1+g)$ | $C\times(1+g)^2$ | | ... | $C\times(1+g)^{T-1}$ | $C\times(1+g)^T$ | $C\times(1+g)^{T+1}$ | $C\times(1+g)^{T+2}...$ |
| Perpetuity B | | | | | | | $C\times(1+g)^T$ | $C\times(1+g)^{T+1}$ | $C\times(1+g)^{T+2}...$ |
| Annuity | C | $C\times(1+g)$ | $C\times(1+g)^2$ | | ... | $C\times(1+g)^{T-1}$ | | | |

The value of perpetuity $A$ is $\frac{C}{r-g}$.

The value of perpetuity $B$ is $\frac{C\times(1+g)^T}{r-g} \times \frac{1}{(1+r)^T}$.

The difference between the two perpetuities is given by (5.15).

EXAMPLE **5.29**

Gilles Lebouder, a second-year MBA student, has just been offered a job at $50,000 a year. He anticipates his salary increasing by 9 percent a year until his retirement in 40 years. Given an interest rate of 20 percent, what is the PV of his lifetime salary?

We simplify by assuming he will be paid his $50,000 salary exactly one year from now, and that his salary will continue to be paid in annual instalments. From (5.15), the calculation is

PV of Gilles's lifetime salary = $50,000 × [1/(0.20 − 0.09)] − [1/(0.20 − 0.09)(1.09/1.20)⁴⁰]
= $444,832

EXAMPLE **5.30**

In Example 5.28, Jon and Gila planned to make 17 identical payments to fund the university education of their daughter, Gabrielle. Alternatively, imagine that they planned to increase their payments at 4 percent per year. What would their first payment be?

The first two steps of Example 5.28 showed that the PV of the university costs was $9,422.91. These two steps would be the same here. However, the third step must be altered. Now we must ask, how much should their first payment be so that if payments increase by 4 percent per year, the PV of all payments will be $9,422.91?

We set the growing annuity formula equal to $9,422.91 and solve for $C$:

$$C\left[\frac{1}{r-g} - \left(\frac{1}{r-g}\right)\left(\frac{1+g}{1+r}\right)^T\right]$$
$$= C\left[\frac{1}{0.14 - 0.04} - \left(\frac{1}{0.14 - 0.04}\right)\left(\frac{1.04}{1.14}\right)^{17}\right]$$
$$= \$9,422.91$$

Here, $C$ = $1,192.75. Thus, the deposit on their daughter's first birthday is $1,192.75, the deposit on the second birthday is $1,240.46 (or 1.04 × $1,192.75), and so on.

***CONCEPT***
*QUESTIONS*

- **What are the formulas for a perpetuity, a growing perpetuity, an annuity, and a growing annuity?**
- **What are three important points concerning the growing perpetuity formula?**
- **What are four tricks concerning annuities?**

# 5.5   WHAT IS A FIRM WORTH?

Suppose you are a business appraiser who determines the value of small companies. The lesson you learned from this chapter is that the PV of a firm depends upon its future cash flows.

Let us consider the example of a firm that is expected to generate net cash flows (cash inflows minus cash outflows) of $5,000 in the first year and $2,000 for each of the next five years. The firm can be sold for $10,000 seven years from now. The owners of the firm would like to be able to make 10 percent on their investment.

The value of the firm is found by multiplying the net cash flow by the appropriate PV factor. The value of the firm is simply the sum of the PVs of the individual net cash flows.

The PV of the net cash flows is given below:

**The Present Value of the Firm**

| End of year | Net cash flow of the firm | Present value factor (10%) | Present value of net cash flows |
|:---:|:---:|:---:|:---:|
| 1 | $ 5,000 | 0.90909 | $ 4,545.45 |
| 2 | 2,000 | 0.82645 | 1,652.90 |
| 3 | 2,000 | 0.75131 | 1,502.62 |
| 4 | 2,000 | 0.68301 | 1,366.02 |
| 5 | 2,000 | 0.62092 | 1,241.84 |
| 6 | 2,000 | 0.56447 | 1,128.94 |
| 7 | 10,000 | 0.51315 | 5,131.58 |
| | | Present value of firm | $16,569.35 |

We can also use the simplifying formula for an annuity to give us

$$\frac{\$5,000}{1.1} + \frac{\$2,000}{1.1} \times A_{0.10}^5 + \frac{\$10,000}{(1.1)^7} = \$16,569.35$$

Suppose you have the opportunity to acquire the firm for $12,000. Should you make this investment? The answer is yes because the NPV is positive.

$$\text{NPV} = \text{PV} - \text{Cost}$$
$$\$4,569.35 = \$16,569.35 - \$12,000$$

The incremental value (NPV) of acquiring the firm is $4,569.35.

**EXAMPLE 5.31**

The Napoli Pizza Company is contemplating investing $1 million in four new outlets in Calgary. Matthew Lee, the firm's chief financial officer, has estimated that the investments will pay out cash flows of $200,000 per year for nine years and nothing thereafter. (The cash flows will occur at the end of each year, and there will be no cash flow after year 9.) Matthew has determined that the relevant discount rate for this investment is 15 percent. This is the rate of return that the firm can earn for comparable projects. Should the Napoli Pizza Company invest in the new outlets?

The decision can be evaluated as

$$\text{NPV} = -\$1,000,000 + \frac{\$200,000}{1.15} + \frac{\$200,000}{(1.15)^2} + \cdots + \frac{\$200,000}{(1.15)^9}$$
$$= -\$1,000,000 + \$200,000 \times A_{0.15}^9$$
$$= -\$1,000,000 + \$954,316.78$$
$$= -\$45,683.22$$

The PV of the four new outlets is only $954,316.78. The outlets are worth less than they cost. The Napoli Pizza Company should not make the investment because the NPV is −$45,683.22. If the Napoli Pizza Company requires a 15 percent rate of return, the new outlets are not a good investment.

## 5.6

# SUMMARY AND CONCLUSIONS

1. Two basic concepts, *future value* and *present value (PV)*, were introduced at the beginning of this chapter. With a 10 percent interest rate, an investor with $1 today can generate a future value of $1.10 in a year, $1.21 [$1 × (1.10)$^2$] in two years, and so on. Conversely, PV analysis places a current value on a later cash flow. With the same 10 percent interest rate, a dollar to be received in one year has a PV of $0.909 ($1/1.10) in year 0. A dollar to be received in two years has a PV of $0.826 [$1/(1.10)$^2$].

2. One commonly expresses the interest rate as, say, 12 percent per year. However, one can speak of the interest rate as 3 percent per quarter. Although the stated annual interest rate remains 12 percent (3 percent × 4), the effective annual interest rate is 12.55 percent [(1.03)$^4$ − 1]. In other words, the compounding process increases the future value of an investment. The limiting case is continuous compounding, where funds are assumed to be reinvested every infinitesimal instant.

3. A basic quantitative technique for financial decision making is NPV analysis. The NPV formula for an investment that generates cash flows ($C_t$) in future periods is

$$\text{NPV} = -C_0 + \frac{C_1}{1 + r} + \frac{C_2}{(1 + r)^2} + \cdots + \frac{C_T}{(1 + r)^T} = -C_0 + \sum_{t=1}^{T} \frac{C_t}{(1 + r)^t}$$

The formula assumes that the cash flow at date 0 is the initial investment (a cash outflow).

4. Frequently, the actual calculation of PV is long and tedious. The computation of the PV of a long-term mortgage with monthly payments is a good example of this. We presented four simplifying formulas:

Perpetuity: $\text{PV} = \dfrac{C}{r}$

Growing prepetuity: $\text{PV} = \dfrac{C}{r - g}$

Annuity: $\text{PV} = C\left[\dfrac{1}{r} - \dfrac{1}{r(1 + r)^T}\right]$

Growing annuity: $\text{PV} = C\left[\dfrac{1}{r - g} - \dfrac{1}{r - g} \times \left(\dfrac{1 + g}{1 + r}\right)^T\right]$

5. We stressed a few practical considerations in the application of these formulas:

   a. The numerator in each of the formulas, *C*, is the cash flow to be received *one full period hence*.

   b. Cash flows are generally irregular in practice. To avoid unwieldy problems, assumptions to create more regular cash flows are made both in this textbook and in practice.

   c. A number of PV problems involve annuities (or perpetuities) beginning a few periods hence. Students should practise combining the annuity (or perpetuity) formula with the discounting formula to solve these problems.

   d. Annuities and perpetuities may have periods of every two or every *n* years, rather than once a year. They may also have shorter periods like one month or one quarter. The annuity and perpetuity formulas can easily handle such circumstances.

   e. One frequently encounters problems where the PV of one annuity must be equated with the PV of another annuity.

**KEY TERMS**

Annual percentage rate   117
Annuity   124
Annuity factor   125
Compounding   107
Compound interest   108
Compound value   105
Continuous
 compounding   119
Discounting   112
Effective annual interest
 rate   117
Future value   105
Growing annuity   130
Growing perpetuity   122
Net present value
 (NPV)   106
Perpetuity   121
Present value (PV)   105
Present value factor   112
Simple interest   108
Stated annual interest
 rate   117

**QUESTIONS & PROBLEMS**

### Simple Interest versus Compound Interest

**5.1** First City Bank pays 8 percent simple interest on its savings account balances, whereas Second City Bank pays 8 percent interest compounded annually. If you made a $5,000 deposit in each bank, how much more money would you earn from your Second City Bank account at the end of 10 years?

### Calculating Future Values

**5.2**   *a.* Compute the future value of $1,000 compounded annually for
  *i.*  10 years at 5 percent.
  *ii.* 10 years at 10 percent.
  *iii.* 20 years at 5 percent.
  *b.* Why is the interest earned in (iii) not twice the amount earned in (i)?

### Calculating Present Values

**5.3** For each of the following, compute the PV:

| Present value | Years | Interest rate | Future value |
|---|---|---|---|
| | 6 | 7% | $ 13,827 |
| | 9 | 15 | 43,852 |
| | 18 | 11 | 725,380 |
| | 23 | 18 | 590,710 |

### Calculating Interest Rates

**5.4** Solve for the unknown interest rate in each of the following:

| Present value | Years | Interest rate | Future value |
|---|---|---|---|
| $   242 | 4 | | $   307 |
| 410 | 8 | | 896 |
| 51,700 | 16 | | 162,181 |
| 18,750 | 27 | | 483,500 |

### Calculating the Number of Periods

**5.5** Solve for the unknown number of years in each of the following:

| Present value | Years | Interest rate | Future value |
|---|---|---|---|
| $   625 | | 9% | $ 1,284 |
| 810 | | 11 | 4,341 |
| 18,400 | | 17 | 402,662 |
| 21,500 | | 8 | 173,439 |

**5.6** At 8 percent interest, how long does it take to double your money? To quadruple it?

### Calculating Present Values

**5.7** Imprudential Inc. has an unfunded pension liability of $750 million that must be paid in 20 years. To assess the value of the firm's stock, financial analysts want to discount this liability back to the present. If the relevant discount rate is 8.2 percent, what is the PV of this liability?

### Calculating Rates of Return

5.8  Although appealing to more refined tastes, art as a collectible has not always performed so profitably. During 2010, Deutscher-Menzies sold *Arkies under the Shower*, a painting by renowned Australian painter Brett Whiteley, at auction for a price of $1,100,000. Unfortunately for the previous owner, he had purchased it three years earlier at a price of $1,680,000. What was his annual rate of return on this painting?

### Perpetuities

5.9  An investor purchasing a British consol is entitled to receive annual payments from the British government forever. What is the price of a consol that pays $150 annually if the next payment occurs one year from today? The market interest rate is 4.6 percent.

### Continuous Compounding

5.10  Compute the future value of $1,900 continuously compounded for

   a.  7 years at a stated annual interest rate of 12 percent.
   b.  5 years at a stated annual interest rate of 10 percent.
   c.  12 years at a stated annual interest rate of 5 percent.
   d.  10 years at a stated annual interest rate of 7 percent.

### Present Value and Multiple Cash Flows

5.11  Conoly Co. has identified an investment project with the following cash flows. If the discount rate is 10 percent, what is the PV of these cash flows? What is the PV at 18 percent? 24 percent?

| Year | Cash flow |
|------|-----------|
| 1 | $   960 |
| 2 | 840 |
| 3 | 935 |
| 4 | 1,350 |

5.12  Investment *X* offers to pay you $4,500 per year for nine years, whereas Investment *Y* offers to pay you $7,000 per year for five years. Which of these cash flow streams has the higher PV if the discount rate is 5 percent? 22 percent?

### Calculating Annuity Present Value

5.13  An investment offers $4,900 per year for 15 years, with the first payment occurring one year from now. If the required return is 8 percent, what is the value of the investment? What would the value be if the payments occurred for 40 years? For 75 years? Forever?

### Calculating Perpetuity Values

5.14  The Perpetual Life Insurance Co. is trying to sell you an investment policy that will pay you and your heirs $20,000 per year forever. If the required return on this investment is 6.5 percent, how much will you pay for the policy? Suppose the Perpetual Life Insurance Co. told you the policy costs $340,000. At what interest rate would this be a fair deal?

### Calculating Effective Annual Rate

5.15  Find the EAR in each of the following cases:

| Stated rate (APR) | Number of times compounded | Effective rate (EAR) |
|-------------------|---------------------------|----------------------|
| 8% | Quarterly | |
| 18 | Monthly | |
| 12 | Daily | |
| 14 | Infinite | |

### Calculating Annual Percentage Rate

5.16  Find the APR, or stated rate, in each of the following cases:

| Stated rate (APR) | Number of times compounded | Effective rate (EAR) |
|---|---|---|
| | Semiannually | 9.8% |
| | Monthly | 19.6 |
| | Weekly | 8.3 |
| | Infinite | 14.2 |

### Calculating Effective Annual Rate

5.17  First National Bank charges 11.2 percent compounded monthly on its business loans. First United Bank charges 11.4 percent compounded semiannually. As a potential borrower, to which bank would you go for a new loan?

### Interest Rates

5.18  Well-known financial writer Andrew Tobias argues that he can earn 177 percent per year buying wine by the case. Specifically, he assumes that he will consume one $10 bottle of fine Bordeaux per week for the next 12 weeks. He can either pay $10 per week or buy a case of 12 bottles today. If he buys the case, he receives a 10 percent discount and, by doing so, earns the 177 percent. Assume he buys the wine and consumes the first bottle today. Do you agree with his analysis? Do you see a problem with his numbers?

### Calculating Number of Periods

5.19  One of your customers is delinquent on his accounts payable balance. You've mutually agreed to a repayment schedule of $700 per month. You will charge 1.3 percent per month interest on the overdue balance. If the current balance is $21,500, how long will it take for the account to be paid off?

### Calculating Effective Annual Rate

5.20  Friendly's Quick Loans Inc. offers you "three for four or I knock on your door." This means you get $3 today and repay $4 when you get your paycheque in one week (or else). What's the EAR Friendly's earns on this lending business? If you were brave enough to ask, what APR would Friendly's say you were paying?

### Future Value

5.21  *a.* What is the future value in six years of $1,000 invested in an account with a stated annual interest rate of 9 percent,

   *i.* Compounded annually?
   *ii.* Compounded semiannually?
   *iii.* Compounded monthly?
   *iv.* Compounded continuously?

   *b.* Why does the future value increase as the compounding period shortens?

### Simple Interest versus Compound Interest

5.22  First Simple Bank pays 5 percent simple interest on its investment accounts. If First Complex Bank pays interest on its accounts compounded annually, what rate should the bank set if it wants to match First Simple Bank over an investment horizon of 10 years?

### Calculating Annuities

5.23  You are planning to save for retirement over the next 30 years. To do this, you will invest $700 a month in a stock account and $300 a month in a bond account. The return of the stock account is expected to be 10 percent, and the bond account will pay 6 percent. When you retire, you will combine your money into an account with an 8 percent return. How much can you withdraw each month from your account, assuming a 25-year withdrawal period?

### Calculating Rates of Return

5.24 Suppose an investment offers to quadruple your money in 12 months (don't believe it). What rate of return per quarter are you being offered?

5.25 You're trying to choose between two different investments, both of which have up-front costs of $65,000. Investment *G* returns $125,000 in six years. Investment *H* returns $185,000 in 10 years. Which of these investments has the higher return?

### Growing Perpetuities

5.26 Mark Weinstein has been working on an advanced technology in laser eye surgery. His technology will be available in the near term. He anticipates his first annual cash flow from the technology to be $215,000, received two years from today. Subsequent annual cash flows will grow at 4 percent in perpetuity. What is the PV of the technology if the discount rate is 10 percent?

### Perpetuities

5.27 A prestigious investment bank designed a new security that pays a quarterly dividend of $4.50 in perpetuity. The first dividend occurs one quarter from today. What is the price of the security if the stated annual interest rate is 6.5 percent, compounded quarterly?

### Annuity Present Values

5.28 What is the PV of an annuity of $6,500 per year, with the first cash flow received three years from today and the last one received 25 years from today? Use a discount rate of 7 percent.

5.29 What is the value today of a 15-year annuity that pays $650 a year? The annuity's first payment occurs six years from today. The annual interest rate is 11 percent for years 1 through 5, and 13 percent thereafter.

### Balloon Payments

5.30 Audrey Sanborn has just arranged to purchase a $450,000 condo in Vancouver with a 20 percent down payment. The mortgage has a 7.5 percent stated annual interest rate, compounded monthly, and calls for equal monthly payments over the next 30 years. Her first payment will be due one month from now. However, the mortgage has an eight-year balloon payment, meaning that the balance of the loan must be paid off at the end of year 8. There were no other transaction costs or finance charges. How much will Audrey's balloon payment be in eight years?

### Calculating Interest Expense

5.31 You receive a credit card application from Shady Banks offering an introductory rate of 2.40 percent per year, compounded monthly for the first six months, increasing thereafter to 18 percent compounded monthly. Assuming you transfer the $7,500 balance from your existing credit card and make no subsequent payments, how much interest will you owe at the end of the first year?

### Perpetuities

5.32 Barrett Pharmaceuticals is considering a drug project that costs $2.5 million today and is expected to generate end-of-year annual cash flows of $227,000, forever. At what discount rate would Barrett be indifferent between accepting and rejecting the project?

### Growing Annuity

5.33 Winnipeg Publishing Company is trying to decide whether to revise its popular textbook, *Financial Psychoanalysis Made Simple.* The company has estimated that the revision will cost $75,000. Cash flows from increased sales will be $21,000 the first year. These cash flows will increase by 4 percent per year. The book will go out of print five years from now. Assume that the initial cost is paid now and revenues are received at the end of each year. If the company requires a 10 percent return for such an investment, should it undertake the revision?

**5.34** Your job pays you only once a year for all the work you did over the previous 12 months. Today, December 31, you just received your salary of $65,000, and you plan to spend all of it. However, you want to start saving for retirement beginning next year. You have decided that one year from today you will begin depositing 5 percent of your annual salary in an account that will earn 10 percent per year. Your salary will increase at 4 percent per year throughout your career. How much money will you have on the date of your retirement 40 years from today?

### Present Value and Interest Rates

**5.35** What is the relationship between the value of an annuity and the level of interest rates? Suppose you just bought a 15-year annuity of $6,800 per year at the current interest rate of 10 percent per year. What happens to the value of your investment if interest rates suddenly drop to 5 percent? What if interest rates suddenly rise to 15 percent?

### Calculating the Number of Payments

**5.36** You're prepared to make monthly payments of $350, beginning at the end of this month, into an account that pays 10 percent interest compounded monthly. How many payments will you have made when your account balance reaches $35,000?

### Calculating Annuity Present Values

**5.37** You want to borrow $65,000 from the bank to buy a new sailboat. You can afford to make monthly payments of $1,320, but no more. Assuming monthly compounding, what is the highest APR you can afford on a 60-month loan?

### Calculating Loan Payments

**5.38** You need a 30-year, fixed-rate mortgage to buy a new home for $250,000. Your bank will lend you the money at a 5.3 percent APR for this 360-month loan. However, you can only afford monthly payments of $950, so you offer to pay off any remaining loan balance at the end of the loan in the form of a single balloon payment. How large will this balloon payment have to be for you to keep your monthly payments at $950?

### Present and Future Values

**5.39** The PV of the following cash flow stream is $7,300 when discounted at 8 percent annually. What is the value of the missing cash flow?

| Year | Cash flow |
| --- | --- |
| 1 | $1,500 |
| 2 | ? |
| 3 | 2,700 |
| 4 | 2,900 |

### Calculating Present Values

**5.40** You just won the Ontario Lottery. You will receive $1 million today plus another 10 annual payments that increase by $275,000 per year. Thus, in one year you receive $1.275 million. In two years, you get $1.55 million, and so on. If the appropriate interest rate is 9 percent, what is the PV of your winnings?

### Effective Annual Rate versus Annual Percentage Rate

**5.41** You have just purchased a new warehouse. To finance the purchase, you've arranged for a 30-year mortgage for 80 percent of the $4,500,000 purchase price. The monthly payment on this loan will be $27,500. What is the APR on this loan? The EAR?

### Present Value and Break-Even Interest

5.42    Consider a firm with a contract to sell an asset for $135,000 three years from now. The asset costs $96,000 to produce today. Given a relevant discount rate on this asset of 13 percent per year, will the firm make a profit on this asset? At what rate does the firm just break even?

### Present Value and Multiple Cash Flows

5.43    What is the PV of $5,000 per year, at a discount rate of 6 percent, if the first payment is received 6 years from now and the last payment is received 25 years from now?

### Variable Interest Rates

5.44    A 15-year annuity pays $1,500 per month, and payments are made at the end of each month. If the interest rate is 12 percent compounded monthly for the first seven years, and 6 percent compounded monthly thereafter, what is the PV of the annuity?

### Comparing Cash Flow Streams

5.45    You have your choice of two investment accounts. Investment $A$ is a 15-year annuity that features end-of-month $1,500 payments and has an interest rate of 8.7 percent compounded monthly. Investment $B$ is an 8 percent continuously compounded lump-sum investment, also good for 15 years. How much money would you need to invest in $B$ today for it to be worth as much as Investment $A$ 15 years from now?

### Calculating the Present Value of a Perpetuity

5.46    Given an interest rate of 6.1 percent per year, what is the value at date $t = 7$ of a perpetual stream of $2,500 annual payments that begins at date $t = 15$?

### Calculating the Effective Annual Rate

5.47    A local finance company quotes a 16 percent interest rate on one-year loans. So, if you borrow $26,000, the interest for the year will be $4,160. Because you must repay a total of $30,160 in one year, the finance company requires you to pay $30,160 divided by 12, or $2,513.33, per month over the next 12 months. Is this a 15 percent loan? What rate would legally have to be quoted? What is the EAR?

### Calculating Present Values

5.48    A five-year annuity of 10 $5,300 semiannual payments will begin 9 years from now, with the first payment coming 9.5 years from now. If the discount rate is 12 percent compounded monthly, what is the value of this annuity five years from now? What is the value three years from now? What is the PV of the annuity?

### Calculating Annuities Due

5.49    Suppose you will receive $20,000 per year for five years. The interest rate is 7 percent.
  a.  What is the PV of the payments if they are in the form of an ordinary annuity? What is the PV if the payments are an annuity due?
  b.  Suppose you plan to invest the payments for five years. What is the future value if the payments are an ordinary annuity? What if the payments are an annuity due?
  c.  Which has the higher PV, the ordinary annuity or the annuity due? Which has the higher future value? Will this always be true?

5.50    You want to buy a new sports car from Muscle Motors for $73,000. The contract is in the form of a 60-month annuity due at a 6.45 percent annual percentage rate. What will your monthly payment be?

5.51 You want to lease a set of golf clubs from Pings Ltd. The lease contract is in the form of 24 equal monthly payments at a 10.4 percent stated annual interest rate, compounded monthly. Because the clubs cost $2,300 retail, Pings wants the PV of the lease payments to equal $2,300. Suppose that your first payment is due immediately. What will your monthly lease payments be?

### Annuities

5.52 You are saving for the university education of your two children. They are two years apart in age; one will begin university 15 years from today and the other will begin 17 years from today. You estimate your children's university expenses to be $45,000 per year per child, payable at the beginning of each school year. The annual interest rate is 7.5 percent. How much money must you deposit in an account each year to fund your children's education? Your deposits begin one year from today. You will make your last deposit when your older child enters university. Assume four years of university.

### Growing Annuities

5.53 Tom Adams has received a job offer from a large investment bank as a clerk to an associate banker. His base salary will be $55,000. He will receive his first annual salary payment one year from the day he begins to work. In addition, he will get an immediate $10,000 bonus for joining the company. His salary will grow at 3.5 percent each year. Each year he will receive a bonus equal to 10 percent of his salary. Tom is expected to work for 25 years. What is the PV of the offer if the discount rate is 9 percent?

### Calculating Annuities

5.54 You have recently won the super jackpot in the Alberta Provincial Lottery. On reading the fine print, you discover that you have the following two options:
   a. You will receive 31 annual payments of $250,000, with the first payment being delivered today. The income will be taxed at a rate of 28 percent. Taxes will be withheld when the cheques are issued.
   b. You will receive $530,000 now, and you will not have to pay taxes on this amount. In addition, beginning one year from today, you will receive $200,000 each year for 30 years. The cash flows from this annuity will be taxed at 28 percent.

   Using a discount rate of 7 percent, which option should you select?

### Calculating Growing Annuities

5.55 You have 30 years left until retirement and want to retire with $2 million. Your salary is paid annually, and you will receive $70,000 at the end of the current year. Your salary will increase at 3 percent per year, and you can earn a 9 percent return on the money you invest. If you save a constant percentage of your salary, what percentage of your salary must you save each year?

### Balloon Payments

5.56 On September 1, 2014, Susan Chao bought a motorcycle for $30,000. She paid $1,000 down and financed the balance with a five-year loan at a stated annual interest rate of 7.2 percent, compounded monthly. She started the monthly payments exactly one month after the purchase (i.e., October 1, 2014). Two years later, at the end of October 2016, Susan got a new job and decided to pay off the loan. If the bank charges her a 1 percent prepayment penalty based on the loan balance, how much must she pay the bank on November 1, 2016?

### Calculating Annuity Values

5.57 Bilbo Baggins wants to save money to meet three objectives. First, he would like to be able to retire 30 years from now with a retirement income of $23,000 per month for 20 years, with the first payment received 30 years and 1 month from now. Second, he would like to purchase a cabin in Regina in 10 years at an estimated cost of $320,000. Third, after he passes on at the end of the 20 years of withdrawals, he would like to leave an inheritance of $1,000,000 to his nephew Frodo. He can afford to save $2,100 per month for the next 10 years. If he can earn an 11 percent EAR before he retires and an 8 percent EAR after he retires, how much will he have to save each month in years 11 through 30?

5.58 After deciding to buy a new car, you can either lease the car or purchase it with a three-year loan. The car you wish to buy costs $31,000. The dealer has a special leasing arrangement where you pay $1,500 today and $405 per month for the next three years. If you purchase the car, you will pay it off in monthly payments over the next three years at a 6 percent APR. You believe that you will be able to sell the car for $20,000 in three years. Should you buy or lease the car? What break-even resale price in three years would make you indifferent between buying and leasing?

5.59 An all-star goaltender is in contract negotiations. The team has offered the following salary structure:

| Time | Salary |
|---|---|
| 0 | $8,500,000 |
| 1 | 3,900,000 |
| 2 | 4,600,000 |
| 3 | 5,300,000 |
| 4 | 5,800,000 |
| 5 | 6,400,000 |
| 6 | 7,300,000 |

All salaries are to be paid in a lump sum. The player has asked you as his agent to renegotiate the terms. He wants a $10 million signing bonus payable today and a contract value increase of $1,500,000. He also wants an equal salary paid every three months, with the first paycheque three months from now. If the interest rate is 5 percent compounded daily, what is the amount of his quarterly cheque? Assume 365 days in a year.

### Discount Interest Loans

5.60 This question illustrates what is known as *discount interest*. Imagine you are discussing a loan with a somewhat unscrupulous lender. You want to borrow $20,000 for one year. The interest rate is 15 percent. You and the lender agree that the interest on the loan will be 0.15 × $20,000 = $3,000. So the lender deducts this interest amount from the loan up front and gives you $17,000. In this case, we say that the discount is $3,000. What's wrong here?

### Calculating Annuity Values

5.61 You are serving on a jury. A plaintiff is suing the city for injuries sustained after a freak street sweeper accident. In the trial, doctors testified that it will be five years before the plaintiff is able to return to work. The jury has already decided in favour of the plaintiff. You are the foreperson of the jury and propose that the jury give the plaintiff an award to cover the following: (1) The PV of two years' back pay. The plaintiff's annual salary for the last two years would have been $37,000 and $39,000, respectively. (2) The PV of five years' future salary. You assume the salary will be $43,000 per year. (3) $150,000 for pain and suffering. (4) $25,000 for court costs. Assume that the salary payments are equal amounts paid at the end of each month. If the interest rate you choose is a 9 percent EAR, what is the size of the settlement? If you were the plaintiff, would you like to see a higher or a lower interest rate?

### Calculating Effective Annual Rate with Points

5.62 You are looking at a one-year loan of $10,000. The interest rate is quoted as 9 percent plus three points. A *point* on a loan is simply 1 percent (one percentage point) of the loan amount. Quotes similar to this one are very common with home mortgages. The interest rate quotation in this example requires the borrower to pay three points to the lender up front and repay the loan later with 9 percent interest. What rate would you actually be paying here? What is the EAR for a one-year loan with a quoted interest rate of 12 percent plus two points? Is your answer affected by the loan amount?

### Effective Annual Rate versus Annual Percentage Rate

5.63 Two banks in the area offer 30-year, $200,000 mortgages at 5.3 percent and charge a $2,400 loan application fee. However, the application fee charged by Insecurity Bank and Trust is refundable if the loan application is denied, whereas that charged by I. M. Greedy and Sons Mortgage Bank is not. The current disclosure law requires that any fees that will be refunded if the applicant is rejected be included in calculating the APR, but this is not required with non-refundable fees (presumably because refundable fees are part of the loan rather than a fee). What are the EARs on these two loans? What are the APRs?

### Calculating Effective Annual Rate with Add-On Interest

5.64 This problem illustrates a deceptive way of quoting interest rates called *add-on interest*. Imagine that you see an advertisement for Crazy Judy's Stereo City that reads something like this: "$1,000 Instant Credit! 18% Simple Interest! Three Years to Pay! Low, Low Monthly Payments!" You're not exactly sure what all this means and somebody has spilled ink over the APR on the loan contract, so you ask the manager for clarification.

Judy explains that if you borrow $1,000 for three years at 18 percent interest, in three years you will owe

$$\$1,000 \times 1.18^3 = \$1,000 \times 1.64303 = \$1,643.03$$

Judy recognizes that coming up with $1,643.03 all at once might be a strain, so she lets you make "low, low monthly payments" of $1,643.03/36 = $45.64 per month, even though this is extra bookkeeping work for her.

Is this a 18 percent loan? Why or why not? What is the APR on this loan? What is the EAR? Why do you think this is called add-on interest?

### Calculating Annuity Payments

5.65 Your friend is celebrating her 30th birthday today and wants to start saving for her anticipated retirement at age 65. She wants to be able to withdraw $100,000 from her savings account on each birthday for 25 years following her retirement, with the first withdrawal on her 66th birthday. Your friend intends to invest her money in the local credit union, which offers 8 percent interest per year. She wants to make equal annual payments on each birthday into the account established at the credit union for her retirement fund.

a. If she starts making these deposits on her 30th birthday and continues to make deposits until she is 65 (the last deposit will be on her 65th birthday), what amount must she deposit annually to be able to make the desired withdrawals at retirement?

b. Suppose your friend has just inherited a large sum of money. Rather than making equal annual payments, she has decided to make one lump-sum payment on her 30th birthday to cover her retirement needs. What amount does she have to deposit?

*c.* Suppose your friend's employer will contribute $1,300 to the account every year as part of the company's profit-sharing plan. In addition, your friend expects a $45,000 distribution from a family trust fund on her 55th birthday, which she will also put into the retirement account. What amount must she deposit annually now to be able to make the desired withdrawals at retirement?

### Calculating the Number of Periods

5.66 Your Christmas ski vacation was great, but it unfortunately ran a bit over budget. All is not lost; you just received an offer in the mail to transfer your $10,000 balance from your current credit card, which charges an annual rate of 18.6 percent, to a new credit card charging a rate of 8.2 percent. How much faster could you pay the loan off by making your planned monthly payments of $200 with the new card? What if there was a 2 percent fee charged on any balances transferred?

### Future Value and Multiple Cash Flows

5.67 An insurance company is offering a new policy to its customers. Typically the policy is bought by a parent or grandparent for a child at the child's birth. The details of the policy are as follows. The purchaser (say, the parent) makes the following six payments to the insurance company:

| | |
|---|---|
| First birthday: | $   500 |
| Second birthday: | $   600 |
| Third birthday: | $   700 |
| Fourth birthday: | $   800 |
| Fifth birthday: | $   900 |
| Sixth birthday: | $1,000 |

After the child's sixth birthday, no more payments are made. When the child reaches age 65, he or she receives $275,000. If the relevant interest rate is 11 percent for the first six years and 7 percent for all subsequent years, is the policy worth buying?

### Annuity Present Values and Effective Rates

5.68 You have just won the lottery. You will receive $2,500,000 today and then receive 40 payments of $1,250,000. These payments will start one year from now and will be paid every six months. A representative from Greenleaf Investments has offered to purchase all the payments from you for $23 million. If the appropriate interest rate is a 9 percent APR compounded daily, should you take the offer? Assume there are 12 months in a year, each with 30 days.

### Calculating Interest Rates

5.69 A financial planning service offers a university savings program. The plan calls for you to make six annual payments of $11,000 each, with the first payment occurring today, your child's 12th birthday. Beginning on your child's 18th birthday, the plan will provide $25,000 per year for four years. What return is this investment offering?

### Break-Even Investment Returns

5.70 Your financial planner offers you two different investment plans. Plan *X* is a $15,000 annual perpetuity. Plan *Y* is a 10-year, $26,000 annual annuity. Both plans will make their first payment one year from today. At what discount rate would you be indifferent between these two plans?

### Perpetual Cash Flows

5.71 What is the value of an investment that pays $30,000 every *other* year forever, if the first payment occurs one year from today and the discount rate is 13 percent compounded daily? What is the value today if the first payment occurs four years from today? Assume 365 days in a year.

### Ordinary Annuities and Annuities Due

5.72  As discussed in the text, an annuity due is identical to an ordinary annuity except that the periodic payments occur at the beginning of each period and not at the end of the period. Show that the relationship between the value of an ordinary annuity and the value of an otherwise equivalent annuity due is

$$\text{Annuity due value} = \text{Ordinary annuity value} \times (1 + r)$$

Show this for both present and future values.

### Calculating the Effective Annual Rate

5.73  A cheque-cashing store is in the business of making personal loans to walk-up customers. The store makes one-week loans at 7 percent interest per week.

   a.  What APR must the store report to its customers? What is the EAR that the customers are actually paying?

   b.  Now suppose the store makes one-week loans at 9 percent discount interest per week (see Problem 5.60). What's the APR now? The EAR?

   c.  The cheque-cashing store also makes one-month add-on interest loans (see Problem 5.64) at 7 percent discount interest per week. Thus, if you borrow $100 for one month (four weeks), the interest will be ($100 \times 1.07^4) - 100 = $31.08. Because this is discount interest, your net loan proceeds today will be $68.92. You must then repay the store $100 at the end of the month. To help you out, though, the store lets you pay off this $100 in instalments of $25 per week. What is the APR of this loan? The EAR?

### Present Value of a Growing Perpetuity

5.74  What is the equation for the PV of a growing perpetuity with a payment of $C$ one period from today if the payments grow by $C$ each period?

### Rule of 72

5.75  A useful rule of thumb for the time it takes an investment to double with discrete compounding is the Rule of 72. To use the Rule of 72, you simply divide 72 by the interest rate to determine the number of periods it takes for a value today to double. For example, if the interest rate is 6 percent, the Rule of 72 says it will take 72/6 = 12 periods to double. This is approximately equal to the actual answer of 11.90 periods. The Rule of 72 can also be applied to determine what interest rate is needed to double money in a specified period. This is a useful approximation for many interest rates and periods. At what rate is the Rule of 72 exact?

### Rule of 69.3

5.76  A corollary to the Rule of 72 is the Rule of 69.3. The Rule of 69.3 is exactly correct except for rounding when interest rates are compounded continuously. Prove the Rule of 69.3 for continuously compounded interest.

# The MBA Decision

Ben Bates graduated from university six years ago with an undergraduate degree in finance. Although he is satisfied with his current job, his goal is to become an investment banker. He feels that an MBA degree would allow him to achieve this goal. After examining schools, he has narrowed his choice to either Atlantic University or Pacific University. Although internships are encouraged by both schools, to get class credit for the internship, no salary can be paid. Other than internships, neither school will allow its students to work while enrolled in its MBA program.

Ben currently works at the money management firm of Dewey and Louis. His annual salary at the firm is $65,000 per year, expected to increase at 3 percent per year until retirement. He is currently 28 years old and expects to work for 40 more years. His current job includes a fully paid health insurance plan, and his current average tax rate is 26 percent. Ben has a savings account with enough money to cover the entire cost of his MBA program.

The Faculty of Management at Atlantic University is one of the top MBA programs in the country. The MBA degree requires two years of full-time enrollment at the university. The annual tuition is $70,000, payable at the beginning of each school year. Books and other supplies are estimated to cost $3,000 per year. Ben expects that after graduation from Atlantic, he will receive a job offer for about $110,000 per year, with a $20,000 signing bonus. The salary at this job will increase at 4 percent per year. Because of the higher salary, his average income tax rate will increase to 31 percent.

The School of Business at Pacific University began its MBA program 16 years ago and is less well known

than Atlantic University's Faculty of Management. Pacific University offers an accelerated, one-year program, with a tuition cost of $85,000 to be paid upon graduation. Books and other supplies for the program are expected to cost $4,500. Ben thinks that he will receive an offer of $92,000 per year upon graduation, with an $18,000 signing bonus. The salary at this job will increase at 3.5 percent per year. His average tax rate at this level of income will be 29 percent.

Both schools offer a health insurance plan that will cost $3,000 per year, payable at the beginning of the year. Ben also estimates that room and board expenses will cost $2,000 more per year at both schools than his current expenses, payable at the beginning of each year. The appropriate discount rate is 6.5 percent.

1.  How does Ben's age affect his decision to get an MBA?

2.  What other, perhaps non-quantifiable, factors affect Ben's decision to get an MBA?

3.  Assuming all salaries are paid at the end of each year, which is the best option for Ben—from a strictly financial standpoint?

4.  Ben believes that the appropriate analysis is to calculate the future value of each option. How would you evaluate this statement?

5.  What initial salary would Ben need to receive to make him indifferent between attending Atlantic University and staying in his current position?

6.  Suppose, instead of being able to pay cash for his MBA, Ben must borrow the money. The current borrowing rate is 5.4 percent. How would this affect his decision?

## Using Financial Calculators

To access Appendix 5A, go to Connect.

**6**

# How to Value Bonds and Stocks

When the stock market closed on February 7, 2014, the common stock of Manulife Financial, a leading financial services company, was trading at $20.22 per share, while athletic apparel company Lululemon closed at $47.38. With the varying stock prices you might expect that of the two companies, Lululemon would be offering a higher dividend, but you would be wrong. In fact, Manulife Financial's annual dividend was $0.52 per share and Lululemon paid no dividends at all!

As we will see in this chapter, current dividends are only one of the primary factors in stock valuation. This chapter will explore dividends, stock values, and the connection between the two. Before discussing stock valuation, however, we will begin with a discussion of how bonds are priced. Since the future cash flows of bonds are known (at least for government bonds and issues of high-quality corporations with minimal default risk), application of net present value (NPV) techniques is fairly straightforward. The uncertainty of future cash flows makes stock valuation more difficult.

## 6.1 DEFINITION AND EXAMPLE OF A BOND

A *bond* is a certificate showing that a borrower owes a specified sum. In order to repay the money, the borrower has agreed to make interest and principal payments on designated dates. For example, imagine that Kreuger Enterprises just issued 100,000 bonds for $1,000 each, each carrying a coupon rate of 5 percent and a maturity of two years. Interest on the bonds is to be paid yearly. This means that

1. $100 million (or 100,000 × $1,000) has been borrowed by the firm.
2. The firm must pay interest of $5 million (or 5% × $100 million) at the end of one year.
3. The firm must pay both $5 million of interest and $100 million of principal at the end of two years.

We now consider how to value a few different types of bonds.

## 6.2 HOW TO VALUE BONDS

### Pure Discount Bonds

The **pure discount bond** is perhaps the simplest kind of bond. It promises a single payment, say $1, at a fixed future date. If the payment is one year from now, it is called a *one-year discount bond*, if it is two years from now, it is called a *two-year discount bond*, and so on. The date when the issuer of the bond makes the last payment is called the **maturity date** of the bond, or just its *maturity* for short. The bond is said to mature or *expire* on the date of its final payment. The payment at maturity ($1 in this example) is termed the bond's **face value**.

Pure discount bonds are often called *zero-coupon bonds* or *zeros* to emphasize the fact that the holder receives no cash payments until maturity. We will use the terms *zero*, *bullet*, and *discount* interchangeably to refer to bonds that pay no coupons.

The first row of Figure 6.1 shows the pattern of cash flows from a four-year pure discount bond. Note that the face value, *F*, is paid when the bond expires in the 48th month. There are no payments of either interest or principal prior to this date.

---

**FIGURE 6.1**

**Different Types of Bonds: *C*, Coupon Paid Every Six Months; *F*, Face Value at Year 4 (maturity for pure discount and coupon bonds)**

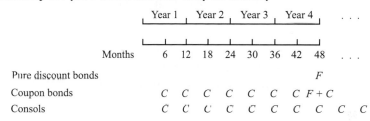

From Chapter 4, we know that the value of an investment is its present value (PV) at a discount rate representing market returns. In Chapter 5, we indicated that one discounts a future cash flow to determine its PV. The PV of a pure discount bond can easily be determined by the techniques of the previous chapter. For short, we sometimes speak of the *value* of a bond instead of its PV.

Consider a pure discount bond that pays a face value of *F* in *T* years, where the interest rate is *r* in each of the *T* years. (We also refer to this rate as the *market interest rate*.) Because the face value is the only cash flow that the bond pays, the PV of this face amount is

**Value of a Pure Discount Bond:**

$$PV = \frac{F}{(1 + r)^T}$$

The PV formula can produce some surprising results. Suppose that the interest rate is 10 percent. Consider a bond with a face value of $1 million that matures in 20 years. Applying the formula to this bond, its PV is given by

$$PV = \frac{\$1 \text{ million}}{(1.1)^{20}} = \$148,644$$

or only about 15 percent of the face value.

## Level-Coupon Bonds

Many bonds, however, are not of the simple, pure discount variety. Typical bonds issued by either governments or corporations offer cash payments not just at maturity, but also at regular times in between. For example, payments on Canadian government issues and Canadian corporate bonds are made every six months until the bond matures. These payments are called the **coupons** of the bond. The middle row of Figure 6.1 illustrates the case of a four-year *level-coupon* bond: the coupon, *C*, is paid every six months and is the same throughout the life of the bond.

Note that the face value of the bond, *F*, is paid at maturity (end of year 4). *F* is sometimes called the *principal* or the *denomination*. Bonds issued in Canada typically have face values of $1,000, though this can vary with the type of bond.

As we mentioned above, the value of a bond is simply the PV of its cash flows. Therefore, the value of a level-coupon bond is merely the PV of its stream of coupon payments plus the PV of its repayment of principal. Because a level-coupon bond is just an annuity of $C$ each period, together with a payment at maturity of $1,000, the value of a level-coupon bond is

**Value of a Level-Coupon Bond:**

$$PV = \frac{C}{1 + r} + \frac{C}{(1 + r)^2} + \cdots + \frac{C}{(1 + r)^T} + \frac{\$1,000}{(1 + r)^T}$$

where $C$ is the coupon, and the face value, $F$, is $1,000. The value of the bond can be rewritten as

**Value of a Level-Coupon Bond:**

$$PV = C \times A_r^T + \frac{\$1,000}{(1 + r)^T}$$

As mentioned in the previous chapter, $A_r^T$ is the PV of an annuity of $1 per period for $T$ eriods at an interest rate per period of $r$.

---

**EXAMPLE 6.1**

Selected bond trading figures for February 7, 2014, appear in Figure 6.2. Suppose an investor was interested in the CHT 3.800 Jun 15/2021. This is jargon that means the bond was issued by Canada Housing Trust, a special purpose trust, and has an annual coupon rate of 3.8 percent.[1] The face value is $1,000, implying that the yearly coupon is $38.00 (3.8% × $1,000). Interest is paid each June and December, implying that the coupon is $19.00 ($38/2) every six months. The face value will be paid out in June 2021. By this we mean that the purchaser obtains claims to the following cash flows:

| June 2014 | December 2014 | June 2015 | December 2015 | June 2016 | | June 2021 |
|---|---|---|---|---|---|---|
| $19.00 | $19.00 | $19.00 | $19.00 | $19.00 | ... | $19.00 + $1,000 |

If today the stated annual interest rate in the market is 2.43 percent, what is the PV of the bond?

The standard North American method of expressing both bond coupons and bond yields is as a stated rate per year, compounded semiannually.[2] Our work on compounding in the previous chapter showed that the interest rate for bonds is semiannually compounding. In the current example, this semiannual rate is 1.215 percent (2.43%/2). Since the coupon payment in each period is $19.00, and there are 15 of these payment dates (from February 2014 to February 2021 there are 14 payments, plus the 1 payment in June 2021), the PV of the bond is

$$PV = \frac{\$19.00}{(1.01215)} + \frac{\$19.00}{(1.01215)^2} + \cdots + \frac{\$19.00}{(1.01215)^{15}} + \frac{\$1,000}{(1.01215)^{15}}$$

$$= \$19.00 \times A_{0.01215}^{15} + \$1,000/(1.01215)^{15}$$

$$= \$259.11 + \$834.31$$

$$= \$1,093.42$$

Traders will generally quote the bond as 109.342, indicating that it is selling at 109.342 percent of the face value of $1,000. This can be seen in Figure 6.2 in the "Bid $" column of our bond. (The small difference in price ($0.202) between our price calculations and the newspaper listing reflects accrued interest arising from the 128 days between February 7 and June 15 and rounding differences.)

---

[1] The coupon rate is specific to the bond and indicates what cash flow should appear in the numerator of the NPV equation. The coupon rate does not appear in the denominator of the NPV equation.

[2] Semiannual compounding also applies to zero-coupon bonds. The example provided earlier, however, was simplified and thus used annual compounding.

FIGURE 6.2

## Sample Bond Quotations

**Sample of a Bond Quotation**

### Federal

| | | | | |
|---|---|---|---|---|
| Canada | 2.000 | 2014-03-01 | 100.05 | 0.96 |
| Canada | 10.250 | 2014-03-15 | 100.85 | 0.94 |
| Canada | 3.000 | 2014-06-01 | 100.62 | 0.93 |
| Canada | 5.000 | 2014-06-01 | 101.22 | 0.93 |
| Canada | 2.250 | 2014-08-01 | 100.62 | 0.94 |
| Canada | 2.000 | 2014-12-01 | 100.84 | 0.95 |
| Canada | 11.250 | 2015-06-01 | 113.27 | 0.97 |
| Canada | 2.500 | 2015-06-01 | 101.97 | 0.97 |
| Canada | 4.500 | 2015-06-01 | 104.55 | 0.97 |
| Canada | 3.000 | 2015-12-01 | 103.58 | 0.99 |
| Canada | 2.000 | 2016-06-01 | 102.24 | 1.02 |
| Canada | 4.000 | 2016-06-01 | 106.79 | 1.01 |
| Canada | 2.750 | 2016-09-01 | 104.21 | 1.07 |
| Canada | 4.000 | 2017-06-01 | 109.02 | 1.2 |
| Canada | 4.250 | 2018-06-01 | 111.48 | 1.48 |
| Canada | 3.750 | 2019-06-01 | 110.43 | 1.09 |
| Canada | 3.500 | 2020-06-01 | 109.73 | 1.86 |
| Canada | 10.500 | 2021-03-15 | 156.26 | 1.96 |
| Canada | 3.250 | 2021-06-01 | 108.28 | 2.02 |
| Canada | 9.750 | 2021-06-01 | 152.66 | 1.97 |
| Canada | 2.750 | 2022-06-01 | 103.83 | 2.24 |
| Canada | 9.250 | 2022-06-01 | 153.39 | 2.18 |
| Canada | 1.500 | 2023-06-01 | 92.52 | 2.4 |
| Canada | 8.000 | 2023-06-01 | 147.36 | 2.31 |
| Canada | 9.000 | 2025-06-01 | 164.19 | 2.46 |
| Canada | 8.000 | 2027-06-01 | 160.26 | 2.61 |
| Canada | 5.750 | 2029-06-01 | 137.5 | 2.73 |
| Canada | 5.750 | 2033-06-01 | 142.36 | 2.87 |
| Canada | 5.000 | 2037-06-01 | 134.58 | 2.94 |
| Canada | 4.000 | 2041-06-01 | 118.42 | 3.01 |
| CHT | 2.200 | 2014-03-15 | 100.11 | 0.99 |
| CHT | 2.750 | 2016-06-15 | 103.65 | 1.17 |
| CHT | 3.800 | 2021-06-15 | 109.14 | 2.43 |

### Provincial

| | | | | |
|---|---|---|---|---|
| BC | 4.700 | 2037-06-18 | 114.5 | 3.76 |
| HydQue | 6.500 | 2035-02-15 | 134.94 | 4.02 |
| HydQue | 6.000 | 2040-02-15 | 130.9 | 4.06 |
| HydQue | 5.000 | 2045-02-15 | 116.08 | 4.08 |
| NovaSc | 6.600 | 2027-06-01 | 132.38 | 3.53 |
| Ontario | 5.000 | 2014-03-08 | 100.28 | 0.99 |
| Ontario | 3.250 | 2014-09-08 | 101.27 | 1 |
| Ontario | 4.500 | 2015-03-08 | 103.64 | 1.06 |
| Ontario | 4.400 | 2016-03-08 | 106.56 | 1.18 |
| Ontario | 4.300 | 2017-03-08 | 108.54 | 1.44 |
| Ontario | 4.200 | 2018-03-08 | 109.28 | 1.82 |
| Ontario | 8.100 | 2023-09-08 | 139.97 | 3.21 |
| Ontario | 6.500 | 2029-03-08 | 132.94 | 3.64 |
| Ontario | 6.200 | 2031-06-02 | 131.01 | 3.75 |
| Ontario | 5.850 | 2033-03-08 | 127.57 | 3.8 |
| Ontario | 5.600 | 2035-06-02 | 125.13 | 3.86 |
| Ontario | 4.700 | 2037-06-02 | 112.27 | 3.89 |
| Quebec | 5.500 | 2014-12-01 | 103.54 | 1.04 |
| Quebec | 5.000 | 2015-12-01 | 106.89 | 1.12 |
| Quebec | 4.500 | 2016-12-01 | 108.52 | 1.39 |
| Quebec | 4.500 | 2017-12-01 | 110.03 | 1.76 |
| Quebec | 4.500 | 2018-12-01 | 110.84 | 2.11 |
| Quebec | 9.375 | 2023-01-16 | 147.69 | 3.19 |
| Quebec | 8.500 | 2026-04-01 | 147.37 | 3.64 |
| Quebec | 6.000 | 2029-10-01 | 125.82 | 3.8 |
| Quebec | 6.250 | 2032-06-01 | 130.26 | 3.92 |
| Quebec | 5.750 | 2036-12-01 | 125.44 | 4.03 |
| Quebec | 5.000 | 2038-12-01 | 114.51 | 4.07 |
| Quebec | 5.000 | 2041-12-01 | 114.79 | 4.1 |

### Corporate

| | | | | |
|---|---|---|---|---|
| Bell | 4.85 | 2014-06-30 | 101.28 | 1.52 |
| Bell | 3.6 | 2015-12-02 | 103.28 | 1.75 |
| Bell | 4.4 | 2018-03-16 | 107.01 | 2.58 |
| Bell | 5 | 2017-02-15 | 108.29 | 2.14 |
| Bell | 6.1 | 2035-03-16 | 114.93 | 4.95 |
| BMO | 4.87 | 2015-04-22 | 103.8 | 1.64 |
| BMO Cap | 4.633 | 2015-12-31 | 105.1 | 1.87 |
| BMO | 5.1 | 2016-04-21 | 106.89 | 1.87 |
| BMO | 6.17 | 2018-03-28 | 114.08 | 2.55 |
| BMO Cap II | 10.221 | 2018-12-31 | 131.89 | 3.13 |
| BNS | 3.43 | 2014-07-16 | 100.94 | 1.24 |
| BNS | 3.34 | 2015-03-25 | 102.12 | 1.42 |
| CIBC | 3.1 | 2015-03-02 | 101.75 | 1.42 |
| CIBC | 3.15 | 2015-11-02 | 102.25 | 1.82 |
| Canadian Tire | 4.95 | 2015-06-01 | 104.18 | 1.69 |
| ENB | 5.17 | 2016-05-19 | 107.42 | 1.81 |

### Corporate Bonds

| | | | | |
|---|---|---|---|---|
| ENB | 4.53 | 2020-03-09 | 108.97 | 2.91 |
| ENB Gas | 5.21 | 2036-02-25 | 112.18 | 4.35 |
| ENB Pipelines | 6.62 | 2018-11-19 | 119.13 | 2.35 |
| ENB Pipelines | 4.45 | 2020-04-06 | 109.78 | 2.71 |
| ENB Pipelines | 5.33 | 2040-04-06 | 115.09 | 4.36 |
| Encana Corp | 5.8 | 2018-01-18 | 111.76 | 2.63 |
| GE CAP | 4.65 | 2015-02-11 | 103.15 | 1.47 |
| GE CAP | 5.1 | 2016-06-01 | 107.64 | 1.7 |
| GE CAP | 5.68 | 2019-09-10 | 115.48 | 2.67 |
| GWLife | 5.691 | 2017-06-21 | 110.37 | 2.45 |
| GWLife | 4.65 | 2020-08-13 | 109.97 | 2.95 |
| HSBC | 4.8 | 2017-04-10 | 107.22 | 2.41 |
| HSBC | 3.558 | 2017-10-04 | 104.77 | 2.19 |
| HydOne | 4.64 | 2016-03-03 | 106.27 | 1.53 |
| HydOne | 5.36 | 2036-05-20 | 114.38 | 4.35 |
| HydOne | 4.89 | 2037-03-13 | 108.16 | 4.33 |
| Loblaw | 4.85 | 2014-05-08 | 100.76 | 1.67 |
| Loblaw | 5.22 | 2020-06-18 | 111.41 | 3.22 |
| Loblaw | 6.05 | 2034-06-09 | 110.66 | 5.19 |
| Loblaw | 5.9 | 2036-01-18 | 108.99 | 5.21 |
| MLI | 4.896 | 2014-06-02 | 101.04 | 1.47 |
| MLI | 7.768 | 2019-04-08 | 123.36 | 2.86 |
| MLI | 5.059 | 2036-12-15 | 100.56 | 5.02 |
| NBC | 4.03 | 2015-05-26 | 103.25 | 1.47 |
| Rogers | 5.8 | 2016-05-26 | 108.67 | 1.91 |
| Rogers | 5.34 | 2021-03-22 | 111.86 | 3.44 |
| Rogers | 6.11 | 2040-08-25 | 112.66 | 5.22 |
| RoyBnk | 4.71 | 2014-12-22 | 102.88 | 1.33 |
| RoyBnk | 3.18 | 2015-03-16 | 101.97 | 1.35 |
| RoyBnk | 3.18 | 2015-11-02 | 102.33 | 1.8 |
| SunLife | 4.95 | 2016-06-01 | 106.09 | 2.22 |
| SunLife | 5.59 | 2018-01-30 | 111.01 | 2.65 |
| Suncor | 5.8 | 2018-05-22 | 113.44 | 2.47 |
| Suncor | 5.39 | 2037-03-26 | 109.36 | 4.72 |
| Toyota Credit | 3.55 | 2016-02-22 | 103.82 | 1.63 |
| TD Bnk | 3.367 | 2015-11-02 | 102.67 | 1.78 |
| TD Bnk | 5.763 | 2017-12-18 | 111.91 | 2.49 |
| Trans-Can Pipelines | 5.05 | 2014-02-14 | 100 | 2.7 |
| Trans-Can Pipelines | 4.65 | 2016-10-03 | 107.65 | 1.68 |
| Trans-Can Pipelines | 8.05 | 2039-02-17 | 152.22 | 4.54 |

Source: www.financialpost.com, February 7, 2014. Used with permission.

One final note concerning level-coupon bonds: Although our example uses government bonds, corporate bonds are identical in form. For example, BMO has a 4.87 percent bond maturing in 2015. This means that BMO will make semiannual payments of $24.35 (4.87%/2 × $1000) between now and 2015 for each face value of $1,000.[3]

## A Note on Bond Price Quotes

As the Canada Housing Trust example showed, when buying a bond between coupon payment dates, the price paid is usually more than the price quoted. The reason is that standard convention in the bond market is to quote prices net of accrued interest, which means that accrued interest is deducted to arrive at the quoted price. This

---

[3] Corporate bonds have a number of features that affect their risk and cash flows, and these features will be discussed in Chapter 21.

quoted price is called the **clean price**. The price actually paid, however, includes the accrued interest. This is the **dirty price**, also known as the full or invoice price.

For example, suppose a bond is bought with a 12 percent annual coupon, payable semiannually. The actual price paid, the dirty price, is $1,080. The next coupon is due four months from the date the bond is purchased. The next coupon will be $60. The accrued interest on a bond is calculated by taking the fraction of the coupon period that has passed, in this case two months out of six, and multiplying this fraction by the next coupon. Thus, accrued interest in this example would be $2/6 \times \$60 = \$20$. The bond's clean price would be $\$1,080 - \$20 = \$1,060$.

## Consols

Not all bonds have a final maturity date. As we mentioned in the previous chapter, consols are bonds that never stop paying a coupon, have no final maturity date, and therefore never mature. Thus, a consol is a perpetuity. In the eighteenth century, the Bank of England issued such bonds, called *English consols*. These were bonds that the Bank of England guaranteed would pay the holder a cash flow forever! Through wars and depressions, the Bank of England continued to honour this commitment, and you can still buy such bonds in London today. The Government of Canada also once sold consols. Even though these Canadian bonds were supposed to last forever and to pay their coupons forever, don't go looking for any. There was a special clause in the bond contract that gave the government the right to buy them back from the holders, and that is what the government did. Clauses like that are called *call provisions*; we will study them later.

An important current Canadian example of a consol is a fixed-rate preferred stock that provides the holder a fixed dividend in perpetuity. If there were never any question that the firm would actually pay the dividend on the preferred stock, such stock would in fact be a consol.

These instruments can be valued by the perpetuity formula of the previous chapter. For example, if the marketwide interest rate is 10 percent, a consol with a yearly interest payment of $50 is valued at

$$\frac{\$50}{0.10} = \$500$$

 **CONCEPT QUESTIONS**
- Define pure discount bonds, level-coupon bonds, and consols.
- Contrast the stated interest rate and the effective annual interest rate for bonds paying semiannual interest.

# 6.3   BOND CONCEPTS

We complete our discussion on bonds by considering three important concepts: the relationship between interest rates and bond prices, the concept of yield to maturity (YTM), and the idea of holding-period return.

## Interest Rates and Bond Prices

The above discussion on level-coupon bonds allows us to relate bond prices to interest rates. Consider Example 6.2.

EXAMPLE **6.2**

The interest rate is 10 percent. A two-year bond with a 10 percent coupon pays interest of $100 (or $1,000 × 10%). For simplicity, we assume that the interest is paid annually. The bond is priced at its face value of $1,000:

$$\$1,000 = \frac{\$100}{1.1} + \frac{\$1,000 + \$100}{(1.1)^2}$$

If the interest rate unexpectedly rises to 12 percent, the bond sells at

$$\$966.20 = \frac{\$100}{1.12} + \frac{\$1,000 + \$100}{(1.12)^2}$$

Because $966.20 is less than $1,000, the bond is said to sell at a **discount**. This is a sensible result. Now that the interest rate is 12 percent, a newly issued bond with a 12 percent coupon rate will sell at $1,000. This newly issued bond will have coupon payments of $120 (or 0.12 × $1,000). Because our bond has interest payments of only $100, investors will pay less than $1,000 for it.

If the interest rate fell to 8 percent, the bond would sell at

$$\$1,035.67 = \frac{\$100}{1.08} + \frac{\$1,000 + \$100}{(1.08)^2}$$

Because $1,035.67 is more than $1,000, the bond is said to sell at a **premium**.

Thus, we find that bond prices fall with a rise in interest rates and rise with a fall in interest rates. Furthermore, the general principle is that a level-coupon bond trades in the following ways:

1. At the face value of $1,000 if the coupon rate is equal to the marketwide interest rate.
2. At a discount if the coupon rate is less than the marketwide interest rate.
3. At a premium if the coupon rate is more than the marketwide interest rate.

## Yield to Maturity

Let us now consider the previous example in reverse. If our bond is selling at $1,035.67, what return is a bondholder receiving? This can be answered by considering the following equation:

$$\$1,035.67 = \frac{\$100}{1 + y} + \frac{\$1,000 + \$100}{(1 + y)^2}$$

The unknown, $y$, is the rate of return that the holder is earning on the bond. Our earlier work implies that $y = 8\%$. Thus, traders state that the bond is yielding an 8 percent return. Equivalently, they say that the bond has a **yield to maturity** (YTM) of 8 percent.[4] The YTM is frequently called the bond's yield for short. So we would say the bond with its 10 percent coupon is priced to yield 8 percent at $1,035.67.

Students get confused between coupon rate and YTM. It is critical to understand the difference between the two in order to gain in-depth knowledge of bond concepts. Coupon rate is the rate at which an investor receives a fixed cash flow every six months, while YTM is the return an investor would receive from his or her entire investment. An easy way to think of YTM is to consider it the rate the market is demanding for investing in that particular bond, considering the riskiness of an asset. YTM and coupon rate are equal for newly issued bonds that sell at their par value.

------

[4] Technically, the YTM calculation assumes that the bond is held to maturity and all coupons are reinvested at $y$.

## Holding-Period Return

Our example of interest rates and bond prices showed how the price of a two-year bond with a 10 percent coupon varied as market yields changed. Suppose that a bond trader bought the bond when its market yield was 12 percent and sold a month later when the yield was 8 percent. This means that the trader succeeded in buying low ($966.20) and selling high ($1,035.67). In this example the trader earned a **holding-period return** of 7.19 percent:

$$\text{Holding-period return} = (\text{Ending price} - \text{Beginning price})/\text{Beginning price}$$
$$= (\$1,035.67 - \$966.20)/\$966.20$$
$$= 7.19\%$$

Holding-period return is a total return received from holding an asset or portfolio of assets. This calculation is on a per-dollar-invested basis, rather than a time basis, which makes it difficult to compare returns on different investments with different time frames. Since the 1980s, corporate bond yields have mostly fallen, rising at a time of financial crisis and then falling again. A bond investor looking to increase holding-period returns would buy low when the rates are high and sell high when they are low.

## The Present Value Formulas for Bonds

**Pure Discount Bonds:**
$$PV = \frac{F}{(1 + r)^T}$$

**Level-Coupon Bonds:**
$$PV = C\left[\frac{1}{r} - \frac{1}{r \times (1 + r)^T}\right] + \frac{F}{(1 + r)^T} = C \times A_r^T + \frac{F}{(1 + r)^T}$$

where $F$ is typically $1,000 for a level-coupon bond.

**Consols:**
$$PV = \frac{C}{r}$$

***CONCEPT QUESTIONS***
- What is the relationship between interest rates and bond prices?
- How does one calculate the YTM on a bond?

# 6.4   THE PRESENT VALUE OF COMMON STOCKS

## Dividends versus Capital Gains

Our goal in this section is to value common stocks. We learned in the previous chapter that an asset's value is determined by the PV of its future cash flows. A stock provides two kinds of cash flows. First, most stocks pay dividends on a regular basis. Second, the shareholder receives the sale price when the stock is sold. Thus, in order to value common stocks, we need to answer an interesting question: is the value of a stock equal to

1. The discounted PV of the sum of next period's dividend plus next period's stock price, or
2. The discounted PV of all future dividends?

This is the kind of question that students would love to see on a multiple-choice exam because both (1) and (2) are correct.

To see that (1) and (2) are the same, we start with an individual who will buy the stock and hold it for one year. In other words, this investor has a one-year *holding period*. In addition, the investor is willing to pay $P_0$ for the stock today:

$$P_0 = \frac{\text{Div}_1}{1+r} + \frac{P_1}{1+r} \qquad (6.1)$$

$\text{Div}_1$ is the dividend paid at year-end and $P_1$ is the price at year-end. $P_0$ is the PV of the common stock investment. The term $r$ in the denominator is the discount rate for the stock. It is the required rate of return for investments of similar risk.

That seems easy enough, but where does $P_1$ come from? $P_1$ is not pulled out of thin air. Rather, there must be a buyer at the end of year 1 who is willing to purchase the stock for $P_1$. This buyer determines price by

$$P_1 = \frac{\text{Div}_2}{1+r} + \frac{P_2}{1+r} \qquad (6.2)$$

Substituting the value of $P_1$ from equation (6.2) into equation (6.1) yields

$$P_0 = \frac{1}{1+r}\left[\text{Div}_1 + \left(\frac{\text{Div}_2 + P_2}{1+r}\right)\right] \qquad (6.3)$$

We can ask a similar question for equation (6.3): where does $P_2$ come from? An investor at the end of year 2 is willing to pay $P_2$ because of the dividend and stock price at year 3. This process can be repeated ad nauseam.[5] At the end, we are left with

$$P_0 = \frac{\text{Div}_1}{1+r} + \frac{\text{Div}_2}{(1+r)^2} + \frac{\text{Div}_3}{(1+r)^3} + \cdots$$

$$= \sum_{t=1}^{\infty} \frac{\text{Div}^t}{(1+r)^t} \qquad (6.4)$$

Thus, the value of a firm's common stock to the investor is equal to the PV of all of the expected future dividends.[6]

This is a very useful result. A common objection to applying PV analysis to stocks is that investors are too shortsighted to care about the long-run stream of dividends. Critics argue that an investor will generally not look past his or her time horizon. Thus, prices in a market dominated by short-term investors will reflect only near-term dividends. However, our discussion shows that a long-run dividend discount model holds even when investors have short-term time horizons. Although an investor may want to cash out early, he or she must find another investor who is willing to buy. The price this second investor pays depends on dividends *after* the date of purchase.

## Valuation of Different Types of Stocks

The discussion to this point shows that the value of the firm is the PV of its future dividends. How do we apply this idea in practice? Equation (6.4) represents a very general model and is applicable regardless of whether the level of expected dividends is growing, fluctuating, or constant. The general model can be simplified if the firm's dividends are expected to follow any of three basic patterns: (1) zero growth, (2) constant growth, and (3) differential growth. These cases are illustrated in Figure 6.3.

---

[5] This procedure reminds us of the physicist lecturing on the origins of the universe. He was approached by an elderly gentleman in the audience who disagreed with the lecture. The attendee said that the universe rests on the back of a huge turtle. When the physicist asked what the turtle rested on, the gentleman said another turtle. Anticipating the physicist's objections, the attendee said, "Don't tire yourself out, young fellow. It's turtles all the way down."

[6] The dividend valuation model is often called the Gordon model in honour of the late Professor Myron Gordon of the University of Toronto, its best-known developer.

FIGURE 6.3

**Zero-Growth, Constant-Growth, and Differential-Growth Patterns**

**Dividend-growth models**

Zero growth: $P_0 = \dfrac{\text{Div}}{r}$

Constant growth: $P_0 = \dfrac{\text{Div}}{r - g}$

Differential growth: $P_0 = \displaystyle\sum_{t=1}^{T} \dfrac{\text{Div}\,(1 + g_1)^t}{(1 + r)^t} + \dfrac{\dfrac{\text{Div}_{T+1}}{r - g_2}}{(1 + r)^T}$

**Case 1 (Zero Growth)**  The value of a stock with a constant dividend is given by

$$P_0 = \frac{\text{Div}_1}{1 + r} + \frac{\text{Div}_2}{(1 + r)^2} + \cdots = \frac{\text{Div}}{r}$$

Here it is assumed that $\text{Div}_1 = \text{Div}_2 = \cdots = \text{Div}$. This is just an application of the perpetuity formula of the previous chapter.

EXAMPLE 6.3

Canadian Products will pay a dividend of $4 per share a year from now. Financial analysts believe that dividends will rise at 6 percent per year for the foreseeable future. What is the dividend per share at the end of each of the first five years?

| End of Year | 1 | 2 | 3 | 4 | 5 |
|---|---|---|---|---|---|
| Dividend | $4.00 | $4 × (1.06) = $4.24 | $4 × (1.06)^2 = $4.4944 | $4 × (1.06)^3 = $4.7641 | $4 × (1.06)^4 = $5.0499 |

The value of a common stock with dividends growing at a constant rate is

$$P_0 = \frac{\text{Div}}{1 + r} + \frac{\text{Div}(1 + g)}{(1 + r)^2} + \frac{\text{Div}(1 + g)^2}{(1 + r)^3} + \frac{\text{Div}(1 + g)^3}{(1 + r)^4} + \cdots$$
$$= \frac{\text{Div}}{r - g}$$

where $g$ is the growth rate. Div is the dividend on the stock at the end of the first period. This is the formula for the PV of a growing perpetuity, which we derived in the previous chapter.

**Case 2 (Constant Growth)**    Dividends grow at rate $g$, as follows:

| End of Year | 1 | 2 | 3 | 4 | ... |
|---|---|---|---|---|---|
| Dividend | Div | Div$(1 + g)$ | Div$(1 + g)^2$ | Div$(1 + g)^3$ | |

Note that Div is the dividend at the end of the first period.

---

EXAMPLE **6.4**

---

Suppose an investor is considering the purchase of a share of the Saskatchewan Mining Company. The stock will pay a $3 dividend a year from today. This dividend is expected to grow at 10 percent per year ($g = 10\%$) for the foreseeable future. The investor thinks that the required return ($r$) on this stock is 15 percent, given her assessment of Saskatchewan Mining's risk. (We also refer to $r$ as the discount rate of the stock.) What is the value of a share of Saskatchewan Mining Company's stock?

Using the constant-growth formula of case 2, we assess the value to be $60:

$$\$60 = \frac{\$3}{0.15 - 0.10}$$

$P_0$ is quite dependent on the value of $g$. If $g$ had been estimated to be 12.5 percent, the value of the share would have been

$$\$120 = \frac{\$3}{0.15 - 0.125}$$

The stock price doubles (from $60 to $120) when $g$ increases only 25 percent (from 10 percent to 12.5 percent). Because of $P_0$'s dependency on $g$, one must maintain a healthy sense of skepticism when using this constant-growth version of the dividend valuation model.

Furthermore, note that $P_0$ is equal to infinity when the growth rate, $g$, equals or exceeds the discount rate, $r$. Because stock prices do not grow infinitely, an estimate of $g$ greater than $r$ implies an error in estimation. More will be said about this later.

---

**Case 3 (Differential Growth)**    In this case, an algebraic formula would be too unwieldy. Instead, we present examples.

---

EXAMPLE **6.5**

---

Consider the stock of Elixir Drug Company, which has a new back-rub ointment and is enjoying rapid growth. The dividend a year from today will be $1.15. During the next four years, the dividend will grow at 15 percent per year ($g_1 = 15\%$). After that, growth ($g_2$) will be equal to 10 percent per year. What is the PV of the stock if the required return ($r$) is 15 percent?

Figure 6.4 displays the growth in the dividends. We need to apply a two-step process to discount these dividends. We first calculate the NPV of the dividends growing at 15 percent per annum. That is, we first calculate the PV of the dividends at the end of each of the first five years. Second, we calculate the PV of the dividends beginning at the end of year 6.

**FIGURE 6.4**

**Growth in Dividends for Elixir Drug Company**

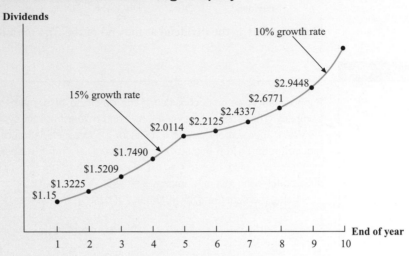

*Calculate the PV of the first five dividends.* The PVs of dividend payments in years 1 through 5 are as follows:

| Future year | Growth rate ($g_1$) | Expected dividend | Present value |
|:-----------:|:-------------------:|:-----------------:|:-------------:|
| 1 | 0.15 | $1.15 | $1 |
| 2 | 0.15 | 1.3225 | 1 |
| 3 | 0.15 | 1.5209 | 1 |
| 4 | 0.15 | 1.7490 | 1 |
| 5 | 0.15 | 2.0114 | 1 |
| Years 1–5 | | Present value of dividends = | $5 |

The growing-annuity formula of the previous chapter could normally be used in this step. However, note that dividends grow at 15 percent, which is also the discount rate. Since $g = r$, the growing-annuity formula cannot be used in this example.

*Calculate the PV of dividends beginning at end of year 6.* This is the procedure for deferred perpetuities and deferred annuities that we mentioned in the previous chapter. The dividends beginning at the end of year 6 are as follows:

| End of year | 6 | 7 | 8 | 9 |
|:-----------:|:-:|:-:|:-:|:-:|
| Dividend | $Div_5 \times (1 + g_2)$ | $Div_5 \times (1 + g_2)^2$ | $Div_5 \times (1 + g_2)^3$ | $Div_5 \times (1 + g_2)^4$ |
| | $2.0114 \times 1.10$ | $2.0114 \times (1.10)^2$ | $2.0114 \times (1.10)^3$ | $2.0114 \times (1.10)^4$ |
| | = $2.2125 | = $2.4337 | = $2.6771 | = $2.9448 |

As stated in the previous chapter, the growing-perpetuity formula calculates PV as of one year prior to the first payment. Because the payment begins at the end of year 6, the PV formula calculates PV as of the end of year 5. The price at the end of year 5 is given by

$$P_5 = \frac{Div_6}{r - g_2} = \frac{\$2.2125}{0.15 - 0.10}$$
$$= \$44.25$$

The PV of $P_5$ at the end of year 0 is

$$\frac{P_5}{(1 + r)^5} = \frac{\$44.25}{(1.15)^5} = \$22$$

The PV of all dividends as of the end of year 0 is $27 (or $22 + $5).

# 6.5 ESTIMATES OF PARAMETERS IN THE DIVIDEND DISCOUNT MODEL

The value of the firm is a function of its growth rate, $g$, and its discount rate, $r$. How does one estimate these variables?

## Where Does $g$ Come From?

The previous discussion on stocks assumed that dividends grow at the rate $g$. We now want to estimate this rate of growth. Consider a business whose earnings next year are expected to be the same as earnings this year unless a *net investment* is made. This situation is likely to occur, because net investment is equal to gross, or total, investment less depreciation. A net investment of zero occurs when *total investment* equals depreciation. If total investment is equal to depreciation, the firm's physical plant is maintained, consistent with no growth in earnings.

Net investment will be positive only if some earnings are not paid out as dividends, that is, only if some earnings are retained.[7] This leads to the following equation:

$$\underset{\text{Increase in earnings}}{\underbrace{\begin{array}{c}\text{Earnings} \\ \text{next year}\end{array} = \begin{array}{c}\text{Earnings} \\ \text{this year}\end{array} + \begin{array}{c}\text{Retained earnings} \\ \text{this year}\end{array} \times \begin{array}{c}\text{Return on} \\ \text{retained earnings}\end{array}}} \tag{6.5}$$

As explained in Chapter 3, the increase in earnings is a function of both the *retained earnings* and the return on the retained earnings.

We now divide both sides of equation (6.5) by earnings this year, yielding

$$\dfrac{\begin{array}{c}\text{Earnings} \\ \text{next year}\end{array}}{\begin{array}{c}\text{Earnings} \\ \text{this year}\end{array}} = \dfrac{\begin{array}{c}\text{Earnings} \\ \text{this year}\end{array}}{\begin{array}{c}\text{Earnings} \\ \text{this year}\end{array}} + \left(\dfrac{\begin{array}{c}\text{Retained earnings} \\ \text{this year}\end{array}}{\text{Earnings this year}}\right) \times \begin{array}{c}\text{Return on} \\ \text{retained earnings}\end{array} \tag{6.6}$$

The left-hand side of equation (6.6) is simply 1 plus the growth rate in earnings, which we write as $1 + g$.[8] The ratio of retained earnings to earnings is called the retention ratio; it can also be referred to as the plowback ratio. Thus, we can write

$$1 + g = 1 + \text{Retention ratio} \times \text{Return on retained earnings} \tag{6.7}$$

It is difficult for a financial analyst to determine the return to be expected on currently retained earnings because the details on forthcoming projects are not generally public information. However, it is frequently assumed that the projects selected in the current year have an anticipated return equal to returns from projects in other years. Here, we can estimate the anticipated return on current retained earnings by the historical **return on equity (ROE)**. After all, ROE is simply the return on the firm's entire equity, which is the return on the cumulation of all the firm's past projects.[9]

---

[7] We ignore the possibility of the issuance of stocks or bonds in order to raise capital. These possibilities are considered in later chapters.

[8] Previously $g$ referred to growth in dividends. However, the growth rate in earnings is equal to the growth rate in dividends in this context because, as we will soon see, the ratio of dividends to earnings is held constant.

[9] Students frequently wonder whether ROE or return on assets (ROA) should be used here. ROA and ROE are identical in our model because debt financing is ignored. However, most real-world firms have debt. Because debt is treated in later chapters, we are not yet able to treat this issue in depth now. Suffice it to say that ROE is the appropriate rate, because both ROE for the firm as a whole and the return to equityholders from a future project are calculated after interest has been deducted.

From equation (6.7), we have a simple way to estimate growth:

**Formula for a Firm's Growth Rate:**

$$g = \text{Retention ratio} \times \text{Return on retained earnings} \qquad (6.8)$$

---

**EXAMPLE 6.6**

Trent Enterprises just reported earnings of $2 million. It plans to retain 40 percent of its earnings. The historical ROE was 0.16, a figure that is expected to continue into the future. How much will earnings grow over the coming year?

We first perform the calculation without reference to equation (6.8). Then we use (6.8) as a check.

*Calculation without reference to equation (6.8).* The firm will retain $800,000 (or 40% × $2 million). Assuming that historical ROE is an appropriate estimate for future returns, the anticipated increase in earnings is

$$\$800,000 \times 0.16 = \$128,000$$

The percentage growth in earnings is

$$\frac{\text{Change in earnings}}{\text{Total earnings}} = \frac{\$128,000}{\$2 \text{ million}} = 0.064$$

This implies that earnings in one year will be $2,128,000 (or $2,000,000 × 1.064).

*Check using equation (6.8).* We use $g$ = Retention ratio × Return on equity. We have

$$g = 0.4 \times 0.16 = 0.064$$

---

## Where Does $r$ Come From?

In this section, we want to estimate $r$, the rate used to discount the cash flows of a particular stock. Two methods have been developed by academics. We present one method below but must defer the second until we give it extensive treatment in later chapters.

The first method begins with the concept that the value of a growing perpetuity is

$$P_0 = \frac{\text{Div}}{r - g}$$

Solving for $r$, we have

$$r = \frac{\text{Div}}{P_0} + g \qquad (6.9)$$

As stated earlier, Div refers to the dividend to be received one year hence.

Thus, the discount rate can be broken into two parts. The ratio $\text{Div}/P_0$ places the dividend return on a percentage basis, frequently called the *dividend yield*. The second term, $g$, is the growth rate of dividends.

Because information on both dividends and stock price is publicly available, the first term on the right-hand side of equation (6.9) can be easily calculated. The second term on the right-hand side, $g$, can be estimated from equation (6.8).

## A Healthy Sense of Skepticism

It is important to emphasize that our approach merely *estimates* $g$; it does not determine $g$ precisely. We mentioned earlier that our estimate of $g$ is based on a number of assumptions. For example, we assume that the return on reinvestment of future retained earnings is equal to the firm's past ROE. We assume that the future retention ratio is equal to the past retention ratio. Our estimate for $g$ will be off if these assumptions prove to be wrong.

Unfortunately, the determination of $r$ is highly dependent on $g$. In our example, if $g$ is estimated to be 0, $r$ equals 12.8 percent ($1.28/$10.00). If $g$ is estimated to be 12 percent, $r$ equals 24.8 percent ($1.28/$10.00 + 12%). Thus, one should view estimates of $r$ with a healthy sense of skepticism.

For this reason, some financial economists generally argue that the estimation error for $r$ for a single security is too large to be practical. Therefore, they suggest calculating the average $r$ for an entire industry. This $r$ would then be used to discount the dividends of a particular stock in the same industry.

One should be particularly skeptical of two polar cases when estimating $r$ for individual securities. First, consider a firm currently paying no dividend. The stock price will be above zero because investors believe that the firm may initiate a dividend at some point or the firm may be acquired at some point. However, when a firm goes from no dividend to a positive number of dividends, the implied growth rate is *infinite*. Thus, equation (6.9) must be used with extreme caution here, if at all—a point we emphasize later in this chapter.

EXAMPLE **6.7**

Trent Enterprises, the company examined in the previous example, has 1,000,000 shares of stock outstanding. The stock is selling at $10. What is the required return on the stock?

Because the retention ratio is 40 percent, the payout ratio is 60 percent (1 − Retention ratio). The **payout ratio** is the ratio of dividends/earnings. Because earnings one year from now will be $2,128,000 (or $2,000,000 × 1.064), dividends will be $1,276,800 (or 0.60 × $2,128,000). Dividends per share will be $1.28 (or $1,276,800/1,000,000). Given our previous result that $g = 0.064$, we calculate $r$ from equation (6.9) as follows:

$$r = 0.192 = \frac{\$1.28}{\$10.00} + 0.064$$

Second, we mentioned earlier that the value of the firm is infinite when $g$ is equal to $r$. Because prices for stocks do not grow infinitely, an analyst whose estimate of $g$ for a particular firm is equal to or greater than $r$ must have made a mistake. Most likely, the analyst's high estimate for $g$ is correct for the next few years. However, firms simply cannot maintain an abnormally high growth rate *forever*. The analyst's error was to use a short-run estimate of $g$ in a model requiring a perpetual growth rate.

In brief, there are a number of difficulties with using the dividend discount model to determine $r$. In practice, analysts use a number of models, including the capital asset pricing model (CAPM), which we present in Chapters 11 and 13.

## 6.6    GROWTH OPPORTUNITIES

We previously spoke of the growth rate of dividends. We now want to address the related concept of growth opportunities. Imagine a company with a level stream of earnings per share (EPS) in perpetuity. The company pays all of these earnings out to shareholders as dividends. Hence,

$$\text{EPS} = \text{Div}$$

A company of this type is frequently called a *cash cow*.

From the perpetuity formula of the previous chapter, the value of a share of stock is

**Value of a Share of Stock When a Firm Acts as a Cash Cow:**

$$\frac{EPS}{r} = \frac{Div}{r}$$

where $r$ is the discount rate on the firm's stock.

The above policy of paying out all earnings as dividends may not be the optimal one. Many firms have *growth* opportunities, that is, opportunities to invest in profitable projects. Because these projects can represent a significant fraction of the firm's value, it would be foolish to forgo them in order to pay out all earnings as dividends.

While firms frequently think in terms of a *set* of growth opportunities, we focus here on only one opportunity, that is, the opportunity to invest in a single project. Suppose the firm retains the entire dividend at date 1 in order to invest in a particular capital budgeting project. The NPV *per share* of the project as of date 0 is *NPVGO*, which stands for the *net present value (per share) of the growth opportunity.*

What is the price of a share of stock at date 0 if the firm decides to take on the project at date 1? Because the per share value of the project is added to the original stock price, the stock price must now be

**Stock Price after a Firm Commits to a New Project:**

$$\frac{EPS}{r} + NPVGO \tag{6.10}$$

Equation (6.10) indicates that the price of a share of stock can be viewed as the sum of two different items. The first term ($EPS/r$) is the value of the firm if it rested on its laurels, that is, if it simply distributed all earnings to the shareholders. The second term is the *additional* value if the firm retained earnings in order to fund new projects.

## NPVGOs of Real Companies

In reality, companies have a whole series of projects, some to be developed in the near term and others to be developed in the long term. The stock price of any real-world company should reflect the market's perception of the NPVs of all of these future projects. In other words, the stock price should reflect the market's estimate of the firm's NPVGO.

Can one estimate NPVGOs for real companies? Yes: while Equation (6.10) may seem conceptual in nature, the equation can easily be used to estimate NPVGOs in the real world. For example, consider Lululemon Athletica Inc. (LL). The company had an EPS of $1.88 in February 2013. With a discount rate of 0.0796,[10] the price of one share of LL, assuming that projected nominal earnings are constant over time and are fully paid out as dividends, is

$$\$1.88/0.11 = \$17.09$$

In other words, a share of LL's stock would be worth $17.09 if no earnings were ever to be retained for investment.

Was LL selling for $17.09 at its February 2013 year-end? No, LL was selling for $67.05. Why the difference? The difference between LL's market price and its per share value as a cash cow is $49.96 ($67.05 − $17.09), which can be viewed as LL's NPVGO. That is, the market expects LL's investment strategy to increase value by $49.96 above the firm's worth as a cash cow. LL's NPVGO, as calculated above, represents 74.51 percent ($49.96/$67.05) of LL's price per share.

---

[10] Recall that discount rates represent expected returns that investors require to invest in a stock. We employ the CAPM (covered in Chapters 11 and 13) under the assumption that the risk-free rate adjusted upward for the impact of easy monetary policy is 5 percent, the expected risk premium of the market portfolio above the risk-free rate is 5 percent, and LL's beta is 1.20, generating a discount rate for LL's stock of

$$r = r_f + B(\text{market risk premium}) = 5\% + 1.20(5\%) = 11.00\%$$

EXAMPLE **6.8**

Nova Scotia Shipping Ltd. expects to earn $1 million per year in perpetuity if it undertakes no new investment opportunities. There are 100,000 shares outstanding, so EPS is $10 (or $1,000,000/100,000). The firm will have an opportunity at date 1 to spend $1,000,000 on a new marketing campaign. The new campaign will increase earnings in every subsequent period by $210,000 (or $2.10 per share). This is a 21 percent return per year on the project. The firm's discount rate is 10 percent. What is the value per share before and after deciding to accept the marketing campaign?

The value of a share of Nova Scotia Shipping before the campaign is

**Value of a Share of Nova Scotia Shipping When the Firm Acts as a Cash Cow:**

$$\frac{EPS}{r} = \frac{\$10}{0.1} = \$100$$

The value of the marketing campaign as of date 1 is

**Value of the Marketing Campaign at Date 1:**

$$-\$1,000,000 + \frac{\$210,000}{0.1} = \$1,100,000 \qquad \textbf{(6.11)}$$

Because the investment is made at date 1 and the first cash inflow occurs at date 2, equation (6.11) represents the value of the marketing campaign as of date 1. We determine the value at date 0 by discounting back one period as follows:

**Value of the Marketing Campaign at Date 0:**

$$\frac{\$1,100,000}{1.1} = \$1,000,000$$

Thus, NPVGO per share is $10 (or $1,000,000/100,000).

The price per share is

$$\frac{EPS}{r} + NPVGO = \$100 + \$10 = \$110$$

The calculation can also be made on a straight NPV basis. Because all the earnings at date 1 are spent on the marketing effort, no dividends are paid to shareholders at that date. Dividends in all subsequent periods are $1,210,000 (or $1,000,000 + $210,000). In this case, $1,000,000 is the annual dividend when Nova Scotia Shipping is a cash cow. The additional contribution to the dividend from the marketing effort is $210,000. Dividends per share are $12.10 (or $1,210,000/100,000). Because these dividends start at date 2, the price per share at date 1 is $121 (or $12.10/0.1). The price per share at date 0 is $110 (or $121/1.1).

Note that value is created in this example because the project earned a 21 percent rate of return when the discount rate was only 10 percent. No value would have been created had the project earned a 10 percent rate of return—the NPVGO would have been zero. Value would have been negative had the project earned a percentage return below 10 percent—the NPVGO would be negative in that case.

Two conditions must be met in order to increase value:

1. Earnings must be retained so that projects can be funded.[11]
2. The projects must have positive NPV.

Surprisingly, a number of companies seem to invest in projects known to have *negative* NPVs. For example, Jensen has pointed out that in the late 1970s, oil

---

[11] Later in the text we discuss issuing stock or debt in order to fund projects.

companies and tobacco companies were flush with cash.[12] Due to declining markets in both industries, high dividends and low investment would have been the rational action. Unfortunately, a number of companies in both industries reinvested heavily in what were widely perceived to be negative-NPVGO projects. A study by McConnell and Muscarella documents this perception.[13] They find that, during the 1970s, the stock prices of oil companies generally decreased on the days that announcements of increases in exploration and development were made.

Canada is not immune to the practice of investing in negative NPV projects. For example, Nortel lost money for investors large and small. Many technology companies have made acquisitions that have subsequently been written down or written off, lowering the value of the companies.

Given that NPV analysis (such as that presented in the previous chapter) is common knowledge in business, why would managers choose projects with negative NPVs? Bad judgment and bad luck are two reasons. Another is that some managers enjoy controlling a large company. Because paying dividends in lieu of reinvesting earnings reduces the size of the firm, some managers find it emotionally difficult to pay high dividends.

## Growth in Earnings and Dividends versus Growth Opportunities

As mentioned earlier, a firm's value increases when it invests in growth opportunities with positive NPVGOs. A firm's value falls when it selects opportunities with negative NPVGOs. However, dividends grow whether projects with positive or negative NPVs are selected. This surprising result can be explained by Example 6.9.

---

**EXAMPLE 6.9**

Lane Supermarkets, a new firm, will earn $100,000 a year in perpetuity if it pays out all its earnings as dividends. However, the firm plans to invest 20 percent of its earnings in projects that earn 10 percent per year. The discount rate is 18 percent. Equation (6.8) tells us that the growth rate of dividends is

$$g = \text{Retention ratio} \times \text{Return on retained earnings} = 0.2 \times 0.10 = 2\%$$

For example, in this first year of the new policy, dividends are $80,000, calculated from $(1 - 0.2) \times \$100,000$. Dividends next year are $81,600 (or $80,000 × 1.02). Dividends the following year are $83,232 or $80,000 × (1.02)^2$, and so on. Because dividends represent a fixed percentage of earnings, earnings must grow at 2 percent a year as well.

However, note that the policy reduces value because the rate of return on the projects of 10 percent is less than the discount rate of 18 percent. That is, the firm would have had a higher value at date 0 if it had a policy of paying all its earnings out as dividends. Thus, a policy of investing in projects with negative NPVs rather than paying out earnings as dividends will lead to growth in dividends and earnings, but will reduce value.

---

## Dividends or Earnings: Which to Discount?

As mentioned earlier, this chapter applied the growing-perpetuity formula to the valuation of stocks. In our application, we discounted dividends, not earnings. This is sensible since investors select a stock for the cash flows they can get out of it. They only get

---

[12] M. C. Jensen, "Agency Costs of Free Cash Flows, Corporate Finance and Takeovers," *American Economic Review* (May 1986).

[13] J. J. McConnell and C. J. Muscarella, "Corporate Capital Expenditure Decisions and the Market Value of the Firm," *Journal of Financial Economics* 14 (1985).

two things out of a stock: dividends and the ultimate sales price, which is determined by what future investors expect to receive in dividends.

The calculated stock price would be too high were earnings to be discounted instead of dividends. As we saw in our estimation of a firm's growth rate, only a portion of earnings goes to the shareholders as dividends. The remainder is retained to generate future dividends. In our model, retained earnings are equal to the firm's investment. To discount earnings instead of dividends would be to ignore the investment that a firm must make today in order to generate future returns.

### The No-Dividend Firm

Students frequently ask the following question: If the dividend discount model is correct, why are no-dividend stocks not selling at zero? This is a good question that addresses the goals of the firm. A firm with many growth opportunities is faced with a dilemma: the firm can pay out dividends now, or it can forgo current dividends to make investments that will generate even greater dividends in the future.[14] This is often a painful choice, because a strategy of dividend deferment may be optimal yet unpopular among certain shareholders.

Many firms choose to pay no dividends—and these firms sell at positive prices.[15] Rational shareholders believe that they will either receive dividends at some point or receive something just as good. That is, the firm will be acquired in a merger, with the shareholders receiving either cash or shares in the acquiring firm.

Of course, the actual application of the dividend discount model is difficult for firms of this type. Clearly, the model for constant growth of dividends does not apply. Though the differential growth model can work in theory, the difficulties of estimating the date of first dividend, the growth rate of dividends after that date, and the ultimate merger price make application of the model quite difficult in reality.

Empirical evidence suggests that firms with high growth rates are likely to pay lower dividends, a result consistent with the above analysis. For example, consider Rogers Communications Inc. The company started in the 1960s and grew rapidly throughout the decades thereafter. It paid the first dividend in its history in July of 2003, though it was a multimillion dollar company prior to that date. Why did it wait so long to pay a dividend? It likely waited because it had so many positive growth opportunities, largely in the form of acquisitions.

Utilities are an interesting contrast because, as a group, historically they have had few growth opportunities. As a result, they pay out a large fraction of their earnings in dividends. For example, Enbridge Inc. targets a payout ratio of 60 to 70 percent.

## 6.7   THE DIVIDEND GROWTH MODEL AND THE NPVGO MODEL (ADVANCED)

This chapter has revealed that the price of a share of stock is the sum of its price as a cash cow plus the per share value of its growth opportunities. The Nova Scotia Shipping example illustrated this formula using only one growth opportunity. We also used the growing-perpetuity formula to price a stock with a steady growth in dividends. When the formula is applied to stocks, it is typically called the *dividend growth model*. A steady growth in dividends results from a continuous investment in growth opportunities, not just investment in a single opportunity. Therefore, it is worthwhile to compare the dividend growth model with the *NPVGO model* when growth occurs through continuous investing.

---

[14] A third alternative is to issue stock so that the firm has enough cash both to pay dividends and to invest. This possibility is explored in a later chapter.

[15] For example, tech stocks like Amazon.com and BlackBerry pay no dividends.

EXAMPLE **6.10**

Prairie Book Publishers has EPS of $10 at the end of the first year, a dividend payout ratio of 40 percent, a discount rate of 16 percent, and a return on its retained earnings of 20 percent. Because the firm retains some of its earnings each year, it is selecting growth opportunities each year. This is different from Nova Scotia Shipping, which had a growth opportunity in only one year. We wish to calculate the price per share using both the dividend growth model and the NPVGO model.

## The Dividend Growth Model

The dividends at date 1 are $0.40 \times \$10 = \$4$ per share. The retention ratio is 0.60 (or $1 - 0.40$), implying a growth rate in dividends of 0.12 (or $0.60 \times 0.20$).

From the dividend growth model, the price of a share of stock is

$$\frac{\text{Div}}{r - g} = \frac{\$4}{0.16 - 0.12} = \$100$$

## The NPVGO Model

Using the NPVGO model, it is more difficult to value a firm with growth opportunities each year (like Prairie) than a firm with growth opportunities in only one year (like Nova Scotia Shipping). To value according to the NPVGO model, we need to calculate on a per share basis (1) the NPV of a single growth opportunity; (2) the NPV of all growth opportunities; and (3) the stock price if the firm acts as a cash cow, that is, the value of the firm without these growth opportunities. The value of the firm is the sum of (2) and (3).

1. *Value per share of a single growth opportunity.* Out of the EPS of $10 at date 1, the firm retains $6 (or $0.6 \times \$10$) at that date. The firm earns $1.20 (or $\$6 \times 0.20$) per year in perpetuity on that $6 investment. The NPV from the investment is

   **Per Share Net Present Value Generated from the Investment at Date 1:**

   $$-\$6 + \frac{\$1.20}{0.16} = \$1.50 \tag{6.12}$$

   That is, the firm invests $6 in order to reap $1.20 per year on the investment. The earnings are discounted at 0.16, implying a value per share from the project of $1.50. Because the investment occurs at date 1 and the first cash flow occurs at date 2, $1.50 is the value of the investment at *date 1*. In other words, the NPV from the date 1 investment has *not* yet been brought back to date 0.

2. *Value per share of all opportunities.* As pointed out earlier, the growth rate of earnings and dividends is 12 percent. Because retained earnings are a fixed percentage of total earnings, retained earnings must also grow at 12 percent a year. That is, retained earnings at date 2 are $6.72 (or $\$6 \times 1.12$), retained earnings at date 3 are $7.5264 (or $\$6 \times (1.12)^2$), and so on.

   Let's analyze the retained earnings at date 2 in more detail. Because projects will always earn 20 percent per year, the firm earns $1.344 (or $\$6.72 \times 0.20$) in each future year on the $6.72 investment at date 2.

   The NPV from the investment is

   **Net Present Value per Share Generated from the Investment at Date 2:**

   $$-\$6.72 + \frac{\$1.344}{0.16} = \$1.68 \tag{6.13}$$

$1.68 is the NPV as of date 2 of the investment made at date 2. The NPV from the date 2 investment has *not* yet been brought back to date 0.

Now consider the retained earnings at date 3 in more detail. The firm earns $1.5053 (or $7.5264 × 0.20) per year on the investment of $7.5264 at date 3. The NPV from the investment is

**Net Present Value per Share Generated from the Investment at Date 3:**

$$-\$7.5264 + \frac{\$1.5053}{0.16} = \$1.882 \tag{6.14}$$

From equations (6.12), (6.13), and (6.14), the NPV per share of all of the growth opportunities, discounted back to date 0, is

$$\frac{\$1.50}{1.16} + \frac{\$1.68}{(1.16)^2} + \frac{\$1.882}{(1.16)^3} + \cdots \tag{6.15}$$

Because it has an infinite number of terms, this expression looks difficult to compute. However, there is an easy simplification. Note that retained earnings are growing at 12 percent per year. Because all projects earn the same rate of return per year, the NPVs in equations (6.12), (6.13), and (6.14) are also growing at 12 percent per year. Hence, we can rewrite equation (6.15) as

$$\frac{\$1.50}{1.16} + \frac{\$1.50 \times 1.12}{(1.16)^2} + \frac{\$1.50 \times (1.12)^2}{(1.16)^3} + \cdots$$

This is a growing perpetuity whose value is

$$\text{NPVGO} = \frac{\$1.50}{0.16 - 0.12} = \$37.50$$

Because the first NPV of $1.50 occurs at date 1, the NPVGO is $37.50 as of date 0. In other words, the firm's policy of investing in new projects from retained earnings has an NPV of $37.50.

3. *Value per share if the firm is a cash cow.* We now assume that the firm pays out all of its earnings as dividends. The dividends would be $10 per year in this case. Since there would be no growth, the value per share would be evaluated by the perpetuity formula:

$$\frac{\text{Div}}{r} = \frac{\$10}{0.16} = \$62.50$$

## Summary

Equation (6.10) states that value per share is the value of a cash cow plus the value of the growth opportunities. This is

$$\$100 = \$62.50 + \$37.50$$

Hence, value is the same whether calculated by a discounted-dividend approach or a growth opportunities approach. The share prices from the two approaches must be equal, because the approaches are different yet equivalent methods of applying concepts of PV.

# 6.8    COMPARABLES

So far in this chapter, we have valued stocks either by discounting dividends or by determining the NPVGO. In addition to these two approaches, practitioners commonly value by comparables as well. The comparables approach is similar to valuation in real estate. If your neighbour's home just sold for $400,000 and it has similar size and amenities to your home, your home is probably worth around $400,000 also. In the stock market, comparable firms are assumed to have similar *multiples*. To see how the comparables approach works, let's look at perhaps the most common multiple, the price–earnings (P/E) multiple, or P/E ratio.

## Price–Earnings Ratio

A stock's P/E ratio is, as the name suggests, the ratio of the stock's price to its EPS. It is generally assumed that similar firms have similar P/E ratios. For example, imagine the average P/E ratio across all publicly traded companies in the specialty retail industry is 12 and a particular company in the industry has earnings of $10 million. If this company is judged to be similar to the rest of the industry, one might estimate that company's value to be $120 million (12 × $10 million).

Valuation via P/E certainly looks easier than valuation via discounted cash flow (DCF), since the DCF approach calls for estimates of yearly cash flows. But is the P/E approach better? That depends on the similarity across comparables.

Our previous discussion stated that

$$\text{Price per share} = \frac{\text{EPS}}{r} + \text{NPVGO}$$

Dividing by EPS yields

$$\frac{\text{Price per share}}{\text{EPS}} = \frac{1}{r} + \frac{\text{NPVGO}}{\text{EPS}}$$

The left-hand side is the formula for the P/E ratio. The equation shows that the P/E ratio is related to the NPV of growth opportunities. As an example, consider two firms, each having just reported EPS of $1. However, one firm has many valuable growth opportunities, while the other firm has no growth opportunities at all. The firm with growth opportunities should sell at a higher price, because an investor is buying both current income of $1 and growth opportunities. Suppose that the firm with growth opportunities sells for $16 and the other firm sells for $8. The $1 EPS number appears in the denominator of the P/E ratio for both firms. Thus, the P/E ratio is 16 for the firm with growth opportunities, but only 8 for the firm without the opportunities.

This explanation seems to hold fairly well in the real world. Biotech and other high-tech stocks generally sell at very high P/E ratios (or *multiples*, as they are often called) because they are perceived to have high growth rates. For example, as we stated in Appendix 2A, in January 2014, Pure Technologies Ltd., a Canadian technology company, traded at a P/E of 67.98. In fact, some technology stocks sell at high prices even though the companies have never earned a profit. The P/E ratios of these companies are infinite. Conversely, utilities and financial services companies sell at lower multiples because of the prospects of lower growth.

Of course, the market is merely pricing *perceptions* of the future, not the future itself. We will argue later in the text that the stock market generally has realistic perceptions of a firm's prospects. However, this is not always true. In the late 1960s, many electronics firms were selling at multiples of 200 times earnings. The high perceived growth rates did not materialize, causing great declines in stock prices during the early 1970s. In earlier decades, fortunes were made in stocks like IBM and Xerox because the high growth rates were not anticipated by investors.

There are two additional factors explaining the P/E ratio. The first is the discount rate, *r*. The above formula shows that the P/E ratio is *negatively* related to the firm's discount rate. We have already suggested that the discount rate is positively linked to the stock's risk or variability. Thus, the P/E ratio is negatively related to the stock's risk. To see that this is a sensible result, consider two firms, *A* and *B*, behaving as cash cows. The stock market *expects* both firms to have annual earnings of $1 per share forever.

However, the earnings of firm *A* are known with certainty, while the earnings of firm *B* are quite variable. A rational shareholder is likely to pay more for a share of firm *A* because of the absence of risk. If a share of firm *A* sells at a higher price and both firms have the same EPS, the P/E ratio of firm *A* must be higher.

The second additional factor concerns the firm's choice of accounting methods. Under current accounting rules, companies are given a fair amount of leeway. For example, consider depreciation accounting, where many different methods may be used. A firm's choice of depreciation method can increase or decrease its earnings in different years. Similar accounting leeway exists for construction costs (completed-contracts versus percentage-of-completion methods).

As an example, consider two identical firms: *C* and *D*. Firm *C* uses straight-line depreciation and reports earnings of $2 per share. Firm *D* uses declining-balance depreciation and reports earnings of $3 per share. The market knows that the two firms are identical and prices both at $18 per share. This P/E ratio is 9 (or $18/$2) for firm *C* and 6 (or $18/$3) for firm *D*. Thus, the firm with the more conservative principles has a higher P/E ratio.

This last example depends on the assumption that the market sees through differences in accounting treatments. A significant portion of the academic community believes in adhering to the hypothesis of *efficient capital markets*, a theory that we explore in great detail later in the text. Though many financial people might be more moderate in their beliefs regarding this issue, the consensus view is certainly that many of the accounting differences are seen through. Thus, the proposition that firms with conservative accountants have high P/E ratios is widely accepted.

In summary, our discussion argued that the P/E ratio is a function of three different factors. A company's ratio or multiple is likely to be high if (1) it has many growth opportunities, (2) it has low risk (reflected in a low discount rate), and (3) its accounting is conservative. While each of the three factors is important, it is our opinion that the first factor is the most important. Thus, our discussion of growth is quite relevant in understanding P/E multiples.

During the tech "bubble" of 1999 and early 2000, Internet stocks like Yahoo and Research in Motion (now BlackBerry) were trading at P/Es over 1000! Clearly the P/E analysis we present could never explain these prices in terms of growth opportunities. Some analysts who recommended buying these stocks developed new measures to justify their recommendation. On the other side, many analysts believed that the market had lost touch with reality. To these analysts, Internet stock prices were the result of speculative fever.

By 2001, it was clear the pessimists were correct that tech stocks were overvalued. Investment dealers on Wall Street and Bay Street were establishing rules to curb possible conflicts of interest on the part of overenthusiastic analysts. Around the same time, a New York investor brought a lawsuit against Merrill Lynch and its star Internet analyst. Merrill Lynch settled out of court without admitting any wrongdoing. The claim criticized "newly minted 'valuation criteria' [that] justify widely inflated price targets and 'buy' recommendations for Internet and technology companies with no profits expected for years."[16]

During the recent (2007–2009) financial crisis, P/E ratios of all stocks fell dramatically. Investors panicked and were demanding a high premium to invest in stock markets. Beginning in April 2009, the stock market regained momentum, leading to higher P/E ratios.

**CONCEPT QUESTIONS**

- What are the three factors determining a firm's P/E ratio?
- How does each affect the P/E ratio, and why?

---

[16] https://variety.com/2001/biz/news/merrill-lynch-s-web-settlement-no-bull-1117850057/.

# 6.9    VALUING THE ENTIRE FIRM

Previously, we valued corporate projects by discounting the projects' cash flows. Similarly, we have discounted dividends to price a single share of stock. As an alternative, one can value entire firms by discounting their cash flows.

As an example, consider Global Harmonic Control Systems (GHCS). Revenues, which are forecast to be $500 million in one year, are expected to grow at 10 percent per year for the two years after that, 8 percent per year for the next two years, and 6 percent per year after that. Expenses including depreciation are 60 percent of revenues. Net investment, including net working capital and capital spending less depreciation, is 10 percent of revenues. Because all costs are proportional to revenues, net cash flow (sometimes referred to as free cash flow) grows at the same rate as do revenues. GHCS is an all-equity firm with 12 million shares outstanding. A discount rate of 16 percent is appropriate for a firm of GHCS's risk.

The relevant numbers for the first five years, rounded to two decimals, are as follows:

| | Year | | | | |
|---|---|---|---|---|---|
| Amount (in $ millions) | 1 | 2 | 3 | 4 | 5 |
| Revenues | 500.0 | 550.0 | 605.0 | 653.4 | 705.67 |
| Expenses | 300.0 | 330.0 | 363.0 | 392.04 | 423.4 |
| Earnings before taxes | 200.0 | 220.0 | 242.0 | 261.36 | 282.27 |
| Taxes (@ 40%) | 80.0 | 88.0 | 96.8 | 104.54 | 112.91 |
| Earnings after taxes | 120.0 | 132.0 | 145.2 | 156.82 | 169.36 |
| Net investment | 50.0 | 55.0 | 60.5 | 65.34 | 70.57 |
| Net cash flow | 70.0 | 77.0 | 84.7 | 91.48 | 98.79 |

Since net cash flow grows at 6 percent per year after year 5, net cash flow in year 6 is forecast to be $104.72 ($98.79 × 1.06). Using the growing-perpetuity formula, we can calculate the PV as of year 5 of all future cash flows to be $1047.2 million ($104.72/ (0.16 − 0.06)).

The PV as of today of that terminal value is

$$\frac{\$1047.2}{(1.16)^5} = \$498.59 \text{ million}$$

The PV of the net cash flows during the first five years is

$$\frac{\$70}{1.16} + \frac{\$77}{(1.16)^2} + \frac{\$84.7}{(1.16)^3} + \frac{\$91.48}{(1.16)^4} + \frac{\$98.79}{(1.16)^5} = \$269.39 \text{ million}$$

Adding in the terminal value, today's value of the firm is $767.98 million ($269.39 + $498.59). Given the number of shares outstanding, the price per share is $64.00 ($767.98/12).

The above calculation assumes a growing perpetuity after year 5. However, we pointed out in the previous section that stocks are often valued by multiples. An investor might estimate the terminal value of GHCS via a multiple, rather than the growing-perpetuity formula. For example, suppose that the P/E ratio for comparable firms in GHCS's industry is 7.

Since earnings after tax in year 5 are $169.36, using the P/E multiple of 7, the value of the firm at year 5 would be estimated as $1185.52 million ($169.36 × 7).

The firm's value today is

$$\frac{\$70}{1.16} + \frac{\$77}{(1.16)^2} + \frac{\$84.7}{(1.16)^3} + \frac{\$91.48}{(1.16)^4} + \frac{\$98.79}{(1.16)^5} + \frac{\$1185.52}{(1.16)^5} = \$833.83 \text{ million}$$

With 12 million shares outstanding, the price per share of GHCS would be $69.49 ($833.83/12).

Now we have two estimates of the value of a share of equity in GHCS. The different estimates reflect the different ways of calculating terminal value. Using the constant-growth DCF method for terminal value, our estimate of the equity value per share of GHCS is $64; using the P/E comparable method, our estimate is $69.49. There is no better method. If the comparable firms were all identical to GHCS, perhaps the P/E method would be better. Unfortunately, firms are not identical. On the other hand, if we were very sure of the terminal date and the growth in subsequent cash flows, perhaps the constant-growth method would be better. In practice, both methods are used.

Conceptually, the dividend discount model, the NPVGO model, and the firm cash flow model are mutually consistent and can be used to determine the value of a share of stock. In practice, the dividend discount model is especially useful for firms paying very steady dividends, and the NPVGO model is useful for firms with attractive growth opportunities. The firm cash flow model is helpful for non–dividend paying firms with external funding needs.

# 6.10    STOCK MARKET REPORTING

Financial websites publish information on a large number of stocks in several different markets. Figure 6.5 produces sample stock listings for the Toronto Stock Exchange (TSX) for February 13, 2014. In Figure 6.5, locate the line for Telus Corporation (TELUS).

The high, low, and close figures are the high, low, and closing prices during the day. Stock prices are quoted in decimals. The net change of 0.26 tells us that the closing price of $37.06 per share is $0.26 higher than the closing price the day before. The next two numbers, $38.96 and $29.52, are the high and low prices for the last 52 weeks. The annual dividend rate is $1.44. Since Telus, like most companies, pays dividends quarterly, this $1.44 is actually the last quarterly dividend multiplied by 4. So the last cash dividend was $1.44/4 = $0.36. The yield column gives the dividend yield based on the current dividend and the closing price. For Telus, this is $1.44/$37.06 = 3.9%, as shown. The column labelled P/E (short for P/E ratio) is the closing price of $37.06 divided by annual EPS (based on the most recent full fiscal year). In the jargon of Bay Street, we might say that Telus "sells for 18.6 times earnings." Finally, the very first column, volume, tells us how many shares traded during the reported day; for example, 884,437 shares changed hands. The dollar volume of transactions was on the order of $37.06 × 884,437 = $32,777,235 worth of Telus stock.

**FIGURE 6.5**

### Sample Stock Market Quotation

| Stock Description | | | Daily Trading | | | | 52 Week | | Dividends | | Earnings |
|---|---|---|---|---|---|---|---|---|---|---|---|
| Company | Ticker | Volume | High/ Ask | Low/ Bid | Close/ Previous | Net Change | High | Low | Annual Dividend | Yield | P/E |
| TD Split Inc | TDS.PR.C | 1,095 | 10.25 | 10.25 | 10.25 | 0 | 10.56 | 10.03 | .... | .... | .... |
| TDb Split Corp | XTD | 3,150 | 4.96 | 4.91 | 4.91 | 0.04 | 5.25 | 2.72 | .... | .... | .... |
| TDb Split Corp | XTD.PR.A | 251 | 10.06 | 10.05 | 10.02 | 0.03 | 10.31 | 9.97 | .... | .... | .... |
| TECSYS Inc | TCS | 2,200 | 5.44 | 5.39 | 5.35 | 0.09 | 6.24 | 3 | 0.07 | 1.3 | 185.8 |
| TELUS Corp | T | 884,437 | 37.71 | 37.26 | 37.06 | 0.26 | 38.96 | 29.52 | 1.44 | 3.9 | 18.6 |
| TMX Group Inc | X | 13,844 | 51.67 | 50.59 | 51.01 | 0.58 | 56.94 | 42.5 | 1.6 | 3.1 | 22.3 |
| TSO3 inc | TOS | 27,120 | 0.5 | 0.49 | 0.5 | -0.01 | 1.1 | 0.48 | .... | .... | .... |
| TVA Group Inc | TVA.B | 500 | 9.46 | 9.46 | 9.5 | -0.04 | 10.52 | 7.5 | .... | .... | 13.4 |
| TVI Pacific Inc | TVI | 59,000 | 0.02 | 0.02 | 0.02 | | 0.04 | 0.02 | .... | .... | 11.9 |
| Taiga Building Prods Ltd | TBL | 1,000 | 0.95 | 0.95 | 0.9 | 0.05 | 1.25 | 0.68 | .... | .... | 5.5 |
| Taiga Building Prods Ltd | TBL.NT | 28,000 | 106 | 105 | 107 | -2 | 112 | 102 | .... | .... | .... |
| Talisman Energy Inc | TLM | 723,704 | 11.92 | 11.74 | 11.92 | -0.14 | 13.83 | 10.68 | 0.28 | 2.4 | 61.3 |
| Talon Metals Corp | TLO | 3,500 | 0.26 | 0.26 | 0.26 | .... | 0.36 | 0.18 | .... | .... | .... |
| Tanzanian Rty Expl Corp | TNX | 8,700 | 2.54 | 2.44 | 2.52 | 0.09 | 4.4 | 1.75 | .... | .... | .... |
| Taseko Mines Ltd | TKO | 158,299 | 2.44 | 2.35 | 2.43 | -0.07 | 3.24 | 1.88 | .... | .... | .... |
| Teck Resources Ltd v | TCK.A | 890 | 27.98 | 27.87 | 28.99 | -1.12 | 35.77 | 22.92 | 0.9 | 3.1 | .... |
| Teck Resources Ltd v | TCK.B | 4,138,413 | 26.95 | 26 | 27.86 | -1.62 | 34.47 | 21.11 | 0.9 | 3.2 | 18.5 |
| Tekmira Phrmctcls Corp | TKM | 16,185 | 17.24 | 16.76 | 17.29 | -0.14 | 17.88 | 4.31 | .... | .... | .... |
| Tembec Inc | TMB | 47,449 | 2.85 | 2.81 | 2.82 | 0.02 | 3.6 | 2.2 | .... | .... | 9.2 |

Source: *www.financialpost.com*, February 13, 2014. Used with permission.

## 6.11

# SUMMARY AND CONCLUSIONS

In this chapter we use general present value (PV) formulas from the previous chapter to price bonds and stock.

1. Pure discount bonds and perpetuities are the polar cases of bonds. The value of a pure discount bond (also called a *zero-coupon bond* or simply a *zero*) is

$$PV = \frac{F}{(1 + r)^T}$$

The value of a perpetuity (also called a *consol*) is

$$PV = \frac{C}{r}$$

2. Level-coupon bonds represent an intermediate case. The coupon payments form an annuity, and the principal repayment is a lump sum. The value of this type of bond is simply the sum of the values of its two parts.

3. The yield to maturity (YTM) on a bond is the single rate that discounts the payments on the bond to its purchase price.

4. A stock can be valued by discounting its dividends. We mention three types of situations:
   a. The case of zero growth of dividends.
   b. The case of constant growth of dividends.
   c. The case of differential growth.

5. An estimate of the growth rate of a stock is needed for case (4b) or (4c) above. A useful estimate of the growth rate is

$$g = \text{Retention ratio} \times \text{Return on retained earnings}$$

6. It is worthwhile to view a share of stock as the sum of its worth if the company behaves as a cash cow (the company does no investing) and the value per share of its growth opportunities. We write the value of a share as

$$\text{Price per share} = \frac{\text{EPS}}{r} + \text{NPVGO}$$

We show that, in theory, share price must be the same whether the dividend growth model or the above formula is used.

7. From accounting, we know that earnings are divided into two parts: dividends and retained earnings. Most firms continuously retain earnings in order to create future dividends. One should not discount earnings to obtain price per share since part of earnings must be reinvested. Only dividends reach the shareholders, and only they should be discounted to obtain share price.

8. We suggested that a firm's price–earnings (P/E) ratio is a function of three factors:
   a. The per share amount of the firm's valuable growth opportunities.
   b. The risk of the stock.
   c. The conservatism of the accounting methods used by the firm.

9. We showed two different methods of valuing the entire firm, which provide different results:
   a. The constant-growth discounted cash flow (DCF) method.
   b. The P/E method.

**KEY TERMS**

| | | |
|---|---|---|
| Clean price   150 | Face value   147 | Premium   151 |
| Coupons   147 | Holding-period return   152 | Pure discount bond   146 |
| Dirty price   150 | Maturity date   146 | Return on equity (ROE)   157 |
| Discount   151 | Payout ratio   159 | Yield to maturity   151 |

**QUESTIONS & PROBLEMS**

### Valuing Bonds

6.1  What is the price of a 15-year, zero-coupon bond paying $1,000 at maturity if the YTM is

 *a.* 5 percent?
 *b.* 10 percent?
 *c.* 15 percent?

6.2  Microhard has issued a bond with the following characteristics:

> Par: $1,000
> Time to maturity: 15 years
> Coupon rate: 7 percent
> Semiannual payments

Calculate the price of this bond if the YTM is

 *a.* 7 percent.
 *b.* 9 percent.
 *c.* 5 percent.

### Bond Yields

6.3  Watters Umbrella Corp. issued 12-year bonds two years ago at a coupon rate of 7.8 percent. The bonds make semiannual payments. If these bonds currently sell for 105 percent of par value, what is the YTM?

### Coupon Rates

6.4  Rhiannon Corporation has bonds on the market with 11.5 years to maturity, a YTM of 7.6 percent, and a current price of $1,060. The bonds make semiannual payments. What must the coupon rate be on these bonds?

### Valuing Bonds

6.5  Even though most corporate bonds in Canada and the United States make coupon payments semiannually, bonds issued elsewhere often have annual coupon payments. Suppose a German company issues a bond with a par value of €1,000, 15 years to maturity, and a coupon rate of 8.4 percent paid annually. If the YTM is 7.6 percent, what is the current price of the bond?

### Bond Yields

6.6  A Japanese company has a bond outstanding that sells for 92 percent of its ¥100,000 par value. The bond has a coupon rate of 2.8 percent paid annually and matures in 21 years. What is the YTM of this bond?

### Bond Price Movements

6.7  Miller Corporation has a premium bond making semiannual payments. The bond pays an 8 percent coupon, has a YTM of 6 percent, and has 13 years to maturity. The Modigliani Company has a discount bond making semiannual payments. This bond pays a 6 percent coupon, has a YTM of 8 percent, and also has 13 years to maturity. If interest rates remain unchanged, what do you expect the price of these bonds to be 1 year from now? 3 years? 8 years? 12 years? 13 years? What's going on here? Illustrate your answers by graphing bond prices versus time to maturity.

### Interest Rate Risk

6.8   Laurel Inc. and Hardy Corp. both have 7 percent coupon bonds outstanding, with semiannual interest payments, and both are priced at par value. The Laurel Inc. bond has 2 years to maturity, whereas the Hardy Corp. bond has 15 years to maturity. If interest rates suddenly rise by 2 percent, what is the percentage change in the price of these bonds? If interest rates were to suddenly fall by 2 percent instead, what would the percentage change in the price of these bonds be then? Illustrate your answers by graphing bond prices versus YTM. What does this problem tell you about the interest rate risk of longer-term bonds?

6.9   The Faulk Corp. has a 6 percent coupon bond outstanding. The Gonas Company has a 14 percent bond outstanding. Both bonds have 12 years to maturity, make semiannual payments, and have a YTM of 10 percent. If interest rates suddenly rise by 2 percent, what is the percentage change in the price of these bonds? What if interest rates suddenly fall by 2 percent instead? What does this problem tell you about the interest rate risk of lower coupon bonds?

### Bond Yields

6.10  Hacker Software has 6.2 percent coupon bonds on the market with nine years to maturity. The bonds make semiannual payments and currently sell for 105 percent of par. What is the current yield on the bonds? The YTM? The effective annual yield?

6.11  Pembroke Co. wants to issue new 20-year bonds for some much-needed expansion projects. The company currently has 7 percent coupon bonds on the market that sell for $1,063, make semiannual payments, and mature in 20 years. What coupon rate should the company set on its new bonds if it wants them to sell at par?

### Finding the Bond Maturity

6.12  Argos Corp. has 9 percent coupon bonds making annual payments with a YTM of 7.81 percent. The current yield on these bonds is 8.42 percent. How many years do these bonds have left until they mature?

### Using Bond Quotes

6.13  Suppose the following bond quote for IOU Corporation appears in the financial pages of today's newspaper. Assume the bond has a face value of $1,000, paying semiannual coupon, and the current date is April 15, 2016. What is the YTM of the bond? What is the current yield?

| Company (ticker) | Coupon | Maturity | Last price | Last yield | Estimated volume (in $ thousands) |
|---|---|---|---|---|---|
| IOU (IOU) | 7.240 | Apr 15, 2025 | 105.312 | ? | 1,827 |

### Finding the Maturity

6.14  You've just found a 10 percent coupon bond on the market that sells for par value. What is the maturity on this bond?

### Components of Bond Returns

6.15  Bond *P* is a premium bond with a 9 percent coupon. Bond *D* is a 5 percent coupon bond currently selling at a discount. Both bonds make annual payments, have a YTM of 7 percent, and have 10 years to maturity. What is the current yield for bond *P*? For bond *D*? If interest rates remain unchanged, what is the expected capital gains yield over the next year for bond *P*? For bond *D*? Explain your answers and the interrelationship among the various types of yields.

**Holding Period Yield**

6.16 The YTM on a bond is the interest rate you earn on your investment if interest rates don't change. If you actually sell the bond before it matures, your realized return is known as the holding period yield (HPY).

    *a.* Suppose that today you buy a 5.6 percent annual coupon bond for $930. The bond has 10 years to maturity. What rate of return do you expect to earn on your investment?

    *b.* Two years from now, the YTM on your bond has declined by 1 percent, and you decide to sell. What price will your bond sell for? What is the HPY on your investment? Compare this yield to the YTM when you first bought the bond. Why are they different?

**Valuing Bonds**

6.17 The Morgan Corporation has two different bonds currently outstanding. Bond *M* has a face value of $30,000 and matures in 20 years. The bond makes no payments for the first six years, then pays $800 every six months over the subsequent eight years, and finally pays $1,000 every six months over the last six years. Bond *N* also has a face value of $30,000 and a maturity of 20 years; it makes no coupon payments over the life of the bond. If the required return on both of these bonds is 8 percent compounded semiannually, what is the current price of bond *M*? Of bond *N*?

**Stock Values**

6.18 The Starr Co. just paid a dividend of $2.15 per share on its stock. The dividends are expected to grow at a constant rate of 5 percent per year, indefinitely. If investors require an 11 percent return on the stock, what is the current price? What will the price be in three years? In 15 years?

6.19 The next dividend payment by ECY Inc. will be $3.20 per share. The dividends are anticipated to maintain a 6 percent growth rate, forever. If ECY stock currently sells for $63.50 per share, what is the required return?

6.20 For the company in Problem 6.19, what is the dividend yield? What is the expected capital gains yield?

6.21 White Wedding Corporation will pay a $3.05 per share dividend next year. The company pledges to increase its dividend by 5.25 percent per year, indefinitely. If you require an 11 percent return on your investment, how much will you pay for the company's stock today?

**Stock Valuation**

6.22 Siblings Inc. is expected to maintain a constant 6.4 percent growth rate in its dividends, indefinitely. If the company has a dividend yield of 4.3 percent, what is the required return on the company's stock?

6.23 Suppose you know that a company's stock currently sells for $72 per share and the required return on the stock is 11.5 percent. You also know that the total return on the stock is evenly divided between a capital gains yield and a dividend yield. If it is the company's policy to always maintain a constant growth rate in its dividends, what is the current dividend per share?

6.24 Gruber Corp. pays a constant $9 dividend on its stock. The company will maintain this dividend for the next 12 years and will then cease paying dividends forever. If the required return on this stock is 10 percent, what is the current share price?

**Valuing Preferred Stock**

6.25 Ayden Inc. has an issue of preferred stock outstanding that pays a $5.90 dividend every year, in perpetuity. If this issue currently sells for $87 per share, what is the required return?

### Growth Rate

6.26 The newspaper reported last week that Bennington Enterprises earned $28 million this year. The report also stated that the firm's ROE is 15 percent. Bennington retains 70 percent of its earnings. What is the firm's earnings growth rate? What will next year's earnings be?

### Stock Valuation

6.27 Universal Laser Inc. just paid a dividend of $3.10 on its stock. The growth rate in dividends is expected to be a constant 6 percent per year, indefinitely. Investors require a 15 percent return on the stock for the first three years, a 13 percent return for the next three years, and then an 11 percent return thereafter. What is the current share price for the stock?

### Non-constant Growth

6.28 Metallica Bearings Inc. is a young start-up company. No dividends will be paid on the stock over the next nine years, because the firm needs to plow back its earnings to fuel growth. The company will pay a $9 per share dividend in 10 years and will increase the dividend by 5.5 percent per year thereafter. If the required return on this stock is 13 percent, what is the current share price?

### Non-constant Dividends

6.29 Bucksnort Inc. has an odd dividend policy. The company has just paid a dividend of $12 per share and has announced that it will increase the dividend by $3 per share for each of the next five years, and then never pay another dividend. If you require a 12 percent return on the company's stock, how much will you pay for a share today?

6.30 North Side Corporation is expected to pay the following dividends over the next four years: $10, $7, $6, and $2.75. Afterwards, the company pledges to maintain a constant 5 percent growth rate in dividends forever. If the required return on the stock is 13 percent, what is the current share price?

### Differential Growth

6.31 Hughes Co. is growing quickly. Dividends are expected to grow at a 20 percent rate for the next three years, with the growth rate falling off to a constant 5 percent thereafter. If the required return is 12 percent and the company just paid a $2.80 dividend, what is the current share price?

6.32 Janicek Corp. is experiencing rapid growth. Dividends are expected to grow at 30 percent per year during the next three years; 18 percent over the following year; and then 8 percent per year, indefinitely. The required return on this stock is 11 percent, and the stock currently sells for $65 per share. What is the projected dividend for the coming year?

### Negative Growth

6.33 Antiques R Us is a mature manufacturing firm. The company just paid a $9 dividend, but management expects to reduce the payout by 4 percent per year, indefinitely. If you require an 11 percent return on this stock, what will you pay for a share today?

### Finding the Dividend

6.34 Mau Corporation stock currently sells for $58.32 per share. The market requires an 11.5 percent return on the firm's stock. If the company maintains a constant 5 percent growth rate in dividends, what was the most recent dividend per share paid on the stock?

**Valuing Preferred Stock**

6.35 Fifth National Bank just issued some new preferred stock. The issue will pay an $8 annual dividend in perpetuity, beginning five years from now. If the market requires a 5.6 percent return on this investment, how much does a share of preferred stock cost today?

**Using Stock Quotes**

6.36 You have found the following stock quote for RJW Enterprises Inc. in the financial pages of today's newspaper. What is the annual dividend? What was the closing price for this stock that appeared in *yesterday's* paper? If the company currently has 25 million shares of stock outstanding, what was net income for the most recent four quarters?

| YTD %chg | Stock | SYM | YLD | P/E | Last | Net chg |
|----------|-------|-----|-----|-----|------|---------|
| −1.1 | RJW Enterp. | RJW | 1.9 | 23 | 26.18 | −0.13 |

**Non-constant Growth and Quarterly Dividends**

6.37 Pasqually Mineral Water Inc. will pay a quarterly dividend per share of $0.80 at the end of each of the next 12 quarters. Thereafter, the dividend will grow at a quarterly rate of 1 percent, forever. The appropriate rate of return on the stock is 10 percent, compounded quarterly. What is the current stock price?

**Finding the Dividend**

6.38 Briley Inc. is expected to pay equal dividends at the end of each of the next two years. Thereafter, the dividend will grow at a constant annual rate of 4 percent, forever. The current stock price is $45. What is next year's dividend payment if the required rate of return is 11 percent?

**Finding the Required Return**

6.39 Juggernaut Satellite Corporation earned $18 million for the fiscal year ending yesterday. The firm also paid out 30 percent of its earnings as dividends yesterday. The firm will continue to pay out 30 percent of its earnings as annual, end-of-year dividends. The remaining 70 percent of earnings is retained by the company for use in projects. The company has 2 million shares of common stock outstanding. The current stock price is $93. The historical ROE of 13 percent is expected to continue in the future. What is the required rate of return on the stock?

**Dividend Growth**

6.40 Four years ago, Bling Diamond Inc. paid a dividend of $1.35 per share. Bling paid a dividend of $1.77 per share yesterday. Dividends will grow over the next five years at the same rate they grew over the last four years. Thereafter, dividends will grow at 5 percent per year. What will Bling Diamond's cash dividend be in seven years?

**Price–Earnings Ratio**

6.41 Consider Pacific Energy Company and Bluechips Inc., both of which reported earnings of $750,000. Without new projects, both firms will continue to generate earnings of $750,000 in perpetuity. Assume that all earnings are paid as dividends and that both firms require a 14 percent rate of return.
   *a.* What is the current P/E ratio for each firm?
   *b.* Pacific Energy Company has a new project that will generate additional earnings of $100,000 each year in perpetuity. Calculate the new P/E ratio of the firm.
   *c.* Bluechips has a new project that will increase earnings by $200,000 in perpetuity. Calculate the new P/E ratio of the firm.

### Growth Opportunities

6.42  The Stambaugh Corporation currently has EPS of $8.25. The company has no growth and pays out all earnings as dividends. It has a new project that will require an investment of $1.60 per share in one year. The project is only a two-year project, and it will increase earnings in the two years following the investment by $2.10 and $2.45, respectively. Investors require a 12 percent return on Stambaugh stock.

    *a.* What is the value per share of the company's stock, assuming the firm does not undertake the investment opportunity?

    *b.* If the firm does undertake the investment, what is the value per share now?

    *c.* Again, assume the firm undertakes the investment. What will the price per share be four years from today?

6.43  Rite Bite Enterprises sells toothpicks. Gross revenues last year were $7.5 million, and total costs were $3.4 million. Rite Bite has 1 million shares of common stock outstanding. Gross revenues and costs are expected to grow at 5 percent per year. Rite Bite pays no income taxes. All earnings are paid out as dividends.

    *a.* If the appropriate discount rate is 13 percent and all cash flows are received at year's end, what is the price per share of Rite Bite stock?

    *b.* Rite Bite has decided to produce toothbrushes. The project requires an immediate outlay of $17 million. In one year, another outlay of $6 million will be needed. The year after that, earnings will increase by $4.2 million. That profit level will be maintained in perpetuity. What effect will undertaking this project have on the price per share of the stock?

6.44  Victoria Real Estate Inc. expects to earn $71 million per year in perpetuity if it does not undertake any new projects. The firm has an opportunity to invest $16 million today and $5 million in one year in real estate. The new investment will generate annual earnings of $11 million in perpetuity, beginning two years from today. The firm has 15 million shares of common stock outstanding, and the required rate of return on the stock is 12 percent. Land investments are not depreciable. Ignore taxes.

    *a.* What is the price of a share of stock if the firm does not undertake the new investment?

    *b.* What is the value of the investment?

    *c.* What is the per-share stock price if the firm undertakes the investment?

6.45  The annual earnings of Avalanche Skis Inc. will be $10 per share in perpetuity if the firm makes no new investments. Under such a situation, the firm would pay out all of its earnings as dividends. Assume the first dividend will be received exactly one year from now.

    Alternatively, assume that three years from now, and in every subsequent year in perpetuity, the company can invest 25 percent of its earnings in new projects. Each project will earn 15 percent at year-end in perpetuity. The firm's discount rate is 13 percent.

    *a.* What is the price per share of Avalanche Skis Inc. stock today without the company making the new investment?

    *b.* If Avalanche announces that the new investment will be made, what will the per-share stock price be today?

### Stock Valuation

6.46  Most corporations pay quarterly dividends on their common stock rather than annual dividends. Barring any unusual circumstances during the year, the board raises, lowers, or maintains the current dividend once a year and then pays this dividend out in equal quarterly instalments to its shareholders.

    *a.* Suppose a company currently pays a $3.20 annual dividend on its common stock in a single annual instalment, and management plans on raising this dividend by

5 percent per year indefinitely. If the required return on this stock is 11 percent, what is the current share price?

b. Now suppose that the company in (a) actually pays its annual dividend in equal quarterly instalments; thus, this company has just paid an $0.80 dividend per share, as it has for the previous three quarters. What is your value for the current share price now? (*Hint:* Find the equivalent annual end-of-year dividend for each year.) Comment on whether or not you think that this model of stock valuation is appropriate.

## Growth Opportunities

6.47 Lewin Skis Inc. (today) expects to earn $8.50 per share for each of the future operating periods (beginning at time 1) if the firm makes no new investments and returns the earnings as dividends to the shareholders. However, Clint Williams, president and CEO, has discovered an opportunity to retain and invest 20 percent of the earnings beginning three years from today. This opportunity to invest will continue for each period indefinitely. He expects to earn 10 percent on this new equity investment, with the return beginning one year after each investment is made. The firm's equity discount rate is 12 percent throughout.

a. What is the price per share of Lewin Skis Inc. stock without making the new investment?

b. If the new investment is expected to be made, per the preceding information, what would the price of the stock be now?

c. Suppose the company could increase the investment in the project by whatever amount it chose. What would the retention ratio need to be to make this project attractive?

## Non-constant Growth

6.48 Storico Co. just paid a dividend of $3.85 per share. The company will increase its dividend by 20 percent next year and will then reduce its dividend growth rate by 5 percentage points per year until it reaches the industry average of 5 percent dividend growth, after which the company will keep a constant growth rate forever. If the required return on Storico stock is 13 percent, what will a share of stock sell for today?

6.49 This one's a little harder. Suppose the current share price for the firm in Problem 6.48 is $78.43, and all the dividend information remains the same. What required return must investors be demanding on Storico stock? (*Hint:* Set up the valuation formula with all the relevant cash flows, and use trial and error to find the unknown rate of return.)

## Growth Opportunities

6.50 Burklin Inc. has earnings of $18 million and is projected to grow at a constant rate of 5 percent forever because of the benefits gained from the learning curve. Currently, all earnings are paid out as dividends. The company plans to launch a new project two years from now that would be completely internally funded and require 30 percent of the earnings that year. The project would start generating revenues one year after the launch of the project, and the earnings from the new project in any year are estimated to be constant at $6.5 million. The company has 7.5 million shares of stock outstanding. Estimate the value of the stock. The discount rate is 10 percent.

# Stock Valuation at Ragan Engines

Larissa Warren has been talking with the company's directors about the future of East Coast Yachts. To this point, the company has used outside suppliers for various key components of the company's yachts, including engines. Larissa has decided that East Coast Yachts should consider the purchase of an engine manufacturer to allow it to better integrate its supply chain and get more control over engine features. After investigating several possible companies, Larissa feels that the purchase of Ragan Engines Inc. is a possibility. She has asked Dan Ervin to analyze Ragan's value.

Ragan Engines Inc. was founded nine years ago by a brother and sister, Carrington and Genevieve Ragan, and has remained a privately owned company. The company manufactures marine engines for a variety of applications. Ragan has experienced rapid growth because of a proprietary technology that increases the fuel efficiency of its engines with very little sacrifice in performance. The company is equally owned by Carrington and Genevieve. The original agreement between the siblings gave each 150,000 shares of stock.

Larissa has asked Dan to determine a value per share of Ragan stock. To accomplish this, Dan has gathered the following information about some of Ragan's competitors that are publicly traded:

| | EPS | DPS | Stock price | ROE | r |
|---|---|---|---|---|---|
| Blue Ribband Motors Corp. | $1.19 | $0.19 | $16.32 | 10.00% | 12.00% |
| Bon Voyage Marine Inc. | 1.26 | 0.55 | 13.94 | 12.00 | 17.00 |
| Nautilus Marine Engines | (0.27) | 0.57 | 23.97 | N/A | 16.00 |
| Industry average | $0.73 | $0.44 | $18.08 | 11.00% | 15.00% |

Nautilus Marine Engines' negative EPS was the result of an accounting write-off last year. Without the write-off, EPS for the company would have been $2.07. Last year, Ragan had an EPS of $5.35 and paid a dividend to Carrington and Genevieve of $320,000 each. The company also had an ROE of 21 percent. Larissa tells Dan that a required return for Ragan of 18 percent is appropriate.

1. Assuming the company continues its current growth rate, what is the value per share of the company's stock?

2. Dan has examined the company's financial statements, as well as examining those of its competitors. Although Ragan currently has a technological advantage, Dan's research indicates that Ragan's competitors are investigating other methods to improve efficiency. Given this, Dan believes that Ragan's technological advantage will last only for the next five years. After that period, the company's growth will likely slow to the industry average. Additionally, Dan believes that the required return the company uses is too high. He believes the industry average required return is more appropriate. Under Dan's assumptions, what is the estimated stock price?

3. What is the industry average P/E ratio? What is Ragan's P/E ratio? Comment on any differences and explain why they may exist.

4. Assume the company's growth rate declines to the industry average after five years. What percentage of the stock's value is attributable to growth opportunities?

5. Assume the company's growth rate slows to the industry average in five years. What future ROE does this imply?

6. Carrington and Genevieve are not sure if they should sell the company. If they do not sell the company outright to East Coast Yachts, they would like to increase the value of the company's stock. In this case, they want to retain control of the company and do not want to sell stock to outside investors. They also feel that the company's debt is at a manageable level and do not want to borrow more money. What steps can they take to increase the price of the stock? Are there any conditions under which this strategy would *not* increase the stock price?

# The Term Structure of Interest Rates

## Spot Rates and Yield to Maturity

In the main body of this chapter, we have assumed that the interest rate is constant over all future periods. In reality, interest rates vary through time. This occurs primarily because inflation rates are expected to differ through time.

To illustrate, we consider two zero-coupon bonds. Bond $A$ is a one-year bond and bond $B$ is a two-year bond. Both have a face value of $1,000. The one-year interest rate, $r_1$, is 8 percent. The two-year interest rate, $r_2$, is 10 percent. These two rates of interest are examples of spot rates. Perhaps this inequality in interest rates occurs because inflation is expected to be higher over the second year than over the first year. The two bonds are depicted in the following time chart:

We can easily calculate the PVs for bond $A$ and bond $B$ as

$$PV_A = \$925.93 = \frac{\$1,000}{1.08}$$

and

$$PV_B = \$826.45 = \frac{\$1,000}{(1.10)^2}$$

Of course, if $PV_A$ and $PV_B$ were observable and the spot rates were not, we could determine the spot rates using the PV formula, because

$$PV_A = \$925.93 = \frac{\$1,000}{(1 + r_1)} \rightarrow r_1 = 8\%$$

and

$$PV_B = \$826.45 = \frac{\$1,000}{(1 + r_2)^2} \rightarrow r_2 = 10\%$$

Now we can see how the prices of more complicated bonds are determined. Try to do Example 6A.1. It illustrates the difference between spot rates and YTMs.

Given the spot rates $r_1 = 8$ percent and $r_2 = 10$ percent, what should a 5 percent coupon, two-year bond cost? The cash flows $C_1$ and $C_2$ are illustrated in the following time chart:

The bond can be viewed as a portfolio of zero-coupon bonds with one- and two-year maturities. Therefore,

$$PV = \frac{\$50}{1 + 0.08} + \frac{\$1,050}{(1 + 0.10)^2} = \$914.06 \qquad \textbf{(6A.1)}$$

$$PV = \frac{\$50}{1 + 0.08} + \frac{\$1,050}{(1 + 0.10)^2} = \$914.06 \qquad \text{(6A.1)}$$

We now want to calculate a single rate for the bond. We do this by solving for $y$ in the following equation:

$$\$914.06 = \frac{\$50}{1 + y} + \frac{\$1,050}{(1 + y)^2} \qquad \text{(6A.2)}$$

In equation (6A.2), $y$ equals 9.95 percent. As mentioned in the chapter, we call $y$ the *yield to maturity* on the bond. Solving for $y$ for a multiyear bond is generally done by means of trial and error.[17] While this can take much time with paper and pencil, it is virtually instantaneous on a hand-held calculator.

It is worthwhile to contrast equation (6A.1) and equation (6A.2). In (6A.1), we use the marketwide spot rates to determine the price of the bond. Once we get the bond price, we use (6A.2) to calculate its YTM. Because equation (6A.1) employs two spot rates whereas only one appears in (6A.2), we can think of YTM as some sort of average of the two spot rates.[18]

Using the above spot rates, the YTM of a two-year coupon bond whose coupon rate is 12 percent and PV equals $1,036.73 can be determined by

$$\$1,036.73 = \frac{\$120}{1 + r} + \frac{\$1,120}{(1 + r)^2} \rightarrow r = 9.89\%$$

As these calculations show, two bonds with the same maturity will usually have different YTMs if the coupons differ.

## Graphing the Term Structure

The *term structure* describes the relationship of spot rates with different maturities. Figure 6A.1 graphs a particular term structure. In Figure 6A.1 the spot rates are increasing with longer maturities; that is, $r_3 > r_2 > r_1$. Graphing the term structure is easy if we can observe spot rates. Unfortunately, this can be done only if there are enough zero-coupon government bonds.

**FIGURE 6A.1**

**The Term Structure of Interest Rates**

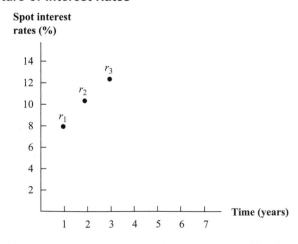

----

[17] The quadratic formula may be used to solve for $y$ for a two-year bond. However, formulas generally do not apply for longer-term bonds.

[18] YTM is not a simple average of $r_1$ and $r_2$. Rather, financial economists speak of it as a time-weighted average of $r_1$ and $r_2$.

A given term structure, such as that in Figure 6A.1, exists for only a moment in time, say, 10:00 AM, January 30, 2016. Interest rates are likely to change in the next minute, so that a different (though quite similar) term structure would exist at 10:01.

**CONCEPT QUESTION**

- What is the difference between a spot interest rate and the YTM?

## Explanations of the Term Structure

Figure 6A.1 showed one of many possible relationships between the spot rate and maturity. We now want to explore the relationship in more detail. We begin by defining a new term, the *forward rate*, and relate it to future interest rates. We also consider alternative theories of the term structure.

### Definition of Forward Rate

Earlier in this appendix, we developed a two-year example where the spot rate over the first year is 8 percent and the spot rate over two years is 10 percent. Here, an individual investing \$1 in a two-year zero-coupon bond would have $\$1 \times (1.10)^2$ in two years.

In order to pursue our discussion, it is worthwhile to rewrite[19]

$$\$1 \times (1.10)^2 = \$1 \times 1.08 \times 1.1204 \tag{6A.3}$$

Equation (6A.3) tells us something important about the relationship between one- and two-year rates. When an individual invests in a two-year zero-coupon bond yielding 10 percent, her wealth at the end of two years is the same as if she received an 8 percent return over the first year and a 12.04 percent return over the second year. This hypothetical rate over the second year, 12.04 percent, is called the *forward rate*. Thus, we can think of an investor with a two-year zero-coupon bond as getting the one-year spot rate of 8 percent and locking in 12.04 percent over the second year. This relationship is presented in Figure 6A.2.

**FIGURE 6A.2**

**Breakdown of a Two-Year Spot Rate into a One-Year Spot Rate and a Forward Rate over the Second Year**

With a two-year spot rate of 10 percent, the investor in the two-year bond receives \$1.21 at date 2.
This is the same return *as if* the investor received the spot rate of 8 percent over the first year and a 12.04 percent return over the second year.

Because both the one-year spot rate and the two-year spot rate are known at date 0, the forward rate over the second year can be calculated at date 0.

---

[19] 12.04 percent is equal to

$$\frac{(1.10)^2}{1.08} - 1$$

when rounding is performed after four digits.

More generally, if we are given spot rates $r_1$ and $r_2$, we can always determine the forward rate, $f_2$, such that

$$(1 + r_2)^2 = (1 + r_1) \times (1 + f_2) \qquad (6A.4)$$

We solve for $f_2$, yielding

$$f_2 = \frac{(1 + r_2)^2}{1 + r_1} - 1 \qquad (6A.5)$$

EXAMPLE **6A.2**

If the one-year spot rate is 7 percent and the two-year spot rate is 12 percent, what is $f_2$?
    We plug into equation (6A.5), yielding

$$f_2 = \frac{(1.12)^2}{1.07} - 1 = 17.23\%$$

Consider an individual investing in a two-year zero-coupon bond yielding 12 percent. We say it is as if he receives 7 percent over the first year and simultaneously locks in 17.23 percent over the second year. Note that both the one-year spot rate and the two-year spot rate are known at date 0. Because the forward rate is calculated from the one-year and two-year spot rates, it can be calculated at date 0 as well.
    Forward rates can be calculated over later years as well. The general formula is

$$f_n = \frac{(1 + r_n)^n}{(1 + r_{n-1})^{n-1}} - 1 \qquad (6A.6)$$

where $f_n$ is the forward rate over the $n$th year, $r_n$ is the $n$-year spot rate, and $r_{n-1}$ is the spot rate for $n - 1$ years.

EXAMPLE **6A.3**

Assume the following set of rates:

| Year | Spot Rate |
|------|-----------|
| 1    | 5%        |
| 2    | 6%        |
| 3    | 7%        |
| 4    | 6%        |

What are the forward rates over each of the four years?
    The forward rate over the first year is, by definition, equal to the one-year spot rate. Thus, we do not generally speak of the forward rate over the first year. The forward rates over the later years are

$$f_2 = \frac{(1.06)^2}{1.05} - 1 = 7.01\%$$

$$f_3 = \frac{(1.07)^3}{(1.06)^2} - 1 = 9.03\%$$

$$f_4 = \frac{(1.06)^4}{(1.07)^3} - 1 = 3.06\%$$

An individual investing $1 in the two-year zero-coupon bond receives $1.1236 [or $1 × $(1.06)^2$] at date 2. She can be viewed as receiving the one-year spot rate of 5 percent over the first year and receiving the forward rate of 7.01 percent over the second year. Another individual investing $1 in a three-year zero-coupon bond receives $1.2250 [or $1 × $(1.07)^3$] at date 3. He can be viewed as receiving the two-year spot rate of 6 percent over the first two years and receiving the forward rate of 9.03 percent over the third year. An individual invest-ing $1 in a four-year zero-coupon bond receives $1.2625 [or $1 × $(1.06)^4$] at date 4. She can be viewed as receiving the three-year spot rate of 7 percent over the first three years and receiving the forward rate of 3.06 percent over the fourth year.

Note that all of the four spot rates in this problem are known at date 0. Because the forward rates are calculated from the spot rates, they can be determined at date 0 as well.

The material in this appendix is likely to be difficult for students exposed to term structure for the first time. In brief, here is what you should know at this point. Given equations (6A.5) and (6A.6), you should be able to calculate a set of forward rates given a set of spot rates. This can simply be viewed as a mechanical computation. In addition to the calculations, you should understand the intuition of Figure 6A.2.

We now turn to the relationship between the forward rate and the expected spot rates in the future.

## Estimating the Price of a Bond at a Future Date

In the example from the body of this chapter, we considered zero-coupon bonds pay-ing $1,000 at maturity and selling at a discount prior to maturity. We now wish to change the example slightly. Now, each bond initially sells for $1,000 so that its pay-ment at maturity is more than $1,000.[20] Keeping the spot rates at 8 percent and 10 per-cent, we have

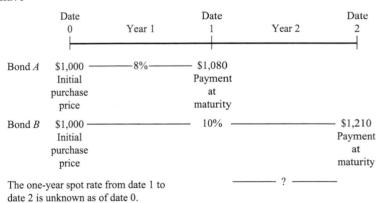

The one-year spot rate from date 1 to date 2 is unknown as of date 0.

The payments at maturity are $1,080 and $1,210 for the one- and two-year zero-coupon bonds, respectively. The initial purchase price of $1,000 for each bond is deter-mined as

$$\$1,000 = \frac{\$1,080}{1.08}$$

$$\$1,000 = \frac{\$1,210}{(1.10)^2}$$

We refer to the one-year bond as bond *A* and the two-year bond as bond *B*.

---

[20] This change in assumptions simplifies our presentation but does not alter any of our conclusions.

There will be a different one-year spot rate when date 1 arrives. This will be the spot rate from date 1 to date 2. We can also call it the spot rate over year 2. This spot rate is not known as of date 0. For example, should the rate of inflation rise between date 0 and date 1, the spot rate over year 2 would likely be high. Should the rate of inflation fall between date 0 and date 1, the spot rate over year 2 would likely be low.

Now that we have determined the price of each bond at date 0, we want to determine what the price of each bond will be at date 1. The price of the one-year bond (bond $A$) must be $1,080 at date 1, because the payment at maturity is made then. The hard part is determining what the price of the two-year bond (bond $B$) will be at that time.

Suppose we find that on date 1, the one-year spot rate from date 1 to date 2 is 6 percent. We state that this is the one-year spot rate over year 2. This means that one can invest $1,000 at date 1 and receive $1,060 (or $1,000 × 1.06) at date 2. Because one year has already passed for bond $B$, the bond has only one year left. Because bond $B$ pays $1,210 at date 2, its value at date 1 is

$$\$1,141.51 = \frac{\$1,210}{1.06} \qquad (6A.7)$$

Note that no one knew ahead of time the price that bond $B$ would sell for on date 1, because no one knew that the one-year spot rate over year 2 would be 6 percent.

Suppose the one-year spot rate beginning at date 1 turned out not to be 6 percent, but to be 7 percent instead. This means that one can invest $1,000 at date 1 and receive $1,070 (or $1,000 × 1.07) at date 2. In this case, the value of bond $B$ at date 1 would be

$$\$1,130.84 = \frac{\$1,210}{1.07} \qquad (6A.8)$$

Finally, suppose that the one-year spot rate at date 1 turned out to be neither 6 percent nor 7 percent, but 14 percent instead. This means that one can invest $1,000 at date 1 and receive $1,140 (or $1,000 × 1.14) at date 2. In this case, the value of bond $B$ at date 1 would be

$$\$1,061.40 = \frac{\$1,210}{1.14}$$

The above possible bond prices are represented in Table 6A.1. The price that bond $B$ will sell for on date 1 is not known before date 1 since the one-year spot rate prevailing over year 2 is not known until date 1.

TABLE 6A.1

### Price of Bond $B$ at Date 1 as a Function of Spot Rate over Year 2

| Price of bond $B$ at date 1 | Spot rate over year 2 |
|---|---|
| $\$1,141.51 = \dfrac{\$1,210}{1.06}$ | 6% |
| $\$1,130.84 = \dfrac{\$1,210}{1.07}$ | 7% |
| $\$1,061.40 = \dfrac{\$1,210}{1.14}$ | 14% |

It is important to re-emphasize that although the forward rate is known at date 0, the one-year spot rate beginning at date 1 is *unknown* ahead of time. Thus, the price of bond *B* at date 1 is unknown ahead of time. Prior to date 1, we can speak only of the amount that bond *B* is *expected* to sell for on date 1. We write this as[21]

**The Amount That Bond *B* Is Expected to Sell for on Date 1:**

$$\frac{\$1,210}{1 + \text{Spot rate expected over year 2}} \tag{6A.9}$$

Making two points is worthwhile now. First, because all individuals are different, the expected value of bond *B* differs across individuals. Later we will speak of a consensus expected value across investors. Second, equation (6A.9) represents the forecast of the price that the bond will be selling for on date 1. The forecast is made ahead of time, that is, on date 0.

## The Relationship between the Forward Rate over the Second Year and the Spot Rate Expected over the Second Year

Given a forecast of bond *B*'s price, an investor can choose one of two strategies at date 0:

1.  Buy a one-year bond. His proceeds at date 1 would be

$$\$1,080 = \$1,000 \times 1.08 \tag{6A.10}$$

2.  Buy a two-year bond but sell at date 1. His *expected* proceeds would be

$$\frac{\$1,000 \times (1.10)^2}{1 + \text{Spot rate expected over year 2}} \tag{6A.11}$$

Given our discussion of forward rates, we can rewrite equation (6A.11) as

$$\frac{\$1,000 \times 1.08 \times 1.1204}{1 + \text{Spot rate expected over year 2}} \tag{6A.12}$$

(Remember that 12.04 percent was the forward rate over year 2, $f_2$.)

Under what condition will the return from strategy 1 equal the expected return from strategy 2? In other words, under what condition will equation (6A.10) equal equation (6A.12)?

The two strategies will yield the same expected return only when

$$12.04\% = \text{Spot rate expected over year 2} \tag{6A.13}$$

In other words, if the forward rate equals the expected spot rate, one would expect to earn the same return over the first year whether one invested in a one-year bond or invested in a two-year bond but sold after one year.

## The Expectations Hypothesis

Equation (6A.13) seems fairly reasonable. That is, it is reasonable that investors would set interest rates so that the forward rate would equal the spot rate expected by the marketplace a year from now.[22] For example, imagine that individuals in the market-

---

[21] Technically, equation (6A.9) is only an approximation due to *Jensen's inequality.* That is, the expected value of

$$\frac{\$1,210}{1 + \text{Spot rate}} > \frac{\$1,210}{1 + \text{Spot rate expected over year 2}}$$

However, we ignore this very minor issue in the rest of the analysis.

[22] Of course, all individuals will have different expectations, so equation (6A.13) cannot hold for all individuals. However, financial economists generally speak of a consensus expectation. This is the expectation of the market as a whole.

place do not concern themselves with risk. If the forward rate, $f_2$, is less than the spot rate expected over year 2, individuals desiring to invest for one year would always buy a one-year bond. That is, our work above shows that an individual investing in a two-year bond but planning to sell at the end of one year would expect to earn less than if he simply bought a one-year bond.

Equation (6A.13) was stated for the specific case where the forward rate was 12.04 percent. We can generalize this to

**Expectations Hypothesis:**

$f_2 = $ Spot rate expected over year 2 $\qquad\qquad$ (6A.14)

Equation (6A.14) says that the forward rate over the second year is set to the spot rate that people expect to prevail over the second year. This is called the *expectations hypothesis*. It states that investors will set interest rates such that the forward rate over the second year is equal to the one-year spot rate expected over the second year.

## Liquidity-Preference Hypothesis

At this point, many students think that equation (6A.14) *must* hold. However, note that we developed (6A.14) by assuming that investors were risk neutral. Suppose, alternatively, that investors are averse to risk.

Which of the following strategies would appear more risky for an individual who wants to invest for one year?

1. Invest in a one-year bond.
2. Invest in a two-year bond but sell at the end of one year.

Strategy 1 has no risk because the investor knows that the rate of return must be $r_1$. Conversely, strategy 2 has more risk; the final return depends on what happens to interest rates.

Because strategy 2 has more risk than strategy 1, no risk-averse investor will choose strategy 2 if both strategies have the same expected return. Risk-averse investors can have no preference for one strategy over the other only when the expected return on strategy 2 is *greater than* the return on strategy 1. Because the two strategies have the same expected return when $f_2$ equals the spot rate expected over year 2, strategy 2 can only have a higher rate of return when

**Liquidity-Preference Hypothesis:**

$f_2 > $ Spot rate expected over year 2 $\qquad\qquad$ (6A.15)

That is, in order to induce investors to hold the riskier two-year bonds, the market sets the forward rate over the second year to be more than the spot rate expected over the second year. Equation (6A.15) is called the *liquidity-preference hypothesis*.

We developed the entire discussion by assuming that individuals are planning to invest over one year. We pointed out that for such individuals, a two-year bond has extra risk because it must be sold prematurely. What about those individuals who want to invest for two years? (We call these people investors with a two-year *time horizon*.)

They could choose one of the following strategies:

3. Buy a two-year zero-coupon bond.
4. Buy a one-year bond. When the bond matures, they immediately buy another one-year bond.

Strategy 3 has no risk for an investor with a two-year time horizon, because the proceeds to be received at date 2 are known as of date 0. However, strategy 4 has risk since the spot rate over year 2 is unknown at date 0. It can be shown that risk-averse investors will prefer neither strategy 3 nor strategy 4 over the other when

$$f_2 < \text{Spot rate expected over year 2} \qquad (6A.16)$$

Note that introducing risk aversion gives contrary predictions. Equation (6A.15) holds for a market dominated by investors with a one-year time horizon. Equation (6A.16) holds for a market dominated by investors with a two-year time horizon. Financial economists have generally argued that the time horizon of the typical investor is generally much shorter than the maturity of typical bonds in the marketplace. Thus, economists view (6A.15) as the better depiction of equilibrium in the bond market with *risk-averse* investors.

However, do we have a market of risk-neutral investors or risk-averse investors? In other words, can the expectations hypothesis of equation (6A.14) or the liquidity-preference hypothesis of equation (6A.15) be expected to hold? As we will learn later in this book, economists view investors as being risk averse for the most part. Yet economists are never satisfied with a casual examination of a theory's assumptions. To them, empirical evidence of a theory's predictions must be the final arbiter.

There has been a great deal of empirical evidence on the term structure of interest rates. Unfortunately (perhaps fortunately for some students), we will not be able to present the evidence in any detail. Suffice it to say that, in our opinion, the evidence supports the liquidity-preference hypothesis over the expectations hypothesis. One simple result might give students the flavour of this research. Consider an individual choosing between one of the following two strategies:

1. Invest in a one-year bond.
2. Invest in a 20-year bond but sell at the end of one year.

(Strategy 2′ is identical to strategy 2 except that a 20-year bond is substituted for a 2-year bond.)

The expectations hypothesis states that the expected returns on both strategies are identical. The liquidity-preference hypothesis states that the expected return on strategy 2′ should be greater than the expected return on strategy 1. Though no one knows what returns are actually expected over a particular time period, actual returns from the past may allow us to infer expectations. The results from January 1926 to December 1999 are illuminating. Over this time period the average yearly return on strategy 1 is 3.8 percent; it is 5.5 percent on strategy 2′.[23] This evidence is generally considered to be consistent with the liquidity-preference hypothesis and inconsistent with the expectations hypothesis.

## Application of Term Structure Theory

In explaining term structure theory, it was convenient to use examples of zero-coupon bonds and spot and forward rates. To see the application, we go back to coupon bonds and YTMs the way that actual bond data is presented in the financial press.

Figure 6A.3 shows a yield curve for Government of Canada bonds, a plot of bond YTMs against time to maturity. Yield curves are observed at a particular date and change shape over time. This yield curve is for February 2014.

---

[23] Taken from *Stocks, Bonds, Bills, and Inflation 2000 Yearbook* (Chicago: Ibbotson Associates). It is important to note that strategy 2′ does not involve buying a 20-year bond and holding it to maturity. Rather, it consists of buying a 20-year bond and selling it 1 year later, that is, when it has become a 19-year bond. This round-trip transaction occurs 63 times in the 63-year sample from January 1926 to December 1999.

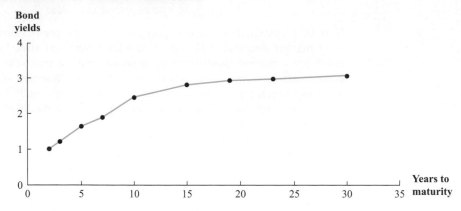

**Government of Canada Yield Curve**

Source: www.bankofcanada.ca, February 14, 2014, and www.financialpost.com, February 14, 2014.

Now suppose you were advising a friend who was renewing a home mortgage. Suppose further that the alternatives were a one-year mortgage at 8.5 percent and a two-year mortgage at 9 percent. We know that on average, over the life of a mortgage, rolling over one-year rates will probably be cheaper because the borrower will avoid paying the liquidity premium. Further, the flat yield curve tells us that the market does not expect interest rates to rise.

## Interest Rate Risk

The risk that arises for bond owners from fluctuating interest rates is called interest rate risk. As interest rates increase, bond prices fall. Conversely, when interest rates decrease, bond prices increase. This inverse relationship occurs because as interest rates increase, bondholders realize that they can earn higher yields by switching to other investments. Accordingly, how much interest rate risk a bond has depends on how sensitive its price is to interest rate changes. This sensitivity directly depends on two things: the time to maturity and the coupon rate. As we will see in a moment, you should keep the following in mind when looking at a bond:

1. All other things being equal, the longer the time to maturity, the greater the interest rate risk.
2. All other things being equal, the lower the coupon rate, the greater the interest rate risk.

Intuitively, shorter-term bonds have less interest rate sensitivity because the face amount is received so quickly. For example, the PV of this amount isn't greatly affected by a small change in interest rates if the amount is received in, say, one year. However, even a small change in the interest rate, once compounded for, say, 30 years, can have a significant effect on PV. As a result, the PV of the face amount will be much more volatile with a longer-term bond.

The other thing to know about interest rate risk is that, like many things in finance and economics, it increases at a decreasing rate. For example, a 10-year bond has much greater interest rate risk than a 1-year bond has. However, a 30-year bond has only slightly greater interest rate risk than a 10-year bond.

The reason that bonds with lower coupons have greater interest rate risk is essentially the same. As we discussed earlier, the value of a bond depends on the PV of both its coupons and its face amount. If two bonds with different coupon rates have the same maturity, the value of the lower-coupon bond is proportionately more dependent on the face amount to be received at maturity. As a result, its value will fluctuate more as interest rates change. Put another way, the bond with the higher coupon has a larger cash flow early in its life, so its value is less sensitive to changes in the discount rate.

To illustrate, at the time of writing in February 2014, bond portfolio managers were expecting interest rates to rise as the U.S. Federal Reserve was tapering off its easy-money policy of quantitative easing. As a result, managers were adjusting their portfolios to reduce their sensitivity to rising rates, thus minimizing expected losses. To do this they replaced long-term low-coupon bonds with short-term high-coupon bonds.

**QUESTIONS & PROBLEMS**

6A.1   Define the forward rate.

6A.2   What is the relationship between the one-year spot rate, the two-year spot rate, and the forward rate over the second year?

6A.3   What is the expectations hypothesis?

6A.4   What is the liquidity-preference hypothesis?

6A.5   What is the difference between a spot interest rate and the YTM?

6A.6   Assume that the five-year spot rate is 10 percent.
   a. If the forward rate over the sixth year is currently at 7.5 percent, what is the six-year spot rate?
   b. If the forward rate over the fifth year is currently at 9 percent, what is the four-year spot rate?

6A.7   The appropriate discount rate for cash flows received one year from today is 11 percent. The appropriate annual discount rate for cash flows received two years from today is 14 percent.
   a. What is the price of a two-year bond that pays an annual coupon of 6 percent?
   b. What is the YTM of this bond?

6A.8   The one-year spot rate equals 8 percent, and the two-year spot rate equals 6.5 percent. What should a 5.1 percent coupon two-year bond cost?

6A.9   If the one-year spot rate is 7.5 percent and the two-year spot rate is 12 percent, what is the forward rate?

6A.10  Assume the following spot rates:

| Maturity | Spot rate (%) |
| --- | --- |
| 1 | 5 |
| 2 | 8 |
| 3 | 14 |

   What are the forward rates over each of the 3 years?

6A.11  Consider the following three zero-coupon bonds:

| Bond | Face value | Time to maturity (years) | Market price |
| --- | --- | --- | --- |
| 1 | $1,000 | 1 | $940.00 |
| 2 | 1,000 | 2 | 820.00 |
| 3 | 1,000 | 3 | 768.00 |

   a. Calculate the one-, two-, and three-year spot rates.
   b. Calculate the forward rate over the second year, and the one corresponding to the third year.
   c. Is the forward rate over the third year the same as the one-year spot rate investors expect to prevail at the end of the second year? Discuss.

6A.12  Consider the bonds from Problem 6.A11.
   a. What price of the third bond would risk-neutral investors expect to prevail at the end of the second year?
   b. Now assume that investors are risk averse with a two-year investment horizon. Further assume that for every year at maturity beyond two years, investors demand a 1.5 percent liquidity premium. What price of the third bond would risk-averse investors expect to prevail at the end of the second year?

# Net Present Value and Other Investment Rules

EXECUTIVE SUMMARY

Chapter 5 examined the relationship between $1 today and $1 in the future. For example, a corporate project generating a set of cash flows can be valued by discounting these flows using the *net present value (NPV)* approach. While we believe that the NPV approach is the best one for evaluating capital budgeting projects, our treatment would be incomplete if we ignored alternative methods. This chapter examines these alternative methods. We first consider the NPV approach as a benchmark. Next we examine four alternatives: payback, average accounting return (AAR), internal rate of return (IRR), and the profitability index (PI).

## 7.1 WHY USE NET PRESENT VALUE?

This chapter, as well as the next two, focuses on *capital budgeting*, the decision-making process for accepting or rejecting projects. This chapter develops the basic capital budgeting methods, leaving much of the practical application to Chapters 8 and 9. But we don't have to develop these methods from scratch. In Chapter 4, we discussed the basic principles of NPV. Further, in Chapter 5, we pointed out that a dollar received in the future is worth less than a dollar received today. The reason, of course, is that today's dollar can be reinvested, yielding a greater amount in the future. And we showed in Chapter 5 that the exact worth of a dollar to be received in the future is its present value. Furthermore, Section 5.1 suggested calculating the *NPV* of any project. That is, the section suggested calculating the difference between the sum of the present values of the project's future cash flows and the initial cost of the project.

The NPV method is the first one to be considered in this chapter. We begin by reviewing the approach with a simple illustration shown in Example 7.1. Next we ask why the method leads to good decisions.

**EXAMPLE 7.1**

The Alpha Corporation is considering investing in a risk-free project costing $100. The project receives $107 in one year and has no other cash flows. The interest rate is 6 percent.

The NPV of the project can easily be calculated as

$$\$0.94 = -\$100 + \frac{\$107}{1.06} \tag{7.1}$$

From Chapter 5, we know that the project should be accepted since its NPV is positive. If the NPV of the project were negative, as would be the case with an interest rate greater than 7 percent, the project should be rejected.

The basic investment rule can be generalized to the following:

Accept a project if the NPV is greater than zero.
Reject a project if the NPV is less than zero.

We refer to this as the NPV rule.

Now why does the NPV rule lead to good decisions? Consider the following two strategies available to the managers of Alpha Corporation:

1. Use $100 of corporate cash to invest in the project. The $107 will be paid as a dividend in one year.
2. Forgo the project and pay the $100 of corporate cash as a dividend today.

If strategy 2 is employed, the shareholder might deposit the dividend in his bank for one year. With an interest rate of 6 percent, strategy 2 would produce cash of $106 ($100 × 1.06) at the end of the year. The shareholder would prefer strategy 1, since strategy 2 produces less than $107 at the end of the year.

Thus, our basic point is as follows:

**Accepting positive NPV projects benefits the shareholders.**

How do we interpret the exact NPV of $0.94? This is the increase in the value of the firm from the project. For example, imagine that the firm today has productive assets worth $V and $100 of cash. If the firm forgoes the project, the value of the firm today is simply

$$\$V + \$100 \tag{7.2}$$

If the firm accepts the project, the firm will receive $107 in one year but will have no cash today. Thus, the firm's value today is

$$\$V + \frac{\$107}{1.06} \tag{7.3}$$

The difference between equation (7.2) and equation (7.3) is just $0.94, the present value of equation (7.1). Thus:

**The value of the firm rises by the NPV of the project.**

Note that the value of the firm is merely the sum of the values of the different projects, divisions, or other entities within the firm. This property, called **value additivity**, is quite important. It implies that the contribution of any project to a firm's value is simply the NPV of the project. As we will see later, alternative methods discussed in this chapter do not generally have this nice property.

One detail remains. We assumed that the project was risk free, a rather implausible assumption. Future cash flows of real-world projects are invariably risky. In other words, cash flows can only be estimated, rather than known. Imagine that the managers of Alpha *expect* the cash flow of the project to be $107 next year. That is, the cash flow could be higher, say $117, or lower, say $97. With this slight change, the project is risky. Suppose the project is about as risky as the stock market as a whole, where the expected return this year is, say, 10 percent. In this case, 10 percent becomes the discount rate, implying that the NPV of the project is

$$-\$2.73 = -\$100 + \frac{\$107}{1.10}$$

Since the NPV is negative, the project should be rejected. This makes sense since a shareholder of Alpha Corporation receiving a $100 dividend today could invest it in the stock market, expecting a 10 percent return. Why accept a project with the same risk as the market but with an expected return of only 7 percent?

Conceptually, the discount rate on a risky project is the return that one can expect to earn on a financial asset of comparable risk. This discount rate is often referred to as an *opportunity cost*, since corporate investment in the project takes away the shareholder's opportunity to invest the dividend in a financial asset. If the actual calculation of the discount rate strikes you as extremely difficult in the real world, you are probably right. While you can call a bank to find out the interest rate, whom do you call to find the expected return on the market this year? And, if the risk of the project differs from that of the market, how do you make the adjustment? However, the calculation is by no means impossible. While we forgo the calculation in this chapter, we present it in later chapters of the text.

Having shown that NPV is a sensible approach, how can we tell whether alternative methods are as good as NPV? The key to NPV is its three attributes:

1. *NPV uses cash flows.* Cash flows from a project can be used for other corporate purposes (e.g., dividend payments, other capital-budgeting projects, or payments of corporate interest). By contrast, earnings are an artificial construct. While earnings are useful to accountants, they should not be used in capital budgeting because they do not represent cash.

2. *NPV uses all the cash flows of the project.* Other approaches ignore cash flows beyond a particular date; beware of these approaches.

3. *NPV discounts the cash flows properly.* Other approaches may ignore the time value of money when handling cash flows. Beware of these approaches as well.

**CONCEPT QUESTIONS**
- What is the NPV rule?
- Why does this rule lead to good investment decisions?

## 7.2    THE PAYBACK PERIOD RULE

### Defining the Rule

One of the most popular alternatives to NPV is the **payback period rule**. Here is how the payback period rule works.

Consider a project with an initial investment of $50,000 (i.e., an initial cash outflow of $50,000). Cash flows are $30,000, $20,000, and $10,000 in the first three years, respectively. These flows are illustrated in Figure 7.1. A useful way of writing down investments like the preceding is with the notation

$$(-\$50,000, \$30,000, \$20,000, \$10,000)$$

The minus sign in front of the $50,000 reminds us that this is a cash outflow for the investor, and the commas between the different numbers indicate that they are received—or if they are cash outflows, that they are paid out—at different times. In this example we are assuming that the cash flows occur one year apart, with the first one occurring the moment we decide to take on the investment.

**FIGURE 7.1**

**Cash Flows of an Investment Project**

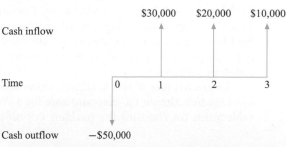

The firm receives cash flows of $30,000 and $20,000 in the first two years, which add up to the $50,000 original investment. This means that the firm has recovered its investment within two years. In this case, two years is the *payback period* of the investment.

The payback period rule for making investment decisions is simple. A particular cut-off time, say two years, is selected. All investment projects that have payback periods of two years or less are accepted, and all of those that pay off in more than two years, if at all, are rejected.

## Problems with the Payback Method

There are at least three problems with the payback method. To illustrate the first two problems, we consider the three projects in Table 7.1. All three projects have the same three-year payback period, so they should all be equally attractive—right?

**TABLE 7.1**

**Expected Cash Flows for Projects *A* through *C***

| Year | *A* | *B* | *C* |
|------|-----|-----|-----|
| 0 | −$100 | −$100 | −$100 |
| 1 | 20 | 50 | 50 |
| 2 | 30 | 30 | 30 |
| 3 | 50 | 20 | 20 |
| 4 | 60 | 60 | 60,000 |
| Payback period (years) | 3 | 3 | 3 |

Actually, they are not equally attractive, as can be seen by a comparison of different *pairs* of projects.

**Problem 1: Timing of Cash Flows within the Payback Period**   Let us compare project *A* with project *B*. In years 1 through 3, the cash flows of project *A* rise from $20 to $50, while the cash flows of project *B* fall from $50 to $20. Because the large cash flow of $50 comes earlier with project *B*, its NPV must be higher. Nevertheless, we saw above that the payback periods of the two projects are identical. Thus, a problem with the payback period is that it does not consider the timing of the cash flows within the payback period. This shows that the payback method is inferior to NPV because, as we pointed out earlier, the NPV approach *discounts the cash flows properly.*

**Problem 2: Payments after the Payback Period**   Now consider projects *B* and *C*, which have identical cash flows within the payback period. However, project *C* is clearly preferred because it has the cash flow of $60,000 in the fourth year. Thus, another problem with the payback method is that it ignores all cash flows occurring after the payback period. This flaw is not present with the NPV approach because, as we pointed out earlier, the NPV approach *uses all the cash flows of the project.* The payback method forces managers to have an artificially short-term orientation, which may lead to decisions not in the shareholders' best interests.

**Problem 3: Arbitrary Standard for Payback Period**   We do not need to refer to Table 7.1 when considering a third problem with the payback approach. Capital markets help us estimate the discount rate used in the NPV method. The risk-free rate, perhaps proxied by the yield on a Treasury instrument, is the appropriate rate for a risk-free investment.

Later chapters of this textbook show how to use historical returns in the capital markets to estimate the discount rate for a risky project. However, there is no comparable guide for choosing the payback cut-off date, so the choice is somewhat arbitrary.

## Managerial Perspective

Despite its shortcomings, the payback method can be acceptable when making relatively small decisions. The decision to build a small warehouse, for example, or to pay for a tune-up for a truck is the sort of decision that is often made by lower-level management. Typically, a manager might reason that a tune-up would cost, say, $200, and if it saved $120 each year in reduced fuel costs, it would pay for itself in less than two years. On such a basis the decision would be made.

Although the treasurer of the company might not have made the decision in the same way, the company endorses such decision making. Why would upper management condone or even encourage such retrograde activity in its employees? One answer would be that it is easy to make decisions using payback. Multiply the tune-up decision into 50 such decisions a month, and the appeal of this simple method becomes clearer.

The payback method also has some desirable features for managerial control. Just as important as the investment decision itself is the company's ability to evaluate the manager's decision-making ability. Under the NPV method, a long time may pass before we can decide whether or not a decision was correct. With the payback method we know in two years whether the manager's assessment of the cash flows was correct.

It has also been suggested that firms with good investment opportunities but no available cash may justifiably use payback. For example, the payback method could be used by small, privately held firms with good growth prospects but limited access to the capital markets. Quick cash recovery enhances the reinvestment possibilities for such firms.

Finally, practitioners often argue that standard academic criticisms of payback overstate any real-world problems with the method. For example, textbooks typically make fun of payback by positing a project with low cash inflows in the early years but a huge cash inflow right after the payback cut-off date. This project is likely to be rejected under the payback method, though its acceptance would, in truth, benefit the firm. Project *C* in our Table 7.1 is an example of such a project. Practitioners point out that the pattern of cash flows in these textbook examples is much too stylized to mirror the real world. In fact, a number of executives have told us that for the overwhelming majority of real-world projects, both payback and NPV lead to the same decision. In addition, these executives indicate that if an investment like project *C* were encountered in the real world, decision makers would almost certainly make *ad hoc* adjustments to the payback rule so that the project would be accepted.

Notwithstanding all of the preceding rationale, it is not surprising to discover that as the decision grows in importance, which is to say, when firms look at bigger projects, NPV becomes the order of the day. When questions of controlling and evaluating the manager become less important than making the right investment decision, payback is used less frequently. For big-ticket decisions, such as whether or not to buy a machine, build a factory, or acquire a company, the payback method is seldom used.

## Summary of Payback

The payback method differs from NPV and is therefore conceptually wrong. With its arbitrary cut-off date and its blindness to cash flows after that date, it can lead to some flagrantly foolish decisions if it is used too literally. Nevertheless, because of its simplicity, as well as its other advantages mentioned above, companies often use it as a screen for making the myriad minor investment decisions they continuously face.

Although this means that you should be wary of trying to change approaches such as the payback method when you encounter them in companies, you should probably be careful not to accept the sloppy financial thinking they represent. After this course, you would do your company a disservice if you used payback instead of NPV when you had a choice.

*CONCEPT QUESTIONS*

- List the problems of the payback method.
- What are some advantages of the payback method?

# 7.3   THE DISCOUNTED PAYBACK PERIOD RULE

Aware of the pitfalls of the payback approach, some decision makers use a variant called the **discounted payback period rule**. Under this approach, we first discount the cash flows. Then we ask how long it takes for the discounted cash flows to equal the initial investment.

For example, suppose that the discount rate is 10 percent and the cash flows on a project are given by

$$(-\$100, \$50, \$50, \$20)$$

This investment has a payback period of two years, because the investment is paid back in that time.

To compute the project's discounted payback period, we first discount each of the cash flows at the 10 percent rate. In discounted terms, then, the cash flows look like

$$[-\$100, \$50/1.1, \$50/(1.1)^2, \$20/(1.1)^3] = (-\$100, \$45.45, \$41.32, \$15.03)$$

The discounted payback period of the original investment is simply the payback period for these discounted cash flows. The payback period for the discounted cash flows is slightly less than three years since the discounted cash flows over the three years are $101.80 (or $45.45 + $41.32 + $15.03). As long as the cash flows are positive, the discounted payback period will never be smaller than the payback period, because discounting will lower the cash flows.

At first glance, the discounted payback may seem like an attractive alternative, but on closer inspection we see that it has some of the same major flaws as the payback. Like payback, discounted payback first requires us to make a somewhat magical choice of an arbitrary cut-off period, and then it ignores all of the cash flows after that date.

If we have already gone to the trouble of discounting the cash flows, any small appeal to simplicity or to managerial control that payback may have has been lost. We might just as well add up the discounted cash flows and use the NPV to make the decision. Although discounted payback looks a bit like the NPV, it is just a poor compromise between the payback method and the NPV.

# 7.4   THE AVERAGE ACCOUNTING RETURN

## Defining the Rule

Another attractive and fatally flawed approach to making financial decisions is the **average accounting return (AAR)**. The AAR is the average project earnings after taxes and depreciation, divided by the average book value of the investment during its life. In spite of its flaws, the AAR method is worth examining because it is still used in business.

EXAMPLE  **7.2**

Consider a company that is evaluating whether or not to buy a store in a newly built mall. The purchase price is $500,000. We will assume that the store has an estimated life of five years and will need to be completely scrapped or rebuilt at the end of that time. The projected yearly sales and expense figures are shown in Table 7.2.

### TABLE 7.2

**Projected Yearly Revenue and Costs for Average Accounting Return**

|  | Year 1 | Year 2 | Year 3 | Year 4 | Year 5 |
|---|---|---|---|---|---|
| Revenue | $433,333 | $450,000 | $266,667 | $200,000 | $133,333 |
| Expenses | 200,000 | 150,000 | 100,000 | 100,000 | 100,000 |
| Before-tax cash flow | 233,333 | 300,000 | 166,667 | 100,000 | 33,333 |
| Depreciation | 100,000 | 100,000 | 100,000 | 100,000 | 100,000 |
| Earnings before taxes | 133,333 | 200,000 | 66,667 | 0 | −66,667 |
| Taxes $(T_c = 0.25)^*$ | 33,333 | 50,000 | 16,667 | 0 | −16,667 |
| Net income | 100,000 | 150,000 | 50,000 | 0 | −50,000 |

*Corporate tax rate = $T_c$. The tax rebate in year 5 of −$16,667 occurs if the rest of the firm is profitable. Here, the loss in the project reduces the taxes of the entire firm.

$$\text{Average net income} = \frac{(\$100,000 + 150,000 + 50,000 + 0 - 50,000)}{5} = \$50,000$$

$$\text{Average investment} = \frac{\$500,000 + 0}{2} = \$250,000$$

$$\text{AAR} = \frac{\$50,000}{\$250,000} = 20\%$$

It is worth looking carefully at Table 7.2. In fact, the first step in any project assessment is a careful look at the projected cash flows. When the store starts up, it is estimated that first-year sales will be $433,333 and that, after expenses, the before-tax cash flow will be $233,333. After the first year, sales are expected to rise and expenses are expected to fall, resulting in a before-tax cash flow of $300,000. After that, competition from other stores and the loss in novelty will drop before-tax cash flow to $166,667, $100,000, and $33,333, respectively, in the next three years.

To compute the AAR on the project, we divide the average net income by the average amount invested. This can be done in three steps.

*Step 1: Determine the average net income.*   The net income in any year is the before-tax net cash flow minus depreciation and taxes. Depreciation is not a cash outflow.[1] Rather, it is a charge reflecting the fact that the investment in the store becomes less valuable every year.

We assume the project has a useful life of five years, at which time it will be worthless. Because the initial investment is $500,000 and because it will be worthless in five years, we will assume that it loses value at a rate of $100,000 each year. This steady loss in value of $100,000 is called *straight-line depreciation*. We subtract both depreciation and taxes from before-tax cash flow to derive the net income, as shown in Table 7.2. The net income over the five years is $100,000 in the first year, $150,000 in year 2, $50,000 in year 3, zero in year 4, and −$50,000 in the last year. The average net income over the life of the project is therefore

**Average Net Income:**
[$100,000 + $150,000 + $50,000 + $0 + (−$50,000)]/5 = $50,000

---

[1] The rates of depreciation and tax used in this example are chosen for simplicity. Leasehold improvements are one of the few asset classes for which tax depreciation in Canada is straight line. We discuss these topics in detail in Appendix 1A and in Chapter 8. Recall from Chapter 2 that depreciation is the special case of amortization applicable to capital assets.

*Step 2: Determine the average investment.*   We stated earlier that due to depreciation, the investment in the store becomes less valuable every year. Because depreciation is $100,000 per year, the value at the end of year zero is $500,000, the value at the end of year 1 is $400,000, and so on. What is the average value of the investment over the life of the investment?

The mechanical calculation is

**Average Investment:**

$$(\$500{,}000 + \$400{,}000 + \$300{,}000 + \$200{,}000 + \$100{,}000 + \$0)/6 = \$250{,}000 \qquad (7.4)$$

We divide by 6 and not 5 because $500,000 is what the investment is worth at the beginning of the five years and $0 is what it is worth at the beginning of the sixth year. In other words, there are six terms in the parentheses of equation (7.4). Note that Table 7.2 arrives at the same answer for average investment by averaging the initial investment and ending value. This works here because we assume straight-line depreciation and zero salvage.

*Step 3: Determine the AAR.*   The AAR is simply

$$\text{AAR} = \frac{\$50{,}000}{\$250{,}000} = 20\%$$

If the firm had a targeted AAR greater than 20 percent, the project would be rejected, and if its targeted AAR were less than 20 percent, it would be accepted.

## Analyzing the Average Accounting Return Method

By now you should be able to see what is wrong with the AAR method. The first and most important flaw with AAR is that it works with the wrong raw materials. It uses net income and book value of the investment, both of which come from the accounting books. Accounting numbers are somewhat arbitrary. For example, certain cash outflows, such as the cost of a building, are depreciated under current accounting rules. Other flows, such as maintenance, are expensed. In real-world situations, the decision to depreciate or expense an item involves judgment. Thus, the basic inputs of the AAR method, income and average investment, are affected by the accountant's judgment. Conversely, the NPV method *uses cash flows.* Accounting judgments do not affect cash flows.

Second, AAR takes no account of timing. In the previous example, the AAR would have been the same if the $100,000 net income in the first year had occurred in the last year. However, delaying an inflow for five years would have lowered the NPV of the investment. As mentioned earlier in this chapter, the NPV approach *discounts properly.*

Third, just as payback requires an arbitrary choice of the cut-off date, the AAR method offers no guidance on what the right targeted rate of return should be. It could be the discount rate in the market. But then again, because the AAR method is not the same as the NPV method, it is not obvious that this would be the right choice.

Given these problems, is the AAR method employed in practice? Like the payback method, the AAR (and variations of it) is frequently used as a backup to discounted cash flow methods. Perhaps this is so because it is easy to calculate and uses accounting numbers readily available from the firm's accounting system. In addition, both shareholders and the media pay a lot of attention to the overall profitability of a firm. Thus, some managers may feel pressured to select projects that are profitable in the near term, even if the projects come up short in terms of NPV. These managers may focus on the AAR of individual projects more than they should.

**CONCEPT QUESTIONS**
- What are the three steps in calculating AAR?
- What are some flaws with the AAR method?

# 7.5  THE INTERNAL RATE OF RETURN

Now we come to the most important alternative to the NPV approach: the internal rate of return, universally known as the IRR. The IRR is about as close as you can get to the NPV without actually being the NPV. The basic rationale behind the IRR is that it tries to find a single number that summarizes the merits of a project. That number does not depend on the interest rate that prevails in the capital market. That is why it is called the internal rate of return; the number is internal or intrinsic to the project and does not depend on anything except the cash flows of the project.

For example, consider the simple project (−$100, $110) in Figure 7.2. For a given rate, the NPV of this project can be described as

$$NPV = -\$100 + \frac{\$110}{1 + r} \tag{7.5}$$

where $r$ is the discount rate.

---

**FIGURE 7.2**

**Cash Flows for a Simple Project**

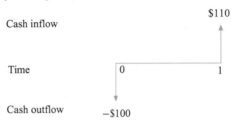

What must the discount rate be to make the NPV of the project equal to zero? We begin by using an arbitrary discount rate of 0.08, which yields

$$\$1.85 = -\$100 + \frac{\$110}{1.08} \tag{7.6}$$

Since the NPV in equation (7.6) is positive, we now try a higher discount rate, say, 0.12. This yields

$$-\$1.79 = -\$100 + \frac{\$110}{1.12} \tag{7.7}$$

Since the NPV in equation (7.7) is negative, we lower the discount rate to, say, 0.10. This yields

$$0 = -\$100 + \frac{\$110}{1.10} \tag{7.8}$$

This trial-and-error procedure tells us that the NPV of the project is zero when $r$ equals 10 percent.[2] Thus, we say that 10 percent is the project's **internal rate of return (IRR)**. In general, the IRR is the rate that causes the NPV of the project to be zero. The implication of this exercise is very simple. The firm should be equally willing to accept or reject the project if the discount rate is 10 percent. The firm should accept the project if the discount rate is less than 10 percent. The firm should reject the project if the discount rate is greater than 10 percent.

---

[2] Of course, we could have directly solved for $r$ in equation (7.5) after setting NPV equal to zero. However, with a long series of cash flows, one cannot generally directly solve for $r$. Instead, one can use either a trial-and-error method or a financial calculator or computer program to solve for $r$.

The general investment rule is clear:

Accept the project if IRR is greater than the discount rate.
Reject the project if IRR is less than the discount rate.

We refer to this as the **basic IRR rule**. Having mastered the basics of the IRR rule, you should recognize that we used the IRR (without defining it) when we calculated the yield to maturity (YTM) of a bond in Chapter 6. In fact, the YTM is the bond's IRR.[3]

Now we can try the more complicated example in Figure 7.3. As we did in equations (7.6) to (7.8), we use trial and error to calculate the IRR.

**FIGURE 7.3**

**Cash Flows for a More Complex Project**

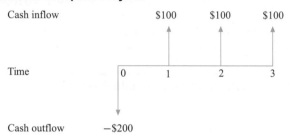

We try 20 percent and 30 percent, yielding the following:

| Discount rate | Net present value |
|---------------|-------------------|
| 20% | $10.65 |
| 30% | −18.39 |

After much more trial and error, we find that the NPV of the project is zero when the discount rate is 23.37 percent. Thus, the IRR is 23.37 percent. With a 20 percent discount rate, the NPV is positive and we accept it. However, if the discount rate is 30 percent, we reject it.

Algebraically, IRR is the unknown in the following equation:[4]

$$0 = -\$200 + \frac{\$100}{1 + IRR} + \frac{\$100}{(1 + IRR)^2} + \frac{\$100}{(1 + IRR)^3}$$

Figure 7.4 illustrates what it means to find the IRR for a project. The figure plots the NPV as a function of the discount rate. The curve crosses the horizontal axis at the IRR of 23.37 percent because this is where the NPV equals zero.

It should also be clear that the NPV is positive for discount rates less than the IRR and negative for discount rates greater than the IRR. This means that if we accept projects like this one when the discount rate is less than the IRR, we will be accepting positive NPV projects. Thus, the IRR rule will coincide exactly with the NPV rule.

---

[3] Strictly speaking, this is true for bonds with annual coupons. Typically, bonds carry semiannual coupons, so YTM is the six-month IRR expressed as a stated rate per year.

[4] One can derive the IRR directly for a problem with an initial outflow and either one or two subsequent inflows. In the case of two subsequent inflows, the quadratic formula is needed. In general, however, only trial and error will work for an outflow and three or more subsequent inflows. Hand-held calculators and computer programs calculate IRR by trial and error, though at lightning speed.

**FIGURE 7.4**

**Net Present Value and Discount Rates for a Relatively Complex Project**

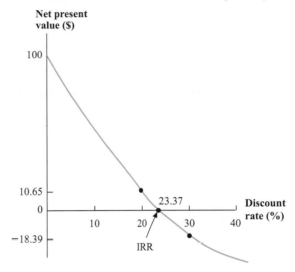

The NPV is positive for discount rates less than the IRR and negative for discount rates greater than the IRR.

If this were all there is to it, the IRR rule would always coincide with the NPV rule. This would be a wonderful discovery because it would mean that just by computing the IRR for a project we would be able to tell where it ranks among all of the projects we are considering. For example, if the IRR rule really worked, a project with an IRR of 20 percent would always be at least as good as one with an IRR of 15 percent.

But the world of finance is not so kind. Unfortunately, the IRR rule and the NPV rule are the same only for simple examples like the ones above. Several problems with the IRR occur in more complicated situations.

**CONCEPT QUESTION**    • How does one calculate the IRR of a project?

## 7.6   PROBLEMS WITH THE INTERNAL RATE OF RETURN APPROACH

### Definition of Independent and Mutually Exclusive Projects

An **independent project** is one whose acceptance or rejection is independent of the acceptance or rejection of other projects. For example, imagine that McDonald's is considering putting another hamburger outlet in Rio de Janeiro to get ready for the 2016 Olympics. Acceptance or rejection of this unit is likely to be unrelated to the acceptance or rejection of any other restaurant in its global system.

Now consider the other extreme, **mutually exclusive investments**. What does it mean for two projects, A and B, to be mutually exclusive? You can accept A or you can accept B or you can reject both of them, but you cannot accept both of them. For example, A might be a decision to build an apartment building on a corner lot that you own, and B might be a decision to build a movie theatre on the same lot.

We now present two general problems with the IRR approach that affect both independent and mutually exclusive projects. Next, we deal with two problems affecting mutually exclusive projects only.

## Two General Problems Affecting Both Independent and Mutually Exclusive Projects

We begin our discussion with project $A$, which has the following cash flows:

$$(-\$100, \$130)$$

The IRR for project $A$ is 30 percent. Table 7.3 provides other relevant information on the project. The relationship between NPV and the discount rate is shown for this project in Figure 7.5. As you can see, the NPV declines as the discount rate rises.

**TABLE 7.3**

### The Internal Rate of Return and Net Present Value

| Dates: | Project A | | | Project B | | | Project C | | |
|---|---|---|---|---|---|---|---|---|---|
| | **0** | **1** | **2** | **0** | **1** | **2** | **0** | **1** | **2** |
| Cash flows | −$100 | $130 | | $100 | −$130 | | −$100 | $230 | −$132 |
| Internal rate of return | | 30% | | | 30% | | 10% | | 20% |
| Net present value at 10% | | $18.2 | | | −$18.2 | | | | |
| Accept if market rate | | < 30% | | | > 30% | | > 10% | | < 20% |
| Financing or investing | | Investing | | | Financing | | | Mixture | |

**FIGURE 7.5**

### Net Present Value and Discount Rates for Projects A, B, and C

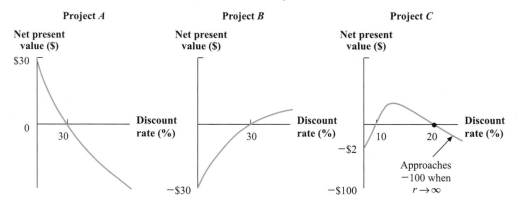

Project $A$ has a cash outflow at date 0 followed by a cash inflow at date 1. Its NPV is negatively related to the discount rate.

Project $B$ has a cash inflow at date 0 followed by a cash outflow at date 1. Its NPV is positively related to the discount rate.

Project $C$ has two changes of sign in its cash flows. It has an outflow at date 0, an inflow at date 1, and an outflow at date 2. Projects with more than one change of sign can have multiple rates of return.

**Problem 1: Investing or Financing?**   Now consider project $B$, with cash flows of

$$(\$100, -\$130)$$

These cash flows are exactly the reverse of the flows for project $A$. In project $B$, the firm receives funds first and then pays out funds later. While unusual, projects of this type do exist. For example, consider a corporation conducting a seminar where the participants pay in advance. Because large expenses are frequently incurred at the seminar date, cash inflows precede cash outflows.

Consider our trial-and-error method to calculate IRR:

$$-\$4 = +\$100 - \frac{\$130}{1.25}$$

$$\$0 = +\$100 - \frac{\$130}{1.30}$$

$$\$3.70 = +\$100 - \frac{\$130}{1.35}$$

As with project A, the IRR is 30 percent. However, notice that the NPV is *negative* when the discount rate is *less than* 30 percent. Conversely, the NPV is positive when the discount rate is more than 30 percent. The decision rule is exactly the opposite of our previous result. For this type of project, the rule is as follows:

Accept the project when IRR is less than the discount rate.

Reject the project when IRR is greater than the discount rate.

This unusual decision rule follows from the graph of project B in Figure 7.5. The curve is upward sloping, implying that NPV is *positively* related to the discount rate.

The graph makes intuitive sense. Suppose that the firm wants to obtain $100 immediately. It can either (1) conduct project B or (2) borrow $100 from a bank. Thus, the project is actually a substitute for borrowing. In fact, because the IRR is 30 percent, taking on project B is tantamount to borrowing at 30 percent. If the firm can borrow from a bank at, say, only 25 percent, it should reject the project. However, if a firm can only borrow from a bank at, say, 35 percent, it should accept the project. Thus, project B will be accepted if and only if the discount rate is *more than* the IRR.[5]

This should be contrasted with project A. If the firm has $100 of cash to invest, it can either (1) conduct project A or (2) lend $100 to the bank. The project is actually a substitute for lending. In fact, because the IRR is 30 percent, taking on project A is tantamount to lending at 30 percent. The firm should accept project A if the lending rate is less than 30 percent. Conversely, the firm should reject project A if the lending rate is greater than 30 percent.

Because the firm initially pays out money with project A but initially receives money with project B, we refer to project A as an investing-type project and project B as a financing-type project. Investing-type projects are the norm. Because the IRR rule is reversed for a financing-type project, we view this type of project as a problem—unless it is understood properly.

**Problem 2: Multiple Rates of Return**    Suppose the cash flows from a project are

$$(-\$100, \$230, -\$132)$$

Because this project has a negative cash flow, a positive cash flow, and another negative cash flow, we say that the project's cash flows exhibit two changes of sign, or flip-flops. While this pattern of cash flows might look a bit strange at first, many projects require outflows of cash after receiving some inflows. An example is a strip-mining project. The first stage in such a project is the initial investment in excavating the mine. Profits from operating the mine are received in the second stage. The third stage involves a further investment to reclaim the land and satisfy the requirements of environmental protection legislation. Cash flows are negative at this stage.

Projects financed by lease arrangements also produce negative cash flows followed by positive ones. We study leasing carefully in a later chapter, but for now we will give

[5] This paragraph implicitly assumes that the cash flows of the project are risk free. In this way, we can treat the borrowing rate as the discount rate for a firm needing $100. With risky cash flows, another discount rate would be chosen. However, the intuition behind the decision to accept when IRR is less than the discount rate would still apply.

you a hint. Using leases for financing can sometimes bring substantial tax advantages. These advantages are often sufficient to make an otherwise bad investment have positive cash flows following an initial outflow. But after a while the tax advantages decline or run out. The cash flows turn negative when this occurs.

It is easy to verify that this project has not one but two IRRs: 10 percent and 20 percent.[6] In a case like this, the IRR does not make any sense. Which IRR are we to use: 10 percent or 20 percent? Because there is no good reason to use one over the other, IRR simply cannot be used here.

Why does this project have multiple rates of return? Project $C$ generates multiple IRRs because both an inflow and an outflow occur after the initial investment. In general, these flip-flops or changes in sign produce multiple IRRs. In theory, a cash flow stream with $K$ changes in sign can have up to $K$ sensible IRRs (greater than $-100\%$).[7] Therefore, since project $C$ has two changes in sign, it can have as many as two IRRs. As we pointed out, projects whose cash flows change sign repeatedly can occur in the real world.

**Net Present Value Rule** Of course, we should not be too worried about multiple rates of return. After all, we can always fall back on the NPV rule. Figure 7.5 plots the NPV of project $C$ ($-\$100$, $\$230$, $-\$132$) as a function of the discount rate. As the figure shows, the NPV is zero at both 10 percent and 20 percent and negative outside the range. Thus, the NPV rule tells us to accept the project if the appropriate discount rate is between 10 percent and 20 percent. The project should be rejected if the discount rate lies outside of this range.

---

[6] The calculations are

$$0 = -\$100 + \frac{\$230}{1.1} - \frac{\$132}{(1.1)^2}$$
$$= -\$100 + \$209.09 - \$109.09$$

and

$$0 = -\$100 + \frac{\$230}{1.2} - \frac{\$132}{(1.2)^2}$$
$$= -\$100 + \$191.67 - \$91.67$$

Thus, we have multiple rates of return. Note that financial calculators only solve for the first IRR of 10 percent.

[7] Those of you who are steeped in algebra might have recognized that finding the IRR is like finding the root of a polynomial equation. For a project with cash flows of ($C_0$, ..., $C_T$), the formula for computing the IRR requires us to find the interest rate, $r$, that makes

$$\text{NPV} = C_0 + C_1/(1 + r) + \cdots + C_T/(1 + r)^T = 0$$

If we let the symbol $x$ stand for the discount factor,

$$x = 1/(1 + r)$$

then the formula for the IRR becomes

$$\text{NPV} = C_0 + C_1 x + C_2 x^2 + \cdots + C_T x^T = 0$$

Finding the IRR, then, is the same as finding the roots of this polynomial equation. If a particular value $x^*$ is a root of the equation, then, because

$$x = 1/(1 + r)$$

it follows that there is an associated IRR:

$$r^* = (1/x^*) - 1$$

From the theory of polynomials, it is well known that an $n$th-order polynomial has $n$ roots. Generally, an IRR more than $-100$ percent is considered sensible. Since each root that is positive generates an IRR greater than $-100$ percent, any positive root can have a sensible IRR associated with it. Applying Descartes' rule of signs gives the result that a stream of $n$ cash flows can have up to $K$ IRRs greater than $-100$ percent, where $K$ is the number of changes in sign for the cash flows.

**Modified Internal Rate of Return**   As an alternative to NPV, we now introduce the **modified IRR (MIRR)** method, which handles the multiple-IRR problem by combining cash flows until only one change in sign remains. To see how it works, consider project $C$ again. With a discount rate of, say, 14 percent, the value of the last cash flow, −$132, is

$$-\$132/1.14 = -\$115.79$$

as of date 1. Since $230 is already received at that time, the "adjusted" cash flow at date 1 is $114.21 ($230 − $115.79). Thus, the MIRR approach produces the following two cash flows for the project:

$$(-\$100, \$114.21)$$

Note that by discounting and then combining cash flows, we are left with only one change in sign. The IRR rule can now be applied. The IRR of these two cash flows is 14.21 percent, implying that the project should be accepted given our assumed discount rate of 14 percent.

Of course, project $C$ is relatively simple to begin with, since it has only three cash flows and two changes in sign. However, the same procedure can easily be applied to more complex projects; that is, just keep discounting and combining the later cash flows until only one change of sign remains.

While this adjustment is correct for multiple IRRs, it appears, at least to us, to violate the spirit of the IRR approach. As stated earlier, the basic rationale behind the IRR method is that it provides a single number summarizing the merits of a project. That number does not depend on the discount rate. In fact, that is why it is called the internal rate of return: the number is *internal*, or intrinsic, to the project and does not depend on anything except the cash flows of the project. By contrast, MIRR is clearly a function of the discount rate. However, this point is not meant to be a criticism of MIRR. A firm using this adjustment will avoid the multiple-IRR problem, just as a firm using the NPV rule will avoid it.

*Are we ever safe from the multiple-IRR problem?*   If the first cash flow for a project is negative—because it is the initial investment—and if all of the remaining flows are positive, there can be only a single, unique IRR, no matter how many periods the project lasts. This is easy to understand by using the concept of the time value of money. For example, it is easy to verify that project $A$ in Table 7.3 has an IRR of 30 percent, because using a 30 percent discount rate gives

$$\begin{aligned} NPV &= -\$100 + \$130/(1.3) \\ &= 0 \end{aligned}$$

How do we know that this is the only IRR? Suppose we tried a discount rate greater than 30 percent. In computing the NPV, changing the discount rate does not change the value of the initial cash flow of −$100 because that cash flow is not discounted. But raising the discount rate can only lower the present value of the future cash flows. In other words, because the NPV is zero at 30 percent, any increase in the rate will push the NPV into the negative range. Similarly, if we try a discount rate of less than 30 percent, the overall NPV of the project will be positive. Though this example has only one positive flow, the above reasoning still implies a single, unique IRR if there are many inflows (but no outflows) after the initial investment.

If the initial cash flow is positive, and if all of the remaining flows are negative, there can only be a single, unique IRR. This result follows from reasoning similar to that above. Both these cases have only one change of sign or flip-flop in the cash flows. Thus, we are safe from multiple IRRs whenever there is only one sign change in the cash flows.

*General rules.* The following chart summarizes our rules:

| Flows | Number of internal rates of return | Internal rate of return criterion | Net present value criterion |
|---|---|---|---|
| First cash flow is negative and all remaining cash flows are positive. | 1 | Accept if IRR $> r$<br>Reject if IRR $< r$ | Accept if NPV $> 0$<br>Reject if NPV $< 0$ |
| First cash flow is positive and all remaining cash flows are negative. | 1 | Accept if IRR $< r$<br>Reject if IRR $> r$ | Accept if NPV $> 0$<br>Reject if NPV $< 0$ |
| Some cash flows after first are positive and some cash flows after first are negative. | May be more than 1 | No valid IRR | Accept if NPV $> 0$<br>Reject if NPV $< 0$ |

Note: $r$ = Discount rate.

Note that the NPV criterion is the same for each of the three cases. In other words, NPV analysis is always appropriate. Conversely, the IRR can be used only in certain cases.

## Problems Specific to Mutually Exclusive Projects

As mentioned earlier, two or more projects are mutually exclusive if the firm can, at most, accept only one of them. We now present two problems dealing with the application of the IRR approach to mutually exclusive projects. These two problems are quite similar, though logically distinct.[8]

**The Scale Problem**  A professor we know motivates class discussions on this topic with the statement, "Students, I am prepared to let one of you choose between two mutually exclusive 'business' propositions. Opportunity 1—You give me $1 now and I'll give you $1.50 back at the end of the class period. Opportunity 2—You give me $10 and I'll give you $11 back at the end of the class period. You can only choose one of the two opportunities. And you cannot choose either opportunity more than once. I'll pick the first volunteer."

Which would you choose? The correct answer is opportunity 2.[9] To see this, look at the following chart:

| | Cash flow at beginning of class | Cash flow at end of class (90 minutes later) | Net present value[*] | Internal rate of return |
|---|---|---|---|---|
| Opportunity 1 | −$ 1 | +$ 1.50 | $0.50 | 50% |
| Opportunity 2 | −10 | +11.00 | 1.00 | 10% |

[*]We assume a zero rate of interest because the class lasted only 90 minutes. It just seemed a lot longer.

As we have stressed earlier in the text, one should choose the opportunity with the higher NPV. This is opportunity 2 in the example. Or, as one of the professor's students explained it, "I trust the professor, so I know I'll get my money back. And I have $10 in my pocket right now so I can choose either opportunity. At the end of the class, I'll be

---

[8] Another problem with IRR occurs either when long-term interest rates differ from short-term rates (that is, when the term structure of interest rates, presented in Appendix 6A, is not flat) or when the riskiness of the cash flows changes over time. In these circumstances, using IRR is inappropriate because no one discount rate is applicable to all the cash flows.

[9] The professor uses real money here. Though many students have done poorly on the professor's exams over the years, no student ever chose opportunity 1. The professor claims that his students are "money players."

able to play two rounds of my favourite electronic game with opportunity 2 and still have my original investment, safe and sound. The profit on opportunity 1 buys only one round."

This business proposition illustrates a defect with the IRR criterion. The basic IRR rule says take opportunity 1, because the IRR is 50 percent. The IRR is only 10 percent for opportunity 2.

Where does IRR go wrong? The problem with IRR is that it ignores issues of scale. While opportunity 1 has a greater IRR, the investment is much smaller. In other words, the high percentage return on opportunity 1 is more than offset by the ability to earn at least a decent return on a much bigger investment under opportunity 2.[10]

Since IRR seems to be misguided here, can we adjust or correct it? We illustrate how in Example 7.3.

EXAMPLE **7.3**

Jack and Ramona have just purchased the rights to *Corporate Finance: The Movie*. They will produce this movie on either a small budget or a big budget. The estimated cash flows are as follows:

|  | Cash flow at date 0 | Cash flow at date 1 | Net present value at 25% | Internal rate of return |
|---|---|---|---|---|
| Small budget | −$10 million | $40 million | $22 million | 300% |
| Large budget | −25 million | 65 million | 27 million | 160% |

Because of high risk, a 25 percent discount rate is considered appropriate. Ramona wants to adopt the large budget because the NPV is higher. Jack wants to adopt the small budget because the IRR is higher. Who is right?

For the reasons espoused in the classroom example above, NPV is correct. Hence, Ramona is right. However, Jack is very stubborn where IRR is concerned. How can Ramona justify the large budget to Jack using the IRR approach?

This is where **incremental IRR** comes in. She calculates the incremental cash flows from choosing the large budget instead of the small budget as follows:

|  | Cash flow at date 0 (in $ millions) | Cash flow at date 1 (in $ millions) |
|---|---|---|
| Incremental cash flows from choosing large budget instead of small budget | −25 − (−10) = −15 | 65 − 40 = 25 |

This chart shows that the incremental cash flows are −$15 million at date 0 and $25 million at date 1. Ramona calculates incremental IRR as

**Formula for Calculating the Incremental IRR:**
$$0 = -\$15 \text{ million} + \frac{\$25 \text{ million}}{1 + IRR}$$

IRR equals 66.67 percent in this equation. Ramona says that the incremental IRR is 66.67 percent. Incremental IRR is the IRR on the incremental investment from choosing the large project instead of the small project.

In addition, we can calculate the NPV of the incremental cash flows:

---
[10] A 10 percent return is more than decent over a 90-minute interval!

**Net Present Value of Incremental Cash Flows:**

$$-\$15 \text{ million} + \frac{\$25 \text{ million}}{1.25} = \$5 \text{ million}$$

We know the small-budget movie would be acceptable as an independent project since its NPV is positive. We want to know whether it is beneficial to invest an additional $15 million in order to make the large-budget movie instead. In other words, is it beneficial to invest an additional $15 million in order to receive an additional $25 million next year? First, the calculations above show the NPV of the incremental investment to be positive. Second, the incremental IRR of 66.67 percent is higher than the discount rate of 25 percent. For both reasons, the incremental investment can be justified. The second reason is what Jack needed to hear to be convinced. Hence, the large-budget movie should be made.

In review, we can handle this example (or any mutually exclusive example) in one of three ways:

1. *Compare the NPVs of the two choices.* The NPV of the large-budget movie is greater than the NPV of the small-budget movie; that is, $27 million is greater than $22 million.

2. *Compare the incremental NPV from making the large-budget movie instead of the small-budget movie.* Because incremental NPV equals $5 million, we choose the large-budget movie.

3. *Compare the incremental IRR to the discount rate.* Because the incremental IRR is 66.67 percent and the discount rate is 25 percent, we take the large-budget movie.

All three approaches always give the same decision. However, we must not compare the IRRs of the two movies. If we did we would make the wrong choice; that is, we would accept the small-budget movie.

While students frequently think that problems of scale are relatively unimportant, the truth is just the opposite. No real-world project comes in one clear-cut size. Rather, the firm has to *determine* the best size for the project. The movie budget of $25 million is not fixed in stone. Perhaps an extra $1 million to hire a bigger star or to film at a better location will increase the movie's gross. Similarly, an industrial firm must decide whether it wants a warehouse of, say, 500,000 square feet or 600,000 square feet. And, earlier in the chapter we imagined McDonald's opening an outlet in Rio de Janeiro. If it does this, it must decide how big the outlet should be. For almost any project, someone in the firm has to decide on its size, implying that problems of scale abound in the real world.

One final note here. Students ask which project should be subtracted from the other in calculating incremental flows. Notice that we are subtracting the smaller project's cash flows from the bigger project's cash flows. This leaves an *outflow* at date 0. We then use the basic IRR rule on the incremental flows.[11]

**The Timing Problem**    In Example 7.4 we illustrate another very similar problem with using the IRR approach to evaluate mutually exclusive projects.

---

[11] Alternatively, we could have subtracted the larger project's cash flows from the smaller project's cash flows. This would have left an *inflow* at date 0, making it necessary to use the IRR rule for financing situations. This would work, but we find it more confusing.

EXAMPLE **7.4**

Suppose that the Kaufold Corporation has two alternative uses for a warehouse. It can store toxic waste containers (investment A) or electronic equipment (investment B). The cash flows are as follows:

| | Year | | | | Net present value | | | |
|---|---|---|---|---|---|---|---|---|
| | **0** | **1** | **2** | **3** | **@ 0%** | **@ 10%** | **@ 15%** | **Internal rate of return** |
| Investment A | −$10,000 | $10,000 | $1,000 | $ 1,000 | $2,000 | $669 | $109 | 16.04% |
| Investment B | −10,000 | 1,000 | 1,000 | 12,000 | 4,000 | 751 | −484 | 12.94 |

We find that the NPV of investment B is higher with low discount rates, and the NPV of investment A is higher with high discount rates. This is not surprising if you look closely at the cash flow patterns. The cash flows of A occur early, whereas the cash flows of B occur later. If we assume a high discount rate, we favour investment A because we are implicitly assuming that the early cash flow (for example, $10,000 in year 1) can be reinvested at that rate. Because most of investment B's cash flows occur in year 3, B's value is relatively high with low discount rates.[12]

The NPVs and IRRs for both projects appear in Figure 7.6. Project A has an NPV of $2,000 at a discount rate of zero. This is calculated by simply adding up the cash flows without discounting them. Project B has an NPV of $4,000 at the zero rate. However, the NPV of project B declines more rapidly as the discount rate increases than does the NPV of project A. As stated above, this is because B's cash flows occur later. Both projects have the same NPV at a discount rate of 10.55 percent. The IRR for a project is the rate at which the NPV equals zero. Because the NPV of B declines more rapidly, B actually has a lower IRR.

FIGURE **7.6**

**Net Present Value and the Internal Rate of Return for Mutually Exclusive Projects**

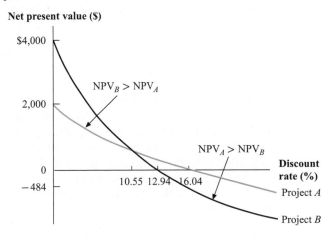

---

[12] It is possible to modify the IRR to specify the reinvestment rate. We do not recommend this modified IRR approach because it does not resolve the timing problem.

As with the movie example presented above, we can select the better project with one of three different methods:

1. *Compare the NPVs of the two projects.* Figure 7.6 aids our decision. If the discount rate is less than 10.55 percent, we should choose project *B* because *B* has a higher NPV. If the rate is more than 10.55 percent, we should choose project *A* because *A* has a higher NPV.

2. *Compare the incremental IRR to the discount rate.* Another way of determining that *B* is a better project is to subtract the cash flows of *A* from the cash flows from *B* and then to calculate the IRR. This is the incremental IRR approach we spoke of earlier.

   The incremental cash flows are as follows:

   |  |  | Year | | | Net present value of incremental cash flows | | | |
   |---|---|---|---|---|---|---|---|---|
   |  | 0 | 1 | 2 | 3 | @ 0% | @ 10% | @ 15% | Internal rate of return |
   | *B − A* | 0 | −$9,000 | 0 | $11,000 | $2,000 | $83 | −$593 | 10.55% |

   This chart shows that the incremental IRR is 10.55 percent. In other words, the NPV on the incremental investment is zero when the discount rate is 10.55 percent. Thus, if the relevant discount rate is less than 10.55 percent, project *B* is preferred to project *A*. If the relevant discount rate is more than 10.55 percent, project *A* is preferred to project *B*.[13]

3. *Calculate the NPV on incremental cash flows.* Finally, we could calculate the NPV on the incremental cash flows. The chart that appears with the previous method displays these NPVs. We find that the incremental NPV is positive when the discount rate is either 0 percent or 10 percent. The incremental NPV is negative if the discount rate is 15 percent. If the NPV is positive on the incremental flows, we should choose *B*. If the NPV is negative, we should choose *A*.

In summary, the same decision is reached whether we compare the NPVs of the two projects, compare the incremental IRR to the relevant discount rate, or examine the NPV of the incremental cash flows. However, as shown earlier, we should not compare the IRR of project *A* with the IRR of project *B*.

We suggested earlier that we should subtract the cash flows of the smaller project from the cash flows of the bigger project. What do we do here, since the two projects have the same initial investment? Our suggestion in this case is to perform the subtraction so that the first nonzero cash flow is negative. In the Kaufold Corporation example, we achieved this by subtracting *A* from *B*. In this way, we can still use the basic IRR rule for evaluating cash flows.

These examples illustrate problems with the IRR approach in evaluating mutually exclusive projects. Both the professor–student example and the movie example illustrate the problem that arises when mutually exclusive projects have different initial investments. The Kaufold Corp. example illustrates the problem that arises when mutually exclusive projects have different cash flow timings. When working with mutually exclusive projects, it is not necessary to determine whether it is the scale problem or the timing problem that exists. Very likely both occur in any real-world situation. Instead, the practitioner should simply use either an incremental IRR or an NPV approach.

---

[13] In this example, we first showed that the NPVs of the two projects are equal when the discount rate is 10.55 percent. We next showed that the incremental IRR is also 10.55 percent. This is not a coincidence; this equality must always hold. The incremental IRR is the rate that causes the incremental cash flows to have zero NPV. The incremental cash flows have zero NPV when the two projects have the same NPV.

### Redeeming Qualities of the Internal Rate of Return

The IRR probably survives because it fills a need that the NPV does not. People seem to want a rule that summarizes the information about a project in a single rate of return. This single rate provides people with a simple way of discussing projects. For example, one manager in a firm might say to another, "Remodelling the north wing has a 20 percent IRR."

To their credit, however, companies that employ the IRR approach seem to understand its deficiencies. For example, companies frequently restrict managerial projections of cash flows to be negative at the beginning and strictly positive later. Perhaps, then, the ability of the IRR approach to capture a complex investment project in a single number and the ease of communicating that number explain the survival of the IRR.

### A Test

To test your knowledge, consider the following two statements:

1. You must know the discount rate to compute the NPV of a project, but you compute the IRR without referring to the discount rate.
2. Hence, the IRR rule is easier to apply than the NPV rule because you don't use the discount rate when applying the IRR.

The first statement is true. The discount rate is needed to *compute* NPV. The IRR is *computed* by solving for the rate where the NPV is zero. No mention is made of the discount rate in the mere computation. However, the second statement is false. In order to *apply* the IRR, you must compare the IRR with the discount rate. Thus, the discount rate is needed to make a decision under either the NPV or the IRR approach.

**CONCEPT QUESTIONS ?**

- What is the difference between independent projects and mutually exclusive projects?
- What are two problems with the IRR approach that apply to both independent and mutually exclusive projects?
- What is the MIRR?
- What are two additional problems applying only to mutually exclusive projects?

## 7.7    THE PROFITABILITY INDEX

Another method that is used to evaluate projects is called the **profitability index** (PI). It is the ratio of the present value of the future expected cash flows *after* initial investment to the amount of the initial investment. The PI can be represented as

$$PI = \frac{\text{PV of cash flows after the initial investment}}{\text{Initial investment}}$$

EXAMPLE **7.5**

Hiram Finnegan Inc. applies a 12 percent cost of capital to two investment opportunities.

| | Cash flow (in $ millions) | | | Present value at 12% of cash flows after the initial investment (in $ millions) | Profitability index | Net present value at 12% (in $ millions) |
|---|---|---|---|---|---|---|
| Project | $C_0$ | $C_1$ | $C_2$ | | | |
| 1 | −20 | 70 | 10 | 70.5 | 3.53 | 50.5 |
| 2 | −10 | 15 | 40 | 45.3 | 4.53 | 35.3 |

For example, the PI is calculated for project 1 as follows. The present value of the cash flows *after* the initial investment is

$$\$70.5 = \frac{\$70}{1.12} + \frac{\$10}{(1.12)^2} \tag{7.9}$$

The PI is calculated by dividing the result of equation (7.9) by the initial investment of $20.[14] This yields

$$3.53 = \frac{\$70.5}{\$20}$$

We consider three possibilities:

1. *Independent projects.* We first assume that we have two independent projects. According to the NPV criterion, both projects should be accepted since NPV is positive in each case. The NPV is positive whenever the PI is greater than 1. Thus, the *PI decision rule* is as follows:

   Accept an independent project if PI > 1.
   Reject if PI < 1.

2. *Mutually exclusive projects.* Let us assume that you can now only accept one project. NPV analysis says accept project 1 because this project has the bigger NPV. Because project 2 has the higher PI, the PI leads to the wrong selection.

   The problem with the PI for mutually exclusive projects is the same as the scale problem with the IRR that we mentioned earlier. Project 2 is smaller than project 1. Because the PI is a ratio, this index misses the fact that project 1 has a larger investment than project 2 has. Thus, like the IRR, the PI ignores differences of scale for mutually exclusive projects.

   However, as with the IRR, the flaw with the PI approach can be corrected using incremental analysis. We write the incremental cash flows after subtracting project 2 from project 1 as follows:

| | Cash flow (in $ millions) | | | Present value at 12% of cash flows after the initial investment (in $ millions) | Profitability index | Net present value at 12% (in $ millions) |
|---|---|---|---|---|---|---|
| Project | $C_0$ | $C_1$ | $C_2$ | | | |
| 1 − 2 | −10 | 55 | −30 | 25.2 | 2.52 | 15.2 |

Because the PI on the incremental cash flows is greater than 1.0, we should choose the bigger project, that is, project 1. This is the same decision we get with the NPV approach.

3. *Capital rationing.* The two cases above implicitly assumed that the firm could always attract enough capital to make any profitable investments. Now we consider the case when a firm does not have enough capital to fund all positive NPV projects. This is the case of **capital rationing**.

Imagine that the firm has a third project, as well as the first two. Project 3 has the following cash flows:

| | Cash flow (in $ millions) | | | Present value at 12% of cash flows after the initial investment ($ in millions) | Profitability index | Net present value at 12% (in $ millions) |
|---|---|---|---|---|---|---|
| Project | $C_0$ | $C_1$ | $C_2$ | | | |
| 3 | −10 | 5 | 60 | 52.3 | 5.23 | 42.3 |

---

[14] For a "borrowing" type of investment, the initial cash flow is an inflow rather than an outflow. In this case, we restate the PI as the present value of the inflows divided by the present value of the outflows.

Further, imagine that the projects of Hiram Finnegan Inc. are independent, but the firm has only $20 million to invest. Because project 1 has an initial investment of $20 million, the firm cannot select both this project and another one. Conversely, because projects 2 and 3 have initial investments of $10 million each, both these projects can be chosen. In other words, the cash constraint forces the firm to choose either project 1 or projects 2 and 3.

What should the firm do? Individually, projects 2 and 3 have lower NPVs than project 1 has. However, when the NPVs of projects 2 and 3 are added, they are more than the NPV of project 1. Thus, common sense dictates that projects 2 and 3 will be accepted.

What does our conclusion have to say about the NPV rule or the PI rule? In the case of limited funds, we cannot rank projects according to their NPVs. Instead, we should rank them according to the ratio of present value to initial investment. This is the PI rule. Both project 2 and project 3 have higher PI ratios than does project 1. Thus, they should be ranked ahead of project 1 when capital is rationed.

Our approach to PI ranking under capital rationing worked because the initial outflows on the two higher-ranked projects exactly used up the budget of $20 million. If some funds were left over, the PI ranking method could break down. In this case, the solution would be to consider all feasible combinations of projects within the budget and to choose the combination with the highest total NPV.

The usefulness of the PI under capital rationing can be explained in terms of the expression "bang for the buck." In capital budgeting, the PI measures the bang (the dollar return) for the buck invested. Hence, it is useful for capital rationing.

It should be noted that the PI does not work if funds are also limited beyond the initial time period. For example, if heavy cash outflows elsewhere in the firm were to occur at date 1, project 3 might need to be rejected. In other words, the PI cannot handle capital rationing over multiple time periods.

**CONCEPT QUESTIONS**

- How does one calculate a project's PI?
- How is the PI applied to independent projects, mutually exclusive projects, and situations of capital rationing?

# 7.8  THE PRACTICE OF CAPITAL BUDGETING

So far, this chapter has asked the question, which capital budgeting methods should companies be using? An equally important question is: which methods *are* companies using? Table 7.4 goes a long way toward answering this question. As can be seen from the table, approximately three-quarters of Canadian companies use the NPV method and nearly 70 percent use the IRR method. This is not surprising, given the theoretical advantages of these approaches. Nearly 70 percent of these companies use the payback method, a rather surprising result given the conceptual problems with this approach. And while discounted payback represents a theoretical improvement over regular payback, the usage here is far less. Perhaps companies are attracted to the user-friendly nature of payback. In addition, the flaws of this approach, as mentioned in the current chapter, may be relatively easy to correct. For example, while the payback method ignores all cash flows after the payback period, an alert manager can make ad hoc adjustments for a project with backloaded cash flows.

One might expect the capital budgeting methods of large firms to be more sophisticated than the methods of small firms. After all, large firms have the financial resources to hire more sophisticated employees. Table 7.5 provides some support for this idea. Here, firms indicate frequency of use of the various capital budgeting methods on a scale of 0 (never) to 4 (always). Both the IRR and payback period methods are used more frequently in large firms than in small firms, while the discounted payback method is used more often by small firms than large. Conversely, large and small firms seem to employ the NPV method about equally.

TABLE 7.4

**Capital Budgeting Techniques Used by Canadian Firms**

|  | % Always or almost always |
|---|---|
| Net present value | 74.6% |
| Internal rate of return | 68.4 |
| Payback period | 67.2 |
| Average accounting return | 39.7 |
| Discounted payback | 24.8 |
| Profitability index | 11.2 |
| Modified internal rate of return | 12.0 |

Source: Table 3 from H. K. Baker, S. Dutta, and S. Saadi, "Corporate Finance Practices in Canada: Where Do We Stand?" *Multinational Finance Journal* 15 (3–4) (2011), p. 157.

TABLE 7.5

**Frequency of Use of Various Capital Budgeting Methods for Canadian Firms**

|  | Large firms | Small firms |
|---|---|---|
| Net present value | 2.92 | 2.95 |
| Internal rate of return | 3.40 | 2.52 |
| Payback period | 3.04 | 2.73 |
| Average accounting return | 2.04 | 1.67 |
| Discounted payback | 0.61 | 1.34 |
| Profitability index | 0.32 | 0.60 |
| Modified internal rate of return | 0.68 | 0.35 |

Firms indicate frequency of use on a scale from 0 (never) to 4 (always). Numbers in table are averages across respondents.

Source: MULTINATIONAL FINANCE JOURNAL by Multinational Finance Society; Rutgers University—Camden School of Business. Reproduced with permission of RUTGERS UNIVERSITY, SCHOOL OF BUSINESS in the format Educational/Instructional Program via Copyright Clearance Center.

The use of quantitative techniques in capital budgeting varies with the industry. As one would imagine, firms that are better able to estimate cash flows precisely are more likely to use NPV. For example, estimation of cash flow in certain aspects of the oil business is quite feasible. Because of this, energy-related firms were among the first to use NPV analysis. Conversely, the flows in the movie business are very hard to project. The grosses of great hits like *The Dark Knight, Frozen, Marvel's The Avengers, Pirates of the Caribbean*, and *Avatar* were far, far greater than anyone imagined. The big failures, like *Green Lantern* and *47 Ronin*, were unexpected as well. Consequently, NPV analysis is frowned upon in the movie business.

Non–cash flow factors may occasionally play a role in capital budgeting decisions. Ego is one example of such a factor. Building extremely tall skyscrapers is usually not as much about economics and practicality as it is about prestige, making a bold statement, and acquiring bragging rights.[15] Another example of a non–cash flow factor is over-optimism when entering the restaurant industry. This initial enthusiasm can be an important factor in taking the plunge into a venture that may not look all that great on paper.

---

[15] *National Post*, Monday, July 23, 2001, pp. A1-2.

## 7.9

# SUMMARY AND CONCLUSIONS

1. In this chapter we covered different investment decision rules. We evaluate the most popular alternatives to the net present value (NPV): the payback period, the average accounting return (AAR), the internal rate of return (IRR), and the profitability index (PI). In doing so, we learned more about the NPV.

2. While we found that the alternatives have some redeeming qualities, when all is said and done, they are not the NPV rule; for those of us in finance, that makes them decidedly second rate.

3. Of the competitors to NPV, IRR must be ranked above either payback or AAR. In fact, IRR always reaches the same decision as NPV in the normal case where the initial outflows of an independent investment project are only followed by a series of inflows.

4. We classified the flaws of IRR into two types. First, we considered the general case applying to both independent and mutually exclusive projects. There appeared to be two problems here.

   a. Some projects have cash inflows followed by one or more outflows. The IRR rule is inverted here: one should accept when the IRR is *less than* the discount rate.

   b. Some projects have a number of changes of sign in their cash flows. Here, there are likely to be multiple IRRs. The practitioner must use either NPV or modified IRR (MIRR) here.

5. Next, we considered the specific problems with the IRR for mutually exclusive projects. We showed that due to differences in either size or timing, the project with the highest IRR need not have the highest NPV. Hence, the IRR rule should not be applied. (Of course, NPV can still be applied.)

   However, we then calculated incremental cash flows. For ease of calculation, we suggested subtracting the cash flows of the smaller project from the cash flows of the larger project. In that way, the incremental initial cash flow is negative.

   One can correctly pick the better of two mutually exclusive projects in three other ways:

   a. Choose the project with the higher NPV.

   b. If the incremental IRR is greater than the discount rate, choose the bigger project.

   c. If the incremental NPV is positive, choose the bigger project.

6. We describe capital rationing as a case where funds are limited to a fixed dollar amount. With capital rationing the PI can be a useful method. Of course, a manager can never go wrong by maximizing the total NPV of all company projects.

**KEY TERMS**

| | | |
|---|---|---|
| Average accounting return (AAR)   196 | Incremental IRR   207 | Mutually exclusive investments   201 |
| Basic IRR rule   200 | Independent project   201 | Payback period rule   193 |
| Capital rationing   212 | Internal rate of return (IRR)   199 | Profitability index (PI)   211 |
| Discounted payback period rule   196 | Modified IRR (MIRR)   205 | Value additivity   192 |

**QUESTIONS & PROBLEMS**

**Calculating Payback Period and Net Present Value**

7.1  Fuji Software Inc. has the following mutually exclusive projects.

| Year | Project *A* | Project *B* |
|---|---|---|
| 0 | −$15,000 | −$18,000 |
| 1 | 9,500 | 10,500 |
| 2 | 6,000 | 7,000 |
| 3 | 2,400 | 6,000 |

*a.* Suppose Fuji's payback period cut-off is two years. Which of these two projects should be chosen?

*b.* Suppose Fuji uses the NPV rule to rank these two projects. Which project should be chosen if the appropriate discount rate is 15 percent?

**Calculating Payback**

7.2 An investment project provides cash inflows of $970 per year for eight years. What is the project payback period if the initial cost is $4,100? $6,200? $8,000?

**Calculating Discounted Payback**

7.3 An investment project has annual cash inflows of $6,000, $6,500, $7,000, and $8,000, and a discount rate of 14 percent. What is the discounted payback period for these cash flows if the initial cost is $8,000? $13,000? $18,000?

7.4 An investment project costs $15,000 and has annual cash flows of $3,800 for six years. What is the discounted payback period if the discount rate is 0 percent? 10 percent? 15 percent?

**Calculating Internal Rate of Return**

7.5 Teddy Bear Planet Inc. has a project with the following cash flows:

| Year | Cash flow ($) |
|---|---|
| 0 | −$11,000 |
| 1 | 5,500 |
| 2 | 4,000 |
| 3 | 3,000 |

The company evaluates all projects by applying the IRR rule. If the appropriate interest rate is 8 percent, should the company accept the project?

7.6 Compute the IRR for the cash flows of the following two projects:

| | Cash flow ($) | |
|---|---|---|
| Year | Project *A* | Project *B* |
| 0 | −$5,300 | −$2,900 |
| 1 | 2,000 | 1,100 |
| 2 | 2,800 | 1,800 |
| 3 | 1,600 | 1,200 |

**Calculating Profitability Index**

7.7 Bill plans to open a self-serve pet grooming centre in a storefront. The grooming equipment will cost $190,000, to be paid immediately. Bill expects after-tax cash inflows of $65,000 annually for seven years, after which he plans to scrap the equipment and retire to the beaches of Nevis. The first cash inflow occurs at the end of the first year. Assume that the required return is 15 percent. What is the project's PI? Should it be accepted?

7.8 Suppose the following two independent investment opportunities are available to Greenplain Inc. The appropriate discount rate is 10 percent.

| Year | Project Alpha | Project Beta |
|---|---|---|
| 0 | −$2,300 | −$3,900 |
| 1 | 1,200 | 800 |
| 2 | 1,100 | 2,300 |
| 3 | 900 | 2,900 |

*a.* Compute the PI for each of the two projects.

*b.* Which project(s) should Greenplain accept based on the PI rule?

### Cash Flow Intuition

7.9   A project has an initial cost of $I$, has a required return of $R$, and pays $C$ annually for $N$ years.

   a. Find $C$ in terms of $I$, $R$, and $N$ such that the project has a payback period just equal to its life.
   b. Find $C$ in terms of $I$, $N$, and $R$ such that this is a profitable project according to the NPV decision rule.
   c. Find $C$ in terms of $I$, $N$, and $R$ such that the project has a benefit–cost ratio of 2.

### Problems with Internal Rate of Return

7.10  Suppose you are offered $7,000 today but must make the following payments:

| Year | Cash flow |
|------|-----------|
| 0 | $7,000 |
| 1 | −3,700 |
| 2 | −2,400 |
| 3 | −1,500 |
| 4 | −1,200 |

   a. What is the IRR of this offer?
   b. If the appropriate discount rate is 10 percent, should you accept this offer?
   c. If the appropriate discount rate is 20 percent, should you accept this offer?
   d. What is the NPV of the offer if the appropriate discount rate is 10 percent? 20 percent?
   e. Are the decisions under the NPV rule in (d) consistent with those of the IRR rule?

### Net Present Value versus Internal Rate of Return

7.11  Consider the following cash flows on two mutually exclusive projects for the B.C. Recreation Corporation (BCRC). Both projects require an annual return of 14 percent.

| Year | Deepwater fishing | New submarine ride |
|------|-------------------|--------------------|
| 0 | −$750,000 | −$2,100,000 |
| 1 | 310,000 | 1,200,000 |
| 2 | 430,000 | 760,000 |
| 3 | 330,000 | 850,000 |

   As a financial analyst for BCRC, you are asked to answer the following questions:

   a. If your decision rule is to accept the project with the greater IRR, which project should you choose?
   b. Because you are fully aware of the IRR rule's scale problem, you calculate the incremental IRR for the cash flows. Based on your computation, which project should you choose?
   c. To be prudent, you compute the NPV for both projects. Which project should you choose? Is it consistent with the incremental IRR rule?

### Problems with Profitability Index

7.12  The Robb Computer Corporation is trying to choose between the following two mutually exclusive design projects:

| Year | Cash flow (I) | Cash flow (II) |
|------|---------------|----------------|
| 0 | −$30,000 | −$12,000 |
| 1 | 18,000 | 7,500 |
| 2 | 18,000 | 7,500 |
| 3 | 18,000 | 7,500 |

a. If the required return is 10 percent and Robb Computer applies the PI decision rule, which project should the firm accept?

b. If the company applies the NPV decision rule, which project should it take?

c. Explain why your answers in (a) and (b) are different.

**Problems with Internal Rate of Return**

7.13  Cutler Petroleum Inc. is trying to evaluate a generation project with the following cash flows:

| Year | Cash flow |
|------|-----------|
| 0 | −$32,000,000 |
| 1 | 57,000,000 |
| 2 | −9,000,000 |

a. If the company requires a 10 percent return on its investments, should it accept this project? Why?

b. Compute the IRR for this project. How many IRRs are there? If you apply the IRR decision rule, should you accept the project or not? What's going on here?

**Comparing Investment Criteria**

7.14  Mario Brothers, a game manufacturer, has a new idea for an adventure game. It can market the game either as a traditional board game or as an interactive smartphone app, but not both. Consider the following cash flows of the two mutually exclusive projects for Mario Brothers. Assume the discount rate for Mario Brothers is 10 percent:

| Year | Board game | App |
|------|-----------|-----|
| 0 | −$600 | −$1,900 |
| 1 | 700 | 1,400 |
| 2 | 150 | 900 |
| 3 | 100 | 400 |

a. Based on the payback period rule, which project should be chosen?

b. Based on the NPV, which project should be chosen?

c. Based on the IRR, which project should be chosen?

d. Based on the incremental IRR, which project should be chosen?

**Profitability Index versus Net Present Value**

7.15  Hanmi Group, a consumer electronics conglomerate, is reviewing its annual budget in wireless technology. It is considering investments in three different technologies to develop wireless communication devices. Consider the following cash flows of the three independent projects for Hanmi. Assume the discount rate for Hanmi is 10 percent. Further, Hanmi Group has only $20 million to invest in new projects this year:

| Year | Cash flow (in $ millions) | | |
|------|------|------|------|
| | CDMA | G4 | Wi-Fi |
| 0 | −$8 | −$12 | −$20 |
| 1 | 11 | 10 | 18 |
| 2 | 7.5 | 25 | 32 |
| 3 | 2.5 | 20 | 20 |

a. Based on the PI decision rule, rank these investments.

b. Based on the NPV, rank these investments.

c. Based on your findings in (a) and (b), what would you recommend to the CEO of Hanmi Group and why?

**Comparing Investment Criteria**

7.16  Consider the following cash flows of two mutually exclusive projects for AZ-Motorcars. Assume the discount rate for AZ-Motorcars is 10 percent:

| Year | AZM Mini-SUV | AZF Full-SUV |
|---|---|---|
| 0 | −$450,000 | −$800,000 |
| 1 | 320,000 | 350,000 |
| 2 | 180,000 | 420,000 |
| 3 | 150,000 | 290,000 |

a. Based on the payback period, which project should be accepted?
b. Based on the NPV, which project should be accepted?
c. Based on the IRR, which project should be accepted?
d. Based on this analysis, is incremental IRR analysis necessary? If yes, conduct the analysis.

7.17  The treasurer of Amaro Canned Fruits Inc. has projected the cash flows of projects A, B, and C as follows:

| Year | Project A | Project B | Project C |
|---|---|---|---|
| 0 | −$150,000 | −$300,000 | −$150,000 |
| 1 | 110,000 | 200,000 | 120,000 |
| 2 | 110,000 | 200,000 | 90,000 |

Suppose the relevant discount rate is 12 percent a year.

a. Compute the PI for each of the three projects.
b. Compute the NPV for each of the three projects.
c. Suppose these three projects are independent. Which project(s) should Amaro accept based on the PI rule?
d. Suppose these three projects are mutually exclusive. Which project(s) should Amaro accept based on the PI rule?
e. Suppose Amaro's budget for these projects is $450,000. The projects are not divisible. Which project(s) should Amaro accept?

7.18  Consider the following cash flows of two mutually exclusive projects for Scotia Rubber Company. Assume the discount rate for Scotia Rubber Company is 10 percent:

| Year | Dry Prepreg | Solvent Prepreg |
|---|---|---|
| 0 | −$1,700,000 | −$750,000 |
| 1 | 1,100,000 | 375,000 |
| 2 | 900,000 | 600,000 |
| 3 | 750,000 | 390,000 |

a. Based on the payback period, which project should be taken?
b. Based on the NPV, which project should be taken?
c. Based on the IRR, which project should be taken?
d. Based on this analysis, is incremental IRR analysis necessary? If yes, conduct the analysis.

**Comparing Investment Criteria**

7.19  Consider two mutually exclusive new product launch projects that Nagano Golf is considering. Assume that the discount rate for Nagano Golf is 15 percent.

Project A. Nagano NP-30. Professional clubs that will take an initial investment of $550,000 at time 0. Next five years (years 1–5) of sales will generate a consistent cash flow of $185,000 per year. Introduction of new product at year 6 will terminate further cash flows from this project.

Project B. Nagano NX-20. High-end amateur clubs that will take an initial investment of $350,000 at time 0. Cash flow at year 1 is $100,000. In each subsequent year, cash flow will grow at 10 percent per year. Introduction of new product at year 6 will terminate further cash flows from this project.

| Year | NP-30 | NX-20 |
|------|-------|-------|
| 0 | −$550,000 | −$350,000 |
| 1 | 185,000 | 100,000 |
| 2 | 185,000 | 110,000 |
| 3 | 185,000 | 121,000 |
| 4 | 185,000 | 133,100 |
| 5 | 185,000 | 146,410 |

Complete the following table:

| | NP-30 | NX-20 | Implications |
|------|-------|-------|--------------|
| Net present value | | | |
| Internal rate of return | | | |
| Incremental internal rate of return | | | |
| Profitability index | | | |

7.20 You are a senior manager at Poeing Aircraft and have been authorized to spend up to $500,000 for projects. The three projects you are considering have the following characteristics:

Project A. Initial investment of $295,000. Cash flow of $190,000 at year 1 and $170,000 at year 2. This is a plant expansion project, where the required rate of return is 12 percent.

Project B. Initial investment of $405,000. Cash flow of $270,000 at year 1 and $240,000 at year 2. This is a new product development project, where the required rate of return is 24 percent.

Project C. Initial investment of $240,000. Cash flow of $160,000 at year 1 and $190,000 at year 2. This is a market expansion project, where the required rate of return is 17 percent.

Assume the corporate discount rate is 12 percent.

Offer your recommendations, backed by your analysis:

| | A | B | C | Implications |
|------|---|---|---|--------------|
| Payback | | | | |
| Internal rate of return | | | | |
| Profitability index | | | | |
| Net present value | | | | |

### Payback and Net Present Value

7.21 An investment under consideration has a payback of six years and a cost of $434,000. If the required return is 12 percent, what is the worst-case NPV? Best-case NPV? Explain. Assume the cash flows are conventional.

### Multiple Internal Rates of Return

7.22 This problem is useful for testing the ability of financial calculators and computer software. Consider the following cash flows. How many different IRRs are there? (*Hint:* Search between 20 percent and 70 percent.) When should we take this project?

| Year | Cash flow |
|------|-----------|
| 0 | −$ 1,008 |
| 1 | 5,724 |
| 2 | −12,140 |
| 3 | 11,400 |
| 4 | −4,000 |

### Net Present Value Valuation

7.23  The Yurdone Corp. wants to set up a private cemetery business. According to the CFO, Barry M. Deep, business is looking up. As a result, the cemetery project will provide a net cash inflow of $115,000 for the firm during the first year, and the cash flows are projected to grow at a rate of 6 percent per year, forever. The project requires an initial investment of $1,400,000.

a. If Yurdone requires a 13 percent return on such undertakings, should the cemetery business be started?

b. The company is somewhat unsure about the assumption of a 6 percent growth rate in its cash flows. At what constant growth rate would the company just break even if it still required a 13 percent return on investment?

### Calculating Internal Rate of Return

7.24  The Aldo Mining Corporation is set to open a gold mine near Edmonton. According to the treasurer, Monty Goldstein, "This is a golden opportunity." The mine will cost $2,400,000 to open and will have an economic life of 11 years. It will generate a cash inflow of $345,000 at the end of the first year, and the cash inflows are projected to grow at 8 percent per year for the next 10 years. After 11 years, the mine will be abandoned. Abandonment costs will be $400,000 at the end of year 11.

a. What is the IRR for the gold mine?

b. The Aldo Mining Corporation requires a 10 percent return on such undertakings. Should the mine be opened?

### Net Present Value and Internal Rate of Return

7.25  Anderson International Ltd. is evaluating a project in Quebec. The project will create the following cash flows:

| Year | Cash flow |
| --- | --- |
| 0 | −$950,000 |
| 1 | 285,000 |
| 2 | 345,000 |
| 3 | 415,000 |
| 4 | 255,000 |

All cash flows will occur in Quebec and are expressed in dollars. In an attempt to improve its economy, the Quebec government has declared that all cash flows created by a foreign company are "blocked" and must be reinvested with the government for one year. The reinvestment rate for these funds is 4 percent. If Anderson uses an 11 percent required return on this project, what are the NPV and IRR of the project? Is the IRR you calculated the MIRR of the project? Why or why not?

### Calculating Internal Rate of Return

7.26  Consider two streams of cash flows, A and B. Stream A's first cash flow is $9,000 and is received three years from today. Future cash flows in stream A grow by 5 percent in perpetuity. Stream B's first cash flow is −$11,000, occurs two years from today, and will continue in perpetuity. Assume that the appropriate discount rate is 12 percent.

a. What is the present value of each stream?

b. Suppose that the two streams are combined into one project, called C. What is the IRR of project C?

c. What is the correct IRR rule for project C?

### Calculating Incremental Cash Flows

7.27  Darin Clay, the CFO of MakeMoney.com, has to decide between the following two projects:

| Year | Project Million | Project Billion |
|------|-----------------|-----------------|
| 0 | −$1,300 | −$I_0 |
| 1 | $I_0 + 260$ | $I_0 + 500$ |
| 2 | 1,060 | 1,300 |
| 3 | 1,300 | 1,700 |

The expected rate of return for either of the two projects is 13 percent. What is the range of initial investment ($I_0$) for which Project Billion is more financially attractive than Project Million?

**Problems with Internal Rate of Return**

7.28  McKeekin Corp. has a project with the following cash flows:

| Year | Cash flow |
|------|-----------|
| 0 | $20,000 |
| 1 | −26,000 |
| 2 | 13,000 |

What is the IRR of the project? What is happening here?

---

**MINICASE**

## Bullock Gold Mining

Serena Bullock, the owner of Bullock Gold Mining, is evaluating a new gold mine in Yellowknife. Dan Dority, the company's geologist, has just finished his analysis of the mine site. He has estimated that the mine would be productive for eight years, after which the gold would be completely mined. Dan has taken an estimate of the gold deposits to Alma Garrett, the company's chief financial officer. Alma has been asked by Serena to perform an analysis of the new mine and present her recommendation on whether the company should open the new mine.

Alma has used the estimates provided by Dan to determine the revenues that could be expected from the mine. She has also projected the expense of opening the mine and the annual operating expenses. If the company opens the mine, it will cost $750 million today and it will have a cash outflow of $75 million nine years from today in costs associated with closing the mine and reclaiming the area surrounding it. The expected cash flows each year from the mine are shown in the following table. Bullock Mining has a 12 percent required return on all of its gold mines:

| Year | Cash Flow |
|------|-----------|
| 0 | −$750,000,000 |
| 1 | 130,000,000 |
| 2 | 180,000,000 |
| 3 | 190,000,000 |
| 4 | 245,000,000 |
| 5 | 205,000,000 |
| 6 | 155,000,000 |
| 7 | 135,000,000 |
| 8 | 95,000,000 |
| 9 | −75,000,000 |

1. Construct a spreadsheet to calculate the payback period, IRR, MIRR, and NPV of the proposed mine. For MIRR, assume that the reinvestment rate and the finance rate are the same.

2. Based on your analysis, should the company open the mine?

3. Bonus question: Most spreadsheets do not have a built-in formula to calculate the payback period. Write a VBA script that calculates the payback period for a project.

---

**connect**     **LEARNSMART**     **SMARTBOOK**

**For more information on the resources available from McGraw-Hill Ryerson, go to www.mheducation.ca/he/solutions.**

# Net Present Value and Capital Budgeting

EXECUTIVE SUMMARY

In January 2014, TransCanada Corporation had plans to invest $38 billion in commercially secured projects to expand its natural gas and oil pipelines and other energy infrastructure. By almost doubling its assets, the company expected to increase earnings before interest and taxes (EBIT) to $9.5 billion by 2020. The decision on whether or not to undertake such an expansion is an example of a capital budgeting decision. TransCanada would not have planned such an enormous investment if it felt that the return from it would be less than the initial costs.

Previous chapters discussed the basics of capital budgeting and the net present value (NPV) approach. We now want to move beyond these basics into the real-world application of these techniques. We want to show you how to use discounted cash flow (DCF) analysis and NPV in capital budgeting decisions.

In this chapter, we show how to identify the relevant cash flows of a project, including initial investment outflows, requirements for working capital, and operating cash flows (OCFs). We look at the effects of depreciation and taxes. We examine the impact of inflation on interest rates and on a project's discount rate, and we show why inflation must be handled consistently in NPV analysis.

## 8.1 INCREMENTAL CASH FLOWS

### Cash Flows—Not Accounting Income

You may not have thought about it, but there is a big difference between corporate finance courses and financial accounting courses. Techniques in corporate finance generally use cash flows, whereas financial accounting generally stresses income or earnings numbers. Certainly, our text has followed this tradition since our NPV techniques discounted cash flows, not earnings. When considering a single project, we discounted the cash flows that the firm receives from the project. When valuing the firm as a whole, we discounted dividends, not earnings, because dividends are the cash flows that an investor receives.

There are many differences between earnings and cash flows. For example, consider a firm buying a building for $100,000 today. The entire $100,000 is an immediate cash outflow. However, assuming straight-line depreciation over 20 years, only $5,000 (or $100,000/20) is considered an accounting expense in the current year.[1] Current earnings are thereby reduced by only $5,000. The remaining $95,000 is expensed over the following 19 years.

Because the seller of the property demands immediate payment, the cost of the project to the firm at date 0 is $100,000. Thus, the full $100,000 figure should be viewed as an immediate outflow for capital budgeting.

---

[1] Recall from Chapter 2 that we use the terms *amortization* and *depreciation* interchangeably throughout this text.

In addition, it is not enough to use cash flows. In calculating the NPV of a project, only cash flows that are *incremental* to the project should be used. **Incremental cash flows** are the changes in the firm's cash flows that occur as a direct consequence of accepting the project. That is, we are interested in the difference between the cash flows of the firm with and without the project.

The use of incremental cash flows sounds easy enough, but pitfalls abound in the real world. In this section we describe how to avoid some of the pitfalls of determining incremental cash flows.

## Sunk Costs

A **sunk cost** is a cost that has already occurred. Because sunk costs are in the past, they cannot be changed by the decision to accept or reject the project. Just as we let bygones be bygones, we should ignore such costs. Sunk costs are not incremental cash outflows.

**EXAMPLE 8.1**

The General Milk Company is currently evaluating the NPV of establishing a line of chocolate milk. As part of the evaluation, the company had paid a consulting firm $100,000 to perform a test marketing analysis. The expenditure was made last year. Is this cost relevant for the capital budgeting decision now confronting the management of General Milk Company?

The answer is no. The $100,000 is not recoverable, so the $100,000 expenditure is a sunk cost, or "spilled milk." Of course, the decision to spend $100,000 for a marketing analysis was a capital budgeting decision itself and was perfectly relevant *before* it was sunk. Our point is that once the company incurred the expense, the cost became irrelevant for any future decision.

## Opportunity Costs

Your firm may have an asset that it is considering selling, leasing, or employing elsewhere in the business. If the asset is used in a new project, potential revenues from alternative uses are lost. These lost revenues can meaningfully be viewed as costs. They are called **opportunity costs** because, by taking the project, the firm forgoes other opportunities for using the assets.

**EXAMPLE 8.2**

Suppose the Pacific Trading Company has an empty warehouse in Vancouver that can be used to store a new line of electronic pinball machines. The company hopes to market the machines to affluent West Coast consumers. Should the cost of the warehouse and land be included in the costs associated with introducing a new line of electronic pinball machines?

The answer is yes. The use of a warehouse is not free; it has an opportunity cost. The cost is the cash that could be raised by the company if the decision to market the electronic pinball machines were rejected and the warehouse and land were put to some other use (or sold). If so, the NPV of the alternative uses becomes an opportunity cost of the decision to sell electronic pinball machines.

## Side Effects

Another difficulty in determining incremental cash flows comes from the side effects of the proposed project on other parts of the firm. A side effect is classified as either **erosion** or **synergy**. Erosion occurs when a new product reduces the sales and, hence, the cash flows of existing products. Synergy occurs when a new project increases the cash flows of existing projects.

### EXAMPLE 8.3

Suppose the Innovative Motors Corporation (IMC) is determining the NPV of a new convertible sports car. Some of the customers who would purchase the car are owners of IMC's compact sedan. Are all sales and profits from the new convertible sports car incremental?

The answer is no, because some of the cash flow represents transfers from other elements of IMC's product line. This is erosion, which must be included in the NPV calculation. Without taking erosion into account, IMC might erroneously calculate the NPV of the sports car to be, say, $100 million. If half the customers are transfers from the sedan and lost sedan sales have an NPV of −$150 million, the true NPV is −$50 million ($100 million − $150 million).

IMC is also contemplating forming a racing team. The team is forecast to lose money for the foreseeable future, with perhaps the best projection showing an NPV of −$35 million for the operation. However, IMC's managers are aware that the team will likely generate great publicity for all of IMC's products. A consultant estimates that the increase in cash flows elsewhere in the firm has a present value (PV) of $65 million. Assuming that the consultant's estimates of synergy are trustworthy, the NPV of the team is $30 million ($65 million − $35 million). The managers should form the team.

## Allocated Costs

Frequently a particular expenditure benefits a number of projects. Accountants allocate this cost across the different projects when determining income. However, for capital budgeting purposes, this **allocated cost** should be viewed as a cash outflow of a project only if it is an incremental cost of the project.

### EXAMPLE 8.4

The Voetmann Consulting Corp. devotes one wing of its suite of offices to a library requiring a cash outflow of $100,000 per a year in upkeep. A proposed capital budgeting project is expected to generate revenue equal to 5 percent of the firm's overall sales. An executive at the firm, H. Sears, argues that $5,000 (5% × 100,000) should be viewed as the proposed project's share of the library's costs. Is this appropriate for capital budgeting?

The answer is no. One must ask the question, what is the difference between the cash flows of the entire firm with the project and the cash flows of the entire firm without the project? The firm will spend $100,000 on library upkeep whether or not the proposed project is accepted. Since acceptance of the proposed project does not affect this cash flow, the cash flow should be ignored when calculating the NPV of the project.

 **CONCEPT QUESTIONS**

- What are the four difficulties in determining incremental cash flows?
- Define sunk costs, opportunity costs, side effects, and allocated costs.

## 8.2     THE MAJESTIC MULCH AND COMPOST COMPANY: AN EXAMPLE

We next consider the example of a proposed investment in machinery and related items. Our example involves the Majestic Mulch and Compost Company (MMCC) and power mulching tools.

The MMCC, originally established 16 years ago to make composting equipment, is now a leading producer of composters. Nine years ago the company introduced "Friends of Grass," its first line of high-performance composters. The MMCC management has sought opportunities in whatever businesses seem to have some potential for cash flow. Recently, Ralph Clean, vice-president of MMCC, identified another segment of the compost market that looked promising and that he felt was not adequately served by larger manufacturers. That market was for power mulching tools, and he believed a large number of composters valued a high-performance mulcher to aid in composting. He also believed that it would be difficult for competitors to take advantage of the opportunity because of MMCC's cost advantages and because of its highly developed marketing skills.

As a result, MMCC decided to evaluate the marketing potential of power mulching tools. MMCC sent a questionnaire to consumers in three markets: Vancouver, Toronto, and Montreal. The results of the three questionnaires were much better than expected and supported the conclusion that the power mulching tools could achieve a 10 to 15 percent share of the market. Of course, some people at MMCC complained about the cost of the test marketing, which was $250,000. However, Ralph argued that it was a sunk cost and should not be included in project evaluation.

In any case, MMCC is now considering investing in a machine to produce power mulching tools. The power mulchers would be produced in a building owned by the firm and located outside Prince George, British Columbia. It is currently vacant and has no resale value due to its location. Working with his staff, Ralph is preparing an analysis of the proposed new product. He summarizes his assumptions as follows. The cost of the tool-making machine is $800,000. The machine has an estimated market value at the end of eight years of $150,000. Production by year during the eight-year life of the machine is expected to be as follows: 6,000 units, 9,000 units, 12,000 units, 13,000 units, 12,000 units, 10,000 units, 8,000 units, and 6,000 units. The price of power mulchers in the first year will be $100. The power mulching tool market is highly competitive, so Ralph believes that the price of power mulchers will increase only 2 percent per year, as compared to the anticipated general inflation rate of 5 percent. Conversely, the materials used to produce power mulchers are becoming more expensive. Because of this, variable production cash outflows are expected to grow 5 percent per year. First-year variable production costs will be $64 per unit, and fixed production costs will be $50,000 each year. The tax rate is 40 percent.

Net working capital is defined as the difference between current assets and current liabilities. Ralph finds that the firm must maintain an investment in working capital. Like any manufacturing firm, it will purchase raw materials before production and sale, giving rise to an investment in inventory. It will maintain cash as a buffer against unforeseen expenditures. Its credit sales will generate accounts receivable. Management believes that the investment in the different items of working capital totals $40,000 in year 0, stays at 15 percent of sales at the end of each year, and falls to $0 by the project's end. In other words, the investment in working capital is completely recovered by the end of the project's life.

Projections based on these assumptions and Ralph's analysis appear in Tables 8.1 through 8.4. In these tables all cash flows are assumed to occur at the *end* of the year. Because of the large amount of data in these tables, it is important to see how the tables are related. Table 8.1 shows the basic data for both investment and income. Supplementary schedules, as presented in Tables 8.2 and 8.3, help explain where the numbers in Table 8.1 come from. Our goal is to obtain projections of cash flow. The information in Table 8.1 is all that is needed to calculate the relevant cash flows, as shown in Table 8.4.

TABLE 8.1

### The Worksheet for Cash Flows of MMCC*

| | Year 0 | Year 1 | Year 2 | Year 3 | Year 4 | Year 5 | Year 6 | Year 7 | Year 8 |
|---|---|---|---|---|---|---|---|---|---|
| **I. Income** | | | | | | | | | |
| (1) Sales revenues | | $600,000 | $918,000 | $1,248,480 | $1,379,570 | $1,298,919 | $1,104,081 | $900,930 | $689,211 |
| (2) Operating costs | | 434,000 | 654,800 | 896,720 | 1,013,144 | 983,509 | 866,820 | 736,129 | 590,327 |
| (3) Capital cost allowance | | 80,000 | 144,000 | 115,200 | 92,160 | 73,728 | 58,982 | 47,186 | 37,749 |
| (4) Earnings before interest and taxes | | 86,000 | 119,200 | 236,560 | 274,266 | 241,682 | 178,278 | 117,615 | 61,136 |
| (5) Taxes | | 34,400 | 47,680 | 94,624 | 109,706 | 96,673 | 71,311 | 47,046 | 24,454 |
| (6) Net income | | 51,600 | 71,520 | 141,936 | 164,560 | 145,009 | 106,967 | 70,569 | 36,682 |
| **II. Investments** | | | | | | | | | |
| (7) Net working capital (end of year) | $40,000 | $ 90,000 | $137,700 | $187,272 | $206,936 | $194,838 | $165,612 | $135,139 | $ 0 |
| (8) Change in net working capital* | $(40,000) | $(50,000) | $(47,700) | $(49,572) | $(19,664) | $12,098 | $29,226 | $30,473 | $135,139 |
| (9) Equipment† | $(800,000) | | | | | | | | |
| (10) After-tax salvage | | | | | | | | | $150,000 |
| (11) Investment cash flow | $(840,000) | $(50,000) | $(47,700) | $(49,572) | $(19,664) | $12,098 | $29,226 | $30,473 | $285,139 |

*All cash flows occur at the end of the year.
†A negative change in net working capital or equipment represents a cash outflow for the company.

TABLE 8.2

### Operating Revenues and Costs of MMCC

| (1) Year | (2) Production | (3) Price* | (4) Sales revenues | (5) Cost per unit† | (6) Variable costs | (7) Fixed costs | (8) Operating costs |
|---|---|---|---|---|---|---|---|
| 1 | 6,000 | $100.00 | $ 600,000 | $64.00 | $384,000 | $50,000 | $ 434,000 |
| 2 | 9,000 | 102.00 | 918,000 | 67.20 | 604,800 | 50,000 | 654,800 |
| 3 | 12,000 | 104.04 | 1,248,480 | 70.56 | 846,720 | 50,000 | 896,720 |
| 4 | 13,000 | 106.12 | 1,379,570 | 74.09 | 963,144 | 50,000 | 1,013,144 |
| 5 | 12,000 | 108.24 | 1,298,919 | 77.79 | 933,509 | 50,000 | 983,509 |
| 6 | 10,000 | 110.41 | 1,104,081 | 81.68 | 816,820 | 50,000 | 866,820 |
| 7 | 8,000 | 112.62 | 900,930 | 85.77 | 686,129 | 50,000 | 736,129 |
| 8 | 6,000 | 114.87 | 689,211 | 90.05 | 540,327 | 50,000 | 590,327 |

*Prices rise 2 percent per year.
†Unit costs rise 5 percent per year.

TABLE 8.3

### Annual Capital Cost Allowance, Power Mulcher Project (Class 8, 20 percent rate*)

| Year | Beginning undepreciated capital cost | Capital cost allowance | Ending undepreciated capital cost |
|------|------|------|------|
| 1 | $400,000 | $ 80,000 | $320,000 |
| 2 | 720,000 | 144,000 | 576,000 |
| 3 | 576,000 | 115,200 | 460,800 |
| 4 | 460,800 | 92,160 | 368,640 |
| 5 | 368,640 | 73,728 | 294,912 |
| 6 | 294,912 | 58,982 | 235,930 |
| 7 | 235,930 | 47,186 | 188,744 |
| 8 | 188,744 | 37,749 | 150,995 |

*See Table 8A.1 in Appendix 8A.

TABLE 8.4

### Incremental Cash Flows for MMCC

| | Year 0 | Year 1 | Year 2 | Year 3 | Year 4 | Year 5 | Year 6 | Year 7 | Year 8 |
|---|---|---|---|---|---|---|---|---|---|
| (1) Sales revenues [line 1, Table 8.1] | | $600,000 | $918,000 | $1,248,480 | $1,379,570 | $1,298,919 | $1,104,081 | $900,930 | $689,211 |
| (2) Operating costs [line 2, Table 8.1] | | 434,000 | 654,800 | 896,720 | 1,013,144 | 983,509 | 866,820 | 736,129 | 590,327 |
| (3) Taxes [line 5, Table 8.1] | | 34,400 | 47,680 | 94,624 | 109,707 | 96,673 | 71,311 | 47,046 | 24,454 |
| (4) Operating cash flow [(1) − (2) − (3)] | | 131,600 | 215,520 | 257,136 | 256,720 | 218,737 | 165,949 | 117,755 | 74,430 |
| (5) Investment cash flow [line 11, Table 8.1] | $(840,000) | (50,000) | (47,700) | (49,572) | (19,664) | 12,098 | 29,226 | 30,473 | 285,139 |
| (6) Total project cash flow [(4) + (5)] | $(840,000) | $ 81,600 | $167,820 | $ 207,564 | $ 237,056 | $230,835 | $ 195,175 | $148,228 | $359,570 |
| Net present value at 4%: $500,135 | | | | | | | | | |
| Net present value at 10%: $188,042 | | | | | | | | | |
| Net present value at 15%: $2,281 | | | | | | | | | |
| Net present value at 20%: ($137,896) | | | | | | | | | |

## An Analysis of the Project

**Investments**    The investment outflows required for the project are summarized in the bottom segment of Table 8.1. They consist of two parts:[2]

1. *The power mulching tool machine.* The purchase requires a cash outflow of $800,000 at year 0. The firm realizes a cash inflow when the machine is sold in year 8. These cash flows are shown in lines 9 and 10 of Table 8.1.

2. *The investment in working capital.* Required working capital appears in line 7. Working capital rises over the early years of the project as expansion occurs. However, all working capital is assumed to be recovered at the end, a common

---

[2] If the vacant building had a resale value, this would be included as a third part to this section. Recall from Section 8.1 the discussion of opportunity costs. A positive resale value would be a cash outflow in year 0.

assumption in capital budgeting. In other words, all inventory is sold by the end, the cash balance maintained as a buffer is liquidated, and all accounts receivable are collected. Increases in working capital in the early years must be funded by cash generated elsewhere in the firm. Hence, these increases are viewed as cash *outflows*. Conversely, decreases in working capital in the later years are viewed as cash inflows. All of these cash flows are presented in line 8. A more complete discussion of working capital is provided later in this section. The total cash flow from the above two investments is shown in line 11.

**Income, Taxes, and Operating Cash Flow**    Next, the determination of income and operating cash flow is presented in the top segment of Table 8.1. While we are ultimately interested in cash flow, not income, we need the income calculation in order to determine taxes. Lines 1 and 2 of Table 8.1 show sales revenues and operating costs, respectively. The projections in these lines are based on the sales revenues and operating costs computed in columns 4 and 8 of Table 8.2. The estimates of revenues and costs follow from assumptions made by the corporate planning staff at MMCC. In other words, the estimates critically depend on the fact that product prices are projected to increase at 2 percent per year and variable costs are projected to increase at 5 percent per year.

Capital cost allowance (CCA, depreciation for tax purposes) of the $800,000 capital investment is based on the amount allowed by the Canada Revenue Agency (CRA).[3] CCA calculations are shown in Table 8.3 and are based on a class 8, 20 percent rate. The column labelled Capital Cost Allowance is reproduced in line 3 of Table 8.1. EBIT is calculated in line 4 of Table 8.1. Taxes are provided in line 5 of this table, and net income is calculated in line 6.

**Project Cash Flow**    Project cash flow is finally determined in Table 8.4. It consists of operating cash flow and investment cash flow. Operating cash flow is determined by subtracting operating costs and taxes from sales revenues as shown in lines 1 through 4 in Table 8.4. Adding investment cash flow from line 11 in Table 8.1 gives total project cash flow on line 6 in Table 8.4.

**Net Present Value**    It is possible to calculate the NPV of the MMCC power mulcher tool project from these cash flows. As can be seen at the bottom of Table 8.4, the NPV is $188,042 if 10 percent is the appropriate discount rate and −$137,896 if 20 percent is the appropriate discount rate. If the discount rate is 15.07 percent, the project will have a zero NPV. In other words, the project's IRR is 15.07 percent. If the discount rate of the MMCC power mulcher tool project is greater than 15.07 percent, it should not be accepted because its NPV is negative.

## Which Set of Books?

It should be noted that the firm's management generally keeps two sets of books, one for the CRA (called the *tax books*) and another for its annual report (called the *shareholders' books*). The tax books follow the rules of the *Income Tax Act*. The shareholders' books follow the rules of the Canadian Institute of Chartered Accountants (CICA), the governing body in accounting. The two sets of rules differ widely in certain areas. For example, deductible expenses as calculated according to CICA rules are often different from the calculations required by the Act.

Such differences result from the different purposes of the two sets of rules. CICA rules seek to represent the accounting income of the firm according to International Financial Reporting Standards (IFRS). Tax rules govern the calculation of corporate income tax. Appendix 8A gives a synopsis of the tax rules on CCA.

---

[3] CCA rules are discussed in detail in Appendix 8A.

Which of the two sets of rules on depreciation do we want in order to create the previous tables for MMCC? Clearly, we're interested in the tax rules. Our purpose is to determine net cash flow, and tax payments are a cash outflow. The CICA regulations determine the calculation of accounting income, not cash flow.

## A Note on Net Working Capital

The investment in net working capital is an important part of any capital budgeting analysis. While we explicitly considered net working capital in line 7 (Table 8.1) as 15 percent of sales, you may be wondering where such numbers come from. An investment in net working capital arises whenever (1) raw materials and other inventory are purchased prior to the sale of finished goods; (2) cash is kept in the project as a buffer against unexpected expenditures; and (3) credit sales are made, generating accounts receivable rather than cash. (The investment in net working capital is offset to the extent that purchases are made on credit, that is, when accounts payable are created.) This investment in net working capital represents a cash outflow, because cash generated elsewhere in the firm is tied up in the project.

To see how the investment in net working capital is built from its component parts, we focus on year 1. We see in Table 8.1 that MMCC's managers predict sales in year 1 to be $600,000 and operating costs to be $434,000. If both the sales and costs were cash transactions, the firm would receive $166,000 (or $600,000 − $434,000).

However, the managers

1. Forecast that $100,000 of the sales will be on credit, implying that cash receipts in year 1 will be only $500,000 (or $600,000 − $100,000). The accounts receivable of $100,000 will be collected in year 2.

2. Believe that they can defer payment on $40,000 of the $434,000 of costs, implying that cash disbursements will be only $394,000 (or $434,000 − $40,000). Of course, MMCC will pay off the $40,000 of accounts payable in year 2.

3. Decide that inventory of $25,000 should be left on hand at year 1 to avoid *stock-outs* (that is, running out of inventory) and other contingencies.

4. Decide that cash of $5,000 should be earmarked for the project at year 1 to avoid running out of cash.

Thus, net working capital in year 1 is

$$\underset{\substack{\text{Accounts}\\\text{receivable}}}{\$100,000} - \underset{\substack{\text{Accounts}\\\text{payable}}}{\$40,000} + \underset{\text{Inventory}}{\$25,000} + \underset{\text{Cash}}{\$5,000} = \underset{\substack{\text{Net working}\\\text{capital}}}{\$90,000}$$

Because $90,000 of cash generated elsewhere in the firm must be used to offset this requirement for net working capital, MMCC's managers correctly view the investment in net working capital as a cash outflow of the project. As the project grows over time, needs for net working capital increase. Changes in net working capital from year to year represent further cash flows, as indicated by the negative numbers for the first few years of line 8 of Table 8.1. However, in the declining years of the project, net working capital is reduced—ultimately to zero. That is, accounts receivable are finally collected, the project's cash buffer is returned to the rest of the corporation, and all remaining inventory is sold off. This frees up cash in the later years, as indicated by positive numbers in years 5, 6, 7, and 8 in line 8.

Typically, corporate worksheets (such as Table 8.1) treat net working capital as a whole. The individual components of net working capital (receivables, inventory, and so on) do not generally appear in the worksheets. However, you should remember that the net working capital numbers in the worksheets are not pulled out of thin air. Rather, they result from a meticulous forecast of the components, just as we illustrated for year 1.

### Interest Expense

It may have bothered you that interest expense was ignored in the MMCC example. After all, many projects are at least partially financed with debt, particularly a power mulcher tool machine that is likely to increase the debt capacity of the firm. As it turns out, our approach of assuming no debt financing is rather standard in the real world. Firms typically calculate a project's cash flows under the assumption that the project is only financed with equity. Any adjustments for debt financing are reflected in the discount rate, not the cash flows. The treatment of debt in capital budgeting will be covered in depth later in the text. Suffice it to say at this time that the full ramifications of debt financing are well beyond our current discussion.

*CONCEPT*
*QUESTIONS*
- What are the items leading to cash flow in any year?
- Why did we determine taxable income when NPV analysis discounts cash flows, not income?
- Why is the increase in net working capital viewed as a cash outflow?

## 8.3    INFLATION AND CAPITAL BUDGETING

*Inflation* is an important fact of economic life, and it must be considered in capital budgeting. We begin by considering the relationship between interest rates and inflation.

### Interest Rates and Inflation

Suppose that the one-year interest rate that a financial institution pays is 10 percent. This means that an individual who deposits $1,000 at date 0 will get $1,100 (or $1,000 × 1.10) in one year. While 10 percent may seem like a handsome return, one can only put it in perspective after examining the rate of inflation.

Suppose that the rate of inflation is 6 percent over the year and it affects all goods equally. For example, a restaurant that charges $1.00 for a hamburger at date 0 charges $1.06 for the same hamburger at the end of the year. You can use your $1,000 to buy 1,000 hamburgers at date 0. Alternatively, if you put all of your money in the bank, you can buy 1,038 (or $1,100/$1.06) hamburgers at date 1. Thus, you are only able to increase your hamburger consumption by 3.8 percent by lending to the bank. Since the prices of all goods rise at this 6 percent rate, lending lets you increase your consumption of any single good or any combination of goods by only 3.8 percent. Thus, 3.8 percent is what you are *really* earning through your savings account, after adjusting for inflation. Economists refer to the 3.8 percent number as the **real interest rate**. Economists refer to the 10 percent rate as the **nominal interest rate** or simply the *interest rate*. The above discussion is illustrated in Figure 8.1.

FIGURE 8.1

**Calculation of Real Rate of Interest**

Hamburgers are used as an illustrative good. 1,038 hamburgers can be purchased at date 1 instead of 1,000 hamburgers at date 0. Real interest rate = 1,038/1,000 − 1 = 3.8%.

We have used an example with a specific nominal interest rate and a specific inflation rate. In general, the equation relating real and nominal interest rates can be written as

$$1 + \text{Nominal interest rate} = (1 + \text{Real interest rate}) \times (1 + \text{Inflation rate})$$

Rearranging terms, we have

$$\text{Real interest rate} = \frac{1 + \text{Nominal interest rate}}{1 + \text{Inflation rate}} - 1 \qquad (8.1)$$

The equation indicates that the real interest rate in our example is 3.8 percent $(1.10/1.06 - 1)$.

This equation determines the real interest rate precisely. The following equation is an approximation:

$$\text{Real interest rate} \approx \text{Nominal interest rate} - \text{Inflation rate} \qquad (8.2)$$

The symbol $\approx$ indicates that the equation is approximately true. This latter equation calculates the real rate in our example as

$$4\% = 10\% - 6\%$$

You should be aware that while equation (8.2) may seem more intuitive than equation (8.1), (8.2) is only an approximation.

This approximation is reasonably accurate for low rates of interest and inflation. In our example, the difference between the approximate calculation and the exact one is only 0.2 percent (4 percent − 3.8 percent). Unfortunately, the approximation becomes poor when rates are higher.

**EXAMPLE 8.5**

The little-known monarchy of Gerberovia recently had a nominal interest rate of 300 percent and an inflation rate of 280 percent. According to equation (8.2), the real interest rate is

$$300\% - 280\% = 20\% \quad \text{(approximate formula)}$$

However, according to equation (8.1), this rate is

$$\frac{1 + 300\%}{1 + 280\%} - 1 = 5.26\% \quad \text{(exact formula)}$$

How do we know that the second formula is indeed the exact one? Let's think in terms of hamburgers again. Had you deposited $1,000 in a Gerberovian bank a year ago, the account would be worth $4,000 [$1,000 × (1 + 300%)] today. However, while a hamburger cost $1 a year ago, it costs $3.80 [$1 × (1 + 280%)] today. Therefore, you would now be able to buy 1052.6 (4,000/3.80) hamburgers, implying a real interest rate of 5.26 percent.

## Cash Flow and Inflation

The above analysis defines two types of interest rates (nominal rates and real rates) and relates them through equation (8.1). Capital budgeting requires data on cash flows as well as on interest rates. Like interest rates, cash flows can be expressed in either nominal or real terms.

A cash flow is expressed in nominal terms if the actual dollars to be received (or paid out) are given. A cash flow is expressed in real terms if the current or date 0 purchasing power of the cash flow is given.

EXAMPLE **8.6**

Ottawa Publishing has just purchased the rights to the next book by famed romance novelist Barbara Musk. Still unwritten, the book should be available to the public in four years. Currently, romance novels sell for $10.00 in paperback. The publishers believe that inflation will be 6 percent per year over the next four years. Since romance novels are so popular, the publishers anticipate that their prices will rise about 2 percent per year more than the inflation rate over the next four years. Not wanting to overprice, Ottawa Publishing anticipates pricing the novel at $13.60 [or $(1.08)^4 \times$ $10.00] four years from now. In other words, the nominal value after four years is the future value calculated using the inflation rate of 6 percent plus the anticipated price rise of 2 percent. The firm anticipates selling 100,000 copies.

The expected cash flow in the fourth year of $1.36 million (or $13.60 × 100,000) is a **nominal cash flow** because the firm expects to receive $1.36 million at that time. In other words, a nominal cash flow reflects the actual dollars to be received in the future.

We determine the purchasing power of $1.36 million in four years as

$$\$1.08 \text{ million} = \frac{\$1.36 \text{ million}}{(1.06)^4}$$

The figure $1.08 million is a **real cash flow** since it is expressed in terms of date 0 purchasing power. Extending our hamburger example, the $1.36 million to be received in four years will only buy 1.08 million hamburgers because the price of a hamburger will rise from $1 to $1.26 [or $1 × $(1.06)^4$] over the period.

EXAMPLE **8.7**

Gatineau Booksellers, a customer of Ottawa Publishing, recently made leasehold improvements to its store for $2,000,000 to be depreciated by the straight-line method over five years. This implies yearly depreciation of $400,000 (or $2,000,000/5). Is this $400,000 figure a real or nominal quantity?

Depreciation is a *nominal quantity* because $400,000 is the actual tax deduction, based on original cost, over each of the next four years. Depreciation becomes a real quantity if it is adjusted for purchasing power.[4] Hence, $289,903 [or $400,000/$(1.06)^5$] is depreciation in the fifth year, expressed as a real quantity.

## Discounting: Nominal or Real?

Our previous discussion showed that interest rates can be expressed in either nominal or real terms. Similarly, cash flows can be expressed in either nominal or real terms. Given these choices, how should one express interest rates and cash flows when performing capital budgeting?

Financial practitioners correctly stress the need to maintain *consistency* between cash flows and discount rates. That is:

*Nominal* cash flows must be discounted at the *nominal* rate.
*Real* cash flows must be discounted at the *real* rate.

As long as one is consistent, either approach is correct. In order to minimize computational error, it is generally advisable in practice to choose the approach that is easier. This idea is illustrated in Examples 8.8 and 8.9.

––––––
[4] We use the word *quantity*, not *cash flow*, because it is the CCA tax shield, not the depreciation itself, that is a cash flow. Tax shields are defined later in this chapter.

EXAMPLE **8.8**

Shields Electric forecasts the following nominal cash flows on a particular project:

| Date | 0 | 1 | 2 |
|------|-----|-----|-----|
| Cash flow | −$1,000 | $600 | $650 |

The nominal interest rate is 14 percent, and the inflation rate is forecast to be 5 percent. What is the value of the project?

*Use nominal quantities.* The NPV can be calculated as

$$\$26.47 = -\$1,000 + \frac{\$600}{1.14} + \frac{\$650}{(1.14)^2}$$

The project should be accepted.

*Use real quantities.* The real cash flows are

| Date | 0 | 1 | 2 |
|------|-----|-----|-----|
| Cash flow | −$1,000 | $571.43 | $589.57 |
|  |  | $\left(\frac{\$600}{1.05}\right)$ | $\left(\frac{\$650}{1.05^2}\right)$ |

The real interest rate is 8.57143 percent ($1.14/1.05 - 1$).

The NPV can be calculated as

$$\$26.47 = -\$1,000 + \frac{\$571.43}{1.0857143} + \frac{\$589.57}{(1.0857143)^2}$$

The NPV is the same when cash flows are expressed in real quantities. It must always be the case that the NPV is the same under the two different approaches.

Because both approaches always yield the same result, which one should be used? Students will be happy to learn the following rule: use the approach that is simpler. In the Shields Electric case, nominal quantities produce a simpler calculation because the problem gave us nominal cash flows to begin with.

EXAMPLE **8.9**

Altshuler Inc. used the following data for a capital budgeting project:

| Year | 0 | 1 | 2 |
|------|-----|-----|-----|
| Capital expenditure | $1,210 |  |  |
| Revenues (in real terms) |  | $1,900 | $2,000 |
| Cash expenses (in real terms) |  | 950 | 1,000 |
| Depreciation (straight-line) |  | 605 | 605 |

The president, Anna Altshuler, estimates inflation to be 10 percent per year over the next two years. In addition, she believes that the cash flows of the project should be discounted at the nominal rate of 15.5 percent. Her firm's tax rate is 40 percent.

Anna forecasts all cash flows in *nominal* terms. Thus, she generates the following spreadsheet:

| Year | 0 | 1 | 2 |
|---|---|---|---|
| Capital expenditure | −$1,210 | | |
| Revenues | | $2,090 $(= 1,900 \times 1.10)$ | $2,420 $(= 2,000 \times (1.10)^2)$ |
| − Expenses | | −1,045 $(= 950 \times 1.10)$ | −1,210 $(= 1,000 \times (1.10)^2)$ |
| − Depreciation | | −605 $(= 1,210/2)$ | −605 |
| Taxable income | | 440 | 605 |
| − Taxes (40%) | | −176 | −242 |
| Income after taxes | | 264 | 363 |
| + Depreciation | | +605 | +605 |
| Cash flow | | $ 869 | $ 968 |

$$NPV = -\$1,210 + \frac{\$869}{1.155} + \frac{\$968}{(1.155)^2} = \$268$$

Anna's sidekick, Stuart Weiss, prefers working in real terms. He first calculates the real rate to be 5 percent $(= 1.155/1.10 - 1)$. Next, he generates the following spreadsheet in *real* quantities:

| Year | 0 | 1 | 2 |
|---|---|---|---|
| Capital expenditure | −$1,210 | | |
| Revenues | | $1,900 | $2,000 |
| − Expenses | | −950 | −1,000 |
| − Depreciation | | −550 $(= 605/1.1)$ | −500 $(= 605/1.1^2)$ |
| Taxable income | | 400 | 500 |
| − Taxes (40%) | | −160 | −200 |
| Income after taxes | | 240 | 300 |
| + Depreciation | | +550 | +500 |
| Cash flow | | $ 790 | $ 800 |

$$NPV = -\$1,210 + \frac{\$790}{1.05} = \frac{\$800}{(1.05)^2} = \$268$$

In explaining his calculations to Anna, Stuart points out the following:

1. Since the capital expenditure occurs at date 0 (today), its nominal value and its real value are equal.

2. Since yearly depreciation of $605 is a nominal quantity, one converts it to a real quantity by discounting at the inflation rate of 10 percent.

3. It is no coincidence that both Anna and Stuart arrive at the same NPV number. Both methods must always give the same NPV. However, Stuart's approach was simpler as the majority of cash flows were already given in real terms.

**CONCEPT QUESTIONS**
- What is the difference between the nominal and the real interest rate?
- What is the difference between nominal and real cash flows?

# 8.4 ALTERNATIVE DEFINITIONS OF OPERATING CASH FLOW

The analysis in the previous section is quite general and can be adapted to just about any capital investment problem. This section discusses the fact that different definitions of project OCF are commonly used, both in practice and in finance texts.

The different approaches to OCF all measure the same thing. If used correctly, every approach will produce the same answer, although one is not necessarily any better or more useful than another. Unfortunately, the fact that alternative definitions are used sometimes leads to confusion. For this reason, we examine several of these variations next to see how they are related.

In the discussion that follows, keep in mind that cash flow literally means dollars in less dollars out. This is all we are concerned with. Different definitions of OCF simply amount to different ways of manipulating basic information about sales, costs, depreciation, and taxes to get at cash flow.

For a particular project and year under consideration, suppose we have the following estimates:

$$\text{Sales} = \$1,500$$
$$\text{Costs} = \$700$$
$$\text{Depreciation} = \$600$$

With these estimates, notice that EBIT is

$$\begin{aligned} \text{EBIT} &= \text{Sales} - \text{Costs} - \text{Depreciation} \\ &= \$1,500 - \$700 - \$600 \\ &= \$200 \end{aligned}$$

Once again, we assume that no interest is paid, so the tax bill is

$$\begin{aligned} \text{Taxes} &= \text{EBIT} \times T_c \\ &= \$200 \times 0.34 = \$68 \end{aligned}$$

where $T_c$, the corporate tax rate, is 34 percent.

When we put all of this together, we see that project OCF is

$$\begin{aligned} \text{OCF} &= \text{EBIT} + \text{Depreciation} - \text{Taxes} \\ &= \$200 + \$600 - \$68 = \$732 \end{aligned}$$

It turns out there are some other ways to determine OCF that could be (and are) used. We consider these next.

## The Bottom-Up Approach

Because we are ignoring any financing expenses, such as interest, in our calculations of project OCF, we can write project net income as

$$\begin{aligned} \text{Project net income} &= \text{EBIT} - \text{Taxes} \\ &= \$200 - \$68 \\ &= \$132 \end{aligned}$$

If we simply add the depreciation to both sides, we arrive at a slightly different and very common expression for OCF:

$$\begin{aligned} \text{OCF} &= \text{Net income} + \text{Depreciation} \\ &= \$132 + \$600 \\ &= \$732 \end{aligned} \tag{8.3}$$

This is the *bottom-up* approach. Begin with the accountant's bottom line (net income) and add back any non-cash deductions such as depreciation. It is crucial to remember that this definition of OCF as net income plus depreciation is correct only if there is no interest expense subtracted in the calculation of net income.

### The Top-Down Approach

Perhaps the most obvious way to calculate OCF is this:

$$OCF = Sales - Costs - Taxes$$
$$= \$1,500 - \$700 - \$68 = \$732 \tag{8.4}$$

This is the *top-down* approach, the second variation on the basic OCF definition. Begin with the top of the comprehensive statement of income with sales, and work down to net cash flow by subtracting costs, taxes, and other expenses. Along the way, simply leave out any strictly non-cash items such as depreciation.

### The Tax Shield Approach

The third variation on our basic definition of OCF is the *tax shield* approach. This approach will be very useful for some problems we consider in the next chapter. The tax shield definition of OCF is

$$OCF = (Sales - Costs) \times (1 - T_c) + Depreciation \times T_c \tag{8.5}$$

where $T_c$ is again the corporate tax rate. Assuming that $T_c = 34$ percent, the OCF works out to be

$$OCF = (\$1,500 - \$700) \times 0.66 + \$600 \times 0.34$$
$$= \$528 + \$204$$
$$= \$732$$

This approach views OCF as having two components. The first part is what the project's cash flow would be if there were no depreciation expense. In this case, this "would-have-been" cash flow is $528. The second part of OCF in this approach is the depreciation deduction multiplied by the tax rate. This is called the **depreciation tax shield**. Knowing that depreciation is a non-cash expense, the only cash flow effect of deducting depreciation is to reduce our taxes. At the current 34 percent corporate tax rate, every dollar in depreciation expense saves 34 cents in taxes. So, in the example, the $600 depreciation deduction saves us $600 \times 0.34 = \$204$ in taxes.

### Conclusion

Now that each approach has been used and it has been shown that all of these approaches are the same, you may be wondering why everyone does not just agree on one of them. One reason is that different approaches are useful in different circumstances. The best one to use is whichever happens to be the most convenient for the problem at hand.

## 8.5    APPLYING THE TAX SHIELD APPROACH TO THE MAJESTIC MULCH AND COMPOST COMPANY PROJECT

If you look back over our analysis of MMCC, you will see that most of the number crunching involved finding CCA, EBIT, and net income figures. The tax shield approach can save us considerable time. To do this, we do the calculations in a different order than in Table 8.4. Instead of adding the cash flow components down the columns for each year and finding the PV of the total cash flows, we find the PV of each source of cash flows and add the PVs. To find the PVs we use a discount rate of 15 percent.

To begin, it will be helpful to define the following:

$$OCF = \text{Operating cash flow}$$
$$R = \text{Revenues}$$
$$E = \text{Expenses (operating costs)}$$
$$D = \text{Depreciation for tax purposes, i.e., CCA}^5$$
$$T_c = \text{Corporate tax rate}$$

The first source of cash flow is $(R - E)(1 - T_c)$, as shown for each year in the first line of Table 8.5. The figure for the first year is $99,600 (the numbers come from Table 8.1):

$$(R - E)(1 - T_c) = (\$600,000 - \$434,000)(1 - 0.40)$$
$$= \$99,600$$

Calculating the PV of the $99,600 for the first year, and adding the PVs of the other $(R - E)(1 - T_c)$ figures in Table 8.5, gives a total PV for this source of $682,696, as seen in the lower part of Table 8.5.

The second term is the tax shield on CCA for the first year. Table 8.6 reproduces the first year's tax shield of $32,000 along with the corresponding tax shield for each year. The total PV of the CCA tax shield is shown as $159,649.

---

**TABLE 8.5**

**Tax Shield Solution, Power Mulcher Project**

|  | Year 0 | Year 1 | Year 2 | Year 3 | Year 4 | Year 5 | Year 6 | Year 7 | Year 8 |
|---|---|---|---|---|---|---|---|---|---|
| (1) $(R - E)(1 - T_c)$ |  | $99,600 | $157,920 | $211,056 | $219,856 | $189,246 | $142,356 | $98,881 | $ 59,331 |
| (2) Changes in net working capital | $(40,000) | (50,000) | (47,700) | (49,572) | (19,664) | 12,098 | 29,226 | 30,473 | 135,139 |
| (3) Equipment expenditure: | (800,000) |  |  |  |  |  |  |  | 150,000 |
| Totals |  |  |  |  |  |  |  |  |  |
| Present value of $(R - E)(1 - T_c)$ | $682,696 |  |  |  |  |  |  |  |  |
| Present value of changes in net working capital | (89,100) |  |  |  |  |  |  |  |  |
| Present value of equipment expenditure | (750,965) |  |  |  |  |  |  |  |  |
| Present value of capital cost allowance tax shield | 159,649 |  |  |  |  |  |  |  |  |
| Net present value | $2,280 |  |  |  |  |  |  |  |  |

---

**TABLE 8.6**

**Present Value of Tax Shield on Capital Cost Allowance**

| Year | Capital cost allowance | 0.40 × Capital cost allowance | Present value at 15 percent |
|---|---|---|---|
| 1 | $ 80,000 | $32,000 | $27,826 |
| 2 | 144,000 | 57,600 | 43,554 |
| 3 | 115,200 | 46,080 | 30,298 |
| 4 | 92,160 | 36,864 | 21,077 |
| 5 | 73,728 | 29,491 | 14,662 |
| 6 | 58,982 | 23,593 | 10,200 |
| 7 | 47,186 | 18,874 | 7,096 |
| 8 | 37,749 | 15,099 | 4,936 |
| | Present value of tax shield on capital cost allowance | | $159,649 |

---

[5] In this discussion we use the terms *depreciation* and *CCA* interchangeably.

The changes in net working capital and equipment expenditure are the same as in Table 8.4. Their PVs are shown in the lower part of Table 8.5. The NPV is the sum of the PVs of the four sources of cash flow. The answer, $2,280, is nearly identical to what we found in Table 8.4 for a discount rate of 15 percent, with the difference due to rounding errors.

## Present Value of the Tax Shield on Capital Cost Allowance

Further time savings are made possible by using a formula that replaces the detailed calculation of yearly CCA. The formula is based on the idea that tax shields from CCA continue in perpetuity as long as there are assets remaining in the CCA class.[6] To calculate the PV of the tax shield on CCA, we first find the PV of an infinite stream of tax shields abstracting from two practical implications: the 50 percent rule for CCA and disposal of the asset. We then adjust the formula. The detailed derivation is in Appendix 8B.

$C =$ Total capital cost of the asset that is added to the pool
$d =$ CCA rate for the asset class
$T_c =$ Company's marginal tax rate
$k =$ Discount rate
$S =$ Salvage or disposal value of the asset
$n =$ Asset life in years

$$\text{PV tax shield on CCA} = \frac{CdT_c}{k+d} \times \frac{1+0.5k}{1+k} - \frac{SdT_c}{k+d} \times \frac{1}{(1+k)^n} \qquad (8.6)$$

Using the first part of (8.6), the PV of the tax shield on MMCC's project is $170,932, assuming that the tax shield goes on in perpetuity:

$$\frac{\$800,000(0.20)(0.40)}{0.15+0.20} \times \frac{1+(0.5)(0.15)}{1+0.15} = \$182,857 \times \frac{1.075}{1.15}$$
$$= \$170,932$$

The adjustment for the salvage value [second part of (8.6)] is

$$-\frac{\$150,000(0.20)(0.40)}{0.15+0.20} \times \frac{1}{(1+0.15)^8} = -\$34,286 \times \frac{1}{(1.15)^8}$$
$$= -\$11,208$$

The PV of the tax shield on CCA is the sum of the two PVs:[7]

$$\text{PV of tax shield from CCA} = \$170,932 - \$11,208$$
$$= \$159,724$$

---

[6] Strictly speaking, the undepreciated capital cost (UCC) for a class remains positive as long as there are physical assets in the class and the proceeds from disposal of assets are less than total UCC for the class.

[7] There is a slight difference between this calculation for the PV of the tax shield on CCA and what we got in Table 8.6 by adding the tax shields over the project life. The difference arises whenever the salvage value of the asset differs from its undepreciated capital cost (UCC). The formula solution is more accurate, as it takes into account the future CCA on this difference. In this case, the asset was sold for $150,000 and had UCC of $150,995. The $995 left in the pool after eight years creates an infinite stream of CCA. At time 8, this stream has a PV of [$995(0.20)(0.40)]/[0.15 + 0.20] = $227.43. At time 0, the PV of this stream, at 15 percent, is about $75. To get the precise estimate of the PV of the CCA tax shield, we need to add this to the approximation in Table 8.6: $159,649 + $75 = $159,724. This adjustment could be made initially by adding another line to Table 8.1.

Now let's turn to machine B. We calculate its EAC from

$$\$916.99 = C \times A_{0.10}^4$$

Because $A_{0.10}^4$ equals 3.1699, $C$ equals $\$916.99/3.1699$, or $\$289.28$.
As we did above for machine A, we can create the following chart for machine B:

| Year | 0 | 1 | 2 | 3 | 4 |
|---|---|---|---|---|---|
| Cash outflows of machine B | $600 | $100 | $100 | $100 | $100 |
| Equivalent annual cost of machine B | | $289.28 | $289.28 | $289.28 | $289.28 |

The decision is easy once the charts of the two machines are compared. Would you rather make annual lease payments of $321.05 or $289.28? Put this way, the problem becomes a no-brainer. Clearly, a rational person would rather pay the lower amount. Thus, machine B is the preferred choice.

Two final remarks are in order. First, it is no accident that we specified the costs of the tennis ball machines in real terms. While B would still have been the preferred machine had the costs been stated in nominal terms, the actual solution would have been much more difficult. As a general rule, always convert cash flows to real terms when working through problems of this type.

Second, the above analysis applies only if one anticipates that both machines can be replaced. The analysis would differ if no replacement were possible. For example, imagine that the only company that manufactured tennis ball throwers just went out of business and no new producers are expected to enter the field. In this case, machine B would generate revenues in the fourth year whereas machine A would not. Here, simple NPV analysis for mutually exclusive projects including both revenues and costs would be appropriate.

## The General Decision to Replace (Advanced)

The previous analysis concerned the choice between machine A and machine B, both of which were new acquisitions. More typically, firms must decide when to replace an existing machine with a new one. This decision is actually quite straightforward. One should replace if the annual cost of the new machine is less than the annual cost of the old machine. As with much else in finance, an example, such as Example 8.11, clarifies this approach better than further explanation.

**EXAMPLE 8.11**

Consider the situation of BIKE, which must decide whether to replace an existing machine. BIKE currently pays no taxes. The replacement machine costs $9,000 now and requires maintenance of $1,000 at the end of every year for eight years. At the end of eight years the machine would be sold for $2,000. All numbers are in real terms.

The existing machine requires increasing amounts of maintenance each year, and its salvage value falls each year, as shown:

| Year | Maintenance | Salvage |
|---|---|---|
| 0 | $     0 | $4,000 |
| 1 | 1,000 | 2,500 |
| 2 | 2,000 | 1,500 |
| 3 | 3,000 | 1,000 |
| 4 | 4,000 | 0 |

This chart tells us that the existing machine can be sold for $4,000 now. If it is sold one year from now, the resale price will be $2,500, and $1,000 must be spent on maintenance during the year to keep it running. For ease of calculation, we assume that this maintenance fee is paid at the end of the year. The machine will last for four more years before it falls apart. In other words, salvage value will be zero at the end of year 4. If BIKE faces an opportunity cost of capital of 15 percent, when should it replace the machine?

As we said above, our approach is to compare the annual cost of the replacement machine with the annual cost of the old machine. The annual cost of the replacement machine is simply its EAC. Let's calculate that first.

**Equivalent Annual Cost of New Machine**    The PV of the cost of the new replacement machine is

$$PV_{costs} = \$9,000 + \$1,000 \times A_{0.15}^8 - \frac{\$2,000}{(1.15)^8}$$

$$= \$9,000 + \$1,000 \times (4.4873) - \frac{\$2,000}{3.059}$$

$$= \$12,833$$

Notice that the $2,000 salvage value is an inflow. It is treated as a *negative* number in the above equation because it *offsets* the cost of the machine.

The EAC of a new replacement machine is

$$\frac{PV}{\text{8-year annuity factor at 15\%}} = \frac{PV}{A_{0.15}^8} = \frac{\$12,833}{4.4873} = \$2,860$$

This calculation implies that buying a replacement machine is financially equivalent to renting this machine for $2,860 per year.

**Cost of Old Machine**    This calculation is a little trickier. If BIKE keeps the old machine for one year, the firm must pay maintenance costs of $1,000 a year from now. But this is not BIKE's only cost from keeping the machine for one year. BIKE will receive $2,500 at date 1 if the old machine is kept for one year but would receive $4,000 today if the old machine were sold immediately. This reduction in sales proceeds is clearly a cost as well.

Thus, the PV of the costs of keeping the machine one more year before selling it is

$$PV_{costs} = \$4,000 + \frac{\$1,000}{1.15} - \frac{\$2,500}{1.15}$$

$$= \$2,696$$

That is, if BIKE holds the old machine for one year, BIKE does *not* receive the $4,000 today. This $4,000 can be thought of as an opportunity cost. In addition, the firm must pay $1,000 a year from now. Finally, BIKE does receive $2,500 a year from now. This last item is treated as a negative number because it offsets the other two costs.

While we normally express cash flows in terms of PV, the analysis to come is made easier if we express the cash flow in terms of its future value one year from now. This future value is

$$FV_{costs} = \$2,696 \times 1.15 = \$3,100$$

In other words, the cost of keeping the machine for one year is equivalent to paying $3,100 at the end of the year.

**Making the Comparison**  Now let's review the cash flows. If we replace the machine immediately, we can view our annual expense as $2,860, beginning at the end of the year. This annual expense occurs forever, if we replace the new machine every eight years. This cash flow stream can be written as

|                                          | Year 1  | Year 2  | Year 3  | Year 4  | ...  |
|------------------------------------------|---------|---------|---------|---------|------|
| Expenses from replacing machine immediately | $2,860  | $2,860  | $2,860  | $2,860  | ...  |

If we replace the old machine in one year, our expense from using the old machine for that final year can be viewed as $3,100, payable at the end of the year. After replacement, our annual expense is $2,860, beginning at the end of two years. This annual expense occurs forever, if we replace the new machine every eight years. This cash flow stream can be written as

|                                                              | Year 1  | Year 2  | Year 3  | Year 4  | ...  |
|--------------------------------------------------------------|---------|---------|---------|---------|------|
| Expenses from using old machine for one year and then replacing it | $3,100  | $2,860  | $2,860  | $2,860  | ...  |

Put this way, the choice is a no-brainer. Anyone would rather pay $2,860 at the end of the year than $3,100 at the end of the year. Thus, BIKE should replace[9] the old machine immediately in order to minimize the expense at year 1.

Two final points should be made on the decision to replace. First, we have examined a situation where both the old machine and the replacement machine generate the same revenues. Because revenues are unaffected by the choice of machine, revenues do not enter our analysis. This situation is common in business. For example, the decision to replace either the heating system or the air conditioning system in one's home office will likely not affect firm revenues. However, sometimes revenues will be greater with a new machine. The above approach can easily be amended to handle differential revenues. Second, we want to stress the importance of the above approach. Applications of the above approach are pervasive in business, since *every* machine must be replaced at some point.

---

**EXAMPLE 8.12**

---

This next example illustrates the use of EACs when the CCA tax shield is considered. You are evaluating two different filtration systems. System *A* costs $1.5 million to install and $65,000, pre-tax, annually, to operate. It would have to be replaced every six years. System *B* costs $2.1 million to install, but only $12,000 per year to operate. It has an effective operating life of nine years.

Both systems are depreciated under the declining-balance method and are expected to sell at the ending undepreciated capital cost (UCC) value at the end of useful life. Which filtration system should be selected if the discount rate is 14 percent? The tax rate is 40 percent. The relevant information is summarized below.[10]

---

[9] One caveat is in order. Perhaps the old machine's maintenance is high in the first year but drops after that. A decision to replace immediately might be premature in that case. Therefore, we need to check the cost of the old machine in future years. The cost of keeping the existing machine a second year is

$$\text{PV of costs at time 1} = \$2{,}500 + \frac{\$2{,}000}{1.15} - \frac{\$1{,}500}{1.15} = \$2{,}935$$

which has future value of $3,375 ($2,935 × 1.15).
The costs of keeping the existing machine for years 3 and 4 are also greater than the EAC of buying a new machine. Thus, BIKE's decision to replace the old machine immediately is still valid.

[10] Note that inflows are positive and outflows are negative.

To decide which filtration system to purchase, we compute the EACs for both systems using the appropriate annuity factors.

| System A | Beginning undepreciated capital cost | Capital cost allowance | Ending undepreciated capital cost |
|---|---|---|---|
| Year 1 | 750,000 | 150,000 | 600,000 |
| Year 2 | 1,350,000 | 270,000 | 1,080,000 |
| Year 3 | 1,080,000 | 216,000 | 864,000 |
| Year 4 | 864,000 | 172,800 | 691,200 |
| Year 5 | 691,200 | 138,240 | 552,960 |
| Year 6 | 552,960 | 110,592 | 442,368 |

| System B | Beginning undepreciated capital cost | Capital cost allowance | Ending undepreciated capital cost |
|---|---|---|---|
| Year 1 | 1,050,000 | 210,000 | 840,000 |
| Year 2 | 1,890,000 | 378,000 | 1,512,000 |
| Year 3 | 1,512,000 | 302,400 | 1,209,600 |
| Year 4 | 1,209,600 | 241,920 | 967,680 |
| Year 5 | 967,680 | 193,536 | 774,144 |
| Year 6 | 774,144 | 154,829 | 619,315 |
| Year 7 | 619,315 | 123,863 | 495,452 |
| Year 8 | 495,452 | 99,090 | 396,362 |
| Year 9 | 396,362 | 79,272 | 317,089 |

| System A | Year 0 | Year 1 | Year 2 | Year 3 | Year 4 | Year 5 | Year 6 | Year 7 | Year 8 | Year 9 |
|---|---|---|---|---|---|---|---|---|---|---|
| After-tax operating cost [Annual operating cost $\times$ $(1 - T_c)$] | | (39,000) | (39,000) | (39,000) | (39,000) | (39,000) | (39,000) | | | |
| Annual capital cost allowance tax shield | | 60,000 | 108,000 | 86,400 | 69,120 | 55,296 | 44,237 | | | |
| Operating cash flow | | 21,000 | 69,000 | 47,400 | 30,120 | 16,296 | 5,237 | | | |
| Capital expenditure | (1,500,000) | | | | | | 442,368 | | | |
| Present value of operating cost | | 18,421 | 53,093 | 31,994 | 17,833 | 8,464 | 2,386 | | | |
| Total present value of operating costs | 132,191 | | | | | | | | | |
| Present value of capital expenditure | (1,298,463) | | | | | | | | | |
| Total present value of cost | (1,166,272) | | | | | | | | | |
| Annuity factor | 3.8887 | | | | | | | | | |
| Equivalent annual cost | (299,913) | | | | | | | | | |

| System B | Year 0 | Year 1 | Year 2 | Year 3 | Year 4 | Year 5 | Year 6 | Year 7 | Year 8 | Year 9 |
|---|---|---|---|---|---|---|---|---|---|---|
| After-tax operating cost [Annual operating cost × $(1 - T_c)$] | | (7,200) | (7,200) | (7,200) | (7,200) | (7,200) | (7,200) | (7,200) | (7,200) | (7,200) |
| Annual capital cost allowance tax shield | | 84,000 | 151,200 | 120,960 | 96,768 | 77,414 | 61,932 | 49,545 | 39,636 | 31,709 |
| Operating cash flow | | 76,800 | 144,000 | 113,760 | 89,568 | 70,214 | 54,732 | 42,345 | 32,436 | 24,509 |
| Capital expenditure | (2,100,000) | | | | | | | | | 317,089 |
| Present value of operating cost | | 67,368 | 110,803 | 76,785 | 53,031 | 36,467 | 24,935 | 16,923 | 11,371 | 7,537 |
| Total present value of operating costs | 405,220 | | | | | | | | | |
| Present value of capital expenditure | (2,002,492) | | | | | | | | | |
| Total present value of cost | (1,597,272) | | | | | | | | | |
| Annuity factor | 4.9464 | | | | | | | | | |
| Equivalent annual cost | (322,916) | | | | | | | | | |

System A has the lower EAC and thus it is selected. The longer life and lower operating cost of System B are not sufficient to offset its higher initial cost of $2.1 million.

**CONCEPT QUESTION**

- What is the EAC method of capital budgeting?

## 8.7

# SUMMARY AND CONCLUSIONS

This chapter discussed a number of practical applications of capital budgeting.

1. Capital budgeting must be conducted on an incremental basis. This means that sunk costs must be ignored, while opportunity costs, side effects, and allocated costs need to be considered.

2. Inflation should be handled consistently. One approach is to express both cash flows and the discount rate in nominal terms. The other approach is to express both cash flows and the discount rate in real terms. Because either approach yields the same net present value (NPV) calculation, the simpler method should be used. Which method is simpler will generally depend on the nature of the capital budgeting problem.

3. In the total project cash flow example, we computed NPV using the following two steps:

   a. Calculate the net cash flow from all sources for each period.

   b. Calculate the NPV using the cash flows calculated above.

   In the tax shield example, we used two different steps:

   c. Calculate the present value (PV) of each source (for example, revenues and capital cost allowance (CCA) tax shield).

d. Add the PVs across the different sources (including initial investment) in order to get NPV.

The second approach has three benefits. Simplifying formulas can often be used. Nominal cash flows and real cash flows can be handled in the same example. Cash flows of varying risk can be used in the same example.

4. A firm should use the equivalent annual cost (EAC) approach when choosing between two machines of unequal lives.

**KEY TERMS**

Allocated cost   225
Depreciation tax shield   237
Erosion   225
Incremental cash flows   224

Nominal cash flow   233
Nominal interest rate   231
Opportunity costs   224
Real cash flow   233

Real interest rate   231
Sunk cost   224
Synergy   225

**QUESTIONS & PROBLEMS**

### Incremental Cash Flows

8.1 Which of the following should be treated as incremental cash flows when computing the NPV of an investment?
   a. The reduction in the sales of the company's other products.
   b. The expenditure on plant and equipment.
   c. The cost of research and development undertaken in connection with the product during the past three years.
   d. The annual CCA expense.
   e. Dividend payments.
   f. The resale value of plant and equipment at the end of the project's life.
   g. Salary and medical costs for production employees on leave.

### Practical Application of Net Present Value to Capital Budgeting (no inflation)

8.2 Suppose Mats Sundin decided to make another comeback with the Toronto Maple Leafs in 2016. The Leafs offer him a two-year contract in January 2016 with the following provisions:
   a. $8 million signing bonus.
   b. $10 million per year for two years.
   c. Seven years of deferred payments of $3 million per year, starting at the end of year 2.
   d. A games-played bonus provision that totals $2 million per year for the two years of the contract.

Assume that Mats achieved his bonus requirements both years and he signed the contract right away on January 1, 2016. Assume that cash flows are discounted at 12.5 percent. Ignore any taxes. Mats' signing bonus was paid on the day the contract was signed. His salary and bonuses, other than the signing bonus, are paid at the end of the year. What was the PV of this contract in January when Mats signed it?

### Comparing Mutually Exclusive Projects

8.3 Victoria Enterprises Inc. is evaluating alternative uses for a three-storey manufacturing and warehousing building that it has purchased for $1,450,000. The company could continue to rent the building to the present occupants for $61,000 per year. These tenants have indicated an interest in staying in the building for at least another 15 years. Alternatively, the company could make improvements to modify the existing structure to use for its own manufacturing and warehousing needs. Victoria's production engineer feels the building could be adapted to handle one of two new product lines. The cost and revenue data for the two product alternatives follow:

| | Product A | Product B |
|---|---|---|
| Initial cash outflow for building modifications | $95,000 | $125,000 |
| Initial cash outflow for equipment | 195,000 | 230,000 |
| Annual pre-tax cash revenues (generated for 15 years) | 180,000 | 215,000 |
| Annual pre-tax cash expenditures (generated for 15 years) | 70,000 | 90,000 |

The building will be used for only 15 years for either product A or product B. After 15 years, the building will be too small for efficient production of either product line. At that time, Victoria plans to rent the building to firms similar to the current occupants. To rent the building again, Victoria will need to restore the building to its present layout. The estimated cash cost of restoring the building if product A has been undertaken is $55,000; if product B has been produced, the cash cost will be $80,000. These cash costs can be deducted for tax purposes in the year the expenditures occur.

Victoria will depreciate the original building shell (purchased for $1,450,000) at a CCA rate of 5 percent, regardless of which alternative it chooses. The building modifications fall into CCA class 13 and are depreciated using the straight-line method over a 15-year life. Equipment purchases for either product are in class 8 and have a CCA rate of 20 percent. The firm's tax rate is 34 percent, and its required rate of return on such investments is 12 percent.

For simplicity, assume all cash flows for a given year occur at the end of the year. The initial outflows for modifications and equipment will occur at $t = 0$, and the restoration outflows will occur at the end of year 15. Also, Victoria has other profitable ongoing operations that are sufficient to cover any losses.

Which use of the building would you recommend to management?

### Valuation of the Firm

8.4   The Regina Wheat Company (RWC) has wheat fields that currently produce annual profits of $750,000. These fields are expected to produce average annual profits of $750,000 in real terms, forever. RWC has no depreciable assets, so the annual cash flow is also $750,000. RWC is an all-equity firm with 320,000 shares outstanding. The appropriate discount rate for its stock is 15 percent. RWC has an investment opportunity with a gross PV of $2.5 million. The investment requires a $1.8 million outflow now. RWC has no other investment opportunities. Assume all cash flows are received at the end of each year. What is the price per share of RWC?

### Capital Budgeting with Inflation

8.5   Consider the following cash flows on two mutually exclusive projects:

| Year | Project A | Project B |
|---|---|---|
| 0 | −$55,000 | −$60,000 |
| 1 | 30,000 | 10,000 |
| 2 | 18,000 | 25,000 |
| 3 | 18,000 | 40,000 |

Cash flows of project A are expressed in real terms, while those of project B are expressed in nominal terms. The appropriate nominal discount rate is 13 percent, and inflation is 5 percent. Which project should you choose?

8.6   Phillips Industries runs a small manufacturing operation. For this year, it expects to have real net cash flows of $275,000. Phillips is an ongoing operation, but it expects competitive pressures to erode its (inflation-adjusted) net cash flows at 8.5 percent per year. The appropriate real discount rate for Phillips is 13 percent. All net cash flows are received at year-end. What is the PV of the net cash flows from Phillips' operations?

8.7    Larry, owner/manager of a small restaurant, is contemplating buying a larger restaurant from its owner, who is retiring. Larry would finance the purchase by selling his existing small restaurant; taking a second mortgage on his house; selling the stocks and bonds that he owns; and, if necessary, taking out a bank loan. Because Larry would have almost all of his wealth in the restaurant, he wants a careful analysis of how much he should be willing to pay for the business. The present owner of the larger restaurant has supplied the following information from the past five years:

| Year | Gross revenue | Profit |
|------|--------------|--------|
| −5   | $   930,000  | $ 75,000 |
| −4   | 945,000      | 37,000 |
| −3   | 917,000      | 11,000 |
| −2   | 985,000      | 103,000 |
| Last | 1,104,000    | 106,000 |

As with many small businesses, the larger restaurant is structured as a sole proprietorship, so no corporate taxes are deducted. The preceding figures have not been adjusted for changes in the price level. There is general agreement that the average profits for the past five years are representative of what can be expected in the future, after adjusting for inflation.

Larry is of the opinion that he could earn at least $5,000 in current dollars per month as a hired manager. Larry feels he should subtract this amount from profits when analyzing the venture. Furthermore, he is aware of statistics showing that for restaurants of this size, approximately 6.5 percent go out of business each year.

Larry has done some preliminary work to value the business. His analysis is as follows:

| Year | Profits | Price-level factor | Profits (current dollars) | Imputed managerial wage | Net profits |
|------|---------|-------------------|---------------------------|-------------------------|-------------|
| −5   | $ 75,000 | 1.28 | $ 96,000 | $45,000 | $ 51,000 |
| −4   | 37,000   | 1.18 | 43,660   | 45,000  | −13,400 |
| −3   | 11,000   | 1.09 | 11,990   | 45,000  | −33,010 |
| −2   | 103,000  | 1.04 | 107,120  | 45,000  | 62,210 |
| Last | 106,000  | 1.00 | 106,000  | 45,000  | 61,000 |

The average net profits for the past five years, expressed in current dollars with a small subjective adjustment, are $28,000. Using this average profit figure, Larry produced the following figures in current dollars:

| Year | Expected profits | Real discount factor 2% | Present value |
|------|-----------------|-------------------------|---------------|
| Next | $28,000 | 0.980 | $27,440 |
| +2   | 26,320  | 0.961 | 25,294 |
| +3   | 24,752  | 0.942 | 23,316 |
| +4   | 23,268  | 0.924 | 21,500 |
| ⋮    | ⋮       | ⋮     | ⋮ |

Based on these calculations, Larry has calculated that the value of the restaurant is $510,000.

a. Do you agree with Larry's assessment of the restaurant? In your answer, consider his treatment of inflation and his deduction of the managerial wage of $45,000 per year.

b. What PV would you place on the revenue stream? In other words, how much would you advise Larry to be willing to pay for the restaurant?

8.8    The Biological Insect Control Corporation (BICC) has hired you as a consultant to evaluate the NPV of its proposed toad ranch. BICC plans to breed toads and sell them as ecologically desirable insect-control mechanisms. It anticipates that the business will continue in perpetuity. Following the negligible start-up costs, BICC expects the following nominal cash flows at the end of the year:

| Revenues | $265,000 |
|----------|----------|
| Labour costs | 185,000 |
| Other costs | 55,000 |

The company will rent machinery for $90,000 per year. The rental payments start at the end of year 1 and are expressed in nominal terms. Revenues will increase by 4 percent per year in real terms. Labour costs will increase by 3 percent per year in real terms. Other costs will increase by 1 percent per year in real terms. The rate of inflation is expected to be 6 percent per year. BICC's required rate of return is 10 percent in real terms. There are no taxes. All cash flows occur at year-end. What is the NPV of BICC's proposed toad ranch today?

8.9    You are asked to evaluate the following project for a corporation with profitable ongoing operations. The required investment on January 1 of this year is $56,000. The firm will depreciate the investment at a CCA rate of 20 percent. The firm is in the 40 percent tax bracket.

The price of the product on January 1 will be $320 per unit. That price will stay constant in real terms. Labour costs will be $14 per hour on January 1. They will increase at 1 percent per year in real terms. Energy costs will be $7.35 per physical unit on January 1; they will increase at 2.5 percent per year in real terms. The inflation rate is 6 percent. Revenue is received and costs are paid at year-end:

|  | Year 1 | Year 2 | Year 3 | Year 4 |
|--|--------|--------|--------|--------|
| Physical production, in units | 100 | 200 | 250 | 100 |
| Labour input, in hours | 2,200 | 2,200 | 2,200 | 2,200 |
| Energy input, physical units | 180 | 180 | 180 | 180 |

The risk-free nominal discount rate is 7 percent. The real discount rate for costs and revenues is 4 percent. Calculate the NPV of this project.

8.10   Sparkling Water Inc. sells 4.6 million bottles of drinking water each year. Each bottle sells for $2, and costs per bottle are $0.45. Sales income and costs occur at year-end. Sales income is expected to rise at 6 percent annually, while costs are expected to rise at 4 percent annually. The relevant discount rate is 12 percent. The corporate tax rate is 34 percent. What is Sparkling worth today?

8.11   International Buckeyes is building a factory that can make 1 million buckeyes a year for five years. The factory costs $9 million. In year 1, each buckeye will sell for $4.50. The price will rise 5 percent each year. During the first year, variable costs will be $0.375 per buckeye and will rise by 2 percent each year. International Buckeyes will depreciate the factory at a CCA rate of 25 percent.

International Buckeyes expects to be able to sell the factory for $750,000 at the end of year 5. The proceeds will be invested in a new factory. The discount rate for risky cash flows is 25 percent. The discount rate for risk-free cash flows is 24 percent. Cash flows, except the initial investment, occur at the end of the year. The corporate tax rate is 38 percent. What is the NPV of this project?

8.12   Marvellous Mining Company (MMC) is negotiating for the purchase of a new piece of equipment for its current operations. MMC wants to know the maximum price that it should be willing to pay for the equipment. That is, how high must the price be for the equipment to have an NPV of zero? You are given the following facts:

1.  The new equipment would replace existing equipment that has a current market value of $35,000.

2. The new equipment would not affect revenues, but before-tax operating costs would be reduced by $12,500 per year for eight years. These savings in cost would occur at year-end.
3. The old equipment is now five years old. It is expected to last for another five years and to have no resale value at the end of those five years. It was purchased for $40,000 and is being depreciated at a CCA rate of 30 percent.
4. The new equipment will also be depreciated at a CCA rate of 30 percent. MMC expects to be able to sell the equipment for $6,000 at the end of five years. At that time, the firm plans to reinvest in new equipment in the same CCA pool.
5. MMC has profitable ongoing operations.
6. The appropriate discount rate is 14 percent.
7. The tax rate is 40 percent.

8.13 After extensive medical and marketing research, Pill Ltd. believes it can penetrate the pain reliever market. It can follow one of two strategies. The first is to manufacture a medication aimed at relieving headache pain. The second strategy is to make a pill designed to relieve headache and arthritis pain. Both products would be introduced at a price of $8.35 per package in real terms. The headache and arthritis remedy would probably sell 4.5 million packages per year, while the headache-only medication is projected to sell 3 million packages per year. Cash costs of production in the first year are expected to be $4.10 per package in real terms for the headache-only brand. Production costs are expected to be $4.65 in real terms for the headache and arthritis pill. All prices and costs are expected to rise at the general inflation rate of 3 percent.

Either strategy would require further investment in plant. The headache-only pill could be produced using equipment that would cost $23 million, last three years, and have no resale value. The machinery required to produce the headache and arthritis remedy would cost $32 million and last three years. At this time the firm would be able to sell it for $1 million (in real terms). The production machinery would need to be replaced every three years at constant real costs.

Suppose that for both projects the firm will use a CCA rate of 25 percent. The firm faces a corporate tax rate of 34 percent. Management believes the appropriate real discount rate is 7 percent. Which pain reliever should Pill Ltd. produce?

8.14 A machine that lasts four years has the following net cash outflows: $12,500 to purchase the machine and $7,500 for the annual year-end operating cost. At the end of four years, the machine is sold for $3,200; thus, the cash flow at year 4, $C_4$, is only $4,300:

| $C_0$ | $C_1$ | $C_2$ | $C_3$ | $C_4$ |
|---|---|---|---|---|
| $12,500 | $7,500 | $7,500 | $7,500 | $4,300 |

The cost of capital is 8 percent. What is the PV of the costs of operating a series of such machines in perpetuity?

### Replacement with Unequal Lives

8.15 Office Automation Inc. must choose between two copiers, XX40 and RH45. XX40 costs less than RH45, but its economic life is shorter. The costs and maintenance expenses of these two copiers are given as follows. These cash flows are expressed in real terms:

| Copier | Year 0 | Year 1 | Year 2 | Year 3 | Year 4 | Year 5 |
|---|---|---|---|---|---|---|
| XX40 | $ 900 | $120 | $120 | $120 | | |
| RH45 | 1,400 | 95 | 95 | 95 | $95 | $95 |

The inflation rate is 5 percent and the nominal discount rate is 14 percent. Assume that revenues are the same regardless of the copier, and that whichever copier the company chooses, it will buy the model forever. Which copier should the company choose? Ignore taxes and depreciation.

8.16 Radio Station CJXT is considering replacing its old, fully depreciated sound mixer. Two new models are available. Mixer X has a cost of $500,000, a five-year expected life, and after-tax cash flow savings of $120,000 per year. Mixer Y has a cost of $650,000, an eight-year life, and after-tax cash flow savings of $140,000 per year. No new technological developments are expected. The cost of capital is 13 percent. Should CJXT replace the old mixer with X or Y?

8.17 Which is better: (1) investing $10,000 in a guaranteed investment certificate (GIC) for one year at 8 percent when expected inflation is 4 percent or (2) investing $10,000 in a GIC at 6 percent when expected inflation is 2 percent? In assessing these alternatives, assume that interest received is taxed at a rate of 32 percent.

8.18 A new electronic process monitor will cost Clarke Designs $145,000. This cost will be depreciated at 25 percent per year (class 9). The monitor will actually be worthless in six years. The new monitor would save Clarke $62,000 per year before taxes in operating costs. If Clarke requires a 13.5 percent return, what is the NPV of the purchase? Assume a tax rate of 38 percent.

8.19 Be Safe Security believes it can sell 15,000 home security devices per year at $28 apiece. They cost $19 each to manufacture (variable cost). Fixed production costs will run $30,000 per year. The necessary equipment costs $180,000 to buy and will be depreciated at a 25 percent CCA rate. The equipment will have zero salvage value after the five-year life of the project. When this project is over, there will still be other assets in the CCA class. Be Safe will need to invest $42,500 in net working capital up front, but no additional net working capital investment will be necessary. The discount rate is 18 percent, and the tax rate is 40 percent. What do you think of the proposal?

8.20 This problem is much easier if you are working with a spreadsheet. Sparky Fireworks Inc. is contemplating the purchase of a $1.2 million computer-based customer order management system. CCA on the system will be calculated at a rate of 25 percent. In five years it will be worth $575,000. When this project is over, there will still be other assets in the CCA class. Sparky would save $440,000 before taxes per year in order processing costs and would reduce working capital by $225,000 (a one-time reduction). What is the DCF return on this investment? The relevant tax rate is 34 percent.

8.21 A proposed cost-saving device has an installed cost of $60,500. It is in class 9 for CCA purposes. (CCA rates are given in Table 8A.1 in Appendix 8A.) It will actually function for six years, at which time it will have no value. When this project is over, there will still be other assets in the CCA class. There are no working capital consequences from the investment; the tax rate is 41 percent.

   a. What must the annual pre-tax cost savings be for a company to favour the investment? The company requires a 13 percent return. *Hint:* This is a variation on the problem of setting a bid price.

   b. Suppose the device will be worth $21,000 in salvage (before taxes). How does this change your answer?

8.22 Klaatu Co. has recently completed a $500,000, two-year marketing study. Based on the results, Klaatu has estimated that 12,000 of its new RUR-class robots could be sold annually over the next eight years at a price of $10,130 each. Variable costs per robot are $8,200; fixed costs total $12 million per year.

   Start-up costs include $39 million to build production facilities, $2.5 million in land, and $10 million in net working capital. The $39 million facility is made up of a building valued at $9 million that will belong to CCA class 3 and $30 million of manufacturing equipment (belonging to CCA class 8). (CCA rates are given in Table 8A.1 in Appendix 8A.) At the end of the project's life, the facilities (including the land) will be sold for an estimated $10.3 million, assuming the building's value will be $4 million. When this project is over, there will still be other assets in the CCA class. The value of the land is not expected to change.

   Finally, start-up would also entail fully deductible expenses of $1.4 million at year 0. An ongoing, profitable business, Klaatu pays taxes at a 40 percent rate. Klaatu uses an 18 percent discount rate on projects such as this one. Should Klaatu produce the RUR-class robots?

8.23 ABC Company is considering purchasing manufacturing equipment from two different suppliers. Equipment *A* has a purchase price of $2.9 million and will cost $80,000, pre-tax, to operate on an annual basis. Equipment *B*, on the other hand, has an initial cost of $5.7 million and costs $69,000, pre-tax, annually. Equipment *A* will have to be replaced every 8 years and has a salvage value of $340,000, while equipment *B* has a useful life of 12 years with a salvage value of $420,000. Both equipment sets are in CCA class 9. The tax rate is 35 percent, and the discount rate is 13 percent. Calculate the EAC for each equipment set, and decide which manufacturing equipment to purchase.

> ### MINICASE

## Beaver Mining Company

Beaver Mining is a mid-sized coal-mining company with 20 mines located in western Canada. The company operates deep mines as well as strip mines. Most of the coal mined is sold under contract, with excess production sold on the spot market.

The coal-mining industry, especially high-sulphur coal operations such as Beaver, has been hard hit by environmental regulations. Recently, however, a combination of increased demand for coal and new pollution reduction technologies has led to an improved market demand for high-sulphur coal. Beaver has just been approached by the Mid-Western Electric Company with a request to supply coal for its electric generators for the next four years. Beaver Mining does not have enough excess capacity at its existing mines to guarantee the contract. The company is considering opening a strip mine in British Columbia on 2,000 hectares of land purchased 10 years ago for $5 million. Based on a recent appraisal, the company feels it could receive $5.5 million on an after-tax basis if it sold the land today.

Strip mining is a process where the layers of topsoil above a coal vein are removed and the exposed coal is removed. Some time ago, the company would simply remove the coal and leave the land in an unusable condition. Changes in mining regulations now force a company to reclaim the land; that is, when the mining is completed, the land must be restored to near its original condition. The land can then be used for other purposes. Because it is currently operating at full capacity, Beaver will need to purchase additional necessary equipment, which will cost $85 million. The equipment is in class 9 for CCA purposes (see Appendix 8A) and will thus depreciate at 25 percent per year. The equipment will be the only asset in the company's CCA class. The equipment will be worthless at the end of seven

years. The contract runs for only four years. At that time the coal from the site will be entirely mined. The company feels that the equipment can be sold for 60 percent of its initial purchase price. However, Beaver plans to open another strip mine at that time and will use the equipment at the new mine. For planning purposes, you believe that assets will remain in the CCA's equipment class regardless of when the equipment is disposed of.

The contract calls for the delivery of 500,000 tonnes of coal per year at a price of $82 per tonne. Beaver Mining feels that coal production will be 620,000 tonnes, 680,000 tonnes, 730,000 tonnes, and 590,000 tonnes, respectively, over the next four years. The excess production will be sold in the spot market at an average of $76 per tonne. Variable costs amount to $31 per tonne, and fixed costs are $4,100,000 per year. The mine will require a net working capital investment of 5 percent of sales. The net working capital will be built up in the year prior to the sales.

Beaver will be responsible for reclaiming the land at termination of the mining. This will occur in year 5. The company uses an outside company for reclamation of all of the company's strip mines. It is estimated the cost of reclamation will be $2.7 million. After the land is reclaimed, the company plans to donate the land to the province for use as a public park and recreation area. This will occur in year 6 and result in a charitable expense deduction of $6 million. Beaver faces a 38 percent tax rate and has a 12 percent required return on new strip mine projects. Assume that a loss in any year will result in a tax credit.

You have been approached by the president of the company with a request to analyze the project. Calculate the NPV for the new strip mine. Should Beaver Mining take the contract and open the mine?

# Goodweek Tires Inc.

After extensive research and development, Goodweek Tires Inc. has recently developed a new tire, the SuperTread, and must decide whether to make the investment necessary to produce and market it. The tire would be ideal for drivers doing a large amount of wet weather and off-road driving in addition to normal highway usage. The research and development costs so far have totalled about $10 million. The SuperTread would be put on the market beginning this year, and Goodweek expects it to stay on the market for a total of four years. Test marketing costing $5 million has shown that there is a significant market for a SuperTread-type tire.

As a financial analyst at Goodweek Tires, you have been asked by your CFO, Alana Smith, to evaluate the SuperTread project and recommend whether to go ahead with the investment. Except for the initial investment, which will occur immediately, assume all cash flows will occur at year-end.

Goodweek must initially invest $160 million in production equipment to make the SuperTread. This equipment can be sold for $65 million at the end of four years. Goodweek intends to sell the SuperTread to two distinct markets:

1. *The original equipment manufacturer (OEM) market.* The OEM market consists primarily of the large automobile companies (like General Motors) that buy tires for new cars. In the OEM market, the SuperTread is expected to sell for $41 per tire. The variable cost to produce each tire is $29.

2. *The replacement market.* The replacement market consists of all tires purchased after the automobile has left the factory. This market

allows higher margins; Goodweek expects to sell the SuperTread for $62 per tire there. Variable costs are the same as in the OEM market.

Goodweek Tires intends to raise prices at 1 percent above the inflation rate; variable costs will also increase at 1 percent above the inflation rate. In addition, the SuperTread project will incur $43 million in marketing and general administration costs the first year. This cost is expected to increase at the inflation rate in the subsequent years.

Goodweek's corporate tax rate is 40 percent. Annual inflation is expected to remain constant at 3.25 percent. The company uses a 13.4 percent discount rate to evaluate new product decisions. Automotive industry analysts expect automobile manufacturers to produce 6.2 million new cars this year and production to grow at 2.5 percent per year thereafter. Each new car needs four tires (the spare tires are undersized and are in a different category). Goodweek Tires expects the SuperTread to capture 11 percent of the OEM market.

Industry analysts estimate that the replacement tire market size will be 32 million tires this year and that it will grow at 2 percent annually. Goodweek expects the SuperTread to capture an 8 percent market share.

The appropriate CCA rate for the equipment is 25 percent. The equipment will be the only asset in the company's CCA class. Assume that assets will still remain in this CCA class after the equipment has been disposed of. The immediate initial working capital requirement is $9 million. Thereafter, the net working capital requirements will be 15 percent of sales. What is the NPV of this project?

# Capital Cost Allowance

Under the *Income Tax Act*, accounting amortization cannot be used in the calculation of income for income tax purposes. Instead, the Act mandates the use of the Capital Cost Allowance (CCA) system.[11] CCA is deducted in determining taxable income. CCA is not the same as depreciation under IFRS, so there is no reason the calculation of a firm's income under tax rules has to be the same as under IFRS. For example, taxable corporate income may often be lower than accounting income because the company uses accelerated CCA rules in computing depreciation for tax purposes while using straight-line depreciation for IFRS reporting.[12]

CCA calculation begins by assigning every asset to a particular class. An asset's class establishes its maximum CCA rate for tax purposes. Leasehold improvements follow straight-line depreciation for CCA. For all other assets, CCA follows the declining-balance method. The CCA for each year is computed by multiplying the asset's book value for tax purposes, called *undepreciated capital cost (UCC)*, by the appropriate rate.

Intangible assets, such as goodwill and patents, are particularly important to knowledge-based firms like software developers and pharmaceutical companies. Such assets are not subject to CCA. Instead, intangible assets are amortized at an effective rate of 5.25 percent on the declining balance.

The CCA system is unique to Canada and differs in many respects from the depreciation method used in the United States. One key difference is that in the Canadian system, the expected salvage value (what we think the asset will be worth when we dispose of it) and the actual expected economic life (how long we expect the asset to be in service) are not considered in the calculation of CCA. (Some typical CCA classes and their respective CCA rates are shown in Table 8A.1.) Another unique feature of the CCA system is the concept of pooling of assets described in detail below. Calculating CCA on pools of assets rather than for each item simplifies the system.

**TABLE 8A.1**

### Common Capital Cost Allowance Classes

| Class | Rate | Asset |
|---|---|---|
| 1 | 4% | Brick buildings (acquired after 1987) |
| 3 | 5 | Brick buildings (acquired prior to 1988) |
| 6 | 10 | Fences and frame buildings |
| 7 | 15 | Canoes and boats, ships |
| 8 | 20 | Manufacturing and processing equipment |
| 9 | 25 | Electrical equipment and aircraft |
| 10 | 30 | Vans, trucks, and tractors |
| 13 | straight-line | Leasehold improvements |
| 16 | 40 | Taxicabs (acquired prior to 1976) and rental cars (acquired prior to 1981) |
| 22 | 50 | Excavating equipment |
| 45 | 45 | Computer equipment |

Source: *Income Tax Act 2014* (98th edition).

[11] Recall from Chapter 2 that we use the terms *amortization* and *depreciation* interchangeably throughout this text.

[12] Where taxable income is less than accounting income, total taxes (calculated from accounting income) are greater than current taxes (calculated from taxable income). The difference, deferred taxes (or future tax liability) for the year, is added to the deferred tax liability account on the balance sheet.

To illustrate how CCA is calculated, suppose your firm is considering buying a van costing $24,000, including any set-up costs that must (by law) be capitalized. (No rational, profitable business would capitalize, for tax purposes, anything that could legally be expensed.) Table 8A.1 shows that vans fall in class 10 with a 30 percent CCA rate. To calculate the CCA, we need to follow the 50 percent rule, which requires us to figure CCA on only one-half of the asset's installed cost in the first year it is put in use. Notice that we add the other half in the second year. The UCC at the beginning of year 2 is

$$\text{Beginning UCC} - \text{CCA} + \text{Remaining half of purchase price}$$

$$\$12,000 - 0.30 \times \$12,000 + \$12,000 = \$20,400$$

Table 8A.2 shows the CCA for our van for the first five years.

## TABLE 8A.2

### Capital Cost Allowance for a Van

| Year | Beginning undepreciated capital cost | Capital cost allowance | Ending undepreciated capital cost |
|------|--------------------------------------|------------------------|-----------------------------------|
| 1 | $12,000* | $3,600 | $ 8,400 |
| 2 | 20,400† | 6,120 | 14,280 |
| 3 | 14,280 | 4,284 | 9,996 |
| 4 | 9,996 | 2,999 | 6,997 |
| 5 | 6,997 | 2,099 | 4,898 |

*One-half of $24,000.

†Year 1 ending balance plus the remaining half of $24,000.

As we pointed out, in calculating CCA under current tax law, the economic life and future market value of the asset are not issues. As a result, an asset's UCC can differ substantially from its actual market value. With our $24,000 van, UCC after the first year is $8,400 (or $12,000 less the first year's CCA of $3,600). The remaining UCC values are summarized in Table 8A.2. After five years, the van's UCC is $4,898.

## Capital Cost Allowance in Practice

Since CCA is deducted in computing taxable income, larger CCA rates reduce taxes and increase cash flows. To illustrate, in a federal budget a few years ago, the minister announced an increase in CCA rates from 30 to 45 percent for computer equipment. The combined federal/provincial corporate tax rate for this sector is 34.5 percent.

## EXAMPLE 8A.1

Mississauga Manufacturing was planning to acquire new processing equipment to enhance efficiency and its ability to compete with U.S. firms. The equipment had an installed cost of $1 million. How much additional tax did the new measure save Mississauga in the first year the equipment was put into use? Assume a tax rate of 34.5 percent.

Under the 50 percent rule, UCC for the first year is $1/2 \times \$1$ million = $500,000. The CCA deductions under the old and new rates are as follows:

Old rate: CCA = $0.30 \times \$500,000 = \$150,000$

New rate: CCA = $0.45 \times \$500,000 = \$225,000$

Because the firm deducts CCA in figuring taxable income, taxable income will be reduced by the incremental CCA of $75,000. With $75,000 less in taxable income, Mississauga Manufacturing's combined tax bill will drop by $75,000 \times 0.345 = \$25,875$.

## Asset Purchases and Sales

When an asset is sold, the UCC in its asset class (or pool) is reduced by the proceeds from disposition or by its original cost, whichever is less. This amount is called the *adjusted cost of disposal* and is frequently referred to as the *lower of cost or proceeds (LOCP) rule*. Suppose that we want to sell the van in our earlier example after five years and find that it is worth $6,000. Since the $6,000 price is less than the original cost, the adjusted cost of disposal is $6,000 and the UCC in class 10 is reduced by this amount.

In this case, the $6,000 removed from the pool is $1,102 (or $6,000 − $4,898) more than the UCC of the van we are selling, and future CCA deductions will be reduced as the pool continues. On the other hand, if we sold the van for, say, $4,000, the UCC in class 10 would be reduced by $4,000, and the $898 excess ($4,898 − $4,000) of UCC over the sale price would remain in the pool. In this case, future CCA increases as the declining-balance calculations depreciate the $898 excess UCC to infinity.

So far, we have focused on CCA calculations for one asset. In practice, firms often buy and sell assets from a given class in the course of a year. In this case, we apply the net acquisitions rule. From the total installed cost of all acquisitions we subtract the adjusted cost of disposal of all assets in the pool. The result is net acquisitions for the asset class. If net acquisitions are positive, we apply the 50 percent rule and calculate CCA as above. If net acquisitions are negative, the 50 percent rule does not apply.

## When an Asset Pool Is Terminated

Suppose your firm decides to contract out all transport and to sell all company vehicles. If the company owns no other class 10 assets, the asset pool in this class is terminated. As before, the adjusted cost of disposal is the net sales proceeds or the total installed cost of all the pool assets, whichever is less. This adjusted cost of disposal is subtracted from the total UCC in the pool. So far, the steps are exactly the same as in our van example, where the pool continued. What happens next is different. Unless the adjusted cost of disposal just happens to equal the UCC exactly, a positive or negative UCC balance remains, which has tax implications.

A positive UCC balance remains when the adjusted cost of disposal is less than UCC before the sale. In this case, the firm has a terminal loss equal to the remaining UCC. The terminal loss represents the fact that the class was underdepreciated and thus is deductible for tax purposes. Because this loss is deductible from income for the year, it results in a tax saving. For example, if we sell the van after two years for $10,000, then the UCC exceeds the market value by $4,280 (or $14,280 − $10,000). In this case, the terminal loss of $4,280—assuming the tax rate is 40 percent—gives rise to a tax saving of $0.40 × $4,280 = $1,712.

A negative UCC balance occurs when the adjusted cost of disposal exceeds UCC in the pool. To illustrate, return to our van example and suppose that this van is the only class 10 asset our company owns when it sells off the pool. In this case, we see that there is a $1,102 excess of adjusted cost of disposal ($6,000 − $4,898) over UCC, so the final UCC balance is −$1,102.

The company must pay tax at its ordinary tax rate on this negative balance. Taxes must be paid in this case since the difference in adjusted cost of disposal and UCC is "excess" CCA recaptured when the asset is sold. We overdepreciated the asset by $6,000 − $4,898 = $1,102. Since we deducted $1,102 too much in CCA, we paid $440.80 ($1,102 × 0.4) too little in taxes, and we simply have to make up the difference.

Notice that this is not a tax on a capital gain. As a general rule, a capital gain only occurs if the market price exceeds the original cost. To illustrate a capital gain, suppose that instead of buying the van, our firm purchased a classic car for $50,000. After five years, the classic car will be sold for $75,000. In this case, the sale price exceeds the purchase price, so the adjusted cost of disposal is $50,000 and the UCC pool is reduced by this amount. The total negative balance left in the UCC pool is $6,123 − $50,000 = −$43,877, which is recaptured CCA. In addition, the firm has a capital gain of $75,000 − $50,000 = $25,000, the difference between the sale price and the original cost.

Staple Supply Ltd. has just purchased a new computerized information system with an installed cost of $160,000. The computer is in class 45 for CCA purposes. What are the yearly CCAs? Based on experience, we think that the system will be worth only $10,000 when we get rid of it in four years. What are the tax consequences of the sale if the company has several other computers that will still be in use in four years? Now suppose that Staple Supply will sell all its assets and wind up the company in four years. What is the total after-tax cash flow from the sale?

In Table 8A.3, at the end of year 4 the remaining balance for the specific computer system will be $20,630.[13] The pool is reduced by $10,000, but it will continue to be "depreciated." There are no tax consequences in year 4. This is only the case when the pool is active. If this is the only computer system, we close the pool and claim a terminal loss of $20,630 − $10,000 = $10,630.

### TABLE 8A.3

**Capital Cost Allowance for a Computer System**

| Year | Beginning undepreciated capital cost | Capital cost allowance | Ending undepreciated capital cost |
|------|--------------------------------------|------------------------|------------------------------------|
| 1 | $ 80,000* | $36,000 | $44,000 |
| 2 | 124,000† | 53,800 | 68,200 |
| 3 | 68,200 | 30,690 | 37,510 |
| 4 | 37,510 | 16,880 | 20,630 |

*One-half of $160,000.
†Year 1 ending balance plus the remaining half of $80,000.

The company must pay tax on this capital gain of $25,000. As explained in Appendix 1A, at the time of writing, a corporation is taxed on 50 percent of any capital gains. Using a marginal corporate tax rate of 40 percent, the tax payable is $5,000 (or $25,000 × 0.50 × 0.40).

8A.1   What is the difference between CCA and IFRS depreciation?

8A.2   A company has just invested $215,500 in new manufacturing equipment (class 8). Develop a CCA and UCC schedule (like Table 8A.2) for the first 10 years.

8A.3   Suppose the company decides to sell the equipment after three years for $60,000 and terminates the asset pool. Calculate the tax results.

---

[13] In actuality, the CCA for the entire pool will be calculated at once, without specific identification of each computer system.

## Derivation of the Present Value of the Capital Cost Allowance Tax Shield Formula

We can use the growing-perpetuity formula from Chapter 5 [equation (5.10)] to derive the PV of the CCA tax shield. Recall that when cash flows grow at a constant rate $g$, the PV of the perpetuity at discount rate $k$ is

$$PV = \frac{\text{1st payment}}{k - g}$$

Since we are temporarily ignoring the half-year rule, the growth rate in CCA payments is equal to $(-d)$, the CCA rate. Since CCA declines over time as the depreciable base (CC) reduces, the growth rate is negative. For example, in Table 8.6,

$$\begin{aligned} CCA_3 &= CCA_2[1 + (-d)] \\ &= 144{,}000[1 + (-0.20)] \\ &= 144{,}000(0.8) = 115{,}200 \end{aligned}$$

Given the growth rate as $(-d)$, we need the first payment to complete the formula. This is the first year's tax shield calculating the CCA at rate $d$ on the total cost of the asset added to the depreciation pool, $C$, and then multiplying by the tax rate, $T_c$:

$$\text{1st payment} = CdT_c$$

We can now complete the formula:

$$\begin{aligned} PV \text{ (CCA tax shield)} &= \frac{\text{1st payment}}{k - g} \\ &= \frac{CdT_c}{k - (-d)} \\ &= \frac{CdT_c}{k + d} \end{aligned}$$

The next step is to extend the formula to adjust for CRA's 50 percent rule. This rule states that a firm must add one-half of the incremental capital cost of a new project in year 1 and the other half in year 2. The result is that we now calculate the PV of the tax shield in two parts. The PV of the stream starting the first year is simply one-half of the original value:

$$PV \text{ of 1st half} = 0.5\left(\frac{CdT_c}{k + d}\right)$$

The PV of the second half (deferred one year) is the same quantity (bracketed term below) discounted back to time zero. The total PV of the tax shield on CCA under the 50 percent rule is the sum of the two PVs:

$$PV \text{ tax shield on CCA} = 0.5\frac{CdT_c}{k + d} + \left(\frac{0.5CdT_c}{k + d}\right)\frac{1}{1 + k}$$

With a little algebra we can simplify the formula to

$$\begin{aligned} PV &= \frac{0.5CdT_c}{k + d}\left(1 + \frac{1}{1 + k}\right) \\ &= \frac{0.5CdT_c}{k + d}\left(\frac{1 + k + 1}{1 + k}\right) \\ &= \frac{CdT_c}{k + d}\left(\frac{1 + 0.5k}{1 + k}\right) \end{aligned}$$

The final adjustment for salvage value begins with the PV in the salvage year, $n$, of future tax shields beginning in year $n + 1$:

$$\frac{SdT_c}{k + d}$$

We discount this figure back to today and subtract it to get the complete formula:[14]

$$\text{PV tax shield on CCA} = \frac{CdT_c}{k + d} \times \frac{1 + 0.5k}{1 + k} - \frac{SdT_c}{k + d} \times \frac{1}{(1 + k)^n} \qquad \text{(8B.1)}$$

---

[14] By not adjusting the salvage value for the 50 percent rule, we assume there will be no new investment in year $n$.

# CHAPTER 9

## Risk Analysis, Real Options, and Capital Budgeting

EXECUTIVE SUMMARY

Chapters 7 and 8 covered the basic principles of capital budgeting, with particular emphasis on the net present value (NPV) approach. However, this is not the end of the story. Real-world practitioners often wonder how much confidence they should place in NPV calculations. This chapter examines sensitivity analysis, scenario analysis, break-even analysis, and Monte Carlo simulations, all of which recognize that because it is based on estimates, NPV is really a distribution, not a single number. These techniques help the practitioner determine the degree of confidence to be placed in a capital budgeting calculation.

Information is uncovered as a project unfolds, allowing a manager to make sequential decisions over the life of the project. This chapter covers decision trees and real options, capital budgeting techniques that specifically take the sequential nature of decision making into account.

## 9.1 DECISION TREES

There is usually a sequence of decisions in NPV project analysis. This section introduces the device of **decision trees** for identifying these sequential decisions.

Imagine you are the treasurer of the Solar Electronics Corporation (SEC), and the engineering group has recently developed the technology for solar-powered jet engines. The jet engine is to be used with 150-passenger commercial airplanes. The marketing staff has proposed that SEC develop some prototypes and conduct test marketing of the engine. A corporate planning group, including representatives from production, marketing, and engineering, estimates that this preliminary phase will take a year and will cost $100 million. Furthermore, the group believes there is a 75 percent chance that the marketing tests will prove successful.

If the initial marketing tests are *successful*, SEC can go ahead with full-scale production. This investment phase will cost $1,500 million. Production and sales will occur over the next five years. The preliminary cash flow projection appears in Table 9.1. If SEC goes ahead with investment and production on the jet engine, the NPV at a discount rate of 15 percent (in millions) will be

$$
\begin{aligned}
\text{NPV} &= -\$1,500 + \sum_{t=1}^{5} \frac{\$900}{(1.15)^t} \\
&= -\$1,500 + \$900 \times A_{0.15}^{5} \\
&= \$1,517
\end{aligned}
$$

sensitive a particular NPV calculation is to changes in underlying assumptions. We illustrate the technique with SEC's solar-powered jet engine from the previous section. As pointed out earlier, the cash flow forecasts for this project appear in Table 9.1. We begin by considering the assumptions underlying revenues, costs, and after-tax cash flows shown in the table.

**Revenues**    Sales projections for the proposed jet engine have been estimated by the marketing department as

| Number of jet engines sold = | Market share | × Size of jet engine market |
|---|---|---|
| 3,000 | = 0.30 | × 10,000 |
| Sales revenues | = Number of jet engines sold × | Price per engine |
| $6,000 million | = 3,000 | × $2 million |

Thus, it turns out that the revenue estimates depend on three assumptions:

1. Market share
2. Size of jet engine market
3. Price per engine

**Costs**    Financial analysts frequently divide costs into two types: variable costs and fixed costs. **Variable costs** change as the output changes, and they are zero when production is zero. Costs of direct labour and raw materials are usually variable. It is common to assume that a variable cost is constant per unit of output, implying that total variable costs are proportional to the level of production. For example, if direct labour is variable and one unit of final output requires $10 of direct labour, then 100 units of final output should require $1,000 of direct labour.

**Fixed costs** do not depend on the amount of goods or services produced during the period. Fixed costs are usually measured as costs per unit of time, such as rent per month or salaries per year. Naturally, fixed costs are not fixed forever. They are only fixed over a predetermined time period.

The engineering department has estimated variable costs to be $1 million per engine. Fixed costs are $1,791 million per year. The cost breakdowns are

| Variable cost | = Variable cost per unit × Number of jet engines sold |
|---|---|
| $3,000 million | = $1 million × 3,000 |

| Total cost before taxes = | Variable cost | + | Fixed cost |
|---|---|---|---|
| $4,791 million | = $3,000 million | + | $1,791 million |

The above estimates for market size, market share, price, variable cost, and fixed cost, as well as the estimate of initial investment, are presented in the middle column of Table 9.2. These figures represent the firm's expectations or best estimates of the different parameters. For comparison, the firm's analysts prepared both optimistic and pessimistic forecasts for the different variables. These are also provided in the table.

TABLE 9.2

**Different Estimates for SEC's Solar Jet Engine**

| Variable | Pessimistic | Expected or best | Optimistic |
|---|---|---|---|
| Market size (per year) | 5,000 | 10,000 | 20,000 |
| Market share | 20% | 30% | 50% |
| Price (per engine)* | $1.9 | $2 | $2.2 |
| Variable cost (per plane)* | $1.2 | $1 | $0.8 |
| Fixed cost (per year)* | $1,891 | $1,791 | $1,741 |
| Investment* | $1,900 | $1,500 | $1,000 |

* In $ millions.

Standard sensitivity analysis calls for an NPV calculation for all three possibilities of a single variable, along with the expected forecast for all other variables. This procedure is illustrated in Table 9.3. For example, consider the NPV calculation of $8,154 million provided in the upper right-hand corner of this table. This occurs when the optimistic forecast of 20,000 units per year is used for market size. However, the expected forecasts from Table 9.2 are employed for all other variables when the $8,154 million figure is generated. Note that the same number—$1,517 million—appears in each row of the middle column of Table 9.3. This occurs because the expected forecast is used for the variable that was singled out, as well as for all other variables.

**TABLE 9.3**

**Net Present Value Calculations as of Date 1 (in $ millions) for the Solar Jet Engine Using Sensitivity Analysis**

|              | Pessimistic | Expected or best | Optimistic |
|--------------|-------------|------------------|------------|
| Market size  | −$1,802*    | $1,517           | $8,154     |
| Market share | −696*       | 1,517            | 5,942      |
| Price        | 853         | 1,517            | 2,844      |
| Variable cost| 189         | 1,517            | 2,844      |
| Fixed cost   | 1,295       | 1,517            | 1,628      |
| Investment   | 1,117       | 1,517            | 2,017      |

Under sensitivity analysis, one input is varied while all other inputs are assumed to meet their expectation. For example, an NPV of −$1,802 occurs when the pessimistic forecast of 5,000 is used for market size. However, the expected forecasts from Table 9.2 are used for all other variables when −$1,802 is generated.

* We assume that the other divisions of the firm are profitable, implying that a loss on this project can offset income elsewhere in the firm, thereby reducing the overall taxes of the firm.

Table 9.3 can be used for a number of purposes. First, taken as a whole, the table can indicate whether NPV analysis should be trusted. In other words, it reduces the false sense of security we spoke of earlier. Suppose that NPV is positive when the expected forecast for each variable is used. However, further suppose that every number in the pessimistic column is highly negative and every number in the optimistic column is highly positive. Even a single error in this forecast greatly alters the estimate, making one leery of the NPV approach. A conservative manager might well scrap the entire NPV analysis in this situation. Fortunately, this does not seem to be the case in Table 9.3, because all but two of the numbers are positive. Managers viewing the table will likely consider NPV analysis to be useful for the solar-powered jet engine.

Second, sensitivity analysis shows where more information is needed. For example, error in the estimate of investment appears to be relatively unimportant because even under the pessimistic scenario, the NPV of $1,117 million is still highly positive. By contrast, the pessimistic forecast for market share leads to a negative NPV of −$696 million, and a pessimistic forecast for market size leads to a substantially negative NPV of −$1,802 million. Since the effect of incorrect estimates on revenues is so much greater than the effect of incorrect estimates on costs, more information on the factors determining revenues might be needed.

Because of these advantages, sensitivity analysis is widely used in practice. Graham and Harvey report that slightly over 50 percent of the 392 firms in their sample subject their capital budgeting calculations to sensitivity analysis.[3] This number is particularly large when one considers that only about 75 percent of the firms in their sample use NPV analysis.

---

[3] See Figure 2 of John Graham and Campbell Harvey, "The Theory and Practice of Corporate Finance: Evidence from the Field," *Journal of Financial Economics* (May/June 2001).

Unfortunately, sensitivity analysis also suffers from some drawbacks. For example, sensitivity analysis may unwittingly *increase* the false sense of security among managers. Suppose all pessimistic forecasts yield positive NPVs. A manager might feel that there is no way the project can lose money. Of course, the forecasters may simply have an optimistic view of a pessimistic forecast. To combat this, some companies do not treat optimistic and pessimistic forecasts subjectively. Rather, their pessimistic forecasts are always, say, 20 percent less than expected. Unfortunately, the cure in this case may be worse than the disease, because a deviation of a fixed percentage ignores the fact that some variables are easier to forecast than others.

In addition, sensitivity analysis treats each variable in isolation when, in reality, the different variables are likely to be related. For example, if ineffective management allows costs to get out of control, it is likely that variable costs, fixed costs, and investment will all rise above expectation at the same time. If the market is not receptive to a solar-powered jet engine, both market share and price should decline together.

Managers frequently perform **scenario analysis**, a variant of sensitivity analysis, to minimize this problem. Simply put, this approach examines a number of different likely scenarios, where each scenario involves a confluence of factors. As a simple example, consider the effect of a few airline crashes. These crashes are likely to reduce flying in total, thereby limiting the demand for any new engines. Furthermore, even if the crashes did not involve solar-powered aircraft, the public could become more averse to any innovative and controversial technologies. Hence, SEC's market share might fall as well. Perhaps the cash flow calculations would look like those in Table 9.4 under the scenario of a plane crash. Given the calculations in the table, the NPV (in millions) would be

$$-\$2,023 = -\$1,500 - \$156 \times A_{0.15}^5$$

A series of scenarios like this might illuminate issues concerning the project better than the standard application of sensitivity analysis would.

TABLE 9.4

**Cash Flow Forecast (in $ millions) under the Scenario of a Plane Crash\***

|  | Year 1 | Years 2–6 |
|---|---|---|
| Revenues |  | $2,800 |
| Variable costs |  | −1,400 |
| Fixed costs |  | −1,791 |
| Depreciation |  | −300 |
| Pre-tax profit |  | −691 |
| Tax ($T_c = 0.34$)† |  | 235 |
| Net profit |  | −456 |
| Cash flow |  | −156 |
| Initial investment cost | −$1,500 |  |

\* Assumptions are

Market size    7,000 (70 percent of expectation)

Market share    20% (2/3 of expectation)

Forecasts for all other variables are the expected forecasts as given in Table 9.2.

† Tax loss offsets income elsewhere in the firm.

## Break-Even Analysis

Our discussion of sensitivity analysis and scenario analysis suggests that there are many ways to examine variability in forecasts. We now present another approach, **break-even analysis**. As its name implies, this approach determines the sales needed to break even. The approach is a useful complement to sensitivity analysis, because it also sheds light on the severity of incorrect forecasts. We calculate the break-even point in terms of both accounting profit and present value (PV).

**Accounting Profit**    Net profit under four different sales forecasts is as follows:

| Unit sales | Net profit (in $ millions) |
|---|---|
| 0 | −$1,380 |
| 1,000 | −720 |
| 3,000 | 600 |
| 10,000 | 5,220 |

A more complete presentation of costs and revenues appears in Table 9.5.

We plot the revenues, costs, and profits under the different assumptions about sales in Figure 9.2. The revenue and cost curves cross at 2,091 jet engines. This is the break-even point—the point where the project generates no profits or losses. As long as sales are above 2,091 jet engines, the project will make a profit.

TABLE 9.5

**Revenues and Costs of Project under Different Sales Assumptions (in $ millions, except unit sales)**

| Year 1 | | | | | | Years 2–6 | | | |
|---|---|---|---|---|---|---|---|---|---|
| Initial investment | Annual unit sales | Revenues | Variable costs | Fixed costs | Depreciation | Taxes* ($T_c$ = 0.34) | Net profit | Operating cash flows | Net present value (evaluated date 1) |
| $1,500 | 0 | $    0 | $    0 | −$1,791 | −$300 | $    711 | −$1,380 | −$1,080 | −$5,120 |
| 1,500 | 1,000 | 2,000 | −1,000 | −1,791 | −300 | 371 | −720 | −420 | −2,908 |
| 1,500 | 3,000 | 6,000 | −3,000 | −1,791 | −300 | −309 | 600 | 900 | 1,517 |
| 1,500 | 10,000 | 20,000 | −10,000 | −1,791 | −300 | −2,689 | 5,220 | 5,520 | 17,004 |

* Loss is incurred in the first two rows. For tax purposes, this loss offsets income elsewhere in the firm.

FIGURE 9.2

**Break-Even Point Using Accounting Numbers**

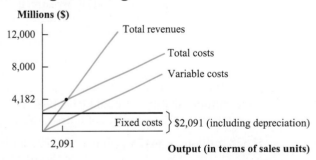

This break-even point can be calculated very easily. Because the sale price is $2 million per engine and the variable cost is $1 million per engine,[4] the after-tax difference per engine is

$$(\text{Sale price} - \text{Variable cost}) \times (1 - T_c) = (\$2 \text{ million} - \$1 \text{ million}) \times (1 - 0.34)$$
$$= \$0.66 \text{ million}$$

---

[4] Though the previous section considered both optimistic and pessimistic forecasts for sale price and variable cost, break-even analysis uses just the expected or best estimates of these variables.

where $T_c$ is the corporate tax rate of 34 percent. This after-tax difference is called the **contribution margin** because each additional engine contributes this amount to after-tax profit.

Fixed costs are $1,791 million and depreciation is $300 million, implying that the after-tax sum of these costs is

$$\text{(Fixed costs + Depreciation)} \times (1 - T_c) = (\$1,791 \text{ million} + \$300 \text{ million}) \times (1 - 0.34)$$
$$= \$1,380 \text{ million}$$

That is, the firm incurs costs of $1,380 million, regardless of the number of sales. Because each engine contributes $0.66 million, sales must reach the following level to offset the above costs:

### Accounting Profit Break-Even Point:

$$\frac{\text{(Fixed costs + Depreciation)} \times (1 - T_c)}{\text{(Sale price − Variable costs)} \times (1 - T_c)} = \frac{\$1,380 \text{ million}}{\$0.66 \text{ million}} = 2,091 \qquad (9.1)$$

Thus, 2,091 engines is the break-even point required for an accounting profit.

**Present Value**   As we stated many times in the text, we are more interested in PV than we are in net profits. Therefore, we must calculate the PV of the cash flows. Given a discount rate of 15 percent, we have

| Unit sales | Net present value (in $ millions) |
|:----------:|:---------------------------------:|
| 0          | −5,120                            |
| 1,000      | −2,908                            |
| 3,000      | 1,517                             |
| 10,000     | 17,004                            |

These NPV calculations are reproduced in the last column of Table 9.5. We can see that the NPV is negative if SEC produces 1,000 jet engines and positive if it produces 3,000 jet engines. Obviously, the zero NPV point occurs between 1,000 and 3,000 jet engines.

The PV break-even point can be calculated very easily. The firm originally invested $1,500 million. This initial investment can be expressed as a five-year equivalent annual cost (EAC), determined by dividing the initial investment by the appropriate five-year annuity factor:

$$\text{EAC} = \frac{\text{Initial investment}}{\text{5-year annuity factor at 15\%}} = \frac{\text{Initial investment}}{A_{0.15}^5}$$
$$= \frac{\$1,500 \text{ million}}{3.3522} = \$447.5 \text{ million}$$

Note that the EAC of $447.5 million is greater than the yearly depreciation of $300 million. This must occur since the calculation of EAC implicitly assumes that the $1,500 million investment could have been invested at 15 percent.

After-tax costs, regardless of output, can be viewed as

$$\$1,528 \text{ million} = \$447.5 \text{ million} + \$1,791 \text{ million} \times \quad 0.66 \quad - \$300 \text{ million} \times 0.34$$
$$= \quad \text{EAC} \quad + \text{ Fixed costs } \times (1 - T_c) - \text{Depreciation} \times \quad T_c$$

That is, in addition to the initial investment's EAC of $447.5 million, the firm pays fixed costs each year and receives a depreciation tax shield each year. The depreciation tax shield is written as a negative number since it offsets the costs in the equation. Because each engine contributes $0.66 million to after-tax profit, it will take the following sales to offset the above costs:

**Present Value Break-Even Point:**

$$\frac{\text{EAC} + \text{Fixed costs} \times (1 - T_c) - \text{Depreciation} \times T_c}{(\text{Sales price} - \text{Variable costs}) \times (1 - T_c)} = \frac{\$1{,}528 \text{ million}}{\$0.66 \text{ million}} = 2{,}315 \quad \textbf{(9.2)}$$

Thus, 2,315 engines is the break-even point from the perspective of PV.

Why is the accounting break-even point (equation (9.1)) different from the financial break-even point in equation (9.2)? When we use accounting profit as the basis for the break-even calculation, we subtract depreciation. Depreciation for the solar jet engines project is $300 million. If 2,091 solar jet engines are sold, SEC will generate sufficient revenues to cover the $300 million depreciation expense plus other costs. Unfortunately, at this level of sales, SEC will not cover the economic opportunity costs of the $1,500 million laid out for the investment. If we take into account that the $1,500 million could have been invested at 15 percent, the true annual cost of the investment is $447.5 million and not $300 million. Depreciation understates the true costs of recovering the initial investment. Thus, companies that break even on an accounting basis are really losing money. They are losing the opportunity cost of the initial investment.

***CONCEPT***
*QUESTIONS*

- What is sensitivity analysis?
- Why is it important to perform a sensitivity analysis?
- What is break-even analysis?
- Describe how sensitivity analysis interacts with break-even analysis.

## Break-Even Analysis, Equivalent Annual Cost, and Capital Cost Allowance

So far, in this chapter and the previous one, all our examples with EAC and break-even analysis have featured straight-line depreciation. While this had the advantage of simplifying the examples, it lacks realism for Canada. Here, Example 9.1 shows how to incorporate capital cost allowance (CCA) into break-even analysis using the EAC approach.

EXAMPLE **13.1**

Nack Trucks Inc. is expanding into the business of buying stripped-down truck platforms, which it plans to customize to client specifications and resell. The company will rent its manufacturing facility for $6,000 per month. Truck platforms cost $20,000 each, and the typical finished product sells for $42,000.

This new business line would require $60,000 in new equipment. This equipment falls into class 8 with a CCA rate of 20 percent and would be worth about $5,000 after four years. Nack's tax rate is 43.5 percent, and the cost of capital is 20 percent.

There is only one major competitor, and Nack's sales staff estimate that they could achieve annual sales of 12 units. In order to determine if this sales level will be profitable, we must find the NPV break-even point.

This problem is very similar to the one we solved for SEC in equation (9.2) above. The key difference is that the depreciation here is based on CCA, so we have to replace the term Depreciation $\times T_c$ in (9.2) with the EAC of the PV of the CCA tax shield (PVCCATS): EAC$_{\text{PVCCATS}}$. This requires first calculating PVCCATS and then converting to an EAC:

$$\text{PVCCATS} = \frac{\$60{,}000(0.20)(0.435)}{0.20 + 0.20} \times \frac{1 + 0.5(0.20)}{1 + 0.20}$$

$$- \frac{\$5{,}000(0.20)(0.435)}{0.20 + 0.20} \times \frac{1}{(1.20)^4} = \$11{,}438$$

$$\text{EAC}_{\text{PVCCATS}} = \frac{\$11{,}438}{A^4_{0.20}} = \frac{\$11{,}438}{2.5887} = \$4{,}418.38$$

Next we find the EAC of the investment as

$$[\$60{,}000 - \$5{,}000/(1.20)^4]/2.5887 = \$22{,}245.90$$

Note that your EAC of the investment may be slightly different due to rounding. Fixed costs after tax are the rent of $6,000 × 12 = $72,000 per year times $(1 - 0.435)$, or $40,680, and the after-tax contribution margin is $(\$42{,}000 - \$20{,}000)(1 - 0.435) = \$12{,}430$.

We can now rewrite equation (9.2) and fill in the numbers:

**Present Value Break-Even Point with Capital Cost Allowance:**

$$\frac{\text{EAC} + \text{Fixed costs} \times (1 - T_c) - \text{EAC}_{\text{PVCCATS}}}{(\text{Sale price} - \text{Variable costs}) \times (1 - T_c)} = \frac{\$22{,}245.90 + \$40{,}680 - \$4{,}418.38}{\$12{,}430}$$

$$= 4.71 \text{ or } 5 \text{ trucks}$$

Our calculations show that the break-even point is 5 trucks. This is well below targeted sales of 12 trucks, so the expansion looks promising.

## 9.3     MONTE CARLO SIMULATION

Both sensitivity analysis and scenario analysis attempt to answer the question, "What if?" However, while both analyses are frequently used in the real world, each has its own limitations. Sensitivity analysis allows only one variable to change at a time. By contrast, many variables are likely to move at the same time in the real world. Scenario analysis follows specific scenarios, such as changes in inflation, government regulation, or the number of competitors. While this methodology is often quite helpful, it cannot cover all sources of variability. In fact, projects are likely to exhibit a lot of variability under just one economic scenario.

**Monte Carlo simulation** is a further attempt to model real-world uncertainty. This approach takes its name from the famous European casino, because it analyzes projects the way one might analyze gambling strategies. Imagine a serious blackjack player who wonders if he should take a third card whenever his first two cards total 16. Most likely, a formal mathematical model would be too complex to be practical here. However, he could play thousands of hands in a casino, sometimes drawing a third card when his first two cards add to 16 and sometimes not drawing that third card. He could compare his winnings (or losses) under the two strategies to determine which was better. Of course, since he would probably lose a lot of money performing this test in a real casino, simulating the results from the two strategies on a computer might be cheaper. Monte Carlo simulation of capital budgeting projects is in this spirit.

Imagine that Backyard Barbecues Inc. (BBI), a manufacturer of both charcoal and gas grills, has the blueprint for a new grill that cooks with compressed hydrogen. The CFO, Ellen H. Comiskey, being dissatisfied with simpler capital budgeting techniques, wants a Monte Carlo simulation for this new grill. A consultant specializing in the Monte Carlo approach, Lester Mauney, takes her through the five basic steps of the method.

## Step 1: Specify the Basic Model

Lester breaks up cash flow into three components: annual revenue, annual costs, and initial investment. The revenue in any year is viewed as

$$\underset{\text{by entire industry}}{\text{Number of grills sold}} \times \underset{\text{hydrogen grill (in percent)}}{\text{Market share of BBI's}} \times \underset{\text{hydrogen grill}}{\text{Price per}} \qquad (9.3)$$

The cost in any year is viewed as

$$\underset{\text{manufacturing costs}}{\text{Fixed}} + \underset{\text{manufacturing costs}}{\text{Variable}} + \underset{\text{costs}}{\text{Marketing}} + \underset{\text{costs}}{\text{Selling}}$$

Initial investment is viewed as

$$\text{Cost of patent} + \text{Test-marketing costs} + \text{Cost of production facility}$$

## Step 2: Specify a Distribution for Each Variable in the Model

Here comes the hard part. Let's start with revenue, which has three components in (9.3). The consultant first models overall market size, that is, the number of grills sold by the entire industry. The trade publication *Outdoor Food* (*OF*) reported that 10 million grills of all types were sold in North America last year and it forecasts sales of 10.5 million next year. Lester, using *OF*'s forecast and his own intuition, creates the following distribution for next year's sales of grills by the entire industry:

| Probability | 20% | 60% | 20% |
|---|---|---|---|
| **Next year's industrywide unit sales** | 10 million | 10.5 million | 11 million |

The tight distribution here reflects the slow but steady historical growth in the grill market. This probability distribution is graphed in Panel A of Figure 9.3.

Lester realizes that estimating the market share of BBI's hydrogen grill is more difficult. Nevertheless, after a great deal of analysis, he determines the distribution of next year's market share to be as follows:

| Probability | 10% | 20% | 30% | 25% | 10% | 5% |
|---|---|---|---|---|---|---|
| **Market share of BBI's hydrogen grill next year** | 1% | 2% | 3% | 4% | 5% | 8% |

While the consultant assumed a symmetrical distribution for industrywide unit sales, he believes a skewed distribution makes more sense for the project's market share. In his mind, there is always the small possibility that sales of the hydrogen grill will really take off. This probability distribution is graphed in Panel B of Figure 9.3.

The above forecasts assume that unit sales for the overall industry are unrelated to the project's market share. In other words, the two variables are *independent* of each other. Lester reasons that while an economic boom might increase industrywide grill sales and a recession might decrease them, the project's market share is unlikely to be related to economic conditions.

Now Lester must determine the distribution of price per grill. Ellen, the CFO, informs him that the price will be in the area of $200 per grill, given what competitors are charging. However, the consultant believes that the price per hydrogen grill will almost certainly depend on the size of the overall market for grills. As in any business, you can usually charge more if demand is high.

After rejecting a number of complex models for price, Lester settles on the following specification:

$$\underset{\text{per hydrogen grill}}{\text{Next year's price}} = \$190 + \$1 \times \underset{\text{(in millions)}}{\text{Industrywide unit sales}} \pm \$3 \qquad (9.4)$$

FIGURE 9.3

**Probability Distributions for Industrywide Unit Sales, Market Share of BBI's Hydrogen Grill, and Price of Hydrogen Grill**

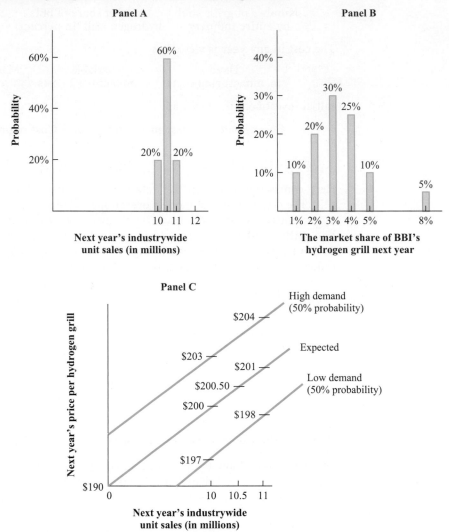

For each of the three variables, a drawing is generated by computer simulation. In addition, price per grill depends on industrywide unit sales.

The grill price in (9.4) depends on the unit sales of the industry. In addition, random variation is modelled via the term "±$3," where a drawing of +$3 and a drawing of −$3 each occur 50 percent of the time. For example, if industrywide unit sales are 11 million, the price per grill will be either

$$\$190 + \$11 + \$3 = \$204 \quad (50\% \text{ probability})$$

or

$$\$190 + \$11 - \$3 = \$198 \quad (50\% \text{ probability})$$

The relationship between the price of a hydrogen grill and industrywide unit sales is graphed in Panel C of Figure 9.3.

The consultant now has distributions for each of the three components of next year's revenue. However, he needs distributions for future years as well. Using forecasts from *OF* and other publications, Lester forecasts the distribution of growth rates for the entire industry over the second year to be as follows:

| Probability | 20% | 60% | 20% |
|---|---|---|---|
| Growth rate of industrywide unit sales in second year | 1% | 3% | 5% |

Given both the distribution of next year's industrywide unit sales and the distribution of growth rates for this variable over the second year, we can generate the distribution of industrywide unit sales for the second year. A similar extension should give Lester a distribution for later years as well, though we won't go into the details here. And, just as the consultant extended the first component of revenue (industrywide unit sales) to later years, he would want to do the same thing for market share and unit price.

The above discussion shows how the three components of revenue can be modelled. Step 2 is complete once the components of cost and of investment are modelled in a similar way. Special attention must be paid to the interactions between variables here, since ineffective management will likely allow the different cost components to rise together. However, since you are probably getting the idea now, we will skip the rest of this step.

## Step 3: The Computer Draws One Outcome

As we said above, next year's revenue in our model is the product of three components. Imagine that the computer randomly picks industrywide unit sales of 10 million, a market share for BBI's hydrogen grill of 2 percent, and a +$3 random price variation. Given these drawings, next year's price per hydrogen grill will be

$$\$190 + \$10 + \$3 = \$203$$

and next year's revenue for BBI's hydrogen grill will be

$$10 \text{ million} \times 0.02 \times \$203 = \$40.6 \text{ million}$$

Of course, we are not done with the entire outcome yet. We would have to perform drawings for revenue in each future year. In addition, we would perform drawings for costs in each future year. Finally, a drawing for initial investment would have to be made as well. In this way, a single outcome would generate a cash flow from the project in each future year.

How likely is it that the specific outcome above would be drawn? We can answer this because we know the probability of each component. Since industry sales of $10 million has a 20 percent probability, a market share of 2 percent also has a 20 percent probability, and a random price variation of +$3 has a 50 percent probability, the probability of these three drawings together in the same outcome is

$$0.02 = 0.20 \times 0.20 \times 0.50 \tag{9.5}$$

Of course, the probability would get even smaller once drawings for future revenues, future costs, and the initial investment were included in the outcome.

This step generates the cash flow for each year from a single outcome. What we are ultimately interested in is the *distribution* of cash flow each year across many outcomes. We ask the computer to randomly draw over and over again to give us this distribution, which is just what is done in the next step.

## Step 4: Repeat the Procedure

While the above three steps generate one outcome, the essence of Monte Carlo simulation is repeated outcomes. Depending on the situation, the computer may be called on to generate thousands or even millions of outcomes. The result of all these drawings is a distribution of cash flow for each future year. This distribution is the basic output of Monte Carlo simulation.

Consider Figure 9.4. Here, repeated drawings have produced the simulated distribution of the third year's cash flow. There would be, of course, a distribution like the one in this figure for each future year. This leaves us with just one more step.

FIGURE 9.4

**Simulated Distribution of the Third Year's Cash Flow for BBI's New Hydrogen Grill**

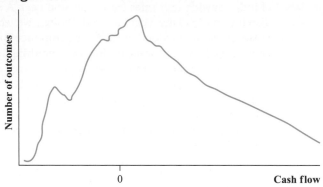

In Monte Carlo simulations, repeated sampling of all the variables from a specific model generates a statistical distribution

## Step 5: Calculate Net Present Value

Given the distribution of cash flow for the third year in Figure 9.4, one can determine the expected cash flow for this year. In a similar manner, one can also determine the expected cash flow for each future year and then calculate the NPV of the project by discounting these expected cash flows at an appropriate rate.

Monte Carlo simulation is often viewed as a step beyond either sensitivity analysis or scenario analysis. Interactions between the variables are explicitly specified in Monte Carlo, so, at least in theory, this methodology provides a more complete analysis. And, as a by-product, having to build a precise model deepens the forecaster's understanding of the project.

Since Monte Carlo simulations have been around for at least 35 years, you might think that most firms would be performing them by now. Surprisingly, this does not seem to be the case. In our experience, executives are frequently skeptical of all the complexity. It is difficult to model either the distributions of all variables or the interactions between variables. For example, a company producing both oil and natural gas in western Canada would require an estimate of the correlation between the prices of oil and natural gas in order to implement simulation. While these prices were highly correlated historically, they have decoupled in recent years as oil prices have gone higher and gas prices have stagnated. While using a historical estimate might seem reasonable, in this case it would have led to serious error. In addition, the computer output is often devoid of economic intuition. Thus, while Monte Carlo simulations are used in certain real-world situations,[5] the approach is not likely to be the wave of the future. In fact, Graham and Harvey report that only about 15 percent of the firms in their sample use capital budgeting simulations.[6]

---

[5] More than perhaps any other, the pharmaceutical industry has pioneered applications of this methodology. For example, see Nancy A. Nichols, "Scientific Management at Merck: An Interview with CFO Judy Lewent," *Harvard Business Review* (January/February 1994).

[6] See Figure 2 of Graham and Harvey, *op. cit.*

# 9.4  REAL OPTIONS

In Chapter 7, we stressed the superiority of NPV analysis over other approaches when valuing capital budgeting projects. However, both scholars and practitioners have pointed out problems with NPV. The basic idea here is that NPV analysis, as well as all the other approaches in Chapter 7, ignores the adjustments that a firm can make after a project is accepted and uncertainty surrounding cash flow estimates is resolved. These adjustments are called **real options**.[7] In this respect, NPV underestimates the true value of a project, particularly in industries such as mining, oil and gas, pharmaceuticals, and biotechnology, where investments are large and uncertainty about future outcomes makes the flexibility in real options valuable.[8] NPV's conservatism here is best explained through a series of examples.

## The Option to Expand

Connie Willig, an entrepreneur, recently learned of a chemical treatment that causes water to freeze at 30°C, rather than 0°C. Of all the many practical applications for this treatment, Connie liked more than anything else the idea of hotels made of ice. Connie estimated the annual cash flows from a single ice hotel to be $2 million, based on an initial investment of $12 million. She felt that 20 percent was an appropriate discount rate, given the risk of this new venture. Assuming that the cash flows were perpetual, Connie determined the NPV of the project to be

$$-\$12{,}000{,}000 + \$2{,}000{,}000/0.20 = -\$2 \text{ million}$$

Most entrepreneurs would have rejected this venture, given its negative NPV. But Connie is not your typical entrepreneur. She reasoned that NPV analysis missed a hidden source of value. While she was pretty sure that the initial investment would cost $12 million, there was some uncertainty concerning annual cash flows. Her cash flow estimate of $2 million per year actually reflected her belief that there was a 50 percent probability that annual cash flows would be $3 million and a 50 percent probability that annual cash flows would be $1 million.

The NPV calculations for the two forecasts are as follows:

> **Optimistic forecast:** $-\$12 \text{ million} + \$3 \text{ million}/0.20 = \$3 \text{ million}$
> **Pessimistic forecast:** $-\$12 \text{ million} + \$1 \text{ million}/0.20 = -\$7 \text{ million}$

On the surface, this new calculation doesn't seem to help Connie very much since an average of the two forecasts yields an NPV for the project of

$$50\% \times \$3 \text{ million} + 50\% \times (-\$7 \text{ million}) = -\$2 \text{ million}$$

(which is just the value she calculated in the first place).

However, if the optimistic forecast turned out to be correct, Connie would want to *expand*. If she believed that there were, say, 10 locations in the country that could support an ice hotel, the true NPV of the venture would be

$$50\% \times 10 \times \$3 \text{ million} + 50\% \times (-\$7 \text{ million}) = \$11.5 \text{ million}$$

The idea here, which is represented in Figure 9.5, is both basic and universal. The entrepreneur has the option to expand if the pilot location is successful. For example, think of all the people who start restaurants, most of them ultimately failing. These

---

[7] To obtain precise estimates of real option value, it is necessary to use the binomial option pricing model. This is covered in depth in Chapter 24. In introducing the topic here, we take a simpler approach based on the probabilities of different scenarios.

[8] H. K. Baker, Shantanu Dutta, and Samir Saadi. "Management Views on Real Options in Capital Budgeting," *Journal of Applied Finance* 21 (1) (2011).

individuals are not necessarily overly optimistic. They may realize the likelihood of failure but go ahead anyway because of the small chance of starting the next McDonald's or Burger King.

FIGURE 9.5

**Decision Tree for Ice Hotel**

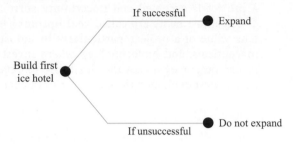

## The Option to Abandon

Managers also have the option to abandon existing projects. While abandonment may seem cowardly, it can often save companies a great deal of money. Because of this, the option to abandon increases the value of any potential project.

The above example on ice hotels, which illustrated the option to expand, can also illustrate the option to abandon. To see this, imagine that Connie now believes that there is a 50 percent probability that annual cash flows will be $6 million and a 50 percent probability that annual cash flows will be −$2 million. The NPV calculations under the two forecasts become

**Optimistic forecast:** −$12 million + $6 million/0.2 = $18 million
**Pessimistic forecast:** −$12 million − $2 million/0.2 = −$22 million

yielding an NPV for the project of

$$50\% \times \$18 \text{ million} + 50\% \times (-\$22 \text{ million}) = -\$2 \text{ million} \qquad (9.6)$$

Furthermore, now imagine that Connie wants to own, at most, just one ice hotel, implying that there is no option to expand. Since the NPV in (9.6) is negative, it looks as if she will not build the hotel.

But things change when we consider the abandonment option. As of date 1, the entrepreneur will know which forecast has come true. If cash flows equal those under the optimistic forecast, Connie will keep the project alive. If, however, cash flows equal those under the pessimistic forecast, she will abandon the hotel. Knowing these possibilities ahead of time, the NPV of the project becomes

$$50\% \times \$18 \text{ million} + 50\% \times (-\$12 \text{ million} - \$2 \text{ million}/1.20) = \$2.17 \text{ million}$$

Since Connie abandons after experiencing the cash flow of −$2 million at date 1, she does not have to endure this outflow in any of the later years. Because the NPV is now positive, Connie will accept the project.

The example here is clearly a stylized one. While many years may pass before a project is abandoned in the real world, our ice hotel was abandoned after just one year. Further, in practice, instead of abandoning a project, a firm can exercise an option to contract by scaling it down. And, while salvage values generally accompany abandonment, we assumed no salvage value for the ice hotel. Nevertheless, abandonment options are pervasive in the real world.

For example, consider the moviemaking industry. As shown in Figure 9.6, movies begin with either the purchase or the development of a script. A completed script might cost a movie studio a few million dollars and potentially lead to actual production. However, the great majority of scripts (perhaps well in excess of 80 percent) are abandoned. Why would studios abandon scripts that they had commissioned in the first place? While the studios know ahead of time that only a few scripts will be promising, they don't know which ones. Thus, they cast a wide net, commissioning many scripts to get a few good ones. And the studios must be ruthless with the bad scripts, since the expenditure here pales in comparison to the huge losses from producing a bad movie.

**FIGURE 9.6**

---

**The Abandonment Option in the Movie Industry**

Movie studios have abandonment options throughout the production of a movie.

The few lucky scripts will then move into production, where costs might be budgeted in the tens of millions of dollars, if not much more. At this stage, the dreaded phrase is that on-location production gets "bogged down," creating cost overruns. But the studios are equally ruthless here. Should these overruns become excessive, production is likely to be abandoned in midstream. Interestingly, abandonment almost always occurs due to high costs, not due to the fear that the movie won't be able to find an audience. Little information on that score will be obtained until the movie is actually released.

Release of the movie is accompanied by significant advertising expenditures, perhaps in the range of $10 to $20 million. Box office success in the first few weeks is likely to lead to further advertising expenditures. Again, the studio has the option, but not the obligation, to increase advertising here. It also has an option to produce a sequel.

Moviemaking is one of the riskiest businesses around, with studios receiving hundreds of millions of dollars in a matter of weeks from a blockbuster while receiving practically nothing during this period from a flop. The above abandonment options contain costs that might otherwise bankrupt the industry.

## Timing Options

One often finds urban land that has been vacant for many years. Yet this land is bought and sold from time to time. Why would anyone pay a positive price for land that has no source of revenue? Certainly one could not arrive at this positive value through NPV analysis. However, the paradox can easily be explained in terms of real options.

Suppose that the land's highest and best use is as an office building. Total construction costs for the building are estimated to be $1 million. Currently, net rents (after all costs) are estimated to be $90,000 per year in perpetuity and the discount rate is 10 percent. The NPV of this proposed building would be

$$-\$1 \text{ million} + \$90,000/0.10 = -\$100,000$$

Since this NPV is negative, one would not currently want to build. In addition, it appears as if the land is worthless. However, suppose that the government is planning a bid for the Summer Olympics. Office rents will likely increase if the bid succeeds. In this case, the property's owner might want to erect the office building after all. Conversely, office rents will remain the same, or even fall, if the bid fails. The owner will not build in this case.

We say that the property owner has a *timing option*. While he does not currently want to build, he will want to build in the future should rents in the area rise substantially. This timing option explains why vacant land often has value. While there are costs, such as taxes, from holding raw land, the value of an office building after a substantial rise in rents may more than offset these holding costs. Of course, the exact value of the vacant land depends on both the probability of success in the Olympic bid and the extent of the rent increase. Figure 9.7 illustrates this timing option.

**FIGURE 9.7**

**Decision Tree for Vacant Land**

Vacant land may have value today, since the owner can erect a profitable office building if rents rise.

Mining operations almost always provide timing options as well. Suppose you own a copper mine where the cost of mining each tonne of copper exceeds the sales revenue. It's a no-brainer to say that you would not want to mine the copper currently. And since there are costs of ownership such as property taxes, insurance, and security, you might actually want to pay someone to take the mine off your hands. However, we would caution you not to do so hastily. Copper prices in the future might very well increase enough so that production is profitable. Given that possibility, you could likely find someone to pay a positive price for the property today.

## Real Options in the Real World

As mentioned previously, common real options include the option to expand, the option to abandon, the option to contract, and the option to delay a project. Although we have explained the value real options add to the capital budgeting decision when faced with uncertainty, it is surprising to see that real options are not readily utilized in practice. In a survey of *Fortune 1000* companies conducted in 2007, it was found that out of the 279 responses received, only 40 managers used real options. The primary reasons given for not using real options were a lack of top management support and the complexity and required expertise needed. These results were duplicated using 847 Canadian firms listed on the Toronto Stock Exchange. In addition to its infrequent usage, it was found that large firms utilized real options more frequently than small firms because they had access to the expertise required to use real options.[9]

For example, Air Canada utilized real options as it emerged from its bankruptcy protection in 2004 and underwent major restructuring. As part of its business restructuring, the airline decided to expand its overseas routes, which required investments in 96 new jetliners. However, due to the riskiness of such investments, instead of immediately buying the entire fleet of planes from Boeing, Air Canada purchased a fraction of the 96 jetliners immediately, followed by an option to purchase the remaining planes in the future, contingent on the success of its initial investments. In this case, real options provided value in facing uncertainty and helped to mitigate risk. Such flexibility is a value that is completely missed by traditional capital budgeting methods like NPV.

**CONCEPT QUESTIONS**

- What are the different types of real options?
- Why does traditional NPV analysis tend to underestimate the true value of a capital project?

# 9.5

# SUMMARY AND CONCLUSIONS

This chapter discusses a number of practical applications of capital budgeting.

1. Though net present value (NPV) is the best capital budgeting approach conceptually, it has been criticized in practice for providing managers with a false sense of security. Sensitivity analysis shows NPV under varying assumptions, giving managers a better feel for the project's risks. Unfortunately, sensitivity analysis modifies only one variable at a time, while many variables are likely to vary together in the real world. Scenario analysis examines a project's performance under different scenarios (e.g., war breaking out or oil prices skyrocketing). Finally, managers want to know how bad forecasts must be before a project loses money. Break-even analysis calculates the sales figure at which the project breaks even. Though break-even analysis is frequently performed on an accounting profit basis, we suggest that an NPV basis is more appropriate.

2. Monte Carlo simulation begins with a model of the firm's cash flows, based on both the interactions between different variables and the movement of each individual variable over time. Random sampling generates a distribution of these cash flows for each period, leading to an NPV calculation.

3. We analyze the hidden options in capital budgeting, such as the option to expand, the option to abandon, the option to contract, and timing options. We return to this topic in Chapter 23.

**KEY TERMS**

| | | |
|---|---|---|
| Break-even analysis 266 | Fixed costs 264 | Scenario analysis 266 |
| Contribution margin 268 | Monte Carlo simulation 270 | Sensitivity analysis 263 |
| Decision trees 261 | Real options 275 | Variable costs 264 |

---

[9] H. K. Baker, Shantanu Dutta, and Samir Saadi, *op. cit.*

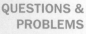

## Sensitivity Analysis and Break-Even Point

**9.1** Lockhart Homebuilders is evaluating a project that costs $724,000, has an eight-year life, and has no salvage value. Assume that depreciation is straight-line to zero over the life of the project. Sales are projected at 75,000 units per year. Price per unit is $39, variable cost per unit is $23, and fixed costs are $850,000 per year. The tax rate is 35 percent, and Lockhart requires a 15 percent return on this project.

    *a.* Calculate the accounting break-even point.

    *b.* Calculate the base-case cash flow and NPV. What is the sensitivity of NPV to changes in the sales figure? Explain what your answer tells you about a 500-unit decrease in projected sales.

    *c.* What is the sensitivity of operating cash flow to changes in the variable cost figure? Explain what your answer tells you about a $1 decrease in estimated variable costs.

## Scenario Analysis

**9.2** In Problem 9.1, suppose the projections given for price, quantity, variable costs, and fixed costs are all accurate to within ±10 percent. Calculate the best-case and worst-case NPV figures.

## Calculating Break-Even

**9.3** In each of the following cases, find the unknown variable. Ignore taxes.

| Accounting break-even | Unit price | Unit variable cost | Fixed costs | Depreciation |
|---|---|---|---|---|
| 95,300 | $41 | $30 | $ 820,000 | ? |
| 143,806 | ? | 56 | 2,750,000 | $1,150,000 |
| 7,835 | 97 | ? | 160,000 | 105,000 |

## Option to Wait

**9.4** Your company is deciding whether to invest in a new machine. The new machine will increase cash flow by $340,000 per year. You believe the technology used in the machine has a 10-year life; in other words, no matter when you purchase the machine, it will be obsolete 10 years from today. The machine is currently priced at $1,800,000. The cost of the machine will decline by $130,000 per year until it reaches $1,150,000, where it will remain. If your required return is 12 percent, should you purchase the machine? If so, when should you purchase it?

## Decision Trees

**9.5** Ang Electronics Inc. has developed a new DVD-R. If the DVD-R is successful, the PV of the payoff (when the product is brought to market) is $22 million. If the DVD-R fails, the PV of the payoff is $9 million. If the product goes directly to market, there is a 50 percent chance of success. Alternatively, Ang can delay the launch by one year and spend $1.5 million to test market the DVD-R. Test marketing would allow the firm to improve the product and increase the probability of success to 80 percent. The appropriate discount rate is 11 percent. Should the firm conduct test marketing?

**9.6** The manager for a growing firm is considering launching a new product. If the product goes directly to market, there is a 50 percent chance of success. For $175,000, the manager can conduct a focus group that will increase the product's chance of success to 65 percent. Alternatively, the manager has the option to pay a consulting firm $390,000 to research the market and refine the product. The consulting firm successfully launches new products 80 percent of the time. If the firm successfully launches the product, the payoff will be $1.9 million. If the product is a failure, the NPV is zero. Which action will result in the highest expected payoff to the firm?

9.7    B&B has a new baby powder ready to market. If the firm goes directly to the market with the product, there is only a 55 percent chance of success. However, the firm can conduct customer segment research, which will take a year and cost $1.2 million. By going through research, B&B will be able to better target potential customers and will increase the probability of success to 70 percent. If successful, the baby powder will bring a PV profit (at time of initial selling) of $19 million. If unsuccessful, the PV payoff is only $6 million. Should the firm conduct customer segment research or go directly to market? The appropriate discount rate is 15 percent.

### Sensitivity Analysis

9.8    Consider a four-year project with the following information: initial fixed asset investment = $480,000; straight-line depreciation to zero over the four-year life; zero salvage value; price = $37; variable costs = $23; fixed costs = $195,000; quantity sold = 90,000 units; tax rate = 34 percent. How sensitive is operating cash flow to changes in quantity sold?

### Project Analysis

9.9    You are considering a new product launch. The project will cost $820,000, have a four-year life, and have no salvage value; depreciation is at a CCA rate of 20%. Sales are projected at 450 units per year, price per unit will be $18,000, variable cost per unit will be $15,400, and fixed costs will be $610,000 per year. The required return on the project is 15 percent, and the relevant tax rate is 35 percent. Assets will remain in the CCA class after the end of the project.

   *a.*    Based on your experience, you think the unit sales, variable cost, and fixed cost projections given here are probably accurate to within ±10 percent. What are the upper and lower bounds for these projections? What is the base-case NPV? What are the best-case and worst-case scenarios?

   *b.*    Evaluate the sensitivity of your base-case NPV to changes in fixed costs.

   *c.*    What is the accounting break-even level of output for this project?

9.10    McGilla Golf has decided to sell a new line of golf clubs. The clubs will sell for $875 per set and have a variable cost of $430 per set. The company has spent $150,000 for a marketing study that determined the company will sell 60,000 sets per year for seven years. The marketing study also determined that the company will lose sales of 12,000 sets of its high-priced clubs. The high-priced clubs sell at $1,100 and have variable costs of $620. The company will also increase sales of its cheap clubs by 15,000 sets. The cheap clubs sell for $400 and have variable costs of $210 per set. The fixed costs each year will be $9,300,000. The company has also spent $1,000,000 on research and development for the new clubs. The plant and equipment required will cost $29,400,000 and qualify for depreciation at a CCA rate of 20 percent. The new clubs will also require an increase in net working capital of $1,400,000 that will be returned at the end of the project. The tax rate is 40 percent, and the cost of capital is 14 percent. Calculate the payback period, the NPV, and the IRR. Assets will remain in the CCA class after the end of the project.

### Sensitivity Analysis

9.11    Refer to Problem 9.10. McGilla Golf would like to know the sensitivity of NPV to changes in the price of the new clubs and the quantity of new clubs sold. What is the sensitivity of the NPV to each of these variables?

### Abandonment Value

9.12    Your company is examining a new project. It expects to sell 9,000 units per year at $35 net cash flow apiece for the next 10 years. In other words, the annual operating cash flow is projected to be $35 × 9,000 = $315,000. The relevant discount rate is 16 percent, and the initial investment required is $1,350,000.

    *a.* What is the base-case NPV?

    *b.* After the first year, the project can be dismantled and sold for $950,000. If expected sales are revised based on the first year's performance, when would it make sense to abandon the investment? In other words, at what level of expected sales would it make sense to abandon the project?

    *c.* Explain how the $950,000 abandonment value can be viewed as the opportunity cost of keeping the project in one year.

### Abandonment

9.13 In Problem 9.12, suppose you think it is likely that expected sales will be revised upward to 11,000 units if the first year is a success and revised downward to 4,000 units if the first year is not a success.

    *a.* If success and failure are equally likely, what is the NPV of the project? Consider the possibility of abandonment in answering.

    *b.* What is the value of the option to abandon?

### Abandonment and Expansion

9.14 In Problem 9.12, suppose the scale of the project can be doubled in one year in the sense that twice as many units can be produced and sold. Naturally, expansion would be desirable only if the project were a success. This implies that if the project is a success, projected sales after expansion will be 22,000. Again, assuming that success and failure are equally likely, what is the NPV of the project? Note that abandonment is still an option if the project is a failure. What is the value of the option to expand?

### Break-Even Analysis

9.15 Your buddy comes to you with a surefire way to make some quick money and help pay off your student loans. His idea is to sell T-shirts with the words "I get" on them. "You get it?" He says, "You see all those bumper stickers and T-shirts that say 'got milk' or 'got surf.' So this says, 'I get.' It's funny! All we have to do is buy a used silk screen press for $5,600 and we are in business!" Assume there are no fixed costs, and you depreciate the $5,600 in the first period. Taxes are 30 percent. What is the accounting break-even point if each shirt costs $4.50 to make and you can sell them for $10 apiece?

### Decision Trees

9.16 Young screenwriter Carl Draper has just finished his first script. It has action, drama, and humour, and he thinks it will be a blockbuster. He takes the script to every movie studio in town and tries to sell it, but to no avail. Finally, ACME studios offers to buy the script for either (a) $12,000 or (b) 1 percent of the movie's profits. The studio will have to make two decisions. First is to decide whether the script is good or bad, and second is to decide whether the movie is good or bad. There is a 90 percent chance that the script is bad. If it is bad, the studio does nothing more and throws the script out. If the script is good, they will shoot the movie. After the movie is shot, the studio will review it, and there is a 70 percent chance that the movie is bad. If the movie is bad, the movie will not be promoted and will not turn a profit. If the movie is good, the studio will promote heavily; the average profit for this type of movie is $20 million. Carl rejects the $12,000 and says he wants the 1 percent of profits. Was this a good decision by Carl?

### Option to Wait

9.17 Hickock Mining is evaluating when to open a gold mine. The mine has 48,000 ounces of gold left that can be mined, and mining operations will produce 6,000 ounces per year. The required return on the gold mine is 12 percent, and it will cost $34 million to open the mine. When the mine is opened, the company will sign a contract that will guarantee the price of gold for the remaining life of the mine. If the mine is opened today, each ounce of gold will generate an after-tax cash flow of $1,400 per ounce. If the company waits one year, there is a 60 percent probability that the contract price will generate an after-tax cash flow of $1,600 per ounce and a 40 percent probability that the after-tax cash flow will be $1,300 per ounce. What is the value of the option to wait?

**Abandonment Decisions**

9.18 Allied Products Inc. is considering a new product launch. The firm expects to have an annual operating cash flow of $10.5 million for the next 10 years. Allied Products uses a discount rate of 13 percent for new product launches. The initial investment is $51 million. Assume that the project has no salvage value at the end of its economic life.

   a. What is the NPV of the new product?
   b. After the first year, the project can be dismantled and sold for $31 million. If the estimates of remaining cash flows are revised based on the first year's experience, at what level of expected cash flows does it make sense to abandon the project?

**Expansion Decisions**

9.19 Applied Nanotech is thinking about introducing a new surface-cleaning machine. The marketing department has estimated that Applied Nanotech can sell 15 units per year at $305,000 net cash flow per unit for the next five years. The engineering department has estimated that developing the machine will take a $15 million initial investment. The finance department has estimated that a 16 percent discount rate should be used.

   a. What is the base-case NPV?
   b. If unsuccessful, after the first year the project can be dismantled and will have an after-tax salvage value of $11 million. Also, after the first year, expected cash flows will be revised up to 20 units per year or to 0 units, with equal probability. What is the revised NPV?

**Scenario Analysis**

9.20 You are the financial analyst for a tennis racquet manufacturer. The company is considering using a graphite-like material in its tennis racquets. The company has estimated the information in the following table about the market for a racquet with the new material. The company expects to sell the racquet for six years. The equipment required for the project has no salvage value. The required return for projects of this type is 13 percent, and the company has a 40 percent tax rate. Should you recommend the project?

|  | Pessimistic | Expected | Optimistic |
|---|---|---|---|
| Market size | 130,000 | 150,000 | 165,000 |
| Market share | 21% | 25% | 28% |
| Selling price | $ 140 | $ 145 | $ 150 |
| Variable costs per unit | $ 102 | $ 98 | $ 94 |
| Fixed costs per year | $1,015,000 | $ 950,000 | $ 900,000 |
| Initial investment | $2,200,000 | $2,100,000 | $2,000,000 |

9.21 Consider a project to supply Hamilton with 35,000 tonnes of machine screws annually for automobile production. You will need an initial $2,900,000 investment in threading equipment to get the project started; the project will last for five years. The accounting department estimates that annual fixed costs will be $495,000 and that variable costs should be $285 per tonne; accounting will depreciate the initial fixed asset investment at a CCA rate of 30 percent over the five-year project life. It also estimates a salvage value of $300,000 after dismantling costs. The marketing department estimates that the automakers will let you have the contract at a selling price of $345 per tonne. The engineering department estimates you will need an initial net working capital investment of $450,000. You require a 13 percent return and face a marginal tax rate of 38 percent on this project. Assets will remain in the CCA class after the end of the project.

a. What is the estimated operating cash flow for this project? The NPV? Should you pursue this project?

b. Suppose you believe that the accounting department's initial cost and salvage value projections are accurate only to within ±15 percent, the marketing department's price estimate is accurate only to within ±10 percent, and the engineering department's net working capital estimate is accurate only to within ±5 percent. What is your worst-case scenario for this project? Your best-case scenario? Do you still want to pursue the project?

**Sensitivity Analysis**

9.22  In Problem 9.21, suppose you're confident about your own projections, but you're a little unsure about Hamilton's actual machine screw requirements. What is the sensitivity of the project operating cash flow to changes in the quantity supplied? What about the sensitivity of NPV to changes in quantity supplied? Given the sensitivity number you calculated, is there some minimum level of output below which you wouldn't want to operate? Why?

**Abandonment Decisions**

9.23  Consider the following project for Hand Clapper Inc. The company is considering a four-year project to manufacture clap-command garage door openers. This project requires an initial investment of $8 million that will be depreciated straight-line to zero over the project's life. An initial investment in net working capital of $950,000 is required to support spare parts inventory; this cost is fully recoverable whenever the project ends. The company believes it can generate $6.85 million in pre-tax revenues with $2.8 million in total pre-tax operating costs. The tax rate is 38 percent, and the discount rate is 16 percent. The market value of the equipment over the life of the project is as follows:

| Year | Market value (in $ millions) |
|------|------------------------------|
| 1 | $5.1 |
| 2 | 3.8 |
| 3 | 3.2 |
| 4 | 0.0 |

a. Assuming Hand Clapper operates this project for four years, what is the NPV?

b. Now compute the project NPVs assuming the project is abandoned after only one year, after two years, and after three years. What economic life for this project maximizes its value to the firm? What does this problem tell you about not considering abandonment possibilities when evaluating projects?

9.24  M.V.P. Games Inc. has hired you to perform a feasibility study of a new video game that requires a $7 million initial investment. M.V.P. expects a total annual operating cash flow of $1.3 million for the next 10 years. The relevant discount rate is 10 percent. Cash flows occur at year-end.

a. What is the NPV of the new video game?

b. After one year, the estimate of remaining annual cash flows will be revised either upward to $2.2 million or downward to $285,000. Each revision has an equal probability of occurring. At that time, the video game project can be sold for $2,600,000. What is the revised NPV given that the firm can abandon the project after one year?

# Bunyan Lumber LLC

Bunyan Lumber LLC harvests timber and delivers logs to timber mills for sale. The company was founded 70 years ago by Pete Bunyan. The current CEO is Paula Bunyan, the granddaughter of the founder. The company is currently evaluating a 5,000-hectare forest it owns in central British Columbia. Paula has asked Steve Boles, the company's finance officer, to evaluate the project. Paula's concern is when the company should harvest the timber.

Lumber is sold by the company for its "pond value." Pond value is the amount a mill will pay for a log delivered to the mill location. The price paid for logs delivered to a mill is quoted in dollars per thousands of board feet (MBF), and the price depends on the grade of the logs. The forest Bunyan Lumber is evaluating was planted by the company 20 years ago and is made up entirely of Douglas fir trees. The table here shows the current price per MBF for the three grades of timber the company feels will come from the stand:

| Timber grade | Price per MBF |
|---|---|
| 1P | $620 |
| 2P | 605 |
| 3P | 595 |

Steve believes that the pond value of lumber will increase at the inflation rate. The company is planning to thin the forest today, and it expects to realize a positive cash flow of $1,000 per hectare from thinning. The thinning is done to increase the growth rate of the remaining trees, and it is always done 20 years after a planting.

The major decision the company faces is when to log the forest. When the company logs the forest, it will immediately replant saplings, which will allow for a future harvest. The longer the forest is allowed to grow, the larger the harvest becomes per hectare. Additionally, an older forest has a higher grade of timber. Steve has compiled the following table with the expected harvest per hectare in thousands of board feet, along with the breakdown of the timber grades:

| Years from today to begin harvest | Harvest (MBF) per hectare | Timber grade | | |
|---|---|---|---|---|
| | | 1P | 2P | 3P |
| 20 | 14.1 | 16% | 36% | 48% |
| 25 | 16.4 | 20 | 40 | 40 |
| 30 | 17.3 | 22 | 43 | 35 |
| 35 | 18.1 | 24 | 45 | 31 |

The company expects to lose 5 percent of the timber it cuts due to defects and breakage.

The forest will be clear-cut when the company harvests the timber. This method of harvesting allows for faster growth of replanted trees. All of the harvesting, processing, replanting, and transportation are to be handled by subcontractors hired by Bunyan Lumber. The cost of the logging is expected to be $140 per MBF. A road system has to be constructed and is expected to cost $50 per MBF on average. Sales preparation and administrative costs, excluding office overhead costs, are expected to be $18 per MBF.

As soon as the harvesting is complete, the company will reforest the land. Reforesting costs include the following:

| | Cost per hectare |
|---|---|
| Excavator piling | $175 |
| Broadcast burning | 310 |
| Site preparation | 150 |
| Planting costs | 225 |

All costs are expected to increase at the inflation rate.

Assume all cash flows occur at the year of harvest. For example, if the company begins harvesting the timber 20 years from today, the cash flow from the harvest will be received 20 years from today. When the company logs the land, it will immediately replant the land with new saplings. The harvest period chosen will be repeated for the foreseeable future. The company's nominal required return is 10 percent, and the inflation rate is expected to be 3.7 percent per year. Bunyan Lumber has a 35 percent tax rate.

Clear-cutting is a controversial method of forest management. To obtain the necessary permits, Bunyan Lumber has agreed to contribute to a conservation fund every time it harvests the lumber. If the company harvested the forest today, the required contribution would be $250,000. The company has agreed that the required contribution will grow by 3.2 percent per year. When should the company harvest the forest?

## PART 3

# CHAPTER

# Risk and Return: Lessons from Market History

We learned in Chapter 5 that risk-free cash flows should be discounted at the risk-free rate of interest. Because most capital budgeting projects involve risky flows, a different discount rate must be used. The next four chapters are devoted to determining the discount rate for risky projects.

Experience indicates that students find the upcoming material among the most difficult in the entire textbook. Because of this, we always teach the material by presenting the results and conclusions first. By seeing where we are going ahead of time, it is easier to absorb the material when we get there. A synopsis of the four chapters follows:

1. Because our ultimate goal is to discount risky cash flows, we must first find a way to measure risk. In the current chapter we measure the variability of an asset by the variance or standard deviation of its returns. If an individual holds only *one* asset, its variance or standard deviation is the appropriate measure of risk.

2. While Chapter 10 considers one type of asset in isolation, Chapter 11 examines a portfolio of many assets. In this case, we are interested in the *contribution* of the security to the risk of the entire portfolio. Because much of an individual security's variance is dispersed in a large, diversified portfolio, neither the security's variance nor its standard deviation can be viewed as the security's contribution to the risk of a large portfolio. Rather, this contribution is best measured by the security's beta ($\beta$). As an example, consider a stock whose returns are high when the returns on a large, diversified portfolio are low—and vice versa. This stock has a negative beta. In other words, it acts as a hedge, implying that the stock actually tends to reduce the risk of the portfolio. However, the stock could have a high variance, implying high risk for an investor holding only this security.

3. Investors will only hold a risky security if its expected return is high enough to compensate for its risk. Given the above, the expected return on a security should be positively related to the security's beta. In fact, the relationship between risk and expected return can be expressed more precisely by the following equation:

$$\begin{matrix}\text{Expected return} \\ \text{on a security}\end{matrix} = \begin{matrix}\text{Risk-free} \\ \text{rate}\end{matrix} + \text{Beta} \times \left( \begin{matrix}\text{Expected return on} \\ \text{market portfolio}\end{matrix} - \begin{matrix}\text{Risk-free} \\ \text{rate}\end{matrix} \right)$$

Because the term in parentheses on the right-hand side is positive, this equation says that the expected return on a security is a positive function of its beta. This equation is frequently referred to as the *capital asset pricing model* (CAPM).

4. We derive the relationship between risk and return in a different manner in Chapter 12. However, many of the conclusions are quite similar. That chapter is based on the *arbitrage pricing theory* (APT).

5. The theoretical ideas in Chapters 10, 11, and 12 are intellectually challenging. Fortunately, Chapter 13, which applies the above theory to the selection of discount rates, is much simpler. In a world where (a) a project has the same risk as the firm, and (b) the firm has no debt, the expected return on the stock should serve as the project's discount rate. This expected return is taken from the CAPM, as presented in Chapter 11.

Because we have a long road ahead of us, the maxim that any journey begins with a single step applies here. We start with the perhaps mundane calculation of a security's return.

# 10.1  RETURNS

## Dollar Earnings

Suppose Canadian Atlantic Enterprises has several thousand shares of stock outstanding. You purchased some of these shares at the beginning of the year. It's now year-end, and you want to determine how well you've done on your investment.

Over the year, a company may pay cash *dividends* to its shareholders. As a shareholder in Canadian Atlantic Enterprises, you are a part owner of the company. If the company is profitable, it may choose to distribute some of its profits to shareholders. (Dividend policy is detailed in Chapter 19.)

In addition to the dividend, the other part of your return is the *capital gain* or *capital loss* on the stock arising from changes in the value of your investment. For example, consider the cash flows illustrated in Figure 10.1. The stock is selling for $37 per share. If you bought 100 shares, you had a total outlay of $3,700. Suppose that over the year the stock paid a dividend of $1.85 per share. By the end of the year, then, you would have received income of

$$\text{Dividend} = \$1.85 \times 100 = \$185$$

FIGURE 10.1

**Dollar Earnings**

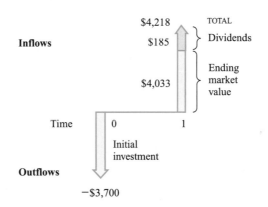

Also, the value of the stock rose to $40.33 per share by the end of the year. Your 100 shares are now worth $4,033, so you have a capital gain of

$$\text{Capital gain} = (\$40.33 - \$37) \times 100 = \$333$$

On the other hand, if the price had dropped to, say, $34.78, you would have had a capital loss of

$$\text{Capital loss} = (\$34.78 - \$37) \times 100 = -\$222$$

Notice that a capital loss is the same thing as a negative capital gain.

The total dollar earnings on your investment is the sum of the dividend and the capital gain:

$$\text{Total earnings} = \text{Dividend income} + \text{Capital gain (or loss)}$$

In our first example, the total dollar earnings is thus given by

$$\text{Total dollar earnings} = \$185 + \$333 = \$518$$

Notice that if you sold the stock at the end of the year, the total amount of cash you would have would be your initial investment plus the total return. In the preceding example, then, you would have

$$\text{Total cash if stock is sold} = \text{Initial investment} + \text{Total dollar earnings}$$
$$= \$3,700 + \$518$$
$$= \$4,218$$

As a check, notice that this is the same as the proceeds from the sale of the stock plus the dividends:

$$\text{Proceeds from stock sale} + \text{Dividends} = \$40.33 \times 100 + \$185$$
$$= \$4,033 + \$185$$
$$= \$4,218$$

Suppose you hold on to your Canadian Atlantic stock and don't sell it at the end of the year. Should you still consider the capital gain as part of your earnings? Isn't this only a paper gain and not really a cash flow if you don't sell it?

The answer to the first question is a strong yes; the answer to the second is an equally strong no. The capital gain is every bit as much a part of your return as the dividend, and you should certainly count it as part of your return. That you actually decided to keep the stock and not sell it or *realize* the gain in no way changes the fact that if you wanted to, you could get the cash value of the stock.[1]

## Percentage Returns or Rate of Return

It is usually more convenient to summarize information about returns in percentage terms, rather than dollar terms, because that way your return does not depend on the amount invested. The question we want to answer is, how much do we get for each dollar we invest?

To answer this question, let $P_t$ be the price of the stock at the beginning of the year and let $D_{t+1}$ be the dividend paid on the stock during the year. Consider the cash flows in Figure 10.2. These are the same as those in Figure 10.1, except that we have now expressed everything on a per share basis.

**FIGURE 10.2**

**Percentage Returns: Dollar Earnings and Per-Share Return**

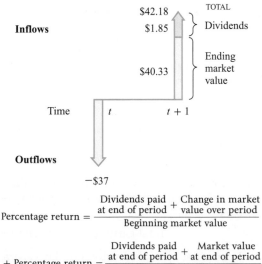

$$\text{Percentage return} = \frac{\text{Dividends paid at end of period} + \text{Change in market value over period}}{\text{Beginning market value}}$$

$$1 + \text{Percentage return} = \frac{\text{Dividends paid at end of period} + \text{Market value at end of period}}{\text{Beginning market value}}$$

---

[1] After all, you could always sell the stock at year-end and immediately reinvest by buying the stock back. There is no difference between doing this and just not selling (assuming, of course, that there are no tax consequences from selling the stock). Again, the point is that whether you actually cash out or reinvest by not selling does not affect the return you earn.

In our example, the price at the beginning of the year was $37 per share and the dividend paid during the year on each share was $1.85. As we discussed in Chapter 6 and Appendix 2A, expressing the dividend as a percentage of the beginning stock price results in the *dividend yield*:

$$\text{Dividend yield} = D_{t+1}/P_t = \$1.85/\$37 = 0.05 = 5\%$$

The second component of our percentage return is the capital gains yield. This is calculated as the change in the price during the year (the capital gain) divided by the beginning price:

$$\text{Capital gains yield} = (P_{t+1} - P_t)/P_t$$
$$= (\$40.33 - \$37)/\$37 = \$3.33/\$37 = 0.09 = 9\%$$

Combining these two results, we find that the *total returns* on the investment in Canadian Atlantic stock during the year, which we will label $R_{t+1}$, were

$$R_{t+1} = \frac{\text{Div}_{t+1}}{P_t} + \frac{(P_{t+1} - P_t)}{P_t} = 5\% + 9\% = 14\%$$

From now on we will refer to returns in percentage terms.

---

**EXAMPLE 10.1**

Suppose a stock begins the year with a price of $25 per share and ends with a price of $35 per share. During the year it paid a $2 dividend per share. What are its dividend yield, its capital gain, and its total return for the year? We can imagine the cash flows in Figure 10.3:

$$R_1 = \frac{\text{Div}_1}{P_0} + \frac{P_1 - P_0}{P_0}$$

$$= \frac{\$2}{\$25} + \frac{\$35 - \$25}{\$25} = \frac{\$12}{\$25}$$

$$= 8\% + \quad 40\% \quad = 48\%$$

Thus, the stock's dividend yield, its capital gain, and its total return are 8 percent, 40 percent, and 48 percent, respectively.

---

**FIGURE 10.3**

**Cash Flow—An Investment Example**

Suppose you had invested $5,000. The total dollar proceeds you would have received on an investment in the stock are $5,000 × 1.48 = $7,400. If you know the total return on the stock, you do not need to know how many shares you would have had to purchase to figure out how much money you would have made on the $5,000 investment. You just use the total return.[2]

**CONCEPT
QUESTIONS**

- What are the two parts of total return?
- Why are unrealized capital gains or losses included in the calculation of returns?
- What is the difference between a dollar return and a percentage return? Why are percentage returns more convenient?

## 10.2    HOLDING-PERIOD RETURNS

Investors look to capital market history as a guide to the risks and returns of alternative portfolio strategies. The data set in Table 10.1 could be used in advising large institutional investors. It draws on two major studies: Roger Ibbotson and Rex Sinquefield's examination of rates of return in U.S. financial markets and James Hatch and Robert White's study of Canadian returns.[3] Our data present year-to-year historical rates of return on five important types of financial investments or asset classes:

1. *Canadian common stocks.* The common stock portfolio is based on a sample of the largest companies (in terms of total market value of outstanding stock) in Canada.[4]

2. *U.S. common stocks.* This portfolio consists of 500 of the largest U.S. companies. The full historical series is given in U.S. dollars and in Canadian dollars, adjusting for shifts in exchange rates.

---

[2] Consider the stock in the previous example. We have ignored the question of when during the year you receive the dividend. Does it make a difference? To explore this question, suppose first that the dividend is paid at the very beginning of the year, and you receive it the moment after you have purchased the stock. Suppose, too, that interest rates are 10 percent, and that immediately after receiving the dividend you lend it out. What will be your total return, including the loan proceeds, at the end of the year?

Alternatively, instead of lending the dividend you could have reinvested it and purchased more of the stock. If that is what you do with the dividend, what will your total return be? (Warning: This does not go on forever, and when you buy more stock with the cash from the dividend on your first purchase, you are too late to get yet another dividend on the new stock.)

Finally, suppose the dividend is paid at year-end. What answer would you get for the total return? As you can see, by ignoring the question of when the dividend is paid when we calculate the return, we are implicitly assuming that it is received at the end of the year and cannot be reinvested during the year. The right way to figure out the return on a stock is to determine exactly when the dividend is received and to include the return that comes from reinvesting the dividend in the stock. This gives a pure stock return without confounding the issue by requiring knowledge of the interest rate during the year.

[3] The two classic studies are R. G. Ibbotson and R. A. Sinquefield, *Stocks, Bonds, Bills, and Inflation* (Charlottesville, VA: Financial Analysts Research Foundation, 1982); and J. Hatch and R. White, *Canadian Stocks, Bonds, Bills, and Inflation: 1950–1983* (Charlottesville, VA: Financial Analysts Research Foundation, 1985). Additional sources used by Mercer Investment Consulting are BMO Nesbitt Burns small-cap index for small stocks, Scotia Capital Markets for Canada Treasury bills and long bonds, and Statistics Canada CANSIM for rates of exchange and inflation.

[4] From 1956 on, the S&P/TSX 60 is used. For earlier years, the data used are a sample provided by the TSX.

**TABLE 10.1**

## Annual Market Index Returns, 1948–2013

| Year | Statistics Canada inflation | Canadian stocks S&P/TSX Composite | DEX 91-day T-bill | Scotia Capital Markets long bonds | U.S. stocks S&P 500 ($CAN) | Nesbitt Burns small stock | S&P/TSX Venture Composite |
|---|---|---|---|---|---|---|---|
| 1948 | 8.88 | 12.25 | 0.40 | −0.08 | 5.50 | | |
| 1949 | 1.09 | 23.85 | 0.45 | 5.18 | 22.15 | | |
| 1950 | 5.91 | 51.69 | 0.51 | 1.74 | 39.18 | | |
| 1951 | 10.66 | 25.44 | 0.71 | −7.89 | 15.00 | | |
| 1952 | −1.38 | 0.01 | 0.95 | 5.01 | 13.68 | | |
| 1953 | 0.00 | 2.56 | 1.54 | 5.00 | −0.99 | | |
| 1954 | 0.00 | 39.37 | 1.62 | 12.23 | 52.62 | | |
| 1955 | 0.47 | 27.68 | 1.22 | 0.13 | 35.51 | | |
| 1956 | 3.24 | 12.68 | 2.63 | −8.87 | 2.35 | | |
| 1957 | 1.79 | −20.58 | 3.76 | 7.94 | −8.51 | | |
| 1958 | 2.64 | 31.25 | 2.27 | 1.92 | 40.49 | | |
| 1959 | 1.29 | 4.59 | 4.39 | −5.07 | 10.54 | | |
| 1960 | 1.27 | 1.78 | 3.66 | 12.19 | 5.15 | | |
| 1961 | 0.42 | 32.75 | 2.86 | 9.16 | 32.85 | | |
| 1962 | 1.67 | −7.09 | 3.81 | 5.03 | −5.77 | | |
| 1963 | 1.64 | 15.60 | 3.58 | 4.58 | 23.19 | | |
| 1964 | 2.02 | 25.43 | 3.73 | 6.16 | 15.75 | | |
| 1965 | 3.16 | 6.67 | 3.79 | 0.05 | 12.58 | | |
| 1966 | 3.45 | −7.07 | 4.89 | −1.05 | −9.33 | | |
| 1967 | 4.07 | 18.09 | 4.38 | −0.48 | 23.61 | | |
| 1968 | 3.91 | 22.45 | 6.22 | 2.14 | 10.26 | | |
| 1969 | 4.79 | −0.81 | 6.83 | −2.86 | −8.50 | | |
| 1970 | 1.31 | −3.57 | 6.89 | 16.39 | −1.96 | −11.69 | |
| 1971 | 5.16 | 8.01 | 3.86 | 14.84 | 13.28 | 15.83 | |
| 1972 | 4.91 | 27.37 | 3.43 | 8.11 | 18.12 | 44.72 | |
| 1973 | 9.36 | 0.27 | 4.78 | 1.97 | −14.58 | −7.82 | |
| 1974 | 12.30 | −25.93 | 7.68 | −4.53 | −26.87 | −26.89 | |
| 1975 | 9.52 | 18.48 | 7.05 | 8.02 | 40.72 | 41.00 | |
| 1976 | 5.87 | 11.02 | 9.10 | 23.64 | 22.97 | 22.77 | |
| 1977 | 9.45 | 10.71 | 7.64 | 9.04 | 0.65 | 39.93 | |
| 1978 | 8.44 | 29.72 | 7.90 | 4.10 | 15.50 | 44.41 | |
| 1979 | 9.69 | 44.77 | 11.01 | −2.83 | 16.52 | 46.04 | |
| 1980 | 11.20 | 30.13 | 12.23 | 2.18 | 35.51 | 42.86 | |
| 1981 | 12.20 | −10.25 | 19.11 | −2.09 | −5.57 | −15.10 | |
| 1982 | 9.23 | 5.54 | 15.27 | 45.82 | 25.84 | 4.55 | |
| 1983 | 4.51 | 35.49 | 9.39 | 9.61 | 24.07 | 44.30 | |
| 1984 | 3.77 | −2.39 | 11.21 | 16.90 | 12.87 | −2.33 | |
| 1985 | 4.38 | 25.07 | 9.70 | 26.68 | 39.82 | 38.98 | |
| 1986 | 4.19 | 8.95 | 9.34 | 17.21 | 16.96 | 12.33 | |
| 1987 | 4.12 | 5.88 | 8.20 | 1.77 | −0.96 | −5.47 | |
| 1988 | 3.96 | 11.08 | 8.94 | 11.30 | 7.21 | 5.46 | |
| 1989 | 5.17 | 21.37 | 11.95 | 15.17 | 27.74 | 10.66 | |
| 1990 | 5.00 | −14.80 | 13.28 | 4.32 | −3.06 | −27.32 | |
| 1991 | 3.78 | 12.02 | 9.90 | 25.30 | 30.05 | 18.51 | |
| 1992 | 2.14 | −1.43 | 6.65 | 11.57 | 18.42 | 13.01 | |
| 1993 | 1.70 | 32.55 | 5.63 | 22.09 | 14.40 | 52.26 | |
| 1994 | 0.23 | −0.18 | 4.76 | −7.39 | 7.48 | −9.21 | |
| 1995 | 1.75 | 14.53 | 7.39 | 26.34 | 33.68 | 13.88 | |
| 1996 | 2.17 | 28.35 | 5.02 | 14.18 | 23.62 | 28.66 | |
| 1997 | 0.73 | 14.98 | 3.20 | 18.46 | 39.18 | 6.97 | |
| 1998 | 1.02 | −1.58 | 4.74 | 12.85 | 37.71 | −17.90 | |
| 1999 | 2.58 | 31.59 | 4.66 | −5.98 | 14.14 | 20.29 | |
| 2000 | 3.23 | 7.41 | 5.49 | 12.97 | −5.67 | −4.29 | |
| 2001 | 0.60 | −12.60 | 4.70 | 8.10 | −6.50 | 0.70 | |
| 2002 | 4.30 | −12.40 | 2.50 | 8.70 | −22.70 | −0.90 | 3.66 |
| 2003 | 1.60 | 26.70 | 2.90 | 6.70 | 5.30 | 42.70 | 63.24 |
| 2004 | 2.40 | 14.50 | 2.30 | 7.20 | 3.30 | 14.10 | 4.40 |
| 2005 | 2.00 | 23.29 | 2.58 | 6.46 | 3.80 | 13.70 | 22.62 |
| 2006 | 1.60 | 17.30 | 4.00 | 4.10 | 15.70 | 20.83 | 33.59 |
| 2007 | 2.10 | 9.80 | 4.40 | 3.70 | −10.50 | −11.38 | −4.94 |
| 2008 | 1.20 | −33.00 | 3.30 | 2.70 | −21.20 | −46.60 | −71.93 |
| 2009 | 1.30 | 34.35 | 0.60 | 5.31 | 9.26 | 86.80 | 90.80 |
| 2010 | 2.40 | 17.27 | 0.50 | 12.10 | 8.10 | 36.10 | 50.45 |
| 2011 | 2.30 | −8.57 | 1.00 | 17.72 | 4.39 | −19.50 | −35.07 |
| 2012 | 1.50 | 7.05 | 1.00 | 3.82 | 13.41 | 10.52 | −17.32 |
| 2013 | 0.90 | 12.71 | 1.00 | −6.53 | 41.06 | 36.55 | −23.14 |

Sources: William M. Mercer Ltd., Bloomberg Financial Services, Fortress Small Cap Equity Fund, BMO, Scotia Capital, and *The Globe and Mail*.

3. *Small stocks.* This portfolio, compiled by BMO Nesbitt Burns, includes the bottom fifth of stocks listed on the Toronto Stock Exchange (TSX). The ranking is by market value of equity capitalization—the price of the stock multiplied by the number of shares outstanding.

4. *Long bonds.* This portfolio includes high-quality, long-term corporate, provincial, and Government of Canada bonds.

5. *Canada Treasury bills.* This portfolio consists of Treasury bills (*T-bills* for short) with a three-month maturity.

6. *S&P/TSX Venture Composite.* This index consists primarily of small oil and gas, mining, IT, and biotechnology companies that do not have the market capitalization to list on the TSX.

These returns are not adjusted for transaction costs, inflation, or taxes; thus, they are nominal, pre-tax returns. In addition to the year-to-year returns on these financial instruments, the year-to-year percentage change in the Statistics Canada Consumer Price Index (CPI) is also computed. This is a commonly used measure of inflation, so we can calculate real returns using this as the inflation rate.

The six asset classes included cover a broad range of investments popular with Canadian individuals and financial institutions. We include U.S. stocks since Canadian investors often invest abroad—particularly in the United States.[5]

Before looking closely at the different portfolio returns, we take a look at the big picture. Figure 10.4 shows what happened to $1 invested in three of these portfolios at the beginning of 1957. We work with a sample period of 1957–2013 for two reasons: the years immediately after World War II do not reflect trends today, and the TSE 300 (predecessor of the TSX) was introduced in 1956, making 1957 the first really comparable year. This decision is somewhat controversial; we return to it later as we draw lessons from our data. The growth in value for each of the different portfolios over the 57-year period ending in 2013 is given separately. Notice that to get everything on a single graph, some modification in scaling is used. As is commonly done with financial series, the vertical axis is on a logarithmic scale such that equal distances measure equal percentage changes (as opposed to equal dollar changes) in values.

Looking at Figure 10.4, we see that the common stock investments did the best overall. Every dollar invested in Canadian stocks grew to $144.89 over the 57 years.

At the other end, the T-bill portfolio grew to only $26.32. Long bonds did better, with an ending value of $79.04. These values are less impressive when we consider inflation over this period. As illustrated, the price level climbed such that $8.40 is needed just to replace the original $1.

Figure 10.4 gives the total value of a $1 investment in the Canadian stock market from 1957 through 2013. In other words, it shows what the total return would have been if the dollar had been left in the stock market and if each year the dividends from the previous year had been reinvested in more stock. If $R_t$ is the return in year $t$ (expressed in decimals), the total you would have from year 1 to year $T$ is the product of the returns in each of the years:

---

[5] Chapter 32 discusses exchange rate risk and other risks of foreign investments.

FIGURE 10.4

**Returns on a $1 Investment, 1957 to 2013**

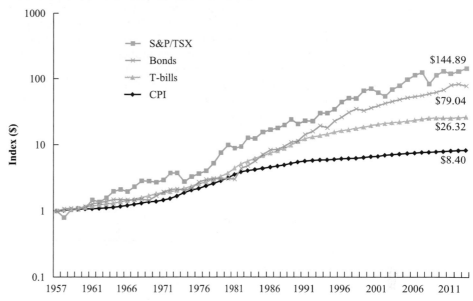

$$(1 + R_1) \times (1 + R_2) \times \cdots \times (1 + R_t) \times \cdots \times (1 + R_T)$$

For example, if the returns were 11 percent, −5 percent, and 9 percent in a three-year period, a $1 investment at the beginning of the period would, at the end of the three years, be worth

$$\begin{aligned}
\text{Initial Investment} \times [(1+R_1) \times (1+R_2) \times (1+R_3)] &= \$1 \times [(1+0.11) \times (1-0.05) \times (1+0.09)] \\
&= \$1 \times (1.11 \times 0.95 \times 1.09) \\
&= \$1.15
\end{aligned}$$

Notice that 0.15 (or 15 percent) is the total return and that it includes the return from reinvesting the first-year dividends in the stock market for two more years and reinvesting the second-year dividends for the final year. The 15 percent is called a three-year holding-period return. Table 10.1 gives annual holding-period returns from 1948 to 2013. From this table you can determine holding-period returns for any combination of years.

***CONCEPT QUESTIONS***

- What was the smallest return observed over the 57 years for each of these investments? When did it occur?
- How many times did large Canadian stocks (common stocks) return more than 30 percent? How many times did they return less than 20 percent?
- What was the longest winning streak (years without a negative return) for large Canadian stocks? For long-term bonds?
- How often did the T-bill portfolio have a negative return?

# 10.3    RETURN STATISTICS

The history of capital market returns is too complicated to be useful in its undigested form. To use the history we must first find some manageable ways of describing it, dramatically condensing the detailed data into a few simple statements.

This is where two important numbers summarizing the history come in. The first and most natural number we want to find is some single measure that best describes the past annual returns on the stock market. In other words, what is our best estimate of the return that an investor could have realized in a particular year over the 1948 through 2013 period? This is the *average return*.

---

**EXAMPLE 10.2**

The returns on Canadian common stocks from 1989 to 1992 were (in decimals) 0.2137, −0.1480, 0.1202, and −0.0143, respectively. The average or mean return over these four years is

$$\overline{R} = \frac{0.2137 - 0.1480 + 0.1202 - 0.0143}{4} = 0.0429$$

---

Figure 10.5 plots the histogram of the yearly stock market returns from 1957 to 2013. This plot is the **frequency distribution** of the numbers. The height of the graph gives the number of sample observations in the range on the horizontal axis.

**FIGURE 10.5**

**Frequency Distribution of Returns on Canadian Common Stocks, 1957 to 2013**

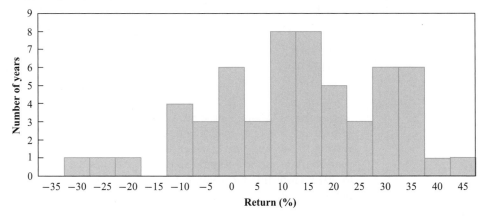

Given a frequency distribution like that in Figure 10.5, we can calculate the **average** or **mean** of the distribution. To compute the arithmetic average of the distribution, we add up all of the values and divide the total number (57 in our case, because we have 57 years of data) by *T*. The bar over the *R* is used to represent the mean, and the formula is the ordinary formula for the average:

$$\text{Mean} = \overline{R} = \frac{(R_1 + \cdots + R_T)}{T}$$

The arithmetic mean of the 57 annual returns from 1957 to 2013 is 10.43 percent. The arithmetic mean return has the advantage of being easy to calculate and interpret, so we use it in Example 10.2 to measure expected return.

• Why are return statistics useful?

# 10.4 AVERAGE STOCK RETURNS AND RISK-FREE RETURNS

Now that we have computed the average return on the stock market, it seems sensible to compare it with the returns on other securities. The most obvious comparison is with the low-variability returns in the government bond market. These are free of most of the volatility we see in the stock market.

The Government of Canada borrows money by issuing bonds, which the investing public holds. As we discussed in an earlier chapter, these bonds come in many forms. The ones we'll look at here are called *Treasury bills*, or *T-bills*. Once a week the government sells some bills at an auction. A typical bill is a pure discount bond that will mature in a year or less. Because the government can raise taxes to pay for the debt it incurs—a trick that many of us would like to be able to perform—this debt is virtually free of risk of default. Thus, we call the yield on T-bills the *risk-free return* over a short time (one year or less).[6]

An interesting comparison, then, is between the virtually risk-free return on T-bills and the very risky return on common stocks. This difference between risky returns and risk-free returns is often called the *excess return on the market portfolio*. It is called *excess* because it is the additional return resulting from the riskiness of common stocks, and it is interpreted as a **risk premium**. It is also known as the market risk premium.

Table 10.2 shows the average stock return, bond return, T-bill return, and inflation rate from 1957 through 2013. From this we can derive risk premiums. We can see that the average risk premium for common stocks for the entire period was 4.46 percent (ranging from 10.43 percent to 5.97 percent).

**TABLE 10.2**

**Average Annual Returns, 1957 to 2013**

| Investment | Arithmetic average return (%) | Risk premium (%) | Standard deviation (%) | Distribution |
|---|---|---|---|---|
| Canadian common stocks | 10.43 | 4.46 | 16.64 | |
| U.S. common stocks ($CAN) | 11.64 | 5.67 | 17.11 | |

*(continued)*

---

[6] A Treasury bill with a 90-day maturity is risk free only during that particular time period.

| Investment | Arithmetic average return (%) | Risk premium (%) | Standard deviation (%) | Distribution |
|---|---|---|---|---|
| Long bonds | 8.38 | 2.41 | 9.81 | |
| Small stocks | 14.16 | 8.19 | 26.25 | |
| Inflation | 3.85 | −2.12 | 3.12 | |
| Treasury bills | 5.97 | 0.00 | 3.81 | |
| S&P/TSX Venture Composite | 9.70 | 3.73 | 47.32 | |

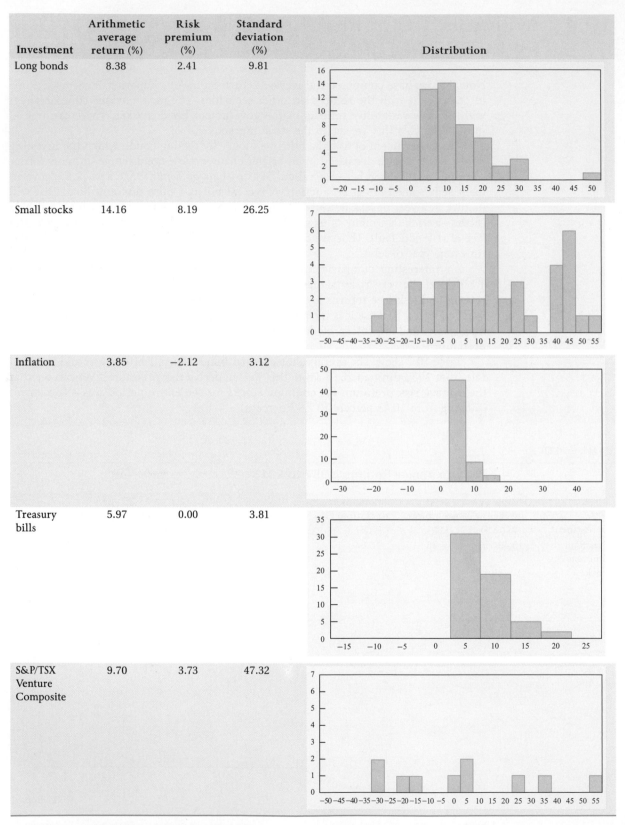

Average returns on small stocks are based on data from 1970 to 2013.

Average returns on the S&P/TSX Venture Composite are based on data from 2002 to 2013.

One of the most significant observations of stock market data is this long-run excess of the stock return over the risk-free return. An investor for this period was rewarded for investment in the stock market with an extra or excess return over what would have been achieved by simply investing in T-bills.

Why was there such a reward? Does it mean that it never pays to invest in T-bills and that someone who invested in them instead of in the stock market needs a course in finance? Complete answers to these questions lie at the heart of modern finance, and Chapter 11 is devoted entirely to them. However, part of the answer can be found in the variability of the various types of investments. We see in Table 10.1 many years when an investment in T-bills achieved higher returns than an investment in common stocks. Also, we note that the returns from an investment in common stocks are frequently negative, whereas an investment in T-bills never produces a negative return.[7] So, we now turn our attention to measuring the variability of returns and an introductory discussion of risk.

By looking more closely at Table 10.2, we see that the standard deviation of T-bills is substantially less than that of common stocks. This suggests that the risk of T-bills is below that of common stocks. Because the answer turns on the riskiness of investments in common stock, we now shift our attention to measuring this risk.

**CONCEPT QUESTIONS**

- What is the major observation about capital markets that we will seek to explain?
- What does the observation tell us about investors for the period from 1957 through 2013?

## 10.5  RISK STATISTICS

The second number that we use to characterize the distribution of returns is a measure of risk. There is no universally agreed upon definition of risk. One way to think about the risk of returns on common stock is in terms of how spread out the frequency distribution in Figure 10.5 is.[8] The spread or dispersion of a distribution is a measure of how much a particular return can deviate from the mean return. If the distribution is very spread out, the returns that will occur are very uncertain. By contrast, a distribution whose returns are all within a few percentage points of each other is tight, and the returns are less uncertain. The measures of risk we will discuss are variance and standard deviation.

**EXAMPLE 10.3**

The returns on Canadian common stocks from 1989 to 1992 were (in decimals) 0.2137, −0.1480, 0.1202, and −0.0143, respectively. The variance and standard deviation (explained below) of this sample are computed as

$$\text{Var} = \frac{1}{T-1}[(R_1 - \bar{R})^2 + (R_2 - \bar{R})^2 + (R_3 - \bar{R})^2 + (R_4 - \bar{R})^2]$$

$$0.0250 = \frac{1}{3}[(0.2137 - 0.0429)^2 + (-0.1480 - 0.0429)^2 + (0.1202 - 0.0429)^2$$
$$+ (-0.0143 - 0.0429)^2]$$

$$\text{SD} = \sqrt{0.0250} = 0.1581 = 15.81\%$$

---

[7] All our returns are nominal and before tax. The real, after-tax return on T-bills can be negative.

[8] Several condensed frequency distributions are also in the far right column of Table 10.2.

## Variance and Standard Deviation

The **variance** and its square root, the **standard deviation**, are the most common measures of variability or dispersion. In Example 10.3, we used Var to denote the variance and SD to represent the standard deviation. This formula tells us just what to do. Take each of the $T$ individual returns ($R_1$, $R_2$, …) and subtract the average return, $\overline{R}$, square the result, and add them all up. Finally, divide this total by the number of returns less 1 ($T - 1$). The standard deviation is always just the square root of the variance.[9]

Using the actual stock returns in Table 10.1 for the 57-year period 1957 through 2013 in the above formula, the resulting standard deviation of stock returns is 16.64 percent. The standard deviation is the standard statistical measure of the spread of a sample, and it will be the measure we use most of the time. Its interpretation is facilitated by a discussion of the normal distribution.

## Normal Distribution and Its Implications for Standard Deviation

A large enough sample drawn from a **normal distribution** looks like the bell-shaped curve drawn in Figure 10.6. As you can see, this distribution is *symmetric* about its mean, not *skewed*, and it has a much cleaner shape than the actual distribution of yearly returns drawn in Figure 10.5.[10] Of course, if we had been able to observe stock market returns for 1,000 years, we might have filled in a lot of the jumps and jerks in Figure 10.5 and had a smoother curve.

In classical statistics, the normal distribution plays a central role, and the standard deviation is the usual way of representing the spread of a normal distribution. For the normal distribution, the probability of having a return that is above or below the mean by a certain amount depends only on the standard deviation. For example, the probability of having a return that is within one standard deviation of the mean of the distribution is approximately 0.68 or close to 2/3, and the probability of having a return that is within two standard deviations of the mean is approximately 0.95.

The 16.64 percent standard deviation we found for Canadian common stock returns from 1957 through 2013 can now be interpreted in the following way. If stock returns are roughly normally distributed, the probability that a yearly return will fall in the range −6.21 percent to 27.07 percent (10.43 percent plus or minus one standard deviation, 16.64 percent) is about 68 percent. This range is illustrated in Figure 10.6. In other words, there is about one chance in three that the return will be *outside* this range. Based on historical experience and assuming that the past is a good guide to the future, investors who buy shares in large Canadian companies should expect to be outside this range in one year out of every three. This reinforces our earlier observations about stock market volatility. However, there is only a 5 percent chance (approximately) that we would end up outside the range −22.85 percent to 43.71 percent (10.43% ± 2 × 16.64%). These points are also illustrated in Figure 10.6.

---

[9] For small samples, as in this example, you can use a financial calculator to compute the variance and standard deviation. For example, using the Sharp Business/Financial calculator, the steps are as follows:
1. Clear the calculator.
2. Set the calculator to statistics mode by pressing *2nd F MODE* until STAT appears on the display.
3. Set the calculator for statistical calculations by pressing *2nd F TAB decimal point*. The calculator responds by displaying 0.
4. Enter the first observation, 0.2137, and press *M+*. The calculator displays 1, showing that it has recorded the first observation.
5. Enter the second observation, −0.1480, using the ± key to enter the sign. The calculator displays 2, showing that it has recorded the second observation.
6. Enter the remaining observations.
7. Ask the calculator for the expected return ($R$ in the formula) by pressing *x*.
8. Ask the calculator for the standard deviation by pressing σ.
For larger samples, you should use the STDEV command in Microsoft Excel.

[10] Some people define risk as the possibility of obtaining a return below the average. Some measures of risk, such as semivariance, use only the negative deviations from the average return. However, for symmetric distributions, such as the normal distribution, this method of measuring downside risk is equivalent to measuring risk with deviations from the mean on both sides.

FIGURE 10.6

**The Normal Distribution**

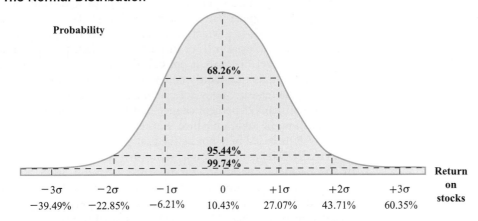

In the case of a normal distribution, there is a 68.26 percent probability that a return will be within one standard deviation of the mean. In this example, there is a 68.26 percent probability that a yearly return will be between −6.21 and 27.07 percent.

There is a 95.44 percent probability that a return will be within two standard deviations of the mean. In this example, there is a 95.44 percent probability that a yearly return will be between −22.85 percent and 43.71 percent.

Finally, there is a 99.74 percent probability that a return will be within three standard deviations of the mean. In this example, there is a 99.74 percent probability that a yearly return will be between −39.49 percent and 60.35 percent.

The distribution in Figure 10.6 is a theoretical distribution, sometimes called the *population*. There is no assurance that the actual distribution of observations in a given sample will produce a histogram that looks exactly like the theoretical distribution. We can see how messy the actual frequency function of historical observations is by observing Figure 10.5. If we were to keep on generating observations for a long enough period of time, however, the aberrations in the sample would disappear, and the actual historical distribution would start to look like the underlying theoretical distribution.

Our comparison illustrates how sampling error exists in any individual sample. In other words, the distribution of the sample only approximates the true distribution; we always measure the truth with some error. For example, we do not know what the true expected return was for common stocks in the 57-year history. However, we are sure that 10.43 percent is a good estimate.

## Value at Risk

Figure 10.6 provides the basis for calculating **value at risk (VaR)**, a popular risk measurement tool used by banks, insurance companies, and other financial institutions. VaR represents the maximum possible loss in dollars for a given confidence level. To explain where VaR comes from, we start with Figure 10.6, which shows that there is a 95.44 percent probability that the annual return on common stock will lie between a loss of −22.85 percent and a gain of 43.71 percent. This means that there is a 4.56 percent probability that the return will lie outside this range. Given that the normal distribution is symmetric, it follows that half that probability (or 2.28 percent) is attached to returns below −22.85 percent. (There is a similar probability of returns higher than 43.71 percent but because we are measuring risk, it is not of concern here.) In brief, if we pick 2.28 percent as our confidence level, Figure 10.6 tells us that returns lower than −22.85 percent will occur only 2.28 percent of the time.

VaR is expressed in dollars, so the final piece of information needed is our total exposure to Canadian equities. Suppose that this is $200 million. Multiplying $200 million by a loss of 22.85 percent gives $45.7 million for VaR. In other words, $45.7 million is the most we can lose in one year on our Canadian equity exposure provided we are willing to accept a 2.28 percent chance that our loss could be higher. Canadian banks are required to report VaR in their annual reports.

Although VaR is a widely used tool in risk management, there are various short-comings with the measure. For instance, VaR often provides a false sense of security as individuals forget that VaR is not calculated at a 100 percent confidence interval. As a result, individuals mistakenly believe that VaR measures the "worst possible loss." Furthermore, the measure does not calculate this maximum loss. In our previous example, there was still a 2.28 percent chance that the losses would be greater than the calculated $45.7 million. In addition, since markets are generally efficient, the historical data on which VaR is based may not be the best predictor of the future exposure to risk.

Finally, VaR assumes a normal return distribution, which may not always be true in the financial markets.[11] For instance, between 2008 and 2009, during the financial crisis, the TSX dropped by 45%.[12] Figure 10.6 shows that this is more than three standard deviations below the mean of 10.43 percent, so the probability of a loss of 45 percent is less than 0.13 percent, calculated as $(100\% - 99.74\%)/2$. According to the normal distribution, this loss should occur only once in 769 years (1/0.0013). However, as history shows, the occurrence of market crashes is more likely than 1 in every 769 years—the last major financial crisis was the Great Depression of the 1930s, only about 80 years ago! This showcases that normality assumptions do not always apply in the markets.

## Further Perspective on Returns and Risk

Table 10.2 presents returns and risks for major asset classes over a reasonably long period of Canadian history. Our discussion of these data suggested that the greater the potential reward, the greater the risk. In particular, the equity risk premium was 4.46 percent over this period for Canadian stocks.

This may strike you as low compared to during the 1990s, as well as in the years immediately after World War II, when double-digit returns on Canadian and U.S. stocks were common, as Table 10.1 shows. Currently, most financial executives and professional investment managers expect lower returns and smaller risk premiums in the future.[13] We agree with their expectation, which relates to our earlier discussion of which data to use to calculate the market risk premium. In Table 10.1 we display returns data back to 1948 but only go back to 1957 when we calculate risk premiums in Table 10.2. This drops off the high returns experienced in many of the post-war years. If we recalculate the returns and risk premiums in Table 10.2 going all the way back to 1948, we arrive at a market risk premium of 6.66 percent. We discuss the relationship between risk and required return in more detail in the next chapter.

Using U.S. data, including the years immediately following World War II and going back to 1926, Appendix 10A (available on Connect) shows a similar result. The risk premium for this period is higher than for other historical periods.

All this suggests that our estimate of around 4 percent is quite reasonable for the future equity risk premium in Canada. However, we must acknowledge that this remains a controversial issue about which experts disagree.

---

[11] A. Damodaran, "Value at Risk (VAR)," NYU Stern School of Business, people.stern.nyu.edu/adamodar/pdfiles/papers/VAR.pdf.

[12] P. Cross, "The Accelerated Pace of the 2008–2009 Downturn," Statistics Canada (May 2010), www.statcan.gc.ca/daily-quotidien/100513/dq100513a-eng.htm.

[13] A survey of academic views on the market risk premium is in I. Welch, "Views of Financial Economists on the Equity Risk Premium and Other Issues," *Journal of Business* (October 2000). William Mercer surveys professional investment managers in Canada in its annual *Fearless Forecast*, available at mercermap.co/.

- Define sample estimates of variance and standard deviation.
- How does the normal distribution help us interpret standard deviation?
- Assuming that long-term bonds have an approximately normal distribution, what is the approximate probability of earning 17 percent or more in a given year? With T-bills, what is this probability?
- Real estate returns appear to be an anomaly, with higher returns and lower standard deviation than common stocks. What factors could explain this?

# 10.6   MORE ON AVERAGE RETURNS

Thus far in this chapter we have looked closely at simple average returns. But there is another way of computing an average return. The fact that average returns are calculated in two different ways leads to some confusion, so our goal in this section is to explain the two approaches and also the circumstances under which each is appropriate.

## Arithmetic versus Geometric Averages

Let's start with a simple example. You buy a particular stock for $100. The first year it falls to $50. The second year it rises back to $100, leaving you right back where you started (no dividends were paid).

What was the average return on this investment? Common sense seems to say that the average return must be exactly zero because you started with $100 and ended with $100. But if we calculate the returns year-by-year, we see that the stock lost 50 percent the first year. The second year, the stock made 100 percent (the stock doubled). The average return over the two years was thus (−50 percent + 100 percent)/2 = 25 percent! So which is correct, 0 percent or 25 percent? The answer is that both are correct; they just answer different questions. The 0 percent is called the geometric average return. The 25 percent is called the arithmetic average return. The geometric average return answers the question, "What was your average compound return per year over a particular period?" The arithmetic average return answers the question, "What was your return in an average year over a particular period?"

Notice that in previous sections, the average returns calculated were all arithmetic averages, so we already know how to calculate them. The following paragraphs will discuss how to calculate geometric averages and under which circumstances one average is more meaningful than the other.

## Calculating Geometric Average Returns

To illustrate how we calculate a geometric average return, suppose a particular investment had annual returns of 10 percent, 12 percent, 3 percent, and −9 percent over the last four years. The geometric average return over this four-year period is calculated as $(1.10 \times 1.12 \times 1.03 \times 0.91)^{1/4} - 1 = 3.66$ percent. In contrast, the average arithmetic return we have been calculating is $(0.10 + 0.12 + 0.03 - 0.09)/4 = 4.0$ percent.

In general, if we have $T$ years of returns, the geometric average return over these $T$ years is calculated using this formula:

$$\text{Geometric average return} = [(1 + R_1) \times (1 + R_2) \times \cdots \times (1 + R_T)]^{1/T} - 1 \quad \textbf{(10.1)}$$

This formula tells us that four steps are required:

1. Add 1 to each of the $T$ annual returns, $R_1, R_2, \ldots, R_T$ (after converting them to decimals).
2. Multiply all the numbers from step 1 together.
3. Take the result from step 2 and raise it to the power of $1/T$.
4. Finally, subtract 1 from the result of step 3. The result is the geometric average return.

In the examples thus far, the geometric average returns seem to be smaller. It turns out that this will always be true (as long as the returns are not all identical, in which case the two "averages" would be the same). To illustrate, Table 10.3 shows the arithmetic averages and standard deviations from Table 10.1, along with the geometric average returns.

**TABLE 10.3**

### Geometric versus Arithmetic Average Returns, 1957 to 2013

| Investment | Average return | | Standard deviation (%) |
|---|---|---|---|
| | Arithmetic (%) | Geometric (%) | |
| Canadian common stocks | 10.43 | 9.12 | 16.64 |
| U.S. common stocks ($CAN) | 11.64 | 10.31 | 17.11 |
| Long bonds | 8.38 | 7.97 | 9.81 |
| Small stocks | 14.16 | 11.08 | 26.25 |
| Inflation | 3.85 | 3.80 | 3.12 |
| Treasury bills | 5.97 | 5.91 | 3.81 |
| S&P/TSX Venture Composite | 9.70 | −0.74 | 45.32 |

Average return on small stocks is based on data from 1970 to 2013. Average return on the TSX Venture is based on data from 2002 to 2013.

EXAMPLE **10.4**

Calculate the geometric average return for S&P 500 large-cap stocks for 1972 through 1976 using the numbers given here. First convert percentages to decimal returns, add 1, and then calculate their product.

| S&P 500 returns | Product |
|---|---|
| 18.12% | 1.1812 |
| −14.58 | × 0.8542 |
| −26.87 | × 0.7313 |
| 40.72 | × 1.4072 |
| 22.97 | × 1.2297 |
| | 1.2768 |

Notice that the number 1.2768 is what our investment is worth after five years if we started with a $1 investment. The geometric average return is then calculated as

$$\text{Geometric average return} = 1.2768^{1/5} - 1 = 0.0501, \text{ or } 5.01\%$$

Thus, the geometric average return is about 5.01 percent in this example. Here is a tip: if you are using a financial calculator, you can put $1 in as the present value (PV), $1.2768 as the future value, and 5 as the number of periods. Then solve for the unknown rate. You should get the same answer.

As shown in Table 10.3, the geometric averages are all smaller, but the magnitude of the difference varies quite a bit. The reason is that the difference is greater for more volatile investments. In fact, there is a useful approximation. Assuming all the numbers are expressed in decimals (as opposed to percentages), the geometric average return is approximately equal to the arithmetic average return minus half the variance. For example, looking at Canadian common stocks, the arithmetic average is 10.43 and the standard deviation is 16.64 percent, implying that the variance is 0.0277. The approximate geometric average is thus $0.1043 - 0.0277/2 = 9.045\%$, which is reasonably close to the actual value.

## Arithmetic Average Return or Geometric Average Return?

When looking at historical returns, the difference between the geometric and arithmetic average returns is not too hard to understand. The geometric average tells you what you actually earned per year on average, compounded annually. The arithmetic average tells you what you earned in a typical year. You should use whichever one answers the question you want answered.

A somewhat trickier question concerns forecasting the future, and there's a lot of confusion about this point among analysts and financial planners. The problem is this: if we have *estimates* of both the arithmetic and geometric average returns, then the arithmetic average is probably too high for longer periods and the geometric average is probably too low for shorter periods.

The good news is that there is a simple way of combining the two averages, which we call *Blume's formula*.[14] Suppose we calculated geometric and arithmetic return averages from $N$ years of data and we wish to use these averages to form a $T$-year average return forecast, $R(T)$, where $T$ is less than $N$. Here's how we do it:

$$R(T) = \frac{T-1}{N-1} \times \text{Geometric average} + \frac{N-T}{N-1} \times \text{Arithmetic average}$$

For example, suppose that from 25 years of annual returns data, we calculate an arithmetic average return of 12 percent and a geometric average return of 9 percent. From these averages, we wish to make 1-year, 5-year, and 10-year average return forecasts. These three average return forecasts are calculated as follows:

$$R(1) = \frac{1-1}{24} \times 9\% + \frac{25-1}{24} \times 12\% = 12\%$$

$$R(5) = \frac{5-1}{24} \times 9\% + \frac{25-5}{24} \times 12\% = 11.5\%$$

$$R(10) = \frac{10-1}{24} \times 9\% + \frac{25-10}{24} \times 12\% = 10.875\%$$

Thus, we see that 1-year, 5-year, and 10-year forecasts are 12 percent, 11.5 percent, and 10.875 percent, respectively. This concludes our discussion of geometric versus arithmetic averages. One last note: In the future, "average return" means arithmetic average unless explicitly stated otherwise.

## 10.7  2008: A YEAR OF FINANCIAL CRISIS

The year 2008 entered the record books as one of the worst years for stock market investors in history. How bad was it? The S&P TSX Index decreased 33 percent and the U.S. S&P 500 dropped 37 percent, in U.S. dollar terms. Of the 500 stocks in the U.S. index, 485 were down for the year. Of the period 1948 through 2013 covered in Table 10.1, the next worst year was 1974, when the S&P TSX posted a loss of 25.93 percent.

The drop in stock prices was a global phenomenon, and many of the world's major markets declined by much more than those in the United States and Canada. China, India, and Russia, for example, all experienced declines of more than 50 percent. The tiny country of Iceland saw share prices drop by more than 90 percent for the year. Trading on the Icelandic exchange was temporarily suspended on October 9, and stocks fell by 76 percent when trading resumed on October 14.

Did any types of securities perform well in 2008? The answer is yes, because as stock values declined, bond values increased, particularly government bonds. As Table 10.1 shows, both long bonds and Treasury bills had positive returns in 2008.

---

[14] This elegant result is due to Marshal Blume, "Unbiased Estimates of Long-Run Expected Rates of Return," *Journal of the American Statistical Association* (September 1974).

In 2009, the S&P TSX returned 35 percent. In the United States, however, the market ended 2009 lower than at the close of 1999. As a result, for the U.S. market, risk premium was negative for the 10 years starting with the tech bubble and running through the crash of 2008 and partial recovery in 2009.

What lessons should investors take away from this very recent bit of capital market history? First, and most obvious, stocks have significant risk. But there is a second, equally important lesson. Depending on the mix, a diversified portfolio of stocks and bonds probably would have suffered in 2008, but the losses would have been much smaller than those experienced by an all-stock portfolio.

## 10.8

# SUMMARY AND CONCLUSIONS

1. This chapter explores capital market history. Such history is useful because it tells us what to expect in the way of returns from risky assets. We summed up our study of market history with two key lessons:

   a. Risky assets, on average, earn a risk premium. There is a reward for bearing risk.

   b. The greater the risk from a risky investment, the greater is the required reward.

   The implications of these lessons for the financial manager are discussed in the chapters ahead.

2. The statistical measures in this chapter are necessary building blocks for the next three chapters. Standard deviation and variance measure the variability of the return on an individual security. We will argue that standard deviation and variance are appropriate measures of the risk of an individual security only if an investor's portfolio is composed exclusively of that security.

KEY TERMS

| | | |
|---|---|---|
| Average (mean) 294 | Risk premium 295 | Variance 298 |
| Frequency distribution 294 | Standard deviation 298 | |
| Normal distribution 298 | Value at risk (VaR) 299 | |

QUESTIONS & PROBLEMS

### Calculating Returns

10.1 Suppose a stock had an initial price of $92 per share, paid a dividend of $1.45 per share during the year, and had an ending share price of $104. Compute the percentage total return.

10.2 Rework Problem 10.1 assuming the ending share price is $67.

10.3 Suppose you bought a 6 percent coupon bond one year ago for $1,040. The bond sells for $1,063 today.

   a. Assuming a $1,000 face value, what was your total dollar return on this investment over the past year?

   b. What was your total nominal rate of return on this investment over the past year?

### Bond Returns

10.4 Using historical returns from Table 10.3, what is the historical real return on Canada Treasury bills? On long-term bonds?

**Calculating Returns and Variability**

10.5 Using the following returns, calculate the average returns, variances, and standard deviations for *X* and *Y*:

| | Returns | |
|---|---|---|
| Year | X | Y |
| 1 | 8% | 12% |
| 2 | 21 | 27 |
| 3 | −27 | −32 |
| 4 | 11 | 18 |
| 5 | 18 | 24 |

**Risk Premiums**

10.6 Refer to Table 10.1 in the text and look at the period from 1973 through 1978.
   *a.* Calculate the arithmetic average returns for common stocks and T-bills over this period.
   *b.* Calculate the standard deviation of the returns for common stocks and T-bills over this period.
   *c.* Calculate the observed risk premium in each year for the common stocks versus the T-bills. What was the arithmetic average risk premium over this period? What was the standard deviation of the risk premium over this period?

**Calculating Returns and Variability**

10.7 You've observed the following returns on Mary Ann Data Corporation's stock over the past five years: 34 percent, 16 percent, 19 percent, −21 percent, and 8 percent.
   *a.* What was the arithmetic average return on Mary Ann's stock over this five-year period?
   *b.* What was the variance of Mary Ann's returns over this period? The standard deviation?

**Holding-Period Return**

10.8  A stock has had returns of 16.12 percent, 12.11 percent, 5.83 percent, 26.14 percent, and −13.19 percent over the past five years, respectively. What was the holding-period return for the stock?

**Calculating Returns**

10.9  You purchased a zero-coupon bond one year ago for $77.81. The market interest rate is now 9 percent. If the bond had 30 years to maturity when you originally purchased it, what was your total return for the past year?

10.10 You bought a share of 4 percent preferred stock for $94.89 last year. The market price for your stock is now $96.12. What was your total return for last year?

**Return Distributions**

10.11 Refer back to Table 10.2. What range of returns would you expect to see 68 percent of the time for small stocks? 95 percent of the time?

10.12 Refer back to Table 10.2. What range of returns would you expect to see 68 percent of the time for T-bills? 95 percent of the time?

**Calculating Returns and Variability**

10.13 You find a certain stock that had returns of 19 percent, −27 percent, 6 percent, and 34 percent for four of the last five years. If the average return of the stock over this period was 11 percent, what was the stock's return for the missing year? What is the standard deviation of the stock's returns?

### Arithmetic and Geometric Returns

10.14 A stock has had returns of 34 percent, 18 percent, 29 percent, −6 percent, 16 percent, and −48 percent over the last six years. What are the arithmetic and geometric returns for the stock?

10.15 A stock has had the following year-end prices and dividends:

| Year | Price | Dividend |
|:----:|:-----:|:--------:|
| 1 | $61.18 | — |
| 2 | 64.83 | $0.72 |
| 3 | 72.18 | 0.78 |
| 4 | 63.12 | 0.86 |
| 5 | 69.27 | 0.95 |
| 6 | 76.93 | 1.08 |

What are the arithmetic and geometric returns for the stock?

### Calculating Returns

10.16 Refer to Table 10.1 in the text and look at the period from 1973 through 1980.
  a. Calculate the average return for Treasury bills and the average annual inflation rate (CPI) for this period.
  b. Calculate the standard deviation of Treasury bill returns and inflation over this period.
  c. Many people consider Treasury bills to be risk free. What do these calculations tell you about the potential risks of Treasury bills?

### Calculating Investment Returns

10.17 You bought one of Bergen Manufacturing Co.'s 7 percent coupon bonds one year ago for $1,080.50. These bonds make annual payments and mature six years from now. Suppose you decide to sell your bonds today when the required return on the bonds is 5.5 percent. What will be your total real return on the investment?

### Using Return Distributions

10.18 Suppose the returns on Canada long bonds are normally distributed. Based on the historical record, what is the approximate probability that your return on these bonds will be less than −3.3 percent in a given year? What range of returns would you expect to see 95 percent of the time? What range would you expect to see 99 percent of the time?

10.19 Assuming that the returns from holding small stocks are normally distributed, what is the approximate probability that your money will double in value in a single year? Triple in value?

### Distributions

10.20 In Problem 10.19, what is the probability that the return is less than −100 percent? (Think.) What are the implications for the distribution of returns?

### Using Probability Distributions

10.21 Suppose the returns on Canadian common stocks are normally distributed. Based on the historical record, use the NORMDIST function in Microsoft Excel to determine the probability that in any given year you will lose money by investing in Canadian common stock.

10.22 Suppose the returns on bonds and T-bills are normally distributed. Based on the historical record, use the NORMDIST function in Microsoft Excel to answer the following questions:
  a. What is the probability that in any given year, the return on bonds will be greater than 10 percent? Less than 0 percent?

*b.* What is the probability that in any given year, the return on T-bills will be greater than 10 percent? Less than 0 percent?

*c.* In 1979, the return on bonds was −4.18 percent. How likely is it that a return this low will recur at some point in the future? T-bills had a return of 10.56 percent in this same year. How likely is it that a return on T-bills this high will recur at some point in the future?

# A Job at Deck Out My Yacht Corporation

You have recently graduated from business school, and your job search led you to Deck Out My Yacht Corporation. Because you felt the company's business was seaworthy, you accepted a job offer. The first day on the job, while you are finishing your employment paperwork, Alvin Jones, who works in Finance, stops by to inform you about the company's retirement plan.

Retirement plans are offered by many companies and are tax-deferred savings vehicles, meaning that any deposits you make into the plan are deducted from your current pre-tax income, so no current taxes are paid on the money. For example, assume your salary will be $50,000 per year. If you contribute $3,000, you will pay taxes on only $47,000 in income. There are also no taxes paid on any capital gains or income while you are invested in the plan, but you do pay taxes when you withdraw money at retirement. As is fairly common, the company also has a 5 percent match. This means that the company will match your contribution up to 5 percent of your salary, but you must contribute to get the match. Assume the risk-free rate is the historical risk-free rate shown in Table 10.2 as the yield on Treasury bills.

This plan has several options for investments, most of which are mutual funds. A mutual fund is a portfolio of assets. When you purchase shares in a mutual fund, you are actually purchasing partial ownership of the fund's assets. The return of the fund is the weighted average of the return of the assets owned by the fund, minus any expenses. The largest expense is typically the management fee, paid to the fund manager. The management fee is compensation for the manager, who makes all of the investment decisions for the fund.

Deck Out My Yacht uses Marshall & McLaren Financial Services as its plan administrator. Here are the investment options offered for employees:

**Company Stock**
One option is stock in Deck Out My Yacht. The company is currently privately held. However, when the owner, Larissa Warren, interviewed you, she informed you that the company stock was expected to go public in the next three to four years. Until then, a company stock price is simply set each year by the board of directors.

**M&M TSX Composite Index Fund**
This mutual fund tracks the TSX Composite. Stocks in the fund are weighted exactly the same as the TSX Composite. This means the fund return is approximately the return on the TSX, minus expenses. Because an index fund purchases assets based on the composition of the index it is following, the fund manager is not required to research stocks and make investment decisions. The result is that the fund expenses are usually low. The M&M TSX Composite Index Fund charges expenses of 0.15 percent of assets per year.

**M&M Small-Cap Fund**
This fund primarily invests in small-cap stocks. As such, the returns of the fund are more volatile. The fund can also invest 10 percent of its assets in companies based outside Canada. This fund charges 1.70 percent in expenses.

**M&M Large-Company Stock Fund**
This fund invests primarily in large-cap stocks of companies based in North America. The fund is managed by Robbie McLaren and has outperformed the market in six of the last eight years. The fund charges 1.50 percent in expenses.

**M&M Bond Fund**
This fund invests in long-term corporate bonds issued by Canadian-domiciled companies. The fund is restricted to investments in bonds with an investment-grade credit rating. This fund charges 1.40 percent in expenses.

**M&M Money Market Fund**
This fund invests in short-term, high–credit quality debt instruments, which include Treasury bills. As such, the return on the money market fund is only slightly higher than the return on Treasury bills.

Because of the credit quality and short-term nature of the investments, there is only a very slight risk of negative return. The fund charges 0.60 percent in expenses.

1. What advantages do the mutual funds offer compared to the company stock?

2. Assume that you invest 5 percent of your salary and receive the full 5 percent match from Deck Out My Yacht. What equivalent annual rate (EAR) do you earn from the match? What conclusions do you draw about matching plans?

3. Assume you decide you should invest at least part of your money in large-cap stocks of companies based in North America. What are the advantages and disadvantages of choosing the M&M Large-Company Stock Fund compared to the M&M TSX Composite Index Fund?

4. The returns on the M&M Small-Cap Fund are the most volatile of all the mutual funds. Why would you ever want to invest in this fund? When you examine the expenses of the mutual funds, you will notice that this fund also has the highest expenses. Does this affect your decision to invest in this fund?

5. A measure of risk-adjusted performance that is often used is the Sharpe ratio. The Sharpe ratio is calculated as the risk premium of an asset divided by its standard deviation. The standard deviation and return of the funds over the past 10 years are listed here. Calculate the Sharpe ratio for each of these funds. Assume that the expected return and standard deviation of the company stock will be 16 percent and 65 percent, respectively. Calculate the Sharpe ratio for the company stock. How appropriate is the Sharpe ratio for these assets? When would you use the Sharpe ratio?

|  | 10-year annual return | Standard deviation |
| --- | --- | --- |
| M&M TSX Composite Index Fund | 9.18% | 20.43% |
| M&M Small-Cap Fund | 14.12 | 25.13 |
| M&M Large-Company Stock Fund | 8.58 | 23.82 |
| M&M Bond Fund | 6.45 | 9.85 |

6. What portfolio allocation would you choose? Why? Explain your thinking carefully.

# The U.S. Equity Risk Premium: Historical and International Perspectives

To access Appendix 10A, go to Connect.

# Risk and Return: The Capital Asset Pricing Model

The previous chapter achieved two purposes. First, we acquainted you with the history of Canadian capital markets. Second, we presented statistics such as expected return, variance, and standard deviation. Our ultimate goal in the next three chapters is to determine the appropriate discount rate for capital budgeting projects. Because the discount rate on a project is a function of its risk, the discussion in the previous chapter on standard deviation is a necessary first step. However, we shall see that standard deviation is not the final word on risk.

Our next step is to investigate the relationship between the risk and the return of individual securities when these securities are part of a large portfolio. This task is taken up in this chapter. The actual treatment of the appropriate discount rate for capital budgeting is reserved for Chapter 13.

The crux of the current chapter can be summarized as follows. An individual who holds one security should use expected return as the measure of the security's return. Standard deviation or variance is the proper measure of the security's risk. An individual who holds a diversified portfolio cares about the *contribution* of each security to the expected return and risk of the portfolio. It turns out that a security's expected return is the appropriate measure of the security's contribution to the expected return on the portfolio. However, neither the security's variance nor the security's standard deviation is an appropriate measure of a security's contribution to the risk of a portfolio. The contribution of a security to the risk of a portfolio is best measured by beta.

## 11.1 INDIVIDUAL SECURITIES

In the first part of this chapter, we will examine the characteristics of individual securities. In particular, we will discuss the following:

1. *Expected return.* This is the return that an individual expects a stock to earn over the next period. Of course, because this is only an expectation, the actual return may be either higher or lower. An individual's expectation may simply be the average return per period a security has earned in the past. Alternatively, it may be based on a detailed analysis of a firm's prospects, on some computer-based model, or on special (or inside) information.

2. *Variance and standard deviation.* There are many ways to assess the volatility of a security's return. One of the most common is variance, which is a measure of the squared deviations of a security's return from its expected return. Standard deviation, which is the square root of the variance, may be thought of as a standardized version of the variance.

3. *Covariance and correlation.* Returns on individual securities are related to one another. Covariance is a statistic measuring the interrelationship between two securities. Alternatively, this relationship can be restated in terms of the correlation between the two securities. Covariance and correlation are building blocks to an understanding of the beta coefficient.

# 11.2   EXPECTED RETURN, VARIANCE, AND COVARIANCE

## Expected Return and Variance

Suppose financial analysts believe that there are four equally likely states of the economy: depression, recession, normal, and boom times. The returns on the Supertech Company are expected to follow the economy closely, while the returns on the Slowpoke Company are not. The return predictions are given below:

|            | Supertech returns, $R_{At}$ | Slowpoke returns, $R_{Bt}$ |
|------------|:---------------------------:|:--------------------------:|
| Depression | −20%                        | 5%                         |
| Recession  | 10                          | 20                         |
| Normal     | 30                          | −12                        |
| Boom       | 50                          | 9                          |

Variance can be calculated in four steps. Calculating expected return is the first step.[1] An additional step is needed to calculate standard deviation. (The calculations are presented in Table 11.1.)

1. Calculate the expected return:

**Supertech:**

$$\frac{-0.20 + 0.10 + 0.30 + 0.50}{4} = 0.175 = 17.5\%$$

**Slowpoke:**

$$\frac{0.05 + 0.20 - 0.12 + 0.09}{4} = 0.055 = 5.5\%$$

2. For each company, calculate the deviation of each possible return from the company's expected return given above. This is presented in the third column of Table 11.1.

3. The deviations we have calculated are indications of the dispersion of returns. However, because some are positive and some are negative, it is difficult to work with them in this form. For example, if we were to add up all the deviations for a single company, we would get zero as the sum.

   To make the deviations more meaningful, we multiply each one by itself. Now all the numbers are positive, implying that their sum must be positive as well. The squared deviations are presented in the last column of Table 11.1.

---

[1] If the probabilities of all the states are not the same, find the expected return (standard deviation) by multiplying each return (deviation) by its probability.

**TABLE 11.1**

### Calculating Variance and Standard Deviation

| (1) State of economy | (2) Rate of return | (3) Deviation from expected return | (4) Squared value of deviation |
|---|---|---|---|
| **Supertech\* (Expected return = 0.175)** | | | |
| | $R_{At}$ | $R_{At} - \overline{R}_A$ | $(R_{At} - \overline{R}_A)^2$ |
| Depression | −0.20 | −0.375 (= −0.20 − 0.175) | 0.140625 [= (−0.375)²] |
| Recession | 0.10 | −0.075 | 0.005625 |
| Normal | 0.30 | 0.125 | 0.015625 |
| Boom | 0.50 | 0.325 | 0.105625 |
| | | | 0.267500 |
| **Slowpoke† (Expected return = 0.055)** | | | |
| | $R_{Bt}$ | $R_{Bt} - \overline{R}_B$ | $(R_{Bt} - \overline{R}_B)^2$ |
| Depression | 0.05 | −0.005 (= 0.05 − 0.055) | 0.000025 [= (−0.005)²] |
| Recession | 0.20 | 0.145 | 0.021025 |
| Normal | −0.12 | −0.175 | 0.030625 |
| Boom | 0.09 | 0.035 | 0.001225 |
| | | | 0.052900 |

\* $\overline{R}_A = \dfrac{-0.20 + 0.10 + 0.30 + 0.50}{4} = 0.175 = 17.5\%$

$Var(R_A) = \sigma_A^2 = \dfrac{0.2675}{4} = 0.066875$

$SD(R_A) = \sigma_A = \sqrt{0.066875} = 0.2586 = 25.86\%$

† $\overline{R}_B = \dfrac{0.05 + 0.20 - 0.12 + 0.09}{4} = 0.055 = 5.5\%$

$Var(R_B) = \sigma_B^2 = \dfrac{0.0529}{4} = 0.013225$

$SD(R_B) = \sigma_B = \sqrt{0.013225} = 0.1150 = 11.50\%$

4. For each company, calculate the average squared deviation, which is the variance:[2]

**Supertech:**

$$\frac{0.140625 + 0.005625 + 0.015625 + 0.105625}{4} = 0.066875$$

**Slowpoke:**

$$\frac{0.000025 + 0.021025 + 0.030625 + 0.001225}{4} = 0.013225$$

Thus, the variance of Supertech is 0.066875, and the variance of Slowpoke is 0.013225.

---

[2] In this example, the four states give rise to four possible outcomes for each stock. Had we used past data, the outcomes would have actually occurred. In that case, statisticians argue that the correct divisor is $N - 1$, where $N$ is the number of observations. Thus, the denominator would be 3 (or $4 - 1$) in the case of past data, not 4. Note that the example in Section 10.5 involved past data and we used a divisor of $N - 1$. While this difference causes grief to both students and textbook writers, it is a minor point in practice. In the real world, samples are generally so large that using $N$ or $N - 1$ in the denominator has virtually no effect on the calculation of variance.

5. Calculate the standard deviation by taking the square root of the variance:

**Supertech:**

$$\sqrt{0.066875} = 0.2586 = 25.86\%$$

**Slowpoke:**

$$\sqrt{0.013225} = 0.1150 = 11.50\%$$

Algebraically, the formula for variance can be expressed as

$$\text{Var}(R) = \text{Expected value of } (R - \overline{R})^2$$

where $\overline{R}$ is the security's expected return and $R$ is the actual return.

A look at the four-step calculation for variance makes it clear why it is a measure of the spread of the sample of returns. For each observation, we square the difference between the actual return and the expected return. We then take an average of these squared differences.

However, because the variance is still expressed in squared terms, it is difficult to interpret. Standard deviation has a much simpler interpretation, which we will provide shortly. Standard deviation is simply the square root of the variance. The general formula for the standard deviation is

$$\text{SD}(R) = \sqrt{\text{Var}(R)}$$

## Covariance and Correlation

The statistical estimates of variance and standard deviation measure the variability of individual stocks. We now wish to measure the relationship between the return on one stock and the return on another. To make our discussion more precise, we need a statistical measure of the relationship between two variables. Enter **covariance** and **correlation**.

Covariance and correlation are ways of measuring whether or not two random variables are related, and how. We explain these terms in Example 11.1, which extends an example presented earlier in this chapter.

**EXAMPLE 11.1**

We have already determined the expected returns and standard deviations for both Supertech and Slowpoke. (The expected returns are 0.175 and 0.055 for Supertech and Slowpoke, respectively. The standard deviations are 0.2586 and 0.1150, respectively.) In addition, we calculated for each firm the deviation of each possible return from the expected return. Using these data, covariance can be calculated in two steps. An extra step is needed to calculate correlation.

1.  For each state of the economy, multiply Supertech's deviation from its expected return and Slowpoke's deviation from its expected return. For example, Supertech's rate of return in a depression is −0.20, which is −0.375 (or −0.20 − 0.175) from its expected return. Slowpoke's rate of return in a depression is 0.05, which is −0.005 (or 0.05 − 0.055) from its expected return. Multiplying the two deviations yields 0.001875 [or (−0.375) × (−0.005)]. The actual calculations are given in the last column of Table 11.2. This procedure can be written algebraically as

$$(R_{At} - \overline{R}_A) \times (R_{Bt} - \overline{R}_B) \tag{11.1}$$

where $R_{At}$ and $R_{Bt}$ are the returns on Supertech and Slowpoke in state $t$. $\overline{R}_A$ and $\overline{R}_B$ are the expected returns on the two securities.

**TABLE 11.2**

**Calculating Covariance and Correlation**

| State of economy | SUPERTECH | | SLOWPOKE | | Product of deviations $(R_{At} - \overline{R}_A) \times$ $(R_{Bt} - \overline{R}_B)$ |
| | Rate of return of $R_{At}$ | Deviation from expected return (= 0.175) $(R_{At} - \overline{R}_A)$ | Rate of return of $R_{Bt}$ | Deviation from expected return (= 0.055) $(R_{Bt} - \overline{R}_B)$ | |
|---|---|---|---|---|---|
| Depression | −0.20 | −0.375 $(= -0.20 - 0.175)$ | 0.05 | −0.005 $(= 0.05 - 0.055)$ | 0.001875 $(= -0.375 \times -0.005)$ |
| Recession | 0.10 | −0.075 | 0.20 | 0.145 | −0.010875 $(= -0.075 \times 0.145)$ |
| Normal | 0.30 | 0.125 | −0.12 | −0.175 | −0.021875 $(= 0.125 \times -0.175)$ |
| Boom | 0.50 | 0.325 | 0.09 | 0.035 | 0.011375 $(= 0.325 \times 0.035)$ |
| | 0.70 | | 0.22 | | −0.0195 |

$$\sigma_{AB} = \text{Cov}(R_A, R_B) = \frac{-0.0195}{4} = -0.004875$$

$$\rho_{AB} = \text{Corr}(R_A, R_B) = \frac{\text{Cov}(R_A, R_B)}{\text{SD}(R_A) \times \text{SD}(R_B)} - \frac{-0.004875}{0.2586 \times 0.1150} = -0.1639$$

2.  Calculate the average value of the four states in the last column. This average is the covariance. That is,[3]

$$\sigma_{AB} = \text{Cov}(R_A, R_B) = \frac{-0.195}{4} = -0.004875$$

Note that we represent the covariance between Supertech and Slowpoke as either $\text{Cov}(R_A, R_B)$ or $\sigma_{AB}$. Equation (11.1) illustrates the intuition of covariance. Suppose Supertech's return is generally above its average when Slowpoke's return is above its average, and Supertech's return is generally below its average when Slowpoke's return is below its average. This indicates a positive dependency or a positive relationship between the two returns. Note that the term in equation (11.1) will be *positive* in any state where both returns are *above* their averages. In addition, (11.1) will still be *positive* in any state where both terms are *below* their averages. Thus, a positive relationship between the two returns will give rise to a positive calculation for covariance.

Conversely, suppose Supertech's return is generally above its average when Slowpoke's return is below its average, and Supertech's return is generally below its average when Slowpoke's return is above its average. This is indicative of a negative dependency or a negative relationship between the two returns. Note that the term in equation (11.1) will be *negative* in any state where one return is above its average and the other return is below its average. Thus, a negative relationship between the two returns will give rise to a negative calculation for covariance.

Finally, suppose there is no relation between the two returns. In this case, knowing whether the return on Supertech is above or below its expected return tells us nothing about the return on Slowpoke. In the covariance formula, then, there will be no tendency for the terms to be positive or negative, and on average they will tend to offset each other and cancel out. This will make the covariance zero.

---

[3] As with variance, we divide by $N$ (4 in this example) because the four states give rise to four possible outcomes. However, had we used past data, the correct divisor would be $N - 1$ (3 in this example).

Of course, even if the two returns are unrelated to each other, the covariance formula will not equal zero exactly in any actual history. This is due to sampling error; randomness alone will make the calculation positive or negative. But for a historical sample that is long enough, if the two returns are not related to each other, we should expect the formula to come close to zero.

The covariance formula seems to capture what we are looking for. If the two returns are positively related to each other, they will have a positive covariance, and if they are negatively related to each other, the covariance will be negative. Last, and very important, if they are unrelated, the covariance should be zero.

The formula for covariance can be written algebraically as[4]

$$\sigma_{AB} = \text{Cov}(R_A, R_B) = \text{Expected value of } [(R_A - \bar{R}_A) \times (R_B - \bar{R}_B)]$$

where $\bar{R}_A$ and $\bar{R}_B$ are the expected returns for the two securities, and $R_A$ and $R_B$ are the actual returns. The ordering of the two variables is unimportant. That is, the covariance of $A$ with $B$ is equal to the covariance of $B$ with $A$. This can be stated more formally as $\text{Cov}(R_A, R_B) = \text{Cov}(R_B, R_A)$ or $\sigma_{AB} = \sigma_{BA}$.

The covariance we calculated is $-0.004875$. A negative number like this implies that the return on one stock is likely to be above its average when the return on the other stock is below its average, and vice versa. However, the size of the number is difficult to interpret. Like the variance figure, the covariance is in squared deviation units. Until we can put it in perspective, we don't know what to make of it.

We solve the problem by computing the correlation.

3.  To calculate the correlation, divide the covariance by the standard deviations of both securities. For our example, we have

$$\rho_{AB} = \text{Corr}(R_A, R_B) = \frac{\text{Cov}(R_A, R_B)}{\sigma_A \times \sigma_B} = \frac{-0.004875}{0.2586 \times 0.1150} = -0.1639 \qquad \textbf{(11.2)}$$

where $\sigma_A$ and $\sigma_B$ are the standard deviations of Supertech and Slowpoke, respectively. Note that we represent the correlation between Supertech and Slowpoke as either $\text{Corr}(R_A, R_B)$ or $\rho_{AB}$. As with covariance, the ordering of the two variables is unimportant. That is, the correlation of $A$ with $B$ is equal to the correlation of $B$ with $A$. More formally, $\text{Corr}(R_A, R_B) = \text{Corr}(R_B, R_A)$ or $\rho_{AB} = \rho_{BA}$.

Because the standard deviation is always positive, the sign of the correlation between two variables must be the same as that of the covariance between the two variables. If the correlation is positive, we say that the variables are *positively correlated*; if it is negative, we say that they are *negatively correlated*; and if it is zero, we say that they are *uncorrelated*. Furthermore, it can be proven that the correlation is always between $+1$ and $-1$. This is due to the standardizing procedure of dividing by the two standard deviations.

We can compare the correlation between different pairs of securities. For example, it turns out that the correlation between Bank of Montreal and Royal Bank of Canada is much higher than the correlation between Bank of Montreal and Telus. Hence, we can state that the first pair of securities is more interrelated than the second pair.

---

[4] The covariance formula can also be written using summation notation:

$$\sigma_{AB} = \text{Cov}(R_A, R_B) = \sum_{t=1}^{4} \left[ P_t (R_{At} - \bar{R}_A)(R_{Bt} - \bar{R}_B) \right]$$

where $P_t$ represents the probability of state $t$ occurring.

Figure 11.1 shows the three benchmark cases for two assets, *A* and *B*. The figure shows two assets with return correlations of $+1$, $-1$, and $0$. This implies perfect positive correlation, perfect negative correlation, and no correlation, respectively. The graphs in the figure plot the separate returns on the two securities through time.

**FIGURE 11.1**

**Examples of Different Correlation Coefficients**

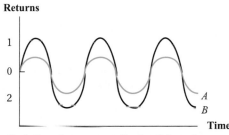

Perfect positive correlation
$\mathrm{Corr}(R_A, R_B) = 1$

Both the return on security *A* and the return on security *B* are higher than average at the same time. Both the return on security *A* and the return on security *B* are lower than average at the same time.

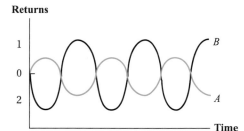

Perfect negative correlation
$\mathrm{Corr}(R_A, R_B) = -1$

Security *A* has a higher-than-average return when security *B* has a lower-than-average return, and vice versa.

Zero correlation
$\mathrm{Corr}(R_A, R_B) = 0$

The return on security *A* is completely unrelated to the return on security *B*.

# 11.3   THE RISK AND RETURN FOR PORTFOLIOS

Suppose that an investor has estimates of the expected returns and standard deviations on individual securities and the correlations between securities. How then does the investor choose the best combination or **portfolio** of securities to hold? Obviously, the investor would like a portfolio with a high expected return and a low standard deviation of return. It is therefore worthwhile to consider the following:

1.  The relationship between the expected return on individual securities and the expected return on a portfolio made up of these securities.
2.  The relationship between the standard deviations of individual securities, the correlations between these securities, and the standard deviation of a portfolio made up of these securities.

## The Example of Supertech and Slowpoke

In order to analyze the above two relationships, we will use the Supertech and Slowpoke example presented previously. The relevant data are in the box below.[5]

### Relevant Data from Example of Supertech and Slowpoke

| Item | Symbol | Value |
|------|--------|-------|
| Expected return on Supertech | $\overline{R}_{Super}$ | $0.175 = 17.5\%$ |
| Expected return on Slowpoke | $\overline{R}_{Slow}$ | $0.055 = 5.5\%$ |
| Variance of Supertech | $\sigma^2_{Super}$ | $0.066875$ |
| Variance of Slowpoke | $\sigma^2_{Slow}$ | $0.013225$ |
| Standard deviation of Supertech | $\sigma_{Super}$ | $0.2586 = 25.86\%$ |
| Standard deviation of Slowpoke | $\sigma_{Slow}$ | $0.1150 = 11.50\%$ |
| Covariance between Supertech and Slowpoke | $\sigma_{Super,\,Slow}$ | $-0.004875$ |
| Correlation between Supertech and Slowpoke | $\rho_{Super,\,Slow}$ | $-0.1639$ |

## The Expected Return on a Portfolio

The formula for expected return on a portfolio is very simple:

> The expected return on a portfolio is simply a weighted average of the expected returns on the individual securities.

**EXAMPLE 11.2**

Consider Supertech and Slowpoke. From the box above, we find that the expected returns on these two securities are 17.5 percent and 5.5 percent, respectively.

The expected return on a portfolio of these two securities alone can be written as

$$\text{Expected return on portfolio} = X_{Super}(17.5\%) + X_{Slow}(5.5\%)$$

where $X_{Super}$ is the proportion of the portfolio in Supertech and $X_{Slow}$ is the proportion of the portfolio in Slowpoke. If the investor with $100 invests $60 in Supertech and $40 in Slowpoke, the expected return on the portfolio can be written as

$$\text{Expected return on portfolio} = 0.6 \times 17.5\% + 0.4 \times 5.5\% = 12.7\%$$

Algebraically, we can write

$$\text{Expected return on portfolio} = X_A\overline{R}_A + X_B\overline{R}_B \qquad (11.3)$$

where $X_A$ and $X_B$ are the proportions of the total portfolio in the assets $A$ and $B$, respectively. (Because our investor can only invest in two securities, $X_A + X_B$ must equal 1 or 100 percent.) $\overline{R}_A$ and $\overline{R}_B$ are the expected returns on the two securities.

Now consider two stocks, each with an expected return of 10 percent. The expected return on a portfolio composed of these two stocks must be 10 percent, regardless of the proportions of the two stocks held. This result may seem obvious at this point, but it will become important later. The result implies that you do not reduce or *dissipate* your expected return by investing in a number of securities. Rather, the expected return on your portfolio is simply a weighted average of the expected returns on the individual assets in the portfolio.

---

[5] See Tables 11.1 and 11.2 for actual calculations.

## Variance and Standard Deviation of a Portfolio

**The Variance**    The formula for the variance of a portfolio composed of two securities, $A$ and $B$, is

**The Variance of the Portfolio:**

$$\text{Var(portfolio)} = X_A^2\sigma_A^2 + 2X_AX_B\sigma_{A,B} + X_B^2\sigma_B^2$$

Note that there are three terms on the right-hand side of the equation. The first term involves the variance of $A$ ($\sigma_A^2$), the second term involves the covariance between the two securities ($\sigma_{A,B}$), and the third term involves the variance of $B$ ($\sigma_B^2$). (It should be noted that $\sigma_{A,B} = \sigma_{B,A}$. That is, the ordering of the variables is not relevant when expressing the covariance between two securities.)

The formula indicates an important point. The variance of a portfolio depends on both the variances of the individual securities and the covariance between the two securities. The variance of a security measures the variability of an individual security's return. Covariance measures the relationship between the two securities. For given variances of the individual securities, a positive relationship or covariance between the two securities increases the variance of the entire portfolio. A negative relationship or covariance between the two securities decreases the variance of the entire portfolio. This important result seems to square with common sense. If one of your securities tends to go up when the other goes down, or vice versa, your two securities are offsetting each other. You are achieving what we call a *hedge* in finance, and the risk of your entire portfolio will be low. However, if both your securities rise and fall together, you are not hedging at all. Hence, the risk of your entire portfolio will be higher.

The variance formula for our two securities, Super and Slow, is

$$\text{Var(portfolio)} = X_{\text{Super}}^2\sigma_{\text{Super}}^2 + 2X_{\text{Super}}X_{\text{Slow}}\sigma_{\text{Super,Slow}} + X_{\text{Slow}}^2\sigma_{\text{Slow}}^2 \qquad \textbf{(11.4)}$$

Given our earlier assumption that an individual with \$100 invests \$60 in Supertech and \$40 in Slowpoke, $X_{\text{Super}} = 0.6$ and $X_{\text{Slow}} = 0.4$. Using this assumption and the relevant data from the box given earlier, the variance of the portfolio is

$$0.023851 = 0.36 \times 0.066875 + 2 \times [0.6 \times 0.4 \times (-0.004875)] + 0.16 \times 0.013225 \quad \textbf{(11.4$'$)}$$

**The Matrix Approach**    Alternatively, equation (11.4) can be expressed in the following matrix format:

|  | Supertech | Slowpoke |
|---|---|---|
| **Supertech** | $X_{\text{Super}}^2\sigma_{\text{Super}}^2$ <br> $0.024075 = 0.36 \times 0.066875$ | $X_{\text{Super}}X_{\text{Slow}}\sigma_{\text{Super,Slow}}$ <br> $-0.00117 = 0.6 \times 0.4 \times (-0.004875)$ |
| **Slowpoke** | $X_{\text{Super}}X_{\text{Slow}}\sigma_{\text{Super,Slow}}$ <br> $-0.00117 = 0.6 \times 0.4 \times (-0.004875)$ | $X_{\text{Slow}}^2\sigma_{\text{Slow}}^2$ <br> $0.002116 = 0.16 \times 0.013225$ |

There are four boxes in the matrix. We can add the terms in the boxes to obtain equation (11.4), the variance of a portfolio composed of the two securities. The term in the upper left-hand corner contains the variance of Supertech. The term in the lower right-hand corner contains the variance of Slowpoke. The other two boxes contain the covariance terms. These two boxes are identical, indicating why the covariance term is multiplied by 2 in equation (11.4).

At this point, students often find the box approach to be more confusing than equation (11.4). However, the box approach is easily generalized to more than two securities, a task we perform later in this chapter.

**Standard Deviation of a Portfolio**    Given equation (11.4$'$), we can now determine the standard deviation of the portfolio's return. This is

$$\sigma_P = \text{SD(portfolio)} = \sqrt{\text{Var(portfolio)}} = \sqrt{0.023851} = 0.1544 = 15.44\% \quad \textbf{(11.5)}$$

The interpretation of the standard deviation of the portfolio is the same as the interpretation of the standard deviation of an individual security. The expected return on our portfolio is 12.7 percent. A return of $-2.74$ percent ($12.7\% - 15.44\%$) is one standard deviation below the mean, and a return of 28.14 percent ($12.7\% + 15.44\%$) is one standard deviation above the mean. If the return on the portfolio is normally distributed, a return between $-2.74$ percent and $+28.14$ percent occurs about 68 percent of the time.[6]

**The Diversification Effect** It is instructive to compare the standard deviation of the portfolio with the standard deviation of the individual securities. The weighted average of the standard deviations of the individual securities is

$$\text{Weighted average of standard deviations} = X_{\text{Super}}\sigma_{\text{Super}} + X_{\text{Slow}}\sigma_{\text{Slow}} \quad (11.6)$$
$$0.2012 = 0.6 \times 0.2586 + 0.4 \times 0.115$$

One of the most important results in this chapter relates to the difference between equations (11.5) and (11.6). In our example, the standard deviation of the portfolio is *less* than the weighted average of the standard deviations of the individual securities.

We pointed out earlier that the expected return on the portfolio is the weighted average of the expected returns on the individual securities. Thus, we get a different type of result for the standard deviation of a portfolio than we do for the expected return on a portfolio.

It is generally argued that our result for the standard deviation of a portfolio is due to diversification. For example, Supertech and Slowpoke are slightly negatively correlated ($\rho = -0.1639$). Supertech's return is likely to be a little below average if Slowpoke's return is above average. Similarly, Supertech's return is likely to be a little above average if Slowpoke's return is below average. Thus, the standard deviation of a portfolio composed of the two securities is less than the weighted average of the standard deviations of the two securities.

The above example has negative correlation. Clearly, there will be less benefit from diversification if the two securities exhibit positive correlation. How high must the positive correlation be before all diversification benefits vanish?

To answer this question, let us rewrite equation (11.4) in terms of correlation rather than covariance. The covariance can be rewritten as[7]

$$\sigma_{\text{Super, Slow}} = \rho_{\text{Super, Slow}}\sigma_{\text{Super}}\sigma_{\text{Slow}} \quad (11.7)$$

The formula states that the covariance between any two securities is simply the correlation between the two securities multiplied by the standard deviations of each. In other words, covariance incorporates both (1) the correlation between the two assets and (2) the variability of each of the two securities as measured by standard deviation.

From our calculations earlier in this chapter, we know that the correlation between the two securities is $-0.1639$. Given the variances used in equation (11.4'), the standard deviations are 0.2586 and 0.115 for Supertech and Slowpoke, respectively. Thus, the variance of a portfolio can be expressed as

### Variance of the Portfolio's Return:

$$\text{Variance of the portfolio's return} = X_{\text{Super}}^2\sigma_{\text{Super}}^2 + 2X_{\text{Super}}X_{\text{Slow}}\rho_{\text{Super,Slow}}\sigma_{\text{Super}}\sigma_{\text{Slow}}$$
$$+ X_{\text{Slow}}^2\sigma_{\text{Slow}}^2 \quad (11.8)$$

$$0.023851 = 0.36 \times 0.066875 + 2 \times 0.6 \times 0.4 \times (-0.1639)$$
$$\times 0.2586 \times 0.115 + 0.16 \times 0.013225$$

---

[6] There are only four equally probable returns for Supertech and Slowpoke, so neither security possesses a normal distribution. Thus, probabilities would be slightly different in our example.

[7] As with covariance, the ordering of the two securities is not relevant when expressing the correlation between the two securities. That is, $\rho_{\text{Super,Slow}} = \rho_{\text{Slow,Super}}$.

The middle term on the right-hand side is now written in terms of correlation, $\rho$, not covariance.

Suppose $\rho_{\text{Super,Slow}} = 1$, the highest possible value for correlation. Assume all the other parameters in the example are the same. The variance of the portfolio's return is

$$\begin{aligned}
\text{Variance of the portfolio's return} &= 0.040466 \\
&= 0.36 \times 0.066875 \\
&\quad + 2(0.6 \times 0.4 \times 1 \times 0.2586 \times 0.115) \\
&\quad + 0.16 \times 0.013225
\end{aligned}$$

The standard deviation is

$$\text{Standard deviation of portfolio's return} = \sqrt{0.040466} = 0.2012 = 20.12\% \quad \textbf{(11.9)}$$

Note that equations (11.9) and (11.6) are equal. That is, the standard deviation of a portfolio's return is equal to the weighted average of the standard deviations of the individual returns when $\rho = 1$. Inspection of equation (11.8) indicates that the variance and hence the standard deviation of the portfolio must drop as the correlation drops below 1. This leads to the following:

> As long as $\rho < 1$, the standard deviation of a portfolio of two securities is less than the weighted average of the standard deviations of the individual securities.

In other words, the diversification effect applies as long as there is less than perfect correlation (as long as $\rho < 1$). Thus, our Supertech–Slowpoke example is a case of overkill. We illustrated diversification with an example with negative correlation. We could have illustrated diversification with an example with positive correlation—as long as it was not perfect positive correlation.

**An Extension to Many Assets**    The preceding insight can be extended to the case of many assets. That is, as long as correlations between pairs of securities are less than 1, the standard deviation of a portfolio of many assets is less than the weighted average of the standard deviations of the individual securities.

Now consider Table 11.3, which shows the standard deviation of the S&P/TSX 60 and the standard deviations of some of the individual securities listed in the index over a recent 25-year period. Note that all of the individual securities in the table have higher standard deviations than that of the index. In general, the standard deviations of most of the individual securities in an index will be above the standard deviation of the index itself, though a few of the securities could have lower standard deviations than that of the index.

**TABLE 11.3**

**Standard Deviations of Annual Returns of Selected TSX Companies over a 25-Year Period**

| | |
|---|---|
| Canadian Tire Corp. | 31.79% |
| Bank of Montreal | 20.12 |
| Bell Canada Enterprises Inc. | 26.03 |
| Canadian Pacific Ltd. | 24.63 |
| Imperial Oil Ltd. | 23.38 |
| WestJet Airlines Ltd. | 46.37 |
| Potash Corporation of Saskatchewan Inc. | 29.96 |
| S&P/TSX 60 | 15.27 |

Source: Calculated from Canadian Financial Markets Research Centre data.

**CONCEPT**
*QUESTIONS*

- What are the formulas for the expected return, variance, and standard deviation of a portfolio of two assets?
- What is the diversification effect?
- What are the highest and lowest possible values for the correlation coefficient?

## 11.4   THE EFFICIENT SET FOR TWO ASSETS

Our results on expected returns and standard deviations are graphed in Figure 11.2. In the figure, there is a dot labelled Slowpoke and a dot labelled Supertech. Each dot represents both the expected return and the standard deviation for an individual security. As can be seen, Supertech has both a higher expected return and a higher standard deviation.

The box or □ in Figure 11.2 represents a portfolio with 60 percent invested in Supertech and 40 percent invested in Slowpoke. You will recall that we have previously calculated both the expected return and the standard deviation for this portfolio.

The choice of 60 percent in Supertech and 40 percent in Slowpoke is just one of an infinite number of portfolios that can be created. The set of portfolios is sketched by the curved line in Figure 11.3.

Consider portfolio 1. This is a portfolio composed of 90 percent Slowpoke and 10 percent Supertech. Because it is weighted so heavily toward Slowpoke, it appears close to the Slowpoke point on the graph. Portfolio 2 is higher on the curve because it is composed of 50 percent Slowpoke and 50 percent Supertech. Portfolio 3 is close to the Supertech point on the graph because it is composed of 90 percent Supertech and 10 percent Slowpoke.

There are a few important points concerning the graph in Figure 11.3:

1. We argued that the diversification effect occurs whenever the correlation between the two securities is less than 1. The correlation between Supertech and Slowpoke is −0.1639. The diversification effect can be illustrated by comparison with the straight line between the Supertech point and the Slowpoke point. The straight line represents points that would have been generated had the correlation coefficient between the two securities been 1. The diversification effect is illustrated in the figure since the curved line is always to the left of the straight line. Consider point 1′. This represents a portfolio composed of 90 percent in Slowpoke and 10 percent in Supertech if the correlation between the two were exactly 1. We argue that there is no diversification effect if $\rho = 1$. However, the diversification effect applies to the curved line, because point 1 has the same expected return as point 1′ but has a lower standard deviation. (Points 2′ and 3′ are omitted to reduce the clutter in Figure 11.3.)

   Though the straight line and the curved line are both represented in Figure 11.3, they do not exist simultaneously. Either $\rho = -0.1639$ and the curve exists or $\rho = 1$ and the straight line exists. In other words, though an investor can choose between different points on the curve if $\rho = -0.1639$, she cannot choose between points on the curve and points on the straight line.

2. The point MV represents the minimum variance portfolio. This is the portfolio with the lowest possible variance. By definition, this portfolio must also have the lowest possible standard deviation. (The term *minimum variance portfolio* is standard in the literature, and we will use that term. Perhaps *minimum standard deviation* would actually be better, because standard deviation, not variance, is measured on the horizontal axis of Figure 11.3.)

**FIGURE 11.2**

**Expected Return and Standard Deviation for (1) Supertech, (2) Slowpoke, and (3) a Portfolio Composed of 60 Percent in Supertech and 40 Percent in Slowpoke**

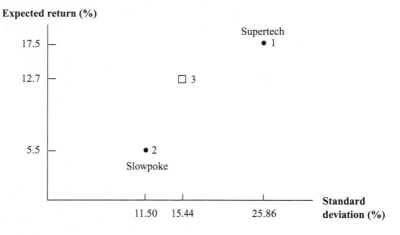

**FIGURE 11.3**

**Set of Portfolios Composed of Holdings in Supertech and Slowpoke (correlation between the two securities is −0.1639)**

Portfolio 1 is composed of 90 percent Slowpoke and 10 percent Supertech ($\rho = -0.1639$).
Portfolio 2 is composed of 50 percent Slowpoke and 50 percent Supertech ($\rho = -0.1639$).
Portfolio 3 is composed of 10 percent Slowpoke and 90 percent Supertech ($\rho = -0.1639$).
Portfolio 1′ is composed of 90 percent Slowpoke and 10 percent Supertech ($\rho = 1$).
Point MV denotes the minimum variance portfolio.

3. An investor considering a portfolio of Slowpoke and Supertech faces an **opportunity set** or **feasible set** represented by the curved line in Figure 11.3. That is, the investor can achieve any point on the curve by selecting the appropriate mix between the two securities. She cannot achieve any points above the curve because she cannot increase the return on the individual securities, decrease the standard deviations of the securities, or decrease the correlation between the two securities. Neither can the investor achieve points below the curve because she cannot lower the returns on the individual securities, increase the standard deviations of the

securities, or increase the correlation. (Of course, the investor would not want to achieve points below the curve, even if it were possible to do so.)

Were the investor relatively tolerant of risk, she might choose portfolio 3. (In fact, the investor could even choose the end point by investing all her money in Supertech.) An investor with less tolerance for risk might choose point 2. An investor wanting as little risk as possible would choose MV, the portfolio with minimum variance or minimum standard deviation.

4. Note that the curve is backward bending between the Slowpoke point and MV. This indicates that for a portion of the feasible set, standard deviation actually decreases as one increases expected return. Students frequently ask, "How can an increase in the proportion of the risky security, Supertech, lead to a reduction in the risk of the portfolio?"

   This surprising finding is due to the diversification effect. The returns on the two securities are negatively correlated. One security tends to go up when the other goes down. Thus, an addition of a small amount of Supertech acts as a hedge to a portfolio composed only of Slowpoke. The risk of the portfolio is reduced, implying a backward-bending curve. Actually, backward bending always occurs if $\rho \leq 0$. It may or may not occur when $\rho > 0$. Of course, the curve bends backward only for a portion of its length. As one continues to increase the percentage of Supertech in the portfolio, the high standard deviation of this security eventually causes the standard deviation of the entire portfolio to rise.

5. No investor would want to hold a portfolio with an expected return below that of the minimum variance portfolio. For example, no investor would choose portfolio 1. This portfolio has less expected return but more standard deviation than the minimum variance portfolio has. We say that portfolios such as portfolio 1 are *dominated* by the minimum variance portfolio.

   Though the entire curve from Slowpoke to Supertech is called the *feasible or opportunity set*, investors only consider the curve from MV to Supertech. Hence, the curve from MV to Supertech is called the **efficient set**.

Figure 11.3 represents the opportunity set when $\rho = -0.1639$. It is worthwhile to examine Figure 11.4, which shows different curves for different correlations. As can be seen, the lower the correlation, the more bend there is in the curve. This indicates that the diversification effect rises as $\rho$ declines. The greatest bend occurs in the limiting case where $\rho = -1$. This is perfect negative correlation. While this extreme case where $\rho = -1$ seems to fascinate students, it has little practical importance. Most pairs of securities exhibit positive correlation. Strong negative correlation, let alone perfect negative correlation, is an unlikely occurrence indeed.[8]

Note that there is only one correlation between a pair of securities. We stated earlier that the correlation between Slowpoke and Supertech is $-0.1639$. Thus, the curve in Figure 11.4 representing this correlation is the correct one and the other curves should be viewed as merely hypothetical.

The graphs we examined are not mere intellectual curiosities. Rather, efficient sets can easily be calculated in the real world. As mentioned earlier, data on returns, standard deviations, and correlations are generally taken from past data, though subjective notions can be used to calculate the values of these statistics as well. Once the statistics have been determined, any one of a whole host of software packages can be purchased to generate an efficient set. However, the choice of the preferred portfolio within the efficient set is up to you. As with other important decisions, like what job to choose, what house or car to buy, and how much time to allocate to this course, there is no computer program to choose the preferred portfolio.

---

[8] A major exception occurs with derivative securities. For example, the correlation between a stock and a put option on the stock is generally strongly negative. Puts will be treated later in the text.

FIGURE 11.4

**Opportunity Sets Composed of Holdings in Supertech and Slowpoke**

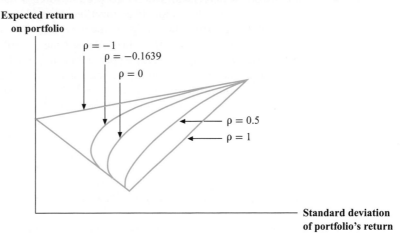

Each curve represents a different correlation. The lower the correlation, the more bend in the curve.

## Application to International Diversification

Research on diversification extends our discussion of historical average risks and returns to include foreign investment portfolios. It turns out that the feasible set looks like Figure 11.5, where points like $U$ and $L$ represent portfolios instead of individual stocks. Portfolio $U$ represents 100 percent investment in Canadian equities and portfolio $L$ represents 100 percent in foreign equities. The domestic stock portfolio is less risky than the foreign portfolio. Does this mean that Canadian portfolio managers should invest entirely in Canada?

FIGURE 11.5

**Efficient Frontier**

The answer is no because the minimum variance portfolio with approximately 20 percent foreign content dominates portfolio *U*, the 100 percent domestic portfolio. Going from 0 percent to around 20 percent foreign content actually reduces portfolio standard deviation due to the diversification effect. However, portfolio MV is not necessarily optimal. Increasing the foreign content beyond around 20 percent increases portfolio risk but also raises expected return. At the time of writing in March 2014, professional investment managers held 30 to 50 percent of their portfolios outside Canada.

Another point worth pondering concerns the potential pitfalls of using only past data to estimate future returns and correlations. The stock markets of many emerging market countries had strong growth early in the first decade of the twenty-first century. Thus, a graph like Figure 11.5 makes a large investment in these foreign markets seem attractive. However, abnormally high returns and low correlations cannot be sustained forever, and the emerging markets—such as India and China—suffered major declines in the financial crisis of 2008–2009. To avoid the forecaster's trap inherent in blind reliance on historical returns, some subjectivity must be used when forecasting expected returns and correlations. Scenario analysis is a useful tool here.

**CONCEPT**
**QUESTION**

- What is the relationship between the shape of the efficient set for two assets and the correlation between the two assets?

## 11.5    THE EFFICIENT SET FOR MANY SECURITIES

The previous discussion concerned two securities. We found that a simple curve sketched out all the possible portfolios. Because investors generally hold more than two securities, we should examine the same feasible set when more than two securities are held. The shaded area in Figure 11.6 represents the opportunity set or feasible set when many securities are considered. The shaded area represents all the possible combinations of expected return and standard deviation for a portfolio. For example, in a universe of 100 securities, point 1 might represent a portfolio of, say, 40 securities. Point 2 might represent a portfolio of 80 securities. Point 3 might represent a different set of 80 securities or the same 80 securities held in different proportions. Obviously, the combinations are virtually endless. However, note that all possible combinations fit into a confined region. No security or combination of securities can fall outside the shaded region. That is, no one can choose a portfolio with an expected return above that given by the shaded region because the expected returns on individual securities cannot be altered. Furthermore, no one can choose a portfolio with a standard deviation below that given in the shaded area. Perhaps more surprisingly, no one can choose an expected return below that given in the curve. In other words, the capital markets actually prevent a self-destructive person from taking on a guaranteed loss.[9]

Figure 11.6 is different from the earlier graphs. When only two securities are involved, all the combinations lie on a single curve. Conversely, with many securities the combinations cover an entire area. However, notice that an individual will want to be somewhere on the upper edge between MV and *X*. The upper edge, which we indicate in Figure 11.6 by a thick line, is called the *efficient set*. Any point below the efficient set would receive less expected return and the same standard deviation as a point on the efficient set. For example, consider *R* on the efficient set and *W* directly below it. If *W* contains the risk you desire, you should choose *R* instead in order to receive a higher expected return.

---

[9] Of course, someone dead set on parting with his money can do so. For example, he can trade frequently without purpose, so that commissions more than offset the positive expected returns on the portfolio.

**FIGURE 11.6**

**The Feasible Set of Portfolios Constructed from Many Securities**

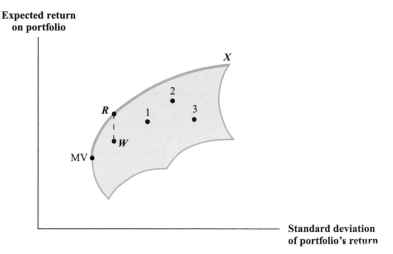

In the final analysis, Figure 11.6 is quite similar to Figure 11.3. The efficient set in Figure 11.3 runs from MV to Supertech. It contains various combinations of the securities Supertech and Slowpoke. The efficient set in Figure 11.6 runs from MV to *X*. It contains various combinations of many securities. The fact that a whole shaded area appears in Figure 11.6 but not in Figure 11.3 is not an important difference; no investor would choose any point below the efficient set in Figure 11.6 anyway.

We mentioned earlier that an efficient set for two securities can be traced out easily in the real world. The task becomes more difficult when additional securities are included because the number of observations grows. For example, using subjective analysis to estimate expected returns and standard deviations for, say, 100 or 500 securities may very well become overwhelming, and the difficulties with correlations may be greater still. There are almost 5,000 correlations between pairs of securities from a universe of 100 securities.

Though much of the mathematics of efficient set computation had been derived in the 1950s,[10] the high cost of computer time restricted application of the principles. In recent years, the cost has been drastically reduced and a number of software packages allow the calculation of an efficient set for portfolios of moderate size. By all accounts, these packages sell quite briskly, so that our discussion above would appear to be important in practice.

## Variance and Standard Deviation in a Portfolio of Many Assets

Earlier, we calculated the formulas for variance and standard deviation in the two-asset case. Because we considered a portfolio of many assets in Figure 11.6, it is worthwhile to calculate the formulas for variance and standard deviation in the many-asset case. The formula for the variance of a portfolio of many assets can be viewed as an extension of the formula for the variance of two assets.

To develop the formula, we employ the same type of matrix that we used in the two-asset case. This matrix is displayed in Table 11.4. Assuming that there are *N* assets, we write the numbers 1 through *N* on the horizontal axis and 1 through *N* on the vertical axis. This creates a matrix of $N \times N = N^2$ boxes.

---

[10] The classic is Harry Markowitz, *Portfolio Selection* (New York: John Wiley & Sons, 1959). Markowitz shared the Nobel Prize in Economics in 1990 (with William Sharpe) for his work on modern portfolio theory.

TABLE 11.4

**Matrix Used to Calculate the Variance of a Portfolio**

| Stock | 1 | 2 | 3 | ... | N |
|-------|---|---|---|-----|---|
| 1 | $X_1^2\sigma_1^2$ | $X_1X_2\text{Cov}(R_1,R_2)$ | $X_1X_3\text{Cov}(R_1,R_3)$ | | $X_1X_N\text{Cov}(R_1,R_N)$ |
| 2 | $X_2X_1\text{Cov}(R_2,R_1)$ | $X_2^2\sigma_2^2$ | $X_2X_3\text{Cov}(R_2,R_3)$ | | $X_2X_N\text{Cov}(R_2,R_N)$ |
| 3 | $X_3X_1\text{Cov}(R_3,R_1)$ | $X_3X_2\text{Cov}(R_3,R_2)$ | $X_3^2\sigma_3^2$ | | $X_3X_N\text{Cov}(R_3,R_N)$ |
| ⋮ | | | | | |
| N | $X_NX_1\text{Cov}(R_N,R_1)$ | $X_NX_2\text{Cov}(R_N,R_2)$ | $X_NX_3\text{Cov}(R_N,R_3)$ | | $X_N^2\sigma_N^2$ |

- The variance of the portfolio is the sum of the terms in all the boxes.
- $\sigma_i$ is the standard deviation of stock $i$.
- $\text{Cov}(R_i, R_j)$ is the covariance between stock $i$ and stock $j$.
- Terms involving the standard deviation of a single security appear on the diagonal. Terms involving covariance between two securities appear off the diagonal.

Consider, for example, the box with a horizontal dimension of 2 and a vertical dimension of 3. The term in the box is $X_3X_2\text{Cov}(R_3, R_2)$. $X_3$ and $X_2$ are the percentages of the entire portfolio that are invested in the third asset and the second asset, respectively. For example, if an individual with a portfolio of $1,000 invests $100 in the second asset, $X_2 = 10\%$ (or $100/$1,000). $\text{Cov}(R_3, R_2)$ is the covariance between the returns on the third asset and the returns on the second asset. Next, note the box with a horizontal dimension of 3 and a vertical dimension of 2. The term in the box is $X_2X_3\text{Cov}(R_2, R_3)$. Because $\text{Cov}(R_3, R_2) = \text{Cov}(R_2, R_3)$, the two boxes have the same value. The second security and the third security make up one pair of stocks. In fact, every pair of stocks appears twice in the table: once in the lower left-hand side and once in the upper right-hand side.

In a large portfolio, the number of terms involving covariance between two securities is much greater than the number of terms involving variance of a single security.

Suppose that the vertical dimension equals the horizontal dimension. For example, the term in the box is $X_1^2\sigma_1^2$ when both dimensions are 1. Here, $\sigma_1^2$ is the variance of the return on the first security.

TABLE 11.5

**Number of Variance and Covariance Terms as a Function of the Number of Stocks in the Portfolio**

| Number of stocks in portfolio | Total number of terms | Number of variance terms (number of terms on diagonal) | Number of covariance terms (number of terms off diagonal) |
|---|---|---|---|
| 1 | 1 | 1 | 0 |
| 2 | 4 | 2 | 2 |
| 3 | 9 | 3 | 6 |
| 10 | 100 | 10 | 90 |
| 100 | 10,000 | 100 | 9,900 |
| ⋮ | ⋮ | | |
| N | $N^2$ | N | $N^2 - N$ |

Thus, the diagonal terms in the matrix contain the variances of the different stocks. The off-diagonal terms contain the covariances. Table 11.5 relates the numbers of diagonal and off-diagonal elements to the size of the matrix. The number of diagonal terms (number of variance terms) is always the same as the number of stocks in the portfolio. The number of off-diagonal terms (number of covariance terms) rises much faster than the number of diagonal terms. For example, a portfolio of 100 stocks has 9,900 covariance terms. Since the variance of a portfolio's returns is the sum of all the boxes, it follows that

> The variance of the return on a portfolio with many securities depends more on the covariances between the individual securities than on the variances of the individual securities

In a large portfolio, the number of terms involving covariance between two securities is much greater than the number of terms involving variance of a single security.

**CONCEPT QUESTIONS**

- What is the formula for the variance of a portfolio for many assets?
- How can the formula be expressed in terms of a box or matrix?

## 11.6   DIVERSIFICATION: AN EXAMPLE

Above we stated that in a portfolio with many securities, the return variances depend more on the covariances between the individual securities than on the variances of the individual securities. This can be illustrated by altering the matrix in Table 11.4 slightly. Suppose that we make the following three assumptions:

1. All securities possess the same variance, which we write as $\overline{\text{var}}$. In other words, $\sigma_i^2 = \overline{\text{var}}$ for every security.

2. All covariances in Table 11.4 are the same. We represent this uniform covariance as $\overline{\text{cov}}$. In other words, $\text{Cov}(R_i, R_j) = \overline{\text{cov}}$ for every pair of securities. It can easily be shown that $\overline{\text{var}} > \overline{\text{cov}}$.

3. All securities are equally weighted in the portfolio. Because there are $N$ assets, the weight of each asset in the portfolio is $1/N$. In other words, $X_i = 1/N$ for each security $i$.

Table 11.6 is the matrix of variances and covariances under these three simplifying assumptions. Note that all of the diagonal terms are identical. Similarly, all of the off-diagonal terms are identical. As with Table 11.4, the variance of the portfolio is the sum of the terms of the boxes in Table 11.6. We know that there are $N$ diagonal terms involving variance. Similarly, there are $N \times (N - 1)$ off-diagonal terms involving covariance. Summing across all the boxes in Table 11.6, we can express the variance of the portfolio as

$$\text{Variance of portfolio} = N \times \left(\frac{1}{N^2}\right)\overline{\text{var}} + N(N-1) \times \left(\frac{1}{N^2}\right)\overline{\text{cov}} \qquad (11.10)$$

| Number of diagonal terms | Each diagonal term | Number of off-diagonal terms | Each off-diagonal term |

$$= \left(\frac{1}{N}\right)\overline{\text{var}} + \left(\frac{N^2 - N}{N^2}\right)\overline{\text{cov}}$$

$$= \left(\frac{1}{N}\right)\overline{\text{var}} + \left(1 - \frac{1}{N}\right)\overline{\text{cov}}$$

Equation (11.10) expresses the variance of our special portfolio as a weighted sum of the average security variance and the average covariance.[11] The intuition is confirmed when we increase the number of securities in the portfolio without limit. The variance of the portfolio becomes

$$\text{Variance of portfolio (when } N \to \infty ) = \overline{\text{cov}} \qquad (11.11)$$

This occurs because (1) the weight on the variance term, $1/N$, goes to 0 as $N$ goes to infinity and (2) the weight on the covariance term, $1 - 1/N$, goes to 1 as $N$ goes to infinity.

---

[11] Equation (11.10) is actually a weighted average of the variance and covariance terms because the weights, $1/N$ and $1 - 1/N$, sum to 1.

**TABLE 11.6**

### Matrix Used to Calculate the Variance of a Portfolio*

| Stock | 1 | 2 | 3 | ... | N |
|-------|---|---|---|-----|---|
| 1 | $(1/N^2)\,\overline{\text{var}}$ | $(1/N^2)\,\overline{\text{cov}}$ | $(1/N^2)\,\overline{\text{cov}}$ | | $(1/N^2)\,\overline{\text{cov}}$ |
| 2 | $(1/N^2)\,\overline{\text{cov}}$ | $(1/N^2)\,\overline{\text{var}}$ | $(1/N^2)\,\overline{\text{cov}}$ | | $(1/N^2)\,\overline{\text{cov}}$ |
| 3 | $(1/N^2)\,\overline{\text{cov}}$ | $(1/N^2)\,\overline{\text{cov}}$ | $(1/N^2)\,\overline{\text{var}}$ | | $(1/N^2)\,\overline{\text{cov}}$ |
| ⋮ | | | | | |
| N | $(1/N^2)\,\overline{\text{cov}}$ | $(1/N^2)\,\overline{\text{cov}}$ | $(1/N^2)\,\overline{\text{cov}}$ | | $(1/N^2)\,\overline{\text{var}}$ |

\* When

   a. All securities possess the same variance, which we represent as $\overline{\text{var}}$.

   b. All pairs of securities possess the same covariance, which we represent as $\overline{\text{cov}}$.

   c. All securities are held in the same proportion, which is $1/N$.

Equation (11.11) provides an interesting and important result. In our special portfolio, the variances of the individual securities completely vanish as the number of securities becomes large. However, the covariance terms remain. In fact, the variance of the portfolio becomes the average covariance, $\overline{\text{cov}}$. We often hear that we should diversify. We should not put all our eggs in one basket. The effect of diversification on the risk of a portfolio can be illustrated in this example. The variances of the individual securities are diversified away, but the covariance terms cannot be diversified away.

The fact that part, but not all, of one's risk can be diversified away should be explored. Consider Jackie Smith, who brings $1,000 to the roulette table at a casino. It would be very risky if she put all her money on one spin of the wheel. For example, imagine that she put the full $1,000 on red at the table. If the wheel showed red, she would get $2,000, but if the wheel showed black, she would lose everything. Suppose, instead, that she divided her money over 1,000 different spins by betting $1 at a time on red. Probability theory tells us that she could count on winning about 50 percent of the time. In other words, she could count on pretty nearly getting all her original $1,000 back.[12]

Now, let's contrast this with our stock market example, which we illustrate in Figure 11.7. The variance of the portfolio with only one security is, of course, $\overline{\text{var}}$, because the variance of a portfolio with one security is the variance of the security. The variance of the portfolio drops as more securities are added, which is evidence of the diversification effect. However, unlike Jackie's roulette example, the portfolio's variance can never drop to zero. Rather it reaches a floor of $\overline{\text{cov}}$, which is the covariance of each pair of securities.[13]

Because the variance of the portfolio asymptotically approaches $\overline{\text{cov}}$, each additional security continues to reduce risk. Thus, if there were neither commissions nor other transaction costs, it could be argued that one can never achieve too much diversification. However, there is a cost to diversification in the real world. Commissions per dollar invested fall as one makes larger purchases in a single stock. Unfortunately, one must buy fewer shares of each security when buying more and more different securities. Comparing the costs and benefits of diversification, Meir Statman argues that a portfolio of about 30 stocks is needed to achieve optimal diversification. Sean Cleary and David Copp find that for Canadian investors, the number of stocks needed is 30 to 50. This higher number is likely because Canadian stocks are more concentrated in a few industries.[14]

---

[12] This example ignores the casino's cut.

[13] Though it is harder to show, this risk reduction effect also applies to the general case where variances and covariances are *not* equal.

[14] Meir Statman, "How Many Stocks Make a Diversified Portfolio?" *Journal of Financial and Quantitative Analysis* (September 1987); Sean Cleary and David Copp, "Diversification with Canadian Stocks: How Much Is Enough?" *Canadian Investment Review* (Fall 1999).

FIGURE 11.7

**Relationship between the Variance of a Portfolio's Return and the Number of Securities in the Portfolio**

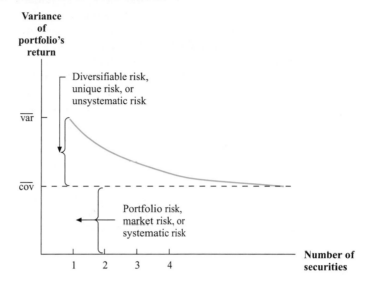

This graph assumes
a.  All securities have constant variance, $\overline{var}$.
b.  All securities have constant covariance, $\overline{cov}$.
c.  All securities are equally weighted in the portfolio.
The variance of a portfolio drops as more securities are added to the portfolio.
However, it does not drop to zero. Rather, $\overline{cov}$ serves as the floor.

We mentioned earlier that $\overline{var}$ must be greater than $\overline{cov}$. Thus, the variance of a security's return can be broken down in the following way:

$$\text{Total risk of individual security} = \text{Portfolio risk} + \text{Unsystematic or diversible risk}$$
$$(\overline{var}) = \quad (\overline{cov}) \quad + \quad (\overline{var} - \overline{cov})$$

*Total risk*, which is $\overline{var}$ in our example, is the risk that one bears by holding one security only. *Portfolio risk* is the risk that one still bears after achieving full diversification, which is $\overline{cov}$ in our example. Portfolio risk is often also called **systematic** or **market risk**. **Diversifiable**, **unique**, or **unsystematic risk** is that risk that can be diversified away in a large portfolio, so it must be $(\overline{var} - \overline{cov})$ by definition.

To an individual who selects a diversified portfolio, the total risk of an individual security is not important. When considering adding a security to a diversified portfolio, the individual cares about that portion of the risk of a security that cannot be diversified away. This risk can alternatively be viewed as the *contribution* of a security to the risk of an entire portfolio. We will talk later about the case where securities make different contributions to the risk of the entire portfolio.

## Risk and the Sensible Investor

Having gone to all this trouble to show that unsystematic risk disappears in a well-diversified portfolio, how do we know that investors even want such portfolios? Suppose they like risk and don't want it to disappear?

We must admit that, theoretically at least, this is possible, but we will argue that it does not describe what we think of as the typical investor. Our typical investor is **risk averse**. Risk-averse behaviour can be defined in many ways, but we prefer the following example. A fair gamble is one with zero expected return; a risk-averse investor would prefer to avoid fair gambles.

Why do investors choose well-diversified portfolios? Our answer is that they are risk averse, and risk-averse people avoid unnecessary risk, such as the unsystematic risk on a stock. If you do not think this is much of an answer to why investors choose well-diversified portfolios and avoid unsystematic risk, consider whether you would take on such a risk. For example, suppose you had worked all summer and had saved $5,000, which you intended to use for university expenses. Now, suppose someone came up to you and offered to flip a coin for the money: heads, you would double your money, and tails, you would lose it all.

Would you take such a bet? Perhaps you would, but the average investor would not. To induce the typical risk-averse investor to take a fair gamble, you must sweeten the pot. For example, you might need to raise the odds of winning from 50–50 to 70–30 or higher. The risk-averse investor can be induced to take fair gambles only if they are sweetened so that they become unfair to the investor's advantage.

Beyond risk aversion, the tremendous growth of mutual funds and exchange-traded funds (ETFs) in recent years strongly suggests that investors want diversified portfolios. *Mutual funds* pool funds from individual investors, allowing them to own units in large, diversified portfolios. ETFs are trusts that track a market index such as the Standard & Poor's 500, the S&P/TSX 60, or the Nikkei. They trade on the New York Stock Exchange and the TSX. By holding such funds, individuals can achieve wide diversification across securities and markets around the world.

**CONCEPT QUESTIONS**

- What are the two components of the total risk of a security?
- Why doesn't diversification eliminate all risk?
- How is risk aversion defined?

## 11.7   RISK-FREE BORROWING AND LENDING

In constructing Figure 11.6, we assume that all the securities on the efficient set are risky. Alternatively, an investor could easily combine a risky investment with an investment in a risk-free security, such as an investment in Canada Treasury bills. This is illustrated in Example 11.3.

---

**EXAMPLE 11.3**

Zoran Sadiq is considering investing in the common stock of Princess Enterprises. In addition, Zoran will either borrow or lend at the risk-free rate. The relevant parameters are as follows:

|  | Expected return on common stock of Princess | Guaranteed return on risk-free asset |
|---|---|---|
| Return | 14% | 3% |
| Standard deviation | 0.20 | 0 |

Suppose Zoran chooses to invest a total of $1,000; $350 is invested in Princess Enterprises and $650 in the risk-free asset. The expected return on his total investment is simply a weighted average of the two returns:

$$\text{Expected return on portfolio composed of one risk-free and one risky asset} = 0.069 = (0.35 \times 0.14) + (0.65 \times 0.03) \quad \textbf{(11.12)}$$

Because the expected return on the portfolio is a weighted average of the expected return on the risky asset (Princess Enterprises) and the risk-free return, the calculation is analogous to the way we treated two risky assets. In other words, equation (11.3) applies here.

Using equation (11.4), the formula for the variance of the portfolio can be written as

$$X^2_{\text{Princess}}\sigma^2_{\text{Princess}} + 2X_{\text{Princess}}X_{\text{Risk free}}\sigma_{\text{Princess, risk free}} + X^2_{\text{Risk free}}\sigma^2_{\text{Risk free}}$$

However, by definition, the risk-free asset has no variability. Thus, both $\sigma_{\text{Princess, Risk-Free}}$ and $\sigma^2_{\text{Risk free}}$ are equal to zero, reducing the above expression to

Variance of portfolio
composed of one risk-free $= X^2_{\text{Princess}}\sigma^2_{\text{Princess}} = (0.35)^2 \times (0.20)^2 = 0.0049$    **(11.13)**
and one risky asset

The standard deviation of the portfolio is

Standard deviation of portfolio
composed of one risk-free $= X_{\text{Princess}}\sigma_{\text{Princess}} = 0.35 \times 0.20 = 0.07$    **(11.14)**
and one risky asset

The relationship between risk and return for one risky and one risk-free asset can be seen in Figure 11.8. Zoran's split of 35–65 percent between the two assets is represented on a *straight* line between the risk-free rate and a pure investment in Princess Enterprises. Note that unlike the case of two risky assets, the opportunity set is straight, not curved.

## FIGURE 11.8

**Relationship between Expected Return and Risk for a Portfolio of One Risky Asset and One Risk-Free Asset**

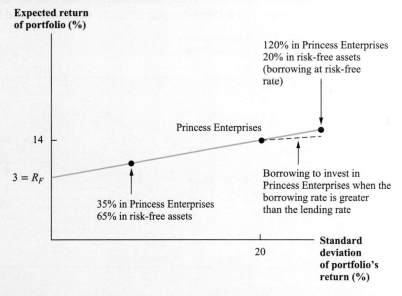

Suppose that, alternatively, Zoran borrows $200 at the risk-free rate. Combining this with his original sum of $1,000, he invests a total of $1,200 in Princess Enterprises. His expected return would be

Expected return on portfolio formed by
borrowing to invest in risky asset $= 16.2\% = 1.20 \times 0.14 + (-0.2) \times 0.03$

Here, he invests 120 percent of his original investment of $1,000 by borrowing 20 percent of his original investment. Note that the return of 16.2 percent is greater than the 14 percent expected return on Princess Enterprises. This occurs because he is borrowing at 3 percent to invest in a security with an expected return greater than 3 percent.

The standard deviation is

$$\text{Standard deviation of portfolio formed} \atop \text{by borrowing to invest in risky asset} = 1.20 \times 0.2 = 0.24$$

The standard deviation of 0.24 is greater than 0.20, the standard deviation of Princess Enterprises, because borrowing increases the variability of the investment. This investment also appears in Figure 11.8.

So far, we have assumed that Zoran is able to borrow at the same rate at which he can lend.[15] Now let us consider the case where the borrowing rate is greater than the lending rate. The dotted line in Figure 11.8 illustrates the opportunity set for borrowing opportunities in this case. The dotted line is below the solid line because a higher borrowing rate lowers the expected return on the investment.

## The Optimal Portfolio

The previous section analyzed a portfolio of one risk-free asset and one risky asset. In reality, an investor is likely to combine an investment in the risk-free asset with a portfolio of risky assets. This is illustrated in Figure 11.9.

FIGURE 11.9

**Relationship between Expected Return and Standard Deviation for an Investment in a Combination of Risky Securities and the Risk-Free Asset**

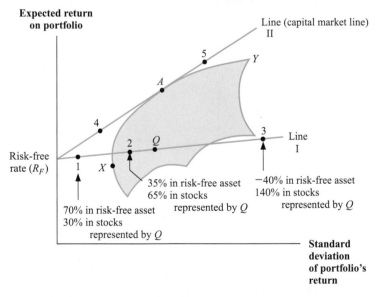

Portfolio $Q$ is composed of 30 percent Telus, 45 percent CIBC, and 25 percent Goldcorp.

---

[15] Surprisingly, this appears to be a decent approximation because a large number of investors are able to borrow on margin when purchasing stocks. The borrowing rate on the margin is very near the risk-free rate of interest, particularly for large investors. More will be said about this in a later chapter. Also note that portfolio weights can be negative when investors sell a stock short. Short selling involves borrowing the stock and selling it today with the plan to cover the short in the future by buying back the stock at a lower price. With short selling, the line in Figure 11.8 extends to the left of the vertical axis.

Consider point $Q$ representing a portfolio of securities. Point $Q$ is in the interior of the feasible set of risky securities. Let us assume the point represents a portfolio of 30 percent in Telus, 45 percent in Canadian Imperial Bank of Commerce (CIBC), and 25 percent in Goldcorp. Individuals combining investments in $Q$ with investments in the risk-free asset would achieve points along the straight line from $R_F$ to $Q$. We refer to this as line $I$. For example, point 1 represents a portfolio of 70 percent in the risk-free asset and 30 percent in stocks represented by $Q$. An investor with $100, choosing point 1 as his portfolio, would put $70 in the risk-free asset and $30 in $Q$. This can be restated as $70 in the risk-free asset, $9 (or 0.3 × $30) in Telus, $13.50 (or 0.45 × $30) in CIBC, and $7.50 (or 0.25 × $30) in Goldcorp. Point 2 also represents a portfolio of the risk-free asset and $Q$ with more (65 percent) being invested in $Q$.

Point 3 is obtained by borrowing to invest in $Q$. For example, an investor with $100 of her own would borrow $40 from the bank or broker in order to invest $140 in $Q$. This can be stated as borrowing $40 and contributing $100 of her own money in order to invest $42 (or 0.3 × $140) in Telus, $63 (or 0.45 × $140) in CIBC, and $35 (or 0.25 × $140) in Goldcorp.

Though any investor can obtain any point on line I, no point on the line is optimal. To see this, consider line II, a line running from $R_F$ through A. Point A represents another portfolio of risky securities. Line II represents portfolios formed by combinations of the risk-free asset and the securities in A. Points between $R_F$ and A are portfolios in which some money is invested in the risk-free asset and the rest is placed in A. Points past A are achieved by borrowing at the risk-free rate to buy more of A than one could with one's original funds alone.

As drawn, line II is tangent to the efficient set of risky securities. Whatever point an individual can obtain on line I, he can obtain a point with the same standard deviation and a higher expected return on line II. In fact, because line II is tangent to the efficient set, it provides the investor with the best possible opportunities. In other words, line II, which is frequently called the **capital market line** (CML), can be viewed as the efficient set of all assets, both risky and risk free. An investor with a fair degree of risk aversion might choose a point between $R_F$ and A, perhaps point 4. An individual with a lower degree of risk aversion might choose a point closer to A or even beyond A. For example, point 5 is achieved when an individual borrows money to increase an investment in A.

The graph illustrates an important point. With risk-free borrowing and lending, the portfolio of risky assets held by any investor would always be point A. Regardless of the investor's tolerance for risk, he would never choose any other point on the efficient set of risky assets (represented by curve $XAY$) or any point in the interior of the feasible region. Rather, the investor would combine the securities of A with the risk-free assets if he had high aversion to risk and would borrow the risk-free asset to invest more funds in A if he had low aversion to risk.

This result establishes what financial economists call the **separation principle**. That is, the investor makes two separate decisions:

1. After estimating (a) the expected return and variances of individual securities and (b) the covariances between pairs of securities, the investor calculates the efficient set of risky assets, represented by curve $XAY$ in Figure 11.9, and determines point A, the tangency between the risk-free rate and the efficient set of risky assets (curve $XAY$). Point A represents the portfolio of risky assets that the investor will hold. This point is determined solely from estimates of returns, variances, and covariances. No personal characteristics, such as degree of risk aversion, are needed in this step.

2. The investor must now determine how to combine point A, the portfolio of risky assets, with the risk-free asset. He could invest some of the funds in the risk-free

asset and some in portfolio *A*. The investor would end up at a point on the line between $R_F$ and *A* in this case. Alternatively, the investor could borrow at the risk-free rate and contribute some personal funds as well, investing the sum in portfolio *A*. He would end up at a point on line II beyond *A*. The investor's position in the risk-free asset (that is, the choice of where on the line he wants to be) is determined by internal characteristics, such as the investor's ability to tolerate risk.

***CONCEPT QUESTIONS***
- What is the formula for the standard deviation of a portfolio composed of one risk-free and one risky asset?
- How does one determine the optimal portfolio among the efficient set of risky assets?

# 11.8 MARKET EQUILIBRIUM

### Definition of the Market Equilibrium Portfolio

The above analysis concerns one investor. Estimates of the expected returns and variances for individual securities and the covariances between pairs of securities are unique to this individual. Other investors would obviously have different estimates of these variables. However, the estimates might not vary much because all investors would be forming expectations from the same data on past price movement and other publicly available information.

Financial economists often imagine a world where all investors possess the same estimates of expected returns, variances, and covariances. Though this can never be literally true, it can be thought of as a useful simplifying assumption in a world where investors have access to similar sources of information. This assumption is called **homogeneous expectations**.[16]

If investors had homogeneous expectations, Figure 11.9 would be the same for all individuals. That is, all investors would sketch out the same efficient set of risky assets because they would be working with the same inputs. This efficient set of risky assets is represented by the curve *XAY*. Because the same risk-free rate would apply to everyone, all investors would view point *A* as the portfolio of risky assets to be held. However, in reality, not everyone has the same risk-free rate since it depends on the individual's investment horizon. This concept is explained later in the chapter.

The point *A* takes on great importance because all investors would purchase the risky securities that it represents. Those investors with a high degree of risk aversion might combine *A* with an investment in the risk-free asset, achieving point 4, for example. Others with low aversion to risk might borrow to achieve, say, point 5. Because this is a very important conclusion, we restate it:

> In a world with homogeneous expectations, all investors would hold the portfolio of risky assets represented by point *A*.

---

[16] The assumption of homogeneous expectations states that all investors have the same beliefs concerning returns, variances, and covariances. It does not say that all investors have the same aversion to risk.

If all investors choose the same portfolio of risky assets, it is possible to determine what that portfolio is. Common sense tells us that it is a market value–weighted portfolio of all existing securities. It is the **market portfolio**.[17]

In practice, financial economists use a broad-based index such as the S&P/TSX 60 as a proxy for the market portfolio. Of course, all investors do not hold the same portfolio in practice. However, we know that a large number of investors hold diversified portfolios, particularly when mutual funds or pension funds are included. A broad-based index is a good proxy for the highly diversified portfolios of many investors.

## Definition of Risk When Investors Hold the Market Portfolio

The previous section states that many investors hold diversified portfolios similar to broad-based indexes. This result allows us to measure the risk of a security in the context of a diversified portfolio as the *beta* of the security. We illustrate beta in Example 11.4.

---

**EXAMPLE 11.4**

Consider the following possible returns both on the stock of Jelco Inc. and on the market:

| State | Type of economy | Return on market | Return on Jelco Inc. |
|-------|-----------------|------------------|----------------------|
| I | Bull | 15% | 25% |
| II | Bull | 15 | 15 |
| III | Bear | −5 | −5 |
| IV | Bear | −5 | −15 |

Though the return on the market has only two possible outcomes (15 percent and −5 percent), the return on Jelco has four possible outcomes. It is helpful to consider the expected return on a security for a given return on the market. Assuming each state is equally likely, we have the following:

| Type of economy | Return on market | Expected return on Jelco Inc. |
|-----------------|------------------|-------------------------------|
| Bull | 15% | $20\% = 25\% \times \frac{1}{2} + 15\% \times \frac{1}{2}$ |
| Bear | −5% | $-10\% = -5\% \times \frac{1}{2} + (-15\%) \times \frac{1}{2}$ |

Jelco Inc. responds to market movements because its expected return is greater in bullish states than in bearish states. We now calculate exactly how responsive the security is to market movements. The market's return in a bullish economy is 20 percent [15% − (−5%)] greater than the market's return in a bearish economy. However, the expected return on Jelco in a bullish economy is 30 percent [20% − (−10%)] greater than its expected return in a bearish state. Thus, Jelco Inc. has a responsiveness coefficient of 1.5 (30%/20%).

This relationship appears in Figure 11.10. The returns for both Jelco and the market in each state are plotted as four points. In addition, we plot the expected return on the security for each of the two possible returns on the market. These two points, each of which we designate by an X, are joined by a line called the **characteristic line** of the security. The slope of the line is 1.5, the number calculated in the previous paragraph. This responsiveness coefficient of 1.5 is the **beta** of Jelco.

---

[17] By "market value–weighted" we mean that the percentage weight of each stock is the market value of the company's equity divided by the total market capitalization.

A good answer might be something like the following:

> A rational, risk-averse investor views the variance (or standard deviation) of his portfolio's return as the proper measure of the risk of his portfolio. If for some reason or another the investor can hold only one security, the variance of that security's return becomes the variance of the portfolio's return. Hence, the variance of the security's return is the security's proper measure of risk.

> If an individual holds a diversified portfolio, she still views the variance (or standard deviation) of her portfolio's return as the proper measure of the risk of her portfolio. However, she is no longer interested in the variance of each individual security's return. Rather, she is interested in the contribution of an individual security to the variance of the portfolio.

Under the assumption of homogeneous expectations, all individuals hold the market portfolio. Thus, we measure risk as the contribution of an individual security to the variance of the market portfolio. This contribution, when standardized properly, is the beta of the security. While very few investors hold the market portfolio exactly, many hold reasonably diversified portfolios. These portfolios are close enough to the market portfolio that the beta of a security is likely to be a reasonable measure of its risk.

**CONCEPT QUESTIONS**

- If all investors have homogeneous expectations, what portfolio of risky assets do they hold?
- What is the formula for beta?
- Why is beta the appropriate measure of risk for a single security in a large portfolio?

# 11.9    RELATIONSHIP BETWEEN RISK AND EXPECTED RETURN (CAPITAL ASSET PRICING MODEL)

It is common to argue that the expected return on an asset should be positively related to its risk. That is, individuals will hold a risky asset only if its expected return compensates for its risk. In this section, we first estimate the expected return on the stock market as a whole. Next, we estimate expected returns on individual securities.

## Expected Return on Market

Financial economists frequently argue that the expected return on the market can be represented as

$$\overline{R}_M = R_F + \text{Risk premium}$$

In words, the expected return on the market is the sum of the risk-free rate and some compensation for the risk inherent in the market portfolio. Note that the equation refers to the *expected* return on the market, not the actual return in a particular month or year. Because stocks have risk, the actual return on the market over a particular period can, of course, be less than $R_F$, or even negative.

Since investors want compensation for risk, the risk premium is presumably positive. But exactly how positive is it? It is generally argued that the best estimate for the risk premium in the future is the average risk premium in the past. As reported in Chapter 10, the expected return on common stocks was 10.43 percent over the period 1957 through 2013. The average risk-free rate on 91-day Treasury bills over the same time interval was 5.97 percent. Thus, the average difference between the two was 4.46 percent (10.43% − 5.97%). Financial economists find this to be a useful estimate of the difference to occur in the future. We will use it frequently in this text.[20]

For example, if the risk-free rate, generally estimated by the yield on a one-year Treasury bill, is 5 percent, the expected return on the market is

$$5\% + 4.46\% = 9.46\%$$

## Expected Return on Individual Security

Now that we have estimated the expected return on the market as a whole, what is the expected return on an individual security? We have argued that the beta of a security is the appropriate measure of risk in a large, diversified portfolio. Since most investors are diversified, the expected return on a security should be positively related to its beta. This is illustrated in Figure 11.11.

**FIGURE 11.11**

**Relationship between Expected Return on an Individual Security and Beta of the Security**

The security market line (SML) is the graphical depiction of the capital asset pricing model (CAPM).
The expected return on a stock with a beta of 0 is equal to the risk-free rate.
The expected return on a stock with a beta of 1 is equal to the expected return on the market.

Actually, financial economists can be more precise about the relationship between expected return and beta. They posit that, under plausible conditions, the relationship between expected return and beta can be represented by the following equation:[21]

**Capital Asset Pricing Model:**

$$\overline{R} = R_F + \beta \times (\overline{R}_M - R_F) \quad (11.17)$$

| Expected return on a security | = | Risk-free rate | + | Beta of the security | × | Difference between expected return on market and risk-free rate |

This formula, which is called the **capital asset pricing model** (or CAPM for short), implies that the expected return on a security is linearly related to its beta. Since the

---

[20] This is not the only way to estimate the market risk premium. In fact, there are several useful ways to estimate the market risk premium. One could argue that the long-term government bond return is the best measure of the long-term historical risk-free rate. With this empirical version of the capital asset pricing model (CAPM), one would use the current long-term government bond return to estimate the current risk-free rate.

[21] This relationship was first proposed independently by John Lintner and William F. Sharpe.

average return on the market has been higher than the average risk-free rate over long periods of time, $\overline{R}_M - R_F$ is presumably positive. Thus, the formula implies that the expected return on a security is *positively* related to its beta. The formula can be illustrated by assuming a few special cases:

*   *Assume that $\beta = 0$.* Here $\overline{R} = R_F$; that is, the expected return on the security is equal to the risk-free rate. Because a security with zero beta has no relevant risk, its expected return should equal the risk-free rate.
*   *Assume that $\beta = 1$.* Equation (11.17) reduces to $\overline{R} = R_M$. That is, the expected return on the security is equal to the expected return on the market. This makes sense since the beta of the market portfolio is also 1.

Equation (11.17) can be represented graphically by the upward-sloping line in Figure 11.11. Note that the line begins at $R_F$ and rises to $\overline{R}_M$ when beta is 1. This line, which graphically represents the CAPM, is frequently called the **security market line** (SML).

As with any (non-vertical) line, the SML has both a slope and an intercept. $R_F$, the risk-free rate, is the intercept. Because the beta of a security is the horizontal axis, $R_M - R_F$ is the slope. The line will be upward sloping as long as the expected return on the market is greater than the risk-free rate. Because the market portfolio is a risky asset, theory suggests that its expected return is more than the risk-free rate. In addition, the empirical evidence of the previous chapter showed that the average return per year on the market portfolio over the past 57 years was 4.46 percent above the risk-free rate.

The stock of Aardvark Enterprises has a beta of 1.2 and that of Zebra Enterprises has a beta of 0.8. The risk-free rate is 5 percent, and the difference between the expected return on the market and the risk-free rate is 4.46 percent. The expected returns on the two securities are

**Expected Return for Aardvark:**

$$10.35\% = 5\% + 1.2 \times 4.46\% \tag{11.18}$$

**Expected Return for Zebra:**

$$8.57\% = 5\% + 0.8 \times 4.46\%$$

Four additional points concerning the CAPM should be mentioned:

1.  *Linearity.* The intuition behind an upwardly sloping curve is clear. Because beta is the appropriate measure of risk, high-beta securities should have an expected return above that of low-beta securities. However, both Figure 11.11 and equation (11.17) show something more than an upwardly sloping curve; the relationship between expected return and beta corresponds to a *straight* line.

    It is easy to show that the line of Figure 11.11 is straight. To see this, consider security *S* with, say, a beta of 0.8. This security is represented by a point below the SML in the figure. Any investor could duplicate the beta of security *S* by buying a portfolio with 20 percent in the risk-free asset and 80 percent in a security with a beta of 1. However, the homemade portfolio would itself lie on the SML. In other words, the portfolio dominates security *S* because the portfolio has a higher expected return and the same beta.

    Now consider security *T* with, say, a beta greater than 1. This security is also below the SML in Figure 11.11. Any investor could duplicate the beta of security *T* by borrowing to invest in a security with a beta of 1. This portfolio must also lie on the SML, thereby dominating security *T*.

Because no one would hold either *S* or *T*, their stock prices would drop. This price adjustment would raise the expected returns on the two securities. The price adjustment would continue until the two securities lay on the SML. The preceding example considered two overpriced stocks and a straight SML. Securities lying above the SML are *underpriced*. Their prices must rise until their expected returns lie on the line. If the SML were itself curved, many stocks would be mispriced. In equilibrium, all securities would be held only when prices changed so that the SML became straight. In other words, linearity would be achieved.

2. *Portfolios as well as securities.* Our discussion of the CAPM considered individual securities. Does the relationship in Figure 11.11 and equation (11.17) hold for portfolios as well?

    Yes. To see this, consider a portfolio formed by investing equally in our two securities, Aardvark and Zebra. The expected return on the portfolio is

    **Expected Return on Portfolio:**

$$9.46\% = 0.5 \times 10.35\% + 0.5 \times 8.57\% \qquad (11.19)$$

The beta of the portfolio is simply a weighted average of the betas of the two securities. Thus we have

    **Beta of Portfolio:**

$$1.0 = 0.5 \times 1.2 + 0.5 \times 0.8$$

Under the CAPM, the expected return on the portfolio is

$$9.46\% = 5\% + 1.0 \times 4.46\% \qquad (11.20)$$

Because the expected return in equation (11.19) is the same as the expected return in equation (11.20), the example shows that the CAPM holds for portfolios as well as for individual securities.

3. *Choice of the risk-free rate.* In our discussion above, we used the one-year Treasury bill rate as the risk-free rate. Because we were calculating the expected return for Canadian securities, we chose Canadian government securities as they are default free in the domestic market. The Canadian government has the power to print Canadian dollars or raise taxes to redeem its securities and, at the time of writing, enjoyed an AAA bond rating—the highest possible. In applying the CAPM in an international context it is common practice to measure the risk-free rate using U.S. Treasury securities, which are commonly regarded as the least risky in the world.

    In addition to zero default risk, we must measure the risk-free rate using a security with zero reinvestment or pricing risk by matching the maturity of the security to the horizon over which we are calculating the expected return. In our examples above, we utilized the CAPM to compute one-year expected returns on securities and so we used a one-year Treasury bill to represent the risk-free rate. In contrast, in Chapter 13 we will use the CAPM to find the cost of equity as input into the weighted average cost of capital (WACC) for capital budgeting. Since capital budgeting involves analysis of long-term investment projects, there we will use the rate of a 10-year Canada bond as the risk-free rate.[22]

---

[22] Aswath Damodaran, "What Is the Riskfree Rate? A Search for the Basic Building Block," Stern School of Business, New York University (December 2008).

4. *A potential confusion.* Students often confuse the SML in Figure 11.11 with line II in Figure 11.9. Actually, the lines are quite different. Line II traces the efficient set of portfolios formed from both risky assets and the risk-free asset. Each point on the line represents an entire portfolio. Point *A* is a portfolio composed entirely of risky assets. Every other point on the line represents a portfolio of the securities in *A* combined with the risk-free asset. The axes on Figure 11.9 are the expected return on a *portfolio* and the standard deviation of a *portfolio*. Individual securities do not lie along line II.

The SML in Figure 11.11 relates expected return to beta. Figure 11.11 differs from Figure 11.9 in at least two ways. First, beta appears on the horizontal axis of Figure 11.11, but standard deviation appears on the horizontal axis of Figure 11.9. Second, the SML in Figure 11.11 holds both for all individual securities and for all possible portfolios, whereas line II in Figure 11.9 holds only for efficient portfolios.

We stated earlier that under homogeneous expectations, point *A* in Figure 11.9 becomes the market portfolio. In this situation, line II is referred to as the capital market line (CML).

**CONCEPT QUESTIONS**

- Why is the SML a straight line?
- What is the CAPM?
- What are the differences between the CML and the SML?

# 11.10

## SUMMARY AND CONCLUSIONS

This chapter sets forth the fundamentals of modern portfolio theory and the pricing of capital assets. Our basic points are these:

1. This chapter shows us how to calculate the expected return and variance for individual securities, and the covariance and correlation for pairs of securities. Given these statistics, the expected return and variance for a portfolio of two securities, *A* and *B*, can be written as

$$\text{Expected return on portfolio} = X_A \overline{R}_A + X_B \overline{R}_B$$

$$\text{Var(portfolio)} = X_A^2 \sigma_A^2 + 2X_A X_B \sigma_{AB} + X_B^2 \sigma_B^2$$

2. In our notation, *X* stands for the proportion of a security in a portfolio. By varying *X*, one can trace out the efficient set of portfolios. We graphed the efficient set for the two-asset case as a curve, pointing out that the degree of curvature or bend in the graph reflects the diversification effect: The lower the correlation between the two securities, the greater the bend. The same general shape of the efficient set holds in a world of many assets.

3. Just as the formula for variance in the two-asset case is computed from a $2 \times 2$ matrix, the variance formula is computed from an $N \times N$ matrix in the *N*-asset case. We show that with a large number of assets, there are many more covariance terms than variance terms in the matrix. In fact, the variance terms are effectively diversified away in a large portfolio, but the covariance terms are not. Thus, a diversified portfolio can only eliminate some of the risk of the individual securities.

4. The efficient set of risky assets can be combined with risk-free borrowing and lending. In this case, a rational investor will always choose to hold the portfolio of risky securities represented by point *A* in Figure 11.9. Then he can either borrow or lend at the risk-free rate to achieve any desired point on line II in the figure.

5. The contribution of a security to the risk of a large, well-diversified portfolio is proportional to the covariance of the security's return with the market's return. This contribution, when standardized, is called the beta. The beta of a security can also be interpreted as the responsiveness of a security's return to that of the market.

6. The capital asset pricing model (CAPM) states that

$$\overline{R} = R_F + \beta(\overline{R}_M - R_F)$$

In other words, the expected return on a security is positively (and linearly) related to the security's beta.

**KEY TERMS**

| | | |
|---|---|---|
| Beta 335 | Diversifiable (unique) | Portfolio 315 |
| Capital asset pricing model | (unsystematic) risk 329 | Risk averse 329 |
| (CAPM) 339 | Efficient set 322 | Security market line (SML) |
| Capital market line 333 | Homogeneous expectations | 340 |
| Characteristic line 335 | 334 | Separation principle 333 |
| Correlation 312 | Market portfolio 335 | Systematic (market) risk 329 |
| Covariance 312 | Opportunity (feasible) set | |
| | 321 | |

**QUESTIONS & PROBLEMS**

### Determining Portfolio Weights

11.1 What are the portfolio weights for a portfolio that has 135 shares of stock A that sell for $47 per share and 105 shares of stock B that sell for $41 per share?

### Portfolio Expected Return

11.2 You own a portfolio that has $1,900 invested in stock A and $2,300 invested in stock B. If the expected returns on these stocks are 10 percent and 15 percent, respectively, what is the expected return on the portfolio?

11.3 You own a portfolio that is 25 percent invested in stock X, 40 percent in stock Y, and 35 percent in stock Z. The expected returns on these three stocks are 11 percent, 17 percent, and 14 percent, respectively. What is the expected return on the portfolio?

11.4 You have $10,000 to invest in a stock portfolio. Your choices are stock X with an expected return of 14 percent and stock Y with an expected return of 9 percent. If your goal is to create a portfolio with an expected return of 12.9 percent, how much money will you invest in stock X? In stock Y?

### Calculating Expected Return

11.5 Based on the following information, calculate the expected return:

| State of economy | Probability of state of economy | Rate of return if state occurs |
|---|---|---|
| Recession | 0.25 | −0.09 |
| Normal | 0.45 | 0.11 |
| Boom | 0.30 | 0.25 |

### Calculating Returns and Standard Deviations

11.6 Based on the following information, calculate the expected return and standard deviation for the two stocks:

| State of economy | Probability of state of economy | Rate of return if state occurs | |
|---|---|---|---|
| | | Stock A | Stock B |
| Recession | 0.20 | 0.06 | −0.20 |
| Normal | 0.55 | 0.07 | 0.13 |
| Boom | 0.25 | 0.11 | 0.33 |

**11.7** Based on the following information, calculate the expected return and standard deviation:

| State of economy | Probability of state of economy | Rate of return if state occurs |
|---|---|---|
| Depression | 0.10 | −0.105 |
| Recession | 0.25 | 0.059 |
| Normal | 0.45 | 0.130 |
| Boom | 0.20 | 0.211 |

### Calculating Expected Returns

**11.8** A portfolio is invested 10 percent in stock $G$, 65 percent in stock $J$, and 25 percent in stock $K$. The expected returns on these stocks are 9 percent, 11 percent, and 14 percent, respectively. What is the portfolio's expected return? How do you interpret your answer?

### Returns and Standard Deviations

**11.9** Consider the following information:

| State of economy | Probability of state of economy | Rate of return if state occurs | | |
|---|---|---|---|---|
| | | Stock A | Stock B | Stock C |
| Boom | 0.65 | 0.07 | 0.15 | 0.33 |
| Bust | 0.35 | 0.13 | 0.03 | −0.06 |

    *a.* What is the expected return on an equally weighted portfolio of these three stocks?

    *b.* What is the variance of a portfolio invested 20 percent each in $A$ and $B$, and 60 per cent in $C$?

**11.10** Consider the following information:

| State of economy | Probability of state of economy | Rate of return if state occurs | | |
|---|---|---|---|---|
| | | Stock A | Stock B | Stock C |
| Boom | 0.20 | 0.24 | 0.45 | 0.33 |
| Good | 0.35 | 0.09 | 0.10 | 0.15 |
| Poor | 0.30 | 0.03 | −0.10 | −0.05 |
| Bust | 0.15 | −0.05 | −0.25 | −0.09 |

    *a.* Your portfolio is invested 30 percent each in $A$ and $C$ and 40 percent in $B$. What is the expected return of the portfolio?

    *b.* What is the variance of this portfolio? The standard deviation?

### Calculating Portfolio Betas

**11.11** You own a stock portfolio invested 10 percent in stock $Q$, 35 percent in stock $R$, 20 percent in stock $S$, and 35 percent in stock $T$. The betas for these four stocks are 0.75, 1.90, 1.38, and 1.16, respectively. What is the portfolio beta?

**11.12** You own a portfolio equally invested in a risk-free asset and two stocks. If one of the stocks has a beta of 1.65 and the total portfolio is equally as risky as the market, what must the beta be for the other stock in your portfolio?

### Using the Capital Asset Pricing Model

**11.13** A stock has a beta of 1.25, the expected return on the market is 12 percent, and the risk-free rate is 5 percent. What must the expected return on this stock be?

**11.14** A stock has an expected return of 10.2 percent, the risk-free rate is 4 percent, and the market risk premium is 7 percent. What must the beta of this stock be?

**11.15** A stock has an expected return of 13.4 percent, its beta is 1.60, and the risk-free rate is 5.5 percent. What must the expected return on the market be?

**11.16** A stock has an expected return of 13.1 percent, its beta is 1.28, and the expected return on the market is 11 percent. What must the risk-free rate be?

**11.17** A stock has a beta of 1.13 and an expected return of 12.1 percent. A risk-free asset currently earns 5 percent.
   *a.* What is the expected return on a portfolio that is equally invested in the two assets?
   *b.* If a portfolio of the two assets has a beta of 0.50, what are the portfolio weights?
   *c.* If a portfolio of the two assets has an expected return of 10 percent, what is its beta?
   *d.* If a portfolio of the two assets has a beta of 2.26, what are the portfolio weights? How do you interpret the weights for the two assets in this case? Explain.

### Using the Security Market Line

**11.18** Asset *W* has an expected return of 12.3 percent and a beta of 1.3. If the risk-free rate is 4 percent, complete the following table for portfolios of asset *W* and a risk-free asset. Illustrate the relationship between portfolio expected return and portfolio beta by plotting the expected returns against the betas. What is the slope of the line that results?

| Percentage of portfolio in asset *W* | Portfolio expected return | Portfolio beta |
|---|---|---|
| 0% | | |
| 25 | | |
| 50 | | |
| 75 | | |
| 100 | | |
| 125 | | |
| 150 | | |

### Portfolio Returns

**11.19** Using information from Table 10.2 in Chapter 10 about capital market history, determine the return on a portfolio that is equally invested in Canadian common stocks and bonds. What is the return on a portfolio that is equally invested in small stocks and Treasury bills?

### The Capital Asset Pricing Model

**11.20** Using the CAPM, show that the ratio of the risk premiums on two assets is equal to the ratio of their betas.

### Portfolio Returns and Deviations

**11.21** Consider the following information about three stocks:

| State of economy | Probability of state of economy | Rate of return if state occurs | | |
|---|---|---|---|---|
| | | Stock *A* | Stock *B* | Stock *C* |
| Boom | 0.30 | 0.20 | 0.25 | 0.60 |
| Normal | 0.45 | 0.15 | 0.11 | 0.05 |
| Bust | 0.25 | 0.01 | −0.15 | −0.50 |

   *a.* If your portfolio is invested 40 percent each in *A* and *B* and 20 percent in *C*, what is the portfolio expected return? The variance? The standard deviation?
   *b.* If the expected T-bill rate is 3.80 percent, what is the expected risk premium on the portfolio?
   *c.* If the expected inflation rate is 3.50 percent, what are the approximate and exact expected real returns on the portfolio? What are the approximate and exact expected real risk premiums on the portfolio?

### Analyzing a Portfolio

**11.22** You want to create a portfolio equally as risky as the market, and you have $1,000,000 to invest. You must invest all of your money. Given this information, fill in the rest of the following table:

| Asset | Investment | Beta |
|-------|-----------|------|
| Stock A | $180,000 | 0.75 |
| Stock B | $290,000 | 1.30 |
| Stock C | | 1.45 |
| Risk-free asset | | |

**11.23** You have $100,000 to invest in a portfolio containing stock X, stock Y, and a risk-free asset. You must invest all of your money. Your goal is to create a portfolio that has an expected return of 11.22 percent and that has only 96 percent of the risk of the over-all market. If X has an expected return of 15.35 percent and a beta of 1.55, Y has an expected return of 9.4 percent and a beta of 0.7, and the risk-free rate is 4.5 percent, how much money will you invest in stock X? How do you interpret your answer?

### Covariance and Correlation

**11.24** Based on the following information, calculate the expected return and standard deviation of each of the following stocks. Assume each state of the economy is equally likely to happen. What are the covariance and correlation between the returns of the two stocks?

| State of economy | Return on stock A | Return on stock B |
|------------------|-------------------|-------------------|
| Bear | 0.102 | −0.045 |
| Normal | 0.115 | 0.148 |
| Bull | 0.073 | 0.233 |

**11.25** Based on the following information, calculate the expected return and standard deviation for each of the following stocks. What are the covariance and correlation between the returns of the two stocks?

| State of economy | Probability of state of economy | Return on stock J | Return on stock K |
|------------------|-------------------------------|-------------------|-------------------|
| Bear | 0.30 | −0.020 | 0.034 |
| Normal | 0.50 | 0.138 | 0.062 |
| Bull | 0.20 | 0.218 | 0.092 |

### Portfolio Standard Deviation

**11.26** Security F has an expected return of 10 percent and a standard deviation of 26 percent per year. Security G has an expected return of 17 percent and a standard deviation of 58 percent per year.

   a. What is the expected return on a portfolio composed of 30 percent of security F and 70 percent of security G?

   b. If the correlation between the returns of security F and security G is 0.25, what is the standard deviation of the portfolio described in (a)?

**11.27** Suppose the expected returns and standard deviations of stocks A and B are $E(R_A) = 0.09$, $E(R_B) = 0.15$, $\sigma_A = 0.36$, and $\sigma_B = 0.62$, respectively.

   a. Calculate the expected return and standard deviation of a portfolio that is composed of 35 percent A and 65 percent B when the correlation between the returns on A and B is 0.5.

   b. Calculate the standard deviation of a portfolio with the same portfolio weights as in part (a) when the correlation coefficient between the returns on A and B is −0.5.

   c. How does the correlation between the returns on A and B affect the standard deviation of the portfolio?

## Correlation and Beta

11.28 You have been provided with the following data about the securities of three firms, the market portfolio, and the risk-free asset:

| Security | Expected return | Standard deviation | Correlation* | Beta |
|---|---|---|---|---|
| Firm A | 0.10 | 0.31 | (i) | 0.85 |
| Firm B | 0.14 | (ii) | 0.50 | 1.40 |
| Firm C | 0.16 | 0.65 | 0.35 | (iii) |
| The market portfolio | 0.12 | 0.20 | (iv) | (v) |
| The risk-free asset | 0.05 | (vi) | (vii) | (viii) |

\* With the market portfolio.

    *a.* Fill in the missing values in the table.

    *b.* Is the stock of firm A correctly priced according to the CAPM? Firm B? Firm C? If these securities are not correctly priced, what is your investment recommendation for someone with a well-diversified portfolio?

## Capital Market Line

11.29 The market portfolio has an expected return of 12 percent and a standard deviation of 19 percent. The risk-free rate is 5 percent.

    *a.* What is the expected return on a well-diversified portfolio with a standard deviation of 7 percent?

    *b.* What is the standard deviation of a well-diversified portfolio with an expected return of 20 percent?

## Beta and the Capital Asset Pricing Model

11.30 A portfolio that combines the risk-free asset and the market portfolio has an expected return of 7 percent and a standard deviation of 10 percent. The risk-free rate is 4 percent, and the expected return on the market portfolio is 12 percent. Assume the CAPM holds. What expected rate of return would a security earn if it had a 0.45 correlation with the market portfolio and a standard deviation of 55 percent?

11.31 Suppose the risk-free rate is 4.8 percent and the market portfolio has an expected return of 11.4 percent. The market portfolio has a variance of 0.0429. Portfolio Z has a correlation coefficient with the market of 0.39 and a variance of 0.1783. According to the CAPM, what is the expected return on portfolio Z?

## Systematic versus Unsystematic Risk

11.32 Consider the following information about stocks I and II:

| State of economy | Probability of state of economy | Rate of return if state occurs | |
|---|---|---|---|
| | | Stock I | Stock II |
| Recession | 0.15 | 0.11 | −0.25 |
| Normal | 0.55 | 0.18 | 0.11 |
| Irrational exuberance | 0.30 | 0.08 | 0.31 |

The market risk premium is 7.5 percent, and the risk-free rate is 4 percent. Which stock has more systematic risk? Which one has more unsystematic risk? Which stock is riskier? Explain.

## Security Market Line

11.33 Suppose you observe the following situation:

| Security | Beta | Expected return |
|---|---|---|
| Pete Corp. | 1.35 | 12.28% |
| Repete Co. | 0.80 | 8.54 |

Assume these securities are correctly priced. Based on the CAPM, what is the expected return on the market? What is the risk-free rate?

## Covariance and Portfolio Standard Deviation

11.34  There are three securities in the market. The following chart shows their possible payoffs:

| State | Probability of outcome | Return on security 1 | Return on security 2 | Return on security 3 |
|-------|-----------------------|---------------------|---------------------|---------------------|
| 1 | 0.15 | 0.20 | 0.20 | 0.05 |
| 2 | 0.35 | 0.15 | 0.10 | 0.10 |
| 3 | 0.35 | 0.10 | 0.15 | 0.15 |
| 4 | 0.15 | 0.05 | 0.05 | 0.20 |

    *a.* What are the expected return and standard deviation of each security?
    *b.* What are the covariances and correlations between the pairs of securities?
    *c.* What are the expected return and standard deviation of a portfolio with half its funds invested in security 1 and half in security 2?
    *d.* What are the expected return and standard deviation of a portfolio with half its funds invested in security 1 and half in security 3?
    *e.* What are the expected return and standard deviation of a portfolio with half its funds invested in security 2 and half in security 3?
    *f.* What do your answers in (a), (c), (d), and (e) imply about diversification?

## Security Market Line

11.35  Suppose you observe the following situation:

| State of economy | Probability of state | Return if state occurs Stock A | Return if state occurs Stock B |
|------------------|---------------------|--------------------------------|--------------------------------|
| Bust | 0.15 | −0.10 | −0.08 |
| Normal | 0.60 | 0.09 | 0.08 |
| Boom | 0.25 | 0.32 | 0.26 |

    *a.* Calculate the expected return on each stock.
    *b.* Assuming the CAPM holds and stock *A*'s beta is greater than stock *B*'s beta by 0.25, what is the expected market risk premium?

## Standard Deviation and Beta

11.36  There are two stocks in the market, stock *A* and stock *B*. The price of stock *A* today is $75. The price of stock *A* next year will be $63 if the economy is in a recession, $83 if the economy is normal, and $96 if the economy is expanding. The probabilities of recession, normal times, and expansion are 0.2, 0.6, and 0.2, respectively. Stock *A* pays no dividends and has a correlation of 0.8 with the market portfolio. Stock *B* has an expected return of 13 percent, a standard deviation of 34 percent, a correlation with the market portfolio of 0.25, and a correlation with stock *A* of 0.48. The market portfolio has a standard deviation of 18 percent. Assume the CAPM holds.

    *a.* If you are a typical, risk-averse investor with a well-diversified portfolio, which stock would you prefer? Why?
    *b.* What are the expected return and standard deviation of a portfolio consisting of 70 percent of stock *A* and 30 percent of stock *B*?
    *c.* What is the beta of the portfolio in (b)?

## Minimum Variance Portfolio

11.37  Assume stocks *A* and *B* have the following characteristics:

| Stock | Expected return | Standard deviation |
|-------|-----------------|--------------------|
| A | 9% | 33% |
| B | 15 | 62 |

The covariance between the returns on the two stocks is 0.001.

    *a.* Suppose an investor holds a portfolio consisting of only stock *A* and stock *B*. Find the portfolio weights, $X_A$ and $X_B$, such that the variance of her portfolio is minimized. (*Hint:* Remember that the sum of the two weights must equal 1.)

    *b.* What is the expected return on the minimum variance portfolio?

    *c.* If the covariance between the returns on the two stocks is −0.05, what are the minimum variance weights?

    *d.* What is the variance of the portfolio in (c)?

## A Job at Deck Out My Yacht, Part 2

You are discussing your retirement plan with Alvin Jones when he mentions that Maureen Buffett, a representative from Marshall & McLaren Financial Services, is visiting Deck Out My Yacht today. You decide that you should meet with Maureen, so Alvin sets up an appointment for you later in the day. When you sit down with Maureen, she discusses the various investment options available in the company's retirement plan. You mention to Maureen that you researched Deck Out My Yacht before you accepted your new job. You are confident in management's ability to lead the company.

Analysis of the company has led to your belief that the company is growing and will achieve a greater market share in the future. You also feel you should support your employer. Given these considerations, along with the fact that you are a conservative investor, you are leaning toward investing 100 percent of your retirement amount in Deck Out My Yacht.

Assume the risk-free rate is the historical average risk-free rate (Chapter 10). The correlation between the bond fund and large-cap stock fund is 0.15. Note that the spreadsheet graphing and "solver" functions may assist you in answering the following questions.

1. Considering the effects of diversification, how should Maureen respond to the suggestion that you invest 100 percent of your retirement savings in Deck Out My Yacht stock?
2. Maureen's response to investing your retirement savings entirely in Deck Out My Yacht stock has convinced you that this may not be the best alternative. Because you are a conservative investor, you tell Maureen that a 100 percent investment in the bond fund may be the best alternative. Is it?
3. Using the returns for the M&M Large-Cap Stock Fund and the M&M Bond Fund, graph the opportunity set of feasible portfolios.
4. After examining the opportunity set, you notice that you can invest in a portfolio consisting of the bond fund and the large-cap stock fund that will have exactly the same standard deviation as the bond fund. This portfolio will also have a greater expected return. What are the portfolio weights and expected return of this portfolio?
5. Examining the opportunity set, notice there is a portfolio that has the lowest standard deviation. This is the minimum variance portfolio. What are the portfolio weights, expected return, and standard deviation of this portfolio? Why is the minimum variance portfolio important?
6. A measure of risk-adjusted performance that is often used is the Sharpe ratio. The Sharpe ratio is calculated as the risk premium of an asset divided by its standard deviation. The portfolio with the highest possible Sharpe ratio on the opportunity set is called the Sharpe optimal portfolio. What are the portfolio weights, expected return, and standard deviation of the Sharpe optimal portfolio? How does the Sharpe ratio of this portfolio compare to the Sharpe ratios of the bond fund and the large-cap stock fund? Do you see a connection between the Sharpe optimal portfolio and the CAPM? What is the connection?

## Is Beta Dead?

To access Appendix 11A, go to Connect.

# An Alternative View of Risk and Return: The Arbitrage Pricing Theory

EXECUTIVE SUMMARY

The previous two chapters showed how variable returns on securities can be. This variability is measured by variance and by standard deviation. Next, we discussed how the returns on securities are interdependent. We measured the degree of interdependence between a pair of securities by covariance and by correlation. This interdependence led to a number of interesting results. First, we showed that diversification in stocks can eliminate some risk. By contrast, we showed that diversification in a casino can eliminate all risk. Second, the interdependence of returns led to the capital asset pricing model (CAPM). This model posits a positive (and linear) relationship between the beta of a security and its expected return.

The CAPM was developed in the early 1960s.[1] An alternative to the CAPM is the *arbitrage pricing theory (APT)*.[2] For our purposes, the differences between the two models stem from the APT's treatment of the interrelationship among the returns on securities.[3] The APT assumes that returns on securities are generated by a number of industrywide and marketwide factors. Correlation between a pair of securities occurs when these two securities are affected by the same factor or factors. By contrast, though the CAPM allows correlation among securities, it does not specify the underlying factors causing the correlation.

Both the APT and the CAPM imply a positive relationship between expected return and risk. In our (perhaps biased) opinion, the APT allows this relationship to be developed in a particularly intuitive manner. In addition, the APT views risk more generally than just as the standardized covariance or beta of a security with the market portfolio. Therefore, we offer this approach as an alternative to the CAPM.

---

[1] In particular, see Jack Treynor, "Toward a Theory of the Market Value of Risky Assets," unpublished manuscript (1961); William F. Sharpe, "Capital Asset Prices: A Theory of Market Equilibrium Under Conditions of Risk," *Journal of Finance* (September 1964); and John Lintner, "The Valuation of Risky Assets and the Selection of Risky Investments in Stock Portfolios and Capital Budgets," *Review of Economics and Statistics* (February 1965).

[2] See Stephen A. Ross, "The Arbitrage Theory of Capital Asset Pricing," *Journal of Economic Theory* (December 1976).

[3] This is by no means the only difference in the assumptions of the two models. For example, the CAPM usually assumes either that the returns on assets are normally distributed or that investors have quadratic utility functions. The APT does not require either assumption. Instead it is based on the more general principle that when assets are priced correctly, it is not possible to make arbitrage profits without taking on risk. While this and other differences are quite important in research, they are not relevant to the material presented in our text.

# 12.1 FACTOR MODELS: ANNOUNCEMENTS, SURPRISES, AND EXPECTED RETURNS

We learned in the previous chapter how to construct portfolios and how to evaluate their returns. We now step back and examine the returns on individual securities more closely. By doing this we will find that the portfolios inherit and alter the properties of the securities they comprise.

To be concrete, let us consider the return on the stock of a company called Quebec Supply. What will determine this stock's return in, say, the coming month?

The return on any stock traded in a financial market consists of two parts. First, the *normal* or *expected return* from the stock is the part of the return that shareholders in the market predict or expect. It depends on all of the information shareholders have that bears on the stock, and it uses all of our understanding of what will influence the stock in the next month.

The second part is the *uncertain* and *risky return* on the stock. This is the portion that comes from information that will be revealed within the month. The list of such information is endless, but here are some examples·

* News about Quebec Supply's research.
* Statistics Canada figures released on the gross domestic product (GDP).
* Announcement of the latest federal deficit reduction plans.
* Discovery that a rival's product has been tampered with.
* News that Quebec Supply's sales figures are higher than expected.
* A sudden drop in interest rates.
* The unexpected retirement of Quebec Supply's founder and president.

A way to write the return on Quebec Supply's stock in the coming month, then, is

$$R = \overline{R} + U$$

where $R$ is the actual total return in the month, $\overline{R}$ is the expected part of the return, and $U$ stands for the unexpected part of the return.

Some care must be exercised in studying the effects of this and other information on the return. For example, Statistics Canada might give us GDP or unemployment figures for this month, but how much of that is new information for shareholders? Surely, at the beginning of the month, shareholders will have some idea or forecast of what the monthly GDP will be. To the extent to which the shareholders had forecast the government's announcement, that forecast should be factored into the expected part of the return, $\overline{R}$, as of the beginning of the month. On the other hand, insofar as the announcement by the government is a surprise and to the extent to which it influences the return on the stock, it will be part of $U$, the unanticipated part of the return.

As an example, suppose shareholders in the market had forecast that the GDP increase this month would be 0.5 percent. If GDP influences our company's stock, this forecast will be part of the information shareholders use to form the expectation, $\overline{R}$, of monthly return. If the actual announcement this month is exactly 0.5 percent, the same as the forecast, then the shareholders learned nothing new, and the announcement is not news. It is like hearing a rumour about a friend when you knew it all along. Another way of saying this is that shareholders had already discounted the announcement. This use of the word *discount* is different from that in computing present value (PV), but the spirit is similar. When we discount a dollar in the future, we say that it is worth less to us because of the time value of money. When we discount an announcement or a news item in the future, we mean that it has less impact on the market because the market already knew much of it.

On the other hand, suppose Statistics Canada announced that the actual GDP increase during the month was 1.5 percent. Now shareholders have learned something—that the increase is one percentage point higher than they had forecast. This difference between the actual result and the forecast, one percentage point in this example, is sometimes called the *innovation* or *surprise*.

Any announcement can be broken into two parts: the anticipated or expected part, and the surprise or innovation:

$$\text{Announcement} = \text{Expected part} + \text{Surprise}$$

The expected part of any announcement is part of the information the market uses to form the expectation, $\overline{R}$, of the return on the stock. The surprise is the news that influences the unanticipated return on the stock, $U$.

To take another example, if shareholders know in January that the president of a firm is going to resign, the official announcement in February will be fully expected and will be discounted by the market. Because the announcement was expected before February, its influence on the stock will have taken place before February. The announcement itself in February will contain no surprise, and the stock's price should not change at all at the announcement in February.

When we speak of news, then, we refer to the surprise part of any announcement and not to the portion that the market has expected and therefore has already discounted.

**CONCEPT QUESTIONS**

- What are the two basic parts of a return?
- Under what conditions will some news have no effect on common stock prices?

## 12.2  RISK: SYSTEMATIC AND UNSYSTEMATIC

The unanticipated part of the return, that portion resulting from surprises, is the true risk of any investment. After all, if we had already got what we had expected, there would be no risk and no uncertainty.

There are important differences, though, among various sources of risk. Look at our previous list of news stories. Some of these stories are directed specifically at Quebec Supply, and some are more general. Which of the news items are of specific importance to Quebec Supply?

Announcements about interest rates or GDP are clearly important for nearly all companies, whereas the news about Quebec Supply's president, its research, its sales, or the affairs of a rival company are of specific interest to Quebec Supply. We will divide these two types of announcements and the resulting risk into two components: a systematic portion, called *systematic risk*, and the remainder, which we call *specific* or *unsystematic risk*. The following definitions describe the difference:

- A *systematic risk* is any risk that affects a large number of assets, each to a greater or lesser degree.
- An *unsystematic risk* is a risk that specifically affects a single asset or a small group of assets.[4]

Uncertainty about general economic conditions, such as GDP, interest rates, or inflation, is an example of systematic risk. These conditions affect nearly all stocks to some degree. An unanticipated or surprise increase in inflation affects wages and the costs of the supplies that companies buy, the value of the assets that companies own, and the prices at which companies sell their products. Forces to which all companies are susceptible are the essence of systematic risk.

In contrast, the announcement of a small oil strike by a company may very well affect that company alone or a few other companies. Certainly, it is unlikely to have

---

[4] In the previous chapter, we briefly mentioned that unsystematic risk is risk that can be diversified away in a large portfolio. This result will also follow from the present analysis.

an effect on the world oil market. To stress that such information is unsystematic and affects only some specific companies, we sometimes call it an *idiosyncratic risk*.

The distinction between a systematic risk and an unsystematic risk is never as exact as we make it out to be. Even the most narrow and peculiar bit of news about a company ripples through the economy. It reminds us of the tale of the war that was lost because one horse lost a shoe; even a minor event may have an impact on the world. But this degree of hair-splitting should not trouble us much. To paraphrase a judge's comment on pornography, we are not able to define systematic and unsystematic risk exactly, but we know them when we see them.

This permits us to break down the risk of Quebec Supply's stock into its two components: the systematic and the unsystematic. As is traditional, we will use the Greek letter epsilon, $\varepsilon$, to represent the unsystematic risk and write

$$R = \bar{R} + U$$
$$= \bar{R} + m + \varepsilon$$

where we have used the letter $m$ to stand for the systematic risk. Sometimes systematic risk is referred to as *market risk*. This emphasizes the fact that $m$ influences all assets in the market to some extent.

The important point about the way we have broken the total risk, $U$, into its two components, $m$ and $\varepsilon$, is that $\varepsilon$, because it is specific to the company, is unrelated to the specific risk of most other companies. For example, the unsystematic risk of Quebec Supply's stock, $\varepsilon_Q$, is unrelated to the unsystematic risk of Bank of Montreal's stock, $\varepsilon_{BMO}$. The risk that Quebec Supply's stock will go up or down because of a discovery by its research team—or its failure to discover something—is probably unrelated to any of the specific uncertainties that affect Bank of Montreal's stock.

Using the terms of the previous chapter, this means that the unsystematic risks of Quebec Supply's stock and Bank of Montreal's stock are unrelated to each other, or uncorrelated. In the symbols of statistics,

$$\text{Corr}(\varepsilon_Q, \varepsilon_{BMO}) = 0$$

 **CONCEPT QUESTIONS**

- Describe the difference between systematic risk and unsystematic risk.
- Why is unsystematic risk sometimes referred to as *idiosyncratic risk*?

## 12.3    SYSTEMATIC RISK AND BETAS

The fact that the unsystematic parts of the returns on two companies are unrelated to each other does not mean that the systematic portions are unrelated. On the contrary, because both companies are influenced by the same systematic risks, individual companies' systematic risks and, therefore, their total returns will be related.

For example, a surprise about inflation will influence almost all companies to some extent. How sensitive is Quebec Supply's stock return to unanticipated changes in inflation? If Quebec Supply's stock tends to go up on news that inflation is exceeding expectations, we say that it is positively related to inflation. If the stock goes down when inflation exceeds expectations and up when inflation falls short of expectations, it is negatively related. In the unusual case where a stock's return is uncorrelated with inflation surprises, inflation has no effect on it.

We capture the influence of a systematic risk like inflation on a stock by using the **beta coefficient**. The beta coefficient, $\beta$, tells us the response of the stock's return to a systematic risk. In the previous chapter, beta measured the responsiveness of a security's return to a specific risk factor, the return on the market portfolio. We used this type of responsiveness to develop the CAPM. Because we now consider many types of systematic risks, our current work can be viewed as a generalization of what we did in the previous chapter.

If a company's stock is positively related to the risk of inflation, that stock has a positive inflation beta. If it is negatively related to inflation, its inflation beta is negative, and if it is uncorrelated with inflation, its inflation beta is zero.

It is not hard to imagine stocks with positive and negative inflation betas. The stock of a company owning gold mines will probably have a positive inflation beta because an unanticipated rise in inflation is usually associated with an increase in gold prices. On the other hand, an automobile company facing stiff foreign competition might find that an increase in inflation means that the wages it pays are higher, but that it cannot raise its prices to cover the increase. This profit squeeze, as the company's expenses rise faster than its revenues, would give its stock a negative inflation beta.

Some companies that have few assets and that act as brokers—buying items in competitive markets and reselling them in other markets—might be relatively unaffected by inflation, because their costs and their revenues would rise and fall together. Their stocks would have an inflation beta of zero.

Some structure is useful at this point. Suppose we have identified three systematic risks on which we want to focus. We may believe that these three are sufficient to describe the systematic risks that influence stock returns. Three likely candidates are inflation, GDP, and interest rates. Thus, every stock will have a beta associated with each of these systematic risks: an inflation beta, a GDP beta, and an interest rate beta. We can write the return on the stock, then, in the following form:

$$
\begin{aligned}
R &= \overline{R} + U \\
&= \overline{R} + m + \varepsilon \\
&= \overline{R} + \beta_I F_I + \beta_{GDP} F_{GDP} + \beta_r F_r + \varepsilon
\end{aligned}
$$

where we have used $\beta_I$ to denote the stock's inflation beta, $\beta_{GDP}$ for its GDP beta, and $\beta_r$ to stand for its interest rate beta. In the equation, $F$ stands for a surprise, whether it be in inflation, GDP, or interest rates.

Let us go through an example to see how the surprises and the expected return add up to produce the total return, $R$, on a given stock. To make it more familiar, suppose that the return is over a horizon of a year and not just a month. Suppose that at the beginning of the year, inflation is forecast to be 5 percent for the year. GDP is forecast to increase by 2 percent, and interest rates are expected not to change. Suppose the stock we are looking at has the following betas:

$$
\begin{aligned}
\beta_I &= \phantom{-}2.0 \\
\beta_{GDP} &= \phantom{-}1.0 \\
\beta_r &= -1.8
\end{aligned}
$$

The magnitude of the beta describes how great an impact a systematic risk has on a stock's returns. A beta of $+1$ indicates that the stock's return rises and falls one for one with the systematic factor. This means, in our example, that because the stock has a GDP beta of 1, it experiences a 1 percent increase in return for every 1 percent surprise increase in GDP. If its GDP beta were $-2$, it would fall by 2 percent when there was an unanticipated increase of 1 percent in GDP, and it would rise by 2 percent if GDP experienced a surprise 1 percent decline.

Next let's suppose that during the year inflation rises by 7 percent, GDP rises by only 1 percent, and interest rates fall by 2 percent. Last, suppose that we learn some good news about the company (perhaps that it's succeeding rapidly with some new business strategy) and that this unanticipated development contributes 5 percent to its return. In other words,

$$
\varepsilon = 5\%
$$

Let us assemble all of this information to find what return the stock had during the year.

First, we must determine what news or surprises took place in the systematic factors. From our information we know that

$$\text{Expected inflation} = 5\%$$
$$\text{Expected GDP change} = 2\%$$
$$\text{Expected change in interest rates} = 0\%$$

This means that the market had discounted these changes, and the surprises will be the difference between what actually takes place and these expectations:

$$
\begin{aligned}
F_I &= \text{Surprise in inflation} \\
&= \text{Actual inflation} - \text{Expected inflation} \\
&= 7\% - 5\% \\
&= 2\%
\end{aligned}
$$

Similarly,

$$
\begin{aligned}
F_{\text{GDP}} &= \text{Surprise in GDP} \\
&= \text{Actual GDP} - \text{Expected GDP} \\
&= 1\% - 2\% \\
&= -1\%
\end{aligned}
$$

and

$$
\begin{aligned}
F_r &= \text{Surprise in change in interest rates} \\
&= \text{Actual change} - \text{Expected change} \\
&= -2\% - 0\% \\
&= -2\%
\end{aligned}
$$

The total effect of the systematic risks on the stock return, then, is

$$
\begin{aligned}
m &= \text{Systematic risk portion of return} \\
&= \beta_I F_I + \beta_{\text{GDP}} F_{\text{GDP}} + \beta_r F_r \\
&= [2 \times 2\%] + [1 \times (-1\%)] + [(-1.8) \times (-2\%)] \\
&= 6.6\%
\end{aligned}
$$

Combining this with the unsystematic risk portion, the total risky portion of the return on the stock is

$$m + \varepsilon = 6.6\% + 5\% = 11.6\%$$

Last, if the expected return on the stock for the year is, say, 4 percent, the total return from all three components is

$$
\begin{aligned}
R &= \overline{R} + m + \varepsilon \\
&= 4\% + 6.6\% + 5\% \\
&= 15.6\%
\end{aligned}
$$

The model we have been looking at is called a **factor model**, and the systematic sources of risk, designated $F$, are called the *factors*. To be perfectly formal, a *k-factor model* is a model where each stock's return is generated by

$$R = \overline{R} + \beta_1 F_1 + \beta_2 F_2 + \cdots + \beta_k F_k + \varepsilon$$

where $\varepsilon$ is specific to a particular stock and uncorrelated with the $\varepsilon$-term for other stocks. In our preceding example, we had a three-factor model. We used inflation, GDP, and the change in interest rates as examples of systematic sources of risk (or factors). Researchers have not settled on what is the correct set of factors. Like so many other questions, this might be one of those matters that are never laid to rest.

In practice, researchers frequently use a one-factor model for returns. They do not use all of the sorts of economic factors we used previously as examples; instead, they use an index of stock market returns—like the S&P/TSX 60 or even a more broadly based index with more stocks in it—as the single factor. Using the single-factor model we can write returns as

$$R = \overline{R} + \beta(R_{\text{S\&P/TSX 60}} - \overline{R}_{\text{S\&P/TSX 60}}) + \varepsilon$$

Where there is only one factor (the returns on the S&P/TSX 60 Index), we do not need to put a subscript on the beta. In this form (with minor modifications) the factor model is called a **market model**. This term is employed because the index that is used for the factor is an index of returns on the whole (stock) market. The market model is written as

$$R = \overline{R} + \beta(R_M - \overline{R}_M) + \varepsilon$$

where $R_M$ is the return on the market portfolio.[5] The single $\beta$ is called the *beta coefficient*.

**CONCEPT QUESTIONS**

- What is an inflation beta? A GDP beta? An interest rate beta?
- What is the difference between a *k*-factor model and the market model?
- Define the beta coefficient.

## 12.4   PORTFOLIOS AND FACTOR MODELS

Now let us see what happens to portfolios of stocks when each of the stocks follows a one-factor model. For this discussion, we will take the coming one-month period and examine returns. We could have used a day, a year, or any other time period. If the period represents the time between decisions, however, we would rather it be short than long—a month is a reasonable time frame to use.

We will create portfolios from a list of $N$ stocks, and we will use a one-factor model to capture the systematic risk. The $i$th stock in the list will therefore have returns

$$R_i = \overline{R}_i + \beta_i F + \varepsilon_i \tag{12.1}$$

where we have subscripted the variables to indicate that they relate to the $i$th stock. Notice that the factor $F$ is not subscripted. The factor that represents systematic risk could be a surprise in GDP, or we could use the market model and let the factor be the difference between the S&P/TSX 60 return and what we expect that return to be, $R_{\text{S\&P/TSX 60}} - \overline{R}_{\text{S\&P/TSX 60}}$. In either case, the factor applies to all stocks.

The $\beta_i$ is subscripted because it represents the unique way the factor influences the $i$th stock. To recapitulate our discussion of factor models, if $\beta_i$ is zero, the returns on the $i$th stock are

$$R_i = \overline{R}_i + \varepsilon_i$$

In words, the $i$th stock's returns are unaffected by the factor $F$ if $\beta_i$ is zero. If $\beta_i$ is positive, positive changes in the factor raise the $i$th stock's returns, and declines lower them. Conversely, if $\beta_i$ is negative, its returns and the factor move in opposite directions.

Figure 12.1 illustrates the relationship between a stock's excess returns, $R_i - \overline{R}_i$, and the factor $F$ for different betas, where $\beta_i > 0$. The lines in Figure 12.1 plot equation (12.1) on the assumption that there has been no unsystematic risk. That is, $\varepsilon_i = 0$. Because we are assuming positive betas, the lines slope upward, indicating that the return on the stock rises with $F$. Notice that if the factor is zero ($F = 0$), the line passes through zero on the *y*-axis.

---

[5] Alternatively, the market model could be written as
$$R = \alpha + \beta R_M + \varepsilon$$
Here alpha ($\alpha$) is an intercept term equal to $\overline{R} - \beta\overline{R}_M$.

FIGURE 12.1

**The One-Factor Model for Stock _i_**

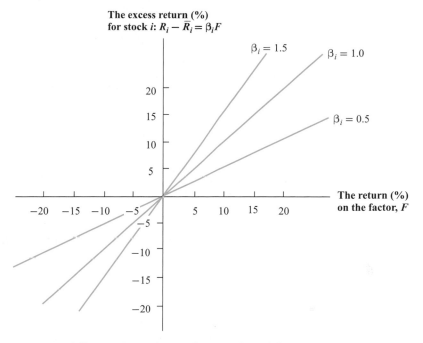

Each line represents a different security, where each security has a different beta.

Now let us see what happens when we create stock portfolios where each stock follows a one-factor model. Let $x_i$ be the proportion of security $i$ in the portfolio. That is, if an individual with a portfolio of $100 wants $20 in TransCanada Pipelines Ltd., we say $X_{TCPL} = 20\%$. Because the $X$'s represent the proportions of wealth we are investing in each of the stocks, we know that they must add up to 100 percent or 1. That is,

$$X_1 + X_2 + X_3 + \cdots + X_N = 1$$

We know that the portfolio return is the weighted average of the returns on the individual assets in the portfolio:

$$R_P = X_1 R_1 + X_2 R_2 + X_3 R_3 + \cdots + X_N R_N \qquad (12.2)$$

Equation (12.2) expresses the return on the portfolio as a weighted average of the returns on the individual assets. We saw from equation (12.1) that each asset's return is determined by both the factor $F$ and the unsystematic risk of $\varepsilon_i$. Thus, by substituting equation (12.1) for each $R_i$ in equation (12.2), we have

$$R_P = \overbrace{X_1(\overline{R}_1 + \beta_1 F + \varepsilon_1)}^{(\text{Return on stock 1})} + \overbrace{X_2(\overline{R}_2 + \beta_2 F + \varepsilon_2)}^{(\text{Return on stock 2})} + \overbrace{X_3(\overline{R}_3 + \beta_3 F + \varepsilon_3)}^{(\text{Return on stock 3})}$$
$$+ \cdots + \underbrace{X_N(\overline{R}_N + \beta_N F + \varepsilon_N)}_{(\text{Return on stock } N)} \qquad (12.3)$$

Equation (12.3) shows us that the return on a portfolio is determined by three sets of parameters:

1. The expected return on each individual security, $\overline{R}_i$.
2. The beta of each security multiplied by the factor $F$.
3. The unsystematic risk of each individual security, $\varepsilon_i$.

We express equation (12.3) in terms of these three sets of parameters as

**Weighted Average of Expected Returns:**

$$R_P = X_1\overline{R}_1 + X_2\overline{R}_2 + X_3\overline{R}_3 + \cdots + X_N\overline{R}_N \tag{12.4}$$

**(Weighted Average of Betas)$F$:**

$$+ (X_1\beta_1 + X_2\beta_2 + X_3\beta_3 + \cdots + X_N\beta_N)F$$

**Weighted Average of Unsystematic Risks:**

$$+ X_1\varepsilon_1 + X_2\varepsilon_2 + X_3\varepsilon_3 + \cdots + X_N\varepsilon_N$$

This rather imposing equation is actually straightforward. The first row is the weighted average of all of the securities' expected returns. The items in the parentheses of the second row represent the weighted average of all of the securities' betas. This weighted average is, in turn, multiplied by the factor $F$. The third row represents a weighted average of the unsystematic risks of the individual securities.

Where does uncertainty appear in equation (12.4)? There is no uncertainty in the first row because only the expected value of each security's return appears there. Uncertainty in the second row is reflected by only one item, $F$. That is, while we know that the expected value of $F$ is zero, we do not know what its value will be over a particular time period. Uncertainty in the third row is reflected by each unsystematic risk, $\varepsilon_i$.

## Portfolios and Diversification

In the previous sections of this chapter, we expressed the return on a single security in terms of our factor model. Portfolios were treated next. Because investors generally hold diversified portfolios, we now want to know what equation (12.4) looks like in a large or diversified portfolio.[6]

As it turns out, something unusual happens to equation (12.4)—the third row actually *disappears* in a large portfolio. To see this, consider the gambler of the previous chapter who divides $1,000 by betting on red over many spins of the roulette wheel. For example, she may participate in 1,000 spins, betting $1 at a time. Though we do not know ahead of time whether a particular spin will yield red or black, we can be confident that red will win about 50 percent of the time. Ignoring the house take, the investor can be expected to end up with just about her original $1,000.

Though we are concerned with stocks, not roulette wheels, the same principle applies. Each security has its own unsystematic risk, where the surprise for one stock is unrelated to the surprise for another stock. By investing a small amount in each security, the weighted average of the unsystematic risks will be very close to zero in a large portfolio.[7]

Although the third row completely vanishes in a large portfolio, nothing unusual occurs in either row 1 or row 2. Row 1 remains a weighted average of the expected returns on the individual securities as securities are added to the portfolio. Because there is no uncertainty at all in the first row, there is no way for diversification to cause this row to vanish. The terms inside the parentheses of the second row remain a weighted average of the betas. They do not vanish, either, when securities are added. Because the factor $F$ is unaffected when securities are added to the portfolios, the second row does not vanish.

---

[6] Technically, we can think of a large portfolio as one where an investor keeps increasing the number of securities without limit. In practice, effective diversification would occur if at least a few dozen securities were held.

[7] More precisely, we say that the weighted average of the unsystematic risk approaches zero as the number of equally weighted securities in a portfolio approaches infinity.

Why does the third row vanish while the second row does not, though both rows reflect uncertainty? The key is that there are many unsystematic risks in row 3. Because these risks are independent of each other, the effect of diversification becomes stronger as we add more assets to the portfolio. The resulting portfolio becomes less and less risky, and the return becomes more certain. However, the systematic risk, $F$, affects all securities because it is outside the parentheses in row 2. Because one cannot avoid this factor by investing in many securities, diversification does not occur in this row.

---

**EXAMPLE 12.1**

The above material can be further explained by an example similar in spirit to the diversification example of the previous chapter. We keep our one-factor model but make three specific assumptions:

1.  All securities have the same expected return of 10 percent. This assumption implies that the first row of equation (12.4) must also equal 10 percent because this row is a weighted average of the expected returns of the individual securities.

2.  All securities have a beta of 1. The sum of the terms inside parentheses in the second row of (12.4) must equal 1 because these terms are a weighted average of the individual betas. Since the terms inside the parentheses are multiplied by $F$, the value of the second row is $1 \times F = F$.

3.  In this example, we focus on the behaviour of one individual, Walter Bagehot. Being a new observer of the economic scene, Walter decides to hold an equally weighted portfolio. That is, the proportion of each security in his portfolio is $1/N$.

We can express the return on Walter's portfolio as

**Return on Walter's Portfolio:**

$$R_P = \underbrace{10\%}_{\substack{\text{From row 1} \\ \text{of (12.4)}}} + \underbrace{F}_{\substack{\text{From row 2} \\ \text{of (12.4)}}} + \underbrace{\left( \frac{1}{N}\varepsilon_1 + \frac{1}{N}\varepsilon_2 + \frac{1}{N}\varepsilon_3 + \cdots + \frac{1}{N}\varepsilon_N \right)}_{\substack{\text{From row 3} \\ \text{of (12.4)}}} \qquad \textbf{(12.4′)}$$

We mentioned above that as $N$ increases without limit, row 3 of (12.4) becomes equal to zero. Thus, the return to Walter's portfolio when the number of securities is very large is

$$RP = 10\% + F \qquad \textbf{(12.4″)}$$

The key to diversification is exhibited in equation (12.4″). The unsystematic risk of row 3 vanishes,[8] while the systematic risk of row 2 remains.

This is illustrated in Figure 12.2. Systematic risk, captured by variation in the factor $F$, is not reduced through diversification. Conversely, unsystematic risk diminishes as securities are added, vanishing as the number of securities becomes infinite. Our result is analogous to the diversification example of the previous chapter. In that chapter, we said that undiversifiable or systematic risk arises from positive covariances between securities. In this chapter, we say that systematic risk arises from a common factor $F$. Because a common factor causes positive covariances, the arguments of the two chapters are parallel.

---

[8] The variance of row 3 is

$$\frac{1}{N^2}\sigma_\varepsilon^2 + \frac{1}{N^2}\sigma_\varepsilon^2 + \frac{1}{N^2}\sigma_\varepsilon^2 + \cdots + \frac{1}{N^2}\sigma_\varepsilon^2 = \frac{1}{N^2}N\sigma_\varepsilon^2$$

where $\sigma_\varepsilon^2$ is the variance of each $\varepsilon$. This can be rewritten as $\sigma_\varepsilon^2/N$, which tends to 0 as $N$ goes to infinity.

**FIGURE 12.2**

**Diversification and the Portfolio Risk for an Equally Weighted Portfolio**

Total risk decreases as the number of securities in the portfolio rises. This drop occurs only in the unsystematic risk component. Systematic risk is unaffected by diversification.

***CONCEPT QUESTIONS***
- How can the return on a portfolio be expressed in terms of a factor model?
- What risk is diversified away in a large portfolio?

## 12.5 BETAS AND EXPECTED RETURNS

### The Linear Relationship

We have argued many times that the expected return on a security compensates for its risk. In the previous chapter we showed that market beta (the standardized covariance of the security's returns with those of the market) was the appropriate measure of risk under the assumptions of homogeneous expectations and risk-free borrowing and lending. The CAPM, which posited these assumptions, implied that the expected return on a security was positively (and linearly) related to its beta. We will find a similar relationship between risk and return in the one-factor model of this chapter.

We begin by noting that the relevant risk in large and well-diversified portfolios is all systematic because unsystematic risk is diversified away. An implication is that when a well-diversified shareholder considers changing holdings of a particular stock, the security's unsystematic risk can be ignored.

Notice that we are not claiming that stocks, like portfolios, have no unsystematic risk. Neither are we saying that the unsystematic risk of a stock will not affect its returns. Stocks do have unsystematic risk, and their actual returns do depend on the unsystematic risk. Because this risk washes out in a well-diversified portfolio, however, shareholders can ignore this unsystematic risk when they consider whether or not to add a stock to their portfolio. Therefore, if shareholders are ignoring the unsystematic risk, only the systematic risk of a stock can be related to its *expected* return.

This relationship is illustrated in the security market line (SML) of Figure 12.3. Points *P*, *C*, *A*, and *L* all lie on the line emanating from the risk-free rate of 10 percent. The points representing each of these four assets can be created by combinations of the risk-free rate and any of the other three assets. For example, since *A* has a beta of 2.0 and *P* has a beta of 1.0, a portfolio of 50 percent in asset *A* and 50 percent in the risk-free rate has the same beta as asset *P*. The risk-free rate is 10 percent and the expected return on security *A* is 35 percent, implying that the combination's return of 22.5 percent [or (10% + 35%)/2] is identical to security *P*'s expected return. Because security *P* has both the same beta and the same expected return as a combination of the risk-free asset and security *A*, an individual is equally inclined to add a small amount of security *P* and to add a small amount of this combination to a portfolio. However, the unsystematic risk of security *P* need not be equal to the unsystematic risk of the combination of security *A* and the risk-free rate because unsystematic risk is diversified away in a large portfolio.

FIGURE 12.3

**A Graph of Beta and Expected Return for Individual Stocks under the One-Factor Model**

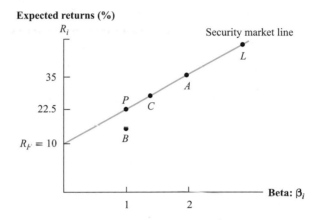

Of course, the potential combinations of points on the SML are endless. One can duplicate *P* by combinations of the risk-free rate and either *C* or *L* (or both of them). One can duplicate *C* (or *A* or *L*) by borrowing at the risk-free rate to invest in *P*. The infinite number of points on the SML that are not labelled can be used as well.

Now consider security *B*. Because its expected return is below the line, no investor would hold it. Instead, the investor would prefer security *P*, a combination of security *A* and the risk-free asset or some other combination. Thus, security *B*'s price is too high. Its price will fall in a competitive market, forcing its expected return back up to the line in equilibrium.

Because we know that the return on any zero-beta asset is $R_F$ and the expected return on asset *P* is $\overline{R}_P$, it can easily be shown that

$$\overline{R} = R_F + \beta(\overline{R}_P - R_F) \tag{12.5}$$

In equation (12.5), $\overline{R}$ can be thought of as the expected return on any security or portfolio lying on the SML. $\beta$ is the beta of that security or portfolio.

## The Market Portfolio and the Single Factor

In the CAPM, the beta of a security measures the security's responsiveness to movements in the market portfolio. In the one-factor model of the APT, the beta of a security measures its responsiveness to the factor. We now relate the market portfolio to the single factor.

A large, diversified portfolio has no unsystematic risk because the unsystematic risks of the individual securities are diversified away. Assuming that no security has a disproportionate market share, the market portfolio is fully diversified and contains no unsystematic risk.[9] In other words, the market portfolio is perfectly correlated with

---

[9] This assumption is generally plausible in the real world. For example, even the market value of a large company like Royal Bank of Canada is only a small fraction of the market value of the S&P/TSX 60 index.

the single factor, implying that the market portfolio is really a scaled-up or scaled-down version of the factor. After scaling properly, we can treat the market portfolio as the factor itself.

The market portfolio, like every security or portfolio, lies on the SML. When the market portfolio is the factor, the beta of the market portfolio is 1 by definition. This is shown in Figure 12.4. (We deleted the securities and the specific expected returns from Figure 12.3 for clarity; the two graphs are otherwise identical.) With the market portfolio as the factor, equation (12.5) becomes

$$\overline{R} = R_F + \beta(\overline{R}_M - R_F)$$

where $\overline{R}_M$ is the expected return on the market. This equation shows that the expected return on any asset, $\overline{R}$, is linearly related to the security's beta. The equation is identical to that of the CAPM, which we developed in the previous chapter.

**FIGURE 12.4**

**A Graph of Beta and Expected Return for Individual Stocks under the One-Factor Model**

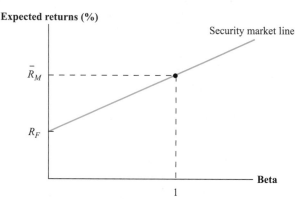

The factor is scaled so that it is identical to the market portfolio.
The beta of the market portfolio is 1.

 **CONCEPT QUESTION**

- What is the relationship between the one-factor model and the CAPM?

## 12.6 THE CAPITAL ASSET PRICING MODEL AND THE ARBITRAGE PRICING THEORY

The CAPM and the APT are alternative models of risk and return. It is worthwhile to consider the differences between the two models, both in terms of pedagogy and in terms of application.

### Differences in Pedagogy

We feel that the CAPM has at least one strong advantage from the student's point of view. The derivation of the CAPM necessarily brings the reader through a discussion of efficient sets. The treatment—beginning with the case of two risky assets, moving to the case of many risky assets, and finishing when a risk-free asset is added to the many risky ones—is of great intuitive value. This sort of presentation is not as easily accomplished with the APT.

However, the APT has an offsetting advantage. The model adds factors until the unsystematic risk of any security is uncorrelated with the unsystematic risk of every other security. Under this formulation, it is easily shown that (1) unsystematic risk steadily falls (and ultimately vanishes) as the number of securities in the portfolio increases but (2) the systematic risks do not decrease. This result was also shown in the CAPM, though the intuition was cloudier because the unsystematic risks could be correlated across securities.

## Differences in Application

One advantage of the APT is that it can handle multiple factors while the CAPM ignores them. Although the bulk of our presentation in this chapter focused on the one-factor model, a multifactor model is probably more reflective of reality. That is, one must abstract from many marketwide and industrywide factors before the unsystematic risk of one security becomes uncorrelated with the unsystematic risks of other securities. Under this multifactor version of the APT, the relationship between risk and return can be expressed as

$$\overline{R} = R_F + (\overline{R}_1 - R_F)\beta_1 + (\overline{R}_2 - R_F)\beta_2 + (\overline{R}_3 - R_F)\beta_3 + \cdots + (\overline{R}_K - R_F)\beta_K \quad \textbf{(12.6)}$$

In this equation, $\beta_1$ stands for the security's beta with respect to the first factor, $\beta_2$ stands for the security's beta with respect to the second factor, and so on. For example, if the first factor is GDP, $\beta_1$ is the security's GDP beta. The term $\overline{R}_1$ is the expected return on a security (or portfolio) whose beta with respect to the first factor is 1 and whose beta with respect to all other factors is zero. Because the market compensates for risk, $(\overline{R}_1 - R_F)$ will be positive in the normal case.[10] (An analogous interpretation can be given for $\overline{R}_2$, $\overline{R}_3$, and so on.)

The equation states that the security's expected return is related to the security's factor betas. The intuition in equation (12.6) is straightforward. Each factor represents risk that cannot be diversified away. The higher a security's beta is with regard to a particular factor, the higher is the risk that the security bears. In a rational world, the expected return on the security should compensate for this risk. The above equation states that the expected return is a summation of the risk-free rate plus the compensation for each type of risk that the security bears.

As an example, consider a classic U.S. study where the factors were monthly growth in industrial production (IP), change in expected inflation ($\Delta EI$), unanticipated inflation (UI), unanticipated change in the risk premium between risky bonds and default-free bonds (URP), and unanticipated change in the difference between the return on long-term government bonds and the return on short-term government bonds (UBR).[11] Using the period 1958 through 1984, the empirical results of the study indicated that the expected monthly return on any stock, $\overline{R}_s$, can be described as

$$\overline{R}_s = 0.0041 + 0.0136\beta_{IP} - 0.0001\beta_{\Delta EI} - 0.0006\beta_{UI} + 0.0072\beta_{URP} - 0.0052\beta_{UBR}$$

Suppose a particular stock had the following betas: $\beta_{IP} = 1.1$, $\beta_{\Delta EI} = 2$, $\beta_{UI} = 3$, $\beta_{URP} = 0.1$, and $\beta_{UBR} = 1.6$. The expected monthly return on that security would be

$$\overline{R}_s = 0.0041 + 0.0136 \times 1.1 - 0.0001 \times 2 - 0.0006 \times 3 + 0.0072 \times 0.1 - 0.0052 \times 1.6$$
$$= 0.0095$$

Assuming that one of the firm's projects has risk equivalent to that of the firm, this value of 0.0095 (i.e., 0.95 percent) can be used as the monthly discount rate for the

---

[10] Actually, $(\overline{R}_i - R_F)$ could be negative in the case where factor $i$ is perceived as a hedge of some sort.

[11] N. Chen, R. Roll, and S. Ross, "Economic Forces and the Stock Market," *Journal of Business* (July 1986).

project.[12] (Because annual data are often supplied for capital budgeting purposes, the annual rate of 0.120 [or $(1.0095)^{12} - 1$] might be used instead.)

A classic Canadian study identified five similar factors:

1. The rate of growth in industrial production.
2. The changes in the slope of the term structure of interest rates (the difference between the returns on long-term and short-term Canada bonds).
3. The default risk premium for bonds (measured as the difference between the yield on long-term Canada bonds and the yield on the ScotiaMcLeod corporate bond index).
4. Inflation (measured as the growth of the consumer price index).
5. The value-weighted return on the market portfolio (S&P/TSX 60).[13]

Using the period 1970 through 1984, the empirical results of the study indicated that expected monthly returns on a sample of 100 TSX stocks could be described as a function of the risk premiums associated with these five factors.

Because many factors appear on the right side of the APT equation, the APT formulation explained expected returns in this Canadian sample more accurately than did the CAPM. However, as we mentioned earlier, one can't easily determine which are the appropriate factors. The factors in the above study were included for reasons of both common sense and convenience. They were not derived from theory, and the choice of factors varies from study to study. A more recent Canadian study, for example, includes changes in a U.S. stock index and in exchange rates as factors.[14]

By contrast, use of the market index in the CAPM formulation is implied by the theory of the previous chapter. We suggested in earlier chapters that the S&P/TSX 60 Index mirrors stock market movements quite well. Using an update of the Hatch and White results first reported in Chapter 10, Chapter 11 easily calculated expected returns on different securities from the CAPM.[15]

**CONCEPT QUESTIONS**

- What are the advantages and disadvantages of the CAPM and the APT?
- What conclusions can be drawn from empirical tests of APT?

## 12.7 PARAMETRIC APPROACHES TO ASSET PRICING

### Empirical Models

The CAPM and the APT by no means exhaust the models and techniques used in practice to measure the expected return on risky assets. Both the CAPM and the APT are *risk-based models*. They each measure the risk of a security by its beta(s) on some

---

[12] Strictly speaking, we must assume that the firm has no debt. We discuss the impact of debt on betas in Chapters 13 and 18.

[13] E. Otuteye, "How Economic Forces Explain Canadian Stock Returns," *Canadian Investment Review* (Spring 1991). An earlier Canadian study supportive of the APT is L. Kryzanowski and M. C. To, "General Factor Models and the Structure of Security Returns," *Journal of Financial and Quantitative Analysis* (March 1983).

[14] L. Kryzanowski, S. Lalancette, and M. C. To, "Performance Attribution Using an APT with Prespecified Macrofactors and Time-Varying Risk Premia and Betas," *Journal of Financial and Quantitative Analysis* (June 1997).

[15] Though many researchers assume that surrogates for the market portfolio are easily found, Richard Roll, "A Critique of the Asset Pricing Theory's Tests," *Journal of Financial Economics* (March 1977), argues that the absence of a universally acceptable proxy for the market portfolio seriously impairs application of the CAPM. After all, the market must include real estate, racehorses, and other assets that are not in the stock market.

systematic factor(s), and they each argue that the expected excess return must be proportional to the beta(s). As we have seen, this is intuitively appealing and has a strong basis in theory, but there are alternative approaches.

Most of these alternatives can be lumped under the broad heading of parametric or empirical methods. The word *empirical* refers to the fact that these approaches are based less on some theory of how financial markets work and more on simply looking for regularities and relations in the history of market data. In these approaches, the researcher specifies some parameters or attributes associated with the securities in question and then examines the data directly for a relation between these attributes and expected returns. For example, Fama and French examine whether the expected return on a firm is related to its size. Is it true that small firms have higher average returns than large firms? Researchers have also examined a variety of accounting measures, such as the ratio of the price of a stock to the accounting earnings, the price–earnings (P/E) ratio, and the closely related ratio of the market value of the stock to the book value of the company, the M/B ratio.[16] Here it might be argued that companies with low P/Es or low M/Bs are "undervalued" and can be expected to have higher returns in the future.

To use the empirical approach to determine the expected return, we would estimate the following equation:

$$\overline{R}_i = R_F + k_{P/E}(P/E)_i + k_{M/B}(M/B)_i + k_{size}(size)_i$$

where $\overline{R}_i$ is the expected return of firm $i$, and where the $k$'s are coefficients that we estimate from stock market data. Notice that this is the same form as equation (12.6), with the firm's attributes in place of betas and with the $k$'s in place of the excess factor portfolio returns.

When tested with data, these parametric approaches seem to do quite well, and when comparisons are made between using parameters and using betas to predict stock returns, the parameters, such as P/E and M/B, seem to work better. There are a variety of possible explanations for these results, and the issues have certainly not been settled. Critics of the empirical approach are skeptical of what they call *data mining*. The particular parameters that researchers work with are often chosen because they have been shown to be related to returns. For instance, suppose that you were asked to explain the change in GMAT test scores over the past 40 years in a particular province. Suppose that to do this you searched through all of the data series you could find. After much searching, you might discover, for example, that the change in the scores was directly related to the jackrabbit population in Alberta. We know that any such relation is purely accidental, but if you search long enough and have enough choices, you will find something even if it's not really there. It's a bit like staring at clouds. After a while you will see clouds that look like anything you want, clowns, bears, or whatever, but all you are really doing is data mining.

Needless to say, the researchers on these matters defend their work by arguing that they have not mined the data and have been very careful to avoid such traps by not snooping at the data to see what will work.

Of course, as a matter of pure theory, since anyone in the market can easily look up the P/E ratio of a firm, one would certainly not expect to find that firms with low P/Es did better than firms with high P/Es simply because they were undervalued. In an efficient market in which prices reflect all public information, such public measures of undervaluation would be quickly exploited and would not be expected to last.

Perhaps a better explanation for the success of empirical approaches lies in a synthesis of the risk-based approaches and the empirical methods. In an efficient market,

---

[16] E. F. Fama and K. R. French, "Common Risk Factors in the Returns on Stocks and Bonds," *Journal of Financial Economics* (February 1993); and "Multifactor Explanations of Asset Pricing Anomalies," *Journal of Finance* (March 1996).

b. Suppose unexpected bad news about the firm was announced that causes the stock price to drop by 2.6 percent. If the expected return on the stock is 10.8 percent, what is the total return on this stock?

12.3 Suppose a factor model is appropriate to describe the returns on a stock. The current expected return on the stock is 10.5 percent. Information about those factors is presented in the following chart:

| Factor | β | Expected value | Actual value |
|---|---|---|---|
| Growth in GDP | 2.04 | 1.80% | 2.6% |
| Interest rates | −1.15 | 4.3 | 4.8 |

a. What is the systematic risk of the stock return?
b. The firm announced that its market share had unexpectedly increased from 23 percent to 27 percent. Investors know from experience that the stock return will increase by 0.45 percent for every 1 percent increase in its market share. What is the unsystematic risk of the stock?
c. What is the total return on this stock?

**Multifactor Models**

12.4 Suppose stock returns can be explained by the following three-factor model:

$$R_i = R_F + \beta_1 F_1 + \beta_2 F_2 - \beta_3 F_3$$

Assume there is no firm-specific risk. The information for each stock is presented here:

| | $\beta_1$ | $\beta_2$ | $\beta_3$ |
|---|---|---|---|
| Stock A | 1.45 | 0.80 | 0.05 |
| Stock B | 0.73 | 1.25 | −0.20 |
| Stock C | 0.89 | −0.14 | 1.24 |

The risk premiums for the factors are 5.5 percent, 4.2 percent, and 4.9 percent, respectively. If you create a portfolio with 20 percent invested in stock A, 20 percent invested in stock B, and the remainder in stock C, what is the expression for the return on your portfolio? If the risk-free rate is 5 percent, what is the expected return on your portfolio?

12.5 Suppose stock returns can be explained by a two-factor model. The firm-specific risks for all stocks are independent. The following table shows the information for two diversified portfolios:

| | $\beta_1$ | $\beta_2$ | E(R) |
|---|---|---|---|
| Portfolio A | 0.70 | 1.13 | 16% |
| Portfolio B | 1.50 | −0.20 | 12 |

If the risk-free rate is 5 percent, what are the risk premiums for each factor in this model?

**Market Model**

12.6 The following three stocks are available in the market:

| | E(R) | β |
|---|---|---|
| Stock A | 10.5% | 1.20 |
| Stock B | 13.0 | 0.98 |
| Stock C | 15.7 | 1.37 |
| Market | 14.2 | 1.00 |

Assume the market model is valid.
a. Write the market model equation for each stock.
b. What is the return on a portfolio with weights of 30 percent stock A, 45 percent stock B, and 25 percent stock C?

   *c.* Suppose the return on the market is 15 percent and there are no unsystematic surprises in the returns. What is the return on each stock? What is the return on the portfolio?

**Portfolio Risk**

12.7 You are forming an equally weighted portfolio of stocks. Many stocks have the same beta of 0.85 for factor 1 and the same beta of 1.75 for factor 2. All stocks also have the same expected return of 13 percent. Assume a two-factor model describes the return on each of these stocks.

   *a.* Write the equation of the returns on your portfolio if you place only five stocks in it.

   *b.* Write the equation of the returns on your portfolio if you place in it a very large number of stocks that all have the same expected returns and the same betas.

**Arbitrage Pricing Theory**

12.8 There are two stock markets, each driven by the same common force, $F$, with an expected value of zero and standard deviation of 10 percent. There are many securities in each market; thus, you can invest in as many stocks as you wish. Due to restrictions, however, you can invest in only one of the two markets. The expected return on every security in both markets is 10 percent.

The returns for each security, $i$, in the first market are generated by the relationship

$$R_{1i} = 0.10 + 1.5F + \varepsilon_{1i}$$

where $\varepsilon_{1i}$ is the term that measures the surprises in the returns of stock $i$ in market 1. These surprises are normally distributed; their mean is zero. The returns on security $j$ in the second market are generated by the relationship

$$R_{2j} = 0.10 + 0.5F + \varepsilon_{2j}$$

where $\varepsilon_{2j}$ is the term that measures the surprises in the returns of stock $j$ in market 2. These surprises are normally distributed; their mean is zero. The standard deviation of $\varepsilon_{1i}$ and $\varepsilon_{2j}$ for any two stocks, $i$ and $j$, is 20 percent.

   *a.* If the correlation between the surprises in the returns of any two stocks in the first market is zero, and if the correlation between the surprises in the returns of any two stocks in the second market is zero, in which market would a risk-averse person prefer to invest? (*Note:* The correlation between $\varepsilon_{1i}$ and $\varepsilon_{1j}$ for any $i$ and $j$ is zero, and the correlation between $\varepsilon_{2i}$ and $\varepsilon_{2j}$ for any $i$ and $j$ is zero.)

   *b.* If the correlation between $\varepsilon_{1i}$ and $\varepsilon_{1j}$ in the first market is 0.85 and the correlation between $\varepsilon_{2i}$ and $\varepsilon_{2j}$ in the second market is zero, in which market would a risk-averse person prefer to invest?

   *c.* If the correlation between $\varepsilon_{1i}$ and $\varepsilon_{1j}$ in the first market is zero and the correlation between $\varepsilon_{2i}$ and $\varepsilon_{2j}$ in the second market is 0.5, in which market would a risk-averse person prefer to invest?

   *d.* In general, what is the relationship between the correlations of the disturbances in the two markets that would make a risk-averse person equally willing to invest in either of the two markets?

12.9 Assume that the following market model adequately describes the return-generating behaviour of risky assets:

$$R_{it} = \alpha_i + \beta_i R_{Mt} + \varepsilon_{it}$$

Here,

   $R_{it}$ = The return on the $i$th asset at time $t$.

   $R_{Mt}$ = The return on a portfolio containing all risky assets in some proportion at time $t$.

   $R_{Mt}$ and $\varepsilon_{it}$ are statistically independent.

Short selling (i.e., negative positions) is allowed in the market. You are given the following information:

| Asset | $\beta_i$ | $E(R_i)$ | $Var(\epsilon_i)$ |
|-------|-----------|----------|-------------------|
| A | 0.7 | 8.41% | 0.0100 |
| B | 1.2 | 12.06 | 0.0144 |
| C | 1.5 | 13.95 | 0.0225 |

The variance of the market is 0.0121, and there are no transaction costs.

    *a.* Calculate the standard deviation of returns for each asset.

    *b.* Calculate the variance of return of three portfolios containing an infinite number of asset types A, B, or C, respectively.

    *c.* Assume the risk-free rate is 5 percent and the expected return on the market is 10.3 percent. Which asset will not be held by rational investors?

    *d.* What equilibrium state will emerge such that no arbitrage opportunities exist? Why?

**12.10** Assume that the returns on individual securities are generated by the following two-factor model:

$$R_{it} = E(R_{it}) + \beta_{i1}F_{1t} + \beta_{i2}F_{2t}$$

Here,

$R_{it}$ is the return on security $i$ at time $t$.

$F_{1t}$ and $F_{2t}$ are market factors with zero expectation and zero covariance.

In addition, assume that there is a capital market for four securities, and the capital market for these four securities is perfect in the sense that there are no transaction costs and short sales (i.e., negative positions) are permitted. The characteristics of the four securities follow:

| Security | $\beta_1$ | $\beta_2$ | $E(R)$ |
|----------|-----------|-----------|--------|
| 1 | 1.0 | 1.5 | 20% |
| 2 | 0.5 | 2.0 | 20 |
| 3 | 1.0 | 0.5 | 10 |
| 4 | 1.5 | 0.75 | 10 |

    *a.* Construct a portfolio containing (long or short) securities 1 and 2, with a return that does not depend on the market factor, $F_{1t}$, in any way. (*Hint:* Such a portfolio will have $\beta_1 = 0$.) Compute the expected return and $\beta_2$ coefficient for this portfolio.

    *b.* Following the procedure in (a), construct a portfolio containing securities 3 and 4 with a return that does not depend on the market factor, $F_{1t}$. Compute the expected return and $\beta_2$ coefficient for this portfolio.

    *c.* There is a risk-free asset with an expected return equal to 4.69 percent, $\beta_1 = 0$, and $\beta_2 = 0$. Describe a possible arbitrage opportunity in enough detail that an investor could implement it.

    *d.* What effect would the existence of these kinds of arbitrage opportunities have on the capital markets for these securities in the short run and long run? Graph your analysis.

# The Fama–French Multifactor Model and Mutual Fund Returns

Dawn Browne, an investment broker, has been approached by client Jack Thomas about the risk of his investments. Dawn has recently read several articles concerning the risk factors that can potentially affect asset returns, and she has decided to examine Jack's mutual fund holdings. Jack is currently invested in the Fidelity Magellan Fund (FMAGX), the Fidelity Low-Priced Stock Fund (FLPSX), and the Baron Small-Cap Fund (BSCFX).

Dawn would like to estimate the well-known multifactor model proposed by Eugene Fama and Kenneth French to determine the risk of each mutual fund. Here is the regression equation for the multifactor model she proposes to use:

$$R_{it} - R_{Ft} = \alpha_i + \beta_1(R_{Mt} - R_{Ft}) + \beta_2(SMB_t) + \beta_3(HML_t) + \varepsilon_t$$

In the regression equation, $R_{it}$ is the return on asset $i$ at time $t$, $R_{Ft}$ is the risk-free rate at time $t$, and $R_{Mt}$ is the return on the market at time $t$. Thus, the first risk factor in the Fama–French regression is the market factor often used with the CAPM.

The second risk factor, SMB, or "small minus big," is calculated by taking the difference in the returns on a portfolio of small-cap stocks and a portfolio of big-cap stocks. This factor is intended to pick up the so-called small-firm effect. Similarly, the third factor, HML, or "high minus low," is calculated by taking the difference in the returns between a portfolio of "value" stocks and a portfolio of "growth" stocks. Stocks with low M/B ratios are classified as value stocks and vice versa for growth stocks. This factor is included because of the historical tendency for value stocks to earn a higher return.

In models such as the one Dawn is considering, the alpha ($\alpha$) term is of particular interest. It is the regression intercept, but, more important, it is also the excess return the asset earned. In other words,

if the alpha is positive, the asset earned a return greater than it should have given its level of risk; if the alpha is negative, the asset earned a return lower than it should have given its level of risk. This measure is called *Jensen's alpha*, and it is a very widely used tool for mutual fund evaluation.

1. For a large-company stock mutual fund, would you expect the betas to be positive or negative for each of the factors in a Fama–French multifactor model?

2. The Fama–French factors and risk-free rates are available at Kenneth French's website: http://mba.tuck.dartmouth.edu/pages/faculty/ken.french/. Download the monthly factors and save the most recent 60 months for each factor. The historical prices for each of the mutual funds can be found on various websites, including http://finance.yahoo.com. Find the price of each mutual fund for the same time as the Fama–French factors and calculate the returns for each month. Be sure to include dividends. For each mutual fund, estimate the multifactor regression equation using the Fama–French factors. How well do the regression estimates explain the variation in the return of each mutual fund?

3. What do you observe about the beta coefficients for the different mutual funds? Comment on any similarities or differences.

4. If the market is efficient, what value would you expect for alpha? Do your estimates support market efficiency?

5. Which fund has performed best considering its risk? Why?

# Risk, Return, and Capital Budgeting

EXECUTIVE SUMMARY

Our text has devoted a number of chapters to net present value (NPV) analysis. We argued that a dollar to be received in the future is worth less than a dollar received today for two reasons. First, there is the simple time value of money argument in a risk-free world. If you have a dollar today, you can invest it in the bank and receive more than a dollar by some future date. Second, a risky dollar is worth less than a risk-free dollar. Consider a firm expecting a $1 cash flow. If actuality exceeds expectations (revenues are especially high or expenses are especially low), perhaps $1.10 or $1.20 will be received. If actuality falls short of expectations, perhaps only $0.80 or $0.90 will be received. This risk is unattractive to the typical firm.

Our work on NPV allowed us to value risk-free cash flows precisely, discounting by the risk-free interest rate. However, because most real-world cash flows in the future are risky, business demands a procedure for discounting risky cash flows. For example, Loblaw Companies Limited has complex capital budgeting decisions due to the size and diversity of projects. Loblaw and its affiliated brand, Joe Fresh, announced in February 2014 that they will extend the brand into 23 new countries spanning the Middle East, North Africa, Europe, and South Korea.[1] This endeavour is clearly risky, with many uncertainties about the outcome of the expansions. Accordingly, it would not make sense to conduct an NPV analysis using the risk-free interest rate. This chapter applies the concept of NPV to risky cash flows.

We begin by reviewing what we learned in previous chapters about NPV. We've learned that the basic NPV formula for an investment that generates incremental cash flows ($C_t$) in future periods is

$$\text{NPV} = C_0 + \sum_{t=1}^{T} \frac{C_t}{(1+r)_t}$$

For risky projects, expected incremental cash flows, $\overline{C}_t$, are placed in the numerator, and the NPV formula becomes

$$\text{NPV} = C_0 + \sum_{t=1}^{T} \frac{\overline{C}_t}{(1+r)_t}$$

The discount rate depends on three sources of capital—equity, debt, and preferred shares. Since equity is the only source that can provide 100 percent of the financing and because it is the most complex of the three, we start with the cost of equity. The costs of debt and preferred shares are considered subsequently.

In this chapter, we will show that the discount rate used to determine the NPV of a risky project can be computed from the capital asset pricing model (CAPM) or arbitrage pricing theory (APT). For example, if an all-equity firm is seeking to value a risky project, such as renovating a warehouse, the firm will determine the required return, $r_S$, on the project by using the security market line (SML). We call $r_S$ the firm's **cost of equity** capital.

When firms finance with both debt and equity, the discount rate to use is the project's overall cost of capital. The overall cost of capital is a weighted average of the cost of debt, the cost of equity, and the cost of preferred shares.

---

[1] "Joe Fresh Launches International Expansion in 23 Countries with Signing of 3 Partnership Agreements," www.loblaw.ca/English/Media-Centre/news-releases/news-release-details/2014/Joe-Fresh-Launches-International-Expansion-in-23-Countries-with-Signing-of-3-Partnership-Agreements/default.aspx, February 20, 2014.

# 13.1   THE COST OF EQUITY CAPITAL

Whenever a firm has extra cash, it can take one of two actions. It can pay out the cash immediately as a dividend or it can invest extra cash in a project, paying out the future cash flows of the project as dividends. Which procedure would the shareholders prefer? If they can reinvest the dividend in a financial asset (a stock or bond) with the same risk as that of the project, the shareholders would desire the alternative with the higher expected return. In other words, the project should be undertaken only if its expected return is greater than that of a financial asset of comparable risk. This is illustrated in Figure 13.1. A very simple capital budgeting rule follows. The discount rate of a project should be the expected return on a financial asset of comparable risk.

**FIGURE 13.1**

**Choices of a Firm with Extra Cash**

Shareholders want the firm to invest in a project only if the expected return on the project is at least as great as that of a financial asset of comparable risk.

From the firm's perspective, the expected return is the cost of equity capital. If we use the CAPM for returns, the expected return on the stock will be

$$\overline{R} = R_F + \beta \times (\overline{R}_M - R_F) \tag{13.1}$$

where $\overline{R}_M - R_F$ is the excess market return and $R_F$ is the risk-free rate.[2]

We now have the tools to estimate a firm's cost of equity capital. To do this, we need to know three things:

- The risk-free rate, $R_F$.
- The market risk premium, $\overline{R}_M - R_F$.
- The company beta, $\beta_i$.

**EXAMPLE 13.1**

Suppose the stock of the Quatram Company, a publisher of university textbooks, has a beta of 1.3. The firm is 100 percent equity financed; that is, it has no debt. Quatram is considering a number of capital budgeting projects that will double its size. Because these new projects are similar to the firm's existing ones, the average beta on the new projects is assumed to be equal to Quatram's existing beta. The market risk premium is 8.5 percent and the risk-free rate is 7 percent. What is the appropriate discount rate for these new projects?

---

[2] Of course, we can use the $k$-factor APT model (Chapter 12) and estimate several beta coefficients. However, for our purposes it is sufficient to estimate a single beta.

Now we can estimate the cost of equity, $r_S$, for Quatram as

$$r_S = 7\% + (8.5\% \times 1.3)$$
$$= 7\% + 11.05\%$$
$$= 18.05\%$$

Two key assumptions were made in this example: (1) the beta risk of the new projects is the same as the risk of the firm, and (2) the firm is all-equity financed. Given these assumptions, it follows that the cash flows of the new projects should be discounted at the 18.05 percent rate.

**EXAMPLE 13.2**

Suppose Alpha Air Freight is an all-equity firm with a beta of 1.21. Further suppose the market risk premium is 4 percent, and the risk-free rate is 6 percent. We can determine the expected return on the common stock of Alpha Air Freight by using the SML of equation (13.1). We find that the expected return is

$$6\% + (1.21 \times 4.0\%) = 10.8\%$$

Because this is the return that shareholders can expect in the financial markets on a stock with a $\beta$ of 1.21, it is the return they expect on Alpha Air Freight's stock.

Further suppose Alpha is evaluating the following independent projects:

| Project | Project's beta ($\beta$) | Project's expected cash flows next year | Project's internal rate of return | Project's net present value when cash flows are discounted at 10.8% | Accept or reject |
|---------|------|------|------|------|------|
| A | 1.21 | $140 | 40% | $26.4 | Accept |
| B | 1.21 | 120 | 20 | 8.3 | Accept |
| C | 1.21 | 109 | 9 | −1.6 | Reject |

Each project initially costs $100 and has a life of one year. All projects are assumed to have the same risk as the firm as a whole. Because the cost of equity capital is 10.8 percent, projects in an all-equity firm are discounted at this rate. Projects A and B have positive NPVs, and C will have a negative NPV. Thus, only A and B will be accepted.[3] This is illustrated in Figure 13.2.

---

[3] In addition to the SML, the dividend valuation model presented in Chapter 6 can be used to represent the firm's cost of equity capital. Using this model, the present value (PV) of the firm's expected dividend payments can be expressed as

$$P = \frac{\text{Div}_1}{(1 + r_S)} + \frac{\text{Div}_2}{(1 + r_S)^2} + \cdots + \frac{\text{Div}_N}{(1 + r_S)^N} + \cdots \qquad (a)$$

where $r_S$ is the required return of shareholders and the firm's cost of equity capital. If the dividends are expected to grow at a constant rate, $g$, equation ($a$) reduces to

$$P = \frac{\text{Div}_1}{r_S - g} \qquad (b)$$

Equation ($b$) can be reformulated as

$$r_S = \frac{\text{Div}_1}{P} + g \qquad (c)$$

We can use equation ($c$) to estimate $r_S$. $\text{Div}_1/P$ is the dividend yield expected over the next year. An estimate of the cost of equity capital is determined from an estimate of $\text{Div}_1/P$ and $g$.

Although there is considerable debate, many consider the dividend valuation model to be both less theoretically sound and more difficult to apply than the SML. Hence, examples in this chapter calculate cost of equity capital using the SML approach.

**FIGURE 13.2**

**Using the Security Market Line to Estimate the Risk-Adjusted Discount Rate for Risky Projects**

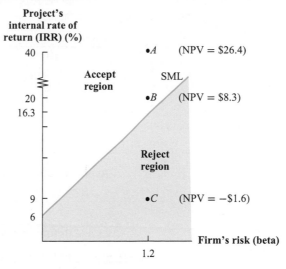

The diagonal line represents the relationship between the cost of equity capital and the firm's beta. An all-equity firm should accept an investment-type project whose IRR is greater than the cost of equity capital, and should reject an investment-type project whose IRR is less than the cost of equity capital. (The above graph assumes that all projects are as risky as the firm.)

**CONCEPT QUESTIONS**

- What choices are available to a firm when extra cash is received?
- When estimating the cost of equity for Quatram, what key assumptions were made?

# 13.2    ESTIMATION OF BETA

In the previous example we assumed that the company beta was known. Of course, beta must be estimated in the real world. We pointed out earlier that the beta of a security is the standardized covariance of a security's return with the return on the market portfolio. The formula for security $i$, first given in Chapter 11 in a slightly different form, is

$$\text{Beta of security } i = \frac{\text{Cov}(R_i,\, R_M)}{\text{Var}(R_M)} = \frac{\sigma_{i,M}}{\sigma_M^2}$$

In words, the beta is the covariance of a security with the market, divided by the variance of the market. Because we calculated both covariance and variance in earlier chapters, calculating beta involves no new material.

EXAMPLE **13.3**

**(ADVANCED)**

Suppose we sample the returns of the General Tool Company and the S&P/TSX 60 Index for four years. They are tabulated as follows:

| Year | General Tool Company $R_G$ | S&P/TSX Index $R_M$ |
|------|------|------|
| 1 | −10% | −40% |
| 2 | 3 | −30 |
| 3 | 20 | 10 |
| 4 | 15 | 20 |

We can calculate beta in six steps:

1. Calculate the average return on each asset:

   **Average Return on General Tool:**

   $$\frac{-0.10 + 0.03 + 0.20 + 0.15}{4} = 0.07 \text{ (or 7\%)}$$

   **Average Return on Market Portfolio:**

   $$\frac{-0.40 - 0.30 + 0.10 + 0.20}{4} = -0.10 \text{ (or } -10\%)$$

2. For each asset, calculate the deviation of each return from the asset's average return, determined above. This is presented in columns 3 and 5 of Table 13.1.

3. Multiply the deviation of General Tool's return by the deviation of the market's return. This is presented in column 6. This procedure is analogous to our calculation of covariance in an earlier chapter. The procedure will be used in the numerator of the beta calculation.

4. Calculate the squared deviation of the market's return. This is presented in column 7. This procedure is analogous to our calculation of variance in Chapter 10. The procedure will be used in the denominator of the beta calculation.

**TABLE 13.1**

**Calculating Beta**

| (1) Year | (2) Rate of return on General Tool ($R_G$) | (3) General Tool's deviation from average return* ($R_G - \overline{R}_G$) | (4) Rate of return on market portfolio | (5) Market portfolio's deviation from average return† ($R_M - \overline{R}_M$) | (6) Deviation of General Tool multiplied by deviation of market portfolio | (7) Squared deviation of market portfolio |
|------|------|------|------|------|------|------|
| 1 | −0.10 | −0.17 | −0.40 | −0.30 | 0.051 | 0.090 |
|   |   | (−0.10 − 0.07) |   |   | [(−0.17) × (−0.30)] | [(−0.30) × (−0.30)] |
| 2 | 0.03 | −0.04 | −0.30 | −0.20 | 0.008 | 0.040 |
| 3 | 0.20 | 0.13 | 0.10 | 0.20 | 0.026 | 0.040 |
| 4 | 0.15 | 0.08 | 0.20 | 0.30 | 0.024 | 0.090 |
|   | Avg = 0.07 |   | Avg = −0.10 |   | Sum: 0.109 | Sum: 0.260 |

Beta of General Tool: $0.419 = \frac{0.109}{0.260}$.

*Average return for General Tool is 0.07.

†Average return for market is −0.10.

5. Take the sum of column 6 and the sum of column 7. They are

**Sum of Deviation of General Tool Multiplied by Deviation of Market Portfolio:**

$$0.051 + 0.008 + 0.026 + 0.024 = 0.109$$

**Sum of Squared Deviation of Market Portfolio:**

$$0.090 + 0.040 + 0.040 + 0.090 = 0.260$$

6. The beta is the sum of column 6 divided by the sum of column 7. This is

**Beta of General Tool:**

$$0.419 = \frac{0.109}{0.260}$$

## Measuring Company Betas

The basic method of measuring company betas is to estimate

$$\frac{\text{Cov }(R_{it},\ R_{Mt})}{\text{Var}(R_{Mt})}$$

using $t = 1, 2, \ldots, T$ observations.

**Problems**

1. Betas may vary over time.
2. The sample size may be inadequate.
3. Betas are influenced by changing financial leverage and business risk.

**Solutions**

1. Problems 1 and 2 (above) can be moderated by more sophisticated statistical techniques.
2. Problem 3 can be lessened by adjusting for changes in business and financial risk.
3. Look at average beta estimates of several comparable firms in the industry.

**CONCEPT**
**QUESTIONS**

- How does one calculate the discount rate from the beta?
- What are the two key assumptions we used when calculating the discount rate?
- What are the six steps needed to calculate beta?

## Beta Estimation in Practice

The General Tool Company discussed in the previous example is fictional. It is instructive to see how betas are determined for real-world companies. Figure 13.3 plots monthly returns for four large firms against monthly returns on the S&P/TSX Composite. As mentioned in Chapter 11, each firm has its own characteristic line. The slope of the characteristic line is beta, as estimated using the technique of Table 13.1. This technique is called *regression*. Though we have not shown it in the table, one can also determine the intercept (commonly called alpha) of the characteristic line by regression. Since a line can be created from its intercept and slope, the regression allows one to estimate the characteristic line of a firm.

We use five years of monthly data for each plot. While this choice is arbitrary, it is in line with calculations performed in the real world. Practitioners know that the accuracy of the beta coefficient is suspect when too few observations are used. Conversely, since firms may change their industry over time, observations from the distant past are out of date.

The mechanics for calculating betas is quite simple. People in business frequently estimate beta by using commercially available computer programs. Certain hand-held calculators are also able to perform the calculation. In addition, a large number of services sell or even give away estimates of beta for different firms.

FIGURE 13.3

**Plots of Five Years of Monthly Returns on Four Individual Securities against Five Years of Monthly Returns of the Broad S&P/TSX Composite Index (2009–2014)**

Source: Bloomberg L.P.

We stated in Chapter 11 that the average beta across all stocks in an index is 1. Of course, this need not be true for a subset of the index. For example, of the four securities in our figure, two have betas substantially above 1, one has a beta below 1, and one has a beta approximately equal to 1. Since beta is a measure of the risk of a single security for someone holding a large, diversified portfolio, our results indicate that Teck Resources Ltd. and BlackBerry have relatively high risk, CGI Group Inc. has relatively low risk, and Bank of Montreal has average risk. A more detailed discussion of the determinants of beta is presented in Section 13.3.

## Stability of Beta

We stated above that the beta of a firm is likely to change if the firm changes its industry. It is also interesting to ask the reverse question: Does the beta of a firm stay the same if its industry stays the same?

Take the case of Imperial Oil, a large firm that for the most part has stayed in the same industries for many decades. While Imperial Oil is just one company, most analysts argue that betas are generally stable for firms remaining in the same industry. However, this is not to say that as long as a firm stays in the same industry, its beta will *never* change. Changes in product line, changes in technology, or changes in the market may affect a firm's beta. For example, the deregulation of the airline industry has increased the betas of airline firms. Furthermore, as we will show in a later section, an increase in the leverage of a firm (i.e., the amount of debt in its capital structure) will increase the firm's beta.

## Using an Industry Beta

Our approach of estimating the beta of a company from its own past data may seem commonsensical to you. However, it is frequently argued that one can better estimate a firm's beta by involving the whole industry. Consider Table 13.2, which shows the betas of some of the more prominent firms in the Canadian financial services industry. The average beta across all of the firms in the table is 0.98. Imagine a financial executive at National Bank of Canada trying to estimate the firm's beta. Because beta estimation is subject to random variation, the executive may be uncomfortable with the estimate of 0.96. However, the error in beta estimation on a single stock is much higher than the error for a portfolio of securities. This is because the error arises from unsystematic risk, which is greatly reduced in a portfolio, as we showed in Chapter 11. Thus, the executive of National Bank may use the industry beta of 0.98 as the estimate of her own firm's beta. (As it turns out, the choice is unimportant here, since the industry beta is quite close to that of the firm.)

**TABLE 13.2**

**Betas for Firms in the Financial Services Industry**

| Company | Beta |
|---|---|
| Bank of Montreal | 1.08 |
| Canadian Imperial Bank of Commerce | 0.94 |
| National Bank of Canada | 0.96 |
| TD-Canada Trust | 1.03 |
| AGF Management Ltd. | 1.66 |
| Power Financial | 1.08 |
| Fairfax Financial | 0.15 |
| Bank of Nova Scotia | 0.96 |
| Investors Group | 0.94 |
| RBC Financial Group | 0.99 |
| Equally weighted portfolio | 0.98 |

Source: www.fpinfomart.ca.

By contrast, consider Fairfax Financial. Using a risk-free rate of 2.44 percent and a risk premium of 4.46 percent, Fairfax Financial might estimate its cost of equity capital as

$$2.44\% + 0.15 \times 4.46\% = 3.11\%$$

However, if Fairfax Financial believed that the industry beta contained less estimation error, it could estimate its cost of equity capital as

$$2.44\% + 0.98 \times 4.46\% = 6.81\%$$

The difference is substantial here, perhaps presenting a difficult choice for a financial executive at Fairfax Financial.

While there is no formula for selecting the right beta, there is a very simple guideline. If one believes that the operations of the firm are similar to the operations of the rest of the industry, one should use the industry beta simply to reduce estimation error.[4] However, if an executive believes that the operations of the firm are fundamentally different from those in the rest of the industry, the firm's beta should be used.

In Canada, we often find large firms, such as Bombardier, Rogers, and Air Canada, that dominate their respective industries. For such firms, industry betas do not work well.

**CONCEPT QUESTIONS**

- What is the disadvantage of using too few observations when estimating beta?
- What is the disadvantage of using too many observations when estimating beta?
- What is the disadvantage of using the industry beta as the estimate of the beta of an individual firm?

## 13.3  DETERMINANTS OF BETA

The regression analysis approach in the previous section does not tell us where beta comes from. The beta of a stock does not come out of thin air. Rather, it is determined by the characteristics of the firm. If the firm is not traded on an exchange because it is a subsidiary of a larger firm or too small to be listed, examining these characteristics may be the best way to estimate beta.[5] We consider three factors: the cyclical nature of revenues, operating leverage, and financial leverage.

### Cyclicality of Revenues

The revenues of some firms are quite cyclical. That is, these firms do well in the expansion phase of the business cycle and poorly in the contraction phase. Empirical evidence suggests high-tech firms, retailers, and mining firms fluctuate with the business cycle. Firms in industries such as utilities and food depend less upon the cycle. Because beta is the standardized covariability of a stock's return with the market's return, it is not surprising that highly cyclical stocks have high betas.

It is worthwhile to point out that cyclicality is not the same as variability. For example, a movie studio has highly variable revenues because hits and flops are not easily predictable. However, because the revenues of a studio depend more on the quality of its releases than on the phase of the business cycle, movie companies are not particularly cyclical. In other words, stocks with high standard deviations need not have high betas, a point we have stressed before.

### Operating Leverage

We distinguished fixed costs from variable costs earlier in the text. At that time, we mentioned that fixed costs do not change as quantity changes. Conversely, variable costs increase as the quantity of output rises. This difference between variable costs and fixed costs allows us to define operating leverage.

---

[4] As we will see later, an adjustment must be made when the debt level in the industry is different from that of the firm.

[5] An interesting example occurred in the debate over the cost of equity for Teleglobe in 1991 hearings before the Canadian Radio-television and Telecommunications Commission. The debate was continued in C. S. Patterson, "The Cost of Equity Capital of a Non-Traded Unique Entity"; in L. Booth, "Estimating the Cost of Equity Capital of a Non-Traded Unique Entity"; and in C. S. Patterson, "Reply"; all in *Canadian Journal of Administrative Sciences* (June 1993).

EXAMPLE **13.4**

Consider a firm that can choose either technology *A* or technology *B* when making a particular product. The relevant differences between the two technologies are displayed below:

| Technology *A* | Technology *B* |
|---|---|
| Fixed cost: $1,000/year | Fixed cost: $2,000/year |
| Variable cost: $8/unit | Variable cost: $6/unit |
| Price: $10/unit | Price: $10/unit |
| Contribution margin: $2 (or $10 − $8) | Contribution margin: $4 (or $10 − $6) |

Technology *A* has lower fixed costs and higher variable costs than does technology *B*. Perhaps technology *A* involves less mechanization than does *B*. Or, the equipment in *A* may be leased whereas the equipment in *B* must be purchased. Alternatively, perhaps technology *A* involves few employees but many subcontractors, whereas *B* involves only highly skilled employees who must be retained in bad times. Because technology *B* has both lower variable costs and higher fixed costs, we say that it has higher **operating leverage**.[6]

Figure 13.4 graphs costs under both technologies. The slope of each total-cost line represents variable costs under a single technology. The slope of *A*'s line is steeper, indicating greater variable costs.

### FIGURE 13.4

**Costs with Two Different Technologies**

Technology *A* has higher variable costs and lower fixed costs than does technology *B*. Technology *B* has higher operating leverage.

Because the two technologies are used to produce the same products, a unit price of $10 applies for both cases. We mentioned in an earlier chapter that contribution margin is the difference between price and variable cost. It measures the incremental profit from one additional unit. The contribution margin in *B* is greater because its technology is riskier. An unexpected sale increases profit by $2 under *A* but increases profit by $4 under *B*. Similarly, an unexpected sale cancellation reduces profit by $2 under *A* but reduces profit by $4 under *B*. This is illustrated in Figure 13.5. This figure shows the change in earnings before interest and taxes (EBIT) for a given change in volume. The slope of the right-hand graph is greater, indicating that technology *B* is riskier.

---

[6] The actual definition of operating leverage is

$$\frac{\text{Change in EBIT}}{\text{EBIT}} \times \frac{\text{Sales}}{\text{Change in sales}}$$

where EBIT is earnings before interest and taxes. That is, operating leverage measures the percentage change in EBIT for a given percentage change in sales or revenues. It can be shown that operating leverage increases as fixed costs rise and as variable costs fall.

**FIGURE 13.5**

**Illustration of the Effect of a Change in Volume on the Change in Earnings before Interest and Taxes**

The cyclicality of a firm's revenues is a determinant of the firm's beta. Operating leverage magnifies the effect of cyclicality on beta. As mentioned earlier, business risk is generally defined as the risk of the firm without financial leverage. Business risk depends both on the responsiveness of the firm's revenues to the business cycle and on the firm's operating leverage.

While the above discussion concerns firms, it applies to projects as well. If one cannot estimate a project's beta in another way, one can examine the project's revenues and operating leverage. Those projects whose revenues appear strongly cyclical and whose operating leverage appears high are likely to have high betas. Conversely, weak cyclicality and low operating leverage imply low betas. As mentioned earlier, this approach is unfortunately qualitative in nature. Because start-up projects have little data, quantitative estimates of their betas generally are not feasible.

## Financial Leverage and Beta

As suggested by their names, operating leverage and financial leverage are analogous concepts. Operating leverage refers to the firm's fixed costs of *production*. Financial leverage is the extent to which a firm relies on debt. Because a levered firm must make interest payments regardless of the firm's sales, financial leverage refers to the firm's fixed costs of *finance*.

In our discussion of beta, we have been implicitly using the firm's **equity beta**. This is the beta of the common stock of the firm. Actually, a firm has an asset beta as well as an equity beta. As the name suggests, the **asset beta** is the beta of the assets of the firm. The asset beta may also be thought of as the beta of the common stock if the firm had been financed with equity only.

Imagine an individual who owns all of the firm's debt and all of its equity. In other words, this individual owns the entire firm. What is the beta of this investor's portfolio of the firm's debt and equity?

As with any portfolio, the beta of this portfolio is a weighted average of the betas of the individual items in the portfolio. Hence, we have

$$\beta_{\text{Portfolio}} = \beta_{\text{Asset}} = \frac{\text{Debt}}{\text{Debt} + \text{Equity}} \times \beta_{\text{Debt}} + \frac{\text{Equity}}{\text{Debt} + \text{Equity}} \times \beta_{\text{Equity}} \quad \textbf{(13.2)}$$

where $\beta_{\text{Equity}}$ is the beta of the equity of the *levered* firm. Notice that the beta of debt is multiplied by Debt/(Debt + Equity), the percentage of debt in the capital structure. Similarly, the beta of equity is multiplied by the percentage of equity in the capital structure. Because the portfolio is the levered firm, the beta of the portfolio is equal to the beta of the levered firm. This is what we refer to as the firm's *asset beta*.

The beta of debt is very low in practice. If we make the common assumption that the beta of debt is zero, we have

$$\beta_{Asset} = \frac{Equity}{Debt + Equity} \times \beta_{Equity} \tag{13.3}$$

Because Equity/(Debt + Equity) must be below 1 for a levered firm, it follows that $\beta_{Asset}$ < $\beta_{Equity}$. In words, the beta of the unlevered firm must be less than the beta of the equity in an otherwise identical levered firm. Rearranging the above equation, we have

$$\beta_{Equity} = \beta_{Asset}\left(1 + \frac{Debt}{Equity}\right)$$

The equity beta will always be greater than the asset beta with financial leverage. It can be shown that the relationship between a firm's asset beta and its equity beta with corporate taxes is

$$\beta_{Equity} = \beta_{Asset}\left[1 + (1 - T_c)\frac{Debt}{Equity}\right]$$

(see Chapter 18 for more details).

EXAMPLE **13.5**

Consider a tree-growing company, Rapid Cedars Inc., which is currently all equity and has a beta of 0.8. The firm has decided to move to a capital structure of one part debt to two parts equity. Because the firm is staying in the same industry, its asset beta should remain at 0.8. However, assuming a zero beta for its debt, its equity beta would become

$$\beta_{Equity} = \beta_{Asset}\left(1 + \frac{Debt}{Equity}\right)$$
$$1.2 = 0.8\left(1 + \frac{1}{2}\right)$$

If the firm had one part debt to one part equity in its capital structure, its equity beta would be

$$1.6 = 0.8(1 + 1)$$

However, as long as it stayed in the same industry, its asset beta would remain at 0.8. The effect of leverage, then, is to increase the equity beta.

**CONCEPT QUESTIONS**

- What are determinants of equity betas?
- What is the difference between an asset beta and an equity beta?

# 13.4    EXTENSIONS OF THE BASIC MODEL

### The Firm versus the Project: *Vive la différence*

We now assume that the risk of a project differs from that of the firm, while keeping the all-equity assumption. We began the chapter by pointing out that each project should be paired with a financial asset of comparable risk. If a project's beta differs from that of the firm, the project should be discounted at the rate commensurate with its own beta. This is a very important point because firms frequently speak of a *corporate discount rate.* (*Hurdle rate, cutoff rate, benchmark,* and *cost of capital* are frequently used synonymously.) Unless all projects in the corporation are of the same risk, choosing the same discount rate for all projects is incorrect.

## The Capital Structure Weights

We use the symbol $S$ (for stock) to stand for the market value of the firm's equity. We calculate this by taking the number of shares and multiplying it by the price per share. The procedure is the same for preferred shares, denoted by the symbol $P$. Similarly, we use the symbol $B$ (for bonds) to stand for the market value of the firm's debt. For long-term debt, we calculate this by multiplying the market price of a single bond by the number of bonds outstanding.

For multiple bond issues (as there normally would be), we repeat this calculation for each and then add the results. If there is debt that is not publicly traded (because it was privately placed with a life insurance company, for example), we must observe the yields on similar, publicly traded debt and estimate the market value of the privately held debt using this yield as the discount rate.

Finally, the symbol $V$ (for value) stands for the combined market value of the debt, equity, and preferred:

$$V = S + B + P$$

If we divide both sides by $V$, we can calculate the percentages of the total capital represented by the debt, equity, and preferred:

$$100\% = S/V + B/V + P/V$$

These percentages can be interpreted just like portfolio weights, and they are often called the capital structure weights.

The correct way to proceed is to use the market values of the debt and equity. We do this because the market values measure management's success in achieving its goal: maximizing shareholder wealth. Under certain circumstances, such as a privately owned company, it may not be possible to get reliable estimates of these quantities. Even for publicly traded firms, market value weights present some difficulties. If there is a major shift in stock or bond prices, market value weights may fluctuate significantly so that the WACC is quite another number by the time a weekend is over. In fact, some practitioners encounter some of these difficulties in computing WACC using market value weights; book values are usually the best alternative when market values are not readily available.

## Taxes and the Weighted Average Cost of Capital

The previous result is called the unadjusted WACC because it does not consider the impact of debt on taxes. When determining the discount rate on after-tax cash flows, the discount rate also needs to be expressed on an after-tax basis.

As discussed previously in Chapter 2, the interest paid by a corporation is deductible for tax purposes. Payments to shareholders, such as dividends paid, are not. Thus, in determining an after-tax discount rate, we need to distinguish between the pre-tax and after-tax cost of debt.

To illustrate, suppose a firm borrows $1 million at 9 percent interest. The corporate tax rate is 40 percent. What is the after-tax interest rate on this loan? The total interest bill would be $90,000 per year. This amount is tax deductible, however, so the $90,000 interest reduces our tax bill by $0.40 \times \$90,000 = \$36,000$. The after-tax interest bill is thus $\$90,000 - \$36,000 = \$54,000$. The after-tax interest rate is $54,000/$1 million = 5.4%.

Notice that the after-tax rate is simply equal to the pre-tax rate multiplied by one minus the tax rate. For example, using the preceding numbers, the after-tax interest rate is $9\% \times (1 - 0.40) = 5.4\%$.

The symbol $T_c$ is used to denote the corporate tax rate. Thus, once the effect of taxes is factored into the WACC, the equation is

$$\text{WACC} = (S/V) \times r_S + (B/V) \times r_B \times (1 - T_c) + (P/V) \times r_P \tag{13.4}$$

This WACC has a very straightforward interpretation. It is the overall return that the firm must earn on its existing assets to maintain the value of its stock. It is also the required return on any investments by the firm that have essentially the same risks as existing operations. So, if the cash flows were being evaluated from a proposed expansion of existing operations, this would be the discount rate used in the evaluation.

---

**EXAMPLE 13.7**

Consider a firm whose debt has a market value of $40 million and whose stock has a market value of $60 million (3 million outstanding shares of stock, each selling for $20 per share). The firm pays a 15 percent rate of interest on its new debt and has a beta of 1.41. The corporate tax rate is 34 percent. (Assume that the SML holds, that the risk premium on the market is 9.5 percent, and that the current Treasury bill rate is 11 percent.) What is this firm's WACC?

To compute the WACC using equation (13.4), we must know (1) the after-tax cost of debt, $r_B \times (1 - T_c)$; (2) the cost of equity, $r_S$; and (3) the proportions of debt and equity used by the firm. These three values are computed below.

1.  The pre-tax cost of debt is 15 percent, implying an after-tax cost of 9.9 percent [15% × (1 − 0.34)].

2.  The cost of equity capital is computed by using the SML:

    $$\begin{aligned}
    r_S &= R_F + \beta \times [\overline{R}_M - R_F] \\
    &= 11\% + 1.41 \times 9.5\% \\
    &= 24.40\%
    \end{aligned}$$

3.  The proportions of debt and equity are computed from the market values of debt and equity. Because the market value of the firm is $100 million ($40 million + $60 million), the proportions of debt and equity are 40 and 60 percent, respectively.

    The cost of equity, $r_S$, is 24.40 percent, and the after-tax cost of debt, $r_B \times (1 - T_c)$, is 9.9 percent. $B$ is $40 million and $S$ is $60 million. Therefore,

    $$\begin{aligned}
    \text{WACC} &= B/V \times r_B \times (1 - T_c) + S/V \times r_S \\
    &= \left(\frac{40}{100} \times 9.9\%\right) + \left(\frac{60}{100} \times 24.40\%\right) = 18.60\%
    \end{aligned}$$

This procedure is presented in chart form next:

| (1) Financing component | (2) Market value | (3) Weight | (4) Cost of capital (after corporate tax) | (5) WACC |
|---|---|---|---|---|
| Debt | $ 40,000,000 | 0.40 | 15% × (1 − 0.34) = 9.9% | 3.96% |
| Equity | 60,000,000 | 0.60 | 11% + 1.41 × 9.5% = 24.40% | 14.64 |
| | $100,000,000 | 1.00 | | 18.60% |

The weights we used in the previous example were market value weights. Market value weights are more appropriate than book value weights because the market values of the securities are closer to the actual dollars that would be received from their sale. Actually, it is useful to think in terms of "target" market weights. These are the market weights expected to prevail over the life of the firm or project.

**EXAMPLE 13.8**

Suppose that a firm has a current and a target debt-to-equity ratio of 0.6, a cost of debt of 15.15 percent, and a cost of equity of 20 percent. The corporate tax rate is 34 percent.

Our first step calls for transforming the debt-to-equity ($B/S$) ratio to a debt-to-value ratio. A $B/S$ ratio of 0.6 implies 6 parts debt for 10 parts equity. Since value is equal to the sum of the debt plus the equity, the debt-to-value ratio is $\dfrac{6}{6 + 10} = 0.375$.

Similarly, the equity-to-value ratio is $\dfrac{10}{6 + 10} = 0.625$. The WACC will then be

$$\text{WACC} = \left(\frac{S}{V}\right) \times r_S + \left(\frac{B}{V}\right) \times r_B \times (1 - T_c)$$
$$= 0.625 \times 20\% + 0.375 \times 15.15\% \times (0.66) = 16.25\%$$

Suppose the firm is considering taking on a warehouse renovation costing $50 million that is expected to yield cost savings of $12 million a year for six years. Using the NPV equation and discounting the six years of expected cash flows from the renovation at the WACC, we have[7]

$$\text{NPV} = -\$50 + \frac{\$12}{(1 + \text{WACC})} + \cdots + \frac{\$12}{(1 + \text{WACC})^6}$$
$$= -\$50 + \$12 \times A^6_{0.1625}$$
$$= -\$50 + (12 \times 3.66)$$
$$= -\$6.07$$

Should the firm take on the warehouse renovation? The project has a negative NPV using the firm's WACC. This means that the financial markets offer superior projects in the same risk class (namely, the firm's risk class). The answer is clear: the firm should reject the project.

***CONCEPT QUESTIONS***
- What is the relationship between the firm's cost of capital and the SML?
- When calculating a firm's WACC, why are market value weights more appropriate than book value weights?

**EXAMPLE 13.9**

Suppose the telephone company Canada Telecom is planning to invest in projects in multimedia applications. The company's debt-to-equity ratio is 0.45. The following information was obtained about other companies related to the multimedia business:

| Company | Equity beta | Debt-to-equity |
|---------|-------------|----------------|
| A | 1.30 | 0.65 |
| B | 1.10 | 1.25 |
| C | 1.05 | 1.40 |
| D | 1.00 | 0.50 |

---

[7] This discussion of WACC has been implicitly based on perpetual cash flows. However, an important paper by J. Miles and R. Ezzel, "The Weighted Average Cost of Capital, Perfect Capital Markets and Project Life: A Clarification," *Journal of Financial and Quantitative Analysis* (September 1980), shows that the WACC is appropriate even when cash flows are not perpetual.

Obtaining asset betas for comparable firms ($T_c = 40\%$), we have the following:

| Company | Equity beta | Debt-to-equity | Asset beta |
|:-------:|:-----------:|:--------------:|:----------:|
| A | 1.30 | 0.65 | 0.94 |
| B | 1.10 | 1.25 | 0.63 |
| C | 1.05 | 1.40 | 0.57 |
| D | 1.00 | 0.50 | 0.77 |

The asset betas are calculated using the equation

$$\beta_{Asset} = Equity/(Debt(1 - T_c) + Equity) \times \beta_{Equity}$$

Using the average asset beta (0.73) of the comparable multimedia firms, we can use Canada Telecom's debt-to-equity ratio to obtain equity beta as follows:

$$\beta_{Equity} = 0.73(1 + (1 - 0.40)0.45) = 0.93$$

We use Canada Telecom's debt-to-equity ratio because multimedia applications appear to be similar to the company's core business. If this is not the case, we should adjust the debt-to-equity ratio.

## EXAMPLE 13.10

**Firm Valuation with $R_{WACC}$** When valuing a complete business enterprise, our approach is the same as the one used for individual capital projects like the warehouse renovation, except that we use a horizon. Specifically, we use the firm's WACC as our discount rate, and we set up the usual discounted cash flow model by forecasting the firm's entire net cash flow up to a horizon along with a terminal value of the firm (TV):

$$PV_0 = \frac{CF_1}{1 + R_{WACC}} + \frac{CF_2}{(1 + R_{WACC})^2} + \frac{CF_3}{(1 + R_{WACC})^3} + \cdots + CF_T + \frac{TV}{(1 + R_{WACC})^T}$$

Here we assume a constant perpetual growth rate for cash flows beyond the horizon, $T$, so that

$$TV_T = \frac{CF_{T+1}}{R_{WACC} - G_{CF}} = \frac{CF_T(1 + G_{CF})}{R_{WACC} - G_{CF}}$$

where $CF$ is the net cash flows, $G_{CF}$ is the growth rate of cash flow beyond $T$, and $R_{WACC}$ is the WACC.

Consider Maple Dining Corporation, a public company headquartered in Vancouver, British Columbia, with 500 restaurants in 50 countries. Maple Dining serves a premium menu focused on freshly caught seafood. The company has $500 million in market-valued debt and $250 million in market-valued common stocks. Its tax rate is 20 percent. Maple Dining has estimated its cost of debt as 5 percent and its cost of equity as 10 percent. Its WACC is equal to the following:

| Financial component | Market value | Weight | Cost of capital | Weighted average |
|:--------------------|:------------:|:------:|:---------------:|:----------------:|
| Debt | $500 million | 0.67 | 5%(1 − 0.2) = 4% | 67% × 4% |
| Equity | $250 million | 0.33 | 10% | 33% × 10% |
| | $750 million | | | 6% = WACC |

Maple Dining is seeking to grow by acquisition of Exquisite Dishes, a private firm and direct competitor. It operates 200 restaurants mostly in North America and Europe with $400 million in debt outstanding (market and book values are the same) and 1 million shares outstanding. Exquisite Dishes expects its EBIT to grow 10 percent a year for the next five years. Increases in net working capital and capital spending are both expected to be 24 percent of EBIT. Depreciation will be 8 percent of EBIT. The perpetual growth rate in cash flow after five years is estimated to be 2 percent.

If Maple Dining acquires Exquisite Dishes, Maple Dining analysts estimate the net cash flows from Exquisite Dishes (in $ millions) will be (rounded to one decimal) as follows:

| Year | 1 | 2 | 3 | 4 | 5 |
|---|---|---|---|---|---|
| Earnings before interest and taxes | 50 | 55 | 60.5 | 66.6 | 73.2 |
| Less: taxes (20%) | 10 | 11 | 12.1 | 13.3 | 14.6 |
| Earnings after taxes | 40 | 44 | 48.4 | 53.3 | 58.6 |
| Add: depreciation | 4 | 4.4 | 4.8 | 5.3 | 5.9 |
| Less: capital spending | 12 | 13.2 | 14.5 | 16.0 | 17.6 |
| Increases in net working capital | 12 | 13.2 | 14.5 | 16.0 | 17.6 |
| Net cash flows (CF) | 20 | 22 | 24.2 | 26.6 | 29.3 |

We start our calculations by computing a terminal value of Exquisite Dishes as

$$TV_5 = \frac{\$29.3(1.02)}{0.06 - 0.02} = \$747.15$$

Next we compute the PV of Exquisite Dishes to be

$$PV_0 = \frac{20}{1.06} + \frac{22}{(1.06)^2} + \frac{24.2}{(1.06)^3} + \frac{26.6}{(1.06)^4} + \frac{29.3}{(1.06)^5} + \frac{747.15}{(1.06)^5} = \$660.04$$

To find the value of equity, we subtract the value of debt, which gives us $660.04 − $400 = $260.04. To find the equity value per share, we divide the value of equity by the number of shares outstanding: $260.04/1 = $260.04. Maple Dining will find Exquisite Dishes an attractive acquisition if it can purchase it for less than $260.04 per share.

Students should note that in this example we have assumed Exquisite Dishes is a pure play for Maple Dining. Our WACC method only works if Exquisite Dishes has the same business risk as Maple Dining and the debt-to-equity ratio will remain the same.

An alternative method applies the same discounted cash flows using WACC, but instead of estimating the terminal value with a growing perpetuity after the time horizon, $T$, the analyst calculates terminal value via an EBITDA multiple (EV/EBITDA). For example, suppose the EV/EBITDA multiple for comparable firms in the food service industry is 10. The EBITDA for Exquisite Dishes in year 5 will be equal to EBIT + depreciation or $79.1 ($73.2 + $5.9). Using the multiple of 10, the value of Exquisite Dishes in year 5 can be estimated as $791. The PV of the company is then

$$PV_0 = \frac{20}{1.06} + \frac{22}{(1.06)^2} + \frac{24.2}{(1.06)^3} + \frac{26.6}{(1.06)^4} + \frac{29.3}{(1.06)^5} + \frac{791}{(1.06)^5} = \$692.81$$

The value of the equity of Exquisite Dishes can be estimated as

PV (of entire firm) less debt = $692.81 − $400 = $292.81

With 1 million shares outstanding, the value of a share of equity is

$292.81/1 = $292.81

Notice how the two values differ depending on how we calculated the terminal value. Using the constant-growth discounted cash flow method for terminal value, our estimate of equity value per share was $260.04. Using the EV/EBITDA multiple, our estimate was $292.81. There is no perfect method. If the comparable firms were all identical to Exquisite Meals, perhaps the EV/EBITDA method would be best. Unfortunately, firms are not identical. On the other hand, if we were very sure of the terminal date and the growth in subsequent cash flows, perhaps the constant-growth method would be best. Both methods are commonly used.

## 13.5 ESTIMATING THE COST OF CAPITAL FOR SUNCOR ENERGY

We will illustrate the practical application of the WACC by calculating it for Suncor Energy Inc. Suncor is an integrated energy company focused on developing Canada's Athabasca oil sands. The company has three operating segments: oil sands, natural gas, and refining and marketing. The company also invests in renewable energy opportunities, partnering in four wind power projects and operating an ethanol plant. It also explores for, acquires, develops, produces, and markets crude oil and natural gas; transports and refines crude oil; and markets petroleum and petrochemical products. In this application, market values for Suncor were observed as of March 5, 2014, and we calculate the WACC for that day.[8]

Complications and compromises arise in applying formulas in practice. As a cross-listed company, Suncor does business in a number of currencies and across many borders; its financing reflects its multinational nature. Ideally, we should calculate the market value of all sources of financing and determine the relative weights of each source. If any difficulties arise in finding the market value of some non-traded bonds for Suncor, we will need to use book values for debt.[9]

A related issue is the degree of precision we can attach to our measures of the cost of capital. Although we will do the computation carrying two decimal points, in reality our estimates are not that precise. When we use the final answer in capital budgeting, sensitivity analysis is highly recommended.

To find the market value weight of equity, we start by finding the total market value of all common stock. The market values are calculated as the number of shares times the share price. The figures for Suncor as of March 5, 2014, were 1,478,659,000 common shares. Multiplying by its price gives the following:

---

[8] Information comes from www.fpinfomart.ca, www.finance.yahoo.com, and Bloomberg. When calculating the cost of capital, it is common to ignore short-term financing, such as payables and accruals. We also ignore short-term debt unless it is a permanent source of financing. For simplicity, leases are not included in long-term debt for this analysis.

[9] It is more important to use the market value for the calculation of equity weights than the calculation of debt weights, as the market value of common equity may differ markedly from its book value. For Suncor, we were fortunate to have access to the market values of the bonds through Bloomberg. Table 13.3 displays a complete list of all 15 bonds that Suncor has outstanding in addition to the amount outstanding, the weights, and the weighted average cost of debt. Some of the yields to maturity were estimated (as indicated) because the information was not present on the Bloomberg Financial Services program. This information enables us to use the market values instead of the book values, which helps to calculate a more applicable cost of debt.

| Security | Shares outstanding (millions) | Market price ($) | Market value (in $ millions) |
|---|---|---|---|
| Common shares | 1,478.659 | 36.33 | 53,719.68 |

To calculate the weighted average cost of debt, we take the percentage of the total debt represented by each issue and multiply by the yield on the issue. We then add to get the overall weighted average debt cost. We use both book values and market values here for comparison. These calculations are shown in Table 13.3.

The purpose of calculating the weighted average cost of debt is to estimate the future cost of debt. Using the amount of debt outstanding calculated in Table 13.3, the relative weighting of the debt and the equity is as follows:

| Security | Market value (in $ millions) | Weight (%) |
|---|---|---|
| Debt | 10,820.31 | 16.77 |
| Equity | 53,719.68 | 83.23 |
| | 64,539.99 | 100 |

As you can see from the weights, Suncor uses common equity for 83.23 percent of its financing needs. Note that the calculation is simplified as both classes of common stock are combined.

As the table shows, Suncor's cost of debt is 3.9 percent on a book value basis and 3.95 percent on a market value basis. This explains why companies frequently use book values for debt in WACC calculations—the differences between book and market value of debt are minuscule. We will, however, use market values in our calculations since they are available to us.

## TABLE 13.3

### Weighted Average Cost of Debt for Suncor Energy Inc.

| Coupon rate | Maturity | Book value (in $ millions) | Percentage of total | Price (as % of par) | Market value (in $ millions) | Percentage of total | Yield to maturity | Book value weights | Market value weights |
|---|---|---|---|---|---|---|---|---|---|
| 6.85% | 2039 | $ 750 | 8.264% | 128.419% | $ 963.14 | 8.901% | 4.879% | 0.40% | 0.43% |
| 6.8 | 2038 | 900 | 9.917 | 125.841 | 1,132.57 | 10.467 | 4.958 | 0.49 | 0.52 |
| 6.5 | 2038 | 1,150 | 12.672 | 120.97 | 1,391.16 | 12.857 | 4.998 | 0.63 | 0.64 |
| 5.95 | 2035 | 600 | 6.612 | 114.424 | 686.54 | 6.345 | 4.852 | 0.32 | 0.31 |
| 5.95 | 2034 | 500 | 5.510 | 115.287 | 576.44 | 5.327 | 4.778 | 0.26 | 0.25 |
| 5.35 | 2033 | 300 | 3.306 | 107.405 | 322.22 | 2.978 | 4.760 | 0.16 | 0.14 |
| 7.15 | 2032 | 500 | 5.510 | 130.481 | 652.41 | 6.029 | 4.626 | 0.25 | 0.28 |
| 6.1 | 2018 | 1,250 | 13.774 | 116.227 | 1,452.84 | 13.427 | 2.066 | 0.28 | 0.28 |
| 6.05 | 2018 | 600 | 6.612 | 115.633 | 693.80 | 6.412 | 2.122 | 0.14 | 0.14 |
| 5 | 2014 | 400 | 4.408 | 102.245 | 408.98 | 3.780 | 1.665 | 0.07 | 0.06 |
| 7 | 2028 | 250 | 2.755 | 126.043 | 315.11 | 2.912 | 4.548 | 0.13 | 0.13 |
| 7.875 | 2026 | 275 | 3.030 | 133.235 | 366.40 | 3.386 | 4.351 | 0.13 | 0.15 |
| 9.25 | 2021 | 300 | 3.306 | 135.631 | 406.89 | 3.760 | 3.803 | 0.13 | 0.14 |
| 5.39 | 2037 | 600 | 6.612 | 109.867 | 659.20 | 6.092 | 4.868 | 0.32 | 0.30 |
| 5.8 | 2018 | 700 | 7.713 | 113.233 | 792.63 | 7.325 | 2.464 | 0.19 | 0.18 |
| | | $9,075 | 100.00% | | $10,820.31 | 100.00% | | 3.90% | 3.95% |

Source: Data drawn from Bloomberg and Suncor 2013 annual report.

The before-tax cost of debt is an estimate of what it would cost Suncor to issue long-term debt today. To convert to an after-tax cost, we use the average tax rate for Suncor during 2013–2014 of 38.66 percent:

$$r_B \times (1 - T_c) = 3.95\%(1 - 0.3866) = 2.42\%$$

To determine the cost of common stock for Suncor, we use the CAPM and the firm beta, as Suncor is unique in Canada:

$$\beta = 1.65^{[10]}$$
$$\text{Market risk premium} = 4.46\%^{[11]}$$
$$\text{Risk-free rate} = 3.44\%^{[12]}$$

$$r_S = r_F + \beta(\text{market risk premium})$$
$$= 3.44\% + 1.65 \times (4.46\%)$$
$$= 10.8\%$$

To find the WACC, we weight the cost of each source:

$$\text{WACC} = \frac{S}{V} \times r_S + \frac{B}{V} \times r_B \times (1 - T_c)$$
$$\text{WACC} = 0.8323 \times 10.8\% + 0.1677 \times 2.42\%$$
$$\text{WACC} = 9.39\%$$

 **CONCEPT QUESTION**

- What compromises are necessary in computing WACC for Suncor?

## 13.6  FLOTATION COSTS AND THE WEIGHTED AVERAGE COST OF CAPITAL

So far, we have not included issue costs in our discussion of the WACC. When projects are funded by stocks and bonds, the firm will incur these costs, which are commonly called *flotation costs*.

Sometimes it is suggested that the firm's WACC should be adjusted upward to reflect flotation costs. This is really not the best approach because the required return on an investment depends on the risk of the investment, not the source of the funds. This is not to say that flotation costs should be ignored. Since these costs arise as a consequence of the decision to undertake a project, they are relevant cash flows. We therefore briefly discuss how to include them in project analysis.

### The Basic Approach

We start with a simple case. The Spatt Company, an all-equity firm, has a cost of equity of 20 percent. Because this firm is 100 percent equity, its WACC and its cost of equity are the same. Spatt is contemplating a large-scale $100 million expansion of its existing operations. The expansion would be funded by selling new stock.

---

[10] From www.fpinfomart.ca.

[11] This is the weighted average of the geometric and arithmetic risk premiums from Chapter 10 for the period 1957 through 2013. Blume's formula, found in Chapter 10, is used to calculate the average for a 10-year forecast horizon using 57 years of past data.

[12] This is the Government of Canada 10-year benchmark bond yield from www.bankofcanada.ca plus an adjustment. The 10-year benchmark bond yield is used because we are assuming that the new project will be long term, having approximately a 10-year life span. In a situation like this, we want to match the project length to that of the appropriate risk-free rate. Further, we add an adjustment of 1.00% to the risk-free rate to reflect the distorting impact of current monetary policy, which is keeping rates artificially low.

Based on conversations with its investment banker, Spatt believes its flotation costs will run 10 percent of the amount issued. This means that Spatt's proceeds from the equity sale will be only 90 percent of the amount sold. When flotation costs are considered, what is the cost of the expansion?

Spatt needs to sell enough equity to raise $100 million *after* covering the flotation costs. In other words

$$\$100 \text{ million} = (1 - 0.10) \times \text{Amount raised}$$
$$\text{Amount raised} = \$100 \text{ million}/0.90 = \$111.11 \text{ million}$$

Spatt's flotation costs are thus $11.11 million, and the true cost of the expansion is $111.11 million, including flotation costs.

Things are only slightly more complicated if the firm uses both debt and equity. For example, suppose Spatt's target capital structure is 60 percent equity, 40 percent debt. The flotation costs associated with equity are still 10 percent, but the flotation costs for debt are less—say, 5 percent.

Earlier, when we had different capital costs for debt and equity, we calculated a WACC using the target capital structure weights. Here, we will do much the same thing. We can calculate an overall or weighted average flotation cost, $f_o$, by multiplying the flotation cost for stock, $f_S$, by the percentage of stock ($S/V$) and the flotation cost for bonds, $f_B$, by the percentage of bonds ($B/V$) and then adding the two together:

$$\begin{aligned} f_o &= (S/V) \times f_S + (B/V) \times f_B \\ &= 60\% \times 0.10 + 40\% \times 0.05 \\ &= 8\% \end{aligned} \qquad (13.5)$$

The weighted average flotation cost is thus 8 percent. What this tells us is that for every dollar in outside financing needed for new projects, the firm must actually raise $1/(1 − 0.08) = $1.087. In our example, the project cost is $100 million when we ignore flotation costs. If we include them, then the true cost is $100 million/$(1 − f_o)$ = $100 million/0.92 = $108.7 million.

In taking issue costs into account, the firm must be careful not to use the wrong weights. The firm should use the target weights, even if it can finance the entire cost of the project with either debt or equity. The fact that a firm can finance a specific project with debt or equity is not directly relevant. If a firm has a target debt-to-equity ratio of 1, for example, but chooses to finance a particular project with all debt, it will have to raise additional equity later on to maintain its target debt-to-equity ratio. To take this into account, the firm should always use the target weights in calculating the flotation cost.

---

**EXAMPLE 13.11**

The Weinstein Corporation has a target capital structure of 80 percent equity and 20 percent debt. The flotation costs for equity issues are 20 percent of the amount raised; the flotation costs for debt issues are 6 percent. If Weinstein needs $65 million for a new manufacturing facility, what is the true cost including flotation costs?

We first calculate the weighted average flotation cost, $f_o$:

$$\begin{aligned} f_o &= S/V \times f_S + B/V \times f_B \\ &= 80\% \times 0.20 + 20\% \times 0.06 \\ &= 17.2\% \end{aligned}$$

The weighted average flotation cost is 17.2 percent. The project cost is $65 million without flotation costs. If we include them, then the true cost is $65 million/$(1 − f_o)$ = $65 million/0.828 = $78.5 million, again illustrating that flotation costs can be a considerable expense.

## Flotation Costs and Net Present Value

To illustrate how flotation costs can be included in an NPV analysis, suppose the Tripleday Printing Company is currently at its target debt-to-equity ratio of 100 percent. It is considering building a new $500,000 printing plant in Nova Scotia. This new plant is expected to generate after-tax cash flows of $73,150 per year, forever. The tax rate is 34 percent. There are two financing options:

1. A $500,000 new issue of common stock. The issuance costs of the new common stock would be about 10 percent of the amount raised. The required return on the company's new equity is 20 percent.

2. A $500,000 issue of 30-year bonds. The issuance costs of the new debt would be 2 percent of the proceeds. The company can raise new debt at 10 percent.

What is the NPV of the new printing plant?

To begin, since printing is the company's main line of business, we will use the company's WACC to value the new printing plant:

$$
\begin{aligned}
\text{WACC} &= S/V \times R_S + B/V \times R_B \times (1 - T_c) \\
&= 0.50 \times 20\% + 0.50 \times 10\% \times (1 - 0.34) \\
&= 13.3\%
\end{aligned}
$$

Because the cash flows are $73,150 per year, forever, the PV of the cash flows at 13.3 percent per year is

$$
\text{PV} = \frac{\$73,150}{0.133} = \$550,000
$$

If we ignore flotation costs, the NPV is

$$
\text{NPV} = \$550,000 - \$500,000 = \$50,000
$$

With no flotation costs, the project generates an NPV that is greater than zero, so it should be accepted.

What about financing arrangements and issue costs? Because new financing must be raised, the flotation costs are relevant. From the information given, we know that the flotation costs are 2 percent for debt and 10 percent for equity. Because Tripleday uses equal amounts of debt and equity, the weighted average flotation cost, $f_o$, is

$$
\begin{aligned}
f_o &= S/V \times f_S + B/V \times f_B \\
&= 0.50 \times 10\% + 0.50 \times 2\% \\
&= 6\%
\end{aligned}
$$

Remember, the fact that Tripleday can finance the project with all debt or all equity is irrelevant. Since Tripleday needs $500,000 to fund the new plant, the true cost, once we include flotation costs, is $500,000/(1 − $f_o$) = $500,000/0.94 = $531,915. Because the PV of the cash flows is $550,000, the plant has an NPV of $550,000 − $531,915 = $18,085, so it is still a good investment. However, its value is less than we initially might have thought.

## Internal Equity and Flotation Costs

Our discussion of flotation costs to this point implicitly assumes that firms always have to raise the capital needed for new investments. In reality, most firms rarely sell equity at all. Instead, their internally generated cash flow is sufficient to cover the equity portion of their capital spending. Only the debt portion must be raised externally.

The use of internal equity doesn't change our approach. However, we now assign a value of zero to the flotation cost of equity because there is no such cost. In our Tripleday example, the weighted average flotation cost would therefore be

$$f_o = S/V \times f_S + B/V \times f_B$$
$$= 0.50 \times 0\% + 0.50 \times 2\%$$
$$= 1\%$$

Notice that whether equity is generated internally or externally makes a big difference, because external equity has a relatively high flotation cost.

# 13.7   REDUCING THE COST OF CAPITAL

Chapters 10 through 13 develop the idea that both the expected return on a stock and the cost of capital of the firm are positively related to risk. A number of academics have argued that expected return and cost of capital are negatively related to liquidity as well.[13] In addition, these scholars make the interesting point that although it is quite difficult to lower the risk of a firm, it is much easier to increase the liquidity of the firm's stock. Therefore, they suggest that a firm can actually lower its cost of capital through liquidity enhancement. We develop this idea next.

## What Is Liquidity?

Anyone who owns his or her own home probably thinks of liquidity in terms of the time it takes to buy or sell the home. For example, condominiums in large metropolitan areas are generally quite liquid. Particularly in good times, a condominium may sell within days of being placed on the market. By contrast, single-family homes in suburban areas may take weeks or months to sell. Special properties, such as multimillion dollar "executive homes," may take longer still.

The concept of liquidity is similar, but not identical, in stocks. Here, we speak of the *cost* of buying and selling instead. That is, those stocks that are expensive to trade are considered less liquid than those that trade cheaply. What do we mean by the cost to trade? We generally think of three costs here: brokerage fees, the bid–ask spread, and market impact costs.

Brokerage fees are the easiest to understand, because you must pay a broker to execute a trade. More difficult is the bid–ask spread. Consider the New York Stock Exchange (NYSE), where all trades on a particular stock must go through the stock's specialist, who is physically on the floor of the exchange.[14] If you want to trade 100 shares of XYZ Co., your broker must get the *quote* from XYZ's specialist. Suppose the specialist provides a quote of 100–100.07. This means that you can buy from the specialist at $100.07 per share and sell to the specialist at $100 per share. Note that the specialist makes money here, since she buys from you at $100 and sells to you (or to someone else) at $100.07. The gain to the specialist is a cost to you, because you are losing $0.07 per share over a round-trip transaction (over a purchase and a subsequent sale).

Finally, we have *market impact costs*. Suppose that a trader wants to sell 10,000 shares instead of just 100 shares. Here, the specialist has to take on extra risk when buying. First, she has to pay out $100,000 (10,000 × $100), cash that may not be easily available to her. Second, the trader may be selling this large amount because he has special information that the stock will fall imminently. The specialist bears the risk of

---

[13] For example, see Y. Amihud and H. Mendelson, "The Liquidity Route to a Lower Cost of Capital," *Journal of Applied Corporate Finance* (Winter 2000); M. J. Brennan and C. Tamarowski, "Investor Relations, Liquidity, and Stock Prices," *Journal of Applied Corporate Finance* (Winter 2000); and G. Jacoby, D. J. Fowler, and A. A. Gottesman, "The Capital Asset Pricing Model and the Liquidity Effect: A Theoretical Approach," *Journal of Financial Markets* 3 (2000).

[14] On the Toronto Stock Exchange, trading is fully automated and there are no specialists. The issue of order execution remains an important one, as shown in L. Kryzanowski, "Trade Costs and Investment Performance," *Canadian Investment Review* (Summer 2001).

losing a lot of money on that trade. Consequently, to compensate for these risks, the specialist may not buy at $100/share but at a lower price. Similarly, the specialist may be willing to sell a large block of stock only at a price above $100.07. The price drop associated with a large sale and the price rise associated with a large purchase are the market impact costs.

## Liquidity, Expected Returns, and the Cost of Capital

The cost of trading an illiquid stock reduces the total return that an investor receives. That is, if one buys a stock for $100 and sells it later for $105, the gain before trading costs is $5. If one must pay a dollar of commission when buying and another dollar when selling, the gain after trading costs is only $3. Both the bid–ask spread and market impact costs would reduce this gain still further.

As we will see later, trading costs vary across securities. In the last four chapters, we have stressed that investors demand a high expected return as compensation when investing in high-risk (e.g., high-beta) stocks. Because the expected return to the investor is the cost of capital to the firm, the cost of capital is positively related to beta. Now, we are saying the same thing for trading costs. Investors demand a high expected return when investing in stocks with high trading costs (i.e., low liquidity). And, this high expected return implies a high cost of capital to the firm. This idea is illustrated in Figure 13.7.

FIGURE 13.7

**Liquidity and the Cost of Capital**

An increase in liquidity, i.e., a reduction in trading costs, lowers a firm's cost of capital.

## Liquidity and Adverse Selection

Liquidity varies across stocks, because the factors determining liquidity vary across stocks. Although there are a number of factors, we focus on just one, *adverse selection*. As mentioned before, the specialist will lose money on a trade if the trader has information that the specialist does not have. If you have special information that the stock is worth $110 in the preceding example, you will want to buy shares at $100.07. The specialist is obliged to sell to you at this price, which is considerably below the true price of $110. Conversely, if you know that the stock is worth only $90 and you currently own 100 shares, you will be happy to sell these shares to the specialist at $100. Again, the specialist loses, since she pays $100/share for a stock worth only $90. In either of these cases, we say that the specialist has been *picked off*, or has been subject to adverse selection.

The specialist must protect herself in some way here. Of course, she cannot forbid informed individuals from trading, because she does not know ahead of time who these investors are. Her next best alternative is to widen the bid–ask spread, thereby increasing the costs of trading to *all* traders—both informed and uninformed. That is, if the spread is widened to, say, 99.98–100.11, each trader pays a round-trip cost of $0.13 per share.

The key here is that the spread should be positively related to the ratio of informed to uninformed traders. That is, informed traders will pick off the specialist and uninformed traders will not. Thus, informed traders in a stock raise the required return on equity, thereby increasing the cost of capital.

### What the Corporation Can Do

The corporation has an incentive to lower trading costs because—given the preceding discussion—a lower cost of capital should result. Amihud and Mendelson (see footnote 13) identify two general strategies for corporations. First, they argue that firms should try to bring in more uninformed investors. Stock splits may be a useful tool here, and we discuss these in Chapter 19. Companies can also attract small investors by facilitating stock purchases through the Internet. Direct stock purchase plans and dividend reinvestment programs handled online give small investors the opportunity to buy securities cheaply.

Second, companies can disclose more information. This narrows the gap between uninformed and informed investors, thereby lowering the cost of capital. Suggestions include providing greater financial data on corporate segments and more management forecasts. An interesting study by Coller and Yohn concludes that the bid–ask spread is reduced after the release of these forecasts.[15]

This section would not be complete without a discussion of security analysts. These analysts are employed by brokerage houses to follow the companies in individual industries. For example, an analyst for a particular brokerage house might follow all the firms in, say, the transportation industry. This analyst distributes reports and other information to the clients of the brokerage house. Virtually all brokerage houses have analysts following the major industries. Again, through dissemination of the information, these analysts narrow the gap between the informed and the uninformed investors, thereby tending to reduce the bid–ask spread.

Although all major industries are covered, the smaller firms in these industries are often ignored, implying a higher bid–ask spread and a higher cost of capital for these firms. Analysts frequently state that they avoid following companies that release little information, pointing out that these companies are more trouble than they are worth. Thus, it behooves companies that are not followed to release as much information as possible to security analysts in the hopes of attracting their interest. Friendliness toward security analysts is very helpful as well. The argument here is not to get the analysts to make buy recommendations. Rather, it is simply to interest the analysts in following the company, thereby reducing the information asymmetry between informed and uninformed investors.

**CONCEPT QUESTIONS**

- What is liquidity?
- What is the relation between liquidity and expected returns?
- What is adverse selection?
- What can a corporation do to lower its cost of capital?

---

[15] M. Coller and T. Yohn, "Management Forecasts and Information Asymmetry: An Examination of Bid-Ask Spreads," *Journal of Accounting Research* (Fall 1997).

**13.8**

# SUMMARY AND CONCLUSIONS

Earlier chapters on capital budgeting assumed that projects generate risk-free cash flows. The appropriate discount rate in those cases is the risk-free interest rate. Of course, most cash flows from real-world capital budgeting projects are risky. This chapter discusses the discount rate when cash flows are risky.

1. A firm with excess cash can either pay a dividend or make a capital expenditure. Because shareholders can reinvest the dividend in risky financial assets, the expected return on a capital budgeting project should be at least as great as the expected return on a financial asset of comparable risk.

2. The expected return on any asset depends upon its beta. Thus, we showed how to estimate the beta of a stock. The appropriate procedure employs regression analysis on historical returns.

3. We considered the case of a project whose beta risk was equal to that of the firm. If the firm is unlevered, the discount rate on the project is equal to

$$R_F + \beta \times (\overline{R}_M - R_F)$$

where $\overline{R}_M$ is the expected return on the market portfolio and $R_F$ is the risk-free rate. In words, the discount rate on the project is equal to the capital asset pricing model's (CAPM's) estimate of the expected return on the security.

4. If the project's beta differs from that of the firm, the discount rate should be based on the project's beta. The project's beta can sometimes be estimated by determining the average beta of the project's industry.

5. The beta of a company is a function of a number of factors. Perhaps the three most important are
   • Cyclicality of revenues.
   • Operating leverage.
   • Financial leverage.

6. Sometimes one should not use the average beta of the project's industry as an estimate of the beta of the project. In this case, one can estimate the project's beta by considering the project's cyclicality of revenues and its operating leverage. This approach is qualitative in nature.

7. If a firm uses debt, the discount rate to use is $r_{WACC}$. In order to calculate $r_{WACC}$, the cost of equity and the cost of debt applicable to a project must be estimated. Assuming a scale-enhancing project, the cost of equity can be estimated using the security market line (SML) for the firm's equity. Conceptually, a dividend growth model could be used as well, though it is likely to be far less accurate in practice. In Chapter 18, three well-known approaches for incorporating debt are presented.

8. A number of academics have argued that expected returns are negatively related to liquidity, where high liquidity is equivalent to low costs of trading. These scholars have further suggested that firms can reduce their cost of capital by lowering these trading costs. Practical suggestions include stock splits, more complete dissemination of information, and more effective assistance to security analysts.

**KEY TERMS**

| | | |
|---|---|---|
| Asset beta  382 | Equity beta  382 | Weighted average cost of |
| Cost of equity  372 | Operating leverage  381 | capital (WACC)  385 |

**Calculating Cost of Equity**

13.1 The Dybvig Corporation's common stock has a beta of 1.21. If the risk-free rate is 3.5 percent and the expected return on the market is 11 percent, what is Dybvig's cost of equity capital?

13.2 The Devon Co. just issued a dividend of $2.35 per share on its common stock. The company is expected to maintain a constant 5 percent growth rate in its dividends—indefinitely. If the stock sells for $52 a share, what is the company's cost of equity?

13.3 Stock in Country Road Industries has a beta of 0.85. The market risk premium is 8 percent, and T-bills are currently yielding 5 percent. The company's most recent dividend was $1.60 per share, and dividends are expected to grow at a 6 percent annual rate indefinitely. If the stock sells for $37 per share, what is your best estimate of the company's cost of equity?

**Calculating Cost of Debt**

13.4 Advance Inc. is trying to determine its cost of debt. The firm has a debt issue outstanding with 17 years to maturity that is quoted at 95 percent of face value. The issue makes semiannual payments and has a coupon rate of 8 percent annually. What is Advance's pre-tax cost of debt? If the tax rate is 35 percent, what is the after-tax cost of debt?

13.5 Shanken Corp. issued a 30-year, 6.2 percent semiannual bond 7 years ago. The bond currently sells for 108 percent of its face value. The company's tax rate is 35 percent.
    *a.* What is the pre-tax cost of debt?
    *b.* What is the after-tax cost of debt?
    *c.* Which is more relevant, the pre-tax or the after-tax cost of debt? Why?

13.6 For the firm in Problem 13.5, suppose the book value of the debt issue is $70 million. In addition, the company has a second debt issue on the market, a zero-coupon bond with 12 years left to maturity; the book value of this issue is $100 million and the bonds sell for 61 percent of par. What is the company's total book value of debt? The total market value? What is your best estimate of the after-tax cost of debt now?

**Calculating Weighted Average Cost of Capital**

13.7 Mullineaux Corporation has a target capital structure of 70 percent common stock and 30 percent debt. Its cost of equity is 15 percent, and the cost of debt is 8 percent. The relevant tax rate is 35 percent. What is Mullineaux's WACC?

**Taxes and Weighted Average Cost of Capital**

13.8 Miller Manufacturing has a target debt-to-equity ratio of 0.55. Its cost of equity is 14 percent, and its cost of debt is 7 percent. If the tax rate is 35 percent, what is Miller's WACC?

**Finding the Capital Structure**

13.9 Fama's Llamas has a WACC of 9.8 percent. The company's cost of equity is 13 percent, and its cost of debt is 6.5 percent. The tax rate is 35 percent. What is Fama's debt-to-equity ratio?

**Book Value versus Market Value**

13.10 Filer Manufacturing has 8.3 million shares of common stock outstanding. The current share price is $53, and the book value per share is $4. Filer Manufacturing also has two bond issues outstanding. The first bond issue has a face value of $70 million and a 7 percent coupon and sells for 108.3 percent of par. The second issue has a face value of $60 million and a 7.5 percent coupon and sells for 108.9 percent of par. The first issue matures in 8 years, the second in 27 years.
    *a.* What are Filer's capital structure weights on a book value basis?

> b. What are Filer's capital structure weights on a market value basis?
> c. Which are more relevant, the book or market value weights? Why?

## Calculating the Weighted Average Cost of Capital

13.11  In Problem 13.10, suppose the company's stock has a beta of 1.2. The risk-free rate is 3.1 percent, and the market risk premium is 7 percent. Assume that the overall cost of debt is the weighted average implied by the two outstanding debt issues. Both bonds make semiannual payments. The tax rate is 35 percent. What is the company's WACC?

## Weighted Average Cost of Capital

13.12  Kose Inc. has a target debt-to-equity ratio of 0.65. Its WACC is 11.2 percent, and the tax rate is 35 percent.

> a. If Kose's cost of equity is 15 percent, what is its pre-tax cost of debt?
> b. If instead you know that the after-tax cost of debt is 6.4 percent, what is the cost of equity?

## Finding the Weighted Average Cost of Capital

13.13  Given the following information for Huntington Power Co., find the WACC. Assume the company's tax rate is 35 percent.

> Debt:          5,000 6 percent coupon bonds outstanding, $1,000 par value, 25 years to maturity, selling for 105 percent of par; the bonds make semiannual payments.
>
> Common stock:  175,000 shares outstanding, selling for $58 per share; the beta is 1.10.
>
> Market:        7 percent market risk premium and 5 percent risk-free rate.

13.14  Titan Mining Corporation has 8.5 million shares of common stock outstanding and 200,000 7.5 percent semiannual bonds outstanding, par value $1,000 each. The common stock currently sells for $34 per share and has a beta of 1.20, and the bonds have 15 years to maturity and sell for 93 percent of par. The market risk premium is 7 percent, T-bills are yielding 5 percent, and Titan Mining's tax rate is 35 percent.

> a. What is the firm's market value capital structure?
> b. If Titan Mining is evaluating a new investment project that has the same risk as the firm's typical project, what rate should the firm use to discount the project's cash flows?

## Security Market Line and Weighted Average Cost of Capital

13.15  An all-equity firm is considering the following projects:

| Project | Beta | Expected return |
|---------|------|-----------------|
| W | 0.75 | 10.0% |
| X | 0.90 | 10.2 |
| Y | 1.20 | 12.0 |
| Z | 1.50 | 15.0 |

The T-bill rate is 5 percent, and the expected return on the market is 11 percent.

> a. Which projects have a higher expected return than the firm's 11 percent cost of capital?
> b. Which projects should be accepted?
> c. Which projects would be incorrectly accepted or rejected if the firm's overall cost of capital were used as a hurdle rate?

### Calculating Flotation Costs

13.16  Suppose your company needs $20 million to build a new assembly line. Your target debt-to-equity ratio is 0.75. The flotation cost for new equity is 7 percent, but the flotation cost for debt is only 3 percent. Your boss has decided to fund the project by borrowing money because the flotation costs are lower and the needed funds are relatively small.

    *a.* What do you think about the rationale behind borrowing the entire amount?

    *b.* What is your company's weighted average flotation cost, assuming all equity is raised externally?

    *c.* What is the true cost of building the new assembly line after taking flotation costs into account? Does it matter in this case that the entire amount is being raised from debt?

13.17  Southern Alliance Company needs to raise $45 million to start a new project and will raise the money by selling new bonds. The company will generate no internal equity for the foreseeable future. The company has a target capital structure of 65 percent common stock, 5 percent preferred stock, and 30 percent debt. Flotation costs for issuing new common stock are 9 percent; for new preferred stock, 6 percent; and for new debt, 3 percent. What is the true initial cost figure Southern Alliance should use when evaluating its project?

### Weighted Average Cost of Capital and Net Present Value

13.18  Och Inc. is considering a project that will result in initial after-tax cash savings of $3.5 million at the end of the first year, and these savings will grow at a rate of 4 percent per year, indefinitely. The firm has a target debt-to-equity ratio of 0.55, a cost of equity of 13 percent, and an after-tax cost of debt of 5.5 percent. The cost-saving proposal is somewhat riskier than the usual projects the firm undertakes; management uses the subjective approach and applies an adjustment factor of +2 percent to the cost of capital for such risky projects. Under what circumstances should Och take on the project?

### Preferred Stock and Weighted Average Cost of Capital

13.19  The Saunders Investment Bank has the following financing outstanding. What is the WACC for the company?

| | |
|---|---|
| *Debt:* | 60,000 bonds with a 6 percent coupon rate and a current price quote of 109.5; the bonds have 20 years to maturity. 230,000 zero-coupon bonds with a price quote of 17.5 and 30 years until maturity. |
| *Preferred stock:* | 150,000 shares of 4 percent preferred stock with a current price of $79 and a par value of $100. |
| *Common stock:* | 2,600,000 shares of common stock; the current price is $65, and the beta of the stock is 1.15. |
| *Market:* | The corporate tax rate is 40 percent, the market risk premium is 7 percent, and the risk-free rate is 4 percent. |

### Flotation Costs

13.20  Goodbye Inc. recently issued new securities to finance a new TV show. The project cost $19 million, and the company paid $1,150,000 in flotation costs. In addition, the equity issued had a flotation cost of 7 percent of the amount raised, whereas the debt issued had a flotation cost of 3 percent of the amount raised. If Goodbye issued new securities in the same proportion as its target capital structure, what is the company's target debt-to-equity ratio?

### Calculating the Cost of Equity

13.21   Floyd Industries stock has a beta of 1.30. The company just paid a dividend of $0.95, and the dividends are expected to grow at 4.5 percent per year. The expected return on the market is 11 percent, and Treasury bills are yielding 4.3 percent. The most recent stock price for Floyd is $64.

a. Calculate the cost of equity using the dividend discount model method.

b. Calculate the cost of equity using the SML method.

c. Why do you think your estimates in (a) and (b) are so different?

### Flotation Costs and Net Present Value

13.22   Photochronograph Corporation (PC) manufactures time series photographic equipment. It is currently at its target debt-to-equity ratio of 0.55. It is considering building a new $50 million manufacturing facility. This new plant is expected to generate after-tax cash flows of $6.7 million a year in perpetuity. The company raises all equity from outside financing. The required equity will be met by the following:

1. *A new issue of common stock.* The flotation costs of the new common stock would be 8 percent of the amount raised. The required return on the company's new equity is 14 percent.

2. *A new issue of 20-year bonds.* The flotation costs of the new bonds would be 4 percent of the proceeds. If the company issues these new bonds at an annual coupon rate of 8 percent, they will sell at par.

3. *Increased use of accounts payable financing.* Because this financing is part of the company's ongoing daily business, it has no flotation costs, and the company assigns it a cost that is the same as the overall firm WACC. Management has a target ratio of accounts payable to long-term debt of 0.20. (Assume there is no difference between the pre-tax and after-tax accounts payable cost.)

What is the NPV of the new plant? Assume that PC has a 35 percent tax rate.

### Flotation Costs

13.23   Trower Corp. has a debt-to-equity ratio of 0.85. The company is considering a new plant that will cost $145 million to build. When the company issues new equity, it incurs a flotation cost of 8 percent. The flotation cost on new debt is 3.5 percent. What is the initial cost of the plant if the company raises all equity externally? What if it typically uses 60 percent retained earnings? What if all equity investments are financed through retained earnings?

### Project Evaluation

13.24   This is a comprehensive project evaluation problem bringing together much of what you have learned in this and previous chapters. Suppose you have been hired as a financial consultant to Defence Electronics Inc. (DEI), a large, publicly traded firm that is the market share leader in radon detection systems (RDSs). The company is looking at setting up a manufacturing plant overseas to produce a new line of RDSs. This will be a five-year project. The company bought some land three years ago for $7.5 million in anticipation of using it as a toxic dump site for waste chemicals, but it built a piping system to safely discard the chemicals instead. The land was appraised last week for $7.1 million. In five years, the after-tax value of the land will be $7.4 million, but the company expects to keep the land for a future project. The company wants to build its new manufacturing plant on this land; the plant and equipment will cost $40 million to build. The following market data on DEI's securities are current:

*Debt:*     260,000 6.8 percent coupon bonds outstanding, 25 years to maturity, selling for 103 percent of par; the bonds have a $1,000 par value each and make semiannual payments.

*Common stock:*    9,500,000 shares outstanding, selling for $67 per share; the beta is 1.25.

*Preferred stock:*    450,000 shares of 5.25 percent preferred stock outstanding, selling for $84 per share and having a par value of $100.

*Market:*    7 percent expected market risk premium; 3.6 percent risk-free rate.

DEI uses G. M. Wharton as its lead underwriter. Wharton charges DEI spreads of 6.5 percent on new common stock issues, 4.5 percent on new preferred stock issues, and 3 percent on new debt issues. Wharton has included all direct and indirect issuance costs (along with its profit) in setting these spreads. Wharton has recommended to DEI that it raise the funds needed to build the plant by issuing new shares of common stock. DEI's tax rate is 35 percent. The project requires $1,400,000 in initial net working capital investment to get operational. Assume DEI raises all equity for new projects externally.

a. Calculate the project's initial time 0 cash flow, taking into account all side effects.

b. The new RDS project is somewhat riskier than a typical project for DEI, primarily because the plant is being located overseas. Management has told you to use an adjustment factor of +2 percent to account for this increased riskiness. Calculate the appropriate discount rate to use when evaluating DEI's project.

c. The manufacturing plant has an eight-year tax life, and DEI uses straight-line depreciation. At the end of the project (that is, the end of year 5), the plant and equipment can be scrapped for $8.5 million. What is the after-tax salvage value of this plant and equipment?

d. The company will incur $7,900,000 in annual fixed costs. The plan is to manufacture 18,000 RDSs per year and sell them at $10,900 per machine; the variable production costs are $9,450 per RDS. What is the annual operating cash flow (OCF) from this project?

e. DEI's controller is primarily interested in the impact of DEI's investments on the bottom line of reported accounting statements. What will you tell him is the accounting break-even quantity of RDSs sold for this project?

f. Finally, DEI's president wants you to throw all your calculations, assumptions, and everything else into the report for the chief financial officer; all she wants to know is what the RDS project's IRR and NPV are. What will you report?

13.25    As a recent graduate, you have been hired by Canadian Communications Inc. (CCI), a large industry leader in the Canadian telecommunications market. CCI is contemplating investing in an upgraded wireless communication service platform known as 5G technology. Based on the company's forecast it is believed that the new investment will last for 3 years before it has to be upgraded with faster speeds. The investment in 5G technology will require an initial net working capital outlay of $175,000,000 and is to be financed using an equal weighting of equity and debt (ignore flotation costs). Its most recent statement of financial position is shown below as well as CCI's list of non-current liabilities:

**Canadian Communications Inc.**
**Statement of Financial Position**
**As of December 31, 20X0 (in $ millions)**

| Assets | | Liabilities and shareholder's equity | |
|---|---|---|---|
| Current assets | $ 5,000 | Current liabilities | $ 7,000 |
| Property, plant, and equipment | 33,000 | Non-current liabilities | 21,000 |
| Other | 2,000 | Total liabilities | $28,000 |
| | | Shareholder's equity | $12,000 |
| Total assets | $40,000 | | $40,000 |

| Issuer | Coupon | Price | Maturity | Yield to maturity | Amount outstanding (in $ millions) |
|---|---|---|---|---|---|
| CCI | 6.8 | 110 | 28/6/20X0 | 1.25 | $    500 |
| CCI | 5.1 | 106.8 | 15/3/20X1 | 4.8 | 3,500 |
| CCI | 6.3 | 109.3 | 20/8/20X1 | 4.7 | 5,000 |
| CCI | 5 | 91.5 | 1/2/20X6 | 5.75 | 12,000 |
| | | | | | $21,000 |

CCI currently has 800,000,000 shares outstanding and was last traded at a price of $23.50 per share. CCI's tax rate is 35%. The CFO is wondering whether the investment in 5G technology is value enhancing and has asked you to provide your analysis. In particular he wants you to do the following:

a. Calculate CCI's market value of equity, market value of debt, and after-tax cost of debt.

b. The CFO has determined that the industry beta contains fewer estimation errors. He has mandated the use of an industry beta comprising the major telecommunication companies in Canada. For reference, find the betas of BCE Inc., TELUS Corporation, Manitoba Telecom Services Inc., and Rogers Communications Inc. to use in the calculation of an industry beta.

c. The current risk-free rate is 2%, and the market risk premium is 4.5%. Calculate the cost of equity.

d. Calculate the WACC.

e. With the completion of the project, CCI will incur estimated annual fixed costs of $90,000,000. CCI forecasts an increase in its service prices, for customers, to an average of $85 per month. Variable service costs incurred per customer are, on average, $10. In addition, the company has forecast an adoption rate of 500,000 users in the first year, 1,000,000 in the second year, and 3,500,000 by the third year. Find the project's projected operating cash flows.

f. What are the project's IRR and NPV? Should the project be undertaken by CCI?

# The Cost of Capital for Goff Communications Inc.

You have recently been hired by Goff Communications Inc. (GCI) in the finance area. GCI was founded 20 years ago by Chris Goff and currently employs over 30,000 workers. GCI is privately owned by Chris and her family and had sales of $8.6 billion last year. GCI provides telecommunication products and services, including wireless, data, Internet, and television, to businesses and households.

GCI's growth to date has been financed from its profits. Whenever the company had sufficient capital, it would open a new store. Relatively little formal analysis has been used in the capital budgeting process. Chris has just read about capital budgeting techniques and has come to you for help. The company has never attempted to determine its cost of capital, and Chris would like you to perform the analysis. Because the company is privately owned, it is difficult to determine the cost of equity for the company. You have determined that to estimate the cost of capital for GCI, you will use Telus Corporation (T) as a representative company. The following steps will allow you to calculate this estimate:

1. Most publicly traded corporations are required to submit quarterly and annual reports to the Ontario Securities Commission (OSC) detailing their financial operations over the previous quarter and year, respectively. These corporate filings are available on the SEDAR website. Go to www.sedar.com and follow the Search Database link and then the Search for Public Company Documents link. Enter the company name, Telus Corporation, and search for filings made by the company. Find and download the company's most recent quarterly or annual report. Look on the balance sheet to find the book value of debt and the book value of equity. If you look farther down the report, you should find a section titled either "Long-Term Debt" or "Long-Term Debt and Interest Rate Risk Management" that will list a breakdown of Telus Corporation's long-term debt.

2. To estimate the cost of equity for Telus, go to www.google.ca/finance and enter "TSE.T," the ticker symbol for Telus. Follow the various links to find answers to the following questions. What is the most recent stock price listed for Telus? What is the market value of equity, or market capitalization? How many shares of stock does Telus have outstanding? What is the beta for Telus? Now go to www.canpxonline.ca/quotes.php and follow the "Canadian Benchmark Yields" link. What is the yield on 3-month Treasury bills? Using a 7 percent market risk premium, what is the cost of equity for CMG using the CAPM?

3. Go to www.reuters.com and find the list of competitors in the industry. Find the beta for each of these competitors, and then calculate the industry average beta. Using the industry average beta, what is the cost of equity? Does it matter if you use the beta for Telus Corporation or the beta for the industry in this case?

4. You now need to calculate the cost of debt for Telus. Go to www.canpxonline.ca/quotes.php; under the "CanPX Trades" link there will be a table listing outstanding Canadian Corporate bonds. Search for "Telus Corp" in the table and find the YTM for each of Telus Corporation's bonds. What is the weighted average cost of debt for Telus using the book value weights and the market value weights? Does it make a difference in this case whether you use book value weights or market value weights?

5. You now have all the necessary information to calculate the WACC for Telus. Calculate the WACC for Telus using book value weights and market value weights, assuming Telus has a 35 percent marginal tax rate. Which cost of capital number is more relevant?

6. You used Telus Corporation as a representative company to estimate the cost of capital for GCI. What are some of the potential problems with this approach in this situation? What improvements might you suggest?

# Economic Value Added and the Measurement of Financial Performance

Chapter 13 shows how to calculate the appropriate discount rate for capital budgeting and other valuation problems. We now consider the measurement of financial performance. We introduce the concept of economic value added (EVA), which uses the same discount rate developed for capital budgeting. We begin with a simple example.

## Calculating Economic Value Added

Many years ago, Henry Bodenheimer started Bodie's Blimps, one of the largest high-speed blimp manufacturers. Because growth was so rapid, Henry put most of his effort into capital budgeting. His approach to capital budgeting paralleled that of Chapter 13. He forecast cash flows for various projects and discounted them at the cost of capital appropriate to the beta of the blimp business. However, these projects have grown rapidly, in some cases becoming whole divisions. He now needs to evaluate the performance of these divisions in order to reward his division managers. How does he perform the appropriate analysis?

Henry is aware that capital budgeting and performance measurement are essentially mirror images of each other. Capital budgeting is forward looking by nature because one must estimate future cash flows to value a project. By contrast, performance measurement is backward looking. As Henry stated to a group of his executives, "Capital budgeting is like looking through the windshield while driving a car. You need to know what lies farther down the road to calculate an NPV. Performance measurement is like looking into the rear-view mirror. You find out where you have been."

Henry first measured the performance of his various divisions by return on assets (ROA), an approach that we treated in Appendix 2A. For example, if a division had earnings after tax of $1,000 and had assets of $10,000, the ROA would be[16]

$$\frac{\$1,000}{\$10,000} = 10\%$$

He calculated the ROA ratio for each of his divisions, paying a bonus to each of his division managers based on the size of that division's ROA. However, while ROA was generally effective in motivating his managers, there were a number of situations where it appeared that ROA was counterproductive.

For example, Henry always believed that Sharon Smith, head of the supersonic division, was his best manager. The ROA of Sharon's division was generally in the high double digits, but the best estimate of the WACC for the division was only 20%. Furthermore, the division had been growing rapidly. However, as soon as Henry paid bonuses based on ROA, the division stopped growing. At that time, Sharon's division had after-tax earnings of $2,000,000 on an asset base of $2,000,000, for an ROA of 100% ($2 million/$2 million).

Henry found out why the growth stopped when he suggested a project to Smith that would earn $1,000,000 per year on an investment of $2,000,000. This was clearly an attractive project with an ROA of 50% ($1 million/$2 million). He thought that Sharon would jump at the chance to place his project into her division, because the ROA of the project was much higher than the cost of capital of 20%. However, Sharon did everything she could to kill the project. And, as Henry later figured out, Sharon was rational to do so. Sharon must have realized that if the project were accepted, the division's ROA would become

---

[16] Earnings after tax is EBIT$(1 - T_c)$, where EBIT is earnings before interest and taxes and $T_c$ is the tax rate. Stern Stewart and other EVA users refer to EBIT$(1 - T_c)$ as net operating profit after tax.

$$\frac{\$2,000,000 + \$1,000,000}{\$2,000,000 + \$2,000,000} = 75\%$$

Thus, the ROA of Sharon's division would fall from 100% to 75% if the project were accepted, with Sharon's bonus falling in tandem.

Henry was later exposed to the EVA approach,[17] which seems to obviate this particular problem. The formula for EVA is

$$[\text{ROA} - \text{WACC}] \times \text{Total capital}$$

Without the new project, the EVA of Sharon's division would be

$$[100\% - 20\%] \times \$2,000,000 = \$1,600,000$$

This is an annual number. That is, the division would bring in $1.6 million above and beyond the cost of capital to the firm each year.

With the new project included, the EVA jumps to

$$[75\% - 20\%] \times \$4,000,000 = \$2,200,000$$

If Sharon knew that her bonus was based on EVA, she would now have an incentive to accept, not reject, the project. Although ROA appears in the EVA formula, EVA differs substantially from ROA. The big difference is that ROA is a percentage number and EVA is a dollar value. In the preceding example, EVA increased when the new project was added even though the ROA actually decreased. In this situation, EVA correctly incorporates the fact that a high return on a large division may be better than a very high return on a smaller division. The situation here is quite similar to the scale problem in capital budgeting that we discussed in Section 7.6.

Further understanding of EVA can be achieved by rewriting the EVA formula. Because ROA multiplied by total capital is equal to earnings after tax, we can write the EVA formula as

$$\text{EVA} = \text{Earnings after tax} - \text{WACC} \times \text{Total capital}$$

Thus, EVA can simply be viewed as earnings after capital costs. Although accountants subtract many costs (including depreciation) to get the earnings number shown in financial reports, they do not subtract out capital costs. One can see the logic of accountants, because the cost of capital is very subjective. By contrast, costs such as COGS (cost of goods sold), SGA (sales, general, and administration), and even depreciation can be measured more objectively.[18] However, even if the cost of capital is difficult to estimate, it is hard to justify ignoring it completely. After all, this textbook argues that the cost of capital is a necessary input to capital budgeting. Shouldn't it also be a necessary input to performance measurement?

This example argues that EVA can increase investment for those firms that are currently underinvesting. However, there are many firms in the reverse situation; the managers are so focused on increasing earnings that they take on projects for which the profits do not justify the capital outlays. These managers either are unaware of capital costs or, knowing these costs, choose to ignore them. Because the cost of capital is right in the middle of the EVA formula, managers will not easily ignore these costs when evaluated on an EVA system.

One other advantage of EVA is that it is so stark; the number is either positive or it is negative. Plenty of divisions have negative EVAs for a number of years. Because these divisions are destroying more value than they are creating, a strong point can be made

---

[17] Stern Stewart & Company have a copyright on the terms *economic value added* and *EVA*. Details on the Stern Stewart & Company EVA can be found in J. M. Stern, G. B. Stewart, and D. A. Chew, "The EVA Financial Management System," *Journal of Applied Corporate Finance* (Summer 1999).

[18] Some EVA users add back depreciation and other non-cash items. A Canadian example is B. A. Schofield, "Evaluating Stocks," *Canadian Investment Review* (Spring 2000).

for liquidating these divisions. Although managers are generally emotionally opposed to this type of action, EVA analysis makes liquidation harder to ignore.

In Example 13A.1, International Trade Corporation has a negative EVA—it is destroying shareholder value. The following paragraph discusses real corporate examples of value creators and value destroyers.

---

**EXAMPLE 13A.1**

Assume the following figures for the International Trade Corporation:

$$EBIT = \$2.5 \text{ billion}$$
$$T_c = 0.4$$
$$r_{WACC} = 11\%$$

$$
\begin{aligned}
\text{Total capital contributed} &= \text{Total debt} + \text{Equity} \\
&= \$10 \text{ billion} + \$10 \text{ billion} \\
&= \$20 \text{ billion}
\end{aligned}
$$

Now we can calculate International Trade's EVA:

$$
\begin{aligned}
EVA &= EBIT(1 - T_c) - r_{WACC} \times \text{Total capital} \\
&= (\$2.5 \text{ billion} \times 0.6) - (0.11 \times \$20 \text{ billion}) \\
&= \$1.5 \text{ billion} - \$2.2 \text{ billion} \\
&= -\$700 \text{ million}
\end{aligned}
$$

---

In 2003, the Corporate Renaissance Group identified Leon's Furniture Limited, Cognos Inc., and Sceptre Investment Counsel Ltd. as the top consistent value creators based on EVA. In comparison, Canlan Ice Sports Corp., Napier Environmental Technologies, and Asia Pacific Resources were identified as the most consistent value destroyers based on EVA performance. The top seven consistent value creators and consistent value destroyers are in Table 13A.1.

**TABLE 13A.1**

**Consistent Value Creators and Value Destroyers Based on Economic Value Added**

| Consistent value creators 1995 to 2002 | Consistent value destroyers 1995 to 2002 |
| --- | --- |
| Leon's Furniture | Canlan Ice Sports Corp. |
| Cognos Inc. | Napier Environmental Technologies |
| Sceptre Investment Counsel Ltd. | Asia Pacific Resources Ltd. |
| Pason Systems Inc. | Ballard Power Systems Inc. |
| Dupont Canada Inc. | F N X Mining Co. Inc. |
| Metro Inc. | Sterlite Gold Ltd. |
| Biovail Corporation | Aldeavision Inc. |

Source: V. Jog, "Value and Wealth Creation in Canada," *Canadian Investment Review* (Winter 2003).

Despite being listed as a consistent value creator, Biovail's stock price had dropped from a high of approximately $90 per share in October of 2002 to $30 per share in May of 2006. The exact opposite of Biovail would be F N X Mining Co. Inc. The company's stock price rose to a high of $16 per share in February 2006 from a low of almost $6 per share in June 2003. These are two examples that show that it is not always possible to predict a share price turnaround by using EVA. It is important to note that Table 13A.1 sets out to compare past EVA with future stock performance.

## Some Caveats on Economic Value Added

The preceding discussion puts EVA in a very positive light. However, one can certainly find much to criticize with EVA as well. We now focus on two well-known problems with EVA. First, the preceding example uses EVA for performance measurement, where we believe it properly belongs. To us, EVA seems a clear improvement over ROA and other financial ratios. However, EVA has little to offer for capital budgeting because EVA focuses only on current earnings. By contrast, NPV analysis uses projections of all future cash flows, where the cash flows will generally differ from year to year. Thus, as far as capital budgeting is concerned, NPV analysis has a richness that EVA does not have. Although supporters may argue that EVA correctly incorporates the WACC, one must remember that the discount rate in NPV analysis is the same as WACC. That is, both approaches take the cost of equity capital based on beta and combine it with the cost of debt to get an estimate of this weighted average.

A second problem with EVA is that it may increase the short-sightedness of managers. Under EVA, a manager will be well rewarded today if earnings are high today. Future losses may not harm the manager, because there is a good chance that she will be promoted or have left the firm by then. Thus, the manager has an incentive to run a division with more regard for short-term than long-term value. By raising prices or cutting quality, the manager may increase current profits (and, therefore, current EVA). However, to the extent that customer satisfaction is reduced, future profits (and therefore future EVA) are likely to fall. However, one should not be too harsh with EVA here, because the same problem occurs with ROA. A manager who raises prices or cuts quality will increase current ROA at the expense of future ROA. The problem, then, is not EVA per se but the use of accounting numbers in general. Because shareholders want the discounted PV of all cash flows to be maximized, managers with bonuses based on some function of current profits or current cash flows are likely to behave in a shortsighted way.

Despite these shortcomings, EVA or something similar is used widely by corporations in the United States and Canada. Table 13A.2 lists some examples.

**TABLE 13A.2**

**Selected Economic Value Added Users**

| United States | Canada |
|---|---|
| Bausch & Lomb | Alcan Aluminum |
| Briggs and Stratton Corp. | Cogeco Inc. |
| Coca-Cola Company | Domtar Inc. |
| Eli Lilly & Co. | Grand & Toy |
| Dun & Bradstreet Corp. | Long Manufacturing |
| J.C. Penney Corp. | Robin Hood Multifoods |
| Monsanto | |
| Rubbermaid Inc. | |
| Sprint | |
| Toys R Us | |
| U.S. Postal Service | |
| Whirlpool | |

Source: Adapted from sternstewart.com.

**CONCEPT QUESTIONS**

- Why is capital budgeting important to a firm?
- What is the major difference between EVA and ROA?
- What are the advantages of using EVA?
- What are the well-known problems of EVA?

**QUESTIONS & PROBLEMS**

13A.1   Last year, Simplex Robotics had $8 million in operating income (EBIT). The company had net depreciation expense of $2 million and an interest expense of $1 million; its corporate tax rate was 32 percent. The company has $12 million in current assets and $5 million in non-interest-bearing current liabilities; it has $18 million in net plant and equipment. It estimates that it has an after-tax cost of capital of 10 percent. Assume that Simplex's only non-cash item is depreciation. What was the company's EVA?

13A.2   You are considering installing an energy-efficient central heating system in your firm's warehouse. The installation will cost $12,000, and you estimate total savings of $3,000 per year. The heating system will depreciate evenly over the next five years, at which point it must be replaced. The cost of capital is 8 percent. What do the NPV and EVA rules indicate about whether or not you should install the heating system?

**LEARNSMART**    **SMARTBOOK**™

## PART 4

# 14

# Corporate Financing Decisions and Efficient Capital Markets

EXECUTIVE SUMMARY

The section of this text on value concentrated on the firm's capital budgeting decisions—the left-hand side of the balance sheet of the firm. This chapter begins our analysis of corporate financing decisions—the right-hand side of the balance sheet. We take the firm's capital budgeting decision as fixed in this section of the text.

The point of this chapter is to introduce the concept of *efficient capital markets* and its implications for corporate finance. Efficient capital markets are those in which market prices reflect available information. This means that market prices reflect the underlying present value (PV) of securities, and there is no way to make unusual or excess profits by using the available information.

This concept has profound implications for financial managers, because market efficiency eliminates many value-enhancing strategies of firms. In particular, we show that in an efficient market:

1. Stock price should not be affected by a firm's choice of accounting method.
2. Financial managers cannot time issues of bonds and stocks.
3. Firms cannot expect to gain through speculation in currency and bond markets.
4. Financial managers should pay attention to the information in market prices.

However, the evidence on market efficiency is not one sided. A very influential school of thought, known as *behavioural finance*, argues that markets are simply not efficient. Ultimately, whether or not capital markets are efficient is an empirical question. We will describe several studies examining efficient markets.

## 14.1 CAN FINANCING DECISIONS CREATE VALUE?

Earlier parts of the book show how to evaluate projects according to the net present value (NPV) criterion. The real world is a competitive place, in which projects with positive NPV are not always easy to come by. However, through hard work or through good fortune, a firm can identify winning projects. For example, to create value from capital budgeting decisions, the firm is likely to do the following:

1. Locate an unsatisfied demand for a particular product or service.
2. Create a barrier to make it more difficult for other firms to compete.
3. Produce products or services at lower cost than the competition.
4. Be the first to develop a new product.

The next five chapters concern *financing* decisions. Typical financing decisions include how much debt and equity to sell, what types of debt and equity to sell, and when to sell debt and equity. Just as the NPV criterion was used to evaluate capital budgeting projects, we now want to use the same criterion to evaluate financing decisions.

Though the procedure for evaluating financing decisions is identical to the procedure for evaluating projects, the results are different. It turns out that the typical firm has many more capital expenditure opportunities with positive NPVs than financing opportunities with positive NPVs. In fact, we later show that some plausible financial models imply that no valuable financial opportunities exist at all.

Though this dearth of profitable financing opportunities will be examined in detail later, a few remarks are in order now. We maintain that there are basically three ways to create valuable financing opportunities:

1. *Fool investors.* Assume that a firm can raise capital either by issuing stock or by issuing a more complex security, say, a combination of stock and warrants. Suppose that, in truth, 100 shares of stock are worth the same as 50 units of our complex security. If investors have a misguided, overly optimistic view of the complex security, perhaps the 50 units can be sold for more than the 100 shares of stock can. Clearly, this complex security provides a valuable financing opportunity because the firm is getting more than fair value for it.

   Financial managers try to package securities to receive the greatest value. A cynic might view this as attempting to fool investors. However, empirical evidence suggests that investors cannot easily be fooled. Thus, one must be skeptical that value can easily be created.

   The theory of efficient capital markets expresses this idea. In its extreme form, it says that all securities are appropriately priced at all times, implying that the market as a whole is very shrewd indeed. Thus, corporate managers should not attempt to create value by fooling investors. Instead, managers must create value in other ways.

2. *Reduce costs or increase subsidies.* We show later in the book that certain forms of financing have greater tax advantages than other forms. Clearly, a firm packaging securities to minimize taxes can increase firm value. In addition, any financing technique involves other costs. For example, investment bankers, lawyers, and accountants must be paid. A firm packaging securities to minimize these costs can also increase firm value.

   Finally, any financing vehicle that provides subsidies is valuable. This last possibility is illustrated in Example 14.1.

---

**EXAMPLE 14.1**

Suppose Mississauga Electronics Company is thinking about relocating its plant to Mexico, where labour costs are lower. In the hope that it can stay in Ontario, the company has submitted an application to the province to guarantee a five-year bank term loan for $2 million. With a provincial guarantee, a chartered bank has offered to make the loan at an interest rate of 5 percent. This is an attractive rate because the normal cost of debt capital for Mississauga Electronics Company is 10 percent. Taxes are ignored for simplicity. What is the NPV of this potential financing transaction?

If the provincial loan guarantee is provided and the term loan is made to Mississauga Electronics Company,

$$\text{NPV} = \$2,000,000 - \left[ \frac{\$100,000}{1.1} + \frac{\$100,000}{(1.1)^2} + \frac{\$100,000}{(1.1)^3} + \frac{\$100,000}{(1.1)^4} + \frac{\$2,100,000}{(1.1)^5} \right]$$

$$= \$2,000,000 - \$1,620,921$$

$$= \$379,079$$

This transaction has a positive NPV. The Mississauga Electronics Company obtains subsidized financing where the amount of the subsidy is $379,079.

3. *Create a new security.* There has been a surge in financial innovation in the past two decades. For example, in a speech on financial innovation, the late Nobel laureate Merton Miller asked the rhetorical question, "Can any twenty-year period in recorded history have witnessed even a tenth as much new development? Where corporations once issued only straight debt and straight common stock, they now issue zero-coupon, inflation-linked bonds, adjustable rate notes, floating rate notes, putable bonds, credit-enhanced debt securities, receivable-backed securities, convertible adjustable preferred stock, and adjustable rate convertible debt—to name just a few!"[1] And financial innovation has occurred even more rapidly in the years following Miller's speech.

Though the advantage of each instrument is different, one general theme is that these new securities cannot easily be duplicated by combinations of existing securities. Thus, a previously unsatisfied clientele may pay extra for a specialized security catering to its needs. For example, putable bonds let the purchaser sell the bond at a fixed price back to the firm. This innovation creates a price floor, allowing the investor to reduce his downside risk. Perhaps risk-averse investors or investors with little knowledge of the bond market would find this feature particularly attractive.

Corporations gain from developing unique securities by issuing these securities at high prices. However, we believe that the value captured by the innovator is small in the long run because the innovator cannot usually patent or copyright the idea. Soon, many firms will be issuing securities of the same kind, forcing prices down as a result.

This brief introduction sets the stage for the next five chapters of the book. The rest of this chapter examines the efficient capital markets hypothesis. We show that if capital markets are efficient, corporate managers cannot create value by fooling investors. This is quite important, because managers must create value in other, perhaps more difficult ways. The following four chapters concern the costs and subsidies of various forms of financing. A discussion of new financing instruments is postponed until later chapters of the text.

**CONCEPT QUESTION**

• List the three ways financing decisions can create value.

## 14.2  A DESCRIPTION OF EFFICIENT CAPITAL MARKETS

An efficient capital market is one in which stock prices fully reflect available information. To illustrate how an efficient market works, suppose the F-stop Camera Corporation (FCC) is attempting to develop a camera that will double the speed of the autofocusing system now available. FCC believes this research has a positive NPV.

Now consider a share of stock in FCC. What determines the willingness of investors to hold shares of FCC at a particular price? One important factor is the probability that FCC will be the company to develop the new autofocusing system first. In an efficient market we would expect the price of the shares of FCC to rise if this probability increases.

---

[1] M. Miller, "Financial Innovation: The Last Twenty Years and the Next," *Journal of Financial and Quantitative Analysis* (December 1986). However, Peter Tufano, "Securities Innovations: A Historical and Functional Perspective," *Journal of Applied Corporate Finance* (Winter 1995), shows that many securities commonly believed to have been invented in the 1970s and 1980s can be traced to as far back as the 1830s.

Suppose a well-known engineer is hired by FCC to help develop the new auto-focusing system. In an efficient market, what will happen to FCC's share price when this is announced? If the well-known scientist is paid a salary that fully reflects her contribution to the firm, the price of the stock will not necessarily change. Suppose, instead, that hiring the scientist is a positive NPV transaction. In this case, the price of shares in FCC will increase because the firm can pay the scientist a salary below her true value to the company.

When will the increase in the price of FCC's shares take place? Assume that the hiring announcement is made in a press release on Wednesday morning. In an efficient market, the price of shares in FCC will *immediately and correctly* adjust to this new information. Investors should not be able to buy the stock on Wednesday afternoon and make a profit on Thursday. This would imply that it took the stock market a day to realize the implication of the FCC press release. The efficient market hypothesis (EMH) predicts that the price of shares of FCC stock on Wednesday afternoon will already reflect the information contained in the Wednesday morning press release.

The **efficient market hypothesis** (EMH) has implications for investors and for firms:

- Because information is reflected in prices immediately, investors should only expect to obtain a normal rate of return. Awareness of information when it is released does an investor no good. The price adjusts before the investor has time to trade on it.

- Firms should expect to receive the fair value for securities that they sell. *Fair* means that the price they receive for the securities they issue is the PV. Thus, valuable financing opportunities that arise from fooling investors are unavailable in efficient capital markets.

EXAMPLE **14.2**

Suppose Cisco announces it has invented a digital switch that is 30 times as fast as existing switches. The price of a share of Cisco should increase immediately to a new equilibrium level.

Figure 14.1 presents three possible adjustments in stock prices in reaction to good news. The solid line represents the path taken by the stock in an efficient market. In this case the price adjusts immediately to the new information so that no further changes take place in the price of the stock. The dotted line depicts a delayed reaction. Here it takes the market 30 days to absorb the information fully. Finally, the broken line illustrates an overreaction and subsequent correction back to the true price. The broken line and the dotted line show the paths that the stock price might take in an inefficient market. If the price of the stock takes several days to adjust, trading profits will be available to investors who bought at the date of the announcement and sold once the price settled back to the equilibrium.[2]

---

[2] Now you should understand the following short story. A student was walking down the hall with his finance professor when they both saw a $20 bill on the floor. As the student bent down to pick it up, the professor shook her head slowly and, with a look of disappointment on her face, said patiently to the student, "Don't bother. If it were really there, someone else would have already picked it up."

The moral of the story reflects the logic of the EMH: If you think you have found a pattern in stock prices or a simple device for picking winners, you probably haven't. If there were such a simple way to make money, someone else would have found it before. Furthermore, if people tried to exploit the information, their efforts would become self-defeating and the pattern would disappear.

**FIGURE 14.1**

**Reaction of a Stock Price to New Information in Efficient and Inefficient Markets**

*Efficient market reaction.* The price instantaneously adjusts to and fully reflects new information; there is no tendency for subsequent increases and decreases.

*Delayed reaction.* The price partially adjusts to the new information; 30 days elapse before the price completely reflects the new information.

*Overreaction.* The price overadjusts to the new information; there is a bubble in the price sequence.

## Foundations of Market Efficiency

Figure 14.1 shows the consequences of market efficiency. But what are the conditions that *cause* market efficiency? Andrei Shleifer argues that there are three conditions, any one of which will lead to efficiency:[3] (1) rationality, (2) independent deviations from rationality, and (3) arbitrage. A discussion of these conditions follows.

**Rationality**    Imagine that all investors are rational. When new information is released in the marketplace, all investors will adjust their estimates of stock prices in a rational way. In our example, investors will use the information in FCC's press release, in conjunction with existing information on the firm, to determine the NPV of FCC's new venture. If the information in the press release implies that the NPV of the venture is $10 million and there are 2 million shares, investors will calculate that the NPV is $5 per share. While FCC's old price might be, say, $40, no one would now transact at that price. Anyone interested in selling would only sell at a price of at least $45 ($40 + $5). And anyone interested in buying would now be willing to pay up to $45.

---

[3] Andrei Shleifer, *Inefficient Markets: An Introduction to Behavioral Finance* (Oxford: Oxford University Press, 2000).

In other words, the price would rise by $5. And the price would rise immediately, since rational investors would see no reason to wait before trading at the new price.

Of course, we all know times when family members, friends, and even ourselves seem to behave less than perfectly rationally. Thus, perhaps it is too much to ask that *all* investors behave rationally. But the market will still be efficient if the following scenario holds.

**Independent Deviations from Rationality**    Suppose that FCC's press release is not all that clear. How many new cameras are likely to be sold? At what price? What is the likely cost per camera? Will other camera companies be able to develop competing products? How long will this likely take? If these and other questions cannot be answered easily, it will be difficult to estimate NPV.

Now imagine that with so many questions going unanswered, many investors do not think clearly. Some investors might get caught up in the romance of a new product, hoping, and ultimately believing, in sales projections well above what is rational. They will overpay for new shares. And if they needed to sell shares (perhaps to finance current consumption), they would do so only at a high price. If these individuals dominate the market, the stock price will likely rise beyond what market efficiency would predict.

However, due to emotional resistance, investors could just as easily react to new information pessimistically. After all, business historians tell us that investors were initially quite skeptical about the benefits of the telephone, the copier, the automobile, and the motion picture. Certainly, they could be overly skeptical about this new camera. If investors were primarily of this type, the stock price would likely rise less than market efficiency would predict.

But suppose that about as many individuals were irrationally optimistic as were irrationally pessimistic. Prices would likely rise in a manner consistent with market efficiency, even though most investors would be classified as less than fully rational. Thus, market efficiency does not require rational individuals, only countervailing irrationalities.

However, this assumption of offsetting irrationalities at *all* times may be unrealistic. Perhaps most investors are swept away at certain times by excessive optimism and caught in the throes of extreme pessimism at other times. But even here, there is an assumption that will produce efficiency.

**Arbitrage**    Imagine a world with two types of individuals: the irrational amateurs and the rational professionals. The amateurs get caught up in their emotions, at times believing irrationally that a stock is undervalued and at other times believing the opposite. If the passions of the different amateurs do not cancel each other out, these amateurs, by themselves, will tend to carry stocks either above or below their efficient prices.

Now let's bring in the professionals. Suppose professionals go about their business methodically and rationally. They study companies thoroughly, they evaluate the evidence objectively, they estimate stock prices coldly and clearly, and they act accordingly. If a stock is underpriced, they buy it. If overpriced, they sell it (or even sell it short.[4]) And their confidence is likely greater than that of the amateurs. While an amateur might risk only a small sum, these professionals might risk large ones, *knowing* as they do that the stock is mispriced. Furthermore, they would be willing to rearrange their entire portfolio in search of a profit. If they find that General Motors is underpriced, they might sell the Ford stock they own (or even sell Ford short) in order to buy GM. *Arbitrage* is the word that comes to mind here, since arbitrage generates

---

[4] When an investor short sells a stock, his position is such that he gains from a fall in the stock and loses from a rise in the stock. Thus, short selling a stock can be viewed as the opposite of buying a stock.

profit from the simultaneous purchase and sale of different, but substitute, securities. If the arbitrage of professionals dominates the speculation of amateurs, markets will still be efficient.[5]

- Define an efficient market.
- Name the three foundations of market efficiency.

# 14.3   THE DIFFERENT TYPES OF EFFICIENCY

In our previous discussion, we assumed that the market responds immediately to all available information. In actuality, certain information may affect stock prices more quickly than other information. To handle differential response rates, researchers separate information into different types. The most common classification system uses three types: information on past prices, publicly available information, and all information. The effect of these three information sets on prices is examined below.

## The Weak Form

Imagine a trading strategy that recommends buying a stock when it has gone up three days in a row and selling a stock when it has gone down three days in a row. This strategy uses only information on past prices. It does not use any other information, such as earnings forecasts, merger announcements, or money supply figures. A capital market is said to be *weakly efficient* or to satisfy **weak-form efficiency** if it fully incorporates the information in past stock prices. Thus, the above strategy would not be able to generate profits if weak-form efficiency held.

Often weak-form efficiency is represented mathematically as

$$P_t = P_{t-1} + \text{Expected return} + \text{Random error}_t \qquad (14.1)$$

Equation (14.1) states that the price today is equal to the sum of the last observed price, the expected return on the stock, and a random component occurring over the interval. The last observed price could have occurred yesterday, last week, or last month, depending on the sampling interval. The expected return is a function of a security's risk and is based on the models of risk and return in previous chapters. The random component is due to new information on the stock. It could be either positive or negative and has an expectation of zero. The random component in any one period is unrelated to the random component in any past period. Hence, this component is not predictable from past prices. If stock prices follow equation (14.1), they are said to follow a **random walk**.[6]

Weak-form efficiency is about the weakest type of efficiency that we would expect a financial market to display because historical price information is the easiest kind of information about a stock to acquire. If it were possible to make extraordinary profits simply by finding the patterns in the stock price movements, everyone would do it, and any profits would disappear in the scramble. An exception to this statement occurred in the hot high-tech market of the late 1990s. Some investors were able to achieve superior returns following momentum strategies based on the idea that stocks that

---

[5] Because Ford and GM are different companies, the arbitrage here is not risk free. For this reason, it is sometimes termed "quasi-arbitrage."

[6] For this text, the random walk can be considered synonymous with weak-form efficiency. Technically, the random walk is a slightly more restrictive hypothesis because it assumes that stock returns are identically distributed through time.

went up yesterday are likely also to go up today. Day trading became very popular in this "momentum market."[7]

The effect of competition can be seen in Figure 14.2. Suppose the price of a stock displayed a cyclical pattern, as indicated by the wavy curve. Shrewd investors would buy at the low points, forcing those prices up. Conversely, they would sell at the high points, forcing prices down. Via competition, the cyclical regularities would be eliminated, leaving only random fluctuations.

FIGURE 14.2

**Investor Behaviour Tends to Eliminate Cyclical Patterns**

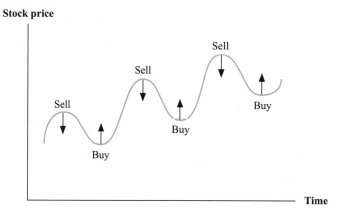

If a stock's price has followed a cyclical pattern, the pattern will quickly be eliminated in an efficient market. A random pattern will emerge as investors buy at the trough and sell at the peak of a cycle.

## The Semistrong and Strong Forms

If weak-form efficiency is controversial, even more contentious are the two stronger types of efficiency: **semistrong-form efficiency** and **strong-form efficiency**. A market is semistrong-form efficient if prices reflect (incorporate) all publicly available information, including published accounting statements for the firm and historical price information. A market is strong-form efficient if prices reflect all information, public or private.

The information set of past prices is a subset of the information set of publicly available information, which in turn is a subset of all information. This is shown in Figure 14.3. Thus, strong-form efficiency implies semistrong-form efficiency, and semistrong-form efficiency implies weak-form efficiency. The distinction between semistrong-form efficiency and weak-form efficiency is that semistrong-form efficiency requires not only that the market be efficient with respect to historical price information, but also that *all* of the information available to the public be reflected in price.

To illustrate the different forms of efficiency, imagine an investor who always sold a particular stock after its price had risen. A market that was only weak-form efficient and not semistrong-form efficient would still prevent such a scheme from generating positive NPV. According to weak-form efficiency, a recent price rise does not imply that the stock is overvalued.

---

[7] A Canadian study on momentum is M. Inglis and S. Cleary, "Momentum in Canadian Stock Returns," *Canadian Journal of Administrative Sciences* (September 1998).

**FIGURE 14.3**

**Relationship among Three Different Information Sets**

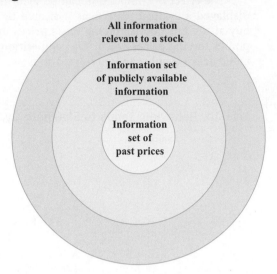

The information set of past prices is a subset of the information set of publicly available information, which in turn is a subset of all information. If today's price reflects only information on past prices, the market is weak-form efficient. If today's price reflects all publicly available information, the market is semistrong-form efficient. If today's price reflects all information, both public and private, the market is strong-form efficient.

Semistrong-form efficiency implies weak-form efficiency and strong-form efficiency implies semistrong-form efficiency.

Now consider a firm reporting increased earnings. An individual might consider investing in the stock after hearing of the news release. However, if the market is semistrong-form efficient, the price should rise immediately upon the news release. Thus, the investor would end up paying the higher price, eliminating all chance for a profit.

At the farthest end of the spectrum is strong-form efficiency, which incorporates the other two types of efficiency. This form says that anything that is pertinent to the value of the stock and that is known to at least one investor is, in fact, fully incorporated into the stock value. A strict believer in strong-form efficiency would deny that an insider who knew whether a company mining operation had struck gold could profit from that information. Such a devotee of the strong-form EMH might argue that as soon as the insider tried to trade on her information, the market would recognize what was happening, and the price would shoot up before she could buy any of the stock. Alternatively, sometimes believers in strong-form efficiency take the view that there is no such thing as a secret and that as soon as the gold is discovered, the secret gets out.

One reason to expect that markets are weak-form efficient is because it is so cheap and easy to find patterns in stock prices. Anyone who can program a computer and knows a little bit of statistics can search for such patterns. It stands to reason that if there were such patterns, people would find and exploit them, causing them to disappear.

Semistrong-form efficiency, though, uses much more sophisticated information and reasoning than weak-form efficiency. An investor must be skilled at economics and statistics and steeped in the idiosyncrasies of individual industries and companies and their products. Furthermore, to acquire and use such skills requires talent, ability, and time. Such an effort is costly, and the ability to be successful at it is probably in scarce supply.

As for strong-form efficiency, this is just farther down the road than semistrong-form efficiency. It is difficult to believe that the market is so efficient that someone with truly valuable inside information cannot prosper by using it. It is also difficult to find direct evidence concerning strong-form efficiency. What we have tends to be unfavourable to this hypothesis of market efficiency. Further, there is a logical paradox that exists with strong-form efficiency that suggests that all pertinent information is already included in the price of a security. If this were true, there would be no incentive to expend resources to gather information and trade on it. As a result, no one would gather information, so how could all the information be incorporated in a security's price? Known as the Grossman–Stiglitz paradox, this suggests that markets cannot be strong-form efficient because analysts have to be able to earn profits to compensate for the costs of conducting market research.[8]

## Some Common Misconceptions about the Efficient Market Hypothesis

No idea in finance has attracted as much attention as that of efficient markets, and not all of the attention has been flattering. To a certain extent this is because much of the criticism has been based on a misunderstanding of what the hypothesis does and does not say. We illustrate three misconceptions below.

**The Efficacy of Dart Throwing**    When the notion of market efficiency was first publicized and debated in the popular financial press, it was often characterized by the following quote: "Throwing darts at the financial page will produce a portfolio that can be expected to do as well as any managed by professional security analysts."[9] This is almost, but not quite, true.

All the EMH really says is that, on average, the manager will not be able to achieve an abnormal or excess return. The excess return is defined with respect to some benchmark expected return that could come from the security market line (SML) of Chapter 11, from the arbitrage pricing theory (APT) of Chapter 12, or from some other asset pricing model. The investor must still decide how risky a portfolio she wants and what expected return it will normally have. A random dart thrower might wind up with all of the darts sticking into one or two high-risk stocks that deal in genetic engineering. Would you really want all of your stock investments in two such stocks? (Beware, though—a professional portfolio manager could do the same.)

The failure to understand this has often led to a confusion about market efficiency. For example, sometimes it is wrongly argued that market efficiency means that it does not matter what you do because the efficiency of the market will protect the unwary. However, as someone once remarked, "The efficient market protects the sheep from the wolves, but nothing can protect the sheep from themselves."

What efficiency does say is that the price a firm will obtain when it sells a share of its stock is a fair price in the sense that it reflects the value of that stock given the information that is available about it. Shareholders need not worry that they are paying too much for a stock with a low dividend or some other characteristic, because the market has already incorporated it into the price. However, investors still have to worry about such things as their level of risk exposure and their degree of diversification.

**Price Fluctuations**    Much of the public is skeptical of efficiency because stock prices fluctuate from day to day. However, this price movement is in no way inconsistent with efficiency, because a stock in an efficient market adjusts to new information by changing price. In fact, the absence of price movements in a changing world might suggest an inefficiency.

---

[8] S. J. Grossman and J. E. Stiglitz, "On the Impossibility of Informationally Efficient Markets," *American Economic Review* (June 1980).

[9] B. G. Malkiel, *A Random Walk down Wall Street*, 8th ed. (New York: Norton, 2003).

**Shareholder Uninterest**   Many laypeople are skeptical that the market price can be efficient if only a fraction of the outstanding shares change hands on any given day. However, the number of traders in a stock on a given day is generally far fewer than the number of people following the stock. This is true because an individual will trade only when his appraisal of the value of the stock differs enough from the market price to justify incurring brokerage commissions and other transaction costs. Furthermore, even if the number of traders following a stock is small relative to the number of out-standing shareholders, the stock can be expected to be efficiently priced as long as a number of interested traders use the publicly available information. That is, the stock price can reflect the available information even if many shareholders never follow the stock and are not considering trading in the near future.

*CONCEPT*
*QUESTIONS*

- How would you describe the three forms of the EMH?
- What could make markets inefficient?
- Does market efficiency mean you can throw darts at a *National Post* listing of TSX stocks to pick a portfolio?
- What does it mean to say that the price you pay for a stock is fair?

# 14.4   THE EVIDENCE

The record on the EMH is extensive, and in large measure it is reassuring to advocates of the efficiency of markets. The studies done by academics fall into broad categories. First, there is evidence on whether changes in stock prices are predictable or random. Second are *event studies*. Third is the record of professionally managed investment firms. Fourth, there are *anomalies* (evidence contrary to the EMH). The final category is tests of whether insiders beat the market.

## The Weak Form

The random walk hypothesis, as expressed in equation (14.1), implies that a stock's price movement in the past is unrelated to its price movement in the future. The work of Chapter 11 allows us to test this implication. In that chapter, we discussed the concept of correlation between the returns on two different stocks. For example, the correlation between the return on U.S. Steel and the return on Dofasco is likely to be high because both stocks are in the steel industry. Conversely, the correlation between the return on Dofasco and the return on the stock of, say, a European fast-food chain is likely to be low.

Financial economists frequently speak of **serial correlation**, which involves only one security. This is the correlation between the current return on a security and the return on the same security over a later period. A positive coefficient of serial correla-tion for a particular stock indicates a tendency toward *continuation*. That is, a higher-than-average return today is likely to be followed by higher-than-average returns in the future. Similarly, a lower-than-average return today is likely to be followed by lower-than-average returns in the future.

A negative coefficient of serial correlation for a particular stock indicates a ten-dency toward *reversal*. A higher-than-average return today is likely to be followed by lower-than-average returns in the future, and so forth. Both significantly positive and significantly negative serial correlation coefficients are indications of market ineffi-ciencies; in either case, returns today can be used to predict future returns.

Serial correlation coefficients for stock returns near zero would be consistent with the random walk hypothesis. Thus, a current stock return that is higher than average is as likely to be followed by lower-than-average returns as by higher-than-average returns. Similarly, a current stock return that is lower than average is as likely to be followed by higher-than-average returns as by lower-than-average returns.

Correlation coefficients can, in principle, vary between −1 and 1, and the reported coefficients are quite small. A Canadian study, for example, found an average correlation coefficient of −0.01 for daily stock returns for TSX stocks.[10] Correlation coefficients like this one are so small relative to both estimation errors and transaction costs that the results are generally considered to be consistent with weak-form efficiency.

The weak form of the EMH has been tested in many other ways as well. Our view of the literature is that the evidence, taken as a whole, is consistent with weak-form efficiency.

This finding raises an interesting question: if price changes are truly random, why do so many technical analysts believe that prices follow patterns? The work of both psychologists and statisticians suggests that most people simply do not know what randomness looks like. For example, consider Figure 14.4. The top graph was generated by a computer using random numbers and equation (14.1). Yet we have found that people examining the chart generally see patterns. Different people see different patterns and forecast different price movements.

---

**FIGURE 14.4**

### Simulated and Actual Stock Price Movements

**A. Price Movements Simulated from Random Walk Process**

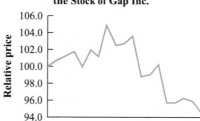

**B. Actual Price Movements for the Stock of Gap Inc.**

Although stock price movements from a random walk process are random by definition, people often see patterns. People may also see patterns in the Gap's price movements. However, the price patterns of the Gap are quite similar to those of the randomly simulated series.

---

However, in our experience, viewers are all quite confident of the patterns they see. Next consider the bottom graph, which tracks actual movements in The Gap's stock price. This graph may look quite non-random to some, suggesting weak-form inefficiency. However, it also bears a close visual resemblance to the simulated series, and statistical tests indicate that it indeed behaves like a purely random series. Thus, in our opinion, people claiming to see patterns in stock price data are probably seeing optical illusions.

---

[10] Stephen R. Foerster, "The Daily and Monthly Return Behaviour of Canadian Stocks," in *Canadian Capital Markets*, Michael J. Robinson and Brian F. Smith, eds. (London, ON: Western Business School, 1993), pp. 1–28.

## The Semistrong Form

The semistrong form of the EMH implies that prices should reflect all publicly available information. We present two types of tests of this form.

**Event Studies**     The *abnormal return (AR)* of a given stock on a particular day can be measured by subtracting the market's return on the same day $(R_m)$—as measured by the market index—from the actual return $(R)$ of the stock on that day.[11] We write this algebraically as

$$AR = R - R_m$$

A way to think of the tests of the semistrong form is to examine the following system of relationships:

Information released at time $t - 1 \rightarrow AR_{t-1}$
Information released at time $t \rightarrow AR_t$
Information released at time $t + 1 \rightarrow AR_{t+1}$

where AR stands for a stock's abnormal return and where the arrows indicate that the return in any time period is related only to the information released during that period.

According to the EMH, a stock's abnormal return at time $t$, $AR_t$, should reflect the release of information at the same time, $t$. Any information released before then, though, should have no effect on abnormal returns in this period, because all of its influence should have been felt before. In other words, an efficient market would already have incorporated previous information into prices. Because a stock's return today cannot depend on what the market does not yet know, the information that will be known only in the future cannot influence the stock's return either. Hence the arrows point in the direction shown, with information in any one time period affecting only that period's abnormal return. *Event studies* are statistical studies that examine whether the arrows are as shown or whether the release of information influences returns on other days.

As an example, consider the study by Szewczyk, Tsetsekos, and Zantout on dividend omissions.[12] Figure 14.5 shows the plot of *cumulative abnormal returns (CARs)* for a sample of companies announcing dividend omissions. Since dividend omissions are generally considered to be bad events, we would expect that abnormal returns would be negative around the time of the announcement. They are, as evidenced by a drop in the CARs on both the day before the announcement (day $-1$) and the day of the announcement (day 0).[13] However, note that there is virtually no movement in the

---

[11] The abnormal return can also be measured by using the market model. In this case the abnormal return is

$$AR = R - (\alpha + \beta R_m)$$

[12] Samuel A. Szewczyk, George P. Tsetsekos, and Zaher Z. Zantout, "Do Dividend Omissions Signal Future Earnings or Past Earnings?" *Journal of Investing* (Spring 1997).

[13] An astute reader may wonder why the abnormal return is negative on day $-1$, as well as on day 0. To see why, first note that the announcement date is generally taken in academic studies to be the publication date of the story in the *Wall Street Journal (WSJ)*. Then consider a company announcing a dividend omission via press release at noon on Tuesday. The stock should fall on Tuesday. The announcement will be reported in the *WSJ* on Wednesday, because the Tuesday edition of the *WSJ* has already been printed. For this firm, the stock price falls on the day *before* the announcement in the *WSJ*. However, as information becomes more readily accessible with the inclusion of online publications, this problem diminishes so that the stock price effect should be seen, more or less, on the day of the announcement.

Alternatively, imagine another firm announcing a dividend omission via press release on Tuesday at 8 p.m. Since the stock market is closed at that late hour, the stock will fall on Wednesday. Because the *WSJ* will report the announcement on Wednesday, the stock price falls on the day of the announcement in the *WSJ*.

Since firms may make announcements either during trading hours or after trading hours, stocks should fall on both day $-1$ and day 0 relative to publication in the *WSJ*.

CARs in the days following the announcement. This implies that the bad news is fully incorporated into the stock price by the announcement day, a result consistent with market efficiency.

**FIGURE 14.5**

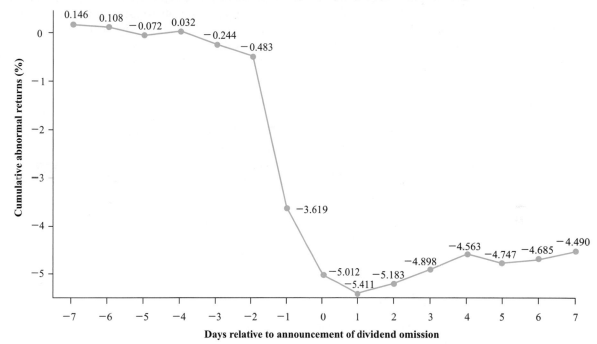

**Cumulative Abnormal Returns for Companies Announcing Dividend Omissions**

CARs fall on both the day before the announcement and the day of the announcement of dividend omissions. CARs have very little movement after the announcement date. This pattern is consistent with market efficiency.

Source: Exhibit 2 in S. H. Szewczyk, George P. Tsetsekos, and Zaher Zantout, "Do Dividend Omissions Signal Future Earnings or Past Earnings?" *Journal of Investing* (Spring 1997).

Over the years, this type of methodology has been applied to a large number of events. Announcements of dividends, earnings, mergers, capital expenditures, and new issues of stock are a few examples of the vast literature in the area.[14] The early event studies generally supported the view that the market is semistrong-form (and therefore also weak-form) efficient. However, a number of more recent studies present evidence that the market does not react to all relevant information immediately. Some conclude from this that the market is not efficient. Others argue that this conclusion is unwarranted, given statistical and methodological problems in the studies. This issue will be addressed in more detail later in the chapter.

**The Record of Mutual Funds**    If the market is efficient in the semistrong form, then no matter what publicly available information mutual fund managers use to pick stocks, their average returns should be the same as those of the average investor in the

---

[14] Some event studies suggest that stock market prices respond to information too slowly for the market to be efficient. For example, see Eli Bartov, Suresh Radhakrishnan, and Itzhak Krinsky, "Investor Sophistication and Patterns in Stock Returns after Earnings Announcements," *The Accounting Review* (January 2000); and V. Mehrotra, W. W. Yu, and C. Zhang, "Market Reactions to the *Financial Post's* 'Hot Stock' Column," *Canadian Journal of Administrative Sciences* (June 1999).

market as a whole. We can test efficiency, then, by comparing the performance of these professionals with that of a market index.

Consider Figure 14.6, which presents the performance of various types of U.S. mutual funds relative to the stock market as a whole. The far left of the figure shows that the universe of all funds covered in the study underperforms the market by 2.13 percent per year, after an appropriate adjustment for risk. Thus, rather than showing outperformance of the market, the evidence shows underperformance. This underperformance holds for a number of types of funds as well. Returns in this study are net of fees, expenses, and commissions, so fund returns would be higher if these costs were added back. However, the study shows no evidence that funds, as a whole, are *beating* the market. Canadian studies of mutual fund performance reach the same conclusion.[15] Canadian pension fund managers also generally fail to outperform the market index.[16]

**FIGURE 14.6**

**Annual Return Performance\* of Different Types of U.S. Mutual Funds Relative to a Broad-Based Market Index (1963–1998)**

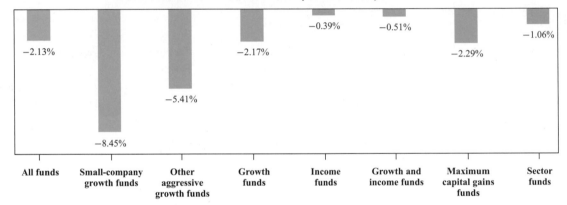

On average, mutual funds do not appear to be outperforming the market.

\* Performance is relative to the market model.

Taken from Table 2 of Lubos Pastor and Robert F. Stambaugh, "Mutual Fund Performance and Seemingly Unrelated Assets," *Journal of Financial Economics* (March 2002).

Perhaps nothing rankles successful stock market investors more than to have some professor tell them that they are not necessarily smart, just lucky. However, while Figure 14.6 represents only one study, there have been a host of papers on mutual funds. The overwhelming evidence here is that mutual funds do not beat broad-based indexes on average.

By and large, mutual fund managers rely on publicly available information. Thus, the finding that they do not outperform the market indexes is consistent with semi-strong-form and weak-form efficiency. This research has two important practical implications. First, it does not imply that mutual funds are bad investments for individuals. Though these funds fail to achieve better returns than some indexes of the market, they do permit the investor to buy a portfolio that has a large number of stocks in it (the phrase "a well-diversified portfolio" is often used). They might also be

---

[15] Two Canadian studies are G. Athanassakos, P. Carayannopoulos, and M. Racine, "Mutual Fund Performance: The Canadian Experience between 1985 and 1996," *Canadian Journal of Financial Planning of the CAFP* (June 2000); and "Canadian Mutual Fund Managers: Missing the Mark(et)!" Milestone Investment Counsel Inc. (August 2005).

[16] Vijay M. Jog, "Investment Performance of Pension Funds—A Canadian Study," *Canadian Journal of Administrative Sciences* (June 1986).

very good at providing a variety of services such as keeping custody and records of all of the stocks.

Second, the research underpins the growth of a particular kind of mutual fund, an index fund, which follows a passive investment strategy of investing in the market index. For example, TD Canadian Index Fund invests in the S&P/TSX Composite Total Return Index, and its performance tracks that of the index. The fund has lower expenses than an actively managed fund because it does not employ analysts to pick stocks. Investors who believe in semistrong-form efficiency prefer index investing because it implies that analysts will not beat the market consistently.

## The Strong Form

Even the most enthusiastic adherents of the EMH would not be surprised to find that markets are inefficient in the strong form. After all, if an individual has information that no one else has, it is likely that she can profit from it. For example, in 2012, the Ontario Securities Commission (OSC) alleged Eda Agueci, executive assistant to the chairman of brokerage at GMP Securities LP, had used her position to gain private information about forthcoming corporate deals, which she then traded on and tipped a network of friends and business contacts on. The OSC also accused Ian Telfer of helping Ms. Agueci hide some of her trades. The insider trading scheme involved eight individuals and amounted to approximately $962,000 in profits.[17] In September 2013, a settlement between the OSC and the accused was made in which Telfer was reprimanded and required to pay $200,000 in costs.[18]

Similarly, looking south of the border, in late 2001, the U.S. Food and Drug Administration (FDA) announced that a key anti-cancer drug produced by ImClone Systems had not passed a regulatory test and the stock dropped sharply. In the days before the announcement, ImClone's ex-CEO, Sam Waksal, and his friend, lifestyle guru Martha Stewart, sold the company's stock. By selling her 3,928 shares before the announcement, Ms. Stewart saved around US$50,000. Mr. Waksal was convicted of insider trading and Ms. Stewart was found guilty of obstructing a criminal investigation. Ironically, ImClone later received FDA approval for the new drug and its stock recovered.

Officers, directors, and major shareholders of a firm are considered insiders who may have information that is not public. In order to promote informational and allocational efficiency, the OSC (and its counterparts in other provinces) and the U.S. Securities and Exchange Commission (SEC) have regulations on insider trading. Insiders are allowed to buy and sell shares in their companies based on their general outlook but are prohibited from trading on specific pieces of information that have not yet become news. To enforce these regulations, the OSC, the SEC, and other securities commissions all require insiders to reveal any trading they might do in their own company's shares.

Researchers have used these records to test the hypothesis of strong-form market efficiency. If the strong form of the EMH holds, insiders should not be able to profit by trading on their information. By examining the record of insider trades, we can see whether they made abnormal returns. A number of studies support the view that these trades were abnormally profitable. Thus, strong-form efficiency does not seem to be substantiated by the evidence.[19]

---

[17] Janet McFarland, Andy Hoffman, and Tim Kiladze, "OSC Unveils Sweeping Insider Trading Case," *The Globe and Mail* (February 7, 2012).

[18] The details of the settlement can be found at www.osc.gov.on.ca/en/Proceedings_set_20130917_agueci-telfer.htm.

[19] H. N. Seyhun, *Investor Intelligence from Insider Trading* (Cambridge, MA: MIT Press, 1998), studies strong-form efficiency on the NYSE. Arturo Bris, "Do Insider Trading Laws Work?" Yale ICF Working Paper No. 00-19, shows that insider trading in Canada offers higher profits than in the United States.

Given the abnormal profitability of insider trading, research has focused on its relationship to the governance structure of a firm. A Canadian study by Jackson, Dutta, and Nitani estimates how the probability of informed (insider) trading depends on various characteristics, like the size of the firm and the level of CEO compensation. Interestingly, they find that only for large firms does the probability of informed trading increase when the CEO's compensation is lower—insider trading profits are seen as a substitute for CEO compensation.[20]

**CONCEPT QUESTIONS**

- The existence of a positive alpha in the capital asset pricing model (CAPM) implies that there are returns in excess of the equilibrium suggested by the return model. Can you conclude that markets are inefficient based on this evidence?
- What conclusions about market efficiency can be drawn from available evidence?

## 14.5 THE BEHAVIOURAL CHALLENGE TO MARKET EFFICIENCY

In Sections 14.2 and 14.3 we presented three conditions, any one of which will lead to market efficiency. In those sections, a case was made that at least one of the conditions is likely to hold in the real world. However, there is definitely disagreement. Many members of the academic community argue that none of the three conditions are likely to hold in reality. This point of view is based on what is called *behavioural finance*. Let us examine the behavioural view of each of these three conditions.

**Rationality**   Are people really rational? Not always. Just travel to Atlantic City or Las Vegas to see people gambling, sometimes with large sums of money. The casino's take implies a negative expected return for the gambler. Because gambling is risky and has a negative expected return, it can never be on the efficient frontier. In addition, gamblers will often bet on black at a roulette table after black has occurred a number of consecutive times, thinking that the run will continue. This strategy is faulty because roulette tables have no memory.

But, of course, gambling is only a sideshow as far as finance is concerned. Is there irrationality in financial markets as well? The answer may well be yes. Many investors do not achieve the degree of diversification that they should. Others trade frequently, generating both commissions and taxes. In fact, taxes can be handled optimally by selling losers and holding onto winners. Although some individuals invest with tax minimization in mind, plenty of them do just the opposite. Many are more likely to sell their winners than their losers, a strategy leading to high tax payments.[21] The behavioural view is not that *all* investors are irrational. Rather, it is that some, perhaps many, investors are.[22]

**Independent Deviations from Rationality**   Are deviations from rationality generally random, thereby likely to cancel out in a whole population of investors? To the contrary, psychologists have long argued that people deviate from rationality in

---

[20] David Jackson, Shantanu Dutta, and Miwako Nitani, "Corporate Governance and Informed Trading," *International Journal of Managerial Finance* 4.4 (2008).

[21] For example, see Brad Barber and Terrance Odean, "The Courage of Misguided Convictions," *Financial Analysts Journal* (November/December 1999).

[22] Irrationality may explain research that shows that stock returns vary directly with the amount of sunlight during different seasons; see Mark J. Kamstra, Lisa A. Kramer, and Maurice D. Levi, "Winter Blues: A SAD Stock Market Cycle," *American Economic Review* (March 2003).

accordance with a number of basic principles. Not all of these principles have an application to finance and market efficiency, but at least two seem to do so.

The first principle, called *representativeness*, can be explained with the gambling example just used. The gambler believing a run of black will continue is in error because the probability of a black spin is still only about 50 percent. Gamblers behaving in this way exhibit the psychological trait of representativeness—drawing conclusions from insufficient data. In other words, the gambler believes the small sample he observed is more representative of the population than it really is.

How is this related to finance? Perhaps a market dominated by representativeness leads to bubbles. People see a sector of the market—for example, Internet stocks—having a short history of high revenue growth and extrapolate that it will continue forever. When the growth inevitably stalls, prices have nowhere to go but down.

The second principle is *conservatism*, which means that people are too slow in adjusting their beliefs to new information. Suppose that your goal since childhood has been to become a dentist. Perhaps you came from a family of dentists, perhaps you liked the security and relatively high income that comes with that profession, or perhaps teeth always fascinated you. As things stand now, you could probably look forward to a long and productive career in that occupation. However, suppose a new drug were developed that would prevent tooth decay. That drug would clearly reduce the demand for dentists. How quickly would you realize the implications as stated here? If you were emotionally attached to dentistry, you might adjust your beliefs slowly. Family and friends could tell you to switch out of pre-dental courses in university, but you might not be psychologically ready to do that. Instead, you might cling to your rosy view of dentistry's future.

Perhaps there is a relationship to finance here. For example, many studies report that prices seem to adjust slowly to the information contained in earnings announcements.[23] Could it be that because of conservatism, investors are slow in adjusting their beliefs to new information? More will be said about this in the next section.

**Arbitrage**  In Section 14.2 we suggested that professional investors, knowing that securities are mispriced, could buy the underpriced ones while selling correctly priced (or even overpriced) substitutes. This might undo any mispricing caused by emotional amateurs.

Trading of this sort is likely to be more risky than it appears at first glance. Suppose professionals generally believed that McDonald's stock was underpriced. They would buy it while selling their holdings in, say, Burger King and Wendy's. However, if amateurs were taking opposite positions, prices would adjust to correct levels only if the positions of amateurs were small relative to those of the professionals. In a world of many amateurs, a few professionals would have to take big positions to bring prices into line, perhaps even engaging heavily in short selling. Buying large amounts of one stock and short selling large amounts of other stocks is quite risky, even if the two stocks are in the same industry. Here, unanticipated bad news about McDonald's and unanticipated good news about the other two stocks would cause the professionals to register large losses.

In addition, if amateurs mispriced McDonald's today, what is to prevent McDonald's from being even *more* mispriced tomorrow? This risk of further mispricing, even in the presence of no new information, may also cause professionals to cut back their arbitrage positions. As an example, imagine a shrewd professional who believed financial stocks were overpriced in 2007. Had she bet on a decline at that time, she would have lost in the near term: prices rose through August 2008. Yet she would have eventually made money because prices later fell. However, near-term risk may reduce the size of arbitrage strategies.

---

[23] For example, see Vijay Singal, *Beyond the Random Walk* (New York: Oxford University Press, 2004), Chapter 4.

In conclusion, the arguments presented here suggest that the theoretical under-pinnings of the EMH, presented in Section 14.2, might not hold in reality. That is, investors may be irrational, irrationality may be related across investors rather than cancelling out across investors, and arbitrage strategies may involve too much risk to eliminate market efficiencies.

## 14.6    EMPIRICAL CHALLENGES TO MARKET EFFICIENCY

Section 14.4 presented empirical evidence supportive of market efficiency. We now present evidence challenging this hypothesis. (Adherents of market efficiency generally refer to results of this type as *anomalies*.)

1. *Limits to arbitrage.* Royal Dutch Petroleum and Shell Transport merged their interests in 1907, with all subsequent cash flows being split on a 60 percent–40 percent basis between the two companies. However, both companies continued to be publicly traded. You might imagine that the market value of Royal Dutch would always be 1.5 (= 60/40) times that of Shell. That is, if Royal Dutch ever became overpriced, rational investors would buy Shell instead of Royal Dutch. If Royal Dutch were underpriced, investors would buy Royal Dutch. In addition, arbitrageurs would go further by buying the underpriced security and selling the overpriced security short.

   However, Figure 14.7 shows that Royal Dutch and Shell have rarely traded at parity (i.e., 60/40) over the 1962 to 2005 period. Why would these deviations occur? As stated in the previous section, behavioural finance suggests that there are limits to arbitrage. That is, an investor buying the overpriced asset and selling the underpriced asset does not have a sure thing. Deviations from parity could actually *increase* in the short run, implying losses for the arbitrageur. The well-known statement, "Markets can stay irrational longer than you can stay solvent," attributed to John Maynard Keynes, applies here. Thus, risk considerations may force arbitrageurs to take positions that are too small to move prices back to parity.

---

**FIGURE 14.7**

**Deviations of the Ratio of the Market Value of Royal Dutch to the Market Value of Shell from Parity**

Apparently arbitrage is unable to keep the ratio of the market value of Royal Dutch to the market value of Shell at parity.

Source: Author calculations.

Academics have documented a number of these deviations from parity. Froot and Dabora show similar results both for the twin companies of Unilever N.V. and Unilever PLC and for two classes of SmithKline Beecham stock.[24] Lamont and Thaler present similar findings for 3Com and its subsidiary Palm Inc.[25] Other researchers find price behaviour in closed-end mutual funds suggestive of parity deviations.

2. *Earnings surprises.* Common sense suggests that prices should rise when earnings are reported to be higher than expected and prices should fall when the reverse occurs. However, market efficiency implies that prices will adjust immediately to the announcement, while behavioural finance would predict another pattern. Kolasinski and Li rank companies by the extent of their *earnings surprise*—that is, the difference between current quarterly earnings and quarterly earnings four quarters ago, divided by the current stock price.[26] They form a portfolio of companies with the most extreme positive surprises and another portfolio of companies with the most extreme negative surprises. Figure 14.8 shows returns from buying the two portfolios, net of the return on the overall market. As can be seen, prices adjust slowly to the earnings announcements, with the portfolio with the positive surprises outperforming the portfolio with the negative surprises over both the next month and the next six months. Many other researchers obtain similar results.

Why do prices adjust slowly? Behavioural finance suggests that investors exhibit conservatism because they are slow to adjust to the information contained in the announcements.

**FIGURE 14.8**

### Returns on Two Investment Strategies Based on Earnings Surprise

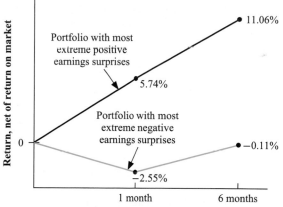

This figure shows returns net of the market return to a strategy of buying stocks with extremely high positive earnings surprise (the difference between current quarterly earnings and quarterly earnings four quarters ago, divided by the current stock price) and to a strategy of buying stocks with extremely high negative earnings surprise. The graph shows a slow adjustment to the information in the earnings announcement.

Source: Adapted from Table 1 of Adam Kolasinski and Xu Li, "Do Managers Detect Mispricing? Evidence from Insider Trading and Post-Earnings-Announcement Drift" (Massachusetts Institute of Technology: unpublished paper, 2005).

---

[24] Kenneth A. Froot and Emil M. Dabora, "How Are Stock Prices Affected by the Location of Trade?" *Journal of Financial Economics* (August 1999).

[25] Owen Lamont and Richard Thaler, "Can the Market Add and Subtract? Mispricing in Tech Stock Carve-Outs," *Journal of Political Economy* (April 2003).

[26] Adam Kolasinski and Xu Li, "Do Managers Detect Mispricing? Evidence from Insider Trading and Post-Earnings-Announcement Drift" (Massachusetts Institute of Technology: unpublished paper, 2005).

3. *Size*. In 1981, two important papers presented evidence that in the United States, the returns on stocks with small market capitalizations were greater than the returns on stocks with large market capitalizations over most of the 20th century.[27] Table 10.3 in Chapter 10 shows that Canadian stocks with small market capitalizations outperformed stocks with large market capitalizations[28] over the period from 1970 to 2013. The difference in returns is perhaps 5 to 10 percent per year. While much of the differential performance is merely compensation for the extra risk of small stocks, a number of researchers have argued that not all of it can be explained by risk differences.[29] In addition, Keim presented evidence that most of the difference in performance occurs in the month of January. Jog shows that this *size effect* (also called the *small capitalization effect* or *January effect*) is international. It has been documented for Canada and in most stock exchanges around the world as occurring immediately after the close of the tax year.[30] While the effect is small relative to commissions on stock purchases and sales, investors who have decided to buy small-capitalization stocks can exploit the anomaly by buying in December rather than in January.

4. *Value versus growth*. A number of papers have argued that stocks with high book value-to-stock price ratios and/or high earnings-to-price ratios (generally called *value stocks*) outperform stocks with low ratios (*growth stocks*). For example, Fama and French find that for 12 of 13 major international stock markets, the average return on stocks with high book value–to–stock price ratios is above the average return on stocks with low book value–to–stock price ratios.[31] Figure 14.9 shows these returns for the world's five largest stock markets. Value stocks have outperformed growth stocks in each of these five markets.

Because the return difference is so large and because these ratios can be obtained so easily for individual stocks, the results may constitute strong evidence against market efficiency. However, a number of papers suggest that the unusual returns are due to biases in the commercial databases, not to a true inefficiency.[32] Since the debate revolves around the details of data collection, we will not pursue the issue further. However, it is safe to say that no conclusion is warranted at this time. As with so many other topics in finance and economics, further research is needed.

---

[27] See R. W. Banz, "The Relationship between Return and Market Value of Common Stocks," *Journal of Financial Economics* (March 1981); and M. R. Reinganum, "Misspecification of Capital Asset Pricing: Empirical Anomalies Based on Earnings Yields and Market Values," *Journal of Financial Economics* (March 1981).

[28] Market capitalization is the price per share of stock multiplied by the number of shares outstanding.

[29] D. B Keim, "Size-Related Anomalies and Stock Return Seasonality: Further Empirical Evidence," *Journal of Financial Economics* (June 1983). See also J. Jaffe, D. Keim, and R. Westerfield, "Earnings Yields, Market Values and Stock Returns," *Journal of Finance* (March 1989). They find that firms with high earnings yields and small market capitalizations have abnormally high returns.

[30] Vijay Jog, "Stock Pricing Anomalies Revisited," *Canadian Investment Review* (Winter 1998); Stephen R. Foerster and David C. Porter, "Calendar and Size-Based Anomalies in Canadian Stock Returns," in *Canadian Capital Markets*, Michael J. Robinson and Brian F. Smith, eds. (London, ON: Western Business School, 1993), pp. 133–140, supports these findings with the TSX–Western database; George Athanassakos, "Seasons for Stocks," *Canadian Investment Review* (Fall 1997), relates the effect of institutional trading; S. Elfakhani, L. J. Lockwood, and R. S. Zaher, "Small Firm and Value Effects in the Canadian Stock Market," *Journal of Financial Research* (Fall 1998).

[31] Taken from Table III of Eugene F. Fama and Kenneth R. French, "Value versus Growth: The International Evidence," *Journal of Finance* (December 1998).

[32] For example, S. P. Kothari, J. Shanken, and R. G. Sloan, "Another Look at the Cross-Section of Expected Stock Returns," *Journal of Finance* (March 1995); document survivorship bias arises because databases do not include the lower returns on companies that went out of business during the sample period.

FIGURE 14.9

**Annual Dollar Returns\* (in percent) on Low Book-to-Price Firms and High Book-to-Price Firms in Selected Countries**

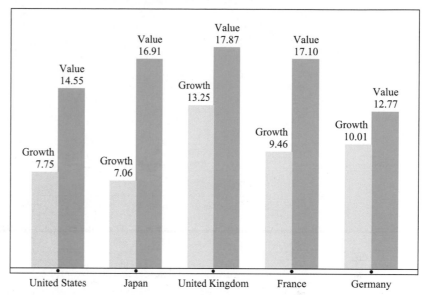

High book-to-price stocks (frequently called value stocks) outperform low book-to-price (growth) stocks in different countries.

\* Dollar returns are expressed as the excess over the return on U.S. Treasury bills.

Source: Eugene F. Fama and Kenneth R. French, "Value versus Growth: The International Evidence," *Journal of Finance* (December 1998).

5. *Crashes and bubbles.* The stock market crash of October 19, 1987, is extremely puzzling. The market dropped between 20 percent and 25 percent on a Monday following a weekend during which little surprising news was released. A drop of this magnitude for no apparent reason is not consistent with market efficiency. Because the crash of 1929 is still an enigma, it is doubtful that the more recent 1987 debacle will be explained any time soon. The recent comments of an eminent historian are apt here. When asked what, in his opinion, the effect of the French Revolution of 1789 was, he replied that it was too early to tell.

Perhaps the two stock market crashes are evidence consistent with the **bubble theory** of speculative markets. That is, security prices sometimes move wildly above their true values. Eventually, prices fall back to their original level, causing great losses for investors. Consider, for example, the behaviour of Internet stocks of the late 1990s. Figure 14.10 shows values of an index of Internet stocks from 1996 through 2002. The index rose over tenfold from January 1996 to its high in March 2000 before retreating to approximately its original level in 2002. For comparison, the figure also shows price movement for the Standard & Poor's 500 index. While this index rose and fell over the same period, the price movement was quite muted relative to that of Internet stocks.

**FIGURE 14.10**

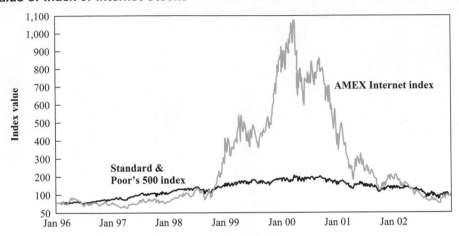

**Value of Index of Internet Stocks**

The index of Internet stocks rose over tenfold from the beginning of 1996 to its high in March 2000 before falling to approximately its original level in 2002.

Many commentators describe the rise and fall of Internet stocks as a *bubble*. Is it correct to do so? Unfortunately, there is no precise definition of the term. Some academics argue that the price movement in the figure is consistent with rationality. Prices rose initially, they say, because it appeared that the Internet would soon capture a large chunk of international commerce. Prices fell when later evidence suggested this would not occur quite so quickly. However, others argue that the initial rosy scenario was never supported by the facts. Rather, prices rose due to nothing more than "irrational exuberance." The emergence of a stable government in India after that country's 2009 elections drove the Bombay Stock Exchange (BSE) to its largest ever single-day gain of 2,110 points, a rise of 20 percent. A rise of this magnitude appears inconsistent with market efficiency.

Recall the market volatility in 2008 and 2009 when the world's financial system nearly collapsed. This was in part due to the irrational belief by investors that pooling and financial engineering had removed the risk of subprime mortgages underlying securitized collateralized debt obligations (CDOs). With interest rates low, investors were quick to take on leverage to buy these new "low-risk" products with high returns.[33] When the irrational housing market bubble burst, investors began to realize that CDOs offered no protection. With the collapse of Lehman brothers, trust became an issue among banks, and the credit crisis ensued.

## 14.7 REVIEWING THE DIFFERENCES

It is fair to say that the controversy over efficient capital markets has not yet been resolved. Rather, academic financial economists have sorted themselves into three camps, with some adhering to market efficiency, some believing in behavioural finance, and others (perhaps the majority) not yet convinced that either side has won the argument. This state of affairs is certainly different from, say, 35 years ago, when market efficiency went unchallenged. In addition, the controversy here is perhaps the most contentious of any area of financial economics. Only in this area do grown-up finance professors come close to fisticuffs over an idea.

---

[33] "The Origins of the Financial Crisis," *The Economist* (September 7, 2013).

Adherents of behavioural finance point out, as discussed in Section 14.5, that the three theoretical foundations of market efficiency appear to be violated in the real world. Second, they stress that there are simply too many anomalies, with a number of them having been replicated in out-of-sample tests.[34] Critics of behavioural finance generally make three points in rebuttal:

1. *The file drawer problem.* Scholars generally submit their papers to academic journals, where independent referees judge whether the work is deserving of publication. Papers either get accepted in a journal, leading to potential influence in the field, or they get rejected, leaving the author to, as the phrase goes, bury the paper "in the file drawer." It has been frequently suggested that, holding quality of research constant, referees are more likely to accept a paper with unusual and interesting results. Critics of behavioural finance argue that since market efficiency has been the received paradigm in finance, any paper challenging efficiency has a higher probability of acceptance that one supporting efficiency. Thus, the publication process may inadvertently favour behavioural finance research.

2. *Risk.* As indicated in Chapter 11, investors try to maximize expected return per unit of risk. However, risk is not always easy to estimate. Efficient market adherents often suggest that some anomalies might disappear if more sophisticated adjustments for risk were made. As an example, we mentioned in the previous section that a number of researchers have argued that the high returns on value stocks can be explained by their higher risk.

3. *Behavioural finance and market prices.* Critics of behavioural finance often argue that even if the data support certain anomalies, it is not clear that these anomalies support behavioural finance. For example, consider representativeness and conservatism, two psychological principles mentioned earlier in this chapter.

   Representativeness implies overweighting the results of small samples, as with the gambler who thinks a few consecutive spins of black on the roulette wheel make black a more likely outcome than red on the next spin. Financial economists argue that representativeness can lead to *overreaction* in stock returns. We mentioned earlier that financial bubbles are likely overreactions to news. Internet companies showed great revenue growth for a short time in the late 1990s, causing many to believe that this growth would continue indefinitely. Stock prices rose (too much) at this point. When at last investors realized that this growth could not be sustained, prices plummeted.

   Conservatism states that individuals adjust their beliefs too slowly to new information. A market composed of this type of investor would likely lead to stock prices that *underreact* in the presence of new information. The example concerning earnings surprises may illustrate this underreaction. Prices rose slowly following announcements of positive earnings surprises. Announcements of negative surprises had a similar, but opposite, reaction.

   Efficient market believers stress that representativeness and conservatism have opposite implications for stock prices. Which principle, they ask, should dominate in any particular situation? In other words, why should investors overreact to news about Internet stocks but underreact to earnings news? Proponents of market efficiency say that unless behaviourists can answer these two questions satisfactorily, we should not reject market efficiency in favour of behavioural finance.[35]

---

[34] Excellent reviews of behavioural finance can be found in Andrei Shleifer, *Inefficient Markets: An Introduction to Behavioral Finance*, op. cit.; and in Nicholas Barberis and Richard Thaler, "A Survey of Behavioral Finance," in *Handbook of the Economics of Finance*, eds. George Constantinides, Milton Harris, and Rene Stulz (Amsterdam: North Holland, 2003).

[35] See, for example, Eugene F. Fama, "Market Efficiency, Long-Term Returns, and Behavioral Finance," *Journal of Financial Economics* (September 1998).

While we have devoted more space in this section to arguments supporting market efficiency than to arguments supporting behavioural finance, you should not take this difference as evidence in favour of efficiency. Rather, the jury, the community of financial economists in this case, is still out here. It does not appear that our textbook, or any textbook, can easily resolve the differing points of view.

# IN THEIR OWN WORDS

## A random talk with Burton Malkiel

**How will the technology bubble be remembered?**
Historians will record the Internet bubble of the late 1990s as one of the greatest bubbles of all time. Valuations became truly unbelievable. During the Nifty Fifty craze, the well-known growth stocks may have sold at 60-, 70- or even 80-times earnings. During the Internet bubble, stocks would sell at 60-, 70- or 80-times sales. Priceline.com, one of the Internet companies that sold discounted airline tickets, was valued at one time with a market capitalization that was larger than the combined market capitalizations of Delta Airlines, American Airlines and United Airlines. At its low, Priceline sold for about a dollar a share. You even had enormous multi-billion-dollar capitalizations from companies that had essentially no sales at all. They were just selling on a promise.

People confused the correct idea that the Internet was real, that it was going to mean some profound changes in the way we live and shop and get information, to saying that the ordinary rules of valuation didn't apply. Whatever business you are in, an asset can only be worth the present value of the cash flows that are going to be generated in the future.

Look at reports that were issued by Wall Street firms. You find statements such as "the old metrics are different this time." That has certainly proved to be wrong. Most of these Internet stocks today are selling at a tiny fraction of their high market valuations. It is not clear that any of them have a business model that is going to allow them to make money. In one sense, Amazon.com is a very successful company. But they have yet to show that they are able to make any money.

To be sure, the same thing happened in our past history. There were many people who laid railroad tracks during the railroad-ization of North America. There was overbuilding and most of them collapsed. We had hundreds of automobile manufacturers at one time.

But what didn't happen in the past were the market valuations assigned to these companies. Why did firms like Morgan Stanley and Merrill Lynch put out buy recommendations on all of these stocks when they were at or near their peaks? The real problem is that their well-known analysts were paid a lot of money, not necessarily to make correct judgments about whether stocks were good buys or not, but rather based on their success in bringing investment banking clients into the firm. Who knows whether they knew better or not? But there was a clear conflict of interest.

Here's another thing—the CNBC effect. You had people talking about these extraordinary gains, and [producers] didn't want a fuddy duddy value manager being interviewed on CNBC. [They] wanted the person who said Amazon.com has a price target of $500 a share. Those were the people who got on those shows. That fed the public enthusiasm. There were some people who got it right. They were generally the value managers who actually underperformed the market as a whole very badly during that period.

**How did institutional investors compare to retail investors?**
The retail investors probably did a bit worse. Some of the institutional investors were sucked up in the enthusiasm and probably did overweight some of these stocks. But I think the real damage occurred with individual investors. It really worries me how sensitive the public money flows are to recent performance.

Having said that, everyone is ranked each quarter in the institutional business versus everyone else. The institutions—not quite to the extent that the public is—are not immune at all. Presumably the savvy institutions should be precisely the ones who lean against the wind. But if you look at the cash balances of mutual fund managers and institutional money managers, you find almost invariably their lowest cash balances are just at the peak of the market. They're almost perfect contrarian indicators.

I can remember arguments that I had with institutional investors in 1999, when I'd talk about the Pricelines of the world. People would say, "You don't understand the value of the first mover. What a brilliant idea Priceline has. Don't worry that they're losing money now." Very clearly, there is soul searching to be done by the institutions.

Burton Malkiel is the Chemical Bank Chairman's Professor of Economics, Emeritus, at Princeton University and author of *A Random Walk down Wall Street*. His comments are excerpted (with permission) from *Canadian Investment Review* (Summer 2001).

# 14.8  IMPLICATIONS FOR CORPORATE FINANCE

## Accounting and Efficient Markets

The accounting profession provides firms with a significant amount of leeway in their reporting practices. For example, companies may choose either the percentage-of-completion or the completed-contracts method for construction projects. They may depreciate physical assets by either accelerated or straight-line depreciation. Financial institutions may exercise considerable judgment in setting aside loan loss provisions.

Accountants have frequently been accused of misusing this leeway in the hopes of boosting earnings and stock prices. For example, U.S. Steel (now USX Corporation) switched from straight-line to accelerated depreciation after World War II, because its high reported profits at that time attracted much government scrutiny. It switched back to straight-line depreciation in the 1960s after years of low reported earnings.

In the 1930s, Canada's largest life insurance company, Sun Life, experienced a major drop in the market value of its common stock portfolio that effectively erased the company's capital. To allow the company to remain in business, federal regulators changed the accounting rules for insurance companies, allowing Sun Life to backdate the prices of its investments until the market improved.[36] This issue arose again during the financial crisis of 2007–2009 when many securities held on banks' balance sheets could not be valued as their markets had disappeared. In April of 2009, the Financial Accounting Standards Board (FASB) voted on and approved new guidelines allowing valuation to be based on a price that would be received in an orderly market rather than in a forced liquidation.

Despite such examples, accounting choice should not affect stock price, provided two conditions hold. First, enough information must be provided in the annual report and other public sources so that financial analysts can construct earnings under the alternative accounting methods. This appears to be the case for many, though not necessarily all, accounting choices. Second, the market must be efficient in the semistrong form. In other words, the market must appropriately use all of this accounting information in determining the market price.

Of course, the issue of whether accounting choice affects stock price is ultimately an empirical matter. A number of academic papers have addressed this issue. Kaplan and Roll found that the switch from accelerated to straight-line depreciation generally did not affect stock prices significantly.[37] Several other accounting procedures have been studied. Hong, Kaplan, and Mandelker found no evidence that the stock market was affected by the artificially higher earnings reported using the pooling method, compared to the purchase method, for reporting mergers and acquisitions.[38] Cheung found no association between security returns and inflation accounting disclosures in Canada.[39] In summary, the above empirical evidence suggests that accounting changes do not fool the market.[40]

---

[36] Lawrence Kryzanowski and Gordon S. Roberts, "Capital Forbearance: A Depression-Era Case Study of Sun Life," *Canadian Journal of Administrative Sciences* (April 1998).

[37] R. S. Kaplan and R. Roll, "Investor Evaluation of Accounting Information: Some Empirical Evidence," *Journal of Business* (April 1972).

[38] H. Hong, R. S. Kaplan, and G. Mandelker, "Pooling vs. Purchase: The Effects of Accounting for Mergers on Stock Prices," *Accounting Review* (January 1978).

[39] J. K. Cheung, "Inflation Accounting Disclosures and Stock Price Adjustments: Some Canadian Results," *Accounting and Finance* (November 1986).

[40] These excellent studies are slightly off the mark for our purposes. They test the hypothesis that, in aggregate, stock prices are invariant to accounting changes. The EMH actually makes a stronger statement. As long as earnings can be reconstructed under alternative accounting methods, each stock should be unaffected by a change in accounting.

Stock price is also likely to be affected if a company either withholds useful information or provides incorrect information that cannot be corrected based on public sources. In many such cases of deliberate misrepresentation, the market obtains more accurate information of its own. One example in which this occurred involved the Northland Bank. Prior to its failure in 1985, the bank used questionable accounting to cover up its exposure to bad energy loans in western Canada. According to the Estey Commission, which investigated the bank failure, "The financial statements became gold fillings covering cavities in the assets and in the earnings of the bank." Yet research on stock prices prior to the collapse has shown that stock market investors were aware that the bank was highly risky.[41]

Companies like Enron, WorldCom, Global Crossing, and Nortel have reported fraudulent numbers. There was no way for financial analysts to construct alternative earnings numbers because these analysts were unaware how the reported numbers were determined.

## The Timing Decision

Imagine a firm whose managers are contemplating the date to issue equity. This decision is frequently called the *timing* decision. If managers believe that their stock is overpriced, they are likely to issue equity immediately. Here, they are creating value for their current stockholders because they are selling stock for more than it is worth. Conversely, if the managers believe that their stock is underpriced, they are more likely to wait, hoping that the stock price will eventually rise to its true value.

However, if markets are efficient, securities are always correctly priced. Since efficiency implies that stock is always sold for its true worth, the timing decision becomes unimportant. Figure 14.11 shows three possible stock price adjustments to the issuance of new stock. Market efficiency implies that the stock price of the issuing firm, on average, neither rises nor falls after issuance of the stock. Of course, market efficiency is ultimately an empirical issue.

**FIGURE 14.11**

**Three Stock Price Adjustments**

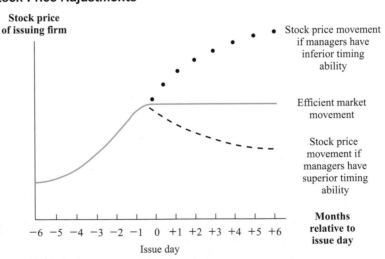

Studies show that stock is more likely to be issued after stock prices have increased. No inferences on market efficiency can be drawn from this result. Market efficiency implies that the stock price of the issuing firm, on average, neither rises nor falls *after* issuance of stock.

---

[41] R. Giammarino, E. Schwartz, and J. Zechner, "Market Valuation of Bank Assets and Deposit Insurance in Canada," *Canadian Journal of Economics* (February 1989).

Surprisingly, a paper has called market efficiency into question. Ritter[42] presents evidence that annual returns over the five years following an IPO are, on average, approximately 3.3 percent less for the issuing company than the return on a non-issuing company of similar market capitalization. In addition, Ritter examines seasoned equity offerings (SEOs), that is, publicly traded companies that issue additional stock. He finds that over the five years following an SEO, the annualized return on the issuing firm's stock is approximately 3.4 percent (see Figure 14.12) less than the return on a comparable non-issuing company. The evidence suggests that corporate managers issue stock when it is overpriced. In other words, they are successfully able to time the market. The evidence that managers time their IPOs is less compelling. Returns following IPOs are closer to those of their control group.

Does the ability of a corporate official to issue an SEO when the security is overpriced indicate that the market is inefficient in the semistrong form or the strong form? The answer is actually somewhat more complex than it may first appear. On one hand, officials are likely to have special information that the rest of us do not have, suggesting that the market need only be inefficient in the strong form. On the other hand, if the market were truly semistrong-form efficient, the price would drop immediately and completely upon the announcement of an upcoming SEO. That is, rational investors would realize that stock is being issued because corporate officials have special information that the stock is overpriced. Indeed, many empirical studies report a price drop on the announcement date. However, Figure 14.12 shows a further price drop in the subsequent years, suggesting that the market is inefficient in the semistrong form.

## Speculation and Efficient Markets

We normally think of individuals and financial institutions as the primary speculators in financial markets. However, industrial corporations speculate as well. For example, many companies make interest rate bets. If the managers of a firm believe that interest rates are likely to rise, they have an incentive to borrow because the PV of the liability will fall with the rate increase. In addition, these managers will have an incentive to borrow long term rather than short term in order to lock in the low rates for a longer period. The thinking can get more sophisticated. Suppose that the long-term rate is already higher than the short-term rate. The manager might argue that this differential reflects the market's view that rates will rise. However, perhaps he anticipates a rate increase even greater than what the market anticipates, as implied by the upward-sloping term structure. Again, the manager will want to borrow long term rather than short term.

Firms also speculate in foreign currencies. Suppose that the CFO of a multinational corporation based in the United States believes that the euro will decline relative to the dollar. She will probably issue euro-denominated debt rather than dollar-denominated debt because she expects the value of the foreign liability to fall. Conversely, she will issue debt domestically if she believes foreign currencies will appreciate relative to the dollar.

We are perhaps getting a little ahead of our story; the subtleties of the term structure and exchange rates are treated in other chapters, not this one. However, the big picture question is, what does market efficiency have to say about such activity? The answer is clear. If financial markets are efficient, managers should not waste their time trying to forecast the movements of interest rates and foreign currencies. Their forecasts will likely be no better than chance. And they will be using up valuable executive time. This is not to say, however, that firms should pick the maturity or the denomination of their debt in a random fashion. A firm must *choose* these parameters carefully. However, the choice should be based on other rationales, not on an attempt to beat the market. For example, a firm with a project lasting five years might decide to issue five-year debt. A firm might issue yen-denominated debt because it anticipates expanding into Japan in a big way.

---

[42] J. R. Ritter, "Investment Banking and Security Issuance," Chapter 9 of *Handbook of the Economics of Finance*, eds. G. Constantinides, M. Harris, and R. Stulz (Amsterdam: North Holland, 2003).

FIGURE 14.12

### Returns on Initial Public Offerings and Seasoned Equity Offerings in Years Following Issue

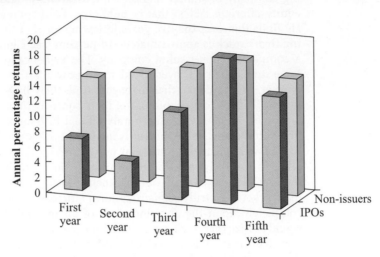

The average returns for 8,464 IPOs from 1970 to 2011 and their matching non-issuing firms during the five years after the issue. The first-year return does not include the return on the day of issue.

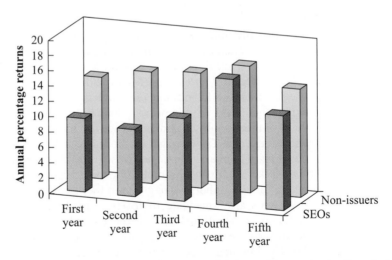

The average returns for 10,208 SEOs from 1970 to 2011 and their matching non-issuing firms during the five years after the issue. The first-year return does not include the return on the day of issue.

On average, IPOs underperform their control groups by about 3.3% per year in the five years following issuance. SEOs underperform by about 3.4% per year.

Original Source: Jay Ritter, "Investment Banking and Security Issuance," Chapter 9 of *Handbook of the Economics of Finance*, eds. George Constantinides, Milton Harris, and Rene Stulz (Amsterdam: North Holland, 2003).

Updated from author websites: Jay Ritter, "Return on IPOs During the Five Years after Issuing, for IPOs from 1970–2011" (April 11, 2013), bear.warrington.ufl.edu/ritter/IPOs2012-5years.pdf; Leming Lin and Jay Ritter, "Return on Seasoned Equity Offerings in the 5 Years After Issuing, from 1970–2011" (June 13, 2011), bear. warrington.ufl.edu/ritter/SEOs.pdf.

The same thinking applies to acquisitions. Many corporations buy up other firms because they think these targets are underpriced. Unfortunately, the empirical evidence suggests that the market is too efficient for this type of speculation to be profitable. And the acquirer never pays just the current market price. The bidding firm must pay a premium above market to induce a majority of shareholders of the target firm to sell their shares. However, this is not to say that firms should never be acquired. Rather, managers should consider an acquisition if there are benefits (synergies) from the union. Improved marketing, economies in production, replacement of bad management, and even tax reduction are typical synergies. These synergies are distinct from the perception that the acquired firm is underpriced.

One final point should be mentioned. We talked earlier about empirical evidence suggesting that SEOs are timed to take advantage of overpriced stock. This makes sense—managers are likely to know more about their own firms than the market does. However, while managers may have special information about their own firms, it is unlikely that they have special information about interest rates, foreign currencies, and other firms. There are simply too many participants in these markets, many of whom are devoting all of their time to forecasting. Managers typically spend most of their effort running their own firms, with only a small amount of time devoted to studying financial markets.

## Information in Market Prices

The previous section argued that it is quite difficult to forecast market prices. However, the current and past prices of any asset are known—and of great use. Consider, for example, Becher's study of bank mergers.[43] The author finds that stock prices of acquired banks rise about 23 percent on average upon the first announcement of a merger. This is not surprising because companies are generally bought out at a premium above current stock price. However, the same study shows that prices of acquiring banks fall almost 5 percent on average upon the same announcement. This is pretty strong evidence that bank mergers do not benefit, and may even hurt, acquiring companies. The reason for this result is unclear, though perhaps acquirers simply overpay for acquisitions. Regardless of the reason, the *implication* is clear. A bank should think deeply before acquiring another bank.

Furthermore, suppose you are the CFO of a company whose stock price drops much more than 5 percent upon announcement of an acquisition. The market is telling you that the merger is bad for your firm. Serious consideration should be given to cancelling the merger, even if, prior to the announcement, you thought the merger was a good idea.

Of course, mergers are only one type of corporate event. Managers should pay attention to the stock price reaction to any of their announcements, whether it concerns a new venture, divestiture, restructuring, or something else.

This is not the only way corporations can use the information in market prices. Suppose you are on the board of directors of a company whose stock price has declined precipitously since the current CEO was hired. In addition, the prices of competitors have risen over the same time. Though there may be extenuating circumstances, this can be viewed as evidence that the CEO is doing a poor job. Perhaps he should be fired. If this seems harsh, consider that Warner, Watts, and Wruck find a strong negative correlation between managerial turnover and prior stock performance.[44] Figure 14.13 shows that stocks fall on average about 40 percent in price (relative to market movements) in the three years prior to the forced departure of a top manager.

---

[43] David A. Becher, "The Valuation Effects of Bank Mergers," *Journal of Corporate Finance* (July 2000).

[44] Jerold B. Warner, Ross L. Watts, and Karen H. Wruck, "Stock Prices and Top Management Changes," *Journal of Financial Economics* (January–March 1988).

**FIGURE 14.13**

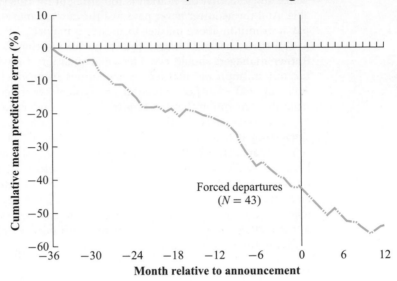

**Stock Performance Prior to Forced Departures of Management**

Stock prices decline on average by more than 40 percent (adjusted for market performance) in the three years prior to forced departures of management.

Source: Adapted from Figure 1 of Warner, Watts, and Wruck, "Stock Prices and Management Changes," *Journal of Financial Economics* (January–March 1988).

If managers are fired for bad stock price performance, perhaps they are rewarded for stock price appreciation. According to Hall and Liebman:

> Our main empirical finding is that CEO wealth often changes by millions of dollars for typical changes in firm value. For example, the median total compensation for CEOs is about $1 million if their firm's stock has a 30th percentile annual return (−7.0 percent) and is $5 million if the firm's stock has a 70th percentile annual return (20.5 percent). Thus, there is a difference of about $4 million in compensation for achieving a moderately above average performance relative to a moderately below average performance.[45]

Market efficiency implies that stock prices reflect all available information. We recommend using this information as much as possible in corporate decisions. And at least with respect to executive firings and executive compensation, it looks as if real-world corporations do pay attention to market prices. The following box summarizes some key issues in the efficient markets debate.

---

[45] Brian J. Hall and Jeffrey B. Liebman, "Are CEOs Really Paid Like Bureaucrats?" *Quarterly Journal of Economics* (August 1998), p. 654.

## Efficient Market Hypothesis: A Summary

**Does Say**
- Prices reflect underlying value.
- Financial managers cannot time stock and bond sales.
- Managers cannot profitably speculate in foreign currencies.
- Managers cannot boost stock prices through creative accounting.

**Does Not Say**
- Prices are uncaused.
- Investors are foolish and too stupid to be in the market.
- All shares of stock have the same expected returns.
- Investors should throw darts to select stocks.
- There is no upward trend in stock prices.

**Why Doesn't Everybody Believe It?**
- There are optical illusions, mirages, and apparent patterns in charts of stock market returns.
- The truth is less interesting.
- There is evidence against efficiency:
  - two different, but financially identical, classes of stock of the same firm selling at different prices
  - earnings surprises
  - small versus large stocks
  - value versus growth stocks
  - crashes and bubbles

**Three Forms**
*Weak form.* Current prices reflect past prices; chartism (technical analysis) is useless.

*Semistrong form.* Prices reflect all public information; most fundamental analysis is useless.

*Strong form.* Prices reflect all that is knowable; nobody consistently makes superior profits.

**CONCEPT QUESTION**
- What are three implications of the EMH for corporate finance?

# 14.9

# SUMMARY AND CONCLUSIONS

1. An efficient financial market processes the information available to investors and incorporates it into the prices of securities. Market efficiency has two general implications. First, in any given time period, a stock's abnormal return depends on information or news received by the market in that period. Second, an investor who uses the same information as the market cannot expect to earn abnormal returns. In other words, systems for playing the market are doomed to fail.

2. What information does the market use to determine prices? The weak form of the EMH says that the market uses the history of prices and is therefore efficient with respect to these past prices. This implies that stock selection based on patterns of past stock price movements is not better than random stock selection.

3. The semistrong form states that the market uses all publicly available information in setting prices.

4. Strong-form efficiency states that the market uses all of the information that anybody knows about stocks, even inside information.

5. Much evidence from different financial markets supports weak-form and semistrong-form efficiency but not strong-form efficiency.

6. Behavioural finance states that the market is not efficient. Adherents argue that
   a. Investors are not rational.
   b. Deviations from rationality are similar across investors.
   c. Arbitrage, being costly, will not eliminate inefficiencies.

7. Behaviourists point to many studies, including those showing that small stocks out-perform large stocks, value stocks outperform growth stocks, and stock prices adjust slowly to earnings surprises, as empirical confirmation of their beliefs.

8. Five implications of market efficiency for corporate finance are as follows:

   a. Managers cannot fool the market through creative accounting.

   b. Firms cannot successfully time issues of debt and equity.

   c. Managers cannot profitably speculate in foreign currencies and other instruments.

   d. Managers can reap many benefits by paying attention to market prices.

   e. A firm can sell as many bonds or shares of stock as it desires without depressing prices significantly.

**KEY TERMS**

Bubble theory  433
Efficient market hypothesis (EMH)  415

Random walk  418
Semistrong-form efficiency  419

Serial correlation  422
Strong-form efficiency  419
Weak-form efficiency  418

**QUESTIONS & PROBLEMS**

### Cumulative Abnormal Returns

14.1 Air Canada, WestJet, and Transat A.T. Inc. announced purchases of planes on July 18 (18/7), February 12 (12/2), and October 7 (7/10), respectively. Given the following information, calculate the CAR for these stocks as a group. Graph the result and provide an explanation. All of the stocks have a beta of 1, and no other announcements are made.

| | Air Canada | | | WestJet | | | Transat A.T. Inc. | |
| Date | Market return | Company return | Date | Market return | Company return | Date | Market return | Company return |
|---|---|---|---|---|---|---|---|---|
| 12/7 | −0.3 | −0.5 | 8/2 | −0.9 | −1.1 | 1/10 | 0.5 | 0.3 |
| 13/7 | 0.0 | 0.2 | 9/2 | −1.0 | −1.1 | 2/10 | 0.4 | 0.6 |
| 16/7 | 0.5 | 0.7 | 10/2 | 0.4 | 0.2 | 3/10 | 1.1 | 1.1 |
| 17/7 | −0.5 | −0.3 | 11/2 | 0.6 | 0.8 | 6/10 | 0.1 | −0.3 |
| 18/7 | −2.2 | 1.1 | 12/2 | −0.3 | −0.1 | 7/10 | −2.2 | −0.3 |
| 19/7 | −0.9 | −0.7 | 15/2 | 1.1 | 1.2 | 8/10 | 0.5 | 0.5 |
| 20/7 | −1.0 | −1.1 | 16/2 | 0.5 | 0.5 | 9/10 | −0.3 | −0.2 |
| 23/7 | 0.7 | 0.5 | 17/2 | −0.3 | −0.2 | 10/10 | 0.3 | 0.1 |
| 24/7 | 0.2 | 0.1 | 18/2 | 0.3 | 0.2 | 13/10 | 0.0 | −0.1 |

14.2 The following diagram shows the CARs for 386 oil exploration companies announcing oil discoveries between 1950 and 1980. Month 0 in the diagram is the announcement month. Assume that no other information is received and the stock market as a whole does not move. Is the diagram consistent with market efficiency? Why or why not?

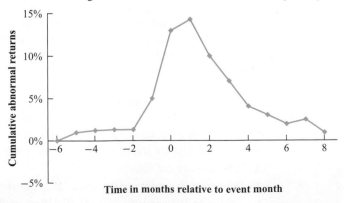

Time in months relative to event month

14.3 The following figures present the results of four CAR studies. Indicate whether the results of each study support, reject, or are inconclusive about the semistrong form of the EMH. In each figure, time 0 is the date of an event.

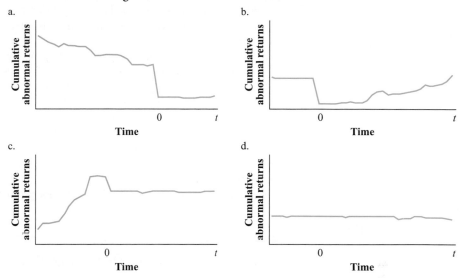

14.4 A study analyzed the behaviour of the stock prices of firms that had lost antitrust cases. Included in the diagram are all firms that lost the initial court decision, even if the decision was later overturned on appeal. The event at time 0 is the initial, pre-appeal court decision. Assume no other information was released, aside from that disclosed in the initial trial. The stock prices all have a beta of 1. Is the diagram consistent with market efficiency? Why or why not?

### Efficient Market Hypothesis

14.5 For each of the following scenarios, discuss whether profit opportunities exist from trading in the stock of the firm under the conditions that (1) the market is not weak-form efficient, (2) the market is weak-form but not semistrong-form efficient, (3) the market is semistrong-form but not strong-form efficient, and (4) the market is strong-form efficient.

    *a.* The stock price has risen steadily each day for the past 30 days.

    *b.* The financial statements for a company were released three days ago, and you believe you've uncovered some anomalies in the company's inventory and cost control reporting techniques that are causing the firm's true liquidity strength to be understated.

    *c.* You observe that the senior management of a company has been buying a lot of the company's stock on the open market over the past week.

14.6 Nanotech, a microchip development and research firm, announced this morning that it has hired the world's most knowledgeable researchers on nanotechnology. Before today, Nanotech's stock had been selling for $100. Assume that no other information is received over the next week and the stock market as a whole does not move.

   *a.* What do you expect will happen to Nanotech's stock?

   *b.* Consider the following scenarios:

      *i.* The stock price jumps to $118 on the day of the announcement. In subsequent days it floats up to $123, then falls back to $116.

      *ii.* The stock price jumps to $116 and remains at that level.

      *iii.* The stock gradually climbs to $116 over the next week.

      Which scenario(s) indicate market efficiency? Which do not? Why?

14.7 Suppose the market is semistrong-form efficient. Can you expect to earn excess returns if you make trades based on each of the following?

   *a.* Your broker's information about record earnings for a stock.

   *b.* Rumours about a merger of a firm.

   *c.* Yesterday's announcement of a successful new product test.

---

## MINICASE

# Your Retirement Plan at Deck Out My Yacht

You have been at your job at Deck Out My Yacht for a week now and have decided you need to sign up for the company's retirement plan. Even after your discussion with the Marshall & McLaren Financial Services representative, you are still unsure which investment option you should choose. Recall that the options available to you are stock in Deck Out My Yacht, the M&M TSX Composite Index Fund, the M&M Small-Cap Fund, the M&M Large-Company Stock Fund, the M&M Bond Fund, and the M&M Money Market Fund.

You have decided that you should invest in a diversified portfolio, with 70 percent of your investment in equity, 25 percent in bonds, and 5 percent in the money market fund. You have also decided to focus your equity investment on large-cap stocks, but you are debating whether to select the TSX/S&P Composite Index Fund or the Large-Company Stock Fund.

In thinking it over, you understand the basic difference in the two funds. One is a purely passive fund that replicates a widely followed large-cap index, the TSX Composite, and has low fees. The other is actively managed with the intention that the skill of the portfolio manager will result in improved performance relative to an index. Fees are higher in the latter fund. You are just not certain which way to go, so you ask Belinda Price, who works in the company's finance area, for advice.

After discussing your concerns, Belinda gives you some information comparing the performance of equity mutual funds and the F&F Passive TSX Composite Fund. The F&F Passive TSX Composite Fund is the largest fictitious equity index mutual fund based on the TSX. It replicates the TSX Composite, and its return is only negligibly different from the TSX Composite. Fees are very low. As a result, the fund is essentially identical to the M&M TSX Composite Index Fund offered in the retirement plan, but it has been in existence for much longer, so you can study its track record for over two decades. The graph below summarizes Belinda's comments by showing the percentage of equity mutual funds that outperformed the fund over the previous 10 years. So, for example, from January 1984 to December 1993, about 75 percent of equity mutual funds outperformed the fund. Belinda suggests that you study the graph and answer the following questions:

1. What implications do you draw from the graph for mutual fund investors?

2. Is the graph consistent or inconsistent with market efficiency? Explain carefully.

3. What investment decision would you make for the equity portion of your retirement plan? Why?

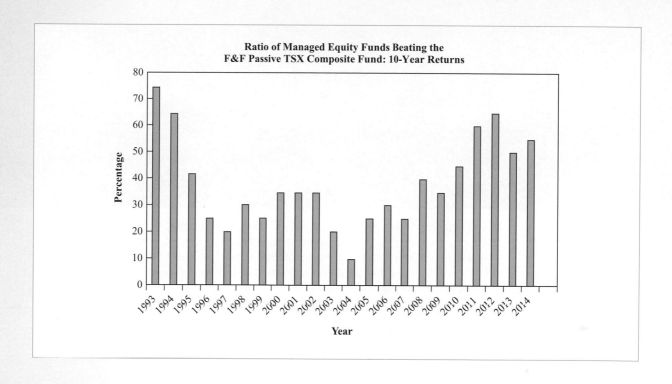

# Long-Term Financing: An Introduction

**EXECUTIVE SUMMARY**

This chapter introduces the basic sources of long-term financing: common stock, preferred stock, and long-term debt. Later chapters discuss these topics in more detail. Perhaps no other area is more perplexing to new students of finance than corporate securities, such as shares of stock, bonds, and debentures. Although the concepts are simple and logical, the language is strange and unfamiliar.

The purpose of this chapter is to describe the basic features of long-term financing. We begin with a look at common stock, preferred stock, and long-term debt and then briefly consider patterns of the different kinds of long-term financing. We also describe the income trust form of organization, which grew rapidly in Canada between 2001 and 2006. Discussion of more complex forms of long-term finance, such as convertibles and leases, is reserved for later chapters.

## 15.1 COMMON STOCK

The term **common stock** (or **common shares**) means different things to different people, but it is usually applied to stock that has no special preference either in dividends or in bankruptcy. A description of the common stock of Enbridge Inc. is presented in the table below:

**Enbridge Inc. Shareholders' Equity at Book Value, 2013**
**(in $ millions)**

| | |
|---|---:|
| **Share capital** | |
| Preferred shares | $ 5,141 |
| Common shares | 5,744 |
| Additional paid-in capital | 746 |
| Retained earnings | 2,550 |
| Accumulated other comprehensive loss | −599 |
| Reciprocal shareholding | −86 |
| **Total shareholder's equity** | **$13,496** |

Source: Enbridge Inc. Annual Report 2013

Owners of common stock in a corporation are referred to as *shareholders* or *stockholders*. They receive stock certificates for the *shares* they own. There can be a stated value on each stock certificate called the *par value*, but more typically in Canada, there is no particular par value assigned to stock.

As we discussed in Chapter 1, common shareholders are protected by *limited liability*. If the company goes bankrupt, the creditors cannot seek payment of the firm's debt from its common shareholders. On the other hand, the common shareholders are the residual claimants and almost always lose 100 percent of their investment if the firm goes bankrupt.

## Authorized versus Issued Common Stock

Shares of common stock are the fundamental ownership units of the corporation. The articles of incorporation of a new corporation must state the number of shares of common stock the corporation is authorized to issue.

The board of directors of the corporation, after a vote of the shareholders, can amend the articles of incorporation to increase the number of shares authorized; there is no legal limit to the number of shares that can be authorized this way. In a recent year, for example, Enbridge Inc. had authorized an unlimited amount of common shares, but had issued 351,800,000 shares. There is no requirement that all of the authorized shares ever be issued.

## Retained Earnings

In 2013, Enbridge Inc. paid out around 70.8 percent of its net income as dividends; the rest is retained in the business and is called **retained earnings**. The cumulative amount of retained earnings (since original incorporation) was $2,550 million in 2013.

The sum of accumulated retained earnings, contributed surplus (if any), share capital, and adjustments to equity is the total shareholders' equity of the firm, which is usually referred to as the firm's **book value of equity** (or *net worth*). The book value of equity represents an accountant's measure of the amount contributed directly and indirectly to the corporation by equity investors.

To illustrate some of these definitions, suppose Western Redwood Corporation was formed in 1976 with 10,000 shares of stock issued and sold for $1 per share. By 2015 the company was profitable and had retained profits of $100,000. Shareholders' equity of Western Redwood Corporation in 2015 is as follows:

| **Western Redwood Corporation Equity Accounts, 2015** | |
|---|---:|
| Common stock (10,000 shares outstanding) | $ 10,000 |
| Retained earnings | 100,000 |
| Total shareholders' equity | $110,000 |

$$\text{Book value per share} = \frac{\$110,000}{10,000} = \$11$$

Now suppose the company has profitable investment opportunities and decides to sell 10,000 shares of new stock to raise the necessary funding. The current market price is $20 per share. The table below shows the effects of the sale of stock on the balance sheet:

| **Western Redwood Corporation, 2015, after Sale of Stock** | |
|---|---:|
| Common stock (20,000 shares outstanding) | $210,000 |
| Retained earnings | 100,000 |
| Total shareholders' equity | $310,000 |

$$\text{Book value per share} = \frac{\$310,000}{20,000} = \$15.50$$

What happened?

1. Since 10,000 shares of new stock were issued at the market value of $20, a total of $200,000 was added to common stock.
2. The book value per share was higher than the previous book value of $11 because the market price of the new stock was higher than the book value.

## Market Value, Book Value, and Replacement Value

The total book value of common equity for Enbridge Inc. in 2013 was $8,355,000,000. The company had outstanding 806,000,000 common shares.

The book value per share was thus

$$\frac{\text{Total common shareholders' equity}}{\text{Shares outstanding}} = \frac{\$8,355,000,000}{806,000,000} = \$10.37$$

Enbridge Inc. is a publicly owned company. Its common stock and preferred stock trade on the Toronto Stock Exchange (TSX); its common stock also trades on the New York Stock Exchange (NYSE). Thousands of shares change hands every day. Market prices of Enbridge's common shares were between $41.87 and $48.65 per share during 2013.[1] Thus, the market prices were above the book value.

In addition to market and book values, you may hear the term *replacement value*. This refers to the current cost of replacing the assets of the firm. Market, book, and replacement value are equal at the time a firm purchases an asset. After that time, these values will diverge. The market-to-book value ratio of common stock, introduced in Appendix 2A, and Tobin's $Q$ (market value of assets/replacement value of assets) are indicators of the success of the firm. A market-to-book value or Tobin's $Q$ ratio greater than 1 indicates the firm has done well with its investment decisions.

## Shareholders' Rights

Shareholders elect directors who, in turn, hire management to carry out their directives. Shareholders, therefore, control the corporation through the right to elect the directors; generally only shareholders have this right.

Directors are elected at an annual shareholders' meeting by a vote of those people who hold a majority of shares present and are entitled to vote. The exact mechanism for electing directors differs across companies. The two most important methods are *cumulative voting* and *straight voting*.[2]

The Canadian Business Incorporation Act Section 24 (3) outlines shareholder rights in corporations that only have one class of shares. As you will soon learn, these rights, in particular voting rights, can be modified in dual or multiclass share structures through explicit specification in the articles of incorporation. For now, we focus on a single class of shares that have the following rights in addition to the right to vote for directors:

1. The right to share proportionally in dividends paid.
2. The right to share proportionally in assets remaining after liabilities have been paid in a liquidation.
3. The right to vote on matters of great importance to shareholders, such as a merger, usually decided at the annual meeting or a special meeting.
4. The right to share proportionally in any new stock sold when approved by the board of directors. Called the *pre-emptive right*, this right is detailed in Chapter 20.

---

[1] Price range obtained by analyzing price quote graphs for the period of January 1, 2013, to December 31, 2013, from quote.morningstar.ca/Quicktakes/Stock/s_ca.aspx?t=ENB.

[2] Outside Canada and the United States, other factors besides proportionate ownership can be important in electing directors. For example, in 1989, T. Boone Pickens, a well-known U.S. takeover specialist, acquired over 20 percent of the shares of Koito, an important auto parts manufacturer in Japan. When Pickens requested that three executives from his firm go on the Koito board, Tamotsu Aoyama, a Koito director, replied, "It is necessary to build a trusting relationship first. In Japan, it is not possible to just say, 'I'm a major shareholder' and get a seat on the board right away." *The Globe and Mail* (April 27, 1989).

**Cumulative Voting**    The effect of **cumulative voting** is to permit minority participation. If cumulative voting is permitted, the total number of votes that each shareholder may cast is determined first. That number is usually calculated as the number of shares (owned or controlled) multiplied by the number of directors to be elected. Each shareholder can distribute these votes as he or she wishes over one or more candidates. Example 15.1 illustrates this concept.

---

**EXAMPLE 15.1**

Imagine that a corporation has two shareholders: MacDonald with 25 shares and Laurier with 75 shares. Both want to be on the board of directors. Laurier does not want MacDonald to be a director. Let us assume that there are four directors to be elected and each shareholder nominates four candidates. MacDonald will get $25 \times 4 = 100$ votes, and Laurier is entitled to $75 \times 4 = 300$ votes. If MacDonald gives all his votes to himself, he is assured of a directorship. It is not possible for Laurier to divide 300 votes among the four candidates to preclude MacDonald's election to the board.

---

In general, if there are $N$ directors up for election, then $1/(N + 1)$ percent of the stock (plus one share) will guarantee you a seat. In our current example, this is $1/(4 + 1)$ = 20%. With cumulative voting, the more seats that are up for election at one time, the easier it is to win one.

**Straight Voting**    If **straight voting** is permitted, MacDonald may cast 25 votes for each candidate and Laurier may cast 75 votes for each. As a consequence, Laurier will elect all of the candidates.

Straight voting can freeze out minority shareholders; that is the rationale for cumulative voting. But devices have been worked out to minimize its impact. One such device is to *stagger* the voting for the board of directors. Staggering permits a fraction of the directorships to come to a vote at a particular time. It has two basic effects:

1. Staggering makes it more difficult for a minority to elect a director when there is cumulative voting.
2. Staggering makes successful takeover attempts less likely by making the election of new directors more difficult.

**Proxy Voting**    A **proxy** is the legal grant of authority by a shareholder to someone else to vote his or her shares. For convenience, the actual voting in large public corporations is usually done by proxy.

Many companies, such as BCE Inc., have hundreds of thousands of shareholders. Shareholders can come to the annual meeting and vote in person, or they can transfer their right to vote to another party by proxy.

Obviously, management always tries to get as many proxies transferred to it as possible. However, if shareholders are not satisfied with management's position on a particular issue or with the corporate governance of the firm, an outside group of shareholders can try to obtain as many votes as possible via proxy. They can vote to direct management actions or more drastically to replace management or change the company's governance. Under the umbrella of the Canadian Coalition for Good Governance, large pension funds, such as the Ontario Teachers' Pension Board and British Columbia Investment Management Corporation, have developed detailed proxy voting guidelines.

## Dividends

A distinctive feature of corporations is that they issue shares of stock and are authorized by law to pay dividends to the holders of these shares. **Dividends** paid to shareholders represent a return on the capital directly or indirectly contributed to the corporation by the shareholders. The payment of dividends is at the discretion of the board of directors.

Here are some important characteristics of dividends:

1. Unless a dividend is declared by the board of directors of a corporation, it is not a liability of the corporation. A corporation cannot *default* on an undeclared dividend. As a consequence, corporations cannot become *bankrupt* because of non-payment of dividends. The amount of the dividend and even whether it is paid are decisions based on the business judgment of the board of directors.

2. The payment of dividends by the corporation is not a business expense. Dividends are not deductible for corporate tax purposes. In short, dividends are paid out of after-tax profits of the corporation.

3. Dividends received by individual shareholders are partially sheltered by a dividend tax credit discussed in detail in Appendix 1A. Canadian corporations that own shares in other companies are permitted to exclude from taxable income 100 percent of the dividend amounts they receive from taxable Canadian corporations. The purpose of this provision is to avoid the double taxation of dividends.

## Classes of Shares

Some firms have more than one class of common shares. Often, the classes are created with unequal voting rights. For example, Canadian Tire Corporation has two classes of common shares, both publicly traded. The majority of the voting common shares were distributed among offspring of the company founder, and the rest are held by Canadian Tire dealers, pension funds, and the general public. The non-voting Canadian Tire A shares are more widely held.[3]

A number of other Canadian corporations have restricted (non-voting or limited-voting) stock. Non-voting shares must receive dividends no lower than dividends on voting shares. Some companies pay a higher dividend on the non-voting shares. In 2013, Canadian Tire's dividend rate was $1.4875 per share on both classes of stock.

A primary reason for creating dual classes of stock has to do with control of the firm. If such stock exists, management of a firm can raise equity capital by issuing non-voting or limited-voting stock while maintaining control. Amoako-Adu and Smith show that firms going public with dual classes of shares in Canada are often family controlled.[4] Examples of such Canadian companies are Bombardier, Rogers Communications, Shaw Communications, and Celestica.

Lease, McConnell, and Mikkelson found the market prices of U.S. stocks with superior voting rights to be about 5 percent higher than the prices of otherwise identical stocks with inferior voting rights.[5] However, DeAngelo and DeAngelo found some evidence that the market value of differences in voting rights may be much higher

---

[3] For example, on one day in mid-2001, 997,200 shares of the non-voting stock traded, but not a single share of the voting stock changed hands.

[4] B. Amoako-Adu and B. Smith, "Dual Class Firms: Capitalization, Ownership Structure and Recapitalization Back into Single Class," *Journal of Banking and Finance* (June 2001).

[5] R. C. Lease, J. J. McConnell, and W. H. Mikkelson, "The Market Value of Control in Publicly Traded Corporations," *Journal of Financial Economics* (April 1983).

when control of the firm is involved.[6] Smith and Amoako-Adu found similar results for TSX stocks.[7] Maynes, Robinson, and White conducted a study of voting rights in Canada that reinforced the importance of control.[8]

One reason for the value of control is that restricted voting shares may allow managers to expropriate benefits from minority shareholders. For example, responding to pressure from institutional shareholders, Magna International Inc. agreed to eliminate its dual-class structure through a shareholder- and court-approved plan of agreement in 2010, as discussed in the In Their Own Words box below. More generally, research by Jog, Zhu, and Dutta on Canadian firms has not found significant agency issues related to dual-class shares.[9]

Since it is only necessary to own 51 percent of the voting stock to control a company, non-voting shareholders could be left out in the cold in the event of a takeover bid for the company. To protect the non-voting shareholders, most companies have a **coattail** provision giving non-voting shareholders the right either to vote or to convert their shares into voting shares that can be tendered to the takeover bid. In the Canadian Tire case, all Class A shareholders become entitled to vote and the coattail provision is triggered if a bid is made for "all or substantially all" of the voting shares.

The effectiveness of coattails was tested in 1986 when the Canadian Tire Dealers Association offered to buy 49 percent of the voting shares from the founding Billes family. In the absence of protection, the non-voting shareholders stood to lose substantially. The dealers bid at a large premium for the voting shares, which were trading at $40 before the bid. Non-voting shares were priced at $14. Further, since the dealers were the principal buyers of Canadian Tire products, control of the company would have allowed them to adjust prices to benefit themselves over the non-voting shareholders.

The key question was whether the bid triggered the coattail. The dealers and the Billes family argued that the offer was for 49 percent of the stock, not for "all or substantially all" of the voting shares. In the end the Ontario Securities Commission (OSC) ruled that the offer was unfair to holders of the A shares (a view upheld in two court appeals). As a result, investors believe that coattails have protective value but remain skeptical that they afford complete protection.[10]

Canadian Tire is not an isolated example. Amoako-Adu and Smith document other cases of shareholder disputes involving dual classes of shares and identify a trend of dual-class firms reclassifying their shares into a single class. Their study suggests that reclassifying the shares makes them more attractive to potential investors.

 *CONCEPT QUESTIONS*

- What is a company's book value?
- What rights do shareholders have?
- What is a proxy?
- Why do firms issue non-voting shares? How are they valued?

---

[6] H. DeAngelo and L. DeAngelo, "Managerial Ownership of Voting Rights: A Study of Public Corporations with Dual Classes of Common Stock," *Journal of Financial Economics* (March 1985).

[7] Brian F. Smith and Ben Amoako-Adu, "Relative Prices of Dual Class Shares," *Journal of Financial and Quantitative Analysis* (June 1995).

[8] Elizabeth Maynes, Chris Robinson, and Alan White, "How Much Is a Share Vote Worth?" *Canadian Investment Review* (Spring 1990).

[9] Vijay Jog, Peng Cheng Zhu, and Shantanu Dutta, "Impact of Restricted Voting Share Structure on Firm Value and Performance," *Corporate Governance: An International Review* (September 2010).

[10] A Canadian study consistent with this conclusion is Chris Robinson, John Rumsey, and Alan White, "Market Efficiency in the Valuation of Corporate Control: Evidence from Dual Class Equity," *Canadian Journal of Administrative Sciences* (September 1996).

# IN THEIR OWN WORDS

## Shares climb as Stronach to give up voting control

Frank Stronach delivered shareholders of Magna International Inc. almost everything they could have asked for Thursday: strong earnings, a reinstated dividend and, perhaps best of all, a chance to control the company.

Magna shares had their best day in almost 20 years Thursday, surging as much as 23 percent on the Toronto Stock Exchange, after Mr. Stronach put forth a proposal to sell all of Stronach Trust's class B multiple-voting shares in exchange for a payout worth about US$863 million in cash and common shares.

If approved by the common shareholders, it would give them ultimate control of the auto-parts giant for the first time. This does not mean Mr. Stronach will lose his influence, however.

"He will be the largest single shareholder," Vincent Galifi, chief financial officer of Magna, said in an interview. "Magna is Frank and Frank is Magna."

Each class B share holds 300 votes, giving Mr. Stronach 66 percent voting control. If the proposal passes, Mr. Stronach would have a stake in the company of about 7.5 percent, each share holding one vote.

Dennis DesRosiers, an expert on the auto industry with DesRosiers Automotive Consultants, told *Bloomberg News* the potential change in control of Magna was a big reason for the share surge.

"The equity markets don't like the control the family has and he has a proven history of hare-brained ideas," he said.

This includes dabbling in horse racing, and taking long looks at the airline industry and even football clubs.

"A number of investors have said to me in the past they wouldn't consider investing in Magna because of the multiple-voting shares," Mr. Tyerman said. "It added an element of risk because it ended up that Mr. Stronach could do things that people wouldn't agree with."

Don Walker, co-chief executive of Magna, said during the conference call that investors had been clamouring for the change for years, but only because it depressed Magna's share value.

"We've been asked for years about what options do we have to get our multiples closer to our peers. I can't answer for Frank why he's open to this now, but we've had a number of discussions over the past few years," he said. "Frank is comfortable with this either way."

Mr. Galifi added that if Magna stock, which trades at a discount, were to trade in line with its competition, its value would rise by as much as 30 percent.

At the Magna annual meeting of shareholders, Mr. Stronach said he had spent so much time thinking about the proposed changes he forgot to put on a tie and was almost late.

"It took a lot of reflecting, soul-searching," Mr. Stronach told a hotel ballroom of about 400 shareholders. "I hope we can go back to a real economy where we make things for a change, and this is why I worked with the board to come up with different proposals to make this company more competitive."

At least part of that stock rally can be attributed to Magna's boffo quarter ended March 31, in which the company earned US$223 million, compared with a loss of US$200 million in the same period last year. The results handily beat analysts' expectations.

"They did much better than I expected and I had expected more than the average. So I'm very happy," David Tyerman, analyst with Genuity Capital Markets, said yesterday. "I imagine a lot of analysts today will go back to their models and wonder, 'Where did I get this wrong?'"

Revenue overall was up 54 percent to US$5.5 billion, beating estimates of US$5.14 billion, and average dollar content per vehicle figures increased by 5 and 15 percent in North America and Europe, to US$953 and US$521, respectively. Production volumes were up 67 percent, to 2.9 million units, in North America and 33 percent, to 3.4 million units, in Europe.

As a result of the return to profitability, the Magna board decided to reinstate the company's quarterly dividend of US$0.18, payable June 15 to shareholders of record as of May 31, Mr. Galifi said.

As for Mr. Stronach, he will be devoting his attention to a new electric-car development project in a co-venture with Magna.

Mr. Stronach, who will take on a 27 percent stake in the venture through an investment of US$80 million of his own money, would assume direction of day-to-day operations.

Material reprinted with the express permission of: National Post, a division of Postmedia Network Inc.

# 15.2    CORPORATE LONG-TERM DEBT: THE BASICS

Securities issued by corporations may be classified roughly as *equity* or *debt*. This distinction is basic to much of the modern theory and practice of corporate finance.

At its crudest level, debt represents something that must be repaid; it is the result of borrowing money. When corporations borrow, they contract to make regularly scheduled interest payments and to repay the original amount borrowed (that is, the *principal*). The person or firm making the loan is called a *creditor* or *lender*.

## Interest versus Dividends

The corporation borrowing the money is called a *debtor* or *borrower*. The amount owed the creditor is a liability of the corporation; however, it is a liability of limited value. The corporation can legally default at any time on its liability (for example, by not paying interest) and hand over the assets to the creditors.[11] This can be a valuable option. The creditors benefit if the assets have a value greater than the value of the liability, but only foolish management would default in this circumstance. On the other hand, the corporation and the equity investors benefit if the value of the assets is less than the value of the liabilities, because equity investors are able to walk away from the liabilities and default on their payment.

From a financial point of view, the main differences between debt and equity are the following:

1. Debt is not an ownership interest in the firm. Creditors do not usually have voting power. The device used by creditors to protect themselves is the loan contract (the *indenture*).

2. The corporation's payment of interest on debt is considered a cost of doing business and is fully tax deductible. Thus, interest expense is paid out to creditors before the corporate tax liability is computed. Dividends on common and preferred stock are paid to shareholders after the tax liability has been determined. Dividends are considered a return to shareholders on their contributed capital. Because interest expense can be used to reduce taxes, the government (that is, the Canada Revenue Agency) is providing a direct tax subsidy on the use of debt when compared to equity. This point is discussed in detail in the next two chapters.

3. Unpaid debt is a liability of the firm. If it is not paid, the creditors can legally claim the assets of the firm. This action may result in *liquidation* and *bankruptcy*. Thus, one of the costs of issuing debt is the possibility of *financial failure*, which does not arise when equity is issued.

## Is It Debt or Equity?

Sometimes it is not clear whether a particular security is debt or equity. For example, suppose a 50-year bond is issued with interest payable solely from corporate income if and only if earned, and repayment is subordinate to all other debts of the business. Corporations are very adept at creating hybrid securities that look like equity but are called *debt*. Obviously, the distinction between debt and equity is important for tax purposes. When corporations try to create a debt security that is really equity, they are trying to obtain the tax benefits of debt while eliminating its bankruptcy costs.

---

[11] In practice, creditors can make a claim against the assets of the firm and a court will administer the legal remedy.

## Basic Features of Long-Term Debt

Long-term corporate debt is usually denominated in $1,000 units called the *principal* or *face value*. Long-term debt is a promise by the borrowing firm to repay the principal amount by a certain date, called the *maturity date*. Long-term debt almost always has a par value equal to the face value, and debt price is often expressed as a percentage of the par value. For example, it might be said that Telus debt is selling at 106.75, which means that a bond with a par value of $1,000 can be purchased for $1,067.50. In this case, the debt is selling at a premium because market price is greater than the par value. Debt can also sell at a discount with respect to par value.

| | **Equity versus Debt** | |
|---|---|---|
| **Feature** | **Equity** | **Debt** |
| Income tax status | Dividends | Interest |
| | Dividends are taxed as personal income. Dividends are not a business expense. | Interest is taxed as personal income. Interest is a business expense, and corporations can deduct interest when computing corporate tax liability. |
| Control | Common stock and preferred stock usually have voting rights. | Control is exercised with a loan agreement. |
| Default | Firms cannot be forced into bankruptcy for non-payment of dividends. | Unpaid debt is a liability of the firm. Non-payment may result in creditors forcing the firm into bankruptcy. |
| Bottom line: | Tax status favours debt, but default favours equity. Control features of debt and equity are different, but one is not better than the other. | |

The borrower using long-term debt generally pays interest at a rate expressed as a fraction of par value. Thus, at $1,000 par value, Telus's 7.5 percent debt means that $75 of interest is paid to holders of debt, usually in semiannual instalments (for example, $37.50 on June 30 and December 31). The payment schedules are in the form of coupons that are detached from the debt certificates and sent to the company for payment.[12] Today most bonds exist in virtual form, with coupon payments made electronically to holders of record.

## Different Types of Debt

Typical debt securities are called *notes*, *debentures*, or *bonds*. In legal language, a debenture is an unsecured corporate debt, whereas a bond is secured by a mortgage on the corporate property. However, in common usage, the word *bond* is used indiscriminately and often refers to both secured and unsecured debt. A note usually refers to a short-term obligation, perhaps less than seven years.

Debentures and bonds are long-term debt. *Long-term debt* is any obligation that is payable more than one year from the date it was originally issued and is sometimes called *funded debt*. Debt that is due in less than one year is unfunded and is accounted for as a current liability. Some debt is perpetual and has no specific maturity.

## Repayment

Bonds can be repaid at maturity or earlier through the use of a sinking fund. A *sinking fund* is an account managed on behalf of the issuer by a bond trustee (generally a trust company) to retire all or part of the bonds prior to their stated maturity. The trustee retires the debt either by buying bonds in the market or by calling some of the debt.

---

[12] Chapter 6 presents valuation formulas for debt.

From an investor's viewpoint, a sinking fund reduces the risk that the company will be unable to repay the principal at maturity. Since it involves regular purchases, a sinking fund also improves the marketability of the bonds.

Debt may be extinguished before maturity through a *call provision* giving the firm the right to pay a specific amount (the *call price*) to *retire* (*extinguish*) the debt before the stated maturity date. The call price is generally higher than the par value of the debt. Debt that is callable at 105 is debt that the firm can buy back from the holder at a price of $1,050 per debenture or bond, regardless of the market value of the debt. Call prices are always specified when the debt is originally issued. However, lenders are given a five- to ten-year call protection period during which the debt cannot be called away.

Many long-term corporate bonds outstanding in Canada have call provisions as we just described. New corporate debt features a different call provision referred to as a **Canada plus call**. This new approach is designed to replace the traditional call feature by making it unattractive for the issuer ever to call the bonds. Unlike the standard call, with the Canada plus call the exact amount of the call premium is not set at the time of issuance. Instead, the Canada plus call stipulates that in the event of a call, the issuer must provide a call premium that will compensate investors for the difference in interest between the original bond and new debt issued to replace it. This compensation cancels the borrower's benefit from calling the debt, and the result is that the call will not occur.

## Seniority

In general terms, **seniority** indicates preference in position over other lenders. Some debt is **subordinated**. In the event of default, holders of subordinated debt must give preference to other specified creditors. Usually, this means that the subordinated lenders will be paid off only after the specified creditors have been compensated. However, debt cannot be subordinated to equity.

## Security

*Security* is a form of attachment to property; it provides that the property can be sold in the event of default to satisfy the debt for which security is given. A mortgage is used for security in tangible property; for example, debt can be secured by mortgages on plant and equipment. Holders of such debt have prior claim on the mortgaged assets in case of default. Debentures are not secured by a mortgage. Thus, if mortgaged property is sold in the event of default, debenture holders will obtain something only if the mortgage bondholders have been fully satisfied.

## Indenture

The written agreement between the corporate debt issuer and the lender, setting forth maturity date, interest rate, and all other terms, is called an *indenture*. We treat this in detail in later chapters. For now, we note the following:

1. The indenture completely describes the nature of the indebtedness.
2. The indenture lists all restrictions placed on the firm by the lenders. These restrictions are placed in *restrictive covenants*. Examples are
   *a.* Restrictions on further indebtedness.
   *b.* A maximum on the amount of dividends that can be paid.
   *c.* A minimum level of working capital.

EXAMPLE **15.2**

The following table shows some of the many long-term debt securities of Rogers Communications Inc., a Canadian leader in wireless communications and broadband services, in December 2013 (in millions):

| | |
|---|---|
| 6.375% secured senior note due 2014 | $ 750 |
| 5.5% secured senior note due 2014 | 350 |
| 7.5% secured senior note due 2015 | 550 |
| 6.75% secured senior note due 2015 | 280 |
| 6.8% secured senior note due 2018 | 1,400 |
| 8.75% secured senior debentures due 2032 | 200 |

As can be seen, Rogers has a number of different notes and debentures, varying in time to maturity, amount, and coupon rate.

**CONCEPT QUESTIONS**

- What is corporate debt? Describe its general features.
- Why is it sometimes difficult to tell whether a particular security is debt or equity?

## 15.3    PREFERRED SHARES

**Preferred shares** have preference over common shares in the payment of dividends and in the distribution of corporate assets in the event of liquidation. *Preference* means that holders of the preferred shares must receive a dividend (in the case of an ongoing firm) before holders of common shares are entitled to anything. If the firm is liquidated, preferred shareholders rank behind all creditors but ahead of common shareholders.

Preferred shares are a form of equity from legal, tax, and regulatory standpoints. However, holders of preferred shares often have no voting privileges.

### Stated Value

Preferred shares have a stated liquidating value, for example, $25 per share. The cash dividend is described in terms of dollars per share. For example, CIBC "$2.25 preferred" translates easily into a dividend yield of 9 percent of the stated $25 value.

### Cumulative and Non-cumulative Dividends

A preferred dividend is not like interest on a bond. The board of directors may decide not to pay the dividends on preferred shares, and the decision may have nothing to do with the current net income of the corporation.

Dividends payable on preferred shares are either *cumulative* or *non-cumulative*; most are cumulative. If preferred dividends are cumulative and are not paid in a particular year, they will be carried forward as an arrearage. Usually both the cumulated (past) preferred dividends and the current preferred dividends must be paid before the common shareholders can receive anything.

Unpaid preferred dividends are not debts of the firm. Directors elected by the common shareholders can defer preferred dividends indefinitely. However, in such cases:

1. Common shareholders must also forgo dividends.
2. Holders of preferred shares are often granted voting and other rights if preferred dividends have not been paid for some time.

Because preferred shareholders receive no interest on the cumulated dividends, some have argued that firms have an incentive to delay paying preferred dividends.

## Are Preferred Shares Really Debt?

A good case can be made that preferred shares are really debt in disguise, a kind of equity bond. Preferred shareholders receive a stated dividend only, and if the corporation is liquidated, they get a stated value. Often, preferreds carry credit ratings much like bonds. Furthermore, preferred shares are sometimes convertible into common shares. Preferreds are often callable by the issuer, and the holder often has the right to sell the preferred shares back to the issuer at a set price.

In addition, in recent years, many new issues of preferred shares have had obligatory sinking funds. Such a sinking fund effectively creates a final maturity, since the entire issue will ultimately be retired.

On top of all of this, preferred shares with adjustable dividends have been offered in recent years. One example is the *CARP* (cumulative, adjustable rate, preferred). Various types of floating rates are preferred, some of which are quite innovative in the way that the dividend is determined. For example, dividends on Royal Bank of Canada First Preferred Shares Series C (old) were set at two-thirds of the bank's average Canadian prime rate with a floor dividend of 6.67 percent per year.

For all these reasons, preferred shares seem to be a lot like debt. In comparison to debt, the yields on preferred shares are generally lower. For example, the Royal Bank of Canada has another series of preferred shares with a $1.25 stated dividend. In October 2013, the market price of the $1 Royal Bank preferred was about $25.00. This gave a yield of about 4 percent, considerably below the yield on Royal Bank long-term debt (about 5.45 percent at that time).

Despite the apparently low yields, corporate investors have an incentive to hold preferred shares issued by other corporations as opposed to holding their debt, since 100 percent of the dividends they receive is exempt from income taxes.[13] Because individual investors do not receive this tax break, most preferred shares in Canada are purchased by corporate investors.[14] Corporate investors pay a premium for preferred shares because of the tax exclusion on dividends; as a consequence, yields are low.

## Preferred Shares and Taxes

Turning to the issuer's point of view, a tax loophole encourages corporations that are lightly taxed or not taxable due to losses or tax shelters to issue preferred shares. Such low-tax companies can make little use of the tax deduction on interest. However, they can issue preferred shares and enjoy lower financing costs since preferred dividends are significantly lower than interest payments.

In 1987, the federal government attempted to close the tax loophole by introducing a tax of 40 percent of the preferred dividends to be paid by the issuer of preferred stock. The tax is refunded (through a deduction) to taxable issuers only. The effect of this and associated tax changes was to narrow, but not close, the loophole.

Table 15.1 shows how Zero Tax Ltd., a corporation not paying any income taxes, can issue preferred shares attractive to Full Tax Ltd., a second corporation taxable at a combined federal and provincial rate of 45 percent. The example assumes that Zero Tax is seeking $1,000 in financing through either debt or preferred stock and that Zero Tax can issue either debt with a 10 percent coupon or preferred stock with a 6.7 percent dividend.[15]

---

[13] In the United States, the corporate dividend exclusion is only for 80 percent. I. Fooladi and G. Roberts, "On Preferred Stock," *Journal of Financial Research* (Winter 1986), argue that this difference in tax law explains why Canadian firms finance much more heavily with preferred shares.

[14] Preferred dividends paid to individual investors qualify for the dividend tax credit.

[15] We set the preferred dividend at around two-thirds of the debt yield to reflect market prices as exemplified by the Royal Bank issue discussed earlier. Further discussion of preferred shares and taxes in Canada appears in I. Fooladi, P. A. McGraw, and G. S. Roberts, "Preferred Share Rules Freeze out the Individual Investor," *CA Magazine* (April 11, 1988).

**TABLE 15.1**

**Tax Loophole on Preferred Stock**

|  | Preferred | Debt |
|---|---|---|
| Issuer: Zero Tax Ltd. | | |
| Preferred dividend/interest paid | $67.00 | $100.00 |
| Dividend tax at 40% | 26.80 | 0.00 |
| Tax deduction on interest | 0.00 | 0.00 |
| Total financing cost | $93.80 | $100.00 |
| After-tax cost | 9.38% | 10.00% |
| Purchaser: Full Tax Ltd. | | |
| Before-tax income | $67.00 | $100.00 |
| Tax | 0.00 | 45.00 |
| After-tax income | $67.00 | $ 55.00 |
| After-tax yield | 6.70% | 5.50% |

Table 15.1 shows that with preferred shares financing, Zero Tax pays out 6.7% × $1,000 = $67.00 in dividends and 40% × $67.00 = $26.80 in tax on the dividends, for a total after-tax outlay of $93.80. This represents an after-tax cost of $93.80/$1,000 = 9.38%. Debt financing is more expensive, with an outlay of $100 and an after-tax cost of 10 percent. So Zero Tax is better off issuing preferred stock.

From the point of view of the purchaser, Full Tax Ltd., the preferred dividend is received tax free, for an after-tax yield of 6.7 percent. If it bought debt issued by Zero Tax instead, Full Tax would pay income tax of $45, for a net after-tax receipt of $55 or 5.5 percent. So again, preferred shares are better than debt.

Of course, if we change the example to make the issuer fully taxable, the after-tax cost of debt will drop to 5.5 percent, making debt financing more attractive. This reinforces our point that the tax motivation for issuing preferred shares is limited to lightly taxed companies.

## Beyond Taxes

For fully taxed firms, the fact that dividends are not an allowable deduction from taxable corporate income is the most serious obstacle to issuing preferred shares, but preferreds are issued for several reasons beyond taxes.

We can start by discussing some supply factors. First, regulated public utilities can pass the tax disadvantage of issuing preferred shares on to their customers because of the way pricing formulas are set up in regulatory environments. Consequently, a substantial amount of straight preferred shares are issued by utilities, particularly in the United States.

Second, firms issuing preferred shares can avoid the threat of bankruptcy that might otherwise exist if debt were relied on. Unpaid preferred dividends are not debts of a corporation, and preferred shareholders cannot force a corporation into bankruptcy because of unpaid dividends.

A third reason for issuing preferred shares concerns control of the firm. Since preferred shareholders often cannot vote, preferreds may be a means of raising equity without surrendering control.

On the demand side, for tax reasons discussed earlier, most preferred shares are owned by corporations. Some of the new types of adjustable-rate preferreds are ideally suited for corporations needing short-term investments for temporarily idle cash.

*CONCEPT*
*QUESTIONS*
- What are preferred shares?
- Why are preferred shares arguably more like debt than equity?
- Why is it attractive for firms that are not paying taxes to issue preferred shares?
- What are three reasons unrelated to taxes that preferred shares are issued?

## 15.4   INCOME TRUSTS

Starting in 2001, the income trust, a non-corporate form of business organization, began to grow in importance in Canada. Within this sector, the fastest-growing component was business income trusts that took this form of business organization, traditionally popular in real estate and oil and gas, and applied it to businesses like telephone listing, container ports, restaurant chains, and other businesses usually organized as corporations. In response to the growing importance of this sector, provincial legislation extended limited liability protection, previously limited to corporate shareholders, to trust unitholders. Along the same lines, at the end of 2005, the TSX began to include income trusts in its benchmark S&P/TSX composite index.

### Income Trust Income and Taxation

Business income trusts were structured so that income was taxed only once in the hands of unitholders. To achieve this, the operating entity (taxed as a corporation) paid the income trust interest, royalties, or lease payments, which are usually tax deductible. Since the operating entity usually paid the income trust enough to reduce operating income to zero, the operating company paid virtually no tax. The interest, royalties, or lease payments received by the trust were not taxable because it was not a corporation but a partnership. Rather, this cash flow was passed through to the unitholders, resulting in the desired level of taxation.

However, at the end of October 2006, the federal government announced plans to tax income trusts as corporations. As a result, companies such as BCE that were in the process of converting to income trusts reversed their decisions. For Telus Corp., the plan to convert to an income trust was already reflected in the stock price. When the federal announcement was made on November 1, 2006, the stock price dropped from $64.93 to $56.15. This shows that before the tax changes, investors were willing to pay an additional $8.78 for the tax advantage offered by an income trust. It also demonstrates the effect that the government can have on dividend policy and capital structure decisions.

In 2011, existing trusts became subject to taxation of approximately 31.5%. This effectively ended any tax advantages of trusts over corporations for investors. Under the current rules, income trust distributions (other than those of Real Estate Investment Trusts) are treated like dividends both at the investor and the corporate level, thus eliminating any motivation for corporations to convert to an income trust or for investors to choose income trusts over other forms of equity investments.

## 15.5   PATTERNS OF LONG-TERM FINANCING

Firms use cash flow for capital spending and net working capital. According to Zyblock's study of financing patterns in the United States and Canada, Canadian firms spent $102.7 billion on capital and working capital in an example year.[16] Of this amount, around two-thirds or $70.1 billion came from **internal financing** (or cash flow), defined as net income plus depreciation minus dividends. Because total spending exceeded internal financing, there was a financial gap. In the year studied, the financial gap was $32.6 billion (i.e., $102.7 billion − $70.1 billion). To fill the financial gap, firms borrowed $12.1 billion in short- and long-term debt and issued new equity (net of share buybacks) of $20.5 billion.

---

[16] M. Zyblock, "Corporate Financial Leverage: A Canada–U.S. Comparison, 1961–1996," Statistics Canada, Analytical Studies Branch, Research Paper Series (December 1997).

Figure 15.1 depicts the financial gap. It shows that Canadian firms generate the majority of their funds internally.

FIGURE 15.1

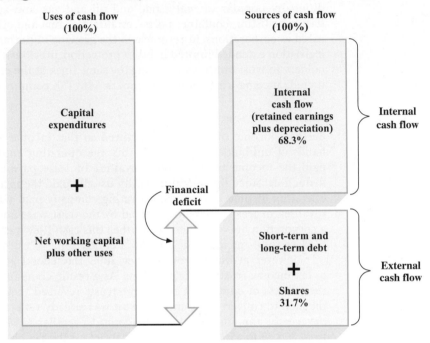

**The Long-Term Financial Gap**

The gap is the difference between long-term financing uses and internal financing.

These data are consistent with the results of a classic survey by Gordon Donaldson on how firms establish long-term financing strategies.[17] He found that

1. The first form of financing used by firms for positive NPV projects is internally generated cash flow (net income plus depreciation minus dividends).
2. When a firm has insufficient cash flow from internal sources, it sells off part of its investment in marketable securities.
3. As a last resort, a firm will use externally generated cash flow. First, debt is used. Common stock is used last.

These observations, when taken together, suggest a pecking order to long-term financing strategy. At the top of the **pecking order** is using internally generated cash flow; at the bottom is issuing new equity.

***CONCEPT QUESTIONS***

- What is the financial gap?
- What are the major sources of corporate financing? What trends have emerged in recent years?

---

[17] G. G. Donaldson, *Corporate Debt Capacity: A Study of Corporate Debt Policy and Determination of Corporate Debt Capacity* (Boston: Harvard Graduate School of Business Administration, 1961). See also S. C. Myers, "The Capital Structure Puzzle," *Journal of Finance* (July 1984).

## 15.6

# SUMMARY AND CONCLUSIONS

The basic sources of long-term financing are long-term debt, preferred stock, and common stock. This chapter describes the essential features of each.

1. We emphasize that common shareholders have
   - Residual risk and return in a corporation.
   - Voting rights.
   - Limited liability if the corporation elects to default on its debt and must transfer some or all of the assets to the creditors.
2. Long-term debt involves contractual obligations set out in indentures. There are many kinds of debt, but the essential feature is that debt involves a stated amount that must be repaid. Interest payments on debt are considered a business expense and are tax deductible.
3. Preferred stock has some of the features of debt and some of the features of common equity. Holders of preferred stock have preference in liquidation and in dividend payments compared to holders of common equity.
4. Firms need financing for fixed assets, current assets, and investment in affiliates along with other uses. Most of the financing is provided from internally generated cash flow. The percentage mix of financing has remained relatively stable in Canada.

**KEY TERMS**

| | | |
|---|---|---|
| Book value of equity 449 | Cumulative voting 451 | Proxy 451 |
| Canada plus call 457 | Dividends 452 | Retained earnings 449 |
| Coattail 453 | Internal financing 461 | Seniority 457 |
| Common stock (common shares) 448 | Pecking order 462 | Straight voting 451 |
| | Preferred shares 458 | Subordinated (debt) 457 |

**QUESTIONS & PROBLEMS**

**Corporate Voting**

15.1  The shareholders of the Unicorn Company need to elect seven new directors. There are 600,000 shares outstanding, currently trading at $39 per share. You would like to serve on the board of directors; unfortunately no one else will be voting for you. How much will it cost you to be certain that you can be elected if the company uses straight voting? How much will it cost you if the company uses cumulative voting?

**Cumulative Voting**

15.2  An election is being held to fill three seats on the board of directors of a firm in which you hold stock. The company has 7,600 shares outstanding. If the election is conducted under cumulative voting and you own 300 shares, how many more shares must you buy to be assured of earning a seat on the board?

15.3  The shareholders of Motive Power Corp. need to elect three new directors to the board. There are 13,000,000 shares of common stock outstanding, and the current share price is $10.50. If the company uses cumulative voting procedures, how much will it cost to guarantee yourself one seat on the board of directors?

**Corporate Voting**

15.4  Power Inc. will elect six board members next month. Betty Brown owns 17.4 percent of the total shares outstanding. How confident can she be of having one of her candidate friends elected under the cumulative voting rule? Will her friend be elected for certain if the voting procedure is changed to the staggering rule, under which shareholders vote on three board members at a time?

**Valuing Callable Bonds**

15.5  KIC Inc. plans to issue $5 million of bonds with a coupon rate of 12 percent paid semi-annually and 30 years to maturity. The current market interest rate on these bonds is 11 percent. In one year, the interest rate on the bonds will be either 14 percent or 7 percent with equal probability. Assume investors are risk neutral.

    *a.* If the bonds are non-callable, what is the price of the bonds today?

    *b.* If the bonds are callable one year from today at $1,450, will their price be greater or less than the price you computed in (a)? Why?

15.6 New Business Ventures Inc. has an outstanding perpetual bond with a 10 percent coupon rate that can be called in one year. The bond makes annual coupon payments. The call premium is set at $150 over par value. There is a 40 percent chance that the interest rate in one year will be 12 percent, and a 60 percent chance that the interest rate will be 7 percent. If the current interest rate is 10 percent, what is the current market price of the bond?

15.7 Bowdeen Manufacturing intends to issue callable, perpetual bonds with annual coupon payments. The bonds are callable at $1,175. One-year interest rates are 9 percent. There is a 60 percent probability that long-term interest rates one year from today will be 10 percent, and a 40 percent probability that they will be 8 percent. Assume that if interest rates fall the bonds will be called. What coupon rate should the bonds have in order to sell at par value?

15.8 Newfoundland Industries has decided to borrow money by issuing perpetual bonds with a coupon rate of 8 percent, payable annually. The one-year interest rate is 8 percent. Next year, there is a 35 percent probability that interest rates will increase to 9 percent, and there is a 65 percent probability that they will fall to 6 percent.

    *a.* What will the market value of these bonds be if they are non-callable?

    *b.* If the company decides instead to make the bonds callable in one year, what coupon will be demanded by the bondholders for the bonds to sell at par? Assume that the bonds will be called if interest rates rise and that the call premium is equal to the annual coupon.

    *c.* What will be the value of the call provision to the company?

**Zero-Coupon Bonds**

15.9 Suppose your company needs to raise $30 million and you want to issue 30-year bonds for this purpose. Assume the required return on your bond issue will be 8 percent, and you're evaluating two issue alternatives: an 8 percent semiannual coupon bond and a zero-coupon bond. Your company's tax rate is 35 percent.

    *a.* How many of the coupon bonds would you need to issue to raise the $30 million? How many of the zeros would you need to issue?

    *b.* In 30 years, what will your company's repayment be if you issue the coupon bonds? What will it be if you issue the zeros?

**Valuing the Call Feature**

15.10 Consider the prices of the following three Treasury issues as of February 24, 2015:

| Coupon | Maturity | Bid | Ask | Change | Yield |
|--------|----------|-----|-----|--------|-------|
| 6.500 | May 2019 | 106:10 | 106:12 | −13 | 5.28 |
| 8.250 | May 2019 | 103:14 | 103:16 | −3 | 5.24 |
| 12.000 | May 2019 | 134:25 | 134:31 | −15 | 5.32 |

The bond in the middle is callable in February 2016. What is the implied value of the call feature? (*Hint:* Is there a way to combine the two non-callable issues to create an issue that has the same coupon as the callable bond?)

**connect**     **LEARNSMART**     **SMARTBOOK**

# Capital Structure: Basic Concepts

EXECUTIVE SUMMARY

Previous chapters of this book examined the capital budgeting decision. We pointed out that this decision concerns the left-hand side of the balance sheet. The previous two chapters began our discussion of the capital structure decision,[1] which deals with the right-hand side of the balance sheet.

In general, a firm can choose among many alternative capital structures. It can issue a large amount of debt or it can issue very little debt. It can issue floating-rate preferred stock, warrants, convertible bonds, caps, and collars. It can arrange lease financing, bond swaps, and forward contracts. Because the number of instruments is so large, the variations in capital structures are endless. We simplify the analysis by considering only common stock and straight debt in this chapter. The "bells and whistles," as they are called on Bay Street, must await later chapters of the text. The capital structure decision we consider is the decision to rely on debt. We examine the factors that are important in the choice of a firm's debt-to-equity ratio.

Our results in this chapter are basic. First, we discuss the capital structure decision in a world with neither taxes nor other capital market imperfections. Surprisingly, we find that the capital structure decision is a matter of *indifference* in this world. We next argue that there is a feature in Canadian tax law that subsidizes debt financing. Finally, we show that an increase in the firm's value from debt financing leads to an increase in the value of the equity.

## 16.1 THE CAPITAL STRUCTURE QUESTION AND THE PIE THEORY

How should a firm choose its debt-to-equity ratio? More generally, what is the best capital structure for the firm? We call our approach to the capital structure question the **pie model**. If you are wondering why we chose this name, just take a look at Figure 16.1. The pie in question is the sum of the financial claims of the firm (debt and equity in this case). We define the value of the firm to be this sum. Hence, the value of the firm, $V$, is

$$V = B + S \tag{16.1}$$

where $B$ is the market value of the debt and $S$ is the market value of the equity. Figure 16.1 presents two possible ways of slicing this pie between stock and debt. If company management's goal is to make the firm as valuable as possible, then the firm should pick the debt-to-equity ratio that makes the pie—the total value, $V$—as big as possible.

[1] It is conventional to refer to choices regarding debt and equity as *capital structure decisions*. However, the term *financial structure decisions* is more accurate. We use the terms interchangeably.

FIGURE 16.1

**Two Pie Models of Capital Structure**

This discussion brings up two important questions:

1. Why should the shareholders in the firm care about maximizing the value of the entire firm? After all, the value of the firm is, by definition, the sum of both the debt and the equity. Instead, why should the shareholders not prefer the strategy that maximizes their interests only?

2. What is the ratio of debt to equity that maximizes the shareholders' interests?

Let us examine each of the two questions in turn.

**CONCEPT QUESTION**

• What is the pie model of capital structure?

## 16.2  MAXIMIZING FIRM VALUE VERSUS MAXIMIZING SHAREHOLDER INTERESTS

The following example illustrates that the capital structure that maximizes the value of the firm is the one that financial managers should choose for the shareholders.

**EXAMPLE 16.1**

Suppose the market value of the J. J. Sprint Company is $1,000. The company currently has no debt, and each of J. J. Sprint's 100 shares of stock sells for $10. A company such as J. J. Sprint, with no debt, is called an unlevered company. Further suppose that J. J. Sprint plans to borrow $500 and pay the $500 proceeds to shareholders as an extra cash dividend of $5 per share. After the issuance of debt, the firm becomes levered. The investments of the firm will not change as a result of this transaction. What will the value of the firm be after the proposed restructuring?

Management recognizes that by definition, only one of three outcomes can occur from restructuring. Firm value after restructuring can be one of the following: (1) greater than the original firm value of $1,000, (2) equal to $1,000, or (3) less than $1,000. After consulting with investment bankers, management believes that restructuring will not change firm value more than $250 in either direction. Thus, it views firm values of $1,250, $1,000, and $750 as the relevant range. The original capital structure and these three possibilities under the new capital structure are presented below:

|  | No debt (original capital structure) | Debt plus dividend (three possibilities after restructuring) | | |
| --- | --- | --- | --- | --- |
|  |  | I | II | III |
| Debt | $    0 | $  500 | $  500 | $500 |
| Equity | 1,000 | 750 | 500 | 250 |
| Firm value | $1,000 | $1,250 | $1,000 | $750 |

Note that the value of equity is less than $1,000 under any of the three possibilities. This can be explained in one of two ways. First, the chart shows the value of the equity *after* the extra cash dividend is paid. Since cash is paid out, a dividend represents a partial liquidation of the firm. Consequently, there is less value in the firm for the equityholders after the dividend payment. Second, in the event of a future liquidation, stockholders will be paid only after bondholders have been paid in full. Thus, the debt is an encumbrance of the firm, reducing the value of the equity.

Of course, management recognizes that there are infinite possible outcomes. These three are to be viewed as *representative* outcomes only. We can now determine the payoff to shareholders under the three possibilities:

| | Payoff to shareholders after restructuring | | |
|---|---|---|---|
| | **I** | **II** | **III** |
| Capital gains | −$250 | −$500 | −$750 |
| Dividends | 500 | 500 | 500 |
| Net gain or loss to shareholders | $250 | $  0 | −$250 |

No one can be sure ahead of time which of the three outcomes will occur. However, imagine that managers believe that outcome I is most likely. They should definitely restructure the firm because the shareholders gain $250. That is, although the value of the stock declines by $250 to $750, they receive $500 in dividends. Their net gain is $250 = −$250 + $500. Also, notice that the value of the firm rises by $250.

Alternatively, imagine that managers believe that outcome III is most likely. In this case, they should not restructure the firm because the shareholders expect a $250 loss. That is, the stock falls by $750 to $250 and they receive $500 in dividends. Their net loss is −$250 = −$750 + $500. Also, notice that the value of the firm falls by $250.

Finally, imagine that the managers believe that outcome II is most likely. Restructuring would not affect the shareholders' interest because the net gain to shareholders in this case is zero. Also, notice that the value of the firm is unchanged if outcome II occurs.

This example explains why managers should attempt to maximize the value of the firm. In other words, it answers question (1) in Section 16.1. In this example, changes in capital structure benefit the shareholders if and only if the value of the firm increases. Conversely, these changes hurt the shareholders if and only if the value of the firm decreases. This result holds generally for capital structure changes of many different types.[2] Thus, managers should choose the capital structure that they believe will have the highest firm value because this capital structure is most beneficial to the firm's shareholders.

Note, however, that the example does not tell us which of the three outcomes is likely to occur. Thus, it does not tell us whether debt should be added to J. J. Sprint's capital structure. In other words, it does not answer question (2) in Section 16.1. This second question is treated in the next section.

**CONCEPT QUESTION**

• Why should financial managers choose the capital structure that maximizes the value of the firm?

_____

[2] This result may not hold exactly in the more complex case where debt has a significant possibility of default, leading to possible agency conflicts between shareholders and bondholders. Issues of default are treated in the next chapter.

## 16.3 FINANCIAL LEVERAGE AND FIRM VALUE: AN EXAMPLE

### Leverage and Returns to Shareholders

The previous section showed that the capital structure producing the highest firm value is the one that maximizes shareholder wealth. In this section, we wish to determine that optimal capital structure. We begin by illustrating the effect of capital structure on returns to shareholders. We will use a detailed example, which we encourage you to study carefully. Once you have mastered this example, you will be ready to determine the optimal capital structure.

Trans Can Corporation currently has no debt in its capital structure. The firm is considering issuing debt to buy back some of its equity. Both its current and proposed capital structures are presented in Table 16.1. The firm's assets are $8,000. There are 400 shares of the all-equity firm, implying a market value per share of $20. The proposed debt issue is for $4,000, leaving $4,000 in equity. The interest rate is 10 percent.

**TABLE 16.1**

### Financial Structure of Trans Can Corporation

|  | Current | Proposed |
|---|---|---|
| Assets | $8,000 | $8,000 |
| Debt | $ 0 | $4,000 |
| Equity (market and book) | $8,000 | $4,000 |
| Interest rate | 10% | 10% |
| Market value/share | $ 20 | $ 20 |
| Shares outstanding | 400 | 200 |

The proposed capital structure has leverage, whereas the current structure is all equity.

The effect of economic conditions on earnings per share (EPS) is shown in Table 16.2 for the current capital structure (all-equity). Consider first the middle column, where earnings are *expected* to be $1,200. Since assets are $8,000, the return on assets (ROA) is 15 percent (= $1,200/$8,000). Because assets equal equity for this all-equity firm, return on equity (ROE) is also 15 percent. EPS is $3.00 (= $1,200/400). Similar calculations yield EPS of $1.00 and $5.00 in the cases of recession and expansion, respectively.

**TABLE 16.2**

### Trans Can's Current Capital Structure: No Debt

|  | Recession | Expected | Expansion |
|---|---|---|---|
| Return on assets | 5% | 15% | 25% |
| Earnings | $ 400 | $1,200 | $2,000 |
| Return on equity = Earnings/Equity | 5% | 15% | 25% |
| Earnings per share | $1.00 | $3.00 | $5.00 |
| Point in Figure 16.2 | A | B | C |

The case of leverage is presented in Table 16.3. ROA in the three economic states is identical in Tables 16.2 and 16.3, because this ratio is calculated before interest is considered. Since debt is $4,000 here, interest is $400 (= 0.10 × $4,000). Thus, earnings after interest are $800 (= $1,200 − $400) in the middle (expected) case. Since equity is $4,000, ROE is 20 percent ($800/$4,000). EPS is $4.00 (= $800/200). Similar calculations yield EPS of $0 and $8.00 for recession and expansion, respectively.

TABLE 16.3

**Trans Can's Proposed Capital Structure: Debt = $4,000**

|  | Recession | Expected | Expansion |
|---|---|---|---|
| Return on assets | 5% | 15% | 25% |
| Earnings before interest and taxes | $400 | $1,200 | $2,000 |
| Interest | −400 | −400 | −400 |
| Earnings after interest | $  0 | $ 800 | $1,600 |
| Return on equity = Earnings after interest/Equity | 0 | 20% | 40% |
| Earnings per share | 0 | $4.00 | $8.00 |
| Point in Figure 16.2 | D | E | F |

Tables 16.2 and 16.3 show that the effect of financial leverage depends on the company's earnings before interest. If earnings before interest are equal to $1,200, the ROE is higher under the proposed structure. If earnings before interest are equal to $400, the ROE is higher under the current structure.

This idea is represented in Figure 16.2. The solid line represents the case of no leverage. The line begins at the origin, indicating that EPS would be zero if earnings before interest and taxes (EBIT) were zero. The EPS rises in tandem with a rise in EBIT. The no-debt line in Figure 16.2 plots points *A*, *B*, and *C*, representing the three cases presented in Table 16.2.

The dotted line represents the case of $4,000 of debt. Here, EPS is negative if EBIT is zero. This follows because $400 of interest must be paid regardless of the firm's profits. The debt line in Figure 16.2 plots points *D*, *E*, and *F*, representing the three cases presented in Table 16.3.

Now consider the slopes of the two lines. The slope of the dotted line (the line with debt) is greater than the slope of the solid line. This occurs because the levered firm has *fewer* shares of stock outstanding than does the unlevered firm. Therefore, any increase in EBIT leads to a greater rise in EPS for the levered firm because the earnings increase is distributed over fewer shares of stock.

Because the dotted line has a lower intercept but a greater slope, the two lines must intersect. The *break-even* point occurs at $800 of EBIT. Were EBIT to be $800, both firms would produce $2 of EPS. Because $800 is break-even, earnings above $800 lead to greater EPS for the levered firm. Earnings below $800 lead to greater EPS for the unlevered firm.

## The Choice between Debt and Equity

Tables 16.2 and 16.3 and Figure 16.2 are important because they show the effect of leverage on EPS. You should study the tables and figure until you feel comfortable with the calculation of each number in them. However, we have not yet presented the punchline. That is, we have not yet stated which capital structure is better for Trans Can.

At this point, many students believe that leverage is beneficial, because EPS is expected to be $4.00 with leverage and only $3.00 without leverage. However, leverage also creates *risk*. Note that in a recession, EPS is higher ($1.00 versus 0) for the unlevered firm. Thus, a risk-averse investor might prefer the all-equity firm, while a risk-neutral (or less risk-averse) investor might prefer leverage. Given this ambiguity, which capital structure *is* better?

Modigliani and Miller (MM) have a convincing argument that a firm cannot change the total value of its outstanding securities by changing the proportions of its capital structure. In other words, the value of the firm is always the same under different capital structures. In still other words, no capital structure is any better or worse than any other capital structure for the firm's shareholders. This rather pessimistic result is the famous **MM Proposition I**.[3]

Their argument compares a simple strategy, which we call strategy *A*, with a two-part strategy, which we call strategy *B*. Both of these strategies for shareholders of Trans Can are illuminated in Table 16.4. Let us now examine the first strategy.

*Strategy A.* Buy 100 shares of the levered equity. This entitles the shareholder to the cash flows from Trans Can supposing that the company goes ahead with adding debt.

The first line in the top panel of Table 16.4 shows EPS for the proposed levered equity in the three economic states. The second line shows the earnings in the three states for an individual buying 100 shares. The next line shows that the cost of these 100 shares is $2,000.

**FIGURE 16.2**

**Financial Leverage: Earnings per Share and Earnings before Interest and Taxes for the Trans Can Corporation**

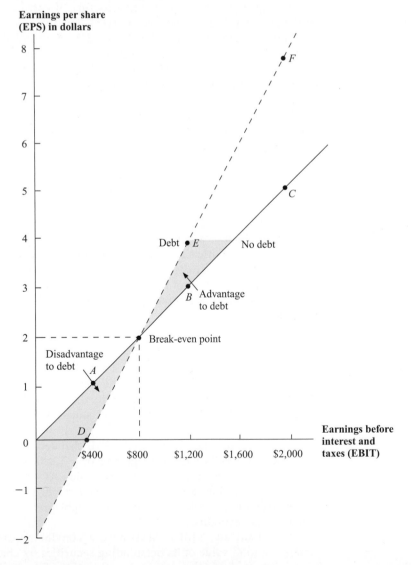

[3] The original paper is F. Modigliani and M. Miller, "The Cost of Capital, Corporation Finance and the Theory of Investment," *American Economic Review* (June 1958).

**TABLE 16.4**

**Payoff and Cost to Shareholders of Trans Can Corporation under the Proposed Structure and under the Current Structure with Homemade Leverage**

| Strategy A: Buy 100 shares of levered equity | Recession | Expected | Expansion |
|---|---|---|---|
| Earnings per share of *levered* equity (taken from last line of Table 16.3) | $0 | $ 4 | $ 8 |
| Earnings per 100 shares | $0 | $400 | $800 |
| Initial cost = 100 shares @ $20/share = $2,000 | | | |

| Strategy B: Homemade leverage | Recession | Expected | Expansion |
|---|---|---|---|
| Earnings per 200 shares in current *unlevered* Trans Can | $1 × 200 = $ 200 | $3 × 200 = $ 600 | $5 × 200 = $ 1,000 |
| Interest at 10% on $2,000 | −200 | −200 | −200 |
| Net earnings | $ 0 | $ 400 | $ 800 |
| Initial cost = 200 shares @ $20/share − $2,000 = $2,000<br>Cost of stock    Amount borrowed | | | |

Let us now consider the second strategy, which has two parts to it.

*Strategy B.* This strategy gives the investor shares in Trans Can assuming no debt is added to the corporate capital structure. The debt goes on the investor's personal balance sheet in proportions chosen to replicate the cash flows from strategy A.

1. Borrow $2,000 from either a bank or, more likely, a brokerage house. (If the brokerage house is the lender, we say that this is *going on margin*.)
2. Use the borrowed proceeds plus your own investment of $2,000 (a total of $4,000) to buy 200 shares of the current unlevered equity at $20 per share.

The bottom panel of Table 16.4 shows payoffs under strategy B, which we call the *homemade leverage* strategy. First, observe the middle column, which indicates that 200 shares of the unlevered equity are *expected* to generate $600 of earnings. Assuming that the $2,000 is borrowed at a 10 percent interest rate, the interest expense is $200 (= 0.10 × $2,000). Thus, the net earnings are expected to be $400. A similar calculation generates net earnings of either $0 or $800 in recession or expansion, respectively.

Now, let us compare these two strategies, in terms of both earnings per year and initial cost. The top panel of the table shows that strategy A generates earnings of $0, $400, and $800 in the three states. The bottom panel of the table shows that strategy B generates the *same* net earnings in the three states.

The top panel of the table shows that strategy A involves an initial cost of $2,000. Similarly, the bottom panel shows an *identical* net cost of $2,000 for strategy B.

This shows a very important result. Both the cost and the payoff from the two strategies are the same. Thus, one must conclude that Trans Can is neither helping nor hurting its shareholders by restructuring. In other words, an investor is not receiving anything from corporate leverage that he could not receive on his own.

Note that, as shown in Table 16.1, the equity of the unlevered firm is valued at $8,000. Since the equity of the levered firm is $4,000 and its debt is $4,000, the value of the levered firm is also $8,000. Now suppose that for whatever reason, the value of the levered firm were actually greater than the value of the unlevered firm. Here, strategy A would cost more than strategy B. In this case, an investor would prefer to borrow on her own account and invest in the stock of the unlevered firm. She would get the same net earnings each year as if she had invested in the stock of the levered firm. However, her cost would be less. The strategy would not be unique to our investor. Given the higher value of the levered firm, no rational investor would invest in the stock of the levered firm. Anyone desiring shares in the levered firm would get the same dollar return more cheaply by borrowing to finance a purchase of the unlevered firm's shares. The equilibrium result would be, of course, that the value of the levered firm would fall and the value of the unlevered firm would rise until they became equal. At this point, individuals would be indifferent between strategy *A* and strategy *B*.

This example illustrates the basic result of Modigliani and Miller and is commonly called their Proposition I. We state this proposition as follows:

> ## MM Proposition I (no taxes):
> The value of the levered firm is the same as the value of the unlevered firm.

This is perhaps the most important result in all of corporate finance. In fact, it is generally considered the beginning point of modern managerial finance. Before Modigliani and Miller, the effect of leverage on the value of the firm was considered complex and convoluted. Modigliani and Miller show a blindingly simple result: if levered firms are priced too high, rational investors will arbitrage by borrowing on their personal accounts to buy shares in unlevered firms. This substitution is often called *homemade leverage*. As long as individuals borrow (and lend) on the same terms as the firms, they can duplicate the effects of corporate leverage on their own.

The example of Trans Can Corporation shows that leverage does not affect the value of the firm. Since we showed earlier that shareholders' welfare is directly related to the firm's value, the example indicates that changes in capital structure cannot affect the shareholders' welfare.

## A Key Assumption

The Modigliani and Miller result hinges on two key assumptions: taxes are zero and individuals can borrow as cheaply as corporations. (We discuss taxes in detail below and focus on borrowing here.) If, alternatively, individuals can only borrow at a higher rate, one can easily show that corporations can increase firm value by borrowing.

Is this assumption of equal borrowing costs a good one? Individuals who want to buy stock and borrow can do so by establishing a margin account with the broker. Under this arrangement, the broker lends the individual a portion of the purchase price. For example, the individual might buy $10,000 of stock by investing $6,000 of his own funds and borrowing $4,000 from the broker. Should the stock be worth $9,000 on the next day, the individual's net worth or equity in the account would be $5,000 = $9,000 − $4,000.[4]

The broker fears that a sudden price drop will cause the equity in the individual's account to be negative, implying that the broker may not get her loan repaid in full. To guard against this possibility, stock exchange rules require that the individual make additional cash contributions (replenish his margin account) as the stock price falls. Because (1) the procedures for replenishing the account have developed over many years, and (2) the broker holds the stock as collateral, there is little default risk to the broker.[5] In particular, if margin contributions are not made on time, the broker can sell the stock in order to satisfy her loan. Therefore, brokers generally charge low interest, with many rates being only slightly above the risk-free rate.

By contrast, corporations frequently borrow using illiquid assets (e.g., plant and equipment) as collateral. The costs to the lender of initial negotiation and ongoing supervision, as well as of working out arrangements in the event of financial distress, can be quite substantial. Thus, it is difficult to argue that individuals must borrow at higher rates than can corporations.[6]

---

[4] We are ignoring the one-day interest charge on the loan.

[5] Had this text been published before October 19, 1987, when stock prices declined by more than 20 percent, we might have used the phrase "virtually no" risk instead of "little."

[6] One caveat is in order. The investor's borrowing is currently limited by law to 50 percent of value. Certain companies, like financial institutions, borrow over 90 percent of their firm's market value. Individuals borrowing against the stock of all-equity corporations cannot duplicate the debt of these highly levered corporations.

CONCEPT
QUESTIONS

- Describe financial leverage.
- What is levered equity?
- How can a shareholder of Trans Can undo the company's financial leverage?

## 16.4   MODIGLIANI AND MILLER: PROPOSITION II (NO TAXES)

### Risk to Equityholders Rises with Leverage

At a Trans Can corporate meeting, a corporate officer said, "Well, maybe it doesn't matter whether the corporation or the individual levers—as long as some leverage takes place. Leverage benefits investors. After all, an investor's expected return rises with the amount of the leverage present." He then pointed out that, as shown in Tables 16.2 and 16.3, the expected return on unlevered equity is 15 percent, while the expected return on levered equity is 20 percent.

However, another officer replied, "Not necessarily. Though the expected return rises with leverage, the *risk* rises as well." This point can be seen by examining Tables 16.2 and 16.3. With EBIT varying between $400 and $2,000, EPS for the shareholders of the unlevered firm varies between $1.00 and $5.00. EPS for the shareholders of the levered firm varies between $0 and $8.00. This greater range for the EPS of the levered firm implies greater risk for the levered firm's shareholders. In other words, levered shareholders have better returns in good times than do unlevered shareholders but have worse returns in bad times. The two tables also show greater range for the ROE of the levered firm's shareholders. The above interpretation concerning risk applies here as well.

The same insight can be taken from Figure 16.2. The slope of the line for the levered firm is greater than the slope of the line for the unlevered firm. This means that the levered shareholders have better returns in good times than do unlevered shareholders, but they have worse returns in bad times, implying greater risk with leverage. In other words, the slope of the line measures the risk to shareholders, since the slope indicates the responsiveness of ROE to changes in firm performance (EBIT).

### Proposition II: Required Return to Equityholders Rises with Leverage

Since levered equity has greater risk, it should have a greater expected return as compensation. In our example, the market *requires* only a 15 percent expected return for the unlevered equity, but it requires a 20 percent expected return for the levered equity.

This type of reasoning allows us to develop **MM Proposition II**. Here, Modigliani and Miller argue that the expected ROE is positively related to leverage, because the risk to equityholders increases with leverage.

To develop this position, recall from Chapter 13 that the firm's weighted average cost of capital (WACC) can be written as[7]

$$\frac{B}{B + S} \times r_B + \frac{S}{B + S} \times r_S \tag{16.2}$$

where

$r_B$ is the interest rate, also called the cost of debt
$r_S$ is the expected return on equity or stock, also called the *cost of equity* or the *required return on equity*

---

[7] Since we do not have taxes here, the cost of debt is $r_B$, not $r_B(1 - T_c)$, as it was in Chapter 13.

$B$ is the value of the firm's debt or bonds

$S$ is the value of the firm's stock or equity

Equation (16.2) is quite intuitive. It simply says that a firm's WACC is a weighted average of its cost of debt and its cost of equity. The weight applied to debt is the proportion of debt in the capital structure, and the weight applied to equity is the proportion of equity in the capital structure. Calculations of WACC from equation (16.2) for both the unlevered and the levered firm are presented in Table 16.5.

**TABLE 16.5**

### Cost of Capital Calculations for Trans Can

$$\text{WACC} = \frac{B}{B + S} \times r_B + \frac{S}{B + S} \times r_S$$

Unlevered firm: $\quad 15\% = \dfrac{0}{\$8{,}000} \times 10\%^* + \dfrac{\$8{,}000}{\$8{,}000} \times 15\%^\dagger$

Levered firm: $\quad 15\% = \dfrac{\$4{,}000}{\$8{,}000} \times 10\%^* + \dfrac{\$4{,}000}{\$8{,}000} \times 20\%^\ddagger$

* 10% is the interest rate.

† From the "Expected" column in Table 16.2, we learn that expected earnings after interest for the unlevered firm are $1,200. From Table 16.1, we learn that equity for the unlevered firm is $8,000. Thus, $r_S$ for the unlevered firm is

$$\frac{\text{Expected earnings after interest}}{\text{Equity}} = \frac{\$1{,}200}{\$8{,}000} = 15\%$$

‡ From the "Expected" column in Table 16.3, we learn that expected earnings after interest for the levered firm are $800. From Table 16.1, we learn that equity for the levered firm is $4,000. Thus, $r_S$ for the levered firm is

$$\frac{\text{Expected earnings after interest}}{\text{Equity}} = \frac{\$800}{\$4{,}000} = 20\%$$

An implication of MM Proposition I is that WACC is a constant for a given firm, regardless of the capital structure.[8] For example, Table 16.5 shows that WACC for Trans Can is 15 percent, with or without leverage.

Let us now define $r_0$ to be the *cost of capital for an all-equity firm*. For Trans Can, $r_0$ is calculated as

$$r_0 = \frac{\text{Expected earnings to unlevered firm}}{\text{Unlevered equity}} = \frac{\$1{,}200}{\$8{,}000} = 15\%$$

As can be seen from Table 16.5, WACC is equal to $r_0$ for Trans Can. In fact, WACC must *always* equal $r_0$ in a world without corporate taxes.

Proposition II states the expected return of equity, $r_S$, in terms of leverage. The exact relationship, derived by setting WACC $= r_0$ and then rearranging equation (16.2), is[9]

---

[8] This statement holds in a world of no taxes. It does not hold in a world with taxes, a point to be brought out later in this chapter (see Figure 16.5).

[9] This can be derived from equation (16.2) by setting $r_{\text{WACC}} = r_0$, yielding

$$\frac{B}{B + S} r_B + \frac{S}{B + S} r_S = r_0 \tag{16.2}$$

Multiplying both sides by $(B + S)/S$ yields

$$\frac{B}{S} r_B + r_S = \frac{B + S}{S} r_0$$

We can rewrite the right-hand side as

$$\frac{B}{S} r_B + r_S = \frac{B}{S} r_0 + r_0$$

Moving $(B/S)r_B$ to the right-hand side and rearranging yields

$$r_S = r_0 + \frac{B}{S}(r_0 - r_B)$$

which is just equation (16.3).

**MM Proposition II (no taxes):**

$$r_S = r_0 + \frac{B}{S}(r_0 - r_B)$$  (16.3)

Equation (16.3) implies that the required ROE is a linear function of the firm's debt-to-equity ratio. Examining equation (16.3), we see that if $r_0$ exceeds the debt rate, $r_B$, then the cost of equity rises with increases in the debt-to-equity ratio, $B/S$. Normally, $r_0$ should exceed $r_B$. That is, because even unlevered equity is risky, it should have an expected return greater than that of risk-free debt. Note that equation (16.3) holds for Trans Can in its levered state:

$$0.20 = 0.15 + \frac{\$\,4,000}{\$\,4,000}(0.15 - 0.10)$$

Figure 16.3 graphs equation (16.3). As you can see, we have plotted the relation between the cost of equity, $r_S$, and the debt-to-equity ratio, $B/S$, as a straight line. What we witness in equation (16.3) and illustrate in Figure 16.3 is the effect of leverage on the cost of equity. As the firm raises the debt-to-equity ratio, each dollar of equity is levered with additional debt. This raises the risk of equity and therefore the required return, $r_S$, on the equity.

---

**FIGURE 16.3**

**The Cost of Equity, the Cost of Debt, and the Weighted Average Cost of Capital: MM Proposition II with No Corporate Taxes**

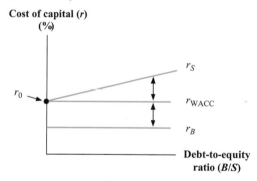

$$r_S = r_0 + \frac{B}{S}(r_0 - r_B)$$

$r_S$ is the cost of equity.
$r_B$ is the cost of debt.
$r_0$ is the cost of capital for an all-equity firm.
$r_{WACC}$ is a firm's WACC.
In a world with no taxes, $r_{WACC}$ for a levered firm is equal to $r_0$.
$r_0$ is a single point, while $r_S$, $r_B$, and $r_{WACC}$ are all entire lines.

The cost of equity capital, $r_S$, is positively related to the firm's debt-to-equity ratio. The firm's WACC is invariant to the firm's debt-to-equity ratio.

---

Figure 16.3 also shows that WACC is unaffected by leverage, a point we made above. (It is important for you to realize that $r_0$, the cost of capital for an all-equity firm, is represented by a single dot on the graph. By contrast, WACC is an entire line.)

| EXAMPLE **16.2** | Example Illustrating Proposition I and Proposition II |

Luteran Motors, an all-equity firm, has an expected cash flow of $10 million per year in perpetuity. There are 10 million shares outstanding, implying an expected annual cash flow of $1 per share. The cost of capital for this unlevered firm is 10 percent. The firm will soon build a new plant for $4 million. The plant is expected to generate additional cash flow of $1 million per year. These figures can be described as follows:

| **Current company** | **New plant** |
| --- | --- |
| Cash flow: $10 million | Initial outlay: $4 million |
| Number of outstanding shares: 10 million | Additional annual cash flow: $1 million |

The project's net present value (NPV) is

$$-\$4 \text{ million} + \frac{\$1 \text{ million}}{0.1} = \$6 \text{ million}$$

assuming that the project is discounted at the same rate as the firm as a whole. Before the market knows of the project, the market value balance sheet of the firm is as follows:

**LUTERAN MOTORS**
**Balance Sheet (all equity)**

| | |
| --- | --- |
| Old assets: $\dfrac{\$10 \text{ million}}{0.1} = \$100$ million | Equity: $100 million (10 million shares of stock) |

The value of the firm is $100 million, because the cash flows of $10 million per year are capitalized at 10 percent. A share of stock sells for $10 (or $100 million/10 million) because there are 10 million shares outstanding.

The market value balance sheet is a useful tool of financial analysis. Because students are often thrown off guard by it initially, we recommend extra study here. The key is that the market value balance sheet has the same form as the balance sheet that accountants use. That is, assets are placed on the left-hand side, whereas liabilities and shareholders' equity are placed on the right-hand side. In addition, the left-hand side and the right-hand side must be equal. The difference is in the numbers. Accountants value items in terms of historical cost (original purchase price less depreciation), whereas financial people value items in terms of market value.

The firm will issue $4 million of either equity or debt. Let us consider the effects of equity and debt financing in turn.

**Share Financing** Imagine that the firm announces that in the near future, it will raise $4 million in equity to build a new plant. The stock price will rise to reflect the positive NPV of the plant. According to efficient markets, the increase occurs immediately. That is, the rise occurs on the day of the announcement, not on the date of either the onset of construction of the power plant or the forthcoming stock offering. The market value balance sheet is now as follows:

**LUTERAN MOTORS**
**Balance Sheet (upon announcement of equity issue to construct plant)**

| | | | |
| --- | --- | --- | --- |
| Old assets | $100 million | Equity | $106 million |
| Net present value of plant: | | | (10 million |
| $-\$4 \text{ million} + \dfrac{\$1 \text{ million}}{0.1} =$ | 6 million | | shares of stock) |
| Total assets | $106 million | | |

Note that the NPV of the plant is included in the market value balance sheet. Because the new shares have not yet been issued, the number of outstanding shares remains 10 million. The price per share has now risen to $10.60 (or $106/10 million) to reflect news concerning the plant.

Shortly thereafter, $4 million of stock is floated. Because the stock is selling at $10.60 per share, 377,358 (or $4 million/$10.60) shares of stock are issued. Imagine that funds are put in the bank *temporarily* before being used to build the plant. The market value balance sheet is now as follows:

### LUTERAN MOTORS
**Balance Sheet (upon issuance of stock but before construction begins on plant)**

| | | | |
|---|---|---|---|
| Old assets | $100 million | Equity | $110 million |
| Net present value of plant | 6 million | | (10,377,358 shares of stock) |
| Proceeds from new issue of stock (currently invested in bank) | 4 million | | |
| Total assets | $110 million | | |

The number of shares outstanding is now 10,377,358 because 377,358 new shares were issued. The price per share is $10.60 ($110,000,000/10,377,358). Note that the price has not changed. This is consistent with efficient capital markets, because the stock price should only move due to new information.

Of course, the funds are placed in the bank only temporarily. Shortly after the new issue, the $4 million is given to a contractor who builds the plant. To avoid problems in discounting, we assume that the plant is built immediately. The balance sheet is then as follows:

### LUTERAN MOTORS
**Balance Sheet (upon completion of plant)**

| | | | |
|---|---|---|---|
| Old assets | $100 million | Equity | $110 million |
| Present value of plant: $\frac{\$1 \text{ million}}{0.1} =$ | 10 million | | (10,377,358 shares of stock) |
| Total assets | $110 million | | |

Though total assets do not change, the composition of the assets does change. The bank account has been emptied to pay the contractor. The present value (PV) of cash flows of $1 million a year from the plant is reflected as an asset worth $10 million. Because the building expenditures of $4 million have already been paid, they no longer represent a future cost. Hence, they no longer reduce the value of the plant. According to efficient capital markets, the price per share of stock remains $10.60.

Expected yearly cash flow from the firm is $11 million, $10 million of which comes from the old assets and $1 million from the new. The expected return to equityholders is

$$r_S = \frac{\$11 \text{ million}}{\$110 \text{ million}} = 0.10$$

Because the firm is all equity, $r_S = r_0 = 0.10$.

**Debt Financing**    Alternatively, imagine that the firm announces that in the near future, it will borrow $4 million at 6 percent to build a new plant. This implies yearly interest payments of $240,000 (or $4,000,000 × 6%). Again, the stock price rises immediately to reflect the positive NPV of the plant. Thus, we have the following:

### LUTERAN MOTORS
**Balance Sheet (upon announcement of debt issue to construct plant)**

| | | | |
|---|---|---|---|
| Old assets | $100 million | Equity | $106 million |
| Net present value of plant: | | | (10 million shares of stock) |
| $-\$4 \text{ million} + \frac{\$1 \text{ million}}{0.1} =$ | 6 million | | |
| Total assets | $106 million | | |

The value of the firm is the same as in the equity financing case because (1) the same plant is to be built and (2) Modigliani and Miller prove that debt financing is neither better nor worse than equity financing.

At some point, $4 million of debt is issued. As before, the funds are placed in the bank temporarily. The market value balance sheet is now as follows:

**LUTERAN MOTORS**
**Balance Sheet (upon debt issuance but before construction begins on plant)**

| | | | |
|---|---|---|---|
| Old assets | $100 million | Debt | $ 4 million |
| Net present value of plant | 6 million | Equity (10 million shares of stock) | 106 million |
| Proceeds from debt issue (currently invested in bank) | 4 million | | |
| Total assets | $110 million | Debt plus equity | $110 million |

Note that debt appears on the right-hand side of the balance sheet. The stock price is still $10.60, in accordance with our discussion of efficient capital markets.

Finally, the contractor receives $4 million and builds the plant. The market value balance sheet is then the following:

**LUTERAN MOTORS**
**Balance Sheet (upon completion of plant)**

| | | | |
|---|---|---|---|
| Old assets | $100 million | Debt | $ 4 million |
| Present value of plant | 10 million | Equity (10 million shares of stock) | 106 million |
| Total assets | $110 million | Debt plus equity | $110 million |

The only change here is that the bank account has been depleted to pay the contractor. The equityholders expect yearly cash flow after interest of

$$10,000,000 \;+\; \$1,000,000 \;-\; \$240,000 \;=\; \$10,760,000$$

Cash flow on    Cash flow on    Interest:
old assets      new assets    $4 million × 6%

The equityholders expect to earn a return of

$$\frac{\$10,760,000}{\$106,000,000} = 10.15\%$$

This return of 10.15 percent for levered equityholders is higher than the 10 percent return for unlevered equityholders. This result is sensible because, as we argued earlier, levered equity is riskier. In fact, the return of 10.15 percent should be exactly what MM Proposition II predicts. This prediction can be verified by plugging values into equation (16.3):

$$r_S = r_0 + \frac{B}{S}(r_0 - r_B)$$

We obtain

$$10.15\% = 10\% + \frac{\$\,4,000,000}{\$106,000,000} \times (10\% - 6\%)$$

This example was useful for two reasons. First, we wanted to introduce the concept of market value balance sheets, which will prove useful elsewhere in the text. Among other things, this technique allows one to calculate the price per share of a new issue of stock. Second, the example illustrates three aspects of Modigliani and Miller:

1. The example is consistent with MM Proposition I because the value of the firm is $110 million after either equity or debt financing.

2. Students are often more interested in stock price than in firm value. We show that the stock price is always $10.60, regardless of whether debt or equity financing is used.

3. The example is consistent with MM Proposition II. The expected return to equity-holders rises from 10 to 10.15 percent, just as equation (16.3) states.

## Modigliani and Miller: An Interpretation

The MM results indicate that managers of a firm cannot change its value by repackaging the firm's securities. Though this idea was considered revolutionary when it was originally proposed in the late 1950s, the MM model and arbitrage proof have since met with wide acclaim.[10]

Modigliani and Miller argue that the firm's overall cost of capital cannot be reduced as debt is substituted for equity, even though debt appears to be cheaper than equity. This is because as the firm adds debt, the remaining equity becomes more risky. As this risk rises, the cost of equity capital rises as a result. The increase in the cost of the remaining equity capital offsets the higher proportion of the firm financed by low-cost debt. In fact, Modigliani and Miller prove that the two effects exactly off-set each other, so that both the value of the firm and the firm's overall cost of capital are invariant to leverage.

Modigliani and Miller use an interesting analogy to food. They consider a dairy farmer with two choices: either she can sell whole milk or, by skimming, she can sell a combination of cream and low-fat milk. Though the farmer can get a high price for the cream, she gets a low price for the low-fat milk, implying no net gain. In fact, imagine that the proceeds from the whole-milk strategy were less than those from the cream–low-fat milk strategy. Arbitrageurs would buy the whole milk, perform the skimming operation themselves, and resell the cream and low-fat milk separately. Competition between arbitrageurs would tend to boost the price of whole milk until proceeds from the two strategies became equal. Thus, the value of the farmer's milk is invariant with how the milk is packaged.

Food found its way into this chapter earlier, when we viewed the firm as a pie.[11] Modigliani and Miller argue that the size of the pie does not change, no matter how shareholders and bondholders divide it. Modigliani and Miller say that a firm's capital structure is irrelevant; it is what it is by some historical accident. The theory implies that firms' debt-to-equity ratios could be anything. They are what they are because of whimsical and random managerial decisions about how much to borrow and how much stock to issue.

Although scholars are always fascinated with far-reaching theories, students are perhaps more concerned with real-world applications. Do real-world managers follow Modigliani and Miller by treating capital structure decisions with indifference? Unfortunately for the theory, virtually all companies in certain industries, such as banking, choose high debt-to-equity ratios. Conversely, companies in other industries, such as pharmaceuticals, choose low debt-to-equity ratios. In fact, almost any industry has a debt-to-equity ratio to which companies in that industry adhere. Thus, companies do not appear to be selecting their degree of leverage in a frivolous or random manner. Because of this, financial economists (including Modigliani and Miller themselves) have argued that real-world factors may have been left out of the theory.

---

[10] Franco Modigliani and Merton Miller each won the Nobel Prize in Economics, in part for their work on capital structure.

[11] Other authors have also brought food into discussions on capital structure. For example, Stewart Myers, in "The Search for Optimal Capital Structure," *Midland Corporate Finance Journal* (Spring 1983), used chicken. Abstracting from the extra costs in cutting up poultry, he argues that all of the chicken parts should, in sum, sell for no more than a whole chicken.

# IN THEIR OWN WORDS

## In Professor Miller's words...

The MM results are not easy to understand fully. This point is related in a story told by Merton Miller.

"How difficult it is to summarize briefly the contribution of the [MM] papers was brought home to me very clearly last October after Franco Modigliani was awarded the Nobel Prize in Economics in part—but, of course, only in part—for the work in finance. The television camera crews from our local stations in Chicago immediately descended upon me. 'We understand,' they said, 'that you worked with Modigliani some years back in developing these M and M theorems and we wonder if you could explain them briefly to our television viewers.'

"'How briefly?' I asked.

"'Oh, take ten seconds,' was the reply.

"Ten seconds to explain the work of a lifetime! Ten seconds to describe two carefully reasoned articles, each running to more than thirty printed pages and each with sixty or so long footnotes! When they saw the look of dismay on my face, they said, 'You don't have to go into details. Just give us the main points in simple, common-sense terms.'

"The main point of the first or cost-of-capital article was, in principle at least, simple enough to make. It said that in an economist's ideal world of complete and perfect capital markets and with full and symmetric information among all market participants, the total market value of all the securities issued by a firm was governed by the earning power and risk of its underlying real assets and was independent of how the mix of securities issued to finance it was divided between debt instruments and equity capital. . . .

"Such a summary, however, uses too many shorthanded terms and concepts, like perfect capital markets, that are rich in connotations to economists but hardly so to the general public. So I thought, instead, of an analogy that we ourselves had invoked in the original paper. . . .

"'Think of the firm,' I said, 'as a gigantic tub of whole milk. The farmer can sell the whole milk as is. Or he can separate out the cream and sell it at a considerably higher price than the whole milk would bring. (That's the analog of a firm selling low-yield and hence high-priced debt securities.) But, of course, what the farmer would have left would be skim milk with low butterfat content and that would sell for much less than whole milk. That corresponds to the levered equity. The M and M proposition says that if there were no costs of separation (and, of course, no government dairy support programs), the cream plus the skim milk would bring the same price as the whole milk.'

"The television people conferred among themselves and came back to inform me that it was too long, too complicated, and too academic.

"'Don't you have anything simpler?' they asked. I thought of another way that the M and M proposition is presented these days, which emphasizes the notion of market completeness and stresses the role of securities as devices for 'partitioning' a firm's payoffs in each possible state of the world among the group of its capital suppliers.

"'Think of the firm,' I said, 'as a gigantic pizza, divided into quarters. If now you cut each quarter in half into eighths, the M and M proposition says that you will have more pieces but not more pizza.'

"Again there was a whispered conference among the camera crew, and the director came back and said:

"'Professor, we understand from the press release that there were two M and M propositions. Can we try the other one?'

[Professor Miller tried valiantly to explain the second proposition, though this was apparently even more difficult to get across. After his attempt:]

"Once again there was a whispered conversation. They shut the lights off. They folded up their equipment. They thanked me for giving them the time. They said that they'd get back to me. But I knew that I had somehow lost my chance to start a new career as a packager of economic wisdom for TV viewers in convenient ten-second bites. Some have the talent for it . . . and some just don't."

Source: GSB Chicago, University of Chicago (Autumn 1986).

---

## Summary of Modigliani–Miller Propositions without Taxes

**Assumptions:**
- No taxes
- No transaction costs
- Individuals and corporations borrow at the same rate
- Complete information
- Perpetual cash flow
- No default risk

**Results:**

Proposition I: $V_L = V_U$ (value of levered firm equals value of unlevered firm)

Proposition II: $r_S = r_0 + \frac{B}{S}(r_0 - r_B)$

**Intuition:**

Proposition I: Through homemade leverage, individuals can either duplicate or undo the effects of corporate leverage.

Proposition II: The cost of equity rises with leverage, because the risk to equity rises with leverage.

---

Though many of our students have argued that individuals can only borrow at rates above the corporate borrowing rate, we disagreed with this argument earlier in the chapter. But when we look elsewhere for unrealistic assumptions in the theory, we find two:[12]

1. Taxes were ignored.
2. Bankruptcy costs and other agency costs were not considered.

We will turn to taxes shortly. Bankruptcy costs and other agency costs will be treated in the next chapter. The boxed section above presents a summary of the main MM results without taxes.

**CONCEPT QUESTIONS**
- Why does the expected ROE rise with firm leverage?
- What is the exact relationship between the expected ROE and firm leverage?
- How are market value balance sheets set up?

# 16.5   TAXES

## The Basic Insight

The previous part of this chapter showed that firm value is unrelated to debt in a world without taxes. We now show that in the presence of corporate taxes, the firm's value is positively related to its debt. The basic intuition can be seen from a pie chart, such as the one in Figure 16.4. Consider the all-equity firm on the left. Here, both equityholders and the Canada Revenue Agency (CRA) have claims on the value of the firm. The value of the all-equity firm is, of course, that owned by the equityholders. The proportion going to taxes is simply a cost.

The pie on the right for the levered firm shows three claims: equityholders, debtholders, and taxes. The value of the levered firm is the sum of the value of the debt and the value of the equity. In selecting between the two capital structures in the picture, a financial manager should select the one with the higher value. Assuming that the total area is the same for both pies, value is maximized for the capital structure paying the least in taxes. In other words, the manager should choose the capital structure that minimizes taxes.

---

[12] Modigliani and Miller were aware of both of these issues, as can be seen in their original paper.

FIGURE 16.4

**Two Pie Models of Capital Structure under Corporate Taxes**

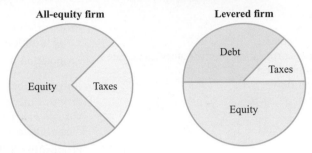

The levered firm pays less in taxes than does the all-equity firm.
Thus, the sum of debt and equity is greater for the levered firm.

We will show that due to Canadian tax law allowing interest to be deducted from taxable income, the proportion of the pie allocated to taxes is less for the levered firm than it is for the unlevered firm. Thus, managers should select high leverage.

---

EXAMPLE 16.3  Taxation of Corporate Income

The Water Products Company has a corporate tax rate, $T_c$, of 40 percent and expected EBIT of $1 million. Its entire earnings after taxes are paid out as dividends.

The firm is considering two alternative capital structures. Under plan I, Water Products would have no debt in its capital structure. Under plan II, the company would have $4,000,000 of debt, $B$. The cost of debt, $r_B$, is 10 percent for both plans.

The CFO for Water Products makes the following calculations:

|  | Plan I | Plan II |
|---|---|---|
| Earnings before interest and taxes (EBIT) | $1,000,000 | $1,000,000 |
| Interest ($r_B B$) | 0 | −400,000 |
| Earnings before taxes = (EBIT − $r_B B$) | 1,000,000 | 600,000 |
| Taxes ($T_c = 0.40$) | −400,000 | −240,000 |
| Earnings after corporate taxes = [(EBIT − $r_B B$) × (1 − $T_c$)] | 600,000 | 360,000 |
| Total cash flow to both shareholders and bondholders [EBIT × (1 − $T_c$) + $T_c r_B B$] | $ 600,000 | $ 760,000 |

The most relevant numbers for our purposes are the two on the bottom line. Here, we see that more cash flow reaches the owners of the firm (both shareholders and bondholders) under plan II. The difference is $160,000 = $760,000 − $600,000. It does not take us long to realize the source of this difference. Water Products pays less in taxes under plan II ($240,000) than it does under plan I ($400,000). The difference here is $160,000 = $400,000 − $240,000.

This difference occurs because interest totally escapes corporate taxation, whereas earnings after interest but before corporate taxes (EBT) are taxed at the 40 percent rate.[13] We express this relationship algebraically in the next section.

---

[13] Note that shareholders actually receive more under plan I ($600,000) than under plan II ($360,000). Students are often bothered by this since it seems to imply that shareholders are better off without leverage. However, remember that there are more shares outstanding in plan I than in plan II. A full-blown model would show that EPS is higher with leverage.

## Present Value of the Tax Shield

The previous example shows a tax advantage to debt or, equivalently, a tax disadvantage to equity. We now want to value this advantage. The dollar interest is

$$\text{Interest} = \underset{\text{Interest rate}}{r_B} \times \underset{\text{Amount borrowed}}{B}$$

This interest is $400,000 (10% × $4,000,000) for Water Products. All this interest is tax deductible. That is, whatever the taxable income of Water Products would have been without the debt, the taxable income is now $400,000 *less* with the debt.

Because the corporate tax rate is 0.40 in our example, the reduction in corporate taxes is $160,000 (0.40 × $400,000). This number is identical to the reduction in corporate taxes calculated previously.

Algebraically, the reduction in corporate taxes is

$$\underset{\text{Corporate tax rate}}{T_c} \times \underset{\text{Dollar amount of interest}}{r_B \times B} \tag{16.4}$$

That is, whatever the taxes that a firm would pay each year without debt, the firm will pay $T_c r_B B$ less with the debt of $B$. Expression (16.4) is often called the *tax shield from debt*. Note that it is an *annual* amount.

As long as the firm expects to be in a positive tax bracket, we can assume that the cash flow in expression (16.4) has the same risk as the interest on the debt. Thus, its value can be determined by discounting at the interest rate, $r_B$. Assuming that the cash flows are perpetual, the PV of the tax shield is

$$\frac{T_c r_B B}{r_B} = T_c B \tag{16.5}$$

## Value of the Levered Firm

We have just calculated the PV of the tax shield from debt. Our next step is to calculate the value of the levered firm. From equation (16.5), the after-tax cash flow to the shareholders and bondholders in the levered firm is

$$\text{EBIT} \times (1 - T_c) + T_c r_B B \tag{16.6}$$

The first term in expression (16.6) is the after-tax cash flow in the unlevered firm. The value of an unlevered firm (that is, a firm with no debt) is the PV of EBIT × (1 − $T_c$),

$$V_U = \frac{\text{EBIT} \times (1 - T_c)}{r_0} \tag{16.7}$$

where

$V_U$ = Present value of an unlevered firm

EBIT × (1 − $T_c$) = Firm cash flows after corporate taxes

$T_c$ = Corporate tax rate

$r_0$ = The cost of capital to an all-equity firm (as can be seen from the formula, $r_0$ now discounts *after-tax* cash flows)

The second part of the cash flows, $T_c r_B B$, is the tax shield. To determine its PV, the tax shield should be discounted at $r_B$.

As a consequence, we have the following:[14]

---

[14] This relationship holds when the debt level is assumed to be constant through time. A different formula would apply if the debt-to-equity ratio were assumed to be constant over time. For a deeper treatment of this point, see J. A. Miles and J. R. Ezzell, "The Weighted Average Cost of Capital, Perfect Capital Markets and Project Life," *Journal of Financial and Quantitative Analysis* (September 1980).

**MM Proposition I (corporate taxes):**

$$V_L = \frac{\text{EBIT} \times (1 - T_c)}{r_0} + \frac{T_c r_B B}{r_B} \qquad (16.8)$$

$$= V_U + T_c B$$

Equation (16.8) is **MM Proposition I under corporate taxes**. The first term in equation (16.8) is the value of the cash flows of the firm with no debt tax shield. In other words, this term is equal to $V_U$, the value of the all-equity firm. The value of the firm is the value of an all-equity firm plus $T_c B$, the tax rate times the value of the debt. $T_c B$ is the PV of the tax shield in the case of perpetual cash flows.[15] Notice how the different cash flows are discounted using different rates. Recall, in our discussion on NPV analysis in previous chapters, that we said that the proper rate to use should reflect the riskiness of the project, hence its future generated cash flows. Similarly, we utilize different discount rates to reflect this concept—the cost of equity, the cost of capital, and the cost of debt.

The Water Products example reveals that because the tax shield increases with the amount of debt, the firm can raise its total cash flow and its value by substituting debt for equity. We now have a clear example of why the capital structure *does* matter. By raising the debt-to-equity ratio, the firm can lower its taxes and thereby increase its total value. The strong forces that operate to maximize the value of the firm would seem to push it toward an all-debt capital structure.

---

**EXAMPLE 16.4**

Divided Airlines is currently an unlevered firm. It is considering a capital restructuring to allow $200 of debt. The company expects to generate $166.67 in cash flows before interest and taxes, in perpetuity. The corporate tax rate is 40 percent, implying after-tax cash flows of $100. Its cost of debt capital is 10 percent. Unlevered firms in the same industry have a cost of equity capital of 20 percent. What will the new value of Divided Airlines be?

The value of Divided Airlines will equal[16]

$$V_L = \frac{\text{EBIT} \times (1 - T_c)}{r_0} + T_c B$$

$$= \frac{\$100}{0.20} + (0.40 \times \$200)$$

$$= \$500 + \$80$$

$$= \$580$$

Because $V_L = B + S$, the value of levered equity, $S$, is equal to $580 − $200 = $380. The value of Divided Airlines as a function of leverage is shown in Figure 16.5.

---

[15] The following example calculates the PV if we assume the debt has a finite life. Suppose the Maxwell Company has $1 million in debt with an 8 percent coupon rate. If the debt matures in two years and the cost of debt capital, $r_B$, is 10 percent, what is the PV of the tax shields if the corporate tax rate is 40 percent? The debt is amortized in equal instalments over two years.

| Year | Loan balance | Interest | Tax shield | Present value of tax shield |
|------|-------------|----------|------------|----------------------------|
| 0 | $1,000,000 | | | |
| 1 | 500,000 | $80,000 | 0.4 × $80,000 | $29,090.91 |
| 2 | 0 | 40,000 | 0.4 × $40,000 | 13,223.14 |
| | | | | $42,314.05 |

The PV of the tax savings is

$$\text{PV} = \frac{0.40 \times \$80,000}{1.10} + \frac{0.40 \times \$40,000}{(1.10)^2} = \$42,314.05$$

The Maxwell Company's value is higher than that of a comparable unlevered firm by $42,314.05. Comparables are discussed in more detail in Chapter 6.

[16] Note that in a world with taxes, $r_0$ is used to discount after-tax cash flows.

**FIGURE 16.5**

**The Effect of Financial Leverage on Firm Value: Modigliani and Miller with Corporate Taxes in the Case of Divided Airlines**

$$V_L = V_U + T_c B$$
$$= \$500 + (0.40 \times \$200)$$
$$= \$580$$

Debt reduces Divided's tax burden. As a result, the value of the firm is positively related to debt.

## Expected Return and Leverage under Corporate Taxes

MM Proposition II under no taxes posits a positive relationship between the expected ROE and leverage. This result occurs because the risk of equity increases with leverage. The same intuition also holds in a world of corporate taxes. The exact formula is[17]

---

[17] This relationship can be shown as follows: Given MM Proposition I under corporate taxes, a levered firm's market value balance sheet can be written as follows:

| $V_U$ = Value of unlevered firm | $B$ = Debt |
|---|---|
| $T_c B$ = Tax shield | $S$ = Equity |

The value of the unlevered firm is simply the value of the assets without benefit of leverage. The balance sheet indicates that the firm's value increases by $T_c B$ when debt of $B$ is added. The expected cash flow from the left-hand side of the balance sheet can be written as

$$V_U r_0 + T_c B r_B \qquad (a)$$

Because assets are risky, their expected rate of return is $r_0$. The tax shield has the same risk as the debt, so its expected rate of return is $r_B$.

The expected cash to bondholders and shareholders together is

$$S r_S + B r_B \qquad (b)$$

Expression (b) reflects the fact that stock earns an expected return of $r_S$ and debt earns the interest rate $r_B$.

Because all cash flows are paid out as dividends in our no-growth perpetuity model, the cash flows going into the firm equal those going to stakeholders. Hence (a) and (b) are equal:

$$S r_S + B r_B = V_U r_0 + T_c B r_B \qquad (c)$$

Dividing both sides of (c) by $S$, subtracting $B r_B$ from both sides, and rearranging yields

$$r_S = \frac{V_U}{S} \times r_0 - (1 - T_c) \times \frac{B}{S} r_B \qquad (d)$$

Because the value of the levered firm, $V_L$, equals $V_U + T_c B = B + S$, it follows that $V_U = S + (1 - T_c) \times B$. Thus, (d) can be rewritten as

$$r_S = \frac{S + (1 - T_c) \times B}{S} \times r_0 - (1 - T_c) \times \frac{B}{S} r_B \qquad (e)$$

Bringing the terms involving $(1 - T_c) \times \frac{B}{S}$ together produces equation (16.9).

**MM Proposition II (Corporate Taxes):**

$$r_S = r_0 + \frac{B}{S} \times (1 - T_c) \times (r_0 - r_B) \qquad (16.9)$$

Applying the **MM Proposition II under corporate taxes** formula to Divided Airlines, we get

$$r_S = 0.2316 = 0.20 + \frac{200}{380} \times (1 - 0.40) \times (0.20 - 0.10)$$

This calculation is illustrated in Figure 16.6.

---

**FIGURE 16.6**

**The Effect of Financial Leverage on the Cost of Debt and Equity Capital**

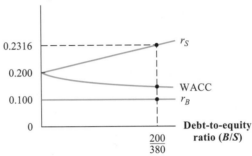

Financial leverage adds risk to the firm's equity. As compensation, the cost of equity rises with the firm's risk:

$$r_S = r_0 + \frac{B}{S}(1 - T_c)(r_0 - r_B)$$
$$= 0.20 + \left( \frac{200}{380} \times 0.60 \times 0.10 \right)$$
$$= 0.2316$$

Whenever $r_0 > r_B$, $r_S$ increases with leverage, a result that we also found in the no-tax case. As stated earlier in this chapter, $r_0$ should exceed $r_B$. That is, since equity (even unlevered equity) is risky, it should have an expected return greater than that on the less risky debt.

We can check this calculation by discounting at $r_S$ to determine the value of the levered equity. The algebraic formula for levered equity is

$$S = \frac{(\text{EBIT} - r_B B) \times (1 - T_c)}{r_S} \qquad (16.10)$$

The numerator is the expected cash flow to levered equity after interest and taxes. The denominator is the rate at which the cash flow to equity is discounted.

For Divided Airlines we get[18]

$$\frac{(\$166.67 - 0.10 \times \$200)(1 - 0.40)}{0.2316} = \$380$$

which is the same result we obtained earlier.

## The Weighted Average Cost of Capital and Corporate Taxes

In Chapter 13, we defined the WACC (with corporate taxes) as

$$\text{WACC} = \frac{B}{V_L} r_B(1 - T_c) + \frac{S}{V_L} r_S$$

---

[18] The calculation suffers slightly from rounding error because we only carried the discount rate, 0.2316, out to four decimal places.

Note that the cost of debt capital, $r_B$, is multiplied by $(1 - T_c)$ because interest is tax deductible at the corporate level. However, the cost of equity, $r_S$, is not multiplied by this factor because dividends are not deductible. In the no-tax case, WACC is not affected by leverage. However, since debt is tax advantaged relative to equity, it can be shown that WACC declines with leverage in a world with corporate taxes. This result can be seen in Figure 16.6.

For Divided Airlines,

$$\text{WACC} = \left( \frac{\$200}{\$580} \times 0.10 \times 0.60 \right) + \left( \frac{\$380}{\$580} \times 0.2316 \right)$$
$$= 0.1724$$

Divided Airlines has reduced its WACC from 0.20 (with no debt) to 0.1724 with reliance on debt. This result is intuitively pleasing because it suggests that when a firm lowers its WACC, the firm's value will increase. Using the WACC approach, we can confirm that the value of Divided Airlines is $580:[19]

$$V_L = \frac{\text{EBIT} \times (1 - T_c)}{\text{WACC}} = \frac{\$166.67(1 - 0.4)}{0.1724}$$
$$= \$580$$

## Stock Price and Leverage under Corporate Taxes

At this point, students often believe the numbers—or at least are too intimidated to dispute them. However, they think we have asked the wrong question. "Why are we choosing to maximize the value of the firm?" they will say. "If managers are looking out for the shareholders' interest, why aren't they trying to maximize stock price?" If this question occurred to you, you have come to the right section.

Our response is twofold. First, we showed in the first section of this chapter that the capital structure that maximizes firm value is also the one that most benefits the interests of the shareholders.[20]

However, that general explanation is not always convincing to students. As a second procedure, we calculate the stock price of Divided Airlines both before and after the exchange of debt for stock. We do this by presenting a set of market value balance sheets. The market value balance sheet for the company in its all-equity form can be represented as follows:

**DIVIDED AIRLINES**
**Balance Sheet (all-equity firm)**

| | | |
|---|---|---|
| Physical assets | Equity | $500 |
| $\frac{\$166.67}{0.20} \times (1 - 0.40) = \$500$ | | (100 shares) |

Assuming that there are 100 shares outstanding, each share is worth $5 = $500/100.

Next, imagine that the company announces that in the near future, it will issue $200 of debt to buy back $200 of stock. We know from our previous discussion that the value of the firm will rise to reflect the tax shield of debt. In efficient capital markets, the increase occurs immediately. That is, the rise occurs on the day of the

---

[19] The WACC is

$$\text{WACC} = \frac{B r_B}{V_L}(1 - T_c) + \frac{S r_S}{V_L}$$

From equation (16.10),

$$S r_S = (\text{EBIT} - r_B B)(1 - T_c)$$

Substituting the value of $S r_S$ in the equation for WACC, we get

$$V_L = \frac{\text{EBIT}(1 - T_c)}{\text{WACC}}$$

[20] At that time, we pointed out that this result may not exactly hold in the more complex case where debt has a significant possibility of default. Issues of default are treated in the next chapter.

announcement, not on the date of the debt-for-equity exchange. The market value balance sheet is now as follows:

**DIVIDED AIRLINES**
**Balance Sheet (upon announcement of debt issue)**

| | | | |
|---|---|---|---|
| Physical assets | $500 | Equity | $580 |
| Present value of tax shield | 80 | | (100 shares) |
| Total assets | $580 | | |

Note that the debt has not yet been issued. Therefore, only equity appears on the right-hand side of the balance sheet. Each share is now worth $580/100 = $5.80, implying that the shareholders have benefited by $80. The equityholders gain because they are the owners of a firm that has improved its financial policy.

The introduction of the tax shield to the balance sheet is frequently perplexing to students. Although physical assets are tangible, the ethereal nature of the tax shield bothers many students. However, remember that an asset is any item with value. The tax shield has value because it reduces the stream of future taxes. The fact that one cannot touch the shield in the way that one can touch a physical asset is a philosophical, not a financial, consideration.

At some point, the exchange of debt for equity occurs. Debt of $200 is issued, and the proceeds are used to buy back shares. How many shares of stock are repurchased? Because shares are now selling at $5.80 each, the number of shares that the firm acquires is $200/$5.80 = 34.48. This leaves 65.52 (or 100 − 34.48) shares of stock outstanding. The market value balance sheet is now as follows:

**DIVIDED AIRLINES**
**Balance Sheet (after exchange has taken place)**

| | | | |
|---|---|---|---|
| Physical assets | $500 | Equity (100 − 34.48 = 65.52 shares) | $380 |
| Present value of tax shield | 80 | Debt | 200 |
| Total assets | $580 | Debt plus equity | $580 |

Each share of stock is worth $380/65.52 = $5.80 after the exchange. Notice that the stock price does not change on the exchange date. As we mentioned above, the stock price moves on the date of the announcement only. Because the shareholders participating in the exchange receive a price equal to the market price per share after the exchange, they do not care whether they exchange their stock or not.

A summary of the main results of Modigliani and Miller with corporate taxes is presented in the following boxed section.

---

## Summary of MM Propositions with Corporate Taxes

**Assumptions:**
- Corporations are taxed at the rate $T_c$ on earnings after interest.
- There are no transaction costs.
- Individuals and corporations borrow at the same rate.
- Information is complete.
- Cash flows are perpetual.
- There is no default risk.

**Results:**
Proposition I: $V_L = V_U + T_c B$
(for a firm with perpetual debt)

Proposition II: $r_S = r_0 + \frac{B}{S}(1 - T_c)(r_0 - r_B)$

**Intuition:**
Proposition I: Since corporations can deduct interest payments but not dividend payments, corporate leverage lowers tax payments.

Proposition II: The cost of equity rises with leverage, because the risk to equity rises with leverage.

The Divided Airlines example was provided for two reasons. First, it shows that an increase in the value of the firm from debt financing leads to an increase in the price of the stock. In fact, the shareholders capture the entire $80 tax shield. Second, we wanted to provide more work with market value balance sheets.

- What makes a levered firm more valuable than an otherwise identical unlevered firm?
- What is MM Proposition I under corporate taxes?
- What is MM Proposition II under corporate taxes?

## 16.6

# SUMMARY AND CONCLUSIONS

1. We began our discussion of the capital structure decision by arguing that the particular capital structure that maximizes the value of the firm can also be the one that provides the most benefit to the shareholders.

2. In a world of no taxes, the famous Proposition I of Modigliani and Miller proves that the value of the firm is unaffected by the debt-to-equity ratio. In other words, a firm's capital structure is a matter of indifference in that world. The authors obtain their results by showing that either a high or a low corporate ratio of debt to equity can be offset by homemade leverage. The result hinges on the assumption that individuals can borrow at the same rate as corporations, an assumption we believe to be quite plausible.

3. MM Proposition II in a world without taxes states

$$r_S = r_0 + \frac{B}{S}(r_0 - r_B)$$

This implies that the expected rate of return on equity (ROE; also called the *cost of equity* or the *required return on equity*) is positively related to the firm's leverage. This makes intuitive sense, because the risk of equity rises with leverage, a point illustrated by the differently sloped lines of Figure 16.2.

4. While the work of Modigliani and Miller is quite elegant, it does not explain the empirical findings on capital structure very well. Modigliani and Miller imply that the capital structure decision is a matter of indifference, while the decision appears to be a weighty one in the real world. Still, learning the MM theory has been far from a waste of time. Modigliani and Miller's arguments are a starting point; they show what does not matter and allow us to relax the assumptions so we can see exactly what does matter in the real world. To achieve real-world relevance, we next considered corporate taxes.

5. In a world with corporate taxes but no bankruptcy costs, firm value is an increasing function of leverage. The formula for the value of the firm is

$$V_L = V_U + T_c B$$

Expected return on levered equity can be expressed as

$$r_S = r_0 + \frac{B}{S} \times (1 - T_c) \times (r_0 - r_B)$$

Here, value is positively related to leverage. This result implies that firms should have a capital structure almost entirely composed of debt. Because real-world firms select more moderate levels of debt, the next chapter considers modifications to the results of this chapter.

KEY TERMS    MM Proposition I 470        MM Proposition II 473        MM Proposition II under
             MM Proposition I under     MM Proposition II              corporate taxes 486
               corporate taxes 484        (no taxes) 475             Pie model 465

QUESTIONS &
PROBLEMS

### Earnings before Interest and Taxes and Leverage

16.1 Money Inc. has no debt outstanding and a total market value of $275,000. EBIT is pro-
jected to be $21,000 if economic conditions are normal. If there is strong expansion
in the economy, then EBIT will be 25 percent higher. If there is a recession, then EBIT
will be 40 percent lower. Money is considering a $99,000 debt issue with an 8 percent
interest rate. The proceeds will be used to repurchase shares of stock. There are currently 5,000 shares outstanding. Ignore taxes for this problem.

   *a.* Calculate EPS under each of the three economic scenarios before any debt is
       issued. Also calculate the percentage changes in EPS when the economy expands
       or enters a recession.
   *b.* Repeat (a) assuming that Money goes through with recapitalization. What do
       you observe?

### Earnings before Interest and Taxes, Taxes, and Leverage

16.2 Repeat (a) and (b) in problem 16.1 assuming Money has a tax rate of 35 percent.

### Return on Equity and Leverage

16.3 Suppose the company in problem 16.1 has a market-to-book ratio of 1.0.

   *a.* Calculate ROE under each of the three economic scenarios before any debt is
       issued. Also calculate the percentage changes in ROE for economic expansion
       and recession, assuming no taxes.
   *b.* Repeat (a) assuming the firm goes through with the proposed recapitalization.
   *c.* Repeat (a) and (b) of this problem assuming the firm has a tax rate of 35 percent.

### Break-Even Earnings before Interest and Taxes

16.4 Rolston Corp. is comparing two different capital structures, an all-equity plan
(plan I) and a levered plan (plan II). Under plan I, Rolston would have 265,000 shares
of stock outstanding. Under plan II, there would be 185,000 shares of stock outstanding and $2.8 million in debt outstanding. The interest rate on the debt is 10 percent
and there are no taxes.

   *a.* If EBIT is $750,000, which plan will result in the higher EPS?
   *b.* If EBIT is $1,500,000, which plan will result in the higher EPS?
   *c.* What is the break-even EBIT?

### MM Model and Stock Value

16.5 In problem 16.4, use MM Proposition I to find the price per share of equity under
each of the two proposed plans. What is the value of the firm?

### Break-Even Earnings before Interest and Taxes and Leverage

16.6 Kolby Corp. is comparing two different capital structures. Plan I would result in 900
shares of stock and $65,700 in debt. Plan II would result in 1,900 shares of stock and
$29,200 in debt. The interest rate on the debt is 10 percent.

   *a.* Ignoring taxes, compare both of these plans to an all-equity plan assuming that
       EBIT will be $8,500. The all-equity plan would result in 2,700 shares of stock out-
       standing. Which of the three plans has the highest EPS? The lowest?
   *b.* In (a), what are the break-even levels of EBIT for each plan as compared to that
       for an all-equity plan? Is one higher than the other? Why?
   *c.* Ignoring taxes, when will EPS be identical for plans I and II?
   *d.* Repeat (a), (b), and (c) assuming that the corporate tax rate is 40 percent. Are the
       break-even levels of EBIT different from before? Why or why not?

**Leverage and Stock Value**

16.7  Ignoring taxes in problem 16.6, what is the price per share of equity under plan I? Plan II? What principle is illustrated by your answers?

**Homemade Leverage**

16.8  Star Inc., a prominent consumer products firm, is debating whether or not to convert its all-equity capital structure to one that is 35 percent debt. Currently there are 6,000 shares outstanding and the price per share is $58. EBIT is expected to remain at $33,000 per year forever. The interest rate on new debt is 8 percent, and there are no taxes.

    *a.* Anita, a shareholder of the firm, owns 100 shares of stock. What is her cash flow under the current capital structure, assuming the firm has a dividend payout rate of 100 percent?

    *b.* What will Anita's cash flow be under the proposed capital structure of the firm? Assume that she keeps all 100 of her shares.

    *c.* Suppose Star does convert, but Anita prefers the current all-equity capital structure. Show how she could unlever her shares of stock to recreate the original capital structure.

    *d.* Using your answer to (c), explain why Star's choice of capital structure is irrelevant.

**Homemade Leverage and Weighted Average Cost of Capital**

16.9  ABC Co. and XYZ Co. are identical firms in all respects except for their capital structure. ABC is all equity financed with $750,000 in stock. XYZ uses both stock and perpetual debt; its stock is worth $375,000 and the interest rate on its debt is 8 percent. Both firms expect EBIT to be $86,000. Ignore taxes.

    *a.* Richard owns $30,000 worth of XYZ's stock. What rate of return is he expecting?

    *b.* Show how Richard could generate exactly the same cash flows and rate of return by investing in ABC and using homemade leverage.

    *c.* What is the cost of equity for ABC? What is it for XYZ?

    *d.* What is the WACC for ABC? For XYZ? What principle have you illustrated?

**MM Model**

16.10  Nina Corp. uses no debt. The WACC is 9 percent. If the current market value of the equity is $37 million and there are no taxes, what is EBIT?

**MM Model and Taxes**

16.11  In question 16.10, suppose the corporate tax rate is 35 percent. What is EBIT in this case? What is the WACC? Explain.

**Calculating Weighted Average Cost of Capital**

16.12  Weston Industries has a debt-to-equity ratio of 1.5. Its WACC is 11 percent, and its cost of debt is 7 percent. The corporate tax rate is 35 percent.

    *a.* What is Weston's cost of equity capital?

    *b.* What is Weston's unlevered cost of equity capital?

    *c.* What would the cost of equity be if the debt-to-equity ratio were 2? 1.0? 0?

16.13  Shadow Corp. has no debt but can borrow at 8 percent. The firm's WACC is currently 11 percent, and the tax rate is 35 percent.

    *a.* What is Shadow's cost of equity?

    *b.* If the firm converts to 25 percent debt, what will its cost of equity be?

    *c.* If the firm converts to 50 percent debt, what will its cost of equity be?

    *d.* What is Shadow's WACC in (b)? (c)?

**MM Model and Taxes**

16.14 Bruce & Co. expects its EBIT to be $185,000 every year, forever. The firm can borrow at 9 percent. Bruce currently has no debt, and its cost of equity is 16 percent. If the tax rate is 35 percent, what is the value of the firm? What will the value be if Bruce borrows $135,000 and uses the proceeds to repurchase shares?

16.15 In problem 16.14, what is the cost of equity after recapitalization? What is the WACC? What are the implications for the firm's capital structure decision?

**MM Proposition I**

16.16 Levered Inc. and Unlevered Inc. are identical in every way except their capital structures. Each company expects to earn $29 million before interest per year in perpetuity, with each company distributing all its earnings as dividends. Levered's perpetual debt has a market value of $91 million and costs 8 percent per year. Levered has 2.3 million shares outstanding, currently worth $105 per share. Unlevered has no debt and 4.5 million shares outstanding, currently worth $80 per share. Neither firm pays taxes. Is Levered's stock a better buy than Unlevered's stock?

**MM Model**

16.17 Tool Manufacturing has an expected EBIT of $57,000 in perpetuity and a tax rate of 35 percent. The firm has $90,000 in outstanding debt at an interest rate of 8 percent, and its unlevered cost of capital is 15 percent. What is the value of the firm according to MM Proposition I with taxes? Should Tool change its debt-to-equity ratio if the goal is to maximize the value of the firm? Explain.

**Firm Value**

16.18 Old School Corporation expects an EBIT of $19,750 every year forever. Old School currently has no debt, and its cost of equity is 15 percent. The firm can borrow at 10 percent. If the corporate tax rate is 35 percent, what is the value of the firm? What will the value be if Old School converts to 50 percent debt? To 100 percent debt?

**MM Proposition I with Taxes**

16.19 The Maxwell Company is financed entirely with equity. The company is considering a loan of $1.8 million. The loan will be repaid in equal instalments over the next two years, and it has an 8 percent interest rate. The company's tax rate is 35 percent. According to MM Proposition I with taxes, what would be the increase in the value of the company after the loan?

**MM Proposition I without Taxes**

16.20 Alpha Corp. and Beta Corp. are identical in every way except their capital structures. Alpha Corporation, an all-equity firm, has 15,000 shares of stock outstanding, currently worth $30 per share. Beta Corporation uses leverage in its capital structure. The market value of Beta's debt is $65,000, and its cost of debt is 9 percent. Each firm is expected to have earnings before interest of $75,000 in perpetuity. Neither firm pays taxes. Assume that every investor can borrow at 9 percent per year.
  a. What is the value of Alpha Corporation?
  b. What is the value of Beta Corporation?
  c. What is the market value of Beta Corporation's equity?
  d. How much will it cost to purchase 20 percent of each firm's equity?
  e. Assuming each firm meets its earnings estimates, what will be the dollar return to each position in (d) over the next year?

    *f.* Construct an investment strategy in which an investor purchases 20 percent of Alpha's equity and replicates both the cost and dollar return of purchasing 20 percent of Beta's equity.

    *g.* Is Alpha's equity more or less risky than Beta's equity? Explain.

### Cost of Capital

16.21  Acetate Inc. has equity with a market value of $23 million and debt with a market value of $7 million. Treasury bills that mature in one year yield 5 percent per year, and the expected return on the market portfolio is 12 percent. The beta of Acetate's equity is 1.15. The firm pays no taxes.

    *a.* What is Acetate's debt-to-equity ratio?

    *b.* What is the firm's WACC?

    *c.* What is the cost of capital for an otherwise identical all-equity firm?

### Homemade Leverage

16.22  The Veblen Company and the Knight Company are identical in every respect except that Veblen is not levered. The market value of Knight Company's 6 percent bonds is $1.4 million. Financial information for the two firms appears here. All earnings streams are perpetuities. Neither firm pays taxes. Both firms distribute all earnings available to common stockholders, immediately.

|  | **Veblen** | **Knight** |
|---|---|---|
| Projected operating income | $ 550,000 | $ 550,000 |
| Year-end interest on debt | — | 84,000 |
| Market value of stock | 4,300,000 | 3,140,000 |
| Market value of debt | — | 1,400,000 |

    *a.* An investor who can borrow at 6 percent per year wishes to purchase 5 percent of Knight's equity. Can she increase her dollar return by purchasing 5 percent of Veblen's equity if she borrows so that the initial net costs of the two strategies are the same?

    *b.* Given the two investment strategies in (a), which will the investor choose? When will this process cease?

### MM Propositions

16.23  Locomotive Corporation is planning to repurchase part of its common stock by issuing corporate debt. As a result, the firm's debt-to-equity ratio is expected to rise from 35 percent to 50 percent. The firm currently has $3.6 million worth of debt outstanding. The cost of this debt is 8 percent per year. Locomotive expects to have an EBIT of $1.35 million per year in perpetuity. Locomotive pays no taxes.

    *a.* What is the market value of Locomotive Corporation before and after the repurchase announcement?

    *b.* What is the expected return on the firm's equity before the announcement of the stock repurchase plan?

    *c.* What is the expected return on the equity of an otherwise identical all-equity firm?

    *d.* What is the expected return on the firm's equity after the announcement of the stock repurchase plan?

### Stock Value and Leverage

16.24  Green Manufacturing Inc. plans to announce that it will issue $2 million of perpetual debt and use the proceeds to repurchase common stock. The bonds will sell at par with a 6 percent annual coupon rate. Green is currently an all-equity firm worth $6.3 million with 400,000 shares of common stock outstanding. After the sale of the bonds, Green will maintain the new capital structure indefinitely. Green currently generates annual pre-tax earnings of $1.5 million. This level of earnings is expected to remain constant in perpetuity. Green is subject to a corporate tax rate of 40 percent.

   a. What is the expected return on Green's equity before the announcement of the debt issue?
   b. Construct Green's market value balance sheet before the announcement of the debt issue. What is the price per share of the firm's equity?
   c. Construct Green's market value balance sheet immediately after the announcement of the debt issue.
   d. What is Green's stock price per share immediately after the repurchase announcement?
   e. How many shares will Green repurchase as a result of the debt issue? How many shares of common stock will remain after the repurchase?
   f. Construct the market value balance sheet after the restructuring.
   g. What is the required return on Green's equity after the restructuring?

### MM Model with Taxes

16.25 Williamson Inc. has a debt-to-equity ratio of 2.5. The firm's WACC is 10 percent, and its pre-tax cost of debt is 6 percent. Williamson is subject to a corporate tax rate of 35 percent.

   a. What is Williamson's cost of equity capital?
   b. What is Williamson's unlevered cost of equity capital?
   c. What would Williamson's WACC be if the firm's debt-to-equity ratio were 0.75? 1.5?

### Weighted Average Cost of Capital

16.26 In a world of corporate taxes only, show that the WACC can be written as WACC $= r_0 \times [1 - T_c(B/V)]$.

### Cost of Equity and Leverage

16.27 Assuming a world of corporate taxes only, show that the cost of equity, $r_S$, is as given in the chapter by MM Proposition II with corporate taxes.

### Business and Financial Risk

16.28 Assume a firm's debt is risk free, so that the cost of debt equals the risk-free rate, $r_f$. Define $\beta_A$ as the firm's *asset* beta—that is, the systematic risk of the firm's assets. Define $\beta_S$ to be the beta of the firm's equity. Use the capital asset pricing model (CAPM) along with MM Proposition II to show that $\beta_S = \beta_A \times (1 + B/S)$, where $B/S$ is the debt-to-equity ratio. Assume the tax rate is zero.

### Stockholder Risk

16.29 Suppose a firm's business operations mirror movements in the economy as a whole very closely—that is, the firm's asset beta is 1.0. Use the result of problem 16.28 to find the equity beta for this firm for debt-to-equity ratios of 0, 1, 5, and 20. What does this tell you about the relationship between capital structure and shareholder risk? How is the shareholders' required ROE affected? Explain.

### Levered Cost of Equity

16.30 Beginning with the cost of capital equation—that is

$$\text{WACC} = \frac{S}{B + S} r_S + \frac{B}{B + S} r_B$$

show that the cost of equity capital for a levered firm can be written as

$$r_S = r_0 + \frac{B}{S}(r_0 - r_B)$$

# Stephenson Real Estate Recapitalization

Stephenson Real Estate Company was founded 25 years ago by the current CEO, Robert Stephenson. The company purchases real estate, including land and buildings, and rents the property to tenants. The company has shown a profit every year for the past 18 years, and the shareholders are satisfied with the company's management. Prior to founding Stephenson Real Estate, Robert was the founder and CEO of a failed alpaca-farming operation. The resulting bankruptcy made him extremely averse to debt financing. As a result, the company is entirely equity financed, with 12 million shares of common stock outstanding. The stock currently trades at $48.50 per share.

Robert is evaluating a plan to purchase a huge tract of land in eastern Canada for $45 million. The land will subsequently be leased to tenant farmers. This purchase is expected to increase Stephenson's annual pre-tax earnings by $11 million in perpetuity. Kim Weyand, the company's new CFO, has been put in charge of the project. Kim has determined that the company's current cost of capital is 11.5 percent. She feels that the company would be more valuable if it included debt in its capital structure, so she is evaluating whether the company should issue debt to entirely finance the project. Based on some conversations with investment banks, she thinks that the company can issue bonds at par value with a 7 percent coupon rate. Based on her analysis, she also believes that a capital structure in the range of 70 percent equity/30 percent debt would be optimal. If the company goes beyond 30 percent debt, its bonds will carry a lower rating and a much higher coupon because the possibility of financial distress and the associated costs will rise sharply. Stephenson has a 40 percent corporate tax rate (provincial and federal).

1. If Stephenson wishes to maximize its total market value, would you recommend that it issue debt or equity to finance the land purchase? Explain.
2. Construct Stephenson's market value balance sheet before it announces the purchase.
3. Suppose Stephenson decides to issue equity to finance the purchase.
   a. What is the NPV of the project?
   b. Construct Stephenson's market value balance sheet after it announces that the firm will finance the purchase using equity. What will be the new price per share of the firm's stock? How many shares will Stephenson need to issue to finance the purchase?
   c. Construct Stephenson's market value balance sheet after the equity issue but before the purchase has been made. How many shares of common stock does Stephenson have outstanding? What is the price per share of the firm's stock?
   d. Construct Stephenson's market value balance sheet after the purchase has been made.
4. Suppose Stephenson decides to issue debt to finance the purchase.
   a. What will the market value of Stephenson be if the purchase is financed with debt?
   b. Construct Stephenson's market value balance sheet after both the debt issue and the land purchase. What is the price per share of the firm's stock?
5. Which method of financing maximizes the per-share stock price of Stephenson's equity?

# Capital Structure: Limits to the Use of Debt

**EXECUTIVE SUMMARY**

A student might ask whether the Modigliani and Miller (MM) theory with taxes predicts the capital structures of typical firms. The answer is, unfortunately, no. The theory states that $V_L = V_U + T_c B$. One can always increase firm value by increasing leverage, implying that firms should issue maximum debt. This is inconsistent with the real world, where firms generally employ only moderate amounts of debt.

However, the MM theory tells us *where to look* when searching for the determinants of capital structure. For example, the theory ignores bankruptcy and its attendant costs. These costs can get out of hand for a highly levered firm like Canwest Global Communications Corporation. The largest media company in Canada filed for bankruptcy in late 2009, when it amassed a debt of $4 billion. The Winnipeg-based company owned a range of broadcasting and printing businesses, including the *National Post* newspaper. As part of the bankruptcy process, Canwest's newspaper arm was sold to a group of creditors led by *National Post* CEO Paul Godfrey, through a newly formed company, Postmedia Network. Canwest's broadcasting arm was sold to Shaw Communications.

In addition, the MM theory ignores personal taxes. In the real world, the *personal* tax rate on interest is higher than the *effective* personal tax rate on equity distributions. Thus, the personal tax penalties to bondholders tend to offset the tax benefits to debt at the corporate level. Even when bankruptcy costs are ignored, this idea can be shown to imply that there is an optimal amount of debt for the economy as a whole. We examine the implications of bankruptcy costs and personal taxes in this chapter.

## 17.1 COSTS OF FINANCIAL DISTRESS

### Bankruptcy Risk or Bankruptcy Cost?

As mentioned throughout the previous chapter, debt provides tax benefits to the firm. However, debt puts pressure on the firm, because interest and principal payments are obligations. If these obligations are not met, the firm may risk some sort of financial distress. The ultimate distress is *bankruptcy*, in which ownership of the firm's assets is legally transferred from the shareholders to the bondholders. These debt obligations are fundamentally different from stock obligations. While shareholders like and expect dividends, they are not legally entitled to dividends in the way bondholders are legally entitled to interest and principal payments.

We show in Example 17.1 that bankruptcy costs or, more generally, financial distress costs, tend to offset the advantages to debt. We begin by positing a simple illustration of bankruptcy. All taxes are ignored to focus only on the costs of debt.

EXAMPLE **17.1**

The Knight Corporation plans to be in business for one more year. It forecasts a cash flow of either $100 or $50 in the coming year, each occurring with 50 percent probability. Previously issued debt requires payments of $49 in interest and principal. The Day Corporation has identical cash flow prospects but has $60 in interest and principal obligations. The cash flows of these two firms can be represented as follows:

|  | Knight Corp. | | Day Corp. | |
|---|---|---|---|---|
|  | **Boom times (prob. 50%)** | **Recession (prob. 50%)** | **Boom times (prob. 50%)** | **Recession (prob. 50%)** |
| Cash flow | $100 | $50 | $100 | $50 |
| Payment of interest and principal on debt | 49 | 49 | 60 | 50 |
| Distribution to shareholders | $ 51 | $ 1 | $ 40 | $ 0 |

The Day Corporation will be bankrupt in a recession. Note that, under the law, corporations have limited liability. Thus, Day's bondholders will receive only $50 in a recession; they cannot get the additional $10 from the shareholders.[1]

We assume that (1) both bondholders and shareholders are risk neutral and (2) the interest rate is 10 percent. Due to this risk neutrality, cash flows to both shareholders and bondholders are to be discounted at the 10 percent rate.[2] We can evaluate the debt, the equity, and the entire firm for both Knight and Day as follows:

$$S_{KNIGHT} = \$23.64 = \frac{\$51 \times \frac{1}{2} + \$1 \times \frac{1}{2}}{1.10} \qquad S_{DAY} = \$18.18 = \frac{\$40 \times \frac{1}{2} + 0 \times \frac{1}{2}}{1.10}$$

$$B_{KNIGHT} = \$44.54 = \frac{\$49 \times \frac{1}{2} + \$49 \times \frac{1}{2}}{1.10} \qquad B_{DAY} = \$50 = \frac{\$60 \times \frac{1}{2} + \$50 \times \frac{1}{2}}{1.10}$$

$$V_{KNIGHT} = \$68.18 \qquad\qquad\qquad V_{DAY} = \$68.18$$

Note that the two firms have the same value, even though Day runs the risk of bankruptcy. Furthermore, notice that Day's bondholders are valuing the bonds with their eyes open. Though the promised payment of principal and interest is $60, the bondholders are willing to pay only $50. Hence, their *promised* return or yield is

$$\frac{\$60}{\$50} - 1 = 20\%$$

Day's debt can be viewed as a *junk bond*, because the probability of default is so high. As with all junk bonds, bondholders demand a high promised yield.

---

[1] There are situations in which the limited liability of a corporation can be "pierced." Typically, fraud or misrepresentation must be present.

[2] Normally, one assumes that investors are averse to risk. In that case, the cost of debt capital, $r_B$, is less than the cost of equity capital, $r_S$, which rises with leverage, as shown in the previous chapter. In addition, $r_B$ may rise when the increase in leverage allows the possibility of default.

For simplicity, we assume *risk neutrality* in this example. This means that investors are indifferent to whether risk is high, low, or even absent. Here, $r_S = r_B$, because risk-neutral investors do not demand compensation for bearing risk. In addition, neither $r_S$ nor $r_B$ rises with leverage. Because the interest rate is 10 percent, our assumption of risk neutrality implies that $r_S = 10\%$ as well.

Though financial economists believe that investors are risk averse, they frequently develop examples based on risk neutrality to isolate a point unrelated to risk. This is our approach, because we want to focus on bankruptcy costs—not bankruptcy risk. The same qualitative conclusions from this example can be drawn in a world of risk aversion, albeit with much more difficulty for the reader.

The Day example is not realistic because it ignores an important cash flow, to be discussed below. A more realistic set of numbers might be the following:

**DAY CORP.**

| | Boom times (prob. 50%) | Recession (prob. 50%) | |
|---|---|---|---|
| Cash flow | $100 | $50 | $S_{\text{DAY}} = \$18.18 = \dfrac{\$40 \times \frac{1}{2} + 0 \times \frac{1}{2}}{1.10}$ |
| Debt repayment | 60 | 35 | $B_{\text{DAY}} = \$43.18 = \dfrac{\$60 \times \frac{1}{2} + \$35 \times \frac{1}{2}}{1.10}$ |
| Distribution to shareholders | $ 40 | $ 0 | $V_{\text{DAY}} = \$61.36$ |

Why do the bondholders receive only $35 in a recession? If cash flow is only $50, bondholders will be informed that they have not been paid in full. These bondholders are likely to hire lawyers to negotiate or even to sue the company. Similarly, the firm is likely to hire lawyers to defend itself. Further costs will be incurred if the case gets to a bankruptcy court. These fees are always paid before the bondholders get paid. In this example, we are assuming that bankruptcy costs total $15 (or $50 − $35).

The value of the firm is now $61.36, an amount below the $68.18 figure calculated earlier. By comparing Day's value in a world with no bankruptcy costs against Day's value in a world with these costs, we make the following conclusion:

> The possibility of bankruptcy has a negative effect on the value of the firm. However, it is not the risk of bankruptcy itself that lowers value. Rather, it is the costs associated with bankruptcy that lower value.

The explanation follows from our pie example. In a world of no bankruptcy costs, the bondholders and the shareholders share the entire pie. However, bankruptcy costs eat up some of the pie in the real world, leaving less for the shareholders and bondholders.

Because the bondholders are aware that they will receive little in a recession, they pay a lower price. In this case, their promised return is

$$\frac{\$60}{\$43.18} - 1 = 39.0\%$$

The bondholders are paying a fair price if they are realistic about both the probability and the cost of bankruptcy. It is the *shareholders* who bear these future bankruptcy costs. To see this, imagine that Day Corp. was originally all equity. The shareholders want the firm to issue debt with a promised payment of $60 and use the proceeds to pay a dividend. If there had been no bankruptcy costs, our results show that bondholders would pay $50 to purchase debt with a promised payment of $60. Hence, a dividend of $50 could be paid to the shareholders. However, if bankruptcy costs existed, bondholders would only pay $43.18 for the debt. In that case, only a dividend of $43.18 could be paid to the shareholders. Because the dividend is less when bankruptcy costs exist, the shareholders are hurt by bankruptcy costs.

**CONCEPT QUESTIONS**

- What does risk neutrality mean?
- Can one have bankruptcy risk without bankruptcy costs?
- Why do we say that shareholders bear bankruptcy costs?

# 17.2  DESCRIPTION OF COSTS

The example above showed that bankruptcy costs can lower the value of the firm. In fact, the same general result holds even if a legal bankruptcy is prevented. Thus, *financial distress costs* may be a better phrase than *bankruptcy costs*. It is worthwhile to describe these costs in more detail.

## Direct Costs of Financial Distress: Legal and Administrative Costs of Liquidation or Reorganization

As mentioned earlier, lawyers are involved throughout the stages before and during bankruptcy. With fees often in the hundreds of dollars an hour, these costs can add up quickly. In addition, administrative and accounting fees can substantially add to the total bill. And if a trial takes place, we must not forget expert witnesses. Each side may hire a number of these witnesses to testify about the fairness of a proposed settlement. Their fees can easily rival those of lawyers or accountants.[3] (However, we personally look upon these witnesses more kindly, because they are frequently drawn from the ranks of finance professors.)

Bankruptcy costs are often quite large. For example, as of June 2009, lawyers and financial advisors working for Lehman Brothers in its bankruptcy case had earned nearly $100 million in the first four months of the case alone. By September 2013, Weil, Gotshal & Manges, Lehman's bankruptcy law firm, had earned over $484 million in fees. In total, the bankruptcy fees amounted to $2.2 billion, a significant difference from the infamous Enron bankruptcy of 2001, where fees totalled only $793 million.[4]

A number of academic studies have measured the direct costs of financial distress. While large in absolute amount, these costs are actually small as a percentage of firm value. White, Altman, and Weiss estimate the direct costs of financial distress to be about 3 percent of market value for U.S. firms. Fisher and Martel find that the costs are closer to 6 percent of firm value for a sample of Canadian bankruptcies.[5] In a study of direct financial distress costs of 20 railroad bankruptcies, Warner finds that net financial distress costs were, on average, 1 percent of the market value of the firm seven years before bankruptcy and were somewhat larger percentages as bankruptcy approached (for example, 2.5 percent of the market value of the firm three years before bankruptcy).[6] Of course, few firms end up in bankruptcy. Thus, the preceding cost estimates must be multiplied by the probability of bankruptcy to yield the *expected* cost of bankruptcy. Warner states:

> Suppose, for example, that a given railroad picks a level of debt such that bankruptcy would occur on average once every 20 years (i.e., the probability of going bankrupt is 5 percent in any given year). Assume that when bankruptcy occurs, the firm would pay a lump sum penalty equal to 3 percent of its now current market value. . . .
>
> [Then], the firm's expected cost of bankruptcy is equal to fifteen one-hundredths of one percent of its now current market value.

---

[3] "The High Cost of Going Bankrupt," *Los Angeles Times Orange County Edition*, December 6, 1995, articles.latimes.com/1995-12-06/news/mn-10861_1_high-cost. All amounts in the article are in U.S. dollars.

[4] James O'Toole, "Five Years Later, Lehman Bankruptcy Fees Hit $2.2 Billion," CNN Money (September 13, 2013), money.cnn.com/2013/09/13/news/companies/lehman-bankruptcy-fees/.

[5] M. J. White, "Bankruptcy Costs and the New Bankruptcy Code," *Journal of Finance* (May 1983); and E. I. Altman, "A Further Empirical Investigation of the Bankruptcy Cost Question," *Journal of Finance* (September 1984). More recently, Lawrence A. Weiss, "Bankruptcy Resolution: Direct Costs and Violation of Priority of Claims," *Journal of Financial Economics* (October 1990), estimates that direct costs of bankruptcy are 3.1 percent of the value of the firm. Canadian bankruptcies are examined in T. C. G. Fisher and J. Martel, "The Bankruptcy Decision: Empirical Evidence from Canada," Working Paper, Wilfrid Laurier University (November 2000).

[6] J. B. Warner, "Bankruptcy Costs: Some Evidence," *Journal of Finance* (May 1977).

## Indirect Costs of Financial Distress

**Impaired Ability to Conduct Business**    Bankruptcy hampers conduct with customers and suppliers. Sales are frequently lost because of both fear of impaired service and loss of trust. For example, after filing for bankruptcy in June 2009, General Motors lost U.S. market share to both Toyota and Ford. Despite receiving billions of dollars in funding from the U.S. federal government, customers questioned whether parts and servicing would be available if GM were to fail. As well, the company was forced to close several plants and discontinue its Pontiac and Saturn lines, losing customers loyal to these brands. Sometimes the taint of impending bankruptcy is enough to drive customers away. For example, gamblers avoided Atlantis casino in Atlantic City after it became technically insolvent. Gamblers are a superstitious bunch. Many reasoned, "If the casino itself cannot make money, how can I expect to make money there?" A particularly outrageous story concerned two unrelated stores, both named Mitchells. When one Mitchells declared bankruptcy, customers stayed away from both stores. In time, the second store was forced to declare bankruptcy as well.

Though these costs clearly exist, it is quite difficult to measure them. Altman has estimated that both direct and indirect costs are frequently greater than 20 percent of firm value.[7]

Andrade and Kaplan estimate total distress costs to be between 10 percent and 20 percent of firm value.[8] Bar-Or estimates expected future distress costs for firms that are currently healthy to be 8 to 10 percent of operating value, a number below the estimates of either Altman or Andrade and Kaplan.[9] However, unlike Bar-Or, these authors consider distress costs for firms already in distress, not expected distress costs for currently healthy firms.

## Agency Costs

When a firm has debt, conflicts of interest arise between shareholders and bondholders, and shareholders are tempted to pursue selfish strategies. These conflicts of interest, which are magnified when financial distress occurs, impose **agency costs** on the firm. We describe three kinds of selfish strategies that shareholders use to hurt the bondholders and help themselves. These strategies are costly because they will lower the market value of the whole firm.

*Selfish investment strategy 1: Incentive to take large risks.*    Firms near bankruptcy often take great chances, because they feel that they are playing with someone else's money. A good example of this occurred in the failure of two banks in western Canada in 1985. Because they were allowed to stay in business although they were economically insolvent, the banks had nothing to lose by taking great risks. Because of these and

---

[7] Additional readings on the cost of financial distress: David M. Cutler and Lawrence H. Summers, "The Costs of Conflict Resolution and Financial Distress: Evidence from the Texaco–Pennzoil Litigation," *Rand Journal of Economics* (Summer 1988), estimate the indirect costs of Texaco's 1987 bankruptcy to be about 9 percent of the firm's value. Steven N. Kaplan, "Campeau's Acquisition of Federated: Value Destroyed or Value Added," *Journal of Financial Economics* (December 1989), finds the indirect costs of financial distress for Campeau to be very small.

The work of L. Lang and R. Stulz, "Contagious and Competitive Intra-Industry Effects of Bankruptcy Announcements: An Empirical Analysis," *Journal of Financial Economics* (August 1992); and T. Opler and S. Titman, "Financial Distress and Corporate Performance," *Journal of Finance* (July 1994), suggest indirect financial distress costs are substantial. T. Opler, "Controlling Financial Distress Costs in LBOs," *Financial Management* (Autumn 1993), shows that leveraged buyout (LBO) financing techniques can be expected to reduce the costs of financial distress.

[8] Gregor Andrade and Steven N. Kaplan, "How Costly Is Financial (Not Economic) Distress? Evidence from Highly Leveraged Transactions That Became Distressed," *Journal of Finance* (October 1998).

[9] Yuval Bar-Or, "An Investigation of Expected Financial Distress Costs," unpublished paper, Wharton School, University of Pennsylvania (March 2000).

other failures, the Canada Deposit Insurance Corporation declared a multibillion-dollar deficit in late 1993.[10]

To see how the incentive to take risk works, imagine a levered firm considering two mutually exclusive projects: a low-risk one and a high-risk one. There are two equally likely outcomes: recession and boom. The firm is in such dire straits that should a recession hit, it will come near to bankruptcy with one project and actually fall into bankruptcy with the other. The cash flows for the firm if the low-risk project is taken can be described as follows:

**Value of entire firm if low-risk project is chosen**

|  | Probability | Value of firm | = | Stock | + | Bonds |
|---|---|---|---|---|---|---|
| Recession | 0.5 | $100 | = | $ 0 | + | $100 |
| Boom | 0.5 | $200 | = | $100 | + | $100 |

If a recession occurs, the value of the firm will be $100, and if a boom occurs, the value of the firm will be $200. The expected value of the firm is $150 (or $0.5 \times \$100 + 0.5 \times \$200$).

The firm has promised to pay bondholders $100. Shareholders will obtain the difference between the total payoff and the amount paid to the bondholders. The bondholders have the prior claim on the payoffs, and the shareholders have the residual claim.

Now suppose that a riskier project can be substituted for the low-risk project. The payoffs and probabilities are as follows:

**Value of entire firm if high-risk project is chosen**

|  | Probability | Value of firm | = | Stock | + | Bonds |
|---|---|---|---|---|---|---|
| Recession | 0.5 | $ 50 | = | $ 0 | + | $ 50 |
| Boom | 0.5 | $240 | = | $140 | + | $100 |

The expected value of the firm is $145 (or $0.5 \times \$50 + 0.5 \times \$240$), which is lower than the expected value with the low-risk project. Thus, the low-risk project would be accepted if the firm were all equity. However, note that the expected value of the stock is $70 (or $0.5 \times \$0 + 0.5 \times \$140$) with the high-risk project, but only $50 (or $0.5 \times \$0 + 0.5 \times \$100$) with the low-risk project. Given the firm's present levered state, shareholders will select the high-risk project.

The key is that relative to the low-risk project, the high-risk project increases firm value in a boom and decreases firm value in a recession. The increase in value in a boom is captured by the shareholders, because the bondholders are paid in full (they receive $100) regardless of which project is accepted. Conversely, the drop in value in a recession is lost by the bondholders, because they are paid in full with the low-risk project but receive only $50 with the high-risk one. The shareholders will receive nothing in a recession anyway, whether the high-risk or low-risk project is selected. Thus, financial economists argue that shareholders expropriate value from bondholders by selecting high-risk projects.

*Selfish investment strategy 2: Incentive toward underinvestment.* Shareholders of a firm with a significant probability of bankruptcy often find that new investment helps the bondholders at the shareholders' expense. The simplest case might be a real estate owner facing imminent bankruptcy. If he took $100,000 out of his own pocket to refurbish the building, he could increase the building's value by, say, $150,000. Though this investment has a positive net present value (NPV), he will turn it down if the increase

---

[10] The same thing happened on a grander scale in the U.S. savings and loan debacle. Edward J. Kane, *The Savings and Loan Mess* (Washington, D.C.: Urban Institute Press, 1989), estimates that closing savings and loans when they first became insolvent, thus preventing them from gambling with deposits insured with taxpayers' money, would have saved half of the over US$100 billion bill for cleaning up the industry.

in value cannot prevent bankruptcy. "Why," he asks, "should I use my own funds to improve the value of a building that the bank will soon repossess?"

This idea is formalized by the following simple example. Consider a firm with $4,000 of principal and interest payments due at the end of the year. It will be pulled into bankruptcy by a recession because its cash flows will be only $2,400 in that state. The firm's cash flows are presented in the left-hand side of Table 17.1. The firm could avoid bankruptcy in a recession by raising new equity to invest in a new project. The project costs $1,000 and brings in $1,700 in either state, implying a positive NPV. Clearly it would be accepted in an all-equity firm.

**TABLE 17.1**

**Example Illustrating Incentive to Underinvest**

|  | Firm without project | | Firm with project | |
|---|---|---|---|---|
|  | **Boom** | **Recession** | **Boom** | **Recession** |
| Firm cash flows | $5,000 | $2,400 | $6,700 | $4,100 |
| Bondholders' claim | 4,000 | 2,400 | 4,000 | 4,000 |
| Shareholders' claim | $1,000 | $    0 | $2,700 | $  100 |

The project has positive NPV. However, much of its value is captured by bondholders. Rational managers, acting in the shareholders' interest, will reject the project.

However, the project hurts the shareholders of the levered firm. To see this, imagine that the old shareholders contribute the $1,000 *themselves*.[11] The expected value of the shareholders' interest without the project is $500 (or $0.5 \times \$1,000 + 0.5 \times \$0$). The expected value with the project is $1,400 (or $0.5 \times \$2,700 + 0.5 \times \$100$). The shareholders' interest rises by only $900 (or $\$1,400 - \$500$), while costing $1,000.

The key is that the shareholders contribute the full $1,000 investment, but the shareholders and bondholders *share* the benefits. The shareholders take the entire gain if boom times occur. Conversely, the bondholders reap most of the cash flow from the project in a recession.

The discussion of selfish strategy 1 is quite similar to the discussion of selfish strategy 2. In both cases, an investment strategy for the levered firm is different from the one for the unlevered firm. Thus, leverage results in distorted investment policy. Whereas the unlevered corporation always chooses projects with positive NPV, the levered firm may deviate from this policy.

*Selfish investment strategy 3: Milking the property.*    Another strategy is to pay out extra dividends or other distributions in times of financial distress, leaving less in the firm for the bondholders. This is known as *milking the property*, a phrase taken from real estate. Strategies 2 and 3 are very similar. In strategy 2, the firm chooses not to raise new equity. Strategy 3 goes one step further, because equity is actually withdrawn through the dividend.

**Summary of Selfish Strategies**    The above distortions occur only when there is a probability of bankruptcy or financial distress. Thus, these distortions *should not* affect, say, Bell Canada Enterprises (BCE) because bankruptcy is not a realistic possibility for a diversified blue-chip firm such as this. In other words, BCE's debt will be virtually risk free, regardless of the projects it accepts. The same argument could be made for regulated utilities, such as TransCanada Corporation, that are protected by federal and provincial energy boards. However, biotechnology firms like Viventia Bio and other high-tech companies might be very affected by these distortions. Viventia

---

[11] The same qualitative results will be obtained if the $1,000 is raised from new shareholders. However, the arithmetic becomes much more difficult since we must determine how many new shares are issued.

has significant future investment opportunities compared to assets in place, and it faces intense competition and uncertain future revenues. Because the distortions are related to financial distress, we included them in the earlier section, "Indirect Costs of Financial Distress."

Who pays the cost of selfish investment strategies? We argue that it is ultimately the shareholders. Rational bondholders know that when financial distress is imminent, they cannot expect help from shareholders. Rather, shareholders are likely to choose investment strategies that reduce the value of the bonds. Bondholders protect themselves accordingly by raising the interest rate that they require on the bonds. Because the shareholders must pay these higher rates, they ultimately bear the costs of selfish strategies.

For firms that face these distortions, debt financing will be difficult and costly to obtain. These firms will have low leverage ratios.

*CONCEPT QUESTIONS*

- What is the main **direct** cost of financial distress?
- What are the indirect costs of financial distress?
- Who pays the costs of selfish strategies?

# 17.3   CAN COSTS OF DEBT BE REDUCED?

Each of the costs of financial distress we mentioned above is substantial in its own right. Their sum may well affect debt financing severely. Thus, managers have an incentive to reduce these costs. We now turn to some of their methods. However, it should be mentioned at the outset that these methods can, at most, reduce the costs of debt. They cannot eliminate them entirely.

## Protective Covenants

Because the shareholders must pay higher interest rates as insurance against their own selfish strategies, they frequently make arrangements with bondholders in hopes of lowering rates. These agreements, called **protective covenants**, are incorporated as part of the loan document (or *indenture*) between shareholders and bondholders. The covenants must be taken seriously since a broken covenant can lead to default. Protective covenants can be classified into two types: negative covenants and positive covenants.

A **negative covenant** limits or prohibits actions that the company may take. Here are some typical negative covenants:

1. Limitations are placed on the amount of dividends a company may pay.
2. The firm may not pledge any of its assets to other lenders.
3. The firm may not merge with another firm.
4. The firm may not sell or lease its major assets without approval by the lender.
5. The firm may not issue additional long-term debt of equal or higher seniority.

A **positive covenant** specifies an action that the company agrees to take or a condition the company must abide by. Here are some examples:

1. The company agrees to maintain its working capital at a minimum level.
2. The company must furnish periodic financial statements to the lender.
3. The company must segregate and maintain specified assets as security for the debt.

These lists of covenants are not exhaustive. We have seen loan agreements with more than 30 covenants. Smith and Warner examined public issues of debt and found that

91 percent of the bond indentures included covenants that restricted the issuance of additional debt, 23 percent restricted dividends, 39 percent restricted mergers, and 36 percent limited the sale of assets.[12] A list of typical bond covenants and their uses appears in Table 17.2.

TABLE 17.2

**Loan Covenants**

| Covenant type | Shareholder action or firm circumstances | Reason for covenant |
|---|---|---|
| Financial statement signals<br>1. Working capital requirement<br>2. Interest coverage<br>3. Minimum net worth | As the firm approaches financial distress, shareholders may want the firm to make high-risk investments. | Shareholders lose value before bankruptcy; bondholders are hurt much more in bankruptcy than shareholders (limited liability); bondholders are hurt by *distortion of investment that leads to increases in risk.* |
| Restrictions on asset disposition<br>1. Limit dividends<br>2. Limit sale of assets<br>3. Collateral and mortgages | Shareholders attempt to transfer corporate assets to themselves. | This limits the ability of shareholders to transfer assets to themselves and to *underinvest.* |
| Restrictions on switching assets | Shareholders attempt to increase the risk of the firm. | Increased firm risk helps shareholders; bondholders are hurt by *distortion of investment that leads to increases in risk.* |
| Dilution<br>1. Limit on leasing<br>2. Limit on further borrowing | Shareholders may attempt to issue new debt of equal or greater priority. | This restricts *dilution of the claim of existing bondholders.* |

Protective covenants should reduce the costs of bankruptcy, ultimately increasing the value of the firm. Thus, shareholders are likely to favour all reasonable covenants. To see this, consider three choices by shareholders to reduce bankruptcy costs:

1. *Issue no debt.* Because of the tax advantages to debt, this is a very costly way of avoiding conflicts.

2. *Issue debt with no restrictive and protective covenants.* In this case, the market price of debt will be much lower (and the cost of debt much higher) than would otherwise be true.

3. *Write protective and restrictive covenants into the loan contracts.* If the covenants are clearly written, the creditors may receive protection without large costs being imposed on the shareholders. They will happily accept a lower interest rate. Roberts and Viscione found that secured debt (bonds with positive covenant item 3 in the list above) carried lower yields than unsecured bonds.[13]

Thus, bond covenants, even if they reduce flexibility, can increase the value of the firm. They can be the lowest-cost solution to the shareholder–bondholder conflict.

---

[12] C. W. Smith and J. B. Warner, "On Financial Contracting: An Analysis of Bond Covenants," *Journal of Financial Economics* (June 1979).

[13] G. S. Roberts and J. A. Viscione, "The Impact of Seniority and Security Covenants on Bond Yields," *Journal of Finance* (December 1984). A similar finding for bank loans is in James R. Booth and Lena C. Booth, "Loan Collateral Decisions and Corporate Borrowing Costs," *Journal of Money, Credit and Banking* (February 2006).

## Consolidation of Debt

One reason that bankruptcy costs are so high is that different creditors (and their lawyers) fight with each other. This problem can be alleviated if one lender or at most a few lenders can shoulder the entire debt. Should financial distress occur, negotiating costs are minimized under this arrangement. In addition, bondholders can purchase stock as well. In this way, shareholders and debtholders are not pitted against each other, because they are not separate entities. This appears to be the approach in Japan, where large banks generally take significant stock positions in the firms to which they lend money.[14] Debt-to-equity ratios in Japan are far higher than those in Canada and the United States.

During the economic recession of 2009, many bailout packages provided firms with much-needed capital through loan provisions. In return, governments not only expected future repayment but were given equity positions. For example, in 2009, the governments of Ontario and Canada contributed $10.5 billion in financial aid to GM. In addition to a return on a portion of their debt, the two governments were given an 11.7 percent equity stake in the restructured company. The Canadian government was also allowed to appoint an independent director to GM's board.[15] Such agreements serve to protect investors against any future financial distress and agency costs.

**CONCEPT QUESTION**

- How can covenants and debt consolidation reduce debt agency costs?

# 17.4 INTEGRATION OF TAX EFFECTS AND FINANCIAL DISTRESS COSTS

Modigliani and Miller argue that the firm's value rises with leverage in the presence of corporate taxes. Because this implies that all firms should choose maximum debt, the theory does not predict the behaviour of firms in the real world. Other authors have suggested that bankruptcy and related costs reduce the value of the levered firm.

The integration of tax effects and distress costs appears in Figure 17.1. At the top of the figure, the diagonal straight line represents the value of the firm in a world without bankruptcy costs. The ∩-shaped curve represents the value of the firm with these costs. This curve rises as the firm moves from all equity to a small amount of debt. Here, the present value (PV) of the distress costs is minimal because the probability of distress is so small. However, as more and more debt is added, the PV of these costs rises at an *increasing* rate. At some point, the increase in the PV of these costs from an additional dollar of debt equals the increase in the PV of the tax shield. This is the debt level maximizing the value of the firm and is represented by $B^*$ in Figure 17.1. In other words, $B^*$ is the optimal amount of debt. Bankruptcy costs increase faster than the tax shield beyond this point, implying a reduction in firm value from further leverage. At the bottom of Figure 17.1, the weighted average cost of capital (WACC) goes down as debt is added to the capital structure. After reaching $B^*$, the WACC goes up. The optimal amount of debt also produces the lowest WACC.

---

[14] Canadian and U.S. banks are becoming increasingly interested in taking equity options when lending to higher-risk firms. Convertible bonds (discussed in Chapter 25) include an equity option partly as a way of controlling agency costs.

[15] "Canada, Ontario commit $10.5B to revamped GM," CBC News, June 1, 2009, www.cbc.ca/news/business/canada-ontario-commit-10-5b-to-revamped-gm-1.806973.

FIGURE 17.1

### The Optimal Amount of Debt and the Value of the Firm

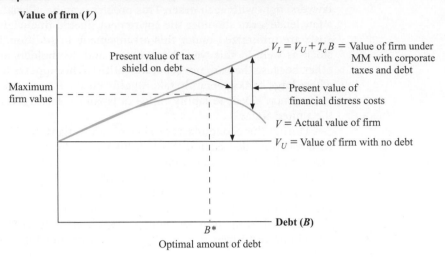

The tax shield increases the value of the levered firm. Financial distress costs lower the value of the levered firm. The two offsetting factors produce an optimal amount of debt at $B^*$.

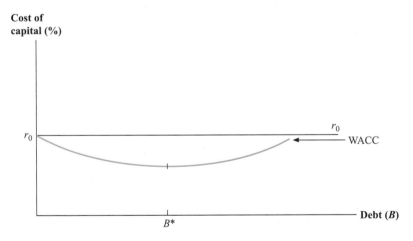

According to the static theory, the WACC falls initially because of the tax advantage of debt. Beyond point $B^*$, it begins to rise because of financial distress costs.

Our discussion implies that a firm's capital structure decisions involve a trade-off between the tax benefits of debt and the costs of financial distress. In fact, this approach is frequently called the *trade-off theory* or the *static trade-off theory* of capital structure. The implication is that there is an optimum amount of debt for any individual firm. This amount of debt becomes the firm's target debt level. (In the real world of finance, this optimum is frequently referred to as the firm's *debt capacity*.) Because financial distress costs cannot be expressed precisely, no formula has yet been developed to determine a firm's optimal debt level exactly. However, the last section of this chapter offers some rules of thumb for selecting a debt-to-equity ratio in the real world. Our situation is reminiscent of a quote of John Maynard Keynes. He reputedly said that although most historians would agree that Queen Elizabeth I was both a better monarch and an unhappier woman than Queen Victoria, no one has yet been able to express the statement in a precise and rigorous formula.

## Pie Again

Critics of the MM theory often say that MM fails when we add such real-world issues as taxes and bankruptcy costs. Taking that view, however, blinds critics to the real value of the MM theory. The pie approach offers a more constructive way of thinking about these matters and the role of capital structure.

Taxes are just another claim on the cash flows of the firm. Let $G$ (for government and taxes) stand for the market value of the government's claim to the firm's taxes. Bankruptcy costs are another claim on the cash flows. Let us label their value with an $L$ (for lawyers). The cash flows to the claim $L$ rise with the debt-to-equity ratio.

The pie theory says that all of these claims are paid from only one source, the cash flows (CF) of the firm. Algebraically, we must have

$$CF = \text{Payments to shareholders}$$
$$+$$
$$\text{Payments to bondholders}$$
$$+$$
$$\text{Payments to the government}$$
$$+$$
$$\text{Payments to lawyers}$$
$$+$$
$$\text{Payments to any and all other claimants to the cash}$$
$$\text{flows of the firms}$$

Figure 17.2 shows the new pie. No matter how many slices we take and no matter who gets them, they must still add up to the total cash flow. The value of the firm, $V_T$, is unaltered by the capital structure. Now, however, we must be broader in our definition of the firm's value:

$$V_T = S + B + G + L$$

We previously wrote the firm's value as

$$S + B$$

when we ignored taxes and bankruptcy costs.

---

**FIGURE 17.2**

**The Pie Model with Real-World Factors**

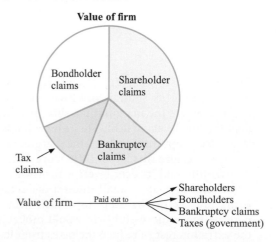

Nor have we even begun to exhaust the list of financial claims to the firm's cash flows. To give an unusual example, everyone reading this book has an economic claim to the cash flows of Ford Motor Company of Canada. After all, if you are injured in an accident, you might sue Ford. Win or lose, Ford will expend resources dealing with the matter. If you think this is far-fetched and unimportant, ask yourself what Ford might be willing to pay every man, woman, and child in the country to have them promise that they would never sue the company, no matter what happened. The law does not permit such payments, but that does not mean that a value to all of those potential claims does not exist. We guess that it would run into billions of dollars, and, for Ford or any other company, there should be a slice of the pie labelled *LS* for "potential lawsuits."

This is the essence of the MM intuition and theory: *V* is *V*(CF) and depends on the total cash flow of the firm. The capital structure cuts it into slices.

There is, however, an important difference between claims such as those of shareholders and bondholders on the one hand and those of government and potential litigants in lawsuits on the other. The first set of claims are **marketed claims**, and the second set are **non-marketed claims**. One difference is that the marketed claims can be bought and sold in financial markets, and the non-marketed claims cannot.

When we speak of the value of the firm, generally we are referring just to the value of the marketed claims, $V_M$, and not the value of non-marketed claims, $V_N$. What we have shown is that the total value,

$$V_T = S + B + G + L$$
$$= V_M + V_N$$

is unaltered. But, as we saw, the value of the marketed claims, $V_M$, can change with changes in the capital structure in general and the debt-to-equity ratio in particular.

By the pie theory, any increase in $V_M$ must imply an identical decrease in $V_N$. In an efficient market, we showed that the capital structure will be chosen to maximize the value of the marketed claims, $V_M$. We can equivalently think of the efficient market as working to minimize the value of the non-marketed claims, $V_N$. These are taxes and bankruptcy costs in the previous example, but they also include all the other non-marketed claims, such as the *LS* claim.

**CONCEPT QUESTIONS**

- List all the claims to the firm's assets.
- Describe marketed claims and non-marketed claims.
- How can a firm maximize the value of its marketed claims?

# 17.5    SIGNALLING

The previous section pointed out that the corporate leverage decision involves a trade-off between a tax subsidy and financial distress costs. This idea was graphed in Figure 17.1, where the marginal tax subsidy of debt exceeds the marginal distress costs of debt for low levels of debt. The reverse holds for high levels of debt. The firm's capital structure is optimized where the marginal subsidy to debt equals the marginal cost.

Let's explore this idea a little more. What is the relationship between a company's profitability and its debt level? A firm with low anticipated profits will likely take on a low level of debt. A small interest deduction is all that is needed to offset all of this firm's pre-tax profits. And, too much debt would raise the firm's expected distress costs. A more successful firm would probably take on more debt. This firm could use the extra interest to reduce the taxes from its greater earnings. And, being more financially secure, this firm would find its extra debt increasing the risk of bankruptcy only slightly. In other words, rational firms raise debt levels (and the concomitant interest payments) when profits are expected to increase.

How do investors react to an increase in debt? Rational investors are likely to infer a higher firm value from a higher debt level. Thus, these investors are likely to bid up a firm's stock price after the firm has, say, issued debt in order to buy back equity. We say that investors view debt as a *signal* of firm value.

Now we get to the incentives of managers to fool the public. Consider a firm whose level of debt is optimal. That is, the marginal tax benefit of debt exactly equals the marginal distress costs of debt. However, imagine that the firm's manager desires to increase the firm's current stock price, perhaps because she knows that many of her shareholders want to sell their stock soon. This manager might want to increase the level of debt just to make investors *think* that the firm is more valuable than it really is. If the strategy works, investors will push up the price of the stock.

The above implies that firms can fool investors by taking on *some* additional leverage. Now let's ask the big question. Are there benefits to extra debt but no costs, implying that all firms will take on as much debt as possible? The answer, fortunately, is that there are costs as well. Imagine that a firm has issued extra debt just to fool the public. At some point the market will learn that the company is not that valuable after all. At this time, the stock price should actually fall *below* what it would have been had the debt never been increased. Why? Because the firm's debt level is now above the optimal level. That is, the marginal tax benefit of debt is below the marginal cost of debt. Thus, if the current shareholders plan to sell, say, half of their shares now and retain the other half, an increase in debt will help them on immediate sales but likely hurt them on later ones.

Now here is the important point. We said earlier that in a world where managers do not attempt to fool investors, valuable firms issue more debt than less valuable ones. It turns out that even when managers attempt to fool investors, the more valuable firms will still want to issue more debt than the less valuable firms. That is, while all firms will increase debt levels somewhat to fool investors, the costs of extra debt prevent the less valuable firms from issuing more debt than the more valuable firms. Thus, investors can still treat debt level as a signal of firm value. In other words, investors can still view an announcement of debt as a positive sign for the firm.

The above is a simplified example of debt signalling, and one can argue that it is too simplified. For example, perhaps the shareholders of some firms want to sell most of their stock immediately, while the shareholders of other firms want to sell only a little of theirs now. It is impossible to tell here whether the firms with the most debt are the most valuable or merely the ones with the most impatient shareholders. Since other objections can be brought up as well, signalling theory is best validated by empirical evidence. And, fortunately, the empirical evidence tends to support the theory.

For example, consider the evidence concerning **exchange offers**. Firms often change their debt levels through exchange offers, of which there are two types. The first type of offer allows shareholders to exchange some of their stock for debt, thereby increasing leverage. The second type allows bondholders to exchange some of their debt for stock, decreasing leverage. Figure 17.3 shows the stock price behaviour of firms that change their proportions of debt and equity via exchange offers. The solid line in the figure indicates that stock prices rise substantially on the date when an exchange offering increasing leverage is announced. (This date is referred to as date 0 in the figure.) Conversely, the dotted line in the figure indicates that stock price falls substantially when an offer decreasing leverage is announced.

The market infers from an increase in debt that the firm is better off, leading to a stock price rise. Conversely, the market infers the reverse from a decrease in debt, implying a stock price fall. Thus, we say that managers signal information when they change leverage.

FIGURE 17.3

**Stock Returns at the Time of Announcements of Exchange Offers**

Exchange offers change the debt-to-equity ratios of firms. The graph shows that stock prices increase for firms whose exchange offers increase leverage. Conversely, stock prices decrease for firms whose offers decrease leverage.

Source: K. Shah, "The Nature of Information Conveyed by Pure Capital Structure Changes," *Journal of Financial Economics* (August 1994).

*CONCEPT*
*QUESTIONS*
- Do managers have an incentive to fool investors by issuing additional debt?
- Is there a cost to issuing additional debt?
- What empirical evidence suggests that managers signal information through debt levels?

## 17.6  SHIRKING, PERQUISITES, AND BAD INVESTMENTS: A NOTE ON AGENCY COST OF EQUITY

The previous section introduced the static trade-off model, in which a rise in debt increases both the tax shield and the costs of distress. We now extend the trade-off model by considering an important agency cost of equity. A discussion of this cost of equity is contained in a well-known quote from Adam Smith:[16]

> The directors of such [joint-stock] companies, however, being the managers rather of other people's money than of their own, it cannot well be expected, that they should watch over it with the same anxious vigilance with which the partners in a private copartnery frequently watch over their own. Like the stewards of a rich man, they are apt to consider attention to small matters as not for their master's honour, and very easily give themselves a dispensation from having it. Negligence and profusion, therefore, must always prevail, more or less, in the management of the affairs of such a company.

This elegant prose can be restated in modern vocabulary. An individual will work harder for a firm if he or she is one of its owners rather than just an employee. In addition, the individual will work harder as the owner of a larger percentage of the company. This idea has an important implication for capital structure, which we illustrate with Example 17.2.

---

[16] Adam Smith, *The Wealth of Nations* [1776], Cannon edition (New York: Modern Library, 1937), p. 700, as quoted in M. C. Jensen and W. Meckling, "Theory of the Firm: Managerial Behavior, Agency Costs, and Ownership Structure," *Journal of Financial Economics* (October 1976).

EXAMPLE **17.2**

Sarah Pagell is an owner–entrepreneur running a computer services firm worth $1 million. She currently owns 100 percent of the firm. Because of the need to expand, she must raise another $2 million. She can either issue $2 million of debt at 12 percent interest or issue $2 million in stock. The cash flows under the two alternatives are presented below:

| | Debt issue | | | | Stock issue | | | |
| | Cash flow | Interest | Cash flow to equity | Cash flow to Sarah (100% of equity) | Cash flow | Interest | Cash flow to equity | Cash flow to Sarah ($33\frac{1}{3}$% of equity) |
|---|---|---|---|---|---|---|---|---|
| 6-hour days | $300,000 | $240,000 | $ 60,000 | $60,000 | $300,000 | 0 | $300,000 | $100,000 |
| 10-hour days | 400,000 | 240,000 | 160,000 | 160,000 | 400,000 | 0 | 400,000 | 133,333 |

Like any entrepreneur, Sarah can choose the degree of intensity with which she works. In our example, she can work either 6 or 10 hours per day. With the debt issue, the extra work brings her $100,000 (or $160,000 − $60,000) more income. However, with a stock issue she retains only a one-third interest in the equity. Thus, the extra work brings her only $33,333 (or $133,333 − $100,000). Being only human, she is likely to work harder if she issues debt. In other words, she has more incentive to *shirk* if she issues equity.

In addition, she is likely to obtain more *perquisites* (a big office, a company car, more expense account meals) if she issues stock. If she is a one-third shareholder, two-thirds of these costs are paid by the other shareholders. If she is the sole owner, any additional perquisites reduce her equity stake.

Finally, if Sarah issues equity, she is more likely to take on capital budgeting projects with negative NPVs. It might seem surprising that a manager with any equity interest at all would take on negative NPV projects, since stock price would clearly fall. However, managerial salaries generally rise with firm size, indicating that managers have an incentive to accept some unprofitable projects after all the profitable ones have been taken on. That is, when an unprofitable project is accepted, the loss in stock value to a manager with only a small equity interest may be less than the increase in salary. In fact, it is our opinion that losses from accepting bad projects are far greater than losses from either shirking or excessive perquisites. Hugely unprofitable projects have bankrupted whole firms, something that even the largest of expense accounts is unlikely to do.

Thus, as the firm issues more equity, our entrepreneur will likely increase leisure time, work-related perquisites, and unprofitable investments. These three items are called agency costs, because managers of the firm are agents of the shareholders.[17]

This example is quite applicable to a small company considering a large stock offering. Because an owner–manager will greatly dilute his share in the total equity in this case, a significant drop in work intensity or a significant increase in fringe benefits is possible. Conversely, consider a large company like Royal Bank of Canada issuing shares for the umpteenth time. The typical manager has such a small percentage stake in the firm that any temptation for negligence is unlikely to change with the share issue.

Who bears the burden of these agency costs? If the new shareholders enter with their eyes open, they do not. Knowing that Sarah may work short hours, they will pay only a low price for the stock. Thus, it is the owner who is hurt by agency costs.

---

[17] As previously discussed, agency costs are generally defined as the costs from the conflicts of interest among shareholders, bondholders, and managers.

We saw earlier that shareholders reduce bankruptcy costs and agency costs of debt through protective covenants. Analogously, owners try to control the agency costs of equity. Firms going public for the first time may allow monitoring by new shareholders. Owners may retain a large portion of the stock to convince new shareholders that no shirking is planned. For large firms, the monitoring role is played by the board of directors, although there is considerable controversy over boards' effectiveness in this role.[18] Another common approach is to use stock options and bonuses linked to stock price performance to bring the interests of management in line with those of the shareholders. However, though these techniques may reduce the agency costs of equity, they are unlikely to eliminate them.

It is commonly suggested that leveraged buyouts (LBOs) significantly reduce the agency costs of equity. In an LBO, a purchaser (sometimes a team of existing management) buys out the shareholders at a price above the current market. In other words, the company goes private since the stock is placed in the hands of only a few people. Because the managers now own a substantial chunk of the business, they are likely to work harder than when they were simply hired hands.

### Effect of Agency Costs of Equity on Debt-to-Equity Financing

Before our discussion of agency costs of equity in the current section, we stated that the change in the value of the firm when debt is substituted for equity is (1) the tax shield on debt minus (2) the increase in the costs of financial distress (including the agency costs of debt). Now, the change in the value of the firm is (1) the tax shield on debt plus (2) the reduction in the agency costs of equity minus (3) the increase in the costs of financial distress (including the agency costs of debt). The optimal debt-to-equity ratio would be higher in a world with agency costs of equity than in a world without these costs. However, because the agency costs of debt are so significant, the costs of equity do not imply 100 percent debt financing.

### Free Cash Flow

Any reader of murder mysteries knows that a criminal must have both motive and opportunity. The above discussion was about motive. Managers with only a small ownership interest have an incentive for wasteful behaviour. For example, they bear only a small portion of the costs of, say, excessive expense accounts, and reap all of the benefits.

Now let's talk about opportunity. A manager can only pad her expense account if the firm has the cash flow to cover it. Thus, we might expect to see more wasteful activity in a firm with a capacity to generate large cash flows than in one with a capacity to generate only small flows. This very simple idea, which is formally called the *free cash flow hypothesis*, has attracted the attention of the academic community.[19]

A fair amount of academic work supports the hypothesis. For example, a frequently cited paper found that firms with high free cash flow are more likely to make bad acquisitions than are firms with low free cash flow.[20] A related Canadian study reports that firms with high free cash flow are more likely to undertake investments with low returns.[21]

---

[18] We discuss agency theory in the context of mergers and acquisitions in Chapter 30.

[19] The seminal article is Michael C. Jensen, "Agency Costs of Free Cash Flow, Corporate Finance, and Takeovers," *American Economic Review* (May 1986).

[20] L. Lang, R. Stulz, and R. Walkling, "Managerial Performance, Tobin's Q and the Gains in Tender Offers," *Journal of Financial Economics* (September 1989).

[21] R. S. Chirinko and H. Schaller, "A Revealed Preference Approach to Understanding Corporate Governance Problems: Evidence from Canada," Center for Economic Studies and Ifo Institute for Economic Research Working Paper 826, Massachusetts Institute of Technology, 2002.

The hypothesis has important implications for capital structure. Since dividends leave the firm, they reduce free cash flow. Thus, according to the free cash flow hypothesis, an increase in dividends should benefit the shareholders by reducing the ability of managers to pursue wasteful activities. Furthermore, since interest and principal also leave the firm, debt reduces free cash flow as well. In fact, interest and principal should have a greater effect than dividends have on the free-spending ways of managers, because bankruptcy will occur if the firm is unable to make future debt payments. By contrast, a future dividend reduction will cause fewer problems to the managers, since the firm has no legal obligation to pay dividends. Because of this, the free cash flow hypothesis argues that a shift from equity to debt will boost firm value.[22]

In summary, the free cash flow hypothesis provides still another reason for firms to issue debt. We previously discussed the costs of equity; new equity dilutes the holdings of managers, increasing their *motive* to waste corporate resources. We now state that debt reduces free cash flow, because the firm must make interest and principal payments. The free cash flow hypothesis implies that debt reduces the *opportunity* for managers to waste resources.

**CONCERT**
*QUESTIONS*

- What are agency costs?
- Why are shirking and perquisites considered an agency cost of equity?
- How do agency costs of equity affect the firm's debt-to-equity ratio?
- What is the free cash flow hypothesis?

## 17.7    THE PECKING-ORDER THEORY

Although the trade-off theory has dominated corporate finance circles for a long time, attention is also being paid to the *pecking-order theory*.[23] To understand this view of the world, let's put ourselves in the position of a corporate financial manager whose firm needs new capital. The manager faces a choice between issuing debt and issuing equity. Previously, we evaluated the choice in terms of tax benefits, distress costs, and agency costs. However, there is one consideration that we have so far neglected: timing.

Imagine the manager saying,

> I want to issue stock in one situation only—when it is overvalued. If the stock of my firm is selling at $50 per share, but I think that it is actually worth $60, I will not issue stock. I would actually be giving new shareholders a gift, because they would receive stock worth $60, but would only have to pay $50 for it. More important, my current shareholders would be upset, because the firm would be receiving $50 in cash, but giving away something worth $60. So if I believed that my stock is undervalued, I would issue bonds. Bonds, particularly those with little or no risk of default, are likely to be priced correctly. Their value is primarily determined by the marketwide interest rate, a variable that is publicly known.
>
> But, suppose that our stock is selling at $70. Now I'd like to issue stock. If I can get some fool to buy our stock for $70 while the stock is really only worth $60, I will be making $10 for our current shareholders.

---

[22] A number of papers provide empirical support for these implications of the free cash flow hypothesis. In particular, see K. Lehn and Poulsen, "Free Cash Flow and Shareholder Value in Going-Private Transactions," *Journal of Finance* (July 1989); L. Lang and R. Litzenberger, "Dividend Announcements: Cash Flow Signalling vs. Free Cash Flow Hypothesis," *Journal of Financial Economics* (September 1989); and T. Nohel and V. Tarhan, "Share Repurchases and Firm Performance: New Evidence on the Agency Costs of Free Cash Flow," *Journal of Financial Economics* (August 1998).

[23] The pecking-order theory is generally attributed to S. C. Myers, "The Capital Structure Puzzle," *Journal of Finance* (July 1984).

Now, although this may strike you as a cynical view, it seems to square well with reality. Before insider trading and disclosure laws were adopted, many managers were alleged to have unfairly trumpeted their firm's prospects prior to equity issuance. And, even today, managers seem more willing to issue equity after the price of their stock has risen than after their stock has fallen in price. For example, in 2001, high-tech stock prices were down from their highs and such well-known firms as PMC-Sierra, Lucent Technologies, and Nortel Networks all issued debt. Thus, timing might be an important motive in equity issuance, perhaps even more important than those motives in the trade-off model. After all, the firm in the preceding example *immediately* makes $10 by properly timing the issuance of equity. Ten dollars' worth of agency costs and bankruptcy cost reduction might take many years to realize.

The key that makes the example work is asymmetric information; in an exception to the efficient market hypothesis (EMH) from Chapter 14, the manager must know more about his firm's prospects than does the typical investor. If the manager's estimate of the true worth of the company is no better than the estimate of a typical investor, any attempts by the manager to time will fail. This assumption of asymmetry is quite plausible. Managers should know more about their company than do outsiders, because managers work at the company every day. (One caveat is that some managers are perpetually optimistic about their firm, blurring good judgment.)

But we are not finished with this example yet; we must consider the investor. Imagine an investor saying,

> I make investments carefully, because it involves my hard-earned money. However, even with all the time I put into studying stocks, I can't possibly know what the managers themselves know. After all, I've got a day job to be concerned with. So I watch what the managers do. If a firm issues stock, the firm was likely overvalued beforehand. If a firm issues debt, it was likely undervalued.

When we look at both issuers and investors, we see a kind of poker game, with each side trying to outwit the other. There are two prescriptions to the issuer in this poker game. The first one, which is fairly straightforward, is to issue debt instead of equity when the stock is undervalued. The second, which is more subtle, is to also issue debt when the firm is *overvalued*. After all, if a firm issues equity, investors will infer that the stock is overvalued. They will not buy it until the stock has fallen enough to eliminate any advantage from equity issuance. In fact, only the most overvalued firms have any incentive to issue equity. Should even a moderately overpriced firm issue equity, investors will infer that this firm is among the *most* overpriced, causing the stock to fall more than is deserved. Thus, the end result is that virtually no one will issue equity.[24]

The result that essentially all firms should issue debt is clearly an extreme one. It is as extreme as (1) the Modigliani–Miller (MM) result that in a world without taxes, firms are indifferent to capital structure, and (2) the MM result that in a world of corporate taxes but no financial distress costs, all firms should be 100 percent debt financed. Perhaps we in finance have a penchant for extreme models!

But, just as one can temper Modigliani and Miller's conclusions by combining financial distress costs with corporate taxes, we can temper those of the pure pecking-order theory. This pure version assumes that timing is the financial manager's only consideration. In reality, a manager must consider taxes, financial distress costs, and agency costs as well. Thus, a firm may issue debt only up to a point. If financial distress becomes a real possibility beyond that point, the firm may issue equity instead.

## Rules of the Pecking Order

For expository purposes, we have oversimplified by comparing equity to *risk-free* debt. Managers cannot use special knowledge of their firm to determine if this type of debt

---

[24] In the interest of simplicity, we have not presented our results in the form of a rigorous model. For a deeper explanation, refer to S. C. Myers. "The Capital Structure Puzzle," *Journal of Finance* (July 1984).

is mispriced, because the price of risk-free debt is determined solely by the market-wide interest rate. However, in reality, corporate debt has the possibility of default. Thus, just as managers have a tendency to issue equity when they think it is overvalued, managers also have a tendency to issue debt when they think it is overvalued.

When would managers view their debt as overvalued? Probably in the same situations when they think their equity is overvalued. For example, if the public thinks that the firm's prospects are rosy but the managers see trouble ahead, these managers will view their debt—as well as their equity—as being overvalued. That is, the public might see the debt as nearly risk free, whereas the managers see a strong possibility of default.

Thus, investors are likely to price a debt issue with the same skepticism that they have when pricing an equity issue. The way managers get out of this box is to finance projects out of retained earnings. You don't have to worry about investor skepticism if you can avoid going to investors in the first place. Thus, the first rule of the pecking order is the following:

**Rule 1**: *Use internal financing.*

However, although investors fear mispricing of both debt and equity, the fear is much greater for equity. Corporate debt still has relatively little risk compared to equity because if financial distress is avoided, investors receive a fixed return. Thus, the pecking-order theory implies that if outside financing is required, debt should be issued before equity.[25] Only when the firm's debt capacity is reached should the firm consider equity.

Of course, there are many types of debt. For example, because convertible debt is more risky than straight debt, the pecking-order theory implies that one should issue straight debt before issuing convertibles. Thus, the second rule of pecking-order theory is as follows:

**Rule 2**: *Issue the safest securities first.*

## Implications

There are a number of implications associated with the pecking-order theory that are at odds with the trade-off theory.

1. *There is no target amount of leverage.* According to the trade-off model, each firm balances the benefits of debt, such as the tax shield, with the costs of debt, such as distress costs. The optimal amount of leverage occurs where the marginal benefit of debt equals the marginal cost of debt.

    By contrast, the pecking-order theory does not imply a target amount of leverage. Rather, each firm chooses its leverage ratio based on financing needs. Firms first fund projects out of retained earnings. This should lower the percentage of debt in the capital structure, because profitable, internally funded projects raise both the book value and the market value of equity. Additional cash needs are met with debt, clearly raising the debt level. However, at some point the debt capacity of the firm may be exhausted, giving way to equity issuance. Thus, the amount of leverage is determined by the happenstance of available projects. Firms do not pursue a target ratio of debt to equity.

2. *Profitable firms use less debt.* Profitable firms generate cash internally, implying less need for outside financing. Because firms desiring outside capital turn to debt first, profitable firms end up relying on less debt. The trade-off model does not have this implication. The greater cash flow of more profitable firms creates greater debt capacity. These firms will use that debt capacity to capture the tax shield and the other benefits of leverage. Two empirical papers find that in the

---

[25] We discuss convertible debt in Chapter 25.

real world, more profitable firms are less levered,[26] a result consistent with the pecking-order theory.

3. *Companies like financial slack.* The pecking-order theory is based on the difficulties of obtaining financing at a reasonable cost. A skeptical investing public thinks a stock is overvalued if the managers try to issue more of it, thereby leading to a stock price decline. Because this happens with bonds, but to a lesser extent, managers rely first on bond financing. However, firms can issue only so much debt before encountering the potential costs of financial distress.

Wouldn't it be easier to have the cash ahead of time? This is the idea behind *financial slack*. Because firms know that they will have to fund profitable projects at various times in the future, they accumulate cash today. Thus, they are not forced to go to the capital markets when a project comes up. However, there is a limit to the amount of cash a firm will want to accumulate. As mentioned earlier in this chapter, too much free cash may tempt managers to pursue wasteful activities.

**CONCEPT QUESTIONS**

- What is the pecking-order theory?
- What are the problems of issuing equity according to this theory?
- What is financial slack?

# 17.8   GROWTH AND THE DEBT-TO-EQUITY RATIO

While the trade-off between the tax shield and bankruptcy costs (as illustrated in Figure 17.1) is the "standard model" of capital structure, it has its critics. For example, some point out that bankruptcy costs in the real world appear to be much smaller than the tax subsidy. Thus, the model implies that the optimal debt-to-value ratio should still be near 100 percent, an implication at odds with reality.[27]

Perhaps the pecking-order theory is more consistent with the real world here. That is, firms are likely to have more equity in their capital structure than implied by the static trade-off theory, because internal financing is preferred to external financing.

In addition, growth can imply significant equity financing, even in a world with low bankruptcy costs.[28] The basic idea is that growth accrues to the shareholders, increasing the value of equity. Because the value of debt does not change, the debt-to-equity ratio falls. To explain the idea, we first consider an example of a no-growth firm. Next, we examine the effect of growth on firm leverage.

### No Growth

Imagine a world of perfect certainty[29] where a firm has earnings before interest and taxes (EBIT) of $100. In addition, the firm has issued $1,000 of debt at an interest rate

---

[26] See L. S. Sunder and S. C. Myers, "Testing Static Trade-off against Pecking Order Models of Capital Structure," *Journal of Financial Economics* (February 1999); and E. F. Fama and K. R. French, "Testing Trade-off and Pecking Order Predictions about Dividends and Debt," *The Review of Financial Studies* (Spring 2002). See also Armen Hovakimian, Tim Opler, and Sheridan Titman, "The Debt–Equity Choice," *Journal of Financial and Quantitative Analysis* (March 2001), which finds that while pecking-order considerations affect firm debt levels in the short run, firms tend to move to target debt ratios in a manner consistent with the trade-off model.

[27] See Merton Miller's Presidential Address to the American Finance Association, reprinted as "Debt and Taxes," *Journal of Finance* (May 1977).

[28] This idea is introduced and analyzed in J. L. Berens and C. L. Cuny, "Inflation, Growth, and Capital Structure," *Review of Financial Studies* (Winter 1995).

[29] The same qualitative results occur under uncertainty, though the mathematics is more troublesome.

of 10 percent, implying interest payments of $100 per year. The cash flows to the firm are as follows:

| Date | 1 | 2 | 3 | 4 | ... |
|---|---|---|---|---|---|
| Earnings before interest and taxes | $100 | $100 | $100 | $100 | ... |
| Interest | −100 | −100 | −100 | −100 | ... |
| Taxable income | $ 0 | $ 0 | $ 0 | $ 0 | ... |

The firm has issued just enough debt so that all EBIT is paid out as interest. Since interest is tax deductible, the firm pays no taxes. In this example, the equity is worthless because shareholders receive no cash flows. Since debt is worth $1,000, the firm is also valued at $1,000. Therefore, the debt-to-value ratio is 100 percent (= $1,000/$1,000).

Had the firm issued less than $1,000 of debt, the corporation would have positive taxable income and, consequently, would have ended up paying some taxes. Had the firm issued more than $1,000 of debt, interest would have exceeded EBIT, causing default. Consequently, the optimal debt-to-value ratio is 100 percent.

## Growth

Now imagine another firm that also has EBIT of $100 at date 1 but is growing at 5 percent per year.[30] To eliminate taxes, this firm also wants to issue enough debt so that interest equals EBIT. Since EBIT is growing at 5 percent per year, interest must also grow at this rate. This is achieved by increasing debt by 5 percent per year.[31] The debt and income levels are as follows:

| Date | 0 | 1 | 2 | 3 | 4 ... |
|---|---|---|---|---|---|
| Debt | $1,000 | $1,050 | $1,102.50 | $1,157.63 ... | |
| New debt issued | | 50 | 52.50 | 55.13 ... | |
| Earnings before interest and taxes | | $ 100 | $ 105 | $ 110.25 | $ 115.76 ... |
| Interest | | −100 | −105 | −110.25 | −115.76 ... |
| Taxable income | | $ 0 | $ 0 | $ 0 | $ 0 |

Note that interest on a particular date is always 10 percent of the debt on the previous date. Debt is set so that interest is exactly equal to EBIT. As in the no-growth case, the levered firm has the maximum amount of debt at each date. Default would occur if interest payments were increased.

Because growth is 5 percent per year, the value of the firm is[32]

$$V_{Firm} = \frac{\$100}{0.10 - 0.05} = \$2,000$$

The equity at date 0 is the difference between the value of the firm at that time, $2,000, and the debt of $1,000. Hence, equity must be equal to $1,000,[33] implying a debt-to-value ratio of 50 percent (= $1,000/$2,000). Note the important difference between the no-growth and the growth example. The no-growth example has no equity; the

---

[30] For simplicity, assume that growth is achieved without earnings retention. The same conclusions would be reached with retained earnings, though the arithmetic would become more involved. Of course, growth without earnings retention is less realistic than growth with retention.

[31] Since the firm makes no real investment, the new debt is used to buy back shares of stock.

[32] The firm can also be valued by a variant of equation (16.7):

$$V_L = V_U + PV \text{ of tax shield}$$

$$= \frac{\$100(1 - T_c)}{0.10 - 0.05} + \frac{T_c \times \$100}{0.10 - 0.05} = \$2,000$$

Because of firm growth, both $V_U$ and $PV$ of the tax shield are growing perpetuities.

[33] Students are often surprised that equity has value when taxable income is zero. Actually, the equityholders are receiving cash flow each period, since new debt is used to buy back stock.

value of the firm is simply the value of the debt. With growth, there is equity as well as debt.

As we mentioned earlier, any further increase in debt would lower the value of the firm in a world with bankruptcy costs. Thus, with growth, the optimal amount of debt is less than 100 percent. Note, however, that bankruptcy costs need not be as large as the tax subsidy. In fact, even with infinitesimally small bankruptcy costs, firm value would decline if promised interest rose above $100 in the first year. The key to this example is that *today's* interest is set equal to *today's* income. While the introduction of future growth opportunities increases firm value, it does not increase the current level of debt needed to shield today's income from today's taxes. Since equity is the difference between firm value and debt, growth increases the value of equity.

The above example captures an essential feature of the real world: growth. The same conclusion is reached in a world of inflation but no growth opportunities.[34] The result of this section, that 100 percent debt financing is suboptimal, holds whether growth opportunities or inflation are present. Since most firms have growth opportunities and since inflation has been with us for most of the last 100 years, this section's example is based on realistic assumptions. The basic point is this: high-growth firms will have lower debt ratios than low-growth firms.

**CONCEPT QUESTION**
- How do growth opportunities decrease the advantage of debt financing?

## 17.9    PERSONAL TAXES

So far in the chapter, we have considered corporate taxes only. Unfortunately, tax law does not let us off that easily. Income to individuals is taxed at federal marginal rates up to 29 percent. Combining the provincial tax rate with the federal tax rate, the marginal rates can be as high as 48 percent.[35] Furthermore, tax law offers a dividend tax credit to individuals. To see the effect of personal taxes on capital structure, we have reproduced our Water Products example (from Section 16.5) below:

|  | Plan I | Plan II |
|---|---|---|
| Earnings before interest and taxes (EBIT) | $1,000,000 | $1,000,000 |
| Interest ($r_B B$) | 0 | (400,000) |
| Earnings before taxes (EBT = EBIT − $r_B B$) | 1,000,000 | 600,000 |
| Taxes ($T_c = 0.40$) | (400,000) | (240,000) |
| Earnings after corporate taxes<br>EAT = (EBIT − $r_B B$) × (1 − $T_c$) | 600,000 | 360,000 |
| Total cash flow to both shareholders and bondholders<br>[EBIT × (1 − $T_c$) + $T_c r_B B$] | $ 600,000 | $ 760,000 |

---

[34] Notice that we restricted the debt to bonds with level-coupon payments. Suppose, instead, that the firm had begun at date 0 by issuing debt-carrying coupons of $105 in year 1, $110.25 in year 2, $115.76 in year 3, and so on. Since there is no uncertainty in our example, these coupons are just the annual EBIT of the firm. At an interest rate of 10 percent such a bond would carry a price of $2,000, which is the entire value of the firm. Thus, the proceeds from the bond issue would equal the value of the firm and the firm would be capitalized as an all-debt firm.

Keep in mind that the important feature of debt is that it is a contractual commitment by the firm to make scheduled payments to the holder. While these payments are usually in the form of level coupons, they may also vary over time. Technically, the same conclusion is reached under an inflation environment similar to that in Canada. But the conclusion will not hold if indexed bonds are issued and/or only real payments are tax deductible.

[35] Appendix 1A gives more detail on taxes.

As presented above, this example considers corporate taxes but not personal taxes. To treat these personal taxes, we first assume that all earnings after taxes are paid out as dividends, and that both dividends and interest are taxed at the same personal rate. (We assume 36 percent.)

|  | Plan I | Plan II |
|---|---|---|
| Dividends | $ 600,000 | $ 360,000 |
| Personal taxes on dividends (personal rate = 36%) | (216,000) | (129,600) |
| Dividends after personal taxes | $ 384,000 | $ 230,400 |
| Interest | 0 | $ 400,000 |
| Taxes on interest | 0 | (144,000) |
| Interest after personal taxes | 0 | 256,000 |
| Total cash flow to both bondholders and shareholders after personal taxes | $ 384,000 | $ 486,400 |

Total taxes paid at both corporate and personal levels are as follows:

Plan I:     $400,000     +     $216,000                              = $616,000
         Corporate taxes    Personal taxes
                            on dividends

Plan II:    $240,000     +     $129,600     +     $144,000     = $513,600
         Corporate taxes    Personal taxes    Personal taxes
                            on dividends       on interest

Total cash flow to all investors after personal taxes is greater under plan II. This must be the case because (1) total cash flow was higher when personal taxes were ignored and (2) all cash flows (both interest and dividends) are taxed at the same personal tax rate. Thus, the conclusion that debt increases the value of the firm still holds.

However, the analysis to this point assumed that all earnings are paid out in dividends, and the personal tax rate on dividends was the same as the personal tax rate on interest. In reality, dividends may be deferred through retention of earnings, and a dividend tax credit exists. Thus, the effective personal tax rate on distributions to shareholders is below the personal tax rate on interest.[36]

To illustrate this tax rate differential, let us assume that the effective personal tax rate on distributions to shareholders, $T_S$, is 10 percent and the personal tax rate on interest, $T_B$, is 50 percent. The cash flows for the two plans are as follows:

|  | Plan I | Plan II |
|---|---|---|
| Distributions to shareholders | $ 600,000 | $ 360,000 |
| Personal taxes on shareholder distributions (at 10% tax rate) | (60,000) | (36,000) |
| Distribution to shareholders after personal taxes | 540,000 | 324,000 |
| Interest | 0 | 400,000 |
| Taxes on interest (at 50% tax rate) | 0 | (200,000) |
| Interest after personal taxes | 0 | 200,000 |
| Add back shareholder distributions after personal taxes | 540,000 | 324,000 |
| Total cash flow to all investors after personal taxes | $ 540,000 | $ 524,000 |

Total taxes paid at both personal and corporate levels are as follows:

Plan I:     $400,000     +     $60,000                              = $460,000
         Corporate taxes    Personal taxes
                            on dividends

Plan II:    $240,000     +     $36,000     +     $200,000     = $476,000
         Corporate taxes    Personal taxes    Personal taxes
                            on dividends      on interest

---

[36] Positive NPV investments financed by deferring dividends will lead to capital gains also taxed at a lower rate. We discuss this in more detail in Chapter 19.

In this scenario, the total cash flows are higher under plan I than under plan II. Though the example is expressed in terms of cash flows, we would expect the value of the firm to be higher under plan I than under plan II because lower total taxes are paid. The increase in corporate taxes under the all-equity plan is more than offset by the decrease in personal taxes.

Interest receives a tax deduction at the corporate level. Equity distributions are taxed at a lower rate than interest at the personal level. The above examples illustrate that total tax at all levels may either increase or decrease with debt, depending on the tax rates and tax credits in effect.

## The Miller Model

**Valuation under Personal and Corporate Taxes**    The previous example calculated *cash flows* for the two plans under personal and corporate taxes. However, we have made no attempt to determine firm value so far. It can be shown that the value of the levered firm can be expressed in terms of an unlevered firm as[37]

$$V_L = V_U + \left[1 - \frac{(1 - T_c) \times (1 - T_S)}{(1 - T_B)}\right] \times B \qquad (17.1)$$

$T_B$ is the personal tax rate on ordinary income, such as interest, and $T_S$ is the personal tax rate on equity distributions.

If we set $T_B = T_S$, equation (17.1) simplifies to

$$V_L = V_U + T_c B \qquad (17.2)$$

which is the result we calculated for a world of no personal taxes. Hence, the introduction of personal taxes does not affect our valuation formula as long as equity distributions are taxed identically to interest at the personal level.

However, the gain from leverage is reduced when $T_S < T_B$. Here, more taxes are paid at the personal level for a levered firm than for an unlevered firm. In fact, imagine that $(1 - T_c) \times (1 - T_S) = 1 - T_B$. Equation (17.1) tells us there is no gain from leverage at all! In other words, the value of the levered firm is equal to the value of the unlevered firm. The gain from leverage disappears because the lower corporate taxes for a levered firm are *exactly* offset by higher personal taxes. Depending on the parameters given, levered firm value can actually be less than the unlevered firm value, resulting in negative values and no benefits to leveraging. These results, known as the Miller model, are presented in Figure 17.4. More details of the Miller model are in Appendix 17B. In addition, we also provide some useful formulas of financial structure in Appendix 17A. Both appendices are available on Connect.

---

[37] Shareholders receive

$$(EBIT - r_B B) \times (1 - T_c) \times (1 - T_S)$$

Bondholders receive

$$r_B B \times (1 - T_B)$$

Thus, the total cash flow to all stakeholders is

$$(EBIT - r_B B) \times (1 - T_c) \times (1 - T_S) + r_B B \times (1 - T_B)$$

which can be rewritten as

$$EBIT \times (1 - T_c) \times (1 - T_S) + r_B B \times (1 - T_B) \times \left[1 - \frac{(1 - T_c) \times (1 - T_S)}{1 - T_B}\right] \qquad (a)$$

The first term in equation (a) is the cash flow from an unlevered firm after all taxes. The value of this stream must be $V_U$, the value of an unlevered firm. An individual buying a bond for $B$ receives $r_B B \times (1 - T_B)$ after all taxes. Thus, the value of the second term in (a) must be

$$B \times \left[1 - \frac{(1 - T_c) \times (1 - T_S)}{1 - T_B}\right]$$

Therefore, the value of the stream in equation (a), which is the value of the levered firm, must be

$$V_U + \left[1 - \frac{(1 - T_c) \times (1 - T_S)}{1 - T_B}\right] \times B$$

FIGURE 17.4

**Gains from Financial Leverage with Both Corporate and Personal Taxes**

$T_c$ is the corporate tax rate.
$T_B$ is the personal tax rate on interest.
$T_S$ is the personal tax rate on dividends and other equity distributions.

Both personal taxes and corporate taxes are included. Bankruptcy costs and agency costs are ignored. The effect of debt on firm value depends on $T_S$, $T_c$, and $T_B$.

EXAMPLE **17.3**

Acme Industries anticipates a perpetual pre-tax earnings stream of $100,000 and faces a 45 percent corporate tax rate. Investors discount the earnings stream after corporate taxes at 15 percent. The personal tax rate on equity distributions is 30 percent, and the personal tax rate on interest is 47 percent. Acme currently has an all-equity capital structure but is considering borrowing $120,000 at 10 percent.

The value of the all-equity firm is[38]

$$V_U = \frac{\$100,000 \times (1 - 0.45)}{0.15} = \$366,667$$

The value of the levered firm is

$$V_L = \$366,667 + \left[1 - \frac{(1 - 0.45) \times (1 - 0.30)}{(1 - 0.47)}\right] \times \$120,000 = \$399,497$$

The advantage to leverage here is $399,497 − $366,667 = $32,830. This is much smaller than $54,000 = 0.45 × $120,000 = $T_c \times B$, which would have been the gain in a world with no personal taxes.

Acme had previously considered the choice years earlier when $T_B$ = 60 percent and $T_S$ = 18 percent. Here

$$V_L = \$366,667 + \left[1 - \frac{(1 - 0.45) \times (1 - 0.18)}{(1 - 0.60)}\right] \times \$120,000 = \$351,367$$

In this case the value of the levered firm $V_L$ is $351,367, which is *less than* the value of the unlevered firm, $V_U$ = $366,667. Hence, Acme was wise not to increase leverage years ago. Leverage causes a loss of value in this case because the personal tax rate on interest is much higher than the personal tax rate on equity distributions. In other words, the reduction in corporate taxes from leverage is more than offset by the increase in taxes from leverage at the personal level.

---

[38] Alternatively, we could have said that investors discount the earnings stream after both corporate and personal taxes at 10.5% = [15% × (1 − 0.30)]:

$$V_U = \frac{\$100,000 \times (1 - 0.45) \times (1 - 0.30)}{0.105} = \$366,667$$

Which one is the most applicable to Canada? While the numbers are different for different firms in different provinces, Chapter 1 showed that interest income is taxed at the full marginal rate, around 43 percent before surtaxes for the top bracket. Equity distributions take the form of either dividends or capital gains, and both are taxed more lightly than interest. As we showed in Appendix 1A, dividend income is sheltered by the dividend tax credit. Capital gains are taxed at 50 percent of the marginal tax rate.

While the exact numbers depend on the type of portfolio chosen, our first scenario for Acme is a reasonable tax scenario for Canadian investors and companies.[39] In Canada, personal taxes reduce, but do not eliminate, the advantage to corporate leverage. This result is still unrealistic. It suggests that firms should add debt, moving out on the second line from the top in Figure 17.4, until 100 percent leverage is reached. Firms do not do this. One reason is that interest on debt is not the firm's only tax shield. Investment tax credits, capital cost allowance (CCA), and depletion allowances give rise to tax shields regardless of the firm's decision on leverage. Because these other tax shields exist, increased leverage brings with it a risk that income will not be high enough to utilize the debt tax shield fully. The result is that firms will use a limited amount of debt.[40]

The results of limited tax deductibility are provided in Figure 17.5. Firm value should rise when debt is first added to the capital structure. However, as more and more debt is issued, the full deductibility of the interest becomes less likely. Firm value still increases, but at a lower and lower rate. At some point, the probability of tax deductibility is low enough that an incremental dollar of debt is as costly to the firm as an incremental dollar of equity. Firm value then decreases with further leverage.

**FIGURE 17.5**

**Value of the Firm under the Miller Model When Interest Deductibility Is Limited to Earnings**

The Miller model with limited deductibility of interest leads to a ∩-shaped graph similar to the one presented in Figure 17.1. The ∩ shape in Figure 17.1 arose from the trade-off between corporate taxes and bankruptcy costs.

---

[39] Support for this scenario comes from M. H. Wilson, "Draft Legislation, Regulations, and Explanatory Notes Respecting Preferred Share Financing" (Ottawa: Department of Finance, April 1988). A survey of 392 CFOs in the United States and Canada found very little evidence that firms directly consider personal taxes when deciding on debt policy: John Graham and Campbell Harvey, "The Theory and Practice of Corporate Finance," *Journal of Financial Economics* (May/June 2001).

[40] This argument was first advanced by H. DeAngelo and R. Masulis, "Optimal Capital Structure under Corporate and Personal Taxation," *Journal of Financial Economics* (March 1980). Empirical testing in Canada has so far failed to find strong support for the argument: A. H. R. Davis, "The Corporate Use of Debt Substitutes in Canada: A Test of Competing Versions of the Substitution Hypothesis," *Canadian Journal of Administrative Sciences* (March 1994).

This graph looks surprisingly like the curve in Figure 17.1, where the trade-off between the tax shield and bankruptcy costs is illustrated. Thus, a key change in assumptions may explain why firms are not 100 percent debt financed under the current tax law.

**CONCEPT QUESTION**

- How do personal taxes change the conclusions of the MM model about capital structure?

## 17.10    HOW FIRMS ESTABLISH CAPITAL STRUCTURE

The theories of capital structure are among the most elegant and sophisticated in the field of finance. Financial economists should (and do!) pat themselves on the back for contributions in this area. However, the practical applications of the theories are less than fully satisfying. Consider that our work on NPV produced an exact formula for evaluating projects. Conversely, the most we can say on capital structure is provided in either Figure 17.1 or Figure 17.5: the optimal capital structure involves a trade-off between taxes and costs of debt. No exact formula is available for evaluating the optimal debt-to-equity ratio. For this reason, we turn to empirical evidence.

The following empirical regularities are worth considering when formulating capital structure policy:

1. *Most Canadian firms have low debt-to-equity ratios.* Figure 17.6 shows the debt-to-equity ratios for non-financial corporations in Australia and the G7 countries. After dropping to historically low levels in 1999, the debt-to-equity ratios in most countries have generally increased. On average, non-financial corporations in Japan, Germany, and Italy have maintained higher debt levels than their international peers. In all countries, firms have historically maintained ratios of less than 3:1. Although most corporations have debt in their capital structures, they still pay substantial taxes. Thus, it is clear that corporations have not issued debt up to the point that tax shelters have been completely used up, and we conclude that there must be limits to the amount of debt corporations can issue.[41]

2. *A number of firms use no debt.* Agrawal and Nagarajan[42] examined approximately 100 firms on the New York Stock Exchange without long-term debt. They found that these firms are averse to leverage of any kind, with little short-term debt as well. In addition, they have levels of cash and marketable securities well above their levered counterparts. Typically, the managers of these firms have high equity ownership. Furthermore, there is significantly greater family involvement in all-equity firms than in levered firms.

   Thus, a story emerges. Managers of all-equity firms are less diversified than the managers of similar, but levered, firms. Because of this, significant leverage represents an added risk that the managers of all-equity firms are loath to accept.

3. *There are differences in the capital structures of different industries.* There are very significant interindustry differences in debt ratios that persist over time. As can be seen in Table 17.3, debt ratios tend to be very low in high-growth industries, such as mining, with ample future investment opportunities—this is true even when the need for external finance is great. Industries with relatively few investment opportunities and slow growth, such as accommodation and food services, tend to use higher levels of debt.

---

[41] For further insight, see John Graham, "How Big Are the Tax Benefits of Debt?" *Journal of Finance* (October 2000).

[42] Anup Agrawal and Nandu Nagarajan, "Corporate Capital Structure, Agency Costs, and Ownership Control: The Case of All-Equity Firms," *Journal of Finance* (September 1990).

FIGURE 17.6

**Debt-to-Equity Ratios for Non-financial Firms, Australia and G7 Countries (1988 Q1–2005 Q4)**

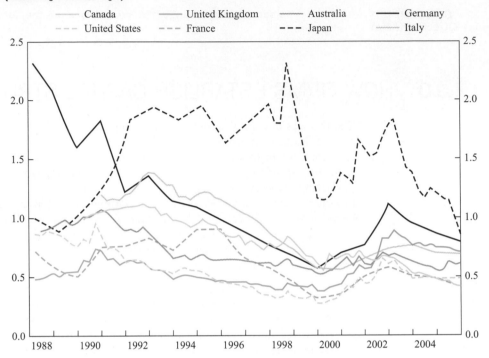

Source: Denise Côté and Christopher Graham, "Corporate Balance Sheets in Developed Economies: Implications for Investment," Working Paper 2007-27, *Bank of Canada* (March 2007).

4. *Most corporations employ target debt-to-equity ratios.* In a survey of 235 corporations in Canada, Europe, and the United States, CFOs were asked whether their firms have implemented target debt-to-equity ratios.[43] Of the firms surveyed, 55 percent used a target, while 35 percent followed the pecking-order theory. Canadian firms were the greatest users of the static trade-off theory, whereas U.S. firms were least likely to use it. In contrast, the pecking-order theory was most popular among U.S. firms and least popular in Canada. With respect to firms using the static trade-off theory, a "flexible target" was most popular, followed by a "somewhat strict target." The findings are similar to those of Graham and Harvey, who surveyed 392 Canadian and U.S. firms.[44]

How should companies establish target debt-to-equity ratios? While there is no mathematical formula for establishing a target ratio, we present three important factors affecting the ratio:

• *Taxes.* As pointed out earlier, firms can only deduct interest for tax purposes to the extent of their profits before interest. Thus, highly profitable firms are more likely to have larger target ratios than less profitable firms.[45]

---

[43] Abe de Jong and Patrick Verwijmeren, "To Have a Target Debt Ratio or Not: What Difference Does It Make?" *Applied Financial Economics* (October 28, 2009).

[44] John Graham and Campbell Harvey, "The Theory and Practice of Corporate Finance," *Journal of Financial Economics* (May/June 2001).

[45] By contrast, the pecking-order theory argues that profitable firms will employ less debt because they can invest out of retained earnings. However, the pecking-order theory argues against the use of *target* ratios in the first place.

**TABLE 17.3**

**Book Value Debt-to-Equity Ratios for Selected Industries in Canada, Fourth Quarter 2013**

|  | Fourth quarter 2013 |
|---|---|
| **Debt to equity** | |
| Total, all industries | **0.855** |
| Total, non-financial industries | **0.883** |
| Agriculture, forestry, fishing, and hunting | 1.009 |
| Oil and gas extraction and support activities | 0.588 |
| Mining and quarrying (except oil and gas) | 0.642 |
| Utilities | 1.245 |
| Construction | 1.267 |
| Manufacturing | 0.705 |
| Wholesale trade | 0.749 |
| Retail trade | 0.845 |
| Transportation and warehousing | 1.39 |
| Information and cultural industries | 1.233 |
| Real estate and rental and leasing | 1.337 |
| Professional, scientific, and technical services | 0.662 |
| Administrative and support, waste management, and remediation services | 0.779 |
| Educational, health care, and social assistance services | 0.741 |
| Arts, entertainment, and recreation | 2.383 |
| Accommodation and food services | 2.269 |
| Repair, maintenance, and personal services | 0.985 |
| Total, finance and insurance industries | **0.784** |
| Non-depository credit intermediation | 2.981 |
| Insurance carriers and related activities | 0.216 |
| Activities related to credit intermediation | 0.581 |
| Depository credit intermediation | 0.885 |
| Securities, commodity contracts, and other financial investments and related activities | 0.587 |

Source: Statistics Canada, "Quarterly Financial Statistics for Enterprises Fourth Quarter 2013," 61-008-X, Fourth Quarter 2013, vol. 24 no. 4, March 17, 2014.

- *Types of assets*. Financial distress is costly, with or without formal bankruptcy proceedings. The costs of financial distress depend on the types of assets that the firm has. For example, if a firm has a large investment in land, buildings, and other tangible assets, it will have smaller costs of financial distress than a firm with a large investment in research and development. Research and development typically have less resale value than land; thus, most of their value disappears in financial distress. Therefore, firms with large investments in tangible assets are likely to have higher target debt-to-equity ratios than firms with large investments in research and development.

- *Uncertainty of operating income*. Firms with uncertain operating income have a high probability of experiencing financial distress, even without debt. Thus, these firms must finance mostly with equity. For example, pharmaceutical firms have uncertain operating income because no one can predict whether today's research will generate new drugs. Consequently, these firms issue little debt. By contrast, the operating income of firms in regulated industries, such as utilities, generally has little uncertainty. Relative to other industries, utilities use a great deal of debt.

5. *Capital structures of individual firms can vary significantly over time.* While Graham and Harvey report that most firms use target leverage ratios, a recent paper nevertheless concludes that capital structures of individual firms often vary widely over time.[46] Taking General Motors, IBM, and Eastman Kodak as examples, the research examines both book leverage (total book value of debt divided by total assets) and market leverage (total book value of debt divided by total book debt plus market value of common stock) for the period 1926 to 2008. Regardless of the measure, all three companies display significant variations in leverage. Large variations in individual firm leverage over time are evidence that variations in individual firm investment opportunities and the need for financing are important determinants of capital structure and the importance of financial slack (i.e., firms borrow money when they have projects worth spending it on).

One final note is in order. Because no formula supports them, the preceding points may seem too nebulous to assist financial decision making. Instead, many real-world firms simply base their capital structure decisions on industry averages. While this may strike some as a cowardly approach, it at least keeps firms from deviating far from accepted practice. After all, the existing firms in any industry are the survivors. Therefore, one should pay at least some attention to their decisions.

CASE **STUDY**

# The Decision to Use More Debt: The Case of Campeau Corporation's Acquisition of Federated

To illustrate the application of capital structure theory, we examine what actually happens when a particular firm decides to use more debt.[47] Let's look at Campeau Corp.'s experiences. Campeau's increased reliance on debt in the acquisition of Federated Department Stores illustrates many important points of this chapter.

On May 3, 1988, after a series of acquisition events, Campeau Corp. purchased Federated Department Stores (a U.S. chain) for $8.17 billion; $7.96 billion (97 percent of the purchase) was financed with debt. In his analysis of this acquisition, Kaplan estimates that after the acquisition, Federated assets increased in value by $1.8 billion. Possible sources of increased value were tax benefits and profits from selling off assets that were undervalued on Federated's balance sheet.

However, even with this large increase in value, Federated had to file for protection under Chapter 11 of U.S. bankruptcy laws in 1990. The biggest reason that Federated filed for bankruptcy was that cash flow was not sufficient to meet the required debt service. Furthermore, Campeau did not have other assets to make up the shortfall. Kaplan argues that if Campeau had financed the acquisition with a mix of debt and equity (as opposed to 97 percent debt), Federated would not have had to file for bankruptcy: "The Federated purchase illustrates that a highly leveraged transaction can increase value, but still not be able to make its debt payments."

---

[46] Harry DeAngelo and Richard Roll, "How Stable Are Corporate Capital Structures?" *Journal of Finance* (Forthcoming 2014).

[47] This section draws on Steven N. Kaplan, "Campeau's Acquisition of Federated: Value Destroyed or Value Added," *Journal of Financial Economics* (December 1989); and a follow-up article (by the same author), "Campeau's Acquisition of Federated: Post-Bankruptcy Results," *Journal of Financial Economics* (February 1994).

**Benefits**

First we examine benefits of Campeau's acquisition of Federated:

1. *Asset sales to more efficient managers.* After purchasing Federated, Campeau proceeded to sell many of the operating divisions. These sales of assets to other department stores and related businesses appear to have increased value. One reason is that Campeau's purchase of Federated came after the stock market crash of 1987; the stock and bond markets may have undervalued Federated. A less convincing argument why value was created is that the purchasers overpaid for the assets sold. In fact, the companies that bought assets showed good post-purchase performance. However, this potential source of value cannot be overlooked.

2. *Lower agency costs.* It is often argued that leverage reduces the agency cost of equity. The new debt from the acquisition forced managers to maximize resources and cash flow.

3. *Tax benefits.* It is well known that new debt can increase a firm's value by reducing taxes. Although Campeau retired some Federated debt with asset sales, most of the asset sales were also financed with debt, and interest tax shields were created and maintained.

**Costs**

Next we examine costs of the acquisition:

1. *Financial distress.* When firms such as Campeau increase their reliance on debt, they also increase the likelihood of financial distress. Financial distress can be formal bankruptcy, which happened to Federated on January 15, 1990. Bankruptcy costs include court costs (direct costs) and loss of market share (indirect costs). According to Kaplan's estimate, bankruptcy costs were relatively modest, reducing Campeau's gain from the acquisition from the original $1.8 billion to $1.6 billion when Federated emerged from bankruptcy in 1992.

2. *Financial slack.* The debt Campeau used to finance the Federated acquisition was well beyond industry norms. In fact, after the purchase, Campeau used up all of Federated's financial slack, which caused the bankruptcy filing. One key area of concern after using up the financial slack is capital expenditures. Cuts in capital expenditures by Federated during the Campeau period may have hurt its assets' market value.

Part of Campeau's purchase of Federated can be analyzed in terms of asset sales, tax benefits, and the costs of financial distress. However, the Campeau experience shows that agency costs and financial slack are also factors in the firm's decision to use more debt.

**CONCEPT QUESTIONS**

- List the empirical regularities we observe for corporate capital structure.
- What are the factors to consider in establishing a debt-to-equity ratio?

## 17.11

# SUMMARY AND CONCLUSIONS

1. We mentioned in the last chapter that according to theory, firms should create all-debt capital structures under corporate taxation. Because firms generally assume moderate amounts of debt in the real world, the theory must have been missing something at that point. We state in this chapter that costs of financial distress cause firms to restrain their issuance of debt. These costs are of two types: direct and indirect. Lawyers' and accountants' fees during the bankruptcy process are examples of direct costs. We mention four examples of indirect costs:

   - Impaired ability to conduct business.
   - Incentive to take on risky projects.
   - Incentive toward underinvestment.
   - Distribution of funds to shareholders prior to bankruptcy.

2. Because the above costs are substantial and the shareholders ultimately bear them, firms have an incentive for cost reduction. We suggest three cost reduction techniques:

   - Protective covenants.
   - Repurchase of debt prior to bankruptcy.
   - Consolidation of debt.

3. Because costs of financial distress can be reduced but not eliminated, firms will not finance entirely with debt. Figure 17.1 illustrates the relationship between firm value and debt. In the figure, firms select the debt-to-equity ratio at which firm value is maximized.

4. Signalling theory argues that profitable firms are likely to increase their leverage, since the extra interest payments will offset some of the pre-tax profits. Rational shareholders will infer higher firm value from a higher debt level. Thus, investors view debt as a signal of firm value.

5. Managers owning a small proportion of a firm's equity can be expected to work less, maintain more lavish expense accounts, and accept more pet projects with negative net present values (NPVs) than managers owning a large proportion of equity. Since new issues of equity dilute a manager's percentage interest in the firm, the above agency costs are likely to increase when a firm's growth is financed through new equity, rather than through new debt.

6. The pecking-order theory implies that managers prefer internal to external financing. If external financing is required, managers tend to choose the safest securities, such as debt. Firms may accumulate slack to avoid external equity.

7. Berens and Cuny argue that significant equity financing can be explained by real growth and inflation, even in a world of low bankruptcy costs.

8. The results so far have ignored personal taxes. If distributions to equityholders are taxed at a lower effective personal tax rate than are interest payments, the tax advantage to debt at the corporate level is partially offset. In fact, the corporate tax advantage to debt is eliminated if

$$(1 - T_c) \times (1 - T_S) = (1 - T_B)$$

9. Debt-to-equity ratios vary across industries. We present three factors determining the target debt-to-equity ratio:

   a. *Taxes.* Firms with high taxable income should rely more on debt than firms with low taxable income.

   b. *Types of assets.* Firms with a high percentage of intangible assets such as research and development should have low debt. Firms with primarily tangible assets should have higher debt.

   c. *Uncertainty of operating income.* Firms with high uncertainty of operating income should rely mostly on equity.

KEY TERMS    Agency costs  500        Negative covenant  503       Protective covenants  503
                       Exchange offers  509      Non-marketed claims  508
                       Marketed claims  508      Positive covenant  503

QUESTIONS &
PROBLEMS

**Firm Value**

17.1  Janetta Corp. has an EBIT rate of $975,000 per year that is expected to continue in perpetuity. The unlevered cost of equity for the company is 14 percent, and the corporate tax rate is 35 percent. The company also has a perpetual bond issue outstanding with a market value of $1.9 million.

    *a.* What is the value of the company?

    *b.* The CFO of the company informs the company president that the value of the company is $4.8 million. Is the CFO correct?

**Agency Costs**

17.2  Tom Scott is the owner, president, and primary salesperson for Scott Manufacturing. Because of this, the company's profits are driven by the amount of work Tom does. If he works 40 hours each week, the company's EBIT will be $400,000 per year; if he works a 50-hour week, the company's EBIT will be $500,000 per year. The company is currently worth $2.5 million. The company needs a cash infusion of $1.2 million, and it can issue equity or issue debt with an interest rate of 8 percent. Assume there are no corporate taxes.

    *a.* What are the cash flows to Tom under each scenario?

    *b.* Under which form of financing is Tom likely to work harder?

    *c.* What specific new costs will occur with each form of financing?

**Capital Structure and Growth**

17.3  Edwards Construction currently has debt outstanding with a market value of $70,000 and a cost of 8 percent. The company has EBIT of $5,600 that is expected to continue in perpetuity. Assume there are no taxes.

    *a.* What is the value of the company's equity? What is the debt-to-value ratio?

    *b.* What are the equity value and debt-to-value ratio if the company's growth rate is 3 percent?

    *c.* What are the equity value and debt-to-value ratio if the company's growth rate is 7 percent?

**Non-marketed Claims**

17.4  Dream Inc. has debt outstanding with a face value of $5 million. The value of the firm if it were entirely financed by equity would be $14.5 million. The company also has 300,000 shares of stock outstanding that sell at a price of $35 per share. The corporate tax rate is 35 percent. What is the decrease in the value of the company due to expected bankruptcy costs?

**Capital Structure and Non-marketed Claims**

17.5  Suppose the president of the company in problem 17.4 stated that the company should increase the amount of debt in its capital structure because of the tax-advantaged status of its interest payments. Her argument is that this action would increase the value of the company. How would you respond?

**Costs of Financial Distress**

17.6  Steinberg Corporation and Dietrich Corporation are identical firms except that Dietrich is more levered. Both companies will remain in business for one more year. The companies' economists agree that the probability of the continuation of the current expansion is 80 percent for the next year, and the probability of a recession is 20 percent. If the expansion continues, each firm will generate EBIT of $2.7 million. If a recession occurs, each firm will generate EBIT of $1.1 million. Steinberg's debt obligation requires the firm to pay $900,000 at the end of the year. Dietrich's debt obligation requires the firm to pay $1.2 million at the end of the year. Neither firm pays taxes. Assume a discount rate of 13 percent.

    *a.* What is the value today of Steinberg's debt and equity? What about that for Dietrich's?

    *b.* Steinberg's CEO recently stated that Steinberg's value should be higher than Dietrich's because the firm has less debt and therefore less bankruptcy risk. Do you agree or disagree with this statement?

### Agency Costs

17.7 Fountain Corp.'s economists estimate that a good business environment and a bad business environment are equally likely for the coming year. The managers of Fountain must choose between two mutually exclusive projects. Assume that the project Fountain chooses will be the firm's only activity and that the firm will close one year from today. Fountain must make a $2,500 payment to bondholders at the end of the year. The projects have the same systematic risk but different volatilities. Consider the following information pertaining to the two projects:

| Economy | Probability | Low-volatility project payoff | High-volatility project payoff |
|---|---|---|---|
| Bad | 0.50 | $2,500 | $2,100 |
| Good | 0.50 | 2,700 | 2,800 |

    *a.* What is the expected value of the firm if the low-volatility project is undertaken? What if the high-volatility project is undertaken? Which of the two strategies maximizes the expected value of the firm?

    *b.* What is the expected value of the firm's equity if the low-volatility project is undertaken? What is it if the high-volatility project is undertaken?

    *c.* Which project would Fountain's stockholders prefer? Explain.

    *d.* Suppose bondholders are fully aware that stockholders might choose to maximize equity value rather than total firm value and opt for the high-volatility project. To minimize this agency cost, the firm's bondholders decide to use a bond covenant to stipulate that the bondholders can demand a higher payment if Fountain chooses to take on the high-volatility project. What payment to bondholders would make stockholders indifferent between the two projects?

### Financial Distress

17.8 Good Time Company is a regional chain department store. It will remain in business for one more year. The probability of a boom year is 60 percent, and the probability of a recession is 40 percent. It is projected that the company will generate a total cash flow of $210 million in a boom year and $85 million in a recession. The company's required debt payment at the end of the year is $120 million. The market value of the company's outstanding debt is $94 million. The company pays no taxes.

    *a.* What payoff do bondholders expect to receive in the event of a recession?

    *b.* What is the promised return on the company's debt?

    *c.* What is the expected return on the company's debt?

### Personal Taxes, Bankruptcy Costs, and Firm Value

17.9 When personal taxes on interest income and bankruptcy costs are considered, the general expression for the value of a levered firm in a world in which the tax rate on equity distributions equals zero is

$$V_L = V_U + \{1 - [(1 - T_c)/(1 - T_B)]\} \times B - C(B)$$

where

$V_L$ = The value of a levered firm.
$V_U$ = The value of an unlevered firm.
$B$ = The value of the firm's debt.
$T_c$ = The tax rate on corporate income.
$T_B$ = The personal tax rate on interest income.
$C(B)$ = The PV of the costs of financial distress.

a. In their no-tax model, what do Modigliani and Miller assume about $T_c$, $T_B$, and $C(B)$? What do these assumptions imply about a firm's optimal debt-to-equity ratio?

b. In their model with corporate taxes, what do Modigliani and Miller assume about $T_c$, $T_B$, and $C(B)$? What do these assumptions imply about a firm's optimal debt-to-equity ratio?

c. Consider an all-equity firm that is certain to be able to use interest deductions to reduce its corporate tax bill. If the corporate tax rate is 34 percent, the personal tax rate on interest income is 20 percent, and there are no costs of financial distress, by how much will the value of the firm change if it issues $1 million in debt and uses the proceeds to repurchase equity?

d. Consider another all-equity firm that will not pay taxes due to large tax loss carryforwards from previous years. The personal tax rate on interest income is 20 percent, and there are no costs of financial distress. What would be the change in the value of this firm from adding $1 of perpetual debt rather than $1 of equity?

e**X**cel    17.10 Overnight Publishing Company (OPC) has $2.5 million in excess cash. The firm plans to use this cash either to retire all of its outstanding debt or to repurchase equity. The firm's debt is held by one institution that is willing to sell it back to OPC for $2.5 million. The institution will not charge OPC any transaction costs. Once OPC becomes an all-equity firm, it will remain unlevered forever. If OPC does not retire the debt, the company will use the $2.5 million in cash to buy back some of its stock on the open market. Repurchasing stock also has no transaction costs. The company will generate $1,300,000 of annual EBIT in perpetuity regardless of its capital structure. The firm immediately pays out all earnings as dividends at the end of each year. OPC is subject to a corporate tax rate of 35 percent, and the required rate of return on the firm's unlevered equity is 20 percent. The personal tax rate on interest income is 25 percent, and there are no taxes on equity distribution. Assume there are no bankruptcy costs.

a. What is the value of OPC if it chooses to retire all of its debt and become an unlevered firm?

b. What is the value of OPC if it decides to repurchase stock instead of retiring its debt? (*Hint:* Use the equation for the value of a levered firm with personal tax on interest income from problem 17.9.)

c. Assume that expected bankruptcy costs have a PV of $400,000. How does this influence OPC's decision?

# McKenzie Restaurants Capital Budgeting

Sally McKenzie is the founder and CEO of McKenzie Restaurants Inc., a regional company. Sally is considering opening several new restaurants. Sam Thornton, the company's CFO, has been put in charge of the capital budgeting analysis. He has examined the potential for the company's expansion and determined that the success of the new restaurants will depend critically on the state of the economy over the next few years.

McKenzie currently has a bond issue outstanding with a face value of $29 million that is due in one year. Covenants associated with this bond issue prohibit the issuance of any additional debt. This restriction means that the expansion will be entirely financed with equity at a cost of $5.7 million. Sam has summarized his analysis in the following table, which shows the value of the company in each state of the economy next year, both with and without expansion:

| Economic growth | Probability | Without expansion | With expansion |
|---|---|---|---|
| Low | 0.30 | $25,000,000 | $27,000,000 |
| Normal | 0.50 | 30,000,000 | 37,000,000 |
| High | 0.20 | 48,000,000 | 57,000,000 |

1. What is the expected value of the company in one year, with and without expansion? Would the company's shareholders be better off with or without expansion? Why?

2. What is the expected value of the company's debt in one year, with and without the expansion?

3. One year from now, how much value creation is expected from the expansion? How much value is expected for shareholders? Bondholders?

4. If the company announces that it is not expanding, what do you think will happen to the price of its bonds? What will happen to the price of the bonds if the company does expand?

5. If the company opts not to expand, what are the implications for the company's future borrowing needs? What are the implications if the company does expand?

6. Because of the bond covenant, the expansion would have to be financed with equity. How would it affect your answer if the expansion were financed with cash on hand instead of new equity?

---

## Some Useful Formulas of Financial Structure

---

## The Miller Model and the Graduated Income Tax

To access Appendix 17A and Appendix 17B, go to Connect.

For more information on the resources available from McGraw-Hill Ryerson, go to www.mheducation.ca/he/solutions.

# 18

# Valuation and Capital Budgeting for the Levered Firm

**EXECUTIVE SUMMARY**

Instructors often structure the basic course in corporate finance around the two sides of the balance sheet. The left-hand side of the balance sheet contains assets. Chapters 5 through 9 discuss capital budgeting, which is a decision concerning the long-term assets of the firm. Chapters 10 through 13 cover the discount rate for a project, so those chapters also concern the left-hand side of the balance sheet. The right-hand side of the balance sheet contains liabilities and shareholders' equity. Chapters 14 through 17 examine the debt-versus-equity decision, which is a decision about the right-hand side of the balance sheet.

While the preceding chapters of this textbook have, for the most part, treated the capital budgeting decision separately from the capital structure decision, the two decisions are actually related. As we will see, a project of an all-equity firm might be rejected, while the same project might be accepted for a levered but otherwise identical firm. This could occur because the cost of capital frequently decreases with leverage, as we saw in Chapter 16, thereby turning some negative net present value (NPV) projects into positive NPV projects.

Chapters 5 through 9 implicitly assumed that the firm is financed with only equity. The goal of this chapter is to value a project, or the firm itself, when leverage is employed. We point out that there are three standard approaches to valuation under leverage: the adjusted present value (APV) method, the flow to equity (FTE) method, and the weighted average cost of capital (WACC) method. These three approaches may seem, at first glance, to be quite different. However, we show that if applied correctly, all three approaches provide the same value estimate.

The three methods discussed below can be used to value either the firm as a whole or a project. The example below discusses project value, though everything we say applies to an entire firm as well.

## 18.1 ADJUSTED PRESENT VALUE APPROACH

The **adjusted present value (APV)** method is best described by the following formula:

$$APV = NPV + NPVF$$

In words, the value of a project to a levered firm (APV) is equal to the value of the project to an unlevered firm (NPV) plus the NPV of the financing side effects (NPVF). There are four major side effects, the first two of which we covered in Chapters 16 and 17:

1. *The tax subsidy to debt.* This was discussed in Chapter 16, where we pointed out that for perpetual debt, the value of the tax subsidy is $T_c B$. ($T_c$ is the corporate tax rate, and $B$ is the value of the debt.) The material on valuation under corporate taxes in Chapter 16 is actually an application of the APV approach.

2. *The costs of financial distress.* The possibility of financial distress, and bankruptcy in particular, arises with debt financing. As stated in the previous chapter, financial distress imposes costs, thereby lowering value.

3. *The costs of issuing new securities.* As we will discuss in detail in Chapter 20, investment bankers participate in the public issuance of corporate debt. These bankers must be compensated for their time and effort, a cost that lowers the value of the project.

4. *Subsidies to debt financing.* The interest rate on debt issued by the provinces and the federal government is substantially below the yield on debt issued by risky private corporations. Frequently, corporations are able to obtain loan guarantees from government, lowering their borrowing costs to a government rate. This subsidy adds value.

While each of these four side effects is important, the tax deduction to debt almost certainly has the highest dollar value in practice. For this reason, the following example considers the tax subsidy, but not the other three side effects.[1]

Consider a project of the Victoria Corporation with the following characteristics:

Sales = $500,000 per year for the indefinite future
Cash costs = 72% of sales
Initial investment = $440,000
$T_c = 40\%$
$r_0 = 20\%$, where $r_0$ is the cost of capital for a project of an all-equity firm

If both the project and the firm are financed with only equity, the project's cash flow is as follows:

| | |
|---|---:|
| Sales | $ 500,000 |
| Cash costs | (360,000) |
| Operating income | 140,000 |
| Corporate tax (40% tax rate) | (56,000) |
| Unlevered cash flow | $  84,000 |

The distinction in Chapter 5 between present value (PV) and NPV is quite important for this example. As pointed out in Chapter 5, the *present value* of a project is determined before the initial investment at date 0 is subtracted. The initial investment is subtracted for the calculation of *net* present value.

Given a discount rate of 20 percent, the PV of the project is the PV of unlevered cash flow (UCF):[2]

$$\frac{\$84,000}{0.20} = \$420,000$$

The project's NPV (that is, its value to an all-equity firm) is

$$\$420,000 - \$440,000 = -\$20,000$$

Since the NPV is negative, the project would be rejected by an all-equity firm.

Now imagine that the firm finances the project with exactly $116,666.67 in debt, so that the remaining investment of $323,333.33 (or $440,000 − $116,666.67) is financed with equity. The *net* present value of the project under leverage, which we call *APV*, is

$$\begin{array}{cccccc} APV = & NPV & + & T_c \times & & B \\ \$26,666.67 = & -\$20,000 & + & 0.40 \times & & \$116,666.67 \end{array}$$

That is, the value of the project when financed with some leverage is equal to the value of the project when financed with all equity plus the tax shield from the debt. Since this number is positive, the project should be accepted.

---

[1] The BDE example of Section 18.5 handles both flotation costs and interest subsidies.

[2] UCF is often referred to as free cash flow.

You may be wondering why we chose such a precise amount of debt. Actually, we chose it so that the ratio of debt to the PV of the project under leverage is 0.25.[3]

In this example, debt is a fixed proportion of the PV of the project, not a fixed proportion of the initial investment of $440,000. This is consistent with the goal of a target debt-to-*market*-value ratio, which we find in the real world. For example, chartered banks typically lend to real estate developers a fixed percentage of the market value of a project, not a fixed percentage of the initial investment.

CONCEPT
QUESTIONS

- How is the APV method applied?
- What additional information beyond NPV does one need to calculate APV?

# 18.2  FLOW TO EQUITY APPROACH

The **flow to equity** (FTE) approach is an alternative capital budgeting approach. The formula simply calls for discounting the cash flow from the project to the equityholders of the levered firm at the cost of equity capital, $r_S$. For a perpetuity, this becomes

$$\frac{\text{Cash flow from project to equityholders of the levered firm}}{r_S}$$

There are three steps to the FTE approach.

## Step 1: Calculating Levered Cash Flow[4]

Assuming an interest rate of 10 percent, the perpetual cash flow to equityholders in our example is as follows:

| | |
|---|---:|
| Sales | $ 500,000.00 |
| Cash costs | −360,000.00 |
| Interest (10% × $116,666.67) | −11,666.67 |
| Income after interest | 128,333.33 |
| Corporate tax (0.40 tax rate) | −51,333.33 |
| Levered cash flow | $  77,000.00 |

Alternatively, one can calculate levered cash flow (LCF) directly from UCF. The key here is that the difference between the cash flow that equityholders receive in an unlevered firm and the cash flow that equityholders receive in a levered firm is the after-tax interest payment. (Repayment of principal does not appear in this example, since the debt is perpetual.) We write this algebraically as

$$\text{UCF} - \text{LCF} = (1 - T_c)r_B B$$

---

[3] We choose 0.25 as an example here. The PV of the project after the initial investment has been made is $466,666.67 (or $26,666.67 + $440,000). Thus, the debt-to-value ratio of the project is 0.25 (or $116,666.67/ $466,666.67).

This level of debt can be calculated directly. Note that

$$\begin{array}{ccc} \text{Present value of} & = \text{Present value of} & + \quad T_c \quad \times B \\ \text{levered project} & \text{unlevered project} & \end{array}$$

$$V_{\text{With debt}} = \qquad \$420{,}000 \qquad + \ 0.40 \times 0.25 \times V_{\text{With debt}}$$

Rearranging the last line, we have

$$V_{\text{With debt}}(1 - 0.40 \times 0.25) = \$420{,}000$$
$$V_{\text{With debt}} = \$466{,}666.67$$

Since debt is 0.25 of value, debt is $116,666.67 (or 0.25 × $466,666.67).

[4] We use the term *levered cash flow (LCF)* for simplicity. A more complete term is *cash flow from the project to the equityholders of a levered firm*. Similarly, a more complete term for *unlevered cash flow (UCF)* is *cash flow from the project to the equityholders of an unlevered firm*.

The term on the right-hand side of this expression is the after-tax interest payment. Thus, since cash flow to the unlevered equityholders (UCF) is $84,000 and the after-tax interest payment is $7,000 [(0.60)0.10 × $116,666.67], cash flow to the levered equityholders (LCF) is

$$\$84,000 - \$7,000 = \$77,000$$

which is exactly the number we calculated earlier.

### Step 2: Calculating $r_S$

The next step is to calculate the discount rate, $r_S$. Note that we assumed that the discount rate on unlevered equity, $r_0$, is 0.20. As we saw in Chapter 16, the formula for $r_S$ is

$$r_S = r_0 + \frac{B}{S}(1 - T_c)(r_0 - r_B)$$

Note that our target debt-to-value ratio of $\frac{1}{4}$ implies a target debt-to-equity ratio of $\frac{1}{3}$. Applying the above formula to this example, we have

$$r_S = 0.20 + \frac{1}{3}(0.60)(0.20 - 0.10) = 0.22$$

### Step 3: Valuation

The PV of the project's LCF is

$$\frac{\text{LCF}}{r_S} = \frac{\$77,000}{0.22} = \$350,000$$

Since the initial investment is $440,000 and $116,666.67 is borrowed, the firm must advance the project $323,333.33 (or $440,000 − $116,666.67) out of its own cash reserves. The *net* present value of the project is simply the difference between the PV of the project's LCF and the investment not borrowed. Thus, the NPV is

$$\$350,000.00 - \$323,333.33 = \$26,666.67$$

which is identical to the result found with the APV approach.

- **How is the FTE method applied?**
- **What information is needed to calculate FTE?**

## 18.3   WEIGHTED AVERAGE COST OF CAPITAL METHOD

Finally, one can value a project using the **weighted average cost of capital (WACC)** method. While this method was discussed in Chapters 13 and 16, it is worthwhile to review it here. The WACC approach begins with the insight that projects of levered firms are simultaneously financed with both debt and equity. The cost of capital is a weighted average of the cost of debt and the cost of equity. As seen in Chapters 13 and 16, the cost of equity is $r_S$. Ignoring taxes, the cost of debt is simply the borrowing rate, $r_B$. However, with corporate taxes, the appropriate cost of debt is $(1 - T_c)r_B$, the after-tax cost of debt.

The formula for determining WACC is

$$\text{WACC} = \frac{S}{S + B}r_S + \frac{B}{S + B}r_B(1 - T_c)$$

The weight for equity, $S/(S + B)$, and the weight for debt, $B/(S + B)$, are target ratios. Target ratios are generally expressed in terms of market values, not book values.

The formula calls for discounting the *unlevered* cash flow of the project (UCF) at the WACC. The NPV of the project can be written algebraically as

$$\sum_{t=1}^{\infty} \frac{\text{UCF}_t}{(1 + \text{WACC})^t} - \text{Initial investment}$$

If the project is a perpetuity, the NPV is

$$\frac{\text{UCF}}{\text{WACC}} - \text{Initial investment}$$

We previously stated that the target debt-to-value ratio of our project is $\frac{1}{4}$ and the corporate tax rate is 0.40, implying that the WACC is

$$\text{WACC} = \frac{3}{4} \times 0.22 + \frac{1}{4} \times 0.10(0.60) = 0.18$$

Note that WACC, 0.18, is lower than the cost of equity capital for an all-equity firm, 0.20. This must always be the case, since debt financing provides a tax subsidy that lowers the average cost of capital.[5]

We previously determined the UCF of the project to be $84,000, implying that the PV of the project is

$$\frac{\$84,000}{0.18} = \$466,666.67$$

Since this initial investment is $440,000, the NPV of the project is

$$\$466,666.67 - \$440,000 = \$26,666.67$$

In this example, all three approaches yield the same value.[6]

**CONCEPT QUESTION**

- How is the WACC method applied?

## 18.4    A COMPARISON OF THE ADJUSTED PRESENT VALUE, FLOW TO EQUITY, AND WEIGHTED AVERAGE COST OF CAPITAL APPROACHES

In this chapter, we provide three approaches to capital budgeting for the levered firm. The APV assumes the dollar amount of debt is known. This approach first values the project on an all-equity basis. That is, the project's after-tax cash flows under all-equity financing (UCF) are placed in the numerator of the capital budgeting equation. The discount rate, assuming all-equity financing, appears in the denominator. At this point, the calculation is identical to that performed in the early chapters of this book. We then add the NPV of the debt. We point out that the NPV of the debt is likely to be the sum of four parameters: tax effects, flotation costs, bankruptcy costs, and interest subsidies.

The FTE approach assumes that debt cash flows are known and that $r_S$ is constant. The FTE approach discounts the after-tax cash flow from a project going to the

---

[5] This is based on MM Proposition I, abstracting from the impact of personal taxes.

[6] The APV, FTE, and WACC approaches yield the same value when using perpetuities only. When, however, evaluating the same project with a limited life (e.g., one year), the three methods yield different results.

equityholders of a levered firm (LCF). LCF is the residual to equityholders after interest has been deducted. The discount rate is $r_S$, the cost of capital to the equityholders of a levered firm. For a firm with leverage, $r_S$ must be greater than $r_0$, the cost of capital for an unlevered firm. This follows from our material in Chapter 16 showing that leverage raises the risk to the equityholders.

The last approach is the WACC method, which assumes the weights (equity and leverage ratios) are constant. This technique calculates the project's after-tax cash flows assuming all-equity financing (UCF). The UCF is placed in the numerator of the capital budgeting equation. The denominator, WACC, is a weighted average of the cost of equity capital and the cost of debt capital. The tax advantage of debt is reflected in the denominator because the cost of debt capital is determined net of corporate tax. The numerator does not reflect debt at all.

All three approaches perform the same task: valuation in the presence of debt financing. And, as illustrated by the previous example, all three provide the same valuation estimate. However, as we saw before, the approaches are markedly different in technique. Because of this, students often ask questions of the following sort: "How can this be? How can the three approaches look so different and yet give the same answer?" We believe that the best way to handle questions like these is through the following two points.

1. *APV versus WACC.* Of the three approaches, APV and WACC display the greatest similarity. After all, both approaches put the UCF in the numerator. However, the APV approach discounts these flows at $r_0$, yielding the value of the unlevered project. Adding the PV of the tax shield gives the value of the project under leverage. The WACC approach discounts UCF at WACC, which is lower than $r_0$.

   Thus, both approaches adjust the basic NPV formula for unlevered firms to reflect the tax benefit of leverage. The APV approach makes this adjustment directly. It simply adds in the PV of the tax shield as a separate term. The WACC approach makes the adjustment in a more subtle way. Here, the discount rate is lowered below $r_0$. Although we do not provide a proof in the textbook, it can be shown that these two adjustments always have the same quantitative effect.

2. *Entity being valued.* The FTE approach appears at first glance to be far different from the other two. For both the APV and the WACC approaches, the initial investment is subtracted out in the final step ($440,000 in our example). However, for the FTE approach, only the firm's contribution to the initial investment ($323,333.33 = $440,000 − $116,666.67) is subtracted out. This occurs because under the FTE approach, only the future cash flows to the levered equityholders (LCF) are valued. By contrast, future cash flows to the unlevered equityholders (UCF) are valued in both the APV and WACC approaches. Thus, since LCFs are net of interest payments, whereas UCFs are not, the initial investment under the FTE approach is correspondingly reduced by debt financing. In this way, the FTE approach produces the same answer that the other two approaches do.

## Caveat: Adjusted Present Value, Flow to Equity, and Weighted Average Cost of Capital Do Not Always Yield the Same Results

Our previous examples (Sections 18.1 to 18.3) produced the same NPV because we assumed the following:

1. A *perpetual cash flow,*
2. A *constant dollar amount of debt* of $116,666.67, and
3. A *constant or target leverage ratio* of $\frac{1}{4}$.

With the absence of the perpetual cash flow assumption, the different methods do not always yield the same results. For instance, having both a constant debt amount and a constant leverage ratio is generally inconsistent because in order to maintain a certain leverage ratio, the amount of debt taken must change. However, in the case of perpetuities, this becomes consistent since the value remains constant over time.[7] Furthermore, in order to have a perpetual cash flow, there has to be a constant dollar amount of debt outstanding. In this case, with a constant interest rate and a constant tax rate, the interest tax shield will be constant and known every year.[8] Finally, if the company manages to maintain a constant leverage ratio, then the interest tax shield is as risky as the firm and should be discounted using $R_{\text{WACC}}$.[9] In the absence of any of these assumptions, the three methods will not yield the same results. Therefore, careful selection of which method to employ is important and is discussed in detail next.

## A Guideline

The key to choosing among capital budgeting methods lies in comparing their assumptions against the facts of the project to be analyzed. However, one method usually provides an easier computation than another, and, in many cases, one or more of the methods are virtually impossible computationally.

To illustrate, consider when it is best to use the WACC and FTE approaches. If the risk of a project stays constant throughout its life, it is plausible to assume that $r_0$ remains constant throughout the project's life. This assumption of constant risk appears to be reasonable for many real-world projects.[10] In addition, if the debt-to-value ratio remains constant over the life of the project, both $r_S$ and WACC will remain constant as well. Under this latter assumption, either the FTE or the WACC approach is easy to apply. However, if the debt-to-value ratio varies from year to year, both $r_S$ and WACC vary from year to year as well. Using the FTE or the WACC approach when the denominator changes every year is computationally quite complex, and when computations become complex, the error rate rises. Thus, both the FTE and WACC approaches present difficulties when the debt-to-value *ratio* changes over time.

The APV approach is based on the *level* of debt in each future period. Consequently, when the debt level can be specified precisely for future periods, the APV approach is quite easy to use. However, when the debt level is uncertain, the APV approach becomes more problematic.[11] For example, when the debt-to-value ratio is a constant, the debt level varies with the value of the project. Since the value of the project in a future year cannot be easily forecast, the level of debt cannot be easily forecast either.

Thus, we suggest the following guideline:

> Use WACC or FTE if the firm's target debt-to-value *ratio* applies to the project over its life. Use APV if the project's *level* of debt is known over the life of the project.

---

[7] L. D. Booth, "Capital Cash Flows, APV and Valuation," *European Financial Management* (January 2007).

[8] R. Stanton and M. S. Seasholes, "The Assumptions and Math behind WACC and APV Calculations," unpublished paper, U. C. Berkeley Haas School of Business (October 2005).

[9] F. Bienfait, "A Note on Valuation Models: CCFs vs. APVs vs. WACC," *International Finance Management*, Harvard Business School, www.learningace.com/doc/88601/4ff752335f8fdd5ae7f8e760030ecba9/bienfait.

[10] Exceptions include projects involving decision trees and real options, discussed in Chapter 9.

[11] For example, when we introduced APV in Section 18.1, we set the optimal debt level at 25 percent of the PV of the project with leverage. In a sense, we "cheated," as this PV was not known at that point. For more on this point, see L. D. Booth, "Capital Budgeting Frameworks for the Multinational Corporation," *Journal of International Business Studies* (Fall 1982).

There are a number of situations where the APV approach is preferred. For example, in a leveraged buyout (LBO), the firm begins with a large amount of debt but rapidly pays down the debt over a number of years. Since the schedule of debt reduction in the future is known when the LBO is arranged, tax shields in every future year can be easily forecast. Thus, the APV approach is easy to use here. By contrast, the WACC and FTE approaches are virtually impossible to apply to LBOs, since the debt-to-equity ratio cannot be expected to be constant over time. In addition, situations involving interest subsidies and flotation costs are much easier to handle with the APV approach. (The BDE example in Section 18.5 applies the APV approach to subsidies and flotation costs.) Finally, the APV approach handles the lease-versus-buy decision much more easily than does either the FTE or the WACC approach. (A full treatment of the lease-versus-buy decision appears in Chapter 22.)

The preceding examples are special cases. Typical capital budgeting situations are more amenable to either the WACC or the FTE approach than to the APV approach. Financial managers generally think in terms of target debt-to-value *ratios*. If a project does better than expected, both its value and its debt capacity will likely rise. The manager will increase debt correspondingly here. Conversely, the manager would be likely to reduce debt if the value of the project were to decline unexpectedly. Of course, because financing is a time-consuming task, the ratio cannot be adjusted on a day-to-day or a month-to-month basis. Rather, the adjustment can be expected to occur over the long run. As mentioned before, the WACC and FTE approaches are more appropriate than is the APV approach when a firm focuses on a target debt-to-value ratio.

---

## The Three Methods of Capital Budgeting with Leverage

1. Adjusted Present Value (APV) Method

$$\sum_{t=1}^{\infty} \frac{UCF_t}{(1 + r_0)^t} + \frac{\text{Additional effects}}{\text{of debt}} - \frac{\text{Initial}}{\text{investment}}$$

$UCF_t$ = The project's cash flow at date $t$ to the equityholders of an unlevered firm

$r_0$ = Cost of capital for project in an unlevered firm

2. Flow to Equity (FTE) Method

$$\sum_{t=1}^{\infty} \frac{LCF_t}{(1 + r_S)^t} - \left( \frac{\text{Initial}}{\text{investment}} - \frac{\text{Amount}}{\text{borrowed}} \right)$$

$LCF_t$ = The project's cash flow at date $t$ to the equityholders of a levered firm

$r_S$ = Cost of equity capital with leverage

3. Weighted Average Cost of Capital (WACC) Method

$$\sum_{t=1}^{\infty} \frac{UCF_t}{(1 + WACC)^t} - \text{Initial investment}$$

**Notes:**

1. The middle term in the APV formula implies that the value of a project with leverage is greater than the value of the project without leverage. Since WACC $< r_0$, the WACC formula implies that the value of a project with leverage is greater than the value of the project without leverage.

2. In the FTE method, cash flow *after interest* (LCF) is used. Initial investment is reduced by the *amount borrowed* as well.

**Guidelines:**

1. Use WACC or FTE if the firm's target debt-to-value *ratio* applies to the project over its life.

2. Use APV if the project's *level* of debt is known over the life of the project.

---

Summing up, we recommend that the WACC and the FTE approaches, rather than the APV approach, be used in most real-world situations. In addition, frequent discussions with business executives have convinced us that the WACC is by far the most widely used method in the real world. Thus, practitioners seem to agree with us that outside the special situations mentioned above, the APV approach is a less important method of capital budgeting.

- What is the main difference between APV and WACC?
- What is the main difference between the FTE approach and the other two approaches?
- When should the APV method be used?
- When should the FTE and WACC approaches be used?

## 18.5   ADJUSTED PRESENT VALUE EXAMPLE

As mentioned above, the APV approach is effective in situations where flotation costs and subsidized financing arise. The FTE and the WACC approaches are less effective in these situations. Example 18.1 illustrates where the APV approach works well.

**EXAMPLE 18.1**

Suppose BDE is considering a $30 million project that will last five years. This investment will be depreciated at a capital cost allowance (CCA) rate of 20 percent. Projected net operating revenue is $5.5 million annually. The tax rate is 40 percent. There is no salvage value at the end of the project. The risk-free rate is 5 percent and the cost of equity is 10 percent. The latter is often called the *cost of unlevered equity* since we assume initially that the firm has no debt.

**All-Equity Value**

Assuming that the project is financed with 100 percent equity, its value is[12]

$$-\$30,000,000 + \frac{\$5,500,000}{0.1}\left[1 - \frac{1}{(1.1)^5}\right] + \text{CCATS}$$

$$= -\$30,000,000 + \$20,849,327 + \frac{\$30,000,000 \times 0.2 \times 0.4}{0.1 + 0.2} \times \frac{1 + 0.5 \times 0.1}{1 + 0.1}$$

$$= -\$30,000,000 + \$20,849,327 + \$7,636,364$$

$$= -\$1,514,309$$

where CCATS is the capital cost allowance tax shield.

An all-equity firm would clearly *reject* this project because the NPV is negative. And equity flotation costs (not considered yet) would only make the NPV more negative. However, debt financing may add enough value to the project to justify acceptance. We consider the effects of debt below.

**Additional Effects of Debt**

BDE can obtain a five-year balloon payment loan for $22,500,000 after flotation costs. The interest rate is the risk-free cost of debt of 5 percent. The flotation costs are 1 percent of the amount raised. We look at three ways in which debt financing alters the NPV of the project.

**Flotation Costs**  The following formula gives us the flotation costs:

$$\$22,500,000 = (1 - 0.01) \times \text{Amount raised}$$

$$\text{Amount raised} = \frac{\$22,500,000}{0.99} = \$22,727,273$$

So flotation costs are $227,273—in the text we added these to the initial outlay, reducing NPV.

The APV method refines the estimate of flotation costs by recognizing that they generate a tax shield. Flotation costs are paid immediately but are deducted from taxes by amortizing over the life of the loan. In this example, the annual tax deduction for flotation costs is $227,273/5 years = $45,455. At a tax rate of 40 percent, the annual tax shield is $45,455 × 0.40 = $18,182.

[12] Notice how we used the cost of equity to discount the CCATS as opposed to the risk-free rate. As a reminder, it is important to use the appropriate rate to reflect the riskiness of cash flows. In this case, since the project is entirely equity financed, the proper rate is the cost of equity.

To find the net flotation costs of the loan, add the PV of the tax shield to the flotation costs:

$$\text{Net flotation costs} = -\$227{,}273 + \frac{\$18{,}182}{0.05} \times \left[1 - \frac{1}{(1.05)^5}\right]$$

$$= -\$227{,}273 + \$78{,}719 = -\$148{,}554$$

The NPV of the project after debt flotation costs but before the benefits of debt is

$$-\$1{,}514{,}309 - \$148{,}554 = -\$1{,}662{,}863$$

**Tax Subsidy** The loan of $22,500,000 is received at date 0. Annual interest at 5 percent is $1,125,000. The interest cost after tax is $675,000 [or $1,125,000 × (1 − 0.40)]. The loan has a balloon payment of the full principal at the end of five years. The loan gives rise to three sets of cash flows: the loan received, the annual interest cost after taxes, and the repayment of principal. The NPV of the loan is simply the sum of three PVs:

$$\text{NPV (loan)} = + \begin{array}{c}\text{Amount}\\\text{borrowed}\end{array} - \begin{array}{c}\text{Present value of after-tax}\\\text{interest payments}\end{array} - \begin{array}{c}\text{Present value of}\\\text{loan repayments}\end{array} \quad \textbf{(18.1)}$$

$$= + \$22{,}500{,}000 - \frac{\$675{,}000}{0.05} \times \left[1 - \frac{1}{(1.05)^5}\right] - \frac{\$22{,}500{,}000}{(1.05)^5}$$

$$= + \$22{,}500{,}000 - \$2{,}922{,}397 - \$17{,}629{,}339$$

$$= \$1{,}948{,}264$$

The NPV of the loan is positive, reflecting the interest tax shield.[13]

The APV of the project with this financing is

$$\text{APV} = \text{All-equity value} - \text{Flotation costs of debt} + \text{NPV (loan)}$$
$$\$285{,}401 = -\$1{,}514{,}309 - \$148{,}554 + \$1{,}948{,}264$$

Though we previously saw that an all-equity firm would reject the project, a firm would *accept* the project if a $22,500,000 loan could be obtained.

Because the loan discussed above was at the market rate of 5 percent, we have considered only two of the three additional effects of debt (flotation costs and tax subsidy) so far. We now examine another loan for which the third effect arises.

**Non-market Rate Financing** In Canada, a number of companies can obtain subsidized financing from federal or provincial governments. For example, in 2001, loan subsidies from the federal government enabled Bombardier to beat its Brazilian rival, Embraer, in winning billion-dollar contracts for its regional jets from Air Wisconsin and Northwest Airlines.[14] Government-subsidized loans are also common in the Canadian softwood lumber industry. Suppose that the BDE project is deemed socially beneficial and a federal minister grants the firm a $22,500,000 loan at 4 percent interest. In addition, the government absorbs all flotation costs. Clearly, the company will choose this loan over the one we previously calculated. At 4 percent interest, annual interest payments are $22,500,000 × 0.04 = $900,000. After-tax payments are $540,000 = $900,000 × (1 − 0.40). Using equation (18.1),

---

[13] The NPV (loan) must be zero in a no-tax world, because interest provides no tax shield there. To check this intuition we calculate

$$0 = \$22{,}500{,}000 - \frac{\$1{,}125{,}000}{0.05}\left[1 - \frac{1}{(1.05)^5}\right] - \frac{\$22{,}500{,}000}{(1.05)^5}$$

[14] K. Leger, "Canada, Brazil both claim win in subsidy war," *National Post*, July 27, 2001.

$$\text{NPV (loan)} = + \begin{array}{c}\text{Amount} \\ \text{borrowed}\end{array} - \begin{array}{c}\text{Present value of after-tax} \\ \text{interest payments}\end{array} - \begin{array}{c}\text{Present value of} \\ \text{loan repayments}\end{array}$$

$$= +\$22,500,000 - \frac{\$540,000}{0.05} \times \left[1 - \frac{1}{(1.05)^5}\right] - \frac{\$22,500,000}{(1.05)^5}$$

$$= +\$22,500,000 - \$2,337,917 - \$17,629,339$$

$$= \$2,532,744$$

Notice that we still discount the cash flows at 5 percent when the firm is borrowing at 4 percent. This is done because 5 percent is the fair market rate (the rate at which the firm could borrow *without* benefit of subsidization). The APV of the subsidized loan is larger than the NPV of the earlier loan because the firm is now borrowing at the below-market rate of 4 percent. Note that the NPV (loan) calculation captures both the tax effect *and* the non-market rate effect.

The APV of the project with subsidized debt financing is

$$\text{APV} = \text{All-equity value} - \text{Flotation costs of debt} + \text{NPV (loan)}$$
$$\$1,018,435 = -\$1,514,309 - \qquad 0 \qquad\qquad + \$2,532,744$$

Subsidized financing has enhanced the NPV substantially. The result is that the government debt subsidy program will likely achieve its result—encouraging the firm to invest in the kind of project the government wishes to encourage.

The above example illustrates the APV approach. The approach begins with the PV of a project for the all-equity firm. Next, the effects of debt are added in. The approach is intuitively appealing because individual components are calculated separately and added together in a simple way. And, if the debt from the project can be specified precisely, the PV of the debt can be calculated precisely.

 **CONCEPT QUESTION**

- How do flotation costs and subsidized financing affect APV?

## 18.6 CAPITAL BUDGETING WHEN THE DISCOUNT RATE MUST BE ESTIMATED

The previous sections of this chapter introduced APV, FTE, and WACC—the three basic approaches to valuing a levered firm. However, one important detail remains. The example in Sections 18.1 through 18.3 *assumed* a discount rate. We now want to show how this rate is determined for real-world firms with leverage, with an application to the three preceding approaches. Example 18.2 brings together the work in Chapters 10 through 13 on the discount rate for unlevered firms with that in Chapter 16 on the effect of leverage on the cost of capital.

EXAMPLE **18.2**

World-Wide Enterprises (WWE) is a large conglomerate thinking of entering the widget business, where it plans to finance projects with a debt-to-value ratio of 25 percent (or, alternatively, a debt-to-equity ratio of $\frac{1}{3}$). As a diversified conglomerate, WWE has a beta approximately equal to 1.0. However, the widget business is more risky than WWE's current operations and requires its own measure of risk. There is currently one firm in the widget industry, Alberta Widgets (AW). This firm is financed with 40 percent debt and 60 percent equity. The beta of AW's equity is 1.5.[15] AW has a borrowing rate of 12 percent, and WWE expects to borrow for its widget venture at 10 percent. The corporate tax rate for both firms is 0.40, the market risk premium is 8.5 percent, and the risk-free interest rate is 8 percent. What is the appropriate discount rate for WWE to use for its widget venture?

As explained in Sections 18.1 through 18.3, a corporation may use one of three capital budgeting approaches: APV, FTE, or WACC. The appropriate discount rates for these three approaches are $r_0$, $r_S$, and WACC, respectively. Since AW is WWE's only competitor in widgets, we look at AW's cost of capital to calculate $r_0$, $r_S$, and WACC for WWE's widget venture. The four-step procedure below will allow us to calculate all three discount rates.

1. *Determining AW's cost of equity capital.* First, we determine AW's cost of equity capital, using the security market line (SML) of Chapter 11:

   **AW's Cost of Equity Capital:**
   $$r_S = R_F + \beta \times (\overline{R}_M - R_F)$$
   $$20.75\% = 8\% + 1.5 \times 8.5\%$$

   where $\overline{R}_M$ is the expected return on the market portfolio and $R_F$ is the risk-free rate.

2. *Determining AW's hypothetical all-equity cost of capital.* However, we must standardize the above number in some way, since AW's and WWE's widget ventures have different target debt-to-value ratios. The easiest approach is to calculate the hypothetical cost of equity capital for AW, assuming all-equity financing. This can be determined from MM's Proposition II under taxes (from Chapter 16):

   **AW's Cost of Capital if All-Equity:**
   $$r_S = r_0 + \frac{B}{S}(1 - T_c)(r_0 - r_B)$$
   $$20.75\% = r_0 + \frac{0.4}{0.6}(0.60)(r_0 - 12\%)$$

   In the examples of Chapter 16, the unknown in this equation was $r_S$.[16] However, for this example, the unknown is $r_0$. By solving the equation, we find that $r_0 = 0.1825$. Of course, $r_0$ is less than $r_S$ because the cost of equity capital would be less when the firm employs no leverage.

   At this point, firms in the real world generally assume that the business risk of their venture is about equal to the business risk of the firms already in the business. Applying this assumption to our problem, we assert that the hypothetical discount rate of WWE's

---

[15] An alternative approach is to estimate beta for the project using projected operating and financial leverage. Cleveland Patterson, "The Cost of Equity Capital of a Non-Traded Entity: A Canadian Study," *Canadian Journal of Administrative Sciences* (June 1993), applies this approach to estimate the cost of equity for Teleglobe Canada Inc. We discussed this in Chapter 13.

[16] In this example we are assuming that the debt betas for AW and WWE are zero. This assumption is not strictly correct because the cost of debt for AW and WWE is assumed to be higher than the risk-free rate. As a practical matter, most academic research suggests debt betas are very close to zero.

widget venture if the venture is all-equity financed is also 0.1825.[17] This discount rate will be employed if WWE uses the APV approach, since the APV approach calls for r0, the project's cost of capital in a firm with no leverage.

3. *Determining $r_S$ for WWE's widget venture.* Alternatively, WWE might use the FTE approach, where the discount rate for levered equity is determined from

**Cost of Equity Capital for WWE's Widget Venture:**

$$r_S = r_0 + \frac{B}{S}(1 - T_c)(r_0 - r_B)$$

$$19.9\% = 18.25\% + \frac{1}{3}(0.60)(18.25\% - 10\%)$$

Note that the cost of equity capital for WWE's widget venture, 0.199, is less than the cost of equity capital for AW, 0.2075. This occurs because AW has a higher debt-to-equity ratio. (As mentioned above, both firms are assumed to have the same business risk.)

4. *Determining WACC for WWE's widget venture.* Finally, WWE might use the WACC approach. The appropriate calculation here is

**WACC for WWE's Widget Venture:**

$$WACC = \frac{B}{S + B}r_B(1 - T_c) + \frac{S}{S + B}r_S$$

$$16.425\% = \frac{1}{4}[10\%(0.60)] + \frac{3}{4} \times 19.9\%$$

The preceding example shows how the three discount rates, $r_0$, $r_S$, and WACC, are determined in the real world. These are the appropriate rates for the APV, FTE, and WACC approaches, respectively. Note that $r_S$ for Alberta Widgets is determined first, because the cost of equity capital can be determined from the beta of the firm's stock. As discussed in Chapter 13, beta can easily be estimated for any publicly traded firm, such as AW.

**CONCEPT QUESTION**

• What adjustments are required in capital budgeting for a project with beta different from the firm's?

# 18.7   BETA AND LEVERAGE

Chapter 13 provides the formula for the relationship between the beta of the common stock and the leverage of the firm in a world without taxes:

**The No-Tax Case:**

$$\beta_{Equity} = \beta_{Asset}\left(1 + \frac{Debt}{Equity}\right) \tag{18.2}$$

As pointed out in Chapter 13, this relationship holds under the assumption that the beta of debt is zero.

---

[17] Alternatively, a firm might assume that its venture would be somewhat riskier since it is a new entrant. Thus, the firm might select a discount rate slightly higher than 0.1825. Of course, no exact formula exists for adjusting the discount rate upward.

Since firms must pay corporate taxes in practice, it is worthwhile to provide the relationship with corporate taxes. It can be shown that the relationship between the beta of the unlevered firm and the beta of the levered equity is[18]

**The Corporate-Tax Case:**

$$\beta_{\text{Equity}} = \left[1 + \frac{(1 - T_c)\text{Debt}}{\text{Equity}}\right]\beta_{\text{Unlevered firm}} \qquad (18.3)$$

when (1) the corporation is taxed at the rate of $T_c$ and (2) the debt has a zero beta.

Because $[1 + (1 - T_c)\text{Debt/Equity}]$ must be more than 1 for a levered firm, it follows that $\beta_{\text{Unlevered firm}} < \beta_{\text{Equity}}$. The corporate tax case of equation (18.3) is quite similar to the no-tax case of equation (18.2), because the beta of levered equity must be greater than the beta of the unlevered firm in either case. The intuition that leverage increases the risk of equity applies in both cases.

However, notice that the two equations are not equal. It can be shown that leverage increases the equity beta less rapidly under corporate taxes. This occurs because, under taxes, leverage creates a *risk-free* tax shield, thereby lowering the risk of the entire firm.

---

**EXAMPLE 18.3**

Alberta Petroleum Ltd. is considering a scale-enhancing project. The market value of the firm's debt is $100 million, and the market value of the firm's equity is $200 million. The debt is considered risk free. The corporate tax rate is 40 percent. Regression analysis indicates that the beta of the firm's equity is 2. The risk-free rate is 10 percent, and the expected market premium is 8.5 percent. What would be the project's discount rate in the hypothetical case that Alberta Petroleum is all-equity?

We can answer this question in two steps:

---

[18] This result—derived in R. Hamada, "The Effect of the Firm's Capital Structure on the Systematic Risk of Common Stocks," *Journal of Finance* (May 1972)—holds only if the beta of debt equals zero. To see this, note that

$$V_U + T_c B = V_L = B + S \qquad (a)$$

where

$V_U$ = Value of unlevered firm
$V_L$ = Value of levered firm
$B$ = Value of debt in a levered firm
$S$ = Value of equity in a levered firm

As we stated in the text, the beta of the levered firm is a weighted average of the debt beta and the equity beta:

$$\frac{B}{B + S} \times \beta_B + \frac{S}{B + S} \times \beta_S$$

where $\beta_B$ and $\beta_S$ are the betas of the debt and the equity of the levered firm, respectively. Because $V_L = B + S$, we have

$$\frac{B}{V_L} \times \beta_B + \frac{S}{V_L} \times \beta_S \qquad (b)$$

The beta of the levered firm can also be expressed as a weighted average of the beta of the unlevered firm and the beta of the tax shield:

$$\frac{V_U}{V_U + T_c B} \times \beta_U + \frac{T_c B}{V_U + T_c B} \times \beta_B$$

where $\beta_U$ is the beta of the unlevered firm. This follows from equation (a). Because $V_L = V_U + T_c B$, we have

$$\frac{V_U}{V_L} \times \beta_U + \frac{T_c B}{V_L} \times \beta_B \qquad (c)$$

We can equate equations (b) and (c) because both represent the beta of a levered firm. Equation (a) tells us that $V_U = S + (1 - T_c) \times B$. Under the assumption that $\beta_B = 0$, equating (b) and (c) and using equation (a) yields equation (18.3).

1.  *Determining the beta of a hypothetical all-equity firm.* Rearranging equation (18.3), we have

**Unlevered Beta:**

$$\frac{\text{Equity}}{\text{Equity} + (1 - T_C) \times \text{Debt}} \times \beta_{\text{Equity}} = \beta_{\text{Unlevered firm}} \qquad \textbf{(18.4)}$$

$$\frac{\$200\ \text{million}}{\$200\ \text{million} + (1 - 0.40) \times \$100\ \text{million}} \times 2 = 1.54$$

2.  *Determining the discount rate.* We calculate the discount rate from the SML as

**Discount Rate:**

$$r_S = R_F + \beta \times [\overline{R}_M - R_F]$$
$$23.09\% = 10\% + 1.54 \times 8.5\%$$

## The Project Is Not Scale Enhancing

Because Example 18.3 assumed that the project is scale enhancing, we began with the beta of the firm's equity. If the project is not scale enhancing, we could begin with the equity betas of firms in the industry of the project. For each firm, the hypothetical beta of the unlevered equity could be calculated by equation (18.4). The SML could then be used to determine the project's discount rate from the average of these betas.

**EXAMPLE 18.4**

The J. Lowes Corporation, which currently manufactures staples, is considering a $1 million investment in a project in the aircraft adhesives industry. The corporation estimates unlevered after-tax cash flows (UCF) of $300,000 per year in perpetuity from the project. The firm will finance the project with a debt-to-value ratio of 0.5 (or, equivalently, a debt-to-equity ratio of 1:1).

The three competitors in this new industry are currently unlevered, with betas of 1.2, 1.3, and 1.4. Assuming a risk-free rate of 5 percent, a market-risk premium of 9 percent, and a corporate tax rate of 40 percent, what is the NPV of the project?

We can answer this question in five steps.

1.  *Calculating the average unlevered beta in the industry.* The average unlevered beta across all three existing competitors in the aircraft adhesives industry is

$$\frac{1.2 + 1.3 + 1.4}{3} = 1.3$$

2.  *Calculating the levered beta for J. Lowes's new project.* Assuming the same unlevered beta for this new project as for the existing competitors, we have, from equation (18.3),

**Levered Beta:**

$$\beta_{\text{Equity}} = \left[1 + \frac{(1 - T_c)\text{Debt}}{\text{Equity}}\right]\beta_{\text{Unlevered firm}}$$

$$2.08 = \left(1 + \frac{0.6 \times 1}{1}\right) \times 1.3$$

3.  *Calculating the cost of levered equity for the new project.* We calculate the discount rate from the SML as

**Discount Rate:**

$$r_S = R_F + \beta \times [\overline{R}_M - R_F]$$

$$0.237 = 0.05 + 2.08 \times 0.09$$

4. *Calculating the WACC for the new project.* The formula for determining the WACC is

$$\text{WACC} = \frac{B}{V}r_B(1 - T_c) + \frac{S}{V}r$$

$$0.134 = \frac{1}{2} \times 0.05 \times 0.6 + \frac{1}{2} \times 0.237$$

5. *Determining the project's value.* Because the cash flows are perpetual, the NPV of the project is

$$\frac{\text{Unlevered cash flows (UCF)}}{\text{WACC}} - \text{Initial investment} = \frac{\$300,000}{0.134} - \$1 \text{ million}$$

$$= \$1.24 \text{ million}$$

**CONCEPT QUESTION**

• How is beta adjusted for leverage and corporate taxes?

# 18.8

# SUMMARY AND CONCLUSIONS

Earlier chapters showed how to calculate net present value (NPV) for projects of all-equity firms. We pointed out in the last two chapters that the introduction of taxes and bankruptcy costs changes a firm's financing decisions and means that rational corporations should employ some debt. Because of the benefits and costs associated with debt, the capital budgeting decision is different for levered firms than for unlevered firms. This chapter has discussed three methods for capital budgeting by levered firms: the adjusted present value (APV), flows to equity (FTE), and weighted average cost of capital (WACC) approaches.

1. The APV formula is

$$\sum_{t=1}^{\infty} \frac{\text{UCF}_t}{(1 + r_0)^t} + \text{Additional effects of debt} - \text{Initial investment}$$

There are four additional effects of debt:

• Tax shield from debt financing.

• Flotation costs.

• Bankruptcy costs.

• Benefit of non-market rate financing.

2. The FTE formula is

$$\sum_{t=1}^{\infty} \frac{\text{LCF}_t}{(1 + r_S)^t} - (\text{Initial investment} - \text{Amount borrowed})$$

3. The WACC formula is

$$\sum_{t=1}^{\infty} \frac{\text{UCF}_t}{(1 + \text{WACC})^t} - \text{Initial investment}$$

4. Corporations frequently follow these guidelines:

• Use WACC or FTE if the firm's target debt-to-value *ratio* applies to the project over its life.

• Use APV if the project's *level* of debt is known over the life of the project.

5. The APV method is used frequently for special situations like interest subsidies, leveraged buyouts (LBOs), and leases. The WACC and FTE methods are commonly used for

more typical capital budgeting situations. The APV approach is less frequently used for typical capital budgeting situations.

6. The beta of the equity of the firm is positively related to the leverage of the firm.

7. The beta of a project is the same as the firm's beta only in the case of scale-enhancing projects. Otherwise, one must begin with unlevered betas for firms in the same industry as the project.

| | | |
|---|---|---|
| **KEY TERMS** | Adjusted present value (APV) 533 | Flow to equity (FTE) 535 | Weighted average cost of capital (WACC) 536 |

**QUESTIONS & PROBLEMS**

### Net Present Value and Adjusted Present Value

18.1 Zoso is a rental car company that is trying to determine whether to add 25 cars to its fleet. The company fully depreciates all its rental cars over five years using the straight-line method. The new cars are expected to generate $140,000 per year in earnings before taxes and depreciation for five years. The company is entirely financed by equity and has a 35 percent tax rate. The required return on the company's unlevered equity is 13 percent, and the new fleet will not change the risk of the company.

   *a.* What is the maximum price that the company should be willing to pay for the new fleet of cars if it remains an all-equity company?

   *b.* Suppose the company can purchase the fleet of cars for $395,000. Additionally, assume the company can issue $260,000 of five-year, 8 percent debt to finance the project. All principal will be repaid in one balloon payment at the end of the fifth year. What is the APV of the project?

### Adjusted Present Value

18.2 Gemini Inc., an all-equity firm, is considering a $1.7 million investment that will be depreciated according to the straight-line method over its four-year life. The project is expected to generate EBIT of $595,000 per year for four years. The investment will not change the risk level of the firm. The company can obtain a four-year, 9.5 percent loan to finance the project from a local bank. All principal will be repaid in one balloon payment at the end of the fourth year. The bank will charge the firm $45,000 in flotation fees, which will be amortized over the four-year life of the loan. If the company financed the project entirely with equity, the firm's cost of capital would be 13 percent. The corporate tax rate is 30 percent. Using the APV method, determine whether the company should undertake the project.

### Flow to Equity

18.3 Milano Pizza Club owns three identical restaurants popular for their specialty pizzas. Each restaurant has a debt-to-equity ratio of 40 percent and makes interest payments of $34,000 at the end of each year. The cost of the firm's levered equity is 19 percent. Each store estimates that annual sales will be $1.2 million, annual cost of goods sold will be $510,000, and annual general and administrative costs will be $340,000. These cash flows are expected to remain the same forever. The corporate tax rate is 40 percent.

   *a.* Use the FTE approach to determine the value of the company's equity.

   *b.* What is the total value of the company?

### Weighted Average Cost of Capital

18.4 If Wild Widgets Inc. were an all-equity company, it would have a beta of 0.85. The company has a target debt-to-equity ratio of 0.40. The expected return on the market portfolio is 11 percent, and Treasury bills currently yield 4 percent. The company has one bond issue outstanding that matures in 20 years and has a 7 percent coupon rate. The bond currently sells for $1,080. The corporate tax rate is 34 percent.

a. What is the company's cost of debt?
b. What is the company's cost of equity?
c. What is the company's WACC?

**Beta and Leverage**

18.5 North Pole Fishing Equipment Corp. and South Pole Fishing Equipment Corp. would have identical equity betas of 1.25 if both were all-equity financed. The market value information for each company is shown here:

|  | North Pole | South Pole |
|---|---|---|
| Debt | $2,900,000 | $3,800,000 |
| Equity | $3,800,000 | $2,900,000 |

The expected return on the market portfolio is 12.40 percent, and the risk-free rate is 5.30 percent. Both companies are subject to a corporate tax rate of 35 percent. Assume the beta of debt is zero.

a. What is the equity beta of each of the two companies?
b. What is the required rate of return on each of the two companies' equity?

**Net Present Value of Loans**

18.6 Danika Kaffe, CFO of Kendrick Enterprises, is evaluating a 10-year, 8 percent loan with gross proceeds of $5,350,000. The interest payments on the loan will be made annually. Flotation costs are estimated to be 1.25 percent of gross proceeds and will be amortized using a straight-line schedule over the 10-year life of the loan. The company has a tax rate of 40 percent, and the loan will not increase the risk of financial distress for the company.

a. Calculate the NPV of the loan excluding flotation costs.
b. Calculate the NPV of the loan including flotation costs.

**Net Present Value for an All-Equity Company**

18.7 Shattered Glass Inc. is an all-equity firm. The cost of the company's equity is currently 11 percent, and the risk-free rate is 3.5 percent. The company is currently considering a project that will cost $11.4 million and last six years. The project will generate revenues minus expenses each year in the amount of $3.2 million. If the company has a tax rate of 40 percent, should it accept the project?

**Weighted Average Cost of Capital**

18.8 National Electric Company (NEC) is considering a $45 million project in its power systems division. Nik Tesla, the company's CFO, has evaluated the project and determined that the project's unlevered cash flows will be $3.1 million per year in perpetuity. Nik has devised two possibilities for raising the initial investment: issuing 10-year bonds or issuing common stock. NEC's pre-tax cost of debt is 6.9 percent, and its cost of equity is 10.8 percent. The company's target debt-to-value ratio is 80 percent. The project has the same risk as NEC's existing businesses, and it will support the same amount of debt. NEC is in the 34 percent tax bracket. Should NEC accept the project?

18.9 Bolero Inc. has compiled the following information on its financing costs:

| Type of financing | Book value | Market value | Cost |
|---|---|---|---|
| Short-term debt | $10,000,000 | $11,000,000 | 6.8% |
| Long-term debt | 3,000,000 | 3,000,000 | 3.5% |
| Common stock | 6,000,000 | 26,000,000 | 14.5% |
| Total | $19,000,000 | $40,000,000 | |

The company is in the 35 percent tax bracket and has a target debt-to-equity ratio of 60 percent. The target short-term debt/long-term debt ratio is 20 percent.

a. What is the company's WACC using book value weights?
b. What is the company's WACC using market value weights?
c. What is the company's WACC using target capital structure weights?
d. What is the difference between WACCs? Which is the correct WACC to use for project evaluation?

**Adjusted Present Value**

18.10 Triad Corp. has established a joint venture with Imperial Road Construction Inc. to build a toll road in southwestern Ontario. The initial investment in paving equipment is $80 million. The equipment will be fully depreciated using the straight-line method over its economic life of five years. Earnings before interest, taxes, and depreciation collected from the toll road are projected to be $12.1 million per annum for 20 years starting from the end of the first year. The corporate tax rate is 35 percent. The required rate of return for the project under all-equity financing is 13 percent. The pre-tax cost of debt for the joint partnership is 8.5 percent. To encourage investment in the country's infrastructure, the Canadian government will subsidize the project with a $25 million, 15-year loan at an interest rate of 5 percent per year. All principal will be repaid in one balloon payment at the end of year 15. What is the APV of this project?

18.11 For the company in problem 18.10, what is the value of being able to issue subsidized debt instead of having to issue debt at the terms it would normally receive? Assume the face amount and maturity of the debt issue are the same.

18.12 MVP Inc. has produced rodeo supplies for over 20 years. The company currently has a debt-to-equity ratio of 50 percent and is in the 40 percent tax bracket. The required return on the firm's levered equity is 16 percent. MVP is planning to expand its production capacity. The equipment to be purchased is expected to generate the following unlevered cash flows:

| Year | Cash flow |
|------|-----------|
| 0 | $(18,000,000) |
| 1 | 5,700,000 |
| 2 | 9,500,000 |
| 3 | 8,800,000 |

The company has arranged a $9.3 million debt issue to partially finance the expansion. Under the loan, the company would pay interest of 9 percent at the end of each year on the outstanding balance at the beginning of the year. The company would also make year-end principal payments of $3,100,000 per year, completely retiring the issue by the end of the third year. Using the APV method, should the company proceed with the expansion?

**Weighted Average Cost of Capital**

18.13 Neon Corp. stock returns have a covariance with the market portfolio of 0.0415. The standard deviation of the returns on the market portfolio is 20 percent, and the expected market risk premium is 7.5 percent. The company has bonds outstanding with a total market value of $55 million and a yield to maturity of 6.5 percent. The company also has 4.5 million shares of common stock outstanding, each selling for $25. The company's CEO considers the firm's current debt-to-equity ratio optimal. The corporate tax rate is 35 percent, and Treasury bills currently yield 3.4 percent. The company is considering the purchase of additional equipment that would cost $42 million. The expected unlevered cash flows from the equipment are $11.8 million per year for five years. Purchasing the equipment will not change the risk level of the firm.

   *a.* Use the WACC approach to determine whether Neon should purchase the equipment.

   *b.* Suppose the company decides to fund the purchase of the equipment entirely with debt. What is the cost of capital for the project now? Explain.

**Adjusted Present Value, Flow to Equity, and Weighted Average Cost of Capital**

18.14 Seger Inc. is an unlevered firm with expected annual earnings before taxes of $21 million in perpetuity. The current required return on the firm's equity is 16 percent, and the firm distributes all of its earnings as dividends at the end of each year. The company has 1.3 million shares of common stock outstanding and is subject to a corporate tax rate of 35 percent. The firm is planning a recapitalization under which it will issue $30 million of perpetual 9 percent debt and use the proceeds to buy back shares.

   *a.* Calculate the value of the company before the recapitalization plan is announced. What is the value of equity before the announcement? What is the price per share?

   *b.* Use the APV method to calculate the company value after the recapitalization plan is announced. What is the value of equity after the announcement? What is the price per share?

   *c.* How many shares will be repurchased? What is the value of equity after the repurchase has been completed? What is the price per share?

   *d.* Use the FTE method to calculate the value of the company's equity after the recapitalization.

18.15 Mojito Mint Company has a debt-to-equity ratio of 0.35. The required return on the company's unlevered equity is 17 percent, and the pre-tax cost of the firm's debt is 9 percent. Sales revenue for the company is expected to remain stable indefinitely at last year's level of $28,900,000. Variable costs amount to 60 percent of sales. The tax rate is 40 percent, and the company distributes all its earnings as dividends at the end of each year.

   *a.* If the company were financed entirely by equity, how much would it be worth?

   *b.* What is the required return on the firm's levered equity?

   *c.* Use the WACC method to calculate the value of the company. What is the value of the company's equity? What is the value of the company's debt?

   *d.* Use the FTE method to calculate the value of the company's equity.

18.16 Lone Star Industries just issued $195,000 of perpetual 9 percent debt and used the proceeds to repurchase stock. The company expects to generate $83,000 of EBIT in perpetuity. The company distributes all its earnings as dividends at the end of each year. The firm's unlevered cost of capital is 15 percent, and the corporate tax rate is 40 percent.

   *a.* What is the value of the company as an unlevered firm?

   *b.* Use the APV method to calculate the value of the company with leverage.

   *c.* What is the required return on the firm's levered equity?

   *d.* Use the FTE method to calculate the value of the company's equity.

**Projects That Are Scale Enhancing**

18.17 Blue Angel Inc., a private firm in the holiday gift industry, is considering a new project. The company currently has a target debt-to-equity ratio of 0.40, but the industry target debt-to-equity ratio is 0.35. The industry average beta is 1.2. The market risk premium is 7 percent, and the risk-free rate is 5 percent. Assume all companies in this industry can issue debt at the risk-free rate. The corporate tax rate is 40 percent. The project requires an initial outlay of $675,000 and is expected to result in a $95,000 cash inflow at the end of the first year. The project will be financed at Blue Angel's target debt-to-equity ratio. Annual cash flows from the project will grow at a constant rate of 5 percent until the end of the fifth year and remain constant forever thereafter. Should Blue Angel invest in the project?

# The Leveraged Buyout of Cheek Products Ltd.

Cheek Products Ltd. (CPL) was founded 53 years ago by James Cheek and originally sold snack foods such as potato chips and pretzels. Through acquisitions, the company has grown into a conglomerate with major divisions in the snack food industry, home security systems, cosmetics, and plastics. Additionally, the company has several smaller divisions. In recent years, the company has been underperforming, but the company's management doesn't seem to be aggressively pursuing opportunities to improve operations (and the stock price).

Meg Whalen is a financial analyst specializing in identifying potential buyout targets. She believes that two major changes are needed at Cheek. First, she thinks that the company would be better off if it sold several divisions and concentrated on its core competencies in snack foods and home security systems. Second, the company is financed entirely with equity. Because the cash flows of the company are relatively steady, Meg thinks the company's debt-to-equity ratio should be at least 0.25. She believes these changes would significantly enhance shareholder wealth, but she also believes that the existing board and company management are unlikely to take the necessary actions. As a result, Meg thinks the company is a good candidate for an LBO.

An LBO is the acquisition by a small group of equity investors of a public or private company. Generally, an LBO is financed primarily with debt. The new shareholders service the heavy interest and principal payments with cash from operations and/or asset sales. Shareholders generally hope to reverse the LBO within three to seven years by way of a public offering or sale of the company to another firm. A buyout is therefore likely to be successful only if the firm generates enough cash to service the debt in the early years and if the company is attractive to other buyers a few years down the road.

Meg has suggested the potential LBO to her partners, Ben Feller and Brenda Flynn. Ben and Brenda have asked Meg to provide projections of the cash flows for the company. Meg has provided the estimates below (in millions).

At the end of five years, Meg estimates that the growth rate in cash flows will be 3.5 percent per year. The capital expenditures are for new projects and the replacement of equipment that wears out. Additionally, the company would realize cash flow from the sale of several divisions. Even though the company will sell these divisions, overall sales should increase because of a more concentrated effort on the remaining divisions.

After plowing through the company's financials and various *pro forma* scenarios, Ben and Brenda feel that in five years they will be able to sell the company to another party or take it public again. They are also aware that they will have to borrow a considerable amount of the purchase price. The interest payments on the debt for each of the next five years if the LBO is undertaken are shown below (in millions):

| | 2015 | 2016 | 2017 | 2018 | 2019 |
|---|---|---|---|---|---|
| Interest payments | $1,927 | $1,859 | $2,592 | $2,526 | $2,614 |

The company currently has a required return on assets of 14 percent. Because of the high debt level, the debt will carry a yield to maturity of 12.5 percent for the next five years. When the debt is refinanced in five years, they believe the new yield to maturity will be 8 percent.

CPL currently has 425 million shares of stock outstanding that sell for $29 per share. The corporate tax rate is 40 percent. If Meg, Ben, and Brenda decide to undertake the LBO, what is the most they should offer per share?

| | 2015 | 2016 | 2017 | 2018 | 2019 |
|---|---|---|---|---|---|
| Sales | $2,749 | $3,083 | $3,322 | $3,400 | $3,539 |
| Costs | 731 | 959 | 1,009 | 1,091 | 1,149 |
| Depreciation | 485 | 516 | 537 | 564 | 575 |
| Earnings before taxes | $1,533 | $1,608 | $1,776 | $1,745 | $1,815 |
| Capital expenditures | $ 279 | $ 242 | $ 304 | $ 308 | $ 304 |
| Change in net working capital | $ (122) | $ (186) | $ 101 | $ 95 | $ 108 |
| Asset sales | $1,419 | $1,028 | | | |

APPENDIX **18A**

## The Adjusted Present Value Approach to Valuing Leveraged Buyouts

To access Appendix 18A, go to Connect.

# 19

# Dividends and Other Payouts

EXECUTIVE SUMMARY

In recent years, Canadian corporations have paid out about 33 percent of their net income as cash dividends. However, a significant number of firms pay no cash dividends, while some pay dividends in excess of their net income. Corporations view the dividend decision as quite important, because it determines what funds flow to investors and what funds are retained by the firm for reinvestment. Dividend policy can also provide information to the shareholder concerning firm performance. For instance, on May 2, 2012, in light of a profitable first quarter, Barrick Gold increased its dividend by 33 percent to US$0.20 per share.[1]

However, dividends cannot be viewed in isolation. Companies currently devote about 40 percent of net income to share repurchases as well, a percentage much higher than that of only a few decades ago. Thus, dividends and repurchases must be seen as alternative payouts competing for corporate cash flows.

This chapter examines corporate policy concerning dividends and other payouts. The first four sections of the chapter deal with two issues. We discuss the practical aspects of both dividends and share repurchases. We also establish the irrelevance of any payout policy in a world of perfect capital markets. We then move on to a world of personal taxes in Section 19.5, where the advantage of repurchases over dividends is presented. This advantage is perhaps the reason for the rapid growth in repurchases in recent years. However, dividends have hardly vanished, leading us to a search for the benefits of a high-dividend policy in Section 19.6.

## 19.1 DIFFERENT TYPES OF DIVIDENDS

The term *dividend* usually refers to cash distributions of earnings. If a distribution is made from sources other than current or accumulated retained earnings, the term *distribution* rather than *dividend* is used. However, it is acceptable to refer to a distribution from earnings as a *dividend* and refer to a distribution from capital as a *liquidating dividend*. More generally, any direct payment by the corporation to the shareholders may be considered part of dividend policy.

The most common type of dividend is in the form of cash. Public companies usually pay **regular cash dividends** four times a year. Sometimes firms pay a regular cash dividend and an *extra cash dividend*. Paying a cash dividend reduces corporate cash and retained earnings shown on the balance sheet—except in the case of a liquidating dividend (where the common shares account may be reduced).[2]

Another type of dividend, paid out in shares of stock, is referred to as a *stock dividend*. It is not a true dividend, because no cash leaves the firm. Rather, a stock dividend increases the number of shares outstanding, thereby reducing the value of each share.

---

[1] "Barrick Gold Announces 33% Dividend Increase," Barrick Gold Corporation Press Release (May 2012).

[2] In Chapter 21 we discuss various bond covenants that may restrict the amount and type of dividends the company can pay.

A stock dividend is commonly expressed as a ratio; for example, with a 2 percent stock dividend, a shareholder receives one new share for every 50 currently owned.

When a firm declares a *stock split*, it increases the number of shares outstanding. For example, in a two-for-one split, each shareholder receives one additional share of stock for each share held originally, so a two-for-one stock split is equivalent to a 100 percent stock dividend.

After a stock split, each share is entitled to a smaller percentage of the firm's cash flow, so the stock price should fall. For example, if the managers of a firm whose stock is selling at $50 declare a two-for-one stock split, the price of a share of stock should fall to about $25. A stock split strongly resembles a stock dividend except it is usually much larger. We talk more about stock dividends and stock splits in Section 19.10.

# 19.2 STANDARD METHOD OF CASH DIVIDEND PAYMENT

The decision of whether to pay a dividend rests in the hands of the board of directors of the corporation. A dividend is distributable to shareholders of record on a specific date. When a dividend has been declared, it becomes a liability of the firm and cannot be easily rescinded by the corporation. The amount of the dividend is expressed as dollars per share (*dividend per share*), as a percentage of the market price (*dividend yield*), or as a percentage of earnings per share (EPS; *dividend payout*).

The mechanics of a dividend payment can be illustrated by the example in Figure 19.1 and the following chronology.

**FIGURE 19.1**

**Example of Procedure for Dividend Payment**

| Thursday, January 15 | Wednesday, January 28 | Friday, January 30 | Monday, February 16 | Date |
|---|---|---|---|---|
| **Declaration date** | **Ex-dividend date** | **Record date** | **Payment date** | |

1. *Declaration date.* The board of directors declares a payment of dividends.

2. *Record date.* The declared dividends are distributable to shareholders of record on a specific date.

3. *Ex-dividend date.* A share of stock becomes ex-dividend on the date the seller is entitled to keep the dividend; under TSX rules, shares are traded ex-dividend on and after the second business day before the record date.

4. *Payment date.* The dividend payments are made to shareholders of record.

1. **Declaration date:** On January 15 (the declaration date), the board of directors passes a resolution to pay a dividend of $1 per share on February 16 to all holders of record on January 30.

2. **Date of record:** The corporation prepares a list on January 30 of all individuals believed to be shareholders as of this date. The word *believed* is important here, because the dividend will not be paid to those individuals whose notification of purchase is received by the company after January 30.

3. **Ex-dividend date:** The procedure on the date of record would be unfair if efficient investment dealers could notify the corporation by January 30 of a trade occurring on January 29, whereas the same trade might not reach the corporation until February 2 if executed by a less efficient dealer. To eliminate this problem, all investment dealers entitle shareholders to receive the dividend if they purchased the stock three business days before the date of record. The second day

before the date of record (Wednesday, January 28, in our example) is called the *ex-dividend date*. Before this date the stock is said to trade *cum dividend* (Latin for "with dividend").[3]

4. **Date of payment:** The dividend payments are made to the shareholders on February 16.

Obviously, the ex-dividend date is important, because an individual purchasing the security before the ex-dividend date will receive the current dividend, whereas another individual purchasing the security on or after this date will not receive the dividend. The stock price should fall on the ex-dividend date.[4] It is worthwhile to note that this drop is an indication of efficiency, not inefficiency, because the market rationally attaches value to a cash dividend. In a world with neither taxes nor transaction costs, the stock price is expected to fall by the amount of the dividend:

$$\text{Before ex-dividend date:} \quad \text{Price} = \$(P + 1)$$
$$\text{On or after ex-dividend date:} \quad \text{Price} = \$P$$

This is illustrated in Figure 19.2.

**FIGURE 19.2**

**Price Behaviour around the Ex-dividend Date for a $1 Cash Dividend**

The stock price will fall by the amount of the dividend on the ex-date (time 0). If the dividend is $1 per share, the price will be equal to $P$ on the ex-date.

$$\text{Before ex-date } (-1) \quad \text{Price} = \$(P + 1)$$
$$\text{Ex-date } (0) \quad \text{Price} = \$P$$

The amount of the price drop is a matter for empirical investigation. Elton and Gruber have argued that due to personal taxes, the stock price should drop by less than the dividend.[5] For example, consider the case with no capital gains taxes. On the day before a stock goes ex-dividend, shareholders must decide either to buy immediately and pay tax on the forthcoming dividend, or to buy tomorrow, thereby missing the dividend. If all investors are in a 30 percent bracket for dividends and the quarterly dividend is $1, the stock price should fall by $0.70 on the ex-dividend date. If the stock price falls by this amount on the ex-dividend date, then purchasers will receive the same return from either strategy.[6]

---

[3] The three-day period between the last *cum dividend* date and the record date is consistent with three-day settlement of stock purchases and sales ($T + 3$) in effect at the time of writing in 2014.

[4] The stock price typically falls within the first few minutes of the ex-dividend day.

[5] N. Elton and M. Gruber, "Marginal Stockholder Tax Rates and the Clientele Effect," *Review of Economics and Statistics* (February 1970).

[6] The situation is more complex when capital gains are considered. The individual pays capital gains taxes upon a subsequent sale. Because the price drops on the ex-dividend date, the original purchase price is higher if the purchase is made before the ex-dividend date, and the individual will reap, and pay taxes on, lower capital gains. Elton and Gruber show that the price drop is increased slightly when capital gains taxes are considered. L. D. Booth and D. J. Johnston, "The Ex-dividend Day Behavior of Canadian Stock Prices: Tax Changes and Clientele Effects," *Journal of Finance* (June 1984), find that personal taxes on dividends are the main factor in determining the price drop with a small adjustment for capital gains tax. We return to personal taxes later in the chapter.

To illustrate a price drop on the ex-dividend date, consider the example of common shares for Bank of Montreal (BMO.TO). The stock went ex-dividend on April 29, 2014, with a total special dividend of $0.76 per share. The following share price chart shows the price of BMO common stock on each of the five days prior to the ex-dividend date and on the ex-dividend date:

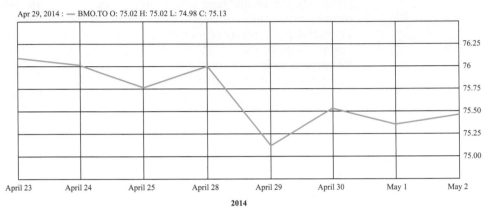

Apr 29, 2014 : — BMO.TO O: 75.02 H: 75.02 L: 74.98 C: 75.13

**2014**

The stock closed at $76.01 on April 28 and opened at $75.02 on April 29, a drop of $0.99.

Source: finance.yahoo.com/q?s=BMO.TO.

**CONCEPT QUESTIONS**

- Describe the procedure of a dividend payment.
- Why should the price of a stock change when it goes ex-dividend?

## 19.3    THE BENCHMARK CASE: AN ILLUSTRATION OF THE IRRELEVANCE OF DIVIDEND POLICY

A powerful argument can be made that dividend policy does not matter. This will be illustrated with the York Corporation, an all-equity firm in existence for 10 years. The financial managers know at the present time (date 0) that the firm will dissolve in one year (date 1). At date 0, the managers are able to forecast cash flows with perfect certainty. The managers know that the firm will receive a cash flow of $10,000 immediately and another $10,000 next year. They believe that York has no additional positive net present value (NPV) projects it can use to its advantage.[7]

### Current Policy: Dividends Set Equal to Cash Flow

At the present time, dividends (Div) at each date are set equal to the cash flow of $10,000. The NPV of the firm can be calculated by discounting these dividends. The firm's value can be expressed as

$$V_0 = \text{Div}_0 + \frac{\text{Div}_1}{1 + r_S}$$

where $\text{Div}_0$ and $\text{Div}_1$ are the cash flows paid out in dividends, and $r_S$ is the discount rate. The first dividend is not discounted because it will be paid immediately.

---

[7] York's investment in physical assets is fixed.

Assuming $r_S = 10\%$, the value of the firm can be calculated by

$$\$19{,}090.91 = \$10{,}000 + \frac{\$10{,}000}{1.1}$$

If 1,000 shares are outstanding, the value of each share is

$$\$19.09 = \$10 + \frac{\$10}{1.1} \tag{19.1}$$

To simplify the example, we assume that the ex-dividend date is the same as the date of payment. After the imminent dividend is paid, the stock price will immediately fall to \$9.09 (or \$19.09 − \$10). Several of York's board members have expressed dissatisfaction with the current dividend policy and have asked you to analyze an alternative policy.

## Alternative Policy: Initial Dividend Is Greater Than Cash Flow

Another policy is for the firm to pay a dividend of \$11 per share immediately, which is, of course, a total dividend of \$11,000. Because the cash runoff is only \$10,000, the extra \$1,000 must be raised in one of a few ways. Perhaps the simplest is to issue \$1,000 of bonds or stock now (at date 0). Assume that stock is issued and the new shareholders will desire enough cash flow at date 1 to let them earn the required 10 percent return on their date 0 investment.[8] The new shareholders will demand \$1,100 of the date 1 cash flow, leaving only \$8,900 to the old shareholders.[9] The dividends to the old shareholders will be as follows:

|                                            | Date 0   | Date 1  |
|--------------------------------------------|----------|---------|
| Aggregate dividends to old shareholders    | \$11,000 | \$8,900 |
| Dividends per share                        | 11.00    | 8.90    |

The present value (PV) of the dividends per share is therefore

$$\$19.09 = \$11 + \frac{\$8.90}{1.1} \tag{19.2}$$

Students often find it instructive to determine the price at which the new stock is issued. Because the new shareholders are not entitled to the immediate dividend, they would pay \$8.09 (or \$8.90/1.1) per share. Thus, 123.61 (or \$1,000/\$8.09) new shares are issued.

## The Indifference Proposition

Note that the NPVs of equations (19.1) and (19.2) are equal. This leads to the initially surprising conclusion that the change in dividend policy did not affect the value of a share of stock. However, upon reflection, the result seems quite sensible. The new shareholders are parting with their money at date 0 and receiving it back with the appropriate return at date 1. In other words, they are taking on a zero-NPV investment. As illustrated in Figure 19.3, old shareholders are receiving additional funds at date 0 but must pay the new shareholders their money with the appropriate return at date 1. Because the old shareholders must pay back principal plus the appropriate return, the act of issuing new stock at date 0 will neither increase nor decrease the value of the old shareholders' holdings. That is, they are giving up a zero-NPV investment to the new shareholders. An increase in dividends at date 0 leads to the necessary reduction of dividends at date 1, so the value of the old shareholders' holdings remains unchanged.

---

[8] The same results would occur after an issue of bonds, though the argument would be less easily resolved.

[9] Because the new shareholders buy at date 0, their first (and only) dividend is at date 1.

FIGURE 19.3

**Current and Alternative Dividend Policies**

**Current dividend policy:**
Old shareholders receive $10,000
at both date 0 and date 1.

**Alternative policy:**
Old shareholders receive
additional $1,000 at date 0
but receive $1,100 less at date 1.

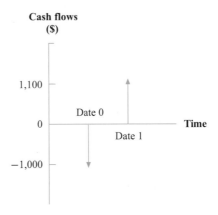

**Alternative policy:**
New shareholders pay in $1,000
at date 0 and receive $1,100 in
dividends at date 1.

This illustration is based on the pioneering work of Miller and Modigliani.[10] Although our presentation is in the form of a numerical example, the Miller and Modigliani paper proves that investors are indifferent to dividend policy in the general algebraic case. Miller and Modigliani make the following assumptions:

1. There are neither taxes nor brokerage fees, and no single participant can affect the market price of the security through his or her trades. Economists say that perfect markets exist when these conditions are met.

2. All individuals have the same beliefs concerning future investments, profits, and dividends. As mentioned in Chapter 11, these individuals are said to have *homogeneous expectations.*

3. The investment policy of the firm is set ahead of time and is not altered by changes in dividend policy.

---

[10] M. H. Miller and F. Modigliani, "Dividend Policy, Growth and the Valuation of Shares," *Journal of Business* (October 1961). Yes, this is the same Miller and Modigliani who gave us a capital structure theory.

## Homemade Dividends

To illustrate the indifference investors have toward dividend policy in our example, we used NPV equations. An alternative, and perhaps more intuitively appealing, explanation avoids the mathematics of discounted cash flows (DCFs).

Suppose individual investor $X$ prefers dividends per share of $10 at both dates 0 and 1. Would she be disappointed when informed that the firm's management is adopting the alternative dividend policy (dividends of $11 and $8.90 on the two dates, respectively)? Not necessarily, because she could easily reinvest the $1 of unneeded funds received on date 0, yielding an incremental return of $1.10 at date 1. Thus, she would receive her desired net cash flow of $11 − $1 = $10 at date 0 and $8.90 + $1.10 = $10 at date 1.

Conversely, imagine investor $Z$, who prefers $11 of cash flow at date 0 and $8.90 of cash flow at date 1, and who finds that management will pay dividends of $10 at both dates 0 and 1. He can sell off shares of stock at date 0 to receive the desired amount of cash flow. That is, if at date 0 he sells off shares (or fractions of shares) totalling $1, his cash flow at date 0 becomes $10 + $1 = $11. Because a sale of $1 of stock at date 0 will reduce his dividends by $1.10 at date 1, his net cash flow at date 1 will be $10 − $1.10 = $8.90.

The example illustrates how investors can make **homemade dividends**. In this instance, corporate dividend policy is being undone by a potentially dissatisfied shareholder. This homemade dividend is illustrated in Figure 19.4. Here the firm's cash flows of $10 at both date 0 and date 1 are represented by point $A$. This point also represents the initial dividend payout. Alternatively, as we just saw, the firm could pay out $11 at date 0 and $8.90 at date 1, a strategy represented by point $B$. Similarly, by either issuing new stock or buying back old stock, the managers of the firm could achieve a dividend payout represented by any point on the diagonal line.

---

**FIGURE 19.4**

**Homemade Dividends: A Trade-off between Dividends at Date 0 and Dividends at Date 1**

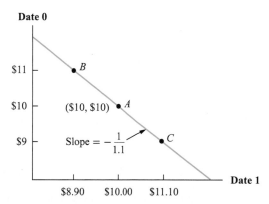

This graph illustrates both (1) how managers can vary dividend policy and (2) how individuals can undo the firm's dividend policy.

*Managers varying dividend policy.* A firm paying out all cash flows immediately is at point $A$ on the graph. The firm could achieve point $B$ by issuing stock to pay extra dividends or achieve point $C$ by buying back old stock with some of its cash.

*Individuals undoing the firm's dividend policy.* Suppose the firm adopts the dividend policy represented by point $B$: dividends of $11 at date 0 and $8.90 at date 1. An investor can reinvest $1 of the dividends at 10 percent, which will place her at point $A$. Suppose, alternatively, the firm adopts the dividend policy represented by point $A$. An individual can sell off $1 of stock at date 0, placing him at point $B$. No matter what dividend policy the firm establishes, a shareholder can undo it.

The same diagonal line also represents the choices available to the shareholder. For example, if the shareholder receives a dividend distribution of ($11, $8.90), he or she can either reinvest some of the dividends to move down and to the right on the graph or sell off shares of stock and move up and to the left.

Many corporations actually assist their shareholders in creating homemade dividend policies by offering *automatic dividend reinvestment plans* (ADPs or DRIPs). As the name suggests, with such a plan, shareholders have the option of automatically reinvesting some or all of their cash dividend in shares of stock.

Under a new-issue dividend reinvestment plan, investors buy new stock issued by the firm and receive a small discount—usually under 5 percent. This makes dividend reinvestment very attractive to investors who do not need cash flow from dividends. Since the 5 percent discount compares favourably with issue costs for new stock (which will be discussed in Chapter 20), dividend reinvestment plans are popular with large companies that periodically seek new common stock.[11]

Investment dealers also use financial engineering to create homemade dividends (or homemade capital gains). **Stripped common shares** entitle holders to receive either all the dividends from one or a group of well-known companies or an instalment receipt that packages any capital gain in the form of a call option. The call option gives the investor the right to buy the underlying shares at a fixed price and so is valuable if the shares appreciate beyond that price.

The implications of Figure 19.4 can be summarized in two sentences:

1. By varying dividend policy, the managers can achieve any payout along the diagonal line in Figure 19.4.
2. Either by reinvesting excess dividends at date 0 or by selling off shares of stock at this date, any individual investor can achieve any net cash payout along the diagonal line.

Thus, because both the corporation and the individual investor can move only along the diagonal line, dividend policy in this model is irrelevant. The changes the managers make in dividend policy can be undone by an individual, who, by either reinvesting dividends or selling off stock, can move to any desired point on the diagonal line.

### A Test

You can test your understanding by examining these true statements:
- Dividends are relevant.
- Dividend policy is irrelevant.

The first statement follows from common sense. Clearly, investors prefer higher dividends to lower dividends at any single date if the dividend level is held constant at every other date. In other words, if the dividend per share at a given date is raised while the dividend per share for each other date is held constant, the stock price will rise. This act can be accomplished by management decisions that improve productivity, increase tax savings, or strengthen product marketing.

The second statement makes sense once we realize that dividend policy cannot raise the dividend per share at one date while holding the dividend level per share constant at all other dates. Rather, dividend policy merely establishes the trade-off between dividends at one date and dividends at another date. As we saw in Figure 19.4, an increase in date 0 dividends can be accomplished only by a decrease in date 1 dividends. The extent of the decrease is such that the PV of all dividends is not affected.

---

[11] Reinvested dividends are still taxable.

Thus, in this simple world, dividend policy does not matter. That is, managers choosing to raise or to lower the current dividend do not affect the current values of their firms. This theory is a powerful one, and the work of Miller and Modigliani is considered a classic in modern finance. With relatively few assumptions, a rather surprising result is shown to be perfectly true.[12] Because we want to examine many real-world factors ignored by Miller and Modigliani, their work is only a starting point in this chapter's discussion of dividends. The next part of the chapter investigates these real-world considerations.

## Dividends and Investment Policy

The argument above shows that an increase in dividends through issuing new shares neither helps nor hurts the shareholders. Similarly, a reduction in dividends through share repurchase neither helps nor hurts shareholders.

What about reducing capital expenditures to increase dividends? Earlier chapters showed that a firm should accept all positive NPV projects. To do otherwise would reduce the value of the firm. Thus, we have an important point:

> Firms should never give up a positive NPV project to increase a dividend (or to pay a dividend for the first time).

This idea was implicitly considered by Miller and Modigliani. As we pointed out, one of the assumptions underlying their dividend-irrelevance proposition was, "The investment policy of the firm is set ahead of time and is not altered by changes in dividend policy."

**CONCEPT**
**QUESTIONS**
- How can an investor make homemade dividends?
- Are dividends irrelevant?
- What assumptions are needed to show that dividend policy is irrelevant?

# 19.4   REPURCHASE OF STOCK

Instead of paying dividends, a firm may use cash to repurchase shares of its own stock. Share repurchases have taken on increased importance in recent years. Over recent years, share repurchases have grown in importance relative to dividends. Figure 19.5 shows that the percentage of Canadian TSX-listed firms paying dividends declined from 80 percent in 1987 to around 30 percent in 2008. Over the same period, the percentage of share repurchasers grew from 12 percent to 25 percent.[13] Following the market crash of 2008 and early 2009, the number of Canadian companies repurchasing shares increased. For example, in February 2012, Tim Hortons announced a program to repurchase $200 million in shares.

---

[12] One of the real contributions of Miller and Modigliani has been to shift the burden of proof. Before Miller and Modigliani, firm value was believed to be influenced by its dividend policy. After Miller and Modigliani, it became clear that establishing a correct dividend policy was not obvious at all.

[13] Chris Mitchell, "Essays on Capital Gains, Household Consumption and Corporate Payout Policy," Electronic Thesis and Dissertation Repository, Paper 687, ir.lib.uwo.ca/etd/687, page 51.

**FIGURE 19.5**

**Dividends and Share Repurchases of Canadian firms: 1987–2008**

Source: Figure 5 of "Essays on Capital Gains, Household Consumption and Corporate Payout Policy," Electronic Thesis and Dissertation Repository, Paper 687, ir.lib.uwo.ca/etd/687, page 51. Repurchase data covering the years 1987–2000 provided by William J. McNally and Brian F. Smith. "Long-Run Returns Following Open Market Share Repurchases," *Journal of Banking and Finance* (March 2007).

Share repurchases are typically accomplished in one of three ways. First, companies may simply purchase their own stock, just as anyone would buy shares of a particular stock. In these *open-market purchases*, the firm does not reveal itself as the buyer. Thus, the seller does not know whether the shares were sold back to the firm or to another investor.

Second, the firm could institute a *tender offer*. Here, the firm announces to all of its shareholders that it is willing to buy a fixed number of shares at a specific price. For example, suppose Arts and Crafts Inc. (A&C) has 1 million shares outstanding, with a price of $50 per share. The firm makes a tender offer to buy back 300,000 shares at $60 per share. A&C chooses a price above $50 to induce shareholders to sell, that is, tender, their shares. In fact, if the tender price is set high enough, shareholders may very well want to sell more than the 300,000 shares. In the extreme case where all outstanding shares are tendered, A&C will buy back 3 out of every 10 shares that a shareholder has. On the other hand, if shareholders do not tender enough shares, the offer can be cancelled. A method related to a tender offer is the *Dutch auction*. Here the firm does not set a fixed price for the shares to be sold. Instead, the firm conducts an auction in which it bids for shares. The firm announces the number of shares it is willing to buy back at various prices, and shareholders indicate how many shares they are willing to sell at the various prices. The firm will then pay the lowest price that will achieve its goal.

Finally, in the United States, firms may repurchase shares from specific individual stockholders, a procedure called a **targeted repurchase**. Companies engage in targeted repurchases for a variety of reasons. In some rare cases, a single large stockholder can be bought out at a price lower than that in a tender offer. The legal fees in a targeted repurchase may also be lower than those in a more typical buyback. In addition, the shares of large stockholders are often repurchased to avoid a takeover unfavourable to management. Securities laws in Canada prohibit targeted repurchases. We now consider an example of a repurchase presented in the theoretical world of a perfect capital market. We next discuss the real-world factors involved in the repurchase decision.

## Dividend versus Repurchase: Conceptual Example

Imagine that Telephonic Industries has excess cash of $300,000 (or $3 per share) and is considering an immediate payment of this amount as an extra dividend. The firm forecasts that after the dividend, earnings will be $450,000 per year, or $4.50 for each of the 100,000 shares outstanding. Because the price–earnings (P/E) ratio is 6 for comparable companies, the shares of the firm should sell for $27 after the dividend is paid. These figures are presented in the top half of Table 19.1. Since the dividend is $3 per share, the stock would have sold for $30 a share *before* payment of the dividend.

**TABLE 19.1**

**Dividend versus Repurchase Example for Telephonic Industries**

|  | For entire firm | Per share |
|---|---|---|
| Extra dividend |  | (100,000 shares outstanding) |
| Proposed dividend | $  300,000 | $ 3.00 |
| Forecast annual earnings after dividend | 450,000 | 4.50 |
| Market value of stock after dividend | 2,700,000 | 27.00 |
| Repurchase |  | (90,000 shares outstanding) |
| Forecast annual earnings after repurchase | $  450,000 | $ 5.00 |
| Market value of stock after repurchase | 2,700,000 | 30.00 |

Alternatively, the firm could use the excess cash to repurchase some of its own stock. Imagine that a tender offer of $30 a share is made. Here, 10,000 shares are repurchased so that the total number of shares remaining is 90,000. With fewer shares outstanding, the EPS will rise to $5. The P/E ratio remains at 6, since both the business and financial risks of the firm are the same in the repurchase case as they were for the dividend case.[14] Thus, the price of a share after the repurchase is $30. These results are presented in the bottom half of Table 19.1.

If commissions, taxes, and other imperfections are ignored in our example, the shareholders are indifferent between a dividend and a repurchase. With dividends, each shareholder owns a share worth $27 and receives $3 in dividends, so that the total value is $30. This figure is the same as both the amount received by the selling shareholders and the value of the stock for the remaining shareholders in the repurchase case.

This example illustrates the important point that in a perfect market, the firm is indifferent between a dividend payment and a share repurchase. This result is quite similar to the indifference propositions established by Miller and Modigliani for debt versus equity financing and for dividends versus capital gains.

You may often read in the popular financial press that a repurchase agreement is beneficial because EPS increases. EPS does rise for Telephonic Industries if a repurchase is substituted for a cash dividend: the EPS is $4.50 after a dividend and $5 after the repurchase. This result holds because the drop in shares after a repurchase implies a reduction in the denominator of the EPS ratio.

However, the financial press frequently places undue emphasis on EPS figures in a repurchase agreement. Given the irrelevance propositions we have discussed, an increase in EPS need not be beneficial. When a repurchase is financed by excess cash, we showed that in a perfect capital market, the total value to the shareholder is the same under the dividend payment strategy as under the repurchase strategy.

---

[14] Chapter 6 discusses use of the P/E ratio to value stocks.

## Dividends versus Repurchases: Real-World Considerations

Why do some firms choose repurchases over dividends? Here are perhaps five of the most common reasons.

1. *Flexibility.* It is well known that firms view dividends as a commitment to their shareholders and are quite hesitant to reduce an existing dividend. Repurchases do not represent a similar commitment. Thus, a firm with a permanent increase in cash flow is likely to increase its dividend. Conversely, a firm whose cash flow increase is only temporary is likely to repurchase shares of stock.[15]

2. *Executive compensation.* Executives are frequently given stock options as part of their overall compensation. Let's revisit the Telephonic Industries example of Table 19.1, where the firm's stock was selling at $30 when the firm was considering either a dividend or a repurchase. Further imagine that Telephonic had granted 1,000 stock options to its CEO, Randee Taylor, two years before the decision was made. At that time the stock price was, say, only $20. This means that Randee can buy 1,000 shares for $20 a share at any time between the grant of the options and their expiration, a procedure called *exercising* the options.[16] Her gain from exercising is directly proportional to the rise in the stock price above $20. As we saw in the example, the price of the stock would fall to $27 following a dividend but would remain at $30 following a repurchase. The CEO would clearly prefer a repurchase to a dividend because the difference between the stock price and the exercise price of $20 would be $10 ($30 − $20) following the repurchase but only $7 ($27 − $20) following the dividend. Existing stock options will always have greater value when the firm repurchases shares instead of paying a dividend,[17] since the stock price will be greater after a repurchase than after a dividend. De Jong, Van Dijk, and Veld surveyed the 500 largest non-financial corporations in Canada on their share repurchase and dividend policies. They found that firms offering significant executive stock options tend to prefer repurchasing shares over paying dividends.[18]

3. *Offset to dilution.* In addition, the exercise of stock options increases the number of shares outstanding. In other words, exercise causes dilution of the stock. Firms frequently buy back shares of stock to offset this dilution. However, it is hard to argue that this is a valid reason for repurchase. As we showed in Table 19.1, repurchase is neither better nor worse for the shareholders than a dividend. Our argument holds whether or not stock options have been exercised previously.[19]

4. *Repurchase as investment.* Many companies buy back stock because they believe that a repurchase is their best investment. This occurs more frequently when managers believe that the stock price is temporarily depressed. Here, it is likely thought that (1) investment opportunities in non-financial assets are few, and (2) the firm's own stock price should rise with the passage of time.

---

[15] See Murali Jagannathan, Clifford P. Stephens, and Michael Weisbach, "Financial Flexibility and the Choice between Dividends and Stock Repurchases," *Journal of Financial Economics* (September 2000); and Wayne Guay and Jarrod Harford, "The Cash-Flow Permanence of Dividend Increases versus Repurchases," *Journal of Financial Economics* (September 2000), for both an explanation of and empirical support for flexibility.

[16] The exercise price of an executive stock option is generally set equal to the market price at the time of the grant.

[17] See George W. Fenn and Nellie Liang, "Corporate Payout Policy and Managerial Stock Incentives," *Journal of Financial Economics* (April 2001).

[18] Abe De Jong, Ronald Van Dijk, and Chris Veld, "The Dividend and Share Repurchase Policies of Canadian Firms: Empirical Evidence Based on a New Research Design," *International Review of Financial Analysis* 12 (4) (2003).

[19] See Kathleen Kahle, "When a Buyback Isn't a Buyback: Open Market Repurchases and Employee Options," *Journal of Financial Economics* (February 2002).

The fact that some companies repurchase their stock when they believe it is undervalued does not imply that the management of the company must be correct; only empirical studies can make this determination. The immediate stock market reaction to the announcement of a stock repurchase is usually quite favourable. In addition, some empirical work has shown that the long-term stock price performance of securities after a buyback is better than the stock price performance of comparable companies that do not repurchase.[20]

5. *Taxes.* Since taxes for both dividends and share repurchases are treated in depth in the next section, suffice it to say at this point that repurchases provide a tax advantage over dividends.

**CONCEPT QUESTIONS**

- In a perfect capital market, are repurchases preferred to dividends?
- What are five reasons for preferring repurchases to dividends in the real world?

## 19.5   PERSONAL TAXES, ISSUANCE COSTS, AND DIVIDENDS

The model we used to determine the level of dividends assumed that there were no taxes, no transaction costs, and no uncertainty. It concluded that dividend policy is irrelevant. Although this model helps us to grasp some fundamentals of dividend policy, it ignores many factors that exist in reality. We begin our investigation of these real-world considerations with the effect of taxes on the level of a firm's dividends.

In Canada, both dividends and capital gains are taxed at effective rates *less than* the marginal tax rate. For dividends, we showed in Chapter 1 that individual investors face a lower tax rate due to the dividend tax credit. Capital gains in the hands of individuals are taxed at 50 percent of the marginal tax rate. Since taxation takes place only when capital gains are realized, capital gains are very lightly taxed in Canada. Thus, for individual shareholders, the *effective* tax rate on dividend income is higher than the tax rate on capital gains.[21]

To facilitate our discussion of dividend policy in the presence of personal taxes, we classify firms into two groups based on whether they have sufficient cash to pay a dividend.

### Firms without Sufficient Cash to Pay a Dividend

It is simplest to begin with a firm without cash owned by a single entrepreneur. If this firm should decide to pay a dividend of $100, it must raise capital. The firm might choose among a number of different stock and bond issues to pay the dividend. However, for simplicity, we assume that the entrepreneur contributes cash to the firm by issuing stock to himself. This transaction, diagrammed in the left-hand side of Figure 19.6, would clearly be a *wash* in a world of no taxes. Here $100 cash goes into the firm when stock is issued and is immediately paid out as a dividend. Thus, the entrepreneur neither benefits nor loses when the dividend is paid, a result consistent with Miller and Modigliani.

---

[20] For Canada, see David Ikenberry, Josef Lakonishok, and Theo Vermaelen, "Stock Repurchases in Canada: Performance and Strategic Trading," *Journal of Finance* (October 2000); and William McNally, Brian F. Smith, and Thomas Barnes, "The Short-Run Impact of Open Market Purchase Trades," Working Paper, Wilfrid Laurier University, 2004.

[21] L. D. Booth and D. J. Johnston, "The Ex-dividend Day Behavior of Canadian Stock Prices: Tax Changes and Clientele Effects," op. cit., found that dividends are taxed more heavily than capital gains for the marginal investor. Subsequent tax reforms have narrowed, but not eliminated, this difference.

FIGURE 19.6

**Firm Issues Stock to Pay a Dividend**

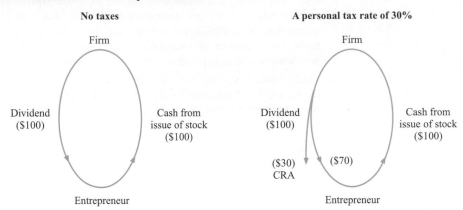

In the no-tax case, the entrepreneur receives the $100 in dividends that he gave to the firm when purchasing stock. The entire operation is called a wash; in other words, it has no economic effect. With taxes, the entrepreneur still receives $100 in dividends. However, he must pay $30 in taxes to CRA. The entrepreneur loses and CRA gains when a firm issues stock to pay a dividend.

Now assume that dividends are taxed at 30 percent. The firm still receives $100 on issuance of stock. However, the $100 dividend is not fully credited to the entrepreneur. Instead, the dividend payment is taxed, implying that the entrepreneur receives only $70 net after tax. Thus, the entrepreneur loses $30. Although our example is a bit simplistic, financial economists generally agree that in a world of personal taxes, one should not issue shares to pay a dividend.

The flotation costs of issuing shares add to this effect. Investment bankers must be paid when new capital is raised. Thus, the net receipts due to the firm from a new issue are less than 100 percent of total capital raised. These costs are examined in a later chapter. Because the size of new issues can be lowered by a reduction in dividends, we have another argument in favour of a low-dividend policy.

Of course, our advice not to finance dividends through new share issues might need to be modified somewhat in the real world. A company with a large and steady cash flow for many years in the past might be paying a regular dividend. If the cash flow unexpectedly dried up for a single year, should new stock be issued so that dividends could be continued? While our previous discussion would imply that new shares should not be issued, many managers might issue the stock anyway for practical reasons. In particular, shareholders might prefer stable dividends. Thus, managers might be forced to issue stock to achieve this stability, knowing full well the adverse tax consequences.

## Firms with Sufficient Cash to Pay a Dividend

The previous discussion argues that in a world with personal taxes, one should not issue stock to pay a dividend. Does the tax disadvantage of dividends imply the stronger policy, "Never pay dividends in a world with personal taxes"?

We argue that this prescription does not necessarily apply to firms with excess cash. To see this, imagine a firm with $1 million in extra cash after selecting all positive NPV projects and determining the level of prudent cash balances. The firm might consider the following alternatives to a dividend:

1. *Select additional capital budgeting projects.* Because the firm has already taken all the available positive NPV projects, it must invest its excess cash in negative NPV projects. This is clearly a policy at variance with the principles of corporate finance and represents an example of the agency costs of equity introduced in Chapter 17. Jensen

has suggested that many managers choose to take on negative NPV projects in lieu of dividends, doing their shareholders a disservice in the process.[22] In support of this view, Li and McNally document positive stock market reaction to Canadian share repurchases when they are seen as an alternative to negative NPV investments.[23]

2. *Acquire other companies.* To avoid paying dividends, a firm might use excess cash to acquire another company. This strategy has the advantage of acquiring profitable assets. However, a firm often incurs heavy costs when it embarks on an acquisition program. In addition, acquisitions are invariably made above the market price. Premiums of 20 to 80 percent are not uncommon. Because of this, a number of researchers have argued that mergers are not generally profitable to the acquiring company, even when firms are merged for a valid business purpose.[24] Therefore, a company making an acquisition merely to avoid a dividend is unlikely to benefit its shareholders.

3. *Purchase financial assets.* The strategy of purchasing financial assets in lieu of a dividend payment is illustrated in Example 19.1.

---

**EXAMPLE 19.1**

The Regional Electric Company has $1,000 of extra cash. It can retain the cash and invest it in Treasury bills yielding 8 percent, or it can pay the cash to shareholders as a dividend. Shareholders can also invest in Treasury bills with the same yield. Suppose, realistically, that the tax rate is 44 percent on ordinary income, such as interest on Treasury bills, for both the company and individual investors, and the individual tax rate *on dividends* is 30 percent. How much cash will investors have after five years under each policy?

If dividends are paid now, shareholders will receive $1,000 before taxes, or $1,000 × (1 − 0.30) = $700 after taxes. This is the amount they will invest. If the rate on T-bills is 8 percent before taxes, then the after-tax return is 8% × (1 − 0.44) = 4.48% per year. Thus, in five years, the shareholders will have

$$\$700 \times (1 + 0.0448)^5 = \$871.49$$

If Regional Electric Company retains the cash, invests in Treasury bills, and pays out the proceeds five years from now, then $1,000 will be invested today. However, since the corporate tax rate is 44 percent, the after-tax return from the T-bills will be 8% × (1 − 0.44) = 4.48% per year. In five years, the investment will be worth

$$\$1,000 \times (1 + 0.0448)^5 = \$1,244.99$$

If this amount is then paid out as a dividend, the shareholders will receive (after tax)

$$\$1,244.99 \times (1 - 0.30) = \$871.49$$

In this case, dividends will be the same after tax whether the firm pays them now or later after investing in Treasury bills. This is because the firm invests exactly as profitably as the shareholders on their own (on an after-tax basis).[25]

---

[22] M. C. Jensen, "Agency Costs of Free Cash Flows, Corporate Finance and Takeovers," *American Economic Review* (May 1986).

[23] Kai Li and William McNally, "The Information Content of Canadian Open Market Repurchase Announcements," *Managerial Finance* 33 (1) (2007).

[24] Richard Roll, "The Hubris Hypothesis of Corporate Turnovers," *Journal of Business* (April 1986), explores this idea in depth.

[25] Personal taxes have no impact on dividend policy in our example because the dividend tax credit reduces the personal tax rate on dividends. For a detailed discussion of this *tax integration* effect, see Robert Beam, Stanley Laiken, and James Barnett, *Introduction to Federal Income Taxation in Canada, 2014-2015*, 35th ed. (Toronto: Wolters Kluwer, 2014).

This example shows that for a firm with extra cash, the dividend payout decision will depend on personal and corporate tax rates. Assuming all other things are the same, when personal tax rates are higher than corporate tax rates, a firm has an incentive to reduce dividend payouts. This would have occurred if we changed our example to have the firm invest in preferred stock instead of T-bills. (Recall from Chapter 1 that corporations enjoy a 100 percent exclusion of dividends from taxable income.) However, if personal tax rates on dividends are lower than corporate tax rates (for investors in lower tax brackets or tax-exempt investors), a firm has an incentive to pay out any excess cash in dividends.

4. *Repurchase shares.* The example we described in the previous section showed that investors are indifferent between share repurchases and dividends in a world without taxes and transaction costs. However, under current tax law, shareholders generally prefer a repurchase to a dividend. A repurchase has a significant tax advantage over a cash dividend. A dividend is taxed, and a shareholder has no choice about whether or not to receive the dividend. In a repurchase, a shareholder pays taxes only if (1) the shareholder actually chooses to sell, and (2) the shareholder has a taxable capital gain on the sale.

### Summary of Personal Taxes

This section suggests that because of personal taxes, firms have an incentive to reduce dividends. For example, they might increase capital expenditures, acquire other companies, or purchase financial assets. However, due to financial considerations and legal constraints, rational firms with large cash flows will likely exhaust these activities with plenty of cash left over for dividends.

It is harder to explain why firms pay dividends instead of repurchasing shares. The tax savings from buybacks are significant. On the other hand, there may be other, more subtle benefits from dividends, and we consider these below.

**CONCEPT QUESTIONS**

- List four alternatives to paying a dividend with excess cash.
- Indicate a problem with each of these alternatives.

## 19.6    REAL-WORLD FACTORS FAVOURING A HIGH-DIVIDEND POLICY

In the previous section, we pointed out that taxes must be paid by the recipient of a dividend. Since the tax rate on dividends is above the *effective* tax rate on capital gains, financial managers will seek out ways to reduce dividends. While we discussed the problems with taking on more capital budgeting projects, acquiring other firms, and hoarding cash, we stated that share repurchase has many of the benefits of a dividend with less of a tax disadvantage. In this section, we consider reasons why a firm might pay its shareholders high dividends, even in the presence of personal taxes on these dividends.

### Desire for Current Income

It has been argued that many individuals desire current income. The classic example is the group of retired people and others living on a fixed income, proverbially known as "widows and orphans." The argument further states that these individuals would bid up the stock price should dividends rise and bid down the stock price should dividends fall.

Miller and Modigliani point out that this argument does not hold in their theoretical model. An individual preferring high current cash flow but holding low-dividend securities could easily sell off shares to provide the necessary funds. Thus, in a world of no transactions costs, a high current dividend policy would be of no value to the shareholder.

However, the current income argument does have relevance in the real world. The sale of stock involves brokerage fees and other transaction costs—direct cash expenses that could be avoided by an investment in high-dividend securities. In addition, the expenditure of one's time when selling securities might further lead many investors to buy high-dividend securities.

However, to put this argument in perspective, one should remember that financial intermediaries such as mutual funds can perform repackaging transactions at low costs. Such intermediaries could buy low-dividend stocks and, by a controlled policy of realizing gains, pay their investors at a higher rate.

## Behavioural Finance

Suppose it turned out that the transaction costs in selling no-dividend securities could not account for the preference of investors for dividends. Would there still be a reason for high dividends? We introduced the topic of behavioural finance in Chapter 14, pointing out that the ideas of behaviourists represent a strong challenge to the theory of efficient capital markets. It turns out that behavioural finance also has an argument for high dividends.

The basic idea here concerns *self-control*, a concept that, though quite important in psychology, has received virtually no emphasis in finance. While we cannot review all that psychology has to say about self-control, let's focus on one example—losing weight. Suppose Al Martin, a university student, just got back from the Christmas break more than a few pounds heavier than he would like. Everyone would probably agree that diet and exercise are the two ways to lose weight. But how should Al put this approach into practice? (We'll focus on exercise, though the same principle would apply to diet as well.) One way, let's call it the economists' way, involves trying to make rational decisions. Each day, Al balances the costs and the benefits of exercising. Perhaps he chooses to exercise on most days, since losing the weight is important to him. However, when he is too busy with exams, he might rationally choose not to exercise because he cannot afford the time. And, he wants to be socially active as well. So he may rationally choose to avoid exercise on days when parties and other social commitments become too time-consuming.

This seems sensible—at first glance. The problem is that he must make a choice every day and there may simply be too many days when his lack of self-control gets the better of him. He may tell himself that he doesn't have the time to exercise on a particular day, simply because he is starting to find exercise boring, not because he really doesn't have the time. Before long, he is avoiding exercise on most days—and overeating in reaction to the guilt from not exercising!

Is there an alternative? One way would be to set rigid rules. Perhaps Al decides to exercise five days a week—*no matter what*. While this is not necessarily the best approach for everyone, there is no question that many of us, perhaps most of us, live by a set of rules. For example, Shefrin and Statman suggest some typical rules:[26]

- —jog at least two miles a day;
- —do not consume more than 1200 calories per day;
- —bank the wife's salary and only spend from the husband's paycheck;
- —save at least 2 percent of every paycheque for children's university education and never withdraw from this fund;
- —never touch a drop.

---

[26] Hersh M. Shefrin and Meir Statman, "Explaining Investor Preference for Cash Dividends," *Journal of Financial Economics* (June 1984).

What does this have to do with dividends? Investors must also deal with self-control. Suppose a retiree wants to consume $20,000 a year from savings, in addition to the Canada Pension Plan and her pension. On one hand, she could buy stocks with a dividend yield high enough to generate $20,000 in dividends. On the other hand, she could place her savings in no-dividend stocks, selling off $20,000 each year for consumption. Though these two approaches seem equivalent financially, the second one may allow for too much leeway. If lack of self-control gets the better of her, she might sell off too much, leaving little for her later years. Better, perhaps, to short-circuit this possibility by investing in dividend-paying stocks, with a firm personal rule of *never* "dipping into principal." While behaviourists do not claim that this approach is for everyone, they argue that enough people think this way to explain why firms pay dividends, even though, as we said earlier, dividends are tax disadvantaged.

Does behavioural finance argue for increased stock repurchases as well as increased dividends? The answer is no, since investors will sell the stock that firms repurchase. As we said above, selling stock involves too much leeway. Investors might sell too many shares of stock, leaving little for the later years. Thus, the behaviourist argument may explain why companies pay dividends in a world with personal taxes.

## Agency Costs

Although shareholders, bondholders, and management form firms for mutually beneficial reasons, one party may later gain at the other's expense. For example, take the potential conflict between bondholders and shareholders. Bondholders would like shareholders to leave as much cash as possible in the firm so that this cash is available to pay the bondholders during times of financial distress. Conversely, shareholders would like to keep this extra cash for themselves. That's where dividends come in. Managers, acting on behalf of the shareholders, may pay dividends simply to keep the cash away from the bondholders. In other words, a dividend can be viewed as a wealth transfer from bondholders to shareholders. There is empirical evidence for this view of things. For example, DeAngelo and DeAngelo find that firms in financial distress are reluctant to cut dividends.[27] Of course, bondholders know of the propensity of shareholders to transfer money out of the firm. To protect themselves, bondholders frequently create protective covenants in loan agreements stating that dividends can be paid only if the firm has earnings, cash flow, and working capital above prespecified levels.

Although the managers may be looking out for the shareholders in any conflict with bondholders, the managers may pursue selfish goals at the expense of shareholders in other situations. For example, as discussed in Chapter 17, managers might pad expense accounts; take on pet projects with negative NPVs; or, more simply, not work very hard. Managers find it easier to pursue these selfish goals when the firm has plenty of free cash flow. After all, one cannot squander funds if the funds are not available in the first place. And that is where dividends come in. Several scholars have suggested that dividends can serve as a way for the board of directors to reduce agency costs.[28] By paying dividends equal to the amount of "surplus" cash flow, a firm can reduce management's ability to squander the firm's resources.[29]

---

[27] H. DeAngelo and L. DeAngelo, "Dividend Policy and Financial Distress: An Empirical Investigation of Troubled NYSE Firms," *Journal of Finance* (December 1990).

[28] Michael Rozeff, "How Companies Set Their Dividend Payout Ratios," in *The Revolution in Corporate Finance*, Joel M. Stern and Donald H. Chew, eds. (New York: Basil Blackwell, 1986). See also Robert S. Hansen, Raman Kumar, and Dilip K. Shome, "Dividend Policy and Corporate Monitoring: Evidence from the Regulated Electric Utility Industry," *Financial Management* (Spring 1994).

[29] Research shows that in many other countries where shareholders have weaker legal rights, the focal agency conflict is not between shareholders and managers but rather between controlling shareholders and other shareholders. In such countries, dividends are seen as a way of prying wealth loose from the hands of controlling shareholders: R. LaPorta, F. Lopez-de-Silanes, A. Schleifer, and R.W. Vishny, "Agency Problems and Dividend Policies around the World," *Journal of Finance* (February 2000).

While the above discussion suggests a reason for increased dividends, the same argument applies to share repurchases as well. Managers, acting on behalf of shareholders, can just as easily keep cash from bondholders through repurchases as through dividends. And the board of directors, also acting on behalf of shareholders, can reduce the cash available to spendthrift managers just as easily through repurchases as through dividends. Thus, the presence of agency costs is not an argument for dividends over repurchases. Rather, agency costs imply firms may well increase either dividends or share repurchases rather than hoard large amounts of cash.

## Information Content of Dividends and Dividend Signalling

**Information Content**  While there are many things researchers do not know about dividends, there is one thing that we know for sure: the stock price of a firm will generally rise when the firm announces an increase in the dividend and will generally fall when a dividend reduction is announced. For example, Asquith and Mullins estimate that stock prices rise following announcements of dividend initiations.[30] Stock prices rose when their sample of U.S. firms started or resumed dividends. Deshpande and Jog obtained the same result for a Canadian sample.[31] Healy and Palepu and Michaely, Thaler, and Womack find that stock prices fall about 7 percent following announcements of dividend omissions.[32]

The question is, how should one *interpret* this empirical evidence? Consider the following three positions on dividends:

1. From the homemade dividend argument of Miller and Modigliani, dividend policy is irrelevant, given that future earnings (and cash flows) are held constant.
2. Because of tax effects, a firm's stock price is negatively related to the current dividend when future earnings (or cash flows) are held constant.
3. Because of shareholders' desire for current income, a firm's stock price is positively related to its current dividend, even when future earnings (or cash flows) are held constant.

At first glance, the empirical evidence that stock prices rise when dividend increases are announced may seem consistent with position 3 and inconsistent with positions 1 and 2. In fact, many writers have argued this. However, other authors have countered that the observation itself is consistent with all three positions. They point out that companies do not like to cut a dividend. Thus, firms will raise the dividend only when future earnings, cash flow, and so on are expected to rise enough so that the dividend is not likely to be reduced later to its original level. A dividend increase is management's *signal* to the market that the firm is expected to do well.

---

[30] P. Asquith and D. Mullins, Jr., "The Impact of Initiating Dividend Payments on Shareholder Wealth," *Journal of Business* (January 1983).

[31] S. D. Deshpande and V. M. Jog, "The Information Content of Dividend Resumptions: The Canadian Evidence," *Proceedings of the Finance Division of the Administrative Sciences Association of Canada* 7 (1986), pp. 151–162. This topic has spawned a large volume of research. Selected examples are G. Charest, "Dividend Information, Stock Returns and Market Efficiency," *Journal of Financial Economics* (June–September 1978); G. Charest, "Returns to Dividend Changing Stocks on the Toronto Stock Exchange," *Journal of Business Administration* (Fall 1980); R. Pettit, "Dividend Announcements, Security Performance, and Capital Market Efficiency," *Journal of Finance* (December 1972); J. Ahroney and I. Swary, "Quarterly Dividend and Earnings Announcements and Stockholders' Returns: An Empirical Analysis," *Journal of Finance* (March 1980); C. Kwan, "Efficient Market Tests of the Informational Content of Dividends: Critique and Extensions," *Journal of Financial and Quantitative Analysis* (June 1981); and F. Adjaoud, "The Information Content of Dividends: A Canadian Test," *Canadian Journal of Administrative Sciences* (December 1984).

[32] P. M. Healy and K. G. Palepu, "Earnings Information Conveyed by Dividend Initiations and Omissions," *Journal of Financial Economics* (September 1988); and R. Michaely, R. H. Thaler, and K. Womack, "Price Reactions to Dividend Initiations and Omissions: Overreactions or Drift," *Journal of Finance* (June 1995).

It is the expectation of good times, and not only the shareholders' affinity for current income, that raises stock price. The rise in the stock price following the dividend signal is called the **information content effect** of the dividend. To recapitulate, imagine that the stock price is unaffected or even negatively affected by the level of dividends, given that future earnings (or cash flows) are held constant. Nevertheless, the information content effect implies that stock price may rise when dividends are raised—if dividends simultaneously cause shareholders to *increase* their expectations of future earnings and cash flows.

**Dividend Signalling**    We just argued that the market infers a rise in earnings and cash flows from a dividend increase, leading to a higher stock price. Conversely, the market infers a decrease in cash flows from a dividend reduction, leading to a fall in stock price. This raises an interesting corporate strategy: could management increase dividends just to make the market *think* that cash flows will be higher, even when management knows that cash flows will not rise?

While this strategy may seem dishonest, academics take the position that managers frequently attempt the strategy. Academics begin with the following accounting identity for an all-equity firm:[33]

$$\text{Cash flow} = \text{Capital expenditures} + \text{Dividends} \qquad (19.3)$$

Equation (19.3) must hold if a firm is neither issuing nor repurchasing stock. That is, the cash flow from the firm must go somewhere. If it is not paid out in dividends, it must be used in some expenditure. Whether the expenditure involves a capital budgeting project or a purchase of Treasury bills, it is still an expenditure.

Imagine that we are in the middle of the year and investors are trying to make some forecast of cash flow over the entire year. These investors may very well use equation (19.3) to estimate cash flow. For example, suppose that the firm announces current dividends will be $50 million and the market believes that capital expenditures are $80 million. The market would then determine cash flow to be $130 million ($50 million + $80 million).

Now, suppose that the firm had, alternatively, announced a dividend of $70 million. The market might assume that cash flow remains at $130 million, implying capital expenditures of $60 million ($130 million − $70 million). Here, the increase in dividends would hurt the stock price, since the market anticipates valuable capital expenditures will be crowded out. Alternatively, the market might assume that capital expenditures remain at $80 million, implying the estimate of cash flow to be $150 million ($70 million + $80 million). Stock price would likely rise here, since stock prices usually increase with cash flow. In general, academics believe that models where investors assume that capital expenditures remain the same are more realistic. Thus, an increase in dividends improves stock price.

Now we come to the incentives of managers to fool the public. Suppose you are a manager who wants to boost stock price, perhaps because you are planning to sell some of your personal holdings of the company's stock immediately. You might increase dividends so that the market would raise its estimate of cash flow, thereby also boosting the current stock price.

If this strategy is appealing, would anything prevent you from raising dividends without limit? The answer is yes, because there is also a *cost* to raising dividends. That is, the firm will have to forgo some of its profitable projects. Remember that cash flow in equation (19.3) is a constant, so that an increase in dividends is obtained only by a reduction in capital expenditures. At some point the market will learn that cash flow has not increased but, instead, profitable capital expenditures have been cut. Once

---

[33] The correct representation of equation (19.3) involves cash flow, not earnings. However, with little loss of understanding, we could discuss dividend signalling in terms of earnings, not cash flow.

the market absorbs this information, stock price should fall below what it would have been had dividends never been raised. Thus, if you plan to sell, say, half of your shares and retain the other half, an increase in dividends should help you on the immediate sale but hurt you when you sell your remaining shares years later. Thus, your decision on the level of dividends will be based, among other things, on the timing of your personal stock sales.

The above is a simplified example of dividend signalling, where the manager sets dividend policy based on maximum benefit for herself.[34] Alternatively, a given manager may have no desire to sell his shares immediately, but knows that at any one time, plenty of ordinary shareholders will want to do so. Thus, for the benefit of shareholders in general, a manager will always be aware of the trade-off between current and future stock price. And this, then, is the essence of signalling with dividends. It is not enough for a manager to set dividend policy in order to maximize the true (or intrinsic) value of the firm. She must also consider the effect of dividend policy on the current stock price, even if the current stock price does not reflect true value.

Does a motive to signal imply that managers will increase dividends rather than share repurchases? The answer is likely no, since most academic models imply that dividends and share repurchases are perfect substitutes.[35] Rather, these models indicate that managers will consider reducing capital spending (even projects with positive NPVs) to increase either dividends or share repurchases.

 *CONCEPT QUESTION*    • What are the real-world factors favouring a high-dividend policy?

## 19.7   THE CLIENTELE EFFECT: A RESOLUTION OF REAL-WORLD FACTORS?

In the previous sections, we pointed out that the existence of personal taxes favours a low-dividend policy, whereas other factors favour high dividends. The financial profession had hoped that it would be easy to determine which of these sets of factors dominates. Unfortunately, after years of research, no one has been able to conclude which of the two is more important. This is surprising, since one might be skeptical that the two sets of factors would cancel each other out so perfectly.

However, one particular idea, known as the *clientele effect*, implies that the two sets of factors are likely to cancel each other out after all. To understand this idea, let's separate those investors in high tax brackets from those in low tax brackets. Individuals in high tax brackets likely prefer either no or low dividends. Low tax bracket investors generally fall into three categories. First, there are individual investors in low brackets. They are likely to prefer some dividends if they desire current income. Second, pension funds pay no taxes on either dividends or capital gains. Because they face no tax consequences, pension funds will also prefer dividends if they prefer current income.

---

[34] Papers examining fully developed models of signalling include S. Bhattacharya, "Imperfect Information, Dividend Policy, and 'The Bird in the Hand' Fallacy," *Bell Journal of Economics* (Spring 1979); S. Bhattacharya, "Nondissipative Signaling Structure and Dividend Policy," *Quarterly Journal of Economics* (August 1980); S. Ross, "The Determination of Financial Structure: The Incentive Signalling Approach," *Bell Journal of Economics* (Spring 1977); M. Miller and K. Rock, "Dividend Policy under Asymmetric Information," *Journal of Finance* (September 1985).

[35] Signalling models where dividends and repurchases are not perfect substitutes are contained in Franklin Allen, Antonio Bernardo, and Ivo Welch, "A Theory of Dividends Based on Tax Clienteles," *Journal of Finance* (December 2000); and John Kose and Joseph Williams, "Dividends, Dilution and Taxes: A Signaling Equilibrium," *Journal of Finance* (September 1985).

Finally, for tax purposes, Canadian corporations can exclude 100 percent of their dividend income received from other Canadian corporations but cannot exclude any of their capital gains. Thus, corporations would prefer to invest in high-dividend stocks, even without a preference for current income.

Suppose that 40 percent of all investors prefer high dividends and 60 percent prefer low dividends, yet only 20 percent of firms pay high dividends while 80 percent pay low dividends. Here, the high-dividend firms will be in short supply; thus their stock should be bid up, while the stock of low-dividend firms should be bid down.

However, the dividend policies of all firms need not be fixed in the long run. In this example, we would expect enough low-dividend firms to increase their payout so that 40 percent of the firms pay high dividends and 60 percent of the firms pay low dividends. After this has occurred, no type of firm will be better off from changing its dividend policy. Once payouts of corporations conform to the desires of shareholders, no single firm can affect its market value by switching from one dividend strategy to another.

**Clienteles** are likely to form in the following way:

| Group | Stocks |
|---|---|
| Individuals in high tax brackets | Zero-to-low-payout stocks |
| Individuals in low tax brackets | Low-to-medium-payout stocks |
| Tax-free institutions | Medium-payout stocks |
| Corporations | High-payout stocks |

To see if you understand the clientele effect, consider the following question: "In spite of the theoretical argument that dividend policy is irrelevant or that firms should not pay dividends, many investors like high dividends. Because of this fact, a firm can boost its share price by having a higher dividend payout ratio." True or false?

The statement is likely to be false. As long as there are already enough high-dividend firms to satisfy dividend-loving investors, a firm will not be able to boost its share price by paying high dividends. A firm can boost its stock price only if an unsatisfied clientele exists. There is no evidence that this is the case.

Our discussion of clienteles followed from the fact that tax brackets vary across investors. If shareholders care about taxes, stocks should attract clienteles based on dividend yield. Is there any evidence that this is the case?

Consider Figure 19.7. Here, John Graham and Alok Kumar rank common stocks by their dividend yields (the ratio of dividend to stock price) and place them into five portfolios, called quintiles.[36] The bottom quintile contains the 20 percent of stocks with the lowest dividend yields, the next quintile contains the 20 percent of stocks with the next lowest dividend yields, and so on. The figure shows the weight of each quintile in the portfolios of low-, medium-, and high-income investors. As can be seen, relative to low-income investors, high-income investors put a greater percentage of their assets into low-dividend securities. Conversely, again relative to low-income investors, high-income investors put a smaller percentage of their assets into high-dividend securities.

**CONCEPT QUESTIONS**

- How does the market react to unexpected dividend changes? What does this tell us about dividends? About dividend policy?
- What is a dividend clientele?
- All things considered, would you expect a risky firm with significant but highly uncertain growth prospects to have a low or high dividend payout?

---

[36] John Graham and Alok Kumar, "Do Dividend Clienteles Exist? Evidence on Dividend Preferences of Retail Investors," *Journal of Finance* (June 2006).

**FIGURE 19.7**

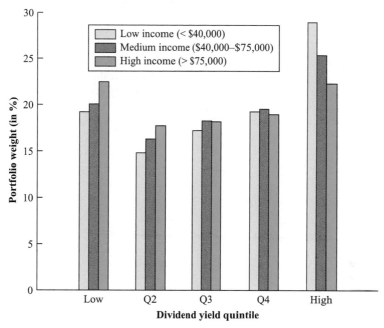

**Preferences of Investors for Dividend Yield**

All stocks are ranked on their dividend yields and placed into five quintile portfolios. The figure shows the weight of each quintile in the portfolios of low-, medium-, and high-income investors. Relative to those with lower income, high-income investors place a greater percentage of their assets in low-dividend stocks and a smaller percentage in high-dividend stocks.

Source: Adapted from Figure 2 of John Graham and Alok Kumar, "Do Dividend Clienteles Exist? Evidence on Dividend Preferences of Retail Investors," *Journal of Finance* (June 2006).

# IN THEIR OWN WORDS

## Why Amazon.com Inc. pays no dividend

Amazon.com Inc. is a U.S-based corporation that focuses on providing an online retail platform for four main customers: consumers, sellers, enterprises, and content creators. Their emphasis on selection, price and convenience has resulted in $20.3 billion in profits in 2013. The company's common shares are listed as AMZN on the NASDAQ. As quoted on their company website, Amazon.com Inc. has "never declared or paid cash dividends on our common stock. We intend to retain all future earnings to finance future growth and, therefore, do not anticipate paying any cash dividends in the foreseeable future." The practice of retaining earnings and not paying cash dividends is common among technology companies.

## Why Rogers Communications pays dividends

Rogers Communications Inc. is Canada's premier cable television provider and generates about $5.1 billion in revenue. The company's common stock is listed as RCI.A on the TSX. In 2003, Rogers Communications announced that it would begin paying a semi-annual dividend to shareholders for the first time in company history. On June 10, 2004, Rogers Communications paid shareholders a cash dividend of $0.10 a share. The company changed its dividend policy in response to its strong financial performance over an extended period of time. At the same time, it wanted to provide its shareholders with an additional opportunity for a return on their investment. Since 2004, Rogers has adopted a quarterly dividend. In 2014, its annual cash dividend was $1.83 per share.

## 19.8   WHAT WE KNOW AND DO NOT KNOW ABOUT DIVIDEND POLICY

### Corporate Dividends Are Substantial

We pointed out earlier in the chapter that shareholder income taxes and new issue flotation costs are two important practical considerations favouring low dividends. Nevertheless, dividends in the United States and Canada are substantial. For example, consider Figure 19.8, which shows the ratio of aggregate dividends to aggregate earnings for all U.S. firms from 1980 to 2010. The ratio was approximately 61 percent in 2010.

**FIGURE 19.8**

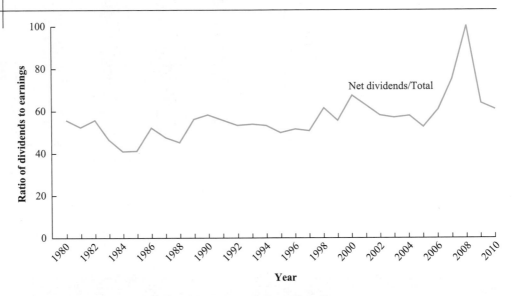

Source: *The Economic Report of the President*, February 2011, Table B-90.

### Fewer Companies Pay Dividends

Although dividends are substantial, Fama and French point out that the percentage of companies paying dividends had fallen over the last few decades of the twentieth century.[37] They argue that the decline was caused primarily by an explosion of small, currently unprofitable companies that had recently listed on various stock exchanges. For the most part, firms of this type do not pay dividends.

This research does not imply that dividends across *all* firms declined. DeAngelo, DeAngelo, and Skinner point out that while small firms have shied away from dividends, the largest firms have substantially increased their dividends over recent decades.[38] For example, this increase has created such concentration in dividends that the top 25 dividend-paying firms accounted for more than 50 percent of aggregate dividends in the United States in 2000. DeAngelo and colleagues conclude (p. 425), "Industrial firms exhibit a two-tier structure in which a small number of firms with very high earnings collectively generates the majority of earnings and dominates the

---

[37] E. F. Fama and K. R. French, "Disappearing Dividends: Changing Firm Characteristics or Lower Propensity to Pay?" *Journal of Financial Economics* (April 2001).

[38] Harry DeAngelo, Linda DeAngelo, and Douglas Skinner, "Are Dividends Disappearing? Dividend Concentration and the Consolidation of Earnings," *Journal of Financial Economics* (June 2004).

dividend supply, while the vast majority of firms has at best a modest collective impact on aggregate earnings and dividends."

Figure 19.5, discussed earlier, shows that the proportion of dividend payers among Canadian firms dropped substantially from 1987 to 2008. The figure also shows an increase starting in 2001. The original decline in dividends can partially be attributed to taxation changes that took place in 1986 and 1987. These changes made dividend income less favourable for investors. Over the 2001 through 2006 period, however, as an increasing number of firms became income trusts, the percentage of firms paying dividends began to increase.[39] In 2006, dividend taxation became more favourable when the government of Canada eliminated double taxation on dividends from large corporations.

## Corporations Smooth Dividends

In 1956, John Lintner made two important observations concerning dividend policy.[40] First, real-world companies typically set long-run target ratios of dividends to earnings. A firm is likely to set a low target ratio if it has many positive NPV projects relative to available cash flow and a high ratio if it has few positive NPV projects. Second, managers know that only part of any change in earnings is likely to be permanent. Because managers need time to assess the permanence of any earnings rise, dividend changes appear to lag earnings changes by a number of periods.

Taken together, Lintner's observations suggest that two parameters describe dividend policy: the target payout ratio ($t$) and the speed of adjustment of current dividends to the target ($s$). Dividend changes will tend to conform to the following model:

$$\text{Div}_1 - \text{Div}_0 = s \times (t\text{EPS}_1 - \text{Div}_0) \tag{19.4}$$

where $\text{Div}_1$ and $\text{Div}_0$ are dividends in the next year and dividends in the current year, respectively. $\text{EPS}_1$ is EPS in the next year.

The limiting cases occur when $s = 1$ and $s = 0$. If $s = 1$, the actual change in dividends will be equal to the target change in dividends. Here, the full adjustment occurs immediately. If $s = 0$, $\text{Div}_1 = \text{Div}_0$. In other words, there is no change in dividends at all. Real-world companies can be expected to set $s$ between 0 and 1.

---

**EXAMPLE 19.2**

Calculator Graphics Inc. (CGI) has a target payout ratio of 0.30. Last year's EPS was $10, and in accordance with the target, CGI paid dividends of $3 per share last year. However, earnings have jumped to $20 this year. Since the managers do not believe that this increase is permanent, they do *not* plan to raise dividends all the way to $6 (0.30 × $20). Rather, their speed of adjustment coefficient, *s*, is 0.5, implying that the *increase* in dividends from last year to this year will be

$$0.5 \times (\$6 - \$3) = \$1.50$$

That is, the increase in dividends is the product of the speed of adjustment coefficient, 0.50, and the difference between what dividends would be with full adjustment [$6 = (0.30 × $20)] and last year's dividends. Since dividends will increase by $1.50, dividends this year will be $4.50 (= $3 + $1.50).

Now, suppose that earnings stay at $20 next year. The increase in dividends next year will be

$$0.5 \times (\$6 - \$4.50) = \$0.75$$

---

[39] Darcey McVanel and Nikita Perevalov, "Financial Constraints and the Cash-Holding Behaviour of Canadian Firms," Discussion Paper 2008-16, Bank of Canada (October 2008).

[40] J. Lintner, "Distribution and Incomes of Corporations among Dividends, Retained Earnings, and Taxes," *American Economic Review* (May 1956).

In words, the increase in dividends from this year to next year will be the speed of adjustment coefficient (0.50) times the difference between what dividends would have been next year with full adjustment ($6) and this year's dividends ($4.50). Since dividends will increase by $0.75, dividends next year will be $5.25 ($4.50 + $0.75). In this way, dividends will slowly rise every year, if earnings in all future years remain at $20. However, dividends will reach $6 only at infinity.

An implication of Lintner's model is that the dividends-to-earnings ratio rises when a company begins a period of bad times, and the ratio falls when a company reaches a period of good times. Thus, dividends display less variability than do earnings. In other words, firms smooth dividends.

## The Pros and Cons of Paying Dividends

| Pros | Cons |
|---|---|
| 1. Cash dividends can underscore good results and provide support to stock price. | 1. Dividends are taxed more heavily than capital gains. |
| 2. Dividends may attract institutional investors that prefer some return in the form of dividends. A mix of institutional and individual investors may allow a firm to raise capital at lower cost because of the ability of the firm to reach a wider market. | 2. Dividends can reduce internal sources of financing. Dividends may force the firm to forgo positive NPV projects or to rely on costly external equity financing. |
| 3. Stock price usually increases with the announcement of a new or increased dividend, which signals optimism about future cash flow. | 3. Once established, dividend cuts are hard to make without adversely affecting a firm's stock price. |
| 4. Dividends absorb excess cash flow and may reduce agency costs that arise from conflicts between management and shareholders. In addition, managers, acting on behalf of shareholders, can pay dividends to keep cash from bondholders. | |
| 5. Behavioural finance argues that investors with limited self-control can meet current consumption needs with high-dividend stocks while adhering to the policy of never dipping into principal. | |

## Some Survey Evidence on Dividends

Baker, Dutta, and Saadi surveyed a large number of Canadian financial executives regarding dividend policy.[41] Table 19.2 shows the top five factors influencing dividend policy.

**TABLE 19.2**

### Factors Influencing Dividend Policy of Canadian Financial Firms

| Factor | Moderate or high level of importance (%) |
|---|---|
| 1. Stability of earnings | 95.7 |
| 2. Pattern of past dividends | 95.7 |
| 3. Level of current earnings | 87.0 |
| 4. Level of expected future earnings | 82.6 |
| 5. Concern about affecting the stock price | 47.8 |

Source: Adapted from Table 2 of H. K. Baker, S. Dutta, and S. Saadi, "Impact of Financial and Multinational Operations on Manager Perceptions of Dividends," *Global Finance Journal* 19 (2) (2008).

---

[41] H. K. Baker, S. Dutta, and S. Saadi, "Impact of Financial and Multinational Operations on Manager Perceptions of Dividends," *Global Finance Journal* 19 (2) (2008).

As shown in Table 19.2, financial managers are highly disinclined to cut dividends. Moreover, they are very conscious of their previous dividends and desire to maintain a relatively steady dividend. In contrast, concerns about dividends affecting the firm's stock price are somewhat less important.

Table 19.3 is drawn from the same survey, but here the responses address the top five reasons for Canadian financial firms paying dividends. Not surprisingly, given the responses in Table 19.2, the primary explanation for paying dividends was to maintain an uninterrupted record of dividend payments. The next several items are also consistent with our previous analysis. Financial managers are very concerned about earnings stability and future earnings levels in making dividend decisions. Survey respondents also believed that the firm should disclose to investors its reasons for changing the cash dividend.

**TABLE 19.3**

### Explanation for Paying Dividends: Canadian Financial Firms

| Policy Statements | Percent who agree or strongly agree (%) |
|---|---|
| 1. A firm should strive to maintain an uninterrupted record of dividend payments. | 96.0 |
| 2. Investors generally regard dividend changes as signals about a firm's prospects. | 95.1 |
| 3. A firm should adequately disclose to investors its reasons for changing its cash dividend. | 91.3 |
| 4. A firm's stock price generally falls when the firm unexpectedly decreases its dividend. | 90.9 |
| 5. A firm's stock price generally rises when the firm unexpectedly increases its dividend. | 87.0 |

Source: Adapted from Table 3 and Table 4 of H. K. Baker, S. Dutta, and S. Saadi, "Impact of Financial and Multinational Operations on Manager Perceptions of Dividends," *Global Finance Journal* 19 (2) (2008).

# 19.9    PUTTING IT ALL TOGETHER

Much of what we have discussed in this chapter (and much of what we know about dividends from decades of research) can be pulled together and summarized in the following six points:[42]

1. Aggregate dividend and stock repurchases are massive, and they have increased steadily in nominal and real terms over the years.
2. Cash dividends and repurchases are heavily concentrated among a relatively small number of large, mature firms.
3. Managers are very reluctant to cut dividends, normally doing so only due to firm-specific problems.
4. Managers smooth dividends, raising them slowly and incrementally as earnings grow.
5. Stock prices react to unanticipated changes in dividends.
6. The magnitude of stock repurchases tends to vary with transitory earnings.

The challenge now is to fit these six pieces into a reasonably coherent picture. With regard to payouts in general, meaning the combination of stock repurchases

---

[42] This list is distilled in part from a longer list in Harry DeAngelo and Linda DeAngelo, "Payout Policy Pedagogy: What Matters and Why," *European Financial Management* (January 2007).

and cash dividends, a simple life cycle theory fits points 1 and 2. The key ideas are straightforward. First, relatively young firms with less available cash generally should not make cash distributions. They need the cash to fund positive NPV projects for growth (and flotation costs discourage the raising of outside cash).

However, as a firm survives and matures, it begins to generate free cash flow (which, you will recall, is internally generated cash flow beyond that needed to fund profitable investment activities). Significant free cash flow can lead to agency problems if it is not distributed. Managers may become tempted to pursue empire building or otherwise spend the excess cash in ways not in the shareholders' best interests. Thus, firms come under shareholder pressure to make distributions rather than hoard cash. Consistent with what we observe, we expect large firms with a history of profitability to make large distributions.

Thus, the life cycle theory says that firms trade off the agency costs of excess cash retention against the potential future costs of external equity financing. A firm should begin making distributions when it generates sufficient internal cash flow to fund its investment needs now and into the foreseeable future.

The more complex issue concerns the type of distributions—cash dividends versus repurchases. The tax argument in favour of repurchases is a clear and strong one. Repurchases are a much more flexible option (and managers greatly value financial flexibility), so the question is: why would firms ever choose a cash dividend?

To answer this question, consider what a cash dividend can accomplish that a share repurchase cannot. One answer is that when a firm makes a commitment to pay a cash dividend now and into the future, it sends a two-part signal to the markets. As we have already discussed, one signal is that the firm anticipates being profitable, with the ability to make ongoing payments. Thus, a cash dividend may let a firm distinguish itself from less profitable rivals.

A second, and more subtle, signal takes us back to the agency problem of free cash flow. By committing to pay cash dividends now and in the future, the firm signals that it won't be hoarding cash (or at least not as much cash), thereby reducing agency costs and enhancing shareholder wealth. This two-part signalling story is consistent with points 3 to 5. The life cycle theory coupled with the two-part signal explanation could explain why the Canadian Big Six Banks continued to pay dividends during the financial crisis. In fact, Toronto-Dominion Bank actually increased its annual dividend in 2008 to $2.36 per share—up from $2.11 in 2007 and $1.78 in 2006.[43]

---

### Characteristics of a Sensible Payout Policy

- Pay out all free cash flows over time.
- Avoid cutting positive NPV projects to pay dividends or buy back shares.
- Do not initiate dividends until the firm is generating substantial free cash flow.
- Set the current regular dividend consistent with a long-run target payout ratio.
- Set the level of dividends low enough to avoid expensive future external financing.
- Use repurchases to distribute transitory cash flow increases.

---

## 19.10   STOCK DIVIDENDS AND STOCK SPLITS

Another type of dividend is paid out in shares of stock. This type of dividend is called a **stock dividend**. A stock dividend is not a true dividend because it is not paid in cash. The effect of a stock dividend is to increase the number of shares that each owner holds. Since there are more shares outstanding, each is simply worth less.

---

[43] *TD Bank Financial Group 2008 Annual Report* (TD Bank Financial Group, 2008).

A stock dividend is commonly expressed as a percentage; for example, a 20 percent stock dividend means that a shareholder receives one new share for every five currently owned (a 20 percent increase). Since every shareholder owns 20 percent more stock, the total number of shares outstanding rises by 20 percent. As we will see in a moment, the result is that each share of stock is worth about 20 percent less.

A **stock split** is essentially the same thing as a stock dividend, except that a split is expressed as a ratio instead of a percentage. When a split is declared, each share is split to create additional shares. For example, Coca-Cola stock split two for one in 2012—each old share was split into two new shares.

## Some Details on Stock Splits and Stock Dividends

Stock splits and stock dividends have essentially the same impacts on the corporation: they increase the number of shares outstanding and reduce the value per share. Also, both options will have a similar impact on future cash dividends. When stocks split, the cash dividend per share is reduced accordingly. The accounting treatment is not the same, however. Under TSX rules, the maximum stock dividend is 25 percent; anything larger is considered a stock split. Further, stock dividends are taxable, but stock splits are not.

**Example of a Stock Dividend**   The Peterson Company, a consulting firm specializing in difficult accounting problems, has 10,000 shares of stock, each selling at $66. The total market value of the equity is $66 × 10,000 = $660,000. With a 10 percent stock dividend, each shareholder receives one additional share for each 10 currently owned, and the total number of shares outstanding after the dividend is 11,000.

Before the stock dividend, the equity portion of Peterson's statement of financial position might look like this:

| | |
|---|---|
| Common stock (10,000 shares outstanding) | $210,000 |
| Retained earnings | 290,000 |
| Total shareholders' equity | $500,000 |

The amount of the stock dividend is transferred from retained earnings to common stock. Since 1,000 new shares are issued, the common stock account is increased by $66,000 (1,000 shares at $66 each). Total shareholders' equity is unaffected by the stock dividend because no cash has come in or out, so retained earnings is reduced by the entire $66,000. The net effect of these machinations is that Peterson's equity accounts now look like this:

| | |
|---|---|
| Common stock (11,000 shares outstanding) | $276,000 |
| Retained earnings | 224,000 |
| Total shareholders' equity | $500,000 |

**Example of a Stock Split**   A stock split is conceptually similar to a stock dividend, but it is commonly expressed as a ratio. For example, in a three-for-two split, each shareholder receives one additional share of stock for each two held originally, so a three-for-two split amounts to a 50 percent stock dividend. Again, no cash is paid out, and the percentage of the entire firm that each shareholder owns is unaffected.

The accounting treatment of a stock split is a little different (and simpler) from that of a stock dividend. Suppose Peterson decides to declare a two-for-one stock split. The number of shares outstanding doubles to 20,000. The shareholders' equity after the split is the same as before the split except the new number of shares is noted.

| | |
|---|---|
| Common stock (20,000 shares outstanding) | $210,000 |
| Retained earnings | 290,000 |
| Total shareholders' equity | $500,000 |

## Value of Stock Splits and Stock Dividends

The laws of logic tell us that stock splits and stock dividends can (1) leave the value of the firm unaffected, (2) increase its value, or (3) decrease its value. Unfortunately, the issues are complex enough that one cannot easily determine which of the three relationships holds.

**The Benchmark Case**    A strong case can be made that stock dividends and splits do not change either the wealth of any shareholder or the wealth of the firm as a whole. In our prior example, the equity was worth a total of $660,000. With the stock dividend, the number of shares increased to 11,000, so that each would be worth $660,000/11,000 = $60.

For example, a shareholder who had 100 shares worth $66 each before the dividend would have 110 shares worth $60 each afterward. The total value of the stock is $6,600 either way, so the stock dividend doesn't really have any economic effect.

With the stock split, there are 20,000 shares outstanding, so each should be worth $660,000/20,000 = $33. In other words, the number of shares doubles and the price halves. From these calculations, it appears that stock dividends and splits are just paper transactions.

Although these results are relatively obvious, reasons are often given to suggest that there may be some benefits to these actions. The typical financial manager is aware of many real-world complexities, and, for that reason, the stock split or stock dividend decision is not treated lightly in practice.

**Trading Range**    Proponents of stock dividends and stock splits frequently argue that a security has a proper **trading range**. When the security is priced above this level, many investors do not have the funds to buy the common trading unit called a *round lot* (usually 100 shares).

Although this argument is a popular one, its validity is questionable for a number of reasons. Mutual funds, pension funds, and other institutions have steadily increased their trading activity since World War II and now handle a sizeable percentage of total trading volume (over half of the trading volume on both the TSX and NYSE). Because these institutions buy and sell in huge amounts, the individual share price is of little concern. Furthermore, we sometimes observe share prices that are quite large without appearing to cause problems. There is evidence, however, that investors attach some weight to the trading range argument. For example, Berkshire Hathaway never split its Class A stock, and it was trading at $190,500 per share on April 24, 2014. Consistent with the trading range argument, the company had Class B shares trading at $126.95 on the same date.

Finally, there is evidence that stock splits may actually decrease the liquidity of the company's shares. Following a two-for-one split, the number of shares traded should more than double if liquidity is increased by the split. This doesn't appear to happen, and the reverse is sometimes observed.

Regardless of the impact on liquidity, firms do split their stock. Some managers believe that keeping the share price within a range attractive to individual investors helps promote Canadian ownership.

## Reverse Splits

A less frequently encountered financial manoeuvre is the **reverse split**. In a one-for-three reverse split, each investor exchanges three old shares for one new share. As mentioned previously with reference to stock splits and stock dividends, a case can be made that a reverse split changes nothing substantial about the company.

Given real-world imperfections, three related reasons are cited for reverse splits. First, transaction costs to shareholders may be less after the reverse split. Second, the liquidity and marketability of a company's stock might be improved when its price is raised to the popular trading range. Third, stocks selling below a certain level are not considered respectable, meaning that investors underestimate these firms' earnings, cash flow, growth, and stability. Some financial analysts argue that a reverse split can achieve instant respectability. As with stock splits, none of these reasons are particularly compelling, especially the third one.

There are two other reasons for reverse splits. First, stock exchanges have minimum price per share requirements. A reverse split may bring the stock price up to such a minimum. Second, companies sometimes perform reverse splits and, at the same time, buy out any shareholders who end up with less than a certain number of shares. This second tactic can be abusive if used to force out minority shareholders.

In the aftermath of the tech bubble, a number of technology firms made the decision to undertake reverse splits. More recently, in 2009, Domtar Corporation, the largest integrated producer of uncoated free sheet paper in North America (based in Montreal), underwent a reverse stock split at a 1-for-12 ratio. Domtar management cited two reasons for undertaking a reverse split—to return the company's share price to a level similar to that of other widely owned companies and to attract a broader range of institutional investors.

**CONCEPT QUESTIONS**

- What is the effect of a stock split on shareholder wealth?
- How does the accounting treatment of a stock split differ from that used with a small stock dividend?

## 19.11

# SUMMARY AND CONCLUSIONS

1. The dividend policy of the firm is irrelevant in a perfect capital market because the shareholder can effectively undo the firm's dividend strategy. If a shareholder receives a greater dividend than desired, he can reinvest the excess. Conversely, if the shareholder receives a smaller dividend than desired, she can sell off extra shares of stock. This argument is due to Miller and Modigliani and is similar to their homemade leverage concept, discussed in Chapter 16.

2. Shareholders will be indifferent between dividends and share repurchases in a perfect capital market.

3. Since dividends in Canada are taxed when paid to individuals, companies should not issue stock to pay out a dividend.

4. Also because of taxes, firms have an incentive to reduce dividends. For example, they might consider increasing capital expenditures, acquiring other companies, or purchasing financial assets. However, due to financial considerations and legal constraints, rational firms with large cash flows will likely exhaust these activities with plenty of cash left over for dividends.

5. In a world with personal taxes, a strong case can be made for repurchasing shares instead of paying dividends.

6. Nevertheless, there are a number of justifications for dividends even in a world with personal taxes:

    a. Investors in no-dividend stocks incur transaction costs when selling off shares for current consumption.

    b. Behavioural finance argues that investors with limited self-control can meet current consumption needs via high-dividend stocks while adhering to a policy of never dipping into principal.

    c. Managers, acting on behalf of shareholders, can pay dividends to keep cash from bondholders. The board of directors, also acting on behalf of shareholders, can use dividends to reduce the cash available to spendthrift managers.

    d. Managers may increase dividends to boost current stock price, even at the expense of projects with positive net present values (NPVs). This strategy is called signalling.

7. The stock market reacts positively to increases in dividends (or an initial payment) and negatively to decreases in dividends. This suggests that there is information content in dividend payments.

8. High- (low-) dividend firms should arise to meet the demands of dividend-preferring (capital gains–preferring) investors. Because of these clienteles, it is not clear that a firm can create value by changing its dividend policy.

<table>
<tr><td rowspan="6">**KEY TERMS**</td><td>Clienteles 576</td><td>Information content</td><td>Stripped common</td></tr>
<tr><td>Date of payment 557</td><td>  effect 574</td><td>  shares 562</td></tr>
<tr><td>Date of record 556</td><td>Regular cash dividends 555</td><td>Targeted repurchase 564</td></tr>
<tr><td>Declaration date 556</td><td>Reverse split 584</td><td>Trading range 584</td></tr>
<tr><td>Ex-dividend date 556</td><td>Stock dividend 582</td><td></td></tr>
<tr><td>Homemade dividends 561</td><td>Stock split 583</td><td></td></tr>
</table>

**QUESTIONS & PROBLEMS**

### Dividends and Taxes

**19.1** Lee Ann Inc. has declared a $5.60 per share dividend. Suppose capital gains are not taxed, but dividends are taxed at 15 percent. Lee Ann sells for $75 per share, and the stock is about to go ex-dividend. What do you think the ex-dividend price will be?

### Stock Dividends

**19.2** The shareholders' equity accounts for Hexagon International are shown here:

| | |
|---|---|
| Common stock ($1 book value) | $ 30,000 |
| Capital surplus | 185,000 |
| Retained earnings | 627,500 |
| Total shareholders' equity | $842,500 |

    a. If Hexagon stock currently sells for $37 per share and a 10 percent stock dividend is declared, how many new shares will be distributed? Show how the equity accounts would change.

    b. If Hexagon declared a 25 percent stock dividend, how would the accounts change?

### Stock Splits

**19.3** For the company in problem 19.2, show how the equity accounts will change in each case.

    a. Hexagon declares a four-for-one stock split. How many shares are outstanding now? What is the new par value per share?

    b. Hexagon declares a one-for-five reverse stock split. How many shares are outstanding now? What is the new par value per share?

### Stock Splits and Stock Dividends

**19.4** Roll Corp. (RC) currently has 260,000 shares of stock outstanding that sell for $78 per share. Assuming no market imperfections or tax effects exist, what will the share price be after

    a. RC has a five-for-three stock split?

    b. RC has a 15 percent stock dividend?

    c. RC has a 42.5 percent stock dividend?

    d. RC has a four-for-seven reverse stock split?

Determine the new number of shares outstanding in (a) through (d).

### Regular Dividends

19.5 The balance sheet for Levy Corp. is shown here in market value terms. There are 12,000 shares of stock outstanding.

**Market Value Balance Sheet**

| Cash | $ 55,000 | | |
|---|---|---|---|
| Fixed assets | 410,000 | Equity | $465,000 |
| Total | $465,000 | Total | $465,000 |

The company has declared a dividend of $1.90 per share. The stock goes ex-dividend tomorrow. Ignoring any tax effects, what is the stock selling for today? What will it sell for tomorrow? What will the balance sheet look like after the dividends are paid?

### Share Repurchase

19.6 In problem 19.5, suppose that Levy has announced it will repurchase $22,800 worth of stock. What effect will this transaction have on the equity of the firm? How many shares will be outstanding? What will the price per share be after the repurchase? Ignoring tax effects, show how the share repurchase is effectively the same as a cash dividend.

### Stock Dividends

19.7 The market value balance sheet for Outbox Manufacturing is shown here. Outbox has declared a 25 percent stock dividend. The stock goes ex-dividend tomorrow (the chronology for a stock dividend is similar to that for a cash dividend). There are 20,000 shares of stock outstanding. What will the ex-dividend price be?

**Market Value Balance Sheet**

| Cash | $295,000 | Debt | $180,000 |
|---|---|---|---|
| Fixed assets | 540,000 | Equity | 655,000 |
| Total | $835,000 | Total | $835,000 |

19.8 The company with the common equity accounts shown here has declared a 15 percent stock dividend when the market value of its stock is $45 per share. What effects on the equity accounts will the distribution of the stock dividend have?

| Common stock ($1 par value) | $ 410,000 |
|---|---|
| Capital surplus | 2,150,000 |
| Retained earnings | 5,320,000 |
| Total shareholders' equity | $7,880,000 |

### Stock Splits

19.9 In problem 19.8, suppose the company instead decides on a five-for-one stock split. The firm's $0.45 per share cash dividend on the new (post-split) shares represents an increase of 10 percent over last year's dividend on the pre-split stock. What effect does this have on the equity accounts? What was last year's dividend per share?

### Dividends and Stock Price

19.10 The Mann Company belongs to a risk class for which the appropriate discount rate is 10 percent. Mann currently has 150,000 outstanding shares selling at $120 each. The firm is contemplating the declaration of a $5 dividend at the end of the fiscal year that just began. Assume there are no taxes on dividends. Answer the following questions based on the Miller and Modigliani (MM) model, which is discussed in the text.

    *a.* What will the price of the stock be on the ex-dividend date if the dividend is declared?

b. What will the price of the stock be at the end of the year if the dividend is not declared?

c. If Mann makes $3 million of new investments at the beginning of the period, earns net income of $1.4 million, and pays the dividend at the end of the year, how many shares of new stock must the firm issue to meet its funding needs?

d. Is it realistic to use the MM model in the real world to value stock? Why or why not?

### Homemade Dividends

19.11 You own 1,000 shares of stock in Avondale Corp. You will receive a $0.95 per share dividend in one year. In two years, Avondale will pay a liquidating dividend of $45 per share. The required return on Avondale stock is 14 percent. What is the current share price of your stock (ignoring taxes)? If you would rather have equal dividends in each of the next two years, show how you can accomplish this by creating homemade dividends. (*Hint:* Dividends will be in the form of an annuity.)

19.12 In problem 19.11, suppose you want only $500 total in dividends the first year. What will your homemade dividend be in two years?

### Stock Repurchase

19.13 Flychucker Corporation is evaluating an extra dividend versus a share repurchase. In either case $3,000 would be spent. Current earnings are $1.50 per share, and the stock currently sells for $58 per share. There are 600 shares outstanding. Ignore taxes and other imperfections in answering (a) and (b).

a. Evaluate the two alternatives in terms of the effect on the price per share of the stock and shareholder wealth.

b. What will be the effect on Flychucker's EPS and P/E ratio under the two different scenarios?

c. In the real world, which of these actions would you recommend? Why?

### Dividends and Firm Value

19.14 The net income of Novis Corp. is $85,000. The company has 25,000 outstanding shares and a 100 percent payout policy. The expected value of the firm one year from now is $1,725,000. The appropriate discount rate for Novis is 12 percent, and the dividend tax rate is zero.

a. What is the current value of the firm assuming the current dividend has not yet been paid?

b. What is the ex-dividend price of Novis's stock if the board follows its current policy?

c. At the dividend declaration meeting, several board members claimed that the dividend is too meagre and is probably depressing Novis's price. They proposed that Novis sell enough new shares to finance a $4.60 dividend.
*i.* Comment on the claim that the low dividend is depressing the stock price. Support your argument with calculations.
*ii.* If the proposal is adopted, at what price will the new shares sell? How many will be sold?

### Dividend Policy

19.15 Gibson Co. has a current-period cash flow of $1.1 million and pays no dividends. The PV of the company's future cash flows is $15 million. The company is entirely financed with equity and has 600,000 shares outstanding. Assume the dividend tax rate is zero.

a. What is the share price of the Gibson stock?

b. Suppose the board of directors of Gibson Co. announces its plan to pay out 50 percent of its current cash flow as cash dividends to its shareholders. How can Jeff Miller, who owns 1,000 shares of Gibson stock, achieve a zero payout policy on his own?

### Dividend Smoothing

19.16  The Sharpe Co. just paid a dividend of $1.50 per share of stock. Its target payout ratio is 40 percent. The company expects to have an EPS of $4.15 one year from now.

a. If the adjustment rate is 0.3 as defined in the Lintner model, what is the dividend one year from now?

b. If the adjustment rate is 0.6 instead, what is the dividend one year from now?

c. Which adjustment rate is more conservative? Why?

### Expected Return, Dividends, and Taxes

19.17  The Gecko Company and the Gordon Company are two firms whose business risk is the same but that have different dividend policies. Gecko pays no dividend, whereas Gordon has an expected dividend yield of 6 percent. Suppose the capital gains tax rate is zero, whereas the dividend tax rate is 35 percent. Gecko has an expected earnings growth rate of 12 percent annually, and its stock price is expected to grow at this same rate. If the after-tax expected returns on the two stocks are equal (because they are in the same risk class), what is the pre-tax required return on Gordon's stock?

### Dividends and Taxes

19.18  As discussed in the text, in the absence of market imperfections and tax effects, we would expect the share price to decline by the amount of the dividend payment when the stock goes ex-dividend. Once we consider the role of taxes, however, this is not necessarily true. One model has been proposed that incorporates tax effects into determining the ex-dividend price:[44]

$$(P_0 - P_X)/D = (1 - t_P)/(1 - t_G)$$

Here $P_0$ is the price just before the stock goes ex, $P_X$ is the ex-dividend share price, $D$ is the amount of the dividend per share, $t_P$ is the relevant marginal personal tax rate on dividends, and $t_G$ is the effective marginal tax rate on capital gains.

a. If $t_P = t_G = 0$, how much will the share price fall when the stock goes ex?

b. If $t_P - 15$ percent and $t_G = 0$, how much will the share price fall?

c. If $t_P = 15$ percent and $t_G = 20$ percent, how much will the share price fall?

d. Suppose the only owners of stock are corporations. In Canada, corporations get a 100 percent exemption from taxation on the dividend income they receive, but they do not get such an exemption on capital gains. If the corporation's income and capital gains tax rates are both 35 percent, what does this model predict the ex-dividend share price will be?

e. What does this problem tell you about real-world tax considerations and the dividend policy of the firm?

### Dividends versus Reinvestment

19.19  National Business Machine Co. (NBM) has $3 million of extra cash after taxes have been paid. NBM has two choices to make use of this cash. One alternative is to invest the cash in financial assets. The resulting investment income will be paid out as a special dividend at the end of three years. In this case, the firm can invest either in Treasury bills yielding 5 percent or in 7 percent preferred stock. Another alternative is to pay out the cash now as dividends. This would allow the shareholders to invest on their own in Treasury bills with the same yield or in preferred stock. The corporate tax rate is 35 percent. Assume the investor has a 31 percent personal income tax rate, which is applied to interest income and preferred stock dividends. The personal dividend tax rate is 15 percent on common stock dividends. The corporate dividend exclusion of 100 percent applies. Should the cash be paid today or in three years? Which of the two options generates the higher after-tax income for the shareholders?

---

[44] N. Elton and M. Gruber, "Marginal Stockholder Tax Rates and the Clientele Effect," *Review of Economics and Statistics* (February 1970).

19.20 After completing its capital spending for the year, Carlson Manufacturing has $1,000 extra cash. Carlson's managers must choose between investing the cash in Treasury bonds that yield 8 percent and paying the cash out to investors, who would invest in the bonds themselves.

   a. If the corporate tax rate is 35 percent, what personal tax rate would make the investors equally willing to receive the dividend or to let Carlson invest the money?
   b. Is the answer to (a) reasonable? Why or why not?
   c. Suppose the only investment choice is a preferred stock that yields 12 percent. The corporate dividend exclusion of 70 percent applies. What personal tax rate will make the stockholders indifferent to the outcome of Carlson's dividend decision?
   d. Is this a compelling argument for a low dividend payout ratio? Why or why not?

### Dividend Signalling and the Life Cycle Hypothesis

19.21 Steady Streams Company went public a month ago. Its owner, Winnie McAbby, briefly learned about the signalling effects of dividends and of maintaining a consistent payout history. Accordingly, she is contemplating whether or not she should declare a dividend. If the dividend is declared, it is unlikely she will be able to abruptly cease dividends without share price ramifications. In light of this dilemma, she has approached you for advice on what course of action to take. Specifically, she wants clarification on the following:

   a. What are the dividend signals Winnie is describing?
   b. Given that her company is young, what are other factors to consider before deciding to pay dividends?
   c. Following the life cycle hypothesis, what should Winnie do?

### Dividends and Taxes

19.22 Marcus purchased 500 shares worth $10,000 of Design Co., a well-established company that provides outsourcing for technological research. On January 8, 2015, Design Co. declared a $2.50 dividend per share. The ex-dividend date is January 23. The dividends are to be paid on March 16, 2015. On January 20, 2015, he sold 100 shares of the company for $40 per share. Marcus's personal tax rate is 35% (federal and provincial tax combined).

   a. Given that capital gains are taxed at 50%, how much tax will Marcus pay for the sale of shares?
   b. Assuming dividends are grossed up at 38% and the total dividend tax credit is equal to 20% of the grossed-up dividends, how much tax will Marcus pay on the cash dividends received from Design Co.?
   c. What is his total tax obligation? Would your answer to part (b) be different if a stock dividend were paid instead of a cash dividend?

# Electronic Timing Ltd.

Electronic Timing Ltd. (ETL) is a small company founded 15 years ago by electronics engineers Jessica Kerr and Tom Miller. ETL manufactures integrated circuits to capitalize on the complex mixed-signal design technology and has recently entered the market for frequency timing generators, or silicon timing devices, which provide the timing signals or "clocks" necessary to synchronize electronic systems. Its clock products were originally used in PC video graphics applications, but the market subsequently expanded to include motherboards, PC peripheral devices, and other digital consumer electronics, such as digital television boxes and game consoles. ETL also designs and markets custom application-specific integrated circuits (ASICs) for industrial customers. The ASIC's design combines analog and digital, or mixed-signal, technology. In addition to Jessica and Tom, Norma Pittman, who provided capital for the company, is the third primary owner. Each owns 25 percent of the 1 million shares outstanding. Several other individuals, including current employees, own the remaining company shares.

Recently, the company designed a new computer motherboard. The company's design is both more efficient and less expensive to manufacture, and the ETL design is expected to become standard in many personal computers. After investigating the possibility of manufacturing the new motherboard, ETL determined that the costs involved in building a new plant would be prohibitive. The owners also decided that they were unwilling to bring in another large outside owner. Instead, ETL sold the design to an outside firm. The sale of the motherboard design was completed for an after-tax payment of $30 million.

1.  Jessica believes the company should use the extra cash to pay a special one-time dividend. How will this proposal affect the stock price? How will it affect the value of the company?

2.  Tom believes the company should use the extra cash to pay off debt and upgrade and expand its existing manufacturing capability. How would Tom's proposals affect the company?

3.  Norma is in favour of a share repurchase. She argues that a repurchase will increase the company's P/E ratio, return on assets (ROA), and return on equity (ROE). Are her arguments correct? How will a share repurchase affect the value of the company?

4.  Another option discussed by Jessica, Tom, and Norma is to begin a regular dividend payment to shareholders. How would you evaluate this proposal?

5.  One way to value a share of stock is the dividend growth, or growing perpetuity, model. Consider the following. The dividend payout ratio is 1 minus $b$, where $b$ is the "retention" or "plowback" ratio. So, the dividend next year will be the earnings next year, $E_1$, times 1 minus the retention ratio. The most commonly used equation to calculate the sustainable growth rate is the ROE times the retention ratio. Substituting these relationships into the dividend growth model, we get the following equation to calculate the price of a share of stock today:

$$P_0 = \frac{E_1(1 - b)}{R_S - \text{ROE} \times b}$$

What are the implications of this result in terms of whether the company should pay a dividend or upgrade and expand its manufacturing capability? Explain.

## PART 5

# CHAPTER 20

# Issuing Equity Securities to the Public

EXECUTIVE SUMMARY

This chapter looks at how corporations issue securities to the investing public. This chapter focuses on equity, but the procedures for debt and equity are basically the same.

Since issuing securities is a specialized activity not undertaken on a daily basis, issuing corporations generally seek assistance from an investment dealer. Depending on the type of security and the alternatives chosen, the assistance from the investment dealer may include a variety of services, including advice on (1) which securities to issue, (2) how to structure and price the deal, and (3) complying with disclosure requirements set by regulators. In addition, investment dealers offer the issuer various forms of protection against receiving substantially less than the issue price or failing to sell the entire issue.

The new securities could be a primary market, which is a public issue sold directly to the public with the help of an investment dealer. Once registered with provincial regulatory authorities, the newly issued securities may be traded on secondary markets (stock exchanges or over the counter (OTC)). In contrast, in a private placement, debt or equity (common or preferred shares) is sold directly to a small number of buyers.

A company's first issue of public equity is called an *initial public offering (IPO)*. IPOs come in cycles: in the late 1990s, dot-com companies dominated the scene. Starting in 2001, income trusts took over. In recent years IPOs of social media firms such as Facebook and Twitter have made headlines. In a public offering of debt or equity, the investment dealer will generally act as an underwriter, taking on some, or all, of the pricing risk in the new issue. The underwriter does this by buying the issue and reselling it. The underwriter takes all the pricing risk in a special type of public offering called a *bought deal*.

Instead of marketing to the general public, a corporation can sell common stock to its existing shareholders by what is called a *rights offer*. Rights offerings[1] are usually cheaper and faster than underwritten public offerings, in part because they are marketed to a narrower audience that has already shown interest in the stock. Through the 1970s, rights offers were easily the most popular method of raising new equity in Canada.

In the 1980s, the Ontario Securities Commission (OSC) introduced a streamlined reporting and registration system for large companies that issue securities regularly, called Prompt Offering Prospectus (POP). With deregulation and the advantages of POP, growing competition among underwriters promoted dramatic growth in the popularity of bought deals over rights offers. Today, the majority of equity dollars raised in Canada use POP and are bought deals.

## 20.1 THE PUBLIC ISSUE

A firm issuing securities must satisfy a number of requirements set out by provincial regulations and statutes and enforced by provincial securities commissions. Regulation of the securities market in Canada is carried out by provincial commissions and through provincial securities acts. However, only eight of the provinces have commissions, due in large part to an absence of exchanges in some provinces. This is in

---

[1] The terms *rights offer* and *rights offering* are used interchangeably.

contrast to the United States, where regulation is handled by a federal body, the Securities and Exchange Commission (SEC). The regulators' goal is to promote the efficient flow of information about securities and the smooth functioning of securities markets.

All companies listed on the Toronto Stock Exchange (TSX) come under the jurisdiction of the OSC. The *Securities Act* sets forth the provincial regulations for all new securities issues involving the province of Ontario and the TSX. The OSC administers the Act. Other provinces have similar legislation and regulating bodies, but the OSC is the most noteworthy because of the TSX's scope.[2] In general terms, the OSC rules seek to ensure that investors receive all material information on new issues in the form of a registration statement and prospectus. The Canadian Securities Administrators (CSA) coordinates regulation under Uniform Securities Legislation, which streamlines practices across jurisdictions. Of particular note is the "passport system," which allows a prospectus that is approved in one province to be immediately approved in all other provinces, making it valid across Canada.

The OSC's responsibility for efficient information flow goes beyond new issues. It continues to regulate the trading of securities after they have been issued to ensure adequate disclosure of information. For example, on May 26, 2014, the OSC announced that it would extend a cease-trade order that stopped trading of all of AFG Flameguard Ltd. shares until further order by the Director. The cease-trade order was made because of the company's failure to file multiple disclosure materials, including audited financial statements, for the year ended December 31, 2013.[3]

Another informational role of the OSC is gathering and publishing insider reports filed by major shareholders, officers, and directors of TSX-listed firms. To ensure efficient functioning of markets, the OSC oversees the training and supervision that investment dealers provide for their personnel. It also monitors investment dealers' capital positions. Increasing market volatility and the popularity of bought deals in which the dealer assumes all the price risk make capital adequacy important. The Investment Industry Regulatory Organization of Canada (IIROC) is a national self-regulatory agency for the securities industry. Its mandate is to set and enforce rules regarding the conduct of dealer firms and their employees and to ensure the integrity of trading on Canadian markets.[4]

## 20.2    THE BASIC PROCEDURE FOR A NEW ISSUE

There is a series of steps involved in issuing securities to the public, which is depicted in Table 20.1. In general terms, the basic procedure is as follows:

1. Management's first step in issuing any securities to the public is to obtain approval from the board of directors. The firm must also engage an underwriter.

2. The firm must prepare and distribute copies of a preliminary **prospectus** to the OSC and to potential investors. The preliminary prospectus contains some of the financial information that will be contained in the final prospectus; it does not contain the price at which the security will be offered. The preliminary prospectus is sometimes called a **red herring**, in part because bold red letters are printed on the cover warning that the OSC has neither approved nor disapproved of the

---

[2] The TSX is Canada's largest stock exchange. The TSX Group, the company that owns and operates the TSX, also operates the TSX Venture Exchange, where smaller companies list their stock because they are not able to meet the TSX requirements, and the Montreal Exchange, which specializes in the trading of derivatives. In addition to equity exchanges, ICE Futures Canada (previously the Winnipeg Commodities Exchange) is focused on trading commodities such as wheat and rice.

[3] Source: cto-iov.csa-acvm.ca/ArticleFile.asp?Instance=101&ID=E6D79EF3FCBB4A2E88B51060C898013E.

[4] Source: www.iiroc.ca.

securities. The OSC studies the preliminary prospectus and notifies the company of any changes required. This process is usually completed within about two weeks.

3. Once the revised, final prospectus meets with the OSC's approval, a price is determined and a full-fledged selling effort gets underway. A final prospectus must accompany the delivery of securities or confirmation of sale, whichever comes first.

TABLE 20.1

**The Process of Raising Capital**

| Steps in public offering | Time | Activities |
| --- | --- | --- |
| 1. Pre-underwriting conferences held | Several months | The amount of money to be raised and the type of security to be issued are discussed. The underwriting syndicate and selling group are put together. The underwriting contract is negotiated. Board approval is obtained. |
| 2. Registration statements filed and approved | A 20-day waiting period | The registration statement contains all relevant financial and business information. |
| 3. Issue priced | Usually not before the last day of the registration period | For seasoned offerings (see later in this section), the price is set close to the prevailing market price. For IPOs, intensive research and analysis are required. |
| 4. Public offering and sale held | Shortly after the last day of the registration period | In a typical firm-commitment contract, the underwriter buys a stipulated amount of stock from the firm and sells it at a higher price. The selling group assists in the sale. |
| 5. Market stabilization occurs | Usually 30 days after the offering | The underwriter stands ready to place orders to buy at a specified price on the market. |

## The Prompt Offering Prospectus System

In 1982, the SEC approved its shelf registration system, which was designed to reduce repetitive filing requirements for large companies. In 1983, the OSC introduced the POP system with a similar goal. The eight provinces with securities commissions all have comparable legislation allowing certain securities issuers prompt access to capital markets without having to prepare a full preliminary and final prospectus prior to a distribution.

The POP system, accessible only by large companies, lets issuers file annual and interim financial statements regardless of whether they issue securities in a given year. To use the POP system, issuers must have been reporting for 36 months and have complied with the continuous disclosure requirements. Because the OSC has an extensive file of information on these companies, only a short prospectus is required when securities are issued. As we stated earlier, POP offerings in the form of bought deals became quite popular in the late 1980s.

In the early 1990s, securities regulators in Canada and the SEC in the United States introduced a Multi-Jurisdictional Disclosure System (MJDS). Under MJDS, large issuers in the two countries are allowed to issue securities in both countries under disclosure documents satisfactory to regulators in the home country. In its day, this was an important simplification of filing requirements for certain large Canadian companies. While MJDS is based on a model of companies issuing securities simultaneously at home and in foreign markets, many Canadian companies are cross-listed on the NYSE or NASDAQ. Cross-listing refers to the practice of listing a firm's shares for trading on other exchanges, usually in foreign countries. For Canadian firms, cross-listing opens up the alternative of issuing in larger U.S. stock markets. Possible advantages for U.S. listing are greater liquidity, lower trading costs, greater visibility, and greater investor protection under more stringent U.S. securities laws, such as Sarbanes–Oxley on corporate governance. U.S. listing also brings possible disadvantages in the form of higher accounting and compliance costs. On balance, it remains undecided whether U.S. listing adds shareholder value.[5]

### Alternative Issue Methods

For equity sales, there are two kinds of public issues: a **general cash offer** and a **rights offer** (or rights offering). With a cash offer, securities are offered to the general public. With a rights offer, securities are initially offered only to existing owners. Rights offers are fairly common in other countries, but they are relatively rare in Canada (and the United States). We therefore focus primarily on cash offers in this chapter.

The first public equity issue made by a company is referred to as an IPO, or an *unseasoned new issue*. This issue occurs when a company decides to go public. Obviously, all IPOs are cash offers. If the firm's existing shareholders wanted to buy the shares, the firm wouldn't have to sell them publicly in the first place.

A **seasoned equity offering** (SEO) is a new issue for a company with securities that have been previously issued. An SEO of common stock can be made by using a cash offer or a rights offer.

**CONCEPT QUESTIONS**

- What are the basic procedures in selling a new issue?
- What is a preliminary prospectus?
- What are the POP system and MJDS, and what advantages do they offer?

## 20.3    THE CASH OFFER

If the public issue of securities is a cash offer, underwriters are usually involved. Underwriters perform the following services for corporate issuers:

1. Formulating the method used to issue the securities.
2. Pricing the new securities.
3. Selling the new securities.

Typically, the underwriter buys the securities for less than the offering price and accepts the risk of not being able to sell them. Because underwriting involves risk, underwriters combine to form an underwriting group called a **syndicate** or a **banking group** to share the risk and to help sell the issue.

In a syndicate, one or more managers arrange or co-manage the offering. The lead manager is typically responsible for packaging and executing the deal. The other underwriters in the syndicate serve primarily to distribute the issue.

The difference between the underwriter's buying price and the offering price is called the **spread** or **discount**. It is the basic compensation received by the underwriter.

In Canada, firms often establish long-term relationships with their underwriters. With the growth in popularity of bought deals, competition among underwriters has increased. At the same time, mergers among investment dealers have reduced the number of underwriters. For example, RBC Dominion Securities grew through merger with six other investment dealers and a major capital injection by the Royal Bank of Canada.

---

[5] A positive view is in Michael R. King and Dan Segal, "Corporate Governance, International Cross Listing and Home Bias," *Canadian Investment Review* (Winter 2003). Usha R. Mittoo challenges the positive view in "The Value of U.S. Listing: Does a U.S. Listing Improve Stock Performance in the Long Run?" *Canadian Investment Review* (Fall 2003). Supporting the challenge, another paper finds that companies tend to cross-list in markets similar to their home country's where diversification benefits are small: Sergei Sarkissian and Michael J. Schill, "The Overseas Listing Decision: New Evidence of Proximity Preference," *Review of Financial Studies* (Fall 2004).

## Types of Underwriting

Two basic types of underwriting are involved in a cash offer: regular underwriting and a bought deal.

**Regular Underwriting**  With **regular underwriting** the banking group of underwriters buys the securities from the issuing firm and resells them to the public for the purchase price plus an underwriting spread. Regular underwriting includes an "out clause," which gives the banking group the option to decline the issue if the price drops dramatically. In this case, the deal is usually withdrawn. The issue might be repriced and/or reoffered at a later date. **Firm-commitment underwriting** is like regular underwriting without the out clause.

A close counterpart to regular underwriting is called **best-efforts underwriting**. The underwriter is legally bound to use "best efforts" to sell the securities at the agreed-upon offering price. Beyond this, the underwriter does not guarantee any particular amount of money to the issuer. This form of underwriting is more common with IPOs.

**Bought Deal**  In a **bought deal**, the issuer sells the entire issue to one investment dealer or to a group that then attempts to resell it. As in firm-commitment underwriting, the investment dealer assumes all the price risk. The dealer has usually "premarketed" the prospective issue to a few large institutional investors. Issuers in bought deals are large, well-known firms that qualify for the use of POP to speed up OSC filings. For these reasons, bought deals are usually executed swiftly. Bought deals are the most popular form of underwriting in Canada today.

## The Selling Period

While the issue is being sold to the public, the underwriting group agrees not to sell securities for less than the offering price until the syndicate dissolves. The principal underwriter is permitted to buy shares if the market price falls below the offering price. The purpose is to support the market and stabilize the price from temporary downward pressure. If the issue remains unsold after a time (for example, 30 days), members can leave the group and sell their shares at whatever price the market will allow.

## The Overallotment Option

Many underwriting contracts contain an *overallotment option* or *Green Shoe provision* that gives members of the underwriting group the option to purchase additional shares at the offering price less fees and commissions.[6] The stated reason for the overallotment option is to cover excess demand and oversubscriptions. The option has a short maturity (around 30 days) and is limited to about 10 percent of the original number of shares issued.

The overallotment option is a benefit to the underwriting syndicate and a cost to the issuer. If the market price of the new issue rises immediately, the overallotment option allows the underwriters to buy additional shares from the issuer and immediately resell them to the public.

## Investment Banks

Investment banks are at the heart of new security issues. They provide advice, market the securities (after investigating the market's receptiveness to the issue), and underwrite the proceeds. They accept the risk that the market price may fall between the date the offering price is set and the time the issue is sold.

---

[6] The term *Green Shoe provision* sounds exotic, but the origin is relatively mundane. It comes from the Green Shoe Company, which once granted such an option.

In addition, investment banks are responsible for pricing fairly. When a firm goes public, particularly for the first time, the buyers know relatively little about the firm's operations. After all, it is not rational for a buyer of, say, only 1,000 shares of stock to study the company at length. Instead, the buyer must rely on the judgment of the investment bank, which has presumably examined the firm in detail. Given this asymmetry of information, what prevents the investment banker from pricing the issued securities too high? While the underwriter has a short-run incentive to price high, it has a long-run incentive to make sure that its customers do not pay too much; they might desert the underwriter in future deals if they lose money on this one. Thus, as long as investment banks plan to stay in business over time, it is in their self-interest to price fairly.

In other words, financial economists argue that each investment bank has a reservoir of "reputation capital."[7] Mispricing of new issues, as well as unethical dealings, is likely to reduce this reputation capital.

One measure of this reputation capital is the pecking order among the investment banks. MBA students are aware of this order because they know that accepting a job with a top-tier firm is universally regarded as more prestigious than accepting a job with a lower-tier firm.

Table 20.2 lists the largest underwriters in Canada ranked by total value of issues. The table shows that RBC Capital Markets was the leading underwriter in 2013.

**TABLE 20.2**

**Canada's Top Equity and Equity-Linked Underwriters, 2013, Ranked by Total Volume Raised**

| Underwriter | Volume (in US$ millions) | Number of deals |
|---|---|---|
| 1. RBC Capital Markets | 6,863 | 80 |
| 2. BMO Capital Markets | 5,154 | 45 |
| 3. Scotiabank | 4,470 | 47 |
| 4. TD Securities | 3,968 | 43 |
| 5. CIBC | 3,330 | 51 |
| 6. GMP Securities | 2,354 | 41 |
| 7. Goldman Sachs and Co. | 2,322 | 2 |
| 8. Barclays | 1,266 | 5 |
| 9. Canaccord Genuity Corp | 990 | 52 |
| 10. National Bank Financial Inc. | 981 | 44 |

Source: Bloomberg L.P.

## The Offering Price and Underpricing

Determining the correct offering price is an underwriter's hardest task. The issuing firm faces a potential cost if the offering price is set too high or too low. If the issue is priced below the true market price, the issuer's existing shareholders will experience an opportunity loss when they sell their shares for less than they are worth. If the issue is priced too high, it may be unsuccessful and have to be withdrawn. Of course, this is the underwriter's problem under a bought deal.

Underpricing is fairly common, and it clearly helps new shareholders earn a higher return on the shares they buy. However, to the existing shareholders of the issuing firm, underpricing is an indirect cost of issuing new securities. In the case of an IPO, underpricing reduces the proceeds received by the original owners.

---

[7] For example, see R. Carter, F. H. Dark, and A. K. Singh, "Underwriter Reputation, Initial Returns and the Long-Run Performance of IPO Stocks," *Journal of Finance* (February 1998); and R. Beatty and J. Ritter, "Investment Banking, Reputation, and the Underpricing of Initial Public Offerings," *Journal of Financial Economics* (January–February 1986).

## The Decision to Go Public

When a private company grows to a certain size, it may consider the advantages of going public by issuing common stock through an **initial public offering (IPO)**. One important advantage is that public firms have greater access to new capital once their shares are valued on secondary markets. Further, publicly traded firms must meet OSC and other disclosure requirements that reduce information risk for potential investors. In addition, going public makes it possible for the firm's principal owners to sell some of their shares and diversify their personal portfolios while retaining control of the company. As a result, most large companies in Canada are public.

However, going public also has disadvantages. For instance, public firms are subject to stricter disclosure and other potentially costly regulatory requirements.

## Pricing Initial Public Offerings

Determining the correct offering price is the most difficult thing the lead investment bank must do for an IPO. The issuing firm faces a potential cost if the offering price is set too high or too low. If the issue is priced too high, it may be unsuccessful and be withdrawn. If the issue is priced below the true market price, the issuer's existing shareholders will experience an opportunity loss.

Table 20.3 draws on studies by Jay R. Ritter at the University of Florida. In general, the studies found that IPOs are underpriced compared to their prices in the aftermarket immediately after the offering period. A dramatic example of underpricing came with the IPO of Tim Hortons in March 2006. The Canadian corporate icon announced the pricing of its IPO of 29 million shares of common stock at a price of $27 per share. The stock closed at $33.10 after one day of trading—a 22.6 percent increase from the IPO price.

**TABLE 20.3**

**Number of Offerings, Average First-Day Return, and Gross Proceeds of Initial Public Offerings, 1960–2013**

| Year | Number of offerings* | Average first-day return, %[†] | Gross proceeds (in $ millions)[‡] |
|---|---|---|---|
| 1960–1969 | 2,661 | 21.2% | 7,988 |
| 1970–1979 | 1,536 | 7.1 | 6,663 |
| 1980–1989 | 2,375 | 6.9 | 60,380 |
| 1990–1999[§] | 4,205 | 21.0 | 296,693 |
| 2000–2013[§] | 1,790 | 22.3 | 423,306 |
| **1960–2013** | **12,567** | **16.9** | **795,030** |

*Beginning in 1975, the number of offerings excludes IPOs with an offer price of less than $5.00, American Depository Receipts (ADRs), best efforts, units, and Regulation A offers (small issues, raising less than $1.5 million during the 1980s and $5 million until 2012), real estate investment trusts (REITs), partnerships, and closed-end funds. Banks and S&Ls and non-CRSP-listed IPOs are included. From 2012 and later, Regulation A offerings (issues raising up to $50 million are eligible) are included.

[†] First-day returns are computed as the percentage return from the offering price to the first closing market price.

[‡] Gross proceeds data are from Securities Data Co. and exclude overallotment options but include the international tranche, if any. No adjustments for inflation have been made.

[§] The years 1990–1999 and 2000–2013 are affected by the Internet bubble. Refer to Table 20.4 for more details.

Source: Professor Jay R. Ritter, University of Florida.

While the international data in Table 20.3 and the Tim Hortons example appear to suggest that IPOs are good short-term investments with positive returns, a study by Lawrence Kryzanowski, Skander Lazrak, and Ian Rakita challenges this conclusion for Canada. They point out that most hot IPOs are *oversubscribed* so that investors will not be able to buy all the shares they want, and the underwriters will allocate the shares among investors. The average investor will only get a small allotment or more likely none of the shares in the hottest IPOs. Their findings suggest that if the investor misses out on about 22 percent of the best-performing IPOs in their sample of 359 Canadian IPOs, the average first-day return is actually −0.64%.[8] An example of this problem occurred in May 2014 with the IPO of PrairieSky Royalty Ltd., a mineral rights royalty company spun off by Encana. This IPO was oversubscribed 15 times, so it was unlikely that many small investors were able to enjoy the 25 percent increase in the share price on the opening day.[9]

However, there is much more to the IPO process. It is not just about what the market will bear at the time but also about trying to get the company launched for the long term and building a good investor base.[10]

## Underpricing: A Possible Explanation

There are several possible explanations for underpricing, but so far there is no agreement among scholars as to which explanation is correct. Two important facts associated with the underpricing puzzle are key to a unifying theory. First, much of the apparent underpricing is concentrated in smaller issues. This point is documented in Table 20.4, which shows that underpricing tends to be attributable to firms with few or no sales in the prior year. These firms tend to be young firms with uncertain prospects. The increased uncertainty in some way probably attracts risk-averse investors only if underpricing exists. Second, when the price of a new issue is too low, the issue is often *oversubscribed*. Although IPOs have positive initial returns on average, a significant fraction of them have price drops. An investor submitting an order for all new issues may find that she will be allocated more shares in issues that go down in price.

**TABLE 20.4**

### Average First-Day Returns, Categorized by Sales, for IPOs: 1980–2013*

| | 1980–1989 | | 1990–1998 | | 1999–2000 | | 2001–2013 | |
|---|---|---|---|---|---|---|---|---|
| | First-day average return | Number of firms | First-day average return | Number of firms | First-day average return | Number of firms | First-day average return | Number of firms |
| 0 ≤ Sales < $10 million | 10.3% | 422 | 17.2% | 741 | 68.9% | 333 | 5.9% | 198 |
| $10 million ≤ Sales < $20 million | 8.7 | 243 | 18.6 | 395 | 81.7 | 137 | 12.1 | 55 |
| $20 million ≤ Sales < $50 million | 7.8 | 500 | 18.8 | 790 | 74.9 | 154 | 14.4 | 177 |
| $50 million ≤ Sales < $100 million | 6.4 | 355 | 12.9 | 588 | 61.2 | 87 | 19.5 | 217 |
| $100 million ≤ Sales < $200 million | 5.1 | 234 | 11.8 | 454 | 35.8 | 56 | 16.3 | 196 |
| $200 million ≤ Sales | 3.4 | 290 | 8.7 | 645 | 25.2 | 90 | 12.0 | 500 |
| All | 7.2 | 2,044 | 14.8 | 3,613 | 64.5 | 857 | 13.3 | 1,343 |

* Data are from Securities Data Co., with corrections by the authors. Sales, measured in millions, are for the last 12 months prior to going public. All sales have been converted into dollars of 2003 purchasing power, using the Consumer Price Index. There are 7,857 IPOs, after excluding IPOs with an offer price of less than $5.00 per share, units, REITs, ADRs, closed-end funds, banks and savings and loans, firms not listed on Center for Research in Security Prices (CRSP) within six months of the offer date, and energy-related limited partnership. The average first-day return is 18 percent.

Source: Professor Jay R. Ritter, University of Florida.

----

[8] L. Kryzanowski, S. Lazrak, and I. Rakita, "The Behavior of Prices, Trades and Spreads for Canadian IPO's," *Multinational Finance Journal* (September–December, 2005).

[9] B. Erman, "PrairieSky makes big splash in largest debut since 2000," *Globe and Mail*, Report on Business, May 30, 2014, p. B1.

[10] Pricing information was obtained through Bloomberg LP. Historical prices and price changes can also be found at finance.yahoo.com.

# IN THEIR OWN WORDS

## Jay Ritter on initial public offering underpricing around the world

The United States is not the only country in which initial public offerings (IPOs) of common stock are underpriced. The phenomenon exists in every country with a stock market, although the extent of underpricing varies from country to country.

In general, countries with developed capital markets have more moderate underpricing than in emerging markets. During the Internet bubble of 1999–2000, however, underpricing in the developed capital markets increased dramatically. In the United States, for example, the average first-day return during 1999–2000 was 65 percent. The underpricing in Chinese IPOs used to be extreme, but in recent years it has moderated. In the 1990s, Chinese government regulations required that the offer price could not be more than 15 times earnings, even when comparable stocks had a price/earnings ratio of 45. In 2010, the average first-day return was 40%, and there were more IPOs in China, raising more money, than any other country. After the bursting of the Internet bubble in mid-2000, the level of underpricing in the United States, Germany, and other developed capital markets has returned to more traditional levels.

The following table gives a summary of the average first-day returns on IPOs in a number of countries around the world, with the figures collected from a number of studies by various authors.

| Country | Sample size | Time period | Average initial return | Country | Sample size | Time period | Average initial return |
|---------|------------|-------------|------------------------|---------|------------|-------------|------------------------|
| Argentina | 26 | 1991–2013 | 4.2% | Jordan | 53 | 1999–2008 | 149.0% |
| Australia | 1,562 | 1976–2011 | 21.8 | Korea | 1,720 | 1980–2013 | 59.3 |
| Austria | 103 | 1971–2013 | 6.4 | Malaysia | 474 | 1980–2013 | 59.3 |
| Belgium | 114 | 1984–2006 | 13.5 | Mexico | 123 | 1987–2012 | 11.6 |
| Brazil | 275 | 1979–2011 | 33.1 | Netherlands | 181 | 1982–2006 | 10.2 |
| Bulgaria | 9 | 2004–2007 | 36.5 | New Zealand | 242 | 1979–2013 | 18.6 |
| Canada | 720 | 1971–2013 | 6.5 | Nigeria | 122 | 1989–2013 | 13.1 |
| Chile | 81 | 1982–2013 | 7.4 | Norway | 209 | 1984–2013 | 8.1 |
| China | 2,512 | 1990–2013 | 118.4 | Philippines | 155 | 1987–2013 | 18.1 |
| Cyprus | 73 | 1997–2012 | 20.3 | Poland | 309 | 1991–2012 | 13.3 |
| Denmark | 164 | 1984–2011 | 7.4 | Portugal | 32 | 1992–2013 | 11.9 |
| Egypt | 62 | 1990–2010 | 10.4 | Russia | 64 | 1999–2013 | 3.3 |
| Finland | 168 | 1971–2013 | 16.9 | Singapore | 609 | 1973–2013 | 25.8 |
| France | 697 | 1983–2010 | 10.5 | South Africa | 316 | 1980–2013 | 17.4 |
| Germany | 736 | 1978–2011 | 24.2 | Spain | 143 | 1986–2013 | 10.3 |
| Greece | 373 | 1976–2013 | 50.8 | Sri Lanka | 105 | 1987–2008 | 33.5 |
| Hong Kong | 1,486 | 1980–2013 | 15.8 | Sweden | 374 | 1980–2011 | 27.2 |
| India | 964 | 1990–2011 | 88.5 | Switzerland | 64 | 1983–2013 | 27.3 |
| Indonesia | 441 | 1990–2013 | 25.0 | Taiwan | 1,620 | 1980–2013 | 38.1 |
| Iran | 279 | 1991–2004 | 22.4 | Thailand | 500 | 1987–2012 | 35.1 |
| Ireland | 38 | 1991–2013 | 21.6 | Turkey | 355 | 1990–2011 | 10.3 |
| Israel | 348 | 1990–2006 | 13.8 | United Kingdom | 4,932 | 1959–2012 | 16.0 |
| Italy | 312 | 1985–2013 | 15.2 | United States | 12,496 | 1960–2013 | 16.9 |
| Japan | 3,236 | 1970–2013 | 41.7 | | | | |

Jay R. Ritter is Cordell Professor of Finance at the University of Florida. An outstanding scholar, he is well known for his insightful analyses of new issues and going public.

Consider this tale of two investors. Ms. Smarts knows precisely what companies are worth when their shares are offered. Mr. Average knows only that prices usually rise one month after the IPO. Armed with this information, Mr. Average decides to buy 1,000 shares of every IPO. Does Mr. Average actually earn an abnormally high average return across all initial offerings?

The answer is no, and at least one reason is Ms. Smarts. For example, because Ms. Smarts knows that company *XYZ* is underpriced, she invests all her money in its IPO. When the issue is oversubscribed, the underwriters must allocate the shares between Ms. Smarts and Mr. Average. If they do this on a pro rata basis and if Ms. Smarts has bid for twice as many shares as Mr. Average, she will get two shares for each one Mr. Average receives. The net result is that when an issue is underpriced, Mr. Average cannot buy as much of it as he wants.

Ms. Smarts also knows that company *ABC* is overpriced. In this case, she avoids its IPO altogether, and Mr. Average ends up with a full 1,000 shares. To summarize, Mr. Average receives fewer shares when more knowledgeable investors swarm to buy an underpriced issue, but he gets all he wants when the smart money avoids the issue. This is called the *winner's curse*, and it largely explains why IPOs have such a large average return. When the average investor wins and gets his allocation, it is because those who knew better avoided the issue. To counteract the winner's curse and attract the average investor, underwriters underprice issues.[11]

- Suppose a stockbroker calls you up out of the blue and offers to sell "all the shares you want" of a new issue. Do you think the issue will be more or less underpriced than average?
- What factors determine the degree of underpricing?

## 20.4 THE ANNOUNCEMENT OF NEW EQUITY AND THE VALUE OF THE FIRM

It seems reasonable to believe that new long-term financing is arranged by firms after positive net present value (NPV) projects are put together. As a consequence, when the announcement of external financing is made, the firm's market value should go up. This is precisely the opposite of what actually happens in the case of new equity financing. Asquith and Mullins, Masulis and Korwar, and Mikkelson and Partch have all found that the market value of existing U.S. equity drops on the announcement of a new issue of common stock.[12] Studies by Mittoo and by Derosiers, L'Her, and Sauriol obtain a similar result for TSX stocks.[13] Plausible reasons for this strange result are as follows:

1. *Managerial information.* If managers have superior information about the market value of the firm, they may know when the firm is overvalued. If they do, they

---

[11] This explanation was first suggested in K. Rock, "Why New Issues Are Underpriced," *Journal of Financial Economics* (January–February 1986).

[12] P. Asquith and D. Mullins, "Equity Issues and Offering Dilution," *Journal of Financial Economics* (January–February 1986); R. Masulis and A. N. Korwar, "Seasoned Equity Offerings: An Empirical Investigation," *Journal of Financial Economics* (January–February 1986); and W. H. Mikkelson and M. M. Partch, "The Valuation Effects of Security Offerings and the Issuance Process," *Journal of Financial Economics* (January–February 1986).

[13] Usha R. Mittoo, "Seasoned Equity Offerings and the Cost of Equity in the Canadian Market," in Paul Halpern, ed., *Financing Growth in Canada* (Calgary, AB: University of Calgary Press, 1997); and Stéphanie Desrosiers, Jean-Francois L'Her, and Lorraine Sauriol, "SEOs: Bearers of Long-Term Bad News," *Canadian Investment Review* (Spring 2004).

might attempt to issue new shares of stock when the market value exceeds the correct value. This will benefit existing shareholders. However, the potential new shareholders are not stupid. They will infer overvaluation from the new issue, thereby bidding down the stock price on the announcement date of the issue.

2. *Debt capacity.* The stereotypical firm chooses a debt-to-equity ratio that balances the tax shield from the debt with the cost of financial distress. When the managers of a firm have special information that the probability of financial distress has risen, the firm is more likely to raise capital through stock than through debt. If the market infers this chain of events, the stock price should fall on the announcement date of an equity issue.

3. *Falling earnings.*[14] When managers raise capital in amounts that are unexpectedly large (as most unanticipated financings will be) and if investors have a reasonable fix on the firm's upcoming investments and dividend payouts (as they do because capital expenditure announcements are often well known, as are future dividends), the unanticipated financings are roughly equal to unanticipated shortfalls in earnings (this follows directly from the firm's sources and uses of funds identity). Therefore, an announcement of a new stock issue will also reveal a future earnings shortfall.

## 20.5   THE COST OF ISSUING SECURITIES

Issuing securities to the public isn't free, and the costs of different methods are important determinants of which method is used. The costs associated with *floating* a new issue are generically called *flotation* costs. In this section, we take a closer look at the flotation costs associated with equity sales to the public.

The costs of selling stock fall into six categories: (1) the spread, (2) other direct expenses, (3) indirect expenses, (4) abnormal returns, (5) underpricing, and (6) the overallotment option. We look at these costs first for American and then for Canadian equity sales:

**The Costs of Issuing Securities**

| | |
|---|---|
| Spread | The spread consists of direct fees paid by the issuer to the underwriting syndicate—the difference between the price the issuer receives and the offer price. |
| Other direct expenses | These are direct costs, incurred by the issuer, that are not part of the compensation to underwriters. These costs include filing fees, legal fees, and taxes—all reported on the prospectus. |
| Indirect expenses | These costs are not reported on the prospectus and include the costs of management time spent working on the new issue. |
| Abnormal returns | In a seasoned issue of stock, the price drops on average by 3 percent on the announcement of the issue. |
| Underpricing | For IPOs, losses arise from selling the stock below the correct value. |
| Overallotment (Green Shoe) option | The Green Shoe option gives the underwriters the right to buy additional shares at the offer price to cover overallotments. |

Table 20.5 reports the direct costs as a percentage of the gross amount raised for IPOs and SEOs over the period from 1990 to 2008 for publicly traded U.S. firms. The percentages in Table 20.5 are as reported in the prospectuses of the issuing companies. These costs include only the spread (underwriter discount) and other direct costs, including legal fees, accounting fees, printing costs, SEC registration costs, and taxes. Not included are indirect expenses, abnormal returns (for SEOs), underpricing (for IPOs), and the overallotment option.

---

[14] Robert S. Haugen and Claire Crutchley, "Corporate Earnings and Financings: An Empirical Analysis," *Journal of Business* (July 1990).

TABLE 20.5

### Direct Costs as a Percentage of Gross Proceeds for Equity (IPOs and SEOs) Offered by U.S. Operating Companies: 1990–2008

| | Equity | | | | | | | |
| | IPOs | | | | SEOs | | | |
| Proceeds (in $ millions) | Number of issues | Gross spread | Other direct expense | Total direct cost | Number of issues | Gross spread | Other direct expense | Total direct cost |
|---|---|---|---|---|---|---|---|---|
| 2–9.99 | 1,007 | 9.40% | 15.82% | 25.22% | 515 | 8.11% | 26.99% | 35.10% |
| 10–19.99 | 810 | 7.39 | 7.30 | 14.69 | 726 | 6.11 | 7.76 | 13.87 |
| 20–39.99 | 1,422 | 6.96 | 7.06 | 14.02 | 1,393 | 5.44 | 4.10 | 9.54 |
| 40–59.99 | 880 | 6.89 | 2.87 | 9.76 | 1,129 | 5.03 | 8.93 | 13.96 |
| 60–79.99 | 522 | 6.79 | 2.16 | 8.95 | 841 | 4.88 | 1.98 | 6.86 |
| 80–99.99 | 327 | 6.71 | 1.84 | 8.55 | 536 | 4.67 | 2.05 | 6.72 |
| 100–199.99 | 702 | 6.39 | 1.57 | 7.96 | 1,372 | 4.34 | 0.89 | 5.23 |
| 200–499.99 | 440 | 5.81 | 1.03 | 6.84 | 811 | 3.72 | 1.22 | 4.94 |
| 500 and up | 155 | 5.01 | 0.49 | 5.50 | 264 | 3.10 | 0.27 | 3.37 |
| Total | 6,265 | 7.19% | 3.18% | 10.37% | 7,587 | 5.02% | 2.68% | 7.69% |

Source: Inmoo Lee, Scott Lochhead, Jay Ritter, and Quanshui Zhao, "The Costs of Raising Capital," *Journal of Financial Research* (Spring 1996); calculations and updates by the authors.

As indicated in Table 20.5, the direct costs alone can be very large, particularly for smaller (less than $10 million) issues. For seasoned offerings, the direct costs, as reported by the companies, average a little more than 35 percent. This means the company, net of costs, receives 65 percent of the proceeds of the sale on average. On a $10 million issue, this is about $3.5 million in direct expenses—a substantial cost.

For IPOs, the effective costs can be much greater because of the indirect costs. Table 20.6 reports the direct costs of going public in Canada as of 2013. These figures understate the total cost because the study did not consider indirect expenses or the overallotment option. Once again we see that the costs of issuing securities can be considerable.

TABLE 20.6

### Costs of Going Public in Canada: 2013

| | Toronto Stock Exchange | TSX Venture Exchange |
|---|---|---|
| Listing fees | $10,000–$200,000 | $7,500–$40,000 |
| Accounting and auditing fees | $75,000–$100,000 | $25,000–$100,000 |
| Legal fees | $400,000–$750,000 | Above $75,000 |
| Underwriters' commission | 4–6% | Up to 12% |

Source: TMX Group, www.tmx.com/en/listings/listing_with_us/faq/index.html.

Overall, three conclusions emerge from our discussion of underwriting:

1. Substantial economies of size are evident. Larger firms can raise equity more easily.
2. The cost associated with underpricing can be substantial and can exceed the direct costs.
3. The issue costs are higher for an IPO than for an SEO.

## The Costs of Going Public: A Case Study

In March 2010, Athabasca Oil Corporation began trading on the TSX. Athabasca, an Alberta-based company, is focused on the sustainable development of oil sands in the Athabasca region in northeastern Alberta and light oil resources in northwestern Alberta.

Athabasca sold 75 million shares at $18 each, generating $1.35 billion after flotation costs. The proceeds of the issue were used to extract tar-like bitumen from the ground using steam-assisted gravity drainage techniques. Morgan Stanley Canada Ltd. and GMP Securities Ltd. were the leading underwriters used in this offering. The underwriters had an overallotment option to purchase up to an additional 11.25 million shares of common stock "at the initial public offering price" that would increase the value of the deal to $1.55 billion.

Even though the IPO raised $1.35 billion, Athabasca got to keep only $1.26 billion after underwriter commissions and other various expenses, which amounted to $81,000,000 and $6,500,000, respectively.[15] As the example shows, an IPO can be costly! In the end, Athabasca's expenses totalled $87,500,000, which represents about 6.5 percent of the issue's gross proceeds.

Despite such initial interest, the Athabasca IPO had a poor debut—shares plummeted[16] to $16.90 on the TSX, nearly a 6 percent drop from the IPO price of $18. The shares were apparently overpriced by $1.10, which means that the company cashed in on an additional $82.5 million. The shares fell an additional 33 percent during the first month of trading, making Athabasca one of the worst Canadian IPOs.[17] The drop in the share price can be attributed to the decrease in crude oil prices, the European debt crisis, and concerns over increasing interest rates. The decrease in crude oil prices exacerbated Athabasca's prospects as it is costly to dig bitumen out of the ground and refine it into usable petroleum products. As of October 3, 2014, Athabasca's shares closed at $5.12, far below its IPO price of $18. The company has never had a stock split, but it did issue warrants on its acquisition of Excelsior Energy back in 2010. As you will learn in Chapter 25, warrants have a dilutive effect on share prices, which may have slightly contributed to the share price decline.

**CONCEPT QUESTIONS**

- What are the different costs associated with security offerings?
- What lessons do we learn from studying issue costs?

## 20.6    RIGHTS

When new shares of common stock are sold to the general public, the proportional ownership of existing shareholders is likely to be reduced. However, if a **pre-emptive right** is contained in the firm's articles of incorporation, then the firm must first offer any new issue of common stock to existing shareholders. If the articles of incorporation do not include a pre-emptive right, the firm can offer the issue of common stock directly to either existing shareholders or the public. In some industries, regulatory authorities set rules concerning rights. For example, prior to the 1980 *Bank Act*, chartered banks were required to raise equity exclusively through rights offerings.

---

[15] The full Athabasca Oil Sands Corp. IPO prospectus can be found here: divestor.com/wp-content/uploads/2010/03/ATH-Final-Prospectus.pdf.

[16] Sacha Peter, "Athabasca Oil Sands—First Day of Trading," *WordPress* (April 2010), divestor.com/2010/04/09/athabasca-oil-sands-ipo-first-day-of-trading/.

[17] Doug Alexander, "Athabasca Oil, Largest Canadian IPO Since 1999, Performs Worst Since 2007," Bloomberg L.P. (May 2010), www.bloomberg.com/news/2010-05-12/athabasca-oil-largest-canadian-ipo-since-1999-performs-worst-since-2007.html.

An issue of common stock offered to existing shareholders is called a *rights offering*. In a rights offering, each shareholder is issued one right for every share owned. The rights give the shareholder an *option* to buy a specified number of new shares from the firm at a specified price within a specified time, after which time the rights are said to expire.

The terms of the rights offering are evidenced by certificates known as *rights*. Such rights are often traded on securities exchanges or OTC.

## The Mechanics of a Rights Offering

To illustrate the various considerations a financial manager has in a rights offering, we will examine the situation faced by the National Power Company, whose abbreviated initial financial statements are given in Table 20.7.

**TABLE 20.7**

**National Power Company Financial Statement before Rights Offering**

| NATIONAL POWER COMPANY | | | |
|---|---|---|---|
| **Balance Sheet** | | | |
| **Assets** | | **Shareholders' equity** | |
| | | Common stock | $ 5,000,000 |
| | | Retained earnings | 10,000,000 |
| Total | $15,000,000 | Total | $15,000,000 |

| Income Statement | |
|---|---|
| Earnings before taxes | $ 3,333,333 |
| Taxes (40%) | $ 1,333,333 |
| Net income | $ 2,000,000 |
| Earnings per share | $        2 |
| Shares outstanding | 1,000,000 |
| Market price per share | $       20 |
| Total market value | $20,000,000 |

As the table shows, National Power earns $2 million after taxes and has 1 million shares outstanding. Earnings per share (EPS) is thus $2. The stock sells for $20 (10 times earnings). To fund a planned expansion, the company intends to raise $5 million of new equity funds by a rights offering.

To execute a rights offering, the financial manager of National Power must answer the following questions:

1. What price should the existing shareholders be allowed to pay for a share of new stock?
2. How many rights will be required to purchase one share of stock?
3. What effect will the rights offering have on the existing price of the stock?

## Subscription Price

In a rights offering, the **subscription price** is the price that existing shareholders are allowed to pay for a share of stock. A rational shareholder will only subscribe to the rights offering if the subscription price is below the market price of the stock on the offer's expiration date. For example, if the stock price at expiration is $13 and the subscription price is $15, no rational shareholder will subscribe. Why pay $15 for something worth $13? National Power chooses a price of $10, which is well below the current market price of $20. As long as the market price does not fall by half before expiration, the rights offering will succeed.

## Number of Rights Needed to Purchase a Share

National Power wants to raise $5 million in new equity. Suppose that the subscription price is set at $10 per share. How National Power arrived at that price is something we will discuss below, but notice that the subscription price is substantially less than the current $20 per share market price.

At $10 per share, National Power will have to issue 500,000 new shares. This can be determined by dividing the total amount of funds to be raised by the subscription price:

$$\text{Number of new shares} = \frac{\text{Funds to be raised}}{\text{Subscription price}} = \frac{\$5,000,000}{\$10} = 500,000 \text{ shares} \quad (20.1)$$

Because shareholders always get one right for each share of stock they own, 1 million rights will be issued by National Power. To determine how many rights will be needed to buy one new share of stock, we can divide the number of existing outstanding shares of stock by the number of new shares:

$$\frac{\text{Number of rights needed}}{\text{to buy a share of stock}} = \frac{\text{Old shares}}{\text{New shares}} = \frac{1,000,000}{500,000} = 2 \text{ rights} \quad (20.2)$$

Thus, a shareholder will need to give up two rights plus $10 to receive a share of new stock. If all shareholders do this, National Power will raise the required $5 million.

It should be clear that the subscription price, the number of new shares, and the number of rights needed to buy a new share of stock are interrelated. For example, National Power can lower the subscription price. If so, more new shares must be issued to raise $5 million in new equity. Several alternatives are worked out here:

| Subscription price | New shares | Rights needed to buy a share of stock |
|---|---|---|
| $20 | 250,000 | 4 |
| 10 | 500,000 | 2 |
| 5 | 1,000,000 | 1 |

## The Value of a Right

Rights clearly have value. In the case of National Power, the right to be able to buy a share of stock worth $20 for $10 is definitely worth something.

Suppose a shareholder of National Power owns two shares of stock just before the rights offering. This situation is depicted in Table 20.8. Initially, National Power costs $20 per share, so the shareholder's total holding is worth 2 × $20 = $40. The National Power rights offer gives shareholders with two rights the opportunity to purchase one additional share for $10. The additional share does not carry a right.

The shareholder who has two shares will receive two rights. The holding of the shareholder who exercises these rights and buys the new share will increase to three shares. The total investment is $40 + $10 = $50 (the $40 initial value plus the $10 paid to the company).

The shareholder now holds three shares, all of which are identical because the new share does not have a right and the rights attached to the old shares have been exercised. Since the total cost of buying these three shares is $40 + $10 = $50, the price per share must end up at $50/3 = $16.67 (rounded to two decimal places).

Table 20.9 summarizes what happens to National Power's stock price. If all shareholders exercise their rights, the number of shares will increase to 1 million + 0.5 million = 1.5 million. The value of the firm will increase to $20 million + $5 million = $25 million. The value of each share will thus drop to $25 million/1.5 million = $16.67 after the rights offering.

**TABLE 20.8**

### The Value of Rights for the Individual Shareholder

| Initial position | |
|---|---|
| Number of shares | 2 |
| Share price | $20 |
| Value of holding | $40 |
| **Terms of offer** | |
| Subscription price | $10 |
| Number of rights issued | 2 |
| Number of rights for a new share | 2 |
| **After offer** | |
| Number of shares | 3 |
| Value of holdings | $50 |
| Share price | $16.67 |
| **Value of a right** | |
| Old price − New price | $20 − $16.67 = $3.33 |

**TABLE 20.9**

### National Power Company Rights Offering

| Initial position | |
|---|---|
| Number of shares | 1 million |
| Share price | $20 |
| Value of firm | $20 million |
| **Terms of offer** | |
| Subscription price | $10 |
| Number of rights issued | 1 million |
| Number of rights for a share | 2 |
| **After offer** | |
| Number of shares | 1.5 million |
| Share price | $16.67 |
| Value of firm | $25 million |
| Value of one right | $20 − $16.67 = $3.33 |

The difference between the old share price of $20 and the new share price of $16.67 reflects the fact that the old shares carried rights to subscribe to the new issue. The difference must equal the value of one right, that is, $20 − $16.67 = $3.33.

Although holding no shares of outstanding National Power stock, an investor who wants to subscribe to the new issue can do so by buying some rights. Suppose an outside investor buys two rights. This will cost $3.33 × 2 = $6.67 (accounting for previous rounding). If the investor exercises the rights at a subscription price of $10, the total cost will be $10 + $6.67 = $16.67. In return for this expenditure, the investor will receive a share of the new stock, which, as we have seen, is worth $16.67.

EXAMPLE 20.1

In the National Power example, suppose the subscription price is set at $8. How many shares will have to be sold? How many rights will you need to buy a new share? What is the value of a right? What will the price per share be after the rights offer?

To raise $5 million, $5 million/$8 = 625,000 shares will need to be sold. There are 1 million shares outstanding, so it will take 1 million/625,000 = 8/5 = 1.6 rights to buy a new share of stock. (You can buy five new shares for every eight you own.) After the rights offer, there will be 1.625 million shares worth $25 million altogether, so the per share value is $25/1.625 = $15.38 each. The value of a right in this case is the $20 original price less the $15.38 ending price ($4.62).

**Theoretical Value of a Right**   We can summarize Example 20.1 with an equation for the theoretical value of a right during the rights-on period:

$$R_0 = (M_0 - S)/(N + 1) \tag{20.3}$$

where

$M_0$ = Common share price during the rights-on period (see below)
$S$ = Subscription price
$N$ = Number of rights required to buy one new share

We illustrate the use of equation (20.3) by checking our answer for the value of one right in the National Power example:

$$R_0 = (\$20 - \$8)/(1.6 + 1) = \$4.62$$

This is the same answer we got earlier.

## Ex-Rights

National Power's rights have a substantial value. In addition, the rights offering will have a large impact on the market price of National Power's stock. It will drop by $3.33 on the day when the shares trade **ex-rights**.

The standard procedure for issuing rights is similar to that for paying a dividend. It begins with the firm's setting a **holder-of-record date**. Following stock exchange rules, the stock typically goes ex-rights four trading days before the holder-of-record date. If the stock is sold before the ex-rights date—rights-on, with rights, or cum rights—the new owner will receive the rights. After the ex-rights date, an investor who purchases the shares will not receive the rights.

EXAMPLE 20.2

The Lagrange Point Co. has proposed a rights offering. The stock currently sells for $40 per share. Under the terms of the offer, shareholders will be allowed to buy one new share for every five that they own at a price of $25 per share. What is the value of a right? What is the ex-rights price?

You can buy five rights-on shares for 5 × $40 = $200 and then exercise the rights for another $25. Your total investment is $225, and you end up with six ex-rights shares. The ex-rights price per share is $225/6 = $37.50 per share. The rights are thus worth $40 − $37.50 = $2.50 apiece.

Using equation (20.3), we have

$$R_0 = (\$40 - \$25)/(5 + 1) = \$2.50$$

## Value of Rights after Ex-Rights Date

When the stock goes ex-rights, its price drops by the value of one right. Until the rights expire, holders can buy one share at the subscription price by exercising $N$ rights. In equation form,[18]

$$M_e = M_0 - R_0 \tag{20.4}$$

$$R_e = (M_e - S)/N \tag{20.5}$$

where $M_e$ is the common share price during the ex-rights period.

Checking the formula using this example gives

$$M_e = \$40 - \$2.50 = \$37.50$$

$$R_e = (\$37.50 - \$25)/5 = \$2.50$$

---

**EXAMPLE 20.3**

In the previous example, suppose you could buy the rights for only $0.25 instead of the $2.50 we calculated. What could you do?

You could get rich quick, because you have found a money machine. Here is the recipe. Buy five rights for $1.25. Exercise them and pay $25 to get a new share. Your total investment to get one ex-rights share is 5 × $0.25 + $25 = $26.25. Sell the share for $37.50 and pocket the $11.25 difference. Repeat as desired.

---

A variation on Example 20.3 actually occurred in the course of a rights offering by a major Canadian chartered bank in the mid-1980s. The bank's employee stock ownership plan had promoted share ownership by tellers and clerical staff who were unfamiliar with the workings of rights offerings. When they received notification of the rights offering, many employees did not bother to respond until they were personally solicited by other, more sophisticated employees who bought the rights for a fraction of their value. We do not endorse the ethics behind such transactions. But the incident does show why it pays for everyone who owns stock to understand the workings of rights offers.

## The Underwriting Arrangements

Rights offerings are typically arranged using **standby underwriting**. In standby underwriting, the issuer makes a rights offering, and the underwriter makes a firm commitment to "take up" (that is, purchase) the unsubscribed portion of the issue. The underwriter usually gets a **standby fee** and additional amounts based on the securities taken up.

Standby underwriting protects the firm against undersubscription. This can occur if investors throw away rights or if bad news causes the stock's market price to fall below the subscription price.

In practice, a small percentage (less than 10 percent) of shareholders fail to exercise valuable rights. This can probably be attributed to ignorance or vacations. Furthermore, shareholders are usually given an **oversubscription privilege**, which enables them to purchase unsubscribed shares at the subscription price. The oversubscription privilege makes it unlikely that the corporate issuer would have to turn to its underwriter for help.

---

[18] During the ex-rights period, a right represents a short-lived option to buy the stock. Equation (20.5) gives the minimum value of this option. The market value of rights is generally higher, as explained in our discussion of options in Chapter 23.

## Effects on Shareholders

Shareholders can exercise their rights or sell them. In either case, the shareholder will not win or lose by the rights offering. The hypothetical holder of two shares of National Power has a portfolio worth $40. If the shareholder exercises the rights, he ends up with three shares worth a total of $50. In other words, by spending $10, the investor's holding increases in value by $10, which means that he is neither better nor worse off.

On the other hand, if the shareholder sells the two rights for $3.33 each, he obtains $3.33 × 2 = $6.67 and ends up with two shares worth $16.67 and the cash from selling the right:

$$
\begin{aligned}
\text{Shares held} &= 2 \times \$16.67 = \$33.33 \\
\text{Rights sold} &= 2 \times \$\ \ 3.33 = \underline{\ \ \ \ 6.67} \\
\text{Total} &\qquad\qquad\ \ = \$40.00
\end{aligned}
$$

The new $33.33 market value plus $6.67 in cash is exactly the same as the original holding of $40. Thus, shareholders cannot lose or gain from exercising or selling rights.

It is obvious that after the rights offering, the new market price of the firm's stock will be lower than it was before the rights offering. As we have seen, however, shareholders have suffered no loss because of the rights offering. The lower the subscription price, the greater is the price decline of a rights offering. It is important to emphasize that because shareholders receive rights equal in value to the price drop, the rights offering does not hurt shareholders.

There is one last issue. How do we set the subscription price in a rights offering? If you think about it, in theory, the subscription price really does not matter. It has to be below the market price of the stock for the rights to have value, but, beyond this, the price is arbitrary. In principle, it can be as low as we care to make it as long as it is not zero.

In practice, however, the subscription price is typically 20 to 25 percent below the prevailing stock price. Once we recognize market inefficiencies and frictions, a subscription price too close to the share price may result in undersubscription due simply to market imperfections.

## Cost of Rights Offerings

Until the early 1980s, rights offerings were the most popular method of raising new equity in Canada for seasoned issuers. (Obviously, rights offerings cannot be used for IPOs.) The reason was lower flotation costs from the simpler underwriting arrangements. In the late 1980s and early 1990s, with the rise of POP, bought deals replaced rights offerings as the prevalent form of equity issue. Even though rights offerings lost some popularity with the advent of POP, they are still widely used by companies to raise capital. For example, in February 2011, Ivanhoe Mines completed one of the largest rights offerings in Canadian history, raising gross proceeds of US$1.18 billion. The proceeds of the rights offering were used to advance construction and development of Ivanhoe Mines' Oyu Tolgoi Copper and Gold Project in southern Mongolia.

In the United States, firms use general cash offers much more often than rights offerings. This reliance on general cash offers has caused considerable debate among researchers because, as in Canada, rights offerings are usually much cheaper in terms of flotation costs. One study has found that firms making underwritten rights offers suffered substantially larger price drops than did firms making underwritten cash offers.[19] This is a hidden cost, and it may be part of the reason that underwritten rights offers are uncommon in the United States. Alternatively, as in Canada, the introduction of streamlined offer procedures through POP is likely a factor.[20]

---

[19] Robert S. Hansen, "The Demise of the Rights Issue," *Review of Financial Studies* (Fall 1988).

[20] This argument is from N. D. Ursel and D. J. Trepanier, "Securities Regulation Reform and the Decline of Rights Offerings," *Canadian Journal of Administrative Science* (June 2001).

**CONCEPT**
**QUESTIONS**

- How does a rights offering work?
- What questions must financial management answer in a rights offering?
- How is the value of a right determined?
- When does a rights offering affect the value of a company's shares?
- Does a rights offering cause a share price decrease? How are existing shareholders affected by a rights offering?

## 20.7   THE PRIVATE EQUITY MARKET

The previous sections of this chapter assumed that a company is big enough, successful enough, and old enough to raise capital in the public equity market. Of course, there are many firms that have not reached this stage and cannot use the public equity market. For start-up firms or firms in financial trouble, the public equity market is often not available.[21] Instead, these firms often raise the required funds through banks and angel investors. This has created a trend toward more private equity buyouts, increasing the profile of private equity firms and the private equity process. In 2014, deal activity in Canada's buyout market continued to play a major role, especially in the oil and gas sector. For instance, in June 2014 Encana Corp. sold assets to Jupiter Resources Inc., a portfolio company of Apollo Capital Management, for US$1.8 billion. As of June 30, 2014, there were 192 buyout private equity transactions totalling nearly $9.7 billion, which is almost triple the $3.2 billion reported in the first half of 2013.[22]

### Private Placement

Private placements avoid the costly procedures associated with the registration requirements that are part of public issues. The OSC and the U.S. SEC restrict private placement issues to no more than a couple of dozen knowledgeable investors, including institutions such as insurance companies and pension funds. The biggest drawback of privately placed securities is that the securities cannot be easily resold. Most private placements involve debt securities, but equity securities can also be privately placed.

### The Private Equity Firm

A large amount of private equity investment is undertaken by professional private equity managers representing large institutional investors such as mutual funds and pension funds. The limited partnership is the dominant form of intermediation in this market. Typically, the institutional investors act as the limited partners and the professional managers act as general partners. The general partners are firms that specialize in funding and managing equity investments in closely held private firms. The private equity market has been important for both traditional start-up companies and established public firms. Thus, the private equity market can be divided into venture equity and non-venture equity markets. A large part of the non-venture market is made up of firms in financial distress. Firms in financial distress are not likely to be able to issue public equity and typically cannot use traditional forms of debt such as bank loans or public debt. For these firms, the best alternative is to find a private equity market firm.

### Venture Capital

**Venture capital** is an important part of the private equity market. The following are three distinctive characteristics of venture capitalists (VCs):

---

[21] S. E. Pratt, "Overview and Introduction to the Venture Capital Industry," *Guide to Venture Capital Sources*, 10th ed. (Laurel Avenue, Box 348, Wellesley Hills, MA 02181: Venture Economics, 1987).

[22] Canada's Buyout & Private Equity Market in Q2 2014, Thomson Reuters, www.cvca.ca/files/News/CVCA_BO___PE_Data_Q2_2014.pdf.

1. *VCs are financial intermediaries that raise funds from outside investors.* VC firms are typically organized as limited partnerships. As with any limited partnership, limited partners invest with the general partner, who makes the investment decisions.

2. *VCs play an active role in overseeing, advising, and monitoring the companies in which they invest.* For example, members of venture capital firms frequently join the board of directors.

3. *VCs generally do not want to own the investment forever. Rather, VCs look for an exit strategy, such as taking the investment public or selling it to another company.* In order for a firm to be sold or go public, the firm must be a certain size. Since the investment is generally small initially, it must possess great growth potential. Out of a study of 11,686 companies first funded in 1991 to 2000, nearly 50 percent had successful exits—went public or were acquired.[23]

## Suppliers of Venture Capital

Venture capital activity varies by industry, with high-tech making up the largest component. There are at least five types of suppliers of venture capital. First, a few old-line, wealthy families have traditionally provided start-up capital to promising businesses. These families have been involved in venture capital since early in the last century, if not before.

Second, a number of private partnerships and corporations have been formed to provide investment funds. The organizer behind the partnership might raise capital from institutional investors, such as insurance companies and pension funds. Alternatively, a group of individuals might provide the funds to be ultimately invested with budding entrepreneurs.

Stories used to abound about how easily an individual could obtain venture capital. Though that may have been the case in an earlier era, it is certainly not the case today. Venture capital firms employ various screening procedures to prevent inappropriate funding. For example, because of the large demand for funds, many VCs have at least one employee whose full-time job consists of reading business plans. Only the very best plans can expect to attract funds. Maier and Walker and Riding indicate that only about 2 to 3 percent of requests actually receive financing.[24]

Third, large industrial or financial corporations have established venture capital subsidiaries. Chartered banks, for example, participate in the venture capital market through affiliates. Other firms, such as Bell Canada Enterprises (BCE), invest in firms developing related technological innovations. Merchant banks such as Onex and Ontario Teachers' Merchant Bank provide venture capital financing.

Fourth, around one-third of venture capital activity has some government involvement. *Crown-related firms* are government owned. Although capital growth is important to these firms, their mandates include investing in depressed areas and targeting particular industries. *Hybrids* have a mix of government and private-sector support. These firms include labour-sponsored venture capital firms. Sponsored by labour unions and established to fund small and medium-sized businesses and promote job creation, these funds offer a 30 percent tax credit to individual investors. Anderson and Tian argue that labour-sponsored funds are unattractive to investors due to poor performance and high fees.[25]

---

[23] "National Venture Capital Association Yearbook 2014," Thomson Reuters (2014), www.nvca.org/index.php?option=com_content&view=article&id=257&Itemid=103.

[24] J. B. Maier and D. Walker, "The Role of Venture Capital in Financing Small Business," *Journal of Business Venturing* (Summer 1987); A. Riding, in "Roundtable on Angel Investment in Canada," *Canadian Investment Review* (Fall 2000).

[25] Scott Anderson and Yisong Tian, "Incentive Fees, Valuation and Performance of Labour Sponsored Investment Funds," *Canadian Investment Review* (Fall 2003).

Fifth, participants in an informal venture capital market have been identified.[26] Rather than belonging to any venture capital firm, these investors (often referred to as *angels*) act as individuals when providing financing. However, they should not, by any means, be viewed as isolated. Wetzel and others indicate that there is a rich network of angels, continuously relying on each other for advice. A number of researchers have stressed that in any informal network, there is likely one knowledgeable and trustworthy individual who, when backing a venture, brings a few less experienced investors in with her. Riding argues that the prototypical angel has income over $175,000, net worth over $1,000,000, and substantial business experience and knowledge. As one might expect, the informal VC is able to tolerate high risks.

Though this informal market may seem small and unimportant, it is perhaps the largest of all sources of venture capital. The size of each contribution is smaller here, typically ranging from $10,000 to $150,000.

## Stages of Financing

Lo identifies five stages in venture capital financing:[27]

1. *Seed-money stage.* A small amount of financing needed to prove a concept or develop a product. Marketing is not included in this stage.

2. *Start-up and first-round financing.* Financing for firms that started within the past year. Funds are likely to pay for marketing and product development expenditures. This also includes additional money to begin sales and manufacturing after a firm has spent its start-up funds.

3. *Second-round financing.* Funds earmarked for working capital for a firm that is currently selling its product but still losing money.

4. *Third-round financing.* Financing for a company that is at least breaking even and is contemplating an expansion. This stage is also known as mezzanine financing.

5. *Fourth-round financing.* Money provided for firms that are likely to go public within half a year. This round is also known as bridge financing.

Although these categories may seem vague to the reader, we have found that the terms are well accepted within the industry. For example, the venture capital firms listed in Pratt's *Guide to Venture Capital* indicate which of the above stages they are interested in financing.

The last stage in venture capital financing is the IPO.[28] VCs are very important participants in IPOS. VCs rarely sell all of the shares they own at the time of the IPO. Instead, they usually sell out in subsequent public offerings. However, there is considerable evidence that VCs can successfully time IPOs by taking firms public when the market values are highest.[29] Venture capital investment in Canada went from $2.65 billion in 1999 to $5.78 billion in 2000 at the height of the tech boom. By 2005, it was back down to $1.83 billion.[30] In general, commitments rose during the bull market years between 2003 and 2006, before dropping in tandem with the more recent economic crisis.

---

[26] See W. E. Wetzel, "The Informal Venture Capital Market: Aspects of Scale and Market Efficiency," *Journal of Business Venturing* (Fall 1987).

[27] Joseph Lo, "Note on Venture Capital," Richard Ivey School of Business, 9B04N005, 2004.

[28] A very influential paper by Christopher Barry, Chris J. Muscarella, John W. Peavey III, and Michael R. Vetsuypens, "The Role of Venture Capital in the Creation of Public Companies: Evidence from the Going Public Process," *Journal of Financial Economics* (October 1990), shows that VCs do not usually sell shares at the time of the IPO, but they usually have board seats and act as advisors to managers.

[29] This successful timing ability adds another anomaly to the efficient markets hypothesis.

[30] Joseph Lo, op. cit. Additional information available at the Canadian Venture Capital and Private Equity Association website. 2005 data were obtained from www.cvca.ca/files/News/RNathan_Presentation_press_conference_Feb_14_2006.pdf.

## Some Venture Capital Realities

Although there is a large venture capital market, the truth is that access to venture capital is very limited. Venture capital companies receive huge numbers of unsolicited proposals, the vast majority of which end up unread. VCs rely heavily on informal networks of lawyers, accountants, bankers, and other VCs to help identify potential investments. As a result, personal contacts are important in gaining access to the venture capital market; it is very much an "introduction" market.

Another simple fact about venture capital is that it is quite expensive. In a typical deal, the VC will demand (and get) 40 percent or more of the equity in the company. VCs frequently hold voting preferred stock, giving them various priorities in the event the company is sold or liquidated. The VC will typically demand (and get) several seats on the company's board of directors and may even appoint one or more members of senior management.

**CONCEPT QUESTIONS**

- What are the different sources of venture capital financing?
- What are the different stages for companies seeking venture capital financing?
- What is the private equity market?

---

## 20.8

# SUMMARY AND CONCLUSIONS

This chapter looks at how corporate securities are issued:

1. The costs of issuing securities can be quite large. They are much lower (as a percentage) for larger issues.

2. For large issues, the bought deal type of underwriting is far more prevalent than regular underwriting. This is probably connected to the savings available through Prompt Offering Prospectuses (POPs) and concentrated selling efforts.

3. Direct and indirect costs of going public can be substantial. However, once a firm is public, it can raise additional capital more easily than private firms.

4. Rights offerings are cheaper than general cash offers. Even so, most new equity issues in the United States are underwritten general cash offers. In Canada, the bought deal is cheaper and dominates the new issue market.

5. Venture capitalists (VCs) are an increasingly important influence on start-up firms and subsequent financing.

**KEY TERMS**

Best-efforts
  underwriting 596
Bought deal 596
Ex-rights 608
Firm-commitment
  underwriting 596
General cash offer 595
Holder-of-record date 608

Initial public offering
  (IPO) 598
Oversubscription
  privilege 609
Pre-emptive right 604
Prospectus 593
Red herring 593
Regular underwriting 596
Rights offer 595

Seasoned equity offering
  (SEO) 595
Spread (discount) 595
Standby fee 609
Standby underwriting 609
Subscription price 605
Syndicate (banking
  group) 595
Venture capital 611

## Rights Offerings

20.1  Again Inc. is proposing a rights offering. There are 450,000 shares outstanding at $90 each. There will be 80,000 new shares offered at $84 each.

    *a.* What is the new market value of the company?

    *b.* How many rights are associated with one of the new shares?

    *c.* What is the ex-rights price?

    *d.* What is the value of a right?

    *e.* Why might a company have a rights offering rather than a general cash offer?

20.2  The Clifford Corp. has announced a rights offer to raise $28 million for a new journal, the *Journal of Financial Excess*. This journal will review potential articles after the author pays a non-refundable reviewing fee of $5,000 per page. The stock currently sells for $27 per share, and there are 2.9 million shares outstanding.

    *a.* What is the maximum possible subscription price? What is the minimum?

    *b.* If the subscription price is set at $25 per share, how many shares must be sold? How many rights will it take to buy one share?

    *c.* What is the ex-rights price? What is the value of a right?

    *d.* Show how a shareholder with 1,000 shares before the offering and no desire (or money) to buy additional shares is not harmed by the rights offer.

## Rights

20.3  Stone Shoe Co. has concluded that additional equity financing will be needed to expand operations and that the needed funds will be best obtained through a rights offering. It has correctly determined that as a result of the rights offering, the share price will fall from $65 to $63.18 ($65 is the rights-on price; $63.18 is the ex-rights price, also known as the *when-issued* price). The company is seeking $15 million in additional funds with a per-share subscription price equal to $50. How many shares are there currently, before the offering? (Assume that the increment to the market value of the equity equals the gross proceeds from the offering.)

## Initial Public Offering Underpricing

20.4  The Woods Co. and the Garcia Co. have both announced IPOs at $40 per share. One of these is undervalued by $8, and the other is overvalued by $5, but you have no way of knowing which is which. You plan on buying 1,000 shares of each issue. If an issue is underpriced, it will be rationed, and only half your order will be filled. If you *could* get 1,000 shares in Woods and 1,000 shares in Garcia, what would your profit be? What profit do you actually expect? What principle have you illustrated?

## Calculating Flotation Costs

20.5  The St. Anger Corp. needs to raise $35 million to finance its expansion into new markets. The company will sell new shares of equity via a general cash offering to raise the needed funds. If the offer price is $31 per share and the company's underwriters charge an 8 percent spread, how many shares need to be sold?

20.6  In Problem 20.5, if the OSC filing fee and associated administrative expenses of the offering are $900,000, how many shares need to be sold?

20.7  The Green Hills Co. has just gone public. Under a firm-commitment agreement, Green Hills received $22.10 for each of the 8 million shares sold. The initial offering price was $24 per share, and the stock rose to $29.50 per share in the first few minutes of trading. Green Hills paid $950,000 in direct legal and other costs and $250,000 in indirect costs. What was the flotation cost as a percentage of funds raised?

## Price Dilution

20.8  Raggio Inc. has 100,000 shares of stock outstanding. Each share is worth $80, so the company's market value of equity is $8,000,000. Suppose the firm issues 20,000 new shares at the following prices: $80, $75, and $65. What will the effect be of each of these alternative offering prices on the existing price per share?

**Stock Offerings**

20.9 The Newton Company has 50,000 shares of stock that each sell for $40. Suppose the company issues 9,000 shares of new stock at the following prices: $40, $20, and $10. What is the effect of each of the alternative offering prices on the existing price per share?

**Rights**

20.10 A company's stock currently sells for $68 per share. Last week the firm issued rights to raise new equity. To purchase a new share, a shareholder must remit $11 and three rights.
 a. What is the ex-rights stock price?
 b. What is the price of one right?
 c. When will the price drop occur? Why will it occur then?

20.11 Summit Corp.'s stock is currently selling at $32 per share. There are 1 million shares outstanding. The firm is planning to raise $2 million to finance a new project. What are the ex-rights stock price, the value of a right, and the appropriate subscription prices under the following scenarios?
 a. Two shares of outstanding stock are entitled to purchase one additional share of the new issue.
 b. Four shares of outstanding stock are entitled to purchase one additional share of the new issue.
 c. How does the stockholders' wealth change from (a) to (b)?

20.12 Hothouse Mfg. is considering a rights offer. The company has determined that the ex-rights price will be $61. The current price is $68 per share, and there are 10 million shares outstanding. The rights offer would raise a total of $60 million. What is the subscription price?

**Value of a Right**

20.13 Show that the value of a right can be written as

$$\text{Value of a right} = P_{RO} - P_X = (P_{RO} - P_S)/(N + 1)$$

where $P_{RO}$, $P_S$, and $P_X$ stand for the rights-on price, the subscription price, and the ex-rights price, respectively, and $N$ is the number of rights needed to buy one new share at the subscription price.

**Selling Rights**

20.14 Wuttke Corp. wants to raise $4,125,000 via a rights offering. The company currently has 750,000 shares of common stock outstanding that sell for $45 per share. Its underwriter has set a subscription price of $25 per share and will charge Wuttke a 6 percent spread. If you currently own 6,000 shares of stock in the company and decide not to participate in the rights offering, how much money can you get by selling your rights?

**Valuing a Right**

20.15 Mitsi Inventory Systems Inc. has announced a rights offer. The company has announced that it will take four rights to buy a new share in the offering at a subscription price of $30. At the close of business the day before the ex-rights day, the company's stock sells for $60 per share. The next morning you notice that the stock sells for $54 per share and the rights sell for $5 each. Are the stock and/or the rights correctly priced on the ex-rights day? Describe a transaction in which you could use these prices to create an immediate profit.

MINICASE

# East Coast Yachts Goes Public

Larissa Warren and Dan Ervin have been discussing the future of East Coast Yachts. The company has been experiencing fast growth, and the future looks like clear sailing. However, the fast growth means that the company's growth can no longer be funded by internal sources, so Larissa and Dan have decided the time is right to take the company public. To this end, they have entered into discussions with the investment bank of Crowe & Mallard. The company has a working relationship with Robin Perry, the underwriter who assisted with the company's previous bond offering. Crowe & Mallard has helped numerous small companies in the IPO process, so Larissa and Dan feel confident with this choice.

Robin begins by telling Larissa and Dan about the process. Although Crowe & Mallard charged an underwriter fee of 4 percent on the bond offering, the underwriter fee is 7 percent on all initial stock offerings of the size of East Coast Yachts' initial offering. Robin tells Larissa and Dan that the company can expect to pay about $1,800,000 in legal fees and expenses, $15,000 in OSC registration fees, and $20,000 in other filing fees. Additionally, to be listed on the TSX, the company must pay $100,000. There are also transfer agent fees of $8,500 and engraving expenses of $525,000. The company should also expect to pay $75,000 for other expenses associated with the IPO.

Finally, Robin tells Larissa and Dan that to file with the OSC, the company must provide three years' worth of audited financial statements. She is unsure of the costs of the audit. Dan tells Robin that the company provides audited financial statements as part of its bond indenture, and the company pays $325,000 per year for the outside auditor.

1. At the end of the discussion Dan asks Robin about the Dutch auction IPO process. What are the differences in the expenses to East Coast Yachts if it uses a Dutch auction IPO versus a traditional IPO? Should the company go public with a Dutch auction or use a traditional underwritten offering?

2. During the discussion of the potential IPO and East Coast Yachts' future, Dan states that he feels the company should raise $75 million. However, Larissa points out that if the company needs more cash soon, a secondary offering close to the IPO would be potentially problematic. Instead, she suggests that the company should raise $100 million in the IPO. How can you calculate the optimal size of the IPO? What are the advantages and disadvantages of increasing the size of the IPO to $100 million?

3. After deliberation, Larissa and Dan have decided that the company should use a firm-commitment offering with Crowe & Mallard as the lead underwriter. The IPO will be for $85 million. Ignoring underpricing, how much will the IPO cost the company as a percentage of the funds received?

4. Many of the employees of East Coast Yachts have shares of stock in the company because of an existing employee stock purchase plan. To sell the stock, the employees can tender their shares to be sold in the IPO at the offering price, or the employees can retain their stock and sell it in the secondary market after East Coast Yachts goes public (once the 180-day lockup period expires). Larissa asks you to advise the employees about which option is best. What would you suggest to the employees?

# Long-Term Debt

**EXECUTIVE SUMMARY**

The previous chapter introduced the mechanics of new long-term financing, with an emphasis on equity. This chapter takes a closer look at long-term debt instruments.

The chapter begins with a review of the basic features of long-term debt and a description of some important aspects of publicly issued long-term bonds. We also discuss forms of long-term financing that are not publicly issued: term loans and private placement bonds. These are directly placed with lending institutions, such as chartered banks and life insurance companies.

All bond agreements have protective covenants. These are restrictions on the firm that protect the bondholder. We present several types of protective covenants in this chapter.

Most publicly issued corporate bonds have call provisions, which enable a company to buy back its bonds at a predetermined call price. This chapter attempts to answer two questions about call provisions:

1. Should firms issue callable bonds?
2. When should such bonds be called?

Financial engineering has produced many different kinds of long-term bonds. We discuss zero-coupon bonds, floating-rate bonds, and other special types of bonds and then analyze what types of bonds are best in different circumstances.

## 21.1  LONG-TERM DEBT: A REVIEW

Long-term debt securities are promises by the issuing firm to repay principal and to pay interest on the unpaid balance. The *maturity* of a long-term debt instrument refers to the length of time the debt remains outstanding with some unpaid balance. Debt securities can be *short term* (maturities of one year or less) or *long term* (maturities of more than one year).[1] Short-term debt is sometimes referred to as *unfunded debt*; long-term debt is sometimes called *funded debt*.[2]

The two major forms of long-term debt are public issue and privately placed debt. We discuss public issue bonds first, and most of what we say about them holds true for privately placed long-term debt as well. The main difference between publicly issued and privately placed debt is that private debt is directly placed with a lending institution.

There are many other attributes of long-term debt, including security, seniority, call features, sinking funds, ratings, and protective covenants. The boxed material below illustrates many of these attributes.

---

[1] In addition, people often refer to *intermediate-term debt*, which has a maturity of more than one year and less than three to five years.

[2] The word *funding* generally implies long term. Thus, a firm planning to *fund* its debt requirements may be replacing short-term debt with long-term debt.

### Features of Suncor Energy Inc.:
### Series 4 Medium-Term Notes (Unsecured) Issue

| Term | | Explanation |
|---|---|---|
| Amount of issue | $700 billion | The company issued $700 billion of bonds. |
| Issue date | May 22, 2008 | The bonds were sold on May 22, 2008. |
| Maturity date | May 22, 2018 | The bonds will be paid in 10 years from the issue date. |
| Annual coupon | 5.8 | Each bondholder will receive $58 per bond per year. |
| Face value | $1,000 | The denomination of the bonds is $1,000. |
| Issue price | 99.925 | The issue price was 99.925% of the $1,000 face value per bond. |
| Yield to maturity | 2.464% | If the bond is held to maturity, bondholders will receive a stated annual rate of return equal to 2.464%. |
| Coupon payment | May 22, November 22 | Coupons of $58/2 = $29 will be paid semiannually on these dates. |
| Security | Unsecured | The bonds are debentures. |
| Call provision | Canada Yield Price at Canada plus 0.525%. | The bonds are redeemable at the company's option at the price calculated to provide a yield to maturity (YTM) equal to Canada yield or equivalent maturity plus 0.525%. |
| Rating | DBRS A− | The bond qualifies for an investment-grade rating. |

Source: Information compiled by the Ontario Securities Commission.

## 21.2    THE PUBLIC ISSUE OF BONDS

The general procedures followed in a **public issue** of bonds are the same as those for stocks. The issue must be registered with the Ontario Securities Commission (OSC) and any other relevant provincial securities commissions, there must be a prospectus, and so on. The registration statement for a public issue of bonds, however, is different from the one for common stock. For bonds, the registration statement must indicate an indenture.

An **indenture** is a written agreement between the corporation (the borrower) and a trust company. It is sometimes referred to as the *deed of trust*.[3] The trust company is appointed by the corporation to represent the bondholders. The trust company must (1) be sure the terms of the indenture are obeyed, (2) manage the sinking fund, and (3) represent bondholders if the company defaults on its payments.

The typical bond indenture can be a document of several hundred pages. It generally includes

1. The basic terms of the bonds.
2. A description of property used as security.
3. The seniority of the bonds.
4. Details of the protective covenants.
5. The sinking fund arrangements.
6. The call provision.

Each of these is discussed below.

---

[3] The terms *loan agreement* and *loan contract* are usually used for privately placed debt and term loans.

## The Basic Terms

Bonds usually have a *face value* of $1,000. This is also called the *principal value* and is stated on the bond certificate. In addition, the *par value* (i.e., initial accounting value) of a bond is the same as the face value.

Transactions between bond buyers and bond sellers determine the market value of the bond. Actual bond market values depend on the general level of interest rates, among other factors, and need not equal the face value. Because the Canadian corporate bond market is quite illiquid, there is a good chance that it is not fully efficient. For this reason, there is likely a good payoff for investment dealers and issuers who pioneer financial engineering innovations. The bond price is quoted as a percentage of the face value. Though interest is paid only twice a year, interest *accrues* continuously over the year. This is illustrated in Example 21.1.

---

**EXAMPLE 21.1**

Suppose the Black Corporation has issued 100 bonds. The amount stated on each bond certificate is $1,000. The total face value or principal value of the bonds is $100,000. Further suppose the bonds are currently *priced* at 100, which means 100 percent of $1,000. This means that buyers and sellers are holding bonds at a price per bond of $1,000. If interest rates rise, the price of the bond might fall to, say, 97, which means 97 percent of $1,000 (or $970).

---

Suppose the bonds have a stated interest rate of 7 percent due on January 1, 2060. The bond indenture might read as follows:

> The bond will mature on January 1, 2060, and will be limited in aggregate principal amount to $100,000. Each bond will bear interest at the rate of 7.0 percent per annum from January 1, 2000, or from the most recent Interest Payment Date to which interest has been paid or provided for. Interest is payable semiannually on July 1 and January 1 of each year.

Suppose an investor bought the bonds on April 1, 2014. Since the last coupon payment on January 1, three months of interest had accrued. These three months (90 days) represented approximately half of a semiannual coupon period. The stated annual rate was 7 percent or 3.5 percent per semiannual period, so accrued interest over the three months is $17.40.[4] Therefore, the buyer of the bond had to pay a price of 100 percent plus accrued interest of $17.40. On July 1, the buyer received an interest payment of $35. This can be viewed as the sum of the $17.40 she paid the seller plus the three months of interest (91 days), $17.60, for holding the bond from April 1 to July 1.

As is typical of corporate bonds, the Black bonds are **registered**. The indenture might read as follows:

> Interest is payable semiannually on July 1 and January 1 of each year to the person in whose name the bond is registered at the close of business on June 15 or December 15, respectively.

This means that the company has a registrar who will record the ownership of each bond. The company will pay the interest and principal directly to the owner of record.

When a bond is registered with attached coupons, the bondholder must separate a coupon from the bond certificate and send it to the company registrar (paying agent). Today most registered bonds pay interest automatically without requiring the owner

---

[4] To be precise, accrued interest in Canada is computed based on a day count. Since 2014 is not a leap year, there are 90 days between the last coupon payment on January 1 and the settlement date on April 1. The coupon period is 181 days. Accrued interest is 90/181 × 3.5% × $1000 = $17.40.

to send in a coupon. Some bonds are in **bearer** form. This means that ownership is not recorded in the company books. As with a registered bond with attached coupons, the holder of the bond certificate separates the coupon and sends it in to the company to receive payment.

There are two drawbacks to bearer bonds. First, they can be easily lost or stolen. Second, because the company does not know who owns its bonds, it cannot notify bondholders of important events. Consider, for example, a couple who go to their safety deposit box and clip the coupon on their 12 percent, $1,000 bond issued by the Black Company. They send the coupon to the paying agent and feel richer. A few days later, a notice comes from the paying agent that the bond was retired and its principal paid off one year earlier. In other words, the bond no longer exists. The couple must forfeit one year of interest. (Of course, they can turn their bond in for $1,000.)

However, bearer bonds have the advantage of secrecy because even the issuing company does not know who the bond's owners are. This secrecy is particularly vexing to taxing authorities because tax collection on interest is difficult if the holder is unknown.

## Security

Debt securities are also classified according to the *collateral* protecting the bondholder. Collateral is a general term for the assets that are pledged as security for payment of debt. For example, *collateral trust bonds* involve a pledge of common stock held by the corporation.

---

**EXAMPLE 21.2**

Suppose Railroad Holding Company owns all of the common stock of Track Inc.; that is, Track Inc. is a wholly owned subsidiary of the Railroad Holding Company. Railroad issues debt securities that pledge the common stock of Track Inc. as collateral. The debts are collateral trust bonds; a trust company will hold them. If Railroad Holding Company defaults on the debt, the trust company will be able to sell the stock of Track Inc. to satisfy Railroad's obligation.

---

*Mortgage securities* are secured by a mortgage on real estate or other long-term assets of the borrower.[5] The legal document that describes such a mortgage is called a *mortgage-trust indenture* or *trust deed*. The mortgage can be *closed end*, so that there is a limit as to the amount of bonds that can be issued. More frequently it is *open end*, without limit to the amount of bonds that may be issued.

---

**EXAMPLE 21.3**

Suppose the Yukon Land Company has buildings and land worth $10 million and a $4 million mortgage on these properties. If the mortgage is closed end, the Yukon Land Company cannot issue more bonds on this property.

If the bond indenture contains no clause limiting the amount of additional bonds that can be issued, it is an open-end mortgage. In this case, the Yukon Land Company can issue additional bonds on its property, making the existing bonds riskier. For example, if additional mortgage bonds of $2 million are issued, the property has been pledged for a total of $6 million of bonds. If Yukon Land Company must liquidate its property for $4 million, the original bondholders will receive 4/6, or 67 percent, of their investment. If the mortgage had been closed end, they would have received 100 percent of the stated value.

---

[5] A set of railroad cars is an example of "other long-term assets" used as security.

The value of a mortgage depends on the market value of the underlying property. For this reason, mortgage bonds sometimes require that the property be properly maintained and insured. Of course, a building and equipment bought in 1914 for manufacturing slide rules might not have much value, no matter how well the company maintains it. The value of any property ultimately depends on its next best economic use. Bond indentures cannot easily insure against losses in economic value.

Sometimes mortgages are on specific property, for example, a single building. More often, blanket mortgages are used. A blanket mortgage pledges many assets owned by the company.

Some bonds represent unsecured obligations of the company. A **debenture** is an unsecured bond, for which no specific pledge of property is made. Debenture holders have a claim on property not otherwise pledged: the property that remains after mortgages and collateral trusts are taken into account. Almost all public bonds issued by industrial and finance companies are debentures. However, most utility bonds are secured by a pledge of assets.

## Seniority

In general terms, *seniority* indicates preference in position over other lenders, and debts are sometimes labelled "senior" or "junior" to indicate seniority. Some debt is *subordinated*, as in, for example, a subordinated debenture.

In the event of default, holders of subordinated debt must give preference to other special creditors. Usually, this means that the subordinated lenders are paid off from cash flow and asset sales only after the specified creditors have been compensated. However, debt cannot be subordinated to equity.

## Protective Covenants

A protective covenant is the part of the indenture or loan agreement that limits certain actions of the borrowing company. **Protective covenants** can be classified into two types: negative covenants and positive covenants. A **negative covenant** limits or prohibits actions that the company may take. Here are some typical examples:

1. Limitations are placed on the amount of dividends a company may pay.
2. The firm cannot pledge any of its assets to other lenders.
3. The firm cannot merge with another firm.
4. The firm may not sell or lease its major assets without approval by the lender.
5. The firm cannot issue additional long-term debt.

A **positive covenant** specifies an action that the company agrees to take or a condition the company must abide by. Here are some examples:

1. The company agrees to maintain its working capital at a minimum level.
2. The company must furnish periodic financial statements to the lender.

The financial implications of protective covenants were treated in detail in the chapters on capital structure. In that discussion, we argued that protective covenants can benefit shareholders because if bondholders are assured that they will be protected in times of financial stress, they will accept a lower interest rate.

## The Sinking Fund

Bonds can be entirely repaid at maturity, at which time the bondholder will receive the stated value of the bond, or they can be repaid before maturity. Early repayment is more typical.

In a direct placement of debt, the repayment schedule is specified in the loan contract. For public issues, the repayment takes place through the use of a sinking fund and a call provision.

A **sinking fund** is an account managed by the bond trustee for the purpose of repaying the bonds. Typically, the company makes yearly payments to the trustee. The trustee can purchase bonds in the market or can select bonds randomly using a lottery and purchase them, generally at face value. There are many different kinds of sinking fund arrangements:

- Most sinking funds start between 5 and 10 years after the initial issuance.
- Some sinking funds establish equal payments over the life of the bond.
- Most high-quality bond issues establish payments to the sinking fund that are not sufficient to redeem the entire issue. As a consequence, there is the possibility of a large *balloon* payment at maturity.

Sinking funds have two opposing effects on bondholders:

1. *Sinking funds provide extra protection to bondholders.* A firm experiencing financial difficulties would have trouble making sinking fund payments. Thus, sinking fund payments provide an early warning system to bondholders.

2. *Sinking funds give the firm an attractive option.* If bond prices fall below the face value, the firm will satisfy the sinking fund by buying bonds at the lower market prices. If bond prices rise above the face value, the firm will buy the bonds back at the lower face value.

## The Call Provision

A *call provision* lets the company repurchase or *call* the entire bond issue at a predetermined price over a specified period.

Historically, the call price was set above the bond's face value of $1,000. The difference between the call price and the face value is the **call premium**. For example, if the call price is 105 (that is, 105 percent of $1,000), the call premium is 50. The amount of the call premium usually becomes smaller over time. One typical arrangement is to set the call premium initially equal to the annual coupon payment and then make it decline to zero over the life of the bond.

Call provisions are not usually operative during the first few years of a bond's life. For example, a company may be prohibited from calling its bonds for the first 10 years. This is referred to as a **deferred call**. During this period, the bond is said to be **call protected**.

Many long-term corporate bonds outstanding in Canada have call provisions as we just described. New corporate debt features a different call provision referred to as a **Canada plus call**. This new approach is designed to replace the traditional call feature by making it unattractive for the issuer ever to call the bonds. Unlike the standard call, with the Canada plus call, the exact amount of the call premium is not set at the time of issuance. Instead, the Canada plus call stipulates that in the event of a call, the issuer must provide a call premium that will compensate investors for the difference in interest between the original bond and new debt issued to replace it. This compensation cancels the borrower's benefit from calling the debt, and the result is that the call will not occur.

The Canada plus call takes its name from the formula used to calculate the difference in the interest; to determine the new, lower interest rate, the formula adds a premium to the yield on Canadas. We give a numerical example of a Canada plus call in Section 21.3.

**CONCEPT QUESTIONS**

- Do bearer bonds have any advantage? Why might Mr. "I Like to Keep My Affairs Private" prefer to hold bearer bonds?
- What advantages and disadvantages do bondholders derive from provisions of sinking funds?
- What is a call provision? What is the difference between the call price and the stated price?

## 21.3   BOND REFUNDING

Replacing all or part of an issue of outstanding bonds is called bond **refunding**. Usually, the first step in a bond refunding is to call the entire issue of bonds at the call price. Bond refunding raises two questions:

1.  Should firms issue callable bonds?
2.  Given that callable bonds have been issued, when should the bonds be called?

We attempt to answer these questions in this section.

### Should Firms Issue Callable Bonds?

Common sense tells us that call provisions have value. First, many publicly issued bonds have call provisions. Second, it is obvious that a call works to the advantage of the issuer. If interest rates fall and bond prices go up, the option to buy back the bonds at the call price is valuable. In bond refunding, firms will typically replace the called bonds with a new bond issue. The new bonds will have a lower coupon rate than the called bonds.

However, bondholders will take the call provision into account when they buy the bond. For this reason, we can expect that bondholders will demand higher interest rates on callable bonds than on non-callable bonds. In fact, financial economists view call provisions as being zero-sum in efficient capital markets.[6] Any expected gains to the issuer from being allowed to refund the bond at lower rates will be offset by higher initial interest rates. We illustrate the zero-sum aspect of callable bonds in Example 21.4.

EXAMPLE **21.4**

Suppose Janine Intercable Company intends to issue perpetual bonds of $1,000 face value at a 10 percent interest rate.[7] Annual coupons have been set at $100. There is an equal chance that by the end of the year, interest rates will either
1. Fall to 6.67 percent, or
2. Increase to 20 percent.
In the first case, the bond price will increase to $1,500. In the second case, the bond price will fall to $500.

**Non-callable Bond**   Suppose the market price of the non-callable bond is the expected price it will have next year plus the coupon, all discounted at the current 10 percent interest rate.[8] The value of the non-callable bond is

**Value of Non-callable Bond:**

$$\frac{\text{First-year coupon} + \text{Expected price at end of year}}{1 + r} = \frac{\$100 + (0.5 \times \$1,500) + (0.5 \times \$500)}{1.10}$$
$$= \$1,000$$

---

[6] See A. Kraus, "An Analysis of Call Provisions and the Corporate Refunding Decision," *Midland Corporate Finance Journal* (Spring 1983).

[7] Recall that perpetual bonds have no maturity date; their market price equals coupon/yield.

[8] We are assuming that the current price of the non-callable bonds is the expected value discounted at the risk-free rate of 10 percent. This is equivalent to assuming that the risk is unsystematic and carries no risk premium.

**Callable Bond**    Now suppose the Janine Intercable Company decides to issue callable bonds. The call premium is set at $100 over par value, and the bonds can be called *only* at the end of the first year.[9] In this case, the call provision will allow the company to buy back its bonds at $1,100 ($1,000 par value plus the $100 call premium). Should interest rates fall, the company will buy for $1,100 a bond that would be worth $1,500 in the absence of a call provision. Of course, if interest rates rise, Janine would not want to call the bonds for $1,100, because they are worth only $500 on the market.

Suppose rates fall and Janine calls the bonds by paying $1,100. If the firm simultaneously issues new bonds with a coupon of $100, it will bring in $1,500 (or $100/0.0667) at the 6.67 percent interest rate. This will allow Janine to pay an extra dividend to shareholders of $400 (or $1,500 − $1,100). In other words, if rates fall from 10 percent to 6.67 percent, exercise of the call will transfer $400 of potential bondholder gains to the shareholders.

When investors purchase callable bonds, they realize that they will forfeit their anticipated gains to shareholders if the bonds are called. As a consequence, they will not pay $1,000 for a callable bond with a coupon of $100.

How high must the coupon on the callable bond be so that it can be issued at the par value of $1,000? We can answer this in three steps.

*Step 1: Determining End-of-Year Value If Interest Rates Drop*    If the interest rate drops to 6.67 percent by the end of the year, the bond will be called for $1,100. The bondholder will receive both this amount and the annual coupon payment. If we let $C$ represent the coupon on the callable bond, the bondholder gets the following at the end of the year:

$$\$1,100 + C$$

*Step 2: Determining End-of-Year Value If Interest Rates Rise*    If interest rates rise to 20 percent, the value of the bondholder's position at the end of the year is

$$\frac{C}{0.20} + C$$

That is, the perpetuity formula tells us that the bond will sell at $C/0.20$. In addition, the bondholder receives the coupon payment at the end of the year.

*Step 3: Solving for $C$*    Because interest rates are equally likely to rise or to fall, the expected value of the bondholder's end-of-year position is

$$(\$1,100 + C) \times 0.5 + \left(\frac{C}{0.20} + C\right) \times 0.5$$

Using the current interest rate of 10 percent, we set the present value (PV) of these payments equal to par:

$$\$1,000 = \frac{(\$1,100 + C) \times 0.5 + \left(\dfrac{C}{0.20} + C\right) \times 0.5}{1.10}$$

$C$ is the unknown in the equation. The equation holds if $C = \$157.14$. In other words, callable bonds can sell at par only if their coupon rate is 15.714 percent.

**The Paradox Restated**    If Janine issues a non-callable bond, it will only need to pay a 10 percent interest rate. By contrast, Janine must pay an interest rate of 15.7 percent on a callable bond. The interest rate differential makes an investor indifferent between the two bonds in our example. Because the expected return to the investor is the same

---

[9] Normally, bonds can be called over a period of many years. Our assumption that the bond can only be called at the end of the first year is introduced for simplicity.

with either bond, the cost of debt capital is the same to Janine with either bond. Thus, our example suggests that there is neither an advantage nor a disadvantage from issuing callable bonds.

If this analysis is correct, why are callable bonds issued in the real world? This question has vexed financial economists for a long time. We now consider four specific reasons that a company might use a call provision:

1. Superior interest rate forecasting.
2. Taxes.
3. Financial flexibility for future investment opportunities.
4. Less interest rate risk.

**Superior Interest Rate Forecasting**     Company insiders may know more about interest rate changes on its bonds than does the investing public. For example, managers may be better informed about potential changes in the firm's credit rating. Thus, a company may prefer the call provision at a particular time because it believes that the expected fall in interest rates (the probability of a fall multiplied by the amount of the fall) is greater than the bondholders believe.

Although this is possible, there is reason to doubt that inside information is the rationale for call provisions. Suppose firms really had superior ability to predict changes that would affect them. Bondholders would infer that a company expected an improvement in its credit rating whenever it issued callable bonds. Bondholders would require an increase in the coupon rate to protect them against a call if this occurred. As a result, we expect that there would be no financial advantage to the firm from callable bonds over non-callable bonds.

Of course, there are many non–company specific reasons interest rates can fall. For example, the interest rate is connected to the anticipated inflation rate. But it is difficult to see how companies could have more information about the general level of interest rates than other participants in the bond markets.

**Taxes**     Call provisions may have tax advantages if the bondholder is taxed at a lower rate than the company. We have seen that callable bonds have higher coupon rates than non-callable bonds. Because the coupons provide a deductible interest expense to the corporation and are taxable income to the bondholder, the corporation will gain more than a bondholder in a low tax bracket will lose. Presumably, some of the tax saving can be passed on to the bondholders in the form of a high coupon.

**Future Investment Opportunities**     As we have explained, bond indentures contain protective covenants that restrict a company's investment opportunities. For example, protective covenants may limit the company's ability to acquire another firm or to sell certain assets (for example, a division of the company). If the covenants are sufficiently restrictive, the cost to the shareholders in lost net present value (NPV) can be large. However, if bonds are callable, the company can buy back the bonds at the call price and take advantage of a superior investment opportunity.[10]

**Less Interest Rate Risk**     The call provision will reduce the sensitivity of a bond's value to changes in the level of interest rates. As interest rates increase, the value of a non-callable bond will fall. Because the callable bond has a higher coupon rate, the value of a callable bond will fall less than the value of a non-callable bond will fall. Kraus has argued that by reducing the sensitivity of a bond's value to changes in interest rates, the call provision may reduce the risk to shareholders as well as

---

[10] This argument is from Z. Bodie and R. A. Taggart, "Future Investment Opportunities and the Value of the Call Provision on a Bond," *Journal of Finance* (September 1978).

bondholders.[11] He argues that because the bond is a liability of the corporation, the equityholders bear risk as the bond changes value over time. Thus, it can be shown that under certain conditions, reducing the risk of bonds through a call provision will also reduce the risk of equity.

## Calling Bonds: When Does It Make Sense?

The value of the company is the value of the stock plus the value of the bonds. From the Modigliani–Miller theory and the pie model in earlier chapters, we know that firm value is unchanged by how it is divided between these two instruments. Therefore, maximizing shareholder wealth means minimizing the value of the callable bonds. In a world with no transaction costs, it can be shown that the company should call its bonds whenever the callable bond value exceeds the call price. This policy minimizes the value of the callable bonds.

The preceding analysis is modified slightly by including the costs from issuing new bonds. These extra costs change the refunding rule to allow bonds to trade at prices above the call price. The objective of the company is to minimize the sum of the value of the callable bonds and new issue costs. It has been observed that many real-world firms do not call their bonds when the market value of the bonds reaches the call price. Perhaps these issue costs are an explanation. Also, when a bond is called, the holder has about 30 days to surrender the bond and receive the call price in cash. In 30 days the market value of the bonds could fall below the call price. If so, the firm is giving away money. To forestall this possibility, it can be argued that firms should wait until the market value of the bond exceeds the call price before calling bonds.

---

**EXAMPLE 21.5**

The Nipigon Lake Mining Co. has a $20 million outstanding bond issue bearing a 16 percent coupon that it issued in 1987. The bonds mature in 2027 but are callable in 2015 for a 6 percent call premium. Nipigon Lake's investment banker has given assurance that up to $30 million of new nine-year bonds maturing in 2024 can be sold carrying a 7 percent coupon. To eliminate timing problems with the two issues, the new bonds will be sold a month before the old bonds are to be called. Nipigon Lake will have to pay the coupons on both issues during this month but can defray some of the cost by investing the issue at 3 percent, the short-term interest rate. Flotation costs for the $20 million new issue would total $1,125,000, and Nipigon Lake's marginal tax rate is 40 percent. Construct a framework to determine whether it is in Nipigon Lake's best interest to call the previous issue.

---

In constructing a framework to analyze a refunding operation, there are three steps: cost of refunding, interest savings, and the NPV of the refunding operation. Following the logic of our capital budgeting analysis in Chapter 8, we calculate the after-tax cash flows from each step and discount them at the after-tax cost of debt. All work described here is illustrated in Table 21.1.

---

[11] A. Kraus, "An Analysis of Call Provisions and the Corporate Refunding Decision," *Midland Corporate Finance Journal* (Spring 1983). Kraus points out that the call provision will not always reduce the equity's interest rate risk. If the firm as a whole bears interest rate risk, more of this risk may be shifted from equityholders to bondholders with non-callable debt. In this case, equityholders may actually bear more risk with callable debt.

**TABLE 21.1**

### Bond Refunding Worksheet

| | Amount before tax | Amount after tax | Time period | 4.2 percent present value factor | Present value |
|---|---|---|---|---|---|
| **Present value cost of refunding** | | | | | |
| Call premium | | $1,200,000 | 0 | 1.0000 | $1,200,000 |
| Flotation costs on new issue | | 1,125,000 | 0 | 1.0000 | 1,125,000 |
| Tax savings on new issue flotation costs | | −90,000 | 1–5 | 4.4269 | −398,423 |
| Extra interest on old issue | $266,667 | 160,000 | 0 | 1.0000 | 160,000 |
| Interest on short-term investment | −50,000 | −30,000 | 0 | 1.0000 | −30,000 |
| Total after-tax investment | | | | | $2,056,577 |
| **Interest savings for the refunding issue: $t = 1$–9** | | | | | |
| Interest on old bond | 3,200,000 | 1,920,000 | | | |
| Interest on new bond | 1,400,000 | 840,000 | | | |
| Net interest savings | $1,800,000 | $1,080,000 | 1–9 | 7.3680 | $7,957,474 |
| **Net present value for refunding operation** | | | | | |
| NPV = PV of interest savings − PV of cost refunding | | | | | $5,900,897 |

**Cost of Refunding** The first step in this framework consists of the call premium, the flotation costs, the related tax savings, and any extra interest that must be paid or can be earned.

*Call Premium* The call premium is $0.06 \times (\$20{,}000{,}000) = \$1{,}200{,}000$. Note that a call premium is not a tax-deductible expense.

*Flotation Costs* Although flotation costs are a one-time expense, for tax purposes they are amortized over the life of the issue or five years, whichever is less. For Nipigon Lake, flotation costs amount to $1,125,000. This results in an annual expense for the first five years after the issue of

$$\$1{,}125{,}000/5 = \$225{,}000$$

Flotation costs produce an annual tax shield of $90,000:

$$\$225{,}000 \times (0.4) = \$90{,}000$$

*Tax Savings* The tax savings on the flotation costs are a five-year annuity and will be discounted at the after-tax cost of debt $(7\%(1 - 0.40) = 4.2\%)$.[12] This amounts to a savings of $398,423. Therefore, the total flotation costs of issuing debt are

| Flotation costs | $1,125,000 |
|---|---|
| Present value of tax savings | (398,423) |
| Total after-tax cost | $ 726,577 |

*Additional Interest* Extra interest paid on the old issue totals[13]

$$\$20{,}000{,}000 \times \left(8\% \times \tfrac{1}{6}\right) = \$266{,}667$$

$$\text{After-tax interest: } \$266{,}667 \times (1 - 0.40) = \$160{,}000$$

---

[12] Since we assume that the refunding costs as well as the principal are financed by the new debt issue, we use the after-tax cost of debt as the discount rate. This is consistent with the adjusted present value (APV) approach as shown in A. R. Ofer and R. A. Taggart, "Bond Refunding: A Clarifying Analysis," *Journal of Finance* (March 1977).

[13] Since we do not know in which month the bond will be called, it is reasonable to assume that it represents 1/6 of a semiannual coupon period.

By investing the proceeds of the new issue at short-term interest rates, some of this expense can be avoided:

$$\$20,000,000 \times \left(3\% \times \tfrac{1}{12}\right) = \$50,000$$

After-tax investment proceeds: $\$50,000 \times (1 - 0.40) = \$30,000$

The total additional interest is

| | |
|---|---|
| Extra interest paid | $160,000 |
| Extra interest earned | (30,000) |
| Total additional interest | $130,000 |

These three items amount to a total after-tax investment of

| | |
|---|---|
| Call premium | $1,200,000 |
| Flotation costs | 726,577 |
| Additional interest | 130,000 |
| Total investment | $2,056,577 |

### Interest Savings on New Issue

$$\text{Interest on old bond} = \$20,000,000 \times 16\% = \$3,200,000$$
$$\text{Interest on new bond} = \$20,000,000 \times 7\% = \$1,400,000$$
$$\text{Annual savings} = \$1,800,000$$
$$\text{After-tax savings} = \$1,800,000 \times (1 - 0.40) = \$1,080,000$$
$$\text{PV of annual savings over 9 years} = \$1,080,000 \times 7.3680 = \$7,957,474$$

### Net Present Value for the Refunding Operation

| | |
|---|---|
| Interest savings | $7,957,474 |
| Investment | (2,056,577) |
| Net present value | $5,900,897 |

Nipigon Lake can save almost $6 million by proceeding with a call on its old bonds. The 16 percent original interest rate used in this example closely follows the actual interest rates during the late 1980s. The example illustrates why firms would want to include a call provision when interest rates are very high.

**Canada Plus Call**   In our example, the Nipigon Lake Mining bond had a traditional call feature. Here we illustrate how a Canada plus call would make calling the debt unattractive. Suppose that when the bonds were issued in 1987, Nipigon debt carried a yield 75 basis points above comparable Canadas. To set up a Canada plus call, Nipigon agreed in 1987 to compensate investors based on a yield of Canada plus 75 basis points if the bonds were ever called.

In our example, by 2015, rates on 10-year Canadas have fallen to 6.25 percent and Nipigon could issue new nine-year debt at 7 percent. Given this information, we can now calculate the annual interest penalty Nipigon would have to pay to call the debt:

$$16\% - (\text{Canada} + 0.75\%) = 16\% - (6.25\% + 0.75\%) = 9.00\%$$

In dollars, this is 9 percent of $20 million or $1.8 million. This $1.8 million is precisely the annual savings from calling the debt with the traditional call calculated earlier. Our example shows that with the Canada plus call, calling the bond will not save Nipigon interest costs. This raises the question of why firms simply do not issue noncallable bonds rather than going to the trouble of setting up a Canada plus call. One answer could be that they wish to retain the flexibility to call debt for other reasons, such as reorganizing their capital structures.

**CONCEPT QUESTIONS**

- What are the advantages to a firm of having a call provision?
- What are the disadvantages to bondholders of having a call provision?
- Why does a Canada plus call effectively make calling debt unattractive?

## 21.4   BOND RATINGS

Firms frequently pay to have their debt rated. The two leading bond-rating firms in Canada are Standard & Poor's (S&P) and Dominion Bond Rating Service (DBRS). Moody's, a large U.S. bond rater, often rates Canadian companies that raise funds in U.S. bond markets.[14] The debt ratings depend upon (1) the likelihood that the firm will default and (2) the protection afforded by the loan contract in the event of default. The ratings are constructed from information supplied by the corporation, primarily the financial statements of the firm. The DBRS rating classes are shown in Table 21.2.

**TABLE 21.2**

### Descriptions of Ratings Used by Dominion Bond Rating Service

The DBRS long-term debt rating scale is meant to indicate the risk that a borrower will not fulfill its full obligations in a timely manner, with respect to both interest and principal commitments. Every DBRS rating is based on quantitative and qualitative considerations relevant to the borrowing entity. Each rating category is denoted by the subcategories "high" and "low." The absence of either a "high" or a "low" designation indicates the rating is in the "middle" of the category. The AAA and D categories do not utilize "high," "middle," and "low" as differential grades.

| | |
|---|---|
| AAA | Long-term debt rated AAA is of the highest credit quality, with exceptionally strong protection for the timely repayment of principal and interest. Earnings are considered stable, the structure of the industry in which the entity operates is strong, and the outlook profitability is favourable. There are few qualifying factors present that would detract from the performance of the entity. The strength of liquidity and coverage ratios is unquestioned, and the entity has established a credible track record of superior performance. Given the extremely high standard that DBRS has set for this category, few entities are able to achieve a AAA rating. |
| AA | Long-term debt rated AA is of superior credit quality, and protection of interest and principal is considered high. In many cases it differs from long-term debt rated AAA only to a small degree. Given the extremely restrictive definition DBRS has for the AAA category, entities rated AA are also considered to be strong credits, typically exemplifying above-average strength in key areas of consideration and unlikely to be significantly affected by reasonably foreseeable events. |
| A | Long-term debt rated A is of satisfactory credit quality. Protection of interest and principal is still substantial, but the degree of strength is less than that of AA-rated entities. While A is a respectable rating, entities in this category are considered to be more susceptible to adverse economic conditions and have greater cyclical tendencies than higher-rated securities. |
| BBB | Long-term debt rated BBB is of adequate credit quality. Protection of interest and principal is considered acceptable, but the entity is fairly susceptible to adverse changes in financial and economic conditions, or there may be other adverse conditions present that reduce the strength of the entity and its rated securities. |
| BB | Long-term debt rated BB is defined to be speculative and non–investment grade, where the degree of protection afforded interest and principal is uncertain, particularly during periods of economic recession. Entities in the BB range typically have limited access to capital markets and additional liquidity support. In many cases, deficiencies in critical mass, diversification, and competitive strength are additional negative considerations. |
| B | Long-term debt rated B is considered highly speculative, with a reasonably high level of uncertainty as to the ability of the entity to pay interest and principal on a continuing basis, especially in periods of economic recession or industry adversity. |
| CCC<br>CC<br>C | Long-term debt rated in any of these categories is very highly speculative and is in danger of default of interest and principal. The degree of adverse elements present is more severe than long-term debt rated B. Long-term debt rated below B often has features that if not remedied may lead to default. In practice, there is little difference between these three categories, with CC and C normally used for lower-ranking debt of companies for which the senior debt is rated in the CCC to B range. |
| D | A security rated D implies the issuer has either not met a scheduled payment of interest or principal or made it clear that it will miss such a payment in the near future. In some cases, DBRS may not assign a D rating under a bankruptcy announcement scenario, as allowances for grace periods may exist in the underlying legal documentation. Once assigned, the D rating will continue as long as the missed payment continues to be in arrears, and until such time as the rating is suspended, discontinued, or reinstated by DBRS. |

Source: Used with permission of Dominion Bond Rating Service, www.dbrs.com.

---

[14] They also rate bonds issued by the individual provinces and the federal government.

The highest rating debt can have is AAA. Debt rated AAA is judged to be the best quality and to have the lowest degree of risk. The lowest rating, C or D, indicates that the firm is in default. Since the 1980s, a growing part of corporate borrowing has taken the form of *low-grade bonds*. These bonds are also known as either *high-yield bonds* or *junk bonds*. Low-grade bonds are corporate bonds that are rated below *investment grade* by the major rating agencies (that is, below BBB for S&P, Fitch, and DBRS or Baa for Moody's).

Bond ratings are important, because bonds with lower ratings tend to have higher interest costs. However, some evidence suggests that bond ratings merely reflect bond risk. There is no conclusive evidence that bond ratings affect risk.[15] It is not surprising that the stock prices and bond prices of firms do not show any unusual behaviour on the days around a rating change. Because the ratings are based on publicly available information, they probably do not, in themselves, supply new information to the market.[16]

Bond ratings can be imperfect measures of risk, as investors found out during the financial crisis of 2007–2008. At that time, asset-backed commercial paper in Canada, rated AAA, found no buyers due to a faulty bank guarantee of backup liquidity. Similarly, in the U.S., mortgage-backed securities with top ratings proved to be highly risky. In both cases, hindsight showed that bond rating agencies were overly optimistic in assigning top ratings to these securities. One contributing factor is likely the business model under which rating agencies receive the bulk of their income from issuers.[17]

## Junk Bonds

The investment community in the United States has labelled bonds with a Standard & Poor's rating of BB and below or a Moody's rating of Ba and below as **junk bonds**. These bonds are also called *high yield* or *low grade*—we shall use all three terms interchangeably. Junk bonds come into existence when investment-grade bonds are downgraded (fallen angels) or through new bond issues rated BB or lower. Issuance of junk bonds has grown greatly in recent years, leading to increased public interest in this form of financing. This interest is not limited to the United States. Although the junk bond market in Canada is not nearly as developed, there has been a rising trend through the 1990s and into the first half of the twenty-first century of more and more companies issuing high-yield debt.[18]

In our opinion, the growth in junk bond financing can better be explained by the activities of one man than by a number of economic factors. While a graduate student at the University of Pennsylvania's Wharton School in the 1970s, Michael Milken observed a large difference between the return on high-yield bonds and the return on safer bonds. Believing that this difference was greater than what the extra default risk would justify, he concluded that institutional investors would benefit from purchases of junk bonds.

His later employment at Drexel Burnham Lambert allowed him to develop the junk bond market. Milken's salesmanship simultaneously increased the demand for junk bonds among institutional investors and the supply of junk bonds among corporations. However, with the collapse of the junk bond market and with Michael Milken's conviction for securities fraud, Drexel had to declare bankruptcy.

---

[15] M. Weinstein, "The Systematic Risk of Corporate Bonds," *Journal of Financial and Quantitative Analysis* (September 1981); J. P. Ogden, "Determinants of Relative Interest Rate Sensitivity of Corporate Bonds," *Financial Management* (Spring 1987); and F. Reilly and M. Joehnk, "The Association between Market-Based Risk Measures for Bonds and Bond Ratings," *Journal of Finance* (December 1976).

[16] M. Weinstein, "The Effect of a Ratings Change Announcement on Bond Price," *Journal of Financial Economics* (December 1977). However, Robert W. Holthausen and Richard W. Leftwich, "The Effect of Bond Rating Changes on Common Stock Prices," *Journal of Financial Economics* (September 1986), find that bond rating downgrades are associated with abnormal negative returns of the stock of the issuing firm.

[17] T. Tedesco and J. Greenwood, "Credit Ratings Storm: DBRS Faces Critics over Role in ABCP Fiasco," *Financial Post*, June 14, 2008.

[18] D. Hamilton and Sharon Ou, "Default Rates of Canadian Corporate Bond Issuers," *Canadian Investment Review* (Summer 2004).

The U.S. junk bond market revived in 1993 with smaller issues by foreign companies and smaller U.S. issuers. This market took on increased importance when junk bonds were used to finance mergers, going-private transactions, and other corporate restructurings. While a firm can only issue a small amount of high-grade debt, the same firm can issue much more debt if low-grade financing is allowed as well. Therefore, the use of junk bonds lets acquirers effect takeovers that they could not do with only traditional bond-financing techniques. Drexel was particularly successful with this technique, primarily because its huge base of institutional clients allowed it to raise large sums of money quickly.

At this time, it is not clear how the great growth in junk bond financing has altered the returns on these instruments. On the one hand, financial theory indicates that the expected return on an asset should be negatively related to its marketability.[19] Because trading volume in junk bonds has greatly increased in recent years, their marketability has risen as well. This should lower the expected return on junk bonds, thereby benefiting corporate issuers. On the other hand, the increased interest in junk bond financing by corporations (the increase in the supply of junk bonds) is likely to raise the expected returns on these assets. The net effect of these two forces is unclear.[20]

Table 21.3 presents data on cumulative global annual default rates on investment-grade bonds (fallen angels) and junk bonds from 1982 through 2011. The table shows that cumulative credit loss increases as rating quality declines, providing validity to the ratings. It also shows that the probability of default increases over time for all bonds. Figure 21.1 presents global defaults over time for all bonds and shows that bond defaults came in cycles, peaking in 1990, 2000–2001, and 2009. This effect was particularly pronounced for junk bonds. In tandem with the collapse of financial markets in 2008, junk bond defaults also peaked in 2009. At the end of 2009, Moody's global speculative-grade bond default rate was 13.076 percent, up from 4.442 percent in 2008.

**TABLE 21.3**

### Average Cumulative Credit Loss Rates by Letter Rating, 1982–2011*

|  | Year 1 | Year 2 | Year 3 | Year 4 | Year 5 |
|---|---|---|---|---|---|
| Aaa | 0.00% | 0.01% | 0.01% | 0.02% | 0.03% |
| Aa | 0.01 | 0.04 | 0.09 | 0.14 | 0.22 |
| A | 0.05 | 0.13 | 0.24 | 0.37 | 0.52 |
| Baa | 0.12 | 0.31 | 0.56 | 0.83 | 1.12 |
| Ba | 0.62 | 1.80 | 3.30 | 4.95 | 6.34 |
| B | 2.62 | 6.30 | 9.93 | 13.05 | 15.77 |
| Caa-C | 10.89 | 18.39 | 24.51 | 29.36 | 33.61 |
| Investment grade | 0.06 | 0.16 | 0.30 | 0.45 | 0.61 |
| Speculative grade | 2.98 | 6.19 | 9.25 | 11.92 | 14.17 |
| All rated | 1.11 | 2.26 | 3.33 | 4.23 | 4.97 |

* Based on average default rates and senior unsecured bond recoveries measured on issuer-weighted basis.

Source: "Annual Default Study: Corporate Default and Recovery Rates, 1920–2011," *Moody's Global Credit Research* (February 2012), p. 26.

---

[19] For example, see Y. Amihud and H. Mendelson, "Asset Pricing and the Bid-Ask Spread," *Journal of Financial Economics* (December 1986).

[20] The actual risk of junk bonds is not known with certainty because it is not easy to measure the default rate. Paul Asquith, David W. Mullins, Jr., and Eric D. Wolff, "Original Issue High Yield Bonds: Aging Analysis of Defaults, Exchanges, and Calls," *Journal of Finance* (September 1989), show that the default rate on junk bonds can be greater than 30 percent over the life of the bond. They look at cumulative default rates and find that of all junk bonds issued in 1977 and 1978, 34 percent had defaulted by December 31, 1988. Edward I. Altman, "Setting the Record Straight on Junk Bonds: A Review of the Research on Default Rates and Returns," *Journal of Applied Corporate Finance* (Summer 1990), shows that yearly default rates of 5 percent are consistent with cumulative default rates of over 30 percent.

FIGURE 21.1

### Global Bond Defaults, 1970–2011

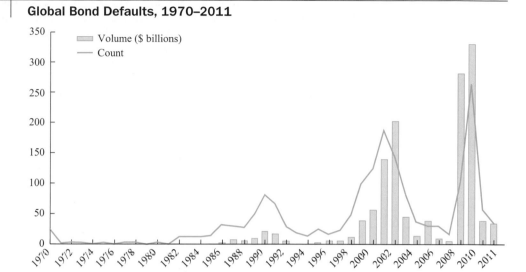

Source: "Annual Default Study: Corporate Default and Recovery Rates, 1920–2011," *Moody's Global Credit Research* (February 2012), p. 4.

TABLE 21.4

### Average Gross Spreads and Total Direct Costs for U.S. Debt Issues, 1990–2008

| | Investment grade | | | Non-investment grade | | |
|---|---|---|---|---|---|---|
| | Number of issues | Gross spread | Total direct cost | Number of issues | Gross spread | Total direct cost |
| **Convertible bonds** | | | | | | |
| 2–9.99 | 0 | — | — | 0 | — | — |
| 10–19.99 | 0 | — | — | 1 | 4.00% | 5.67% |
| 20–39.99 | 0 | — | — | 11 | 3.47 | 5.02 |
| 40–59.99 | 3 | 1.92% | 2.43% | 21 | 3.33 | 4.48 |
| 60–79.99 | 4 | 1.65 | 2.09 | 47 | 2.78 | 3.40 |
| 80–99.99 | 3 | 0.89 | 1.16 | 9 | 2.54 | 3.19 |
| 100–199.99 | 28 | 2.22 | 2.55 | 50 | 2.57 | 3.00 |
| 200–499.99 | 26 | 1.99 | 2.18 | 17 | 2.62 | 2.85 |
| 500 and up | 12 | 1.96 | 2.09 | 1 | 2.50 | 2.57 |
| Total | 76 | 1.99% | 2.26% | 157 | 2.81% | 3.47% |
| **Straight bonds** | | | | | | |
| 2–9.99 | 40 | 0.62% | 1.90% | 0 | — | — |
| 10–19.99 | 68 | 0.50 | 1.35 | 2 | 2.74% | 4.80% |
| 20–39.99 | 119 | 0.58 | 1.21 | 13 | 3.06 | 4.36 |
| 40–59.99 | 132 | 0.39 | 0.86 | 12 | 3.01 | 3.93 |
| 60–79.99 | 68 | 0.57 | 0.97 | 43 | 2.99 | 4.07 |
| 80–99.99 | 100 | 0.66 | 0.94 | 56 | 2.74 | 3.66 |
| 100–199.99 | 341 | 0.55 | 0.80 | 321 | 2.71 | 3.39 |
| 200–499.99 | 173 | 0.50 | 0.81 | 156 | 2.49 | 2.90 |
| 500 and up | 97 | 0.28 | 0.38 | 20 | 2.45 | 2.71 |
| Total | 1,138 | 0.51% | 0.91% | 623 | 2.68% | 3.35% |

Source: Inmoo Lee, Scott Lochhead, Jay Ritter, and Quanshui Zhao, "The Costs of Raising Capital," *Journal of Financial Research* (Spring 1996); calculations and updates by the authors.

We discussed the costs of issuing securities in Chapter 20 and established that the costs of issuing debt are substantially less than the costs of issuing equity. Table 21.4 clarifies several questions regarding the costs of issuing debt securities. It contains a breakdown of direct costs for bond issues in the United States after the investment and non-investment grades have been separated.

First, there are substantial economies of scale here as well. Second, investment-grade issues have much lower direct costs, particularly for straight bonds. Finally, there are relatively few non–investment grade issues in the smaller size categories.

**CONCEPT QUESTIONS**

- List and describe the different bond-rating classes.
- Why don't bond prices change when bond ratings change?
- Are the costs of bond issues related to their ratings?

## 21.5    SOME DIFFERENT TYPES OF BONDS

Thus far, we have mostly considered "plain vanilla" bonds. In this section, we look at two more-unusual types, the products of financial engineering: zero-coupon bonds and floating-rate bonds.[21] We discuss convertible bonds with embedded call options in Chapter 25.

### Zero-Coupon Bonds

A bond that pays no coupons at all must be offered at a price that is much lower than its stated value. Such bonds are called **zero-coupon bonds** or just **zeros**.[22]

Suppose the DDB Company issues a $1,000 face value five-year zero-coupon bond. The initial price is set at $713. It is straightforward to check that at this price, the bonds yield 7 percent to maturity. The total interest paid over the life of the bond is $1,000 − $713 = $287.

For tax purposes, the issuer of a zero-coupon bond deducts interest every year even though no interest is actually paid. Similarly, the owner must pay taxes on interest accrued every year as well, even though no interest is actually received.[23] This second tax feature makes taxable zero-coupon bonds less attractive to taxable investors. However, they are still a very attractive investment for tax-exempt investors with long-term dollar-denominated liabilities, such as pension funds, because the future dollar value is known with relative certainty. Zero-coupon bonds, often in the form of stripped coupons or Guaranteed Investment Certificates (GICs), are attractive to individual investors for tax-sheltered Registered Retirement Savings Plans (RRSPs).

Because zero-coupon bonds have no intermediate coupon payments, they are quite attractive to certain investors and quite unattractive to others. For example, consider an insurance company forecasting death benefit payments of $1,000,000 five years from today. The company would like to be sure that it will have the funds to pay off the liability in five years. It could buy five-year zero-coupon bonds with a face value of $1,000,000. The company is matching assets with liabilities here, a procedure that eliminates interest rate risk. That is, regardless of the movement of interest rates, the firm's set of zeros will always be able to pay off the $1,000,000 liability.

---

[21] For more on financial engineering, see John D. Finnerty, "Financial Engineering in Corporate Finance: An Overview," in *Handbook of Financial Engineering*, C. W. Smith and C. W. Smithson, eds. (New York: Harper Business, 1990).

[22] A bond issued with a very low coupon rate (as opposed to a zero-coupon rate) is an original-issue, discount (OID) bond.

[23] Calculation of yearly interest on a zero-coupon bond is governed by tax law and is not necessarily the true compound interest.

Conversely, the firm would be at risk if it bought coupon bonds instead. For example, if it bought five-year coupon bonds, it would need to reinvest the coupon payments through to the fifth year. Because interest rates in the future are not known with certainty today, one cannot be sure if the sum of bond principal and coupon accumulation will be worth more or less than $1,000,000 by the fifth year. This type of risk is called reinvestment risk.

Consider a couple saving for their child's university education in 15 years. They *expect* that, with inflation, four years of university should cost $150,000 in 15 years. Thus, they buy 15-year zero-coupon bonds with a face value of $150,000.[24] If they have forecast inflation perfectly (and if costs keep pace with inflation), their child's tuition will be fully funded. However, if inflation rises more than expected, the tuition will be more than $150,000. Because the zero-coupon bonds produce a shortfall, the child might end up working her way through school. As an alternative, the parents might have considered rolling over Treasury bills. Because the yields on Treasury bills rise and fall with the inflation rate, this simple strategy is likely to cause less risk than the strategy with zeros.

The key to these examples is the distinction between nominal and real quantities. The insurance company's liability is $1,000,000 in *nominal* dollars. Because the face value of a zero-coupon bond is a nominal quantity, the purchase of zeros eliminates risk. However, it is easier to forecast university costs in real terms than in nominal terms. Thus, a zero-coupon bond is a poor choice to reduce the financial risk of a child's university education.

## Floating-Rate Bonds

The conventional bonds discussed in this chapter have *fixed dollar obligations* because the coupon rate is set as a fixed percentage of the par value. Similarly, the principal is set equal to the par value. Under these circumstances, the coupon payment and principal are completely fixed.

With **floating-rate bonds** (**floaters**), the coupon payments are adjustable. The adjustments are tied to the Treasury bill rate or another short-term interest rate. For example, in 2009 RBC Financial Group had outstanding $224 million in floating-rate notes maturing in 2083. The coupon rate was set at 40 basis points over the 30-day Bankers' Acceptance rate.

The majority of these *floaters* have put provisions and floor-and-ceiling provisions:

1. With a *put provision* the holder has the right to redeem his note at par on the coupon payment date. Frequently, the investor is prohibited from redeeming at par during the first few years of the bond's life.
2. With *floor-and-ceiling provisions* the coupon rate is subject to a minimum and maximum. For example, the minimum coupon rate might be 8 percent and the maximum rate might be 14 percent.

The popularity of floating-rate bonds is connected to *inflation risk*. When inflation is higher than expected, issuers of fixed-rate bonds tend to make gains at the expense of lenders, and when inflation is less than expected, lenders make gains at the expense of borrowers. Because the inflation risk of long-term bonds is borne by both issuers and bondholders, it is in their interests to devise loan agreements that minimize inflation risk.[25]

Floaters reduce inflation risk because the coupon rate is tied to the current interest rate, which, in turn, is influenced by the rate of inflation. This can most clearly be seen by considering the formula for the PV of a bond. As inflation increases the interest rate (the denominator of the formula), inflation increases a floater's coupon rate (the numerator of the formula). Hence, bond value is hardly affected by inflation.

---

[24] A more precise strategy would be to buy zeros maturing in years 15, 16, 17, and 18, respectively. In this way, the bonds might mature just in time to meet tuition payments. Further, taxes are ignored in this example.

[25] See B. Cornell, "The Future of Floating Rate Bonds," in *The Revolution in Corporate Finance*, J. M. Stern and D. H. Chew, Jr., eds. (New York: Basil Blackwell, 1986).

Conversely, the coupon rate of fixed-rate bonds cannot change, implying that the prices of these bonds are at the mercy of inflation.

As an alternative, an individual who is concerned with inflation risk can invest in short-term notes, such as Treasury bills, and *roll them over*.[26] The investor can accomplish essentially the same objective by buying a floater that is adjusted to the London Interbank Offered Rate (LIBOR) or T-bill rate. However, the purchaser of a floater can reduce transaction costs relative to rolling over short-term Treasury bills because floaters are long-term bonds. The same type of reduction in transaction costs makes floaters attractive to some corporations.[27] They benefit from issuing a floater instead of issuing a series of short-term notes.

In an earlier section, we discussed callable bonds. Because the coupon on floaters varies with marketwide interest rates, floaters always sell at or near par. Therefore, it is not surprising that floaters do not generally have call features.

## Financial Engineering and Bonds

Since bonds are financial contracts, the possible features are only limited by the imagination of the parties involved. As a result, bonds can be fairly exotic, particularly some more recent issues. We discuss a few of the more common features and types next.

**Income bonds** are similar to conventional bonds, except that coupon payments depend on company income. Specifically, coupons are paid to bondholders only if the firm's income is sufficient. In Canada, income bonds are usually issued by firms that are reorganizing to overcome financial distress. The firm can skip the interest payment on an income bond without being in default. Interest paid on income bonds is not tax deductible by the issuer. Since firms in financial distress generally have little taxable income, this disadvantage is reduced. Purchasers of income bonds must pay tax on interest received.

A **convertible bond** can be swapped for a fixed number of shares of stock any time before maturity at the holder's option. Convertibles are a debt/equity hybrid that allow the holder to profit if the issuer's stock price rises.

A **retractable bond** or **put bond** allows the holder to force the issuer to buy the bond back at a stated price. As long as the issuer remains solvent, the put feature sets a floor price for the bond. It is, therefore, just the reverse of the call provision. Canada Savings Bonds (CSBs) are an example of retractable bonds. Holders of CSBs may sell them back to the Bank of Canada at any time (through any financial institution) at their par value plus accrued interest.

A **stripped real-return bond** is a zero-coupon bond with inflation protection. These bonds, issued by the Government of Canada for the first time in 1993, have their principal indexed to inflation. Investors receive a known amount in real terms. This feature is designed to make zeros more attractive to investors such as the couple saving for their child's university education in our earlier example.[28]

An **asset-backed bond** is backed by a diverse pool of assets, such as accounts receivable collections, credit card debt, or mortgages. If an issuing company defaults on its bond debt payments, bondholders become legally entitled to cash flows generated from these pools of assets. Asset backing or securitization reduces risk, provided

---

[26] That is, the investor could buy a bill, receive the face value at maturity, use these proceeds to buy a second bill, receive the face value from the second bill at maturity, and so on.

[27] J. Cox, J. Ingersoll, and S. A. Ross, "An Analysis of Variable Rate Loan Contracts," *Journal of Finance* (May 1980), developed a framework for pricing floating-rate notes.

[28] Barry Critchley, "Indexing Gives These Bonds a Real Return," *The Financial Post* (November 27, 1993), p. 17.

that the assets are of high quality. As we mentioned earlier, in the credit crisis of 2007–2008, bonds backed by sub-prime mortgages to risky borrowers lost most of their value.

**CONCEPT QUESTIONS**
- Why might a zero-coupon bond be attractive to investors?
- How might a put feature affect a bond's coupon? How about a convertibility feature? Why?
- What is the attraction of a floating-rate bond?

## 21.6   DIRECT PLACEMENT COMPARED TO PUBLIC ISSUES

Earlier in this chapter, we described the mechanics of issuing debt to the public. However, a large portion of debt is privately placed. There are two basic forms of direct private long-term financing: term loans and private placements.

**Term loans** are direct business loans. These loans have maturities of one to five years. Most term loans are repayable during the life of the loan. The lenders include chartered banks, insurance companies, trust companies, and other lenders that specialize in corporate finance. The interest rate on a term loan may be either a fixed or floating rate.

**Private placements** are very similar to term loans except that the maturity is longer. Unlike term loans, privately placed debt usually employs an investment dealer. The dealer facilitates the process but does not underwrite the issue. A private placement does not require a full prospectus. Instead, the firm and its investment dealer only need to draw up an offering memorandum briefly describing the issuer and the issue. Most privately placed debt is sold to *exempt purchasers*. These are large insurance companies, pension funds, and other institutions that, as sophisticated market participants, do not require the protection provided by studying a full prospectus.

The following are important differences between direct private long-term financing (term loans and private debt placements) and public issues of debt:

1. Registration costs are lower for direct financing. A term loan avoids the cost of OSC registration altogether. Private debt placements require an offering memorandum, but this is cheaper than preparing a full prospectus.
2. Direct placement is likely to have more restrictive covenants.
3. It is easier to renegotiate a term loan or a private placement in the event of a default. It is harder to renegotiate a public issue because hundreds of holders are usually involved.
4. Life insurance companies and pension funds dominate the private placement segment of the bond market. Chartered banks are significant participants in the term loan market.
5. The costs of distributing bonds are lower in the private market because fewer buyers are involved and the issue is not underwritten.

The interest rates on term loans and private placements are usually higher than those on an equivalent public issue. This reflects the trade-off between a higher interest rate and more flexible arrangements in the event of financial distress, as well as the lower costs and lower liquidity associated with private placements.

**CONCEPT QUESTIONS**
- What are the differences between private and public bond issues?
- A private placement is more likely to have restrictive covenants than is a public issue. Why?

## 21.7   LONG-TERM SYNDICATED BANK LOANS

Most bank loans are for less than a year. They serve as a short-term "bridge" for the acquisition of inventory and are typically self-liquidating—that is, when the firm sells the inventory, the cash is used to repay the bank loan. We talk about the need for short-term bank loans in Chapter 27. For now we focus on long-term bank loans.

First, we introduce the concept of commitment. Most bank loans are made with a commitment to a firm. That commitment establishes a line of credit and allows the firm to borrow up to a predetermined limit. Most commitments are in the form of a revolving credit commitment (i.e., a revolver) with a fixed term of up to three years or even more. Revolving credit commitments are drawn when they are used by the borrower or undrawn, depending on whether the firm has a current need for the funds. These loans typically charge a commitment fee on the unused portion of the revolver in addition to interest paid on the actual amount borrowed.

Now we turn to the concept of syndication. Very large banks, such as Citigroup and Royal Bank of Canada, typically have a larger demand for loans than they can supply, and smaller banks frequently have more funds on hand than they can profitably lend to existing customers. Basically, they cannot generate enough good loans with the funds they have available. As a result, a very large bank may arrange a loan with a firm or country and then sell portions of it to a syndicate of other banks. With a syndicated loan, each bank has a separate loan agreement with the borrowers.

A syndicated loan is a corporate loan made by a group (or syndicate) of banks and other institutional investors. The syndicate is generally composed of a lead arranger and participant lenders. As the name suggests, the lead arranger takes the lead, creating the relationship with the borrower and negotiating the specifics of the loan. The participant lenders are typically not involved in the negotiation process. The lead arranger works with the participant lenders to determine shares of the loan and generally lends the most. While all lenders receive interest and principal payments, the lead arranger also receives an up-front fee as compensation for its additional responsibilities.

Syndicated loans are generally rated investment grade. However, a *leveraged* syndicated loan is rated speculative grade (i.e., it is "junk"). Every week, the *Wall Street Journal* reports on the number of syndicated loan deals, credit costs, and yields. In addition, syndicated loan prices are reported for a group of publicly traded loans.

While there is no exchange for the public trading of syndicated loans, banks in the United States have created loan trading desks and a secondary market for syndicated loans. The Loan Syndications and Trading Association sets regulations and practices for this market.[29]

Syndicated loans are comparable to bonds in many respects. Altman and Suggitt report slightly higher default rates for syndicated loans. Gottesman and Roberts show that features like maturity and security affect rates on syndicated loans similarly to bonds.[30]

**CONCEPT QUESTION**

- What are the features of syndicated bank loans?

---

[29] J. Armstrong, "The Syndicated Loan Market: Developments in the North American Context," Bank of Canada, *Financial System Review*, vol. 24 (2000), www.banqueducanada.ca/wp-content/uploads/2010/02/wp03-15.pdf.

[30] A. Gottesman and G. S. Roberts, "Loan Rates and Collateral," *Financial Review* (August 2007); and "Maturity and Corporate Loan Pricing," *Financial Review* (February 2004).

# 21.8

# SUMMARY AND CONCLUSIONS

This chapter describes important aspects of long-term debt financing.

1. The written agreement describing the details of the long-term debt contract is called an *indenture*. Some of the main provisions are security, repayment, protective covenants, and call provisions.

2. Shareholders can take advantage of bondholders in many ways. Protective covenants are designed to protect bondholders from management decisions that favour shareholders at bondholders' expense.

3. Unsecured bonds are called *debentures* or *notes*. They are general claims on the company's value. Most public corporate bonds are unsecured. In contrast, utility bonds are usually secured. Mortgage bonds are secured by tangible property, and collateral trust bonds are secured by financial securities such as stocks and bonds. If the company defaults on secured bonds, the trustee can repossess the assets. This makes secured bonds more valuable.

4. Long term bonds usually provide for repayment of principal before maturity. This is accomplished by a sinking fund. With a sinking fund, the company retires a certain number of bonds each year. A sinking fund protects bondholders because it reduces the average maturity of the bond, and its payment signals the financial condition of the company.

5. Most publicly issued bonds are callable. A callable bond is less attractive to bondholders than a non-callable bond. A callable bond can be bought back by the company at a call price that is less than the true value of the bond. As a consequence, callable bonds are priced to obtain higher stated interest rates for bondholders than non-callable bonds.

   Generally, companies should exercise the call provision whenever the bond's value is greater than the call price.

   There is no single reason for call provisions. Sensible reasons include taxes, greater flexibility, management's ability to predict interest rates, and the fact that callable bonds are less sensitive to interest rate changes.

6. There are many different types of bonds, including floating-rate bonds, deep-discount bonds, and income bonds. This chapter also compares private placement with public issuance.

**KEY TERMS**

Asset-backed bond 636
Bearer bond 621
Call premium 623
Call protected 623
Canada plus call 623
Convertible bond 636
Debenture 622
Deferred call 623
Floating-rate bonds
  (floaters) 635

Income bonds 636
Indenture 619
Junk bonds 631
Negative covenant 622
Positive covenant 622
Private placements 637
Protective covenants 622
Public issue 619
Refunding 624
Registered bond 620

Retractable (put) bond 636
Sinking fund 623
Stripped real-return
  bond 636
Term loans 637
Zero-coupon bonds
  (zeros) 634

**Public Issue of Bonds**

21.1 Raeo Corp. bonds trade at 100 today. The bonds pay semiannual interest on January 1 and July 1. The coupon on the bonds is 7 percent. How much will you pay for a Raeo bond if today is
   *a.* April 1?
   *b.* September 1?
   *c.* July 1?
   *d.* August 15?

21.2 Sinking funds have both positive and negative characteristics to the bondholders. Why?

21.3 Which of the following are characteristics of public issues, and which are characteristics of direct financing?
   *a.* OSC registration.
   *b.* Higher interest cost.
   *c.* Higher fixed cost.
   *d.* Quicker access to funds.
   *e.* Active secondary market.
   *f.* Easy renegotiation.
   *g.* Lower flotation costs.
   *h.* Regular amortization.
   *i.* Ease of repurchase at favourable prices.
   *j.* High total cost to small borrowers.
   *k.* Flexible terms.
   *l.* Less intensive investigation.

21.4 What is a call premium? During what period of time is a bond said to be call protected?

21.5 What is a Canada plus call? How does it remove the issuer's incentive to call debt?

21.6 A company is contemplating a long-term bond issue. It is debating whether to include a call provision. What are the benefits to the company from including a call provision? What are the costs? How do these answers change for a put provision?

21.7 How does a bond issuer decide on the appropriate coupon rate to set on its bonds? Explain the difference between the coupon rate and the required return on a bond.

21.8 Companies pay rating agencies to rate their bonds, and the costs can be substantial. However, companies are not required to have their bonds rated in the first place; doing so is strictly voluntary. Why do you think they do it?

21.9 Recently several companies have issued bonds with 100-year maturities. Critics charge that the issuers are really selling equity in disguise. What are the issues here? Why would a company want to sell "equity in disguise"?

**Bond Refunding**

21.10 Bowdeen Manufacturing intends to issue callable, perpetual bonds with annual coupon payments. The bonds are callable at $1,175. One-year interest rates are 9 percent. There is a 60 percent probability that long-term interest rates one year from today will be 10 percent, and a 40 percent probability that long-term interest rates will be 8 percent. Assume that if interest rates fall, the bonds will be called. What coupon rate should the bonds have in order to sell at par value?

21.11 Bobcaygeon Industries has decided to borrow money by issuing perpetual bonds with a coupon rate of 7 percent, payable annually. The one-year interest rate is 7 percent. Next year, there is a 40 percent probability that interest rates will increase to 9 percent, and there is a 60 percent probability that they will fall to 5 percent.
   *a.* What will the market value of these bonds be if they are non-callable?
   *b.* If the company instead decides to make the bonds callable in one year, what coupon will be demanded by the bondholders for the bonds to sell at par?

Assume that the bonds will be called if interest rates rise and that the call premium is equal to the annual coupon.

    *c.* What will be the value of the call provision to the company?

21.12 Old Business Ventures Inc. has an outstanding perpetual bond with a 11 percent coupon rate that can be called in one year. The bonds make annual coupon payments. The call premium is set at $150 over par value. There is a 35 percent chance that the interest rate in one year will be 12 percent and a 65 percent chance that the interest rate will be 8 percent. If the current interest rate is 11 percent, what is the current market price of the bond?

21.13 In 2012, Whitby Enterprises issued $5 million in bonds. At issue, the bonds carried a yield of 80 basis points above comparable Government of Canada bonds yielding 7.35 percent. When Whitby originally issued the debt, the company agreed to compensate investors on a yield of Canada plus 80 basis points if the bonds were ever called. By 2015, rates on comparable Canadas fell to 5.5 percent and Whitby could issue new debt at 6.4 percent. Given this information, calculate the annual interest penalty Whitby would have to pay to call the debt. Is calling the debt in the best interests of Whitby?

 21.14 An outstanding issue of Executive Airlines debentures has a call provision attached. The total principal value of the bonds is $170 million, and the bonds have an annual coupon rate of 8 percent. The total cost of refunding would be 12 percent of the principal amount raised. The appropriate tax rate for the company is 39 percent. How low does the borrowing cost need to drop to justify refunding with a new bond issue?

21.15 KIC Inc. plans to issue $5 million of bonds with a coupon rate of 8 percent and 30 years to maturity. The coupons are paid semiannually and the current market interest rate on these bonds is 7 percent. In one year, the interest rate on the bonds will be either 10 percent or 6 percent with equal probability. Assume investors are risk neutral.

    *a.* If the bonds are non-callable, what is the price of the bonds today?

    *b.* If the bonds are callable one year from today at $1,080, will their price be greater than or less than the price you computed in (a)? Why?

 21.16 Margret Kimberly, CFO of Georgia Strait Associates, is considering whether or not to refund the two currently outstanding corporate bonds of the firm. The first one is a 7 percent perpetual bond with a $1,000 face value with $125 million outstanding. The second one is an 8 percent perpetual bond with the same face value with $132 million outstanding. The call premiums for the two bonds are 7.5 percent and 8.5 percent of the face value, respectively. The transaction costs of the refundings are $11.5 million and $13 million, respectively. The current interest rates for the two bonds are 6.25 percent and 7.1 percent, respectively. The tax rate is 35 percent. Which, if either, bond should Margret recommend be refunded? What is the NPV of the refunding?

## Some Different Types of Bonds

21.17 What is a junk bond? What are some of the controversies created by junk-bond financing?

21.18 Describe the following types of bonds.

    *a.* Floating-rate.

    *b.* Deep discount.

    *c.* Income.

## General Topics

21.19 *a.* In an efficient market, callable and non-callable bonds will be priced so that there will be no advantage or disadvantage to the call provision. Comment.

    *b.* If interest rates fall, will the price of non-callable bonds move up higher than that of callable bonds? Why or why not?

## Financing the Expansion of East Coast Yachts with a Bond Issue

Larissa Warren, the owner of East Coast Yachts, the main competitor to Deck Out My Yacht, has decided to expand her operations. She asked her newly hired financial analyst, Dan Ervin, to enlist an underwriter to help sell $40 million in new 25-year bonds to finance new construction. Dan has entered into discussions with Wilson Molina, an underwriter from the firm of Molina, Molina, & Rodriguez, about which bond features East Coast Yachts should consider and also what coupon rate the issue will likely have. Although Dan is aware of bond features, he is uncertain of the costs and benefits of some features, so he is not sure how each feature would affect the coupon rate of the bond issue.

1. You are Wilson's assistant, and he has asked you to prepare a memo to Dan describing the effect of each of the following bond features on the coupon rate of the bond. He would also like you to list any advantages or disadvantages of each feature.

    a. The security of the bond—that is, whether the bond has collateral.

    b. The seniority of the bond.

    c. The presence of a sinking fund.

    d. A call provision with specified call dates and call prices.

    e. A deferred call accompanying the call provision in (d).

    f. A Canada plus call provision.

    g. Any positive covenants. Also, discuss several possible positive covenants East Coast Yachts might consider.

    h. Any negative covenants. Also, discuss several possible negative covenants East Coast Yachts might consider.

    i. A conversion feature. (*Note:* East Coast Yachts is not a publicly traded company.)

    j. A floating-rate coupon.

    Dan is also considering whether to issue coupon-bearing bonds or zero-coupon bonds. The YTM on either bond issue will be 7 percent. The coupon bond will have a 6 percent coupon rate and is paid semiannually. The company's tax rate is 38 percent.

2. How many of the semiannual coupon bonds must East Coast Yachts issue to raise the $40 million? How many of the zeros must it issue?

3. In 25 years, what will be the principal repayment due if East Coast Yachts issues the coupon bonds? What if it issues the zeros?

4. What are the company's considerations in issuing a coupon bond compared to a zero-coupon bond?

5. Suppose East Coast Yachts issues the coupon bonds with a Canada plus call provision. The call rate is the T-bill rate plus 0.45 percent. If East Coast calls the bonds in 9 years when the T-bill rate is 5.2 percent, what is the call price of the bond? What if the rate is 7.7 percent?

6. Are investors really fully compensated with a Canada plus call provision?

7. After considering all the relevant factors, would you recommend a zero-coupon issue or a regular coupon issue? Why? Would you recommend an ordinary call feature or a Canada plus call feature? Why?

# Leasing

EXECUTIVE SUMMARY

Long-term leasing is a method of financing property, plant, and equipment. For example, as of December 31, 2013, 91 out of 183 aircraft in Air Canada's mainline fleet were leased.[1] The aircraft industry is particularly suited to leasing rather than buying, and over one-third of commercial jetliners worldwide are leased.

Every lease contract has two parties: the **lessee** and the **lessor**. The lessee is the user of the equipment, and the lessor is the owner. Typically, the lessee first decides on the asset needed and then negotiates a lease contract with a lessor. From the lessee's standpoint, long-term leasing is similar to buying the equipment with a secured loan. The terms of the lease contract are compared to what a banker might arrange with a secured loan. Thus, long-term leasing is a form of financing.

Many questionable advantages are claimed for long-term leasing, such as "leasing provides 100 percent financing," or "leasing conserves capital." However, the principal benefit of long-term leasing is tax reduction. Leasing allows those who need equipment, but cannot take full advantage of the tax benefits associated with ownership, to transfer the tax benefits to a party who can. If the corporate income tax were repealed, long-term leasing would decline dramatically.

## 22.1 TYPES OF LEASES

### The Basics

A **lease** is a contractual agreement between a lessee and a lessor. The agreement establishes that the lessee has the right to use an asset and in return must make periodic payments to the lessor, the owner of the asset. The lessor is either the asset's manufacturer or an independent leasing company.[2] If the lessor is an independent leasing company, it must buy the asset from a manufacturer and deliver it to the lessee.

As far as the lessee is concerned, it is the use of the asset that is important, not the ownership. The use of an asset can be obtained by a lease contract. Because the user can also buy the asset, leasing and buying involve alternative financing arrangements for the use of an asset. This is illustrated in Figure 22.1.

---

[1] More information about the company's lease terms and arrangements can be found on page 40 of Air Canada's 2013 annual report.

[2] Independent of the manufacturer, the leasing company may be owned by a chartered bank. Under the current *Bank Act*, banks are allowed to own leasing subsidiaries but prohibited from leasing vehicles through their branch networks.

**FIGURE 22.1**

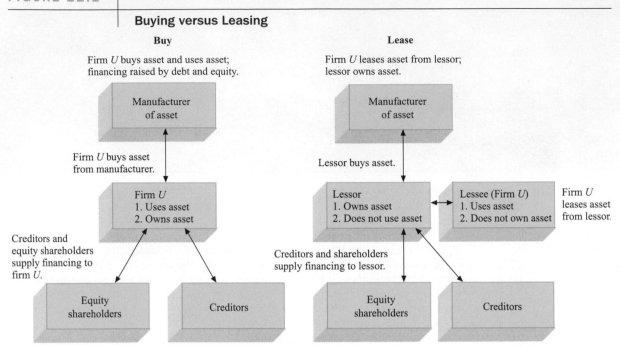

**Buying versus Leasing**

The example in Figure 22.1 is common in the computer industry. Firm *U*, the lessee, might be a hospital, a law firm, or any other firm that uses computers. The lessor is an independent leasing company that purchased the equipment from a manufacturer such as IBM or Apple. Leases of this type are called **direct leases**. In the figure, the lessor issued both debt and equity to finance the purchase.

Of course, a manufacturer like IBM could lease its *own* computers, though we do not show this situation in the example. Leases of this type are called **sales-type leases**. In this case, IBM would compete with the independent computer-leasing company.

## Operating Leases

Years ago, a lease that provided an operator along with the equipment was called an **operating lease**. Today, an operating lease (or service lease) is difficult to define precisely, but this form of leasing has several important characteristics:

1. Operating leases are usually not fully amortized. This means that the payments required under the terms of the lease are not enough to recover the full cost of the asset for the lessor. This occurs because the term or life of the operating lease is usually less than the economic life of the asset. Thus, the lessor must expect to recover the costs of the asset by renewing the lease or by selling the asset for its residual value.

2. Operating leases usually require the lessor to maintain and insure the leased assets.

3. Perhaps the most interesting feature of an operating lease is the cancellation option. This option gives the lessee the right to cancel the lease contract before the expiration date. If the option to cancel is exercised, the lessee must return the equipment to the lessor. The value of a cancellation clause depends on whether future technological and/or economic conditions are likely to make the value of the asset to the lessee less than the value of the future lease payments under the lease.

To leasing practitioners, these characteristics constitute an operating lease. However, accountants use the term in a slightly different way, as we will see shortly.

## Financial Leases

**Financial leases** are the exact opposite of operating leases, as is seen from their important characteristics:

1. Financial leases do not provide for maintenance or service by the lessor.
2. Financial leases are fully amortized.
3. The lessee usually has a right to renew the lease on expiration.
4. Generally, financial leases cannot be cancelled. In other words, the lessee must make all payments or face the risk of bankruptcy.

The characteristics of a financial lease (particularly the fact that it is fully amortized) make it very similar to debt financing, so the name is a sensible one. Two special types of financial leases are the sale and lease-back arrangement and the leveraged lease.

**Sale and Lease-Back**   A **sale and lease-back** occurs when a company sells an asset it owns to another firm and immediately leases it back. In a sale and lease back, two things happen:

1. The lessee receives cash from the sale of the asset.
2. The lessee makes periodic lease payments, thereby retaining use of the asset.

For example, in July 2009, Air Canada arranged a sale and lease-back of three Boeing 777-300ER aircraft. The purchaser was GE Capital Aviation, and the transaction proceeds of $122 million provided immediate cash for the airline during the financial crisis. With a sale and lease-back, the lessee may have the option to repurchase the leased assets at the end of the lease.

**Leveraged Leases**   A **leveraged lease** is a three-sided arrangement among the lessee, the lessor, and the lenders:

1. As in other leases, the lessee uses the assets and makes periodic lease payments.
2. As in other leases, the lessor purchases the assets, delivers them to the lessee, and collects the lease payments. However, the lessor puts up no more than 40 to 50 percent of the purchase price.
3. The lenders supply the remaining financing and receive interest payments from the lessor. Thus, the arrangement on the right-hand side of Figure 22.1 would be a leveraged lease if the bulk of the financing were supplied by creditors.

The lenders in a leveraged lease typically use a non-recourse loan. This means that the lessor is not obliged to the lender in case of a default. However, the lender is protected in two ways:

1. The lender has a first lien on the asset.
2. In the event of loan default, the lease payments are made directly to the lender.

The lessor puts up only part of the funds but gets the lease payments and all of the tax benefits of ownership. Lease payments are used to service the non-recourse loan. The lessee benefits because in a competitive market, the lease payment is lowered when the lessor saves taxes.

**CONCEPT QUESTIONS**

- What are the differences between an operating lease and a financial lease?
- What is a sale and lease-back agreement?
- How does a leveraged lease work?

## 22.2 ACCOUNTING AND LEASING

Under the International Financial Reporting Standards (IFRS) rules for lease accounting (IAS 17), the basic idea is that all financial leases must be "capitalized." These rules for *capital leases* originated under Canadian GAAP CICA 3065 and continue under IFRS. While Canadian GAAP remains an allowable accounting standard for private corporations, our main interest here is in IFRS. Still, we comment briefly on how the rules have evolved in order to make a point about the underlying motivation of corporations. Both sets of rules require that the present value (PV) of the lease payments be calculated and reported along with debt and other liabilities on the right-hand side of the lessee's statement of financial position.[3] The same amount must be shown as an asset on the left-hand side of that statement. Operating leases are not disclosed on the statement of financial position. Instead, only the lease expenses are recognized on a straight-line basis over the lease term. Exactly what constitutes a financial or operating lease for accounting purposes is discussed below.

IFRS require recognition of an asset (by way of acquisition) and an assumption of an obligation (to pay future lease payments), based on the lower of the PV of the minimum lease payments and the fair value of the leased asset. Subsequent to initial recognition, the asset is amortized over its expected useful life according to the lessee's depreciation policy for other similar assets. Lease payments are apportioned between a finance charge and a reduction of the outstanding liability.

The accounting implications of CICA 3065 and IAS 17 are similar and are illustrated in Table 22.1. Imagine a firm that has $100,000 in assets and no debt, implying that the equity is also $100,000. The firm needs a truck costing $100,000 that it can lease or buy. The top of the table shows the balance sheet assuming that the firm borrows the money and buys the truck.

**TABLE 22.1**

**Leasing and the Statement of Financial Position[4]**

| Statement of Financial Position | | | |
|---|---|---|---|
| 1. Initial statement of financial position (the company buys a $100,000 truck with debt) | | | |
| Truck | $100,000 | Debt | $100,000 |
| Other assets | 100,000 | Equity | 100,000 |
| Total assets | $200,000 | Total debt plus equity | $200,000 |
| 2. Operating lease (the company has an operating lease for the truck) | | | |
| Truck | $   0 | Debt | $   0 |
| Other assets | 100,000 | Equity | 100,000 |
| Total assets | $100,000 | Total debt plus equity | $100,000 |
| 3. Capital (finance) lease (the company has a capital/finance lease for the truck) | | | |
| Assets under capital/finance lease | $100,000 | Obligations under capital lease | $100,000 |
| Other assets | 100,000 | Equity | 100,000 |
| Total assets | $200,000 | Total debt plus equity | $200,000 |

In the first case, a $100,000 truck is purchased with debt. In the second case, an operating lease is used; no statement of financial position entries are created. In the third case, a capital (financial) lease is used; the lease payments are capitalized as a liability, and the leased truck appears as an asset.

---

[3] The statement of comprehensive income is also affected. The asset created is amortized over the lease life, and reported income is adjusted downward.

[4] We use the terms *balance sheet* and *statement of financial position* interchangeably throughout this text.

If the firm leases the truck, then one of two things will happen. If the lease is an operating lease, then the statement of financial position will look like the one in the centre of the table. In this case, neither the asset (the truck) nor the liability (the lease payments) appears. If the lease is a capital (finance) lease, then the balance sheet will look like the one at the bottom of the table, where the truck is shown as an asset and the PV of the lease payments is shown as a liability.

Accountants generally argue that a firm's financial strength is inversely related to the amount of its liabilities. Since the lease liability is hidden with an operating lease, the balance sheet of a firm with an operating lease *looks* stronger than the balance sheet of a firm with an otherwise identical capital lease. Given the choice, firms would probably classify all their leases as operating leases. Because of this tendency, GAAP-ASPE CICA 3065 states that a lease must be classified as a capital lease if at least one of the following four criteria is met:

1. The lease transfers ownership of the property to the lessee by the end of the term of the lease.
2. The lessee has an option to purchase the asset at a price below fair market value (bargain purchase price option) when the lease expires.
3. The lease term is *75 percent* or more of the estimated economic life of the asset.
4. The PV of the lease payments is *at least 90 percent* of the asset's fair market value at the start of the lease.[5]

Under IFRS IAS 17, the first four standards are similar to those under CICA 3065. However, IAS 17 removes the cut-offs of 75 percent and 90 percent for criteria 3 and 4 respectively because these cut-offs also provided firms with the ability to negotiate lease contracts so that they would be classified as operating leases. For instance, a firm might be tempted to try to cook the books by taking advantage of the somewhat arbitrary distinction between operating leases and capital leases. Suppose a trucking firm wants to lease the $100,000 truck in our example in Table 22.1. The truck is expected to last for 15 years. A (perhaps unethical) financial manager could try to negotiate a lease contract for 10 years with lease payments having a PV of $89,000. These terms would get around criteria 3 and 4. If criteria 1 and 2 are similarly circumvented, the arrangement would be an operating lease and would not show up on the balance sheet. To address this possibility, IAS 17 incorporates standards that provide room for professional judgment by replacing 75 percent in criterion 3 with *the major part* and 90 percent in criterion 4 with *substantially all*. IAS 17 also adds four additional criteria. Meeting at least one of these eight criteria constitutes a finance lease under IAS 17:

5. The leased assets are of such a specialized nature that only the lessee can use them without major modifications.
6. Gains or losses from the fluctuation in the fair value of the residual accrue to the lessee.
7. The lessee can continue the lease for a secondary period at a rent that is substantially lower than market rent.
8. If the lessee can cancel the lease, the lessor's associated losses are borne by the lessee.[6]

Does this sort of gimmickry pay? The semistrong form of the efficient capital markets hypothesis implies that stock prices reflect all publicly available information. As we discussed earlier in this text, the empirical evidence generally supports this form of the hypothesis. Though operating leases do not appear in the firm's balance sheet, information on these leases must be disclosed elsewhere in the annual report.

---

[5] For more accounting information on leases, see T. H. Beechy, J. E. D. Conrod, and E. Farrell, Chapter 17: "Leases," in *Intermediate Accounting*, Vol. II, 5th ed. (Whitby, ON: McGraw-Hill Ryerson, 2011).

[6] "IFRS at a Glance—IAS 17 Leases," *BDO* (January 2014).

All of this suggests that attempts to keep leases off the balance sheet will not affect stock price in an efficient capital market.

**CONCEPT**
**QUESTIONS**
- Define the terms *capital/finance lease* and *operating lease*.
- How are capital/finance leases reported in a firm's financial statements?

## 22.3    TAXES AND LEASES

The lessee can deduct lease payments for income tax purposes if the lease is qualified under tax law. The tax shields associated with lease payments are critical to the economic viability of a lease, so guidelines are an important consideration. Tax rules on leasing have changed considerably in the past few years, and further changes may occur. The discussion that follows summarizes the rules in force at the time of writing.

Essentially, the Canada Revenue Agency (CRA) requires that a lease be primarily for business purposes and not merely for tax avoidance. In particular, the CRA is on the lookout for leases that are really conditional sales agreements in disguise. The reason is that, in a lease, the lessee gets a tax deduction on the full lease payment. In a conditional sales agreement, only the interest portion of the payment is deductible. If CRA detects one or more of the following, the lease will be disallowed:[7]

1. The lessee automatically acquires title to the property after payment of a specified amount in the form of rentals.
2. The lessee is required to buy the property from the lessor during or at the termination of the lease.
3. The lessee has the right during or at the expiration of the lease to acquire the property at a price less than fair market value.

These rules also apply to sale and lease-back agreements. CRA auditors will rule that a sale and lease-back is really a secured loan if they find one of the above clauses in the agreement.

Once leases are qualified for tax purposes, lessors must still be aware of further tax regulations limiting their use of capital cost allowance (CCA) tax shields on leased assets. Current regulations allow lessors to deduct CCA from leasing income only. Any unused CCA tax shields cannot be passed along to other companies owned by the same parent holding company.

CCA rules limit the tax advantages of sale and lease-backs. The rules place strict limits on a lessor's CCA write-offs on expensive assets, such as aircraft. The result is that big deals are done offshore, such as through U.S. lessors, where the restriction does not apply.

**CONCEPT**
**QUESTIONS**
- Why is the CRA concerned about leasing?
- What are some standards the CRA uses in evaluating a lease?

## 22.4    THE CASH FLOWS OF FINANCIAL LEASING

To begin our analysis of the leasing decision, we need to identify the relevant cash flows. The first part of this section illustrates how this is done. A key point, and one to watch for, is that taxes are a very important consideration in a lease analysis.

---

[7] Note that the CRA tax rules are different from the CICA's accounting rules. For more details on these conditions, see Interpretation Bulletin IT-233R and updates.

## The Incremental Cash Flows

Consider the business decision facing TransCanada Taxis, a firm that provides taxi services in major cities throughout Canada. In addition to traditional taxi dispatchers, the company recently introduced a new taxi app, which allows customers to hail taxis from anywhere in the operating cities using their smartphones. Since the introduction, business has been growing, so the firm needs 50 more taxicabs. The type of car required can be purchased wholesale for $20,000. TransCanada Taxis has determined that each car can be expected to generate $72,000 per year in added sales for the next five years.

TransCanada Taxis has a corporate tax rate (combined federal and provincial) of 40 percent. The cars would qualify for a CCA rate of 40 percent and, due to the hard-driving habits of TransCanada Taxis' staff, the cars would have no residual value after five years. Financial Lease Co. has offered to lease the cars to TransCanada Taxis for lease payments of $5,000 per year for each car over the five-year period. Lease payments are made at the beginning of the year. With the lease, TransCanada Taxis would remain responsible for maintenance, insurance, and operating expenses.

Susan Smart, a recently hired MBA, has been asked to compare the direct incremental cash flows from leasing the cars to the cash flows associated with buying them. The first thing she realizes is that because TransCanada Taxis will have the cars either way, the $72,000 sales increase will be realized whether the cars are leased or purchased. Thus, this sales increase and any other operating costs or revenues can be ignored in the analysis because they are not incremental.

Upon reflection, Susan concludes that there are only three important cash flow differences between financial leasing and buying:[8]

1. If the cars are leased, TransCanada Taxis must make a lease payment of $5,000 each year. However, lease payments are fully tax deductible, so there is a tax shield of $2,000 on each lease payment. The after-tax lease payment is $5,000 − $2,000 = $3,000. This is a cost of leasing instead of buying.[9]

2. If the cars are leased, TransCanada Taxis does not own them and cannot depreciate them for tax purposes.

3. If the cars are leased, TransCanada Taxis does not have to spend $20,000 apiece today to buy them. This is a benefit to leasing.

Table 22.2 shows the CCA and undepreciated capital cost (UCC) schedule for one car. Notice that under the half-year rule the eligible UCC is only $10,000 when the car is put in use in period 0.[10] Table 22.2 also shows the tax shield on CCA for each year. For example, in period 0, the tax shield is $4,000 × 0.40 = $1,600. The tax shields for years 1 through 4 are calculated in the same way. In year 5, the car is scrapped for a zero salvage value. We assume that the asset pool is closed at this time, so there is a tax shield on the terminal loss of $2,074 × 0.40 = $830.[11] All of these tax shields are lost to TransCanada Taxis if it leases, so they are a cost of leasing.

---

[8] There is fourth consequence that we do not discuss here. If the car has a non-trivial salvage value and we lease, we give up that salvage value. This is another cost of leasing instead of buying.

[9] Lease payments are made at the beginning of the year, as shown in Table 22.3. Firms pay taxes later, but our analysis ignores this difference for simplicity.

[10] The purchased car is put in use in period 0 to be consistent with the leasing alternative under which the first payment is made in period 0. Note that the UCC starts in period 0 here. In Chapter 8, the UCC starts at period 1 but does not include period 0. Both labelling methods are accurate and will result in the same CCA calculations.

[11] If the pool were continued, the remaining UCC of $2,074 would be depreciated to infinity, as explained in Appendix 8A. To make the example simple and easy to follow, we assume that the asset pool will be closed. In practice, however, it is unrealistic to assume that the asset pool will be closed and depreciated to infinity. We illustrate this later.

**TABLE 22.2**

### Tax Shield on Capital Cost Allowance for Car

| Year | Undepreciated capital cost | Capital cost allowance | Tax shield |
|------|---------------------------|------------------------|-----------|
| 0 | $10,000 | $4,000 | $1,600 |
| 1 | 16,000 | 6,400 | 2,560 |
| 2 | 9,600 | 3,840 | 1,536 |
| 3 | 5,760 | 2,304 | 922 |
| 4 | 3,456 | 1,382 | 553 |
| 5 | 2,074 | | 830 |

The cash flows from leasing instead of buying are summarized in Table 22.3. Notice that the car's cost is positive in year 0, reflecting the fact that TransCanada Taxis *saves* $15,400 by leasing instead of buying. We could have expressed the cash flows from the purchase relative to the cash flows from leasing. These cash flows would be as follows:

| | Year | | | | | |
|---|---|---|---|---|---|---|
| | **0** | **1** | **2** | **3** | **4** | **5** |
| Net cash flows from purchase alternative relative to lease alternative | −$15,400 | $5,560 | $4,536 | $3,922 | $3,553 | $830 |

Of course, the cash flows here are the opposite of those in the bottom line of Table 22.3. Depending on our purpose, we may look at the purchase relative to the lease or vice versa. You should become comfortable with either viewpoint.

**TABLE 22.3**

### Incremental Cash Flows for TransCanada Taxis from Leasing One Car Instead of Buying

| | Year | | | | | |
|---|---|---|---|---|---|---|
| | **0** | **1** | **2** | **3** | **4** | **5** |
| Investment | $20,000 | | | | | |
| Lease payment | −5,000 | −$5,000 | −$5,000 | −$5,000 | −$5,000 | |
| Payment shield | 2,000 | 2,000 | 2,000 | 2,000 | 2,000 | |
| Forgone tax shield | −1,600 | −2,560 | −1,536 | −922 | −553 | −$830 |
| Total cash flow | $15,400 | −$5,560 | −$4,536 | −$3,922 | −$3,553 | −$830 |

Now that we have the cash flows, we can make our decision by discounting the flows properly. However, because the discount rate is tricky, we take a detour in the next section before moving back to the TransCanada Taxis case. There we show that cash flows in the lease-versus-buy decision should be discounted at the after-tax interest rate—the after-tax cost of debt capital.

**CONCEPT QUESTIONS**
- What are the cash flow consequences of leasing instead of buying?
- Explain why the $15,400 in Table 22.3 is positive.

## 22.5  A DETOUR ON DISCOUNTING AND DEBT CAPACITY WITH CORPORATE TAXES

The analysis of leases is difficult, so both financial practitioners and academics have made conceptual errors. These errors revolve around taxes. We hope to avoid their mistakes by beginning with the simplest type of example, a loan for one year. Though this example is unrelated to our lease-versus-buy situation, principles developed here will apply directly to lease-versus-buy analysis.

### Present Value of Risk-Free Cash Flows

Consider a corporation that lends $100 for a year. If the interest rate is 11 percent, the firm will receive $111 at the end of the year. Of this amount, $11 is interest and the remaining $100 is the original principal. A corporate tax rate of 40 percent implies taxes on the interest of $4.40 (or 0.40 × $11). Thus, the firm ends up with $106.60 (or $111 − $4.40) after taxes on a $100 investment.

Now, consider a company that borrows $100 for a year. With an 11 percent interest rate, the firm must pay $111 to the bank at the end of the year. However, the borrowing firm can take the $11 of interest as a tax deduction. The corporation pays $4.40 (or 0.40 × $11) less in taxes than it would have paid had it not borrowed the money at all. Thus, considering this reduction in taxes, the firm must pay $106.60 (or $111 − $4.40) on a $100 loan. The cash flows from both lending and borrowing are displayed in Table 22.4.

**TABLE 22.4**

**Lending and Borrowing in a World with Corporate Taxes (11 percent interest rate and 40 percent corporate tax rate)**

| Date 0 | Date 1 | |
|---|---|---|
| **Lending example** | | |
| Lend −$100 | Receive | +$100.00 of principal |
| | Receive | +$ 11.00 of interest |
| 11.0% lending rate | Pay | $\frac{-\$\ \ 4.40}{+\$106.60}$ (= −0.40 × $11) in taxes |
| After-tax lending rate is 6.6%. | | |
| **Borrowing example** | | |
| Borrow +$100 | Pay | −$100.00 of principal |
| | Pay | −$ 11.00 of interest |
| 11.0% borrowing rate | Receive | $\frac{+\$\ \ 4.40}{-\$106.60}$ (= 0.40 × $11) as a tax rebate. |
| After-tax borrowing rate is 6.6%. | | |

General principle: In a world with corporate taxes, risk-free cash flows should be discounted at the after-tax interest rate.

The above two paragraphs show a very important result: the firm is indifferent between receiving $100 today and $106.60 next year. If it receives $100 today, it can lend it out, thereby receiving $106.60 after corporate taxes at the end of the year. Conversely, if it knows today that it will receive $106.60 at the end of the year, it can borrow $100 today. The after-tax interest and principal payments on the loan will be paid with the $106.60 that the firm will receive at the end of the year. Because of the interchangeability illustrated above, we say that a payment of $106.60 next year has a PV of $100. Because $100 = $106.60/1.066, a risk-free cash flow should be discounted at the after-tax interest rate of 0.066 [or 0.11 × (1 − 0.40)].

Our discussion considers a specific example. The general principle is as follows:

> In a world with corporate taxes, the firm should discount risk-free cash flows at the after-tax risk-free rate of interest.

### Optimal Debt Level and Risk-Free Cash Flows (Advanced)

In addition, our simple example can illustrate a related point concerning the optimal debt level. Consider a firm that has just determined that the current level of debt in its capital structure is optimal. Immediately following that determination, the firm is surprised to learn that it will receive a guaranteed payment of $106.60 in one year from, say, a tax-exempt government lottery. This future windfall is an asset that, like any asset, should raise the firm's optimal debt level. How much does this payment raise the firm's optimal level?

Our analysis above implies that the firm's optimal debt level must be $100 more than it previously was. That is, the firm could borrow $100 today, perhaps paying the entire amount out as a dividend. It would owe the bank $111 at the end of the year. However, because it receives a tax rebate of $4.40 (or $0.40 \times \$11$), its net repayment will be $106.60. Thus, its borrowing of $100 today is fully offset by next year's government lottery proceeds of $106.60. In other words, the lottery proceeds act as an irrevocable trust that can service the increased debt. Note that we need not know the optimal debt level before the lottery was announced. We are merely saying that whatever this pre-lottery optimal level was, the optimal debt level is $100 more after the lottery announcement.

Of course, this is just one example. The general principle is as follows:[12]

> In a world with corporate taxes, one determines the increase in the firm's optimal debt level by discounting a future guaranteed after-tax inflow at the after-tax risk-free interest rate.

Conversely, suppose that a second and unrelated firm is surprised to learn that it must pay $106.60 next year to the government for back taxes. Clearly, this additional liability impinges on the second firm's debt capacity. By the same reasoning, it follows that the second firm's optimal debt level must be lowered by exactly $100.

**CONCEPT QUESTION**

• How should one discount a risk-free cash flow?

## 22.6    NET PRESENT VALUE ANALYSIS OF THE LEASE-VERSUS-BUY DECISION

The detour leads to a simple method for evaluating leases: discount all cash flows at the after-tax interest rate. From the bottom line of Table 22.3, TransCanada Taxis' incremental cash flows from leasing versus purchasing are as follows:

|  | Year | | | | | |
| --- | --- | --- | --- | --- | --- | --- |
|  | 0 | 1 | 2 | 3 | 4 | 5 |
| Net cash flows from lease alternative relative to purchase alternative | $15,400 | −$5,560 | −$4,536 | −$3,922 | −$3,553 | −$830 |

---

[12] This principle holds for risk-free or guaranteed cash flows only. Unfortunately, there is no easy formula for determining the increase in optimal debt level from a *risky* cash flow.

Let us assume that TransCanada Taxis can either borrow or lend at the 11 percent interest rate. If the corporate tax rate is 40 percent, the correct discount rate is the after-tax rate of 6.6 percent we used earlier [11% × (1 − 0.40)]. When 6.6 percent is used to compute the net present value (NPV) of the lease, we have

$$NPV = \$15,400 - \frac{\$5,560}{(1.066)} - \frac{\$4,536}{(1.066)^2} - \frac{\$3,922}{(1.066)^3} - \frac{\$3,553}{(1.066)^4} - \frac{\$830}{(1.066)^5}$$

$$= -\$399.61$$

(22.1)

Because the NPV of the incremental cash flows from leasing relative to purchasing is negative, TransCanada Taxis prefers to purchase.

Equation (22.1) is the correct approach to a lease-versus-buy analysis. However, students are often bothered by three things. First, they question whether the cash flows in Table 22.3 are truly risk free. Second, they wonder how the cash flow and calculations would change when the asset pool stays open and salvage value is not zero. We examine these two issues next. Third, they feel that this approach lacks intuition. We address this concern a little later.

## The Discount Rate

Because we discounted at the after-tax risk-free rate of interest, we have implicitly assumed that the cash flows in the TransCanada Taxis example are risk free. Is this appropriate?

A lease payment is like the debt service on a secured bond issued by the lessee, and the discount rate should be approximately the same as the interest rate on such debt. In general, this rate will be slightly higher than the risk-free rate considered in the previous section. The various tax shields could be somewhat riskier than the lease payments for two reasons. First, the value of the CCA tax benefits depends on TransCanada Taxis' ability to generate enough taxable income to use them. Second, the corporate tax rate may change. For these two reasons, a firm might be justified in discounting the CCA tax benefits at a rate higher than that used for the lease payments. However, our experience is that, in practice, companies discount both the CCA shield and lease payments at the same rate. This implies that financial practitioners view the above two risks as minor. We adopt the pragmatic convention of discounting the two flows at the same rate—the after-tax interest rate on secured debt issued by the lessee.

At this point some students still ask the question, why not use weighted average cost of capital (WACC) as the discount rate in a lease-versus-buy analysis? WACC should not be used for lease analysis because the cash flows are more like debt service cash flows than operating cash flows, so the risk is much less. The discount rate should reflect the risk of the incremental cash flows.

## Asset Pool and Salvage Value

The TransCanada Taxis example, where the asset pool is assumed to close and the salvage value of the vehicle is assumed to be zero at the end of four years, is simplistic. In reality, this may occur in some circumstances, but in most situations the asset pool will remain open and the car will have some resale value. To illustrate, we assume that the vehicle will have approximately a $1,000 resale value.

Assuming that the asset pool will not close after the lease is complete, Table 22.5 shows the incremental cash flows for TransCanada Taxis excluding the forgone tax shield.

The PV of these payments, using the 6.6 percent discount rate calculated earlier, is

$$PV = \$17,000.00 - \frac{\$3,000.00}{1.066} - \frac{\$3,000.00}{(1.066)^2} - \frac{\$3,000.00}{(1.066)^3} - \frac{\$3,000.00}{(1.066)^4} - \frac{\$1,000.00}{(1.066)^5}$$

$$= \$6,019.46$$

**TABLE 22.5**

**Incremental Cash Flows for TransCanada Taxis from Leasing One Car Instead of Buying**

|  | 0 | 1 | 2 | 3 | 4 | 5 |
|---|---|---|---|---|---|---|
| Investment | $20,000 | | | | | |
| Lease payment | −5,000 | −$5,000 | −$5,000 | −$5,000 | −$5,000 | |
| Payment shield | 2,000 | 2,000 | 2,000 | 2,000 | 2,000 | |
| Salvage value | | | | | | −1,000 |
| | $17,000 | −$3,000 | −$3,000 | −$3,000 | −$3,000 | −1,000 |

Assuming that the salvage value for the vehicle is $1,000 at the end of five years, the PV of the CCA tax shield is

$$\text{PV} = \frac{CdT_c}{k + d} \times (1 + 0.5k) - \frac{SdT_c}{k + d} \times \frac{1}{(1 + k)^n}$$

$$= \frac{(\$20,000)(0.40)(0.40)}{0.066 + 0.40} \times [1 + 0.5(0.066)] - \frac{(\$1,000)(0.40)(0.40)}{0.066 + 0.40} \times \frac{1}{(1 + 0.066)^5}$$

$$= \$6,866.95 \times 1.033 - \$343.35 \times 0.7265$$

$$= \$6,844.13$$

These revised calculations show that the NPV of leasing one car instead of buying amounts to $6,019.46 − $6,844.13 = −$824.67 when the vehicle has a salvage value of $1,000. Given that the NPV is negative, it would be better to buy the vehicle than to lease.

# 22.7    DEBT DISPLACEMENT AND LEASE VALUATION

### The Basic Concept of Debt Displacement (Advanced)

The previous analysis allows us to calculate the right answer in a simple manner. Although simplicity is an important benefit, the analysis has little intuitive appeal. To remedy this, we hope to make lease-versus-buy analysis more intuitive by considering the issue of debt displacement.

A firm that purchases equipment will generally issue debt to finance the purchase, and the debt becomes a liability of the firm. A lessee incurs a liability equal to the PV of all future lease payments. This comparison suggests that leases displace debt. The balance sheets in Table 22.6 illustrate how leasing might affect debt.

Suppose a firm initially has $100,000 of assets and a 150 percent optimal debt-to-equity ratio. The firm's debt is $60,000, and its equity is $40,000. Suppose the firm must use a new $10,000 machine. The firm has two alternatives:

1. *The firm can purchase the machine.* If it does, it will finance the purchase with a secured loan and with equity. The debt capacity of the machine is assumed to be the same as for the firm as a whole.

2. *The firm can lease the asset and get 100 percent financing.* That is, the PV of the future lease payments is $10,000.

If the firm finances the machine with both secured debt and new equity, its debt will increase by $6,000 and its equity by $4,000. Its optimal debt-to-equity ratio of 150 percent will be maintained.

**TABLE 22.6**

**Debt Displacement Elsewhere in the Firm When a Lease Is Instituted**

| Assets | | Liabilities | |
|---|---|---|---|
| **Initial situation** | | | |
| Current | $ 50,000 | Debt | $ 60,000 |
| Fixed | 50,000 | Equity | 40,000 |
| Total | $100,000 | Total | $100,000 |
| **Buy with secured loan** | | | |
| Current | $ 50,000 | Debt | $ 66,000 |
| Fixed | 50,000 | Equity | 44,000 |
| Machine | 10,000 | | |
| Total | $110,000 | Total | $110,000 |
| **Lease** | | | |
| Current | $ 50,000 | Lease | $ 10,000 |
| Fixed | 50,000 | Debt | 56,000 |
| Machine | 10,000 | Equity | 44,000 |
| Total | $110,000 | Total | $110,000 |

This example shows that leases reduce the level of debt elsewhere in the firm. Though the example illustrates a point, it is not meant to show a *precise* method for calculating debt displacement.

Conversely, consider the lease alternative. Because the lessee views the lease payment as a liability, the lessee thinks in terms of a *liability-to-equity* ratio, not just a debt-to-equity ratio. As mentioned above, the PV of the lease liability is $10,000. If the leasing firm is to maintain a liability-to-equity ratio of 150 percent, debt elsewhere in the firm must fall by $4,000 when the lease is instituted. Because debt must be repurchased, net liabilities only rise by $6,000 (or $10,000 − $4,000) when $10,000 of assets is placed under lease.[13]

**Debt displacement** is a hidden cost of leasing. If a firm leases, it will not use as much regular debt as it would otherwise. The benefits of debt capacity will be lost, particularly the lower taxes associated with interest expense.

## Optimal Debt Level in the TransCanada Taxis Example (Advanced)

The previous section showed that leasing displaces debt. Though the section illustrated a point, it was not meant to show the precise method for calculating debt displacement. Below, we describe the precise method for calculating the difference in optimal debt levels between purchase and lease in the TransCanada Taxis example.

From the last line of Table 22.3, we know that the cash flows from the *purchase* alternative relative to the cash flows from the lease alternative are as follows:[14]

| | Year | | | | | |
|---|---|---|---|---|---|---|
| | **0** | **1** | **2** | **3** | **4** | **5** |
| Net cash flows from purchase alternative relative to lease alternative | −$15,400 | $5,560 | $4,536 | $3,922 | $3,553 | $830 |

[13] In practice, growing firms will generally not repurchase debt when instituting a lease. Rather, they will issue less debt in the future than they would have without the lease.

[14] The last line of Table 22.3 presents the cash flows from the lease alternative relative to the purchase alternative. As pointed out earlier, our cash flows are now reversed because we are now presenting the cash flows from the purchase alternative relative to the lease alternative.

An increase in the optimal debt level at year 0 occurs because the firm learns at that time of guaranteed cash flows beginning at year 1. Our detour on discounting and debt capacity taught us to calculate this increased debt level by discounting the future risk-free cash inflows at the after-tax interest rate. Thus, the additional debt level of the purchase alternative relative to the lease alternative is

$$\begin{array}{l} \text{Increase in optimal debt level} \\ \text{from purchase alternative} \end{array} = \$15{,}799.61$$

$$= \frac{\$5{,}560}{(1.066)} + \frac{\$4{,}536}{(1.066)^2} + \frac{\$3{,}922}{(1.066)^3} + \frac{\$3{,}553}{(1.066)^4} + \frac{\$830}{(1.066)^5}$$

That is, whatever the optimal amount of debt under the lease alternative, it will be $15,799.61 higher under the purchase alternative.

This result can be stated in another way. Imagine there are two identical firms except that one firm purchases a corporate car and the other leases it. From Table 22.3, we know that the purchasing firm generates more cash flow after taxes in each of the five years than does the leasing firm. Further, imagine that the same bank lends money to both firms. The bank should lend the purchasing firm more money because it has a greater cash flow each period. How much extra money should the bank lend the purchasing firm so that the incremental loan can be paid off by the extra cash flows shown in Table 22.3? The answer is exactly $15,799.61—the increase in the optimal debt level we calculated earlier.

To see this, Table 22.7 works through the example on a year-by-year basis. Because the purchasing firm borrows $15,799.61 more at year 0 than does the leasing firm, the purchasing firm will pay interest of $1,737.96 (or $15,799.61 × 0.11) at year 1 on the additional debt. The interest allows the firm to reduce its taxes by $695.18 (or $1,737.96 × 0.40), leaving an after-tax interest expense of $1,042.78 (or $1,737.96 − $695.18) at year 1.

**TABLE 22.7**

### Calculation of Increase in Optimal Debt Level If TransCanada Taxis Purchases Instead of Leases

|  | Year | | | | | |
| --- | --- | --- | --- | --- | --- | --- |
|  | **0** | **1** | **2** | **3** | **4** | **5** |
| Outstanding balance of loan | $15,799.61 | $11,282.38* | $7,491.02 | $4,063.43 | $ 778.62 | $  0.00 |
| Interest |  | 1,737.96 | 1,241.06 | 824.01 | 446.98 | 85.65 |
| Tax deduction on interest |  | 695.18 | 496.42 | 329.60 | 178.79 | 34.26 |
| After-tax interest expenses |  | 1,042.77 | 744.64 | 494.41 | 268.19 | 51.39 |
| Extra cash that purchasing firm generates over leasing firm (from Table 22.3) |  | 5,560.00 | 4,536.00 | 3,922.00 | 3,553.00 | 830.00 |
| Repayment of loan |  | $ 4,517.23** | $3,791.36 | $3,427.59 | $3,284.81 | $778.61 |

\* $11,282.38 = $15,799.61 − $4,517.23

\*\* $4,517.23 = $5,560.00 − $1,042.77

We know from Table 22.3 that the purchasing firm generates $5,560 more cash at year 1 than does the leasing firm. Because the purchasing firm has the extra $5,560 coming in at year 1 but must pay interest on its loan, how much of the loan can the firm repay at year 1 and still have the same cash flow as the leasing firm has? The purchasing firm can repay $4,517.33 of the loan at year 1 and still have the same net cash flow that the leasing firm has. After the repayment, the purchasing firm will have a remaining balance of $11,282.38 (or $15,799.61 − $4,517.33) at year 1. For each of the five years, this sequence of cash flows is displayed in Table 22.7. The outstanding balance goes to zero over the five years. Thus, the cash flows shown at the bottom of Table 22.3, which represent the extra cash from purchasing instead of leasing, fully amortize the loan of $15,799.61.

Our analysis of debt capacity has two purposes. First, we want to show the additional debt capacity from purchasing, and we just completed this task. Second, we want to determine whether or not the lease is preferred to the purchase. This decision rule follows easily from our discussion. By leasing the equipment and having $15,799.61 less debt than under the purchase alternative, the firm has exactly the same cash flow in years 1 to 5 that it would have through a levered purchase. Thus, we can ignore cash flows beginning in year 1 when comparing the lease alternative with the purchase-with-debt alternative. However, the cash flows differ between the alternatives at year 0. These differences are as follows:

1. *The purchase cost at year 0 of $15,400 is avoided by leasing.* This should be viewed as a cash inflow under the leasing alternative.
2. *The firm borrows $15,799.61 less at year 0 under the lease alternative than it can under the purchase alternative.* This should be viewed as a cash outflow under the leasing alternative.

Because the firm borrows $15,799.61 less by leasing but saves only $15,400 on the equipment, the lease alternative requires an extra cash outflow at year 0, relative to the purchase alternative, of −$399.61 (or $15,400 − $15,799.61). Because cash flows in later years from leasing are identical to those from purchasing with debt, the firm should purchase.

This conclusion can be expressed another way by looking at the cash flows of the purchase alternative relative to those from the lease. Point 2 means that these incremental cash flows can service a loan of $15,799.61. However, buying instead of leasing requires an outlay of only $15,400 in year 0. Therefore, buying instead of leasing generates a surplus in year 0 (NPV) of $399.61.

This is exactly the same answer we got earlier in this chapter when we discounted all cash flows at the after-tax interest rate. Of course, this is no coincidence because the increase in the optimal debt level is also determined by discounting all flows at the after-tax interest rate. The following box presents both methods. (The numbers in the box are in terms of the NPV of the lease relative to the purchase. Thus, a negative NPV indicates that the purchase alternative should be taken.)

---

### Two Methods for Calculating Net Present Value of Lease Relative to Purchase

Method 1: Discount all cash flows at the after-tax interest rate:

$$-\$399.61 = \$15,\!400 - \text{PV (cash flows) at } 6.6\%$$
$$= \$15,\!400 - \$15,\!799.61$$

Method 2: Compare the purchase price with the reduction in optimal debt level under the leasing alternative:

$$-\$399.61 = \underset{\substack{\text{Purchase} \\ \text{price}}}{\$15,\!400} - \underset{\substack{\text{Reduction in optimal} \\ \text{debt level if leasing}}}{\$15,\!799.61}$$

*Note:* Because we are calculating the NPV of the lease relative to the purchase, a negative value indicates that the purchase alternative is preferred.

## 22.8   DOES LEASING EVER PAY? THE BASE CASE

We previously looked at the lease-versus-buy decision from the perspective of the potential lessee, TransCanada Taxis. We now turn things around and look at the lease from the perspective of the lessor, Financial Leasing. The cash flows associated with the lease from the lessor's perspective are shown in Table 22.8. First, the lessor must buy each car for $20,000, so there is a $20,000 outflow today. Next, Financial Leasing depreciates the machine at a CCA rate of 40 percent to obtain the CCA tax shields shown. Finally, the lessor receives a lease payment of $5,000 each year on which it pays taxes at a 40 percent tax rate. The after-tax lease payment received is $3,000.

**TABLE 22.8**

**Cash Flows to the Lessor**

|  | Year | | | | | |
|---|---|---|---|---|---|---|
|  | **0** | **1** | **2** | **3** | **4** | **5** |
| Investment | −$20,000.00 | | | | | |
| Lease payment | 5,000.00 | $5,000 | $5,000 | $5,000 | $5,000 | |
| Payment shield | −2,000.00 | −2,000 | −2,000 | −2,000 | −2,000 | |
| Forgone tax shield | 1,600.00 | 2,560 | 1,536 | 922 | 553 | $830 |
| Total cash flow | −$15,400.00 | $5,560 | $4,536 | $3,922 | $3,553 | $830 |
| Net present value | $    399.61 | | | | | |

Now examine the total cash flows to Financial Leasing, as displayed in the second-last line of Table 22.8. Readers with a good memory will notice something very interesting. These cash flows are exactly the opposite of those of TransCanada Taxis, as displayed in the bottom line of Table 22.3. Readers with a healthy sense of skepticism may be thinking something very interesting: "If the cash flows of the lessor are exactly the opposite of those of the lessee, the combined cash flow of the two parties must be zero each year. Thus, there does not seem to be any joint benefit to this lease. Because the NPV to the lessee was −$399.61, the NPV to the lessor must be $399.61. The joint NPV is $0 (or −$399.61 + $399.61). There does not appear to be any way for the NPV of both the lessor and the lessee to be positive at the same time. Because one party would inevitably lose money, the leasing deal could never fly."

This is one of the most important results of leasing. Though Table 22.8 concerns one particular leasing deal, the principle can be generalized. As long as (1) both parties are subject to the same interest and tax rates and (2) transaction costs are ignored, there can be no leasing deal that benefits both parties. However, there is a lease payment for which both parties would calculate an NPV of zero. For that lease payment, TransCanada Taxis would be indifferent to whether it leased or bought, and Financial Leasing would be indifferent to whether it leased or not. To find the indifference lease payment, we rerun our leasing spreadsheet from Table 22.8, setting the NPV of leasing equal to zero. Table 22.9 shows that the indifference lease payment is $4,849.25.

The skeptical student might say, "This textbook appears to be arguing that leasing is not beneficial. Yet, we know that leasing occurs frequently in the real world. Maybe, just maybe, the textbook is wrong." Although we will not admit to being wrong (what textbook would!), we freely admit to being incomplete at this point. The next section considers factors that create benefits to leasing.

**TABLE 22.9**

**Indifference Lease Payments**

| | Year | | | | | |
|---|---|---|---|---|---|---|
| | **0** | **1** | **2** | **3** | **4** | **5** |
| Investment | $20,000.00 | | | | | |
| Lease payment | −4,849.25 | −$4,849.25 | −$4,849.25 | −$4,849.25 | −$4,849.25 | |
| Payment shield | 1,939.70 | 1,939.70 | 1,939.70 | 1,939.70 | 1,939.70 | |
| Forgone tax shield | −1,600.00 | −2,560.00 | −1,536.00 | −922.00 | −553.00 | −$830.00 |
| Total cash flow | $15,490.45 | −$5,469.55 | −$4,445.55 | −$3,831.55 | −$3,462.55 | −$830.00 |
| Net present value | $      0.00 | | | | | |

# 22.9   REASONS FOR LEASING

Proponents of leasing make many claims about why firms should lease assets rather than buy them. Some of the reasons given to support leasing are good, and some are not. We discuss here the reasons for leasing we think are good and some that we think are not so good.

## Good Reasons for Leasing

If leasing is a good choice, it is because one or more of the following is true:

1.  Taxes may be reduced by leasing.
2.  The lease contract may reduce certain types of uncertainty.
3.  Transaction costs can be higher for buying an asset and financing it with debt or equity than for leasing the asset.

**Tax Advantages**   By far the most important reason for long-term leasing is tax avoidance. If the corporate income tax were repealed, long-term leasing would become much less important. A lease contract is not a zero-sum game between the lessee and lessor when their effective tax rates differ. In this case, the lease can be structured so that both sides benefit. Any tax benefits from leasing can be split between the two firms by setting the lease payments at the appropriate level, and the shareholders of both firms will benefit from this tax transfer arrangement.

This works because a lease contract swaps two sets of tax shields. The lessor obtains the CCA tax shields due to ownership. The lessee receives the tax shield on lease payments made. In a full-payout lease, the total dollar amounts of the two sets of tax shields may be roughly the same, but the critical difference is the timing. CCA tax shields are accelerated deductions reducing the tax burden in early years. Lease payments, on the other hand, reduce taxes by the same amount in every year. As a result, the ownership tax shields often have a greater PV provided the firm is fully taxed.

The basic logic behind structuring a leasing deal makes a firm in a high tax bracket want to act as the lessor. Low-tax (or untaxed) firms will be lessees, because they will not be able to use the tax advantages of ownership, such as CCA and debt financing. These ownership tax shields are worth less to the lessee in this case because the lessee faces a lower tax rate or may not have enough taxable income to absorb the accelerated tax shields in the early years.

Overall, less tax is paid by the lessee and lessor combined, and this tax savings occurs sooner rather than later. The lessor gains on the tax side; the lessee may lose but the amount of any loss is less than the lessor gains. To make the lease attractive, the lessor must pass on some of the tax savings in the form of lower lease payments. In the end, the lessor gains by keeping part of the tax savings, the lessee gains through a lower lease payment, and both gains are paid for through a reduction in tax revenue.

To see how this would work in practice, recall the example of Section 22.8 and the situation of Financial Leasing. The value of the lease it proposed to TransCanada Taxis was $399.61. However, the value of the lease to TransCanada Taxis was exactly the opposite, −$399.61. Since the lessor's gains came at the expense of the lessee, no deal could be arranged. However, if TransCanada Taxis paid no taxes and the lease payments were reduced to $4,874 from $5,000, both Financial Leasing and TransCanada Taxis would find there is positive NPV in leasing.

To see this, we can rework Table 22.8 with a zero tax rate. This would occur when TransCanada Taxis has enough alternative tax shields to reduce taxable income to zero for the foreseeable future.[15] In this case, notice that the cash flows from leasing are simply the lease payments of $4,874 because no CCA tax shield is lost and the lease payment is not tax deductible. The cash flows from leasing are thus as follows:

|  | Year | | | | | |
|---|---|---|---|---|---|---|
|  | 0 | 1 | 2 | 3 | 4 | 5 |
| Cost of car | $20,000 |  |  |  |  |  |
| Lease payment | −4,874 | −$4,874 | −$4,874 | −$4,874 | −$4,874 | 0 |
| Cash flow | $15,126 | −$4,874 | −$4,874 | −$4,874 | −$4,874 | 0 |

The value of the lease for TransCanada Taxis is

$$\text{NPV} = \$15,126 - \$4,874 \times A^4_{0.11}$$
$$= \$4.68$$

which is positive. Notice that the discount rate here is 11 percent because TransCanada Taxis pays no taxes; in other words, this is both the pre-tax and the after-tax rate.

From Table 22.10, the value of the lease to Financial Leasing can be worked out as +$65.60. The discount rate for Financial Leasing is the after-tax rate of 6.6 percent.

**TABLE 22.10**

**Revised Cash Flows to Lessor**

|  | Year | | | | | |
|---|---|---|---|---|---|---|
|  | 0 | 1 | 2 | 3 | 4 | 5 |
| Cost of car | −$20,000.00 |  |  |  |  |  |
| Lease payment | 4,874.00 | $4,874.00 | $4,874.00 | $4,874.00 | $4,874.00 |  |
| Payment shield | −1,949.60 | −1,949.60 | −1,949.60 | −1,949.60 | −1,949.60 |  |
| CCA tax shield | 1,600.00 | 2,560.00 | 1,536.00 | 922.00 | 553.00 | $830.00 |
| Total cash flow | −$15,475.60 | $5,484.40 | $4,460.40 | $3,846.40 | $3,477.40 | $830.00 |
| Net present value lessor | $    65.60 |  |  |  |  |  |

As a consequence of different tax rates, the lessee (TransCanada Taxis) gains $4.68, and the lessor (Financial Leasing) gains $65.60. What this example shows is that the lessor and the lessee can gain if their tax rates are different. The lease contract allows

---

[15] Strictly speaking, the UCC of the cars would be carried on the books until the firm was able to claim CCA. However, the PV of this deferred CCA tax shield would be low, so for the sake of simplicity, we ignore it here.

the lessor to take advantage of the CCA and interest tax shields that cannot be used by the lessee. Some of the tax gains to the lessor are passed on to the lessee in the form of lower lease payments.

Because both parties can gain when tax rates differ, the lease payment is agreed upon through negotiation. Before negotiation begins, each party needs to know the *reservation* payment of both parties. This is the payment such that one party will be indifferent to whether it entered the lease deal or not. In other words, this is the payment such that the value of the lease is zero. These payments are calculated below.

*Reservation Payment of Lessee*   We now solve for $L_{MAX}$, the payment such that the value of the lease to the lessee is zero. When the lessee is in a zero tax bracket, its cash flows, in terms of $L_{MAX}$, are as follows:

|  | Year | | | | | |
| --- | --- | --- | --- | --- | --- | --- |
|  | **0** | **1** | **2** | **3** | **4** | **5** |
| Cost of taxicab | $20,000 | | | | | |
| Lease payment | $-L_{MAX}$ | $-L_{MAX}$ | $-L_{MAX}$ | $-L_{MAX}$ | $-L_{MAX}$ | |

This chart implies that

$$\text{Value of lease} = \$20{,}000 - L_{MAX} \times A^5_{0.11} \times 1.11$$

The value of the lease equals zero when

$$L_{MAX} = \frac{\$20{,}000}{A^5_{0.11} \times 1.11} = \$4{,}875.14$$

Because the lease payments are an annuity in advance, we multiply the annuity factor by one plus the discount rate. After performing this calculation, the lessor knows that it will never be able to charge a payment above $4,875.14.

*Reservation Payment of Lessor*   We now solve for $L_{MIN}$, the payment such that the value of the lease to the lessor is zero. The cash flows to the lessor, in terms of $L_{MIN}$, are as follows:

|  | Year | | | | | |
| --- | --- | --- | --- | --- | --- | --- |
|  | **0** | **1** | **2** | **3** | **4** | **5** |
| Cost of taxicab | −$20,000 | | | | | |
| CCA tax shield | $ 1,600 | $2,560 | $1,536 | $922 | $533 | $830 |
| After-tax lease payment ($T_c = 0.40$) | $L_{MIN} \times (0.60)$ | $L_{MIN} \times (0.60)$ | $L_{MIN} \times (0.60)$ | $L_{MIN} \times (0.60)$ | $L_{MIN} \times (0.60)$ | |

This chart implies that

$$\text{Value of lease} = -\$20{,}000 + \text{PV}_{\text{CCA Tax Shield}} + L_{MIN} \times (0.60) \times A^5_{0.066} \times 1.066$$

The value of the lease equals zero when

$$L_{MIN} = \frac{\$20{,}000 - \$7{,}130.05}{0.60 \times A^5_{0.066} \times 1.066}$$

$$= \frac{\$12{,}869.95}{2.487 \times 1.066}$$

$$= \$4{,}855.09$$

After performing this calculation, the lessee knows that the lessor will never agree to a lease payment below $4,855.09. Note that the lease payment we found earlier, $4,874.00, is close to $L_{MAX}$ and consistent with the previous small NPV of leasing, only $4.68, for TransCanada Taxis.

**A Reduction of Uncertainty**   We have noted that the lessee does not own the property when the lease expires. The value of the property at this time is called the *residual value* and belongs to the lessor. When the lease contract is signed, there may be

### Why Are Leases Offered by Both Manufacturers and Third-Party Lessors?

The offsetting effects of taxes can explain why both manufacturers and third-party lessors offer leases:

1. For manufacturer lessors, the basis for determining CCA is the manufacturer's cost. For third-party lessors, the basis is the sales price that the lessor paid to the manufacturer. Because the sales price is generally greater than the manufacturer's cost, this is an advantage to third-party lessors.

2. However, the manufacturer must recognize a profit for tax purposes when selling the asset to the third-party lessor. The manufacturer's profit for some equipment can be deferred if the manufacturer becomes the lessor. This provides an incentive for manufacturers to lease.

### Why Are Some Assets Leased More Commonly Than Others?

Certain assets appear to be leased more frequently than others. Smith and Wakeman and Johnson, Schneider, and Waldman have looked at non-tax incentives affecting leasing.[21] Their analysis suggests that asset and firm characteristics are important in the lease-versus-buy decision:

1. Ownership provides a better incentive to conduct maintenance than does leasing. The more sensitive the value of an asset to use and maintenance decisions, the more likely it is that the asset will be purchased instead of leased. This is likely an important reason that car leasing has grown in recent decades as new cars have become more reliable and less dependent on maintenance.

2. Price discrimination opportunities may be important. Leasing may be a way for a manufacturer to charge a lower price to one group of customers who lease its product while keeping prices up for other customers who buy.

## 22.11

## SUMMARY AND CONCLUSIONS

A large fraction of equipment is leased rather than purchased. This chapter describes the institutional arrangements surrounding leases and shows how to evaluate leases financially.

1. Leases can be separated into two types: financial and operating. Financial leases are generally longer term, fully amortized, and not cancellable. In effect, the lessor obtains economic but not legal ownership. Operating leases are usually shorter term, partially amortized, and cancellable and can be likened to a rental agreement.

2. When a firm purchases an asset with debt, both the asset and the liability appear on the firm's balance sheet. If a lease meets at least one of a number of criteria, it must be capitalized. This means that the present value (PV) of the lease appears as both an asset and a liability. A lease escapes capitalization if it does not meet any of these criteria. Leases not meeting the criteria are called *operating leases*, though the accountant's definition differs somewhat from the practitioner's definition. Operating leases do not appear on the balance sheet. For cosmetic reasons, many firms prefer that a lease be called *operating*.

---

[21] C. W. Smith, Jr., and L. M. Wakeman, "Determinants of Corporate Leasing Policy," *Journal of Finance* (July 1985); and J. P. Johnson, H. S. Schneider, and M. Waldman, "The Role and Growth of New Car Leasing: Theory and Evidence," *Journal of Law and Economics* (April 2014), works. bepress.com/henry_schneider/5/.

3. Firms generally lease for tax purposes. To protect its interests, the Canada Revenue Agency (CRA) allows financial arrangements to be classified as leases only if a number of criteria are met.

4. We showed that risk-free cash flows should be discounted at the after-tax, risk-free rate. Because both lease payments and capital cost allowance (CCA) tax shields are nearly risk free, all relevant cash flows in the lease-versus-buy decision should be discounted at a rate near this after-tax rate. We use the practical convention of discounting at the after-tax interest rate on the lessee's secured debt.

5. Though this method is simple, it lacks certain intuitive appeal. In an optional section, we present an alternative, more intuitively appealing method. Relative to a lease, a purchase generates debt capacity. This increase in debt capacity can be calculated by discounting the difference between the cash flows of the purchase and the cash flows of the lease using the after-tax interest rate. The increase in debt capacity from a purchase is compared to the extra outflow at year 0 from a purchase.

6. If the lessor is in the same tax bracket as the lessee, the cash flows to the lessor are exactly the opposite of the cash flows to the lessee. Thus, the value of the lease to the lessee plus the value of the lease to the lessor must be zero. While this suggests that leases can never fly, there are actually at least three good reasons for leasing:

   a. Differences in tax brackets between lessor and lessee.

   b. Shift of risk bearing to the lessor.

   c. Minimization of transactions costs.

   We also document a number of bad reasons for leasing.

**KEY TERMS**

Debt displacement  655
Direct lease  644
Financial lease  645
Lease  643

Lessee  643
Lessor  643
Leveraged lease  645
Operating lease  644

Sale and lease-back  645
Sales-type lease  644

**QUESTIONS & PROBLEMS**

Use the following information to work Problems 22.1 through 22.5. You work for a nuclear research laboratory that is contemplating leasing a diagnostic scanner (leasing is a common practice with expensive, high-tech equipment). The scanner costs $4,500,000, and it would be depreciated straight-line to zero over four years. Because of radiation contamination, it will actually be completely valueless in four years. You can lease it for $1,350,000 per year for four years.

**Lease or Buy**

22.1 Assume that the tax rate is 35 percent. You can borrow at 8 percent before taxes. Should you lease or buy?

**Leasing Cash Flows**

22.2 What are the cash flows from the lease from the lessor's viewpoint? Assume a 35 percent tax bracket.

**Finding the Break-Even Payment**

22.3 What would the lease payment have to be for both the lessor and the lessee to be indifferent about the lease?

**Taxes and Leasing Cash Flows**

22.4 Assume that your company does not contemplate paying taxes for the next several years. What are the cash flows from leasing in this case?

**Setting the Lease Payment**

22.5 In Problem 22.4, over what range of lease payments will the lease be profitable for both parties?

**Lease or Buy**

22.6  Super Sonics Entertainment is considering buying a machine that costs $435,000. The machine will be depreciated over five years by the straight-line method and will be worthless at that time. The company can lease the machine with year-end payments of $107,500. The company can issue bonds at a 9 percent interest rate. If the corporate tax rate is 35 percent, should the company buy or lease?

**Setting the Lease Payment**

22.7  Quartz Corporation is a relatively new firm. Quartz has experienced enough losses during its early years to provide it with at least eight years of tax loss carryforwards. Thus, Quartz's effective tax rate is zero. Quartz plans to lease equipment from New Leasing Company. The term of the lease is five years. The purchase cost of the equipment is $780,000. New Leasing Company is in the 35 percent tax bracket. There are no transaction costs to the lease. Each firm can borrow at 7 percent.

   a. What is Quartz's reservation price?
   b. What is New Leasing Company's reservation price?
   c. Explain why these reservation prices determine the negotiating range of the lease.

Use the following information to work Problems 22.8 through 22.10. The Wildcat Oil Company is trying to decide whether to lease or buy a new computer-assisted drilling system for its oil exploration business. Management has decided that it must use the system to stay competitive; it will provide $2.6 million in annual pre-tax cost savings. The system costs $8.4 million and will be depreciated at a CCA rate of 20 percent over five years. Wildcat's tax rate is 34 percent, and the firm can borrow at 9 percent. Lambert Leasing Company has offered to lease the drilling equipment to Wildcat for payments of $1,950,000 per year. Lambert's policy is to require its lessees to make payments at the start of the year.

**Lease or Buy**

22.8  What is the NPV of leasing for Wildcat? What is the maximum lease payment that would be acceptable to the company?

**Leasing and Salvage Value**

22.9  Suppose it is estimated that the equipment will have an after-tax salvage value of $700,000 at the end of the lease. What is the maximum lease payment acceptable to Wildcat now?

**Deposits in Leasing**

22.10  Many lessors require a security deposit in the form of a cash payment or other pledged collateral. Suppose Lambert requires Wildcat to pay a $500,000 security deposit at the inception of the lease. If the lease payment is still $1,950,000, is it advantageous for Wildcat to lease the equipment now?

**Lease or Buy**

22.11  Wolfson Corporation has decided to purchase a new machine that costs $5.1 million. The machine will be depreciated at a CCA rate of 30 percent and will be worthless after four years. The corporate tax rate is 35 percent. The Sur Bank has offered Wolfson a four-year loan for $5.1 million. The repayment schedule is four yearly principal repayments of $1,275,000 and an interest charge of 9 percent on the outstanding balance of the loan at the beginning of each year. Both principal repayments and interest are due at the end of each year. Cal Leasing Corporation offers to lease the same machine to Wolfson. Lease payments of $1.5 million per year are due at the beginning of each of the four years of the lease.

   a. Should Wolfson lease the machine or buy it with bank financing?
   b. What is the annual lease payment that will make Wolfson indifferent to whether it leases the machine or purchases it?

### Setting the Lease Price

22.12  An asset costs $330,000 and will be depreciated in a straight-line manner over its three-year life. It will have no salvage value. The lessor can borrow at 7 percent, and the lessee can borrow at 9 percent. The corporate tax rate is 34 percent for both companies.

  a. How does the fact that the lessor and lessee have different borrowing rates affect the calculation of the NPV of leasing?

  b. What set of lease payments will make the lessee and the lessor equally well off?

  c. Assume that the lessee pays no taxes and the lessor is in the 34 percent tax bracket. For what range of lease payments does the lease have a positive NPV for both parties?

### Automobile Lease Payments

22.13  Automobiles are often leased, and there are several terms unique to auto leases. Suppose you are considering leasing a car. The price you and the dealer agree on for the car is $36,000. This is the base capitalized cost. Other costs added to the capitalized cost price include the acquisition (bank) fee, insurance, or extended warranty. Assume these costs are $450. Capitalization cost reductions include any down payment, credit for trade-in, or dealer rebate. Assume you make a down payment of $2,000, and there is no trade-in or rebate. If you drive 20,000 kilometres per year, the lease-end residual value for this car will be $21,000 after three years. The lease or "money" factor, which is the interest rate on the loan, is the annual percentage rate (APR) of the loan divided by 2,400. (We're not really sure where the 2,400 comes from either.) The lease factor the dealer quotes you is 0.00285. The monthly lease payment consists of three parts: a depreciation fee, a finance fee, and sales tax. The CCA rate is 30 percent. The net capitalization cost is the cost of the car minus any cost reductions plus any additional costs. The finance fee is the net capitalization cost plus the residual times the money factor, and the monthly sales tax is simply the monthly lease payment times the tax rate. What APR is the dealer quoting you? What is your monthly lease payment for a 36-month lease if the sales tax is 7 percent?

### Lease versus Borrow

22.14  Return to the case of the diagnostic scanner discussed in Problems 22.1 through 22.5. Suppose the entire $4.5 million purchase price of the scanner is borrowed. The rate on the loan is 8 percent, and the loan will be repaid in equal instalments. Create a lease-versus-buy analysis that explicitly incorporates the loan payments. Show that the NPV of leasing instead of buying is not changed from what it was in Problem 22.1. Why is this so?

### Lease versus Buy

22.15  High electricity costs have made Farmer Corporation's chicken-plucking machine economically worthless. Only two machines are available to replace it. The International Plucking Machine (IPM) model is available only on a lease basis. The lease payments will be $65,000 for five years, due at the beginning of each year. This machine will save Farmer $15,000 per year through reductions in electricity costs in every year. As an alternative, Farmer can purchase a more energy-efficient machine from Basic Machine Corporation (BMC) for $330,000. This machine will save $25,000 per year in electricity costs. The bank has offered to finance the machine with a $330,000 loan. The interest rate on the loan will be 10 percent on the remaining balance and will require five annual principal payments of $66,000. Farmer has a target debt-to-asset ratio of 67 percent. Farmer is in the 34 percent tax bracket. After five years, both machines will be worthless. The machines qualify for a 30 percent CCA rate.

  a. Should Farmer lease the IPM machine or purchase the more efficient BMC machine?

  b. Does your answer depend on the form of financing for direct purchase?

  c. How much debt is displaced by this lease?

# The Decision to Lease or Buy at Warf Computers Ltd.

Warf Computers Ltd. has decided to proceed with the manufacture and distribution of the virtual keyboard (VK) the company has developed. To undertake this venture, the company needs to obtain equipment for the production of the microphone for the keyboard. Because of the required sensitivity of the microphone and its small size, the company needs specialized equipment for production.

Nick Warf, the company president, has found a vendor for the equipment. Clapton Acoustical Equipment has offered to sell Warf Computers the necessary equipment at a price of $4 million. Because of the rapid development of new technology, the equipment falls in CCA class 20 for depreciation. At the end of four years, the market value of the equipment is expected to be $480,000.

Alternatively, the company can lease the equipment from Hendrix Leasing. The lease contract calls for four annual payments of $1,040,000, due at the beginning of the year. Additionally, Warf Computers must make a security deposit of $240,000 that will be returned when the lease expires. Warf Computers can issue bonds with a yield of 11 percent, and the company has a marginal tax rate of 35 percent.

1. Should Warf buy or lease the equipment?
2. Nick mentions to James Hendrix, the president of Hendrix Leasing, that although the company will need the equipment for four years, he would like a lease contract for two years instead. At the end of the two years, the lease could be renewed. Nick would also like to eliminate the security deposit, but he would be willing to increase the lease payments to

$1,840,000 for each of the two years. When the lease is renewed in two years, Hendrix would consider the increased lease payments in the first two years when calculating the terms of the renewal. The equipment is expected to have a market value of $1.6 million in two years. Why might Nick prefer this lease? What are the potential ethical issues concerning the new lease terms?

3. In the leasing discussion, James informs Nick that the contract could include a purchase option for the equipment at the end of the lease. Hendrix Leasing offers three purchase options:

    a. An option to purchase the equipment at the fair market value.

    b. An option to purchase the equipment at a fixed price. The price will be negotiated before the lease is signed.

    c. An option to purchase the equipment at a price of $200,000.

   How would the inclusion of a purchase option affect the value of the lease?

4. James also informs Nick that the lease contract can include a cancellation option. The cancellation option would allow Warf Computers to cancel the lease on any anniversary date of the contract. In order to cancel the lease, Warf Computers would be required to give 30 days' notice prior to the anniversary date. How would the inclusion of a cancellation option affect the value of the lease?

# Adjusted Present Value Approach to Leasing

To access Appendix 22A, go to Connect.

**Mc Graw Hill Education** connect    **Mc Graw Hill Education** LEARNSMART®    **Mc Graw Hill Education** SMARTBOOK™

**For more information on the resources available from McGraw-Hill Ryerson, go to www.mheducation.ca/he/solutions.**

## PART 6

# 23

## CHAPTER

# Options and Corporate Finance: Basic Concepts

**EXECUTIVE SUMMARY**

On July 2013, AT&T announced that it would acquire prepaid wireless provider Leap Wireless International Inc. for $15 per share in cash. In addition to the cash offer, the deal included a contingent value right (CVR) entitling shareholders of Leap Wireless International Inc. to the net proceeds of AT&T's planned sale of Leap's 700-MHz "A Block" spectrum.[1] The acquisition deal was approved and closed on March 13, 2014. Although CVRs may seem arcane, they are really straightforward applications of options, a topic to be examined in this chapter.

Options are special contractual arrangements giving the owner the right to buy or sell an asset at a fixed price any time on or before a given date. Stock options, the most familiar type, are options to buy and sell shares of common stock. Ever since 1973, stock options have been traded on organized exchanges.

Corporate securities are very similar to the stock options that are traded on organized exchanges. Almost every issue of corporate bonds and stocks has option features. In addition, capital structure decisions and capital budgeting decisions can be viewed in terms of options.

We start this chapter with a description of different types of publicly traded options. We identify and discuss the factors that determine their values. Next, we show how common stocks and bonds can be thought of as options on the underlying value of the firm. This leads to several new insights concerning corporate finance. For example, we show how certain corporate decisions can be viewed as options. AT&T's issuance of a CVR is one of these corporate decisions, and we return to this example at the end of the chapter

## 23.1 OPTIONS

An **option** is a contract giving its owner the right to buy or sell an asset at a fixed price on or before a given date. For example, an option on a building might give the buyer the right to buy the building for $1 million on, or any time before, the Saturday prior to the third Wednesday in January 2016. Options are a unique type of financial contract because they give the buyer the right, but not the *obligation*, to do something. The buyer uses the option only if it is advantageous; otherwise the option can be discarded.

There is a special vocabulary associated with options. Here are some important definitions:

1. **Exercising the option.** The act of buying or selling the underlying asset via the option contract is referred to as *exercising the option*.

2. **Strike or exercise price.** The fixed price in the option contract at which the holder can buy or sell the underlying asset is called the *strike price* or *exercise price*.

3. **Expiration date.** The maturity date of the option is referred to as the *expiration date*. After this date, the option is dead.

---

[1] "AT&T Completes Acquisition of Leap Wireless," AT&T News Room, AT&T, March 13, 2014, about.att.com/story/att_completes_acquisition_of_leap_wireless.html.

4. **American and European options.** An *American option* may be exercised at any time up to and including the expiration date. A *European option* differs from an American option in that it can be exercised only on the expiration date.

## 23.2   CALL OPTIONS

The most common type of option is a **call option.** A call option gives the owner the right to buy an asset at a fixed price during a particular time period. There is no restriction on the kind of asset, but the most common options traded on exchanges are on stocks and bonds. Usually the assets involved are shares of common stock.

For example, call options on Bank of Nova Scotia are traded on the Montreal Exchange and cleared through the Canadian Derivatives Clearing Corporation (CDCC). Bank of Nova Scotia does not issue (that is, sell) call options on its common stock. Instead, individual investors are the original buyers and sellers of these options. A representative call option on Bank of Nova Scotia stock enables an investor to buy 100 shares of Bank of Nova Scotia from the option seller (or writer) on or before January 15, 2016, at an exercise price of $70. Like all options traded on the CDCC, the Bank of Nova Scotia calls are American options, which can be exercised at any time during their life. This is a valuable option if there is some probability that the price of Bank of Nova Scotia common stock will exceed $70 on or before January 15, 2016.

Virtually all stock option contracts specify that the exercise price and number of shares be adjusted for stock splits and stock dividends. To illustrate, suppose that Bank of Nova Scotia stock was selling for $66 on the day the option was purchased. Further, suppose that the next day it split three for one. Each share would drop in price to $22, and the probability that the stock would rise to over $66 per share in the near future would become very remote. To protect the option holder from such an occurrence, call options are typically adjusted for stock splits and stock dividends. In the case of a three-for-one split, the exercise price would become $23.33 (or $70/3). Furthermore, the option contract would now include 300 shares, instead of the original 100 shares.[2]

### The Value of a Call Option at Expiration

What is the value of a call option contract on common stock at expiration? The answer depends on the value of the underlying stock when the option expires.

We define $S_T$ as the market price of the underlying common stock on the expiration date, *T.* Of course, this price is not known prior to expiration. Suppose that a particular call option can be exercised at an exercise price of $50. If the value of the common stock at expiration, $S_T$, is greater than the exercise price of $50, the option will be worth the difference, $S_T - \$50$. When $S_T > \$50$, the call is said to be *in the money.*

For example, suppose that the stock price on expiration day is $60. The option holder has the right to buy the stock from the option seller for $50.[3] Because the stock is selling in the market for $60, the option holder will exercise the option, that is, buy the stock for $50. The holder can then sell the stock for $60 and pocket the difference of $10 (or $60 − $50).[4]

Of course, it is also possible that the value of the common stock will turn out to be less than the exercise price. If $S_T < \$50$, the call is *out of the money.* The holder will

---

[2] No adjustment is made for the payment by Bank of Nova Scotia of cash dividends to shareholders. This failure to adjust hurts holders of call options, but, of course, they should know the terms of option contracts before buying.

[3] We use the words *buyer, owner,* and *holder* interchangeably.

[4] This example assumes that the call lets the holder purchase one share of stock at $50. In reality, a call lets the holder purchase 100 shares at $50 per share. The profit would then equal $1,000 [or ($60 − $50) × 100].

not exercise in this case. For example, if the stock price at the expiration date is $40, no rational investor would exercise. Why pay $50 for stock worth only $40? An option holder has no obligation to exercise the call and can *walk away* from the option. As a consequence, if $S_T < \$50$ on the expiration date, the value of the call option is 0. In this case, the value of the call option is not $S_T - \$50$, as it would be if the holder of the call option had the *obligation* to exercise the call.

The payoff of a call option at expiration is as follows:

|  | Payoff on the Expiration Date | |
|---|---|---|
|  | If $S_T \leq \$50$ | If $S_T > \$50$ |
| Call option value | 0 | $S_T - \$50$ |

Figure 23.1 plots the value of the call at expiration against the value of the stock. It is referred to as the *hockey stick diagram* of call option values. If $S_T < \$50$, the call is out of the money and worthless. If $S_T > \$50$, the call is in the money and rises one-for-one with increases in the stock price. Notice that the call can never have a negative value. It is a *limited liability instrument*, which means that all the holder can lose is the initial amount paid for it.

**FIGURE 23.1**

### The Value of a Call Option on the Expiration Date

If $S_T > \$50$, then call option value = $S_T - \$50$. If $S_T \leq \$50$, then call option value = 0.

A call option gives the owner the right to buy an asset at a fixed price during a particular time period.

**EXAMPLE 23.1**

Suppose Mr. Optimist holds a one-year call option for 100 shares of Bank of Nova Scotia common stock. It is a European call option and can be exercised at $70 per share. Assume that the expiration date has arrived. What is the value of the Bank of Nova Scotia call option on the expiration date? If Bank of Nova Scotia is selling for $82 per share, Mr. Optimist can exercise the option—purchase 100 shares of Bank of Nova Scotia at $70 per share—and then immediately sell the shares at $82. Mr. Optimist will have made $1,200 (or 100 shares × $12).

Alternatively, assume that Bank of Nova Scotia is selling for $30 per share on the expiration date. If Mr. Optimist still holds the call option, he will throw it away. The value of the Bank of Nova Scotia call on the expiration date will be zero in this case.

**CONCEPT**
**QUESTIONS**
- What is a call option?
- How is a call option's price related to the underlying stock price at the expiration date?

# 23.3    PUT OPTIONS

A **put option** can be viewed as the opposite of a call option. Just as a call gives the holder the right to buy the stock at a fixed price, a put gives the holder the right to *sell* the stock for a fixed exercise price during the life of the option.

## The Value of a Put Option at Expiration

The circumstances that determine the value of a put option are the opposite of those for a call option, because a put option gives the holder the right to sell shares. Let us assume that the exercise price of the put is $50. If the price, $S_T$, of the underlying common stock at expiration is greater than the exercise price, it is foolish to exercise the option and sell shares at $50. In other words, the put option is worthless if $S_T > \$50$. The put is out of the money in this case. However, if $S_T < \$50$, the put is in the money. In this case, it pays to buy shares at $S_T$ and use the option to sell them at the exercise price of $50. For example, if the stock price at expiration is $40, the holder should buy the stock in the open market at $40. By immediately exercising, she receives $50 for the sale. Her profit is $10 (or $50 − $40).

The payoff of a put option at expiration is as follows:

|  | Payoff on the Expiration Date | |
| --- | --- | --- |
|  | If $S_T < \$50$ | If $S_T \geq \$50$ |
| Put option value | $50 − S_T$ | 0 |

Figure 23.2 plots the values of a put option for all possible values of the underlying stock. It is instructive to compare Figure 23.2 with Figure 23.1 for the call option. The call option is valuable whenever the stock price is above the exercise price, and the put is valuable when the stock price is below the exercise price.

---

**EXAMPLE 23.2**

In 2001, the shares of Bombardier, the world's largest manufacturer of plane and train equipment, traded at $25.10. By the time of writing in May 2014, Bombardier's share price was driven down below $4 with news that the company's biggest customer for CSeries jets was considering whether to take the planes after a change in airline strategy.[5] Suppose that Ms. Pessimist foresaw Bombardier's troubles and bought one put contract allowing the sale of 100 Bombardier shares at $12 each through May 2014. At the expiration date, Ms. Pessimist exercised her put contract, which was then in the money. She bought 100 shares of Bombardier for $4 and, on the same day, sold the shares at the exercise price of $12 per share. Her profit was $800 [or 100 shares × ($12 − $4)]. The value of the put contract at expiration was $800. Similarly, if put options were not available to Ms. Pessimist, she could have short sold the Bombardier stock to achieve a comparable result.

---

**CONCEPT QUESTIONS**

- What is a put option?
- How is a put option's price related to the underlying stock price at the expiration date?

---

[5] M. Schlangenstein and F. Tomesco, "Bombardier Inc Shares Fall as Biggest CSeries Customer Turns Cold on Jets," *Financial Post* (21 May 2014), business.financialpost.com/2014/05/21/bombardier-inc-shares-fall-as-biggest-cseries-customer-turns-cold-on-jets/.

**FIGURE 23.2**

### The Value of a Put Option on the Expiration Date

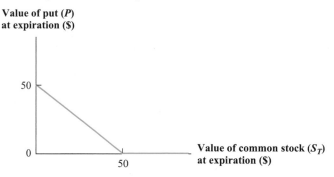

If $S_T \geq \$50$, then put option value $= 0$. If $S_T < \$50$, then put option value $= \$50 - S_T$.

A put option gives the owner the right to *sell* an asset at a fixed price during a particular time period.

## 23.4    SELLING OPTIONS

An investor who sells (or *writes*) a call on common stock promises to deliver the shares if required to do so by the call option holder. Notice that the seller is *obliged* to deliver if the option is exercised. The seller of a call option obtains a cash payment from the holder (or buyer) at the time the option is bought. If, at the expiration date, the price of the common stock is below the exercise price, the call option will not be exercised and the seller's liability is zero.

If, at the expiration date, the price of the common stock is greater than the exercise price, the holder will exercise the call and the seller must give the holder shares of stock in exchange for the exercise price. Here the seller loses the difference between the stock price and the exercise price. For example, assume that the stock price is $60 and the exercise price is $50. Knowing that exercise is imminent, the option seller buys stock in the open market at $60. By being obliged to sell at $50, the option seller loses $10 (or $50 − $60).

Conversely, an investor who sells a put on common stock agrees to purchase shares of common stock if the put holder should so request. The seller loses on this deal if the stock price falls below the exercise price and the holder puts the stock to the seller. For example, assume that the stock price is $40 and the exercise price is $50. The holder of the put will exercise in this case. In other words, the holder will sell the underlying stock at the exercise price of $50. This means that the seller of the put must buy the underlying stock at the exercise price of $50. Because the stock is worth only $40, the loss here is $10 (or $40 − $50).

The values of the "sell-a-call" and "sell-a-put" positions are depicted in Figure 23.3. The graph on the left-hand side of the figure shows that the seller of a call loses nothing when the stock price at the expiration date is below $50. However, the seller loses a dollar for every dollar that the stock rises above $50. The graph in the centre of the figure shows that the seller of a put loses nothing when the stock price at the expiration date is above $50. However, the seller loses a dollar for every dollar that the stock falls below $50.

FIGURE 23.3

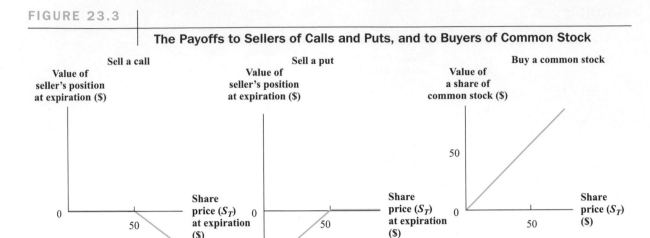

**The Payoffs to Sellers of Calls and Puts, and to Buyers of Common Stock**

It is worthwhile to spend a few minutes comparing the graphs in Figure 23.3 to those in Figures 23.1 and 23.2. The graph of selling a call (the graph on the left-hand side of Figure 23.3) is the mirror image over the horizontal axis of the graph of buying a call (Figure 23.1). This occurs because options are a zero-sum game. The seller of a call loses what the buyer makes. Similarly, the graph of selling a put (the middle graph in Figure 23.3) is the mirror image of the graph of buying a put (Figure 23.2). Again, the seller of a put loses what the buyer makes.

Figure 23.3 also shows the value at expiration of simply buying common stock. Notice that buying the stock is the same as buying a call option on the stock with an exercise price of zero. This is not surprising. If the exercise price is 0, the call holder can buy the stock for nothing, which is really the same as owning it.

## 23.5   STOCK OPTION QUOTATIONS

Now that we understand the definitions for calls and puts, let's look at the exchanges where they are traded. In the 1970s and 1980s, organized trading in options grew from literally zero into some of the world's largest markets. The tremendous growth in interest in derivative securities resulted from the greatly increased volatility in financial markets we discussed in Chapter 1.[6] Exchange trading in options began in 1973 on the Chicago Board Options Exchange (CBOE). The CBOE is still the largest organized options market, and options are traded in a number of other places today, including London, Paris, Tokyo, and Hong Kong.

Option trading in Canada began in 1975. Today, options are traded on the Montreal Exchange and cleared through the CDCC. The CDCC stands between option buyers and sellers. Put and call options involving stock in some of the best-known corporations in Canada are traded daily. Almost all such options are American (as opposed to European).

To illustrate how options are quoted on the CDCC, Table 23.1 presents information on some of the options of Bank of Nova Scotia and Barrick Gold Corporation.

---

[6] Our discussion of trends in options trading draws on L. Gagnon, "Exchange-Traded Financial Derivatives in Canada: Finally off the Launching Pad," *Canadian Investment Review* (Fall 1990).

**TABLE 23.1**

## Options Quotations: Thursday, May 22, 2014

BNS—Bank of Nova Scotia (The)
Last update: May 22, 2014 at 11:50 am (Data 15 minutes delayed)
Last price: 67.980    Net change: 0.390    Bid price: 67.970    Ask price: 67.980    30-day historical volatility: 6.82%

| | Calls | | | | | | | Puts | | | | | |
|---|---|---|---|---|---|---|---|---|---|---|---|---|---|
| Month / Strike | Bid price | Ask price | Last price | Impl. vol. | Open int. | Vol. | Month / Strike | Bid price | Ask price | Last price | Impl. vol. | Open int. | Vol. |
| 14 JUN 52.000 | 15.95 | 16.05 | 15.7 | 59.90% | 0 | 0 | 14 JUN 52.000 | 0 | 0.07 | 0.07 | 43.10% | 0 | 0 |
| 14 JUN 66.000 | 2.19 | 2.26 | 2 | 15.20% | 325 | 10 | 14 JUN 66.000 | 0.18 | 0.23 | 0.18 | 10.60% | 258 | 10 |
| 14 JUN 68.000 | 0.75 | 0.79 | 0.79 | 11.50% | 2,664 | 413 | 14 JUN 68.000 | 0.73 | 0.77 | 0.97 | 8.20% | 44 | 0 |
| 14 JUN 70.000 | 0.1 | 0.14 | 0.09 | 9.80% | 20 | 342 | 14 JUN 70.000 | 2.08 | 2.16 | 2.5 | — | 10 | 0 |
| 14 JUN 72.000 | 0 | 0.07 | 0.07 | 10.50% | 0 | 0 | 14 JUN 72.000 | 3.95 | 4.05 | 4.45 | — | 0 | 0 |
| 14 JUL 48.000 | 19.95 | 20.1 | 19.7 | 57.90% | 0 | 0 | 14 JUL 48.000 | 0 | 0.09 | 0.09 | 40.10% | 0 | 0 |
| 14 JUL 60.000 | 8 | 8.1 | 7.75 | 25.50% | 88 | 0 | 14 JUL 60.000 | 0.04 | 0.11 | 0.12 | 17.70% | 966 | 0 |
| 14 JUL 68.000 | 0.89 | 0.94 | 0.88 | 10.10% | 2,356 | 60 | 14 JUL 68.000 | 1.31 | 1.39 | 1.5 | 11.00% | 84 | 5 |
| 14 JUL 70.000 | 0.18 | 0.2 | 0.16 | 8.40% | 384 | 0 | 14 JUL 70.000 | 2.72 | 2.81 | 3.2 | 11.70% | 53 | 0 |
| 14 JUL 72.000 | 0.01 | 0.11 | 0.11 | 9.10% | 20 | 0 | 14 JUL 72.000 | 4.55 | 4.7 | 5.1 | 14.80% | 10 | 0 |
| 14 JUL 82.000 | 0 | 0.09 | 0.09 | 20.50% | 0 | 0 | 14 JUL 82.000 | 14.55 | 14.65 | 15.05 | 32.10% | 0 | 0 |
| 14 OCT 50.000 | 17.95 | 18.1 | 17.7 | 40.10% | 0 | 0 | 14 OCT 50.000 | 0.04 | 0.16 | 0.16 | 24.50% | 0 | 0 |
| 14 OCT 60.000 | 8 | 8.15 | 7.8 | 20.80% | 50 | 0 | 14 OCT 60.000 | 0.32 | 0.39 | 0.44 | 15.20% | 285 | 0 |
| 14 OCT 68.000 | 1.45 | 1.53 | 1.45 | 10.90% | 2,060 | 30 | 14 OCT 68.000 | 2.33 | 2.42 | 2.63 | 11.40% | 90 | 0 |
| 14 OCT 70.000 | 0.65 | 0.72 | 0.61 | 10.00% | 268 | 15 | 14 OCT 70.000 | 3.6 | 3.7 | 4 | 11.30% | 25 | 0 |
| 14 OCT 72.000 | 0.23 | 0.29 | 0.26 | 9.40% | 10 | 0 | 14 OCT 72.000 | 5.2 | 5.35 | 5.7 | 11.60% | 0 | 0 |
| 14 OCT 82.000 | 0 | 0.13 | 0.13 | 13.90% | 0 | 0 | 14 OCT 82.000 | 14.95 | 15.1 | 15.45 | 20.70% | 0 | 0 |
| 15 JAN 48.000 | 19.9 | 20.1 | 19.75 | 39.60% | 70 | 0 | 15 JAN 48.000 | 0.11 | 0.2 | 0.21 | 22.80% | 1,960 | 0 |
| 15 JAN 60.000 | 8.05 | 8.25 | 7.9 | 19.60% | 561 | 0 | 15 JAN 60.000 | 0.77 | 0.88 | 0.96 | 15.20% | 1,825 | 0 |
| 15 JAN 66.000 | 3.2 | 3.3 | 3.1 | 13.50% | 947 | 0 | 15 JAN 66.000 | 2.32 | 2.46 | 2.64 | 12.90% | 407 | 0 |
| 15 JAN 68.000 | 2 | 2.12 | 1.93 | 12.20% | 580 | 0 | 15 JAN 68.000 | 3.2 | 3.4 | 3.25 | 12.10% | 49 | 2 |
| 15 JAN 70.000 | 1.17 | 1.25 | 1.15 | 11.40% | 519 | 10 | 15 JAN 70.000 | 4.45 | 4.6 | 4.85 | 12.00% | 20 | 0 |
| 15 JAN 72.000 | 0.61 | 0.65 | 0.65 | 10.70% | 594 | 20 | 15 JAN 72.000 | 5.9 | 6.1 | 6.4 | 11.60% | 86 | 0 |
| 15 JAN 82.000 | 0 | 0.13 | 0.13 | 11.30% | 0 | 0 | 15 JAN 82.000 | 15.3 | 15.45 | 15.85 | 14.50% | 0 | 0 |
| 16 JAN 52.000 | 15.6 | 16.3 | 16 | 27.60% | 138 | 0 | 16 JAN 52.000 | 0.97 | 1.19 | 1.24 | 17.30% | 2,040 | 0 |
| 16 JAN 60.000 | 8.4 | 8.9 | 8.55 | 18.80% | 177 | 0 | 16 JAN 60.000 | 2.57 | 2.93 | 3.05 | 15.10% | 1,379 | 0 |
| 16 JAN 66.000 | 4.35 | 4.75 | 4.55 | 15.30% | 260 | 0 | 16 JAN 66.000 | 4.9 | 5.25 | 5.45 | 13.80% | 397 | 0 |
| 16 JAN 68.000 | 3.3 | 3.65 | 3.55 | 14.40% | 140 | 0 | 16 JAN 68.000 | 5.85 | 6.3 | 6.6 | 13.20% | 23 | 0 |
| 16 JAN 70.000 | 2.45 | 2.7 | 2.55 | 13.70% | 85 | 5 | 16 JAN 70.000 | 7.1 | 7.5 | 7.8 | 12.50% | 25 | 0 |
| 16 JAN 72.000 | 1.85 | 2.08 | 2.05 | 13.40% | 197 | 1 | 16 JAN 72.000 | 8.35 | 8.8 | 9.05 | 12.30% | 18 | 0 |
| 17 JAN 54.000 | 13.3 | 14.75 | 14.5 | 24.20% | 0 | 0 | 17 JAN 54.000 | 2.37 | 3.05 | 3.05 | 16.70% | 16 | 0 |
| 17 JAN 66.000 | 5.1 | 5.9 | 5.7 | 16.70% | 0 | 0 | 17 JAN 66.000 | 6.7 | 7.55 | 7.7 | 13.40% | 0 | 0 |
| 17 JAN 68.000 | 4.15 | 4.95 | 4.8 | 16.10% | 22 | 0 | 17 JAN 68.000 | 7.7 | 8.6 | 8.75 | 12.80% | 0 | 0 |
| 17 JAN 70.000 | 3.55 | 3.9 | 3.65 | 15.40% | 10 | 0 | 17 JAN 70.000 | 8.85 | 9.75 | 9.9 | 12.50% | 0 | 0 |
| 17 JAN 72.000 | 2.63 | 3.35 | 3.25 | 15.00% | 0 | 0 | 17 JAN 72.000 | 10.1 | 11 | 11.2 | 11.60% | 0 | 0 |

ABX—Barrick Gold Corporation
Last update: May 22, 2014 at 11:40 am (data 15 minutes delayed)
Last price: 18.080   Net change: −0.240   Bid price: 18.070   Ask price: 18.080   30-day historical volatility: 25.61%

| | Calls | | | | | | | Puts | | | | | |
|---|---|---|---|---|---|---|---|---|---|---|---|---|---|
| Month / Strike | Bid price | Ask price | Last price | Impl. vol. | Open int. | Vol. | Month / Strike | Bid price | Ask price | Last price | Impl. vol. | Open int. | Vol. |
| 14 JUN 14.000 | 4.05 | 4.1 | 4.35 | 45.50% | 0 | 0 | 14 JUN 14.000 | 0 | 0.05 | 0.04 | 48.30% | 0 | 0 |
| 14 JUN 16.000 | 2.07 | 2.11 | 2.36 | 24.40% | 12 | 0 | 14 JUN 16.000 | 0.03 | 0.06 | 0.06 | 29.60% | 1,050 | 0 |
| 14 JUN 18.000 | 0.52 | 0.55 | 0.53 | 24.80% | 221 | 110 | 14 JUN 18.000 | 0.48 | 0.52 | 0.45 | 26.10% | 138 | 40 |
| 14 JUN 20.000 | 0.04 | 0.08 | 0.11 | 26.70% | 416 | 10 | 14 JUN 20.000 | 1.99 | 2.05 | 1.83 | 29.60% | 31 | 0 |
| 14 JUN 22.000 | 0 | 0.06 | 0.05 | 46.20% | 65 | 0 | 14 JUN 22.000 | 3.95 | 4 | 3.8 | 46.20% | 40 | 0 |
| 14 JUL 14.000 | 4.05 | 4.1 | 4.35 | 31.60% | 0 | 0 | 14 JUL 14.000 | 0.01 | 0.06 | 0.06 | 36.60% | 0 | 0 |
| 14 JUL 16.000 | 2.16 | 2.21 | 2.34 | 27.70% | 0 | 2 | 14 JUL 16.000 | 0.12 | 0.14 | 0.12 | 28.30% | 29 | 0 |
| 14 JUL 18.000 | 0.77 | 0.81 | 0.95 | 26.20% | 41 | 0 | 14 JUL 18.000 | 0.71 | 0.75 | 0.65 | 26.90% | 788 | 10 |
| 14 JUL 20.000 | 0.18 | 0.22 | 0.23 | 27.30% | 362 | 10 | 14 JUL 20.000 | 2.12 | 2.17 | 1.97 | 28.50% | 341 | 0 |
| 14 JUL 22.000 | 0.03 | 0.09 | 0.11 | 31.30% | 548 | 0 | 14 JUL 22.000 | 3.95 | 4.05 | 3.8 | 34.90% | 199 | 0 |
| 14 OCT 14.000 | 4.2 | 4.3 | 4.5 | 33.30% | 14 | 0 | 14 OCT 14.000 | 0.12 | 0.16 | 0.14 | 30.80% | 0 | 0 |
| 14 OCT 16.000 | 2.54 | 2.62 | 2.82 | 30.20% | 1 | 0 | 14 OCT 16.000 | 0.48 | 0.51 | 0.47 | 29.60% | 111 | 0 |
| 14 OCT 18.000 | 1.35 | 1.4 | 1.39 | 29.70% | 17 | 3 | 14 OCT 18.000 | 1.25 | 1.3 | 1.21 | 28.70% | 228 | 0 |
| 14 OCT 20.000 | 0.63 | 0.68 | 0.78 | 29.60% | 369 | 0 | 14 OCT 20.000 | 2.53 | 2.59 | 2.42 | 28.70% | 428 | 0 |
| 14 OCT 22.000 | 0.29 | 0.34 | 0.38 | 30.40% | 214 | 0 | 14 OCT 22.000 | 4.15 | 4.25 | 4.05 | 29.80% | 231 | 0 |
| 15 JAN 14.000 | 4.4 | 4.5 | 4.7 | 33.80% | 21 | 0 | 15 JAN 14.000 | 0.3 | 0.35 | 0.32 | 31.20% | 170 | 0 |
| 15 JAN 16.000 | 2.88 | 2.97 | 3.15 | 31.50% | 100 | 0 | 15 JAN 16.000 | 0.79 | 0.83 | 0.77 | 30.00% | 290 | 0 |
| 15 JAN 18.000 | 1.73 | 1.83 | 1.98 | 30.70% | 128 | 0 | 15 JAN 18.000 | 1.62 | 1.69 | 1.58 | 29.20% | 155 | 10 |
| 15 JAN 20.000 | 1.01 | 1.08 | 1.19 | 30.50% | 455 | 0 | 15 JAN 20.000 | 2.87 | 2.94 | 2.81 | 29.20% | 429 | 0 |
| 15 JAN 22.000 | 0.57 | 0.64 | 0.69 | 30.90% | 321 | 0 | 15 JAN 22.000 | 4.4 | 4.55 | 4.3 | 29.50% | 26 | 0 |
| 16 JAN 14.000 | 5 | 5.5 | 5.5 | 35.70% | 316 | 0 | 16 JAN 14.000 | 0.84 | 1.19 | 1.19 | 31.50% | 153 | 0 |
| 16 JAN 16.000 | 3.8 | 4.35 | 4.45 | 35.00% | 22 | 0 | 16 JAN 16.000 | 1.57 | 2.03 | 2 | 31.50% | 12 | 0 |
| 16 JAN 18.000 | 3.1 | 3.5 | 3.45 | 36.50% | 32 | 0 | 16 JAN 18.000 | 2.55 | 3.05 | 2.6 | 31.20% | 215 | 5 |
| 16 JAN 20.000 | 2.08 | 2.53 | 2.59 | 33.50% | 20 | 0 | 16 JAN 20.000 | 3.75 | 4.25 | 4.25 | 30.70% | 176 | 0 |
| 16 JAN 22.000 | 1.53 | 1.97 | 2.08 | 33.60% | 25 | 0 | 16 JAN 22.000 | 5.15 | 5.65 | 5.6 | 30.50% | 30 | 0 |
| 17 JAN 16.000 | 4.65 | 5.45 | 5.6 | 37.80% | 0 | 0 | 17 JAN 16.000 | 2.14 | 2.85 | 3.85 | 30.90% | 63 | 0 |
| 17 JAN 18.000 | 3.7 | 4.5 | 4.65 | 36.50% | 0 | 0 | 17 JAN 18.000 | 3.1 | 3.9 | 4.5 | 29.10% | 0 | 5 |
| 17 JAN 20.000 | 3 | 3.75 | 3.85 | 36.10% | 8 | 0 | 17 JAN 20.000 | 4.3 | 4.8 | | | | |
| 17 JAN 21.000 | 2.59 | 3.35 | 3.4 | 35.20% | 2 | 0 | 17 JAN 21.000 | 4.95 | 5.75 | 5.65 | 30.20% | 0 | 0 |

Source: www.m-x.ca. Used with permission.

The first thing listed in Table 23.1 is the company identifier, Bank of Nova Scotia (BNS). This tells us that these options involve the right to buy or sell shares of stock in Bank of Nova Scotia, which are listed on the Toronto Stock Exchange (TSX). Beside the company identifier is the stock's last price. Bank of Nova Scotia's last price was $67.980.

On the next line is the expiration date. JUN means the option expires in June. At the bottom is an option marked JAN, meaning it expires in January. All CDCC options expire on the third Friday of the expiration month. Right beside the expiration date is the strike price. The Bank of Nova Scotia options listed here have exercise prices ranging from $48 to $82.

For Barrick Gold, the company listed below Bank of Nova Scotia, the first option (under the call table) would be described as the "Barrick Gold, $14 call." The price for this option is approximately $4.075 (estimated centre value between the "Bid" and "Ask"). If you pay the $4.075, then you have the right any time between now and the third Friday of June to buy one share of Barrick Gold stock for $14. Actually, trading takes place in round lots (multiples of 100 shares), so one option contract costs $4.075 × 100 = $407.50.

The other quotations are similar. For example, the $20 October call option costs approximately $0.655. If you pay $0.655 × 100 = $65.50, then you have the right to buy 100 shares of Barrick Gold stock at any time between now and the third Friday in October at a price of $20 per share.

## Long-Term Equity Anticipation Securities

The Montreal Exchange also offers long-lived options called LEAPS (long-term equity anticipation securities). LEAPS are exactly the same as the call or put options already discussed except that they have much longer lives.

Table 23.1 shows quotes for Bank of Nova Scotia LEAPS expiring in 2016 and 2017. When these quotations were made in May 2014, the Bank of Nova Scotia LEAPS had maturities of 18 months or more.

## 23.6   COMBINATIONS OF OPTIONS

Puts and calls can serve as building blocks for more complex option contracts. For example, Figure 23.4 illustrates the payoff from buying a put option on a stock and simultaneously buying the stock.

**FIGURE 23.4**

Payoff to the Combination of Buying Puts and Buying Stock

If the share price is greater than the exercise price, the put option is worthless, and the value of the combined position is equal to the value of the common stock. If instead the exercise price is greater than the share price, the decline in the value of the shares will be exactly offset by the rise in value of the put.

The strategy of buying a put and buying the underlying stock is called a *protective put*. It is as if one is buying insurance for the stock. The stock can always be sold at the exercise price, regardless of how far the market price of the stock falls.

Note that the combination of buying a put and buying the underlying stock has the same *shape* in Figure 23.4 as the call purchase in Figure 23.1. To pursue this point, let's consider the graph for buying a call, which is shown at the far left of Figure 23.5. This graph is the same as Figure 23.1. Now, let's try the strategy of

(Leg A) Buying a call.

(Leg B) Buying a zero-coupon bond with a face value of $50 that matures on the same day that the option expires.

**FIGURE 23.5**

### Payoff to the Combination of Buying a Call and Buying a Zero-Coupon Bond

The graph of buying a call and buying a zero-coupon bond is the same as the graph of buying a put and buying the stock in Figure 23.4.

We have drawn the graph of Leg A of this strategy at the far left of Figure 23.5, but what does the graph of Leg B look like? It looks like the middle graph of the figure. That is, anyone buying this zero-coupon bond will be guaranteed to get $50, regardless of the price of the stock at expiration.

What does the graph of *simultaneously* buying both Leg A and Leg B of this strategy look like? It looks like the far-right graph of Figure 23.5. That is, the investor receives a guaranteed $50 from the bond, regardless of what happens to the stock. In addition, the investor receives a payoff from the call of $1 for every $1 that the price of the stock rises above the exercise price of $50.

The far-right graph of Figure 23.5 looks *exactly* like the far-right graph of Figure 23.4. Thus, an investor gets the same payoff from the strategy of Figure 23.4 and the strategy of Figure 23.5, regardless of what happens to the price of the underlying stock. In other words, the investor gets the same payoff from

1. Buying a put and buying the underlying stock.
2. Buying a call and buying a zero-coupon bond.

If investors have the same payoffs from the two strategies, the two strategies must have the *same* cost. Otherwise, all investors will choose the strategy with the lower cost and avoid the strategy with the higher cost. This leads to the interesting result that

$$\underbrace{\text{Price of underlying stock} + \text{Price of put}}_{\text{Cost of first strategy}} = \underbrace{\text{Price of call} + \text{PV of exercise price}}_{\text{Cost of second strategy}} \quad \text{(23.1)}$$

This relationship is known as **put–call parity** and is one of the most fundamental relationships concerning options. It says that there are two ways of buying a protective put. You can buy a put and buy the underlying stock simultaneously. Here, your total cost is the price of the underlying stock plus the price of the put. Or you can buy the call and buy a zero-coupon bond. Here, your total cost is the price of the call plus the price of the zero-coupon bond. The price of the zero-coupon bond is equal to the present value (PV) of the exercise price, that is, the PV of $50 in our example.

Equation (23.1) is a very precise relationship. It holds only if the put and the call have both the same exercise price and the same expiration date. In addition, the maturity date of the zero-coupon bond must be the same as the expiration date of the options. Also, we are assuming that the underlying stock pays no dividends and that the call and the put are European.[7]

---

[7] These assumptions can be relaxed, but doing so would take us beyond the scope of this text.

To see how fundamental put–call parity is, let's rearrange the formula, yielding

Price of underlying stock = Price of call − Price of put + PV of exercise price

This relationship now states that you can replicate the purchase of a share of stock by buying a call, selling a put, and buying a zero-coupon bond. (Note that because a minus sign comes before "Price of put," the put is sold, not bought.) Investors in this three-legged strategy are said to have purchased a *synthetic* stock.

Let's do one more transformation:

### Covered-Call Strategy

Price of underlying stock − Price of call = −Price of put + PV of exercise price

Many investors like to buy a stock and write the call on the stock simultaneously. This is a conservative strategy known as *selling a covered call*. The preceding put–call parity relationship tells us that this strategy is equivalent to selling a put and buying a zero-coupon bond. Figure 23.6 develops the graph for the **covered-call strategy**. You can verify that the covered call can be replicated by selling a put and simultaneously buying a zero-coupon bond.

**FIGURE 23.6**

**Payoff to the Combination of Buying a Stock and Writing a Call**

Of course, there are other ways of rearranging the basic put–call relationship. For each rearrangement, the strategy on the left-hand side is equivalent to the strategy on the right-hand side. The beauty of put–call parity is that it shows how any strategy in options can be achieved in two different ways.

**CONCEPT QUESTION**

- What is put–call parity?

## 23.7    VALUING OPTIONS

In the last section, we determined what options are worth on the expiration date. Now we wish to evaluate the value of options when you buy them well before expiration.[8] We begin by considering the upper and lower bounds on the value of a call.

---

[8] Our discussion in this section is of American options, because they are traded in the real world. As necessary, we will indicate differences for European calls.

## Bounding the Value of an American Call

**Lower Bound**    Consider an American call that is in the money prior to expiration. For example, assume that the stock price is $60 and the exercise price is $50. In this case, the option cannot sell below $10. To see this, note the simple strategy if the option sells at, say, $9:

| Date | Transaction | |
|------|-------------|---|
| Today | (1) Buy call. | −$ 9 |
| Today | (2) Exercise call, that is, buy underlying stock at exercise price. | −$50 |
| Today | (3) Sell stock at current market price. | +$60 |
| Arbitrage profit | | +$ 1 |

The type of profit that is described in this transaction is an *arbitrage profit*. Arbitrage profits come from transactions that have no risk or cost and cannot occur regularly in normal, well-functioning financial markets.[9] The excess demand for these options would quickly force the option price up to at least $10 (or $60 − $50).[10]

In practice, the price of the option is likely to be above $10. Investors will rationally pay more than $10 because of the possibility that the stock will rise above $60 before expiration.

**Upper Bound**    Is there an upper bound for the option price as well? It turns out that the upper bound is the price of the underlying stock. That is, an option to buy common stock cannot have a greater value than the common stock itself. A call option can be used to buy common stock with a payment of an exercise price. It would be foolish to buy stock this way if the stock could be purchased directly at a lower price. The upper and lower bounds are represented in Figure 23.7. In addition, these bounds are summarized in the bottom half of Table 23.2.

**FIGURE 23.7**

**The Upper and Lower Bounds of Call Option Values**

The precise option value will depend on five factors:
1. Exercise price.
2. Expiration date.
3. Stock price.
4. Risk-free interest rate.
5. Variance of the stock.

---

[9] Paul Halpern and Stuart Turnbull, "Empirical Tests of Boundary Conditions for Toronto Stock Exchange Options," *Journal of Finance* (June 1985), tested these boundary conditions for options on Canadian stocks in the late 1970s when Canadian options trading was relatively new. While they detected arbitrage opportunities, it is unlikely that these persist today.

[10] Note that this lower bound is strictly true for an American option but not for an European option.

TABLE 23.2

**Factors Affecting American Option Values**

| Increase in | Call option | Put option |
| --- | :---: | :---: |
| Value of underlying asset (stock price) | + | − |
| Exercise price | − | + |
| Stock volatility | + | + |
| Interest rate | + | − |
| Time to exercise date | + | + |

In addition to the preceding, we have presented the following four relationships for American calls:
1.  The call price can never be greater than the stock price (*upper bound*).
2.  The call price can never be less than either zero or the difference between the stock price and the exercise price (*lower bound*).
3.  The call is worth zero if the stock is worth zero.
4.  When the stock price is much greater than the exercise price, the call price tends toward the difference between the stock price and the PV of the exercise price.

## The Factors Determining Call Option Values

The previous discussion indicated that the price of a call option must fall somewhere in the shaded region of Figure 23.7. We now determine more precisely where in the shaded region it should be. The factors that determine a call's value can be broken into two sets. The first set contains the features of the option contract. The two basic contractual features are the expiration date and the exercise price. The second set of factors affecting the call price reflects characteristics of the stock and the market.

**Exercise Price**    An increase in the exercise price reduces the value of the call. For example, imagine that there are two calls on a stock selling at $60. The first call has an exercise price of $50 and the second one has an exercise price of $40. Which call would you rather have? Clearly, you would rather have the call with an exercise price of $40, because that one is $20 ($60 − $40) in the money. In other words, the call with an exercise price of $40 should sell for more than an otherwise identical call with an exercise price of $50.

**Expiration Date**    The value of an American call option must be at least as great as the value of an otherwise identical option with a shorter term to expiration. Consider two American calls: one has a maturity of nine months and the other expires in six months. The nine-month call offers the same rights as the six-month call, and also has an additional three months within which these rights can be exercised. It cannot be worth less and will generally be more valuable.[11]

**Stock Price**    Other things being equal, the higher the stock price, the more valuable the call option will be. For example, if a stock is worth $80, a call with an exercise price of $100 isn't worth very much. If the stock soars to $120, the call becomes much more valuable.

Now consider Figure 23.8, which shows the relationship between the call price and the stock price prior to expiration. The curve indicates that the call price increases as the stock price increases. Furthermore, it can be shown that the relationship is represented, not by a straight line, but by a *convex* curve. That is, the increase in the call price for a given change in the stock price is greater when the stock price is high than when the stock price is low.

---

[11] This relationship need not hold for a European call option. Consider a firm with two otherwise identical European call options, one expiring at the end of May and the other expiring a few months later. Further, assume that a *huge* dividend is paid in early June. If the first call is exercised at the end of May, its holder will receive the underlying stock. If he does not sell the stock, he will receive the large dividend shortly thereafter. However, the holder of the second call will receive the stock through exercise after the dividend is paid. Because the market knows that the holder of this option will miss the dividend, the value of the second call option could be less than the value of the first.

FIGURE 23.8

**Value of a Call as a Function of Stock Price**

The call price is positively related to the stock price. In addition, the change in the call price for a given change in the stock price is greater when the stock price is high than when it is low.

There are two special points on the curve in Figure 23.8:

1. *The stock is worthless.* The call must be worthless if the underlying stock is worthless. That is, if the stock has no chance of attaining any value, it is not worthwhile to pay the exercise price in order to obtain the stock.

2. *The stock price is* very *high relative to the exercise price.* In this situation, the owner of the call knows that she will end up exercising the call. She can view herself as the owner of the stock now, with one difference. She must pay the exercise price at expiration.

Thus, the value of her position, i.e., the value of the call, is

$$\text{Stock price} - \text{PV of exercise price}$$

These two points on the curve are summarized in the bottom half of Table 23.2.

**The Key Factor: The Variability of the Underlying Asset** The greater the variability of the underlying asset, the more valuable the call option will be. Consider the following example. Suppose that just before the call expires, the stock price will be either $100 with probability 0.5 or $80 with probability 0.5. What will be the value of a call with an exercise price of $110? Clearly, it will be worthless because no matter what happens to the stock, its price will always be below the exercise price.

Now let us see what happens if the stock is more variable. Suppose that we add $20 to the best case and take $20 away from the worst case. Now the stock has a one-half chance of being worth $60 and a one-half chance of being worth $120. We have spread the stock returns, but, of course, the expected value of the stock has stayed the same:

$$\left(\tfrac{1}{2} \times \$80\right) + \left(\tfrac{1}{2} \times \$100\right) = \$90 = \left(\tfrac{1}{2} \times \$60\right) + \left(\tfrac{1}{2} \times \$120\right)$$

Notice that the call option has value now because there is a one-half chance that the stock price will be $120, or $10 above the exercise price of $110. This illustrates a very important point. There is a fundamental distinction between holding an option on an underlying asset and holding the underlying asset. If investors in the marketplace are risk averse, a rise in the variability of the stock will decrease its market value. However, the holder of a call receives payoffs from the positive tail of the probability distribution. As a consequence, a rise in the variability in the underlying stock increases the market value of the call.

This result can also be seen from Figure 23.9. Consider two stocks, *A* and *B*, each of which is normally distributed. For each security, the figure illustrates the probability of different stock prices on the expiration date.[12] As we see, stock *B* has more volatility than does stock *A*. This means that stock *B* has higher probability of both abnormally high returns and abnormally low returns. Let us assume that options on each of the two securities have the same exercise price. To option holders, a return much below average on stock *B* is no worse than a return only moderately below average on stock *A*. In either situation, the option expires out of the money. However, to option holders, a return much above average on stock *B* is better than a return only moderately above average on stock *A*. Because a call's price at the expiration date is the difference between the stock price and the exercise price, the value of the call on *B* at expiration will be higher in this case.

**FIGURE 23.9**

**Distribution of Common-Stock Price at Expiration for Both Security *A* and Security *B*, Whose Options Have the Same Exercise Price**

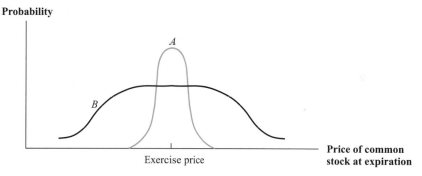

The call on stock *B* is worth more than the call on stock *A* because stock *B* is more volatile. At expiration, a call that is way in the money is more valuable than a call that is way out of the money. However, at expiration, a call way out of the money is worth zero, just as is a call only slightly out of the money.

**The Interest Rate**    Call prices are also a function of the level of interest rates. The higher the risk-free rate, the more the call is worth. Normally, we think of asset values going down as rates rise. In this case, the exercise price is a cash outflow, a liability. The current value of that liability goes down as the discount rate goes up. This makes the call worth more.

## A Quick Discussion of Factors Determining Put Option Values

Given our extended discussion of the factors influencing a call's value, we can easily examine these factors' effect on puts. Table 23.2 summarizes the five factors influencing prices of both American calls and American puts, holding other factors constant. The effects of three factors on puts are the opposite of the effects of these three factors on calls:

1. The put's market price *decreases* as the stock price increases because puts are in the money when the stock sells below the exercise price.
2. The market value of a put with a high exercise price is *greater* than the value of an otherwise identical put with a low exercise price for the reason given in (1) above.
3. A high interest rate *adversely* affects the value of a put. The ability to sell a stock at a fixed exercise price some time in the future is worth less if the PV of the exercise price is diminished by a high interest rate.

---

[12] This graph assumes that for each security, the exercise price is equal to the expected stock price. This assumption is employed merely to facilitate the discussion. It is not needed to show the relationship between a call's value and the volatility of the underlying stock.

The effect of the other two factors on puts is the same as the effect of these factors on calls:

4.  The value of an American put with a distant expiration date is greater than an otherwise identical put with an earlier expiration.[13] The longer time to maturity gives the put holder more flexibility, just as it did in the case of a call.

5.  The volatility of the underlying stock increases the value of the put. The reasoning is analogous to that for a call. At expiration, a put that is deep in the money is more valuable than a put only slightly in the money. However, at expiration, a put way out of the money is worth zero, just as is a put only slightly out of the money.

CONCEPT
QUESTIONS
- List the factors that determine the value of options.
- Why does a stock's variability affect the value of options written on it?

## 23.8    AN OPTION PRICING FORMULA

We have explained *qualitatively* that the value of a call option is a function of five variables:

1.  The current price of the underlying asset, which for stock options is the price of the shares of common stock.
2.  The exercise price.
3.  The time to the expiration date.
4.  The variance of the underlying asset.
5.  The risk-free interest rate.

It is time to replace the qualitative model with a precise option valuation model. The model we choose is the famous Black–Scholes option pricing model. Myron Scholes and Robert Merton shared the 1997 Nobel Prize in Economics for their pioneering work on option pricing models. You can put numbers into the Black–Scholes model and get values back.

The Black–Scholes model is represented by a rather imposing formula. A derivation of the formula is simply not possible in this textbook, as students will be happy to learn. However, some appreciation for the achievement as well as some intuitive understanding is in order.

In the early chapters of this book, we showed how to discount capital budgeting projects using the net present value (NPV) formula. We also used this approach to value stocks and bonds. Why, students sometimes ask, can't the same NPV formula be used to value puts and calls? It is a good question because the earliest attempts at valuing options used NPV. Unfortunately, the attempts were simply not successful because no one could determine the appropriate discount rate. An option is generally riskier than the underlying stock, but no one knew exactly how much riskier.

Black and Scholes attacked the problem by pointing out that a strategy of borrowing to finance a stock purchase duplicates the risk of a call. Then, knowing the price of a stock already, one can determine the price of a call such that its return is identical to that of the stock-with-borrowing alternative.

We illustrate the intuition behind the Black–Scholes approach by considering a simple example in which a combination of a call and a stock eliminates all risk. This example works because we let the future stock price be one of only two values. Hence, the example is called a *two-state option model*. By eliminating the possibility that the stock price can take on other values, we are able to duplicate the call exactly.

---

[13] Though this result must hold in the case of an American put, it need not hold for a European put.

## A Two-State Option Model

Consider the following example. Suppose the current market price of a stock is $50 and the stock will be either $60 or $40 at the end of the year. Further, imagine a call option on this stock with a one-year expiration date and a $50 exercise price. Investors can borrow at 10 percent. Our goal is to determine the value of the call.

In order to value the call correctly, we need to examine two strategies. The first is to simply buy the call. The second is to

a.    Buy one-half share of stock.
b.    Borrow $18.18, implying a payment of principal and interest at the end of the year of $20 ($18.18 × 1.10).

As you will see shortly, the cash flows from the second strategy exactly match the cash flows from buying a call. (A little later we will show how we came up with the exact fraction of a share of stock to buy and the exact borrowing amount.) Because the cash flows match, we say that we are *duplicating* the call with the second strategy.

At the end of the year, the future payoffs are set out as follows:

| | Future payoffs | |
| Initial transactions | If stock price is $60 | If stock price is $40 |
| --- | --- | --- |
| 1.  Buy a call | $60 − $50 =    $10 | 0 |
| 2.  Buy $\frac{1}{2}$ share of stock | $\frac{1}{2}$ × $60 =    $30 | $\frac{1}{2}$ × $40 =    $20 |
| Borrow $18.18 at 10% | −($18.18 × 1.10) = −$20 | −$20 |
| Total from stock and borrowing strategy | $10 | 0 |

Note that the future payoff structure of the "buy-a-call" strategy is duplicated by the strategy of "buy stock" and "borrow." That is, under either strategy, an investor would end up with $10 if the stock price rose and $0 if the stock price fell. Thus, these two strategies are equivalent as far as traders are concerned.

Now, if two strategies always have the same cash flows at the end of the year, how must their initial costs be related? The two strategies must have the *same* initial cost. Otherwise, there will be an arbitrage possibility. We can easily calculate this cost for our strategy of buying stock and borrowing. This cost is

$$\begin{array}{lll} \text{Buy } \tfrac{1}{2} \text{ share of stock} & \tfrac{1}{2} \times \$50 = & \$25.00 \\ \text{Borrow } \$18.18 & & -\$18.18 \\ \hline & & \$\ 6.82 \end{array}$$

Because the call option provides the same payoffs at expiration as does the strategy of buying stock and borrowing, the call must be priced at $6.82. This is the value of the call option in a market without arbitrage profits.

We left two issues unexplained in the preceding example.

**Determining the Delta**    How did we know to buy one-half share of stock in the duplicating strategy? Actually, the answer is easier than it might at first appear. The call price at the end of the year will be either $10 or $0, whereas the stock price will be either $60 or $40. Thus, the call price has a potential swing of $10 ($10 − $0) next period, whereas the stock price has a potential swing of $20 ($60 − $40). We can write this in terms of the following ratio:

**Delta**

$$\frac{\text{Swing of call}}{\text{Swing of stock}} = \frac{\$10 - \$0}{\$60 - \$40} = \frac{1}{2}$$

This ratio is called the *delta* of the call. In words, a $1 swing in the price of the stock gives rise to a $\$\frac{1}{2}$ swing in the price of the call. Because we are trying to duplicate the call with the stock, it seems sensible to buy one-half share of stock instead of buying one call. In other words, the risk of buying one-half share of stock should be the same as the risk of buying one call.

**Determining the Amount of Borrowing**   How did we know how much to borrow? Buying one-half share of stock brings us either $30 or $20 at expiration, which is exactly $20 more than the payoffs of $10 and $0, respectively, from the call. To duplicate the call through a purchase of stock, we should also borrow enough money so that we have to pay back exactly $20 of interest and principal. This amount of borrowing is merely the PV of $20, which is $18.18 ($20/1.10).

Now that we know how to determine both the delta and the amount borrowed, we can write the value of the call as

$$\text{Value of call} = \text{Stock price} \times \text{Delta} - \text{Amount borrowed} \qquad (23.2)$$
$$\$6.82 = \$50 \qquad\qquad \times \quad \tfrac{1}{2} \quad - \qquad \$18.18$$

We will find this intuition very useful in explaining the Black–Scholes model.

**Risk-Neutral Valuation**   Before leaving this simple example, we should comment on a remarkable feature. We found the exact value of the option without even knowing the probability that the stock would go up or down! If an optimist thought the probability of an up move was very high and a pessimist thought it was very low, they would still agree on the option value. How could that be? The answer is that the current $50 stock price already balances the views of the optimists and the pessimists. The option reflects that balance because its value depends on the stock price.

This insight provides us with another approach to valuing the call. If we don't need the probabilities of the two states to value the call, perhaps we can select *any* probabilities we want and still come up with the right answer. Suppose we selected probabilities such that the return on the stock is equal to the risk-free rate of 10 percent. We know the stock return given a rise is 20 percent ($60/$50 − 1) and the stock return given a fall is −20 percent ($40/$50 − 1). Thus, we can solve for the probability of a rise necessary to achieve an expected return of 10 percent as

$$10\% = \text{Probability of a rise} \times 20\% + (1 - \text{Probability of rise}) \times (-20\%)$$

Solving this formula, we find that the probability of a rise is $\tfrac{3}{4}$ and the probability of a fall is $\tfrac{1}{4}$. If we apply these probabilities to the call, we can value it as

$$\text{Value of call} = \frac{\tfrac{3}{4} \times \$10 + \tfrac{1}{4} \times \$0}{1.10} = \$6.82$$

which is the same value that we got from the duplicating approach.

Why did we select probabilities such that the expected return on the stock was 10 percent? We wanted to work with the special case where investors are *risk neutral*. This case occurs when the expected return on *any* asset (including both the stock and the call) is equal to the risk-free rate. In other words, this case occurs when investors demand no additional compensation beyond the risk-free rate, regardless of the risk of the asset in question.

What would have happened if we had assumed that the expected return on a stock was greater than the risk-free rate? The value of the call would still be $6.82. However, the calculations would be difficult. For example, if we assumed that the expected return on the stock was, say, 11 percent, we would have had to derive the expected return on the call. Although the expected return on the call would be higher than 11 percent, it would take a lot of work to determine it precisely. Why do any more work than you have to? Because we can't think of any good reason, we (and most other financial economists) choose to assume risk-neutrality.

Thus, the preceding material allows us to value a call in the following two ways:

1. Determine the cost of a strategy to duplicate the call. This strategy involves an investment in a fractional share of stock financed by partial borrowing.

2. Calculate the probabilities of a rise and a fall under the assumption of risk-neutrality. Use these probabilities, in conjunction with the risk-free rate, to discount the payoffs of the call at expiration.

## The Black–Scholes Model

The above example illustrates the duplicating strategy. Unfortunately, such a two-state (or binomial) strategy will not work in the real world over, say, a one-year time frame, because there are many more than two possibilities for next year's stock price. However, the number of possibilities is reduced as the time period is shortened. In fact, the assumption that there are only two possibilities for the stock price over the next infinitesimal instant is quite plausible.[14]

In our opinion, the fundamental insight of Black and Scholes is to shorten the time period. They show that a specific combination of stock and borrowing can indeed duplicate a call over an infinitesimal time horizon. Because the price of the stock will change over the first instant, another combination of stock and borrowing is needed to duplicate the call over the second instant, and so on. By adjusting the combination from moment to moment, they can continually duplicate the call. It may boggle the mind that a formula can (1) determine the duplicating combination at any moment and (2) value the option based on this duplicating strategy. Suffice it to say that their dynamic strategy allows them to value a call in the real world just as we showed how to value the call in the two-state model.

This is the basic intuition behind the Black–Scholes model. Because the actual derivation of their formula is, alas, far beyond the scope of this text, we simply present the formula itself. The formula is

**Black–Scholes Model:**

$$C = SN(d_1) - Ee^{-rt}N(d_2)$$

where

$$d_1 = \frac{\ln(S/E) + \left(r + \frac{1}{2}\sigma^2\right)t}{\sqrt{\sigma^2 t}}$$

$$d_2 = d_1 - \sqrt{\sigma^2 t}$$

This formula for the value of a call, $C$, is one of the most complex in finance. However, it involves only five parameters:

1. $S$ = Current stock price.
2. $E$ = Exercise price of call.
3. $r$ = Continuously compounded risk-free rate of return (annualized).
4. $\sigma^2$ = Variance (per year) of the continuous return on the stock.
5. $t$ = Time (in years) to expiration date.

In addition, there is the statistical concept

$N(d)$ = Probability that a standardized, normally distributed, random variable will be less than or equal to $d$

Rather than discuss the formula in its algebraic state, we illustrate it with Example 23.3.

---

[14] A full treatment of this assumption can be found in John C. Hull, *Options, Futures and Other Derivatives*, 7th ed. (Upper Saddle River, NJ: Prentice Hall 2009).

EXAMPLE **23.3**

Consider Private Equipment Company (PEC). On October 4, of year 0, the PEC April $49 call option had a closing value of $4. The stock itself was selling at $50. On October 4 the option had 199 days to expiration (maturity date is April 21, year 1). The annual risk-free interest rate (continuously compounded) is 7 percent.

The above information determines three variables directly:

1. The stock price, $S$, is $50.
2. The exercise price, $E$, is $49.
3. The risk-free rate, $r$, is 0.07.

In addition, the time to maturity, $t$, can be calculated quickly. The formula calls for $t$ to be expressed in years.

4. We express the 199-day interval in years as $t = 199/365$.

In the real world, an option trader would know $S$ and $E$ exactly. Traders generally view Canada Treasury bills as risk free, so a current quote would be obtained for the interest rate. The trader would also know (or could count) the number of days to expiration exactly. Thus, the fraction of a year to expiration, $t$, could be calculated quickly.

The problem comes in determining the variance of the stock's return. The formula calls for the variance measured between the purchase date of October 4 and the expiration date. Unfortunately, this represents the future, so the correct value for variance is simply not available. Instead, traders frequently estimate variance from past data, just as we calculated variance in an earlier chapter. In addition, some traders may use intuition to adjust their estimate. For example, if anticipation of an upcoming event is currently increasing the volatility of the stock, the trader might adjust the estimate of variance upward. (This problem was most severe right after the October 19, 1987, crash. The stock market was quite risky in the aftermath, so estimates using precrash data were too low.)

The above discussion was intended merely to mention the difficulties in variance estimation, not to present a solution.[15] For our purposes, we assume that a trader has come up with an estimate of variance.

5. The variance of PEC has been estimated to be 0.09 per year.

Using the above five parameters, we calculate the Black–Scholes value of the PEC option in three steps:

*Step 1: Calculate $d_1$ and $d_2$.* These values can be determined by a straightforward, albeit tedious, insertion of our parameters into the basic formula. We have

$$d_1 = \frac{\ln(S/E) + \left(r + \frac{1}{2}\sigma^2\right)t}{\sqrt{\sigma^2 t}}$$

$$= \frac{\ln(50/49) + \left(0.07 + \frac{1}{2} \times 0.09\right) \times (199/365)}{\sqrt{0.09 \times (199/365)}}$$

$$= \frac{0.0202 + 0.0627}{0.2215} = 0.3742$$

$$d_2 = d_1 - \sqrt{\sigma^2 t}$$
$$= 0.1527$$

---

[15] A more in-depth attempt to estimate variance can be found in John C. Hull, op. cit.

*Step 2: Calculate $N(d_1)$ and $N(d_2)$.* The values $N(d_1)$ and $N(d_2)$ can best be understood by examining Figure 23.10. The figure shows the normal distribution with an expected value of 0 and a standard deviation of 1. This is frequently called the **standardized normal distribution**. We mentioned in an earlier chapter that the probability that a drawing from this distribution will be between −1 and +1 (within one standard deviation of its mean, in other words) is 68.26 percent.

FIGURE 23.10

**Graph of Cumulative Probability**

The shaded area represents cumulative probability. Because the probability is 0.6459 that a drawing from the standard normal distribution will be below 0.3742, we say that N(0.3742) = 0.6459. That is, the cumulative probability of 0.3742 is 0.6459.

Now, let us ask a different question. What is the probability that a drawing from the standardized normal distribution will be *below* a particular value? For example, the probability that a drawing will be below 0 is clearly 50 percent because the normal distribution is symmetric. Using statistical terminology, we say that the **cumulative probability** of 0 is 50 percent. Statisticians say N(0) = 50%. It turns out that

$$N(d_1) = N(0.3742) = 0.6459$$
$$N(d_2) = N(0.1527) = 0.5607$$

The first value means that there is a 64.59 percent probability that a drawing from the standardized normal distribution will be below 0.3742. The second value means that there is a 56.07 percent probability that a drawing from the standardized normal distribution will be below 0.1527. More generally, N(d) is the notation that a drawing from the standardized normal distribution will be below *d*. In other words, N(d) is the cumulative probability of *d*. Note that $d_1$ and $d_2$ in our example are slightly positive, so $N(d_1)$ and $N(d_2)$ are slightly greater than 0.50.

We can determine the cumulative probability from Table 23.3.[16] For example, consider $d = 0.37$. This can be found in the table as 0.3 on the vertical and 0.07 on the horizontal. The value in the table for $d = 0.37$ is 0.1443. This value is *not* the cumulative probability of 0.37. One must first make an adjustment to determine cumulative probability. That is,

---

[16] The following website is a useful normal distribution function cumulative probabilities calculator: stattrek.com/online-calculator/normal.aspx. There are four input boxes: (1) Standard score (z), (2) Cumulative probability (Z ≤ z), (3) Mean, and (4) Standard deviation. To find any cumulative probability, input *d* into the Standard score (z) box, leave the cumulative probability box empty, and input 0 as the mean and 1 as the standard deviation. The tool will calculate the cumulative probability (second box).

$$N(0.37) = 0.50 + 0.1443 = 0.6443$$
$$N(-0.37) = 0.50 - 0.1443 = 0.3557$$

Unfortunately, our table only handles two significant digits, whereas our value of 0.3742 has four significant digits. Hence, we must interpolate to find N(0.3742). Because N(0.37) = 0.6443 and N(0.38) = 0.6480, the difference between the two values is 0.0037 (0.6480 − 0.6443). Because 0.3742 is 42 percent of the way between 0.37 and 0.38, we interpolate as[17]

$$N(0.3742) = 0.6443 + 0.42 \times 0.0037 = 0.6459$$

**TABLE 23.3**

## Cumulative Probabilities of the Standard Normal Distribution Function

| $d$ | 0.00 | 0.01 | 0.02 | 0.03 | 0.04 | 0.05 | 0.06 | 0.07 | 0.08 | 0.09 |
|-----|------|------|------|------|------|------|------|------|------|------|
| 0.0 | 0.0000 | 0.0040 | 0.0080 | 0.0120 | 0.0160 | 0.0199 | 0.0239 | 0.0279 | 0.0319 | 0.0359 |
| 0.1 | 0.0398 | 0.0438 | 0.0478 | 0.0517 | 0.0557 | 0.0596 | 0.0636 | 0.0675 | 0.0714 | 0.0753 |
| 0.2 | 0.0793 | 0.0832 | 0.0871 | 0.0910 | 0.0948 | 0.0987 | 0.1026 | 0.1064 | 0.1103 | 0.1141 |
| 0.3 | 0.1179 | 0.1217 | 0.1255 | 0.1293 | 0.1331 | 0.1368 | 0.1406 | 0.1443 | 0.1480 | 0.1517 |
| 0.4 | 0.1554 | 0.1591 | 0.1628 | 0.1664 | 0.1700 | 0.1736 | 0.1772 | 0.1808 | 0.1844 | 0.1879 |
| 0.5 | 0.1915 | 0.1950 | 0.1985 | 0.2019 | 0.2054 | 0.2088 | 0.2123 | 0.2157 | 0.2190 | 0.2224 |
| 0.6 | 0.2257 | 0.2291 | 0.2324 | 0.2357 | 0.2389 | 0.2422 | 0.2454 | 0.2486 | 0.2517 | 0.2549 |
| 0.7 | 0.2580 | 0.2611 | 0.2642 | 0.2673 | 0.2704 | 0.2734 | 0.2764 | 0.2794 | 0.2823 | 0.2852 |
| 0.8 | 0.2881 | 0.2910 | 0.2939 | 0.2967 | 0.2995 | 0.3023 | 0.3051 | 0.3078 | 0.3106 | 0.3133 |
| 0.9 | 0.3159 | 0.3186 | 0.3212 | 0.3238 | 0.3264 | 0.3289 | 0.3315 | 0.3340 | 0.3365 | 0.3389 |
| 1.0 | 0.3413 | 0.3438 | 0.3461 | 0.3485 | 0.3508 | 0.3531 | 0.3554 | 0.3577 | 0.3599 | 0.3621 |
| 1.1 | 0.3643 | 0.3665 | 0.3686 | 0.3708 | 0.3729 | 0.3749 | 0.3770 | 0.3790 | 0.3810 | 0.3830 |
| 1.2 | 0.3849 | 0.3869 | 0.3888 | 0.3907 | 0.3925 | 0.3944 | 0.3962 | 0.3980 | 0.3997 | 0.4015 |
| 1.3 | 0.4032 | 0.4049 | 0.4066 | 0.4082 | 0.4099 | 0.4115 | 0.4131 | 0.4147 | 0.4162 | 0.4177 |
| 1.4 | 0.4192 | 0.4207 | 0.4222 | 0.4236 | 0.4251 | 0.4265 | 0.4279 | 0.4292 | 0.4306 | 0.4319 |
| 1.5 | 0.4332 | 0.4345 | 0.4357 | 0.4370 | 0.4382 | 0.4394 | 0.4406 | 0.4418 | 0.4429 | 0.4441 |
| 1.6 | 0.4452 | 0.4463 | 0.4474 | 0.4484 | 0.4495 | 0.4505 | 0.4515 | 0.4525 | 0.4535 | 0.4545 |
| 1.7 | 0.4554 | 0.4564 | 0.4573 | 0.4582 | 0.4591 | 0.4599 | 0.4608 | 0.4616 | 0.4625 | 0.4633 |
| 1.8 | 0.4641 | 0.4649 | 0.4656 | 0.4664 | 0.4671 | 0.4678 | 0.4686 | 0.4693 | 0.4699 | 0.4706 |
| 1.9 | 0.4713 | 0.4719 | 0.4726 | 0.4732 | 0.4738 | 0.4744 | 0.4750 | 0.4756 | 0.4761 | 0.4767 |
| 2.0 | 0.4773 | 0.4778 | 0.4783 | 0.4788 | 0.4793 | 0.4798 | 0.4803 | 0.4808 | 0.4812 | 0.4817 |
| 2.1 | 0.4821 | 0.4826 | 0.4830 | 0.4834 | 0.4838 | 0.4842 | 0.4846 | 0.4850 | 0.4854 | 0.4857 |
| 2.2 | 0.4861 | 0.4866 | 0.4830 | 0.4871 | 0.4875 | 0.4878 | 0.4881 | 0.4884 | 0.4887 | 0.4890 |
| 2.3 | 0.4893 | 0.4896 | 0.4898 | 0.4901 | 0.4904 | 0.4906 | 0.4909 | 0.4911 | 0.4913 | 0.4916 |
| 2.4 | 0.4918 | 0.4920 | 0.4922 | 0.4925 | 0.4927 | 0.4929 | 9.4931 | 0.4932 | 0.4934 | 0.4936 |
| 2.5 | 0.4938 | 0.4940 | 0.4941 | 0.4943 | 0.4945 | 0.4946 | 0.4948 | 0.4949 | 0.4951 | 0.4952 |
| 2.6 | 0.4953 | 0.4955 | 0.4956 | 0.4957 | 0.4959 | 0.4960 | 0.4961 | 0.4962 | 0.4963 | 0.4964 |
| 2.7 | 0.4965 | 0.4966 | 0.4967 | 0.4968 | 0.4969 | 0.4970 | 0.4971 | 0.4972 | 0.4973 | 0.4974 |
| 2.8 | 0.4974 | 0.4975 | 0.4976 | 0.4977 | 0.4977 | 0.4978 | 0.4979 | 0.0479 | 0.4980 | 0.4981 |
| 2.9 | 0.4981 | 0.4982 | 0.4982 | 0.4982 | 0.4984 | 0.4984 | 0.4985 | 0.4985 | 0.4986 | 0.4986 |
| 3.0 | 0.4987 | 0.4987 | 0.4987 | 0.4988 | 0.4988 | 0.4989 | 0.4989 | 0.4989 | 0.4990 | 0.4990 |

N($d$) represents areas under the standard normal distribution function. Suppose that $d_1 = 0.24$. This table implies a cumulative probability of $0.5000 + 0.0948 = 0.5948$. If $d_1$ is equal to 0.2452, we must estimate the probability by interpolating between N(0.25) and N(0.24).

---

[17] This method is called *linear interpolation*. It is only one of a number of possible methods of interpolation.

*Step 3: Calculate C.* We have

$$C = S \times [N(d_1)] - Ee^{-rt} \times [N(d_2)]$$
$$= \$50 \times [N(d_1)] - \$49 \times [e^{-0.07 \times (199/365)}] \times N(d_2)$$
$$= (\$50 \times 0.6459) - (\$49 \times 0.9626 \times 0.5607)$$
$$= \$32.295 - \$26.447$$
$$= \$5.85$$

The estimated price of $5.85 is greater than the $4 actual price, implying that the call option is underpriced. A trader believing in the Black–Scholes model would buy a call. Of course, the Black–Scholes model is fallible. Perhaps the disparity between the model's estimate and the market price reflects an error in the model's estimate of variance.

The previous example stressed the calculations involved in using the Black–Scholes formula. Is there any intuition behind the formula? Yes, and that intuition follows from the stock purchase and borrowing strategy in our binomial (two-state) example.[18] The first line of the Black–Scholes equation is

$$C = S \times N(d_1) - Ee^{-rt}N(d_2)$$

which is exactly analogous to equation (23.2),

$$\text{Value of call} = \text{Stock price} \times \text{Delta} - \text{Amount borrowed} \qquad (23.2)$$

which we presented in the two-state example. It turns out that $N(d_1)$ is the delta in the Black–Scholes model. $N(d_1)$ is 0.6459 in the previous example. In addition, $Ee^{-rt}N(d_2)$ is the amount that an investor must borrow to duplicate a call. In the previous example, this value is $26.45 ($49 × 0.9626 × 0.5607). Thus, the model tells us that we can duplicate the call of the preceding example by both

1. Buying 0.6459 share of stock, and
2. Borrowing $26.45.

It is no exaggeration to say that the Black–Scholes formula is among the most important contributions in finance. It allows anyone to calculate the value of an option given a few parameters. The attraction of the formula is that four of the parameters are observable: the current price of the stock, $S$; the exercise price, $E$; the interest rate, $r$; and the time to expiration, $t$. Only one of the parameters must be estimated: the variance of return, $\sigma^2$.

To see how truly attractive this formula is, note what parameters are *not* needed. First, the investor's risk aversion does not affect value. The formula can be used by anyone, regardless of willingness to bear risk. Second, it does not depend on the expected return on the stock! Investors with different assessments of the stock's expected return will nevertheless agree on the call price. As in the two-state example, this is because the call depends on the stock price, and that price already balances investors' divergent views.

- How does the two-state option model work?
- What is the formula for the Black–Scholes option pricing model?

---

[18] Another intuitive approach to the Black–Scholes formula views $N(d_1)$ and $N(d_2)$ as probabilities that the option will expire in the money and be exercised. For example, when the stock price is high, these probabilities are close to unity and the call value is the stock price minus the PV of the exercise price. At the other extreme, when the stock price is low, the probabilities are near zero and the call is almost worthless. For more on this intuition, see Z. Bodie, A. Kane, A. J. Marcus, S. Perrakis, and P. J. Ryan, *Investments*, 7th Canadian ed. (Whitby, ON: McGraw-Hill Ryerson, 2011), p. 641.

## 23.9    STOCKS AND BONDS AS OPTIONS

The previous material in this chapter described, explained, and valued publicly traded options. This is important material to any finance student because much trading occurs in these listed options. The study of options has another purpose for the student of corporate finance.

You may have heard the one-liner about the elderly gentleman who was surprised to learn that he had been speaking prose all of his life. The same can be said about the corporate finance student and options. Although options were formally defined for the first time in this chapter, many corporate policies discussed earlier in the text were actually options in disguise. Though it is beyond the scope of this chapter to recast all of corporate finance in terms of options, the rest of the chapter considers two topics in which implicit options play an important role:

1.  Stocks and bonds as options.
2.  Capital budgeting decision as options.

We begin by illustrating the implicit options in stocks and bonds through Example 23.4.

EXAMPLE **23.4**

The Popov Company has been awarded the concessions at next year's Ice Games in Antarctica. Because the firm's principals live in Antarctica and because there is no other concession business on that continent, their enterprise will disband after the games. The firm has issued debt to help finance this venture. Interest and principal due on the debt next year will be $800, at which time the debt will be paid off in full. The firm's cash flows next year are forecast as follows:

| | Popov's Cash Flow Schedule | | | |
|---|---|---|---|---|
| | Very successful games | Moderately successful games | Moderately unsuccessful games | Outright failure |
| Cash flow before interest and principal | $1,000 | $850 | $700 | $550 |
| Interest and principal | 800 | 800 | 700 | 550 |
| Cash flow to shareholders | $ 200 | $ 50 | $ 0 | $ 0 |

As can be seen, the principals forecast four equally likely scenarios. If either of the first two scenarios occurs, the bondholders will be paid in full. The extra cash flow goes to the shareholders. However, if either of the last two scenarios occurs, the bondholders will not be paid in full. Instead, they will receive the firm's entire cash flow, leaving the shareholders with nothing.

This example is similar to the bankruptcy examples presented in our chapters on capital structure. Our new insight is that the relationship between the common stock and the firm can be expressed in terms of options. We consider call options first because the intuition is easier. The put option scenario is treated after that.

### The Firm Expressed in Terms of Call Options

**Shareholders**    We now show that stock can be viewed as a call option on the firm. To illustrate this, Figure 23.11 graphs the cash flow to the shareholders as a function of the cash flow to the firm. The shareholders receive nothing if the firm's cash flows are less than $800; here, all of the cash flows go to the bondholders. However, the shareholders earn a dollar for every dollar that the firm receives above $800. The graph looks exactly like the call option graph (Figure 23.5) that we considered earlier in this chapter.

**FIGURE 23.11**

**Cash Flow to Shareholders of Popov Corporation as a Function of Cash Flow of the Firm**

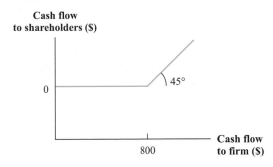

But what is the underlying asset upon which the stock is a call option? The underlying asset is the firm itself. That is, we can view the bondholders as owning the firm. However, the shareholders have a call option on the firm with an exercise price of $800.

If the firm's cash flow is above $800, the shareholders will choose to exercise this option. In other words, they will buy the firm from the bondholders for $800. Their net cash flow is the difference between the firm's cash flow and their $800 payment. This will be $200 (or $1,000 − $800) if the games are very successful and $50 (or $850 − $800) if the games are moderately successful.

If the value of the firm's cash flows is less than $800, the shareholders will not choose to exercise their option. Instead, they will walk away from the firm, as would any call option holder. The bondholders then receive the firm's entire cash flow.

This view of the firm is a novel one, and students are frequently bothered by it on first exposure. However, we encourage you to keep looking at the firm in this way until the view becomes second nature.

**Bondholders**   What about the bondholders? Our earlier cash flow schedule showed that they get the entire cash flow of the firm if it is less than $800. Should the firm earn more than $800, the bondholders receive only $800. That is, they are entitled only to interest and principal. This schedule is graphed in Figure 23.12.

**FIGURE 23.12**

**Cash Flow to Bondholders as a Function of Cash Flow of the Firm**

In keeping with our view that the shareholders have a call option on the firm, what does the bondholders' position consist of? The bondholders' position can be described by two claims:

1. They own the firm.
2. They have written a call against the firm with an exercise price of $800.

As we mentioned above, the shareholders walk away from the firm if cash flows are less than $800. Thus, the bondholders retain ownership in this case. However, if the cash flows are greater than $800, the shareholders exercise their option. They call the stock away from the bondholders for $800.

## The Firm Expressed in Terms of Put Options

The above analysis expresses the positions of the shareholders and the bondholders in terms of call options. We can now express the situation in terms of put options.

**Shareholders**     The shareholders' position can be expressed by three claims:

1. They own the firm.
2. They owe $800 in interest and principal to the bondholders.

If the debt were risk free, these two claims would fully describe the shareholders' situation. However, because of the possibility of default, we have a third claim as well:

3. The shareholders own a put option on the firm with an exercise price of $800. The group of bondholders is the seller of the put.

Now consider two possibilities.

*Cash Flow Is Less Than $800*     Because the put has an exercise price of $800, the put is in the money. The shareholders "put" (that is, sell) the firm to the bondholders. Normally, the holder of a put receives the exercise price when the asset is sold. However, the shareholders already owe $800 to the bondholders. Thus, the debt of $800 is simply cancelled—and no money changes hands—when the stock is delivered to the bondholders. Because the shareholders give up the stock in exchange for extinguishing the debt, the shareholders end up with nothing if the cash flow is below $800.

*Cash Flow Is Greater Than $800*     Because the put is out of the money in this case, the shareholders do not exercise. Thus, the shareholders retain ownership of the firm but pay $800 to the bondholders as interest and principal.

**Bondholders**     The bondholders' position can be described by two claims:

1. The bondholders are owed $800.
2. They have sold a put option on the firm to the shareholders with an exercise price of $800.

*Cash Flow Is Less Than $800*     As mentioned above, the shareholders will exercise the put in this case. This means that the bondholders are obliged to pay $800 for the firm. Because they are owed $800, the two obligations offset each other. Thus, the bondholders simply end up with the firm.

*Cash Flow Is Greater Than $800*     Here, the shareholders do not exercise the put. Thus, the bondholders merely receive the $800 that is due them.

Expressing the bondholders' position in this way is illuminating. With a risk- and default-free bond, the bondholders are owed $800. Thus, we can express the risky bond in terms of a risk-free bond and a put:

$$\begin{matrix} \text{Value of} \\ \text{risky bond} \end{matrix} = \begin{matrix} \text{Value of} \\ \text{default-free bond} \end{matrix} - \begin{matrix} \text{Value of} \\ \text{put option} \end{matrix}$$

That is, the value of the risky bond is the value of the default-free bond less the value of the shareholders' option to sell the company for $800.

## A Resolution of the Two Views

We have argued above that the positions of the shareholders and the bondholders can be viewed either in terms of calls or in terms of puts. These two viewpoints are summarized in Table 23.4.

**TABLE 23.4**

**Positions of Shareholders and Bondholders in Popov Company in Terms of Calls and Puts**

| Shareholders | Bondholders |
|---|---|
| **Positions viewed in terms of call options** | |
| 1. Shareholders own a call on the firm with an exercise price of $800. | 1. Bondholders own the firm. |
| | 2. Bondholders have sold a call on the firm to shareholders. |
| **Positions viewed in terms of put options** | |
| 1. Shareholders own the firm. | 1. Bondholders are owed $800 in interest and principal. |
| 2. Shareholders owe $800 in interest and principal to bondholders. | 2. Bondholders have sold a put on the firm to shareholders. |
| 3. Shareholders own a put option on the firm with an exercise price of $800. | |

We have found from experience that it is generally harder for students to think of the firm in terms of puts than in terms of calls. Thus, it would be helpful if there were a way to show that the two viewpoints are equivalent. Fortunately there is *put–call parity.* In an earlier section we presented the put–call parity relationship as equation (23.1), which we now repeat in a slightly different form:

$$\underset{\text{common stock}}{\text{Value of}} + \underset{\text{on common stock}}{\text{Value of put}} - \underset{\text{on common stock}}{\text{Value of call}} = \underset{\text{exercise price}}{\text{PV of}} \quad \textbf{(23.1)}$$

Using the results of this section, equation (23.1) can be rewritten as

$$\underbrace{\underset{\text{on firm}}{\text{Value of call}}}_{\substack{\text{Shareholders' position in} \\ \text{terms of call options}}} = \underbrace{\underset{\text{firm}}{\text{Value of}} + \underset{\text{on firm}}{\text{Value of put}} - \underset{\text{default-free bond}}{\text{Value of}}}_{\substack{\text{Shareholders' position} \\ \text{in terms of put options}}} \quad \textbf{(23.3)}$$

Going from equation (23.1) to equation (23.3) involves a few steps. First, we treat the firm, not the stock, as the underlying asset in this section. Second, the exercise price is now $800, the principal and interest on the firm's debt. Taking the PV of this amount at the risk-free rate yields the value of a default-free bond. Third, the order of the terms in equation (23.1) is rearranged in equation (23.3).

Note that the left-hand side of equation (23.3) is the shareholders' position in terms of call options, as shown in Table 23.4. The right-hand side of equation (23.3) is the shareholders' position in terms of put options, as shown in the table. Thus, put–call parity shows that viewing the shareholders' position in terms of call options is equivalent to viewing the shareholders' position in terms of put options.

Now, let's rearrange terms in equation (23.3) to yield

$$\underbrace{\underset{\text{firm}}{\text{Value of}} - \underset{\text{on firm}}{\text{Value of call}}}_{\substack{\text{Bondholders' position in} \\ \text{terms of call options}}} = \underbrace{\underset{\text{default-free bond}}{\text{Value of}} - \underset{\text{on firm}}{\text{Value of put}}}_{\substack{\text{Bondholders' position in} \\ \text{terms of put options}}} \quad \textbf{(23.4)}$$

The left-hand side of equation (23.4) is the bondholders' position in terms of call options, as shown in Table 23.4. The right-hand side of the equation is the bondholders' position in terms of put options, as shown in Table 23.4. Thus, put–call parity shows that viewing the bondholders' position in terms of call options is equivalent to viewing the bondholders' position in terms of put options.

## A Note on Loan Guarantees

In the Popov example above, the bondholders bore the risk of default. Of course, bondholders generally ask for an interest rate that is high enough to compensate them for bearing risk. When firms experience financial distress, they can no longer attract new debt at moderate interest rates. Thus, firms experiencing distress have frequently sought loan guarantees from the government. Our framework can be used to understand these guarantees.

If the firm defaults on a guaranteed loan, the government must make up the difference. In other words, a government guarantee converts a risky bond into a risk-free bond. What is the value of this guarantee?

Recall that with option pricing,

$$\text{Value of default-free bond} = \text{Value of risky bond} + \text{Value of put option}$$

This equation shows that the government is assuming an obligation that has a cost equal to the value of a put option.

Our analysis differs from that of either politicians or company spokespersons. They generally say that the guarantee will cost the taxpayer nothing because the guarantee enables the firm to attract debt, thereby staying solvent. However, it should be pointed out that though solvency may be a strong possibility, it is never a certainty. Thus, at the time the guarantee is made, the government's obligation has a cost in terms of PV. To say that a guarantee costs the government nothing is like saying that a put on the stock of, say, Royal Bank, has no value because the stock is *likely* to rise in price.

Federal and provincial governments guarantee bank loans to companies whose survival is considered important to the public interest. Who benefits from a typical loan guarantee?

1. If existing risky debt is guaranteed, all gains accrue to the existing bondholders or creditors. The shareholders gain nothing because the limited liability of corporations absolves the shareholders of any obligation in bankruptcy.

2. If new debt is being issued and guaranteed, the new debtholders do not gain. Rather, in a competitive market, they must accept a low interest rate because of the debt's low risk. The shareholders gain here because they are able to issue debt at a low interest rate. In addition, some of the gains accrue to the old bondholders because the firm's value is greater than would otherwise be true. Therefore, if shareholders want all the gains from loan guarantees, they should renegotiate or retire existing bonds before the guarantee is in place.

**Deposit Insurance as a Loan Guarantee**    When you lend money to a financial institution (by making a deposit), your loan is guaranteed (up to $100,000) by the federal government provided your institution is a member of the Canada Deposit Insurance Corporation (CDIC). As we argued above, loan guarantees are not cost free. This point was made abundantly clear to the government when two banks (the Canadian Commercial Bank and the Northland Bank of Canada) in western Canada collapsed in 1985, the Principal Group collapsed in 1987, and Central Guaranty Trust collapsed in 1992.

We also pointed out that since the put option allows a risky firm to borrow at subsidized rates, it is an asset to the shareholders. The more volatile the firm, the greater the value of the put option and the more the guarantee is worth to the shareholders.

Following this logic, Giammarino, Schwartz, and Zechner modified the Black–Scholes model to value the put option in CDIC deposit insurance for Canadian banks in the mid-1980s. They found that financial markets provided early warning of bank failures as the value of the put option increased significantly before bank failure occurred. Their research also showed that by charging the same premium for all financial institutions regardless of risk, the CDIC subsidized riskier banks and likely encouraged risk-taking.[19]

One result is that accountants in Canada, urged on by the auditor general, are forcing government agencies to report guarantees and other contingent liabilities in their financial statements. This may induce greater caution in extending guarantees in the first place.

***CONCEPT QUESTIONS***

- How can the firm/value be expressed in terms of call options?
- How can the firm/value be expressed in terms of put options?
- How does put–call parity relate these two expressions?
- Why are government loan guarantees not free? Why do such guarantees often encourage firms to increase their risk?

## 23.10    INVESTMENT IN REAL PROJECTS AND OPTIONS

Our discussion begins with a quick review of the material on capital budgeting presented earlier in the text. We first considered projects where forecasts for future cash flows were made at date 0. The expected cash flow in each future period was discounted at an appropriate risky rate, yielding an NPV calculation. For independent projects, a positive NPV meant acceptance and a negative NPV meant rejection.

This approach treated risk through the discount rate. We later considered decision-tree analysis, an approach that handles risk in a more sophisticated way. We pointed out that the firm will make investment and operating decisions on a project over its entire life. We value a project today, assuming that future decisions will be optimal. However, we do not yet know what these decisions will be, because much information remains to be discovered. The firm's ability to delay its investment and operating decisions until the release of information is an option. We now illustrate this option through Example 23.5.

**EXAMPLE 23.5**

Exoff Oil Corporation is considering the purchase of an oil field in a remote northern area. The seller has listed the property for $10,000 and is eager to sell immediately. Initial drilling costs are $500,000. The firm anticipates that 10,000 barrels of oil can be extracted each year for many decades. Because the termination date is so far in the future and so hard to estimate, the firm views the cash flow stream from the oil as a perpetuity. With oil prices at $93 per barrel and extraction costs at $89 a barrel, the firm anticipates a net margin of $4 per barrel. Because the firm budgets capital in real terms, it assumes that its cash flow per barrel will always be $4 in real terms. The appropriate real discount rate is 10 percent. The firm has enough tax credits from bad years in the past so that it will not need to pay taxes on any profits from the oil field. Should Exoff buy the property?

---

[19] R. Giammarino, E. Schwartz, and J. Zechner, "Market Valuation of Bank Assets and Deposit Insurance in Canada," *Canadian Journal of Economics* (February 1989).

The NPV of the oil field to Exoff is

$$-\$110,000 = -\$10,000 - \$500,000 + \frac{\$4 \times 10,000}{0.10} \qquad \textbf{(23.5)}$$

According to this analysis, Exoff should not purchase the land.

Though this approach uses the standard capital budgeting techniques of this and other textbooks, it is actually inappropriate for this situation. To see this, consider the analysis of Kirtley Thornton, a consultant to Exoff. He agrees that the price of oil is *expected* to rise at the rate of inflation. However, he points out that the next year is quite perilous for oil prices. On the one hand, OPEC is considering a long-term agreement that would raise oil prices to $108 per barrel in real terms for many years into the future. On the other hand, National Motors recently indicated that cars using a mixture of sand and water for fuel are currently being tested. Thornton argues that oil will be priced at $5 in real terms for many years, should this development prove successful. Full information on both these developments will be released in exactly one year.

Should oil prices rise to $108 a barrel, the NPV of the project will be

$$\$1,390,000 = -\$10,000 - \$500,000 + \frac{(\$108 - \$89) \times 10,000}{0.10}$$

However, should oil prices fall to $5 a barrel, the NPV of the oil field will be even more negative than it is today.

Kirtley makes two recommendations to Exoff's board:

1.  The land should be purchased.
2.  The drilling decision should be delayed until information on both OPEC's new agreement and National Motors' new automobile are developed.

He explains his recommendations to the board by first assuming that the land has already been purchased. He argues that under this assumption, the drilling decision should be delayed. Second, he investigates his assumption that the land should have been purchased in the first place. This approach, examining the second decision (whether to drill) after assuming that the first decision (to buy the land) has been made, was also used in our earlier presentation on decision trees. Let us now work through Kirtley's analysis.

*Assume that the land has already been purchased.* If the land has already been purchased, should drilling begin immediately? If drilling begins immediately, the NPV is −$110,000. If the drilling decision is delayed until new information is released in a year, the optimal choice can be made at that time. If oil prices drop to $5 a barrel, Exoff should not drill. Instead, the firm walks away from the project, losing nothing beyond its $10,000 purchase price for the land. If oil prices rise to $108, drilling should begin.

Kirtley points out that by delaying, the firm will only invest the $500,000 of drilling costs if oil prices rise. Thus, by delaying, the firm saves $500,000 in the case where oil prices drop. He concludes that once the land is purchased, the drilling decision should be delayed.[20]

---

[20] Actually, there are three separate effects here. First, the firm avoids drilling costs in the case of low oil prices by delaying the decision. This is the effect discussed by Kirtley. Second, the PV of the $500,000 payment is less when the decision is delayed, even if drilling eventually takes place. Third, the firm loses one year of cash inflows through delay.

The first two arguments support delaying the decision. The third argument supports immediate drilling. In this example, the first argument greatly outweighs the other two arguments. Thus, Kirtley avoided the second and third arguments in his presentation.

> *Should the land have been purchased in the first place?* We now know that if the land is purchased, it is optimal to defer the drilling decision until the release of information. Given that we know this optimal decision concerning drilling, should the land be purchased in the first place? Without knowing the exact probability that oil prices will rise, Kirtley is nevertheless confident that the land should be purchased. The NPV of the project at $108 oil prices is $1,390,000, whereas the cost of the land is only $10,000. Kirtley believes that an oil price rise is possible, though by no means probable. Even so, he argues that the high potential return is clearly worth the risk.

This example presents an approach that is similar to our decision-tree analysis of the Solar Electronics Corporation in Chapter 9. Our purpose here is to discuss this type of decision in an option framework. When Exoff purchases the land, it is actually purchasing a call option. That is, once the land has been purchased, the firm has an option to buy an active oil field at an exercise price of $500,000. As it turns out, one should generally not exercise a call option immediately.[21] In this case, the firm delays exercise until relevant information concerning future oil prices is released.

This section points out a serious deficiency in classical capital budgeting: NPV calculations typically ignore the flexibility that real-world firms have. In our example, the standard techniques generated a negative NPV for the land purchase. Yet, by allowing the firm the option to change its investment policy according to new information, the land purchase can easily be justified.

We urge you to look for hidden options in projects. Because options are beneficial, managers are shortchanging their firm's projects if capital budgeting calculations ignore flexibility.

**CONCEPT QUESTION**

- Why are the hidden options in projects valuable?

## 23.11 CONTINGENT VALUE RIGHTS, MERGERS, AND CORPORATE DECISIONS

Mergers are structured either as *cash-for-stock* transactions or as *stock-for-stock* transactions. The selling shareholders receive cash from the buyer in the first type of transaction and receive stock in the buying company in the second. As discussed earlier, AT&T announced, in July 2013, its intent to acquire Leap Wireless International Inc., then trading at $5.83, for a premium cash offer of $15 per share. When the deal closed on March 13, 2014, Leap had 79.8 million shares outstanding, which amounted to a hefty acquisition price of $1.2 billion (79.8 million shares outstanding × $15 per share). In addition to an already premium price, AT&T assumed Leap's net debt worth $2.8 billion, for a total deal of nearly $4 billion.[22] Despite an already premium acquisition,

---

[21] Actually, it can be shown that a call option on a stock that pays no dividend should never be exercised before expiration. However, for a dividend-paying stock, it may be optimal to exercise prior to the ex-dividend date. The analogy applies to our example of an option in real assets.

The firm would receive cash flows from oil earlier if drilling began immediately. This is equivalent to the benefit from exercising a call on a stock prematurely in order to capture the dividend. However, in our example, this dividend effect is far outweighed by the benefits from waiting.

[22] Our discussion draws on A. Weissberger, "Analysis of AT&T's Bid to Acquire Leap Wireless," ComSoc Communities, IEEE Communications Society, July 16, 2013, community.comsoc.org/blogs/ alanweissberger/analysis-att%E2%80%99s-bid-acquire-leap-wireless; and P. A. Sokoloff, "Sokoloff & Company Case Study: AT&T Acquires Leap Wireless," *Transaction Case Studies* (Peter A. Sokoloff & Co, n.d.), www.sokoloffco.com/transactioncasestudy/07-12-13.php.

AT&T also offered a CVR, which allowed Leap to sell its 700-MHz spectrum, which it acquired for $204 million, and distribute the net proceeds to its existing shareholders. Assuming the spectrum sells at cost in the worst case, which is highly unlikely due to the limited nature of wireless spectrums, each CVR is worth $2.56 ($204 million divided by 79.8 million shares outstanding). Therefore, the total suggested acquisition price is $17.56 ($15 per share offered + $2.56 CVR value).

Having examined the details of the acquisition, you may be wondering why AT&T would issue a CVR in addition to the already high premium (more than double) over the original share price. As mentioned in the opening of the chapter, the issuance of CVRs is part of corporate strategy. The main motivation for AT&T's acquisition of Leap was to tap into the prepaid wireless market and to acquire spectrum, with the latter being more important. Given the fact that spectrum is limited (much like real estate), obtaining control over a wider spectrum would provide AT&T with a competitive advantage over rivals like T-Mobile and Sprint. Shortly after AT&T's offer, Leap's shares rose to $17 and settled around $16. Many financial journalists assumed the higher prices were indicative of an impending competing offer. Given the necessity of consolidating and obtaining spectrum to be successful in the wireless telecom industry and the possibility that AT&T's offer could have been topped, the issuance of a CVR was strategically made to seal the deal.

 **CONCEPT QUESTION**

- How can a CVR plan assist in a merger?

## 23.12

# SUMMARY AND CONCLUSIONS

This chapter introduces options.

1. The most familiar options are puts and calls. These options give the holder the right to sell or buy shares of common stock at a given exercise price. American options can be exercised at any time up to and including the expiration date. European options can be exercised only on the expiration date.

2. Options can be held either in isolation or in combination. We focused on the strategy of
   - Buying a put
   - Buying the stock
   - Selling a call

   where the put and call have both the same exercise price and the same expiration date. This strategy yields a risk-free return because the gain or loss on the call precisely offsets the gain or loss on the stock-and-put combination. In equilibrium, the return on this strategy must be exactly equal to the risk-free rate. From this, the put–call parity relationship was established:

$$\frac{\text{Value of}}{\text{stock}} + \frac{\text{Value of}}{\text{put}} - \frac{\text{Value of}}{\text{call}} = \frac{\text{PV of}}{\text{exercise price}}$$

3. The value of an option depends on five factors:
   - The price of the underlying asset.
   - The exercise price.
   - The expiration date.
   - The variability of the underlying asset.
   - The interest rate on risk-free bonds.

   The Black–Scholes model can determine the intrinsic price of an option from these five factors.

4.  Much of corporate financial theory can be presented in terms of options. In this chapter, we pointed out that
    a.  Common stock can be represented as a call option on the firm.
    b.  Shareholders enhance the value of their call by increasing the risk of their firm.
    c.  Real projects have hidden options that enhance value.

KEY TERMS

American options  670
Call option  670
Covered-call strategy  679
Cumulative probability  689
European options  670

Exercising the option  669
Expiration date  669
Option  669
Put–call parity  678
Put option  672

Standardized normal
  distribution  689
Strike or exercise price  669

QUESTIONS &
PROBLEMS

**Two-State Option Pricing Model**

23.1  T bills currently yield 4.8 percent. Stock in Nina Manufacturing is currently selling for $63 per share. There is no possibility that the stock will be worth less than $61 per share in one year.
    a.  What is the value of a call option with a $60 exercise price? What is the intrinsic value?
    b.  What is the value of a call option with a $50 exercise price? What is the intrinsic value?
    c.  What is the value of a put option with a $60 exercise price? What is the intrinsic value?

**Understanding Option Quotes**

23.2  Use the option quote information shown here to answer the questions that follow. The stock is currently selling for $83.

| Option and TSX close | Expiration | Strike price | Calls | | Puts | |
|---|---|---|---|---|---|---|
| | | | Vol. | Last | Vol. | Last |
| RWJ | March | 80 | 230 | 2.80 | 160 | 0.80 |
| | April | 80 | 170 | 6.00 | 127 | 1.40 |
| | July | 80 | 139 | 8.05 | 43 | 3.90 |
| | October | 80 | 60 | 10.20 | 11 | 3.65 |

    a.  Are the call options in the money? What is the intrinsic value of an RWJ Corp. call option?
    b.  Are the put options in the money? What is the intrinsic value of an RWJ Corp. put option?
    c.  Two of the options are clearly mispriced. Which ones? At a minimum, what should the mispriced options sell for? Explain how you could profit from the mispricing in each case.

**Calculating Payoffs**

23.3  Use the option quote information shown here to answer the questions that follow. The stock is currently selling for $114, and the size of each contract is 100 shares.

| Option and TSX close | Expiration | Strike price | Calls | | Puts | |
|---|---|---|---|---|---|---|
| | | | Vol. | Last | Vol. | Last |
| Macrosoft | February | 110 | 85 | 7.60 | 40 | 0.60 |
| | March | 110 | 61 | 8.80 | 22 | 1.55 |
| | May | 110 | 22 | 10.25 | 11 | 2.85 |
| | August | 110 | 3 | 13.05 | 3 | 4.70 |

a. Suppose you buy 10 contracts of the February 110 call option. How much will you pay, ignoring commissions?

b. In (a), suppose that Macrosoft stock is selling for $140 per share on the expiration date. How much is your options investment worth? What if the terminal stock price is $125? Explain.

c. Suppose you buy 10 contracts of the August 110 put option. What is your maximum gain? On the expiration date, Macrosoft is selling for $104 per share. How much is your options investment worth? What is your net gain?

d. In (c), suppose you *sell* 10 of the August 110 put contracts. What is your net gain or loss if Macrosoft is selling for $103 at expiration? For $132? What is the break-even price—that is, the terminal stock price that results in a zero profit?

**Two-State Option Pricing Model**

ecel    23.4  The price of Ervin Corp. stock will be either $65 or $85 at the end of the year. Call options are available with one year to expiration. T-bills currently yield 6 percent.

a. Suppose the current price of Ervin stock is $70. What is the value of the call option if the exercise price is $60 per share?

b. Suppose the exercise price is $80 in (a). What is the value of the call option now?

23.5  The price of Tara Inc. stock will be either $50 or $70 at the end of the year. Call options are available with one year to expiration. T-bills currently yield 5 percent.

a. Suppose the current price of Tara stock is $62. What is the value of the call option if the exercise price is $35 per share?

b. Suppose the exercise price is $60 in (a). What is the value of the call option now?

**Put–Call Parity**

ecel    23.6  A stock is currently selling for $47 per share. A call option with an exercise price of $45 sells for $3.80 and expires in three months. If the risk-free rate of interest is 2.6 percent per year, compounded continuously, what is the price of a put option with the same exercise price?

23.7  A put option that expires in six months with an exercise price of $65 sells for $4.89. The stock is currently priced at $61, and the risk-free rate is 3.6 percent per year, compounded continuously. What is the price of a call option with the same exercise price?

23.8  A put option and a call option with an exercise price of $85 and three months to expiration sell for $2.40 and $5.09, respectively. If the risk-free rate is 4.8 percent per year, compounded continuously, what is the current stock price?

23.9  A put option and a call option with an exercise price of $55 expire in two months and sell for $2.65 and $5.32, respectively. If the stock is currently priced at $57.30, what is the annual continuously compounded rate of interest?

**Black–Scholes**

ecel    23.10  What are the prices of a call option and a put option with the following characteristics?

Stock price = $46
Exercise price = $50
Risk-free rate = 6% per year, compounded continuously
Maturity = 3 months
Standard deviation = 54% per year

**23.11**  What are the prices of a call option and a put option with the following characteristics?

$$Stock\ price = \$93$$
$$Exercise\ price = \$90$$
$$Risk\text{-}free\ rate = 4\%\ per\ year,\ compounded\ continuously$$
$$Maturity = 5\ months$$
$$Standard\ deviation = 62\%\ per\ year$$

### Delta

**23.12**  What are the deltas of a call option and a put option with the following characteristics? What does the delta of the option tell you?

$$Stock\ price = \$67$$
$$Exercise\ price = \$70$$
$$Risk\text{-}free\ rate = 5\%\ per\ year,\ compounded\ continuously$$
$$Maturity = 9\ months$$
$$Standard\ deviation = 49\%\ per\ year$$

### Black–Scholes and Asset Value

**23.13**  You own a lot in Montreal that is currently unused. Similar lots have recently sold for $1.9 million. Over the past five years, the price of land in the area has increased 12 percent per year, with an annual standard deviation of 25 percent. A buyer has recently approached you and wants an option to buy the land in the next 12 months for $2.1 million. The risk-free rate of interest is 5 percent per year, compounded continuously. How much should you charge for the option?

**23.14**  In Problem 23.13, suppose you wanted the option to sell the land to the buyer in one year. Assuming all the facts are the same, describe the transaction that would occur today. What is the price of the transaction today?

### Time Value of Options

**23.15**  You are given the following information concerning options on a particular stock:

$$Stock\ price = \$83$$
$$Exercise\ price = \$80$$
$$Risk\text{-}free\ rate = 6\%\ per\ year,\ compounded\ continuously$$
$$Maturity = 6\ months$$
$$Standard\ deviation = 53\%\ per\ year$$

*a.* What is the intrinsic value of the call option? The put option?
*b.* What is the time value of the call option? The put option?
*c.* Does the call or the put have the larger time value component? Would you expect this to be true in general?

### Risk-Neutral Valuation

**23.16**  A stock is currently priced at $73. The stock will either increase or decrease by 15 percent over the next year. There is a call option on the stock with a strike price of $70 and one year until expiration. If the risk-free rate is 8 percent, what is the risk-neutral value of the call option?

**23.17**  In Problem 23.16, assume the risk-free rate is only 5 percent. What is the risk-neutral value of the option now? What happens to the risk-neutral probabilities of a stock price increase and a stock price decrease?

### Black–Scholes

23.18  A call option matures in six months. The underlying stock price is $75, and the stock's return has a standard deviation of 30 percent per year. The risk-free rate is 4 percent per year, compounded continuously. If the exercise price is $0, what is the price of the call option?

23.19  A call option has an exercise price of $80 and matures in six months. The current stock price is $84, and the risk-free rate is 5 percent per year, compounded continuously. What is the price of the call if the standard deviation of the stock is 0 percent per year?

23.20  A stock is currently priced at $35. A call option with an expiration of one year has an exercise price of $50. The risk-free rate is 7 percent per year, compounded continuously, and the standard deviation of the stock's return is infinitely large. What is the price of the call option?

### Equity as an Option

23.21  Sunburn Sunscreen has a zero-coupon bond issue outstanding with a $15,000 face value that matures in one year. The current market value of the firm's assets is $15,800. The standard deviation of the return on the firm's assets is 38 percent per year, and the annual risk-free rate is 5 percent per year, compounded continuously. Based on the Black–Scholes model, what is the market value of the firm's equity and debt?

### Equity as an Option and Net Present Value

23.22  Suppose the firm in Problem 23.21 is considering two mutually exclusive investments. Project *A* has an NPV of $1,200, and project *B* has an NPV of $1,600. As a result of taking project *A*, the standard deviation of the return on the firm's assets will increase to 55 percent per year. If project *B* is taken, the standard deviation will fall to 34 percent per year.
  *a.* What is the value of the firm's equity and debt if project *A* is undertaken? If project *B* is undertaken?
  *b.* Which project would the shareholders prefer? Can you reconcile your answer with the NPV rule?
  *c.* Suppose the shareholders and bondholders are, in fact, the same group of investors. Would this affect your answer to (b)?
  *d.* What does this problem suggest to you about shareholder incentives?

### Equity as an Option

23.23  Frostbite Thermalwear has a zero-coupon bond issue outstanding with a face value of $30,000 that matures in one year. The current market value of the firm's assets is $36,400. The standard deviation of the return on the firm's assets is 53 percent per year, and the annual risk-free rate is 5 percent per year, compounded continuously. Based on the Black–Scholes model, what is the market value of the firm's equity and debt? What is the firm's continuously compounded cost of debt?

### Mergers and Equity as an Option

23.24  Suppose Sunburn Sunscreen and Frostbite Thermalwear in Problems 23.21 through 23.23 have decided to merge. Because the two companies have seasonal sales, the combined firm's return on assets (ROA) will have a standard deviation of 29 percent per year.
  *a.* What is the combined value of equity in the two existing companies? The value of debt?
  *b.* What is the value of the new firm's equity? The value of debt?
  *c.* What was the gain or loss for shareholders? For bondholders?
  *d.* What happened to shareholder value here?

### Equity as an Option and Net Present Value

23.25  A company has a single zero-coupon bond outstanding that matures in 10 years with a face value of $15 million. The current value of the company's assets is $13.4 million, and the standard deviation of the return on the firm's assets is 39 percent per year. The risk-free rate is 6 percent per year, compounded continuously.

    *a.* What is the current market value of the company's equity?

    *b.* What is the current market value of the company's debt?

    *c.* What is the company's continuously compounded cost of debt?

    *d.* The company has a new project available. The project has an NPV of $1.2 million. If the company undertakes the project, what will be the new market value of equity? Assume volatility is unchanged.

    *e.* Assuming the company undertakes the new project and does not borrow any additional funds, what is the new continuously compounded cost of debt? What is happening here?

### Two-State Option Pricing Model

23.26  Kate is interested in buying a European call option written on EastJet Airlines Ltd., a non–dividend paying common stock, with a strike price of $75 and one year until expiration. Currently EastJet's stock sells for $78 per share. In one year Kate knows that EastJet's stock will be trading at either $93 per share or $65 per share. Kate can borrow and lend at the risk-free equivalent annual rate (EAR) of 2.5 percent.

    *a.* What should the call option sell for today?

    *b.* If no options currently trade on the stock, is there a way to create a synthetic call option with identical payoffs to the call option just described? If there is, how would you do it?

    *c.* How much does the synthetic call option cost? Is this greater than, less than, or equal to what the actual call option costs? Does this make sense?

23.27  Rob wishes to buy a European put option on BioLabs Inc., a non–dividend paying common stock, with a strike price of $40 and six months until expiration. BioLabs' common stock is currently selling for $30 per share, and Rob expects that the stock price will either rise to $60 or fall to $15 in six months. Rob can borrow and lend at the risk-free EAR of 5 percent.

    *a.* What should the put option sell for today?

    *b.* If no options currently trade on the stock, is there a way to create a synthetic put option with identical payoffs to the put option just described? If there is, how would you do it?

    *c.* How much does the synthetic put option cost? Is this greater than, less than, or equal to what the actual put option costs? Does this make sense?

23.28  Maverick Manufacturing Ltd. must purchase gold in three months for use in its operations. Maverick's management has estimated that if the price of gold were to rise above $1,530 per ounce, the firm would go bankrupt. The current price of gold is $1,450 per ounce. The firm's CFO believes that the price of gold will either rise to $1,605 per ounce or fall to $1,340 per ounce over the next three months. Management wishes to eliminate any risk of the firm going bankrupt. Maverick can borrow and lend at the risk-free EAR of 6.50 percent.

    *a.* Should the company buy a call option or a put option on gold? To avoid bankruptcy, what strike price and time to expiration would the company like this option to have?

    *b.* How much should such an option sell for in the open market?

    *c.* If no options currently trade on gold, is there a way for the company to create a synthetic option with identical payoffs to the option just described? If there is, how would the firm do it?

    *d.* How much does the synthetic option cost? Is this greater than, less than, or equal to what the actual option costs? Does this make sense?

### Black–Scholes and Collar Cost

23.29 An investor is said to take a position in a "collar" if she buys the asset, buys an out-of-the-money put option on the asset, and sells an out-of-the-money call option on the asset. The two options should have the same time to expiration. Suppose Marie wishes to purchase a collar on Hollywood Inc., a non–dividend paying common stock, with six months until expiration. She would like the put to have a strike price of $55 and the call to have a strike price of $95. The current price of Hollywood's stock is $70 per share. Marie can borrow and lend at the continuously compounded risk-free rate of 7 percent per annum, and the annual standard deviation of the stock's return is 50 percent. Use the Black–Scholes model to calculate the total cost of the collar that Marie is interested in buying.

### Debt Valuation and Time to Maturity

23.30 McLemore Industries has a zero-coupon bond issue that matures in two years with a face value of $50,000. The current value of the company's assets is $29,000, and the standard deviation of the ROA is 60 percent per year.
   a. Assume the risk-free rate is 5 percent per year, compounded continuously. What is the value of a risk-free bond with the same face value and maturity as the company's bond?
   b. What price would the bondholders have to pay for a put option on the firm's assets with a strike price equal to the face value of the debt?
   c. Using your answers from (a) and (b), what is the value of the firm's debt? What is the continuously compounded yield on the company's debt?
   d. From an examination of the value of the assets of McLemore Industries, and the fact that the debt must be repaid in two years, it seems likely that the company will default on its debt. Management has approached bondholders and proposed a plan whereby the company would repay the same face value of debt, but the repayment would not occur for five years. What is the value of the debt under the proposed plan? What is the new continuously compounded yield on the debt? Explain why this occurs.

### Debt Valuation and Asset Variance

23.31 Brozik Corp. has a zero-coupon bond that matures in five years with a face value of $60,000. The current value of the company's assets is $57,000, and the standard deviation of its ROA is 50 percent per year. The risk-free rate is 6 percent per year, compounded continuously.
   a. What is the value of a risk-free bond with the same face value and maturity as the current bond?
   b. What is the value of a put option on the firm's assets with a strike price equal to the face value of the debt?
   c. Using your answers from (a) and (b), what is the value of the firm's debt? What is the continuously compounded yield on the company's debt?
   d. Assume the company can restructure its assets so that the standard deviation of its ROA increases to 60 percent per year. What happens to the value of the debt? What is the new continuously compounded yield on the debt? Reconcile your answers in (c) and (d).
   e. What happens to bondholders if the company restructures its assets? What happens to shareholders? How does this create an agency problem?

### Two-State Option Pricing and Corporate Valuation

23.32 Strudler Real Estate Ltd., a construction firm financed by both debt and equity, is undertaking a new project. If the project is successful, the value of the firm in one year will be $280 million, but if the project is a failure, the firm will be worth only $190 million. The current value of Strudler is $230 million, a figure that includes the prospects for the new project. Strudler has outstanding zero-coupon bonds due in one year with a face value of $260 million. Treasury bills that mature in one year yield a 7 percent EAR. Strudler pays no dividends.

    *a.* Use the two-state option pricing model to find the current value of Strudler's debt and equity.

    *b.* Suppose Strudler has 500,000 shares of common stock outstanding. What is the price per share of the firm's equity?

    *c.* Compare the market value of Strudler's debt to the PV of an equal amount of debt that is risk free with one year until maturity. Is the firm's debt worth more than, less than, or the same as the risk-free debt? Does this make sense? What factors might cause these two values to be different?

    *d.* Suppose that in place of the preceding project, Strudler's management decides to undertake a project that is even more risky. The value of the firm will either increase to $315 million or decrease to $175 million by the end of the year. Surprisingly, management concludes that the value of the firm today will remain at exactly $230 million if this risky project is substituted for the less risky one. Use the two-state option pricing model to determine the values of the firm's debt and equity if the firm plans on undertaking this new project. Which project do bondholders prefer?

### Black–Scholes and Dividends

23.33 In addition to the five factors discussed in the chapter, dividends also affect the price of an option. The Black–Scholes option pricing model with dividends is

$$C = S \times e^{-dt} \times N(d_1) - E \times e^{-Rt} \times N(d_2)$$

$$d_1 = \frac{\ln(S/E) + (R - d + \sigma^2/2) \times t}{\sqrt{\sigma^2 t}}$$

$$d_2 = d_1 - \sqrt{\sigma^2 t}$$

All of the variables are the same as the Black–Scholes model without dividends except for the variable *d*, which is the continuously compounded dividend yield on the stock.

    *a.* What effect do you think the dividend yield will have on the price of a call option? Explain.

    *b.* A stock is currently priced at $93 per share; the standard deviation of its return is 50 percent per year; and the risk-free rate is 5 percent per year, compounded continuously. What is the price of a call option with a strike price of $90 and a maturity of six months if the stock has a dividend yield of 2 percent per year?

### Put–Call Parity and Dividends

23.34 The put-call parity condition is altered when dividends are paid. The dividend-adjusted put-call parity formula is

$$S \times e^{-dt} + P = E \times e^{-Rt} + C$$

where *d* is again the continuously compounded dividend yield.

    *a.* What effect do you think the dividend yield will have on the price of a put option? Explain.

    *b.* From Problem 23.33(b), what is the price of a put option with the same strike price and time to expiration as the call option?

### Put Delta

23.35 In the chapter we noted that the delta for a put option is $N(d_1) - 1$. Is this the same thing as $-N(-d_1)$? (*Hint:* Yes, but why?)

### Black–Scholes Put Pricing Model

23.36 Use the Black–Scholes model for pricing a call, put-call parity, and the result of Problem 23.35 to show that the Black-Scholes model for directly pricing a put can be written as follows:

$$P = E \times e^{-Rt} \times N(-d_2) - S \times N(-d_1)$$

### Black–Scholes

23.37 A stock is currently priced at $50. The stock will never pay a dividend. The risk-free rate is 12 percent per year, compounded continuously, and the standard deviation of the stock's return is 60 percent. A European call option on the stock has a strike price of $100 and no expiration date, meaning that it has an infinite life. Based on Black–Scholes, what is the value of the call option? Do you see a paradox here? Do you see a way out of the paradox?

**Delta**

23.38    You purchase one call and sell one put with the same strike price and expiration date. What is the delta of your portfolio? Why?

## Clissold Industries Options

You are currently working for Clissold Industries. The company, which went public five years ago, designs, produc-es, and distributes lighting equipment and specialty products worldwide. Because of recent events, Mal Clissold, the company president, is concerned about the company's risk, so he asks for your input.

In your discussion with Mal, you explain that the capital asset pricing model (CAPM) proposes that the market risk of the company's stock is the determinant of its expected return. Even though Mal agrees with this, he argues that his portfolio consists entirely of Clissold Industry stock and options, so he is concerned with the total risk, or standard deviation, of the company's stock. Furthermore, even though he has calculated the standard deviation of the company's stock for the past five years, he would like an estimate of the stock's future volatility.

Mal states that you can find the estimated volatility of the stock for future periods by calculating the implied standard deviation of option contracts on the company stock. When you examine the factors that affect the price of an option, all of the factors except the standard deviation of the stock are directly observable in the market. Mal states that because you can observe all of the option factors except the standard deviation, you can simply solve the Black–Scholes model and find the implied standard deviation.

To help you find the implied standard deviation of the company's stock, Mal has provided you with the following option prices on four call options that expire in six months. The risk-free rate is 4 percent, and the current stock price is $68:

| Strike price | Option price |
| --- | --- |
| $65 | $18.73 |
| 70 | 15.69 |
| 75 | 11.06 |
| 80 | 7.36 |

1. How many different volatilities would you expect to see for the stock?

2. Unfortunately, solving for the implied standard deviation is not as easy as Mal suggests. In fact, there is no direct solution for the standard deviation of the stock even if we have all the other variables for the Black–Scholes model. Mal would still like you to estimate the implied standard deviation of the stock. To do this, set up a spreadsheet using the Solver function in Microsoft Excel to calculate the implied volatility for each of the op-tions.

3. Are all of the implied volatilities for the options the same? (*Hint:* No.) What are the possible reasons that can cause different volatilities for these options?

4. After you discuss the importance of volatility on option prices, your boss mentions that he has heard of the VIX. What is the VIX and what does it represent? You might need to visit the Chicago Board Options Exchange (CBOE) at www.cboe.com to help with your answer.

5. When you are on the CBOE website, look for the option quotes for the VIX. What does the implied volatility of a VIX option represent?

# CHAPTER

# Options and Corporate Finance: Extensions and Applications

This chapter extends the analysis of options in Chapter 23. We describe four different types of options found in common corporate finance decisions:

- Executive stock options and compensation.
- The embedded option in a start-up company.
- The options in simple business contracts.
- The option to shut down and reopen a project.

Option features are pervasive in corporate finance decisions. They are involved in decisions of whether to build, expand, or close a factory; to buy productive assets like trucks or machines; to drill for oil or mine for gold; or to construct a building. Sometimes they are involved in decisions about how to pay managers and other employees. In this chapter we do not argue that the net present value (NPV) approach should be completely jettisoned. In fact, many decisions have few embedded options and, in these cases, optionality can be ignored. However, in many cases, options are an important aspect of the decision and must be separately valued. In practice, there is a decision continuum. At one end of the continuum are decisions with little optionality, and at the other are decisions with significant optionality.

In the previous chapter, we presented a few examples of options in corporate finance. We saw that stock is a call option on the firm. We showed that the value of this option could be increased by selecting high-risk rather than low-risk projects. We discussed the embedded option in oil exploration.

However, although the previous chapter presented these options, we made no attempt to *value* them. In this chapter, we will value four embedded options. The first two are handled with the Black–Scholes model. We use the binomial (two-state) model to value the last two options. Although the Black–Scholes model is more well known, the binomial model is probably used more frequently in the real world. The Black–Scholes model works well on only a narrow set of problems. The flexibility of the binomial model allows it to be applied to a wider range of situations. However, binomial approaches often use complex numerical analyses involving large amounts of computer time when applied to portfolios of options in actual companies. In this regard, binomial approaches are less elegant than the Black–Scholes approach.

EXECUTIVE SUMMARY

## 24.1 EXECUTIVE STOCK OPTIONS

### Why Options?

Executive compensation is usually made up of base salary plus some or all of the following elements:

- Long-term compensation.
- Annual bonuses.
- Retirement contributions.
- Options.

The final component of compensation, options, is a sizable part of total compensation for many top executives at major Canadian corporations, including Barrick Gold,

Rogers Communications, Agrium, and Magna International. For example, in 2013, Gerald Schwartz, CEO of Onex Corp., a large Canadian private equity firm, received option grants worth $61,399,347, far in excess of his salary and bonus of $26,517,679.[1] Knowing the face value of an option does not automatically allow us to determine the market value of the option. We also need to know the exercise price before valuing the option according to either the Black–Scholes model or the binomial model. However, the exercise price is generally set equal to the market price of the stock on the date the executive receives the options. In the next section, we value options under the assumption that the exercise price is equal to the market price of the underlying stock.

Starting in the late 1990s, options in the stock of the company were increasingly granted to executives as an alternative to increases in base pay. Ninety percent of firms listed on the Toronto Stock Exchange (TSX) had a bonus plan and used stock options.[2] Some of the reasons given for using options follow:

1. Options make executives share the interests of the shareholders. By aligning their interests, it is argued that executives will make decisions that benefit the shareholders.

2. Using options allows the company to lower the executive's base pay. This removes pressures on morale caused by great disparities between the salaries of executives and those of other employees.

3. Options put an executive's pay at risk, rather than guaranteeing it independent of the performance of the firm.

4. In principle, under current U.S. and Canadian tax laws, options are a tax-efficient way to pay employees. Under current tax law, if an executive is given options to purchase the company stock and the options are "at the money," they are not considered part of taxable income. The options are taxed only when they are eventually exercised.

## Executive Compensation: Where Are We Now?

Until recently, options had the advantage of creating no charge against earnings and were popular for this reason with start-up companies short of cash. This changed for Canadian public companies in 2004 when the Canadian Accounting Standards Board began to require stock options to be expensed.

Research studies in the United States, Canada, and other countries find that, over the 1990s, the use of executive stock options generally served its goal of helping to tie executive compensation to company performance.[3] Still, options have come in for considerable criticism. Corporate governance experts worry that options sometimes encourage executives to focus too much on short-term actions to raise share prices. For example, in September 2004, Molson and Coors proposed a friendly merger supported by top executives at both companies. Critics of the proposed merger discounted the support by Dan O'Neill, Molson CEO, pointing out that the merger would increase the value of his stock options by $2.6 million.[4] More generally, recent research

---

[1] "CEO Compensation," Report on Business, *Globe and Mail*, June 2, 2014, page B4.

[2] X. Zhou, "CEO Pay, Firm Size, and Corporate Performance: Evidence from Canada," *Canadian Journal of Economics* 33 (2000), pages 213–251.

[3] The most current study for Canada is X. Zhou, "CEO Pay, Firm Size, and Corporate Performance: Evidence from Canada," University of Sydney, Australia, October 2000. A widely cited U.S. study is K. J. Murphy, "Executive Compensation," in *Handbook of Labor Economics*, vol. 3, O. Ashenfelter and D. Card, eds. (Amsterdam: North Holland, 1999).

[4] D. Decloet, "Merger Would Pay Millions to Molson, Coors Chiefs," Report on Business, *The Globe and Mail*, September 20, 2004, B1.

by Yuval Deutsch, Thomas Keil, and Tomi Laamanen demonstrates that the award of options is associated with increased risk-taking.[5]

# IN THEIR OWN WORDS

## Jim Middlemiss on options backdating

Research undertaken by London, Ontario, law firm Siskinds two years ago into possible stock-option backdating at Canadian public companies continues to pay dividends for securities class action lawyers Dimitri Lascaris and Charles Wright.

The research, released in the fall of 2007 and conducted in conjunction with Michael Wright of Cavalluzzo Hayes Shilton McIntyre & Cornish of Toronto, found that a number of Canadian-listed companies likely engaged in stock-option backdating, or at least flouted Toronto Stock Exchange rules governing the granting of options to senior executives.

The statistical analysis determined a greater-than-95-percent probability that at least 50 TSX-listed companies manipulated their option grants to senior executives between Jan. 1, 1987, and Dec. 31, 2006. The likelihood of manipulation exceeded 99 percent for at least 10 of the companies, which the firm declined to name.

Siskinds and its local counsel in various provinces then contacted boards of more than 20 public companies, calling on them to conduct an "independent and thorough" investigation of stock-option practices on behalf of clients who held shares in the companies.

Last Friday, the latest of those firms involved in that research came forward. Trican Well Service Ltd. announced a review of its option-granting practices between 1998 and 2007 and found that some stock options "had been improperly priced with retroactively selected grant dates."

Trican formed a special committee of the board last year after being contacted by Alberta law firm May Jensen Shawa Solomon, which works with the Ontario-based Siskinds on class actions.

The special committee concluded that, "while Trican's historical option-granting practice was inappropriate, it was a practice adopted for a period of time in good-faith reliance upon external legal advice and was not found to have been motivated by personal gain."

The special committee said that, "all unexercised option grants that were identified as having been issued using incorrect dates will be repriced according to correct grant dates. The company will pursue all reasonable avenues for recovery of costs related to the review and the improper pricing of options."

Trican reported that directors and officers who received unintended benefits totalling approximately $1.1 million from incorrectly dated stock options have voluntarily agreed to repay the full amount of those benefits.

Other companies that have addressed their option-granting practices, spurred on by the Siskinds research, include Research In Motion [now BlackBerry], Savanna Energy Services Corp., and Com Dev International Ltd. TVI Pacific Inc. settled a class suit brought by Siskinds for $2.1 million without admitting liability. A special committee of TVI's board of directors found "no intentional misconduct in relation to prior grants of options by the company."

In the settlement notice, TVI "agreed to make efforts to reprice certain outstanding stock options and to adopt measures targeted at eliminating the potential for future stock option manipulation."

Mr. Lascaris said his firm is involved in a number of "ongoing" discussions with corporations about stock-option grants. While it's been two years since the research, he said a lot of the cases involved boards undertaking a "detailed forensic exam going back 20 years. A lot of the results of [his firm's initial research] are only coming to light now." He expects there will be "further disclosures" involving companies that were contacted.

Material reprinted with the express permission of *National Post*, a division of Postmedia Network Inc.

---

[5] Y. Deutsch, Thomas Keil, and Tomi Laamanen, "A Dual Agency View of Board Compensation: The Joint Effects of Outside Director and CEO Stock Options on Firm Risk," *Strategic Management Journal* (February 2011).

Further, after the end of the tech bubble, the decline in stock prices, especially in the technology sector, had made options granted earlier almost worthless in motivating employees. In response, many companies are currently emphasizing cash compensation. More controversially, others are offering employees an opportunity to exchange their options for new ones with exercise prices at or near the current, lower share price. Compensation plans are supposed to motivate executives and provide an incentive for future performance that will enrich both shareholders and the executive. When companies issue stock options that are already in the money to executives, the incentive to increase shareholder value and business performance is not there.

In response to the criticism of stock options, some companies are switching to rewarding their employees with shares. The idea is to retain the alignment of interests while getting away from the short-term focus of options. However, this incentive compensation scheme is also criticized for encouraging imprudent risk-taking and was labelled as a contributing factor to the 2007–2008 financial crisis. In line with similar research on executive compensation, Raviv and Sisli-Ciamarra demonstrate that executives, particularly in the banking industry, exhibit a positive correlation between risk-taking and the state of the economy, holding their level of equity-based compensation constant.[6] In other words, given the same level of equity-based compensation, executives were found to target higher (lower) levels of asset risk during good (bad) states of the economy. For example, in the context of the booming U.S. housing market before the 2007–2008 financial crisis, it is easy to see this correlation, as banks were adopting riskier business policies and providing riskier loans.

With the corporate governance failures in designing executive compensation packages, a "say-on-pay" movement ensued, which looks to shareholders for approval of executive compensation. A vote on executive compensation during shareholder meetings was made mandatory for all U.S.-listed companies by the U.S. Congress in July 2010. Although not mandatory in Canada, the movement is growing, with 80 percent of the largest 60 firms listed on the TSX voluntarily adopting this practice.[7] As seen from this discussion, executive compensation is an issue far from being resolved and is still an intensely debated topic in the corporate world.

## Valuing Executive Compensation

In this section, we value executive stock options. Not surprisingly, the complexity of the total compensation package often makes valuation a difficult task. The economic value of the options depends on factors such as the volatility of the underlying stock and the exact terms of the option grant.

We attempt to estimate the economic value of the options held by the executives listed in Table 24.1. To do so, we employ the Black–Scholes option-pricing formula from Chapter 23. Of course, we are missing many features of the particular plans, and the best we can hope for is a rough estimate. Simple matters, such as requiring the executive to hold the option for a fixed period—the freeze-out period—before exercising, can significantly diminish the value of a standard option. Equally important, the Black–Scholes formula has to be modified if the stock pays dividends and is no longer applicable if the volatility of the stock changes randomly over time. Intuitively, a call option on a dividend-paying stock is worth less than a call on a stock that pays no dividends. All other things being equal, the dividends will lower the stock price. Nevertheless, let us see what we can do.

[6] A. Raviv and E. Sisli-Ciamarra, "Executive Compensation, Risk Taking and the State of the Economy," *Journal of Financial Stability* (April 2013).

[7] Theresa Tedesco, "Say-on-Pay Movement on the Rise in Canada, but Is It Changing Anything?" *Financial Post*, Postmedia Network Inc., business.financialpost.com/2014/03/12/say-on-pay-movement-on-the-rise-in-canada-but-is-it-changing-anything/.

**TABLE 24.1**

**Value of 2011–2012 Top 10 Option Grants***

| Company | CEO | Grant value of options granted (in $ millions)[†] | Annual stock volatility, % | As reported option value (in $ millions)[‡] |
|---|---|---|---|---|
| Oracle Corporation | L. Ellison | $227.01 | 30% | $62.81 |
| CBS Corp. | L. Moonves | 50.31 | 41 | 16.45 |
| Walt Disney Co. | R. Iger | 28.37 | 28 | 10.38 |
| Chevron Corp. | J. Watson | 45.25 | 31 | 10.08 |
| Hewlett-Packard Co. | M. Whitman | 31.74 | 41 | 9.97 |
| Medco Health Solutions Inc. | D. Snow | 37.30 | 25 | 9.93 |
| Honeywell International Inc. | D. Cote | 41.91 | 28 | 9.17 |
| The Coca-Cola Co. | M. Kent | 62.13 | 19 | 8.67 |
| General Dynamics Corp. | J. Johnson | 33.70 | 30 | 7.11 |
| Procter & Gamble Co. | R. McDonald | 35.29 | 16 | 6.41 |

* Based on the 200 largest U.S. industrial and service corporations that filed proxy statements for fiscal year 2011–2012. Includes mega-grants that were annualized over their respective vesting periods.

[†] Grant value of options granted equals the number of options times the stock price.

[‡] Option value is FAS 123(R) value as reported by each company. For prior-year mega-grants, grant date Black–Scholes value is used when "As Reported" value was not available. Grants are annualized over their respective vesting periods.

Source: Pearl Meyer & Partners.

**EXAMPLE 24.1**

**Options at United Express Corporation** According to the proxy statement filed in fiscal year 2013, Rich Pettit, the CEO of United Express Corporation, was granted 1.662 million stock options. The average exercise price of the options was $50.99, and we will assume that all of the options were granted at the money. We'll also assume that the options expire in five years and that the risk-free rate is 5 percent. This information implies that

1.  The stock price, $S$, equals the exercise price, $E$, $50.99, so $\ln(S/E) = \ln(1) = 0$ in the formula.
2.  The risk-free rate, $r$, equals 0.05.
3.  The time interval, $t$, equals 5.

In addition, the stock volatility, $\sigma$, is given as 37.46 percent per year, which implies that the variance, $\sigma^2$, equals $(0.3746)^2 = 0.1403$.

We now have enough information to estimate the value of Rich's options using the Black–Scholes model:

$$C = SN(d_1) - Ee^{-rt}N(d_2)$$

$$d_1 = \frac{(r + \frac{1}{2}\sigma^2)t}{\sqrt{\sigma^2 t}} = 0.7173$$

$$d_2 = d_1 - \sqrt{\sigma^2 t} = -0.1203$$

$$N(d_1) = 0.7634$$

$$N(d_2) = 0.4521$$

$$e^{-rt} = 0.7788$$

$$C = \$50.99 \times 0.7634 - \$50.99 \times (0.7788 \times 0.4521) = \$20.97$$

Since Rich was granted options on 1.662 million shares, and since each option is worth $20.97, the market value of his options by the above calculations is 1.662 million × $20.97 = $34.9 million.

Table 24.1 shows the grant value as well as the actual option values as reported by each of the companies. Most of these companies use the Black–Scholes method to value the options, but they take into account the special features of their plans and their stock, including whether or not it pays dividends. As can be seen, these values, while large by ordinary standards, are significantly less than the corresponding grant values. Notice that the ordering by grant value is not the same as that by economic value. For example, whereas the CEO of Coca-Cola Co. ranks second in grant value, Table 24.1 shows that he ranks eighth in Black–Scholes value—the difference being caused by Coca-Cola's relatively low standard deviation.

The values computed in Table 24.1 are the economic values of the options if they were to trade in the market. The real question is, whose value are we talking about? Are these the costs of the options to the company? Are they the values of the options to the executives?

Suppose that a company computes the fair market value of the options as we have done; suppose, for purposes of illustration, that we ignore warrant dilution;[8] and suppose that the options are in the money and are worth $25 each. Suppose, further, that the CEO holds 1 million such options for a total value of $25 million. This is the amount that the options would trade at in the financial markets and the amount that traders and investors would be willing to pay. If the company were very large, it would not be unreasonable for it to view this as the cost of granting the options to the CEO. Of course, in return, the company expects the CEO to improve the value of the company to its shareholders by more than this amount. As we have seen, perhaps the main purpose of options is to align the interests of management with those of the shareholders of the firm. Under no circumstances, though, is the $25 million necessarily a fair measure of what they are worth to the CEO.

As an illustration, suppose that the CEO of ABC has options on 1 million shares with an exercise price of $30 per share and that the current price of ABC is $50 per share. If the options were exercised today, they would be worth $20 million (an underestimate of their market value). Suppose, in addition, the CEO owns $5 million in company stock and has $5 million in other assets. The CEO clearly has a very undiversified personal portfolio. By the standards of modern portfolio theory, having 25/30 or about 83 percent of your personal wealth in one stock and its options is unnecessarily risky.

While the CEO is wealthy by most standards, significant shifts in the stock value will have dramatic impacts on her economic well-being. If the value drops from $50 per share to $30 per share, the current exercise value of the options on 1 million shares drops from $20 million to zero. Ignoring the fact that if the options have more time to mature, they will not lose all of this value, we nevertheless have a rather startling decline in the CEO's net worth from about $30 million to $8 million ($5 million in other assets plus stock that is now worth $3 million). But that is the very purpose of the options and the stock holdings given to the CEO, namely to make the CEO's fortunes rise and fall with those of the company. That is why the company requires executives to hold the options, at least for a freeze-out period, and not simply sell them to realize their value.

The implication is that when options are a large portion of an executive's net worth and the executive is forced by the company to be undiversified, the total value of the position is worth less to the executive than the fair financial market value. As a purely financial matter, an executive might be happier with $5 million in cash rather than $20 million in options. At the least, the executive could then diversify her personal portfolio.

**CONCEPT QUESTION**

• Why do companies issue options to executives if they cost the company more than they are worth to the executive? Why not just give cash and split the difference? Wouldn't that make both the company and the executive better off?

---

[8] See Chapter 25 for a discussion of warrant dilution.

## 24.2  VALUING A START-UP

Michel Normand was not your typical MBA student. Since childhood, he had had one ambition: to open a restaurant that sold wild game and other exotic meats prepared in a French style. He went to business school because he realized that although he knew 101 ways to cook rabbit, he didn't have the business skills necessary to run a restaurant. He was extremely focused, with each course at graduate school being important to him only to the extent that it could further his dream.

While taking his school's course on entrepreneurship, he began to develop a business plan for his restaurant, which he now called Chez Michel. He thought about marketing; he thought about raising capital; he thought about dealing with future employees. He even devoted a great deal of time to designing the physical layout of the restaurant. Of course, his business plan would not be complete without financial projections. After much thought, he came up with the projections shown in Table 24.2.

**TABLE 24.2**

**Financial Projections for Chez Michel**

|  | Year 1 | Year 2 | Year 3 | Year 4 | All future years |
|---|---|---|---|---|---|
| (1) Sales | $300,000 | $600,000 | $900,000 | $1,000,000 | $1,000,000 |
| (2) Cash flows from operations | −$100,000 | −$ 50,000 | +$ 75,000 | +$ 250,000 | +$ 250,000 |
| (3) Increase in working capital | $ 50,000 | $ 20,000 | $ 10,000 | $ 10,000 | 0 |
| (4) Net cash flows (2) − (3) | −$150,000 | −$ 70,000 | $ 65,000 | $ 240,000 | $ 250,000 |
| Present value of net cash flows in years 1–4 (discounted at 20%) | | | −$ 20,255 | | |
| Present value of terminal value $\left[\dfrac{\$250,000}{0.20} \times \dfrac{1}{(1.20)^4}\right]$ | | | +$602,816 | | |
| Present value of restaurant | | | $582,561 | | |
| − Cost of building | | | −$700,000 | | |
| Net present value of restaurant | | | −$117,439 | | |

The table starts with sales projections, which rise from $300,000 in the first year to a steady state of $1 million a year. Cash flows from operations are shown in the next line, although we leave out the intermediate calculations needed to move from line 1 to line 2. After subtracting working capital, the table shows net cash flows in line 4. Net cash flows are negative initially, as is quite common in start-ups, but they become positive by year 3. However, the rest of the table presents the unfortunate truth. The cash flows from the restaurant yield a present value (PV) of $582,561, assuming a discount rate of 20 percent. Unfortunately, the cost of the building is greater, at $700,000, implying a negative *net* present value of −$117,439.

The projections indicate that Michel's lifelong dream may not come to pass. He cannot expect to raise the capital needed to open his restaurant, and if he did obtain the funding, the restaurant would likely go under anyway. Michel checked and rechecked the numbers, hoping vainly to discover either a numerical error or a cost-saving omission that would move his venture from the red to the black. In fact, Michel saw that, if anything, his forecasts are generous, because a 20 percent discount rate and an infinitely long-lived building are on the optimistic side.

It wasn't until Michel took a course on corporate strategy that he realized the hidden value in his venture. In that course, his instructor repeatedly stated the importance of positioning a firm to take advantage of new opportunities. Although Michel didn't see the connection at first, he finally realized the implications for Chez Michel. His financial projections were based on expectations. There was a 50 percent probability that wild game would be more popular than he thought, in which case actual cash flows would exceed projections. And, there was a 50 percent probability that the meat would be less popular, in which case the actual flows would fall short of projections.

If the restaurant did poorly, it would probably fold in a few years, because he would not want to keep losing money forever. However, if the restaurant did well, he would be in a position to expand. If wild game proved popular in one locale, it would likely prove popular in other locales as well. Thus, he noticed two options: the option to abandon under bad conditions and the option to expand under good conditions. Although both options can be valued according to the principles of the previous chapter, we focus on the option to expand because it is probably much more valuable.

Michel reasoned that consumer reaction to wild game and exotic meats would be mixed. Some more adventurous individuals would welcome the chance to try new dishes, while others would likely be won over once they understood that these meats are far lower in cholesterol than traditional meats are. Still, some consumers would undoubtedly resist the idea of eating the meat of wild animals. He forecast that although he could expand quickly if the first restaurant proved successful, the market would limit him to 30 additional restaurants.

Michel believes that this expansion will occur about four years from now. He believes that he will need three years of operating the first restaurant to (1) get the initial restaurant running smoothly and (2) have enough information to place an accurate value on the restaurant. If the first restaurant is successful enough, he will need another year to obtain outside capital. Thus, he will be ready to build the 30 additional units around the fourth year.

Michel will value his enterprise, including the option to expand, according to the Black–Scholes model. From Table 24.2, we see that each unit costs $700,000, implying a total cost over the 30 additional units of $21,000,000 (30 × $700,000). The PV of the cash inflows from these 30 units is $17,476,830 (30 × $582,561), according to the table. However, because the expansion will occur around the fourth year, this PV calculation is provided from the point of view of four years in the future. The PV as of today is $8,428,255 [$17,476,830/(1.20)$^4$], assuming a discount rate of 20 percent per year. Thus, Michel views his potential restaurant business as an option, where the exercise price is $21,000,000 and the value of the underlying asset is $8,428,255. The option is currently out of the money, a result that follows from the negative value of a typical restaurant, as calculated in Table 24.2. Of course, Michel is hoping that the option will move into the money within four years.

Michel needs three additional parameters to use the Black–Scholes model: $r$, the annual continuously compounded interest rate; $t$, the time to maturity; and $\sigma$, the standard deviation of the underlying asset. Michel uses the yield on a four-year zero-coupon bond, which is 3.5 percent, as the estimate of the interest rate. The time to maturity is four years. The estimate of standard deviation is a little trickier, because there are no historical data on wild game restaurants. Michel finds that the average annual standard deviation of the returns on publicly traded restaurants is 0.35. Because Chez Michel is a new venture, he reasons that the risk here would be somewhat greater. He finds that the average annual standard deviation for restaurants that have gone public in the last few years is 0.45. Because Michel's restaurant is newer still, he uses a standard deviation of 0.50.

There are now enough data to value Michel's venture. The value according to the Black–Scholes model is $1,454,269.[9] The actual calculations are shown in Table 24.3. This value should be used with caution as it is not as precise as it looks. The Black–Scholes model is based on a number of assumptions that hold quite well for short-lived options on exchange-listed stocks but are more difficult to justify for real options like opening a restaurant.[10]

---

[9] The exact value may vary slightly depending on the degree of rounding in the calculation.

[10] In particular, the underlying asset is not traded; its price does not follow a continuous process; the variance may not be constant over the extended life of the option and the option cannot be exercised without delay. For more on how violations of these assumptions affect valuation of real options, see A. Damodaran, *Investment Valuation* (New York: John Wiley & Sons, 1996), pp. 375–376.

**TABLE 24.3**

**Valuing a Start-Up Firm (Chez Michel) as an Option**

| Facts |
| --- |

1.  The value of a single restaurant is negative, as indicated by the NPV calculation in Table 24.2 of −$117,439. Thus, the restaurant would not be funded if there were no possibility of expansion.

2.  If the pilot restaurant is successful, Michel plans to create 30 additional restaurants around year 4. This leads to the following observations:

    a.  The total cost of 30 units is $21,000,000 (30 × $700,000).

    b.  The PV of future cash flows as of year 4 is $17,476,830 (30 × $582,561).

    c.  The PV of these cash flows today is $8,428,255 [$17,476,830/(1.20)$^4$].

    Here, we assume that cash flows from the project are discounted at 20% per annum.

    Thus, the business is essentially a call option, where the exercise price is $21,000,000 and the underlying asset is worth $8,428,255.

3.  Michel estimates the standard deviation of the return on Chez Michel's stock to be 0.50.

    Parameters of the Black–Scholes model:

    $$S \text{ (stock price)} = \$8,428,255$$
    $$F \text{ (exercise price)} = \$21,000,000$$
    $$t \text{ (time to maturity)} = 4 \text{ years}$$
    $$\sigma \text{ (standard deviation)} = 0.50$$
    $$r \text{ (continuously compounded interest rate)} = 3.5\%$$

    Calculation from the Black–Scholes model:

    $$C = SN(d_1) - Ee^{-rt}N(d_2)$$
    $$d_1 = \frac{\ln(S/E) + (r + \frac{1}{2}\sigma^2)t}{\sqrt{\sigma^2 t}}$$
    $$d_2 = d_1 - \sqrt{\sigma^2 t}$$
    $$d_1 = \left[\ln\frac{8,428,255}{21,000,000} + (0.035 + \tfrac{1}{2}(0.50)^2)4\right] \Big/ \sqrt{(0.50)^2 \times 4} = -0.27293$$
    $$d_2 = -0.27293 - \sqrt{(0.50)^2 \times 4} = -1.27293$$
    $$N(d_1) = N(-0.27293) = 0.39245$$
    $$N(d_2) = N(-1.27293) = 0.10152$$
    $$C = \$8,428,255 \times 0.39245 - \$21,000,000 \times e^{-0.035 \times 4} \times 0.10152$$
    $$= \$1,454,269$$

    Value of business including cost of pilot restaurant = $1,454,269 − $117,439
    = $1,336,830

Of course, Michel must start his pilot restaurant before he can take advantage of this option. Thus, the net value of the call option less the negative NPV of the pilot restaurant is $1,336,830 ($1,454,269 − $117,439). Because this value is large and positive, Michel decides to stay with his dream of Chez Michel. He knows that the probability that the restaurant will fail is greater than 50 percent. Nevertheless, the option to expand is important enough that his restaurant business has value. And, if he needs outside capital, he can probably attract the necessary investors.

This finding leads to the appearance of a paradox. If Michel approaches investors to invest in a single restaurant with no possibility of expansion, he will probably not be able to attract capital. After all, Table 24.2 shows an NPV of −$117,439. However, if Michel thinks bigger, he will likely be able to attract all the capital that he needs. But this is really not a paradox at all. By thinking bigger, Michel is offering investors the option, not the obligation, to expand.

The example we have chosen may seem frivolous, and, certainly, we added offbeat characteristics for interest. However, if you think that business situations involving options are unusual or unimportant, let us state emphatically that nothing can be further from the truth. The notion of embedded options is at the heart of business. There are two possible outcomes for virtually every business idea. On the one hand, the business may fail, in which case the managers will probably try to shut it down in the most cost-efficient way. On the other hand, the business may prosper, in which case the managers will try to expand. Thus, virtually every business has both the option to abandon and the option to expand. You may have read pundits claiming that the NPV approach to capital budgeting is wrong or incomplete. Although criticism of this type frequently irritates the finance establishment, the pundits definitely have a point. If virtually all projects have embedded options, only an approach such as the one we have outlined can be appropriate. Ignoring the options is likely to lead to serious undervaluation.

**CONCEPT QUESTIONS**

- **What are the two options that many businesses have?**
- **Why does a strict NPV calculation typically understate the value of a firm or project?**

## 24.3    MORE ABOUT THE BINOMIAL MODEL

Earlier in this chapter, we examined two applications of options: executive compensation and the start-up decision. In both cases we valued an option using the Black–Scholes model. Although this model is justifiably well known, it is not the only approach to option valuation. As mentioned in the previous chapter, the two-state, or binomial, model is an alternative and—in some situations—a superior approach to valuation. The rest of this chapter examines two applications of the binomial model.

### Heating Oil

**Two-Date Example**    Consider Antonia Meyer, a typical heating oil distributor, whose business consists of buying heating oil at the wholesale level and reselling the oil to homeowners at a somewhat higher price. Most of her revenue comes from sales during the winter. Today, September 1, heating oil sells for $2.00 per gallon. In this example, Antonia hedges her risk using options on heating oil. These options are traded on the New York Mercantile Exchange denominated in U.S. dollars and expressing quantities of heating oil in U.S. gallons. For this reason, we use gallons here, and, when we refer to dollars, we mean U.S. dollars.[11] Of course, this price is not fixed. Rather, oil prices will vary from September 1 until December 1, the time when her customers will probably make their big winter purchases of heating oil. Let's simplify the situation by assuming that Antonia believes that oil prices will be at either $2.74 or $1.46 on December 1. Figure 24.1 portrays this possible price movement. This potential price range represents a great deal of uncertainty because Antonia has no idea which of the two possible prices will actually occur. However, this price variability does not translate into that much risk because she can pass price changes on to her customers. That is, she will charge her customers more if she ends up paying $2.74 per gallon than if she ends up paying $1.46 per gallon.

Of course, Antonia is avoiding risk by passing on that risk to her customers. Her customers accept the risk, perhaps because they are each too small to negotiate a better deal. This is not the case with CECO, a large electric utility in her area. CECO approaches Antonia with the following proposition. The utility would like to be able to buy *up to* 6 million gallons of oil from her at $2.10 per gallon on December 1.

---

[11] Technically speaking, the underlying asset for the options is a futures contract on heating oil. We discuss futures in Chapter 26.

**FIGURE 24.1**

**Movement of Heating Oil Prices from September 1 to December 1 in a Two-Date Example**

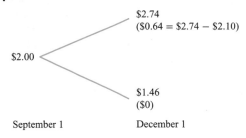

The price of heating oil on December 1 will be either $2.74 or $1.46. Because the price on September 1 is $2.00, we say that $u = 1.37$ (= $2.74/$2.00) and $d = 0.73$ (= $1.46/$2.00). The loss per gallon to Antonia (or, equivalently, the gain per gallon to CECO) of $0.64 in the up state or $0 in the down state is shown in parentheses.

Although this arrangement represents a lot of oil, both Antonia and CECO know that Antonia can expect to lose money on it. If prices rise to $2.74 per gallon, the utility will happily buy all 6 million gallons at only $2.10 per gallon, clearly creating a loss for the distributor. However, if oil prices decline to $1.46 per gallon, the utility will not buy any oil. After all, why should CECO pay $2.10 per gallon to Antonia when the utility can buy all the oil it wants at $1.46 per gallon in the open market? In other words, CECO is asking for a *call option* on heating oil. To compensate Antonia for the risk of loss, the two parties agree that CECO will pay her $1,000,000 up front for the right to buy up to 6 million gallons of oil at $2.10 per gallon.

Is this a fair deal? Although small distributors may evaluate a deal like this by gut feel, we can evaluate it more quantitatively by using the binomial model described in the previous chapter. In that chapter, we pointed out that option problems can be handled most easily by assuming *risk-neutral pricing*. In this approach, we first note that oil will either rise 37 percent (= $2.74/$2.00 − 1) or fall −27 percent (= $1.46/$2.00 − 1) from September 1 to December 1. We can think of these two numbers as the possible returns on heating oil. In addition, we introduce two new terms, $u$ and $d$. We define $u$ as $1 + 0.37 = 1.37$ and $d$ as $1 − 0.27 = 0.73$.[12] Using the methodology of the previous chapter, we value the contract in the following two steps.

**Step 1: Determining the Risk-Neutral Probabilities**    We determine the probability of a price rise such that the expected return on oil exactly equals the risk-free rate. Assuming an 8 percent annual interest rate, which implies a 2 percent rate over the next three months, we can solve for the probability of a rise as follows:[13]

$$2\% = \text{Probability of rise} \times 0.37 + (1 − \text{Probability of rise}) \times (−0.27)$$

Solving this equation, we find that the probability of a rise is approximately 45 percent, implying that the probability of a fall is 55 percent. In other words, if the probability of a price rise is 45 percent, the expected return on heating oil is 2 percent. In accordance with what we said in the previous chapter, these are the probabilities that are consistent with a world of risk neutrality. That is, under risk neutrality, the expected return on any asset would equal the risk-free rate of interest. No one would demand an expected return above this risk-free rate, because risk-neutral individuals do not need to be compensated for bearing risk.

---

[12] As we will see later, $u$ and $d$ are consistent with a standard deviation of the annual return on heating oil of 0.63.

[13] For simplicity, we ignore both storage costs and a convenience yield.

**Step 2: Valuing the Contract**    If the price of oil rises to $2.74 on December 1, CECO will want to buy oil from Antonia at $2.10 per gallon. Antonia will lose $0.64 per gallon because she buys oil in the open market at $2.74 per gallon, only to resell it to CECO at $2.10 per gallon. This loss of $0.64 is shown in parentheses in Figure 24.1. Conversely, if the market price of heating oil falls to $1.46 per gallon, CECO will not buy any oil from Antonia. That is, CECO would not want to pay $2.10 per gallon to her when the utility could buy heating oil in the open market at $1.46 per gallon. Thus, we can say that Antonia neither gains nor loses if the price drops to $1.46. The gain or loss of zero is placed in parentheses under the price of $1.46 in Figure 24.1. In addition, as mentioned earlier, Antonia receives $1,000,000 up front.

Given these numbers, the value of the contract to Antonia can be calculated as

$$\underbrace{[0.45 \times (\$2.10 - \$2.74) \times 6 \text{ million} + 0.55 \times \$0]/1.02}_{\text{Value of the call option}} + \$1,000,000 = -\$694,118 \quad \text{(24.1)}$$

As in the previous chapter, we are valuing an option using risk-neutral pricing. The cash flows of −$0.64 (= $2.10 − $2.74) and $0 per gallon are multiplied by their risk-neutral probabilities. The entire first term in equation (24.1) is then discounted at 1.02 because the cash flows in that term occur on December 1. The $1,000,000 is not discounted because Antonia receives it today, September 1. Because the PV of the contract is negative, Antonia would be wise to reject the contract.

As stated before, the distributor has sold a call option to CECO. The first term in the preceding equation, which equals −$1,694,118, can be viewed as the value of this call option. It is a negative number because the equation looks at the option from Antonia's point of view. Therefore, the value of the call option would be +$1,694,118 to CECO. On a per-gallon basis, the value of the option to CECO is

$$[0.45(\$2.74 - \$2.10) + 0.55 \times \$0]/1.02 = \$0.282 \quad \text{(24.2)}$$

Equation (24.2) shows that CECO will gain $0.64 (= $2.74 − $2.10) per gallon in the up state because CECO can buy heating oil worth $2.74 for only $2.10 under the contract. By contrast, the contract is worth nothing to CECO in the down state because the utility will not pay $2.10 for oil selling for only $1.46 in the open market. Using risk-neutral pricing, the formula tells us that the value of the call option on one gallon of heating oil is $0.282.

**Three-Date Example**    Although the preceding example captures a number of aspects of the real world, it has one deficiency. It assumes that the price of heating oil can take on only two values on December 1. This is clearly not plausible; oil can take on essentially any value, in reality. Although this deficiency seems glaring at first glance, it is actually easily correctable. All we have to do is introduce more intervals over the three-month period of our example.

For example, consider Figure 24.2, which shows the price movement of heating oil over two intervals of $1\frac{1}{2}$ months each.[14] As shown in the figure, the price will be either $2.50 or $1.60 on October 15. We refer to $2.50 as the price in the *up state* and $1.60 as the price in the *down state*. Thus, heating oil has returns of 25 percent (= $2.50/$2.00) and −20 percent (= $1.60/$2.00) in the two states.

We assume the same variability as we move forward from October 15 to December 1. That is, given a price of $2.50 on October 15, the price on December 1 will be either $3.12 (= $2.50 × 1.25) or $2 (= $2.50 × 0.80). Similarly, given a price of $1.60 on October 15, the price on December 1 will be either $2 (= $1.60 × 1.25) or $1.28 (= $1.60 × 0.80). This assumption of constant variability is quite plausible because the rate of new information impacting heating oil (or most commodities or assets) is likely to be similar from month to month.

---

[14] Though it is not apparent at first glance, we will see later that the price movement in Figure 24.2 is consistent with the price movement in Figure 24.1.

FIGURE 24.2

**Movement of Heating Oil Prices in a Three-Date Model**

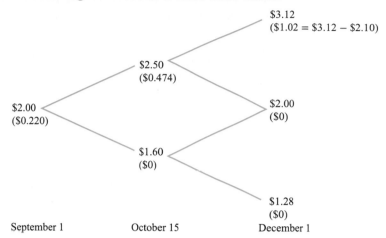

The figure shows the prices of a gallon of heating oil on three dates, given $u = 1.25$ and $d = 0.80$. There are three possible prices for heating oil on December 1. For each one of these three prices, we calculate the price on December 1 of a call option on a gallon of heating oil with an exercise price of $2.10. These numbers are in parentheses. Call prices at earlier dates are determined by the binomial model and are also shown in parentheses.

Note that there are three possible prices on December 1, but there are two possible prices on October 15. Also, note that there are two paths to a price of $2 on December 1. The price could rise to $2.50 on October 15 before falling back down to $2 on December 1. Alternatively, the price could fall to $1.60 on October 15 before going back up to $2 on December 1. In other words, the model has symmetry, where an up movement followed by a down movement yields the same price on December 1 as a down movement followed by an up movement.

How do we value CECO's option in this three-date example? We employ the same procedure that we used in the two-date example, although we now need an extra step because of the extra date.

**Step 1: Determining the Risk-Neutral Probabilities**    As we did in the two-date example, we determine what the probability of a price rise would be such that the expected return on heating oil exactly equals the risk-free rate. However, in this case we work with an interval of $1\frac{1}{2}$ months. Assuming an 8 percent annual rate of interest, which implies a 1 percent rate over a $1\frac{1}{2}$-month interval,[15] we can solve for the probability of a rise:

$$1\% = \text{Probability of rise} \times 0.25 + (1 - \text{Probability of rise}) \times (-0.20)$$

Solving the equation, we find that the probability of a rise here is 47 percent, implying that the probability of a fall is 53 percent. In other words, if the probability of a rise is 47 percent, the expected return on heating oil is 1 percent per $1\frac{1}{2}$-month interval. Again, these probabilities are determined under the assumption of risk-neutral pricing.

Note that the probabilities of 47 percent and 53 percent hold for both the interval from September 1 to October 15 and the interval from October 15 to December 1. This is the case because the return in the up state is 25 percent and the return in the down state is −20 percent for each of the two intervals. Thus, the preceding equation must apply to each of the intervals separately.

---

[15] For simplicity, we ignore interest compounding.

**Step 2: Valuing the Option as of October 15**    As indicated in Figure 24.2, the option to CECO will be worth $1.02 per gallon on December 1 if the price of heating oil has risen to $3.12 on that date. That is, CECO can buy oil from Antonia at $2.10 when it would otherwise have to pay $3.12 in the open market. However, the option will be worthless on December 1 if the price of a gallon of heating oil is either $2 or $1.28 on that date. Here, the option is out of the money because the exercise price of $2.10 is above both $2 and $1.28.

Using these option prices on December 1, we can calculate the value of the call option on October 15. If the price of a gallon of heating oil is $2.50 on October 15, Figure 24.2 shows us that the call option will be worth either $1.02 or $0 on December 1. Thus, if the price of heating oil is $2.50 on October 15, the value of the option on one gallon of heating oil at that time is

$$[0.47 \times \$1.02 + 0.53 \times \$0]/1.01 = \$0.474$$

Here we are valuing an option using the same risk-neutral pricing approach that we used in the earlier two-date example. This value of $0.474 is shown in parentheses in Figure 24.2.

We also want to value the option on October 15 if the price at that time is $1.60. However, the value here is clearly zero, as indicated by the calculation

$$[0.47 \times \$0 + 0.53 \times \$0]/1.01 = 0$$

This is obvious once we look at Figure 24.2. We see from the figure that the call must end up out of the money on December 1 if the price of heating oil is $1.60 on October 15. Thus, the call must have zero value on October 15 if the price of heating oil is $1.60 on that date.

**Step 3: Valuing the Option on September 1**    In the previous step, we saw that the price of the call on October 15 would be $0.474 if the price of a gallon of heating oil was $2.50 on that date. Similarly, the price of the option on October 15 would be $0 if oil was selling at $1.60 on that date. From these values, we can calculate the call option value on September 1 as

$$[0.47 \times \$0.474 + 0.53 \times \$0]/1.01 = \$0.220$$

Notice that this calculation is completely analogous to the calculation of the option value in the previous step, as well as the calculation of the option value in the two-date example that we presented earlier. In other words, the same approach applies regardless of the number of intervals used. As we will see later, we can move to many intervals, which produces greater realism, yet still maintain the same basic methodology.

The previous calculation has given us the value to CECO of its option on one gallon of heating oil. Now we are ready to calculate the value of the contract to Antonia. Given the calculations from the previous equation, the contract's value can be written as

$$-\$0.220 \times 6,000,000 + \$1,000,000 = -\$320,000$$

That is, Antonia is giving away an option worth $0.220 for each of the 6 million gallons of heating oil. In return, she is receiving only $1,000,000 up front. Overall, she is losing $320,000. Of course, the value of the contract to CECO is the opposite, so the value to this utility is $320,000.

**Extension to Many Dates**    We have looked at the contract between CECO and Antonia using both a two-date example and a three-date example. The three-date case is more realistic because more possibilities for price movements are allowed here. However, why stop at just three dates? Moving to 4 dates, 5 dates, 50 dates, 500 dates, and so on should give us even more realism. Note that as we move to more dates, we are merely shortening the interval between dates without increasing the overall time period of three months (September 1 to December 1).

For example, imagine a model with 90 dates over the three months. Here, each interval is approximately one day long because there are about 90 days in a three-month period. The assumption of two possible outcomes in the binomial model is more plausible over a one-day interval than it is over a $1\frac{1}{2}$-month interval, let alone a three-month interval. Of course, we could probably achieve greater realism still by going to an interval of, say, one hour or one minute.

How do we adjust the binomial model to accommodate increases in the number of intervals? It turns out that two simple formulas relate $u$ and $d$ to the standard deviation of the return on the underlying asset:[16]

$$u = e^{\sigma/\sqrt{n}} \quad \text{and} \quad d = 1/u$$

where $\sigma$ is the standard deviation of the annualized return on the underlying asset (heating oil, in this case) and $n$ is the number of intervals over a year.

When we created the heating oil example, we assumed that the annualized standard deviation of the return on heating oil was 0.63 (or, equivalently, 63 percent). Because there are four quarters in a year, $u = e^{0.63/\sqrt{4}} = 1.37$ and $d = 1/1.37 = 0.73$, as shown in the two-date example of Figure 24.1. In the three-date example of Figure 24.2, where each interval is $1\frac{1}{2}$ months long, $u = e^{0.63/\sqrt{8}} = 1.25$ and $d = 1/1.25 = 0.80$. Thus, the binomial model can be applied in practice if the standard deviation of the return of the underlying asset can be estimated.

We stated earlier that the value of the call option on a gallon of heating oil was estimated to be $0.282 in the two-date model and $0.220 in the three-date model. How does the value of the option change as we increase the number of intervals while keeping the time period constant at three months (from September 1 to December 1)? We have calculated the value of the call for various time intervals in Table 24.4.[17] The realism increases with the number of intervals because the restriction of only two possible outcomes is more plausible over a short interval than over a long one. Thus, the value of the call when the number of intervals is 99 or infinity is likely more realistic than this value when the number of intervals is, say, 1 or 2.

**TABLE 24.4**

**Value of a Call on One Gallon of Heating Oil**

| Number of intervals* | Call value |
|---|---|
| 1 | $0.282 |
| 2 | 0.220 |
| 3 | 0.244 |
| 4 | 0.232 |
| 6 | 0.228 |
| 10 | 0.228 |
| 20 | 0.228 |
| 30 | 0.228 |
| 40 | 0.228 |
| 50 | 0.226 |
| 99 | 0.226 |
| Black–Scholes infinity | 0.226 |

In this example, the value of the call according to the binomial model varies as the number of intervals increases. However, the value of the call converges rapidly to the Black–Scholes value. Thus, the binomial model, even with only a few intervals, appears to be a good approximation of Black–Scholes.

* The number of intervals is always one less than the number of dates.

---

[16] See John C. Hull, *Options, Futures, and Other Derivatives*, 7th ed. (Upper Saddle River, NJ: Prentice Hall, 2009), for a derivation of these formulas.

[17] In this discussion, we have used both *intervals* and *dates*. To keep the terminology straight, remember that the number of intervals is always one less than the number of dates. For example, if a model has two dates, it has only one interval.

However, a very interesting phenomenon can be observed from the table. Although the value of the call changes as the number of intervals increases, convergence occurs quite rapidly. The call's value with 6 intervals is almost identical to the value with 99 intervals. Thus, a small number of intervals appears serviceable for the binomial model. Six intervals in a three-month period implies that each interval is two weeks long. Of course, the assumption that heating oil can take on only one of two prices in two weeks is simply not realistic. The paradox is that this unrealistic assumption still produces a realistic call price.

What happens when the number of intervals goes to infinity, implying that the length of the interval goes to zero? It can be proven mathematically that we end up with the value of the Black–Scholes model. This value is also presented in Table 24.4. Thus, we can argue that the Black–Scholes model is the best approach to value the heating oil option. It is also quite easy to apply. We can use a calculator to value options with Black–Scholes, whereas we must generally use a computer program for the binomial model. However, as shown in Table 24.4, the values from the binomial model, even with relatively few intervals, are quite close to the Black–Scholes value. Thus, although Black–Scholes may save us time, it does not materially affect our estimate of value.

At this point it seems as if the Black–Scholes model is preferable to the binomial model. Who wouldn't want to save time and still get a slightly more accurate value? However, this is not always the case. There are plenty of situations where the binomial model is preferred to the Black–Scholes model. One such situation is presented in the next section.

# 24.4    SHUTDOWN AND REOPENING DECISIONS

Some of the earliest and most important examples of special options occur in the natural resources and mining industries.

## Valuing a Gold Mine

The Woe Is Me gold mine was founded in 1882 on one of the richest veins of gold in the West. Thirty years later, by 1912, the mine had closed, but occasionally, depending on the price of gold, it is reopened. Currently, gold is not actively mined at Woe Is Me, but its stock is still trading on the exchange under the ticker symbol WOE. WOE has no debt and, with 20 million outstanding shares, its market value exceeds $6 billion. WOE owns about 160 acres of land surrounding the mine and has a 100-year government lease to mine gold on the land. However, land in that area has a market value of only a few thousand dollars. WOE holds cash and securities and other assets worth about $30 million. What could possibly explain why a company with $30 million in assets and a closed gold mine that was producing no cash flows whatsoever has a market value of more than $6 billion?

The answer lies in the options that WOE implicitly owns in the gold mine. Assume that the current price of gold is about $1,300 per ounce and the cost of extraction and processing at the mine is about $1,400 per ounce.[18] It is no wonder that the mine is closed. Every ounce of gold extracted would cost $1,400 and could be sold for only $1,300, for a loss of $100 per ounce. Presumably if the price of gold were to rise, the mine could be opened. It costs $20 million to open the mine, and when it is opened, production is 50,000 ounces per year. Geologists believe that the amount of gold in the mine is essentially unlimited, and WOE has the right to mine it for the next hundred years. Under the terms of its lease, WOE cannot stockpile gold and each year it must sell all the gold it mines that year. Closing the mine requires equipment to be moth-

---

[18] Gold is quoted in U.S. dollars, so all the prices in this example are in U.S. dollars.

balled and some environmental precautions to be put in place, which costs $10 million. We will refer to the $20 million required to open the mine as the entry fee or investment and the $10 million to close it as the closing or abandonment cost. (There is no way to avoid the abandonment cost by simply keeping the mine open and not operating.)

From a financial perspective, WOE is really just a package of options on the price of gold disguised as a company and a mine. The basic option is a call on the price of gold where the exercise price is the $1,400 extraction cost. The option is complicated by having an exercise fee of $20 million—the opening cost—whenever it is exercised and a closing fee of $10 million when it is abandoned. It is also complicated by the fact that it is a perpetual option with no final maturity.

## The Abandonment and Opening Decisions

Before trying to figure out the exact value of the option implicit in WOE or, for that matter, in any real option problem, it is useful to see what we can glean by just applying common sense. To begin with, the mine should only be opened when the price of gold is sufficiently above the extraction cost of $1,400 per ounce. Because it costs $20 million to open the mine, the mine should not be opened whenever the price of gold is only slightly above $1,400. At a gold price of, say, $1,401, the mine would not be opened because the $1 profit per ounce translates into $50,000 per year (50,000 ounces × $1/ounce). This would not even be close to covering the $20 million opening costs. More significantly, though, the mine probably would not be opened if the price rose to $1,450 per ounce even though a $50 profit per ounce—$2,500,000 per year—would pay the $20 million opening costs at any reasonable discount rate. The reason is that here, as in all option problems, volatility (in this case the volatility of gold) plays a significant role. Because the gold price is volatile, the price has to rise sufficiently above $1,400 per ounce to make it worth opening the mine. If the price at which the mine is opened is too close to the extraction price of $1,400 per ounce, say $1,450 per ounce, then we would wind up opening the mine every time the price jogged above $1,450 and find ourselves operating at a loss or facing a closing decision whenever the price jogged back down $50 per ounce (only 3 percent) to $1,400.

The estimated volatility of the return on gold is about 25 percent per year. This means that a single annual standard deviation movement in the gold price is 25 percent of $1,300 or $325 per year. Surely, with this amount of random movement in the gold price, a threshold of, for example, $1,405 is much too low to open the mine. A similar logic applies to the closing decision. If the mine is open, then we will clearly keep it open as long as the gold price is above the extraction cost of $1,400 per ounce since we are profiting on every ounce of gold mined. But, we will also not close the mine down simply because the gold price drops below $1,400 per ounce. We will tolerate a running loss to keep alive the possibility that the gold price will rise above $1,400 and to avoid the necessity of having to pay the $10 million abandonment cost only to have to then pay another $20 million to reopen the mine.

To summarize, if the mine is currently closed, then it will be opened—at a cost of $20 million—whenever the price of gold rises sufficiently above the extraction cost of $1,400 per ounce. If the mine is currently operating, then it will be closed down—at a cost of $10 million—whenever the price of gold falls sufficiently below the extraction cost of $1,400 per ounce. Our problem is to first find these two threshold prices at which we open a closed mine and close an open mine. We call these prices $p_{open}$ and $p_{close}$, respectively, where

$$p_{open} > \$1,400/\text{ounce} > p_{close}$$

In other words, we open the mine if the gold price option is sufficiently in the money and we close it when the option is sufficiently out of the money.

## Valuing the Simple Gold Mine

Here is what has to be done in order to determine both $p_{open}$ and $p_{close}$ and to value the mine:

*Step 1.* Find the risk-free interest rate and the volatility. We will use a semiannual interest rate of 3.4 percent and a volatility of 25 percent per year for gold.

*Step 2.* Construct a binomial tree and fill it in with gold prices. Suppose, for example, that we set the steps of the tree six months apart. If the annual volatility is 25 percent, $u$ is equal to $e^{0.25/\sqrt{2}}$, which is approximately equal to 1.19. The other parameter, $d$, is 0.84 (1/1.19). Figure 24.3 illustrates the tree. Starting at the current price of $1,300, the first 19 percent increase takes the price to $1,551 in six months. The first 16 percent decrease takes the price to $1,089. Subsequent steps are up 19 percent or down 16 percent from the previous price. The tree extends for the 100-year life of the lease or 200 six-month steps.

**FIGURE 24.3**

**A Binomial Tree for Gold Prices**

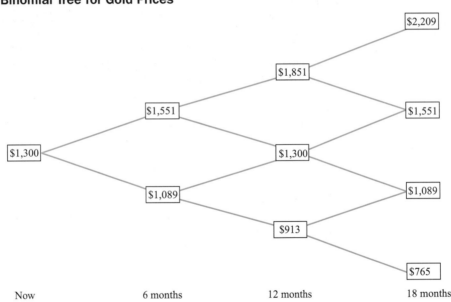

| Now | 6 months | 12 months | 18 months |

Steps of the binomial tree are six months apart. For each step, $u$ is equal to 1.19 and $d$ is equal to 0.84. Note that $u$ and $d$ are rounded to two decimal places.

Using our analysis from the previous section, we now compute the risk-adjusted probability for each step. Given a semiannual interest rate of 3.4 percent, we have

$$3.4\% = \text{Probability of a rise} \times 0.19 + (1 - \text{Probability of a rise}) \times (-0.16)$$

Solving this equation gives us 0.55 for the probability of a rise, implying that the probability of a fall is 0.45. These probabilities are the same for each six-month interval. In other words, if the probability of a rise is 0.55, the expected return on gold is 3.4 percent per six-month interval. These probabilities are determined under the assumption of risk-neutral pricing. In other words, if investors are risk neutral, they will be satisfied with an expected return equal to the risk-free rate, because the extra risk of gold will not concern them.

*Step 3.* Now we turn on the computer and let it simulate, say, 5,000 possible paths through the tree. At each node, the computer has a 0.55 probability of picking an up movement in the price and a corresponding 0.45 probability of picking a down movement in the price. A typical path might be represented by whether the price rose or fell each six-month period over the next 100 years and it would be a list like

up, up, down, up, down, down, . . . , down

where the first "up" meant the price rose from $1,300 to $1,551 in the first six months, the next "up" meant it again went up in the second half of the year from $1,551 to $1,851, and so on, ending with a down move in the last half of year 100.

  With 5,000 such paths, we will have a good sample of all the future possibilities for movement in the gold price.

*Step 4.* Next we consider possible choices for the threshold prices, $p_{open}$ and $p_{close}$. For $p_{open}$, we let the possibilities be

$$p_{open} = \$1,500 \text{ or } \$1,600 \text{ or } \ldots \text{ or } \$2,900$$

a total of 15 values. For $p_{close}$ we let the possibilities be

$$p_{close} = \$1,300 \text{ or } \$1,200 \text{ or } \ldots \text{ or } \$400$$

a total of 10 values.

  We picked these choices because they seemed reasonable and because increments of $100 for each seemed sensible. To be precise, though, we should let the threshold prices change as we move through the tree and get closer to the 100-year end. Presumably, for example, if we decided to open the mine with one year left on the lease, the price of gold should be at least high enough to cover the $20 million opening costs in the coming year. Since we mine 50,000 ounces per year, in year 99 we will only open the mine if the gold price is at least $400 above the extraction cost, or $1,800.

  While this will become important at the end of the lease, using a constant threshold shouldn't have too big an impact on the value with 100 years to go and we will stick with our approximation of constant threshold prices.

*Step 5.* We calculate the value of the mine for each pair of choices of $p_{open}$ and $p_{close}$. For example, if $p_{open} = \$2,200$ and $p_{close} = \$1,100$, we use the computer to keep track of the cash flows if we opened the mine whenever it was closed and the gold price rose to $2,200, and closed the mine whenever it was open and the gold price fell to $1,100. We do this for each of the 5,000 paths we simulated in step 3.

  For example, consider the path illustrated in Figure 24.4 of

up, up, down, up, up, down, down, down, down

As can be seen from the figure, the price reaches a peak of $2,209 in $2\frac{1}{2}$ years, only to fall to $1,089 over the following four six-month intervals. If $p_{open} = \$2,200$ and $p_{close} = \$1,100$, the mine will be opened when the price reaches $2,209, necessitating a cost of $20 million. However, the firm can sell 25,000 ounces of gold at $2,209 at that time, producing a cash flow of $20.225 million [25,000 × ($2,209 − $1,400)]. When the price falls to $1,851 six months later, the firm sells another 25,000 ounces, yielding a cash flow of $11.275 million [25,000 × ($1,851 − $1,400)]. The price continues to fall, with the price reaching $1,300 a year later. Here, the firm realizes a cash outflow, because production costs are $1,400 per ounce. Next, the price falls to $1,089. Because this is below $p_{close}$ of $1,100, the mine is closed at a cost of $10 million. Of course, the price of gold will fluctuate in further years, leading to the possibility of future mine openings and closings.

  This path is just a possibility. It may or may not occur in any simulation of 5,000 paths. For each of these 5,000 paths that the computer simulated, we have a sequence of semiannual cash flows using a $p_{open}$ of $2,200 and a $p_{close}$ of $1,100. We calculate the PV of each of these cash flows, discounting at the interest rate of 3.4 percent. Summing up across all the cash flows, we have the PV of the gold mine for one path.

**FIGURE 24.4**

**A Possible Path for the Price of Gold**

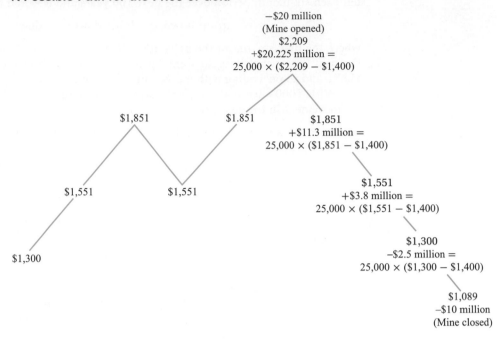

Imagine that this path is one of the 5,000 simulated price paths for gold. Because $p_{open}$ = $2,200 and $p_{close}$ = $1,100, the mine is opened when the price reaches $2,209. This mine is closed when the price reaches $1,089.

We then take the average PV of the gold mine across all the 5,000 simulated paths. This number is the expected value of the mine from following a policy of opening the mine whenever the gold price hits $2,200 and closing it at a price of $1,100.

*Step 6.*   The final step is to compare the different expected discounted cash flows from step 5 for the range of possible choices for $p_{open}$ and $p_{close}$ and to pick the highest one. This is the best estimate of the expected value of the mine. The values for $p_{close}$ and $p_{open}$ corresponding to this estimate are our best estimate of the points at which to open a closed mine and to close an open one.

As mentioned in step 4, there are 15 different values for $p_{open}$ and 10 different values for $p_{close}$, implying 150 (15 × 10) different pairs. Consider Table 24.5, which shows the PVs associated with the 20 best pairs. The table indicates that the best pair is $p_{open}$ = $2,900 and $p_{close}$ = $1,200, with a PV of $6.629 billion. This number represents the average PV across 5,000 simulations, all assuming the preceding values of $p_{open}$ and $p_{close}$. The next best pair is $p_{open}$ = $2,200 and $p_{close}$ = $1,300, with a PV of $6.557 billion. The third best pair has a somewhat lower PV still, and so on.

Of course, our estimate of the value of the mine is $6.629 billion, the PV of the best pair of choices. The market capitalization (price × number of shares outstanding) of WOE should reach this value if the market makes the same assumptions that we did. Note that the value of the firm is quite high using an option framework. However, as stated earlier, WOE would appear worthless if a regular discounted cash flow approach were used. This occurs because the initial price of gold of $1,300 is below the extraction cost of $1,400.

**TABLE 24.5**

**Valuation of Woe Is Me (WOE) Gold Mine for the 20 Best Choices of $p_{open}$ and $p_{close}$**

| $p_{open}$ | $p_{close}$ | Estimated value of gold mine (in $ millions) |
|---|---|---|
| $2,900 | $1,200 | $6,629 |
| 2,200 | 1,300 | 6,557 |
| 2,000 | 1,000 | 6,428 |
| 2,000 | 1,200 | 6,288 |
| 1,800 | 1,400 | 6,168 |
| 2,900 | 500 | 6,140 |
| 2,800 | 500 | 6,103 |
| 2,900 | 900 | 6,055 |
| 3,000 | 1,100 | 6,054 |
| 2,600 | 900 | 6,050 |
| 2,600 | 600 | 6,038 |
| 3,000 | 500 | 6,033 |
| 1,900 | 1,400 | 5,958 |
| 2,100 | 700 | 5,939 |
| 2,300 | 500 | 5,934 |
| 2,200 | 1,400 | 5,928 |
| 1,800 | 800 | 5,895 |
| 2,300 | 600 | 5,892 |
| 2,400 | 1,100 | 5,862 |
| 1,900 | 500 | 5,855 |

For our simulation, WOE opens the mine whenever the gold price rises above $p_{open}$ and closes the mine whenever the gold price falls below $p_{close}$.

This example is not easy, neither in concepts nor in terms of implementation. However, we believe that the extra work involved in mastering this example is worth it, because it illustrates the type of modelling that actually occurs in corporate finance departments in the real world.

Furthermore, the example illustrates the benefits of the binomial approach. One merely calculates the cash flows associated with each of a number of simulations, discounts the cash flows from each simulation, and averages PVs across the simulations. Because the Black–Scholes model is not amenable to simulations, it cannot be used for this type of problem. In addition, there are a number of other situations where the binomial model is more appropriate than the Black–Scholes model. For example, it is well known that the Black–Scholes model cannot properly handle options with dividend payments prior to the expiration date. This model also does not adequately handle the valuation of an American put. By contrast, the binomial model can easily handle both these situations.

Thus, any student of corporate finance should be well versed in both models. The Black–Scholes model should be used whenever appropriate, because it is simpler to use than is the binomial model. However, for the more complex situations where the Black–Scholes model breaks down, the binomial model becomes a necessary tool.

## 24.5

# SUMMARY AND CONCLUSIONS

This chapter extends the intuition of one of the most significant concepts in finance: option pricing theory. We described four different types of special options:

- Executive stock options.
- The embedded option in a start-up company.
- The option in simple business contracts.
- The option to shut down and reopen a project.

We tried to keep the presentation simple and straightforward from a mathematical point of view. We extended the binomial approach to option pricing in Chapter 23 to many periods. This adjustment brings us closer to the real world, because the assumption of only two prices at the end of an interval is more plausible when the interval is short.

**QUESTIONS &
PROBLEMS**

**Employee Stock Options**

24.1 Gary Levin is the CEO of Mountainbrook Trading Company. The board of directors has just granted Gary 30,000 at-the-money European call options on the company's stock, which is currently trading at $50 per share. The stock pays no dividends. The options will expire in five years, and the standard deviation of the returns on the stock is 56 percent. Treasury bills that mature in five years currently yield a continuously compounded interest rate of 6 percent.

    *a.* Use the Black–Scholes model to calculate the value of the stock options.

    *b.* You are Gary's financial adviser. He must choose between the previously mentioned stock option package and an immediate $750,000 bonus. If he is risk neutral, which would you recommend?

    *c.* How would your answer to (b) change if Gary were risk averse and he could not sell the options prior to expiration?

24.2 Jessica Lazarus has just been named the new CEO of BluBell Fitness Centres Inc. In addition to an annual salary of $375,000, her three-year contract states that her compensation will include 15,000 at-the-money European call options on the company's stock that expire in three years. The current stock price is $34 per share, and the standard deviation of the returns on the firm's stock is 74 percent. The company does not pay a dividend. Treasury bills that mature in three years yield a continuously compounded interest rate of 5 percent. Assume that Jessica's annual salary payments occur at the end of the year and that these cash flows should be discounted at a rate of 9 percent. Using the Black–Scholes model to calculate the value of the stock options, determine the total value of the compensation package on the date the contract is signed.

**Binomial Model**

24.3 Gasworks Inc. has been approached to sell up to 40 litres of gasoline in three months at a price of $1.00 per litre. Gasoline is currently selling on the wholesale market at $0.90 per litre and has a standard deviation of 52 percent. If the risk-free rate is 41 percent per year, what is the value of this option?

**Real Options**

24.4 The Webber Company is an international conglomerate with a real estate division that owns the right to erect an office building on a parcel of land in downtown Calgary over the next year. This building would cost $20 million to construct. Due to low demand for office space in the downtown area, such a building is worth approximately $18.5 million today. If demand increases, the building will be worth $22.4 million a year from today. If demand decreases, the same office building will be worth only $17.5 million in a year. The company can borrow and lend at the risk-free annual effective rate of 4.8 percent. A local competitor in the real estate business has recently offered $750,000 for the right to build an office building on the land. Should the company accept this offer? Use a two-state model to value the real option.

24.5 Jet Black is an international conglomerate with a petroleum division and is currently competing in an auction to win the right to drill for crude oil on a large piece of land in one year. The current market price of crude oil is $58 per barrel, and the land is believed to contain 375,000 barrels of oil. If found, the oil would cost $35 million to extract. Treasury bills that mature in one year yield a continuously compounded interest rate of 4 percent, and the standard deviation of the returns on the price of crude oil is 50 percent. Use the Black–Scholes model to calculate the maximum bid that the company should be willing to make at the auction.

24.6 Sardano Corp. is a large, publicly held company that is considering leasing a warehouse. One of the company's divisions specializes in manufacturing steel, and this particular warehouse is the only facility in the area that suits the firm's operations. The current price of steel is $670 per tonne. If the price of steel falls over the next six months, the company will purchase 500 tonnes of steel and produce 55,000 steel rods. Each steel rod will cost $18 to manufacture, and the company plans to sell the rods for $29 each. It will take only a matter of days to produce and sell the steel rods. If the price of steel rises or remains the same, it will not be profitable to undertake the project, and the company will allow the lease to expire without producing any steel rods. Treasury bills that mature in six months yield a continuously compounded interest rate of 4.5 percent, and the standard deviation of the returns on steel is 45 percent. Use the Black–Scholes model to determine the maximum amount that the company should be willing to pay for the lease.

24.7 Wet for the Summer Inc. manufactures filters for swimming pools. The company is deciding whether to implement a new technology in its pool filters. One year from now the company will know whether the new technology is accepted in the market. If the demand for the new filters is high, the PV of the cash flows in one year will be $13.4 million. Conversely, if the demand is low, the value of the cash flows in one year will be $7 million. The value of the project today under these assumptions is $11.6 million, and the risk-free rate is 6 percent. Suppose that in one year, if the demand for the new technology is low, the company can sell the technology for $8.2 million. What is the value of the option to abandon?

## Binomial Model

24.8 There is a European put option on a stock that expires in two months. The stock price is $58, and the standard deviation of the stock returns is 70 percent. The option has a strike price of $65, and the risk-free interest rate is a 5 percent annual percentage rate (APR). What is the price of the put option today using one-month steps? (*Hint:* How will you find the value of the option if it can be exercised early? When would you exercise the option early?)

## Real Options

24.9 You are in discussions to purchase an option on an office building with a strike price of $63 million. The building is currently valued at $60 million. The option will allow you to purchase the building either six months from today or one year from today. Six months from today, accrued rent payments from the building in the amount of $900,000 will be made to the owners. If you exercise the option in six months, you will receive the accrued rent payments; otherwise, the payment will be made to the current owners. A second accrued rent payment of $900,000 will be paid one year from today with the same payment terms. The standard deviation of the value of the building is 30 percent, and the risk-free rate is a 6 percent APR. What is the price of the option today using six-month steps? (*Hint:* The value of the building in six months will be reduced by the accrued rent payment if you do not exercise the option at that time.)

# Exotic Cuisines Employee Stock Options

As a newly minted MBA, you've taken a management position with Exotic Cuisines Ltd., a restaurant chain that just went public last year. The company's restaurants specialize in exotic main dishes, using ingredients such as buffalo and ostrich. A concern you had going in was that the restaurant business is very risky. However, after some due diligence, you discovered a common misperception about the restaurant industry. It is widely thought that 90 percent of new restaurants close within three years; however, recent evidence suggests the failure rate is closer to 60 percent over three years. So it is a risky business, although not as risky as you originally thought.

During your interview process, one of the benefits mentioned was employee stock options. Upon signing your employment contract, you received options with a strike price of $50 for 10,000 shares of company stock. As is fairly common, your stock options have a three-year vesting period and a 10-year expiration, meaning that you cannot exercise the options for three years, and you lose them if you leave before they vest. After the three-year vesting period, you can exercise the options at any time. Thus, the employee stock options are European (and subject to forfeit) for the first three years and American afterward. Of course, you cannot sell the options, nor can you enter into any sort of hedging agreement. If you leave the company after the options vest, you must exercise within 90 days or forfeit.

Exotic Cuisines stock is currently trading at $38.15 per share, a slight increase from the initial offering price last year. There are no market-traded options on the company's stock. Because the company has been traded for only about a year, you are reluctant to use the historical returns to estimate the standard deviation of the stock's return. However, you have estimated that the average annual standard deviation for restaurant company stocks is about 55 percent. Because Exotic Cuisines is a newer restaurant chain, you decide to use a 60 percent standard deviation in your calculations. The company is relatively young, and you expect that all earnings will be reinvested in the company for the near future. Therefore, you expect no dividends will be paid for at least the next 10 years. A three-year Treasury note currently has a yield of 3.8 percent, and a 10-year Treasury note has a yield of 4.4 percent.

1. You're trying to value your options. What minimum value would you assign? What is the maximum value you would assign?

2. Suppose that in three years the company's stock is trading at $60. At that time, should you keep the options or exercise them immediately? What are some of the important determinants in making such a decision?

3. Your options, like most employee stock options, are not transferable or tradable. Does this have a significant effect on the value of the options? Why?

4. Why do you suppose employee stock options usually have a vesting provision? Why must they be exercised shortly after you depart the company even after they vest?

5. A controversial practice with employee stock options is repricing. What happens is that a company experiences a stock price decrease, which leaves employee stock options far out of the money or "underwater." In such cases, many companies have "repriced" or "restruck" the options, meaning that the company leaves the original terms of the option intact but lowers the strike price. Proponents of repricing argue that because the option is very unlikely to end in the money because of the stock price decline, the motivational force is lost. Opponents argue that repricing is in essence a reward for failure. How do you evaluate this argument? How does the possibility of repricing affect the value of an employee stock option at the time it is granted?

6. As we have seen, much of the volatility in a company's stock price is due to systematic or marketwide risks. Such risks are beyond the control of a company and its employees. What are the implications for employee stock options? In light of your answer, can you recommend an improvement over traditional employee stock options?

# Warrants and Convertibles

EXECUTIVE SUMMARY

In this chapter, we study two financing instruments: warrants and convertibles. A warrant gives the holder the right to buy common stock for cash. In this sense, it is very much like a call. Warrants are generally issued with privately placed bonds, though they are also packaged with new issues of common stock and preferred stock. In the case of new issues of common stock, warrants are sometimes given to investment bankers as compensation for underwriting services.

A convertible bond gives the holder the right to exchange the bond for common stock. It is therefore a mixed security that blurs the traditional line between stocks and bonds. There is also convertible preferred stock.

The chapter describes the basic features of warrants and convertibles. It also discusses some of the most important questions concerning these securities:

1. How can warrants and convertibles be valued?
2. What impact do warrants and convertibles have on the value of the firm?
3. What are the differences among warrants, convertibles, and call options?
4. Why do some companies issue bonds with warrants and convertible bonds?
5. Under what circumstances are warrants and convertibles converted into common stock?

## 25.1 WARRANTS

**Warrants** are securities that give holders the right, but not the obligation, to buy shares of common stock directly from a company at a fixed price for a given period of time. Each warrant specifies the number of shares that the holder can buy, the exercise price, and the expiration date.

The preceding description of warrants makes it clear that they are similar to call options. The differences in contractual features between warrants and the call options that trade through the Montreal Exchange and the Canadian Derivatives Clearing Corporation (CDCC) are small. For example, warrants have longer maturity periods.[1] Some warrants are actually perpetual, meaning that they never expire at all.

Warrants are referred to as *equity kickers* because they are usually issued in combination with privately placed bonds.[2] In most cases, warrants are attached to the bonds when issued. The loan agreement will state whether the warrants are detachable from the bond, that is, whether they can be sold separately. Usually, the warrant can be detached immediately.

Including warrants with an issue of securities makes the issue more attractive. With the growth of financial engineering, warrant issuers are creating new varieties. Some warrant issues give investors the right to buy the issuers' bonds instead of their stock. In addition, warrants are issued on their own instead of as sweeteners in a bond issue.

---

[1] Warrants are usually protected against stock splits and stock dividends in the same way that call options are.

[2] Warrants are also issued with publicly distributed bonds and new issues of common and preferred shares.

An important recent example is provided by the warrants in several financial institutions that the U.S. Treasury received in exchange for the US$700 billion government rescue package enacted in the aftermath of the 2008 financial meltdown. In March 2010, the U.S. Treasury sold its warrants to purchase shares of Bank of America (BofA). The Treasury sold 121.8 million Group B warrants with an exercise price of $30.79 per share. The warrants, which were sold at a price of $2.55, expire in October 2018. BofA shares were selling at $16.43 per share at the time of the announcement.

The relationship between the value of BofA's warrants and its stock price can be viewed as similar to the relationship between a call option and the stock price, described in Chapter 23. Figure 25.1 depicts the relationship for BofA Group B warrants. The lower limit on the value of the warrants is zero if the stock price for BofA is below $30.79 per share. If the price of BofA stock rises above $30.79 per share, the lower limit is the stock price minus $30.79. The upper limit is the price of BofA stock. A warrant to buy one share of stock cannot sell at a price above the price of the underlying stock.

**FIGURE 25.1**

**Bank of America Group B Warrants on March 4, 2010**

The price of BofA Group B warrants on March 4, 2010, was higher than the lower limit. How far the warrant price lies above the lower limit will depend on

1. The variance of BofA's stock returns.
2. The time to the warrant's expiration date.
3. The risk-free rate of interest.
4. The stock price of BofA.
5. The exercise price.

These are the same factors that determine the value of a call option.

Table 25.1 provides some examples of warrants listed on the TSX and TSX-Venture. Many issuing companies are probably unknown to most students and exhibit high volatility. Not surprisingly, warrants are typically highly speculative investments and are common during corporate restructuring. For instance, Birchcliff Energy Ltd, an Alberta-based intermediate oil and gas company, raised $50 million in equity via preferred shares and warrant issues to reduce indebtedness. The warrants had an exercise price of $8.30, which was about a 25 percent premium over the trading price of the shares on the day the deal was announced back in July 2012.[3]

---

[3] B. Critchley, "Birchcliff Energy Raises $50-million through Potentially Dilutive Issue," *Financial Post*, Postmedia Network Inc., July 20, 2012, business.financialpost.com/2012/07/20/birchcliff-raises-50-million-through-potentially-dilutive-issue/.

**TABLE 25.1**

**Warrants Trading on the TSX and TSX-V**

| Warrants at 2014.05.01 | | | | | | | Warrant | | | | | |
| Company | Stock close | Bid/ ask | Symbol | Stock exch. | Exercise price | Recent close | Bid/ ask | Intrinsic value | Time value | Lev'ge | Years left | Expiry date |
|---|---|---|---|---|---|---|---|---|---|---|---|---|
| Adherex Technologies unit | n.a. | | AHX.WT | TSX | 1.44 | 0.6302 | | 0 | 0 | n.a. | 1.9 | 30-Mar-16 |
| Alamos Gold Inc | 10.250 | | AGI.WT | TSX | 29.48 | 0.970 | | −19.23 | 0.97 | 10.57 | 4.3 | 30-Aug-18 |
| Amaya Gaming Group Inc | 6.950 | | AYA.WT | TSX | 3 | 4.200 | | 3.95 | 0.25 | 1.65 | 1.0 | 30-Apr-15 |
| | 6.950 | | AYA.WT.A | TSX | 6.25 | 2.050 | | 0.7 | 1.35 | 3.39 | 1.8 | 31-Jan-16 |
| Aston Hill Oil & Gas Incm | 5.450 | | OGF.WT | TSX | 5.25 | 0.200 | | 0.2 | 0 | 27.25 | 0.1 | 10-Jun-14 |
| Aston Hill VIP Income Fd | 10.260 | | VIP.WT | TSX | 10.16 | 0.110 | | 0.1 | 0.01 | 93.27 | 0.1 | 10-Jun-14 |
| Birchcliff Energy Ltd | 12.710 | | BIR.WT | TSX | 8.3 | 4.480 | | 4.41 | 0.07 | 2.84 | 0.3 | 8-Aug-14 |
| Brand Leaders Income Fund | 11.800 | | HBL.WT | TSX | 11.74 | 0.1102 | Bid | 0.06 | 0.05 | 107.27 | 0.3 | 15-Aug-14 |
| Cdn Life Cos Split Corp unit | n.a. | | LFE.WT.B | TSX | n.a. | 1.600 | | 0 | 0 | n.a. | 0.1 | 02-Jun-14 |
| Crocodile Gold Corp | 0.235 | | CRK.WT | TSX | 2.25 | 0.020 | Bid | −2.015 | 0.02 | 11.75 | 1.9 | 24-Mar-16 |
| Dalradian Resources Inc | 0.900 | | DNA.WT | TSX | 0.9 | 0.145 | | 0 | 0.145 | 6.21 | 0.8 | 19-Feb-15 |
| Delta Gold Corp | 0.020 | Bid | DLT.WT | TSX-VEN | 0.17 | 0.010 | Ask | −0.15 | 0.01 | 2 | 3.4 | 14-Sep-17 |
| Dunav Resources Ltd | 0.075 | | DNV.WT | TSX-VEN | 0.5 | 0.005 | Bid | −0.425 | 0.005 | 15 | 1.8 | 6-Mar-16 |
| Dundee Precious Mtls Inc | 3.640 | | DPM.WT.A | TSX | 3.25 | 1.290 | | 0.39 | 0.9 | 2.82 | 1.6 | 20-Nov-15 |

Most warrant issuers are energy or resource related and exhibit high volatility. As a result, warrants are typically highly speculative.

Source: Material reprinted with the express permission of *National Post*, a division of Postmedia Network Inc.

**CONCEPT QUESTION**

- In March 2010, BofA also sold 150.4 million Group A warrants with a per-share exercise price of $13.30. The warrants were sold for $8.35 each. If BofA shares were trading at $16.43 per share, what were the upper and lower limits of the Group A warrants?

## 25.2 THE DIFFERENCE BETWEEN WARRANTS AND CALL OPTIONS

From the holder's point of view, warrants are similar to call options on common stock. A warrant, like a call option, gives its holder the right to buy common stock at a specified price. Warrants usually have an expiration date, though in most cases they are issued with longer lives than call options. From the firm's point of view, however, a warrant is very different from a call option on the company's common stock.

The most important difference between call options and warrants is that call options are issued by individuals and warrants are issued by firms. When a warrant is exercised, a firm must issue new shares of stock. Each time a warrant is exercised, the number of shares outstanding increases.

To illustrate, suppose the Endrun Company issues a warrant giving holders the right to buy one share of common stock at $25. Further, suppose the warrant is exercised. Endrun must print one new stock certificate. In exchange for the stock certificate, it receives $25 from the holder.

In contrast, when a call option is exercised, there is no change in the number of shares outstanding. Suppose Ms. Eager holds a call option on the common stock of the Endrun Company. The call option gives Ms. Eager the right to buy one share of the common stock for $25. If Ms. Eager chooses to exercise the call option, a seller, say Mr. Swift, is obliged to give her one share of Endrun's common stock in exchange for $25. If Mr. Swift does not already own a share, he must enter the stock market and buy one. The call option is a side bet between buyers and sellers on the value of the Endrun Company's common stock. When a call option is exercised, one investor gains and the other loses. The total number of shares outstanding of the Endrun Company remains constant, and no new funds are made available to the company.

## EXAMPLE 25.1

To see how warrants affect the value of the firm, imagine that Mr. Canuck and Ms. America are two investors who have together purchased six ounces of platinum. At the time they bought the platinum, Mr. Canuck and Ms. America each contributed one-half of the cost, which we will assume was $3,000 for six ounces, or $500 an ounce. (They each contributed $1,500.) They incorporated, printed two share certificates, and named the firm the CA Company. Each certificate represents a one-half claim to the platinum. Mr. Canuck and Ms. America each own one certificate. They have formed a company with platinum as its only asset.

### A Call Is Issued

Suppose Mr. Canuck later decides to sell to Ms. North a call option issued on Mr. Canuck's share. The call option gives Ms. North the right to buy Mr. Canuck's share for $1,800 within the next year. If the price of platinum rises above $600 per ounce, the firm will be worth more than $3,600 and each share will be worth more than $1,800. If Ms. North decides to exercise her option, Mr. Canuck must turn over his stock certificate and receive $1,800.

How will the firm be affected by the exercise? The number of shares will remain the same. There will still be two shares, now owned by Ms. America and Ms. North. If the price of platinum rises to $700 an ounce, each share will be worth $2,100 (or $4,200/2). If Ms. North exercises her option at this price, she will profit by $300.

### A Warrant Is Issued Instead

This story changes if a warrant is issued. Suppose that Mr. Canuck does not sell a call option to Ms. North. Instead, Mr. Canuck and Ms. America have a shareholders' meeting. They vote that CA Company will issue a warrant and sell it to Ms. North. The warrant will give Ms. North the right to receive a share of the company at an exercise price of $1,800.[4] If Ms. North decides to exercise the warrant, the firm will issue another share certificate and give it to Ms. North in exchange for $1,800.

From Ms. North's perspective, the call option and the warrant seem to be the same. The exercise prices of the warrant and the call are the same: $1,800. It is still advantageous for Ms. North to exercise the option when the price of platinum exceeds $600 per ounce. However, we will show that Ms. North actually makes less in the warrant situation due to dilution.

The CA Company must also consider dilution. Suppose the price of platinum increases to $700 an ounce and Ms. North exercises her warrant. Two things will occur:

1. Ms. North will pay $1,800 to the firm.
2. The firm will print one share certificate and give it to Ms. North. The certificate will represent a one-third claim on the platinum of the firm.

---

[4] The sale of the warrant brings cash into the firm. We assume that the sale proceeds immediately leave the firm through a cash dividend to Mr. Canuck and Ms. America. This simplifies the analysis, because the firm with warrants then has the same total value as the firm without warrants.

Because Ms. North contributes $1,800 to the firm, the value of the firm increases. It is now worth

New value of firm = Value of platinum + Contribution by Ms. North

= $4,200 + $1,800

= $6,000

Because Ms. North has a one-third claim on the firm's value, her share is worth $2,000 (or $6,000/3). By exercising the warrant, Ms. North gains $2,000 − $1,800 = $200. This is illustrated in Table 25.2.

TABLE 25.2

**Effect of Call Option and Warrant on the CA Company**

|  | Price of platinum per share | |
|---|---|---|
| Value of firm | $ 700 | $ 600 |
| No warrant or option: | | |
| Mr. Canuck's share | $2,100 | $1,800 |
| Ms. America's share | 2,100 | 1,800 |
| Firm | $4,200 | $3,600 |
| Call option: | | |
| Mr. Canuck's claim | $ 0 | $1,800 |
| Ms. America's claim | 2,100 | 1,800 |
| Ms. North's claim | 2,100 | 0 |
| Firm | $4,200 | $3,600 |
| Warrant: | | |
| Mr. Canuck's share | $2,000 | $1,800 |
| Ms. America's share | 2,000 | 1,800 |
| Ms. North's share | 2,000 | 0 |
| Firm | $6,000 | $3,600 |

If the price of platinum is $700, the value of the firm is equal to the value of six ounces of platinum plus the excess dollars paid into the firm by Ms. North. This amount is $4,200 + $1,800 = $6,000.

**Dilution**

Why does Ms. North only gain $200 in the warrant case while gaining $300 in the call option case? The key is dilution, that is, the creation of another share. In the call option case, she contributes $1,800 and receives one of the two outstanding shares. That is, she receives a share worth $2,100 (or $\frac{1}{2}$ × $4,200). Her gain is $300 (or $2,100 − $1,800). We rewrite this gain as

**Gain on Exercise of Call:**

$$\frac{\$4,200}{2} - \$1,800 = \$300 \tag{25.1}$$

In the warrant case, she contributes $1,800 and receives a newly created share. She now owns one of the three outstanding shares. Because the $1,800 remains in the firm, her share is worth $2,000 [($4,200 + $1,800)/3]. Her gain is $200 ($2,000 − $1,800). We rewrite this gain as

**Gain on Exercise of Warrant:**

$$\frac{\$4,200 + \$1,800}{2 + 1} - \$1,800 = \$200 \tag{25.2}$$

Warrants also affect accounting numbers. Warrants and (as we shall see) convertible bonds cause the number of shares to increase. This causes the firm's net income to be spread over a larger number of shares, thereby decreasing earnings per share (EPS). Firms with significant amounts of warrants and convertible issues must report earnings on a *primary* basis and a *fully* diluted basis.

### How the Firm Can Hurt Warrant Holders

The platinum firm owned by Mr. Canuck and Ms. America has issued a warrant to Ms. North that is *in the money* and about to expire. One way that Mr. Canuck and Ms. America can hurt Ms. North is to pay themselves a large dividend. This could be funded by selling a substantial amount of platinum. The value of the firm would fall, and the warrant would be worth much less.

**CONCEPT**
**QUESTIONS**

- What is the key difference between a warrant and a traded call option?
- Why does dilution occur when warrants are exercised?
- How can the firm hurt warrant holders?

## 25.3   WARRANT PRICING AND THE BLACK–SCHOLES MODEL (ADVANCED)

We now wish to express the gains from exercising a call and a warrant in more general terms. The gain on a call can be written as

**Gain from Exercising a Single Call:**

$$\underbrace{\frac{\text{Firm's value net of debt}}{N}}_{\text{(Value of a share of stock)}} - \text{Exercise price} \tag{25.3}$$

Equation (25.3) generalizes equation (25.1). We define the *firm's value net of debt* to be the total firm value less the value of the debt. The total firm value is \$4,200 in our example, and there is no debt. The $N$ stands for the number of shares outstanding, which is 2 in our example. The ratio on the left is the value of a share of stock.

The gain on a warrant can be written as

**Gain from Exercising a Single Warrant:**

$$\underbrace{\frac{\text{Firm's value net of debt} + \text{Exercise price} \times N_w}{N + N_w}}_{\text{(Value of a share of stock after warrant is exercised)}} - \text{Exercise price} \tag{25.4}$$

Equation (25.4) generalizes equation (25.2). The numerator of the left-hand term is the firm's value net of debt *after* the warrant is exercised. It is the sum of the firm's value net of debt *prior* to the warrant's exercise plus the proceeds the firm receives from the exercise. The proceeds equal the product of the exercise price and the number of warrants. The number of warrants appears as $N_w$. (Our analysis uses the plausible assumption that all warrants in the money will be exercised.) Note that $N_w = 1$ in our numerical example. The denominator, $N + N_w$, is the number of shares outstanding after the exercise of the warrants. The ratio on the left is the value of a share of stock after exercise. By rearranging terms, equation (25.4) can be rewritten as[5]

**Gain from Exercising a Single Warrant:**

$$\frac{N}{N + N_w} \times \underbrace{\left( \frac{\text{Firm's value net of debt}}{N} - \text{Exercise price} \right)}_{\text{(Gain from a call on a firm with no warrants)}} \tag{25.5}$$

---

[5] To derive equation (25.5), we should separate "Exercise price" in equation (25.4). This yields

$$\frac{\text{Firm's value net of debt}}{N + N_w} - \frac{N}{N + N_w} \times \text{Exercise price}$$

By rearranging terms, we obtain equation (25.5).

Equation (25.5) relates the gain on a warrant to the gain on a call. Note that the term within parentheses is equation (25.3). Thus, the gain from exercising a warrant is a proportion of the gain from exercising a call in a firm without warrants. The proportion $N/(N + N_w)$ is the ratio of the number of shares in the firm without warrants to the number of shares after all the warrants have been exercised. This ratio must always be less than 1. Thus, the gain on a warrant must be less than the gain on an identical call in a firm without warrants. Note that $N/(N + N_w) = 200/300 = \frac{2}{3}$ in our example, which explains why Ms. North gains $300 on her call yet gains only $200 on her warrant.

Our discussion to this point implies that the Black–Scholes model must be adjusted for warrants. When a call option is issued to Ms. North, we know that the exercise price is $1,800 and the time to expiration is one year. Though we have not posited the price of the stock, the variance of the stock, or the interest rate, we could easily provide these data for a real-world situation. Thus, we could use the Black–Scholes model to value Ms. North's call.

Suppose that the warrant is to be issued tomorrow to Ms. North. We know the number of warrants to be issued, the warrant's expiration date, and the exercise price. Using our assumption that the warrant proceeds are immediately paid out as a dividend, we could use the Black–Scholes model to value the warrant. We would first calculate the value of an identical call. The warrant price is the call price multiplied by the ratio $N/(N + N_w)$. As stated earlier, this ratio is $\frac{2}{3}$ in our example.

• How can the Black–Scholes model be used to value warrants?

## 25.4    CONVERTIBLE BONDS

A **convertible bond** is similar to a bond with warrants. The most important difference is that a bond with warrants can be separated into distinct securities, but a convertible bond cannot. A convertible bond gives the holder the right to exchange it for a given number of shares of stock at any time up to and including the maturity date of the bond.

Preferred stock can frequently be converted into common stock. A share of convertible preferred stock is the same as a convertible bond except that it has no maturity date. Table 25.3 provides examples of convertible bonds. Much like with warrants, many issuers are from the resource or mining industries.

**TABLE 25.3**

### Convertible Bonds*

| Issuer | Symbol | Coupon | Maturity | Last price | Parity | Yield to maturity | Premium | Conversion ratio | Conversion price | Symbol | Share price |
|---|---|---|---|---|---|---|---|---|---|---|---|
| Advantage Energy | AAV.DB.H | 5.00% | 30-Jan-15 | 102 | 71.63 | 2.88% | 40.20% | 11.63 | 8.6 | AAV | 6.22 |
| Aecon Group Inc. | ARE.DB | 7.00% | 30-Sep-14 | 102.3 | 86.42 | 0.26% | 18.23% | 5.26 | 19 | ARE | 16.44 |
| Aecon Group Inc. | ARE.DB.A | 6.25% | 31-Oct-15 | 107.1 | 86.42 | 1.20% | 23.78% | 5.26 | 19 | ARE | 16.44 |
| Aecon Group Inc. | ARE.DB.B | 5.50% | 31-Dec-18 | 111.5 | 82.1 | 2.81% | 35.64% | 5 | 20 | ARE | 16.44 |
| Ag Growth Intl | AFN.DB.A | 5.25% | 31-Dec-18 | 106.5 | 83.18 | 3.70% | 27.34% | 1.82 | 55 | AFN | 46 |
| Algoma Central Corp | ALC.DB | 6.00% | 31-Mar-18 | 113 | 100.32 | 2.43% | 12.63% | 6.49 | 15.4 | ALC | 15.45 |
| Altus Group | AIF.DB | 5.75% | 31-Dec-17 | 113.8 | 110.75 | 1.77% | 2.70% | 5.38 | 18.6 | AIF | 20.61 |
| Altus Group | AIF.DB.A | 6.75% | 30-Jun-17 | 207.6 | 206 | −17.81% | 0.73% | 10 | 10 | AIF | 20.61 |
| Anderson Energy | AXL.DB | 7.50% | 31-Jan-16 | 84.75 | 14.52 | 19.88% | 471.78% | 64.52 | 1.55 | AXL | 0.23 |
| Anderson Energy | AXL.DB.B | 7.25% | 30-Jun-17 | 76.01 | 13.24 | 17.64% | 474.30% | 58.82 | 1.7 | AXL | 0.23 |
| Boralex | BLX.DB | 6.75% | 30-Jun-17 | 118.59 | 110 | 0.66% | 6.65% | 8 | 12.5 | BLX | 13.9 |
| CargoJet | CJT.DB.A | 6.50% | 30-Mar-17 | 180 | 179.57 | −15.03% | 0.24% | 8.51 | 11.75 | CJT | 21.1 |

* Data retrieved on May 29, 2014. Material reprinted with the express permission of *National Post*, a division of Postmedia Network Inc.

EXAMPLE **25.2**

Oceandoor Technology is one of the most important manufacturers of rigid magnetic disk drives for computers. Its stock is traded over the counter (OTC).

On November 1, 2014, Oceandoor raised $300 million by issuing 6.75 percent convertible subordinated debentures due in 2030. It planned to use the proceeds to invest in new plant and equipment. Like typical debentures, they had a sinking fund and were callable. Oceandoor's bonds differed from other debentures in their convertible feature. Each bond was convertible into 23.53 shares of common stock of Oceandoor any time before maturity. The number of shares received for each bond (23.53 in this example) is called the **conversion ratio**.

Bond traders also speak of the **conversion price** of the bond. This is calculated as the ratio of the face value of the bond to the conversion ratio. Because the face value of each Oceandoor bond was $1,000, the conversion price was $42.50 (= $1,000/23.53). The bondholders of Oceandoor could give up bonds with a face value of $1,000 and receive 23.53 shares of Oceandoor common stock. This was equivalent to paying $42.50 (= $1,000/23.53) for each share of Oceandoor common stock received.

When Oceandoor issued its convertible bonds, its common stock was trading at $22.625 per share. The conversion price of $42.5 was 88 percent higher than the actual common stock price. This 88 percent is referred to as the **conversion premium**. It reflects the fact that the conversion option in Oceandoor convertible bonds was *out of the money*. This conversion premium is typical.

Convertibles are almost always protected against stock splits and stock dividends. If Oceandoor's common stock had been split two for one, the conversion ratio would have increased from 23.53 to 47.06.

*Conversion ratio, conversion price,* and *conversion premium* are well-known terms in the financial community. For that reason alone, you should master the concepts they represent. However, conversion price and conversion premium implicitly assume that the bond is selling at par. If the bond is selling at another price, the terms have little meaning. By contrast, *conversion ratio* can have a meaningful interpretation regardless of the price of the bond.

 CONCEPT QUESTION

• What are the conversion ratio, the conversion price, and the conversion premium?

# 25.5 THE VALUE OF CONVERTIBLE BONDS

The value of a convertible bond can be described in terms of three components: straight bond value, conversion value, and option value.[6] We examine these three components below.

## Straight Bond Value

The straight bond value is what the convertible bonds would sell for if they could not be converted into common stock. It will depend on the general level of interest

---

[6] For a similar treatment, see Richard Brealey and Stewart Myers, *Principles of Corporate Finance*, 10th ed. (Boston: McGraw-Hill, 2010), Chapter 22; and James C. Van Horne, *Financial Market Rates and Flows*, 6th ed. (Englewood Cliffs, NJ: Prentice-Hall, 2001), Chapter 11.

rates and on the default risk. Suppose that straight debentures issued by Oceandoor had been rated A, and A-rated bonds were priced to yield 4 percent per six months on November 1, 2014. The straight bond value of Oceandoor convertible bonds can be determined by discounting the $33.75 semiannual coupon payment and principal amount at 4 percent:

$$\text{Straight bond} = \sum_{t=1}^{32} \frac{33.75}{1.04^t} + \frac{\$1,000}{(1.04)^{32}}$$
$$= \$33.75 \times A_{0.04}^{32} + \frac{\$1,000}{(1.04)^{32}}$$
$$= \$603.23 + \$285.06$$
$$= \$888.29$$

The straight bond value of a convertible bond is a minimum value. The price of Oceandoor's convertible could not have gone lower than the straight bond value.

Figure 25.2 illustrates the relationship between straight bond value and stock price. In Figure 25.2 we have been somewhat dramatic and implicitly assumed that the convertible bond is default free. In this case the straight bond value does not depend on the stock price, so it is graphed as a straight line.

**FIGURE 25.2**

**Minimum Value of a Convertible Bond versus the Value of the Stock for a Given Interest Rate**

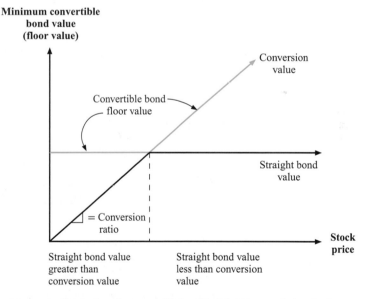

As shown, the minimum, or floor, value of a convertible bond is either its straight bond value or its conversion value, whichever is greater.

## Conversion Value

The value of convertible bonds depends on conversion value. **Conversion value** is what the bonds would be worth if they were immediately converted into common stock at current prices. Typically, we compute conversion value by multiplying the number of shares of common stock that will be received when the bond is converted by the current price of the common stock.

On November 1, 2014, each Oceandoor convertible bond could have been converted into 23.53 shares of Oceandoor common stock. Oceandoor common stock was selling for $22.625. Thus, the conversion value was $23.53 \times \$22.625 = \$532.37$. A convertible cannot sell for less than its conversion value. Arbitrage prevents this from happening. If Oceandoor's convertible sold for less than $532.37, investors would buy the bonds and convert them into common stock and sell the stock. The profit would be the difference between the value of the stock sold and the bond's conversion value.

Thus, convertible bonds have two minimum values: the straight bond value and the conversion value. The conversion value is determined by the value of the firm's underlying common stock. This is illustrated in Figure 25.2. As the value of common stock rises and falls, the conversion value rises and falls with it. When the value of Oceandoor's common stock increased by $1, the conversion value of its convertible bonds increased by $23.53.

## Option Value

The value of a convertible bond will generally exceed both the straight bond value and the conversion value.[7] This occurs because holders of convertibles need not convert immediately. Instead, by waiting they can take advantage of whichever is greater in the future: the straight bond value or the conversion value. This option to wait has value, and it raises the value over both the straight bond value and the conversion value.

When the value of the firm is low, the value of convertible bonds is most significantly influenced by their underlying value as straight debt. However, when the value of the firm is very high, the value of convertible bonds is mostly determined by their underlying conversion value. In the language of Bay Street, the convertible is "trading off the stock." This is illustrated in Figure 25.3.

FIGURE 25.3

**Value of a Convertible Bond versus the Value of the Stock for a Given Interest Rate**

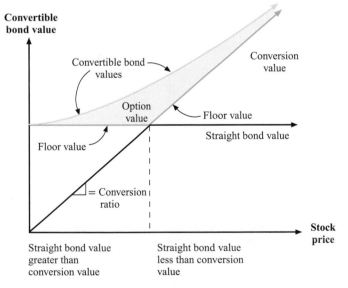

As shown, the value of a convertible bond is the sum of its floor value and its option value (highlighted region).

---

[7] The most plausible exception is when conversion would provide the investor with a dividend much greater than the interest available prior to conversion. The optimal strategy here could very well be to convert immediately, implying that the market value of the bond would exactly equal the conversion value. Other exceptions occur when the firm is in default or the bondholders are forced to convert.

The bottom portion of the figure implies that the value of a convertible bond is the maximum of its straight bond value and its conversion value, plus its option value:

$$\begin{array}{c} \text{Value of} \\ \text{convertible bond} \end{array} = \begin{array}{c} \text{The greater of (straight bond} \\ \text{value and conversion value)} \end{array} + \begin{array}{c} \text{Option} \\ \text{value} \end{array}$$

Suppose the Moulton Company has outstanding 1,000 shares of common stock and 100 bonds. Each bond has a face value of $1,000 at maturity. They are pure discount bonds and pay no coupons. At maturity each bond can be converted into 10 shares of newly issued common stock.

What circumstances will make it advantageous for holders of Moulton's convertible bonds to convert to common stock at maturity?

If the holders of the convertible bonds convert, they will receive $100 \times 10 = 1,000$ shares of common stock. Because there were already 1,000 shares, the total number of shares outstanding becomes 2,000 upon conversion. Thus, converting bondholders own 50 percent of the value of the firm, $V$. If they do not convert, they will receive $100,000 or $V$, whichever is less. The choice for the holders of Moulton's bonds is obvious. They should convert if 50 percent of $V$ is greater than $100,000. This will be true whenever $V$ is greater than $200,000. This is illustrated as follows:

**Payoff to Convertible Bondholders and Stockholders of the Moulton Company**

|  | (1)<br>$V \leq \$100,000$ | (2)<br>$\$100,000 < V \leq \$200,000$ | (3)<br>$V > \$200,000$ |
|---|---|---|---|
| Decision: | Bondholders will<br>not convert | Bondholders will<br>not convert | Bondholders<br>will convert |
| Convertible bondholders | $V$ | $100,000 | $0.5\,V$ |
| Stockholders | 0 | $V - \$100,000$ | $0.5\,V$ |

## 25.6   REASONS FOR ISSUING WARRANTS AND CONVERTIBLES

The reasons for issuing convertible debt and warrants are a topic with great potential for confusion. To separate fact from fantasy, we present a rather structured argument. In this section and the next one we focus on convertible debt. Given the similarities between convertible debt and warrants, discussed in Section 25.4, the arguments apply to warrants as well. We first compare convertible debt with straight debt. Then we compare convertible debt with equity. For each comparison, we ask, in what situations is the firm better off with convertible debt and in what situations is it worse off?

### Convertible Debt versus Straight Debt

Convertible debt pays a lower interest rate than does otherwise identical straight debt. For example, if the interest rate is 10 percent on straight debt, the interest rate on convertible debt might be 9 percent. Investors will accept a lower interest rate on a convertible because of the potential gain from conversion.

Imagine a firm that seriously considers both convertible debt and straight debt and then finally decides to issue convertibles. When will this decision benefit the firm and when will it hurt the firm? We consider two situations.

**The Stock Price Later Rises So That Conversion Is Indicated**    The firm clearly likes to see the stock price rise. However, it would have benefited even more had it previously issued straight debt instead of a convertible. While the firm paid out a lower interest rate than it would have with straight debt, it will be obliged to sell the convertible holders a chunk of the equity below its current market price.

**The Stock Price Later Falls or Does Not Rise Enough to Justify Conversion**    The firm hates to see the stock price fall. However, as long as the stock price does fall, the firm is glad that it had previously issued convertible debt instead of straight debt. This is because the interest rate on convertible debt is lower. Because conversion does not take place, our comparison of interest rates is all that is needed.

**Summary**    Compared to straight debt, the firm is worse off having issued convertible debt if the underlying stock subsequently does well. The firm is better off having issued convertible debt if the underlying stock subsequently does poorly. In an efficient market, one cannot predict stock prices. Thus, we cannot argue that convertibles either dominate or are dominated by straight debt.

## Convertible Debt versus Common Stock

Next, imagine a firm that seriously considers both convertible debt and common stock and then finally decides to issue convertibles. When will this decision benefit the firm and when will it hurt the firm? We consider our two situations.

**The Stock Price Later Rises So That Conversion Is Indicated**    The firm is better off having previously issued a convertible instead of equity. To see this, consider the Oceandoor case. The firm could have issued stock for $22.625. Instead, by issuing a convertible, the firm effectively received $42.50 for a share upon conversion.[8]

**The Stock Price Later Falls or Does Not Rise Enough to Justify Conversion**    No firm wants to see the stock price fall. However, given that the price did fall, the firm would have been better off if it had previously issued stock instead of a convertible. The firm would have benefited by issuing stock above its later market price. That is, the firm would have received more than the subsequent worth of the stock. However, the drop in stock price did not affect the value of the convertible much because the straight bond value serves as a floor.

**Summary**    Compared with equity, the firm is better off having issued convertible debt if the underlying stock subsequently does well. The firm is worse off having issued convertible debt if the underlying stock subsequently does poorly. One cannot predict future stock price in an efficient market. Thus, we cannot argue that issuing convertibles is better or worse than issuing equity. The above analysis is summarized in Table 25.4.

Modigliani and Miller (MM) pointed out that abstracting from taxes and bankruptcy costs, the firm is indifferent between issuing stock and issuing debt. The MM relationship is a quite general one. Their pedagogy could be adjusted to show that the firm is indifferent to whether it issues convertibles or issues other instruments. To conserve space (and the patience of students), we have omitted a full-blown proof of MM in a world with convertibles. However, the above results are perfectly consistent with MM. Now we turn to the real-world view of convertibles.

---

[8] This $42.50 is based on the conversion price in reference to the bond's issue value at par.

**TABLE 25.4**

**The Cases for and against Convertible Bonds**

|  | If firm subsequently does poorly | If firm subsequently prospers |
|---|---|---|
| Convertible bonds (CBs) | No conversion occurs because of low stock price. | Conversion occurs because of high stock price. |
| Compared to: | | |
| Straight bonds | CBs provide cheap financing because coupon rate is lower. | CBs provide expensive financing because bonds are converted, which dilutes existing equity. |
| Common stock | CBs provide expensive financing because firm could have issued common stock at high prices. | CBs provide cheap financing because firm issues stock at high prices when bonds are converted. |

## The "Free Lunch" Story

The previous discussion suggests that issuing a convertible bond is no better and no worse than issuing other instruments. Unfortunately, many corporate executives fall into the trap of arguing that issuing convertible debt is actually better than issuing alternative instruments. This is a free lunch type of explanation, of which we are quite critical.

**EXAMPLE 25.4**

The stock price of RW Company is $20. Suppose that this company can issue subordinated debentures at 10 percent. It can also issue convertible bonds at 6 percent with a conversion value of $800. The conversion value means that the holders can convert a convertible bond into 40 (or $800/$20) shares of common stock.

A company treasurer who believes in free lunches might argue that convertible bonds should be issued because they represent a cheaper source of financing than either subordinated bonds or common stock. The treasurer will point out that if the company does poorly and the price does not rise above $20, the convertible bondholders will not convert the bonds into common stock. In this case, the company will have obtained debt financing at below-market rates by attaching worthless equity kickers. On the other hand, if the firm does well and the price of its common stock rises to $25 or above, convertible holders will convert. The company will issue 40 shares. The company will receive a bond with face value of $1,000 in exchange for issuing 40 shares of common stock, implying a conversion price of $25. The company will have issued common stock *de facto* at $25 per share, or 20 percent above the $20 common stock price prevailing when the convertible bonds were issued. This enables it to lower its cost of equity capital. Thus, the treasurer happily points out, regardless of whether the company does well or poorly, convertible bonds are the cheapest form of financing.

Although this argument may sound quite plausible at first glance, there is a flaw. The treasurer is comparing convertible financing *with straight debt* when the stock subsequently falls. However, the treasurer compares convertible financing *with common stock* when the stock subsequently rises. This is an unfair mixing of comparisons. By contrast, our analysis of Table 25.4 was fair, because we examined both stock increases and stock decreases when comparing a convertible with each alternative instrument. We found that no single alternative dominated convertible bonds in both up and down markets.

## The "Expensive Lunch" Story

Suppose we stand the treasurer's argument on its head by comparing (1) convertible financing with straight debt when the stock rises and (2) convertible financing with equity when the stock falls.

From Table 25.4, we see that convertible debt is more expensive than straight debt when the stock subsequently rises. The firm's obligation to sell convertible holders a chunk of the equity at a below-market price more than offsets the lower interest rate on a convertible.

Also from Table 25.4, we see that convertible debt is more expensive than equity when the stock subsequently falls. Had the firm issued stock, it would have received a price higher than its subsequent worth. Therefore, the expensive lunch story implies that convertible debt is an inferior form of financing. Of course, we dismiss both the free lunch and the expensive lunch arguments.

## A Reconciliation

In an efficient financial market there is neither a free lunch nor an expensive lunch. Convertible bonds can be neither cheaper nor more expensive than other instruments. A convertible bond is a package of straight debt and an option to buy common stock. The difference between the market value of a convertible bond and the value of a straight bond is the price investors pay for the call option feature. In an efficient market this is a fair price.

In general, if a company prospers, issuing convertible bonds will turn out to be worse than issuing straight bonds and better than issuing common stock. In contrast, if a company does poorly, convertible bonds will turn out to be better than issuing straight bonds and worse than issuing common stock.

- What is wrong with the simple view that it is cheaper to issue a bond with a warrant or a convertible feature because the required coupon is lower than on straight debt?
- What is wrong with the free lunch story?
- What is wrong with the expensive lunch story?

# 25.7    WHY ARE WARRANTS AND CONVERTIBLES ISSUED?

Research on firms that issue convertible bonds and warrants shows that they are different from other firms. Here are some of the differences:

1. The bond ratings of firms using convertibles are lower than those of other firms.[9]
2. Convertibles tend to be used by smaller firms with high growth rates and more financial leverage.[10]
3. Convertibles are usually subordinated and unsecured.

As we showed in Tables 25.1 and 25.3, in Canada, junior mining and resource companies frequently finance with convertibles and warrants. The kind of company that uses these securities provides clues to why they are issued. Sensible explanations involve matching cash flows, risk synergy, and agency costs.

## Matching Cash Flows

If financing is costly, it makes sense to issue securities whose cash flows match those of the firm. A young, risky, aspiring growth firm might prefer to issue convertibles

---

[9] E. F. Brigham, "An Analysis of Convertible Debentures," *Journal of Finance* (March 1966).

[10] W. H. Mikkelson, "Convertible Calls and Security Returns," *Journal of Financial Economics* (September 1981), established this result for U.S. convertible bonds. R. G. Storey and C. R. Dipchand, "Factors Related to the Conversion Record of Convertible Securities," *Journal of Financial Research* (Winter 1978), studied the conversion record in Canada over the period 1946–1975. They found that 70 percent of the convertible issues were converted, suggesting that most issuers experienced growth.

or bonds with warrants because these will have lower initial interest costs. When the firm is successful, the convertibles (or warrants) will be converted. This causes expensive dilution, but it occurs when the firm can best afford it.

## Risk Synergy

Another argument for convertible bonds and bonds with warrants is that they are useful when it is very costly to assess the risk of the issuing company. Suppose you are evaluating a new product offered by a start-up company. The new product is a biogenetic virus that may increase the yields of corn crops in northern climates. It may also cause cancer. This type of product is difficult to value properly. Thus, the risk of the company is very hard to determine—it may be high, or it may be low. If you could be sure the risk of the company was high, you would price the bonds for a high yield, say 15 percent. If it was low, you would price them at a lower yield, say 10 percent.

Convertible bonds and bonds with warrants can protect somewhat against mistakes of risk evaluation. Convertible bonds and bonds with warrants have two components: a straight bond and a call option on the company's underlying stock. If the company turns out to be a low-risk company, the straight bond component will have high value and the call option will have low value. However, if the company turns out to be a high-risk company, the straight bond component will have low value and the call option will have high value. This is illustrated in Table 25.5.

**TABLE 25.5**

### A Hypothetical Case of the Yields on Convertible Bonds

|  | Firm risk | |
|---|---|---|
|  | Low | High |
| Straight bond yield | 10% | 15% |
| Convertible bond yield | 6 | 7 |

The yields on straight bonds reflect the risk of default. The yields on convertibles are not sensitive to default risk.

However, although risk has effects on value that cancel each other out in convertibles and bonds with warrants, the market and the buyer nevertheless must assess the firm's potential in order to value securities. It is not clear that the effort involved is that much less than is required for a straight bond.

## Agency Costs

Convertible bonds can resolve agency problems associated with raising money. In Chapter 23, we showed that a straight bond is like a risk-free bond minus a put option on the assets of the firm. This creates an incentive for creditors to force the firm into low-risk activities. In contrast, holders of common stock have incentives to adopt high-risk projects. High-risk projects with negative net present value (NPV) transfer wealth from bondholders to shareholders.

If these conflicts cannot be resolved, the firm may be forced to pass up profitable investment opportunities. However, because convertible bonds have an equity component, less expropriation of wealth can occur when convertible debt is issued instead of straight debt.[11] In other words, convertible bonds mitigate agency costs. One implication of this approach is that convertible bonds should have fewer restrictive debt covenants than do straight bonds. Casual empirical evidence seems to bear this out.

---

[11] A. Barnea, R. A. Haugen, and L. Senbet, *Agency Problems and Financial Contracting*, Prentice-Hall Foundations of Science Series (New York: Prentice-Hall, 1985), Chapter VI.

## Backdoor Equity

A popular theory of convertibles views them as backdoor equity.[12] The basic story is that young, small, high-growth firms cannot usually issue debt on reasonable terms due to high financial distress costs. However, the owners may be unwilling to issue equity if current stock prices are too low. This is the same as the argument in Table 25.4 that convertibles offer cheap financing relative to common stock if the firm subsequently prospers. It also suggests that issuing convertibles signals that a firm expects high growth.

Lewis, Ragolski, and Seward examine the risk shifting and backdoor equity theories of convertible bond debt. They find evidence for both theories.

In May 2004, Gemini Energy Corp. issued $10 million of convertible debt. The issue had a 10-year maturity and a coupon rate of 10 percent. The bonds were convertible to common shares at $4. At the time of issue, Gemini was trading in Toronto at $3.60 a share. There are many explanations for why convertible debt made sense for Gemini. One of the biggest reasons is that, although it is far from a small firm, it faced high financing costs. Moreover, with its share value lower than years before (in 2000, the shares traded at over $100), convertibles were viewed as backdoor equity.

 • **Why do firms issue convertible bonds and bonds with warrants?**

## 25.8  CONVERSION POLICY

There is one aspect of convertible bonds that we have omitted so far. Firms are frequently granted a call option on the bond. The typical arrangements for calling a convertible bond are simple. When the bond is called, the holder has about 30 days to choose between the following:

1. Converting the bond to common stock at the conversion ratio.
2. Surrendering the bond and receiving the call price in cash.

What should bondholders do? It should be clear that if the conversion value of the bond is greater than the call price, conversion is better than surrender, and if the conversion value is less than the call price, surrender is better than conversion. If the conversion value is greater than the call price, the call is said to **force conversion**.

What should financial managers do? Calling the bonds does not change the value of the firm as a whole. However, an optimal call policy can benefit the shareholders at the expense of the bondholders. Because we are speaking of dividing a pie of fixed size, the optimal call policy is very simple: do whatever the bondholders do not want you to do.

Bondholders would love the shareholders to call the bonds when the bonds' market value is below the call price. Shareholders would be giving bondholders extra value. Alternatively, should the value of the bonds rise above the call price, the bondholders would love the shareholders not to call the bonds, because bondholders would be allowed to hold onto a valuable asset.

There is only one policy left. This is the policy that maximizes shareholder value and minimizes bondholder value. This policy is as follows:

Call the bond when its value is equal to the call price.

---

[12] J. Stein, "Convertible Bonds as Backdoor Equity Financing," *Journal of Financial Economics* (August 1992). See also Craig M. Lewis, Richard J. Ragolski, and James K. Seward, "Understanding the Design of Convertible Debt," *The Journal of Applied Corporate Finance* (Spring 1998).

It is a puzzle that firms do not always call convertible bonds when the conversion value reaches the call price. Ingersoll examined the call policies of 124 firms between 1968 and 1975.[13] In most cases he found that the company waited to call the bonds until the conversion value was much higher than the call price. The median company waited until the conversion value of its bonds was 44 percent higher than the call price. This is not even close to the above strategy. Why?

The reason is that if firms attempt to implement the above optimal strategy, it may not be truly optimal. Recall that bondholders have 30 days to decide whether to convert bonds to common stock or to surrender bonds for the call price in cash. In 30 days the stock price could drop, forcing the conversion value below the call price. If so, the convertible is "out of the money" and the firm is giving away money. The firm would be giving up cash for common stock worth much less. Because of this possibility, firms in the real world usually wait until the conversion value is substantially above the call price before they trigger the call.[14] This is sensible.

**CONCEPT QUESTIONS**

- Why will convertible bonds not be voluntarily converted to stock before expiration?
- When should firms force conversion of convertibles? Why?

## 25.9

# SUMMARY AND CONCLUSIONS

1. A warrant gives the holder the right to buy shares of common stock at an exercise price for a given period of time. Typically, warrants are issued in a package with privately placed bonds. Afterward, they become detached and trade separately.

2. A convertible bond is a combination of a straight bond and a call option. The holder can give up the bond in exchange for shares of stock.

3. Convertible bonds and warrants are like call options. However, there are some important differences:

   a. Warrants and convertible securities are issued by corporations. Call options are traded between individual investors.

      i. Warrants are usually issued privately and are combined with a bond. In most cases, the warrants can be detached immediately after the issue. In some cases, warrants are issued with preferred stock, with common stock, in executive compensation programs, or as stand-alone issues.

      ii. Convertibles are bonds that can be converted into common stock.

---

[13] J. Ingersoll, "An Examination of Corporate Call Policies on Convertible Bonds," *Journal of Finance* (May 1977). See also M. Harris and A. Raviv, "A Sequential Signalling Model of Convertible Debt Policy," *Journal of Finance* (December 1985). Harris and Raviv describe a signalling equilibrium that is consistent with Ingersoll's result. They show that managers with favourable information will delay calls to avoid depressing stock prices.

[14] See Paul Asquith, "Convertible Bonds Are Not Called Late," *Journal of Finance* (September 1995). On the other hand, the stock market usually reacts negatively to the announcement of a call. For example, see A. K. Singh, A. R. Cowan, and N. Nayan, "Underwritten Calls of Convertible Bonds," *Journal of Financial Economics* (March 1991); and M. A. Mazzeo and W. T. Moore, "Liquidity Costs and Stock Price Response to Convertible Security Calls," *Journal of Business* (July 1992).

Ederington, Caton, and Campbell test various theories on when it is optimal to call convertibles. They find evidence consistent for the preceding 30-day "safety margin" theory. They also find that calls of in-the-money convertibles are highly unlikely if dividends to be received (after conversion) exceed the company's interest payment. See Louis H. Ederington, Gary L. Caton, and Cynthia J. Campbell, "To Call or Not to Call Convertible Debt," *Financial Management* (Spring 1997).

      iii. Call options are sold separately by individual investors (called *writers* of call options).

   b. Warrants and call options are exercised for cash. The holder of a warrant gives the company cash and receives new shares of the company's stock. The holder of a call option gives another individual cash in exchange for shares of stock. When someone converts a bond, it is exchanged for common stock. As a consequence, bonds with warrants and convertible bonds have different effects on corporate cash flow and capital structure.

   c. Warrants and convertibles cause dilution to the existing shareholders. When warrants are exercised and convertible bonds converted, the company must issue new shares of common stock. The percentage ownership of the existing shareholders will decline. New shares are not issued when call options are exercised.

4. Many arguments, both plausible and implausible, are given for issuing convertible bonds and bonds with warrants. One plausible rationale for such bonds has to do with risk. Convertibles and bonds with warrants are associated with risky companies. Lenders can do several things to protect themselves from high-risk companies:

   a. Require high yields.

   b. Lend less or not at all to firms whose risk is difficult to assess.

   c. Impose severe restrictions on such debt.

Another useful way to protect against risk is to issue bonds with equity kickers. This gives the lenders the chance to benefit from risks and reduces the conflicts between bondholders and shareholders concerning risk.

5. A puzzle particularly vexes financial researchers: convertible bonds usually have call provisions. Companies appear to delay calling convertibles until the conversion value greatly exceeds the call price. From the shareholders' standpoint, the optimal call policy is to call the convertibles when the conversion value equals the call price.

---

**KEY TERMS**

| | | |
|---|---|---|
| Conversion premium 740 | Conversion value 741 | Warrants 733 |
| Conversion price 740 | Convertible bond 739 | |
| Conversion ratio 740 | Force conversion 748 | |

---

**QUESTIONS & PROBLEMS**

### Conversion Price

25.1  A convertible bond has a conversion ratio of 24.6. What is the conversion price?

### Conversion Ratio

25.2  A convertible bond has a conversion price of $61.50. What is the conversion ratio of the bond?

### Conversion Premium

25.3  Eckely Inc. recently issued bonds with a conversion ratio of 17.5. If the stock price at the bond issue date was $48.53, what was the conversion premium?

### Convertible Bonds

25.4  Hannon Home Products Inc. recently issued $2 million worth of 8 percent convertible debentures. Each convertible bond has a face value of $1,000. Each convertible bond can be converted into 18.5 shares of common stock anytime before maturity. The stock price is $38.20, and the market value of each bond is $1,070.

   *a.* What is the conversion ratio?

   *b.* What is the conversion price?

   *c.* What is the conversion premium?

   *d.* What is the conversion value?

   *e.* If the stock price increases by $2, what is the new conversion value?

**Warrant Value**

25.5 A warrant gives its owner the right to purchase three shares of common stock at an exercise price of $41 per share. The current market price of the stock is $47. What is the minimum value of the warrant?

**Convertible Bond Value**

25.6 An analyst has informed you that at the issuance of a company's convertible bonds, one of the two following sets of relationships existed:

|  | Scenario A | Scenario B |
|---|---|---|
| Face value of bond | $1,000 | $1,000 |
| Straight value of convertible bond | 900 | 950 |
| Market value of convertible bond | 1,000 | 900 |

Assume the bonds are available for immediate conversion. Which of the two scenarios do you believe is more likely? Why?

25.7 Sportime Fitness Centre Inc. issued convertible bonds with a conversion price of $51. The bonds are available for immediate conversion. The current price of the company's common stock is $44 per share. The current market price of the convertible bonds is $990. The convertible bonds' straight value is not known.

    *a.* What is the minimum price for the convertible bonds?
    *b.* Explain the difference between the current market price of each convertible bond and the value of the common stock into which it can be immediately converted.

**Convertible Bonds**

25.8 You own a callable, convertible bond with a conversion ratio of 24.25. The stock is currently selling for $48 per share. The issuer of the bond has announced a call at a call price of $110. What are your options? What should you do?

**Warrant Value**

25.9 General Modems has five-year warrants that currently trade in the open market. Each warrant gives its owner the right to purchase one share of common stock for an exercise price of $55.

    *a.* Suppose the stock is currently trading for $51 per share. What is the lower limit on the price of the warrant? What is the upper limit?
    *b.* Suppose the stock is currently trading for $58 per share. What is the lower limit on the price of the warrant? What is the upper limit?

**Convertible Bonds**

25.10 Flaherty Corp. has just issued a 30-year, callable, convertible bond with 6 percent annual coupon payments. The bond has a conversion price of $130. The company's stock is selling for $26 per share. The owner of the bond will be forced to convert if the bond's conversion value is ever greater than or equal to $1,100. The required return on an otherwise identical non-convertible bond is 11 percent.

    *a.* What is the minimum value of the bond?
    *b.* If the stock price were to grow by 13 percent per year forever, how long would it take for the bond's conversion value to exceed $1,100?

25.11 Rob Stevens is the CEO of Isner Construction Inc. and owns 950,000 shares of stock. The company currently has 6 million shares of stock and convertible bonds with a face value of $40 million outstanding. The convertible bonds have a conversion price of $38, and the stock is currently selling for $45.

    *a.* What percentage of the firm's common stock does Rob own?

   *b.* If the company decides to call the convertible bonds and force conversion, what percentage of the firm's common stock will Rob own? He does not own any convertible bonds.

**Warrants**

25.12 Survivor Inc., an all-equity firm, has eight shares of stock outstanding. Yesterday, the firm's assets consisted of nine ounces of platinum, currently worth $850 per ounce. Today, the company issued Anna Wu a warrant for its fair value of $850. The warrant gives Anna the right to buy a single share of the firm's stock for $1,000 and can be exercised only on its expiration date one year from today. The firm used the proceeds from the issue to immediately purchase an additional ounce of platinum.

   *a.* What was the price of a single share of stock *before* the warrant was issued?

   *b.* What was the price of a single share of stock immediately *after* the warrant was issued?

   *c.* Suppose platinum is selling for $975 per ounce on the warrant's expiration date in one year. What will be the value of a single share of stock on the warrant's expiration date?

25.13 The capital structure of Ricketti Enterprises Inc. consists of 15 million shares of common stock and 1 million warrants. Each warrant gives its owner the right to purchase one share of common stock for an exercise price of $19. The current stock price is $25, and each warrant is worth $7. What is the new stock price if all warrant holders decide to exercise today?

**Convertible Calculations**

25.14 You have been hired to value a new 25-year, callable, convertible bond. The bond has a 6.80 percent coupon rate, payable annually. The conversion price is $150, and the stock currently sells for $35.50. The stock price is expected to grow at 12 percent per year. The bond is callable at $1,150, but based on prior experience, it won't be called unless the conversion value is $1,250. The required return on this bond is 9 percent. What value would you assign to this bond?

**Warrant Value**

25.15 Superior Clamps Inc. has a capital structure consisting of 6 million shares of common stock and 750,000 warrants. Each warrant gives its owner the right to purchase one share of newly issued common stock for an exercise price of $20. The warrants are European and will expire one year from today. The market value of the company's assets is $105 million, and the annual variance of the returns on the firm's assets is 0.15. Treasury bills that mature in one year yield a continuously compounded interest rate of 7 percent. The company does not pay a dividend. Use the Black–Scholes model to determine the value of a single warrant.

25.16 Omega Airline's capital structure consists of 3.2 million shares of common stock and zero-coupon bonds with a face value of $18 million that mature in six months. The firm just announced that it will issue warrants with an exercise price of $75 and six months until expiration to raise the funds to pay off its maturing debt. Each warrant can be exercised only at expiration and gives its owner the right to buy a single newly issued share of common stock. The firm will place the proceeds from the warrant issue immediately into Treasury bills. The market value balance sheet shows that the firm will have assets worth $210 million after the announcement. The company does not pay dividends. The standard deviation of the returns on the firm's assets is 50 percent, and Treasury bills with a six-month maturity yield 6 percent. How many warrants must the company issue today to be able to use the proceeds from the sale to pay off the firm's debt obligation in six months?

# S&S Air's Convertible Bond

Christine Guthrie was recently hired by S&S Air Inc. to assist the company with its short-term financial planning and to evaluate the company's performance. Christine graduated from university five years ago with a finance degree. She has been employed in the finance department of a Fortune 500 company since then.

S&S Air was founded 10 years ago by two friends, Mark Sexton and Tammy Story. The company has manufactured and sold light airplanes over this period, and the company's products have received excellent reviews for safety and reliability. The company has a niche market in that it sells primarily to individuals who own and fly their own airplanes. The company has two models: the Birdie, which sells for $53,000, and the Eagle, which sells for $78,000.

S&S Air is not publicly traded, but the company needs new funds for investment opportunities. In consultation with Tony Jones of underwriter Raines and Warren, Christine decides that a convertible bond issue with a 20-year maturity is the way to go. She meets with the owners, Mark and Tammy, and presents her analysis of the convertible bond issue. Because the company is not publicly traded, Christine looks at comparable publicly traded companies and determines that the average price–earnings (P/E) ratio for the industry is 17.5. EPS for the company is $1.75. With this in mind, Christine concludes that the conversion price should be $45 per share.

Several days later, Tammy, Mark, and Christine meet again to discuss the potential bond issue. Both Tammy and Mark have researched convertible bonds and have questions for Christine. Tammy begins by asking Christine if the convertible bond issue will have a lower coupon rate than a comparable bond without a conversion feature. Christine replies that to sell the bond at par value, the convertible bond issue requires a 5 percent coupon rate with a conversion value of $680.56, while a plain vanilla bond would have an 8 percent coupon rate. Tammy nods in agreement, and she explains that the convertible bonds are a win–win form of financing. She states that if the value of the company stock does not rise above the conversion price, the company will have

issued debt at a cost below the market rate (5 percent instead of 8 percent). If the company's stock does rise to the conversion value, the company will have effectively issued stock at above the current value.

Mark immediately disagrees, arguing that convertible bonds are a no-win form of financing. He argues that if the value of the company stock rises to $45, the company is forced to sell stock at the conversion price. This means the new shareholders (those who bought the convertible bonds) benefit from a bargain price. Put another way, if the company prospers, it would have been better to have issued straight debt so that the gains would not be shared.

Christine goes back to Tony for help. As Tony's assistant, you are asked to prepare another memo answering the following questions:

1. Why do you think Christine is suggesting a conversion price of $45? Given that the company is not publicly traded, does it even make sense to talk about a conversion price?
2. What is the floor value of the S&S Air convertible bond?
3. What is the conversion ratio of the bond?
4. What is the conversion premium of the bond?
5. What is the value of the option?
6. Is there anything wrong with Tammy's argument that it is cheaper to issue a bond with a convertible feature because the required coupon is lower?
7. Is there anything wrong with Mark's argument that a convertible bond is a bad idea because it allows new shareholders to participate in gains made by the company?
8. How can you reconcile the arguments made by Tammy and Mark?
9. During the debate, a question comes up concerning whether the bonds should have an ordinary (not Canada plus) call feature. Christine confuses everybody by stating, "The call feature lets S&S Air force conversion, thereby minimizing the problem Mark has identified." What is she talking about? Is she making sense?

# 26

# Derivatives and Hedging Risk

EXECUTIVE SUMMARY

Managing risk is one of the most important tasks confronting corporate management, and financial markets are always willing to introduce new products to meet a need, either real or perceived. Consider credit derivatives, also known as credit default swaps (CDSs). A credit derivative is an option-like instrument that allows the seller of the derivative to put an underlying bond to the purchaser if a credit event, such as bankruptcy, occurs. Credit derivatives were practically unheard of in 2000, but according to the International Swaps and Derivatives Association (ISDA), the notional value of these instruments had grown to US$54.6 trillion by July 2008. After the global financial crisis, however, the value of credit derivatives fell, and by July 2010, their notional value was US$26.3 trillion, a 13.7 percent decrease from $30.4 trillion at the end of 2009. The market for interest rate derivatives, which includes interest rate and cross-currency swaps, had grown larger, however, with a notional value of $434.1 trillion in July 2010. This was a 1.7 percent increase from $426.8 trillion at year-end 2009. In this chapter, we explore a variety of derivative contracts that allow a company's management to control risk.

## Derivatives, Hedging, and Risk

The name *derivatives* is self-explanatory. A derivative is a financial instrument whose payoffs and values are derived from, or depend on, something else. Often we speak of the thing that the derivative depends on as the *primitive* or the *underlying*. For example, in Chapter 23 we studied how options work. An option is a derivative. The value of a call option depends on the value of the underlying stock on which it is written. Actually, call options are quite complicated examples of derivatives. The vast majority of derivatives are simpler than call options. Most derivatives are forward or futures agreements or what are called swaps, and we will study each of these in some detail.

Why do firms use derivatives? The answer is that derivatives are tools for changing the firm's risk exposure. Derivatives are to finance what scalpels are to surgery. By using derivatives, the firm can cut away unwanted portions of risk exposure and even transform the exposures into quite different forms. A central point in finance is that risk is undesirable. In our chapters on risk and return, we pointed out that individuals would choose risky securities only if the expected return compensated for the risk. Similarly, a firm should accept a project with high risk only if the return on the project compensates for this risk. Not surprisingly, then, firms are usually looking for ways to reduce their risk. When the firm reduces its risk exposure, it is said to be **hedging**. Hedging offsets the firm's risk, such as the risk in a project, by one or more transactions in the financial markets.

Derivatives can also be used merely to change or even increase the firm's risk exposure. When this occurs, the firm is *speculating* on the movement of some economic variables—those that underlie the derivative. For example, if a derivative is purchased that will rise in value if interest rates rise, and if the firm has no offsetting exposure to interest rate changes, then the firm is speculating that interest rates will rise and result in a profit on its derivatives position. Using derivatives to translate an opinion about whether interest rates or some other economic variable will rise or fall is the opposite of hedging—it is risk enhancing. Speculating on your views on the economy and using derivatives to profit if that view turns out to be correct is not necessarily wrong. However, the speculator should always remember that sharp tools cut deep. If the opinions on which the derivatives position is based turn out to be incorrect, then the consequences can prove costly. Efficient market theory teaches how difficult it is to predict what markets will do. Many unfavourable experiences with derivatives occur not from their use as instruments for hedging and offsetting risk, but, rather, from speculation.

## The Impact of Financial Risk: The Credit Crisis of 2007–2009

The greatest credit crisis since the Great Depression of the 1930s started in the U.S. housing market and spread around the world. After recovering from the collapse of the dot-com bubble, the U.S. economy enjoyed a period of low interest rates and easy access to financing. Optimistic about growth and eager to obtain higher returns, investors and financial institutions took on increased credit and liquidity risks. Expansion of the U.S. mortgage market resulted.

Financial markets provided a favourable setting for financial engineering focused on credit risk in the form of structured securitization products. One example is the growth and seizure of the Canadian market for asset-backed commercial paper. Another example is the market for CDSs, a type of derivative discussed later in this chapter, which grew from approximately US$900 billion in 2001[1] to around US$54.6 trillion in July 2008. A good part of this growth was due to investors misusing CDSs to implement "bets" on the credit default of issuers as opposed to hedging risk.

The confidence of investors in the United States and globally was also shaken by the collapse and rescue of several financial institutions in the United Kingdom and the United States in early 2008. Panic resulted in the autumn of 2008 when Lehman Brothers was allowed to fail. At the time of its collapse and bankruptcy filing, Lehman Brothers was the fourth-largest U.S. investment bank and largest bankruptcy filing to that point. Lehman's collapse greatly intensified the 2008 credit crisis and contributed to the evaporation of nearly US$10 trillion in market capitalization from global equity markets in October 2008.

The credit crisis led to a global recession and the implementation of bailout packages tallying in the billions of dollars. Governments around the world have since implemented an ambitious set of changes to financial institution regulation aimed at controlling excessive risk-taking. At the time of writing in July 2014, the European economy is still recovering from the crisis and the sovereign debt crisis that followed.

## 26.1    FORWARD CONTRACTS

We can begin our discussion of hedging by considering forward contracts. You have probably been dealing in forward contracts your whole life without knowing it. To illustrate, suppose you walk into a bookstore on, say, February 1 to buy the best-seller *Eating Habits of the Rich and Famous*. The cashier tells you that the book is currently sold out, but he takes your phone number, saying that he will reorder it for you. He says the book will cost $10. If you agree on February 1 to pick up and pay $10 for the book when called, you and the cashier have engaged in a **forward contract**. That is, you have agreed both to pay for the book and to pick it up when the bookstore notifies you. Since you are agreeing to buy the book at a later date, you are *buying* a forward contract on February 1. In commodity parlance, you will be **taking delivery** when you pick up the book. The book is called the **deliverable instrument**.

---

[1] Yves Smith, "Credit Default Swaps and Bank Leverage," Naked Capitalism, April 16, 2008, www.nakedcapitalism.com/2008/04/credit-default-swaps-and-bank-leverage.html.

The cashier, acting on behalf of the bookstore, is selling a forward contract. (Alternatively, we say that he is writing a forward contract.) The bookstore has agreed to turn the book over to you at the predetermined price of $10 as soon as it arrives. The act of turning the book over to you is called **making delivery**. Table 26.1 illustrates the book purchase. Note that the agreement takes place on February 1. The price and the conditions for sale are set at that time. In this case, the sale will occur when the book arrives. In other cases, an exact date of sale would be given. However, *no* cash changes hands on February 1; cash changes hands only when the book arrives.

**TABLE 26.1**

**Illustration of Book Purchase as a Forward Contract**

|  | February 1 | Date book arrives |
|---|---|---|
| | Buyer agrees to | Buyer |
| | 1.  Pay purchase price of $10. | 1.  Pays purchase price of $10. |
| | 2.  Receive book when it arrives. | 2.  Receives book. |
| | Seller agrees to | Seller |
| | 1.  Give up book. | 1.  Gives up book. |
| | 2.  Accept payment of $10 when book arrives. | 2.  Accepts payment of $10. |

Note that cash does not change hands on February 1. Cash changes hands when the book arrives.

Though forward contracts may have seemed exotic to you before you began this chapter, you can see that they are quite common. Forward contracts occur frequently in business. Every time a firm orders an item that cannot be delivered immediately, a forward contract takes place. Sometimes, particularly when the order is small, an oral agreement will suffice. Other times, particularly when the order is larger, a written agreement is necessary.

Note that a forward contract is not an option. Both the buyer and the seller are obliged to perform under the terms of the contract. In contrast, the buyer of an option *chooses* whether or not to exercise the option.

A forward contract should be contrasted with a **cash transaction**, that is, a transaction where exchange is immediate. Had the book been on the bookstore's shelf, your purchase of it would have been a cash transaction.

**CONCEPT QUESTIONS**

- What is a forward contract?
- Give examples of forward contracts in your life.

# 26.2   FUTURES CONTRACTS

A variant of the forward contract takes place on financial exchanges. Contracts on exchanges are usually called **futures contracts**. There are a number of futures exchanges around the world, with the CME Group among the largest, combining the old Chicago Mercantile Exchange (CME) and the Chicago Board of Trade (CBT). However, the two are still separate trading platforms. The New York Mercantile Exchange (NYM) is also now owned by the CME Group. Another notable exchange is the London International Financial Futures and Options Exchange (LIFFE).

Table 26.2 gives a partial *Wall Street Journal* listing for selected futures contracts. Taking a look at the corn contracts in the left portion of the table, note that the contracts trade on the CBT, one contract calls for the delivery of 5,000 bushels of corn, and prices are quotes in cents per bushel. The months in which the contracts mature are given in the first column.

**TABLE 26.2**

## Data on Futures Contracts, Wednesday, June 4, 2014

**Futures Contracts | WSJ.com/commodities**

### Metal & Petroleum Futures

| | Open | High | Low | Settle | Chg | Open Int |
|---|---|---|---|---|---|---|
| **Copper-High (CMX)-25,000 lbs.; $ per lb.** | | | | | | |
| 14-Jun | 3.0965 | 3.1 | 3.091 | 3.0935 | -0.052 | 1,327 |
| 15-Jan | 3.103 | 3.103 | 3.0905 | 3.089 | -0.037 | 196 |
| **Gold (CMX)-100 troy oz.; $ per troy oz.** | | | | | | |
| 14-Dec | 1245.8 | 1250 | 1243.5 | 1245 | -0.2 | 53,925 |
| 15-Feb | 1248.4 | 1248.4 | 1244.3 | 1245.5 | -0.2 | 7,055 |
| 15-Dec | 1248.7 | 1248.7 | 1248.7 | 1249 | -0.1 | 11,531 |
| 16-Dec | 1262.4 | 1262.4 | 1262.4 | 1262.3 | -0.1 | 5,464 |
| **miNY Gold (CMX) - 50 troy oz.; $ per troy oz.** | | | | | | |
| 14-Aug | 1245.25 | 1248.25 | 1242.75 | 1244.25 | -0.25 | 526 |
| 14-Oct | 1254 | 1254 | 1244.75 | 1244.5 | -0.25 | 1 |
| **Palladium (NYM) - 50 troy oz.; $ per troy oz.** | | | | | | |
| 14-Sep | 837.7 | 838 | 832.7 | 837.15 | 0.45 | 40,163 |
| 14-Dec | 833.7 | 836.9 | 833.7 | 837.1 | 0.45 | 534 |
| **Platinum (NYM)-50 troy oz.; $ per troy oz.** | | | | | | |
| 14-Oct | 1431.1 | 1441.7 | 1422.6 | 1434.2 | 0.3 | 8,681 |
| 15-Jan | 1431.3 | 1431.3 | 1424.5 | 1434.5 | 0.3 | 96 |
| **Silver (CMX)-5,000 troy oz.; $ per troy oz.** | | | | | | |
| 14-Jun | 18.79 | 18.81 | 18.765 | 18.766 | 0.034 | 9 |
| 14-Dec | 18.88 | 18.955 | 18.81 | 18.878 | 0.03 | 16,913 |
| 15-Jan | 18.885 | 18.9 | 18.885 | 18.893 | 0.03 | 1,873 |
| **miNY Silver (CMX) - 2500 troy oz.; $ per troy oz.** | | | | | | |
| 14-Jly | 18.775 | 18.825 | 18.775 | 18.788 | 0.025 | 142 |
| 14-Sep | 18.85 | 18.85 | 18.85 | 18.825 | 0.025 | 12 |
| **Crude Oil, Light Sweet (NYM)-1,000 bbls.; $ per bbl.** | | | | | | |
| 14-Jly | 102.79 | 103.69 | 102.34 | 102.64 | -0.02 | 281,888 |
| 14-Aug | 102.05 | 102.94 | 101.63 | 101.93 | -0.04 | 185,985 |
| 14-Sep | 101.31 | 101.98 | 100.73 | 101.01 | -0.06 | 150,516 |
| 14-Dec | 98.36 | 98.98 | 97.88 | 98.15 | -0.1 | 236,469 |
| 15-Dec | 90.89 | 91.32 | 90.44 | 90.67 | -0.22 | 135,579 |
| **Heating Oil No. 2 (NYM)-42,000 gal.; $ per gal.** | | | | | | |
| 14-Dec | 2.8976 | 2.9049 | 2.8791 | 2.8815 | -0.0135 | 27,534 |
| 15-Jan | 2.9045 | 2.9045 | 2.8805 | 2.8848 | -0.0126 | 11,239 |
| **Gasoline-NY RBOB (NYM)-42,000 gal.; $ per gal.** | | | | | | |
| 14-Dec | 2.6312 | 2.6434 | 2.6186 | 2.6211 | -0.0124 | 25,559 |
| 15-Jan | 2.618 | 2.6271 | 2.6036 | 2.6059 | -0.0125 | 9,379 |
| **Natural Gas (NYM)-10,000 MMBtu.; $ per MMBtu.** | | | | | | |
| 14-Dec | 4.685 | 4.723 | 4.661 | 4.712 | 0.016 | 73,473 |
| 15-Jan | 4.754 | 4.779 | 4.715 | 4.768 | 0.016 | 69,936 |
| 15-Feb | 4.717 | 4.745 | 4.686 | 4.735 | 0.017 | 29,250 |
| 15-Mar | 4.634 | 4.637 | 4.582 | 4.628 | 0.014 | 53,070 |

### Agricultural Futures

| | Open | High | Low | Settle | Chg | Open Int |
|---|---|---|---|---|---|---|
| **Corn (CBT)-5,000 bu.; cents per bu.** | | | | | | |
| 14-Dec | 454 | 456.75 | 450.5 | 453.5 | -0.75 | 428,829 |
| 15-Mar | 464.25 | 466 | 460 | 463.25 | -0.25 | 66,166 |
| **Ethanol (CBT)-29,000 gal.; $ per gal.** | | | | | | |
| 14-Dec | 1.81 | 1.828 | 1.779 | 1.787 | -0.04 | 572 |
| 15-Jan | 1.778 | 1.778 | 1.739 | 1.745 | -0.04 | 467 |
| **Oats (CBT)-5,000 bu.; cents per bu.** | | | | | | |
| 14-Dec | 332 | 333.25 | 326.5 | 327.75 | -5 | 2,761 |
| 15-Mar | 323 | 323 | 319.25 | 320.5 | -3.5 | 218 |
| **Soybeans (CBT)-5,000 bu.; cents per bu.** | | | | | | |
| 15-Jan | 1227.5 | 1233.5 | 1220.5 | 1223.25 | -4.5 | 25,122 |
| 15-Mar | 1232 | 1237 | 1225 | 1227.5 | -4.25 | 11,148 |
| **Soybean Meal (CBT)-100 tons; $ per ton.** | | | | | | |
| 14-Dec | 397.9 | 399.4 | 390.5 | 391.3 | -6.6 | 83,485 |
| 15-Jan | 396.4 | 397.6 | 389.6 | 390 | -6.5 | 9,865 |
| **Soybean Oil (CBT)-60,000 lbs.; cents per lb.** | | | | | | |
| 14-Dec | 38.71 | 39.49 | 38.56 | 39.4 | 0.69 | 103,044 |
| 15-Jan | 38.82 | 39.67 | 38.77 | 39.59 | 0.68 | 9,823 |
| **Rough Rice (CBT)-2,000 cwt.; $ per cwt.** | | | | | | |
| 14-Nov | 1426 | 1434.5 | 1405.5 | 1406 | -20 | 941 |
| 15-Jan | 1438 | 1439 | 1421 | 1419 | -20 | 19 |
| **Wheat (CBT)-5,000 bu.; cents per bu.** | | | | | | |
| 14-Dec | 644.5 | 651.5 | 643 | 646.5 | 1.25 | 75,308 |
| 15-Mar | 663.75 | 668.75 | 662.75 | 664 | 0.75 | 25,188 |
| **Wheat (KC)-5,000 bu.; cents per bu.** | | | | | | |
| 14-Dec | 725.5 | 735.5 | 725 | 732.25 | 5.5 | 35,261 |
| 15-Mar | 738 | 742 | 735.5 | 737.5 | 5.25 | 4,398 |
| **Wheat (MPLS)-5,000 bu.; cents per bu.** | | | | | | |
| 14-Dec | 706 | 712.75 | 703.75 | 709 | 4 | 18,506 |
| 15-Mar | 718 | 721.75 | 715.75 | 717.5 | 3 | 5,465 |
| **Cattle-Feeder (CME)-50,000 lbs.; cents per lb.** | | | | | | |
| 14-Nov | 198.7 | 199.2 | 197.5 | 199.1 | 0.475 | 3,656 |
| 15-Mar | 192.75 | 193.375 | 192.475 | 193.3 | 0.4 | 694 |
| **Cattle-Live (CME)-40,000 lbs.; cents per lb.** | | | | | | |
| 14-Dec | 146.425 | 147.05 | 145.85 | 146.825 | 0.45 | 38,751 |
| 15-Feb | 147.925 | 148.7 | 147.45 | 148.45 | 0.475 | 16,660 |
| **Hogs-Lean (CME)-40,000 lbs.; cents per lb.** | | | | | | |
| 14-Dec | 94.55 | 94.7 | 93.1 | 94.275 | -0.475 | 36,961 |
| 15-Feb | 89.5 | 89.6 | 88.65 | 89.6 | -0.075 | 13,006 |
| **Lumber (CME)-110,000 bd. ft.; $ per 1,000 bd. ft.** | | | | | | |
| 14-Sep | 312.1 | 312.1 | 308.3 | 310 | -1 | 2,379 |
| 14-Nov | 312.1 | 315 | 311.6 | 311.8 | -2.2 | 194 |
| **Milk (CME)-200,000 lbs., cents per lb.** | | | | | | |
| 14-Nov | 19.5 | 19.53 | 19.39 | 19.42 | -0.03 | 2,053 |
| 14-Dec | 19 | 19.01 | 18.95 | 18.95 | 0.01 | 1,940 |
| **Cocoa (ICE-US)-10 metric tons; $ per ton.** | | | | | | |
| 14-Dec | 3,068 | 3,093 | 3,068 | 3,089 | 14 | 47,705 |
| 15-Mar | 3,072 | 3,089 | 3,065 | 3,087 | 18 | 27,363 |

| | Open | High | Low | Settle | Chg | Open Int |
|---|---|---|---|---|---|---|
| **Coffee (ICE-US)-37,500 lbs.; cents per lb.** | | | | | | |
| 14-Dec | 177.4 | 177.4 | 173.4 | 176 | -1 | 30,683 |
| 15-Mar | 180.25 | 180.25 | 176.15 | 178.7 | -1.05 | 16,287 |
| **Sugar-World (ICE-US)-112,000 lbs.; cents per lb.** | | | | | | |
| 15-Mar | 19.02 | 19.1 | 18.92 | 18.98 | -0.08 | 137,519 |
| 15-May | 18.93 | 19.07 | 18.92 | 18.97 | -0.05 | 26,503 |
| **Sugar-Domestic (ICE-US)-112,000 lbs.; cents per lb.** | | | | | | |
| 15-Mar | 26.5 | 26.5 | 26.25 | 26.33 | -0.05 | 962 |
| 15-May | 26.99 | 26.99 | 26.99 | 26.13 | -0.12 | 727 |
| **Cotton (ICE-US)-50,000 lbs.; cents per lb.** | | | | | | |
| 14-Dec | 78.1 | 78.33 | 77.22 | 77.88 | -0.22 | 80,152 |
| 15-Mar | 78.04 | 78.26 | 77.51 | 78.16 | 0.04 | 9,528 |
| **Orange Juice (ICE-US)-15,000 lbs.; cents per lb.** | | | | | | |
| 15-Jan | 168 | 168.8 | 167.5 | 167.95 | 0.45 | 333 |
| 15-Mar | 169.25 | 169.25 | 169.25 | 168.9 | 0.05 | 6 |

### Interest Rate Futures

| | Open | High | Low | Settle | Chg | Open Int |
|---|---|---|---|---|---|---|
| **Treasury Bonds (CBT)-$100,000; pts 32nds of 100%** | | | | | | |
| 14-Jun | 136-070 | 136-180 | 135-280 | 136-010 | -6 | 53,080 |
| 14-Sep | 135-090 | 135-230 | 134-310 | 135-050 | -6 | 665,617 |
| **Treasury Notes (CBT)-$100,000; pts 32nds of 100%** | | | | | | |
| 14-Jun | 125-065 | 125-145 | 125-015 | 125-050 | -3.5 | 72,490 |
| 14-Sep | 124-115 | 124-200 | 124-060 | 124-100 | -3.5 | 2,508,226 |
| **5 Yr. Treasury Notes (CBT)-$100,000; pts 32nds of 100%** | | | | | | |
| 14-Jun | 119-307 | 120-030 | 119-282 | 119-305 | -1 | 73,063 |
| 14-Sep | 119-057 | 119-105 | 119-030 | 119-057 | -0.7 | 1,970,658 |
| **2 Yr. Treasury Notes (CBT)-$200,000; pts 32nds of 100%** | | | | | | |
| 14-Jun | 110-032 | 110-037 | 110-020 | 110-022 | -0.5 | 67,003 |
| 14-Sep | 109-262 | 109-272 | 109-257 | 109-262 | 0.2 | 1,031,176 |
| **30 Day Federal Funds (CBT)-$5,000,000; 100 - daily avg.** | | | | | | |
| 14-Nov | 99.885 | 99.885 | 99.875 | 99.88 | -0.005 | 14,217 |
| 14-Dec | 99.88 | 99.88 | 99.865 | 99.875 | -0.005 | 32,350 |
| **10 Yr. Int. Rate Swaps (CBT)-$100,000; pts 32nds of 100%** | | | | | | |
| 14-Jun | 102-175 | 102-240 | 102-100 | 102-125 | -6.5 | 48,591 |
| **1 Month Libor (CME)-$3,000,000; pts of 100%** | | | | | | |
| 14-Jly | 99.85 | 99.85 | 99.85 | 99.85 | ... | 713 |
| 14-Oct | 99.84 | 99.84 | 99.84 | 99.845 | 0.0025 | 301 |
| **Eurodollar (CME)-$1,000,000; pts of 100%** | | | | | | |
| 14-Dec | 99.735 | 99.735 | 99.73 | 99.735 | ... | 902,464 |
| 15-Mar | 99.655 | 99.665 | 99.65 | 99.66 | ... | 978,608 |
| 16-Mar | 98.795 | 98.835 | 98.79 | 98.81 | 0.005 | 1,012,782 |

### Currency Futures

| | Open | High | Low | Settle | Chg | Open Int |
|---|---|---|---|---|---|---|
| **Japanese Yen (CME)-¥12,500,000; $ per 100¥** | | | | | | |
| 14-Sep | 0.9758 | 0.9767 | 0.9734 | 0.9743 | -0.0019 | 6,914 |
| 14-Dec | 0.9744 | 0.9768 | 0.9744 | 0.9749 | -0.0019 | 153 |
| **Canadian Dollar (CME)-CAD 100,000; $ per CAD** | | | | | | |
| 14-Dec | 0.911 | 0.9123 | 0.9089 | 0.9101 | -0.0021 | 2,930 |
| 15-Mar | 0.91 | 0.9103 | 0.91 | 0.9081 | -0.0021 | 518 |
| **British Pound (CME)-£62,500; $ per £** | | | | | | |
| 14-Sep | 1.6735 | 1.6755 | 1.669 | 1.673 | -0.0002 | 12,215 |
| 14-Dec | 1.6728 | 1.674 | 1.6717 | 1.6716 | -0.0002 | 88 |
| **Swiss Franc (CME)-CHF 125,000; $ per CHF** | | | | | | |
| 14-Jun | 1.1155 | 1.1175 | 1.1134 | 1.1147 | -0.0005 | 46,210 |
| 14-Sep | 1.1161 | 1.1179 | 1.1146 | 1.1157 | -0.0006 | 2,547 |
| **Australian Dollar (CME)-AUD 100,000; $ per AUD** | | | | | | |
| 14-Jun | 0.9258 | 0.9294 | 0.9244 | 0.927 | 0.0021 | 106,733 |
| 14-Sep | 0.9202 | 0.9242 | 0.9188 | 0.9212 | 0.0021 | 4,142 |
| **Mexican Peso (CME)-MXN 500,000; $ per MXN** | | | | | | |
| 14-Jun | 0.07713 | 0.07733 | 0.07703 | 0.07713 | -0.00003 | 129,378 |
| 14-Dec | 0.07625 | 0.07625 | 0.07625 | 0.07608 | -0.00002 | 231 |
| **Euro (CME)-€125,000; $ per €** | | | | | | |
| 14-Dec | 1.3621 | 1.3636 | 1.3602 | 1.3604 | -0.0023 | 5,864 |
| 15-Mar | 1.3617 | 1.3633 | 1.3617 | 1.3608 | -0.0024 | 290 |

### Index Futures

| | Open | High | Low | Settle | Chg | Open Int |
|---|---|---|---|---|---|---|
| **DJ Industrial Average (CBT)-$10 x index** | | | | | | |
| 14-Sep | 16595 | 16595 | 16595 | 16645 | 5 | 13 |
| **Mini DJ Industrial Average (CBT)-$5 x index** | | | | | | |
| 14-Jun | 16715 | 16733 | 16662 | 16718 | 5 | 125,898 |
| 14-Sep | 16643 | 16659 | 16590 | 16645 | 5 | 1,885 |
| **S & P 500 Index (CME)-$250 x index** | | | | | | |
| 14-Sep | 1914 | 1919.7 | 1910.7 | 1918.3 | 3.6 | 3,327 |
| 14-Dec | 1903 | 1912 | 1903 | 1910.6 | 3.6 | 3,432 |
| **Mini S & P 500 (CME)-$50 x index** | | | | | | |
| 14-Sep | 1915.75 | 1919.5 | 1908.75 | 1918.25 | 3.5 | 86,475 |
| 14-Dec | 1906.5 | 1911.25 | 1901.5 | 1910.5 | 3.5 | 5,184 |
| **Mini S & P Midcap 400 (CME)-$100 x index** | | | | | | |
| 14-Jun | 1381.1 | 1388.1 | 1375.7 | 1387.6 | 6.4 | 91,599 |
| **Nasdaq 100 (CME)-$100 x index** | | | | | | |
| 14-Jun | 3731 | 3751 | 3714 | 3743.25 | 12.5 | 16,270 |
| 14-Sep | 3734 | 3740 | 3722 | 3735.75 | 12.25 | 274 |
| **Mini Nasdaq 100 (CME)-$20 x index** | | | | | | |
| 14-Jun | 3732.8 | 3749.3 | 3714 | 3743.3 | 12.5 | 356,791 |
| 14-Sep | 3722 | 3741.8 | 3706.5 | 3735.8 | 12.3 | 11,686 |
| **Mini Russell 2000 (ICE-US)-$100 x index** | | | | | | |
| 14-Jun | 1123.7 | 1130.8 | 1116.6 | 1129.4 | 5.7 | 319,720 |
| 14-Sep | 1117.5 | 1125 | 1112.4 | 1124.5 | 5.5 | 2,116 |
| **Mini Russell 1000 (ICE-US)-$100 x index** | | | | | | |
| 14-Jun | 1070 | 1075.2 | 1068.7 | 1074.6 | 2.8 | 9,590 |
| **U.S. Dollar Index (ICE-US)-$1,000 x index** | | | | | | |
| 14-Jun | 80.6 | 80.72 | 80.51 | 80.71 | 0.11 | 48,903 |
| 14-Sep | 80.73 | 80.83 | 80.63 | 80.82 | 0.11 | 4,859 |

For the corn contract with a March maturity, the first number in the row is the opening price (464.25 cents per bushel), the next number is the high price for the day (466), and the following number is the low price for the day (460). The *settlement price* is the fourth number (463.25), and it is the closing price for the day. For purposes of marking to market, this is the figure used. The change, listed next, is the movement in the settlement price since the previous trading session (−0.25 cents). Finally, the *open interest* (66,166), the number of contracts outstanding at the end of the day, is shown.

To see how large futures trading can be, look at the CBT Treasury bond contracts (under the interest rate heading). One contract is for long-term Treasury bonds with a face, or par, value of $100,000. The total open interest for all months is about 718,700 contracts. The total face value outstanding is therefore $71.87 billion for this one type of contract!

Though we are discussing a futures contract, let us work with a forward contract first. Suppose you wrote a *forward* contract for December wheat at $6.46 on the CBT. From our discussion of forward contracts, this would mean that you would agree to turn over an agreed-upon number of wheat bushels for $6.46 per bushel on some specified date later in the month of December.

A futures contract differs somewhat from a forward contract. First, the seller can choose to deliver the wheat on any day during the delivery month, that is, the month of December. This gives the seller leeway that he would not have with a forward contract. When the seller decides to deliver, he notifies the exchange clearinghouse that he wants to do so. The clearinghouse then notifies an individual who bought a December wheat contract that she must stand ready to accept delivery within the next few days. Though each exchange selects the buyer in a different way, the buyer is generally chosen randomly. Because there are so many buyers at any one time, the buyer selected by the clearinghouse to take delivery almost certainly did not originally buy the contract from the seller now making delivery.

Second, futures contracts are traded on an exchange, whereas forward contracts are generally traded off an exchange. Because of this, there is generally a liquid market in futures contracts. A buyer can net out her futures position with a sale. A seller can net out his futures position with a purchase. This procedure is analogous to the *netting-out* process in the options markets. However, the buyer of an options contract can also walk away from the contract by not exercising it. If the buyer of a futures contract does not subsequently sell her contract, she must take delivery. In practice, over 95 percent of futures contracts are not settled through delivery. Most are offset by other contracts before the delivery date.

Third, and most important, the prices of futures contracts are **marked to the market** on a daily basis. That is, suppose that the price falls to $6.44 on Friday's close. Because all buyers lost two cents per bushel on that day, they each must turn over the two cents per bushel to their brokers within 24 hours, who subsequently remit the proceeds to the clearinghouse. Because all sellers gained two cents per bushel on that day, they each receive two cents per bushel from their brokers. Their brokers are subsequently compensated by the clearinghouse. Because there is a buyer for every seller, the clearinghouse must break even every day.

Now suppose that the price rises to $6.51 on the close of the following Monday. Each buyer receives seven cents ($6.51 − $6.44) per bushel and each seller must pay seven cents per bushel. Finally, suppose that, on Monday, a seller notifies his broker of his intention to deliver.[2] The delivery price will be $6.51, which is Monday's close.

---

[2] He will deliver on Wednesday, two days later.

## Illustration of Example Involving Marking to Market in Futures Contracts

Both buyer and seller originally transact at Thursday's closing price. Delivery takes place at Monday's closing price.[*]

| | Thursday, December 18 | Friday, December 19 | Monday, December 22 | Delivery (notification given by seller on Monday) |
|---|---|---|---|---|
| Closing price: | $6.46 | $6.44 | $6.51 | |
| Buyer | Buyer purchases futures contract at closing price of $6.46 /bushel. | Buyer must pay two cents/bushel to clearinghouse within one business day. | Buyer receives seven cents/ bushel from clearinghouse within one business day. | Buyer pays $6.51/bushel and receives wheat. |

Buyer's net payment of −$6.46 (or −$0.02 + $0.07 − $6.51) is the same as if buyer purchased a forward contract for $6.46/bushel.

| | | | | |
|---|---|---|---|---|
| Seller | Seller sells futures contract at closing price of $6.46/bushel. | Seller receives two cents/ bushel from clearinghouse within one business day. | Seller pays seven cents/bushel to clearinghouse within one business day. | Seller receives $6.51/bushel and delivers wheat within one business day. |

Seller's net receipts of $6.46 (or $0.02 − $0.07 + $6.51) are the same as if seller sold a forward contract for $6.46/bushel.

[*] For simplicity, we assume that buyer and seller both (1) initially transact at the same time and (2) meet in the delivery process. This is actually very unlikely to occur in the real world because the clearinghouse randomly assigns the buyer to take delivery.

There are clearly many cash flows in futures contracts. However, after all the dust settles, the *net price* to the buyer must be the price at which she bought originally. That is, an individual buying at Thursday's closing price of $6.46 and being called to take delivery on Monday pays two cents per bushel on Friday, receives seven cents per bushel on Monday, and takes delivery at $6.51. Her net outflow per bushel is −$6.46 (−$0.02 + $0.07 − $6.51), which is the price at which she contracted on Thursday. (Our analysis ignores the time value of money.) Conversely, an individual selling at Thursday's closing price of $6.46 and notifying his broker concerning delivery the following Monday receives two cents per bushel on Friday, pays seven cents per bushel on Monday, and makes delivery at $6.51. His net inflow per bushel is $6.46 ($0.02 − $0.07 + $6.51), which is the price at which he contracted on Thursday.

These details are presented in the box above. For simplicity, we assumed that the buyer and seller who initially transact on Thursday's close meet in the delivery process.[3] The point in the example is that the buyer's net payment of $6.46 per bushel is the same as if she purchased a forward contract for $6.46. Similarly, the seller's net receipt of $6.46 per bushel is the same as if he sold a forward contract for $6.46 per bushel. The only difference is the timing of the cash flows. The buyer of a forward contract knows that she will make a single payment of $6.46 on the expiration date. She will not need to worry about any other cash flows in the interim. Conversely, though the cash flows to the buyer of a futures contract will net to exactly $6.46 as well, the pattern of cash flows is not known ahead of time.

---

[3] As pointed out earlier, this is actually very unlikely to occur in the real world.

The mark-to-the-market provision on futures contracts has two related effects. The first concerns differences in net present value (NPV). For example, a large price drop immediately following purchase means an immediate outpayment for the buyer of a futures contract. Though the net outflow of $6.46 is still the same as under a forward contract, the present value (PV) of the cash outflows is greater to the buyer of a futures contract. Of course, the PV of the cash outflows is less to the buyer of a futures contract if a price rise followed purchase.[4] Though this effect could be substantial in certain theoretical circumstances, it appears to be of quite limited importance in the real world.[5]

Second, the firm must have extra liquidity to handle a sudden outflow prior to expiration. This added risk may make the futures contract less attractive.

Students frequently ask, "Why in the world would managers of the commodity exchanges ruin perfectly good contracts with these bizarre mark-to-the-market provisions?" Actually, the reason is a very good one. Consider the forward contract of Table 26.1 concerning the bookstore. Suppose that the public quickly loses interest in *Eating Habits of the Rich and Famous*. By the time the bookstore calls the buyer, other stores may have dropped the price of the book to $6. Because the forward contract was for $10, the buyer has an incentive not to take delivery on the forward contract. Conversely, should the book become a hot item selling at $15, the bookstore may simply not call the buyer.

As indicated, forward contracts have a very big flaw. Whichever way the price of the deliverable instrument moves, one party has an incentive to default. There are many cases in which defaults have occurred. One famous case concerned Coca-Cola. When the company began in the early twentieth century, Coca-Cola made an agreement to supply its bottlers and distributors with cola syrup at a constant price *forever*. Of course, subsequent inflation would have caused Coca-Cola to lose large sums of money had it honoured the contract. After much legal effort, Coke and its bottlers inserted an *inflation escalator clause* in the contract. Another famous case concerned Westinghouse. It seems the firm had promised to deliver uranium to certain utilities at a fixed price. The price of uranium skyrocketed in the 1970s, making Westinghouse lose money on every shipment. Westinghouse defaulted on its agreement. The utilities took Westinghouse to court but did not recover anything near what Westinghouse owed them.

The mark-to-the-market provisions minimize the chance of default on a futures contract. If the price rises, the seller has an incentive to default on a forward contract. However, after paying the clearinghouse, the seller of a futures contract has little reason to default. If the price falls, the same argument can be made for the buyer. Because changes in the value of the underlying asset are recognized daily, there is no accumulation of loss, and the incentive to default is reduced.

Because of this default issue, forward contracts generally involve individuals and institutions who know and can trust each other. But as early-twentieth-century film actor W. C. Fields said, "Trust everybody, but cut the cards." Lawyers earn a handsome living writing supposedly airtight forward contracts, even among friends. The genius of the mark-to-the-market system is that it can prevent default where it is most likely to occur—among investors who do not know each other. Early textbooks on futures contracts usually included a statement such as "No major default has ever occurred on the commodity exchanges." No textbook published after the Hunt brothers defaulted

---

[4] The direction is reversed for the seller of a futures contract. However, the general point that the NPV of cash flows may differ between forward and futures contracts holds for sellers as well.

[5] See John C. Cox, John E. Ingersoll, and Steven A. Ross, "The Relation between Forward Prices and Futures Prices," *Journal of Financial Economics* (December 1981).

on silver contracts in 1980 can make that claim.[6] Nevertheless, the extremely low default rate in futures contracts is truly impressive.

**CONCEPT**
**QUESTIONS**
- What is a futures contract?
- How is a futures contract related to a forward contract?
- Why do exchanges require futures contracts to be marked to market?

## 26.3 HEDGING

Now that we have determined how futures contracts work, we turn to hedging. There are two types of hedges: long and short. We discuss the short hedge first in Example 26.1.

---

**EXAMPLE 26.1**

In June, WildCan, an Alberta junior oil producer, anticipates pumping 1 million barrels of oil for the quarter closing at the end of September. WildCan's CFO, Michael Oleschuk, has two alternatives:

1. *Write futures contracts against anticipated production.* The September crude oil contract (1,000 barrels) on the New York Mercantile Exchange is trading at US$37.80 a barrel on June 1. The CFO executes the following transaction:

| Date of transaction | Transaction | Price per barrel |
|---|---|---|
| June 1 | Write 1,000 September futures contracts | US$37.80 |

2. *Produce the oil without writing a futures contract.* Alternatively, the CFO could have pumped the oil without benefit of a futures contract. The risk would be quite great here since no one knows what the cash price in September will be. If prices rise, he will profit. Conversely, he will lose if prices fall.

We say that strategy 2 is an unhedged position because there is no attempt to use the futures markets to reduce risk. Conversely, strategy 1 involves a hedge. That is, a position in the futures market offsets the risk of a position in the physical (that is, the actual) commodity.

Though hedging may seem quite sensible to you, it should be mentioned that not everyone hedges. The CFO of WildCan might reject hedging for at least two reasons.

First, he may simply be uninformed about hedging. Not everyone in business understands the hedging concept. Some executives do not want to use futures markets for hedging their inventories because they feel that the risks are too great.[7] However, we disagree. While there are large price fluctuations in these markets, hedging actually reduces the risk that an individual holding inventories bears.

---

[6] Amid political and inflationary pressure, the Hunt brothers sought to hedge themselves against the rampant printing of U.S. dollars by investing in silver and silver futures (they amassed over 200 million ounces of silver, about half of the world's supply). By 1980, silver prices rose from $5 to $55 per ounce, only to decline to around $10 by the end of March. The fall in the speculative asset forced the Hunt brothers into bankruptcy, as they could not pay the $135 million margin call. The government had to force the banks to bail the brothers out to prevent widespread failures. See www.traderslog.com/hunt-brothers-silver/ for more information.

[7] B. Kalymon, *Global Innovation and the Impact on Canada's Financial Markets* (Toronto: Wiley, 1989), Chapter 1, found that many Canadian managers expressed this view when hedging markets were relatively new.

Second, the CFO may have a special insight or some special information that commodity prices will rise. He would not be wise to lock in a price of US$37.80 if he expects the cash price in September to be well above this price.

Strategy 1 is called a **short hedge**, because WildCan reduces its risk by taking a short position in a futures contract. The short hedge is very common in business. It occurs whenever someone either anticipates receiving inventory or is holding inventory. WildCan was anticipating the production of crude oil. A refiner of gasoline may hold large quantities of crude, which are already paid for. However, the price to be received for gasoline is not known because no one knows what the market price will be when it is produced. The manufacturer may write futures contracts to lock in a sales price.

A mortgage officer may assemble mortgages slowly before selling them in bulk to a financial institution. Movements of interest rates affect the value of the mortgages during the time they are in inventory. The mortgage officer could sell Government of Canada bond futures contracts in order to offset this interest rate risk. (This last example is treated later in this chapter.)

---

**EXAMPLE 26.2**

---

On April 1, Alberta Chemical agreed to sell petrochemicals to a major customer in the future. The delivery dates and the prices have been determined. Because oil is a basic ingredient of the production process, Alberta Chemical will need to have large quantities of oil on hand. The firm can get the oil in one of two ways:

1. *Buy the oil as the firm needs it.* This is an unhedged position because, as of April 1, the firm does not know the prices it will later have to pay for the oil. Oil is quite a volatile commodity, so Alberta Chemical is bearing a good bit of risk. The key to this risk bearing is that the sales price has already been fixed. Thus, Alberta Chemical cannot pass on increased costs to the consumer.

2. *Buy futures contracts.*[8] The firm can buy futures contracts with expiration months corresponding to the dates on which inventory is needed. A futures contract locks in the purchase price to Alberta Chemical. Because there is a crude oil futures contract for every month, selecting the correct futures contract is not difficult. Many other commodities have only five contracts per year, frequently necessitating buying contracts one month away from the month of production.

As mentioned earlier, Alberta Chemical is interested in hedging the risk of fluctuating oil prices because it cannot pass any cost increases on to the consumer. Suppose, alternatively, that Alberta Chemical was not selling petrochemicals on fixed contract. Instead, imagine that the petrochemicals were to be sold at currently prevailing prices. The price of petrochemicals should move directly with oil prices, because oil is a major component. Because cost increases are likely to be passed on to the consumer, Alberta Chemical would probably not want to hedge in this case. Instead, the firm is likely to choose strategy 1, buying oil as it is needed. If oil prices increase between April 1 and September 1, Alberta Chemical will, of course, find that its inputs have become quite costly. However, in a competitive market, its revenues are likely to rise as well.

---

[8] Alternatively, the firm could buy the oil on April 1 and store it. This would eliminate the risk of price movement, because the firm's oil costs would be fixed upon the immediate purchase. However, this strategy is often inferior to strategy 2 because storage costs often exceed the difference between the futures contract quoted on April 1 and the April 1 cash price.

Strategy 2 is called a **long hedge** because one takes a long position in a futures contract to reduce risk. In other words, one takes a long position in the futures market. In general, a firm institutes a long hedge when it is committed to a fixed purchase price. One class of situations involves actual written contracts with customers, such as Alberta Chemical had. Alternatively, a firm may find that it cannot easily pass on costs to consumers or does not want to pass on these costs.

For example, a group of students opened a small meat market called What's Your Beef near the University of Pennsylvania in the late 1970s.[9] This was a time of volatile consumer prices, especially food prices. Knowing that their fellow students were particularly budget conscious, the owners vowed to keep food prices constant, regardless of price movements in either direction. They accomplished this by purchasing futures contracts in various agricultural commodities.

## Hedging with Futures versus Hedging with Options

When comparing hedging with futures to hedging with options, there are two key differences between the contracts. The first is that a futures contract creates an obligation between both parties to complete the transaction. One party must deliver the asset and the other party must pay for it. With an option, the transaction occurs only if the owner of the option chooses to exercise it.

The second difference between an option contract and a futures contract is that the buyer of an option contract gains a valuable right and must pay the seller for that right. The price of the option is frequently called the option premium. With a futures contract, the buyer sets up the account with the investment dealer and the value in the account changes as the price of the asset fluctuates from changes in the market.

**CONCEPT QUESTIONS**

- Define *short* and *long hedges*.
- Under what circumstances is each of the two hedges used?

# 26.4  INTEREST RATE FUTURES CONTRACTS

In this section, we consider interest rate futures contracts. Our examples deal with futures contracts on Government of Canada bonds because of their high popularity. We first price Canada bonds and Canada bond forward contracts. Differences between futures contracts and forward contracts are explored. We then provide hedging examples using Canada government bond (CGB) futures traded on the Montreal Exchange.

## Pricing of Government of Canada Bonds

As explained in Chapter 6, a Government of Canada bond pays semiannual interest over its life. In addition, the face value of the bond is paid at maturity. Consider a 20-year, 8 percent coupon bond that was issued on March 1. The first payment is to occur in six months, that is, on September 1. The value of the bond can be determined as

**Pricing of a Canada Bond:**

$$P_{CGB} = \frac{\$40}{1 + r_1} + \frac{\$40}{(1 + r_2)^2} + \cdots + \frac{\$40}{(1 + r_{39})^{39}} + \frac{\$1,040}{(1 + r_{40})^{40}} \tag{26.1}$$

---

[9] Ordinarily, an unusual firm name in this textbook is a tipoff that it is fictional. This, however, is a true story.

Because this 8 percent coupon bond pays interest of $80 a year, the semiannual coupon is $40. Principal is paid at maturity along with the last semiannual coupon. The price of the Canada bond, $P_{CGB}$, is determined by discounting each payment at the appropriate spot rate. Because the payments are semiannual, each spot rate is expressed in semiannual terms. That is, imagine a flat term structure where the effective annual yield is 12 percent for all maturities. Because each spot rate, $r$, is expressed in semiannual terms, each spot rate is $\sqrt{1.12} - 1 = 5.83\%$. Because coupon payments occur every six months, there are 40 spot rates over the 20-year period.

## Pricing of Forward Contracts

Now, imagine a *forward* contract where, on March 1, you agree to buy a new 20-year, 8 percent coupon Canada bond in six months, that is, on September 1. As with typical forward contracts, you will pay for the bond on September 1, not March 1. The cash flows from both the Canada bond issued on March 1 and the forward contract that you purchase on March 1 are presented in Figure 26.1. The cash flows on the Canada bond begin exactly six months earlier than do the cash flows on the forward contract. The bond is purchased with cash on March 1 (date 0). The first coupon payment occurs on September 1 (date 1). The last coupon payment occurs at date 40, along with the face value of $1,000. The forward contract compels you to pay $P_{FORW.CONT.}$, the price of the forward contract, on September 1 (date 1). You receive a new Canada bond at that time. The first coupon payment from the bond you receive occurs on March 1 of the following year (date 2). The last coupon payment occurs at date 41, along with the face value of $1,000.

**FIGURE 26.1**

**Cash Flows for Both a Canada Bond and a Forward Contract on a Canada Bond**

Given the 40 spot rates, equation (26.1) showed how to price a Canada bond. How does one price the forward contract on a Canada bond? Just as we saw earlier in the text that NPV analysis is used to price bonds, we will now show that NPV analysis can be used to price forward contracts. Given the cash flows for the forward contract in Figure 26.1, the price of the forward contract must satisfy the following equation:

$$\frac{P_{FORW.CONT.}}{1 + r_1} = \frac{\$40}{(1 + r_2)^2} + \frac{\$40}{(1 + r_3)^3} + \cdots + \frac{\$40}{(1 + r_{40})^{40}} + \frac{\$1,040}{(1 + r_{41})^{41}} \qquad (26.2)$$

The right-hand side of equation (26.2) discounts all the cash flows from the delivery instrument (the Canada bond issued on September 1) back to date 0 (March 1). Because the first cash flow occurs at date 2 (March 1 of the subsequent year), it is discounted by $1/(1 + r_2)^2$. The last cash flow of $1,040 occurs at date 41, so it is discounted by $1/(1 + r_{41})^{41}$. The left-hand side represents the cost of the forward contract as of date 0. Because the actual payment occurs at date 1, it is discounted by $1/(1 + r_1)$.

Students often ask, "Why are we discounting everything back to date 0, when we are actually paying for the forward contract on September 1?" The answer is simply that we apply the same techniques to equation (26.2) that we apply to all capital budgeting problems; we want to put everything in today's (date 0's) dollars. Given that the spot rates are known in the marketplace, traders should have no more trouble pricing a forward contract by equation (26.2) than they would have pricing a bond by equation (26.1).

Forward contracts are similar to the underlying bonds themselves. If the entire term structure of interest rates unexpectedly shifts upward on March 2, the Canada bond issued the previous day should fall in value. This can be seen from equation (26.1). A rise in each of the spot rates lowers the PV of each of the coupon payments. Hence, the value of the bond must fall. Conversely, a fall in the term structure of interest rates increases the value of the bond.

The same relationship holds with forward contracts, as can be seen from rewriting equation (26.2) as

$$P_{\text{FORW.CONT.}} = \frac{\$40 \times (1 + r_1)}{(1 + r_2)^2} + \frac{\$40 \times (1 + r_1)}{(1 + r_3)^3} + \cdots + \frac{\$40 \times (1 + r_1)}{(1 + r_{40})^{40}}$$
$$+ \frac{\$1,040 \times (1 + r_1)}{(1 + r_{41})^{41}} \qquad (26.3)$$

We went from equation (26.2) to equation (26.3) by multiplying both the left- and the right-hand sides by $(1 + r_1)$. If the entire term structure of interest rates unexpectedly shifts upward on March 2, the first term on the right-hand side of equation (26.3) should fall in value.[10] That is, both $r_1$ and $r_2$ will rise an equal amount. However, $r_2$ enters as a *squared* term, $1/(1 + r_2)^2$, so an increase in $r_2$ more than offsets the increase in $r_1$. As we move farther to the right, an increase in any spot rate, $r_i$, more than offsets an increase in $r_1$. Here, $r_i$ enters as the $i$th power, $1/(1 + r_i)^i$. Thus, as long as the entire term structure shifts upward by an equal amount on March 2, the value of a forward contract must fall on that date. Conversely, as long as the entire term structure shifts downward by an equal amount on March 2, the value of a forward contract must rise.

## Futures Contracts

Our discussion so far has concerned a forward contract in Canada bonds, that is, a forward contract where the deliverable instrument is a Canada bond. What about a futures contract on such a bond?[11] We stated earlier that futures contracts and forward contracts are quite similar, though there are a few differences between the two.

First, futures contracts are generally traded on exchanges, whereas forward contracts are not traded on an exchange. In this case, the Canada bond futures contract is traded on the Montreal Exchange. Table 26.3 shows a listing for CGB 10-year futures. The terminology is similar to what we presented earlier for wheat futures. For the bond futures contract, the delivery month is June 2014. The delivery vehicle is a CGB with maturity between 7.75 and 9.75 years, and the face value is $100,000. The listing shows that the settle (closing) price for the futures contract was $132.040 per $100 of par value. Open interest shows that 24,067 contracts were outstanding at this time.

---

[10] We are assuming that each spot rate shifts by the same amount. For example, suppose that on March 1, $r_1 = 5\%$, $r_2 = 5.4\%$, and $r_3 = 5.8\%$. Assuming that all rates increase by 0.5 percent on March 2, $r_1$ becomes 5.5 percent (5% + 0.5%), $r_2$ becomes 5.9 percent, and $r_3$ becomes 6.3 percent.

[11] Futures contracts on bonds are also called interest rate futures contracts.

**TABLE 26.3**

**Listing for Government of Canada Bonds (CGB), 10-Year Futures**

| Ten-year Government of Canada Bond futures, June 2014 (CGBM14) | | | |
|---|---|---|---|
| Bid size | 50 | Bid price | 132.040 |
| Ask size | 3 | Ask price | 132.170 |
| Last price | 131.910 | Net change | −0.610 |
| Volume | 9,903 | Implied volatility (%) | N/A |
| Open interest | 24,067 | | |
| High | 132.370 | Low | 131.910 |
| Settlement price | 132.040 | Open | 132.370 |

Source: Montreal Exchange.

Second, futures contracts generally allow the seller a period of time in which to deliver, whereas forward contracts generally call for delivery on a particular day. The seller of a Canada bond futures contract can choose to deliver on any business day during the delivery month.[12] Third, futures contracts are subject to the mark-to-the-market convention, whereas forward contracts are not. Traders in Canada bond futures contracts must adhere to this convention. Fourth, there is generally a liquid market for futures contracts, allowing contracts to be quickly netted out. That is, a buyer can sell a futures contract at any time and a seller can buy back a futures contract at any time. On the other hand, because forward markets are generally quite illiquid, traders cannot easily net out their positions. The popularity of the Canada bond futures contract has produced a reasonably liquid market, and positions of some size can be netted out quite easily.

Our discussion is not intended to be an exhaustive list of differences between forward contracts and futures contracts on Canada bonds. Rather, it is intended to show that the two types of contracts share fundamental characteristics. Though there are differences, the two instruments should be viewed as variations of the same species, not different species. Thus, the pricing equation of (26.3), which is exact for the forward contract, should be a decent approximation for the futures contract.

## Hedging in Interest Rate Futures

Now that we have covered the basic institutional details of bond futures, we are ready for examples of hedging. Our examples feature bond futures rather than forward contracts because the greater liquidity of futures, discussed above, makes them better suited for hedging.

EXAMPLE **26.3**

Peter James is a mortgage officer for a small credit union. On March 1, he made a commitment to lend $1 million on May 1 in a mortgage on a piece of commercial property. The loan is a 10-year mortgage at 6 percent, the going interest rate on mortgages at the time. Thus, the mortgage is made at par. Though the borrower would not use the term, we could say that Peter is buying a forward contract on a mortgage. That is, he agrees on March 1 to give $1 million to the borrower on May 1 in exchange for principal and interest every month for the next 10 years.

---

[12] Delivery occurs two days after the seller notifies the clearinghouse of the intention to deliver.

Like many small mortgage lenders, Peter has no intention of keeping the $1 million loan on his credit union's balance sheet. Rather, he intends to sell the mortgage to an insurance company. Thus, the insurance company will actually lend the funds and will receive principal and interest over the next 10 years. Peter sets April 30 as a deadline for making the sale because the borrowers expect the funds on the following day.

Suppose that Peter sells the mortgage to the Great Saskatchewan Life Insurance Company on April 15. What price will the insurance company pay for the mortgage?

You may think that it is obvious that the insurance company will pay $1 million. However, suppose interest rates have risen above 6 percent by April 15. The insurance company will buy the mortgage at a discount. For example, suppose the insurance company agrees to pay only $940,000 for the mortgage. Because the mortgage officer agreed to lend a full $1 million to the borrower, the difference of $60,000 (or $1 million − $940,000) represents a loss to the credit union.

Alternatively, suppose that interest rates fall below 6 percent by April 15. The mortgage can be sold at a premium under this scenario. If the insurance company buys the mortgage at $1.05 million, the mortgage officer will have made an unexpected profit of $50,000 (or $1.05 million − $1 million).

Because Peter cannot forecast interest rates, this risk is something that he would like to avoid. The risk is summarized in Table 26.4.

## TABLE 26.4

### Effects of Changing Interest Rate on Peter James, Mortgage Officer

| Mortgage interest rate on April 15 | Above 6% | Below 6% |
|---|---|---|
| Sale price to Great Saskatchewan Life Insurance Company | Below $1 million (we assume $940,000) | Above $1 million (we assume $1.05 million) |
| Effect on mortgage officer | He loses because he must lend full $1 million to borrowers. | He gains because he lends only $1 million to borrowers. |
| Dollar gain or loss | Loss of $60,000 ($1 million − $940,000) | Gain of $50,000 ($1.05 million − $1 million) |

The interest rate on March 1, the date when the loan agreement was made with the borrowers, was 6 percent. April 15 is the date the mortgages were sold to Great Saskatchewan Life Insurance Company.

Seeing the interest rate risk, you may ask, "What does the mortgage officer get out of this loan to offset his risk-bearing?" Peter wants to sell the mortgage to the insurance company so that he can get two fees. The first is an *origination fee*, which is paid to the mortgage officer from the insurance company on April 15, that is, on the date the loan is sold. An industry standard in certain locales is 1 percent of the value of the loan, that is, $10,000 (or 1% × $1 million). In addition, Peter will act as a collection agent for the insurance company. For this service, he will receive a small portion of the outstanding balance of the loan each month. For example, if he is paid 0.03 percent of the loan each month, he will receive $300 (0.03% × $1 million) in the first month. As the outstanding balance of the loan declines, he will receive less.

Though Peter will earn profitable fees on the loan, he bears interest rate risk. He loses money if interest rates rise after March 1, and he profits if interest rates fall after March 1. To hedge this risk, he writes June Government of Canada bond futures contracts on March 1. As with mortgages, Government of Canada bond futures contracts fall in value if interest rates rise. Because he *writes* the contract, he makes money on these contracts if they fall in value. Therefore, with an interest rate rise, the loss he endures in the mortgages is offset by his gain in the futures market.

In the opposite case, Government of Canada bond futures contracts rise in value if interest rates fall. Because he writes the contracts, he suffers losses on them when rates fall. With an interest rate fall, the profit he makes on the mortgages is offset by the loss he suffers in the futures markets.

The details of this hedging transaction are presented in Table 26.5. The column on the left is labelled "Cash Markets," because the deal in the mortgage market is transacted off an exchange. The column on the right shows the offsetting transactions in the futures markets. Consider the first row. The mortgage officer enters into a forward contract on March 1. He simultaneously writes Government of Canada bond futures contracts. Ten contracts are written because the deliverable instrument on each contract is $100,000 of Government of Canada bonds. The total is $1 million (or 10 × $100,000), which is equal to the value of the mortgages. Peter would prefer to write May Government of Canada bond futures contracts. Here, Government of Canada bonds would be delivered on the futures contract during the same month that the loan is funded. Because there is no May Government of Canada bond futures contract, Peter achieves the closest match through a June contract.[13]

**TABLE 26.5**

**Illustration of Hedging Strategy for Peter James, Mortgage Officer**

|  | Cash markets | Futures markets |
|---|---|---|
| March 1 | Mortgage officer makes forward contract to lend $1 million at 6 percent for 10 years. The loans are to be funded on May 1. No cash changes hands on March 1. | Mortgage officer writes 10 June Government of Canada bond futures contracts. |
| April 15 | Loans are sold to Great Saskatchewan Life Insurance Company. Mortgage officer will receive sale price from Great Saskatchewan on the May 1 funding date. | Mortgage officer buys back all the futures contracts. |
| If interest rates rise: | Loans are sold at a price below $1 million. Mortgage officer *loses* because he receives less than the $1 million he must give to borrowers. | Each futures contract is bought back at a price below the sales price, resulting in *profit*. Mortgage officer's profit in futures market offsets loss in cash market. |
| If interest rates fall: | Loans are sold at a price above $1 million. Mortgage officer *gains* because he receives more than the $1 million he must give to borrowers. | Each futures contract is bought back at a price above the sales price, resulting in *loss*. Mortgage officer's loss in futures market offsets gain in cash market. |

If held to maturity, the June contract would oblige the mortgage officer to deliver Government of Canada bonds in June. Interest rate risk ends in the cash market when the loans are sold. Interest rate risk must be terminated in the futures market at that time. Thus, Peter nets out his position in the futures contract as soon as the loan is sold to Great Saskatchewan Life Insurance.

Risk is clearly reduced via an offsetting transaction in the futures market. However, is risk totally eliminated? The answer would be yes if losses in the cash markets were exactly offset in the futures markets and vice versa. This is unlikely to happen because mortgages and Government of Canada bonds are not identical instruments. First, mortgages may have different maturities than Government of Canada bonds.

---

[13] The Government of Canada bond futures contract is by no means the only instrument available to use for hedging. In Canada, there are also futures on banker's acceptances, which are short-term paper. These futures can be used to hedge interest rate risk in the same way that Government of Canada bond futures are used. As well, the expiration months vary with the instrument.

Second, Government of Canada bonds have a different payment stream than do mortgages. Principal is only paid at maturity on Government of Canada bonds, whereas principal is paid every month on mortgages. Because mortgages pay principal continuously, these instruments have a shorter *effective* time to maturity than do Government of Canada bonds of equal maturity.[14] Third, mortgages have default risk, whereas Government of Canada bonds do not. The term structure applicable to instruments with default risk may change even when the term structure for risk-free assets remains constant. Fourth, mortgages may be paid off early and hence have a shorter *expected maturity* than Canada bonds of equal maturity.

Because mortgages and Government of Canada bonds are not identical instruments, they are not identically affected by interest rates.[15] If Canada bonds are less volatile than mortgages, a financial consultant may advise Peter to write more than 10 Government of Canada bond futures contracts. Conversely, if these bonds are more volatile, the consultant may state that fewer than 10 futures contracts are required. An optimal ratio of futures contracts to mortgages will reduce risk as much as possible. However, because the price movements of mortgages and Government of Canada bonds are not perfectly correlated, Peter's hedging strategy cannot eliminate all risk.

The strategy we described is called a *short hedge* because Peter sells futures contracts in order to reduce risk. Though it involves an interest rate futures contract, this short hedge is analogous to short hedges in agricultural and metallurgical futures contracts. We argued at the beginning of this chapter that individuals and firms institute short hedges to offset inventory price fluctuation. Once Peter makes a contract to lend money, the mortgage effectively becomes his inventory. He writes a futures contract to offset the price fluctuation of his inventory.

We now consider a long hedge in Example 26.4.

---

**EXAMPLE 26.4**

Canada Wide Ltd. is a large conglomerate with thousands of employees. Nadia Comeau manages the firm's pension fund. In the next three months, Canada Wide's pension fund is expecting to purchase $25 million in long-term Government of Canada bonds because the pension fund managers have been selling securities for the past month, and they feel that they have too much cash on hand. Nadia's pension fund group faces problems similar to those facing Peter's firm. However, in this case, we will be dealing with a long hedge instead of a short hedge.

As with Peter, changing interest rates will affect Nadia. If interest rates fall before she purchases the long-term Canada bonds, the price of the bonds will increase, and she will be paying more than was expected. Conversely, if interest rates rise, the price of long-term Canada bonds will fall, and the bonds can be purchased for less than expected.

The details are provided in the middle column of Table 26.6. Like Peter, Nadia finds the risk excessive. Therefore, she offsets her decision to purchase bonds with a transaction in the futures markets. Because she loses in the cash market when interest rates fall, she buys futures contracts to reduce the risk. When interest rates fall, the value of her futures contracts increases. The gain in the futures market offsets the loss in the cash market. Conversely, she gains in the cash markets when interest rates rise. The value of her futures contracts decreases when interest rates rise, offsetting her gain.

---

[14] Alternatively, we can say that mortgages have shorter duration than do Government of Canada bonds of equal maturity. A precise definition of duration is provided later in this chapter.

[15] In formal terminology, this type of risk is called *basis risk*. When Peter hedges mortgages with Government of Canada bond futures, he is said to be cross-hedging his position, because he is not using identical instruments.

**TABLE 26.6**

**Illustration of Futures Hedge for Nadia Comeau, Pension Fund Manager**

|  | **Cash markets** | **Futures markets** |
|---|---|---|
| March 1 | Nadia decides to purchase $25 million in long-term bonds over the next three months. | Nadia buys 250 Government of Canada bond futures contracts. |
| April 15 | Nadia purchases $25 million in long-term Canada bonds. | Nadia sells all futures contracts. |
| If interest rates rise: | Nadia gains because the price of bonds will have fallen. | Futures contracts are sold at a price below purchase price, resulting in loss. Nadia's loss in futures market offsets gain in cash market. |
| If interest rates fall: | Nadia loses because the price of bonds will have risen. | Futures contracts are sold at a price above purchase price, resulting in gain. Nadia's gain in futures market offsets loss in cash market. |

We call this a *long hedge* because Nadia offsets risk in the cash markets by buying a futures contract. Though it involves an interest rate futures contract, this long hedge is analogous to long hedges in agricultural and metallurgical futures contracts. We argued at the beginning of this chapter that individuals and firms institute long hedges when their finished goods are to be sold at a fixed price. Once Nadia decides to purchase Government of Canada bonds, she can fix her purchase price. She buys a futures contract to offset the price fluctuation of the bonds.

**CONCEPT QUESTIONS**
- How are forward contracts on bonds priced?
- What are the differences between forward contracts on bonds and futures contracts on bonds?
- Give examples of hedging with futures contracts on bonds.

# 26.5  DURATION HEDGING

The prior section concerned the risk of interest rate changes. We now wish to explore this risk more precisely. In particular, we want to show that the concept of duration is a prime determinant of interest rate risk. We begin by considering the effect of interest rate movements on bond prices.

## The Case of Zero-Coupon Bonds

Suppose that interest rates are 10 percent across all maturities. A one-year pure discount bond pays $110 at maturity. A five-year pure discount bond pays $161.05 at maturity. Both of these bonds are worth $100, as given by[16]

---

[16] Alternatively, we could have chosen bonds that pay $100 at maturity. Their values would be $90.91 (or $100/1.10) and $62.09 [or $100/(1.10)$^5$]. However, our comparisons to come are made easier if both have the same initial price.

**Value of One-Year Pure Discount Bond:**
$$\$100 = \frac{\$110}{1.10}$$

**Value of Five-Year Pure Discount Bond:**
$$\$100 = \frac{\$161.05}{(1.10)^5}$$

Which bond value will change more when interest rates move? To find out, we calculate the values of these bonds when interest rates are either 8 or 12 percent. The results are presented in Table 26.7. As can be seen, the five-year bond has greater price swings than does the one-year bond. That is, both bonds are worth $100 when interest rates are 10 percent. The five-year bond is worth more than the one-year bond when interest rates are 8 percent and worth less than the one-year bond when interest rates are 12 percent. We state that the five-year bond is subject to greater price volatility. This point, which was mentioned in passing in an earlier section of the chapter, is not difficult to understand. The interest rate term in the denominator, $1 + r$, is taken to the fifth power for a five-year bond and only to the first power for the one-year bond. Thus, the effect of a changing interest rate is magnified for the five-year bond. The general rule is the following:

The percentage price changes in long-term pure discount bonds are greater than the percentage price changes in short-term pure discount bonds.

**TABLE 26.7**

### Value of a Pure Discount Bond as a Function of Interest Rate

| Interest rate | One-year pure discount bond | Five-year pure discount bond |
|---------------|------------------------------|-------------------------------|
| 8% | $\$101.85 = \dfrac{\$110}{1.08}$ | $\$109.61 = \dfrac{\$161.05}{(1.08)^5}$ |
| 10% | $\$100.00 = \dfrac{\$110}{1.10}$ | $\$100.00 = \dfrac{\$161.05}{(1.10)^5}$ |
| 12% | $\$98.21 = \dfrac{\$110}{1.12}$ | $\$91.38 = \dfrac{\$161.05}{(1.12)^5}$ |

For a given interest rate change, a five-year pure discount bond fluctuates more in price than does a one-year pure discount bond.

## The Case of Two Bonds with the Same Maturity but with Different Coupons

The previous example concerned pure discount bonds of different maturities. We now want to see the effect of different coupons on price volatility. To abstract from the effect of differing maturities, we consider two bonds with the same maturity but with different coupons.

Consider a five-year 10 percent coupon bond and a five-year 1 percent coupon bond. When interest rates are 10 percent, the bonds are priced as follows:

**Value of Five-Year 10-Percent Coupon Bond:**
$$\$100 = \frac{\$10}{1.10} + \frac{\$10}{(1.10)^2} + \frac{\$10}{(1.10)^3} + \frac{\$10}{(1.10)^4} + \frac{\$110}{(1.10)^5}$$

**Value of Five-Year 1-Percent Coupon Bond:**
$$\$65.88 = \frac{\$1}{1.10} + \frac{\$1}{(1.10)^2} + \frac{\$1}{(1.10)^3} + \frac{\$1}{(1.10)^4} + \frac{\$101}{(1.10)^5}$$

Which bond value will experience greater change in percentage terms if interest rates change?[17] To find out, we calculate the values of these bonds when interest rates are either 8 or 12 percent. The results are presented in Table 26.8. As we would expect, the 10 percent coupon bond always sells for more than the 1 percent coupon bond. Also, as we would expect, each bond is worth more when the interest rate is 8 percent than when the interest rate is 12 percent.

**TABLE 26.8**

**Value of Coupon Bonds at Different Interest Rates**

| Interest rate | Five-year 10% coupon bond |
|---|---|
| 8% | $107.99 = \dfrac{\$10}{1.08} + \dfrac{\$10}{(1.08)^2} + \dfrac{\$10}{(1.08)^3} + \dfrac{\$10}{(\$1.08)^4} + \dfrac{\$110}{(1.08)^5}$ |
| 10% | $100.00 = \dfrac{\$10}{1.10} + \dfrac{\$10}{(1.10)^2} + \dfrac{\$10}{(1.10)^3} + \dfrac{\$10}{(1.10)^4} + \dfrac{\$110}{(1.10)^5}$ |
| 12% | $92.79 = \dfrac{\$10}{1.12} + \dfrac{\$10}{(1.12)^2} + \dfrac{\$10}{(1.12)^3} + \dfrac{\$10}{(1.12)^4} + \dfrac{\$110}{(1.12)^5}$ |

| Interest rate | Five-year 1% coupon bond |
|---|---|
| 8% | $72.05 = \dfrac{\$1}{1.08} + \dfrac{\$1}{(1.08)^2} + \dfrac{\$1}{(1.08)^3} + \dfrac{\$1}{(1.08)^4} + \dfrac{\$101}{(1.08)^5}$ |
| 10% | $65.88 = \dfrac{\$1}{1.10} + \dfrac{\$1}{(1.10)^2} + \dfrac{\$1}{(1.10)^3} + \dfrac{\$1}{(1.10)^4} + \dfrac{\$101}{(1.10)^5}$ |
| 12% | $60.35 = \dfrac{\$1}{1.12} + \dfrac{\$1}{(1.12)^2} + \dfrac{\$1}{(1.12)^3} + \dfrac{\$1}{(1.12)^4} + \dfrac{\$101}{(1.12)^5}$ |

We calculate percentage price changes for both bonds as the interest rate changes from 10 to 8 percent and from 10 to 12 percent. These percentage price changes are as follows:

|  | 10% coupon bond | 1% coupon bond |
|---|---|---|
| Interest rate changes from 10% to 8% | $7.99\% = \dfrac{\$107.99}{\$100} - 1$ | $9.37\% = \dfrac{\$72.05}{\$65.88} - 1$ |
| Interest rate changes from 10% to 12% | $-7.21\% = \dfrac{\$92.79}{\$100} - 1$ | $-8.39\% = \dfrac{\$60.35}{\$65.88} - 1$ |

As can be seen, the 1 percent coupon bond has a greater percentage price increase than does the 10 percent coupon bond when the interest rate falls. Similarly, the 1 percent coupon bond has a greater percentage price decrease than does the 10 percent coupon bond when the interest rate rises. Thus, we say that the percentage price changes on the 1 percent coupon bond are greater than are the percentage price changes on the 10 percent coupon bond.

## Duration

The question, of course, is "Why?" We can answer this question only after we have explored a concept called **duration**. We begin by noticing that any coupon bond is actually a combination of pure discount bonds. For example, the five-year 10 percent coupon bond is made up of five pure discount bonds:

1. A pure discount bond paying $10 at the end of year 1.
2. A pure discount bond paying $10 at the end of year 2.
3. A pure discount bond paying $10 at the end of year 3.
4. A pure discount bond paying $10 at the end of year 4.
5. A pure discount bond paying $110 at the end of year 5.

---

[17] The bonds are at different prices initially. Thus, we are concerned with percentage price changes, not absolute price changes.

Similarly, the five-year 1 percent coupon bond is made up of five pure discount bonds. Because the price volatility of a pure discount bond is determined by its maturity, we would like to determine the average maturity of the five pure discount bonds that make up a five-year coupon bond. This leads us to the concept of duration.

We calculate average maturity in three steps. For the 10 percent coupon bond, we do the following:

1. *Calculate the PV of each payment.* We do this as follows:

| Year | Payment | Present value of payment by discounting at 10% |
|------|---------|-----------------------------------------------|
| 1 | $ 10 | $  9.091 |
| 2 | 10 | 8.264 |
| 3 | 10 | 7.513 |
| 4 | 10 | 6.830 |
| 5 | 110 | 68.302 |
| | | $100.00 |

2. *Express the PV of each payment in relative terms.* We calculate the relative value of a single payment as the ratio of the PV of the payment to the value of the bond. The value of the bond is $100. We have the following:

| Year | Payment | Present value of payment | Relative value = $\dfrac{\text{Present value of payment}}{\text{Value of bond}}$ |
|------|---------|--------------------------|-------------------------------------------------------------------------------|
| 1 | $ 10 | $  9.091 | $9.091/$100 = 0.09091 |
| 2 | 10 | 8.264 | 0.08264 |
| 3 | 10 | 7.513 | 0.07513 |
| 4 | 10 | 6.830 | 0.06830 |
| 5 | 110 | 68.302 | 0.68302 |
| | | $100.00 | 1.0 |

The bulk of the relative value, 68.302 percent, occurs at year 5 because the principal is paid back at that time.

3. *Weight the maturity of each payment by its relative value.* We have

4.1699 years = 1 year × 0.09091 + 2 years × 0.08264 + 3 years × 0.07513 + 4 years × 0.06830 + 5 years × 0.68302

There are many ways to calculate the average maturity of a bond. We have calculated it by weighting the maturity of each payment by the percentage of total PV received at that maturity. We find that the *effective* maturity of the bond is 4.1699 years. *Duration* is a commonly used word for effective maturity. Thus, the bond's duration is 4.1699 years. Note that duration is expressed in units of time.[18]

Because the five-year 10 percent coupon bond has a duration of 4.1699 years, its percentage price fluctuations should be the same as those of a zero-coupon bond with a duration of 4.1699 years.[19] It turns out that the five-year 1 percent coupon bond has

---

[18] The mathematical formula for duration is

$$\text{Duration} = \frac{\text{PV}(C_1)1 + \text{PV}(C_2)2 + \cdots + \text{PV}(C_T)T}{\text{PV}}$$

and

$$\text{PV} = \text{PV}(C_1) + \text{PV}(C_2) + \cdots + \text{PV}(C_T)$$

$$\text{PV}(C_T) = \frac{C_T}{(1 + r)^T}$$

where $C_T$ is the cash to be received at time $T$ and $r$ is the current discount rate.

Also note that in the above numerical example we discounted each payment by the interest rate of 10 percent. This was done because we wanted to calculate the duration of the bond before a change in the interest rate occurred. After a change in the rate to, say, 8 or 12 percent, all three of our steps would need to reflect the new interest rate. In other words, the duration of a bond is a function of the current interest rate.

[19] Actually, this relationship only holds exactly in the case of a one-time shift in a flat yield curve, where the change in the spot rate is identical for all different maturities.

a duration of 4.8742 years. Because the 1 percent coupon bond has a higher duration than the 10 percent bond, the 1 percent coupon bond should be subject to greater price fluctuations. This is exactly what we found earlier. In general:

> The percentage price changes of a bond with high duration are greater than the percentage price changes of a bond with low duration.

A final question: why does the 1 percent bond have a greater duration than the 10 percent bond, even though they have the same five-year maturity? As mentioned earlier, duration is an average of the maturity of the bond's cash flows, weighted by the PV of each cash flow. The 1 percent coupon bond receives only $1 in each of the first four years. Thus, the weights applied to years 1 through 4 in the duration formula will be low. Conversely, the 10 percent coupon bond receives $10 in each of the first four years. The weights applied to years 1 through 4 in the duration formula will be higher.

## Matching Liabilities with Assets

Earlier in this chapter, we argued that firms can hedge risk by trading in futures. Because some firms are subject to interest rate risk, we showed how they can hedge with interest rate futures contracts. Firms may also hedge interest rate risk by matching liabilities with assets. This approach follows from our discussion of duration.

---

**EXAMPLE 26.5**

The Colonist Bank of Canada has the following market value balance sheet:

**THE COLONIST BANK OF CANADA**
**Market Value Balance Sheet**

|  | Market value | Duration |
|---|---|---|
| **Assets** | | |
| Overnight money | $     35 million | 0 |
| Accounts receivable–backed loans | 500 million | 3 months |
| Inventory loans | 275 million | 6 months |
| Industrial loans | 40 million | 2 years |
| Mortgages | 150 million | 14.8 years |
|  | $1,000 million | |
| **Liabilities and shareholders' equity** | | |
| Chequing and savings accounts | $   400 million | 0 |
| Guaranteed Investment Certificates | 300 million | 1 year |
| Long-term financing | 200 million | 10 years |
| Equity | 100 million | |
|  | $1,000 million | |

The bank has $1,000 million of assets and $900 million of liabilities. Its equity is the difference between the two: $100 million (or $1,000 million − $900 million). Both the market value and the duration of each individual item are provided in the balance sheet. Both overnight money and chequing and savings accounts have a duration of zero. This is because the interest paid on these instruments adjusts immediately to changing interest rates in the economy.

The bank's executives think that interest rates are likely to be volatile in the coming months. Because they do not know in which direction rates will move, they are worried that their bank's equity value is vulnerable to changing rates. They call in a consultant, Robert Charest, to determine hedging strategy.

Robert first calculates the duration of the assets and the duration of the liabilities:[20]

**Duration of Assets:**

$$2.56 \text{ years} = 0 \text{ years} \times \frac{\$35 \text{ million}}{\$1,000 \text{ million}} + \frac{1}{4} \text{ year} \times \frac{\$500 \text{ million}}{\$1,000 \text{ million}}$$

$$+ \frac{1}{2} \text{ year} \times \frac{\$275 \text{ million}}{\$1,000 \text{ million}} + 2 \text{ years} \times \frac{\$40 \text{ million}}{\$1,000 \text{ million}} \qquad \textbf{(26.4)}$$

$$+ 14.8 \text{ years} \times \frac{\$150 \text{ million}}{\$1,000 \text{ million}}$$

**Duration of Liabilities:**

$$2.56 \text{ years} = 0 \text{ years} \times \frac{\$400 \text{ million}}{\$900 \text{ million}} + 1 \text{ year} \times \frac{\$300 \text{ million}}{\$900 \text{ million}}$$

$$+ 10 \text{ years} \times \frac{\$200 \text{ million}}{\$900 \text{ million}} \qquad \textbf{(26.5)}$$

The duration of the assets, 2.56 years, equals the duration of the liabilities. Because of this, Robert argues that the firm is immune to interest rate risk.

Just to be on the safe side, the bank calls in a second consultant, Gail Ellert. Gail argues that it is incorrect simply to match durations, because assets total $1,000 million and liabilities total only $900 million. If both assets and liabilities have the same duration, the price change on a dollar of assets should be equal to the price change on a dollar of liabilities. However, the total price change will be greater for assets than for liabilities, because there are more assets than liabilities. The firm will be immune to interest rate risk only when the duration of the liabilities is greater than the duration of the assets. Gail states that the following relationship must hold if the bank is to be **immunized**, that is, immune to interest rate risk:

$$\begin{array}{c} \text{Duration of} \\ \text{assets} \end{array} \times \begin{array}{c} \text{Market value of} \\ \text{assets} \end{array} = \begin{array}{c} \text{Duration of} \\ \text{liabilities} \end{array} \times \begin{array}{c} \text{Market value} \\ \text{of liabilities} \end{array} \qquad \textbf{(26.6)}$$

She says that the bank should not equate the duration of the liabilities with the duration of the assets. Rather, using equation (26.6), the bank should match the duration of the liabilities to the duration of the assets. She suggests two ways to achieve this match:

1.  *Increase the duration of the liabilities without changing the duration of the assets.* Gail argues that the duration of the liabilities could be increased to

    $$\text{Duration of assets} \times \frac{\text{Market value of assets}}{\text{Market value of liabilities}} = 2.56 \text{ years} \times \frac{\$1,000 \text{ million}}{\$900 \text{ million}}$$
    $$= 2.84 \text{ years}$$

    Equation (26.6) then becomes

    $$2.56 \times \$1 \text{ billion} = 2.84 \times \$900 \text{ million}$$

2.  *Decrease the duration of the assets without changing the duration of the liabilities.* Alternatively, Gail points out that the duration of the assets could be decreased to

    $$\text{Duration of liabilities} \times \frac{\text{Market value of liabilities}}{\text{Market value of assets}} = 2.56 \text{ years} \times \frac{\$900 \text{ million}}{\$1,000 \text{ million}}$$
    $$= 2.30 \text{ years}$$

    Equation (26.6) then becomes

    $$2.30 \times \$1 \text{ billion} = 2.56 \times \$900 \text{ million}$$

    Though we agree with Gail's analysis, the bank's current mismatch was small anyway.

---

[20] Note that the duration of a group of items is an average of the durations of the individual items, weighted by the market value of each item. This is a simplifying step that greatly increases duration's practicality.

## Duration in Practice

Huge mismatches have occurred between the durations of assets and liabilities of financial institutions. Probably the most famous example occurred in the U.S. savings and loan (S&L) industry. S&Ls invested large portions of their assets in mortgages. The durations of these mortgages were over 10 years. Many of the funds available for mortgage lending were financed by short-term credit, especially savings accounts. The duration of such instruments is quite small. A thrift institution in this situation faced major interest rate risk, because any increase in interest rates greatly reduced the value of the mortgages. Because an interest rate rise only reduced the value of the liabilities slightly, the equity of the firm fell. As interest rates rose over much of the 1960s and 1970s, many S&Ls found that the market value of their equity turned negative. Allowed to stay in business by regulators, these "zombie thrifts" increased the eventual clean-up costs by engaging in risky investments.[21]

Duration and the accompanying immunization strategies are useful in other areas of finance. For example, many firms establish pension funds to meet obligations to retirees. If the assets of a pension fund are invested in bonds and other fixed-income securities, the duration of the assets can be computed. Similarly, the firm views the obligations to retirees as analogous to interest payments on debt. The duration of these liabilities can be calculated as well. The manager of a pension fund could choose pension assets so that the duration of the assets is matched with the duration of the liabilities. In this way, changing interest rates would not affect the net worth of the pension fund.

Life insurance companies receiving premiums today are legally obliged to provide death benefits in the future. Actuaries view these future benefits as analogous to interest and principal payments of fixed-income securities. The duration of these expected benefits can be calculated. Insurance companies frequently invest in bonds where the duration of the bonds is matched to the duration of the future death benefits.

The business of a leasing company is quite simple. The firm issues debt to purchase assets, which are then leased. The lease payments have a duration, as does the debt. Leasing companies frequently structure debt financing so that the duration of the debt matches the duration of the lease. If the firm did not do this, the market value of its equity could be eliminated by a sudden change in interest rates.

Duration can also be used to speculate on interest rate movements. Bond managers for mutual funds and pension funds routinely calculate the duration of their portfolios. Applying the basic duration principle that bond price volatility is higher for bonds with high durations, fund managers lengthen duration when they predict that falling interest rates will boost bond prices. When they expect rates to rise, managers shorten duration to shield portfolios against losses. In contrast, other managers believe that accurately forecasting interest rates is impossible. These managers simply match the duration of their portfolio with the duration of their liabilities. Research on duration concludes that such duration strategies have been effective in controlling interest rate risk in Canadian bond portfolios.[22]

**CONCEPT**
*QUESTIONS*

- What is duration?
- How is the concept of duration used to reduce interest rate risk?

---

[21] This behaviour is a good example of a selfish investment strategy from Chapter 17. Firms near bankruptcy often take great chances, because they feel that they are playing with someone else's money. In this case, deposit insurance allowed S&Ls to play with taxpayers' money. The example also illustrates our discussion of deposit insurance as a put option in Chapter 23.

[22] I. J. Fooladi and G. S. Roberts, "How Effective Are Duration-Based Bond Strategies in Canada?" *Canadian Investment Review* (Spring 1989); "Duration Analysis and Its Applications," *FINECO* (February 1999); and "Bond Portfolio Immunization: Canadian Tests," *Journal of Economics and Business* (February 1992).

## 26.6    SWAP CONTRACTS

A swap contract is an agreement between two parties to exchange, or swap, specified cash flows at specific intervals. **Swaps** were first introduced to the public in 1981 when IBM and the World Bank entered into a swap agreement. The growth in the use of this financing instrument clearly indicates its growing importance for today's corporations. By mid-2010, the value of outstanding CDSs was $26.3 trillion. Interest rate derivatives, which include interest rate swaps and options and cross-currency swaps, amounted to $434.1 trillion.[23]

Swaps are similar to forward and futures contracts. A swap contract is essentially just a portfolio of forward contracts. With a swap, the only difference is that there are multiple exchanges instead of just one. In principle, a swap contract could be tailored to exchange anything. In practice, most swap contracts fall into one of three basic categories: currency swaps, interest rate swaps, and commodity swaps.

### Interest Rate Swaps

Like other derivatives, swaps are tools that firms can easily use to change their risk exposures and their balance sheets.[24] Consider a firm that has borrowed and carries on its books an obligation to repay a 10-year loan for $100 million of principal with a 9 percent coupon rate paid annually. Ignoring the possibility of calling the loan, the firm expects to have to pay coupons of $9 million every year for 10 years and a balloon payment of $100 million at the end of the 10 years. Suppose, though, that the firm is uncomfortable with having this large fixed obligation on its books. Perhaps the firm is in a cyclical business where its revenues vary and could, conceivably, fall to a point where it would be difficult to make the debt payment.

Suppose, too, that the firm earns a lot of its revenue from financing the purchase of its products. Typically, for example, a manufacturer might help its customers finance their purchase of its products through a leasing or credit subsidiary. Usually these loans are for relatively short time periods and are financed at some premium over the prevailing short rate of interest. This puts the firm in the position of having revenues that move up and down with interest rates while its costs are relatively fixed.

This is a classic situation where a swap can be used to offset the risk. When interest rates rise, the firm would have to pay more on the loan, but it would be making more on its product financing. What the firm would really prefer is to have a floating-rate loan rather than a fixed-rate loan. It can use a swap to accomplish this.

Of course, the firm could also just go into the capital markets and borrow $100 million at a variable interest rate and then use the proceeds to retire its outstanding fixed-rate loan. While this is possible, it is generally quite expensive, requiring underwriting a new loan and repurchasing the existing loan. The ease of entering into a swap is its inherent advantage.

The particular swap would be one that exchanged its fixed obligation for an agreement to pay a floating rate. Every six months it would agree to pay a coupon based on whatever the prevailing interest rate was at that time in exchange for an agreement from a counterparty to pay the firm's fixed coupon.

A common reference point for floating-rate commitments is called LIBOR (London Interbank Offered Rate), and it is the rate that most international banks charge one another for dollar-denominated loans in the London market. LIBOR is commonly used as the reference rate for a floating-rate commitment, and, depending on the

---

[23] For more information and statistics on swaps, visit the ISDA website at www.isda.org.

[24] Under current accounting rules, derivatives do not usually show up on firms' balance sheets since they do not have a historical cost (i.e., the amount a bank would pay on the initial transaction day).

creditworthiness of the borrower, the rate can vary from LIBOR to LIBOR plus one percentage point or more.

If we assume that our firm has a credit rating that requires it to pay LIBOR plus 50 basis points, then in a swap it would be exchanging its fixed 9 percent obligation for the obligation to pay whatever the prevailing LIBOR rate is plus 50 basis points. Table 26.9 displays how the cash flows on this swap would work. In the table we have assumed that LIBOR starts at 8 percent and rises for four years to 11 percent and then drops to 7 percent. As the table illustrates, the firm would owe a coupon of 8.5% × $100 million = $8.5 million in year 1, $9.5 million in year 2, $10.5 million in year 3, and $11.5 million in year 4. The precipitous drop to 7 percent lowers the annual payments to $7.5 million thereafter. In return, the firm receives the fixed payment of $9 million each year. Actually, rather than swapping the full payments, the cash flows would be netted. Since the firm is paying variable amounts and receiving fixed amounts—which it uses to pay its lender—in the first year, for example, the firm owes $8.5 million and is owed by its counterparty, who pays a fixed amount of $9 million. Hence, net, the firm would receive a payment of $0.5 million. Since the firm has to pay its lender $9 million but gets a net payment from the swap of $0.5 million, it really only pays out the difference, or $8.5 million. In each year, then, the firm would effectively pay only LIBOR plus 50 basis points.

**TABLE 26.9**

**Fixed-for-Floating Swap: Cash Flows (in $ millions)**

| | | | | | Coupons | | | | | |
|---|---|---|---|---|---|---|---|---|---|---|
| | Year 1 | 2 | 3 | 4 | 5 | 6 | 7 | 8 | 9 | 10 |
| **A. Swap** | | | | | | | | | | |
| Fixed obligation | 9 | 9 | 9 | 9 | 9 | 9 | 9 | 9 | 9 | 9 |
| LIBOR floating | −8.5 | −9.5 | −10.5 | −11.5 | −7.5 | −7.5 | −7.5 | −7.5 | −7.5 | −7.5 |
| **B. Original loan** | | | | | | | | | | |
| Fixed obligation | −9 | −9 | −9 | −9 | −9 | −9 | −9 | −9 | −9 | −9 |
| Net effect | 8.5 | 9.5 | 10.5 | 11.5 | 7.5 | 7.5 | 7.5 | 7.5 | 7.5 | 7.5 |

Notice, too, that the entire transaction can be carried out without any need to change the terms of the original loan. In effect, by swapping, the firm has found a counterparty who is willing to pay its fixed obligation in return for the firm paying a floating obligation.

## Currency Swaps

FX stands for foreign exchange, and currency swaps are sometimes called FX swaps. Currency swaps are swaps of obligations to pay cash flows in one currency for obligations to pay in another currency.

Currency swaps arise as a natural vehicle for hedging the risks in international trade. For example, suppose a U.S. firm sells a broad range of its product line in the German market. Every year the firm can count on receiving revenue from Germany in euros. We will study international finance later in this book, but for now we can just observe that the fluctuation of exchange rates subjects the firm to considerable risk.

If the firm produces its products in the United States and exports them to Germany, then the firm has to pay its workers and its suppliers in dollars. But it is receiving some of its revenues in euros. The exchange rate between dollars and euros changes over time. As the euro rises in value, the German revenues are worth more dollars, but as it falls they decline. Suppose that the firm can count on selling 100 million euros of goods each year in Germany. If the exchange rate is one euro for each dollar, then the firm will receive $100 million. But if the exchange rate were to rise to two euros for each dollar, the firm would only receive $50 million for its 100 million euros. Naturally the firm would like to protect itself against these currency swings.

To do so the firm can enter into a currency swap. We will learn more later about exactly what the terms of such a swap might be, but for now we can assume that the swap is for five years at a fixed term of 100 million euros for $100 million each year. Now, no matter what happens to the exchange rate between euros and dollars over the next five years, as long as the firm makes 100 million euros each year for the sale of its products, it will swap this for $100 million each year.

We have not addressed the question of how the market prices swaps, either interest rate swaps or currency swaps. In the fixed-for-floating example and in the currency swap, we just quoted some terms. We won't go into great detail on exactly how it is done, but we can stress the most important points.

Swaps, like forwards and futures, are essentially zero-sum transactions, which is to say that in both cases the market sets prices at a fair level, and neither party has any substantial bargain or loss at the moment the deal is struck. For example, in the currency swap, the swap rate is some average of the market expectation of what the exchange rate will be over the life of the swap. In the interest rate swap, the rates are set as the fair floating and fixed rates for the creditor, taking account of the creditworthiness of the counterparties. We can actually price swaps fairly once we know how to price forward contracts. In our interest rate swap example, the firm swapped LIBOR plus 50 basis points for a 9 percent fixed rate, all on a principal amount of $100 million. This is equivalent to a series of forward contracts extending out the life of the swap. In year 1, for example, having made the swap, the firm is in the same position that it would be if it had sold a forward contract entitling the buyer to receive LIBOR plus 50 basis points on $100 million in return for a fixed payment of $9 million (9 percent on $100 million). Similarly, the currency swap can also be viewed as a series of forward contracts.

**CONCEPT QUESTION**

• Show that a currency swap is equivalent to a series of forward contracts.

## Credit Default Swaps

CDSs, along with other credit derivatives, make up one of the fastest growing markets in the financial world. A CDS is a contract that pays off when a credit event occurs—default by a particular company, termed the reference entity. In this case, the buyer of the CDS has the right to sell corporate bonds issued by the reference entity to the CDS seller at their face value. Since bonds in default trade at a deep discount, the right to sell bonds at their face value becomes quite valuable when a default occurs.

CDSs are an important risk management tool for financial institutions. By buying a CDS on a borrower, a bank sets up a payment in the event the borrower defaults on its loan. In effect, CDSs are a form of insurance against credit losses.[25]

The collapse of major corporations, beginning in September 2008, served to test the systems and procedures used to settle CDSs. The bankruptcy of Lehman Brothers was a credit event triggering enormous liabilities to participants in the CDS market. CDS sellers were obliged to assume Lehman's credit and compensate CDS buyers for their full investment in the debt. Lehman's debt was auctioned off for 8.625 cents on the dollar, meaning that the debt was worth only $8.625 per $100 of initial par value. Thus, the sellers of Lehman's CDSs were required to compensate buyers with the

[25] For more on CDSs, see John C. Hull, *Fundamentals of Futures and Options Markets*, 7th ed. (Upper Saddle River, NJ: Pearson Prentice Hall, 2009), Chapter 21.

remaining $91.375 in exchange for the debt. Because swaps are traded over the counter (OTC), there is no exchange to backstop the credit risk of the swap participants. This **counterparty risk** became overwhelming and motivated the bailout of AIG.

The Lehman Brothers collapse is just one recent example illustrating the potentially devastating effects that CDSs create for CDS sellers. In light of such events, the United States adopted new regulations for credit default and other swaps, aimed in part at protecting CDS sellers such as AIG. We discuss these rules later in this chapter.

## Exotics

Up to now we have dealt with the meat and potatoes of the derivatives markets: swaps, options, forwards, and futures. **Exotics** are the complicated blends of these that often produce surprising results for the buyers.

One of the more interesting types of exotics is called an *inverse floater*. In our fixed-for-floating swap, the floating payments fluctuated with LIBOR. An inverse floater is one that fluctuates inversely with some rate, such as LIBOR. For example, the floater might pay interest of 20 percent minus LIBOR. If LIBOR is 9 percent, then the inverse pays 11 percent, and if LIBOR rises to 12 percent, the payments on the inverse would fall to 8 percent. Clearly the purchaser of an inverse profits from the inverse if interest rates fall.

Both floaters and inverse floaters have a supercharged version called *superfloaters* and *superinverses* that fluctuate more than one for one with movements in interest rates. As an example of a superinverse floater, consider a floater that pays an interest rate of 30 percent minus *twice* LIBOR. When LIBOR is 10 percent, the inverse pays

$$30\% - 2 \times 10\% = 30\% - 20\% = 10\%$$

and if LIBOR falls by 3 percent to 7 percent, then the return on the inverse rises by 6 percent from 10 percent to 16 percent,

$$30\% - 2 \times 7\% = 30\% - 14\% = 16\%$$

Sometimes derivatives are combined with options to bound the impact of interest rates. The most important of these instruments are called *caps* and *floors*. A cap is so named because it puts an upper limit, or a cap, on the impact of a rise in interest rates. A floor, conversely, provides a floor below which the interest rate impact is insulated.

To illustrate the impact of these, consider a firm that is borrowing short term and is concerned that interest rates might rise. For example, using LIBOR as the reference interest rate, the firm might purchase a 7 percent cap. The cap pays the firm the difference between LIBOR and 7 percent on some principal amount, provided that LIBOR is greater than 7 percent. As long as LIBOR is below 7 percent, the holder of the cap receives no payments.

By purchasing the cap, the firm has assured itself that even if interest rates rise above 7 percent, it will not have to pay more than a 7 percent rate. Suppose that interest rates rise to 9 percent. While the firm is borrowing short term and paying 9 percent rates, this is offset by the cap, which is paying the firm the difference between 9 percent and the 7 percent limit. For any LIBOR rate above 7 percent, the firm receives the difference between LIBOR and 7 percent, and, as a consequence, it has capped its cost of borrowing at 7 percent.

On the other side, consider a financial firm that is in the business of lending short term and is concerned that interest rates—and, consequently, its revenues—might fall. The firm could purchase a floor to protect itself from such declines. If the limit on the floor is 7 percent, then the floor pays the difference between 7 percent and LIBOR whenever LIBOR is below 7 percent, and nothing if LIBOR is above 7 percent. Thus, if interest rates were to fall to, say, 5 percent, while the firm is only receiving 5 percent from its lending activities, the floor is paying it the difference between 7 percent and

5 percent, or an additional 2 percent. By purchasing the floor, the firm has assured itself of receiving no less than 7 percent from the combination of the floor and its lending activities.

We have only scratched the surface of what is available in the world of derivatives. Derivatives are designed to meet marketplace needs, and the only binding limitation is the human imagination. Nowhere should the buyer's warning *caveat emptor* be taken more seriously than in the derivatives markets, and this is especially true for the exotics. If swaps are the meat and potatoes of the derivatives markets, then caps and floors are the meat and potatoes of the exotics. As we have seen, they have obvious value as hedging instruments. But much attention has been focused on truly exotic derivatives, some of which appear to have arisen more as the residuals that were left over from more straightforward deals. We won't examine these in any detail, but suffice it to say that some of these are so volatile and unpredictable that market participants have dubbed them "toxic waste."

### Movement toward Exchange Trading for Swaps

Swaps typically trade **over the counter** (OTC), which refers to trades made via a dealer network as opposed to a centralized exchange. Many blamed the lack of regulation and transparency in pricing and risk associated with OTC derivatives trading as an important cause of the 2007–2009 global financial crisis.

In the past, swap trading took place OTC directly between a seller and buyer, without the exchange and the regulations it conveyed. However, in response to the financial crisis, the U.S. Dodd–Frank Act was created, bringing comprehensive regulation to the OTC swaps market. Many swaps transactions are now required to trade on electronic venues, also known as swap execution facilities, and be submitted for clearing in clearinghouses.[26] This change eliminates the counterparty risk inherent in OTC swap trading, which, under the new regulations, is likely to become more costly.

With increased OTC trading costs, a recent movement has seen many swaps, which were previously traded OTC, migrate toward being traded on futures exchanges like CME Group Inc. and the Intercontinental Exchange. However, there are still critics of the movement, who argue that swaps traded on futures exchanges limit and remove the customized risk-hedging nature of OTC swaps.[27] Nevertheless, this movement is another result of financial product innovation and regulatory response.

## 26.7    ACTUAL USE OF DERIVATIVES

Historically, under Canadian GAAP, firms have not been required to disclose the value of their derivatives on the face of financial statements. This holds true for many other reporting standards as well. Consequently, it has been much more difficult to observe firm use of derivatives as opposed to, say, bank debt. Thus, much of our knowledge of corporate derivative use comes from academic surveys. With the implementation of IFRS, however, adhering firms must record derivatives on their statements, and their use will become much clearer in the future.

Most surveys report that derivative use is widespread among large publicly traded firms. It appears that around 50 percent of all publicly traded non-financial firms in the United States and Canada use derivatives of some kind, and this percentage jumps

---

[26] "Evolution of the OTC Swaps Market," Bloomberg L. P. (2013), www.bloomberg.com/professional/content/uploads/sites/2/2013/07/54104667-fi-us-garp-wnar-idoc.pdf.

[27] Jay Taylor, "Futurisation of Swaps under New Trading Rules," *Euromoney Handbooks* (May 21, 2013), taylorlouis.files.wordpress.com/2013/07/taylor-pb-blog-euromoney-article-skt-july-16-2013.pdf

# IN THEIR OWN WORDS

## Robert A. Jarrow on an expensive education

The recent credit crisis [2007–2009] offers an opportunity to reflect upon the success and failure of existing risk management tools, putting the spotlight on two in particular: traded derivatives to hedge credit risk and risk management models to quantify credit risk. Did these risk management tools fail?

The financial press has pointed to these newfangled derivatives—especially those on subprime mortgages—and the risk management models as the cause of the crisis. Warren Buffett admonished both models and quantitative researchers in a *Wall Street Journal* report, warning, "All I can say is, beware of geeks. . .bearing formulas" (*WSJ*, November 3, 2008). Before we can form a judgment, we need to dispel three myths appearing repeatedly in the financial press claiming that (1) derivatives are new, (2) derivatives are bad, and (3) using risk models is bad.

Contrary to common belief, the first myth is false. Derivatives are not new. Derivatives have been trading for thousands of years. The "modern" era of derivatives really began in the 1600s in Amsterdam with the trading of options and futures. Even then, derivatives were blamed for high commodity prices and enabling manipulation. Does this sound familiar?

But if derivatives are not new, why have they existed for so long? The answer to this question brings us to our second myth—that derivatives are bad.

### Defending Derivatives

Derivatives are not bad. The reason derivatives have existed for so long and why they are so pervasive today is that they improve individual welfare by enabling the hedging of financial risks. To understand why this is true, one just needs to recognize that financial derivatives are really types of insurance contracts.

Similar to a put option, all derivatives have characteristics of insurance contracts. For example, the credit derivatives—credit default swaps (CDS)—that were so visible during the crisis are precisely insurance contracts written to insure the value of bonds issued by various corporations and financial trusts (Collateralized Default Obligations [CDOs] on subprime mortgages). As insurance contracts, these derivatives enable the insured to hedge financial risks. And everyone understands the benefits of obtaining insurance.

The provider of the insurance, the insurer, is willing to sell the insurance and bear the risk of a loss because they receive a risk premium for this activity. Insurance contracts are good, and they increase society's welfare

as long as the insurer can fulfill the terms of the contract if the insured event occurs; that is, of course, if the insurer is well capitalized and has sufficient funds set aside to cover any losses incurred by the insured. If not, then insurance doesn't reduce risk, but it magnifies it; when the loss event occurs, both the insured and the insurer suffer losses. In this latter case, insurance, although good in concept, fails in practice.

How much capital does the insurer need? It depends on the risks involved. For standard insurance risks that are familiar to households (auto, home, life), little capital is needed because the loss events are well understood. Long histories of losses are available to analyze in great detail. In addition, the losses are usually independent (and identically distributed) across the insured, so the law of large numbers applies. The insurer can calculate their expected losses very accurately, and determine the appropriate amount of capital to hold. Furthermore, the actual losses will be close to their expected values and, therefore, the capital will be sufficient due to the law of large numbers. In this case, insurance works.

### A Short History of Loss Events

For credit derivatives (insuring default), however, the situation is quite different. There is not a long history of loss events, because the current financial system (including corporations and CDO bonds on subprime mortgages) is different from the past. The loss events are not independent (nor identically distributed); in fact, there is significant correlation in defaults, called systemic risk. Firm defaults are correlated with the business cycle and therefore correlated to each other. For the insurer, it is, therefore, very difficult to determine the expected losses and the amount of capital to hold to pay claims against default.

Furthermore, since defaults are not independent events, the law of large numbers does not hold. Capital is needed not just to cover the expected losses, but losses at a higher than 95 or 99 percent level. And if not enough capital is held, the insurance does not work. The insurers will not be able to pay claims against the insurance policies and the risk in the financial system is magnified. Unfortunately, this is what happened with credit derivatives during the credit crisis.

Why did this happen? Well, this brings us to the third myth: risk models are bad. The truth is that risk management models are good. The uneducated use of poor risk models is what's bad.

Using risk models is analogous to using prescription medical drugs. If used correctly, drugs are of immense benefit to the user. If used incorrectly, they can be dangerous, even deadly. Proper use requires extensive testing, proper education in their use, and care. The same is true of risk management models.

## Inadequate Models, Uneducated Use

Unfortunately, uneducated use of poor risk management models did help cause the financial crisis. Two inadequate models were relied upon: value-at-risk (VAR) and the Gaussian copula. Since these models were so crucial to the crisis, we explain both of these in more detail below.

Unfortunately, it is—and was already before the crisis—well known that VAR is not a good risk measure. It has many problems. First of all, it ignores the magnitude of the loss beyond the VAR level. Secondly, it only considers a single time horizon (10 days above); what happens if the loss occurs over 20 days, instead? Thirdly, it penalizes diversification; it can be shown that a diversified bond portfolio can have a higher VAR, and thus require more capital, than a single bond portfolio (all else equal). Lastly, it is very difficult to compute, due to the fact that one is estimating a "rare event," that is, an event that almost never occurs. As such, these are hard to estimate because there is little historical data, as there is with credit risk. Consequently, as a flawed risk measure, VAR does not provide good estimates of the economic capital needed to insure the risk of default.

A Gaussian copula is a model used for computing the level of systemic risk in defaults across a portfolio of bonds for use in VAR. It uses as inputs the probabilities that any single bond will default. These are observable using CDS prices. To access joint default across bonds, it assumes a normal distribution to characterize the correlation in defaults across firms. Furthermore, standard practice is to assume a very simple correlation structure. That is, that the correlation between any two bonds defaulting is identical across all bonds in the portfolio, regardless of the firms' industries. Of course, these assumptions are not true.

The Gaussian copula models were, unfortunately, also used to value the CDO bonds on subprime mortgages. For the reasons cited, the Gaussian copula model did not perform well. Default risks were understated, and the Gaussian copula significantly overvalued CDO subprime mortgage bonds. As a result, these subprime mortgage–backed bonds looked very attractive to market participants, paying high yields for what appeared to be low risks. They looked "too good to be true" and they, in fact, were.

Both of these models (VAR and Gaussian copula) were inadequate, and both of these models were too simple for the complexity of the credit risks involved. These failings were well known at the time and better models existed, but better models were not used by the industry. Is this the models' fault, or the fault of the users? I would argue—the fault of the users, just as the poor use of prescription drugs is the fault of the user and not of the prescription drugs.

## Credit Rating Agencies: Underestimating Risk

The most visible poor users of these inadequate models were the credit rating agencies where use of these models resulted in the underestimation of default risk for individual firms as well as structured products (the subprime mortgage–backed CDOs). This is particularly egregious because the *investment* community looked to the counsel of credit rating agencies to assess the risks of default correctly. The credit agencies failed in this regard.

So, what caused the crisis? I would say that it was partly caused by the uneducated use of poor risk management models. Why did this happen? It happened because the players in the financial system had the wrong set of incentives. The players were the money managers, credit rating agencies, mortgage originators of subprime loans, creators of the subprime CDO trusts, and financial regulators.

Money managers investing in subprime-backed securities had the wrong incentives. They were compensated mostly via short-term bonuses. As long as they were making money, money managers didn't need to worry about a possible financial crisis. In addition, there was an overreliance on the credit rating agencies' ratings by these money managers. The subprime-backed securities they invested in were quite complex, so responsibility was delegated to the credit rating agencies. Consequently, the money managers did not perform independent due diligence of the risks involved.

The credit rating agencies had the wrong incentives as well. They had an incentive to provide high ratings for these subprime CDO bonds because they were paid by the entities that they rated. High ratings were needed by their clients to create the CDO trusts. And, the creation of the CDO trusts generated

# IN THEIR OWN WORDS *(Continued)*

a guarantee of receiving significant future revenues. The CDO asset trust pools had to be continuously monitored by the rating agencies, which were paid for these services.

The CDO equityholders in search of profits created the CDO trusts. In the process, they played the "rating arbitrage" game, turning "junk" into "gold." They succeeded where alchemists for centuries could not. By paying the credit agencies for their rating services, the CDO equityholders could guarantee that they received the ratings they needed to issue the CDO bonds—the desired AAA stamp—based on pools of junk bonds issued against subprime mortgages.

The entities originating the subprime mortgage loans underlying the CDO bonds, the mortgage originators, found that their incentives were also skewed. By selling the loans to the CDO trust pools, they removed the risks of the mortgages' defaulting from their own bottom lines. Their profits increased with the volume of loans issued, not on the performance of the mortgage loans with respect to whether or not the borrowers could make the loan payments. Of course, as is now well known, most mortgage borrowers were not well qualified, and this created much of the subsequent difficulty in the economy.

And, where were the regulatory agencies in all of this? Well, there was fragmented coverage, split between the SEC, the CFTC [U.S. Commodity Futures Trading Commission], and the Federal Reserve. Most of this subprime mortgage activity fell between the cracks. And if the financial system is not broken, the standard response in government—due to entrenched interests—is, why fix it?

It was the "perfect storm" of all the failings of the system converging at one point in time to create a financial crisis.

## Better Education

So what did we learn from all of this? We can safely say that, if the correct models had been used, and the financial risk had been correctly quantified, then adequate capital would have been in the system and the credit crisis would have been avoided.

This is particularly true of the credit rating agencies. If the credit rating agencies had quantified the risks correctly, then the money managers would not have taken such large, risky positions, and the losses would have been dramatically reduced. Furthermore, rating arbitrage would not have existed, the CDOs would not have been created, and mortgage loans to unqualified borrowers would not have been issued.

So, how can we prevent future crises? We need to be better educated in the use of risk management models so that we can use them correctly. Furthermore, we need to fix the perverse incentives in the system. First of all, we need to change the money managers' payment scheme so that it depends on long-term performance, and not short-term profits. Secondly, we need to change the way that credit agencies are compensated; they should not receive their revenues directly from the entities that they rate. In addition, the use of credit ratings should not be mandated by government regulations. And thirdly, we need the regulatory agencies to set proper capital standards. All of these changes are possible, but only with the educated use of risk management models and traded derivatives.

Robert A. Jarrow is professor of finance and economics at Cornell University in Ithaca, New York. His comments are excerpted with permission from the *Canadian Investment Review*, Winter 2009.

Reprinted with permission, Rogers Media, *Canadian Investment Review.*

to 89 percent for companies with annual revenue over US$5 billion.[28] For firms implementing derivatives, the use of foreign exchange and interest rate derivatives is the most common, followed by commodity derivatives. For instance, Tim Hortons, which operates in the United States, Ireland, and the United Kingdom as well as in Canada, uses foreign exchange derivatives to manage the impact of foreign exchange fluctuations on U.S. dollar purchases and payments for coffee and intercompany transactions. As of December 29, 2013, Tim Hortons had forward currency contracts totalling US$147.4 million.[29]

---

[28] Meg Waters, "Real-World Impact of Derivatives Reforms," *Treasury & Risk* (November 21, 2013), www.treasuryandrisk.com/2013/11/21/real-world-impact-of-derivatives-reforms.

[29] More information regarding Tim Hortons' exposure to foreign exchange risk and their derivatives can be found on pages 70, 86, and 100–101 of their 2013 annual report.

Canadian multinational companies are more likely to use derivatives than national firms. Their use is also greater for companies with higher exposure to commodity price risk. Consequently, Agrium, a retail supplier of agricultural products and services, utilizes various derivatives, such as seed forwards, swaps, and options, to manage its commodity price risk.[30] Recent research by Bartram, Brown, and Conrad shows that derivatives can be very helpful in reducing the variability of firm cash flows, which, in turn, reduces the various costs associated with financial distress. Therefore, it is somewhat puzzling that large firms use derivatives more often than small firms—because large firms tend to have less cash flow variability than small firms. Also, some surveys report that firms occasionally use derivatives when they want to speculate about future prices and not just to hedge risks.

However, most of the evidence is consistent with the theory that derivatives are most frequently used by firms where financial distress costs are high and access to the capital markets is constrained.[31]

---

[30] A full list of derivatives used by Agrium to hedge against various risks can be found on pages 129–135 of their 2013 annual report.

[31] Sohnke M. Bartram, Gregory W. Brown, and Jennifer Conrad, "The Effects of Derivatives on Firm Risk and Value," *Journal of Financial and Quantitative Analysis* (August 2011).

## 26.8

# SUMMARY AND CONCLUSIONS

1. Firms hedge to reduce risk. This chapter shows a number of hedging strategies.

2. A forward contract is an agreement by two parties to sell an item for cash at a later date. The price is set at the time the agreement is signed. However, cash changes hands on the date of delivery. Forward contracts are generally not traded on organized exchanges.

3. Futures contracts are also agreements for future delivery. They have certain advantages, such as liquidity, that forward contracts do not. An unusual feature of futures contracts is the mark-to-the-market convention. If the price of a futures contract falls on a particular day, every buyer of the contract must pay money to the clearinghouse. Every seller of the contract receives money from the clearinghouse. Everything is reversed if the price rises. The mark-to-the-market convention prevents defaults on futures contracts.

4. We divided hedges into two types: short hedges and long hedges. An individual or firm that sells a futures contract to reduce risk is instituting a short hedge. Short hedges are generally appropriate for holders of inventory. An individual or firm that buys a futures contract to reduce risk is instituting a long hedge. Long hedges are typically used by firms with contracts to sell finished goods at a fixed price.

5. An interest rate futures contract employs a bond as the deliverable instrument. Because of their popularity, we worked with Government of Canada bond futures contracts. We showed that Government of Canada bond futures contracts can be priced using the same type of net present value (NPV) analysis that is used to price Canada bonds themselves.

6. Many firms face interest rate risk. They can reduce this risk by hedging with interest rate futures contracts. As with other commodities, a short hedge involves the sale of a futures contract. Firms that are committed to buying mortgages or other bonds are likely to institute short hedges. A long hedge involves the purchase of a futures contract. Firms that have agreed to sell mortgages or other bonds at a fixed price are likely to institute long hedges.

7. Duration measures the average maturity of all the cash flows in a bond. Bonds with high duration have high price variability. Firms frequently try to match the duration of their assets with the duration of their liabilities.

8. Swaps are agreements to exchange cash flows over time. The first major type is an interest rate swap, in which one pattern of coupon payments, say fixed payments, is exchanged for another, say, coupons that float with LIBOR. The second major type is a currency swap, in which an agreement is struck to swap payments in one currency for payments in another currency over time.

**KEY TERMS**

Cash transaction 756
Counterparty risk 780
Deliverable instrument 755
Duration 772
Exotics 780
Forward contract 755

Futures contract 756
Hedging 754
Immunized 775
Long hedge 763
Making delivery 756
Marked to the market 758

Over the counter 781
Short hedge 762
Swaps 777
Taking delivery 755

### Futures Quotes

26.1 Refer to Table 26.2 in the text to answer this question. Suppose you purchase a December wheat futures contract, traded on the KC, on June 4, 2014, at the last price of the day. What will your profit or loss be if wheat prices turn out to be $7.44 per bushel at expiration?

26.2 Refer to Table 26.2 in the text to answer this question. Suppose you sell five March wheat futures contracts, traded on the CBT, on June 4, 2014, at the last price of the day. What will your profit or loss be if wheat prices turn out to be $6.56 per bushel at expiration? What if wheat prices are $6.90 per bushel at expiration?

### Put and Call Payoffs

26.3 Suppose a financial manager buys call options on 50,000 barrels of oil with an exercise price of $95 per barrel. She simultaneously sells a put option on 50,000 barrels of oil with the same exercise price of $95 per barrel. Consider her gains and losses if oil prices are $90, $92, $95, $98, and $100. What do you notice about the payoff profile?

### Marking to the Market

26.4 You are long 10 gold futures contracts, established at an initial settle price of $951 per ounce, where each contract represents 100 ounces. Over the subsequent four trading days, gold settles at $943, $946, $953, and $957, respectively. Compute the cash flows at the end of each trading day, and compute your total profit or loss at the end of the trading period.

26.5 You are short 25 gasoline futures contracts, established at an initial settle price of $1.41 per litre, where each contract represents 42,000 litres. Over the subsequent four trading days, gasoline settles at $1.37, $1.42, $1.45, and $1.51, respectively. Compute the cash flows at the end of each trading day, and compute your total profit or loss at the end of the trading period.

### Duration

26.6 What is the duration of a bond with three years to maturity and a coupon of 8 percent paid annually if the bond sells at par?

26.7 What is the duration of a bond with four years to maturity and a coupon of 8 percent paid annually if the bond sells at par?

26.8 Blue Steel Community Bank has the following market value balance sheet:

| Asset or liability | Market value (in $ millions) | Duration (in years) |
|---|---|---|
| Federal funds deposits | $ 31 | 0 |
| Accounts receivable | 590 | 0.20 |
| Short-term loans | 340 | 0.65 |
| Long-term loans | 98 | 5.25 |
| Mortgages | 485 | 12.85 |
| Chequing and savings deposits | 645 | 0 |
| Guaranteed Investment Certificates | 410 | 1.60 |
| Long-term financing | 336 | 9.80 |
| Equity | 153 | N/A |

a. What is the duration of the assets?
b. What is the duration of the liabilities?
c. Is the bank immune to interest rate risk?

### Hedging with Futures

26.9 Refer to Table 26.2 in the text to answer this question. Suppose today is June 4, 2014, and your firm produces breakfast cereal and needs 140,000 bushels of wheat in March 2015 for an upcoming promotion. You would like to lock in your costs today because you are concerned that wheat prices might go up between now and March. You are looking at wheat future contracts traded on the MPLS.

    *a.* How could you use wheat futures contracts to hedge your risk exposure? What price would you effectively be locking in based on the closing price of the day?

    *b.* Suppose wheat prices are $7.20 per bushel in March 2015. What is the profit or loss on your futures position? Explain how your futures position has eliminated your exposure to price risk in the corn market.

### Duration

26.10 Ted and Alice have a son who will begin university seven years from today. School expenses of $30,000 will need to be paid at the beginning of each of the four years that their son plans to attend university. What is the duration of this liability to the couple if they can borrow and lend at the market interest rate of 9 percent?

26.11 What is the duration of a bond with two years to maturity if the bond has a coupon rate of 7 percent paid semiannually, and the market interest rate is 5 percent?

### Forward Pricing

26.12 You enter into a forward contract to buy a 10-year zero-coupon bond that will be issued in one year. The face value of the bond is $1,000, and the 1-year and 11-year spot interest rates are 5 percent and 7 percent, respectively.

    *a.* What is the forward price of your contract?

    *b.* Suppose both the 1-year and 11-year spot rates unexpectedly shift downward by 2 percent. What is the new price of the forward contract?

26.13 This morning you agreed to buy a one-year Treasury bond in six months. The bond has a face value of $1,000. Use the spot interest rates listed here to answer the following questions:

| Time | Equivalent annual rate |
| --- | --- |
| 6 months | 3.61% |
| 12 months | 4.05 |
| 18 months | 4.73 |
| 24 months | 5.42 |

    *a.* What is the forward price of this contract?

    *b.* Suppose shortly after you purchased the forward contract all rates increased by 30 basis points. For example, the six-month rate increased from 3.61 percent to 3.91 percent. What is the price of a forward contract otherwise identical to yours given these changes?

### Financial Engineering

26.14 Suppose there were call options and forward contracts available on coal, but no put options. Show how a financial engineer could synthesize a put option using the available contracts. What does your answer tell you about the general relationship between puts, calls, and forwards?

# Williamson Mortgage Inc.

Jennifer Williamson recently quit her job as an investment banker and has decided to enter the mortgage brokerage business. Rather than work for someone else, she has decided to open her own shop. Her cousin Jerry has approached her about a mortgage for a house he is building. The house will be completed in three months, and he will need the mortgage at that time. Jerry wants a 25-year fixed-rate mortgage in the amount of $500,000 with monthly payments.

Jennifer has agreed to lend Jerry the money in three months at the current market rate of 5.5 percent. Because Jennifer is just starting out, she does not have $500,000 available for the loan, so she approaches Maxine Cabell, the president of MC Insurance Corporation, about purchasing the mortgage from her in three months. Maxine has agreed to purchase the mortgage in three months, but she is unwilling to set a price on the mortgage. Instead, she has agreed in writing to purchase the mortgage at the market rate in three months. There are CGB futures contracts available for delivery in three months. A CGB bond contract is for $100,000 in face value of bonds.

1.  What is the monthly mortgage payment on Jerry's mortgage?
2.  What is the most significant risk Jennifer faces in this deal?
3.  How can Jennifer hedge this risk?
4.  Suppose that in the next three months the market rate of interest rises to 6.2 percent.
    a.  How much will Maxine be willing to pay for the mortgage?
    b.  What will happen to the value of CGB futures contracts? Will the long or short position increase in value?
5.  Suppose that in the next three months the market rate of interest falls to 4.6 percent.
    a.  How much will Maxine be willing to pay for the mortgage?
    b.  What will happen to the value of CGB futures contracts? Will the long or short position increase in value?
6.  Are there any possible risks Jennifer faces in using CGB futures contracts to hedge her interest rate risk?

## PART 7

# Short-Term Finance and Planning

EXECUTIVE SUMMARY

Up to now we have described many of the decisions of long-term finance: capital budgeting, dividend policy, and capital structure. This chapter introduces short-term finance. Short-term finance is an analysis of decisions that (1) affect current assets and current liabilities and (2) will frequently have an impact on the firm within a year.

The term *net working capital* is often associated with short-term financial decision making. Net working capital is the difference between current assets and current liabilities. The focus of short-term finance on net working capital seems to suggest that it is an accounting subject. However, making net working capital decisions still relies on cash flow and net present value (NPV).

There is no universally accepted definition of short-term finance. The most important difference between short-term and long-term finance is the timing of cash flows. Short-term financial decisions involve cash inflows and outflows within a year or less. For example, a short-term financial decision is involved when a firm orders raw materials, pays in cash, and anticipates selling finished goods in one year for cash, as illustrated in Figure 27.1. A long-term financial decision is involved when a firm purchases a special machine that will reduce operating costs over the next five years, as illustrated in Figure 27.2.

Here are some questions related to short-term finance:

1. What is a reasonable level of cash to keep on hand (in a bank) to pay bills?
2. How much raw material should be ordered?
3. How much credit should be extended to customers?

This chapter introduces the basic elements of short-term financial decisions. First, we describe the short-term operating activities of the firm, and then we identify alternative short-term financial policies. Finally, we outline the basic elements in a short-term financial plan and describe short-term financing instruments.

## 27.1 TRACING CASH AND NET WORKING CAPITAL

In this section we trace the components of cash and net working capital as they change from one year to the next. Our goal is to describe the short-term operating activities of the firm and their impact on cash and working capital.

*Current assets* are cash and other assets that are expected to be converted to cash within the year. Current assets are presented in the statement of financial position in order of their **liquidity**—the ease with which they can be converted to cash at a fair price and the time it takes to do so. Table 27.1 gives the statement of financial position and the statement of comprehensive income of the Tradewinds Manufacturing Corporation for 2015 and 2014. The four major items found in the current assets section of Tradewinds' statement of financial position are cash, marketable securities, accounts receivable, and inventories.

**FIGURE 27.1**

**Short-Term Financial Decision**

**FIGURE 27.2**

**Long-Term Financial Decision**

As a counterpart to their investment in current assets, firms use several kinds of short-term debt called *current liabilities*. Current liabilities are obligations that are expected to require cash payment within one year or within the operating cycle, whichever is shorter.[1] The major items found as current liabilities are accounts payable, accrued wages, taxes, other expenses payable, and notes payable.

## 27.2    DEFINING CASH IN TERMS OF OTHER ELEMENTS

Now we will define cash in terms of the other elements of the statement of financial position. The statement of financial position equation is

$$\text{Net working capital} + \text{Fixed assets} = \text{Long-term debt} + \text{Equity} \tag{27.1}$$

Net working capital is cash plus the other elements of net working capital; that is,

$$\text{Net working capital} = \text{Cash} + \text{Other current assets} - \text{Current liabilities} \tag{27.2}$$

Substituting equation (27.2) into equation (27.1) yields

$$\text{Cash} + \text{Other current assets} - \text{Current liabilities} = \text{Long-term debt} + \text{Equity} - \text{Fixed assets} \tag{27.3}$$

Rearranging, we find that

$$\text{Cash} = \text{Long-term debt} + \text{Equity} - \text{Net working capital (excluding cash)} - \text{Fixed assets} \tag{27.4}$$

The natural interpretation of equation (27.4) is that increasing long-term debt and equity and decreasing fixed assets and net working capital (excluding cash) will increase cash to the firm.

---

[1] As we will learn in this chapter, the operating cycle begins when inventory is received and ends when cash is collected from the sale of the inventory.

**TABLE 27.1**

## Financial Statements

### TRADEWINDS MANUFACTURING CORPORATION
### December 31, 2015, and December 31, 2014
### Statement of Financial Position

|  | 2015 | 2014 |
|---|---|---|
| **Assets** | | |
| Current assets: | | |
| Cash | 500,000 | 500,000 |
| Marketable securities (at cost) | 500,000 | 450,000 |
| Accounts receivable less allowance for bad debts | 2,000,000 | 1,600,000 |
| Inventories | 3,000,000 | 2,000,000 |
| Total current assets | 6,000,000 | 4,550,000 |
| Fixed assets (property, plant, and equipment): | | |
| Land | 450,000 | 450,000 |
| Building | 4,000,000 | 4,000,000 |
| Machinery | 1,500,000 | 800,000 |
| Office equipment | 50,000 | 50,000 |
| Less: Accumulated depreciation | 2,000,000 | 1,700,000 |
| Net fixed assets | 4,000,000 | 3,600,000 |
| Prepayments and deferred charges | 400,000 | 300,000 |
| Intangibles | 100,000 | 100,000 |
| Total assets | $10,500,000 | $ 8,550,000 |
| **Liabilities** | | |
| Current liabilities: | | |
| Accounts payable | $ 1,000,000 | $    750,000 |
| Notes payable | 1,500,000 | 500,000 |
| Accrued expenses payable | 250,000 | 225,000 |
| Taxes payable | 250,000 | 225,000 |
| Total current liabilities | 3,000,000 | 1,700,000 |
| Long-term liabilities: | | |
| First mortgage bonds, 5% interest, due 2018 | 3,000,000 | 3,000,000 |
| Deferred taxes | 600,000 | 600,000 |
| Total liabilities | $ 6,600,000 | $ 5,300,000 |
| **Shareholders' equity** | | |
| Common stock: authorized, issued, and outstanding 300,000 shares | $ 1,500,000 | $ 1,500,000 |
| Capital surplus | 500,000 | 500,000 |
| Accumulated retained earnings | 1,900,000 | 1,250,000 |
| Total shareholders' equity | 3,900,000 | 3,250,000 |
| Total liabilities and shareholders' equity | $10,500,000 | $ 8,550,000 |
| **Statement of Comprehensive Income** | | |
| Net sales | $11,500,000 | $10,700,000 |
| Cost of sales and operating expenses: | | |
| Cost of goods sold | 8,200,000 | 7,684,000 |
| Depreciation | 300,000 | 275,000 |
| Selling and administrative expenses | 1,400,000 | 1,325,000 |
| Operating profit | 1,600,000 | 1,416,000 |
| Other income: | | |
| Dividends and interest | 50,000 | 50,000 |
| Total income from operations | 1,650,000 | 1,466,000 |
| Less: Interest on bonds and other liabilities | 300,000 | 150,000 |
| Income before provision for income tax | 1,350,000 | 1,316,000 |
| Provision for income tax | 610,000 | 600,000 |
| Net profit | $    740,000 | $    716,000 |
| Dividends paid out | $     90,000 | $    132,000 |
| Retained earnings | $    650,000 | $    584,000 |

## The Sources and Uses of Cash Statement

We first introduced the cash flow statement in Chapter 2. This is the accounting statement that describes the sources and uses of cash. In this section we look at where cash comes from and how it is used. From the right-hand side of equation (27.4), we can see that an increase in long-term debt or equity leads to an increase in cash. Moreover, an increase in net working capital or fixed assets leads to a decrease in cash. In addition, the sum of net income and depreciation increases cash, whereas dividend payments decrease cash.[2] This reasoning allows an accountant to create a sources and uses of cash statement, which shows all the transactions that affect a firm's cash position.

Let us trace the changes in cash for Tradewinds during the year. Notice that Tradewinds' cash balance remained constant during 2015, even though cash flow from operations was $1.04 million (net income plus depreciation). Why did cash remain the same? The answer is simply that the sources of cash were equal to the uses of cash. From the firm's sources and uses of cash statement (Table 27.2), we find that Tradewinds generated cash as follows:

1. Generated cash flow from operations of $1.04 million.
2. Increased its accounts payable by $250,000. This is the same as increasing borrowing from suppliers.
3. Increased its borrowing from banks by $1 million. This shows up as an increase in notes payable.
4. Increased accrued expenses by $25,000.
5. Increased taxes payable by $25,000, in effect borrowing from the Canada Revenue Agency.

**TABLE 27.2**

**Sources and Uses of Cash Statement**

| TRADEWINDS MANUFACTURING CORPORATION Sources and Uses of Cash (in $ thousands) | |
| --- | --- |
| **Sources of cash:** | |
| Cash flow from operations: | |
| Net income | $ 740 |
| Depreciation | 300 |
| Total cash flow from operations | $1,040 |
| Decrease in net working capital: | |
| Increase in accounts payable | 250 |
| Increase in notes payable | 1,000 |
| Increase in accrued expenses | 25 |
| Increase in taxes payable | 25 |
| Total sources of cash | $2,340 |
| **Uses of cash:** | |
| Increase in fixed assets | 700 |
| Increase in prepayments | 100 |
| Dividends | 90 |
| Increase in net working capital: | |
| Investment in inventory | 1,000 |
| Increase in accounts receivable | 400 |
| Increase in marketable securities | 50 |
| Total uses of cash | $2,340 |
| Change in cash balance | $ 0 |

---

[2] Depreciation is not really a source of cash; it is added back as a correction because it was originally a non-cash deduction from net income.

Tradewinds used cash for the following purposes:

1. Invested $700,000 in fixed assets.
2. Increased prepayments by $100,000.
3. Paid a $90,000 dividend.
4. Invested in inventory worth $1 million.
5. Lent its customers additional money. Hence, accounts receivable increased by $400,000.
6. Purchased $50,000 worth of marketable securities.

This example illustrates the difference between a firm's cash position on the statement of financial position and cash flows from operations.

**CONCEPT**
**QUESTIONS**

- What is the difference between net working capital and cash?
- Will net working capital always increase when cash increases?
- List the potential uses of cash.
- List the potential sources of cash.

## 27.3  THE OPERATING CYCLE AND THE CASH CYCLE

Short-term finance is concerned with the firm's **short-run operating activities**. A typical manufacturing firm's short-run operating activities consist of a sequence of events and decisions:

| Event | Decision |
|---|---|
| 1. Buying raw materials | 1. How much inventory should we order? |
| 2. Paying cash for purchases | 2. Should we borrow or draw down the cash balance? |
| 3. Manufacturing the product | 3. What choice of production technology should we use? |
| 4. Selling the product | 4. Should we offer cash terms or credit terms to customers? |
| 5. Collecting cash | 5. How can we collect cash? |

These activities create patterns of cash inflows and cash outflows that are both unsynchronized and uncertain. They are unsynchronized because the payment of cash for raw materials does not happen at the same time as the receipt of cash from selling the product. They are uncertain because future sales and costs are not known with certainty.

Figure 27.3 depicts the short-term operating activities and cash flows for a typical manufacturing firm along the **cash flow timeline**. The **operating cycle** is the time interval between the arrival of inventory stock and the date when cash is collected from receivables. The **cash cycle** begins when cash is paid for materials and ends when cash is collected from receivables. The cash flow timeline consists of an operating cycle and a cash cycle. The need for short-term financial decision making is suggested by the gap between the cash inflows and cash outflows. This is related to the lengths of the operating cycle and the accounts payable period. This gap can be filled either by borrowing or by holding a liquidity reserve for marketable securities. The gap can be shortened by changing the inventory, receivable, and payable periods. Now we take a closer look at the operating cycle.

The length of the operating cycle is equal to the sum of the lengths of the inventory and accounts receivable periods. The *inventory period* is the length of time required to order, produce, and sell a product. The *accounts receivable period* is the length of time required to collect cash receipts.

FIGURE 27.3

**Cash Flow Timeline and the Short-Term Operating Activities of a Typical Manufacturing Firm**

The *operating cycle* is the time period from the arrival of stock until the receipt of cash. (Sometimes the operating cycle is defined to include the time from placement of the order until arrival of the stock.) The *cash cycle* begins when cash is paid for materials and ends when cash is collected from receivables.

The *cash cycle* is the time between cash disbursement and cash collection. It can be thought of as the operating cycle less the accounts payable period:

$$\text{Cash cycle} = \text{Operating cycle} - \text{Accounts payable period}$$

The *accounts payable period* is the length of time the firm is able to delay payment on the purchase of various resources, such as wages and raw materials.

In practice, the inventory period, the accounts receivable period, and the accounts payable period are measured by days in inventory, days in receivables, and days in payables, respectively. We illustrate how the operating cycle and the cash cycle can be measured in Example 27.1.

EXAMPLE **27.1**

Tradewinds Manufacturing is a diversified manufacturing firm with the statement of financial position and the statement of comprehensive income shown in Table 27.1 for 2014 and 2015. The operating cycle and the cash cycle can be determined for Tradewinds after calculating the appropriate ratios for inventory, receivables, and payables. Consider inventory first:

$$\text{Average inventory} = \frac{\$3 \text{ million} + \$2 \text{ million}}{2} = \$2.5 \text{ million}$$

The terms in the numerator are the ending inventory in the second and first years, respectively.

We next calculate the inventory turnover ratio:

$$\text{Inventory turnover ratio} = \frac{\text{Cost of goods sold}}{\text{Average inventory}} = \frac{\$8.2 \text{ million}}{\$2.5 \text{ million}} = 3.3$$

This implies that the inventory cycle occurs 3.3 times a year. Finally, we calculate days in inventory:

$$\text{Days in inventory} = \frac{365 \text{ days}}{3.3} = 110.6 \text{ days}$$

Our calculation implies that the inventory cycle is about 111 days. We perform analogous calculations for receivables and payables:[3]

$$\text{Average accounts receivable} = \frac{\$2.0 \text{ million} + \$1.6 \text{ million}}{2} = \$1.8 \text{ million}$$

$$\text{Average receivables turnover} = \frac{\text{Credit sales}}{\text{Average accounts receivable}} = \frac{\$11.5 \text{ million}}{\$1.8 \text{ million}} = 6.4$$

$$\text{Days in receivables} = \frac{365 \text{ days}}{6.4} = 57 \text{ days}$$

$$\text{Average payables} = \frac{\$1.0 \text{ million} + \$0.75 \text{ million}}{2} = \$0.875 \text{ million}$$

$$\text{Accounts payable deferral period} = \frac{\text{Cost of goods sold}}{\text{Average payables}} = \frac{\$8.2 \text{ million}}{\$0.875 \text{ million}} = 9.4$$

$$\text{Days in payables} = \frac{365 \text{ days}}{9.4} = 38.8 \text{ days}$$

These calculations allow us to determine both the operating cycle and the cash cycle:

$$\text{Operating cycle} = \text{Days in inventory} + \text{Days in receivables}$$
$$= 110.6 \text{ days} + 57 \text{ days} = 167.6 \text{ days}$$

$$\text{Cash cycle} = \text{Operating cycle} - \text{Days in payables}$$
$$= 167.6 \text{ days} - 38.8 \text{ days} = 128.8 \text{ days}$$

## Interpreting the Cash Cycle

Our examples show how the cash cycle depends on the inventory, receivables, and payables periods. The cash cycle increases as the inventory and receivables periods get longer. It decreases if the company is able to stall payment of payables, lengthening the payables period. Suppose a firm could purchase inventory, sell its product, collect receivables (perhaps selling for cash), and then pay suppliers all on the same day. This firm would have a cash cycle of zero days.

Some firms may meet this description, but it is hard to think of examples. Most firms have a positive cash cycle. Such firms require some additional financing for inventories and receivables. The longer the cash cycle, the more financing is required, other things being equal. Since bankers are conservative and dislike surprises, they monitor the firm's cash cycle. A lengthening cycle may indicate obsolete, unsaleable inventory or problems in collecting receivables. Unless these problems are detected and solved, the firm may require emergency financing or face insolvency.

Our calculations of the cash cycle used financial ratios introduced in Chapter 2. We can use some other ratio relationships from Chapter 2 to see how the cash cycle relates to profitability and sustainable growth. A good place to start is with the Du Pont equation for profitability as measured by return on assets (ROA):

$$\text{ROA} = \text{Profit margin} \times \text{Total asset turnover}$$

$$\text{Total asset turnover} = \frac{\text{Sales}}{\text{Total assets}}$$

Go back to the case of the firm with a lengthening cash cycle. Increased inventories and receivables that caused the cash cycle problem also reduce total asset turnover. The result is lower profitability. In other words, with more assets tied up over a longer cash cycle, the firm is less efficient and therefore less profitable. And, as if its troubles were not enough already, this firm suffers a drop in its sustainable growth rate.

---

[3] We assume that Tradewinds Manufacturing makes no cash sales.

Chapter 3 showed that total asset turnover is directly linked to sustainable growth. Reducing total asset turnover lowers sustainable growth. This makes sense because our troubled firm must divert its financial resources into financing excess inventory and receivables.

**CONCEPT QUESTIONS**
- What does it mean to say that a firm has an inventory turnover ratio of 4?
- Describe the operating cycle and cash cycle. What are the differences between them?

# 27.4    SOME ASPECTS OF SHORT-TERM FINANCIAL POLICY

The policy that a firm adopts for short-term finance will be composed of at least two elements:

1. *The size of the firm's investment in current assets.* This is usually measured relative to the firm's level of total operating revenues. A flexible or accommodative short-term financial policy would maintain a high ratio of current assets to sales. A restrictive short-term financial policy would entail a low ratio of current assets to sales.

2. *The financing of current assets.* This is measured as the proportion of short-term debt to long-term debt. A restrictive short-term financial policy means a high proportion of short-term debt relative to long-term financing, and a flexible policy means less short-term debt and more long-term debt.

## The Size of the Firm's Investment in Current Assets

Flexible short-term financial policies include the following:

1. Keeping large balances of cash and marketable securities.
2. Making large investments in inventory.
3. Granting liberal credit terms, which result in a high level of accounts receivable.

Restrictive short-term financial policies are as follows:

1. Keeping low cash balances and no investment in marketable securities.
2. Making small investments in inventory.
3. Allowing no credit sales and no accounts receivable.

Determining the optimal investment level in short-term assets requires identifying the different costs of alternative short-term financing policies. The objective is to trade off the cost of restrictive policies against the cost of flexible policies to arrive at the best compromise.

Current asset holdings are highest with a flexible short-term financial policy and lowest with a restrictive policy. Thus, flexible short-term financial policies are costly in that they require higher cash outflows to finance cash and marketable securities, inventory, and accounts receivable. However, future cash inflows are highest with a flexible policy. Sales are stimulated by the use of a credit policy that provides liberal financing to customers. A large amount of inventory on hand ("on the shelf") provides a quick delivery service to customers and increases sales.[4] In addition, the firm can probably charge higher prices for the quick delivery service and the liberal credit terms of flexible policies. A flexible policy may also result in fewer production stoppages because of inventory shortages.[5]

Managing current assets can be thought of as involving a trade-off between costs that rise with the level of investment and costs that fall with the level of investment. Costs that rise with the level of investment in current assets are called **carrying costs**. Costs that fall with increases in the level of investment in current assets are called **shortage costs**.

---

[4] This is true of some types of finished goods.

[5] This is true of inventory of raw material but not of finished goods.

Carrying costs are generally of two types. First, because the rate of return on current assets is low compared with that of other assets, there is an opportunity cost. Second, there is the cost of maintaining the economic value of the item. The cost of warehousing inventory is an example.

Shortage costs are incurred when the investment in current assets is low. If a firm runs out of cash, it will be forced to sell marketable securities. If a firm runs out of cash and cannot readily sell marketable securities, it may need to borrow or default on an obligation. (This general situation is called a *cash-out*.) If a firm has no inventory (a *stock-out*) or if it cannot extend credit to its customers, it will lose business.

There are two kinds of shortage costs:

1. *Trading or order costs.* Order costs are the costs of placing an order for more cash (*brokerage costs*) or more inventory (*production set-up costs*).

2. *Costs related to safety reserves.* These are costs of lost sales, lost customer goodwill, and disruption of production schedules.

Figure 27.4 illustrates the basic nature of carrying costs. The total costs of investing in current assets are determined by adding the carrying costs and the shortage costs. The minimum point on the total cost curve (CA*) reflects the optimal balance of current assets. The curve is generally quite flat at the optimum, and it is difficult, if not impossible, to find the precise optimal balance of shortage and carrying costs. Usually we are content with a choice near the optimum.

If carrying costs are low or shortage costs are high, the optimal policy calls for substantial current assets. In other words, the optimal policy is a flexible one. This is illustrated in the middle graph of Figure 27.4.

If carrying costs are high or shortage costs are low, the optimal policy is a restrictive one. That is, the optimal policy calls for modest current assets. This is illustrated in the bottom graph of the figure.

Opler, Pinkowitz, Stulz, and Williamson examine the determinants of holdings of cash and marketable securities by publicly traded firms.[6] They find evidence that firms behave according to the static trade-off model of short-term financial policy described earlier. Their study focuses only on liquid assets (i.e., cash and market securities), so that carrying costs are the opportunity costs of holding liquid assets and shortage costs are the risks of not having cash when investment opportunities are good.

---

### Determinants of Corporate Liquid Asset Holdings

| Firms with high holdings of liquid assets will have | Firms with low holdings of liquid assets will have |
|---|---|
| High growth opportunities | Low growth opportunities |
| High-risk investments | Low-risk investments |
| **Firms with high holdings of liquid assets will be** | **Firms with low holdings of liquid assets will be** |
| Small firms | Large firms |
| Low-credit firms | High-credit firms |

Firms will hold more-liquid assets (i.e., cash and marketable securities) to ensure that they can continue investing when cash flow is low relative to positive NPV investment opportunities. Firms that have good access to capital markets will hold less-liquid assets.

Source: Tim Opler, Lee Pinkowitz, René Stulz, and Rohan Williamson, "The Determinants and Implications of Corporate Cash Holdings," *Journal of Financial Economics* (April 1999).

---

[6] Tim Opler, Lee Pinkowitz, René Stulz, and Rohan Williamson, "The Determinants and Implications of Corporate Cash Holdings," *Journal of Financial Economics* (April 1999).

FIGURE 27.4

**Carrying Costs and Shortage Costs**

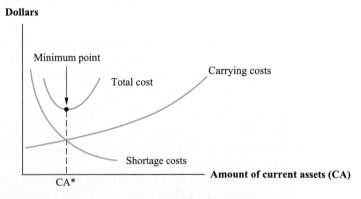

*Carrying costs* increase with the level of investment in current assets. They include both opportunity costs and the costs of maintaining the asset's economic value. *Shortage costs* decrease with increases in the level of investment in current assets. They include trading costs and the costs of running out of the current asset (for example, being short of cash).

*The optimal amount of current assets. This point minimizes costs.

## Alternative Financing Policies for Current Assets

In the previous section we examined the level of investment in current assets. Now we turn to the level of current liabilities, assuming the investment in current assets is optimal.

**An Ideal Model**   In an ideal economy, short-term assets can always be financed with short-term debt, and long-term assets can be financed with long-term debt and equity. In this economy, net working capital is always zero.

Imagine the simple case of a grain elevator operator. Grain elevator operators buy crops after harvest, store them, and sell them during the year. They have high inventories of grain after the harvest and end with low inventories just before the next harvest.

Bank loans with maturities of less than one year are used to finance the purchase of grain. These loans are paid with the proceeds from the sale of grain.

The situation is shown in Figure 27.5. Long-term assets are assumed to grow over time, whereas current assets increase at the end of the harvest and then decline during the year. Short-term assets end at zero just before the next harvest. These assets are financed by short-term debt, and long-term assets are financed with long-term debt and equity. Net working capital—current assets minus current liabilities—is always zero.

**FIGURE 27.5**

**Financing Policy for an Idealized Economy**

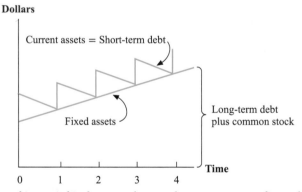

In an ideal world, net working capital is always zero because short-term assets are financed by short-term debt.

**Different Strategies in Financing Current Assets**   Current assets cannot be expected to drop to zero in the real world because a long-term rising level of sales will result in some permanent investment in current assets. A growing firm can be thought of as having a permanent requirement for both current assets and long-term assets. This total asset requirement will exhibit balances over time, reflecting (1) a secular growth trend, (2) a seasonal variation around the trend, and (3) unpredictable day-to-day and month-to-month fluctuations. This is depicted in Figure 27.6. (We have not tried to show the unpredictable day-to-day and month-to-month variations in the total asset requirement.)

Now, let us look at how this asset requirement is financed. First, consider the strategy (strategy *F* in Figure 27.7) where long-term financing covers more than the total asset requirement, even at seasonal peaks. The firm will have excess cash available for investment in marketable securities when the total asset requirement falls from peaks. Because this approach implies chronic short-term cash surpluses and a large investment in net working capital, it is considered a flexible strategy.

When long-term financing does not cover the total asset requirement, the firm must borrow in the short term to make up the deficit. This restrictive strategy is labelled strategy *R* in Figure 27.7.

FIGURE 27.6

**The Total Asset Requirement over Time**

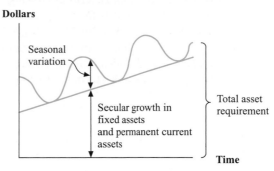

FIGURE 27.7

**Alternative Asset-Financing Policies**

Strategy *F* always implies a short-term cash surplus and a large investment in cash and marketable securities.

Strategy *R* uses long-term financing for secular asset requirements only, and short-term borrowing for seasonal variations.

**Which Is Better?**    Which is the more appropriate amount of short-term borrowing? There is no definitive answer. Several considerations must be included in a proper analysis:

1. *Cash reserves.* The flexible financing strategy implies surplus cash and little short-term borrowing. This strategy reduces the probability that a firm will experience financial distress. Firms may not need to worry as much about meeting recurring, short-run obligations. However, investments in cash and marketable securities are zero NPV investments at best.

2. *Maturity hedging.* Most firms finance inventories with short-term bank loans but pay for fixed assets with long-term financing. Firms tend to avoid financing long-lived assets with short-term borrowing. This type of maturity mismatching would necessitate frequent refinancing and is inherently risky because short-term interest rates are more volatile than longer-term rates.

3. *Term structure.* Short-term interest rates are normally lower than long-term interest rates. This implies that, on average, it is more costly to rely on long-term borrowing than on short-term borrowing.

## Current Assets and Liabilities in Practice

Table 27.3 shows that current assets made up approximately 58.54 percent of all assets for Canadian Tire in 2013. For small firms, especially in the retailing and service sectors, current assets make up an even larger portion of total assets.

**TABLE 27.3**

**Current Assets and Current Liabilities as Percentages of Total Assets for Canadian Tire, 2012–2013**

|  | 2013 | 2012 |
|---|---|---|
| **Current assets** | | |
| Cash and cash equivalents | 4.72% | 7.68% |
| Short-term investments | 3.06 | 1.28 |
| Trade and other receivables | 5.56 | 5.67 |
| Loans receivable | 33.53 | 32.25 |
| Merchandise inventories | 10.87 | 11.36 |
| Income taxes recoverable | 0.23 | 0.36 |
| Prepaid expenses and deposits | 0.50 | 0.30 |
| Assets classified as held for sale | 0.07 | 0.04 |
| Total current assets | 58.54% | 58.94% |
| **Current liabilities** | | |
| Bank indebtedness | 0.51% | 0.65% |
| Deposits | 8.65 | 9.91 |
| Trade and other payables | 13.33 | 12.33 |
| Provisions | 1.44 | 1.40 |
| Short-term borrowings | 0.88 | 0.90 |
| Loans payable | 4.48 | 4.71 |
| Income taxes payable | 0.42 | 0.40 |
| Current portion of long-term debt | 2.00 | 5.00 |
| Total current liabilities | 31.71% | 35.30% |

Source: Calculated from Canadian Tire's Annual Report, 2013.

Over time, advances in technology will change the way Canadian firms manage current assets. With new techniques such as just-in-time inventory and business-to-business e-business (B2B) sales, industrial firms are moving away from flexible policies and toward a more restrictive approach to current assets.

Current liabilities are also declining as a percentage of total assets. Firms are practising maturity hedging as they match lower current liabilities with decreased current assets. In addition to these differences over time, there are differences between industries in policies on current assets and liabilities.

The cash cycle is longer in some industries than in others, while various products and industry practices require different levels of inventory and receivables. This is why we saw in Appendix 2A that industry average ratios are not the same. For example, the aircraft industry carries more than five times as much inventory as printing and publishing carries. Does this mean that aircraft manufacturers are less efficient? Most likely the higher inventory consists of airplanes under construction. Because building planes takes more time than most printing processes, it makes sense that aircraft manufacturers carry higher inventories than printing and publishing firms.

**CONCEPT**
*QUESTIONS*

- What keeps the real world from being an ideal one where net working capital can always be zero?
- What considerations determine the optimal compromise between flexible and restrictive net working capital policies?

## 27.5   CASH BUDGETING

The **cash budget** is a primary tool of short-run financial planning. It allows the financial manager to identify short-term financing needs (and opportunities). It will tell the manager the required borrowing in the short term. It is a way of identifying the cash flow gap on the cash flow time line. The idea of the cash budget is simple: it records estimates of cash receipts and disbursements. We illustrate cash budgeting in Example 27.2.

**EXAMPLE 27.2**

All of Fun Toys' cash inflows come from the sale of toys. Cash budgeting for Fun Toys starts with a sales forecast for the next year, by quarter:

|  | First quarter | Second quarter | Third quarter | Fourth quarter |
|---|---|---|---|---|
| Sales (in $ millions) | $100 | $200 | $150 | $100 |

Fun Toys' fiscal year starts on July 1. Fun Toys' sales are seasonal and are usually very high in the second quarter, due to Christmas sales. But Fun Toys sells to department stores on credit, and sales do not generate cash immediately. Instead, cash comes later from collections on accounts receivable. Fun Toys has a 90-day collection period, and 100 percent of sales are collected the following quarter. In other words,

$$\text{Collections} = \text{Last quarter's sales}$$

This relationship implies that

$$\text{Accounts receivable at end of last quarter} = \text{Last quarter's sales} \qquad \textbf{(27.5)}$$

We assume that sales in the fourth quarter of the previous fiscal year were $100 million. From equation (27.5), we know that accounts receivable at the end of the fourth quarter of the previous fiscal year were $100 million and collections in the first quarter of the current fiscal year are $100 million.

The first-quarter sales of the current fiscal year of $100 million are added to the accounts receivable, but $100 million of collections is subtracted. Therefore, Fun Toys ended the first quarter with accounts receivable of $100 million. The basic relation is

$$\text{Ending accounts receivable} = \text{Starting accounts receivable} + \text{Sales} - \text{Collections}$$

Table 27.4 shows cash collections for Fun Toys for the next four quarters. Though collections are the only source of cash here, this need not always be the case. Other sources of cash could include sales of assets, investment income, and long-term financing.

**TABLE 27.4**

**Sources of Cash (in $ millions)**

|  | First quarter | Second quarter | Third quarter | Fourth quarter |
|---|---|---|---|---|
| Sales | $100 | $200 | $150 | $100 |
| Cash collections | 100 | 100 | 200 | 150 |
| Starting receivables | 100 | 100 | 200 | 150 |
| Ending receivables | 100 | 200 | 150 | 100 |

## Cash Outflow

Next, we consider the cash disbursements. They can be put into four basic categories, as shown in Table 27.5:

1. *Payments of accounts payable.* These are payments for goods or services, such as raw materials. These payments will generally be made after purchases. Purchases will depend on the sales forecast. In the case of Fun Toys, assume that

$$\text{Payments} = \text{Last quarter's purchases}$$
$$\text{Purchases} = 1/2 \text{ of next quarter's sales forecast}$$

2. *Wages, taxes, and other expenses.* This category includes all other normal costs of doing business that require actual expenditures. Depreciation, for example, is often thought of as a normal cost of business, but it requires no cash outflow.
3. *Capital expenditures.* These are payments of cash for long-lived assets. Fun Toys plans a major capital expenditure in the fourth quarter.
4. *Long-term financing.* This category includes interest and principal payments on long-term outstanding debt and dividend payments to shareholders.

The total forecast outflow appears in the last line of Table 27.5.

**TABLE 27.5**

**Disbursement of Cash (in $ millions)**

|  | First quarter | Second quarter | Third quarter | Fourth quarter |
|---|---|---|---|---|
| Sales | $100 | $200 | $150 | $100 |
| Purchases | 100 | 75 | 50 | 50 |
| Uses of cash: |  |  |  |  |
| Payments of accounts payable | 50 | 100 | 75 | 50 |
| Wages, taxes, and other expenses | 20 | 40 | 30 | 20 |
| Capital expenditures | 0 | 0 | 0 | 100 |
| Long-term financing expenses: interest and dividends | 10 | 10 | 10 | 10 |
| Total uses of cash | $ 80 | $150 | $115 | $180 |

## The Cash Balance

The net cash balance appears in Table 27.6, and a large net cash outflow is forecast in the second quarter. This large outflow is not caused by an inability to earn a profit. Rather, it results from delayed collections on sales. This results in a cumulative cash shortfall of $30 million in the second quarter.

**TABLE 27.6**

**The Cash Balance (in $ millions)**

|  | First quarter | Second quarter | Third quarter | Fourth quarter |
|---|---|---|---|---|
| Total cash receipts | $100 | $100 | $200 | $150 |
| Total cash disbursements | 80 | 150 | 115 | 180 |
| Net cash flow | 20 | (50) | 85 | (30) |
| Cumulative excess cash balance | 20 | (30) | 55 | 25 |
| Minimum cash balance | 5 | 5 | 5 | 5 |
| Cumulative finance surplus (deficit) requirement | 15 | (35) | 50 | 20 |

Fun Toys had established a minimum operating cash balance equal to $5 million to facilitate transactions and to protect against unexpected contingencies. This means that it has a cash shortfall in the second quarter equal to $35 million.

**CONCEPT QUESTIONS**

- How would you conduct a sensitivity analysis for Fun Toys' net cash balance?
- What could you learn from such an analysis?

## 27.6 THE SHORT-TERM FINANCIAL PLAN

### Short-Term Planning and Risk

The short-term financial plan represents Fun Toys' "best guess" for the future. Large firms go beyond the "best guess" to ask "what if" questions using scenario analysis, sensitivity analysis, and simulation. We introduced these techniques in Chapter 9's discussion of project analysis. They are tools for assessing the degree of forecasting risk and identifying those components that are most critical to a financial plan's success or failure.

Recall that scenario analysis involves varying the base case plan to create several others: a best case, worst case, and so on. Each will produce different financing needs to give the financial manager a first look at risk.

Sensitivity analysis is a variation on scenario analysis that is useful in pinpointing areas where forecasting risk is especially severe. The basic idea of sensitivity analysis is to freeze all variables except one and then see how sensitive our estimate of financing needs is to changes in that one variable. If our projected financing turns out to be very sensitive to, say, sales, then we know that extra effort in refining the sales forecast will pay off.

Since the original financial plan was almost surely developed on a computer spreadsheet, scenario and sensitivity analyses are quite straightforward and widely used.

Simulation analysis combines features of scenario and sensitivity analysis, varying all variables over a range of outcomes simultaneously. Simulation analysis yields a probability distribution of financing needs.

Air Canada uses simulation analysis in forecasting its cash needs. The simulation is useful in capturing the variability of cash flow components in Canada's airline industry. Bad weather, for example, causes delays and cancelled flights with unpredictable dislocation payments to travellers and crew overtime. This and other risks are reflected in a probability distribution of cash needs, giving the treasurer better information for planning borrowing needs.

### Short-Term Borrowing

Fun Toys has a short-term financing problem. It cannot meet the forecast cash outflows in the second quarter from internal sources. In addition, much of the cash deficit comes from the large capital expenditure. Arguably, this is a candidate for long-term financing. If it chose equity financing through an initial public offering (IPO), Fun Toys would be following the example of Chapters Online. As the firm's Internet division,

Chapters Online sold books, CD ROMs, DVDs, and videos through its website. In September 1999, Chapters Online went public, raising equity at an offering price of $13.50 per share. A little under a year later, in August 2000, analysts calculated Chapters Online's "burn rate," the rate at which the firm was using cash, to determine its cash position. Given that the stock price had fallen from the offering price of $13.50 to $2.80 per share, a further equity offering seemed unlikely and the discussion of the firm's financial health focused on the availability of short-term borrowing.

Here we concentrate on two short-term borrowing alternatives: (1) unsecured borrowing and (2) secured borrowing.

**Operating Loans**    The most common way to finance a temporary cash deficit is to arrange a short-term **operating loan** from a chartered bank. This is an agreement under which a firm is authorized to borrow up to a specified amount for a given period, usually one year (much like a credit card). Operating loans can be either unsecured or secured by collateral. Large corporations with excellent credit ratings usually structure the facility as an unsecured line of credit. Because unsecured credit lines are backed only by projections of future cash flows, bankers offer this "cash flow" lending only to top-drawer credits.

Short-term lines of credit are classified as either *committed* or *non-committed*. The latter is an informal arrangement. Committed lines of credit are more formal, legal arrangements and usually involve a commitment fee paid by the firm to the bank. (Usually the fee is on the order of 0.25 percent of the total committed funds per year.) A firm that pays a commitment fee for a committed line of credit is essentially buying insurance to guarantee that the bank cannot back out of the arrangement (absent some material change in the borrower's status).

*Compensating the Bank*    The interest rate on an operating loan is typically set equal to the bank's prime lending rate plus an additional percentage, and the rate will usually float. For example, suppose that the prime rate is 3 percent when the loan is initiated and the loan is at prime plus 1.5 percent. The original rate charged to the borrower is 4.5 percent. If after, say, 125 days, prime increases to 3.5 percent, the company's borrowing rate goes up to 5 percent and interest charges are adjusted accordingly.

The premium charged over prime will reflect the banker's assessment of the borrower's risk. Risks related to management appear most often, since poor management is considered the major risk with small businesses. There is a trend among bankers to look more closely at industry and economic risk factors. A similar set of risk factors applies to loans to large corporations.

Banks are in the business of lending mainly to low-risk borrowers. For this reason, bankers generally prefer to decline risky business loans that would require an interest rate above prime plus 3 percent. Many of the loan requests that banks turn down are from small businesses, especially start-ups. Around 60 percent of these "turn-downs" find financing elsewhere. Alternative sources include venture capital financing (discussed in Chapter 20) and federal and provincial government programs to assist small businesses.

In addition to charging interest, banks also levy fees for account activity and loan management. Small businesses may also pay application fees to cover the costs of processing loan applications. Fees are becoming increasingly important in bank compensation.[7] Fees and other details of any short-term business lending arrangements are highly negotiable. Banks will generally work with firms to design a package of fees and interest.

**Letters of Credit**    A **letter of credit** is a common arrangement in international finance. With a letter of credit, the bank issuing the letter promises to make a loan if

---

[7] U.S. banks sometimes require that the firm keep some account of money on deposit. This is called a *compensating balance*. A compensating balance is some of the firm's money kept by the bank in low-interest or non–interest bearing accounts. By leaving these funds with the bank and receiving no interest, the firm further increases the effective interest rate earned by the bank on the line of credit, thereby compensating the bank.

certain conditions are met. Typically, the letter guarantees payment on a shipment of goods provided that the goods arrive as promised. A letter of credit can be revocable (subject to cancellation) or irrevocable (not subject to cancellation if the specified conditions are met).

**Secured Loans**   Banks and other financial institutions often require *security* for a loan. Security for short-term loans usually consists of accounts receivable or inventories. In addition, banks routinely limit risk through loan conditions called **covenants**.

Under **accounts receivable financing**, receivables are either *assigned* or *factored*. Under assignment, the lender not only has a lien on the receivables but also has recourse to the borrower. Factoring involves the sale of accounts receivable. The purchaser, who is called a *factor*, must then collect on the receivables. The factor assumes the full risk of default on bad accounts.

Financial engineers have come up with a new approach to receivables financing. When Superior Plus Corp (TSX: SPB) securitized receivables, it sold them to Superior Plus LP, a wholly owned subsidiary. Under the terms of the securitization program, Superior Plus LP may sell up to $130 million of certain accounts receivable on a 30-day revolving basis to a Canadian chartered bank to finance a portion of its working capital requirements. Since receivables are liquid, Superior Plus LP debt is less risky than lending to Superior Plus Corp., and the company benefits through interest savings.[8]

As the name implies, an **inventory loan** uses inventory as collateral. Some common types of inventory loans are as follows:

1. *Blanket inventory lien.* The blanket inventory lien gives the lender a lien against all the borrower's inventories.

2. *Trust receipt.* Under this arrangement, the borrower holds the inventory in trust for the lender. The document acknowledging the loan is called the *trust receipt*. Proceeds from the sale of inventory are remitted immediately to the lender.

3. *Field warehouse financing.* In field warehouse financing, a public warehouse company supervises the inventory for the lender.

When a firm purchases supplies on credit, the increase in accounts payable is a source of funds and automatic financing. As compared with bank financing, **trade credit** has the advantage of arising automatically from the firm's business. It does not require a formal financing agreement with covenants that may restrict the borrower's business activities. Suppliers offer credit to remain competitive; in many industries, the terms of credit include a cash discount for paying within a certain period.

**Other Sources**   Corporations obtain short-term funds from a variety of other sources. The most important of these are the issuance of **commercial paper** and financing through **banker's acceptances**.

Commercial paper consists of short-term notes issued by large and highly rated firms. Firms issuing commercial paper in Canada generally have borrowing needs over $20 million. Rating agencies—the Dominion Bond Rating Service and Standard & Poor's (discussed in Chapter 21)—rate commercial paper similarly to bonds. Typically, these notes are of short maturity, ranging from 30 to 90 days, with some maturities up to 365 days. Commercial paper is offered in denominations of $100,000 and up. Because the firm issues paper directly and because it usually backs the issue with a special bank line of credit, the interest rate the firm obtains is below the rate a bank would charge for a direct loan (usually by around 1 percent). Another advantage is that commercial paper offers the issuer flexibility in tailoring the maturity and size of the borrowing.

Banker's acceptances are a variant on commercial paper. When a bank "accepts" paper, it charges a stamping fee in return for a guarantee of the paper's principal and

---

[8] "Superior Plus Corp. Extends Its Accounts Receivable Securitization Program," July 2, 2010, marketwired.com/press-release/superior-plus-corp-extends-its-accounts-receivable-securitization-program-tsx-spb-1285259.htm.

interest. Stamping fees vary from 0.20 percent to 0.75 percent. Banker's acceptances are more widely used than commercial paper in Canada because Canadian chartered banks enjoy stronger credit ratings than all but the largest corporations.[9] The main buyers of banker's acceptances and commercial paper are institutions, including mutual funds, insurance companies, and banks.

A disadvantage of borrowing through banker's acceptances or commercial paper is the risk that the market might temporarily dry up when it comes time to "roll over" the paper.

**CONCEPT QUESTIONS**

- What are the two basic forms of short-term financing?
- Describe two types of secured loans.

## In the Absence of Short-Term Borrowing

Throughout this chapter, we explained the importance of short-term financing for everyday operations. Without short-term financing, otherwise solvent businesses would not have the liquid assets needed for current obligations, like paying employee wages or repaying a loan. This was the global environment all businesses faced in the financial crisis of 2007–2009—a world without short-term borrowing. As we discussed earlier in this book, the financial crisis was triggered by a mixture of a housing market bubble, risky derivatives, lenient lending policies, and overoptimism on the part of the credit rating agencies. When the bubble burst and reality set in, the clouds were already gathering for the perfect storm. As prominent companies like Lehman Brothers filed for bankruptcy, the market lost confidence and the credit markets froze. In an attempt to mitigate a global crisis, one of the first responses of central banks around the world was to cut rates to support liquidity and lending. Between June 2007 and June 2009, the Canadian target overnight rate declined from 4.50 percent to 0.25 percent.[10]

The central bank's emphasis on lowering rates stresses the importance of maintaining ample liquidity in the markets. Without liquidity, businesses cannot operate and performance will decline, leading to eventual bankruptcy. Air Canada is one of many prominent Canadian corporations that faced significant challenges during the recession because of liquidity issues. For instance, in 2008, Air Canada recorded a $1.025 billion loss attributable to a spike in oil prices, adverse fluctuations in foreign exchange, liquidity requirements, and the weakening demand for air travel. In particular, the airline noted the need to plan for liquidity required to meet continuing interest and debt payments.[11] As the example shows, all companies have short-term obligations. Without short-term borrowing, operating is virtually impossible.

Learning from the recession, many corporations have steadily accumulated a growing amount of cash reserves to deal with future uncertainties. For instance, Canadian non-financial corporations held a total of $600 billion in unused, idle cash in 2012.[12]

---

[9] The reverse situation prevails in the United States.

[10] Historical data drawn from bankofcanada.ca/rates/interest-rates/canadian-interest-rates/.

[11] Air Canada's management discusses liquidity risks during the recession as well as their course of preventative action on pages 38–40 of their 2008 annual report.

[12] John Shmuel, "Stop Sitting on Your Cash Piles, Carney Tells Corporate Canada," Financial Post, August 22, 2012, business.financialpost.com/2012/08/22/dont-blame-the-loonie-for-weak-exports-carney-tells-caw/.

# 27.7

# SUMMARY AND CONCLUSIONS

1. This chapter introduces the management of short-term finance. Short-term finance involves short-lived assets and liabilities. We trace and examine the short-term sources and uses of cash as they appear on the firm's financial statements. We see how current assets and current liabilities arise in the short-term operating activities and the cash cycle of the firm. From an accounting perspective, short-term finance involves net working capital.

2. Managing short-term cash flows involves minimizing costs. The two major costs are carrying costs (the interest and related costs incurred by overinvesting in short-term assets such as cash) and shortage costs (the costs of running out of short-term assets). The objective of managing short-term finance and of short-term financial planning is to find the optimal trade-off between these two costs.

3. In an ideal economy, the firm could perfectly predict its short-term uses and sources of cash, and net working capital could be kept at zero. In the real world, net working capital provides a buffer that lets the firm meet its ongoing obligations. The financial manager seeks the optimal level of each of the current assets.

4. The financial manager can use the cash budget to identify short-term financial needs. The cash budget tells the manager what borrowing is required or what lending will be possible in the short run. The firm has available to it a number of possible ways of acquiring funds to meet short-term shortfalls, including unsecured and secured loans.

**KEY TERMS**

| | | |
|---|---|---|
| Accounts receivable financing   807 | Commercial paper   807 | Shortage costs   798 |
| Banker's acceptance   807 | Covenant   807 | Short-run operating activities   794 |
| Carrying costs   798 | Inventory loan   807 | Target cash balance 817 |
| Cash budget   803 | Letter of credit   806 | Trade credit   807 |
| Cash cycle   794 | Liquidity   790 | |
| Cash flow timeline   794 | Operating cycle   794 | |
| | Operating loan   806 | |

**QUESTIONS & PROBLEMS**

## Changes in the Cash Account

27.1 Indicate the impact of the following corporate actions on cash, using the letter *I* for an increase, the letter *D* for a decrease, or the letter *N* when no change occurs.

   *a.* A dividend is paid with funds received from a sale of debt.
   *b.* Real estate is purchased and paid for with short-term debt.
   *c.* Inventory is bought on credit.
   *d.* A short-term bank loan is repaid.
   *e.* Next year's taxes are prepaid.
   *f.* Preferred stock is redeemed.
   *g.* Sales are made on credit.
   *h.* Interest on long-term debt is paid.
   *i.* Payments for previous sales are collected.
   *j.* The accounts payable balance is reduced.
   *k.* A dividend is paid.
   *l.* Production supplies are purchased and paid for with a short-term note.
   *m.* Utility bills are paid.
   *n.* Cash is paid for raw materials purchased for inventory.
   *o.* Marketable securities are sold.

### Cash Equation

27.2 McConnell Corp. has a book net worth of $10,380. Long-term debt is $7,500. Net working capital, other than cash, is $2,105. Fixed assets are $15,190. How much cash does the company have? If current liabilities are $1,450, what are current assets?

### Changes in the Operating Cycle

27.3 Indicate the effect that the following will have on the operating cycle. Use the letter *I* to indicate an increase, the letter *D* for a decrease, or the letter *N* for no change.

   a. Receivables average goes up.
   b. Credit repayment times for customers are increased.
   c. Inventory turnover goes from 3 times to 6 times.
   d. Payables turnover goes from 6 times to 11 times.
   e. Receivables turnover goes from 7 times to 9 times.
   f. Payments to suppliers are accelerated.

### Changes in Cycles

27.4 Indicate the impact of the following on the cash and operating cycles, respectively. Use the letter *I* to indicate an increase, the letter *D* for a decrease, or the letter *N* for no change.

   a. The terms of cash discounts offered to customers are made less favourable.
   b. The cash discounts offered by suppliers are increased; thus, payments are made earlier.
   c. An increasing number of customers begin to pay in cash instead of with credit.
   d. Fewer raw materials than usual are purchased.
   e. A greater percentage of raw material purchases are paid for with credit.
   f. More finished goods are produced for inventory instead of for order.

### Calculating Cash Collections

27.5 The Litzenberger Co. has projected the following quarterly sales amounts for the coming year:

|        | Q1    | Q2    | Q3    | Q4    |
|--------|-------|-------|-------|-------|
| Sales  | $700  | $630  | $810  | $930  |

   a. Accounts receivable at the beginning of the year are $275. Litzenberger has a 45-day collection period. Calculate cash collections in each of the four quarters by completing the following:

|                      | Q1 | Q2 | Q3 | Q4 |
|----------------------|----|----|----|----|
| Beginning receivables |    |    |    |    |
| Sales                 |    |    |    |    |
| Cash collections      |    |    |    |    |
| Ending receivables    |    |    |    |    |

   b. Rework (a) assuming a collection period of 60 days.
   c. Rework (a) assuming a collection period of 30 days.

### Calculating Cycles

27.6 Consider the following financial statement information for the Bulldog Icers Corp.:

| Item                | Beginning | Ending    |
|---------------------|-----------|-----------|
| Inventory           | $15,382   | $16,147   |
| Accounts receivable | 12,169    | 12,682    |
| Accounts payable    | 13,408    | 14,108    |
| Net sales           | $143,625  |           |
| Cost of goods sold  | 105,817   |           |

Calculate the operating and cash cycles. How do you interpret your answer?

## Calculating Payments

**27.7** Lewellen Products has projected the following sales for the coming year:

|  | Q1 | Q2 | Q3 | Q4 |
|---|---|---|---|---|
| Sales | $620 | $555 | $705 | $780 |

Sales in the year following this one are projected to be 15 percent greater in each quarter.

    *a.* Calculate payments to suppliers assuming that Lewellen places orders during each quarter equal to 30 percent of projected sales for the next quarter. Assume that the company pays immediately. What is the payables period in this case?

|  | Q1 | Q2 | Q3 | Q4 |
|---|---|---|---|---|
| Payment of accounts | $ | $ | $ | $ |

    *b.* Rework (a) assuming a 90-day payables period.
    *c.* Rework (a) assuming a 60-day payables period.

 **27.8** The Thakor Corp.'s purchases from suppliers in a quarter are equal to 75 percent of the next quarter's forecast sales. The payables period is 60 days. Wages, taxes, and other expenses are 20 percent of sales, and interest and dividends are $73 per quarter. No capital expenditures are planned.

Here are the projected quarterly sales:

|  | Q1 | Q2 | Q3 | Q4 |
|---|---|---|---|---|
| Sales | $830 | $1,050 | $970 | $860 |

Sales for the first quarter of the following year are projected at $970. Calculate the company's cash outlays by completing the following:

|  | Q1 | Q2 | Q3 | Q4 |
|---|---|---|---|---|
| Payment of accounts |  |  |  |  |
| Wages, taxes, and other expenses |  |  |  |  |
| Long-term financing expenses (interest and dividends) |  |  |  |  |
| Total |  |  |  |  |

## Calculating Cash Collections

**27.9** The following is the sales budget for Shleifer Inc. for the first quarter of 2016:

|  | January | February | March |
|---|---|---|---|
| Sales budget | $234,800 | $249,300 | $271,000 |

Credit sales are collected as follows:

    65 percent in the month of the sale.
    20 percent in the month after the sale.
    15 percent in the second month after the sale.

The accounts receivable balance at the end of the previous quarter was $106,800 ($76,300 of which was uncollected December sales).

    *a.* Compute the sales for November.
    *b.* Compute the sales for December.
    *c.* Compute the cash collections from sales for each month from January through March.

### Calculating the Cash Budget

27.10   Here are some important figures from the budget of Cornell Inc. for the second quarter of 2015:

|  | April | May | June |
|---|---|---|---|
| Credit sales | $547,200 | $570,240 | $630,720 |
| Credit purchases | 211,680 | 252,720 | 288,450 |
| Cash disbursements |  |  |  |
| Wages, taxes, and expenses | 57,240 | 69,422 | 72,432 |
| Interest | 16,416 | 16,416 | 16,416 |
| Equipment purchases | 119,520 | 131,040 | 0 |

The company predicts that 5 percent of its credit sales will never be collected, 35 percent of its sales will be collected in the month of the sale, and the remaining 60 percent will be collected in the following month. Credit purchases will be paid in the month following the purchase.

In March 2015, credit sales were $302,400 and credit purchases were $224,640. Using this information, complete the following cash budget:

|  | April | May | June |
|---|---|---|---|
| Beginning cash balance | $403,200 |  |  |
| Cash receipts |  |  |  |
| Cash collections from credit sales |  |  |  |
| Total cash available |  |  |  |
| Cash disbursements |  |  |  |
| Purchases |  |  |  |
| Wages, taxes, and expenses |  |  |  |
| Interest |  |  |  |
| Equipment purchases |  |  |  |
| Total cash disbursements |  |  |  |
| Ending cash balance |  |  |  |

### Sources and Uses

27.11   Here are the most recent statements of financial position for Country Kettles Inc. Excluding accumulated depreciation, determine whether each item is a source or a use of cash, and the amount:

**COUNTRY KETTLES INC.**
**Statement of Financial Position**
**December 31, 2015**

|  | 2014 | 2015 |
|---|---|---|
| **Assets** |  |  |
| Cash | $ 48,180 | $ 45,815 |
| Accounts receivable | 100,155 | 105,413 |
| Inventories | 83,600 | 89,716 |
| Property, plant, and equipment | 225,992 | 249,086 |
| Less: accumulated depreciation | (77,194) | (85,579) |
| Total assets | $380,733 | $404,451 |
| **Liabilities and equity** |  |  |
| Accounts payable | $ 72,522 | $ 50,396 |
| Accrued expenses | 10,980 | 9,840 |
| Long-term debt | 49,500 | 45,000 |
| Common stock | 25,000 | 30,000 |
| Accumulated retained earnings | 222,731 | 269,215 |
| Total liabilities and equity | $380,733 | $404,451 |

## Cash Budgeting

27.12 The sales budget for your company in the coming year is based on a 10 percent quarterly growth rate with the first-quarter sales projection at $225 million. In addition to this basic trend, the seasonal adjustments for the four quarters are 0, −$16 million, −$8 million, and $21 million, respectively. Generally, 50 percent of the sales can be collected within the quarter and 45 percent in the following quarter; the rest of the sales are bad debt. The bad debts are written off in the second quarter after the sales are made. The beginning accounts receivable balance is $104 million. Assuming all sales are on credit, compute the cash collections from sales for each quarter.

## Calculating the Cash Budget

27.13 Wildcat Inc. has estimated sales (in millions) for the next four quarters as follows:

|  | Q1 | Q2 | Q3 | Q4 |
|---|---|---|---|---|
| Sales | $105 | $90 | $122 | $140 |

Sales for the first quarter of the year after this one are projected at $120 million. Accounts receivable at the beginning of the year were $34 million. Wildcat has a 45-day collection period.

Wildcat's purchases from suppliers in a quarter are equal to 45 percent of the next quarter's forecast sales, and suppliers are normally paid in 36 days. Wages, taxes, and other expenses run about 30 percent of sales. Interest and dividends are $6 million per quarter.

Wildcat plans a major capital outlay in the second quarter of $40 million. Finally, the company started the year with a $32 million cash balance and wishes to maintain a $15 million minimum balance.

a. Complete a cash budget for Wildcat by filling in the following:

**WILDCAT INC.**
**Cash Budget**
**(in $ millions)**

|  | Q1 | Q2 | Q3 | Q4 |
|---|---|---|---|---|
| Beginning cash balance | $15 |  |  |  |
| Net cash inflow |  |  |  |  |
| Ending cash balance |  |  |  |  |
| Minimum cash balance | 15 |  |  |  |
| Cumulative surplus (deficit) |  |  |  |  |

b. Assume that Wildcat can borrow any needed funds on a short-term basis at a rate of 3 percent per quarter and can invest any excess funds in short-term marketable securities at a rate of 2 percent per quarter. Prepare a short-term financial plan by filling in the following schedule. What is the net cash cost (total interest paid minus total investment income earned) for the year?

**WILDCAT INC.**
**Short-Term Financial Plan**
**(in $ millions)**

|  | Q1 | Q2 | Q3 | Q4 |
|---|---|---|---|---|
| Beginning cash balance | $15 | | | |
| Net cash inflow | | | | |
| New short-term investments | | | | |
| Income from short-term investments | | | | |
| Short-term investments sold | | | | |
| New short-term borrowing | | | | |
| Interest on short-term borrowing | | | | |
| Short-term borrowing repaid | | | | |
| Ending cash balance | | | | |
| Minimum cash balance | 15 | | | |
| Cumulative surplus (deficit) | | | | |
| Beginning short-term investments | | | | |
| Ending short-term investments | | | | |
| Beginning short-term debt | | | | |
| Ending short-term debt | | | | |

### Cash Management Policy

27.14 Rework Problem 27.13 assuming the following:
   a. Wildcat maintains a minimum cash balance of $20 million.
   b. Wildcat maintains a minimum cash balance of $10 million.

Based on your answers in (a) and (b), do you think the firm can boost its profit by changing its cash management policy? Should other factors be considered as well? Explain.

### Short-Term Finance Policy

27.15 Calgary Compressor and Pnew Brunswick Pneumatic are competing manufacturing firms. Their financial statements are printed here.
   a. How are the current assets of each firm financed?
   b. Which firm has the larger investment in current assets? Why?
   c. Which firm is more likely to incur carrying costs, and which is more likely to incur shortage costs? Why?

**CALGARY COMPRESSOR**
**Statement of Financial Position**

|  | 2014 | 2015 |
|---|---|---|
| **Assets** | | |
| Current assets: | | |
| Cash | $ 16,339 | $ 13,862 |
| Net accounts receivable | 25,778 | 23,887 |
| Inventory | 43,287 | 54,867 |
| Total current assets | $ 85,404 | $ 92,616 |
| Fixed assets: | | |
| Plant, property, and equipment | 99,615 | 101,543 |
| Less: accumulated depreciation | (31,957) | (34,331) |
| Net fixed assets | $ 67,658 | $ 67,212 |
| Prepaid expenses | 1,791 | 1,914 |
| Other assets | 13,138 | 13,052 |
| Total assets | $167,991 | $174,794 |
| **Liabilities and equity** | | |
| Current liabilities: | | |
| Accounts payable | $  4,893 | $  6,494 |
| Notes payable | 11,617 | 10,483 |
| Accrued expenses | 7,227 | 7,422 |
| Other taxes payable | 8,460 | 9,924 |
| Total current liabilities | 32,197 | 34,323 |
| Long-term debt | 22,036 | 22,036 |
| Total liabilities | $ 54,233 | $ 56,359 |
| Equity: | | |
| Common stock | 38,000 | 38,000 |
| Paid-in capital | 12,000 | 12,000 |
| Retained earnings | 63,758 | 68,435 |
| Total equity | 113,758 | 118,435 |
| Total liabilities and equity | $167,991 | $174,794 |

**CALGARY COMPRESSOR**
**Statement of Comprehensive Income 2015**

| | |
|---|---|
| **Income:** | |
| Sales | $162,749 |
| Other income | 1,002 |
| Total income | $163,751 |
| **Operating expenses:** | |
| Cost of goods sold | 103,570 |
| Selling and administrative expenses | 28,495 |
| Depreciation | 2,274 |
| Total expenses | $134,339 |
| Pre-tax earnings | 29,412 |
| Taxes | 14,890 |
| Net earnings | $ 14,522 |
| Dividends | $  9,845 |
| Retained earnings | $  4,677 |

## PNEW BRUNSWICK PNEUMATIC
### Statement of Financial Position

|  | 2014 | 2015 |
|---|---|---|
| **Assets** | | |
| **Current assets:** | | |
| Cash | $ 5,794 | $ 3,307 |
| Net accounts receivable | 26,177 | 22,133 |
| Inventory | 46,463 | 44,661 |
| Total current assets | $78,434 | $70,101 |
| **Fixed assets:** | | |
| Plant, property, and equipment | 31,842 | 31,116 |
| Less: accumulated depreciation | (19,297) | (18,143) |
| Net fixed assets | $12,545 | $12,973 |
| Prepaid expenses | 763 | 688 |
| Other assets | 1,601 | 1,385 |
| Total assets | $93,343 | $85,147 |
| **Liabilities and equity** | | |
| **Current liabilities:** | | |
| Accounts payable | $ 6,008 | $ 5,019 |
| Bank loans | 3,722 | 645 |
| Accrued expenses | 4,254 | 3,295 |
| Other taxes payable | 5,688 | 4,951 |
| Total current liabilities | $19,672 | $13,910 |
| **Equity:** | | |
| Common stock | 20,576 | 20,576 |
| Paid-in capital | 5,624 | 5,624 |
| Retained earnings | 48,598 | 46,164 |
| Less: Treasury stock | (1,127) | (1,127) |
| Total equity | $73,671 | $71,237 |
| Total liabilities and equity | $93,343 | $85,147 |

## PNEW BRUNSWICK PNEUMATIC
### Statement of Comprehensive Income 2015

| | |
|---|---|
| **Income:** | |
| Sales | $91,374 |
| Other income | 1,067 |
| Total income | $92,441 |
| **Operating expenses:** | |
| Cost of goods sold | 59,042 |
| Selling and administrative expenses | 18,068 |
| Depreciation | 1,154 |
| Total expenses | $78,264 |
| Pre-tax earnings | 14,177 |
| Taxes | 6,838 |
| Net earnings | $ 7,339 |
| Dividends | $ 4,905 |
| Retained earnings | $ 2,434 |

# Keafer Manufacturing Working Capital Management

You have recently been hired by Keafer Manufacturing to work in its established treasury department. Keafer Manufacturing is a small company that produces highly customized cardboard boxes in a variety of sizes for different purchasers. Adam Keafer, the owner of the company, works primarily in the sales and production areas of the company. Currently, the company basically puts all receivables in one pile and all payables in another, and a part-time bookkeeper periodically comes in and attacks the piles. Because of this disorganized system, the finance area needs work, and that's what you've been brought in to do.

The company currently has a cash balance of $210,000, and it plans to purchase new machinery in the third quarter at a cost of $390,000. The purchase of the machinery will be made with cash because of the discount offered for a cash purchase. Adam wants to maintain a minimum cash balance of $135,000 to guard against unforeseen contingencies. All of Keafer's sales to customers and purchases from suppliers are made with credit, and no discounts are offered or taken.

The company had the following sales each quarter of the year just ended:

|  | Q1 | Q2 | Q3 | Q4 |
|---|---|---|---|---|
| Gross sales | $1,102,000 | $1,141,000 | $1,125,000 | $1,063,000 |

After some research and discussions with customers, you're projecting that sales will be 8 percent higher in each quarter next year. Sales for the first quarter of the following year are also expected to grow at 8 percent. You calculate that Keafer currently has an accounts receivable period of 57 days and an accounts receivable balance of $675,000. However, 10 percent of the accounts receivable balance is from a company that has just entered bankruptcy, and it is likely that this portion will never be collected.

You've also calculated that Keafer typically orders supplies each quarter in the amount of 50 percent of the next quarter's projected gross sales, and suppliers are paid in 53 days on average. Wages, taxes, and other costs run about 25 percent of gross sales. The company has a quarterly interest payment of $185,000 on its long-term debt. Finally, the company uses a bank for its short-term financial needs. It currently pays 1.2 percent per quarter on all short-term borrowing and maintains a money market account that pays 0.5 percent per quarter on all short-term deposits.

Adam has asked you to prepare a cash budget and short-term financial plan for the company under the current policies. He has also asked you to prepare additional plans based on changes in several inputs.

1.  Use the numbers given to complete the cash budget and short-term financial plan.

2.  Rework the cash budget and short-term financial plan assuming Keafer changes to a minimum cash balance of $90,000.

3.  Rework the sales budget assuming an 11 percent growth rate in sales and a 5 percent growth rate in sales. Assume a $135,000 **target cash balance**.

4.  Assuming the company maintains its target cash balance at $135,000, what sales growth rate would result in a zero need for short-term financing? Explain what your answer implies about the likely need for short-term financing. To answer these questions, you may need to set up a spreadsheet and use the "Solver" function.

# 28

# Cash Management

**EXECUTIVE SUMMARY**

Most large corporations hold some of their assets in highly liquid form—in cash and marketable securities. For example, in 2013, Magna International Inc., Canadian supplier of automotive components, held around US$1,554 million or 8.6 percent of its assets in cash and cash equivalents. Major U.S. technology firms were the largest holders of cash in 2013. For example, at the end of its fiscal year in September 2013, Apple held cash and marketable securities totalling US$146.8 billion, making up 70.9 percent of total assets.

This chapter is about how firms manage cash. The basic objective in cash management is to keep the investment in cash as low as possible while still operating the firm's activities efficiently and effectively. As we explained in the previous chapter, this is becoming an issue as corporations are trending toward holding large reserves of cash as a precaution against an uncertain future coming out of the financial crisis of 2007–2009. The chapter separates cash management into two steps:

1. Collecting and disbursing cash efficiently.
2. Investing excess cash in marketable securities.

The firm must establish procedures so that cash is collected and disbursed as efficiently as possible.

Firms must invest temporarily idle cash in short-term marketable securities. These securities can be bought and sold in the *money market*. Money market securities have very little risk of default and are highly marketable.

Cash management is not as complex and conceptually challenging as other topics, such as capital budgeting and asset pricing. Still, cash management is very important, and financial managers in many companies, especially in the retail and services industries, spend a significant portion of their time on this activity.

## 28.1 REASONS FOR HOLDING CASH

John Maynard Keynes, in his classic work *The General Theory of Employment, Interest, and Money*, identified three motives for liquidity: the speculative motive, the precautionary motive, and the transaction motive. We discuss these next.

### The Speculative and Precautionary Motives

The **speculative motive** is the need to hold cash to be able to take advantage of, for example, bargain purchases that might arise, attractive interest rates, and (in the case of international firms) favourable exchange rate fluctuations.

For most firms, reserve borrowing ability and marketable securities can be used to satisfy speculative motives. Thus, there might be a speculative motive for maintaining liquidity, but not necessarily for holding cash per se. Think of it this way: if you have a credit card with a very large credit limit, then you can probably take advantage of any unusual bargains that come along without carrying any cash.

This is also true, to a lesser extent, for precautionary motives. The **precautionary motive** is the need for a safety supply to act as a financial reserve. Once again, there is probably a precautionary motive for maintaining liquidity. However, given that the value of money market instruments is relatively certain and that instruments such as T-bills are extremely liquid, there is no real need to hold substantial amounts of cash for precautionary purposes.

## The Transaction Motive

Cash is needed to satisfy the **transaction motive**: the need to have cash on hand to pay bills. Transaction-related needs come from the normal disbursement and collection activities of the firm. The disbursement of cash includes the payment of wages and salaries, trade debts, taxes, and dividends.

Cash is collected from product sales, the selling of assets, and new financing. The cash inflows (collections) and outflows (disbursements) are not perfectly synchronized, and some level of cash holdings is necessary to serve as a buffer.

As electronic funds transfers and other high-speed, "paperless" payment mechanisms continue to develop, even the transaction demand for cash may all but disappear. Even if it does, however, there will still be a demand for liquidity and a need to manage it efficiently.

## Costs of Holding Cash

When a firm holds cash in excess of some necessary minimum, it incurs an opportunity cost. The opportunity cost of excess cash (held in currency or bank deposits) is the interest income that could be earned by the next best use, such as investment in marketable securities.

Given the opportunity cost of holding cash, why would a firm hold cash in excess of its requirements? The answer is that a cash balance must be maintained to provide the liquidity necessary for transaction needs—paying bills. If the firm maintains too small a cash balance, it may run out of cash. If this happens, the firm may have to raise cash on a short-term basis. This could involve, for example, selling marketable securities or borrowing.

Activities such as selling marketable securities and borrowing involve various costs. As we've discussed, holding cash has an opportunity cost. To determine the appropriate cash balance, the firm must weigh the benefits of holding cash against these costs. We discuss this subject in more detail in the sections that follow.

## Cash Management versus Liquidity Management

Before we move on, we should note that it is important to distinguish between true cash management and a more general subject, liquidity management. The distinction is a source of confusion because the word *cash* is used in practice in two different ways. First of all, it has its literal meaning, actual cash on hand. However, financial managers frequently use the word to describe a firm's holdings of cash along with its marketable securities, and marketable securities are sometimes called *cash equivalents*, or *near-cash*.

The distinction between liquidity management and cash management is straightforward. Liquidity management concerns the optimal quantity of liquid assets a firm should have on hand, and it is one particular aspect of the current asset management policies we discussed in Chapter 27. Cash management is much more closely related to optimizing mechanisms for collecting and disbursing cash, and it is this subject that we primarily focus on in this chapter.

In general, the firm needs to balance the benefits of holding cash to meet transactions and avoid insolvency against the opportunity costs of lower returns. A sensible cash management policy is to have enough cash on hand to meet the obligations that may arise in the ordinary course of business and to invest some excess cash in marketable securities for precautionary purposes. All other excess cash should be invested in the business or paid out to investors.[1] By considering the trade-off of holding cash as well as evaluating future cash flow obligations, firms decide on a target cash balance.

**CONCEPT QUESTIONS**

- What is the transaction motive, and how does it lead firms to hold cash?
- What is the cost to firms of holding excess cash?
- What is a target cash balance?

# 28.2  MANAGING THE COLLECTION AND DISBURSEMENT OF CASH

A firm's cash balance as reported in its financial statements (*book cash* or *ledger cash*) is not the same thing as the balance shown in its bank account (*bank cash* or *collected bank cash*). The difference between bank cash and book cash is called **float** and represents the net effect of cheques in the process of collection.

---

**EXAMPLE 28.1**

Imagine that General Mechanics Inc. (GMI) has $100,000 on deposit with its bank. It purchases some raw materials, paying its vendors with a cheque written on July 8 for $100,000. The company's books (that is, ledger balances) are changed to show the $100,000 reduction in the cash balance. But the firm's bank will not find out about this cheque until it has been deposited at the vendor's bank and has been presented to the firm's bank for payment on, say, July 15. Until the cheque's presentation, the firm's bank cash is greater than its book cash, and it has *positive float*:

**Position Prior to July 8:**

$$\text{Float} = \text{Firm's bank cash} - \text{Firm's book cash}$$
$$= \$100,000 - \$100,000$$
$$= 0$$

**Position from July 8 through July 14:**

$$\text{Disbursement float} = \text{Firm's bank cash} - \text{Firm's book cash}$$
$$= \$100,000 - 0$$
$$= \$100,000$$

During the period of time that the cheque is *outstanding*, GMI has a balance with the bank of $100,000. Cheques written by the firm generate *disbursement float*, causing an immediate decrease in book cash but no immediate change in bank cash.

---

[1] There is some evidence that corporate governance has some role in the cash holdings of U.S. firms. Jarrad Harford, Sattar A. Mansi, and William F. Maxwell, in "Corporate Governance and Firm Cash Holdings in the U.S.," *Journal of Financial Economics* (March 2008), find that firms with weaker corporate governance systems have larger cash reserves. The combination of excess cash and weak governance leads to more capital spending and more acquisitions.

EXAMPLE **28.2**

Imagine that GMI receives a cheque from a customer for $100,000. Assume, as before, that the company has $100,000 deposited at its bank and has a *neutral float position*. It processes the cheque through the bookkeeping department and increases its book balance by $100,000 to $200,000. However, the additional cash is not available to GMI until the cheque is deposited in the firm's bank. This will occur on, say, November 9, the next day. In the meantime, the cash position at GMI will reflect a collection float of $100,000:

**Position Prior to November 8:**

$$\text{Float} = \text{Firm's bank cash} - \text{Firm's book cash}$$
$$= \$100,000 - \$100,000$$
$$= 0$$

**Position from November 8 to November 9:**

$$\text{Collection float} = \text{Firm's bank cash} - \text{Firm's book cash}$$
$$= \$100,000 - \$200,000$$
$$= -\$100,000$$

Cheques received by the firm represent *collection float*, which increases book cash immediately but does not immediately change bank cash. The firm is helped by disbursement float and is hurt by collection float. The sum of disbursement float and collection float is *net float*.

A firm should be more concerned with net float and bank cash than with book cash. If a financial manager knows that a cheque will not clear for several days, he will be able to keep a lower cash balance at the bank. Good float management can generate a great deal of money. For example, the average daily sales of Exxon are about $248 million. If Exxon speeds up the collection process or slows down the disbursement process by one day, it frees up $248 million, which can be invested in marketable securities. With an interest rate of 3 percent compounded daily, this represents overnight interest of $20,384 [or $248 million × (0.03/365)].

Float management involves controlling the collection and disbursement of cash. The objective in cash collection is to reduce the lag between the time customers pay their bills and the time the cheques are collected. The objective in cash disbursement is to slow down payments, thereby increasing the time between when cheques are written and when cheques are presented. Of course, to the extent that the firm succeeds in doing this, the customers and suppliers lose money, and the trade-off is the effect on the firm's relationship with them.

Collection float can be broken down into three parts: mail float, in-house processing float, and availability float.

1. *Mail float* is the time during which cheques are trapped in the postal system.
2. *In-house processing float* is the time it takes the receiver of a cheque to process the payment and deposit it in a bank for collection.
3. *Availability float* refers to the time required to clear a cheque through the banking system. In the Canadian banking system, availability float cannot exceed one day and is often zero, so this is the least important part.

EXAMPLE **28.3**

A cheque for $1,000 is mailed by a customer on Monday, September 1. Because of mailing, processing, and clearing delays, it is not credited as available cash in the firm's bank until the following Monday, seven days later. The float for this cheque is

$$\text{Float} = \$1,000 \times 7 \text{ days}$$
$$= \$7,000$$

Another cheque for $7,000 is mailed on September 1. It is available on the next day. The float for this cheque is

$$\text{Float} = \$7,000 \times 1 \text{ day}$$
$$= \$7,000$$

The measurement of float depends on the time lag and the dollars involved. The cost of float is an opportunity cost, because the cash is unavailable for use during the time cheques are tied up in the collection process. The cost of float can be determined by (1) estimating the average daily receipts, (2) calculating the average delay in obtaining the receipts, and (3) discounting the average daily receipts by the *delay-adjusted cost of capital*.

EXAMPLE **28.4**

Suppose that Concepts Inc. received two items each month:

|        | Amount      | Number of days delay | Float        |
|--------|-------------|----------------------|--------------|
| Item 1 | $5,000,000  | × 3 =                | $15,000,000  |
| Item 2 | 3,000,000   | × 5 =                | 15,000,000   |
| Total  | $8,000,000  |                      | $30,000,000  |

The average daily float over the month is calculated as follows:

**Average Daily Float:**

$$\frac{\text{Total float}}{\text{Total days}} = \frac{\$30,000,000}{30}$$
$$= \$1,000,000$$

Another procedure that can be used to calculate average daily float is to determine average daily receipts and multiply by the average daily delay:

**Average Daily Receipts:**

$$\frac{\text{Total receipts}}{\text{Total days}} = \frac{\$8,000,000}{30}$$
$$= \$266,666.67$$

$$\text{Weighted average delay} = (5/8) \times 3 \text{ days} + (3/8) \times 5 \text{ days}$$
$$= 1.875 \text{ days} + 1.875 \text{ days}$$
$$= 3.75 \text{ days}$$

$$\text{Average daily float} = \text{Average daily receipts} \times \text{Weighted average delay}$$
$$= \$266,666.67 \times 3.75$$
$$= \$1,000,000$$

EXAMPLE **28.5**

Suppose Concepts Inc. has average daily receipts of $266,667. The float results in this amount being delayed 3.75 days. The present value (PV) of the delayed cash flow is

$$V = \frac{\$266,667}{1 + r_B}$$

where $r_B$ is the cost of debt capital for Concepts, adjusted to the relevant time frame for daily compounding. Suppose the annual cost of debt capital is 6 percent. Then

$$r_B = 0.06 \times (3.75/365) = 0.0006$$

and

$$V = \frac{\$266,667}{1 + 0.0006} = \$266,507.10$$

Thus, the net present value (NPV) of the delay float is $266,507.10 − $266,667 = −$159.90 per day. For a year, this is −$159.90 × 365 = −$58,363.50.

## Electronic Data Interchange: The End of Float?

*Electronic data interchange* (EDI) is a general term that refers to the growing practice of direct electronic information exchange between all types of businesses. One important use of EDI, often called financial EDI, or FEDI, is to electronically transfer financial information and funds between parties, thereby eliminating paper invoices, paper cheques, mailing, and handling. It is even possible to arrange to have your chequing account directly debited each month to pay many types of bills, and corporations now routinely directly deposit paycheques into employee accounts. More generally, EDI allows a seller to send a bill electronically to a buyer, thereby avoiding the mail. The buyer can then authorize payment, which also occurs electronically. Its bank then transfers the funds to the seller's account at a different bank. The net effect is that the length of time required to initiate and complete a business transaction is shortened considerably, and much of what we normally think of as float is reduced or eliminated. As the use of FEDI increases, float management will evolve to focus much more on issues surrounding computerized information exchange and fund transfers.

One of the drawbacks of EDI (and FEDI) is that it is expensive and complex to set up. For this reason, the use of extranet portals is gaining use over EDI, especially in the electronics and high-tech industries.[2] Original equipment manufacturers (OEMs) are putting pressure on manufacturing suppliers to abandon EDI for Web-based business-to-business (B2B) extranets. One example of a B2B platform is RosettaNet, a non-profit consortium of 40 of the largest high-tech companies, including Motorola, IBM, and Sony. Another of the drawbacks that firms face in switching away from EDI (and FEDI) is that they would be losing efficiency in the switch because the extranets require more manual work compared to EDI. Because of security concerns and lack of standardization, don't look for e-commerce and extranets to completely eliminate the need for EDI anytime soon. In fact, it appears these complementary systems will most likely be used in tandem as the future unfolds.

## Accelerating Collections

Based on our discussion above, we depict the basic parts of the cash collection process in Figure 28.1. The total time in this process is made up of mailing time, cheque-processing time, and the bank's cheque-clearing time. The amount of time that cash spends in each part of the cash collection process depends on where the firm's customers are located and how efficient the firm is at collecting cash.

---

[2] Extranet portals are private networks that use Internet protocol and public telecommunication systems to securely share information with certain stakeholders, while EDI implies direct computer-to-computer transactions into the vendors' databases and ordering systems.

**FIGURE 28.1**

**The Cash Collection Process**

Coordinating the firm's efforts in all areas is its cash flow information system. Tracking payments through the system and providing the cash manager with up-to-date daily cash balances and investment rates are its key tasks. Linking the manager's computer with the bank's online, real-time system gives the manager access to account balances and transactions plus information on money market rates.

Since it is the corporate equivalent of a bank machine, the cash management system has security features to prevent unauthorized use. Different passwords or smart cards allow access to each level of authority. For example, a receivables clerk could have access to deposit activity files but not to payroll.

We next discuss several techniques used to accelerate collections and reduce collection time: systems to expedite mailing and cheque processing as well as concentration banking.

**Lockboxes**    Lockboxes are special post office boxes set up to intercept accounts receivable payments. Figure 28.2 illustrates a lockbox system. The collection process is started by having business and retail customers mail their cheques to a post office box instead of sending them to the firm. The lockbox is maintained at a local bank branch. Large corporations may maintain a number of lockboxes, one in each significant market area. The location depends on a trade-off between bank fees and savings on mailing time.

In the typical lockbox system, the local bank branch collects the lockbox cheques from the post office daily. The bank deposits the cheques directly to the firm's account. Details of the operation are recorded (in some computer-usable form) and sent to the firm.

A lockbox system reduces mailing time because cheques are received at a nearby post office instead of at corporate headquarters. Lockboxes also reduce the processing time because the corporation does not have to open the envelopes and deposit cheques for collection. In all, a bank lockbox should enable a firm to get its receipts processed, deposited, and cleared faster than if it were to receive cheques at its headquarters and deliver them itself to the bank for deposit and clearing.[3]

**Electronic Collection Systems**    Lockbox systems are standard ways to reduce mail and processing float time. They are used by almost all large firms in Canada that can benefit from them. Newer approaches focus on reducing float virtually to zero by replacing cheques with electronic funds transfer. Examples used in Canada are preauthorized payments, point-of-sale transfers, and electronic trade payables. We discuss the first two here and the third later when we look at disbursement systems.

---

[3] An example of lockbox services currently offered by one Canadian bank is at cibc.com/ca/lrg-corporate/cash-management/lockbox.html.

**FIGURE 28.2**

**Overview of Lockbox Processing**

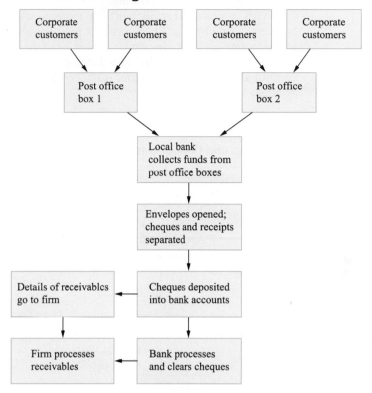

The flow starts when a corporate customer mails remittances to a post office box number instead of to the corporation. Several times a day the bank collects the lockbox receipts from the post office. The cheques are then put into the company bank accounts.

*Preauthorized payments* are paperless transfers of contractual or instalment payments from the customer's account directly to the firm's. Common applications are mortgage payments and instalment payments for insurance, rent, and TV services. This system eliminates all paperwork in invoices as well as in deposit and reconciliation of cheques. There is no mail or processing float. The system is currently limited mainly to annuity payments, but the technology could handle any payments.

*Point-of-sale systems* use **debit cards** to transfer funds directly from a customer's bank account to a retailer's. Unlike with a credit card, the funds are transferred immediately. Point-of-sale systems are widely used across Canada.

The next generation of cards for point-of-sale applications is the smart card mentioned earlier in its role of security for corporate cash management systems. Consumers can download small amounts of money (usually under $300) directly to the card and then spend it at point-of-sale terminals for small purchases at retailers like Starbucks.

More recently, the mobile wallet has been gaining popularity around the world, especially in Asia and Europe, as a convenient method of payment. Mobile wallet technology allows consumers to use their smartphones to make both in-store and online payments; manage their credit, debit, and reward cards; and receive special offers directly on their phones.

**Cash Concentration**    Using lockboxes or other collection systems helps firms collect cheques from customers and rapidly deposit them. But the job is not finished yet, since those systems give the firm cash at a number of widely dispersed branches. Until it is concentrated in a central account, the cash is of little use to the firm for paying bills, reducing loans, or investing.

With a **concentration banking** system, sales receipts are processed at bank branches providing lockbox services; they are then deposited locally. Surplus funds are transferred from the various local branches to a single, central concentration account. This process is illustrated in Figure 28.3, where concentration accounts are combined with over-the-counter (OTC) collection and lockboxes in a total cash management system.

**FIGURE 28.3**

### Lockboxes and Concentration Banks in a Cash Management System

Large firms in Canada may manage collections across the country through one chartered bank. Chartered banks offer a concentrator account, which automatically electronically transfers deposits at any branch in Canada to the firm's concentration account. These funds receive **same-day value**. This means that the firm has immediate use of the funds even though it takes 24 hours for a cheque to clear in Canada. If the concentration involves branches of more than one bank, electronic transfers will take place between banks.

Once the funds are in the concentration account, the bank can make automatic transfers to pay down the firm's credit line or, if there is a surplus, to an investment account. Transfers are made in units of minimum size agreed in advance; common practice is units of $5,000. Mid-sized firms lacking money market expertise may invest in bank accounts at competitive interest rates. The largest firms are able to purchase money market instruments electronically.

## Controlling Disbursements

Accelerating collections is one method of cash management; slowing down disbursements is another. This can be a sensitive area—some practices exist that we do not recommend. For example, some small firms that are short of working capital make disbursements on the "squeaky wheel principle." Payables invoices are processed prior to their due dates and cheques printed. When the cheques are ready, the firm's controller puts them all in a desk drawer. As suppliers phone and ask for their money, the cheques come out of the drawer and go in the mail! We do not recommend the desk-drawer method because it is bad for supplier relations and borders on being unethical.

## Ethical and Legal Questions

The cash manager must work with collected bank cash balances and not the firm's book balance (which reflects cheques that have been deposited but not collected). If this is not done, a cash manager could be drawing on uncollected cash as a source for making short-term investments. Most banks charge a penalty rate for the use of uncollected funds. The issue is minor in Canada since there can be a maximum of only one day's deposit float. In the United States, however, smaller banks' accounting and control procedures may not be accurate enough to make them fully aware of the use of uncollected funds. This raises some ethical and legal questions for firms doing business across the border.

**Controlling Disbursements in Practice**    As we have seen, float in terms of slowing down payments comes from mail delivery, cheque-processing time, and collection of funds. As we just showed, in the United States, disbursement float can be increased by writing a cheque on a geographically distant bank. Because there are significant ethical (and legal) issues associated with deliberately delaying disbursements in these and similar ways, such strategies appear to be disappearing. In Canada, banks provide same-day availability, so the temptation is easy to resist.

For these reasons, the goal is to control rather than simply to delay disbursements. A treasurer should try to pay payables on the last day appropriate for net terms or a discount.[4] The traditional way is to write a cheque and mail it, timing it to arrive on the due date. With the cash management system we described earlier, the payment can be programmed today for electronic transfer on the future due date. This eliminates paper along with guesswork about mail times.

The electronic payment is likely to come from a disbursement account, kept separate from the concentration account to ease accounting and control. Firms keep separate accounts for payroll, vendor disbursements, customer refunds, and so on. This makes it easy for the bank to provide each cost or profit centre with its own statement.

Firms use **zero-balance accounts** to avoid carrying extra balances in each disbursement account. With a zero-balance account, the firm, in cooperation with its bank, transfers in just enough funds to cover cheques presented that day. Figure 28.4 illustrates how such a system might work. In this case, the firm maintains two disbursement accounts: one for suppliers and one for payroll. As shown, if the firm does not use zero-balance accounts, then each of these accounts must have a safety stock of cash to meet unanticipated demands. If the firm does use zero-balance accounts, then it can keep one safety stock in a master account and transfer in the funds to the two subsidiary accounts as needed. The key is that the total amount of cash held as a buffer is smaller under the zero-balance arrangement, thereby freeing up cash to be used elsewhere.

Firms also use sweep accounts to increase interest earned. Excess cash is automatically transferred into an interest-bearing account or money market fund at the close of each business day.

---

[4] We discuss credit terms in depth in Chapter 29.

FIGURE 28.4

**Zero-Balance Accounts**

*CONCEPT*
*QUESTIONS*

- Describe collection and disbursement float.
- What are lockboxes? Concentration banking? Zero-balance accounts?
- How do computer and communications technologies aid in cash management by large corporations?

## 28.3    INVESTING IDLE CASH

If a firm has a temporary cash surplus, it can invest in short-term, or money market, securities. Short-term financial assets that trade in the money market have maturities of one year or less.

Most large firms manage their own short-term financial assets, transacting through banks and investment dealers. Some smaller firms use money market funds that invest in short-term financial assets for a management fee. The management fee is compensation for the professional expertise and diversification provided by the fund manager. Canadian chartered banks compete with money market funds, offering arrangements in which the bank takes all excess available funds at the close of each business day and invests them for the firm.

Firms have temporary cash surpluses for these reasons: to help finance seasonal or cyclical activities of the firm, to help finance planned expenditures of the firm, and to provide for unanticipated contingencies.

## Seasonal or Cyclical Activities

Some firms have a predictable cash flow pattern. They have surplus cash flows during part of the year and deficit cash flows the rest of the year. For example, Toys "R" Us, a retail toy firm, has a seasonal cash flow pattern influenced by Christmas. Such a firm may buy marketable securities when surplus cash flows occur and sell marketable securities when deficits occur. Of course, bank loans are another short-term financing device. Figure 28.5 illustrates the use of bank loans and marketable securities to meet temporary financing needs.

**FIGURE 28.5**

**Seasonal Cash Demands**

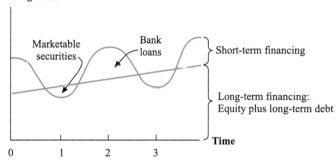

Time 1: A surplus cash flow exists. Seasonal demand for investing is low. The surplus cash flow is invested in short-term marketable securities. Time 2: A deficit cash flow exists. Seasonal demand for investing is high. The financial deficit is financed by selling marketable securities and by bank borrowing.

## Planned Expenditures

Firms frequently accumulate temporary investments in marketable securities to provide the cash for a plant construction program, dividend payment, or other large expenditures. Thus, firms may issue bonds and stocks before the cash is needed, investing the proceeds in short-term marketable securities and then selling the securities to finance the expenditures.

## Characteristics of Short-Term Securities

Given that a firm has some temporarily idle cash, a variety of short-term securities are available for investing. Their most important characteristics are maturity, default risk, marketability, and taxability.

**Maturity**    *Maturity* refers to the time period over which interest and principal payments are made. For a given change in the level of interest rates, the prices of longer-maturity securities will change more than those for shorter-maturity securities. Our discussion of duration in Chapter 26 explored this relationship in detail. As a consequence, firms that invest in long-term securities are accepting greater risk than firms that invest in securities with short-term maturities. This type of risk is usually called *interest-rate risk*. Most firms limit their investments in marketable securities to those maturing in less than 90 days. Of course, the expected return on securities with short-term maturities is usually less than the expected return on securities with longer maturities.

EXAMPLE **28.6**

Suppose you are the treasurer of a firm that needs $10 million to make a major capital investment after 90 days. You have decided to invest in Government of Canada obligations to eliminate all possible default risk. The newspaper (or your computer screen) lists securities and rates (Figure 28.6). The safest investment is three-month Treasury bills yielding 0.93 percent. Because this matches the maturity of the investment with the planned holding period, there is no interest rate risk. After three months, the Treasury bills will mature for a certain future cash flow of $10 million.[5]

### FIGURE 28.6

## Money Market Quotations

### YIELDS

**CANADIAN YIELDS**

| | Latest | Previous Day | Week Ago | 4 Weeks Ago |
|---|---|---|---|---|
| **T-bills** | | | | |
| 1-month | 0.92 | 0.92 | 0.92 | 0.91 |
| 3-month | 0.93 | 0.93 | 0.92 | 0.92 |
| 6-month | 0.95 | 0.95 | 0.95 | 0.94 |
| 1-year | 0.99 | 0.99 | 0.99 | 0.98 |
| **Bonds** | | | | |
| 2-year | 1.077 | 1.08 | 1.064 | 1.044 |
| 5-year | 1.609 | 1.608 | 1.612 | 1.564 |
| 7-year | 2.347 | 2.346 | 2.35 | 2.289 |
| 10-year | 2.866 | 2.864 | 2.862 | 2.834 |
| 30-year | 4.07 | 4.09 | 4.08 | 4.05 |
| **Banker's Acceptances (ask Price)** | | | | |
| 1-month | 1.25 | 1.25 | 1.25 | 1.25 |
| 3-month | 1.28 | 1.28 | 1.28 | 0.93 |
| 6-month | 1.38 | 1.38 | 1.38 | 1.38 |
| **3-mth Forward Rate Agreement** | | | | |
| 3-month | 1.25 | 1.25 | 1.25 | 1.25 |
| 6-month | 1.25 | 1.25 | 1.25 | 1.25 |
| 9-month | 1.27 | 1.28 | 1.26 | 1.27 |

**U.S. YIELDS**

| | Latest | Previous Day | Week Ago | 4 Weeks Ago |
|---|---|---|---|---|
| **T-bills** | | | | |
| 1-month | 0.023 | 0.023 | 0.036 | 0.003 |
| 3-month | 0.033 | 0.033 | 0.03 | 0.02 |
| 6-month | 0.06 | 0.05 | 0.05 | 0.05 |
| **Bonds** | | | | |
| 2-year | 0.43 | 0.43 | 0.4 | 0.38 |
| 5-year | 1.7 | 1.71 | 1.64 | 1.61 |
| 10-year | 2.63 | 2.64 | 2.6 | 2.61 |
| 30-year | 3.46 | 3.47 | 3.44 | 3.44 |
| **Commercial Paper** | | | | |
| 1-month | 0.05 | 0.05 | 0.06 | 0.07 |
| 3-month | 0.1 | 0.09 | 0.1 | 0.09 |
| 6-month | 0.22 | 0.22 | 0.22 | 0.22 |
| **3-mth Forward Rate Agreement** | | | | |
| 3-month | 0.22 | 0.22 | 0.22 | 0.21 |
| 6-month | 0.25 | 0.25 | 0.24 | 0.24 |
| 9-month | 0.33 | 0.32 | 0.31 | 0.3 |

**INTERNATIONAL RATES**

| | | Latest | Prev. Day | Week Ago | 4 Weeks Ago |
|---|---|---|---|---|---|
| **Euro-Deposit Rates (Bid)** | | | | | |
| US$ | 1-month | 0.03 | 0.11 | 0.14 | 0.03 |
| | 3-month | 0.1 | 0.21 | 0.25 | 0.1 |
| | 6-month | 0.34 | 0.36 | 0.38 | 0.34 |
| CS | 3-month | 1.03 | 1.06 | 1.09 | 1.03 |
| euro | 3-month | 0.11 | 0.12 | 0.22 | 0.11 |
| Yen | 3-month | 0.06 | 0.02 | 0.06 | 0.06 |
| £ | 3-month | 0.52 | 0.51 | 0.49 | 0.52 |

**London Interbank Offer Rate US$**

| | | Latest | Prev. Day | Week Ago | 4 Weeks Ago |
|---|---|---|---|---|---|
| US$ | 1-month | 0.15 | 0.15 | 0.15 | 0.15 |
| | 3-month | 0.23 | 0.23 | 0.23 | 0.23 |
| | 6-month | 0.32 | 0.32 | 0.32 | 0.32 |

**CANADA BANK RATES**

| | |
|---|---|
| Bank of Canada | 1.25 |
| Overright Money Market Financing | 0.98 |
| Prime | 3 |
| Car Loan Average | 0.95 |

**U.S. BANK RATES**

| | |
|---|---|
| Discount | 0.75 |
| Prime | 3.25 |
| Federal Funds | 0.07 |

Source: Material reprinted with the express permission of *National Post*, a division of Postmedia Network Inc.

If instead you invest in 10-year Canada bonds, the expected return will be higher, but so will the risk. If interest rates rise over the next three months, the bond will drop in price. The resulting capital loss will reduce the yield, possibly below the 0.93 percent on Treasury bills.

**Default Risk**    Default risk refers to the probability that interest and principal will not be paid in the promised amounts on the due dates. In Chapter 21, we observed that bond rating agencies, such as Dominion Bond Rating Service (DBRS) and Standard & Poor's (S&P), compile and publish ratings of various corporate and public securities. These ratings are connected to default risk. Of course, some securities have negligible default risk, such as Canada Treasury bills. Given the purposes of investing idle corporate cash, firms typically avoid investing in marketable securities with significant default risk.

---

[5] Treasury bills are sold on a discount basis, so the future cash flow includes principal and interest.

Small variations in default risk are reflected in the rates in Figure 28.6. For example, look at the rates on two alternative 90-day (three-month) Canadian investments. Since the maturities are the same, they differ only in default risk. In increasing order of default risk the securities are Treasury bills (0.93 percent yield) and banker's acceptances (1.28 percent yield). Both are unsecured paper. Treasury bills (the less risky) are backed by the credit of the Government of Canada. Banker's acceptances are guaranteed by a chartered bank as well as by the issuing corporation.

**Marketability**   *Marketability* refers to how easy it is to convert an asset to cash. Sometimes marketability is referred to as *liquidity*. It has two characteristics:

1. *No price-pressure effect.* If an asset can be sold in large amounts without changing the market price, it is marketable. Price-pressure effects are those that come about when the price of an asset must be lowered to facilitate the sale.

2. *Time.* If an asset can be sold quickly at the existing market price, it is marketable. In contrast, a Renoir painting or antique desk appraised at $1 million will likely sell for much less if the owner must sell quickly on short notice.

In general, marketability is the ability to sell an asset for its face market value quickly and in large amounts. Perhaps the most marketable of all securities are Canada Treasury bills.

**Taxability**   Interest earned on money market securities is subject to federal and provincial corporate income taxes. Capital gains and dividends on common and preferred shares are taxed more lightly, but these long-term investments are subject to significant price fluctuations; most managers consider them too risky for the marketable securities portfolio.

One exception is the strategy of **dividend capture**. Under this strategy, portfolio managers purchase high-grade preferred stock or blue chip common stock just prior to a dividend payment. They hold the stock only long enough to receive the dividend. In this way, firms willing to tolerate price risk for a short period can benefit from the dividend exclusion allowing corporations to receive tax-free dividends from other Canadian corporations.

To mitigate price risk and to make their firms' preferred shares more attractive to managers seeking to capture dividends, financial engineers have invented various forms of floating-rate preferred shares. The idea is to make the dividends adjust to changes in market yields, keeping the price of the preferred share near par.[6]

## Some Different Types of Money Market Securities

The money market securities listed in Figure 28.6 are generally highly marketable and short term. They usually have low risk of default. These securities are issued by the federal government (for example, Treasury bills), domestic and foreign banks (for example, certificates of deposit), and business corporations (for example, commercial paper). There are many types in all, and we only illustrate a few of the most common here.

Treasury bills are obligations of the federal government that mature in one month, three months, six months, or one year. They are sold at weekly auctions and traded actively OTC by banks and investment dealers.

---

[6] The zero-growth formula of Chapter 6 values preferred shares as $P =$ Dividend rate $\times$ Par value/Discount rate. For floating-rate preferreds, as the discount rate changes with market conditions, the dividend rate adjusts to remain equal to the discount rate. As a result, the price remains at par value. Since there is some lag in adjustment, the price can move away from the par value somewhat. Also, since all preferred shares bear some default risk, the floating rate does not protect investors from price declines arising from the downgrading of the issuer's credit rating.

# IN THEIR OWN WORDS

## Credit crisis made in Canada

Canadian banks are struggling to contain a credit crisis that could spiral out of control here more than it has elsewhere because of a lax regulatory regime, sources have told the *National Post*.

The crisis relates to the market for a complex type of short-term funding known as asset-backed commercial paper (ABCP), which had grown out of proportion in this country partly thanks to Canadian rules that were not as tough as in other nations.

"It's a made-in-Canada problem," said Claude Lamoureux, head of Ontario Teachers' Pension Plan. Many people in the market "didn't know or didn't ask questions," because they were making more profits than elsewhere, he added.

The Canadian ABCP market attracted a flood of foreign financial institutions such as Barclays Bank and Deutsche Bank, who exploited the gaps in the Canadian ABCP rules to make big profits at lower risk to themselves, sources said.

"They were effectively able to earn fees from supplying liquidity without ever having to supply the liquidity or set aside capital," said a source.

In the worst-case scenario, if global financial players lose confidence in the Canadian ABCP system altogether, the crisis could spread to Canada's big banks, leaving them on the hook for tens of billions of dollars.

ABCP is a package of debt obligations—anything from car loans to credit card debt. The product grew in popularity in recent years among everyone from pension funds to corporate treasury departments to banks, because ABCP offered higher returns than, for example, a corporate bond or treasury bill.

Typically, ABCP products also involve liquidity support from a supplier, usually a major bank. In simple terms, it is an agreement to buy the ABCP in the event of a disruption to the market.

In Canada, the market grew more quickly than in other countries, doubling between the years 2000 and 2007 to $120 billion, because the Canadian definition of disruption to the market was much narrower than elsewhere.

In Canada, liquidity suppliers did not have to provide funding except in catastrophic circumstances.

Also, the Canadian banking regulator, unlike regulators in other countries, did not ask the liquidity supplier, the bank, to set aside any capital, so they could use it to grow other lines of business.

"ABCP growth outstripped traditional personal and commercial loan growth," and was "meaningfully

---

*Commercial paper* refers to short-term securities issued by finance companies, banks, and corporations. Typically, commercial paper is unsecured.[7] Maturities range from a few weeks to three months. There is no active secondary market in commercial paper. As a consequence, the marketability is low; however, firms that issue commercial paper will often repurchase it directly before maturity. The default risk of commercial paper depends on the financial strength of the issuer. DBRS and S&P publish quality ratings for commercial paper. These ratings are similar to the bond ratings we discussed in Chapter 21.

As explained earlier, *banker's acceptances* are a form of corporate paper stamped by a chartered bank that adds its guarantee of principal and interest.

*Marketable certificates of deposit*, also called bearer deposit notes (BDNs), are short-term loans to chartered banks. Rates quoted are for BDNs in excess of $100,000. There are active markets in BDNs of three-month, six-month, nine-month, and twelve-month maturities. BDNs are called certificates of deposit (CDs) in the United States.

*Dollar swaps* are foreign currency deposits that will be converted or swapped back into Canadian dollars at a predetermined rate by chartered banks. They allow the

---

[7] Commercial paper and banker's acceptances are sources of short-term financing for their issuers. We discussed them in more detail in Chapter 27.

above the pace of U.S. ABCP market expansion," said Blackmont Capital banking analyst Brad Smith.

In addition, Canadian debt rating agency Dominion Bond Rating Service gave a rating to Canadian ABCP even though other rating agencies such as Moody's and Standard & Poor's shied away from doing so.

By June of this year, Canada's ABCP market was about 10 percent of the size of the market in the United States, although the overall U.S. financial system is proportionately far larger than Canada's.

When concerns surfaced in August about the underlying assets in ABCP, many of which in the U.S. have included troubled mortgage loans, some owners of ABCP were caught off guard. Owners of ABCP were under the belief that they could convert it to cash or another similar product at the end of 30 or 60 days, but, instead, they were left holding the product.

Canadian investment bank Coventree Capital Inc. became one of the first major victims of the global credit crunch when it was unable to trade the ABCP it was holding because of the general seizing up of credit markets around the world.

Following Coventree's collapse, Canadian non-bank owners of $40 billion of troubled asset-backed commercial paper—pension funds and corporate treasury departments—were forced into an unprecedented joining of forces known as the Montréal Accord to try to salvage their holdings.

Canada's bank regulator, the Office of the Superintendent of Financial Institutions, did not return calls from the *National Post* seeking comment for this story. However, in an email, the regulator indicated that the rules enforced in Canada were in accordance with international guidelines.

## How It Works

A bank packages a collection of mortgages, credit card balances, or lines of credit into an ABCP that matures in 30 days. The bank sells ABCP for a fee to an intermediary that assumes all the risk associated with the underlying assets. The intermediary sells pieces of the ABCP to investors, including pension funds or corporations or individuals. Investors are paid interest and assume there will be a buyer for their piece of the ABCP after 30 days. For a fee, the bank supplies funds to buy the ABCP if there are no other buyers; in Canada, this feature did not work in August when investors could not find a buyer.

Excerpted with permission from *National Post*, September 27, 2007.

Canadian treasurer to place funds in major money markets outside Canada without incurring foreign exchange risk.

Our brief look at money markets illustrates the challenges and opportunities for treasurers today. Securitization has produced dramatic growth in banker's acceptances and commercial paper. The accompanying box discusses a failed securitization product: asset-backed commercial paper. Currency swaps are a financial engineering product driven by globalization of financial markets.

**CONCEPT QUESTIONS**

- Why do firms find themselves with idle cash?
- What are some types of money market securities?

## 28.4

# SUMMARY AND CONCLUSIONS

1. A firm holds cash to conduct transactions and to compensate banks for the various services they render.

2. The optimal amount of cash for a firm to hold depends on the opportunity cost of holding cash and the uncertainty of future cash inflows and outflows.

3. The firm can make use of a variety of procedures to manage the collection and disbursement of cash to speed up the collection of cash and slow down payments. Some methods to speed up collection are lockboxes, concentration banking, and electronic collection systems.

4. Because of seasonal and cyclical activities, to help finance planned expenditures, or as a reserve for unanticipated needs, firms temporarily find themselves with cash surpluses. The money market offers a variety of possible vehicles for parking this idle cash.

**KEY TERMS**
Concentration banking  826   Lockbox  824             Transaction motive  819
Debit card  825                Precautionary motive  819   Zero-balance account  827
Dividend capture  831          Same-day value  826
Float  820                     Speculative motive  818

**QUESTIONS & PROBLEMS**

**Calculating Float**

28.1 In a typical month, the Jeremy Corp. receives 80 cheques totalling $156,000. These are delayed four days on average. What is the average daily float?

**Calculating Net Float**

28.2 Each business day, on average, a company writes cheques totalling $17,000 to pay its suppliers. The usual clearing time for the cheques is four days. Meanwhile, the company is receiving payments from its customers each day, in the form of cheques, totalling $28,500. The cash from the payments is available to the firm after two days.
   a. Calculate the company's disbursement float, collection float, and net float.
   b. How would your answer to (a) change if the collected funds were available in one day instead of two?

**Costs of Float**

28.3 Purple Feet Wine Inc. receives an average of $16,000 in cheques per day. The delay in clearing is typically three days. The current interest rate is 0.018 percent per day.
   a. What is the company's float?
   b. What is the most Purple Feet should be willing to pay today to eliminate its float entirely?
   c. What is the highest daily fee the company should be willing to pay to eliminate its float entirely?

**Float and Weighted Average Delay**

28.4 Your neighbour goes to the post office once a month and picks up two cheques: one for $11,000 and one for $3,400. The larger cheque takes four days to clear after it is deposited; the smaller one takes five days.
   a. What is the total float for the month?
   b. What is the average daily float?
   c. What are the average daily receipts and weighted average delay?

### Net Present Value and Collection Time

28.5  Your firm has an average receipt size of $117. A bank has approached you concerning a lockbox service that will decrease your total collection time by two days. You typically receive 6,500 cheques per day. The daily interest rate is 0.015 percent. If the bank charges a fee of $160 per day, should the lockbox project be accepted? What would the net annual savings be if the service were adopted?

### Using Weighted Average Delay

28.6  A mail-order firm processes 5,300 cheques per month. Of these, 60 percent are for $55 and 40 percent are for $80. The $55 cheques are delayed two days on average; the $80 cheques are delayed three days on average.

   *a.* What is the average daily collection float? How do you interpret your answer?
   *b.* What is the weighted average delay? Use the result to calculate the average daily float.
   *c.* How much should the firm be willing to pay to eliminate the float?
   *d.* If the interest rate is 7 percent per year, calculate the daily cost of the float.
   *e.* How much should the firm be willing to pay to reduce the weighted average float by 1.5 days?

### Value of Lockboxes

28.7  Paper Submarine Manufacturing is investigating a lockbox system to reduce its collection time. It has determined the following:

| | |
|---|---|
| Average number of payments per day | 385 |
| Average value of payment | $1,105 |
| Variable lockbox fee (per transaction) | $0.50 |
| Daily interest rate on money market securities | 0.02% |

The total collection time will be reduced by three days if the lockbox system is adopted.

   *a.* What is the PV of adopting the system?
   *b.* What is the NPV of adopting the system?
   *c.* What is the net cash flow per day from adopting? Per cheque?

### Lockboxes and Collections

28.8  It takes Cookie Cutter Modular Homes Inc. about five days to receive and deposit cheques from customers. Cookie Cutter's management is considering a lockbox system to reduce the firm's collection times. It is expected that the lockbox system will reduce receipt and deposit times to three days total. Average daily collections are $135,000, and the required rate of return is 9 percent per year.

   *a.* What is the reduction in outstanding cash balance as a result of implementing the lockbox system?
   *b.* What is the dollar return that could be earned on these savings?
   *c.* What is the maximum monthly charge Cookie Cutter should pay for this lockbox system if the payment is due at the end of the month? What if the payment is due at the beginning of the month?

### Value of Delay

28.9  No More Pencils Inc. disburses cheques every two weeks that average $93,000 and take seven days to clear. How much interest can the company earn annually if it delays transfer of funds from an interest-bearing account that pays 0.015 percent per day for these seven days? Ignore the effects of compounding interest.

### Lockboxes and Collection Time

28.10   Bird's Eye Treehouses Inc. has determined that a majority of its customers are located in the Winnipeg area. It therefore is considering using a lockbox system offered by a bank in Manitoba. The bank has estimated that use of the system will reduce collection time by two days. Based on the following information, should the lockbox system be adopted?

| | |
|---|---|
| Average number of payments per day | 850 |
| Average value of payment | $630 |
| Variable lockbox fee (per transaction) | $0.22 |
| Annual interest rate on money market securities | 7% |

How would your answer change if there were a fixed charge of $5,000 per year in addition to the variable charge?

### Calculating Transactions Required

28.11   Cow Chips Inc., a large fertilizer distributor based in Saskatchewan, is planning to use a lockbox system to speed up collections from its customers on the east coast. A local bank branch will provide this service for an annual fee of $20,000 plus 10 cents per transaction. The estimated reduction in collection and processing time is one day. If the average customer payment in this region is $5,300, how many customers are needed, on average, each day to make the system profitable for Cow Chips? Treasury bills are currently yielding 5 percent per year.

MINICASE

## Cash Management at Richmond Ltd.

Richmond Ltd. was founded 20 years ago by its president, Daniella Richmond. The company originally began as a mail-order company but has grown rapidly in recent years, in large part due to its website. Because of the wide geographical dispersion of the company's customers, it currently employs a lockbox system with collection centres in Toronto, Calgary, Montreal, and Vancouver.

Steve Dennis, the company's treasurer, has been examining the current cash collection policies. On average, each lockbox centre handles $185,000 in payments each day. The company's current policy is to invest these payments in short-term marketable securities daily at the collection centre banks. Every two weeks, the investment accounts are swept, and the proceeds are wire-transferred to Richmond's headquarters in Winnipeg to meet the company's payroll. The investment accounts each pay 0.068 percent per day, and the wire transfers cost 0.20 percent of the amount transferred.

Steve has been approached by Manitoba National Bank, located just outside Winnipeg, about the possibility of setting up a concentration banking system for Richmond Ltd. Manitoba National will accept the lockbox centre's daily payments via automated clearinghouse (ACH) transfers in lieu of wire transfers. The ACH-transferred funds will not be available for use for one day. Once cleared, the funds will be deposited in a short-term account, which will yield 0.075 percent per day. Each ACH transfer will cost $200. Daniella has asked Steve to determine which cash management system will be the best for the company. Steve has asked you, his assistant, to answer the following questions.

1.  What is Richmond Ltd.'s total net cash flow from the current lockbox system that is available to meet payroll?

2.  Under the terms outlined by Manitoba National Bank, should the company proceed with the concentration banking system?

3.  What cost of ACH transfers would make the company indifferent between the two systems?

**connect**   **LEARNSMART**®   **SMARTBOOK**™

29

# Credit Management

EXECUTIVE SUMMARY

When a firm sells goods and services, it can (1) be paid in cash immediately or (2) wait for a time to be paid, that is, extend credit to customers. Granting credit is investing in a customer, an investment tied to the sale of a product or service. This chapter examines the firm's decision to grant credit.

An account receivable is created when credit is granted. These receivables include credit granted to other firms, called *trade credit*, and credit granted to consumers, called *consumer credit*. About 15 percent of all the assets of Canadian industrial firms are in the form of accounts receivable. For retail firms, the figure is much higher. Trade credit extended by a firm's supplier to the firm appears as an account payable. Figure 29.1 illustrates this aspect of trade credit.

The investment in accounts receivable for any firm depends on both the amount of credit sales and the average collection period. For example, if a firm's daily credit sales are $1,000 and its average collection period is 30 days, its accounts receivable will be $30,000. Thus, a firm's investment in accounts receivable depends on factors influencing credit sales and collection. A firm's credit policy affects these factors.

The following are the components of credit policy:

1.  **Terms of the sale.** A firm must decide on certain conditions when selling its goods and services for credit. The terms of sale may specify the credit period, the cash discount, and the type of credit instrument.
2.  **Credit analysis.** When granting credit, a firm tries to distinguish between customers who will pay and those who will not. Firms use a number of devices and procedures to determine the probability that customers will pay.
3.  **Collection policy.** Firms that grant credit must establish a policy for collecting the cash when it becomes due.

This chapter discusses each of the components of credit policy that make up the decision to grant credit.

In some ways, the decision to grant credit is connected to the cash collection process described in the previous chapter. This is illustrated with a cash flow diagram in Figure 29.2.

The typical sequence of events when a firm grants credit is (1) the credit sale is made, (2) the customer sends a cheque to the firm, (3) the firm deposits the cheque, and (4) the firm's account is credited for the amount of the cheque.

**FIGURE 29.1**

**Trade Credit**

Trade credit extended to a customer by a firm appears as an account receivable.

Trade credit extended by the firm's supplier to the firm appears as an account payable.

FIGURE 29.2

**The Cash Flows of Granting Credit**

## 29.1   TERMS OF THE SALE

The terms of sale refer to the period for which credit is granted, the cash discount, and the type of credit instrument. Within a given industry, the terms of sale are usually fairly standard, but across industries these terms vary quite a bit. In many cases, the terms of sale are remarkably archaic and literally date to previous centuries. Organized systems of trade credit that resemble current practice can easily be traced to the great fairs of medieval Europe, and they almost surely existed long before then.

### Why Trade Credit Exists

Set aside the venerable history of trade credit for a moment and ask yourself why it should exist.[1] It is quite easy to imagine that all sales could be for cash, which, from the firm's viewpoint, would get rid of receivables' carrying costs and collection costs. Bad debts would be zero (assuming that the firm was careful to accept no counterfeit money).

Imagine this cash-only economy in the context of perfectly competitive product and financial markets. Competition would force companies to lower their prices to pass the savings from immediate collections on to customers. Any company that then granted credit to its customers would have to raise its prices accordingly to survive. If a purchaser needed financing over the operating cycle, it could borrow from a bank or the money market. In this "perfect markets" environment, it would make no difference to the seller or the buyer whether credit was granted.

But, in practice, firms spend significant resources setting credit policy and managing its implementation. So deviations from perfect markets—market imperfections—must explain why trade credit exists. We look briefly at several imperfections and how trade credit helps to overcome them.

In practice, buyers and sellers have imperfect information. Buyers lack perfect information on the quality of the product. For this reason, the buyer may prefer credit terms that give time to return the product if it is defective or unsuitable. When the seller offers credit, it "signals" potential customers that the product is of high quality and likely to provide satisfaction.[2]

In addition, in practice, any firm granting credit lacks perfect information on the creditworthiness of the borrower. Although it is costly for a bank or other third-party

---

[1] Our discussion of trade credit draws on N. C. Hill and W. S. Sartoris, *Short-Term Financial Management* (New York: Macmillan, 1988), Chapter 14.

[2] This use of signalling is very similar to dividend signalling, discussed in Chapter 19. There, corporations signalled the quality of projected cash flows by maintaining dividends even when earnings were down.

lender to acquire this information, a seller that has been granting trade credit to a purchaser likely has it already. Further, the seller may have superior information on the resale value of the product serving as collateral. These information advantages may allow the seller to offer more attractive, more flexible credit terms and to be more liberal in authorizing credit.

Finally, perfect markets have zero transaction costs, but, in reality, it is costly to set up a bank borrowing facility or to borrow in money markets. We discussed some of the costs in Chapter 27. It may be cheaper to utilize credit from the seller.

## The Basic Form

Suppose a customer is granted credit with terms of 2/10, net 30. This means that the customer has 30 days from the invoice date within which to pay. (An **invoice** is a bill written by a seller of goods or services and submitted to the buyer. The invoice date is usually the same as the shipping date.) In addition, a cash discount of 2 percent from the stated sales price is to be given if payment is made in 10 days. If the stated terms are net 60, the customer has 60 days from the invoice date to pay and no discount is offered for early payment.

When sales are seasonal, a firm might use seasonal dating. O. M. Scott and Sons is a manufacturer of lawn and garden products with a seasonal dating policy that is tied to the growing season. Payments for winter shipments of fertilizer might be due in the spring or summer. A firm offering 3/10, net 60, May 1 dating is making the effective invoice date May 1. The stated amount must be paid on June 30, regardless of when the sale is made. The cash discount of 3 percent can be taken until May 10.

## Credit Period

The **credit period** is the basic length of time for which credit is granted. The credit period varies widely from industry to industry, but it is almost always between 30 and 120 days. If a cash discount is offered, then the credit period has two components: the net credit period and the cash discount period.

The net credit period is the length of time the customer has to pay. The cash discount period is the time during which the discount is available. With 2/10, net 30, for example, the net credit period is 30 days and the cash discount period is 10 days.

**Length of the Credit Period**    Several factors influence the length of the credit period. Two important ones are the *buyer's* inventory period and operating cycle. All else equal, the shorter these are, the shorter the credit period will be.

From Chapter 27, the operating cycle has two components: the inventory period and the receivables period. The buyer's inventory period is the time it takes the buyer to acquire inventory (from us), process it, and sell it. The buyer's receivables period is the time it then takes the buyer to collect on the sale. Note that the credit period we offer is effectively the buyer's payables period.

By extending credit, we finance a portion of our buyer's operating cycle and thereby shorten that buyer's cash cycle (see Figure 27.3). If our credit period exceeds the buyer's inventory period, then we are financing not only the buyer's inventory purchases, but part of the buyer's receivables as well.

Furthermore, if our credit period exceeds our buyer's operating cycle, then we are effectively providing financing for aspects of our customer's business beyond the immediate purchase and sale of our merchandise. The reason is that the buyer effectively has a loan from us even after the merchandise is resold, and the buyer can use that credit for other purposes. For this reason, the length of the buyer's operating cycle is often cited as an appropriate upper limit to the credit period.

A number of other factors influence the credit period. Many of these also influence our customer's operating cycles; so, once again, these are related subjects. Among the most important are these:

1. *Perishability and collateral value.* Perishable items have relatively rapid turnover and relatively low collateral value. Credit periods are thus shorter for such goods. For example, a food wholesaler selling fresh fruit and produce might use net seven days. Alternatively, jewellery might be sold for 5/30, net four months.

2. *Consumer demand.* Products that are well established generally have more rapid turnover. Newer or slower-moving products will often have longer credit periods associated with them to entice buyers. Also, as we have seen, sellers may choose to extend much longer credit periods for off-season sales (when customer demand is low).

3. *Cost, profitability, and standardization.* Relatively inexpensive goods tend to have shorter credit periods. The same is true for relatively standardized goods and raw materials. These all tend to have lower markups and higher turnover rates, both of which lead to shorter credit periods. However, there are exceptions. Auto dealers, for example, generally pay for cars as they are received.

4. *Credit risk.* The greater the credit risk of the buyer, the shorter the credit period is likely to be (if credit is granted at all).

5. *Size of the account.* If an account is small, the credit period may be shorter because small accounts cost more to manage, and the customers are less important.

6. *Competition.* When the seller is in a highly competitive market, the longer credit periods may be offered as a way of attracting customers.

7. *Customer type.* A single seller might offer different credit terms to different buyers. A food wholesaler, for example, might supply groceries, bakeries, and restaurants. Each group would probably have different credit terms. More generally, sellers often have both wholesale and retail customers, and they frequently quote different terms to the two types.

## Cash Discounts

**Cash discounts** are often part of the terms of sale. One reason they are offered is to speed up the collection of receivables. The firm must balance this against the cost of the discount.

---

**EXAMPLE 29.1**

---

Edward Manalt, the CFO of Charlottetown Grocers, is considering the request of the company's largest customer, who wants to take a 3 percent discount for payment within 20 days on a $10,000 purchase. In other words, the customer intends to pay $9,700 [or $10,000 × (1 − 0.03)]. Normally, this customer pays in 30 days with no discount. The after-tax cost of short-term debt capital for Charlottetown is 3 percent and represents the opportunity cost of investing in receivables. Edward has worked out the cash flow implications, which are illustrated in Figure 29.3. He assumes that the time required to cash the cheque when the firm receives it is the same under both credit arrangements. He has calculated the present value (PV) of the two proposals:

**Current Policy:**

$$PV = \frac{\$10,000}{(1 + 0.03)^{30/365}} = \$9,975.73$$

**Proposed Policy:**

$$PV = \frac{\$9,700}{(1 + 0.03)^{20/365}} = \$9,684.30$$

## FIGURE 29.3

**Cash Flows for Different Credit Terms**

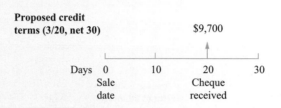

Current situation: Customers usually pay 30 days from the sale date and receive no discount.

Proposed situation: Customer will pay 20 days from the sale date at a 3 percent discount from the $10,000 purchase price.

His calculation shows that granting the discount would cost the Charlottetown firm $291.43 (or $9,975.73 − $9,684.30) in PV. Consequently, Charlottetown is better off with the current credit arrangement.[3]

In the previous example, we implicitly assumed that granting credit had no side effects. However, the decision to grant credit may generate higher sales and involve a different cost structure. Example 29.2 illustrates the impact of changes in the level of sales and costs in the credit decision.

**EXAMPLE 29.2**

Suppose that Charlottetown Grocers has variable costs of $0.50 per $1 of sales. If offered a discount of 3 percent, customers will increase their order size by 10 percent. This new information is shown in Figure 29.4. That is, the customer will increase its order size to $11,000 and, with the 3 percent discount, will remit $10,670 [or $11,000 × (1 − 0.03)] to Charlottetown in 20 days. It will cost more to fill the larger order because variable costs are $5,500. The net present values (NPVs) are worked out here:

**Current Policy:**

$$\text{NPV} = -\$5,000 + \frac{\$10,000}{(1.03)^{30/365}} = \$4,975.73$$

---

[3] We can reinforce this calculation by calculating a *customer's* rate of return from taking the discount if it were offered. With the cash discount, a customer pays $9,700 instead of $10,000. By passing on the discount, the customer takes a loan for 10 days and pays 3/97 = 3.09% more for the order. By adopting the policy, the customer takes 365/10 = 36.5 loans per year. By investing, say, one dollar at 3.09 percent per period for 36.5 periods, the customer receives a future value at the end of one year of $(1.0309)^{36.5} = 3.037$—a return of 203.7 percent annually.

**Proposed Policy:**

$$NPV = -\$5,500 + \frac{\$10,670}{(1.03)^{20/365}} = \$5,152.73$$

**FIGURE 29.4**

**Cash Flows for Different Credit Terms: The Impact of New Sales and Costs**

Now it is clear that the firm is better off with the proposed credit policy. This increase is the net effect of several different factors, including the larger initial costs, the earlier receipt of the cash inflows, the increased sales level, and the discount.

## Credit Instruments

Most credit is offered on *open account*. This means that the only formal **credit instrument** is the invoice, which is sent with the shipment of goods, and which the customer signs as evidence that the goods have been received. Afterward, the firm and its customers record the exchange on their books.

When the order is large or the firm anticipates a problem in collections, it may require that the customer sign a *promissory note* or IOU. Promissory notes can prevent future controversies about the existence of a credit agreement.

However, promissory notes are signed after delivery of the goods. One way to obtain a credit commitment from a customer before the goods are delivered is through the use of a *commercial draft*. The selling firm typically writes a commercial draft calling for the customer to pay a specific amount by a specified date. The draft is then sent to the customer's bank with the shipping invoices. The bank has the buyer sign the draft before turning over the invoices. The goods can then be shipped to the buyer. If immediate payment is required, it is called a *sight draft*. Here, funds must be turned over to the bank before the goods are shipped.

Frequently, even the signed draft is not enough for the seller. In this case, the seller might demand that the banker pay for the goods and collect the money from the customer. When the banker agrees to do so in writing, the document is called a *banker's acceptance*. That is, the banker *accepts* responsibility for payment. Because banks are generally well-known and well-respected institutions, the banker's acceptance becomes a liquid instrument. In other words, the seller can then sell (*discount*) the banker's acceptance in the secondary market.

A firm can also use a *conditional sales contract* as a credit instrument. This is an arrangement where the firm retains legal ownership of the goods until the customer has completed payment. Conditional sales contracts are usually paid off in instalments and have interest costs built into them.

**CONCEPT QUESTIONS**

- **What considerations enter into the determination of the terms of sale?**
- **Explain the design of common credit instruments.**

# 29.2    THE DECISION TO GRANT CREDIT: RISK AND INFORMATION

Locust Industries has been in existence for two years. It is one of several successful firms that develop computer programs. The financial managers have set out two alternative credit strategies: the firm can offer credit, or the firm can refuse credit.

Suppose Locust has determined that if it offers no credit to its customers, it can sell its existing computer software for $50 per program. It estimates that the costs to produce a typical computer program are $20 per unit.

The alternative is to offer credit. In this case, customers of Locust will pay one period later. With some probability, Locust has determined that if it offers credit, it can charge higher prices and expect higher sales.

*Strategy 1: Refuse credit.*  If Locust refuses to grant credit, cash flows will not be delayed, and period 0 net cash flows, NCFs, will be

$$P_0 Q_0 - C_0 Q_0 = \text{NCF}$$

The subscripts denote the time when the cash flows are incurred, where

$$P_0 = \text{Price per unit received at time 0}$$
$$C_0 = \text{Cost per unit incurred at time 0}$$
$$Q_0 = \text{Quantity sold at time 0}$$

The NCFs at period 1 are zero, and the NPV to Locust of refusing credit will simply be the period 0 NCF:

$$\text{NPV} = \text{NCF}$$

For example, if credit is not granted and $Q_0 = 100$, the NPV can be calculated as

$$\$50 \times 100 - \$20 \times 100 = \$3{,}000$$

*Strategy 2: Offer credit.*  Alternatively, let us assume that Locust grants credit to all customers for one period. The factors that influence the decision are listed below:

|  | Strategy 1: Refuse credit | Strategy 2: Offer credit |
| --- | --- | --- |
| Price per unit | $P_0 = \$50$ | $P_0' = \$50$ |
| Quantity sold | $Q_0 = 100$ | $Q_0' = 200$ |
| Cost per unit | $C_0 = \$20$ | $C_0' = \$25$ |
| Probability of payment | $h = 1$ | $h = 0.90$ |
| Credit period | 0 | 1 period |
| Discount rate | 0 | $r_B = 0.01$ |

The prime (′) denotes the variables under the second strategy. If the firm offers credit and the new customers pay, the firm will receive revenues of $P_0' Q_0'$ one period hence, but its costs, $C_0' Q_0'$, are incurred in period 0. If new customers do not pay, the firm incurs costs $C_0' Q_0'$ and receives no revenues. The probability that customers will pay, $h$, is 0.90 in the example. Quantity sold is higher with credit, because new customers are attracted. The cost per unit is also higher with credit because of the costs of operating a credit policy.

The expected cash flows for each policy are set out as follows:

|  | Expected cash flows | |
| --- | :---: | :---: |
|  | Time 0 | Time 1 |
| Refuse credit | $P_0 Q_{-0} - C_0 Q_{-0}$ | 0 |
| Offer credit | $-C_0' Q_0'$ | $h \times P_0' Q_0'$ |

Note that granting credit produces delayed expected cash inflows equal to $h \times P_0' Q_0'$. The costs are incurred immediately and require no discounting. The NPV if credit is offered is

$$
\begin{aligned}
\text{NPV (offer)} &= \frac{h \times P_0' Q_0'}{1 + r_B} - C_0' Q_0' \\
&= \frac{0.9 \times \$50 \times 200}{1.01} - \$5{,}000 \\
&= \$3{,}910.89
\end{aligned}
$$

Locust Software's decision should be to adopt the proposed credit policy. The NPV of granting credit is higher than that of refusing credit. This decision is very sensitive to the probability of payment. If it turns out that the probability of payment is 81 percent, Locust Software is indifferent to whether it grants credit or not. In this case, the NPV of granting credit is $3,000, which we previously found to be the NPV of not granting credit:

$$
\begin{aligned}
\$3{,}000 &= h \times \frac{\$50 \times 200}{1.01} - \$5{,}000 \\
\$8{,}000 &= h \times \frac{\$50 \times 200}{1.01} \\
h &= 80.8\%
\end{aligned}
$$

The decision to grant credit depends on four factors:

1. The delayed revenues from granting credit, $P_0' Q_0'$.
2. The immediate costs of granting credit, $C_0' Q_0'$.
3. The probability of payment, $h$.
4. The appropriate required rate of return for delayed cash flows, $r_B$. This rate is the after-tax cost of debt, which represents the opportunity cost of investing in receivables.

## The Value of New Information about Credit Risk

Obtaining a better estimate of the probability that a customer will default can lead to a better decision. How can a firm determine when to acquire new information about the creditworthiness of its customers?

It may be sensible for Locust Software to determine which of its customers are most likely not to pay. The overall probability of non-payment is 10 percent. But credit checks by an independent firm show that 90 percent of Locust's customers (computer stores) have been profitable over the past five years and that these customers have never defaulted on payments. The less profitable customers are much more likely to default. In fact, 100 percent of the less profitable customers have defaulted on previous obligations.

Locust would like to avoid offering credit to the deadbeats. Consider its projected number of customers per year of $Q_0' = 200$ if credit is granted. Of these customers, 180 have been profitable over the past five years and have never defaulted on past obligations. The remaining 20 have not been profitable. Locust Software expects that all of these less profitable customers will default. This information is set out in a table:

| Type of customer | Number | Probability of non-payment | Expected number of defaults |
|---|---|---|---|
| Profitable | 180 | 0 | 0 |
| Less profitable | 20 | 100% | 20 |
| Total customers | 200 | 10% | 20 |

The NPV of granting credit to the customers who default is

$$\frac{hP_0'Q_0'}{1 + r_B} - C_0'Q_0' = \frac{0 \times \$50 \times 20}{1.01} - \$25 \times 20 = -\$500$$

This is the cost of providing them with the software. If Locust could identify these customers without cost, it would certainly deny them credit.

In fact, it actually costs Locust \$3 per customer to figure out whether a customer has been profitable over the past five years. The expected payoff of the credit check on its 200 customers is then

$$\begin{array}{ccc} \text{Cost savings from} & - & \text{Cost of} \\ \text{not extending credit} & & \text{credit checks} \\ \$500 & - & \$3 \times 200 & = -\$100 \end{array}$$

For Locust, credit is not worth checking. It would need to pay \$600 to avoid a \$500 loss.

## Future Sales

Up to this point, Locust has not considered the possibility that offering credit will permanently increase the level of sales in future periods (beyond next month). In addition, payment and non-payment patterns in the current period will provide credit information that is useful for the next period. These two factors should be analyzed.

In the case of Locust, there is a 90 percent probability that the customer will pay in period 1. But, if payment is made, there will be another sale in period 2. The probability that the customer will pay in period 2, if the customer has paid in period 1, is 100 percent. Locust can refuse to offer credit in period 2 to customers that have refused to pay in period 1. This is diagrammed in Figure 29.5.

**FIGURE 29.5**

**Future Sales and the Credit Decision**

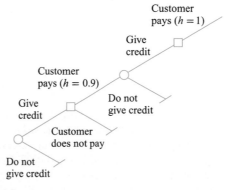

There is a 90 percent probability that a customer will pay in period 1. However, if payment is made, there will be another sale in period 2. The probability that the customer will pay in period 2 is 100 percent—if the customer has paid in period 1.

**CONCEPT QUESTION**    • List the factors that influence the decision to grant credit.

## 29.3   OPTIMAL CREDIT POLICY

So far we have discussed how to compute NPV for two alternative credit policies. However, we have not discussed the optimal amount of credit. At the optimal amount of credit, the incremental cash flows from increased sales are exactly equal to the carrying costs from the increase in accounts receivable.

Consider a firm that does not currently grant credit. This firm has no bad debts, no credit department, and relatively few customers. Now consider another firm that grants credit. This firm has lots of customers, a credit department, and a bad-debt expense account.

It is useful to think of the decision to grant credit in terms of carrying costs and opportunity costs:

1. *Carrying costs* are the costs associated with granting credit and making an investment in receivables. Carrying costs include the delay in receiving cash, the losses from bad debts, and the costs of managing credit.

2. *Opportunity costs* are the lost sales from refusing to offer credit. These costs drop as credit is granted.

We represent these costs in Figure 29.6.

**FIGURE 29.6**

**The Costs of Granting Credit**

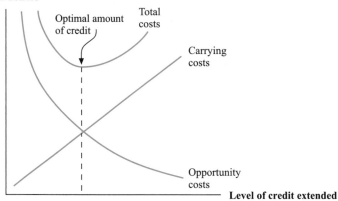

*Carrying costs* are the costs that must be incurred when credit is granted. They are positively related to the amount of credit extended.

*Opportunity costs* are the lost sales from refusing credit. These costs drop when credit is granted.

The sum of the carrying costs and the opportunity costs of a particular credit policy is called the *total credit cost curve*. A point is identified as the minimum of the total credit cost curve. If the firm extends more credit than the minimum of the total credit cost curve, the additional NCF from new customers will not cover the carrying costs of the higher investment in receivables.

The concept of optimal credit policy in the context of modern principles of finance should be somewhat analogous to the concept of the optimal capital structure discussed earlier in the text. In perfect financial markets, there should be no optimal credit policy. Alternative amounts of credit for a firm should not affect the value of the firm. Thus, the decision to grant credit would be a matter of indifference to financial managers.

---

# The Decision to Grant Credit

Trade credit is more likely to be granted by the selling firm if the following things are true about the selling firm.

1. The selling firm has a cost advantage over other lenders.

   *Example:* The Canadian Manufacturing Co. produces widgets. In a default, it is easier for the Canadian Manufacturing Co. to repossess widgets and resell them than for a finance company with no experience in selling widgets to arrange for it.

2. The selling firm can engage in price discrimination.

   *Example:* National Motors can offer below-market interest rates to lower-income customers who must finance a large portion of the purchase price of cars. Higher-income customers pay the list price and do not generally finance a large part of the purchase.

3. The selling firm can obtain favourable tax treatment.

   *Example:* The A.B. Production Company offers long-term credit to its best customers. This form of financing may qualify as an instalment plan and allow the A.B. Production Co. to book profits of the sale over the life of the loan. This may save taxes because the PV of the tax payments will be lower if spread over time.

4. The selling firm has no established reputation for quality products or services.

   *Example:* Advanced Micro Instruments (AMI) manufactures sophisticated measurement instruments for controlling electrical systems on commercial airplanes. The firm was founded by two engineering graduates from the University of Toronto in 1997. It became a public firm in 1998. To hedge their bets, aircraft manufacturers will ask for credit from AMI. It is very difficult for customers of AMI to assess the quality of its instruments until the instruments have been in place for some time.

5. The selling firm perceives a long-term strategic relationship.

   *Example:* Food.com is a fast-growing, cash-constrained Internet food distributor. It is currently not profitable. Acme Food will grant Food.com credit for food purchased, because Food.com will generate profits in the future.

Sources: Shezad I. Mian and Clifford W. Smith, "Extending Trade Credit and Financing Receivables," *Journal of Applied Corporate Finance* (Spring 1994); Marc Deloof and Marc Jegers, "Trade Credit, Product Quality and Intragroup Trade: Some European Evidence," *Financial Management* (Autumn 1996); Michael Long, I. B. Malitz, and S. A. Ravid, "Trade Credit, Quality Guarantees, and Product Marketability," *Financial Management* (Winter 1993); Mitchell A. Petersen and Raghuram G. Rajan, "Trade Credit: Theories and Evidence," *The Review of Financial Studies* (Autumn 1997).

---

Just as with optimal capital structure, we could expect taxes, bankruptcy costs, and agency costs to be important in determining an optimal credit policy in a world of imperfect financial markets. For example, customers in high tax brackets would be better off borrowing and taking advantage of cash discounts offered by firms than would customers in low tax brackets. Corporations in low tax brackets would be less able to offer credit, because borrowing would be relatively more expensive than for firms in high tax brackets.

In general, a firm will extend trade credit if it has a comparative advantage in doing so. Trade credit is likely to be advantageous if the selling firm has a cost advantage over other potential lenders, if the selling firm has monopoly power it can exploit, if the selling firm can reduce taxes by extending credit, and if the product quality of the selling firm is difficult to determine. Firm size may be important if there are size economies in managing credit.

The optimal credit policy depends on characteristics of particular firms. Assuming that the firm has more flexibility in its credit policy than in the prices it charges, firms with excess capacity, low variable operating costs, high tax brackets, and repeat customers should extend credit more liberally than others.

## Credit Insurance

Firms that run strictly internal credit operations are self-insured against default risk. An alternative is to buy credit insurance through an insurance company. The insurance company offers coverage up to a preset dollar limit for accounts. As you would expect, accounts with a higher credit rating merit higher insurance limits. Exporters may qualify for credit insurance through Export Development Canada (EDC), a Crown corporation of the federal government. In 2013, EDC played a major role in helping Canadian businesses access supply chains in India. For example, EDC provided a US$100 million financing agreement to Tata Steel as well as a US$500 million financing agreement to Aditya Birla Group, the Indian multinational conglomerate. These and similar efforts helped generate close to $2 billion of Canadian business in India in 2013.[4]

**CONCEPT QUESTION**

- What are the advantages of credit insurance?

# 29.4 CREDIT ANALYSIS

When granting credit, a firm tries to distinguish between customers who will pay and those who will not pay. There are a number of sources of information for determining creditworthiness.

## Credit Information

Information commonly used to assess creditworthiness includes the following:

1. *Financial statements.* A firm can ask a customer to supply financial information such as balance sheets and income statements. Minimum standards and rules of thumb based on financial ratios like the ones we discussed in Appendix 2A can then be used as a basis for extending or refusing credit.

2. *Credit reports on customer's payment history with other firms.* Several organizations sell information on the credit strength and credit history of business firms. D&B Canada and Creditel provide subscribers with credit references and credit reports on individual firms. Ratings and information are available for a huge number of firms, including very small ones.

3. *Banks.* Banks will generally assist their business customers in obtaining information on the creditworthiness of other firms.

4. *The customer's payment history with the firm.* The most obvious way to obtain information about the likelihood of a customer's not paying is to examine whether the customer paid up in the past and how much trouble collecting turned out to be.

## Credit Evaluation and Scoring

Once information has been gathered, the firm faces the hard choice of either granting or refusing credit. Many firms use the traditional and subjective guidelines referred to as the "five Cs of credit":

1. *Character.* The customer's willingness to meet credit obligations.

2. *Capacity.* The customer's ability to meet credit obligations out of operating cash flows.

---

[4] More information about EDC's initiatives and performance can be found in its 2013 annual report. The discussion regarding financing agreements with India is on page 17 of the report, available at edc.ca/EN/About-Us/Corporate-Reports/Documents/annual-report-2013.pdf.

3. *Capital.* The customer's financial reserves, or how much net worth the customer has.
4. *Collateral.* A pledged asset in the case of default.
5. *Conditions.* General business conditions, which affect the customer's ability to repay.

**Credit scoring** refers to the process of (1) calculating a numerical rating for a customer based on information collected and then (2) granting or refusing credit based on the result. For example, a firm might rate a customer on a scale of 1 (very poor) to 10 (very good) on each of the five Cs of credit using all the information available about the customer. A credit score could then be calculated based on the total. From experience, a firm might choose to grant credit only to customers with a score of more than, say, 30 out of a possible 50 points.

Financial institutions have developed elaborate statistical models for credit scoring. This approach has the advantage of being objective as compared to scoring based on judgments on the five Cs. Usually, all legally relevant and observable characteristics of a large pool of customers are studied to find their historic relation to default rates. Based on the results, it is possible to determine the variables that best predict whether or not a customer will pay; then, a credit score based on those variables is calculated.

Because credit-scoring models and procedures determine who is and who is not creditworthy, it is not surprising that they have been the subject of government regulation. In particular, the kinds of background and demographic information that can be used in the credit decision are limited. For example, suppose a consumer applicant was formerly bankrupt but had discharged all obligations. After a waiting period, which varies from province to province, this information cannot be used in the credit decision.

Credit scoring is used for business customers by Canadian chartered banks. Scoring for small business loans is a particularly attractive application because the technique offers the advantages of objective analysis without taking more of the lending officer's time than could be justified for a small account.

**CONCEPT QUESTIONS**

- What is credit analysis?
- What are the five Cs of credit?
- What are credit-scoring models, and how are they used?

# 29.5    COLLECTION POLICY

*Collection* refers to obtaining payment of past-due accounts. The credit manager keeps a record of payment experience with each customer.

## Average Collection Period

Acme Smartphones sells 100,000 smartphones a year at $300 each. All sales are for credit with terms of 2/20, net 60.

Suppose that 80 percent of Acme customers take the discounts and pay on day 20; the rest pay on day 60. The **average collection period** (ACP) measures the average amount of time required to collect an account receivable. The ACP for Acme is 28 days:

$$0.8 \times 20 \text{ days} + 0.2 \times 60 \text{ days} = 28 \text{ days}$$

(The average collection period is frequently referred to as *days' sales outstanding* or *days in receivables.*)

Of course, this is an idealized example where customers pay on either one of two dates. In reality, payments arrive in a random fashion, so that the ACP must be calculated differently.

To determine the ACP in the real world, firms first calculate average daily sales. The **average daily sales (ADS)** equal annual sales divided by 365. The ADS of Acme is

$$ADS = \frac{\$300 \times 100,000}{365 \text{ days}}$$

$$= \$82,192/\text{day}$$

If receivables today are \$2,301,376, the ACP is

$$ACP = \frac{\text{Accounts receivable}}{\text{ADS}}$$

$$= \frac{\$2,301,376}{\$82,192/\text{day}}$$

$$= 28 \text{ days}$$

In practice, firms observe sales and receivables on a daily basis. Consequently, an ACP can be computed and compared to the stated credit terms. For example, suppose Acme had computed its ACP at 40 days for several weeks, versus its credit terms of 2/20, net 60. With a 40-day ACP, some customers are paying later than usual. It may be that some accounts are overdue.

However, firms with seasonal sales will often find the *calculated* ACP changing during the year, making the ACP a somewhat flawed tool. This occurs because receivables are low before the selling season and high after the season. Thus, firms may keep track of seasonal movement in the ACP over past years. In this way, they can compare the ACP for today's date with the average ACP for that date in previous years. To supplement the information in the ACP, the credit manager may make up an accounts receivable aging schedule.

## Aging Schedule

The **aging schedule** tabulates receivables by age of account. In the following schedule, 75 percent of the accounts are on time, but a significant number are more than 60 days past due. This signifies that some customers are in arrears:

**Aging schedule**

| Age of account | Percentage of total value of accounts receivable |
|---|---|
| 0–20 days | 50 |
| 21–60 days | 25 |
| 61–80 days | 20 |
| Over 80 days | 5 |
| | 100 |

The aging schedule changes during the year. To avoid confusion, the aging schedule is often augmented by the payments pattern. The *payments pattern* describes the lagged collection pattern of receivables. Like a mortality table that describes the probability that a 23-year-old will live to be 24, the payments pattern describes the probability that a 67-day-old account will still be unpaid when it is 68 days old.

## Collection Effort

The firm usually employs a sequence of procedures for customers that are overdue:

1. Send a delinquency letter informing the customer of the past-due status of the account.
2. Make a telephone call to the customer.
3. Employ a collection agency.
4. Take legal action against the customer.

At times, a firm may refuse to grant additional credit to customers until arrearages are paid. This may antagonize a normally good customer, and it points to a potential conflict of interest between the collections department and the sales department.

One last point should be stressed. We have presented the elements of credit policy as though they were somewhat independent of each other. In fact, they are closely interrelated. For example, the optimal credit policy is not independent of collection and monitoring policies. A tighter collection policy can reduce the probability of default, which in turn can raise the NPV of a more liberal credit policy.

**CONCEPT**
**QUESTION**

- What tools can a manager use to analyze a collection policy?

## 29.6    OTHER ASPECTS OF CREDIT POLICY

### Factoring

A *factor* is an independent company that acts as "an outside credit department" for the client. It checks the credit of new customers, authorizes credit, and handles collection and bookkeeping. As the accounts are collected, the factor pays the client the face amount of the invoice less a 1 or 2 percent discount. If any accounts are late, the factor still pays the selling firm on an average maturity date determined in advance. The legal arrangement is that the factor purchases the accounts receivable from the firm. Thus, factoring provides insurance against bad debts, since any bad accounts are the factor's problem.

**Factoring** in Canada is conducted by independent firms whose main customers are small businesses that might not otherwise qualify for financing.[5] Factoring is popular with manufacturers of retail goods—especially in the apparel business—because it allows outside professionals to handle the headaches of credit.

What we have described so far is *maturity factoring* and does not involve a formal financing arrangement. What factoring does is remove receivables from the balance sheet, so, indirectly, it reduces the need for financing. It may also reduce the costs associated with granting credit. Since factors do business with many firms, they may be able to achieve scale economies, reduce risks through diversification, and carry more clout in collection.

Firms financing their receivables through a chartered bank may also use the services of a factor to improve the receivables' collateral value. In this case, the factor buys the receivables and assigns them to the bank. This is called maturity factoring with assignment of equity. Or, the factor will provide an advance on the receivables and charge interest at prime plus 2.5 to 3 percent. In this case of advance factoring, the factor is providing financing as well as other services.

### How to Finance Trade Credit

In addition to unsecured debt instruments described earlier in this chapter, there are three general ways of financing accounting receivables: secured debt, a captive finance company, and securitization.

Use of secured debt is usually referred to as asset-based receivables financing. This is the predominant form of receivables financing. Many lenders will not lend without security to firms with substantive uncertainty or little equity. With secured debt, if the borrower gets into financial difficulty, the lender can repossess the asset and sell it for its fair market value.

---

[5] Leora F. Klapper, "The Role of Factoring for Financing Small and Medium Enterprises" (May 2005). World Bank Policy Research Working Paper No. 3593. Available at SSRN, ssrn.com/abstract=748344.

Many large firms with good credit ratings use captive finance companies. The captive finance companies are subsidiaries of the parent firm. This is similar to the use of secured debt because the creditors of the captive finance company have a claim on its assets and, as a consequence, the accounts receivable of the parent firm. A captive finance company is attractive if economies of scale are important and if an independent subsidiary with limited liability is warranted.[6]

**CONCEPT QUESTION**

- What services do factors provide?

---

[6] The trend toward securitization of receivables through wholly owned subsidiaries discussed in Chapter 28 is supporting evidence. For more on finance captives, see G. S. Roberts and J. A. Viscione, "Captive Finance Subsidiaries and the M-Form Hypothesis," *Bell Journal of Economics* (Spring 1981); and S. Mian and C. Smith, "Extending Trade Credit and Financing Receivables," *Journal of Applied Corporate Finance* (Spring 1994).

## 29.7

# SUMMARY AND CONCLUSIONS

1. The three components of a firm's credit policy are the terms of sale, the credit analysis, and the collection policies.

2. The terms of sale describe the amount and period of time for which credit is granted and the type of credit instrument.

3. The decision to grant credit is a straightforward net present value (NPV) decision and can be improved by additional information about the payment characteristics of the customers. Additional information about the customers' probability of defaulting is valuable, but this value must be traded off against the expense of acquiring the information.

4. The optimal amount of credit the firm offers is a function of the competitive conditions in which it finds itself. These conditions will determine the carrying costs associated with granting credit and the opportunity costs of the lost sales from refusing to offer credit. The optimal credit policy minimizes the sum of these two costs.

5. We have seen that knowledge of the probability that customers will default is valuable. To enhance its ability to assess customers' default probability, a firm can score credit. This relates the default probability to observable characteristics of customers.

6. The collection policy is the method of dealing with past-due accounts. The first step is to analyze the average collection period (ACP) and to prepare an aging schedule that relates the age of accounts to the proportion of the accounts receivable they represent. The next step is to decide on the collection method and to evaluate the possibility of factoring, that is, selling the overdue accounts.

**KEY TERMS**

| | | |
|---|---|---|
| Aging schedule   850 | Cash discount   840 | Credit scoring   849 |
| Average collection period | Collection policy   837 | Factoring   851 |
| (ACP)   849 | Credit analysis   837 | Invoice   839 |
| Average daily sales | Credit instrument   842 | Terms of the sale   837 |
| (ADS)   850 | Credit period   839 | |

**QUESTIONS & PROBLEMS**

### Cash Discounts

29.1 You place an order for 400 units of inventory at a unit price of $125. The supplier offers terms of 1/10, net 30.

    *a.* How long do you have to pay before the account is overdue? If you take the full period, how much should you remit?

    *b.* What is the discount being offered? How quickly must you pay to get the discount? If you do take the discount, how much should you remit?

    *c.* If you don't take the discount, how much interest are you paying implicitly? How many days' credit are you receiving?

### Size of Accounts Receivable

29.2 The Tate Corp. has annual sales of $34 million. The ACP is 33 days. What is the average investment in accounts receivable as shown on the balance sheet?

### Average Collection Period and Accounts Receivable

29.3 Kyoto Joe Inc. sells earnings forecasts for Japanese securities. Its credit terms are 2/10, net 30. Based on experience, 65 percent of all customers will take the discount.

   a. What is the average collection period for Kyoto Joe?
   b. If Kyoto Joe sells 1,300 forecasts every month at a price of $1,700 each, what is its average balance sheet amount in accounts receivable?

### Size of Accounts Receivable

29.4 Tidwell Inc. has weekly credit sales of $27,500, and the average collection period is 27 days. The cost of production is 75 percent of the selling price. What is the average accounts receivable figure?

### Terms of Sale

29.5 A firm offers terms of 1/10, net 30. What effective annual interest rate does the firm earn when a customer does not take the discount? What will happen to this effective rate if

   a. The discount is changed to 2 percent.
   b. The credit period is increased to 60 days.
   c. The discount period is increased to 15 days.

### Average Collection Period and Receivables Turnover

29.6 Lipman Inc. has an ACP of 39 days. Its average daily investment in receivables is $47,500. What are annual credit sales? What is the receivables turnover?

### Size of Accounts Receivable

29.7 Essence of Skunk Fragrances Ltd. sells 4,900 units of its perfume collection each year at a price per unit of $495. All sales are on credit with terms of 1/10, net 40. The discount is taken by 40 percent of the customers. What is the total amount of the company's accounts receivable? In reaction to sales by its main competitor, Sewage Spray, Essence of Skunk is considering a change in its credit policy to terms of 2/10, net 30 to preserve its market share. How will this change in policy affect accounts receivable?

29.8 The Arizona Bay Corp. sells on credit terms of net 30. Its accounts are, on average, six days past due. If annual credit sales are $9.3 million, what is the company's balance sheet amount in accounts receivable?

### Evaluating Credit Policy

29.9 Air Spares is a wholesaler that stocks engine components and test equipment for the commercial aircraft industry. A new customer has placed an order for eight high-bypass turbine engines, which increase fuel economy. The variable cost is $1.6 million per unit, and the credit price is $1.87 million each. Credit is extended for one period, and based on historical experience, payment for about 1 out of every 200 such orders is never collected. The required return is 2.9 percent per period.

   a. Assuming that this is a one-time order, should it be filled? The customer will not buy if credit is not extended.
   b. What is the break-even probability of default in (a)?
   c. Suppose that customers who don't default become repeat customers and place the same order every period forever. Further assume that repeat customers never default. Should the order be filled? What is the break-even probability of default?
   d. Describe in general terms why credit terms will be more liberal when repeat orders are a possibility.

## Credit Policy Evaluation

29.10  Lealos Inc. is considering a change in its cash-only sales policy. The new terms of sale would be net one month. Based on the following information, determine if Lealos should proceed or not. Describe the buildup of receivables in this case. The required return is 0.95 percent per month.

|                       | Current policy | New policy |
|-----------------------|:--------------:|:----------:|
| Price per unit        | $720           | $720       |
| Cost per unit         | $495           | $495       |
| Unit sales per month  | 1,100          | 1,140      |

29.11  The Harrington Corp. is considering a change in its cash-only policy. The new terms would be net one period. Based on the following information, determine if Harrington should proceed or not. The required return is 2.5 percent per period.

|                       | Current policy | New policy |
|-----------------------|:--------------:|:----------:|
| Price per unit        | $91            | $94        |
| Cost per unit         | $47            | $47        |
| Unit sales per month  | 3,850          | 3,940      |

29.12  Happy Times currently has an all-cash policy. It is considering making a change in the credit policy by going to terms of net 30 days. Based on the following information, what do you recommend? The required return is 0.95 percent per month.

|                       | Current policy | New policy |
|-----------------------|:--------------:|:----------:|
| Price per unit        | $295           | $302       |
| Cost per unit         | $230           | $234       |
| Unit sales per month  | 1,105          | 1,125      |

## Credit Policy

29.13  The Silver Spokes Bicycle Shop has decided to offer credit to its customers during the spring selling season. Sales are expected to be 500 bicycles. The average cost to the shop of a bicycle is $490. The owner knows that only 96 percent of the customers will be able to make their payments. To identify the remaining 4 percent, the company is considering subscribing to a credit agency. The initial charge for this service is $450, with an additional charge of $5 per individual report. Should it subscribe to the agency?

## Break-Even Quantity

29.14  In Problem 29.11, what is the break-even quantity for the new credit policy?

## Credit Markup

29.15  In Problem 29.11, what is the break-even price per unit that should be charged under the new credit policy? Assume that the sales figure under the new policy is 4,100 units and all other values remain the same.

29.16  In Problem 29.12, what is the break-even price per unit under the new credit policy? Assume all other values remain the same.

## Credit Policy at Braam Industries

Tricia Haltiwinger, the president of Braam Industries, has been exploring ways of improving the company's financial performance. Braam Industries manufactures and sells office equipment to retailers. The company's growth has been relatively slow in recent years, but with an expansion in the economy, it appears that sales may increase more quickly in the future. Tricia has asked Andrew Preston, the company's treasurer, to examine Braam's credit policy to see if a different credit policy can help increase profitability.

The company currently has a policy of net 30. As with any credit sales, default rates are always of concern. Because of Braam's screening and collection process, the default rate on credit is currently only 2.1 percent. Andrew has examined the company's credit policy in relation to other vendors, and he has determined that three options are available.

The first option is to relax the company's decision on when to grant credit. The second option is to increase the credit period to net 45, and the third option is a combination of the relaxed credit policy and the extension of the credit period to net 45. On the positive side, each of the three policies under consideration would increase sales. The three policies have the drawbacks that default rates would increase, the administrative costs of managing the firm's receivables would increase, and the receivables period would increase. The credit policy change would impact all four of these variables to different degrees. Andrew has prepared a table (see below) outlining the effect on each of these variables.

Braam's variable costs of production are 45 percent of sales, and the relevant interest rate is a 6 percent effective annual rate. Which credit policy should the company use? Also, notice that in option 2 the default rate and administrative costs are below those in option 3. Is this plausible? Why or why not?

| | Annual sales (millions) | Default rate (% of sales) | Administrative costs (% of sales) | Receivables period |
|---|---|---|---|---|
| Current policy | $116 | 1.90% | 1.60% | 38 days |
| Option 1 | 130 | 2.60 | 2.40 | 41 |
| Option 2 | 129 | 2.20 | 1.90 | 51 |
| Option 3 | 132 | 2.50 | 2.10 | 49 |

## Inventory Management

To access Appendix 29A, go to Connect.

# 30

# Mergers and Acquisitions

There are no more dramatic or controversial activities in corporate finance than the acquisition of one firm by another and the merger of two firms. This chapter addresses two basic questions: Why does a firm choose to merge with or acquire another firm, and how does it happen?

The acquisition of one firm by another is, of course, an investment made under uncertainty. The basic principle of valuation applies; that is, a firm should be acquired if it generates a positive net present value (NPV) to the shareholders of the acquiring firm. However, because the NPV of an acquisition candidate is very difficult to determine, mergers and acquisitions are interesting topics in their own right. Here are some of the special features of this area of finance:

1. The benefits from acquisitions are called *synergies*. It is hard to estimate synergies using discounted cash flow (DCF) techniques.
2. There are complex accounting, tax, and legal effects when one firm is acquired by another.
3. Acquisitions are an important control device of shareholders. It appears that some acquisitions are a consequence of an underlying conflict between the interests of management and of shareholders. Agreeing to be acquired by another firm is one way that shareholders can remove managers with whom they are unhappy.
4. Acquisition analysis frequently focuses on the total value of the firms involved. But usually an acquisition will affect the relative values of stocks and bonds as well as their total value.
5. Mergers and acquisitions sometimes involve unfriendly transactions. Thus, when one firm attempts to acquire another, it does not always involve quiet negotiations. The sought-after firm may use defensive tactics, including poison pills, greenmail, and white knights.

This chapter starts by introducing the basic legal, accounting, and tax aspects of acquisitions. When one firm acquires another, it must choose the legal framework, the accounting method, and the tax status. These choices will be explained throughout the chapter.

The chapter discusses how to determine the NPV of an acquisition candidate. The NPV of an acquisition candidate is the difference between the synergy from the merger and the premium to be paid. We consider the following types of synergy: (1) revenue enhancement, (2) cost reduction, (3) lower taxes, and (4) lower cost of capital. The premium paid for an acquisition is the price paid minus the market value of the acquisition prior to the merger. The premium depends on whether cash or securities are used to finance the offer price.

## 30.1 THE BASIC FORMS OF ACQUISITIONS

There are three basic legal procedures that one firm can use to acquire another firm: (1) merger or consolidation, (2) acquisition of stock, and (3) acquisition of assets.

### Merger or Consolidation

A **merger** refers to the absorption of one firm by another. The acquiring firm retains its name and identity and acquires all of the assets and liabilities of the acquired firm. After a merger, the acquired, or target, firm ceases to exist as a separate business entity.

A **consolidation** is the same as a merger except that an entirely new firm is created. In a consolidation, both the acquiring firm and the acquired firm terminate their previous legal existence and become part of the new firm. In a consolidation, the distinction between the acquiring and the acquired firm is not important. However, the rules for mergers and consolidations are basically the same. Acquisitions by merger and consolidation result in combinations of the assets and liabilities of acquired and acquiring firms.

There are some advantages and some disadvantages to using a merger to acquire a firm:

1. A merger is legally straightforward and does not cost as much as other forms of acquisition. It avoids the necessity of transferring title of each individual asset of the acquired firm to the acquiring firm.

2. A primary disadvantage is that a merger must be approved by a vote of the shareholders of each firm.[1] Typically, two-thirds (or even more) of the share votes are required for approval. Obtaining the necessary votes can be time-consuming and difficult. Furthermore, as we discuss in greater detail below, the cooperation of the target firm's existing management is almost a necessity for a merger. This cooperation may not be easily or cheaply obtained.

**EXAMPLE 30.1**

Suppose firm $A$ acquires firm $B$ in a merger. Further, suppose firm $B$ shareholders are given one share of firm $A$'s stock in exchange for two shares of firm $B$'s stock. From a legal standpoint, firm $A$'s shareholders are not directly affected by the merger. However, firm $B$'s shares cease to exist. In a consolidation, the shareholders of firm $A$ and firm $B$ exchange their shares for the shares of a new firm (firm $C$). Because the differences between mergers and consolidations are minor for our purposes, we shall refer to both types of reorganizations as *mergers*.

## Acquisition of Stock

A second way to acquire another firm is to purchase the firm's voting stock in exchange for cash, shares of stock, or other securities. This process will often start as a private offer from the management of one firm to another. At some point the offer is taken directly to the target firm's shareholders through a tender offer. A **tender offer** is a public offer to buy shares made by one firm directly to the shareholders of another firm.

If the shareholders choose to accept the offer, they tender their shares by exchanging them for cash or securities (or both), depending on the offer. A tender offer is frequently contingent on the bidder's obtaining some percentage of the total voting shares. If not enough shares are tendered, then the offer might be withdrawn or reformulated.

The takeover bid is communicated to the target firm's shareholders by public announcements such as newspaper advertisements. Takeover bids may be either by **circular bid** mailed directly to the target's shareholders or by **stock exchange bid** (through the facilities of the TSX or other exchange). In either case, Ontario securities law requires that the bidder mail a notice of the proposed share purchase to shareholders. Furthermore, the management of the target firm must also respond to the bid, including its recommendation to accept or to reject the bid. In the case of a circular bid, the response must be mailed to shareholders. If the bid is made through a stock exchange, the response is through a press release.

---

[1] As we discuss later, obtaining majority assent is less of a problem in Canada than in the United States because fewer Canadian corporations are widely held.

The following are factors involved in choosing between an acquisition of stock and a merger:

- In an acquisition of stock, shareholder meetings do not need to be held and no vote is required. If the shareholders of the target firm do not like the offer, they are not required to accept it and they will not tender their shares.
- In an acquisition of stock, the bidding firm can deal directly with the shareholders of a target firm by using a tender offer. The target firm's management and board of directors can be bypassed.
- Acquisition of stock is often unfriendly and is used in an effort to circumvent the target firm's management, which is usually actively resisting acquisition. Resistance by the target firm's management often makes the cost of acquisition by stock higher than the cost by merger.
- Sometimes a minority of shareholders will hold out in a tender offer, and thus the target firm cannot be completely absorbed.
- Complete absorption of one firm by another requires a merger. Many acquisitions of stock end with a formal merger later.

## Acquisition of Assets

One firm can acquire another by buying all of its assets. A formal vote of the shareholders of the selling firm is required. This approach to acquisition will avoid the potential problem of having holdout minority shareholders, which can occur in an acquisition of stock. But, acquisition of assets involves a costly legal process of transferring title.

## A Classification Scheme

Financial analysts typically classify acquisitions into three types:

1. *Horizontal acquisition.* This is an acquisition of a firm in the same industry as the acquiring firm. The firms compete with each other in their product market. For instance, Petro-Canada was a Canadian Crown Corporation until 2009, when it merged with Suncor Energy.
2. *Vertical acquisition.* A vertical acquisition involves firms at different stages of the production process. A vertical acquisition occurred when BCE Inc., provider of cable TV, acquired Astral Media, an owner of radio and TV stations, in 2013.
3. *Conglomerate acquisition.* The acquiring firm and the acquired firm are not related to each other. The acquisition of Federated Department Stores by Campeau Corporation, a real estate company, was considered a conglomerate acquisition.

## A Note on Takeovers

*Takeover* is a general and imprecise term referring to the transfer of control of a firm from one group of shareholders to another.[2] The bidder offers to pay cash or securities to obtain the stock or assets of another company. If the offer is accepted, the target firm will give up control over its stock or assets to the bidder in exchange for the *consideration*—the bidder's stock, debt, or cash.[3]

For example, when a bidding firm acquires a target firm, the right to control the operating activities of the target firm is transferred to a newly elected board of directors of the acquiring firm. This is a takeover by acquisition.

Takeovers can occur by acquisition, proxy contests, and going-private transactions. Thus, as shown in Figure 30.1, takeovers encompass a broader set of activities than acquisitions.

---

[2] *Control* may be defined as having a majority vote on the board of directors.

[3] Audra L. Boone and J. Harold Mulherin, in "How Are Firms Sold?" *Journal of Finance* (April 2007), look closely at the takeover process and the chain of negotiations and competitive bidding.

FIGURE 30.1

**Varieties of Takeovers**

If a takeover is achieved by acquisition, it will be by merger, tender offer for shares of stock, or purchase of assets. In mergers and tender offers, the acquiring firm buys the voting common stock of the acquired firm.

Takeovers can occur with **proxy contests** in which a group of shareholders attempts to gain controlling seats on the board of directors by voting in new directors. A *proxy* authorizes the proxyholder to vote on all matters in a shareholders' meeting. In a proxy contest, proxies from the rest of the shareholders are solicited by an insurgent group of shareholders.

In **going-private transactions**, all of the equity shares of a public firm are purchased by a small group of investors. Usually, the group includes members of incumbent management and some outside investors. Such transactions have come to be known generically as **leveraged buyouts** (**LBOs**) because a large percentage of the money needed to buy up the stock is usually borrowed. Such transactions are also termed **management buyouts** (**MBOs**) when existing management is heavily involved. The shares of the firm are delisted from stock exchanges and can no longer be purchased in the open market.

There have been a large number of mergers and acquisitions in recent years, many of them involving very familiar companies. Table 30.1 lists some recent examples of mergers involving Canadian companies. Some of these mergers failed, while others were successful. For instance, the acquisition of Shoppers Drug Mart Corporation by Loblaw Companies Limited provided Loblaw with an advantage over U.S. retail competitors like Wal-Mart and Target, which face obstacles opening stores in the inner cities due to the scarcity and cost of real estate. The acquisition of Shoppers allowed Loblaw to gain 1,240 small-format stores within busy downtown areas across the country. This enabled the company to sell more groceries in Shoppers Drug Mart stores, expand its own pharmaceuticals section, and expand its market reach.[4] In contrast, CNOOC Limited's 2012 acquisition of Calgary-based Nexen Inc. hurt its financial performance. CNOOC Limited's average companywide return on investment is 11 percent. However, the return on Nexen Inc.'s assets was only 3.5 percent.[5]

EXAMPLE 30.2

In 2008, Royal Bank of Canada (RBC) announced the successful takeover of Philips, Hager & North Investment Management Ltd. (PH&N) in a $1.4 billion all-stock deal that made RBC the largest institutional manager in Canada. Based on their respective year-ends, RBC and PH&N had a combined total of $160 billion in assets under management.

---

[4] Ari Altstedter and Katia Dmitrieva, "Loblaw Gains Inner-City Advantage with $12.4B Shoppers Drug Mart Deal," Retail & Marketing, *National Post*, 16 July 2013, business.financialpost.com/2013/07/16/loblaw-walmart-target-cities/.

[5] Nathan VanderKlippe, "Nexen Deal Comes Back to Haunt CNOOC," *The Globe and Mail*, 3 December 2013, theglobeandmail.com/report-on-business/international-business/asian-pacific-business/nexen-acquisition-hurting-cnoocs-performance/article15742860/.

**TABLE 30.1**

### Twelve Large Mergers and Acquisitions Involving Canadian Companies

| Rank | Year | Value (in $ billions) | Target company | Acquiring company |
|------|------|------------------------|-----------------|-------------------|
| 1 | 2007 | $39.83 | Alcan Inc. | Rio Tinto Group |
| 2 | 2000 | $39.72 | The Seagram Company Ltd. | Vivendi S.A. |
| 3 | 2009 | $23.90 | Petro-Canada | Suncor Energy Inc. |
| 4 | 2006 | $19.87 | Inco Limited | Companhia Vale do Rio Doce |
| 5 | 2006 | $19.20 | Falconbridge Limited | Xstrata plc |
| 6 | 2007 | $18.98 | Reuters Group PLC | The Thomson Corporation |
| 7 | 1998 | $15.37 | Polygram N.V. | The Seagram Company Ltd. |
| 8 | 2012 | $15.35 | Nexen Inc. | CNOOC Limited |
| 9 | 2003 | $15.00 | John Hancock Financial Services Inc. | Manulife Financial Corporation |
| 10 | 2008 | $14.44 | Fording Canadian Coal Trust | Teck Cominco Limited |
| 11 | 2013 | $12.30 | Shoppers Drug Mart Corporation | Loblaw Companies Limited |
| 12 | 2005 | $11.88 | Placer Dome Inc. | Barrick Gold Corporation |

Source: FP Infomart.

As these examples show, the success or failure of merger transactions often depends on the presence of synergies, which we devote Sections 30.4 and 30.5 to discussing.

*CONCEPT QUESTIONS*

- What is a merger? How does a merger differ from other forms of acquisition?
- What is a takeover?

## 30.2    THE TAX FORMS OF ACQUISITIONS

If one firm buys another firm, the transaction may be taxable or tax free. In a *taxable acquisition*, the shareholders of the target firm are considered to have sold their shares, and they may have realized capital gains or losses that will be taxed. In a *tax-free acquisition*, since the acquisition is considered an exchange instead of a sale, no realized capital gain or loss occurs.

### Determinants of Tax Status

The general requirements for tax-free status are that (1) the acquisition involve two Canadian corporations subject to corporate income tax and (2) there be a continuity of equity interest. In other words, the shareholders in the target firm must retain an equity interest in the bidder.

The specific requirements for a tax-free acquisition depend on the legal form of the acquisition, but, in general, if the buying firm offers the selling firm cash for its equity, it will be a taxable acquisition. If shares of stock are offered, it will be a tax-free acquisition.

In a tax-free acquisition, the selling shareholders are considered to have exchanged their old shares for new ones of equal value, and no realized capital gains or losses are experienced.

### Taxable versus Tax-Free Acquisitions

There are two factors to consider when comparing a tax-free acquisition and a taxable acquisition: the capital gains effect and the write-up effect. The *capital gains effect* refers to the fact that the target firm's shareholders may have to pay capital gains taxes in a taxable acquisition. They may demand a higher price as compensation, thereby increasing the cost of the merger. This is a cost of a taxable acquisition.

The bidder's shareholders may be willing to pay this cost because the bidder enjoys a *write-up effect* in a taxable acquisition. The tax status of an acquisition also affects the appraised value of the assets of the selling firm. In a taxable acquisition, the assets of the selling firm are revalued or "written up" from their historic book value to their estimated current market value. This is the write-up effect, and it is important because the depreciation expense on the acquired firm's assets can be increased in taxable acquisitions. Remember that an increase in depreciation is a non-cash expense, but it has the desirable effect of reducing taxes.

**CONCEPT QUESTIONS**

- What factors influence the choice between a taxable and a tax-free acquisition?
- What is the write-up effect in a taxable acquisition?

# 30.3 ACCOUNTING FOR ACQUISITIONS

Earlier in this text we mentioned that firms keep two distinct sets of books: the shareholders' books and the tax books. The previous section concerned the effect of acquisitions on the tax books. We now consider the shareholders' books. When one firm acquires another firm, the acquisition is treated as a purchase on the shareholders' books. The following section provides a basic example of the accounting treatment under the acquisition method, which is required under IFRS 3 for all business combinations.

## The Acquisition Method

The **acquisition method** requires that the identifiable assets of the acquired firm, the liabilities assumed, and any non-controlling interest in the target be reported on the books of the acquirer. The assets and liabilities should be measured at their acquisition-date fair market value. This allows the acquirer to establish a new cost basis for the acquired assets.

In a purchase, an accounting entry called *goodwill* is created. **Goodwill** is the excess of the purchase price over the net value of assets acquired.[6] For simplicity, we exclude any discussion on non-controlling interests.

**EXAMPLE 30.3**

Suppose firm *A* acquires firm *B*, creating a new firm, *AB*. Firm *A*'s and firm *B*'s financial positions at the date of the acquisition are shown in Table 30.2. The book value of firm *B* on the date of the acquisition is $10 million. This is the sum of $8 million in buildings and $2 million in cash. However, an appraiser states that the sum of the fair market values of the individual buildings is $14 million. With $2 million in cash, the sum of the market values of the individual assets in firm *B* is $16 million. This represents the value to be received if the firm is liquidated by selling off the individual assets separately.

---

[6] Another accounting method formerly used in mergers and acquisitions was pooling of interests, under which the balance sheet items of two companies were added together. This method was preferred because it did not result in creation of goodwill and led to higher reported earnings. The method was abandoned in Canada with the restructuring of IASB standards prior to the adoption of IFRS.

**TABLE 30.2**

**Accounting for Acquisitions: Purchase (in $ millions)**

| Firm A | | | | Firm B | | |
|---|---|---|---|---|---|---|
| Cash | $ 4 | Equity | $20 | Cash | $ 2 | Equity | $10 |
| Land | 16 | | | Land | 0 | | |
| Buildings | 0 | | | Buildings | 8 | | |
| Total | $20 | | $20 | Total | $10 | | $10 |
| **Firm AB** | | | | | | |
| | | Cash | $ 6 | Debt | $19 | |
| | | Land | 16 | Equity | 20 | |
| | | Buildings | 14 | | | |
| | | Goodwill | 3 | | | |
| | | Total | $39 | | $39 | |

The assets of the acquired firm (firm B) appear in the combined firm's books at their fair market value.

However, the whole is often worth more than the sum of the parts in business. Firm A pays $19 million in cash for firm B. This difference of $3 million (or $19 million − $16 million) is goodwill. It represents the increase in value by keeping the firm intact as an ongoing business. Firm A issued $19 million in new debt to finance the acquisition. The last balance sheet in Table 30.2 shows what happens under the acquisition method of accounting.

1.  The total assets of firm AB increase to $39 million. The buildings of firm B appear in the new balance sheet at their current market value. That is, the market value of the assets of the acquired firm becomes part of the book value of the new firm. However, the assets of the acquiring firm (firm A) remain at their old book value. They are not revalued upward when the new firm is created.

2.  The excess of the purchase price over the sum of the fair market values of the individual assets acquired is $3 million. This amount is reported as goodwill. Financial analysts generally ignore goodwill because it has no cash flow consequences. The current accounting practice says that each year firms must assess the value of goodwill on their balance sheets. If the value goes down (this is called *impairment* in accounting speak), the firm must deduct the decrease from earnings; otherwise no amortization is required.

 **CONCEPT QUESTION**

• What is the role of goodwill in purchase accounting for mergers?

# 30.4   DETERMINING THE SYNERGY FROM AN ACQUISITION

Suppose firm A is contemplating acquiring firm B. The value of firm A is $V_A$, and the value of firm B is $V_B$. (It is reasonable to assume that for public companies, $V_A$ and $V_B$ can be determined by observing the market prices of the outstanding securities.) The difference between the value of the combined firm ($V_{AB}$) and the sum of the values of the firms as separate entities is the *synergy* from the acquisition:

$$\text{Synergy} = V_{AB} - (V_A + V_B)$$

The acquiring firm must generally pay a premium for the acquired firm. For example, if stock of the target is selling for $50, the acquirer might need to pay $60 a share, implying a premium of $10 or 20 percent. From 1990 to 2007, the average premiums paid for public acquisitions were 45.79 percent, 42.02 percent, and 37.01 percent in the United States, the United Kingdom, and Canada, respectively, compared to 31.91 percent in the rest of the world.[7] The acquirer's willingness to pay a premium for a target firm makes it more challenging to create value for the acquiring firm's shareholders. A study by Robert Eccels, Kersten Lanes, and Thomas Wilson[8] finds that acquisitions typically do not create any value for an acquiring firm's shareholders because of irrational exuberance about the strategic importance of the target, weakness in integration, and the overpayment for the target. We return to the idea of value creation in Section 30.10, but we would simply like to emphasize here that premiums are common and usually expected in merger transactions.

Given that high premiums are common, acquirers need to be certain that the potential synergy values are enough to justify the premium—there is little margin for error. Accordingly, firm $A$ will want to determine the synergy before entering into negotiations with firm $B$ on the premium.

The synergy of an acquisition can be determined from the usual DCF model:

$$\text{Synergy} = \sum_{t=1}^{T} \frac{\Delta\text{CF}_t}{(1 + r)^t}$$

where $\Delta\text{CF}_t$ is the difference between the cash flows at date $t$ of the combined firm and the sum of the cash flows of the two separate firms. In other words, $\Delta\text{CF}_t$ is the incremental cash flow at date $t$ from the merger. The term $r$ is the risk-adjusted discount rate appropriate for the incremental cash flows. This is generally considered to be the required rate of return on the equity of the target, reflecting the risk of the target's incremental cash flows.

From the chapters on capital budgeting, we know that the incremental cash flows can be separated into four parts:

$$\Delta\text{CF}_t = \Delta\text{Rev}_t - \Delta\text{Costs}_t - \Delta\text{Taxes}_t - \Delta\text{Capital requirements}_t$$

where $\Delta\text{Rev}_t$ is the incremental revenue of the acquisition, $\Delta\text{Costs}_t$ is the incremental costs of the acquisition, $\Delta\text{Taxes}_t$ is the incremental acquisition taxes, and $\Delta\text{Capital requirements}_t$ is the incremental new investment required in working capital and fixed assets.

# 30.5   SOURCES OF SYNERGY FROM ACQUISITIONS

It follows from our classification of incremental cash flows that the possible sources of synergy fall into four basic categories: revenue enhancement, cost reduction, lower taxes, and lower cost of capital.

## Revenue Enhancement

One important reason for acquisitions is that a combined firm may generate greater revenues than two separate firms. Increased revenues may come from marketing gains, strategic benefits, and market power.

**Marketing Gains**   It is frequently claimed that mergers and acquisitions can produce greater operating revenues from improved marketing. Improvements can be made in

1. Previously ineffective media programming and advertising efforts.

[7] G. Alexandridis, D. Petmezas, and N. G. Travlos, "Gains from Mergers and Acquisitions around the World: New Evidence," *Financial Management Association International* (Winter 2010).

[8] Robert G. Eccels, Kersten L. Lanes, and Thomas C. Wilson, "Are You Paying Too Much for That Acquisition?" *Harvard Business Review* (July–August 1999).

2. A weak existing distribution network.

3. An unbalanced product mix.

**Strategic Benefits**    Some acquisitions promise a *strategic* advantage. This is an opportunity to take advantage of the competitive environment if certain situations materialize. In this regard, a strategic benefit is more like an option than like a standard investment opportunity. For example, imagine that a computer company acquired an automotive manufacturing company. The firm would be well positioned if traffic law changes allowed computer-driven cars in the future. Michael Porter has used the word *beachhead* in his description of the process of entering a new industry to exploit perceived opportunities. The beachhead is used to spawn new opportunities based on *intangible* relationships. He views Procter & Gamble's initial acquisition of the Charmin Paper Company as a beachhead that allowed Procter & Gamble to develop a highly interrelated cluster of paper products: disposable diapers, paper towels, feminine hygiene products, and bathroom tissue.

**Market or Monopoly Power**    One firm may acquire another to increase its market share and market power. Profits can be enhanced through higher prices and reduced competition for customers. In theory, such mergers are controlled by law. In practice, however, horizontal mergers are far more common in Canada than in the United States due to weaker legal restrictions against combinations of competitors that might limit market competition. For instance, Loblaw Companies Limited obtained approval from the Competition Bureau for its acquisition of Shoppers Drug Mart Corporation.

## Cost Reduction

One of the most basic reasons to merge is that a combined firm may operate more efficiently than two separate firms. A merger or acquisition can increase a firm's operating efficiency in several different ways: economies of scale, economies of vertical integration, complementary resources, and elimination of inefficient management.

**Economies of Scale**    If the average cost of production falls while the level of production increases, there is said to be an economy of scale. Figure 30.2 illustrates that economies of scale result while the firm grows to its optimal size. Beyond this size, diseconomies of scale occur. In other words, average cost increases with further firm growth. The phrase *spreading overhead* is frequently used in connection with economies of scale from horizontal mergers. This refers to the sharing of central facilities such as corporate headquarters, top management, and a large mainframe computer.

**FIGURE 30.2**

**Economies of Scale and the Optimal Size of the Firm**

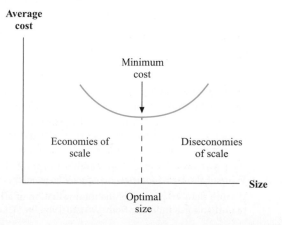

**Economies of Vertical Integration**     Operating economies can be gained from vertical as well as horizontal combinations. The main purpose of vertical acquisitions is to make coordination of closely related operating activities easier. This is probably why most forest product firms that cut timber also own sawmills and hauling equipment. Economies from vertical integration probably explain why most airline companies own airplanes; it also may explain why some airline companies have purchased hotels and car rental companies.

Technology transfers are another reason for vertical integration. Consider the merger of General Motors and Hughes Aircraft in 1985. An automobile manufacturer might well acquire an advanced electronics firm if the special technology of the electronics firm can improve the quality of the automobile.

**Complementary Resources**     Some firms acquire others to make better use of existing resources or to provide the missing ingredient for success. Think of a ski equipment store that could merge with a tennis equipment store to produce more even sales over both the winter and summer seasons—and better use of store capacity. Along the same lines, management know-how, systems, and brands can add value in mergers. Measuring such organizational capital by capitalized selling, general, and administrative expenses, Li, Qiu, and Shen show that U.S. acquirers with more organizational capital enjoy greater revenue and are better able to cut capital costs after mergers.[9]

**Elimination of Inefficient Management**     There are firms whose value could be increased with a change in management. For example, Jensen and Ruback argue that acquisitions can occur because of changing technology or market conditions that require a restructuring of the corporation.[10] Incumbent managers in some cases do not understand changing conditions. They have trouble abandoning strategies and styles they have spent years formulating.

The oil industry is an example of managerial inefficiency cited by Jensen. In the late 1970s, changes in the oil industry included reduced expectations of the future price of oil, increased exploration and development costs, and increased real interest rates. As a result of these changes, substantial reductions in exploration and development were called for. However, many oil company managers were unable to downsize their firms. For example, a study by McConnell and Muscarella reports that the stock prices of oil companies tended to drop upon announcements of increases in exploration and development expenditures in the period 1975–1981.[11] By 1999, changes in the economic landscape resulted in the $81.38 billion acquisition of Mobil Corp. by Exxon Corp. One of the main forces propelling this merger forward was that throughout the 1990s the oil industry had been cutting costs to remain competitive, and analysts projected $2.8 billion in annual cost savings.

Acquiring companies sought out oil firms in order to reduce the investment levels of these oil companies.[12] For example, T. Boone Pickens of Mesa Petroleum perceived the changes taking place in the oil industry and attempted to buy several oil companies: Unocal, Phillips, and Getty. The results of these attempted acquisitions were reduced expenditures on exploration and development and huge gains to the shareholders of the affected firms.

---

[9] K. Li, B. Qiu, and R. Shen, "Organizational Capital and Mergers and Acquisitions," Working Paper, April 2014. Available at business.illinois.edu/finance/papers/2014/Li.K.pdf.

[10] M. C. Jensen and R. S. Ruback, "The Market for Corporate Control: The Scientific Evidence," *Journal of Financial Economics* (April 1983); and M. C. Jensen, "Agency Costs of Free Cash Flow, Corporate Finance and Takeovers," *American Economic Review* (May 1986).

[11] J. J. McConnell and C. J. Muscarella, "Corporate Capital Expenditure Decisions and the Market Value of the Firm," *Journal of Financial Economics* (September 1985).

[12] More than 26 percent of the total valuation of all takeover transactions involved a selling firm in the oil and gas industry from 1981 to 1984 [W. T. Grimm, *Mergerstat Review* (1985), p. 41].

Mergers and acquisitions can be viewed as part of the labour market for top management. Jensen and Ruback have used the phrase *market for corporate control*, in which alternative management teams compete for the rights to manage corporate activities.

**The Negative Side of Takeovers**    While most financial analysts would likely agree that competition for corporate control can enhance efficiency, there is concern over whether the cost is too high. Critics of takeovers (and especially of LBOs) are concerned that social costs are not counted when the post-takeover search for efficiency gains leads to plant closures and layoffs. When plants close or move, workers and equipment can be turned to other uses only at some cost to society. For example, taxpayers may need to subsidize retraining and relocation programs for workers or tax incentives for investment. In an extreme case, suppose a mine is closed down in a rural area where there is no other large employer. All capital goods that cannot be moved may become worthless.

Critics of takeovers argue that they reduce trust between management and labour, thus reducing efficiency and increasing costs. They point to Japan, Germany, and Korea (where there are few takeovers) as examples of more efficient economies. They argue that, as an alternative to takeovers, a strong board of outside directors could maximize management's efficiency.[13]

## Tax Gains

Tax gains are often a powerful incentive for acquisitions. Possible tax gains from an acquisition include

1. The use of tax losses.
2. The use of unused debt capacity.
3. The use of surplus funds.

**Net Operating Losses**    Firms that lose money on a pre-tax basis will not pay taxes. Such firms can end up with tax losses that they cannot use. These tax losses are referred to as *NOL* (an acronym for *net operating losses*).

A firm with NOL may be an attractive merger partner for a firm with significant tax liabilities. Barring any other effects, the combined firm will have a lower tax bill than the two firms considered separately. This is a good example of how a firm can be more valuable merged than standing alone. For example, tax savings made possible by Dome Petroleum's large losses were an important attraction to Amoco when it bought Dome in 1988.

There is an important qualification to our NOL discussion. Canadian tax laws permit firms that experience periods of profit and loss to even things out through loss carryback and carryforward provisions. A firm that has been profitable in the past but has a loss in the current year can obtain refunds of income taxes paid in the three previous years. After that, losses can be carried forward for up to 20 years. Thus, a merger to exploit unused tax shields must offer tax savings over and above what can be accomplished by firms via carryovers.

**Unused Debt Capacity**    We argued earlier in the text that the optimal debt-to-equity ratio is the one where the marginal tax benefit from additional debt is equal to the marginal increase in the financial distress costs from additional debt. Because some diversification occurs when firms merge, the cost of financial distress is likely to be less for the combined firm than is the sum of these present values (PVs) for the two

---

[13] This section draws on C. Robinson's arguments in C. Robinson versus W. Block, "Are Corporate Takeovers Good or Bad? A Debate," *Canadian Investment Review* (Fall 1991); and on a piece by W. S. Allen, "Relegating Corporate Takeovers to the 'Campeaust' Heap: A Proposal," *Canadian Investment Review* (Spring 1990).

separate firms. Thus, the acquiring firm might be able to increase its debt-to-equity ratio after a merger, creating additional tax benefits—and additional value.[14,15]

**Surplus Funds**   Another quirk in the tax laws involves surplus funds. Consider a firm that has *free cash flow*—cash flow available after all taxes have been paid and after all positive net present value (NPV) projects have been financed.

In this situation, aside from purchasing fixed income securities, the firm has several ways to spend the free cash flow, including

1. Pay dividends.
2. Buy back its own shares.
3. Acquire shares in another firm.

We discussed the first two options in Chapter 19 and showed that an extra dividend will increase the income tax paid by some investors. And, under Canada Revenue Agency (CRA) regulations, share repurchase seldom reduces the taxes paid by shareholders when compared to paying dividends.

To avoid these problems, the firm can buy another firm. This avoids the tax problem associated with paying a dividend. Of course, if the purchase is a negative NPV investment, this action exemplifies inefficient management and may make the bidder into a target.

### The Cost of Capital

The cost of capital can often be reduced when two firms merge because the costs of issuing securities are subject to economies of scale. As we observed in earlier chapters, the costs of issuing both debt and equity are much lower for larger issues than for smaller issues.

**CONCEPT QUESTION**    • What are sources of possible synergy in acquisitions?

## 30.6   CALCULATING THE VALUE OF THE FIRM AFTER AN ACQUISITION

Now that we have listed the possible sources of synergy from a merger, we examine how to value these sources. Consider two firms. Gamble Inc. manufactures and markets soaps and cosmetics. The firm has a reputation for its ability to attract, develop, and keep talented people and has successfully introduced several major products in the past two years. It would like to enter the over-the-counter drug market to round out its product line. Shapiro Inc. is a well-known maker of cold remedies. Alma Shapiro, the great-granddaughter of the founder of Shapiro Inc., became chair of the firm last year. Unfortunately, Alma knows nothing about cold remedies, and as a consequence Shapiro Inc. has had lacklustre financial performance. For the most recent year, pre-tax cash flow fell by 15 percent. The firm's stock price is at an all-time low.

The financial management of Gamble finds Shapiro an attractive candidate. It believes that the cash flows from the combined firms would be far greater than what

---

[14] While unused debt capacity can be a valid reason for a merger, hindsight shows that many mergers in the 1980s overused debt financing. We discuss this in more detail later.

[15] Michael C. Jensen, "Agency Costs of Free Cash Flow, Corporate Finance and Takeovers," *American Economic Review* (May 1986), offers another reason that debt is frequently used in mergers and acquisitions. He argues that using more debt provides incentives for the new management to create efficiencies so that debt can be repaid.

each firm would have alone. The anticipated cash flows and PVs from the acquisition are shown in Table 30.3. The increased cash flows ($CF_t$) come from three benefits:

1. *Tax gains.* If Gamble acquires Shapiro, Gamble will be able to use some tax-loss carryforwards to reduce its tax liability. The additional cash flows from tax gains should be discounted at the cost of debt capital because they can be determined with very little uncertainty. The financial management of Gamble estimates that the acquisition will reduce taxes by $1 million per year in perpetuity. The relevant discount rate is 5 percent, the after-tax cost of debt, and the PV of the tax reduction is $20 million.

2. *Operating efficiencies.* The financial management of Gamble has determined that Gamble can take advantage of some of the unused production capacity of Shapiro. At times, Gamble has been operating at full capacity with a large backlog of orders. Shapiro's manufacturing facilities, with a little reconfiguration, can be used to produce Gamble's soaps. Thus, more soaps and cold remedies can be produced without adding to the combined firm's capacity and cost. These operating efficiencies will increase after-tax cash flows by $1.5 million per year. Using Shapiro's discount rate and assuming perpetual gains, the PV of the unused capacity is determined to be $10 million.

3. *Strategic fit.* The financial management of Gamble has determined that the acquisition of Shapiro will give Gamble a strategic advantage. The management of Gamble believes that the addition of the Shapiro Bac-Rub ointment for sore backs to its existing product mix will give it a better chance of launching successful new skin care products if these markets develop in the future. Management of Gamble estimates that there is a 50 percent probability that $6 million in after-tax cash flow can be generated with the new skin care products. These opportunities are contingent on factors that cannot be easily quantified. Because of the lack of precision here, the managers decided to use a high discount rate. Gamble chooses a 20 percent rate, and it estimates that the PV of the strategic factors is $15 million (or $0.50 \times \$6$ million/0.20).

**TABLE 30.3**

**Acquisition of Shapiro Inc. by Gamble Inc.**

|  | Net cash flow per year (perpetual) | Discount rate | Value |
|---|---|---|---|
| Gamble Inc. | $10.0 million | 0.10 | $100 million |
| Shapiro Inc. | 4.5 million | 0.15 | 30 million* |
| **Benefits from acquisition:** |  |  |  |
| Strategic fit | 3.0 million | 0.20 | 15 million |
| Tax shelters | 1.0 million | 0.05 | 20 million |
| Operating efficiencies | 1.5 million | 0.15 | 10 million |
| Total benefits from acquisition | 5.5 million | 0.122 | 45 million |
| Gamble–Shapiro | 20.0 million | 0.114 | 175 million |

* The market value of Shapiro's outstanding common stock is $30 million; 1 million shares are outstanding.

## Avoiding Mistakes

The Gamble–Shapiro illustration is very simple and straightforward. It is deceptive because the incremental cash flows have already been determined. In practice, an analyst must estimate these cash flows and determine the proper discount rate. Valuing the benefits of a potential acquisition is harder than valuing benefits for standard capital budgeting projects. Many mistakes can be made. Here are some general rules:

1. *Do not ignore market values.* In many cases it is very difficult to estimate values using DCFs. Because of this, an expert business appraiser should know the market prices of comparable opportunities. In an efficient market, prices should reflect value. Because the market value of Shapiro is $30 million, we use this estimate of Shapiro's current value.

2. *Estimate only incremental cash flows.* Only incremental cash flows from an acquisition will add value to the acquiring firm. Thus, it is important to estimate the cash flows that are incremental to the acquisition.

3. *Use the correct discount rate.* The discount rate should be the required rate of return for the incremental cash flows associated with the acquisition.[16] It should reflect the risk associated with the *use* of funds, not their *source*. It would be a mistake for Gamble to use its own cost of capital to value the cash flows from Shapiro.

4. *If Gamble and Shapiro combine, there will be transaction costs.* These will include fees to investment bankers, legal fees, and costs of disclosure requirements.

# 30.7    A COST TO SHAREHOLDERS FROM REDUCTION IN RISK

The previous section discussed gains to the firm from a merger. In a firm with debt, these gains are likely to be shared by both bondholders and shareholders. We now consider how a merger could benefit the bondholders at the expense of the shareholders.

When two firms merge, the variability of their combined values is usually lower than if the firms remained separate entities. The variability of firm values can fall if the values of the two firms are less than perfectly correlated. The resulting reduction in the cost of borrowing will make the creditors better off than before because the probability of financial distress is reduced by the merger.

Unfortunately, the shareholders are likely to be worse off. The gains to creditors are at the expense of the shareholders if the total value of the firm does not change. The relationship among the value of the merged firm, debt capacity, and risk is very complicated. We now consider two examples.

## The Base Case

Consider a base case where two all-equity firms merge. Table 30.4 gives the NPVs of firm *A* and firm *B* in three possible states of the economy: prosperity, average, and depression. The market value of firm *A* is $60, and the market value of firm *B* is $40. The market value of each firm is the weighted average of the values in each of the three states. For example, the value of firm *A* is

$$\$60 = \$80 \times 0.5 + \$50 \times 0.3 + \$25 \times 0.2$$

The values in each of the three states for firm *A* are $80, $50, and $25, respectively. The probabilities of each of the three states occurring are 0.5, 0.3, and 0.2, respectively.

When firm *A* merges with firm *B*, the combined firm *AB* will have a market value of $100. There is no synergy from this merger, and consequently the value of firm *AB* is the sum of the values of firm *A* and firm *B*. Shareholders of *B* receive stock with a value of $40, and therefore shareholders of *A* will receive stock with a value of $100 − $40 = $60. Thus, shareholders of *A* and *B* are indifferent to the proposed merger.

---

[16] Recall that the required rate of return is sometimes referred to as the *cost of capital* or the opportunity cost of capital.

**TABLE 30.4**

### Stock-Swap Mergers

| | Net present value | | | Market value |
|---|---|---|---|---|
| | State 1 | State 2 | State 3 | |
| **Base case: two all-equity firms before merger:** | | | | |
| Firm $A$ | $80 | $50 | $25 | $60 |
| Firm $B$ | $50 | $40 | $15 | $40 |
| Probability | 0.5 | 0.3 | 0.2 | |
| After merger* | | | | |
| Firm $AB$ | $130 | $90 | $40 | $100 |
| **Firm $A$, equity and risky debt before merger:** | | | | |
| **Firm $B$, all-equity before merger:** | | | | |
| Firm $A$ | $80 | $50 | $25 | $60 |
| Debt | $40 | $40 | $25 | $37 |
| Equity | $40 | $10 | $0 | $23 |
| Firm $B$ | $50 | $40 | $15 | $40 |
| **After merger:†** | | | | |
| Firm $AB$ | $130 | $90 | $40 | $100 |
| Debt | $40 | $40 | $40 | $40 |
| Equity | $90 | $50 | $0 | $60 |

Value of debt rises after merger. Value of original stock in acquiring firm falls correspondingly.

\* Shareholders in $B$ receive stock value of $40. Therefore, shareholders of $A$ have a value of $100 − $40 = $60 and are *indifferent to merger*.

† Because firm $B$'s shareholders receive stock in firm $A$ worth $40, original shareholders in firm $A$ have stock worth $20 (or $60 − $40). Gains and losses from merger are

$20 − $23 = −$3; therefore, shareholders of $A$ lose $3

$40 − $37 = $3; therefore, bondholders of $A$ gain $3

## The Case Where One Firm Has Debt

Alternatively, imagine firm $A$ has some debt and some equity outstanding before the merger.[17] Firm $B$ is an all-equity firm. Firm $A$ will default on its debt in state 3 because the NPV of firm $A$ in this state is $25, and the value of the debt claim is $40. As a consequence, the full value of the debt claim cannot be paid by firm $A$. The creditors take this into account, and the value of the debt is $37 (or $40 × 0.5 + $40 × 0.3 + $25 × 0.2).

Though default occurs without a merger, no default occurs with a merger. To see this, notice that when the two firms are separate, firm $B$ does not guarantee firm $A$'s debt. That is, if firm $A$ defaults on its debt, firm $B$ does not help the bondholders of firm $A$. However, after the merger, the bondholders can draw on the cash flows from both $A$ and $B$. When one of the divisions of the combined firm fails, creditors can be paid from the profits of the other division. This mutual guarantee, which is called the *coinsurance effect*, makes the debt less risky and more valuable than before.

The bonds are worth $40 after the merger. Thus, the bondholders of $AB$ gain $3 (or $40 − $37) from the merger.

The shareholders of firm $A$ lose $3 (or $20 − $23) from the merger. That is, firm $A$'s stock is worth $23 prior to the merger. The stock is worth $60 after the merger. However, shareholders in firm $B$ receive $40 of stock in firm $A$. Hence, those individuals who were shareholders in firm $A$ prior to the merger have stock worth only $20 (or $60 − $40) after the merger.

There is no net benefit to the firm as a whole. The bondholders gain the coinsurance effect, and the shareholders lose the coinsurance effect. Some general conclusions emerge from the preceding analysis:

---

[17] This example was provided by David Babbel.

1. Bondholders in the aggregate will usually be helped by mergers and acquisitions. The size of the gain to bondholders depends on the reduction of bankruptcy risk after the combination. That is, the less risky the combined firm, the greater are the gains to bondholders.

2. Shareholders of the acquiring firm will be hurt by the amount that bondholders gain.

3. The conclusions apply to mergers and acquisitions where no synergy is present. In the case of synergistic combinations, much depends on the size of the synergy.

### How Can Shareholders Reduce Their Losses from the Coinsurance Effect?

The coinsurance effect allows some mergers to increase bondholder values by reducing shareholder values. However, there are at least two ways that shareholders can reduce or eliminate the coinsurance effect. First, the shareholders in firm *A* could retire its debt *before* the merger announcement date and reissue an equal amount of debt after the merger. Because debt is retired at the low, pre-merger price, this type of refinancing transaction can neutralize the coinsurance effect to the bondholders.

Also, note that the debt capacity of the combined firm is likely to increase because the acquisition reduces the probability of financial distress. Thus, the shareholders' second alternative is simply to issue more debt after the merger. An increase in debt following the merger will have two effects, even without the prior action of debt retirement. The interest deduction from new corporate debt raises firm value. In addition, an increase in debt after merger raises the probability of financial distress, thereby reducing or eliminating the bondholders' gain from the coinsurance effect.

 **CONCEPT QUESTION**

- How is the distribution of merger gains complicated if one of the firms has debt outstanding?

## 30.8  TWO "BAD" REASONS FOR MERGERS

### Earnings Growth

An acquisition can create the appearance of earnings growth, which may fool investors into thinking that the firm is worth more than it really is. Suppose Global Resources Ltd. acquires Regional Enterprises. The financial positions of Global and Regional before the acquisition are shown in Table 30.5. Regional has had very poor earnings growth and sells at a price–earnings (P/E) ratio much lower than that of Global. The merger creates no additional value. If the market is smart, it will realize that the combined firm is worth the sum of the values of the separate firms. In this case, the market value of the combined firm will be $3,500, which is equal to the sum of the values of the separate firms before the merger.

At these values, Global will acquire Regional by exchanging 40 of its shares for 100 Regional shares, so that Global will have 140 shares outstanding after the merger.[18] Because the stock price of Global is unchanged by the merger, the P/E ratio must fall. This is true because the market is smart and recognizes that the total market value has not been altered by the merger. This scenario is represented by the third column of Table 30.5.

Let us now consider the possibility that the market is fooled. One can see from Table 30.5 that the acquisition enables Global to increase its earnings per share (EPS) from $1 to $1.43. If the market is fooled, it might mistake the 43 percent increase in EPS for true growth. In this case, the P/E ratio of Global may not fall after the merger. Suppose the P/E ratio of Global remains equal to 25. The total value of the combined firm will increase to $5,000 (or 25 × $200), and the stock price per share of Global will increase to $35.71 (or $5,000/140). This is reflected in the last column of Table 30.5.

---

[18] This ratio implies a fair exchange because a share of Regional is selling for 40 percent ($10/$25) of the price of a share of Global.

**TABLE 30.5**

**Financial Positions of Global Resources and Regional Enterprises**

| | Global Resources before merger | Regional Enterprises before merger | Global Resources after merger | |
| --- | --- | --- | --- | --- |
| | | | The market is "smart" | The market is "fooled" |
| Earnings per share | $   1.00 | $   1.00 | $   1.43 | $   1.43 |
| Price per share | $ 25.00 | $ 10.00 | $ 25.00 | $ 35.71 |
| Price–earnings ratio | 25 | 10 | 17.5 | 25 |
| Number of shares | 100 | 100 | 140 | 140 |
| Total earnings | $ 100.00 | $ 100.00 | $ 200.00 | $ 200.00 |
| Total value | $2,500.00 | $1,000.00 | $3,500.00 | $5,000.00 |

Exchange ratio: 1 share in Global for 2.5 shares in Regional.

This is earnings growth magic. Like all good magic, it is just illusion. For it to work, the shareholders of Global and Regional must receive something for nothing. This may work for a while, but in the long run the efficient market will work its wonders and the value will decline.

## Diversification

Diversification is often mentioned as a benefit of one firm's acquiring another. For example, U.S. Steel included diversification as a benefit in its acquisition of Marathon Oil. In 1982, U.S. Steel was a cash-rich company. (Over 20 percent of its assets were in the form of cash and marketable securities.) It is not uncommon to see firms with surplus cash articulating a need for diversification.

However, we argue that diversification, by itself, cannot produce increases in value. To see why, recall that a business's variability of return can be separated into two parts: (1) what is specific to the business and called *unsystematic* and (2) what is *systematic* because it is common to all businesses.

Systematic variability cannot be eliminated by diversification, so mergers will not eliminate this risk at all. In contrast, unsystematic risk can be diversified away through mergers. However, the investor does not need widely diversified companies such as Onex and Brascan to eliminate unsystematic risk. Shareholders can diversify more easily than corporations by simply purchasing common stock in different corporations. For example, the shareholders of U.S. Steel could have purchased shares in Marathon if they believed there would be diversification gains in doing so. Thus, diversification through conglomerate merger may not benefit shareholders.[19]

---

[19] Evidence suggests that diversification can actually hurt shareholders. Randall Morck, Andrei Shleifer, and Robert W. Vishney, "Do Managerial Objectives Drive Bad Acquisitions?" *Journal of Finance* (March 1990), show that shareholders did poorly in firms that diversified by acquisition in the 1980s. There is also evidence that diversified firms trade at a discount relative to a portfolio of single-segment firms, most recently from Karl Lins and Henri Servaes, "The International Evidence on the Value of Corporate Diversification," *Journal of Finance* (December 1999). On the other hand, Matsusaka and Hubbard and Palia find some benefits to diversification in internal capital allocation. See John Matsusaka, "Takeover Motives during the Conglomerate Merger Wave," *Rand Journal of Economics* (Autumn 1993). See also R. Glenn Hubbard and Darius Palia, "A Reexamination of the Conglomerate Merger Wave in the 1960s: An Internal Capital Markets View," *Journal of Finance* (June 1999).

One interesting study reports a positive relationship between focus and value for diversified firms. See P. G. Berger and E. Ofek, "Diversification's Effect on Firm Value," *Journal of Financial Economics* (January 1995). Also see P. G. Berger and E. Ofek, "Causes and Effects of Corporate Refocusing Program," *Review of Financial Studies* (April 1999).

Diversification can produce gains to the acquiring firm only if two things are true:

1. Diversification decreases the unsystematic variability at lower costs than investors could via adjustments to personal portfolios. This seems very unlikely.
2. Diversification reduces risk and thereby increases debt capacity. This possibility was mentioned earlier in the chapter.

**CONCEPT QUESTIONS**

- Why can a merger create the appearance of earnings growth?
- Why is diversification generally a poor motive for a merger?

# 30.9   THE NET PRESENT VALUE OF A MERGER

Firms typically use NPV analysis when making acquisitions. The analysis is relatively straightforward when the consideration is cash. The analysis becomes more complex when the consideration is stock.

## Cash

Suppose firm $A$ and firm $B$ have values as separate entities of $500 and $100, respectively. They are both all-equity firms. If firm $A$ acquires firm $B$, the merged firm $AB$ will have a combined value of $700 due to synergies of $100. The board of firm $B$ has indicated that it will sell firm $B$ if it is offered $150 in cash.

Should firm $A$ acquire firm $B$? Assuming that firm $A$ finances the acquisition out of its own retained earnings, its value after the acquisition is[20]

$$\text{Value of firm } A \text{ after the acquisition} = \text{Value of combined firm} - \text{Cash paid}$$
$$= \qquad \$700 \qquad - \qquad \$150$$
$$= \$550$$

Because firm $A$ was worth $500 prior to the acquisition, the NPV to firm $A$'s shareholders is

$$\$50 = \$550 - \$500 \tag{30.1}$$

Assuming that there are 25 shares in firm $A$, each share of the firm is worth $20 (or $500/25) prior to the merger and $22 (or $550/25) after the merger. These calculations are displayed in the first and third columns of Table 30.6. Looking at the rise in stock price, we conclude that firm $A$ should make the acquisition.

We spoke earlier of both the synergy and the premium of a merger. We can also value the NPV of a merger to the acquirer as

$$\text{NPV of merger to firm } A = \$100 - \$50 = \$50$$

Because the value of the combined firm is $700 and the pre-merger values of $A$ and $B$ were $500 and $100, respectively, the synergy is $100 [or $700 − ($500 + $100)]. The premium is $50 (or $150 − $100). Thus, the NPV of the merger to the acquirer is

$$\text{NPV of merger to firm } A = \$100 - \$50 = \$50$$

---

[20] The analysis will be essentially the same if new stock is issued. However, it will differ if new debt is issued to fund the acquisition because of the tax shield to debt. An adjusted present value (APV) approach would be necessary here.

**TABLE 30.6**

**Cost of Acquisition: Cash versus Common Stock**

| | Before acquisition | | | After acquisition: Firm $A$ | |
|---|---|---|---|---|---|
| | (1)<br>Firm $A$ | (2)<br>Firm $B$ | (3)<br>Cash* | (4)<br>Common stock:<br>Exchange ratio<br>(0.75:1) | (5)<br>Common stock:<br>Exchange ratio<br>(0.6819:1) |
| Market value ($V_A$, $V_B$) | $500 | $100 | $550 | $ 700 | $ 700 |
| Number of shares | 25 | 10 | 25 | 32.5 | 31.819 |
| Price per share | $ 20 | $ 10 | $ 22 | $21.54 | $ 22 |

<table>
<tr><td>

* Value of firm $A$ after acquisition—cash:

$$V_A = V_{AB} - \text{Cash}$$
$$\$550 = \$700 - \$150$$

</td><td>

* Value of firm $A$ after acquisition—common stock:

$$V_A = V_{AB}$$
$$\$700 = \$700$$

</td></tr>
</table>

One caveat is in order. This textbook has consistently argued that the market value of a firm is the best estimate of its true value. However, we must adjust our analysis when discussing mergers. If the true price of firm $A$ *without the merger* is $500, the market value of firm $A$ may actually be above $500 when merger negotiations take place. This occurs because the market price reflects the possibility that the merger will occur. For example, if the probability is 60 percent that the merger will take place, the market price of firm $A$ will be

| Market value of firm $A$ with merger | × | Probability of merger | + | Market value of firm $A$ without merger | × | Probability of no merger |
|---|---|---|---|---|---|---|
| $530 = 550 | × | 0.60 | + | $500 | × | 0.40 |

The managers would underestimate the NPV from merger in equation (30.1) if the market price of firm $A$ were used. Thus, managers are faced with the difficult task of valuing their own firm without the acquisition.

## Common Stock

Of course, firm $A$ could purchase firm $B$ with common stock instead of cash. Unfortunately, the analysis is not as straightforward here. In order to handle this scenario, we need to know how many shares are outstanding in firm $B$. We assume that there are 10 shares outstanding, as indicated in column 2 of Table 30.6.

Suppose firm $A$ exchanges 7.5 of its shares for the entire 10 shares of firm $B$. We call this an exchange ratio of 0.75:1. The value of each share of firm $A$'s stock before the acquisition is $20. Because $7.5 × \$20 = \$150$, this exchange *appears* to be the equivalent of purchasing firm $B$ in cash for $150.

This is incorrect; the true cost is greater than $150. To see this, note that firm $A$ has 32.5 (or 25 + 7.5) shares outstanding after the merger. Firm $B$ shareholders own 23 percent (7.5/32.5) of the combined firm. Their holdings are valued at $161 (or 23% × $700). Because these shareholders receive stock in firm $A$ worth $161, the cost of the merger to firm $A$'s shareholders must be $161, not $150.

This result is shown in column 4 of Table 30.6. The value of each share of firm $A$'s stock after a stock-for-stock transaction is only $21.54 (or $700/32.5). We found out earlier that the value of each share is $22 after a cash-for-stock transaction. The difference is that the cost of the stock-for-stock transaction to firm $A$ is higher.

This non-intuitive result occurs because the exchange ratio of 7.5 shares of firm $A$ for 10 shares of firm $B$ was based on the *pre-merger* prices of the two firms. However, since the stock of firm $A$ rises after the merger, firm $B$ shareholders receive more than $150 in firm $A$ stock.

What should the exchange ratio be so that firm $B$ shareholders receive only $150 of firm $A$'s stock? We begin by defining $\alpha$, the proportion of the shares in the combined firm that firm $B$'s shareholders own. Because the combined firm's value is $700, the value to firm $B$ shareholders after the merger is

**Value to Firm $B$ Shareholders after Merger:**

$$\alpha \times \$700$$

Setting $\alpha \times \$700 = \$150$, we find that $\alpha = 21.43\%$. In other words, firm $B$'s shareholders will receive stock worth $150 if they receive 21.43 percent of the firm after the merger.

Now we determine the number of shares issued to firm $B$'s shareholders. The proportion, $\alpha$, that firm $B$'s shareholders have in the combined firm can be expressed as

$$\alpha = \frac{\text{New shares issued}}{\text{Old shares} + \text{New shares issued}} = \frac{\text{New shares issued}}{25 + \text{New shares issued}}$$

Plugging our value of $\alpha$ into the equation yields

$$0.2143 = \frac{\text{New shares issued}}{25 + \text{New shares issued}}$$

Solving for the unknown, we have

$$\text{New shares} = 6.819 \text{ shares}$$

Total shares outstanding after the merger is 31.819 (or $25 + 6.819$). Because 6.819 shares of firm $A$ are exchanged for 10 shares of firm $B$, the exchange ratio is 0.6819:1.

Results at the exchange ratio of 0.6819:1 are displayed in column 5 of Table 30.6. Each share of common stock is worth $22, exactly what it is worth in the stock-for-cash transaction. Thus, given that the board of firm $B$ will sell its firm for $150, this is the fair exchange ratio, not the ratio of 0.75:1 used earlier.

## Cash versus Common Stock

In this section, we have examined both cash deals and stock-for-stock deals. Our analysis leads to the following question: when do bidders want to pay with cash and when do they want to pay with stock? There is no easy formula. The decision hinges on a few variables, with perhaps the most important being the price of the bidder's stock.

In the example of Table 30.6, firm $A$'s market price per share prior to the merger was $20. Let's now assume that at the time firm $A$'s managers believed the "true" price was $15. In other words, the managers believed that their stock was overvalued. Is it likely for managers to have a different view than that of the market? Yes—managers often have more information than does the market. After all, managers deal with customers, suppliers, and employees daily and are likely to obtain private information.

Now imagine that firm $A$'s managers are considering acquiring firm $B$ with either cash or stock. The overvaluation would have no impact on the merger terms in a cash deal; firm $B$ would still receive $150 in cash. However, the overvaluation would have a big impact on a stock-for-stock deal. Although firm $B$ receives $150 worth of $A$'s stock as calculated at market prices, firm $A$'s managers know that the true value of the stock is less than $150.

How should firm $A$ pay for the acquisition? Clearly, firm $A$ has an incentive to pay with stock because it would end up giving away less than $150 of value. This conclusion might seem rather cynical because firm $A$ is, in some sense, trying to cheat firm $B$'s shareholders. However, both theory and empirical evidence suggest that firms are more likely to acquire with stock when their own stocks are overvalued.[21]

---

[21] The theoretical ideas presented here are from a classic article by S. Myers and N. Majluf, "Corporate Financing and Investment Decisions When Firms Have Information That Investors Do Not Have," *Journal of Financial Economics* (June 1984).

The story is not quite this simple. Just as the managers of firm *A* think strategically, firm *B*'s managers will likely think this way as well. Suppose that in the merger negotiations, firm *A*'s managers push for a stock-for-stock deal. This might tip off firm *B*'s managers that firm *A* is overpriced. Perhaps firm *B*'s managers will ask for better terms than firm *A* is currently offering. Alternatively, firm *B* may resolve to accept cash or not sell at all.

And just as firm *B* learns from the negotiations, the market learns also. Empirical evidence shows that the acquirer's stock price generally falls upon the announcement of a stock-for-stock deal.[22]

However, this discussion does not imply that mistakes are never made. For example, consider the stock-for-stock merger in January 2001 between AOL, an Internet service provider, and Time Warner (TW), a media firm. Although the deal was presented as a merger of equals and the combined company is now called Time Warner, AOL appears, in retrospect, to have been the acquirer. The merger was one of the biggest of all time, with a combined market capitalization between the two firms of about $350 billion at the time of the announcement in January 2000. (The delay of about a year between merger announcement and merger completion was due to regulatory review.) It is also considered one of the worst deals of all time, with Time Warner having a market value of about $36 billion in May 2010.

AOL was in a precarious position at the time of the merger, providing narrowband Internet service when consumers were hungering for broadband. Also, at least in retrospect, Internet stocks were greatly overpriced. The deal allowed AOL to offer its inflated stock as currency for a company not in the technology industry and, therefore, not nearly as overpriced, if overpriced at all. Had TW looked at the deal in this way, it might have simply called it off. (Alternatively, it could have demanded cash, though it is unlikely that AOL had the financial resources to pay in this way.)

Just as TW's managers did not understand all the implications of the merger right away, it appears that the market did not either. TW's stock price rose over 25 percent relative to the market in the week following the merger announcement.

**CONCEPT QUESTION**

- In an efficient market with no tax effects, should an acquiring firm use cash or stock?

## Defensive Tactics

Target firm managers frequently resist takeover attempts. Resistance usually starts with press releases and mailings to shareholders presenting management's viewpoint. It can eventually lead to legal action and solicitation of competing bids. Managerial action to defeat a takeover attempt may make target shareholders better off if it elicits a higher offer premium from the bidding firm or another firm. Of course, management resistance may simply reflect pursuit of self-interest at the expense of shareholders—the target firm's managers may resist a takeover to preserve their jobs. In this section, we describe various defensive tactics that have been used by target firm managements to resist unfriendly takeover attempts.

## Divestitures

Target firm managers considering the prospect of a takeover may decide that a narrowing of strategic focus can increase stock price, thereby making a takeover too expensive. If so, they will consider the pros and cons of four kinds of divestitures: a sale of assets, a spin-off, a carve-out, and the issuance of a tracking stock.

---

[22] For example, see G. Andrade, M. Mitchell, and E. Stafford, "New Evidence and Perspectives on Mergers," *Journal of Economic Perspectives* (Spring 2001); and R. Heron and E. Lie, "Operating Performance and the Method of Payment in Takeovers," *Journal of Financial and Quantitative Analysis* (March 2002).

The most basic type of divestiture is the *sale* of a division, business unit, segment, or set of assets to another company. The buyer generally, but not always, pays in cash. A number of reasons are provided for sales. First, asset sales can act as a defence against hostile takeovers. Sales often improve corporate focus, leading to greater overall value for the seller. This same rationale applies when the selling company does not have additional bidders or, in other words, is not "in play." Second, asset sales provide needed cash to liquidity-poor firms. Third, it is often argued that the paucity of data about individual business segments makes large, diversified firms hard to value. Investors may discount the firm's overall value because of this lack of transparency. Sell-offs streamline a firm, making it easier to value. However, this argument is inconsistent with market efficiency because it implies that large, diversified firms sell below their true value. Fourth, firms may simply want to sell unprofitable divisions. However, unprofitable divisions are likely to have low values to anyone. A division should be sold only if its value is greater to the buyer than to the seller. For example, as of 2012, Rona Inc. had recorded five straight years of earnings decline and was subject to takeover offers, including Lowe's offer of $14.50 per share. However, Rona Inc. declined the offer due to the belief that the company would be selling at a low. In 2013 it sold its commercial and professional division, for $215 million, in an attempt to streamline the business, improve liquidity, and focus on its core competencies.[23]

There has been a fair amount of research on sell-offs, with academics reaching two conclusions. First, event studies show that returns on the seller's stock are positive around the time of the announcement of sale, suggesting that sell-offs create value to the seller. Second, acquisitions are often sold off down the road. For example, Kaplan and Weisbach found that over 40 percent of acquisitions were later divested, a result that does not reflect well on mergers.[24] The average time between acquisition and divestiture was about seven years.

In a spin-off a parent firm turns a division into a separate entity and distributes shares in this entity to the parent's stockholders. For instance, in 2013, Canadian Tire Corporation created a real estate spin-off that would hold its diverse portfolio of some 250 properties largely comprising Canadian Tire retail stores, retail developments, and one distribution centre. Spin-offs differ from sales in at least two ways. First, the parent firm receives no cash from a spin-off: shares are sent for free to the shareholders. Second, the initial shareholders of the spun-off division are the same as the parent's shareholders. By contrast, the buyer in a sell-off is most likely another firm. However, because the shares of the division are publicly traded after the spin-off, the identities of the shareholders will change over time.

At least four reasons are generally given for a spin-off. First, as with a sell-off, the spin-off may increase corporate focus. Second, because the spun-off division is now publicly traded, the Ontario Securities Commission (OSC) requires additional information to be disseminated, so investors may find it easier to value the parent and subsidiary after the spin-off. Third, corporations often compensate executives with shares of stock in addition to cash. The stock acts as an incentive: good performance from managers leads to stock price increases. However, prior to the spin-off, executives can receive stock only in the parent company. If the division is small relative to the entire firm, price movement in the parent's stock will be less related to the performance of the manager's division than to the performance of the rest of the firm. Thus, divisional managers may see little relation between their effort and stock appreciation. However, after the spin-off, the manager can be given stock in the subsidiary. The manager's

---

[23] Nicolas Van Praet, "Rona to Sell Commercial and Professional Division for $215M as Part of Profitability Drive," *Financial Post*, June 20, 2013, business.financialpost.com/2013/06/20/rona-to-sell-commercial-and-professional-division-for-215m-as-part-of-profitability-drive/.

[24] Steven Kaplan and Michael Weisbach, "The Success of Acquisitions: Evidence from Divestitures," *Journal of Finance* (March 1992).

effort should directly impact price movement in the subsidiary's stock. Fourth, the tax consequences from a spin-off are generally better than from a sale because the parent receives no cash from a spin-off.

In a carve-out, the firm turns a division into a separate entity and then sells shares in the division to the public. Generally, the parent retains a large interest in the division. This transaction is similar to a spin-off, and the first three benefits listed for a spin-off apply to a carve-out as well. However, the big difference is that the firm receives cash from a carve-out, but not from a spin-off. The receipt of cash can be both good and bad. On the one hand, many firms need cash. Michaely and Shaw find that large, profitable firms are more likely to use carve-outs, whereas small, unprofitable firms are more likely to use spin-offs.[25] One interpretation is that firms generally prefer the cash that comes with a carve-out. However, small and unprofitable firms have trouble issuing stock. They must resort to a spin-off, where stock in the subsidiary is merely given to their own stockholders. In 2009, Calgary based EnCana Corporation announced a carve-out that would split itself into two distinct energy companies—Cenovus Energy Inc. and EnCana (GasCo).

Unfortunately, on the other hand, there is also a harmful side to cash, as developed in the free cash flow hypothesis. That is, firms with cash exceeding that needed for profitable capital budgeting projects may spend it on unprofitable ones. Allen and McConnell find that the stock market reacts positively to announcements of carve-outs if the cash is used to reduce debt.[26] The market reacts neutrally if the cash is used for investment projects.

A parent corporation issues tracking stock to "track" the performance of a specific division of the corporation. For example, if the tracking stock pays dividends, the size of the dividend depends on the division's performance. However, although "trackers" trade separately from the parent's stock, the division stays with the parent. By contrast, the subsidiary separates from the parent in a spin-off.

The first tracking stock was tied to the performance of EDS, a subsidiary of General Motors. Later, large firms such as Walt Disney and Sony issued trackers. However, few companies have issued tracking stocks in recent years, and parents have pulled most of those issued in earlier times. Perhaps the biggest problem with tracking stocks is their lack of clearly defined property rights. An optimistic accountant can increase the earnings of a particular division, leading to a larger dividend. A pessimistic accountant will have the reverse effect. Although accountants affect the earnings of regular companies, a change in earnings will not directly impact dividends.

## The Control Block and the Corporate Charter

If one individual or group owns 51 percent of a company's stock, this **control block** makes a hostile takeover virtually impossible. In the extreme, one interest may own all the stock. Examples are privately owned companies like Irving Oil and Crown corporations like Export Development Canada (EDC). Many Canadian companies are subsidiaries of foreign corporations that own control blocks. Many domestically owned companies have controlling shareholders.[27]

As a result, control blocks are typical in Canada, although they are the exception in the United States. Table 30.7 shows that only 15 percent of the top 100 corporations

---

[25] Roni Michaely and Wayne Shaw, "The Choice of Going Public: Spinoffs vs. Carveouts," *Financial Management* (Autumn 1995).

[26] Jeffrey Allen and John McConnell, "Equity Carve-outs and Managerial Discretion," *Journal of Finance* (February 1998).

[27] Important exceptions are chartered banks. As we stated in Chapter 1, the *Bank Act* prohibits any one interest from owning more than 10 percent of the shares.

in Canada were widely held in 1989 versus 73 percent for the United States.[28] One important implication is that minority shareholders need protection in Canada. One key group of minority shareholders comprises pension funds and other institutional investors. They are becoming increasingly vocal in opposing defensive tactics that are seen to be entrenching management at the expense of shareholders. We will discuss several examples below.

**TABLE 30.7**

**Ownership Makeup of the Top 100 Corporations**

|                  | Canada | United States |
| ---------------- | :----: | :-----------: |
| Widely held      | 15     | 73            |
| Control block    | 50     | 25            |
| Privately owned  | 28     | 2             |
| Government owned | 7      | 0             |

Source: D. H. Thain and D. S. R. Leighton, "Ownership Structure and the Board," *Canadian Investment Review* (Fall 1991).

For widely held companies, the corporate charter establishes the conditions that allow for a takeover. The *corporate charter* refers to the articles of incorporation and corporate bylaws that establish the governance rules of the firm. Firms can amend corporate charters to make acquisitions more difficult. For example, usually two-thirds of the shareholders of record must approve a merger. Firms can make it more difficult to be acquired by changing this to a higher percentage. This is called a *supermajority amendment*. Many charters with supermajority provisions have what is known as a *board out* clause as well. Here, supermajority does not apply if the board of directors approves the merger. This clause makes sure that the provision hinders only hostile takeovers.

Another device is to stagger the election of the board members. This makes it more difficult to elect a new board of directors quickly. In examining samples of U.S. adopting firms, DeAngelo and Rice, and Linn and McConnell, found that antitakeover amendments to corporate charters had no adverse effect on stock prices.[29]

## Standstill Agreements

Managers of target firms may simultaneously negotiate standstill agreements. *Standstill agreements* are contracts under which the bidding firm agrees to limit its holdings of another firm. These agreements usually lead to cessation of takeover attempts, and announcements of such agreements have had a negative effect on stock prices.

In the United States, standstill agreements often occur at the same time that a targeted repurchase is arranged. In a targeted repurchase, also known as greenmail, a firm buys a certain amount of its own stock from an individual investor, usually at a substantial premium. These premiums can be thought of as payments to potential bidders to eliminate unfriendly takeover attempts. Critics of such payments view them as bribes and label them as greenmail (compare "blackmail"). Paying greenmail may harm minority shareholders if it heads off a takeover that would also raise the stock price. Standstill agreements also occur in takeover attempts in Canada, but without greenmail, which is ruled out by securities laws.

---

[28] The list of top 100 corporations in Canada is from the *Financial Post* 500. The U.S. corporations list comes from *Fortune* 500.

[29] H. DeAngelo and E. M. Rice, "Antitakeover Charter Amendments and Stockholder Wealth," *Journal of Financial Economics* (April 1983); and S. G. Linn and J. J. McConnell, "An Empirical Investigation of the Impact of Antitakeover Amendments on Common Stock Prices," *Journal of Financial Economics* (April 1983).

EXAMPLE **30.4**

In February 2008, Lake Shore Gold entered into a strategic alliance with Hochschild Mining Plc ("Hochschild"), which resulted in Hochschild becoming a significant shareholder of Lake Shore Gold and a strategic partner for future projects. Lake Shore Gold and Hochschild entered into an agreement governing the future relationship, including terms with respect to Hochschild's representation on the company's board of directors and its shareholding percentage. Both companies entered into a standstill agreement, which restricted Hochschild from owning more than 40 percent of Lake Shore until November 22, 2010, after which it could buy as much stake as it wanted.

## Exclusionary Offers and Non-voting Stock

An *exclusionary offer* is a tender offer for a given amount of its own shares while excluding targeted shareholders.

A well-known example occurred in 1986 when the Canadian Tire Dealers Association offered to buy 49 percent of the company's voting shares from the founding Billes family. The dealers' bid was at $169 per share for voting shares trading at $40 before the bid. The non-voting shares were priced at $14. Further, since the dealers were the principal buyers of Canadian Tire products, control of the company would have allowed them to adjust prices to benefit themselves over the non-voting shareholders.

The offer was voided by the OSC, and it appears that any future exclusionary offers are likely to be viewed as an illegal form of discrimination against one group of shareholders.

## Going Private and Leveraged Buyouts

Going-private transactions and LBOs have much in common with mergers, and it is worthwhile to discuss them in this chapter. A publicly traded firm *goes private* when a private group, usually composed of existing management, purchases its stock. As a consequence, the firm's stock is taken off the market (if it is an exchange-traded stock, it is delisted) and is no longer traded. Thus, in going-private transactions, shareholders of publicly held firms are forced to accept cash for their shares.

Going-private transactions are frequently LBOs. In an LBO the cash offer price is financed with large amounts of debt. Part of the appeal of LBOs is that the arrangement calls for little equity capital. This equity capital is generally supplied by a small group of investors, some of whom are likely to be managers of the firm being purchased.

The selling shareholders are invariably paid a premium above market price in an LBO, just as in a merger. As with a merger, the acquirer profits only if the synergy created is greater than the premium. Synergy is quite plausible in a merger of *two* firms, and we delineated a number of types of synergy earlier in the chapter. However, it is more difficult to explain synergy in an LBO because only *one* firm is involved.

Two reasons are generally given for value creation in an LBO. First, the extra debt provides a tax deduction, which, as earlier chapters suggested, leads to an increase in firm value. Most LBOs are on firms with stable earnings and with low to moderate debt. The LBO may simply increase the firm's debt to its optimum level.

The second source of value comes from increased efficiency and is often explained in terms of "the carrot and the stick." Managers become owners under an LBO, giving them an incentive to work hard. This incentive is commonly referred to as the carrot, and the carrots in some LBOs have been huge. For example, consider the buyout of Metals USA by Apollo Global Management LLC, the LBO firm run by Leon Black. The Fort Lauderdale, Florida–based company was taken private in 2005. When it went public again in April 2010, shares of Metals USA sold at $21 a share, and the value of the initial public offering (IPO) was close to $240 million.

Interest payments from the high level of debt constitute the stick. Large interest payments can easily turn a profitable firm before an LBO into an unprofitable one after the LBO. Management must make changes, either through revenue increases or cost reductions, to keep the firm in the black. Agency theory, a topic discussed later in this chapter, suggests that managers can be wasteful with a large free cash flow. Interest payments reduce this cash flow, forcing managers to curb the waste.

Though it is easy to measure the additional tax shields from an LBO, it is difficult to measure the gains from increased efficiency. Nevertheless, this increased efficiency is considered at least as important as the tax shield in explaining the LBO phenomenon.

Academic research suggests that LBOs have, on average, created value. First, premiums are positive, as they are with mergers, implying that selling shareholders benefit. Second, studies indicate that LBOs that eventually go public generate high returns for the management group. In our earlier example of the Metals USA buyout, Apollo Global Management LLC quadrupled its investment. Finally, other studies show that operating performance increases after the LBO. However, we cannot be completely confident of value creation because researchers have difficulty obtaining data about LBOs that do not go public. If these LBOs generally destroy value, the sample of firms going public will be a biased one.

Regardless of the average performance of firms undertaking an LBO, we can be sure of one thing: because of the great leverage involved, the risk is huge. On the one hand, LBOs have created many large fortunes, a prominent example being Metals USA. On the other hand, a number of bankruptcies and near-bankruptcies have occurred as well, perhaps the most infamous being Revco's LBO. Revco was taken private near the end of 1986, but it is still talked about extensively today. In retrospect, the management group overpaid (a premium almost 50 percent above market price) and overlevered (a debt-to-value ratio of 97 percent). Revco was also not an ideal LBO candidate, though it seemed to be at the time. As mentioned earlier, firms with stable cash flows can best handle the high leverage of LBOs. Revco, a chain of about 1,400 drugstores, seemed to fit the bill here because sales in this retail industry are relatively unresponsive to the business cycle. However, Revco planned to add about 100 stores a year, a strategy necessitating large capital expenditures. The combination of high leverage and large capital commitments provided little margin for error. The firm went under about a year and a half after the LBO. Perhaps the depressed Christmas season of 1987 or the rise of the discounters pushed Revco over the edge. Because of the size of the transaction (total LBO financing over $1.4 billion) and the embarrassment to the LBO specialist (it was Salomon Brothers' first large LBO), pundits are still arguing about the cause of Revco's demise.

## Other Defensive Devices

As corporate takeovers become more common, other colourful terms have become popular:

- **Golden parachutes.** Some target firms provide compensation to top-level management if a takeover occurs. This can be viewed as a payment to management to make it less concerned for its own welfare and more interested in shareholders when considering a takeover bid. Alternatively, the payment can be seen as an attempt to enrich management at the shareholders' expense.
- **Crown jewels.** Firms often sell major assets—crown jewels—when faced with a takeover threat. This is sometimes referred to as the *scorched-earth strategy*.
- **White knight.** Target firms sometimes seek a competing bid from a friendly bidder—a white knight—who promises to maintain the jobs of existing management and to refrain from selling off the target's assets.

A Canadian example of a white knight rescue occurred when Great-West Lifeco placed a bid of $7.3 billion for Canada Life Financial in February of 2003, protecting that company from its rival Manulife. A hostile offer from Manulife had caused

Canada Life Financial's board of directors and management to explore several take-over defences. Within a month, Canada Life Financial announced the white knight offer, which was 15 percent higher than that lodged by Manulife, and the board recommended acceptance to its shareholders. The white knight rescue plan made the combined company the second largest insurer in Canada, behind Sunlife, overtaking Manulife with the rejection of its two bids for Canada Life Financial.

- **Poison pill.** Poison pill is a term taken from the world of espionage. Agents are supposed to bite a pill of cyanide rather than permit capture. Presumably this prevents enemy interrogators from learning important secrets. In finance, poison pills are used to make a stock repellent to others. A poison pill, also termed a shareholder rights plan, is generally a right to buy shares in the merged firm at a bargain price. The right is granted to the target firm's shareholders, contingent on another firm acquiring control. The right dilutes the stock so much that the bidding firm loses money on its shares. Thus, wealth is transferred from the bidder to the target.[30]

EXAMPLE **30.5**

In 2010, the Vancouver-based film studio Lionsgate rejected an unsolicited partial-tender offer from the Icahn group. The group's offer was to purchase up to 13,164,420 common shares of Lionsgate for $6.00 per share. Lionsgate urged its shareholders to adopt a poison pill as a means of deflecting Icahn's takeover bid for the company. The company stated that Icahn's offer was "financially inadequate and coercive, and not in the best interests of Lionsgate, its shareholders, and other stakeholders."[31] Despite this action, the Icahn group subsequently succeeded in gaining control of Lionsgate.

**CONCEPT QUESTION**
- What can a firm do to make a takeover less likely?

# 30.10   SOME EVIDENCE ON ACQUISITIONS

One of the most controversial issues surrounding our subject is whether mergers and acquisitions benefit shareholders.

## Do Acquisitions Benefit Shareholders?

Much research has attempted to estimate the effect of mergers and takeovers on stock prices of the bidding and target firms. These studies are called *event studies* because they estimate abnormal stock price changes on and around the offer announcement date (the event). Abnormal returns are usually defined as the difference between actual stock returns and a market index, to take account of the influence of market-wide effects on the returns of individual securities.

Table 30.8 summarizes the results of numerous studies that look at the effects of merger and tender offers on stock prices in the United States. Table 30.9 shows high points of studies on mergers in Canada. Both tables are relevant, since firms from one country often purchase companies in the other.

---

[30] In Canada, the wealth transfer is mitigated by intervention of provincial commissions such as the OSC, which rule on the acceptability of poison pills. In many cases, the result has been to extend the waiting period and increase shareholder value. Still, most large Canadian institutional investors vote against the introduction of poison pills. For example, see otpp.com/documents/10179/20940/Good+Governance+is+Good+Business/cfca9682-9368-4cf4-96ce-fe5381d5647e.

[31] Source: dmwmedia.com/news/2010/03/26/lionsgate-urges-shareholders-adopt-poison-pill-icahn-bid.

TABLE 30.8

### Percentage and Dollar Returns for U.S. Mergers

| Time period | Gain or loss to merger (both acquired and acquiring firms) | | Gain or loss to acquiring firms | |
| --- | --- | --- | --- | --- |
| | Abnormal percentage return | Aggregate dollar gain or loss | Abnormal percentage return | Aggregate dollar gain or loss |
| 1980–2001 | 0.0135 | −$ 79 billion | 0.0110 | −$220 billion |
| 1980–1990 | 0.0241 | $ 12 billion | 0.0064 | −$  4 billion |
| 1991–2001 | 0.0104 | −$ 90 billion | 0.0120 | −$216 billion |
| 1998–2001 | 0.0029 | −$134 billion | 0.0069 | −$240 billion |

Source: Modified from Sara Moeller, Frederik Schlingemann, and Rene Stulz, "Wealth Destruction on a Massive Scale? A Study of Acquiring-Firm Returns in the Recent Merger Wave," *Journal of Finance* (April 2005), Table 1.

TABLE 30.9

### Abnormal Returns in Successful Canadian Mergers

| | Target | Bidder |
| --- | --- | --- |
| 1,271 aquired, 242 targets, 1994–2000** | 10% | 1% |
| 1,930 mergers, 1964–1983* | 9 | 3 |
| 119 mergers, 1963–1982[†] | 23 | 11 |
| 173 going-private transactions, 1977–1989[‡] | 25 | N/A |
| Minority buyouts | 27 | |
| Non-controlling bidder | 24 | |
| 1,300 acquisitions, 1993–2002*** | N/A | 0% |

* From B. Espen Eckbo, "Mergers and the Market for Corporate Control: The Canadian Evidence," *Canadian Journal of Economics* (May 1986). The test for bidders excluded firms involved in multiple mergers.

[†] From A. L. Calvet and J. Lefoll, "Information Asymmetry and Wealth Effect of Canadian Corporate Acquisitions," *Financial Review* (November 1987).

[‡] Modified from B. Amoako-Adu and B. Smith, "How Do Shareholders Fare in Minority Buyouts?" *Canadian Investment Review* (Fall 1991).

** From A. Yuce and A. Ng, "Effects of Private and Public Canadian Mergers," *Canadian Journal of Administrative Sciences* (June 2005).

*** From S. Dutta and V. Jog, "The Long-Term Performance of Acquiring Firms: A Re-examination of an Anomaly," *Journal of Banking and Finance* (August 2009).

The tables show that shareholders of target companies in successful takeovers gain substantially. Starting with U.S. takeovers in Table 30.8, the average abnormal percentage return across all mergers from 1980 to 2001 is 0.0135. This number combines the returns on both the acquiring company and the acquired company. Because 0.0135 is positive, the market believes that mergers on average create value. The other three returns in the first column are positive as well, implying value creation in the different subperiods. Many other academic studies have provided similar results. Thus, it appears from this column that the synergies we mentioned earlier show up in the real world.

However, the next column tells us something different. Across all U.S. mergers from 1980 to 2001, the aggregate dollar change around the day of merger announcement is −$79 billion. This means that the market is, on average, *reducing* the combined stock value of the acquiring and acquired companies around the merger announcement date. Though the difference between the two columns may seem confusing, there is an explanation. Although most mergers have created value, mergers involving the very largest U.S. firms have lost value. The abnormal percentage return is an unweighted average in which the returns on all mergers are treated equally. A positive return here reflects all those small mergers that created value. However, losses in a few large mergers cause the aggregate dollar change to be negative.

But there is more. The rest of the second column indicates that the aggregate dollar losses occurred only in the 1998 to 2001 period. While there were losses of −$134 billion in this period, there were gains of $12 billion from 1980 to 1990. And interpolation of the table indicates that there were gains of $44 billion (= $134 − $90) from 1991 through 1997. Thus, it appears that some large U.S. mergers lost a great deal of value from 1998 to 2001.

The results in a table such as Table 30.8 are, unfortunately, ambiguous. On the one hand, you could focus on the first column, saying that mergers create value on average. Proponents of this view might argue that the great losses in the few large mergers were flukes, not likely to occur again. On the other hand, we cannot easily ignore the fact that over the entire period, mergers destroyed more value than they created.

The preceding results combined returns on both bidders and targets. Investors want to separate the bidders from the targets. Columns 3 and 4 of Table 30.8 provide returns for U.S. acquiring companies alone. The third column shows that abnormal percentage returns for bidders have been positive for the entire sample period and for each of the individual subperiods—a result similar to that for bidders and targets combined. The fourth column indicates aggregate dollar losses, suggesting that large mergers did worse than small ones.

Although the U.S. evidence just presented for both the combined entity and the bidder alone is ambiguous, the evidence for targets is crystal clear. Acquisitions benefit the target's shareholders. Consider the following table, which shows the median merger *premium* over different periods in the United States:[32]

| Time period | 1973–1998 | 1973–1979 | 1980–1989 | 1990–1998 |
|---|---|---|---|---|
| Premium | 42.1% | 47.2% | 37.7% | 34.5% |

The premium is the difference between the acquisition price per share and the target's pre-acquisition share price, divided by the target's pre-acquisition share price. The average premium is quite high for the entire sample period and for the various subsamples. For example, a target stock selling at $100 per share before the acquisition that is later acquired for $142.1 per share generates a premium of 42.1 percent. Clearly, shareholders of any firm trading at $100 would love to be able to sell their holdings for $142.1 per share.

Turning to Canadian research in Table 30.9, we find that bidders experience modest returns here as well—on the order of 1 percent in the most recent study. As in the United States, targets do much better than bidders, with an average return of 10 percent for mergers between 1994 and 2000. Canadian research also suggests that bidding firms do poorly over a longer, three-year period after the merger.[33] The other studies found that target firm shareholders in going-private transactions enjoyed an abnormal return of 25 percent, a figure consistent with the U.S. results in Table 30.8.

The Canadian study of going-private transactions also looked at whether minority shareholders suffer. You can see from Table 30.9 that the answer is no. Returns to minority shareholders hardly differ from returns occurring when firms went private with no majority shareholder.[34]

For both countries, these gains are a reflection of the merger premium that is typically paid by the acquiring firm. These gains are excess returns, that is, returns over and above what the shareholders would normally have earned.

What conclusions can be drawn from Tables 30.8 and 30.9? First, the evidence strongly suggests that shareholders of successful target firms achieve substantial gains from takeovers.

---

[32] Taken from Gregor Andrade, Mark Mitchell, and Erik Stafford, "New Evidence and Perspectives on Mergers," *Journal of Economic Perspectives* (Spring 2001), Table 1.

[33] P. André, M. Kooli, and J-F L'Her, "The Long-Run Performance of Mergers and Acquisitions: Evidence from the Canadian Stock Market," *Financial Management* (Winter 2004).

[34] In contrast, in a later study of takeovers and dual-class shares in Canada, Smith and Amoako-Adu find that shareholders with superior voting shares enjoy higher returns: B. F. Smith and B. Amoako-Adu, "A Comparative Analysis of Takeovers of Single and Dual Class Firms," *Financial Review* (February 1994).

The second conclusion we can draw is that shareholders of bidding firms earn significantly less from takeovers. The balance is more level for Canadian mergers than for U.S. ones. This may be because there is less competition among bidders in Canada. Two reasons for this are that the Canadian capital market is smaller, and there are federal government agencies to review foreign investments.[35]

A caveat is needed here because the previous discussion focused solely on short-term returns on or around the offer announcement date. When Dutta and Jog study long-term performance of 1,300 mergers and acquisitions involving TSX-listed bidders from 1993 to 2002, they find that Canadian markets react positively to acquisitions.[36] However, this return quickly diminishes as markets correct within a short period of time—around 15 days. As a result, Canadian acquisitions do not show any evidence of value destruction or overpayment in the long run.

## The Managers versus the Shareholders

**Managers of Bidding Firms**   The preceding discussion was presented from the shareholders' point of view. Because, in theory, shareholders pay the salaries of managers, we might think that managers would look at things from the shareholders' point of view. However, it is important to realize that individual shareholders have little clout with managers. For example, the typical shareholder is simply not in a position to pick up the phone and give the managers a piece of his or her mind. It is true that the shareholders elect the board of directors, which monitors the managers. However, an elected director has little contact with individual shareholders.

Thus, it is fair to ask whether managers are held fully accountable for their actions. This question is at the heart of what economists call *agency theory*. Researchers in this area often argue that managers work less hard, get paid more, and make worse business decisions than they would if shareholders had more control over them. And there is a special place in agency theory for mergers. Managers frequently receive bonuses for acquiring other companies. In addition, their pay is often positively related to the size of their firm. Finally, managers' prestige is also tied to firm size. Because firm size increases with acquisitions, managers are disposed to look favourably on acquisitions, perhaps even ones with negative NPV.

A fascinating study compared companies where managers received a lot of options on their own company's stock as part of their compensation package with companies where the managers did not.[37] Because option values rise and fall in tandem with the firm's stock price, managers receiving options have an incentive to forgo mergers with negative NPVs. The paper reported that the acquisitions by firms where managers receive lots of options (termed *equity-based compensation* in the paper) create more value than the acquisitions by firms where managers receive few or no options.

Agency theory may also explain why the biggest merger failures have involved large firms. Managers owning a small fraction of their firm's stock have less incentive to behave responsibly because the great majority of any losses are borne by other shareholders. Managers of large firms likely have a smaller percentage interest in their firm's stock than do managers of small firms (a large percentage of a large firm is too costly to acquire). Thus, the merger failures of large acquirers may be due to the small percentage ownership of the managers.

---

[35] Paul Halpern, "Poison Pills: Some Insights from the Canadian Experience," Working paper series 6, Carleton University, School of Business, 1992, p. 66; and A. L. Calvet and J. Lefoll, "Information Asymmetry and Wealth Effect of Canadian Corporate Acquisitions," *Financial Review* (November 1987).

[36] Shantanu Dutta and Vijay Jog, "The Long-Term Performance of Acquiring Firms: A Re-examination of an Anomaly," *Journal of Banking and Finance* (August 2009).

[37] Sudip Datta, Mai Iskandar-Datta, and Kartil Raman, "Executive Compensation and Corporate Acquisition Decisions," *Journal of Finance* (December 2001).

Earlier, in Chapter 17 of this text, we discussed the free cash flow hypothesis. The idea here is that managers can spend only what they have. Managers of firms with low cash flow are likely to run out of cash before they run out of good (positive NPV) investments. Conversely, managers of firms with high cash flow are likely to have cash on hand even after all the good investments are taken. Managers are rewarded for growth, so managers with cash flow above that needed for good projects have an incentive to spend the remainder on bad (negative NPV) projects. A paper tested this conjecture, finding that "cash-rich firms are more likely than other firms to attempt acquisitions . . . cash-rich bidders destroy seven cents in value for every dollar of cash reserves held . . . consistent with the stock return evidence, mergers in which the bidder is cash-rich are followed by abnormal declines in operating performance."[38]

The previous discussion has considered the possibility that some managers were knaves—more interested in their own welfare than in the welfare of their shareholders. However, Malmendier and Tate entertained the idea that other managers were more fools than knaves. They classified certain CEOs as overconfident, either because they refused to exercise stock options on their own company's stock when it was rational to do so or because the press portrayed them as confident or optimistic.[39] The authors find that these overconfident managers are more likely to make acquisitions than are other managers. In addition, the stock market reacts more negatively to announcements of acquisitions when the acquiring CEO is overconfident.

The divergence between shareholders' interests and management merger motivation became more extreme during the Internet bubble of 1997 to 2001. Using their firms' overvalued stock as currency, tech company management often could not resist going on a buying spree. For example, during this period Nortel Networks spent over $33 billion buying 19 companies. Later, Nortel's stock fell by 95 percent and most of the acquired companies were written off and their employees laid off. The result was large-scale destruction of shareholder value through mergers.[40]

However, that is only half of the story. Shareholders of target firms may have just as hard a time controlling their managers. While there are many ways that managers of target firms can put themselves ahead of their shareholders, two seem to stand out. First, we said earlier that because premiums are positive, takeovers are beneficial to the target's shareholders. However, if managers may be fired after their firms are acquired, they may resist these takeovers.[41] Tactics employed to resist takeover, generally called defensive tactics, were discussed in an earlier section of this chapter. Second, managers who cannot avoid takeover may bargain with the bidder, getting a good deal for themselves at the expense of their shareholders.

Consider Wulf's fascinating work on *mergers of equals* (MOEs).[42] Some deals are announced as MOEs, primarily because both firms have equal ownership in and equal representation on the board of directors of the merged entity. AOL and Time Warner, Daimler-Benz and Chrysler, Morgan Stanley and Dean Witter, and Fleet Financial Group and BankBoston are generally held out as examples of MOEs. Nevertheless,

---

[38] From Jarrad Harford, "Corporate Cash Reserves and Acquisitions," *Journal of Finance* (December 1999), p. 1969.

[39] Ulrike Malmendier and Geoffrey Tate, "Who Makes Acquisitions? CEO Overconfidence and the Market's Reaction," unpublished paper, Stanford University (December 2003).

[40] For more on value destruction through mergers during the Internet bubble, see M. C. Jensen, "Agency Costs of Overvalued Equity," Finance Working Paper No. 39/2004, European Corporate Governance Institute, ssrn.com/abstract=480421; and S. B. Moeller, F. P. Schlingemann, and R. M. Stulz, "Wealth Destruction on a Massive Scale? A Study of Acquiring Firm Returns in the Recent Merger Wave," *Journal of Finance* (April 2005).

[41] However, as stated earlier, managers may resist takeovers to raise the offer price, not to prevent the merger.

[42] Julie Wulf, "Do CEOs in Mergers Trade Power for Premium? Evidence From 'Mergers of Equals,'" *Journal of Law, Economics, and Organization* (Spring 2004).

authorities point out that in any deal one firm is typically "more equal" than the other. That is, the target and the bidder can usually be distinguished in practice. For example, while the two companies were still together, Daimler-Benz was commonly classified as the bidder and Chrysler as the target in their merger. In 2007, the Chrysler division was sold and the merger ceased.

Wulf finds that targets get a lower percentage of the merger gains, as measured by abnormal returns around the announcement date, in MOEs than in other mergers. And the percentage of the gains going to the target is negatively related to the representation of the target's officers and directors on the post-merger board. These and other findings led Wulf to conclude, "They [the findings of the paper] suggest that CEOs trade power for premium in merger of equals transactions."

### Real Productivity

There are many potential synergies from mergers and acquisitions. Unfortunately, it is very hard to precisely measure synergy. In the previous section, we focused on stock market gains or losses to the shareholders of the acquiring and acquired firms. In very general terms, we found that target firm shareholders experience stock market gains and acquiring firm shareholders experience stock market losses. There appear to be net gains to shareholders. This would suggest that mergers can increase real productivity. In fact, several studies suggest that mergers can increase real productivity. Healey, Palepu, and Ruback report that merged companies' after-tax returns increased substantially after the mergers. They trace this gain to an increase in selling activity (turnover). They find no evidence that merged firms cut back on positive NPV capital expenditures.[43]

**CONCEPT QUESTION**

- What does the evidence say about the distribution of benefits of mergers and acquisitions?

---

## 30.11

# SUMMARY AND CONCLUSIONS

1. One firm can acquire another in several different ways. The three legal forms of acquisition are merger and consolidation, acquisition of stock, and acquisition of assets. Mergers and consolidations are the least costly to arrange from a legal standpoint, but they require a vote of approval by the shareholders. Acquisition of stock does not require a shareholder vote and is usually done via a tender offer. However, it is difficult to obtain 100 percent control with a tender offer. Acquisition of assets is comparatively costly because it requires a more difficult transfer of asset ownership.

2. Mergers and acquisitions require an understanding of complicated tax and accounting rules. Mergers and acquisitions can be taxable or tax-free transactions. In a taxable transaction, each selling shareholder must pay taxes on the stock's capital appreciation. Should the acquiring firm elect to write up the assets, additional tax implications arise. However, acquiring firms do not generally elect to write up the assets for tax purposes. The selling shareholders do not pay taxes at the time of a tax-free acquisition.

---

[43] P. Healey, K. Palepu, and R. Ruback, "Does Corporate Performance Improve after Mergers?" *Journal of Financial Economics* (April 1992).

3. The synergy from an acquisition is defined as the value of the combined firm ($V_{AB}$) less the value of the two firms as separate entities ($V_A$ and $V_B$):

$$\text{Synergy} = V_{AB} - (V_A + V_B)$$

The shareholders of the acquiring firm will gain if the synergy from the merger is greater than the premium.

4. The possible benefits of an acquisition come from
   a. Revenue enhancement.
   b. Cost reduction.
   c. Lower taxes.
   d. Lower cost of capital.

   In addition, the reduction in risk from a merger may actually help bondholders and hurt shareholders.

5. Some of the most colourful language of finance stems from defensive tactics in acquisition battles. *Poison pills, golden parachutes, crown jewels, white knights,* and *greenmail* are terms that describe various antitakeover tactics discussed in this chapter.

6. The empirical research on mergers and acquisitions is extensive. Its basic conclusions are that, on average, the shareholders of acquired firms fare very well, while the shareholders of acquiring firms do not gain much. However, in the long run, market effi ciency generally prevails.

KEY TERMS

| | | |
|---|---|---|
| Acquisition method   862 | Golden parachute   882 | Poison pill   883 |
| Circular bid   858 | Goodwill   862 | Proxy contest   860 |
| Consolidation   858 | Leveraged buyout | Stock exchange bid   858 |
| Control block   879 |   (LBO)   860 | Tender offer   858 |
| Crown jewels   882 | Management buyout | White knight   882 |
| Going-private |   (MBO)   860 | |
|   transaction   860 | Merger   857 | |

QUESTIONS & PROBLEMS

### Calculating Synergy

30.1 Evan Inc. has offered $620 million cash for all of the common stock in Tanner Corporation. Based on recent market information, Tanner is worth $585 million as an independent operation. If the merger makes economic sense for Evan, what is the minimum estimated value of the synergistic benefits from the merger?

### Balance Sheets for Mergers

30.2 Consider the following pre-merger information about firm $X$ and firm $Y$:

| | Firm $X$ | Firm $Y$ |
|---|---|---|
| Total earnings | $90,000 | $52,200 |
| Shares outstanding | 46,800 | 36,000 |
| Per-share values: | | |
|   Market | $    53 | $    19 |
|   Book | $    21 | $    9 |

Assume that firm $X$ acquires firm $Y$ by paying cash for all the shares outstanding at a merger premium of $5 per share. Assuming that neither firm has any debt before or after the merger, construct the post-merger balance sheet for firm $X$ assuming the use of purchase accounting methods.

30.3 Assume that the following balance sheets are stated at book value. Construct a post-merger balance sheet assuming that Jurion Co. purchases James Inc. through the pooling of interests method.

### Jurion Co.

| | | | |
|---|---|---|---|
| Current assets | 8,000 | Current liabilities | $4,500 |
| Net fixed assets | $23,000 | Long-term debt | 8,500 |
| | | Equity | 18,000 |
| Total | $31,000 | Total | $31,000 |

### James Inc.

| | | | |
|---|---|---|---|
| Current assets | 2,600 | Current liabilities | $1,900 |
| Net fixed assets | $7,100 | Long-term debt | 1,200 |
| | | Equity | 6,600 |
| Total | $9,700 | Total | $9,700 |

### Incorporating Goodwill

30.4 In Problem 30.3, suppose the fair market value of James's fixed assets is $12,000 versus the $7,100 book value shown. Jurion pays $17,000 for James and raises the needed funds through an issue of long-term debt. Construct the post-merger balance sheet now.

### Balance Sheets for Mergers

30.5 Silver Enterprises has acquired All Gold Mining in a merger transaction. Construct the balance sheet for the new corporation if the merger is treated as a pooling of interests for accounting purposes. The following balance sheets represent the pre-merger book values for both firms:

### Silver Enterprises

| | | | |
|---|---|---|---|
| Current assets | $ 8,600 | Current liabilities | $ 5,200 |
| Other assets | 1,800 | Long-term debt | 3,700 |
| Net fixed assets | 15,800 | Equity | 17,300 |
| Total | $26,200 | Total | $26,200 |

### All Gold Mining

| | | | |
|---|---|---|---|
| Current assets | $2,500 | Current liabilities | $2,300 |
| Other assets | 850 | Long-term debt | 0 |
| Net fixed assets | 5,800 | Equity | 6,850 |
| Total | $9,150 | Total | $9,150 |

### Incorporating Goodwill

30.6 In Problem 30.5, construct the balance sheet for the new corporation, assuming that the transaction is treated as a purchase for accounting purposes. The market value of All Gold Mining's fixed assets is $5,800; the market values for current and other assets are the same as the book values. Assume that Silver Enterprises issues $10,500 in new long-term debt to finance the acquisition.

### Cash versus Stock Payment

30.7 Penn Corp. is analyzing the possible acquisition of Teller Company. Both firms have no debt. Penn believes the acquisition will increase its total after-tax annual cash flow by $1.1 million indefinitely. The current market value of Teller is $45 million, and that of Penn is $62 million. The appropriate discount rate for the incremental cash flows is 12 percent. Penn is trying to decide whether it should offer 40 percent of its stock or $48 million in cash to Teller's shareholders.

    *a.* What is the cost of each alternative?
    *b.* What is the NPV of each alternative?
    *c.* Which alternative should Penn choose?

### Earnings per Share, Price–Earnings Ratio, and Mergers

30.8 The shareholders of Flannery Company have voted in favour of a buyout offer from Stultz Corporation. Information about each firm is given here:

|  | Flannery | Stultz |
|---|---|---|
| Price-earnings ratio | 6.35 | 12.70 |
| Shares outstanding | 73,000 | 146,000 |
| Earnings | $230,000 | $690,000 |

Flannery's shareholders will receive one share of Stultz stock for every three shares they hold in Flannery.

 a. What will the EPS of Stultz be after the merger? What will the P/E ratio be if the NPV of the acquisition is zero?
 b. What must Stultz feel is the value of the synergy between these two firms? Explain how your answer can be reconciled with the decision to go ahead with the takeover.

### Merger Rationale

30.9 Cholern Electric Company (CEC) is a public utility that provides electricity to central Ontario. Recent events at its Spruce Nuclear Station have been discouraging. Several shareholders have expressed concern over last year's financial statements.

| Statement of Comprehensive Income last year (in $ millions) | | Balance Sheet end of year (in $ millions) | |
|---|---|---|---|
| Revenue | $110 | Assets | $400 |
| Fuel | 50 | Debt | 300 |
| Other expenses | 30 | Equity | 100 |
| Interest | 30 | | |
| Net income | $ 0 | | |

Recently, a wealthy group of individuals has offered to purchase half of CEC's assets at fair market price. Management recommends that this offer be accepted because "We believe our expertise in the energy industry can be better exploited by CEC if we sell our electricity-generating and transmission assets and enter the telecommunications business. Although telecommunications is a riskier business than providing electricity as a public utility, it is also potentially very profitable."

Should management approve this transaction? Why or why not?

### Cash versus Stock as Payment

30.10 Consider the following pre-merger information about a bidding firm (firm *B*) and a target firm (firm *T*). Assume that both firms have no debt outstanding:

|  | Firm *B* | Firm *T* |
|---|---|---|
| Shares outstanding | 2,900 | 1,400 |
| Price per share | $39 | $26 |

Firm *B* has estimated that the value of the synergistic benefits from acquiring firm *T* is $5,500.

 a. If firm *T* is willing to be acquired for $29 per share in cash, what is the NPV of the merger?
 b. What will the price per share of the merged firm be, assuming the conditions in (a)?
 c. In (a), what is the merger premium?
 d. Suppose firm *T* is agreeable to a merger by an exchange of stock. If *B* offers three of its shares for every five of *T*'s shares, what will the price per share of the merged firm be?
 e. What is the NPV of the merger assuming the conditions in (d)?

**30.11** In Problem 30.10, are the shareholders of firm *T* better off with the cash offer or the stock offer? At what exchange ratio of *B* shares to *T* shares would the shareholders in *T* be indifferent between the two offers?

### Effects of a Stock Exchange

**30.12** Consider the following pre-merger information about firm *A* and firm *B*:

|  | Firm *A* | Firm *B* |
|---|---|---|
| Total earnings | $1,600 | $700 |
| Shares outstanding | 600 | 250 |
| Price per share | $ 50 | $ 20 |

Assume that firm *A* acquires firm *B* via an exchange of stock at a price of $22 for each share of *B*'s stock. Both *A* and *B* have no debt outstanding.

a. What will the EPS of firm *A* be after the merger?

b. What will firm *A*'s price per share be after the merger if the market incorrectly analyzes this reported earnings growth (that is, the P/E ratio does not change)?

c. What will the P/E ratio of the post-merger firm be if the market correctly analyzes the transaction?

d. If there are no synergy gains, what will the share price of *A* be after the merger? What will the P/E ratio be? What does your answer for the share price tell you about the amount *A* bid for *B*? Was it too high? Too low? Explain.

### Merger Net Present Value

**30.13** Show that the NPV of a merger can be expressed as the value of the synergistic benefits, $\Delta V$, less the merger premium.

**30.14** Fly-by-Night Couriers is analyzing the possible acquisition of Flash-in-the-Pan Restaurants. Neither firm has debt. The forecasts of Fly-by-Night show that the purchase would increase its annual after-tax cash flow by $390,000, indefinitely. The current market value of Flash-in-the-Pan is $7 million. The current market value of Fly-by-Night is $22 million. The appropriate discount rate for the incremental cash flows is 8 percent. Fly-by-Night is trying to decide whether it will offer 30 percent of its stock or $9 million in cash to Flash-in-the-Pan.

a. What is the synergy from the merger?

b. What is the value of Flash-in-the-Pan to Fly-by-Night?

c. What is the cost to Fly-by-Night of each alternative?

d. What is the NPV to Fly-by-Night of each alternative?

e. Which alternative should Fly-by-Night use?

**30.15** Harolds PLC has a market value of £400 million and 30 million shares outstanding. Selfishes Department Store has a market value of £160 million and 18 million shares outstanding. Harolds is contemplating acquiring Selfishes. Harolds' CFO concludes that the combined firm with synergy will be worth £590 million, and Selfishes can be acquired at a premium of £15 million.

a. If Harolds offers 12 million shares of its stock in exchange for the 18 million shares of Selfridges, what will the stock price of Harolds be after the acquisition?

b. What exchange ratio between the two stocks would make the value of the stock offer equivalent to a cash offer of £175 million?

### Mergers and Shareholder Value

**30.16** Bentley Corp. and Rolls Manufacturing are considering a merger. The possible states of the economy and each company's value in that state are shown here:

| State | Probability | Bentley | Rolls |
|---|---|---|---|
| Boom | 0.70 | $280,000 | $250,000 |
| Recession | 0.30 | $100,000 | $ 70,000 |

Bentley currently has a bond issue outstanding with a face value of $125,000. Rolls is an all-equity company.

 *a.* What is the value of each company before the merger?

 *b.* What are the values of each company's debt and equity before the merger?

 *c.* If the companies continue to operate separately, what are the total values of the companies, the equity, and the debt?

 *d.* What would be the value of the merged company? What would be the value of the merged company's debt and equity?

 *e.* Is there a transfer of wealth in this case? Why?

 *f.* Suppose that the face value of Bentley's debt were $90,000. Would this affect the transfer of wealth?

### Calculating Net Present Value

30.17 Plant Inc. is considering making an offer to purchase Palmer Corp. Plant's vice-president of finance has collected the following information:

| | Plant | Palmer |
|---|---|---|
| Price–earnings ratio | 14.5 | 10 |
| Shares outstanding | 1,500,000 | 750,000 |
| Earnings | $4,200,000 | $960,000 |
| Dividends | 1,050,000 | 470,000 |

 Plant also knows that securities analysts expect the earnings and dividends of Palmer to grow at a constant rate of 4 percent each year. Plant management believes that the acquisition of Palmer will provide the firm with some economies of scale that will increase this growth rate to 6 percent per year.

 *a.* What is the value of Palmer to Plant?

 *b.* What would Plant's gain be from this acquisition?

 *c.* If Plant were to offer $20 in cash for each share of Palmer, what would the NPV of the acquisition be?

 *d.* What is the most Plant should be willing to pay in cash per share for the stock of Palmer?

 *e.* If Plant were to offer 225,000 of its shares in exchange for the outstanding stock of Palmer, what would the NPV be?

 *f.* Should the acquisition be attempted? If so, should it be as in (c) or as in (e)?

 *g.* Plant's outside financial consultants think that the 6 percent growth rate is too optimistic and a 5 percent rate is more realistic. How does this change your previous answers?

### Mergers and Shareholder Value

30.18 The Chocolate Ice Cream Company and the Vanilla Ice Cream Company have agreed to merge and form Fudge Swirl Consolidated. Both companies are exactly alike except that they are located in different towns. The end-of-period value of each firm is determined by the weather, as shown below. There will be no synergy to the merger.

| State | Probability | Value |
|---|---|---|
| Rainy | 0.1 | $250,000 |
| Warm | 0.4 | 425,000 |
| Hot | 0.5 | 875,000 |

 The weather conditions in each town are independent of those in the other. Furthermore, each company has an outstanding debt claim of $425,000. Assume that no premiums are paid in the merger.

 *a.* What are the possible values of the combined company?

 *b.* What are the possible values of end-of-period debt and stock after the merger?

 *c.* Show that the bondholders are better off and the stockholders are worse off in the combined firm than they would have been if the firms had remained separate.

# The Birdie Golf–Hybrid Golf Merger

Birdie Golf Ltd. has been in merger talks with Hybrid Golf Company for the past six months. After several rounds of negotiations, the offer under discussion is a cash offer of $352 million for Hybrid Golf. Both companies have niche markets in the golf club industry, and the companies believe a merger will result in significant synergies due to economies of scale in manufacturing and marketing, as well as significant savings in general and administrative expenses.

Bryce Bichon, the CFO for Birdie, has been instrumental in the merger negotiations. Bryce has prepared the following pro forma financial statements for Hybrid Golf assuming the merger takes place. The financial statements include all synergistic benefits from the merger:

|  | 2016 | 2017 | 2018 | 2019 | 2020 |
|---|---|---|---|---|---|
| Sales | $512,000,000 | $576,000,000 | $640,000,000 | $720,000,000 | $800,000,000 |
| Production costs | 359,200,000 | 403,200,000 | 448,000,000 | 505,600,000 | 564,000,000 |
| Depreciation | 48,000,000 | 51,200,000 | 52,800,000 | 53,120,000 | 53,600,000 |
| Other expenses | 51,200,000 | 57,600,000 | 64,000,000 | 72,320,000 | 77,600,000 |
| Earnings before interest and taxes | $53,600,000 | $64,000,000 | $75,200,000 | $88,960,000 | $104,800,000 |
| Interest | 12,160,000 | 14,080,000 | 15,360,000 | 16,000,000 | 17,280,000 |
| Taxable income | $41,440,000 | $49,920,000 | $59,840,000 | $72,960,000 | $ 87,520,000 |
| Taxes (40%) | 16,576,000 | 19,968,000 | 23,936,000 | 29,184,000 | 35,008,000 |
| Net income | $24,864,000 | $29,952,000 | $35,904,000 | $43,776,000 | $ 52,512,000 |

Bryce is also aware that the Hybrid Golf division will require investments each year for continuing operations, along with sources of financing. The following table outlines the required investments and sources of financing:

|  | 2016 | 2017 | 2018 | 2019 | 2020 |
|---|---|---|---|---|---|
| **Investments:** | | | | | |
| Net working capital | $12,800,000 | $16,000,000 | $16,000,000 | $19,200,000 | $19,200,000 |
| Fixed assets | 9,600,000 | 16,000,000 | 11,520,000 | 76,800,000 | 4,480,000 |
| Total | $22,400,000 | $32,000,000 | $27,520,000 | $96,000,000 | $23,680,000 |
| **Sources of financing:** | | | | | |
| New debt | $22,400,000 | $10,240,000 | $10,240,000 | $ 9,600,000 | $ 7,680,000 |
| Profit retention | 0 | 21,760,000 | 17,280,000 | 17,280,000 | 16,000,000 |
| Total | $22,400,000 | $32,000,000 | $27,520,000 | $26,880,000 | $23,680,000 |

The management of Birdie Golf feels that the capital structure at Hybrid Golf is not optimal. If the merger takes place, Hybrid Golf will immediately increase its leverage with a $71 million debt issue, which would be followed by a $96 million dividend payment to Birdie Golf. This will increase Hybrid's debt-to-equity ratio from 0.50 to 1.00. Birdie Golf will also be able to use a $16 million tax loss carryforward in 2017 and 2018 from Hybrid Golf's previous operations. The total value of Hybrid Golf is expected to be $576 million in five years, and the company will have $192 million in debt at that time.

Stock in Birdie Golf currently sells for $94 per share, and the company has 11.6 million shares of stock outstanding. Hybrid Golf has 5.2 million shares of stock outstanding. Both companies can borrow at an 8 percent interest rate. The risk-free rate is 6 percent, and the expected return on the market is 13 percent. Bryce believes the current cost of capital for Birdie Golf is 11 percent. The beta for Hybrid Golf stock at its current capital structure is 1.30.

Bryce has asked you to analyze the financial aspects of the potential merger. Specifically, he has asked you to answer the following questions:

1. Suppose Hybrid shareholders will agree to a merger price of $68.75 per share. Should Birdie proceed with the merger?
2. What is the highest price per share that Birdie should be willing to pay for Hybrid?

3. Suppose Birdie is unwilling to pay cash for the merger but will consider a stock exchange. What exchange ratio would make the merger terms equivalent to the original merger price of $68.75 per share?
4. What is the highest exchange ratio Birdie would be willing to pay and still undertake the merger?

# 31

# Financial Distress

EXECUTIVE SUMMARY

This chapter discusses financial distress, private workouts, and bankruptcy. A firm that does not generate enough cash flow to pay interest or other contractually required payments will experience financial distress. If it defaults on a required payment, a firm may be forced to liquidate its assets. More often, a defaulting firm will reorganize its financial structure. Financial restructuring involves replacing old financial claims with new ones; it takes place with private workouts or legal bankruptcy. Private workouts are voluntary arrangements to restructure a company's debt, such as postponing a payment or reducing the size of the payment. Sometimes a private workout is not possible and formal bankruptcy is required. Canwest Global Communications Corporation, one of Canada's largest international media companies, went through all of these stages, as shown in the chronology of Figure 31.1.

## 31.1 WHAT IS FINANCIAL DISTRESS?

**Financial distress** is surprisingly hard to define precisely—partly because of the variety of events befalling firms under financial distress. The list of events is almost endless but includes the following:

- Dividend reductions
- Plant closings
- Losses
- Layoffs
- CEO resignations
- Plummeting stock prices

Financial distress occurs when a firm's operating cash flows (OCFs) are not sufficient to satisfy current obligations (such as trade credits or interest expenses) and the firm is forced to take corrective action.[1] Financial distress may lead a firm to default on a contract, and it may involve financial restructuring among the firm, its creditors, and its equity investors. Usually, the firm is forced to take actions that it would not have taken if it had had sufficient cash flow. For example, Figure 31.1 shows that Canwest had to sell its TV stations in Montreal, Hamilton, and Victoria and shut down its TV outlet in Red Deer. The chronology also shows how financial distress led the company to sell its stake in an international media company as well as set up private workouts on interest payments to creditors.

Our definition of financial distress can be expanded somewhat by linking it to insolvency. *Insolvency* is defined in *Black's Law Dictionary* as follows:

> Inability to pay one's debts; lack of means of paying one's debts. Such a condition of [one's] assets and liability that the former made immediately available would be insufficient to discharge the latter.[2]

---

[1] This definition is close to the one used by Karen Wruck, "Financial Distress: Reorganization and Organization Efficiency," *Journal of Financial Economics* (October 1990).

[2] *Black's Law Dictionary*, 5th ed. (St. Paul, MN: West, 1979), p. 716.

FIGURE 31.1

## Canwest: A Chronology

- **1975:** Izzy Asper launches Winnipeg television station CKND.
- **1980:** Canwest adds stations in British Columbia, Saskatchewan, and the Maritimes.
- **1989:** Canwest completes acquisition of 100 percent of Global.
- **1991:** Canwest begins trading on the Toronto Stock Exchange. The same year, it acquires a 20 percent stake in TV3, New Zealand.
- **1992:** Asper purchases a controlling stake in Network Ten, Australia.
- **1996:** Canwest lists on the New York Stock Exchange.
- **1999:** Izzy's son Leonard becomes CEO.
- **2000:** Canwest acquires Western International Communications (WIC) to form a national network. The same year, Canwest borrows heavily to acquire the former Southam chain of 14 newspapers from Conrad Black's Hollinger Group, paying $3.2 billion.
- **October 7, 2003:** Izzy Asper, 71, dies at home in Winnipeg.
- **August 15, 2007:** Canwest buys Alliance-Atlantis Communications to boost its stake in specialty TV channels.
- **October 4, 2007:** Canwest announces it will cut 200 Global TV newsroom jobs across Canada.
- **November 12, 2008:** Canwest cuts 560 jobs Canada-wide.
- **November 14, 2008:** Canwest reports a $1.02 billion loss in its fourth quarter.
- **March 2009:** Canwest Media Inc. defaults on US$30.4 million interest payments to bondholders.
- **April 14, 2009:** Canwest gets the first of many extensions of interest payment deadlines from key creditors.
- **May 29, 2009:** Canwest LP fails to meet interest payments of $10 million owed to senior creditors.
- **June 29, 2009:** Canwest says it will sell TV stations in Montreal and Hamilton to an affiliate of Channel Zero, an independent Canadian broadcaster.
- **July 22, 2009:** Canwest announces it will shut down TV outlets in Victoria and Red Deer by the end of August. On September 4, it makes a deal with local investors to sell the Victoria station, CHEK.
- **September 24, 2009:** Canwest sells its stake in Australia's Network Ten.
- **October 6, 2009:** Canwest announces that some of its business units, including the *National Post* newspaper and Global Television, have obtained court protection from their creditors.

- **October 28, 2009:** Canwest secures court approval to move the *National Post* into its existing newspaper division, Canwest Limited Partnership, an arm that was not in creditor protection.
- **November 13, 2009:** After its shares were suspended from trading on the TSX, they are officially delisted and, soon after, begin trading instead on the TSX Venture exchange.
- **January 8, 2010:** An Ontario court approves an order placing Canwest's newspaper division under creditor protection, paving the way for the company to begin looking for buyers for Canada's biggest newspaper chain.
- **January 11, 2010:** Four potential suitors weigh a hefty investment in Canwest Global Communications Corp., but Corus Entertainment Inc., Shaw Communications Inc., Fairfax Financial Holdings Ltd., and Jim Pattison Group all face considerable obstacles to cutting a deal with the owner of specialty and conventional television networks.
- **February 9, 2010:** David and Gail Asper, the son and daughter of Canwest Global Communications founder Izzy Asper, resign from the board to pursue other interests and help shrink the board's size as the company restructures. Leonard Asper remains as chief executive and a director of Canwest. Lisa Pankratz, president of Mackenzie Cundill Investment Management Ltd., also resigns her position on the board. The empty positions on Canwest's board are not filled.
- **February 12, 2010:** Canwest finds an investor, Shaw Communications, to buy a controlling stake in the company and help it emerge from creditor protection. The Calgary-based company's investment will help Canwest pay back its creditors.
- **February 20, 2010:** Asper Family and Goldman Sachs make their own bid of $120 million to retake Canwest in competition with the bid proposed by Shaw Communications.
- **February 25, 2010:** Shaw Communications wins a court battle to continue its plans to purchase assets and voting shares from Canwest.
- **May 4, 2010:** Torstar, backed by Fairfax Financial Holdings, bids for print and digital assets of Canwest.
- **June 11, 2010:** Bondholders of the company buy Canwest newspaper division for $1.1 billion.
- **October 27, 2010:** Canwest renamed 2737469 Canada Inc.
- **May 27, 2013:** 2737469 Canada Inc., formerly Canwest Global Communications Corporation, is dissolved and ceases to exist.

Sources: cbc.ca/news/business/canwest-timeline-the-empire-izzy-asper-built-1.815086, ic.gc.ca/app/scr/cc/CorporationsCanada/fdrlCrpDtls.html?corpId=2737469.

This definition has two general themes: stocks and flows.[3] These two ways of thinking about insolvency are depicted in Figure 31.2. *Stock-based insolvency* occurs when a firm has negative net worth, so the value of its assets is less than the value of its debts. *Flow-based insolvency* occurs when OCF is insufficient to meet current obligations. Flow-based insolvency refers to the inability to pay one's debts. Insolvency may lead to bankruptcy. Some examples of Canadian bankruptcies are in Table 31.1.

The two kinds of insolvency usually occur together, but this is not always the case. For example, a firm that had no current obligations could remain in business even if its debt exceeded its assets. Such a firm would be solvent according to the flow-based measure but insolvent by the stock-based measure. When this occurs, firms often resort to creative accounting to hide their stock-based insolvency and increase their risk to try to increase the value of assets. This represents an agency cost of debt, as we discussed in Chapter 17.

**FIGURE 31.2**

**Insolvency**

**A. Stock-based insolvency**

**B. Flow-based insolvency**

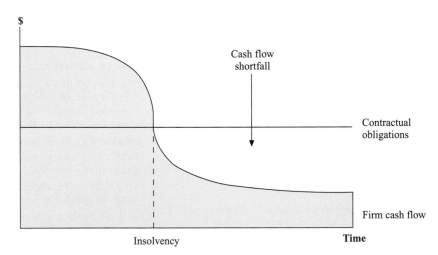

Stock-based insolvency occurs when the value of the assets of a firm is less than the value of the debts. This implies negative equity. Flow-based insolvency occurs when firm cash flows are insufficient to cover contractually required payments.

---

[3] Edward Altman was one of the first to distinguish between stock-based insolvency and flow-based insolvency. See Edward Altman, *Corporate Financial Distress: A Complete Guide to Predicting, Avoiding and Dealing with Bankruptcy*, 2nd ed. (New York: John Wiley & Sons, 1993).

**TABLE 31.1**

**Canadian Bankruptcies**

| Firm | Liabilities as reported on latest available annual reports (in $ millions) | Bankruptcy date |
|---|---|---|
| Campeau Corporation | $ 7,000.00 | Early 1990s |
| Consumers Distributing* | N/A | 1996 |
| Gandalf Technologies Inc.* | N/A | July 25, 1997 |
| Eaton's | $   437.29 | August 1999 |
| Sam the Record Man* | N/A | October 30, 2001 |
| Air Canada | $ 4,700.00 | April 1, 2003 |
| Quebecor World Inc. | $ 4,331.40 | January 21, 2008 |
| Icefloe Technologies Inc. | $3.42 | January 31, 2008 |
| Nortel Networks Corporation | $11,966.00† | January 14, 2009 |
| Canwest | $ 4,000.00 | October 6, 2009 |
| Sino-Forest Corporation | $ 2,479.37† | March 30, 2012 |

\* Liabilities figures were not available either because the company was private or due to a lack of financial records.

† All figures in Canadian dollars except these two, which are in U.S. dollars.

Sources: Bloomberg L.P., forbes.com, cbc.ca, theguardian.com, and the companies' respective annual reports and MD&A when available.

**CONCEPT**
**QUESTIONS**
- Describe financial distress.
- What are stock-based insolvency and flow-based insolvency?

## 31.2   WHAT HAPPENS IN FINANCIAL DISTRESS?

In 2009, Canwest, one of Canada's largest international media companies, experienced financial distress. Canwest's various acquisitions took a significant financial toll. The company trimmed its workforce, sold its stake in Australia's Network Ten, and shut down TV outlets and TV stations. In October 2009, Canwest filed for creditor protection under the *Companies' Creditors Arrangement Act* (CCAA) to restructure its $4 billion debt, with plans to emerge as a going concern. In late February 2010, the company announced that Shaw Communications would buy 80 percent voting interest and 20 percent equity interest in the restructured entity. The company newspapers were not part of the Shaw transaction and were expected to sell separately.[4] Two months later, Torstar, backed by Fairfax Financial Holdings, bid for print and digital assets of Canwest. In June 2010, bondholders of the company bought Canwest's newspaper division for $1.1 billion. With most of its operating assets sold, Canwest was renamed 2737469 Canada Inc. on October 27, 2010, and was finally dissolved on May 27, 2013. Generalizing from the Canwest example, firms deal with financial distress in many ways, such as

1. Selling major assets.
2. Reducing capital spending as well as research and development.
3. Negotiating with banks and other creditors.
4. Exchanging equity for debt.
5. Filing for bankruptcy.

Items (1) and (2) concern the firm's assets. Items (3), (4), and (5) involve the right-hand side of the firm's balance sheet and are examples of financial restructuring. Financial distress may involve both asset restructuring and financial restructuring—changes on both sides of the balance sheet.

---

[4] Our discussion draws on the chronology in Figure 31.1.

Some firms may actually benefit from financial distress by restructuring their assets. A recent example is General Motors (GM). In June 2008, GM reported second-quarter net income of −$15 million and lost money in 2005 and 2007. In addition, the company steadily lost market share to rivals such as Toyota, BMW, and Honda. Its stock price decreased from $50 in late 2003 to about $1 in 2009. GM struggled to increase sales and cut costs, attempted to sell assets (e.g., the Hummer line), drew down bank debt, and arranged for more long-term financing. GM was clearly a firm experiencing financial distress. The company eventually filed for bankruptcy on June 1, 2009, and would emerge from bankruptcy protection six weeks later, on July 10, 2009. The stay in bankruptcy reorganization left the company with lower costs, a lighter debt load, new strategic initiatives, and four automotive brands instead of eight. The company received substantial government assistance amounting to nearly $50 billion in bailout money, which gave the U.S. and Canadian governments approximately 70 percent ownership. By November 2010, the U.S. government began selling its shares of GM, with the remainder sold on December 9, 2013.[5] GM shares were trading on the New York Stock Exchange for $36.67 on June 23, 2014, far above their $1 low. The GM example shows that for some firms, financial distress may bring about new organizational forms and new operating strategies. However, in this chapter we focus on financial restructuring.

Figure 31.3 shows how firms move through financial distress in Canada. Previously, most legal bankruptcies in this country ended with liquidation. However, changes to the bankruptcy process are encouraging restructurings, reorganizations, and private workouts.

**FIGURE 31.3**

**What Happens in Financial Distress**

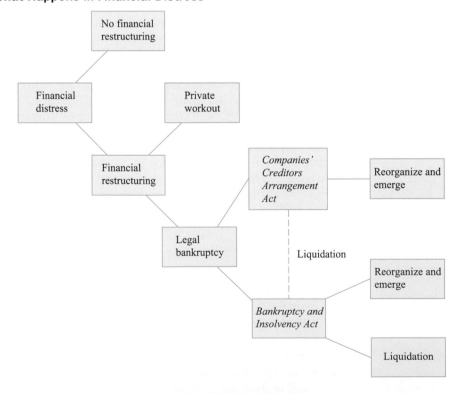

---

[5] Eric Beech, "U.S. Government Says It Lost $11.2 Billion on GM Bailout," Thomson Reuters, April 30, 2014, reuters.com/article/2014/04/30/us-autos-gm-treasury-idUSBREA3T0MR20140430.

Financial distress can serve as a firm's early-warning system for trouble. Firms with more debt will experience financial distress earlier than firms with less debt. However, firms that experience financial distress earlier will have more time for private workouts and reorganization. Firms with low leverage will experience financial distress later and, in many instances, be forced to liquidate.

- Why doesn't financial distress always cause firms to die?
- What is a benefit of financial distress?

## 31.3  BANKRUPTCY LIQUIDATION AND REORGANIZATION

Firms that cannot or choose not to make contractually required payments to creditors have two basic options: liquidation and reorganization. **Liquidation** means termination of the firm as a going concern, and it involves selling off the assets of the firm. The proceeds, net of selling costs, are distributed to creditors in order of established priority. **Reorganization** is the option of keeping the firm a going concern; it often involves issuing new securities to replace old ones. Liquidation or reorganization is the result of a bankruptcy proceeding. Which occurs depends on whether the firm is worth more "dead" or "alive."

Liquidation and reorganization are covered under the *Bankruptcy and Insolvency Act* (1993); reorganization is also covered under the CCAA. In late 1992, after intense criticism of the inherent difficulties of reorganization under the old law, the federal government introduced wide-ranging changes to the *Bankruptcy and Insolvency Act* to make it "debtor friendly." The changes have met with mixed reviews, but most industry experts agree that the changes facilitate corporate restructurings.

### Bankruptcy Liquidation

Liquidation occurs when the court directs sale of all assets of the firm. The following sequence of events is typical:

1. A petition is filed in a federal court. Corporations may file a voluntary petition, or involuntary petitions may be filed against the corporation by creditors. Creditors must give 10 days' notice before filing a petition.
2. A trustee-in-bankruptcy is elected by the creditors to take over the assets of the debtor corporation. The trustee will attempt to liquidate the assets.
3. When the assets are liquidated, after payment of the bankruptcy administration costs, the proceeds are distributed among the creditors.
4. If any assets remain, after expenses and payments to creditors, they are distributed to the shareholders.

The distribution of the proceeds of the liquidation occurs according to the following priority. (The higher a claim is on this list, the more likely it is to be paid. In many of these categories, there are various limitations and qualifications that we omit for the sake of brevity.[6])

1. Administrative expenses associated with the bankruptcy.
2. Other expenses arising after the filing of an involuntary bankruptcy petition but before the appointment of a trustee.
3. Wages, salaries, and commissions.
4. Municipal tax claims.

---

[6] Our discussion draws on R. Klapstein, *Legal Aspects of Financial Counselling* (Montreal: Institute of Canadian Bankers, 1994), Chapter 16.

5. Rent.

6. Claims resulting from employee injuries that are not covered by workers' compensation.

7. Unsecured creditors.

8. Preferred shareholders.

9. Common shareholders.

Three qualifications to this list are in order. The first concerns unpaid federal source deductions such as income tax and employment insurance premiums. These funds are beyond the grasp of the bankruptcy trustee and must be paid to the government ahead of any payments to the claimants on our list. (Provincial source deductions have the same status only if the bankrupt company had kept them in a separate bank account.)

The second qualification concerns secured creditors. Such creditors are entitled to the proceeds from the sale of the security and are outside this ordering. However, if the secured property is liquidated and provides insufficient cash to cover the amount owed, the secured creditors join with unsecured creditors in dividing the remaining liquidated value. In contrast, if the secured property is liquidated for proceeds greater than the secured claim, the net proceeds are used to pay unsecured creditors and others.

The third qualification is that, in reality, courts have a great deal of freedom in deciding what actually happens and who actually gets what in the event of bankruptcy. As a result, the priority set out above is not always followed.

---

**EXAMPLE 31.1**

The B. O. Drug Company is to be liquidated. Bonds worth $1.5 million are secured by a mortgage on the B. O. Drug Company corporate headquarters building, which is sold for $1 million; $200,000 is used to cover administrative costs and other claims (including unpaid wages, pension benefits, consumer claims, and taxes). This leaves an amount of $2.5 million available to pay secured and unsecured creditors. This is less than the $4 million of unpaid debt. Following our list of priorities, all creditors must be paid before shareholders, and the mortgage bondholders have first claim on the $1 million obtained from the sale of the headquarters building.

The trustee has proposed the following distribution:

| Type of claim | Prior claim | Cash received under liquidation |
|---|---|---|
| Bonds (secured by mortgage) | $ 1,500,000 | $1,500,000 |
| Subordinated debentures | 2,500,000 | 1,000,000 |
| Common shareholders | 10,000,000 | 0 |
| Total | $14,000,000 | $2,500,000 |

**Calculation of the distribution**

| | |
|---|---|
| Cash received from sale of assets available for distribution | $2,500,000 |
| Cash paid to secured bondholders on sale of mortgaged property | 1,000,000 |
| Available to bond and debenture holders | $1,500,000 |
| Total claims remaining ($4,000,000 less payment of $1,000,000 on secured bonds) | $3,000,000 |

Distribution of remaining $1,500,000 to cover total remaining claims of $3,000,000:

| Type of claim remaining | Claim on liquidation proceeds | Cash received |
|---|---|---|
| Bonds | $ 500,000 | $ 500,000 |
| Debentures | 2,500,000 | 1,000,000 |
| Total | $3,000,000 | $1,500,000 |

## Bankruptcy Reorganization

The general objective of corporate reorganization is to plan to restructure the corporation with some provision for repayment of creditors. The new provisions introduced to the *Bankruptcy and Insolvency Act* in 1992 were intended to facilitate the corporate reorganization process. Here is a typical sequence of events:

1. A voluntary petition can be filed by the corporation, or an involuntary petition can be filed by creditors. Under the new legislation, creditors must provide the insolvent company with 10 days' notice before filing the petition.

2. A federal judge either approves or denies the petition. If the petition is approved, a time for filing proofs of claims is set. A debtor files a notice of intention to make a proposal (reorganization plan), and a stay of proceedings of 30 days is effected against all creditors. A further 21 days is added until the creditors meet to vote on the proposal. The court can add a maximum of five months to the stay period.

3. In almost all cases, the corporation (the "debtor in possession") continues to run the business. While the stay of proceedings is in effect, the new legislation has included several safeguards intended to prevent the collapse of the business.

4. The corporation is required to submit a proposal, which is the reorganization plan.

5. Creditors and shareholders are divided into classes. A class of creditors accepts the plan if a majority of the class (in dollars or in number) agrees. The secured creditors must vote before the unsecured creditors. The debtor decides on the classes of secured creditors and can force proposals on uncooperative creditors.

6. After acceptance by creditors, the plan is confirmed by the court.

7. Payments in cash, property, and securities are made to creditors and shareholders. The plan may provide for the issuance of new securities.

---

**EXAMPLE 31.2**

---

Suppose B. O. Drug Co. decides to reorganize under the *Bankruptcy and Insolvency Act*. Generally, senior claims are honoured in full before various other claims receive anything. Assume that the "going-concern" value of B. O. Drug Co. is $3 million and that its balance sheet is as shown:

| | |
|---|---|
| Assets | $3,000,000 |
| Liabilities: | |
| Mortgage bonds | 1,500,000 |
| Subordinated debentures | 2,500,000 |
| Shareholders' equity | −1,000,000 |

The firm has proposed the following reorganization plan:

| Old security | Old claim | New claim with reorganization plan |
|---|---|---|
| Mortgage bonds | $1,500,000 | $1,500,000 |
| Subordinated debentures | 2,500,000 | 1,500,000 |

and a distribution of new securities under the new claim with the reorganization plan:

| Old security | Receives under proposed reorganization plan |
|---|---|
| Mortgage bonds | $1,000,000 in 9% senior debentures |
| | $500,000 in 11% subordinated debentures |
| Debentures | $1,000,000 in 8% preferred stock |
| | $500,000 in common stock |

The corporation may wish to allow the old shareholders to retain some participation in the firm. Needless to say, this may lead to protests by the holders of unsecured debt.

*Companies' Creditors Arrangement Act.*   The CCAA—federal legislation originally enacted during the 1930s—allows for the reorganization and continuation of insolvent businesses.[7] Some important differences between the CCAA and the *Bankruptcy and Insolvency Act* are as follows:

1. The *Bankruptcy and Insolvency Act* is primarily restricted to dealing with unsecured creditors, but the CCAA can deal with any or all creditors.
2. The CCAA is a brief statute that is silent on the framework for proceeding with an arrangement (reorganization plan). Therefore, a series of court orders must be used to develop an appropriate framework.
3. When a company applies for protection under the CCAA, there is no provision for the debtor to be placed in bankruptcy for failing to carry out the agreed-upon terms.

In the 1980s, the CCAA became a popular statute for major reorganizations. The advantage that it gives debtors in dealing with secured creditors makes this statute invaluable for certain corporate restructurings. In this regard, the CCAA is similar to Chapter 11 of the U.S. *Federal Bankruptcy Reform Act* of 1978, popularly referred to as just Chapter 11. Later in the chapter we will look at this statute's use in the reorganization of Canwest.

### Agreements to Avoid Bankruptcy

When a firm defaults on an obligation, it may still be able to avoid bankruptcy. Because the legal process of bankruptcy can be lengthy and expensive, it is often in everyone's best interest to devise a *private workout* that avoids a bankruptcy filing. Much of the time, creditors can work with the management of a company that has defaulted on a loan contract. Voluntary arrangements to restructure the company's debt can be and often are made. This may involve *extension*, which postpones the date of payment, or *composition*, which involves a reduced payment.

**CONCEPT QUESTIONS**

- What is bankruptcy?
- What is the difference between liquidation and reorganization?
- What is the *Companies' Creditors Arrangement Act*?

# 31.4   CURRENT ISSUES IN FINANCIAL DISTRESS

In this section we examine two important tactics in financial distress: private workouts and prepackaged bankruptcies. It is expected that these responses to financial distress, prevalent in the United States, will grow in importance in Canada under the current legislation. For this reason, this section relates U.S. experience to the current Canadian law.

### Private Workout or Bankruptcy: Which Is Better?

A firm that defaults on its debt payments will need to restructure its financial claims. The firm will have two choices: formal bankruptcy or **private workout**. The previous section described two types of formal bankruptcies: liquidation and reorganization. This section compares private workouts with bankruptcy reorganizations. Both types of financial restructuring involve exchanging new financial claims for old financial claims. Usually senior debt is replaced with junior debt, and debt is replaced with

---

[7] An excellent description of the CCAA is provided in E. B. Leonard, *Guide to Commercial Insolvency in Canada* (Toronto: Butterworths Canada, 1988), pp. 20-1 to 20-6.

equity. Much academic research in the United States has described what happens in private workouts and formal bankruptcies:[8]

- Historically, one-half of financial restructurings have been private, but recently formal bankruptcy has dominated.
- Firms that emerge from private workouts experience stock price increases that are much greater than those for firms emerging from formal bankruptcies.
- The direct costs of private workouts are only about 10 percent of the costs of formal bankruptcies.
- Top management usually loses pay and sometimes jobs in both private workouts and formal bankruptcies.

These facts, when taken together, seem to suggest that a private workout is much better than a formal bankruptcy. In Canada, the *Bankruptcy and Insolvency Act* has added increased costs and time commitments to the formal bankruptcy proceedings. Therefore, direct negotiations (private workouts) between creditors and debtors can be expected to increase. In some cases, however, formal bankruptcy is the better alternative.

## Holdouts

Bankruptcy is usually better for equity investors than for creditors because equity investors can usually hold out for a better deal in bankruptcy. The priority of claims, which favours creditors over equity investors, is usually violated in formal bankruptcies. One study found that in 81 percent of recent U.S. bankruptcies, equity investors obtained some compensation.[9]

## Complexity

A firm with a complicated capital structure will have more trouble putting together a private workout. Firms with secured creditors and trade creditors will usually use formal bankruptcy because it is too difficult to reach an agreement with many different types of creditors.

## Lack of Information

There is an inherent conflict of interest between equity investors and creditors, and the conflict is accentuated when both have incomplete information about the circumstances of financial distress. When a firm initially experiences a cash flow shortfall, it may not know whether the shortfall is permanent or temporary. If the shortfall is permanent, creditors will push for a formal reorganization or liquidation. However, if the cash flow shortfall is temporary, formal reorganization or liquidation may not be necessary, and equity investors will take this viewpoint. This conflict of interest cannot easily be resolved.

These last two points are especially important. They suggest that financial distress will be more expensive if complexity is high and information is incomplete. Complexity and lack of information make cheap workouts less likely.

---

[8] For example, see Stuart Gilson, "Managing Default: Some Evidence on How Firms Choose between Workouts and Bankruptcy," *Journal of Applied Corporate Finance* (Summer 1991); and Stuart C. Gilson, Kose John, and Larry N. P. Lang, "Troubled Debt Restructuring: An Empirical Study of Private Reorganization of Firms in Defaults," *Journal of Financial Economics* (October 1990).

[9] Lawrence A. Weiss, "Bankruptcy Dissolution: Direct Costs and Violation of Priority and Claims," *Journal of Financial Economics* (October 1990). However, W. Beranek, R. Boehmer, and B. Smith, "Much Ado about Nothing: Absolute Priority Deviations in Chapter 11," *Financial Management* (Autumn 1996), find 33.8 percent of bankruptcy reorganizations leave the shareholders with nothing. They also point out that deviations from the absolute priority role are to be expected because the Bankruptcy Code allows creditors to waive their rights if they perceive a waiver to be in their best interest.

## Prepackaged Bankruptcy

On January 19, 2010, Morris Publishing, owner of 13 daily newspapers, filed for protection from its creditors under Chapter 11 of the U.S bankruptcy code.[10] This company was the latest in a string of newspapers that sought bankruptcy protection amid a downturn in advertising. The company planned to exchange $100 million in new debt for $278 million in existing debt, if approved by the court. Less than a month later, the company emerged from the bankruptcy protection. This surprised many people because, traditionally, bankruptcy has been costly and often takes many years to emerge from. Morris Publishing avoided lengthy bankruptcy by gaining overwhelming support from its creditors before the bankruptcy filing date.

This alternative reorganization arrangement has been called prepackaged bankruptcy. **Prepackaged bankruptcy** is a combination of private workout and legal bankruptcy. In prepackaged bankruptcy, the firm and most of its creditors agree to private reorganization outside formal bankruptcy. After the private reorganization is put together, the firm files a formal bankruptcy.

Prepackaged bankruptcy arrangements require that most creditors reach agreement privately. Prepackaged bankruptcy does not seem to work when there are thousands of reluctant trade creditors, such as in the case of retail trading firms.

The main benefit of prepackaged bankruptcy is that it forces holdouts to accept a bankruptcy reorganization. If a large fraction of a firm's creditors can agree privately to a reorganization plan, the holdout problem may be avoided. This makes a reorganization plan in formal bankruptcy easier to put together.

A study by McConnell, Lease, and Tashjian reports that U.S. prepackaged bankruptcies offer many of the advantages of a formal bankruptcy; moreover, they are also more efficient. Their results suggest that the time spent and the direct costs of resolving financial distress are less in a prepackaged bankruptcy than in a formal bankruptcy.[11]

 ***CONCEPT QUESTIONS***

- • What are two ways a firm can restructure its finances?
- • Why do firms use formal bankruptcy?
- • What is prepackaged bankruptcy?
- • What is the main benefit of prepackaged bankruptcy?

## 31.5    THE DECISION TO SEEK COURT PROTECTION: THE CASE OF CANWEST GLOBAL COMMUNICATIONS CORPORATION

Canwest Global Communications Corporation, headquartered in Winnipeg, was one of Canada's largest international media companies. As shown in Figure 31.1, Canwest's various acquisitions took a significant financial toll. The company was highly leveraged and too dependent on advertising for its revenue. The financial distress was caused by issuing $4 billion in debt to fund various ambitious acquisitions that became unmanageable when the company's cash flows were insufficient to cover its debt obligations. Revenue fell due to a secular trend toward getting news on the Internet and a steep decline in advertising caused by the global economic downturn.

---

[10] Chapter 11 is the U.S. version of Canada's reorganization laws.

[11] John J. McConnell, Ronald Lease, and Elizabeth Tashjian, "Prepacks as a Mechanism for Resolving Financial Distress: The Evidence," *Journal of Applied Corporate Finance* (Winter 1996).

On October 6, 2009, Canwest filed for court protection in Canada under the CCAA, with plans to emerge as a going concern. Due to the complex structure of the organization, there were assets that were not filed for creditors' protection, as shown in Figure 31.4. On January 8, 2010, an Ontario court approved an order placing Canwest's newspaper division under creditors' protection, paving the way for the company to begin looking for buyers for Canada's largest newspaper chain. As Figure 31.1 documented earlier, after several competing bids, the bondholders bought the newspaper division for $1.1 billion.

**FIGURE 31.4**

---

**Canwest Assets Not Included in October 6, 2009, Filing for Creditor Protection**

> **Newspapers:** All publishing and online operations of newspapers, including the former Southam dailies in Vancouver, Montreal, Ottawa, Edmonton, Calgary, Windsor, and Victoria, as well as Saskatchewan's two main dailies, in Regina and Saskatoon, acquired from the Sifton family.
>
> **Online:** Ten websites, including *Canada.com*, *FPinfomart.ca*, *Working.com*, *Driving.ca*, and *Dose.ca*.
>
> **CW Media Inc.:** Numerous specialty TV channels acquired from Alliance Atlantis, including Showcase, Slice, History Television, HGTV Canada, and Food Network Canada.
>
> **Other television:** TVtropolis, Mystery TV, and Men TV.
>
> Source: cbc.ca/news/business/canwest-wins-court-shelter-for-global-tv-post-1.774693.

Costs of the Canwest restructuring included the following:

1. *Direct costs of restructuring.* Formal protection can be time-consuming and expensive. In the case of Canwest, "for the first six months, the cost of restructuring at Canwest Media Inc., which runs the broadcast side, has run to $87.7 million. Professional fees account for $25.5 million, according to court documents. On the newspaper side, which entered court protection two months later, the cost of reorganizing its business has run to $40 million, of which $19.2 million has been for professional fees."[12]

2. *Indirect costs of restructuring.* There are many indirect costs of financial distress, including management distraction, loss of customers, and loss of reputation. Indirect costs may occur whether or not formal bankruptcy is declared.

3. *Costs of a complicated financial structure.* Firms such as Canwest that have bank loans, senior subordinated debt, and junior subordinated debt with many different creditors will have a difficult time getting all claimholders to agree to an out-of-court settlement. It is axiomatic that the more complicated a firm's financial structure, the more difficult it will be to work out private arrangements to avoid bankruptcy. Conflicts between managers, shareholders, and creditors make reaching a private agreement difficult. There is a tendency for each group to try to gain value at the expense of the others.

**CONCEPT QUESTIONS**

- Was Canwest's insolvency stock based or flow based?
- What are some costs of the Canwest bankruptcy?

---

[12] Fees were drawn from thestar.com/business/2010/04/15/corporate_restructurings_cost_millions.html.

## 31.6

# SUMMARY AND CONCLUSIONS

This chapter examines what happens when firms experience financial distress.

1. Financial distress occurs when a firm's operating cash flow (OCF) is not sufficient to cover contractual obligations. Financially distressed firms are often forced to take corrective action and to undergo financial restructuring. Financial restructuring involves exchanging new financial claims for old ones.

2. Financial restructuring can be accomplished with a private workout or formal bankruptcy. Financial restructuring can involve liquidation or reorganization. However, liquidation is becoming less common in Canada.

3. Two important tactics in restructuring are private workouts and prepackaged bankruptcies. Both are expected to increase in Canada with the advent of "debtor-friendly" legislation.

4. In the example of Canwest's filing for court protection to avoid bankruptcy proceedings, we see how a complicated financial structure can make it hard to achieve agreement among creditors.

**KEY TERMS**

| | | |
|---|---|---|
| Financial distress  896 | Prepackaged | Private workout  904 |
| Liquidation  901 | bankruptcy  906 | Reorganization  901 |

**QUESTIONS & PROBLEMS**

### Companies' Creditors Arrangement Act

31.1 When the Beacon Computer Company filed for bankruptcy under CCAA, it had the following balance sheet information:

| Liquidating value | | Claims | |
|---|---|---|---|
| | | Trade credit | $ 4,800 |
| | | Secured mortgage notes | 8,000 |
| | | Senior debentures | 10,000 |
| | | Junior debentures | 15,000 |
| Total assets | $28,500 | Equity | −9,300 |

Assuming there are no legal fees associated with the bankruptcy, as a trustee, what distribution of liquidating value do you propose?

31.2 When the Master Printing Company filed for bankruptcy, it filed under CCAA. Key information is shown here:

| Assets | | Claims | |
|---|---|---|---|
| | | Mortgage bonds | $19,000 |
| | | Senior debentures | 9,500 |
| | | Junior debentures | 7,500 |
| Going-concern value | $27,000 | Book equity | −9,000 |

Assume that the mortgage bonds are fully recognized as senior debentures, the senior debentures will receive junior debentures in the value of 65 cents on the dollar, and the junior debentures will receive any remaining value as equity. As a trustee, which reorganization plan would you accept?

31.3 The A&Z Real Estate Co. is to be liquidated. The book value of its assets is $52 billion. Bonds with a face value of $28 billion are secured by a mortgage on the company's Toronto and New York buildings. A&Z has subordinated debentures outstanding in the amount of $35 billion; shareholders' equity has a book value of $9 billion; $4.4 billion is used to cover administrative costs and other claims (including unpaid wages, pension benefits, legal fees, and taxes).

The company has a liquidating value of $30 billion. Of this amount, $14 billion represents the proceeds from the sale of the Toronto and New York buildings.

As the trustee in bankruptcy, you wish to follow the bankruptcy law strictly. What is your proposed distribution?

31.4 Now suppose that the A&Z Real Estate Company in Problem 31.3 wishes to reorganize instead of liquidate. In this case the company has a going-concern value of $37 billion. Which proposal would you recommend? How does this proposal differ from your solution in the case of liquidation? Explain briefly.

31.5 The Southeast Asia Corporation (SAC) is to be liquidated. The market value of its assets is $16.3 million. Bonds with a face value of $5.6 million are unsecured. SAC has no subordinated debentures outstanding; shareholders' equity has a market value of $1.95 million; $850,000 is used to cover administrative costs and other claims (including unpaid wages, pension benefits, legal fees, and taxes).

The company has a liquidating value of $14 million. Of this amount, $8 million represents the proceeds from the sale of their flagship Indonesian resort.

As a trustee in bankruptcy, you wish to follow the bankruptcy law strictly. What is your proposed distribution?

---

APPENDIX **31A**

## Predicting Corporate Bankruptcy: The Z-Score Model

To access Appendix 31A, go to Connect.

# 32

# International Corporate Finance

**EXECUTIVE SUMMARY**

Canada has an open economy linked very closely by a free trade agreement to its largest trading partner, the United States. There are also important economic and financial ties to Mexico under NAFTA, to Europe, to the Pacific Rim, and to other major economies worldwide.

Corporations that have significant foreign operations are often referred to as *international corporations* or *multinationals*. International corporations must consider many financial factors that do not directly affect purely domestic firms. These include foreign exchange rates, different interest rates from country to country, complex accounting methods for foreign operations, foreign tax rates, and foreign government intervention. These topics are also of interest to many smaller Canadian businesses.

Smaller corporations do not qualify as multinationals in the league of Alcan or McCain, but their financial managers must know how to manage foreign exchange risk.

The basic principles of corporate finance apply to international corporations. Like domestic companies, international ones seek to (1) invest in projects that create more value for the shareholders than they cost and (2) arrange financing that raises cash at the lowest possible cost. That is, the net present value (NPV) principle holds for both foreign and domestic operations. However, it is usually more complicated to apply the NPV principle to foreign operations.

Perhaps the most important complication of international finance is foreign exchange. The foreign exchange markets provide information and opportunities for an international corporation when it undertakes capital budgeting and financing decisions. The relationship among foreign exchange, interest rates, and inflation is defined by the basic theories of exchange rates: purchasing power parity, interest rate parity, and the expectations theory.

Typically, international financing decisions involve a choice of three basic approaches:

1. Export domestic cash to the foreign operations.
2. Borrow in the country where the investment is located.
3. Borrow in a third country.

We will discuss the merits of each approach.

## 32.1 TERMINOLOGY

A common buzzword across all business school subjects is *globalization*. The first step in learning about the globalization of financial markets is to conquer the new vocabulary. Here are some of the most common terms used in international finance and in this chapter:

1. The **European currency unit (euro)** was devised in 1979 and intended to serve as a monetary unit for the *European Monetary System (EMS)*. Effective January 2002, the euro replaced a basket of 10 domestic European currencies. As of November 2014, the Euro is used by 18 of the 28 European Union countries, with Lithuania to adopt the currency on January 1, 2015.

2. The **cross rate** is the exchange rate between two foreign currencies, generally neither of which is the U.S. dollar. The U.S. dollar, however, is used as an interim step

in determining the cross rate. For example, if an investor wants to sell Canadian dollars and buy Swiss francs, he would sell Canadian dollars against U.S. dollars and then buy francs with those U.S. dollars. So, although the transaction is designed to be Canadian dollars for francs, the U.S. dollar's exchange rate serves as a benchmark.

3. **Eurobonds** are bonds denominated in a particular currency and issued simultaneously in the bond markets of several countries. For many international companies and governments, they have become an important way to raise capital. Eurobonds are issued outside the restrictions that apply to domestic offerings and are typically syndicated in London. Trading can and does take place anywhere there is a buyer and a seller.

4. **Eurocurrency** is money deposited in a financial centre outside of the country whose currency is involved. For instance, Eurodollars—the most widely used Eurocurrency—are U.S. dollars deposited in banks outside the United States.

5. **Foreign bonds**, unlike Eurobonds, are issued in a single country and are usually denominated in that country's currency. Often, the country in which these bonds are issued will draw distinctions between them and bonds issued by domestic issuers, including different tax laws, restrictions on the amount issued, and tougher disclosure rules.

   Foreign bonds often are nicknamed for the country where they are issued: Yankee bonds (United States), Samurai bonds (Japan), Rembrandt bonds (the Netherlands), and Bulldog bonds (Britain). Partly because of tougher regulations and disclosure requirements, the foreign bond market has not grown in past years with the vigour of the Eurobond market. A substantial portion of all foreign bonds are issued in Switzerland.

6. An **American Depository Receipt** (ADR) is a security issued in the United States to represent shares of a foreign stock, allowing that stock to be traded in the United States. Foreign companies use ADRs, which are issued in U.S. dollars, to expand the pool of potential U.S. investors. ADRs are available in two forms for about 690 foreign companies: company-sponsored, which are listed on an exchange, and unsponsored, which are usually held by the investment bank that makes a market in the ADR. Both forms are available to individual investors, but only company-sponsored issues are quoted daily in newspapers.

7. The **London Interbank Offered Rate (LIBOR)** is the rate that most international banks charge one another for loans of Eurodollars overnight in the London market. As discussed in Chapter 26, LIBOR is a cornerstone in the pricing of money market issues and other short-term debt issues by both governments and corporate borrowers. Less creditworthy issuers will often borrow at a rate above LIBOR.

8. As discussed in Chapter 26, there are two basic kinds of **swaps**: interest rate and currency. An interest rate swap occurs when two parties exchange debt with a floating-rate payment for debt with a fixed-rate payment, or vice versa. Currency swaps are agreements to deliver one currency against another currency. Often, both types of swaps are used in the same transaction when debt denominated in different currencies is swapped.

9. **Export Development Canada (EDC)** is a federal Crown corporation with a mandate to promote Canadian exports. EDC provides long-term financing for foreign companies that purchase Canadian exports. To qualify for EDC support, exporters must produce or market goods with a minimum Canadian content of 60 percent.

Another government program to support exports is the federal Global Opportunities for Association (GOA), formerly known as the Program for Export Market Development (PEMD), which reimburses part of the costs of developing export markets and a variety of provincial programs.

 **CONCEPT QUESTION**

• What is the difference between a Eurobond and a foreign bond?

## 32.2   FOREIGN EXCHANGE MARKETS AND EXCHANGE RATES

The **foreign exchange market** is undoubtedly the world's largest financial market. It is the market where one country's currency is traded for another's. Most of the trading takes place in a few currencies: the U.S. dollar ($), euro (€), British pound sterling (£), Japanese yen (¥), and Swiss franc (SF).

The foreign exchange market is an over-the-counter (OTC) market. There is no single location where traders get together. Instead, traders are located in the major banks around the world. They communicate using computer terminals, telephones, and other telecommunication devices.

The many different types of participants in the foreign exchange market include the following:

1. Importers who convert their domestic currency to foreign currency to pay for goods from foreign countries.
2. Exporters who receive foreign currency and may want to convert to the domestic currency.
3. Portfolio managers who buy and sell foreign stocks and bonds.
4. Foreign exchange brokers who match buy and sell orders.
5. Traders who make the market in foreign exchange.

The value of currency constantly changes, reflecting market conditions. For instance, on January 29, 2008, the Canadian dollar was valued at US$1.0005. The above-parity rate was attributed to the U.S Federal Reserve cutting their key interest rate to prevent the economy from falling into a recession and to the increase in commodity prices on light, sweet crude, which Canada exports to the United States.[1] Six years later, on January 22, 2014, the closing rate was US$0.9033 per Canadian dollar, attributed to the strengthening U.S economy, a slowing Canadian economy, competition in the retail industry, and lower than expected inflation in Canada.[2]

As the example shows, currency values fluctuate because of economic and political stability, inflation and interest rates, and economic growth expectations relative to other nations. Other factors include the employment outlook, trade balance, and central bank actions. Although many factors affect currency value and their demand, we focus primarily on the effects of interest rates and inflation in this chapter.

### Exchange Rates

An **exchange rate** is the price of one country's currency expressed in terms of another country's currency. In practice, almost all trading of currencies worldwide takes place in terms of the U.S. dollar.

Figure 32.1A reproduces exchange rate quotations. The first section represents major currencies. The first part of this section is labelled "per US$" and gives the amount of foreign currency it takes to buy one U.S. dollar. For example, the Canadian dollar spot rate is quoted at 1.0747, which means that you could buy one U.S. dollar today with 1.0747 Canadian dollars.[3] The second part under major currencies is labelled "per CDN$"[4] and gives the amount of foreign currency it takes to buy one

---

[1] "Loonie Closes above U.S. Parity," Thestar.com, *Toronto Star*, January 29, 2008, thestar.com/business/2008/01/29/loonie_closes_above_us_parity.html.

[2] David Friend, "Canadian Dollar Drops Half a Cent after Bank of Canada Rate Decision," CTVNews, January 21, 2014, ctvnews.ca/business/canadian-dollar-drops-half-a-cent-after-bank-of-canada-rate-decision-1.1648644.

[3] The spot rate is for immediate trading. Forward rates are for future transactions and are discussed in detail later. When we write *today*, we refer to the date the rates were quoted in June 2014.

[4] The symbols CDN$ and CAD are commonly used to represent Canadian dollars in various sources. For this chapter, we use them interchangeably.

Canadian dollar. For example, the U.S. dollar spot rate is quoted here at 0.93049, so you could get 0.93049 U.S. dollars for one Canadian dollar. Naturally, this second exchange rate is just the reciprocal of the first one, $1/1.0747 = 0.93049$.

Figure 32.1B shows cross rates for major currencies: U.S. and Canadian dollars, European euros, Japanese yen, and U.K. pounds. Notice that each of the cross rates *under* the diagonal has a counterpart *above* the diagonal that is symmetrical and equals the reciprocal. For example, in the fourth column it is shown that one U.K. pound equals $1.8205 Canadian (fourth column, sixth row). By looking at its counterpart in the sixth column, we realize that one Canadian dollar equals 0.5492 U.K. pounds (sixth column, eighth row), which is the reciprocal of its counterpart, $1/1.8205 = 0.5492$.

There are two reasons for quoting all foreign currencies in terms of the U.S. dollar. First, it reduces the number of possible cross-currency quotes. For example, with five major currencies, there would potentially be 10 exchange rates instead of just four.[5] Second, it makes **triangular arbitrage** more difficult. If all currencies were traded against each other, it would make inconsistencies more likely. That is, the exchange rate of the British pound against the Canadian dollar would be compared to the exchange rate between the U.S. dollar and the Canadian dollar. This implies a particular rate between the British pound and the U.S. dollar to prevent triangular arbitrage.

FIGURE 32.1A

### Exchange Rate Quotations

## FOREIGN EXCHANGE

Supplied by Thomson Reuters. Listing indicative of late afternoon rates. Charts based on close.

| Per US$ | Latest | Previous Day | 4 weeks Ago | Day % change | Week % change | 4 week % change |
|---|---|---|---|---|---|---|
| Canada $ | 1.0747 | 1.0732 | 1.0856 | 0.1% | −1.1% | −1.0% |
| Euro | 0.7351 | 0.7353 | 0.7334 | nil | −0.4% | 0.2% |
| Japan Yen | 101.915 | 101.903 | 101.975 | nil | −0.3% | −0.1% |
| UK Pound | 0.589 | 0.5874 | 0.5948 | 0.3% | −0.1% | −1.0% |
| Swiss Franc | 0.894 | 0.8945 | 0.8966 | −0.1% | −10.1% | −0.3% |
| Australia $ | 1.0683 | 1.0612 | 1.0794 | 0.7% | −0.3% | −1.0% |
| Mexico Peso | 13.0675 | 13.0337 | 12.8588 | 0.3% | −0.3% | 1.6% |
| Hong Kong | 7.7516 | 7.7512 | 7.7528 | nil | nil | 0.0% |
| Singapore $ | 1.2495 | 1.2494 | 1.2563 | nil | −0.3% | −0.5% |
| China Renminbi | 6.2325 | 6.2255 | 6.2475 | 0.1% | 0.1% | −0.2% |
| India Rupee | 60.13 | 60.19 | 58.98 | −0.1% | −0.3% | 1.9% |
| Russia Rouble | 33.837 | 34.098 | 34.415 | −0.8% | −2.9% | −1.7% |
| Brazil Real | 2.2243 | 2.2212 | 2.239 | 0.1% | −1.7% | −0.7% |

| Per CDN$ | Latest | Previous Day | 4 weeks Ago | Day % change | Week % change | 4 week % change |
|---|---|---|---|---|---|---|
| US $ | 0.93049 | 0.93179 | 0.92115 | −0.1% | 1.1% | 1.0% |
| Euro | 0.684 | 0.68515 | 0.67557 | −0.2% | 0.7% | 1.2% |
| Japan Yen | 94.83112 | 94.95248 | 93.93423 | −0.1% | 0.8% | 1.0% |
| UK Pound | 0.54806 | 0.54734 | 0.5479 | 0.1% | 1.0% | 0.0% |
| Swiss Franc | 0.83186 | 0.83349 | 0.8259 | −0.2% | 0.5% | 0.7% |
| Australia $ | 0.99404 | 0.98882 | 0.99429 | 0.5% | 0.8% | 0.0% |
| Mexico Peso | 12.15921 | 12.14471 | 11.84488 | 0.1% | 0.8% | 2.7% |
| Hong Kong | 7.2128 | 7.22251 | 7.14149 | −0.1% | 1.1% | 1.0% |
| Singapore $ | 1.16265 | 1.16344 | 1.15724 | −0.1% | 0.8% | 0.5% |
| China Renminbi | 5.79929 | 5.80088 | 5.75488 | nil | 1.2% | 0.8% |
| India Rupee | 55.9505 | 56.08461 | 54.3294 | −0.2% | 0.8% | 3.0% |
| Russia Rouble | 31.48507 | 31.77227 | 31.70136 | −0.9% | −1.8% | −0.7% |
| Brazil Real | 2.06969 | 2.0697 | 2.06245 | nil | −0.7% | 0.4% |

Quotations are closing rates of June 24, 2014.

Source: Compiled data from www.fx-exchange.com/.

[5] There are four exchange rates instead of five because one exchange rate would involve the exchange rate for a currency with itself. More generally, it might seem there should be 25 exchange rates with five currencies. There are 25 different combinations, but, of these, five involve the exchange rate of a currency for itself. Of the remaining 20, half of them are redundant because they are just the reciprocals of the exchange rate. Of the remaining 10, six can be eliminated by using a common denominator.

FIGURE 32.1B

## Currency Cross Rates

| | Per USD | Per EUR | Per JPY | Per GBP | Per CHF | Per CAD | Per AUD | Per RUB | Per HKD | Per MXN | Per BRL |
|---|---|---|---|---|---|---|---|---|---|---|---|
| BRL Brazilian Real | 2.2097 | 3.0132 | 0.0217 | 3.7493 | 2.4758 | 2.0592 | 2.0740 | 0.0654 | 0.2848 | 0.1696 | 1 |
| MXN Mexican Peso | 13.0240 | 17.7570 | 0.1279 | 22.1040 | 14.5980 | 12.1420 | 12.2290 | 0.3856 | 1.6799 | 1 | 5.8978 |
| HKD Hong Kong Dollar | 7.7517 | 10.5700 | 0.0762 | 13.1610 | 8.6914 | 7.2291 | 7.2810 | 0.2296 | 1 | 0.5952 | 3.5102 |
| RUB Russian | 33.7690 | 46.0490 | 0.3318 | 57.3300 | 37.8580 | 31.4900 | 31.7150 | 1 | 4.3559 | 2.5927 | 15.2900 |
| AUD Australian Dollar | 1.0646 | 1.4515 | 0.0105 | 1.8074 | 1.1936 | 0.9928 | 1 | 0.0315 | 0.1373 | 0.0817 | 0.4820 |
| CAD Canadian Dollar | 1.0722 | 1.4619 | 0.0105 | 1.8205 | 1.2023 | 1 | 1.0074 | 0.0318 | 0.1384 | 0.0823 | 0.4857 |
| CHF Swiss Franc | 0.8918 | 1.2160 | 0.0088 | 1.5143 | 1 | 0.8317 | 0.8377 | 0.0264 | 0.1151 | 0.0685 | 0.4039 |
| GBP British Pound | 0.5889 | 0.8031 | 0.0058 | 1 | 0.6604 | 0.5492 | 0.5531 | 0.0174 | 0.0760 | 0.0452 | 0.2666 |
| JPY Japanese Yen | 101.7800 | 138.7700 | 1 | 172.8100 | 114.1200 | 94.9017 | 95.6020 | 3.0143 | 13.1300 | 7.8144 | 46.0880 |
| EUR Euro | 0.7334 | 1 | 0.0072 | 1.2453 | 0.8223 | 0.6839 | 0.6889 | 0.0217 | 0.0946 | 0.0563 | 0.3321 |
| USD US Dollar | 1 | 1.3634 | 0.0098 | 1.6979 | 1.1212 | 0.9325 | 0.9393 | 0.0296 | 0.1290 | 0.0768 | 0.4528 |

Quotes have been rounded to the fourth decimal for clarity; quotations are trading rates of June 25, 2014.

Source: Bloomberg L.P. Used with permission.

EXAMPLE 32.1

What if the pound traded for €4 in Frankfurt and US$1.60 in London? If the U.S. dollar traded for €2 in Frankfurt, there would be a triangular arbitrage opportunity. Starting with US$1.60, a trader could purchase £1 in London. This pound could then be used to buy €4 in Frankfurt. With the U.S. dollar trading at €2, the €4 could then be traded for US$2 in Frankfurt, as illustrated in Figure 32.2. The net gain from going around this "triangle" would be (in U.S. dollars) $2.00 – $1.60 = $0.40. Imagine what the return would be on an initial US$1 billion purchase.

### FIGURE 32.2

**Triangular Arbitrage**

$1.60 / £

€2 / US$    €4 / £

## Types of Transactions

Three types of trades take place in the foreign exchange market: spot, forward, and swap. **Spot trades** involve an agreement on the exchange rate today for settlement in two days. The rate is called the **spot exchange rate**. **Forward trades** involve an agreement on exchange rates today for settlement in the future. The rate is the **forward exchange rate**. As seen in Figure 32.1C, maturities for forward trades range from one month to five years. A swap is the sale (purchase) of a foreign currency with a simultaneous agreement to repurchase (resell) it some time in the future. The difference between the sale price and the repurchase price is called the **swap rate**.

EXAMPLE 32.2

On October 11, bank *A* pays Canadian dollars to bank *B*'s account at a Toronto bank and *A* receives pounds sterling in its account at a bank in London. On November 11, as agreed on October 11, the transaction is reversed. *A* pays the sterling back to *B*, while *B* pays back the dollars to *A*. This is a swap. In effect, *A* has borrowed pounds sterling while giving up the use of Canadian dollars to *B*.

**FIGURE 32.1C**

**Forward Exchange Rate Quotations**

## FORWARD EXCHANGE

| Per US$ | 1 month | 3 months | 6 months | 1 year | 2 years | 3 years | 4 years | 5 years |
|---|---|---|---|---|---|---|---|---|
| C$ | 1.0753 | 1.0769 | 1.0794 | 1.0842 | 1.0906 | 1.0915 | 1.0891 | 1.0869 |
| Euro* | 0.7349 | 0.7348 | 0.7344 | 0.7335 | 0.7277 | 0.7161 | 0.702 | 0.6887 |
| Yen | 101.9495 | 101.911 | 101.8449 | 101.64 | 100.5045 | 98.3086 | 95.4422 | 92.3128 |
| £* | 0.5889 | 0.5892 | 0.5898 | 0.5918 | 0.5967 | 0.5994 | 0.5998 | 0.5989 |

| Per CDN$ | 1 month | 3 months | 6 months | 1 year | 2 years | 3 years | 4 years | 5 years |
|---|---|---|---|---|---|---|---|---|
| US$ | 0.9300 | 0.9286 | 0.9264 | 0.9223 | 0.9169 | 0.9162 | 0.9182 | 0.9200 |
| Euro* | 0.6834 | 0.6822 | 0.6804 | 0.6765 | 0.6674 | 0.6561 | 0.6446 | 0.6334 |
| Yen | 94.812 | 94.626 | 94.35 | 93.74 | 92.156 | 90.066 | 87.6272 | 84.933 |
| £* | 0.5476 | 0.5471 | 0.5464 | 0.5458 | 0.5472 | 0.5493 | 0.5507 | 0.5511 |

Quotations are closing rates of June 24, 2014.

Source: Bloomberg L.P. Used with permission.

**CONCEPT QUESTION**

- What are the three kinds of foreign exchange transactions?

## 32.3 THE LAW OF ONE PRICE AND PURCHASING POWER PARITY

What determines the level of the spot exchange rate? One answer is the **law of one price (LOP)**. The LOP says that a commodity will cost the same regardless of the country in which it is purchased.[6] More formally, let $S_£(t)$ be the spot exchange rate, that is, the number of Canadian dollars needed to purchase a British pound at time $t$. Let $P^{CDN}(t)$ and $P^{UK}(t)$ be the current Canadian and British prices of a particular commodity, say, apples. The LOP says that

$$P^{CDN}(t) = S_£(t)P^{UK}(t)$$

for apples.

The rationale behind the LOP is similar to that of triangular arbitrage. If the LOP did not hold, arbitrage would be possible by moving apples from one country to another. For example, suppose that apples in Toronto are selling for $4 per bushel, while in London the price is £3 per bushel. Then the LOP implies that

$$\$4 = S_£(t) \times \£3$$

and

$$S_£(t) = \$1.33/\£$$

That is, the spot exchange rate implied by the LOP is $1.33 per pound.

Figure 32.1B shows that the actual exchange rate is $1.8205 per pound. Starting with $4, a trader could buy a bushel of apples in Toronto, ship it to London, and sell it there for £3. The pounds sterling could then be converted into dollars at the exchange rate, $1.8205/£, yielding a total of $5.4615 for a gain of $1.4615 (or $5.4615 − $4).

The rationale of the LOP is that if the exchange rate is not $1.33/£ but is instead $1.8205/£, then forces would be set in motion to change the rate and/or the price of apples. In our example, tonnes of apples would be flying from Toronto to London. Thus,

---

[6] In practice, the LOP may not always be applicable. The main flaw is that it is not easy to move commodities from one country to another. In some cases, it is illegal to do so. Such restrictions on the movement of some commodities can have an impact on the price from one country or region to the next.

demand for apples in Toronto would raise the dollar price for apples there, and the supply in London would lower the pound sterling price. The apple traders converting pounds sterling into dollars, that is, supplying pounds sterling and demanding Canadian dollars, would also put pressure on the exchange rate to drop from $1.8205/£.

As you can see, for the LOP to be strictly true, three assumptions are needed:

1. The transaction costs of trading apples—shipping, insurance, wastage, and so on—must be zero.
2. No barriers to trading apples, such as tariffs or taxes, can exist.
3. Finally, an apple in Toronto must be identical to an apple in London. It won't do for you to send red apples to London if Londoners eat only green apples.

Given the reality that transaction costs are not zero and that the other conditions are rarely met exactly, the LOP is really applicable only to traded goods, and then only to very uniform ones. The LOP does not imply that a Mercedes costs the same as a Ford or that a nuclear power plant in France costs the same as one in Ontario. In the case of the cars, they are not identical. In the case of the power plants, even if they were identical, they are expensive and very difficult to ship.

Because consumers purchase many goods, economists refer to **purchasing power parity (PPP)**, the idea that the exchange rate adjusts so that a *market basket* of goods costs the same regardless of the country in which it is purchased. In addition, a relative version of PPP has evolved. **Relative purchasing power parity (RPPP)** says that the rate of change in the price level of commodities in one country relative to the rate of change in the price level in another determines the rate of change of the exchange rate between the two countries. Formally,

$$\frac{P^{\text{CDN}}(t+1)}{P^{\text{CDN}}(t)} = \frac{S_{\pounds}(t+1)}{S_{\pounds}(t)} \times \frac{P^{\text{UK}}(t+1)}{P^{\text{UK}}(t)}$$

$$1 + \frac{\text{Canadian}}{\text{inflation rate}} = \left(1 + \frac{\text{Change in foreign}}{\text{exchange rate}}\right) \times \left(1 + \frac{\text{British}}{\text{inflation rate}}\right)$$

This states that the rate of inflation in Canada relative to that in the United Kingdom determines the rate of change in the value of the dollar relative to that of the pound during the interval $t$ to $t + 1$. It is common to write $\Pi_{\text{CDN}}$ as the rate of inflation in Canada. $1 + \Pi_{\text{CDN}}$ is equal to $P^{\text{CDN}}(t+1)/P^{\text{CDN}}(t)$. Similarly, $\Pi_{\text{UK}}$ is the rate of inflation in the United Kingdom. $1 + \Pi_{\text{UK}}$ is equal to $P^{\text{UK}}(t+1)/P^{\text{UK}}(t)$.

The above equation can be rearranged as

$$\frac{1 + \Pi_{\text{CDN}}}{1 + \Pi_{\text{UK}}} = \frac{S_{\pounds}(t+1)}{S_{\pounds}(t)} \tag{32.1}$$

We can rewrite this in an approximate form as

$$\Pi_{\text{CDN}} \approx \Pi_{\text{UK}} + \frac{\dot{S}_{\pounds}}{S_{\pounds}}$$

where $\dot{S}_{\pounds}/S_{\pounds}$ now stands for the rate of change in the dollars-per-pound exchange rate.

As an example, suppose that inflation in the European Union during the year is equal to 4 percent and inflation in Canada is equal to 10 percent. Then, according to RPPP, the price of the euro in terms of the Canadian dollar should rise; that is, the Canadian dollar declines in value in terms of the euro. Using our approximation, the dollars-per-euro exchange rate should rise by

$$\frac{\dot{S}_{\euro}}{S_{\euro}} \approx \Pi_{\text{CDN}} - \Pi_{\euro}$$
$$= 10\% - 4\%$$
$$= 6\%$$

where $\dot{S}_\epsilon/S_\epsilon$ stands for the rate of change in the dollars-per-euro exchange rate. That is, if the euro is worth \$0.70 at the beginning of the period, it should be worth approximately \$0.742 (or \$0.70 × 1.06) at the end of the period.

RPPP says that the change in the ratio of domestic commodity prices of two countries must be matched in the exchange rate. This version of the LOP suggests that to estimate changes in the spot rate of exchange, it is necessary to estimate the differences in relative inflation rates. In other words, we can express our formula in expectational terms as

$$E\left(\frac{\dot{S}_\epsilon}{S_\epsilon}\right) = E(\Pi_{CDN}) - E(\Pi_\epsilon)$$

If we expect the Canadian inflation rate to exceed the EU inflation rate, we should expect the dollar price of euros to rise, which is the same as saying that the dollar is expected to fall against the euro.

The more exact relationship of equation (32.1) can be expressed in expectational terms as

$$\frac{E(1 + \Pi_{CDN})}{E(1 + \Pi_{UK})} - \frac{E[S_{\pounds}(t + 1)]}{S_{\pounds}(t)} \qquad (32.2)$$

**CONCEPT QUESTIONS**
- What is the LOP? What is PPP?
- What is the relationship between inflation and exchange rate movements?

## 32.4   INTEREST RATES AND EXCHANGE RATES

The forward exchange rate and the spot exchange rate are tied together by the same sort of arbitrage that underlies the LOP. To explain the link, we begin with some useful terminology. If forward exchange rates are greater than the spot exchange rate in a particular currency, the forward foreign currency is said to be at a *premium*. (This implies that the domestic currency is at a discount.) If the values of forward exchange rates are less than the spot exchange rate, the forward rate on foreign currency is at a discount.

For example, in Figure 32.1A, the spot U.S. dollar rate is US\$0.93049 = CDN\$1, and the one-month forward U.S. dollar rate is US\$0.9300 = CDN\$1 in Figure 32.1C. Because less in U.S. dollars is needed to buy a Canadian dollar at the forward rate than is needed to buy at the spot rate, the U.S. dollar is less valuable in the spot market than in the forward market. This means that the one-month forward U.S. dollar is at a premium. Of course, the forward standing of the U.S. dollar must be opposite that of the Canadian dollar. In this example, the Canadian dollar is at a discount because its forward value is less than the spot value. Forward exchange is quoted in terms of the premium or discount that is to be added onto the spot rate.

Whether forward rates are at a premium or a discount when compared to a domestic currency depends on the relative interest rates in the foreign and domestic currency markets. The **interest rate parity theorem** states that if interest rates are higher domestically than in a particular foreign country, the foreign country's currency will be selling at a premium in the forward market, and if interest rates are lower domestically, the foreign currency will be selling at a discount in the forward market.

We need some notation to develop the interest rate parity theorem. Let $S(0)$ be the current domestic currency price of spot foreign exchange (current time is denoted by 0). If the domestic currency is the Canadian dollar and the foreign currency is the euro, we might observe $S(0) = \$1.4619/\epsilon$, as shown in Figure 32.1B. $S(0)$ is in direct terms. Let $F(0, 1)$ be the current domestic currency price of forward exchange for a contract that matures in six months. Thus, the contract is for forward exchange six months hence. Let $i$ and $i^*$ be the yearly rates of interest paid on Eurocurrency deposits denominated in the domestic ($i$) and foreign ($i^*$) currencies, respectively. Of course, the maturity of the deposits can be chosen to coincide with the maturity of the forward contract.

Now consider a trader who has access to the interbank market in foreign exchange and Eurocurrency deposits. Suppose the trader has some dollars to invest for six months. The trader can make a dollar loan or a euro loan. The annual interest rate is 6.4 percent in euros and 7.5 percent in dollars. Which is better?

### The Dollar Investment

Given an annual interest rate of 7.5 percent, the six-month rate of interest is 3.75 percent, assuming semiannual compounding. If the trader invests $1 million now, she will get $1 million $\times$ 1.0375 = $1,037,500 million at the end of six months. Here is an illustration:

| Time 0 | Time 1 |
|---|---|
| Lend 1 unit of dollars | Obtain $1 + i \times (1/2)$ units of domestic currency |
| $1,000,000 | $1,000,000 $\times$ (1 + 0.0375) = $1,037,500 |

### The Euro Investment

From Figure 32.1B, the current spot rate is $1.4619/€. This means the trader can currently obtain $1 million/1.4619 = €684,041. The rate of interest on one-year euro loans is 6.4 percent. For six months, the interest rate is 0.064/2 = 0.032. Thus, at the end of six months the trader will obtain €684,041 $\times$ 1.032 = €705,930. Of course, if the trader wants dollars at the end of the month, she must convert the euro back into dollars. The trader can fix the exchange rate for six-month conversion. Figure 32.1C shows that the six-month forward rate is €0.6804/CDN$1, which is equivalent to CDN$1.4697/€ (CDN$1/€0.6804). Then the trader can sell euros forward. This will ensure that the trader gets €705,930 $\times$ 1.4697 = $1,037,505 at the end of the month.[7] The general relationships are set forth here:

| Time 0 | Time 1 |
|---|---|
| Purchase 1 unit $[1/S(0)]$ of foreign exchange. | Deposit matures and pays $[1/S(0)] \times [1 + i \times (1/2)]$ units of foreign exchange: €684,041 $\times$ 1.032 = €705,930 |

| Time 0 | Time 1 |
|---|---|
| Sell forward $[1/S(0)] \times [1 + i^* \times (1/2)]$ units of forward exchange at the forward rate $F(0, 1)$. | Deliver foreign exchange in fulfillment of forward contract, receiving $[1/S(0)] \times [1 + i^* \times (1/2)] \times [F(0, 1)]$ = €684,041 $\times$ 1.032 $\times$ 1.4697 = $1,037,505 |

In our example, the investments earned the same rate of return and $1 + i \times (1/2) = [1/S(0)] \times [1 + i^* \times (1/2)] \times [F(0, 1)]$, with the small difference due to rounding. In competitive financial markets, this must be true for risk-free investments. When the trader makes the euro loan, the interest rate is lower. But the return is the same because the euro must be sold forward at a higher price than it can be exchanged for initially. If the domestic interest rate were different from the covered foreign interest rate, the trader would have arbitrage opportunities.

To summarize, to prevent arbitrage possibilities from existing, we must have equality of the Canadian interest rate and covered foreign interest rates:

---

[7] Due to rounding, we are off by $5.

$$1 + i = \frac{1}{S(0)} \times (1 + i^*) \times F(0, 1)$$

or

$$\frac{1 + i}{1 + i^*} = \frac{F(0, 1)}{S(0)} \tag{32.3}$$

The last equation is the famous interest rate parity theorem. It relates the forward exchange rate and the spot exchange rate to interest rate differentials. Notice that if $i > i^*$, the spot rate (expressed as dollars per unit of foreign currency) will be less than the forward rate.

EXAMPLE **32.3**

Figure 32.1B shows the spot rate $1.4619/€ and Figure 32.1C shows the one-year forward rate $F(0, 1) = \$1.4782/€$ ($1/€0.6765). Let the one-year rates on euro-Canadian dollar deposits and euro deposits be, respectively, $i = 6.00\%$ and $i^* = 5.05\%$. Then, comparing the return on domestic borrowing with the return on covered foreign lending,

$$\$(1 + 0.06) = \$1.06$$
$$\$[1/S(0)] \times (1 + i^*) \times F(0, 1) = \$(1/1\ 4619 \times 1.0505) \times (1.4782)$$
$$= \$1.06$$

For each dollar borrowed domestically, a trader must repay $1.06. The return from using the $1.00 to buy spot foreign exchange, placing the deposit at the foreign rate of interest, and selling the total return forward is $1.06. These two amounts are equal, so it is not worth anyone's time to try to exploit the difference. In this case, interest parity can be said to hold.

## The Forward Discount and Expected Spot Rates

A close connection exists between forward exchange rates and expected spot rates. A trader's buy and sell decisions in today's forward market are based on the trader's market expectation of the future spot rate. In fact, if traders were completely indifferent to risk, the forward rate of exchange would depend solely on expectations about the future spot rate. For example, the one-year forward rate on the euro is $1.4782/€ [that is, $F(0, 1) = \$1.4782/€$]. This must mean that traders expect the spot rate to be $1.4782/€ in one year [$E(S(1)) = \$1.4782/€$]. If they thought it would be higher, there would be an arbitrage opportunity. Traders would buy euros forward at the low price and sell euros one year later at the expected higher price. This implies that the forward rate of exchange is equal to the expected spot, or (in general terms)

$$F(0, 1) = E[S(1)]$$

and

$$\frac{F(0, 1)}{S(0)} = \frac{E[S(1)]}{S(0)} \tag{32.4}$$

An equilibrium is achieved only when the forward discount (or premium) equals the expected change in the spot exchange rate.

## Exchange Rate Risk

Exchange rate risk is the natural consequence of international operations in a world where foreign currency values move up and down. International firms usually enter into some contracts that require payments in different currencies. For example, suppose that the treasurer of an international firm knows that one month from today, the firm must pay £2 million for goods it will receive in England. The current exchange rate, shown in Figure 32.1A, is £0.54806/CDN$, which is equivalent to $1.8246/£ ($1/£0.54806), and if that rate prevails in one month, the dollar cost of the goods to the firm will be $1.8246/£ × £2 million = $3.65 million. The treasurer in this case is obliged to pay pounds in one month. (Alternatively, we say that he is *short* in pounds.) A net short or long position of this type can be very risky. If, during the month, the pound rises to $2/£, the treasurer must pay $2/£ × £2 million = $4 million, an extra $350,000.

This is the essence of foreign exchange risk. The treasurer may want to hedge his position. When forward markets exist, the most convenient means of hedging is the purchase or sale of forward contracts. In this example, the treasurer may want to consider buying £2 million one month forward. If the one-month forward rate quoted today is also $1.8246/£, the treasurer will fulfill the contract by exchanging $3.65 million for £2 million in one month. The £2 million he receives from the contract can then be used to pay for the goods. By hedging today, he fixes the outflow one month from now to exactly $3.65 million.

Should the treasurer hedge or speculate? Building on our discussion in Chapter 26, we can identify two reasons the treasurer should usually hedge:

1. In an efficient foreign exchange market, speculation is a zero-NPV activity. Unless the treasurer has special information, nothing will be gained from foreign exchange speculation.

2. The costs of hedging are not large. The treasurer can use forward contracts to hedge, and if the forward rate is equal to the expected spot, the costs of hedging are negligible. Of course, there are ways to hedge foreign exchange risk other than with forward contracts. For example, the treasurer can borrow dollars, buy pounds sterling in the spot market today, and lend them for one month in London. By the interest rate parity theorem, this will be the same as buying the pounds sterling forward.

**Which Firms Hedge Exchange Rate Risk?**   Not all firms with exchange rate risk exposure hedge. A recent survey found that 89 percent of large firms with annual revenues over US$5 billion hedge their currency risks but that this percentage drops dramatically for smaller firms. An older survey by Géczy, Minton, and Schrand[8] finds that larger firms with greater growth opportunities are more likely to use currency derivatives to hedge exchange rate risk than smaller firms with fewer investment opportunities. This suggests that some firms hedge to make sure that they have enough cash on hand to finance their growth opportunities. In addition, firms with greater growth opportunities will tend to have higher indirect bankruptcy costs. For these firms, hedging exchange rate risk will reduce indirect bankruptcy costs and increase the probability that they will not default on their debt obligations.

The fact that larger firms are more likely to use hedging techniques suggests that the costs of hedging are not insignificant. There may be fixed costs of establishing a hedging operation, in which case, economies of scale may explain why smaller firms hedge less than larger firms.

## More Advanced Short-Term Hedges

Currency swaps, currency options, and other financially engineered products are taking considerable business away from the forward exchange market.[9] As introduced in Chapter 26, a **currency swap** is an arrangement among a borrower, a second borrower (called a *counterparty*), and a bank. The borrower and the counterparty each raise funds in a different currency and then swap liabilities. The bank guarantees the borrower's

---

[8] M. Waters, "Real-World Impact of Derivatives Reforms," *Treasury & Risk* (November 21, 2013), treasuryandrisk.com/2013/11/21/real-world-impact-of-derivatives-reforms; and C. Géczy, B. Minton, and C. Schrand, "Why Firms Use Currency Derivatives," *Journal of Finance* (September 1997). See also D. R. Nance, C. Smith, Jr., and C. W. Smithson, "On the Determinants of Corporate Hedging," *Journal of Finance* (March 1993).

[9] Our discussion of currency swaps in practice draws on B. Critchley, "Explosion of New Products Cuts Foreign Currency Risk," *The Financial Post* (September 14, 1987).

and counterparty's credit as in a banker's acceptance. The result is that the borrower obtains funds in the desired currency at a lower rate than for direct borrowing.

For example, in 1986, the federal government of Canada made an ¥80 billion bond issue and swapped part of it into U.S. dollars. The interest rate was six-month LIBOR, and the ending liability was in U.S. dollars, not yen. The interest cost turned out to be 54 basis points below the cost of direct borrowing in the United States.

Currency options are similar to options on stock (discussed in Chapter 23) except the exercise price is an exchange rate. They are exchange traded in the United States with exercise prices in various currencies, including the Canadian dollar. Currency options can be exercised at any time prior to maturity. In the jargon of options, they are **American options**. A call option on the Canadian dollar gives the holder the right, but not the obligation, to buy Canadian dollars at a fixed exercise price in U.S. dollars. The call increases in value as the Canadian dollar exchange rate in U.S. dollars. A put option allows the holder to sell Canadian dollars at the exercise price. A put becomes more valuable when the Canadian dollar declines against the U.S. dollar.

The basic idea behind hedging with options is to take an options position opposite to the cash position. For this reason, hedge analysis starts by looking at the unhedged position of the business. For example, suppose an exporter expects to collect receivables totalling US$1 million in 30 days. Suppose the present Canadian dollar exchange rate is US$0.90. If the rate remains at 90 cents, the exporter will receive US$1 million/0.90 = CDN$1,111,111 after 30 days. The exporter is at risk if the exchange rate rises so that the US$1 million will buy fewer Canadian dollars. For example, if the exchange rate rises to 0.92, the exporter will receive only US$1 million/0.92 = CDN$1,086,957. The loss of CDN$24,154 comes out of profits.

Since the exporter loses if the exchange rate rises, buying call options is an appropriate hedge. Calls on the Canadian dollar will increase in value if the exchange rate rises. The profit on the calls will help offset the loss on exchange. To implement this strategy, the exporter will likely seek expert advice on how many calls to buy.

## The Hedging Decision in Practice

Hedging the exchange rate for the U.S. dollar is important for the Toronto Blue Jays.[10] When they won the World Series for the second consecutive year in 1993, the Blue Jays had the highest payroll in major league baseball—US$48.3 million. Players' contracts are negotiated in U.S. dollars and paid over the baseball season. The team receives some revenues in U.S. dollars from television contracts and gate receipts for games on the road, but the majority of its income—receipts at the Rogers Centre and Canadian television contracts—is in Canadian dollars. As a result, the team is exposed to currency losses if the Canadian dollar falls. According to one estimate, the Jays lose CDN$800,000 for every one-cent drop in the Canadian dollar.

Blue Jays management has used both forward contracts and currency options to hedge its exposure. At the start of the baseball season of 1994, management was tracking the results of its earlier decision not to hedge. As the Canadian dollar fell from around US 80 cents in 1993 to under 73 cents, locking in the exchange rate looked more and more attractive. As the risk of a players' strike loomed large, the ideal hedge would have been with options, because options would have allowed the Jays to get out of the hedge when payroll obligations ceased.

**CONCEPT QUESTIONS**

- What is the interest rate parity theorem?
- Why is the forward rate related to the expected future spot rate?
- How can one offset foreign exchange risk through a transaction in the forward markets?
- How can firms hedge using currency swaps or currency options?

---

[10] Our discussion is based on L. Millson, "Jays Fortunes Ride on Shaky Canuck Buck," *The Globe and Mail* (April 8, 1994), p. A12.

## 32.5 INTERNATIONAL CAPITAL BUDGETING

Kihlstrom Equipment, a Canadian-based international company, is evaluating an investment in France. Kihlstrom's exports of drill bits have increased to such an extent that it is considering operating a plant there. The project will cost €1.8 million; it is expected to produce cash flows of €1.2 million a year for the next three years. The current spot exchange rate for euros is $S(0) = €0.684/CDN\$$ from Figure 32.1A, which is equivalent to $\$1.462/€$ ($\$1/€0.684$). How should Kihlstrom calculate the NPV of the projects in Canadian dollars?

Although the investment is made abroad, this does not alter Kihlstrom's NPV criterion. The firm must identify incremental cash flows and discount them at the appropriate cost of capital. After making the required discounted cash flow (DCF) calculations, Kihlstrom should undertake projects with positive NPVs. However, two major factors complicate such international NPV calculations: foreign exchange conversion and repatriation of funds.

### Foreign Exchange Conversion

The simplest way for Kihlstrom to calculate the NPV of the investment is to convert all euro cash flows to Canadian dollars. This involves a three-step process:

Step 1. Estimate future cash flows in euros.
Step 2. Convert to Canadian dollars at the predicted exchange rate.
Step 3. Calculate NPV using the cost of capital in Canadian dollars.

In Table 32.1 we apply these three steps to Kihlstrom's French investment. Notice here that Kihlstrom's euro cash flows were converted to dollars by multiplying the foreign cash flows by the predicted foreign exchange rate.

**TABLE 32.1**

**Net Present Value of Foreign Cash Flows: Kihlstrom Equipment**

| | End of year | | | |
|---|---|---|---|---|
| | 0 | 1 | 2 | 3 |
| Incremental cash flows (CF$_€$)<br>(in € millions) | −1.8 | 1.2 | 1.2 | 1.2 |
| Foreign exchange rate ($/€)* | 1.462 | 1.4782 | 1.4984 | 1.5242 |
| Foreign exchange rate conversion | 1.8 × 1.462 | 1.2 × 1.4782 | 1.2 × 1.4984 | 1.2 × 1.5242 |
| Incremental cash flows (in $ millions) | −2.6316 | 1.7738 | 1.7981 | 1.8290 |

* Figure 32.1A gives the rates as (€/$). To get to ($/€) we take the inverse:

$T_0 = \$1/€0.684$, $T_1 = \$1/€0.6765$, $T_2 = \$1/€0.6674$, $T_3 = \$1/€0.6561$

NPV at 15% = $1.4731 million.

How might Kihlstrom predict future exchange rates? Kihlstrom could calculate NPV using the foreign exchange market's implicit predictions—the forward rates. Finally, the NPV of the project is computed:

$$NPV = \sum_{t=0}^{3} \frac{CF_€(t) \times E[S_€(t)]}{(1 + r^*)^t}$$

where $CF_€(t)$ refers to the euros forecast to be received in each of the next three years. The discount rate we use is Kihlstrom's Canadian cost of capital. We do not use the Canadian risk-free rate because Kihlstrom's project is risky; a risk-adjusted discount rate must be used. Because the NPV at 15 percent is $1,473,100, Kihlstrom should invest in a subsidiary in France.

In this example, we used the foreign exchange market's implicit forecast as contained in the forward exchange rates in Figure 32.1C. Why not use management's own forecast of foreign exchange rates in the calculations? Suppose that the financial management of Kihlstrom feels optimistic about the euro. If its forecasts are sufficiently pessimistic and they are used, Kihlstrom's investment in a French subsidiary will generate a negative NPV. But, in general, it is a good idea to separate the economic prospects of an investment from the foreign exchange prospects, and it is unwise to use the latter projections in the NPV calculation. If Kihlstrom wishes to speculate on an increase in the euro relative to the Canadian dollar, the best way to do this is to buy euros in the forward foreign exchange market. By using the forward exchange rates implicit in the domestic and foreign interest rates, the firm is using the actual dollar flows that it could, in principle, lock in today by borrowing in the foreign currency. This makes the foreign cash flows equivalent to domestic cash flows.

## Unremitted Cash Flows

The previous example assumed that all after-tax cash flows from the foreign investment were remitted to the parent firm. The remittance decision is similar to the dividend decision for a purely domestic firm. Substantial differences can exist between the cash flows of a project and the amount that is actually remitted to the parent firm. Of course, the NPV of a project will not be changed by deferred remittance if the unremitted cash flows are reinvested at a rate of return equal (as adjusted for exchange rates) to the domestic cost of capital.

A foreign subsidiary can remit funds to a parent in many ways, including the following:

1. Dividends.
2. Management fees for central services.
3. Royalties on the use of trade names and patents.

International firms must pay special attention to remittance for two reasons. First, there may be present and future exchange controls. Many governments are sensitive to the charge of being exploited by foreign firms. Therefore, governments are tempted to limit the ability of international firms to remit cash flows. Funds that cannot be remitted are sometimes said to be blocked.

Another reason is taxes. It is always necessary to determine what taxes must be paid on profits generated in a foreign country. International firms must usually pay foreign taxes on their foreign profits. The total taxes paid by an international firm may be a function of the time of remittance. For example, Kihlstrom's French subsidiary would need to pay taxes in France on the profits it earns in France. Kihlstrom will also pay taxes on dividends it remits to Canada. In most cases, Kihlstrom can offset the payment of foreign taxes against the Canadian tax liability. Thus, if the French corporate income tax is 40 percent, Kihlstrom will not be liable for additional Canadian taxes.

## The Cost of Capital for International Firms

An important question for firms with international investments is whether the required return for international projects should be different from that of similar domestic projects.

**Lower Cost of Capital from International Firm Diversification**    In Chapter 30, we expressed some skepticism concerning the benefits of diversification. We can make a stronger case for diversification in international firms than for purely domestic firms. Suppose barriers prevented shareholders in Canada from holding foreign securities; the financial markets of different countries would be segmented. Further suppose that Canadian firms were not subject to the same barriers. In such a case, a firm engaging in international investing could provide indirect diversification for

Canadian shareholders that they could not achieve by investing within Canada. This could lead to the lowering of the risk premium on international projects. In general, if the costs of investing abroad are lower for a firm than for its shareholders, there is an advantage to international diversification by firms, and this advantage will be reflected in a lower risk-adjusted discount rate.

Alternatively, if there were no barriers to international investing for shareholders, shareholders could obtain the benefit of international diversification for themselves by buying foreign securities. In this case, the project cost of capital for a firm in Canada would not depend on whether the project was in Canada or in a foreign country. In practice, holding foreign securities involves substantial expenses. These expenses include taxes, the costs of obtaining information, and trading costs. This implies that although Canadian investors are free to hold foreign securities, they will not be perfectly internationally diversified.

Financial engineering is aiding investors in avoiding some of these costs. As a result, as investors diversify globally, the cost of capital advantage to firms will likely decline.

An *index participation* (*IP*) is a current example of a financially engineered vehicle for international diversification.[11] An IP on the Standard & Poor's 500 Index, for example, gives an investor an asset that will track this well-known U.S. market index. IPs are highly liquid, thus reducing trading costs. Information costs are also reduced since the holder need not research each of the 500 individual stocks that make up the index.

International diversification for Canadian investors was made easier by the lowering of an important barrier. In 2001, the maximum allowable foreign holding for pension funds and RRSPs was raised to 30 percent. Increased demand fuelled the development of global mutual funds and related new products to exploit this opportunity.

**Lower Cost of Capital from International Shareholder Diversification**    Recall our discussion of the capital asset pricing model (CAPM) and the market portfolio. Consider the Canadian stock market and a Canadian investor who is not internationally diversified but, instead, is invested only in Canadian stocks. From our previous discussion of diversification, we know this investor would be bearing more risk than if she were able to diversify in the stocks of different countries. Now imagine she can invest in many foreign stocks by diversifying internationally. She should be able to reduce the variance (or standard deviation) of her portfolio significantly.

For this investor, the market risk premium will be lower than for investors who cannot diversify internationally. In internationally integrated markets, investors with internationally diversified portfolios will measure the risk of an individual stock in terms of a world-market portfolio and global betas. Therefore, the cost of capital of a particular firm will be in terms of a global CAPM, such as

$$E(R_I) = r_F + B_G \left[ E(R_G) - r_F \right]$$

where $R_I$ is the required return on a stock when markets are global, $r_F$ is the risk-free rate, $B_G$ is the global beta, and $R_G$ is the return on the world-market portfolio. A firm with internationally diversified investors will have a cost of capital with a lower market risk premium [i.e., $E(R_G) - r_F$] and a lower global beta when compared to a firm with investors that cannot diversify internationally.

Solnik has presented evidence that suggests that international diversification significantly reduces risk for shareholders.[12] He shows that the variance of an internationally

[11] G. Axford and Y. Lin, "Surprise! Currency Risk Improves International Investment," *Canadian Treasury Management Review*, Royal Bank of Canada (March–April 1990).

[12] B. H. Solnik, "Why Not Diversify Internationally Rather Than Domestically?" *Financial Analysts Journal* (July–August 1974). An estimate of the benefits of international diversification can be found in Georgio DeSantis and Bruno Gerard, "International Asset Pricing and Portfolio Diversification with Time-Varying Risk," *Journal of Finance* (December 1997). They estimate that an internationally diversified portfolio will reduce standard deviation by 20 percent when compared to investing in U.S. stocks only.

diversified portfolio of common stocks is about 33 percent of the variance of individual securities. A diversified portfolio of U.S. stocks will reduce variance by only 50 percent. Table 32.2 shows that a world portfolio has lower risk than a portfolio of stocks within a single country. For example, a citizen of Hong Kong can reduce risk from 12.8 percent to 4.2 percent by investing in a world portfolio. This evidence is consistent with a lower global-market risk premium than is a purely domestic-market risk premium. Global betas will be different than purely domestic betas. Stulz has argued that the preceding claim for why internationalization reduces the cost of capital doesn't capture the complete picture. He agrees that the global-market risk premium is likely to be substantially lower than the risk premium for an isolated country. In addition, he argues that global investing is likely to improve corporate governance and reduce agency costs. Firms in countries with less-developed financial markets will need to improve their governance so that they can raise capital in well-developed capital markets such as the United States and Canada. Foreign firms raising capital in the United States or Canada must appeal to more sophisticated investors and better market architectures with superior monitoring abilities.[13] Table 32.2 also shows that the systematic risk of foreign stock investment can be very low, as is the case in Austria, or very high, as is the case in Hong Kong. The United States and Canada have betas very close to unity because the United States is an economic colossus and Canada is closely integrated with it.[14]

**TABLE 32.2**

**Risk Measures for Foreign-Market Portfolios**

|  | Beta | Monthly standard deviation (%) |
|---|---|---|
| Hong Kong | 2.08 | 12.8% |
| Japan | 1.42 | 6.1 |
| Sweden | 0.73 | 6.2 |
| Norway | 0.57 | 5.3 |
| Belgium | 1.06 | 6.0 |
| Netherlands | 1.01 | 5.6 |
| United Kingdom | 1.38 | 7.9 |
| Denmark | 0.49 | 5.5 |
| France | 0.69 | 7.4 |
| Austria | 0.19 | 5.4 |
| Germany | 0.70 | 6.0 |
| Switzerland | 0.83 | 5.7 |
| Australia | 1.39 | 8.2 |
| Canada | 1.04 | 5.9 |
| United States | 0.97 | 4.7 |
| World | 1.00 | 4.2 |

Source: Campbell R. Harvey, "The World Price of Covariance Risk," *Journal of Finance* (March 1991), from Table I, p. 122, and Table VI, p. 140.

***CONCEPT*** • **What problems do international projects pose for the use of NPV techniques?**
*QUESTIONS* • **How is international capital budgeting affected by growing investor interest in international diversification?**

---

[13] René M. Stulz, "Globalization, Corporate Finance, and the Cost of Capital," *Journal of Applied Corporate Finance* (Fall 1999). See also Ronald M. Schramm and Henry N. Wang, "Measuring the Cost of Capital in an International CAPM Framework," *Journal of Applied Corporate Finance* (Fall 1999); and Thomas J. O'Brien, "The Global CAPM and a Firm's Cost of Capital in Different Currencies," *Journal of Applied Corporate Finance* (Fall 1999).

[14] The betas in Table 32.2 are calculated using the Morgan Stanley value-weighted index as the world-market portfolio.

# 32.6  INTERNATIONAL FINANCING DECISIONS

An international firm can finance foreign projects in three basic ways:

1. Raise cash in the home country and export it to finance the foreign project.
2. Raise cash by borrowing in the foreign country where the project is located.
3. Borrow in a third country where the cost of debt is lowest.

If a Canadian firm raises cash for its foreign projects by borrowing in Canada, it faces exchange rate risk. If the foreign currency depreciates, the Canadian parent firm will experience an exchange rate loss when the foreign cash flow is remitted to Canada. Of course, the Canadian firm may sell foreign exchange forward to hedge this risk. However, for many currencies, it is difficult to sell forward contracts beyond one year.

Firms may borrow in the country where the foreign project is located. This is the usual way of hedging long-term foreign exchange risk up to the amount borrowed. Any residual (equity) would not be hedged. Thus, if Kihlstrom Equipment wishes to invest €20 million in France, it may attempt to raise much of the cash in France. Toyota took this approach and financed assembly plants in the United States in U.S. dollars during the early 1970s. Volkswagen also built plants in the United States, but financed them in deutsche marks. During the late 1970s, the U.S. dollar dropped against both the yen and the deutsche mark. Toyota was unaffected on the financing side, but Volkswagen faced increased costs, putting it at a disadvantage in selling low-end cars.

Another alternative is to find a country where interest rates are low. However, foreign interest rates may be lower because of lower expected foreign inflation. Thus, financial managers must be careful to look beyond nominal interest rates to real interest rates.

---

**EXAMPLE 32.4**

The two bridges spanning the Halifax Harbour are the responsibility of the Halifax–Dartmouth Bridge Commission.[15] In 1969, the commission, then chaired by A. Murray MacKay, decided to combine $3 million in outstanding debt from building the MacDonald Bridge in the mid-1950s with new borrowings of $39 million for the MacKay Bridge to be built in 1970.

Because Canadian interest rates were high in 1970, the commission decided to borrow in deutsche marks (DM). The exchange rate at the time was around DM3.5 per Canadian dollar, so the $42 million loan translated into approximately DM150 million. Borrowing in deutschemarks left the commission exposed because its revenues (bridge tolls) were in Canadian dollars. In the 1970s and 1980s the deutsche mark strengthened dramatically, reaching DM1.47 per dollar by 1989. At this exchange rate the original DM150 million was worth $102 million—far more than the original cost of the loan. A refinancing in Swiss francs experienced the same problem. Only in 1991 was the debt converted to Canadian dollars and stabilized.

---

## Short-Term and Medium-Term Financing

In raising short-term and medium-term cash, Canadian international firms have a choice between borrowing from a chartered bank at the Canadian rate or borrowing Euro-Canadian (or other Eurocurrency) from a bank outside Canada through the Euro-currency market.

A **Eurodollar** is a dollar deposited in a bank outside the United States. For example, dollar deposits in Paris are Eurodollars. The Eurocurrency markets are the banks

---

[15] Our example is based on J. Myrden, "Bridges of Debt," Halifax Chronicle Herald (January 18, 1992), p. C1.

(**Eurobanks**) that make loans and accept deposits in foreign currencies. Most Eurocurrency trading involves the borrowing and lending of time deposits at Eurobanks. For example, a Eurobank receives a Eurodollar deposit from a domestic U.S. bank. Afterward, the Eurobank will make a dollar-denominated loan to a borrowing party. This is the Eurocurrency market. It is not a retail bank market. The customers are corporations and governments.

One important characteristic of the Eurocurrency market is that loans are made on a floating-rate basis. The interest rates are set at a fixed margin above the LIBOR for the given period and currency involved. For example, if the margin is 0.5 percent for dollar loans and the current LIBOR is 8 percent for dollar loans, the dollar borrower will pay an interest rate of 8.5 percent. This rate is usually changed every six months. The dollar loans will have maturities ranging from 3 to 10 years.

It is obvious that in a perfectly competitive financial market the interest rate on a Eurodollar loan in a Eurocurrency market must be the same as the interest rate in the U.S. loan market. If the interest rate on a Eurodollar loan were higher than that on a domestic-dollar loan, arbitrageurs would borrow in the domestic-dollar market and lend in the Eurodollar market. This type of arbitrage trading would force interest rates to be the same in both dollar markets. However, from time to time there are differences between the Eurodollar loan rate and the domestic loan rate. Risk, government regulations, and taxes explain most of the differences.

## International Bond Markets

The worldwide bond market is made up of approximately US$88 trillion in bonds issued in many currencies. Table 32.3 shows that bonds issued by the United States and the euro area make up nearly 52 percent of the total. The total worldwide bond market can be divided into domestic bonds and international bonds. Domestic bonds are those issued by a firm in its home country. International bonds are those issued by firms in a currency other than the currency of the home country.

**TABLE 32.3**

### Value of the World Bond Market, 2013 (in US$ billions)

| Market | Bonds | |
|---|---|---|
| United States | $8,245 | 9.3% |
| Eurozone | 37,448 | 42.3% |
| China (including Hong Kong, excluding Chinese Taipei) | 769 | 0.9% |
| Japan | 775 | 0.9% |
| United Kingdom | 13,545 | 15.3% |
| Canada | 2,918 | 3.3% |
| Australia | 2,420 | 2.7% |
| India | 89 | 0.1% |
| Brazil | 617 | 0.7% |
| Switzerland | 123 | 0.1% |
| Nordic area (Norway, Sweden, Denmark, and Iceland) | 3,693 | 4.2% |
| Korea | 661 | 0.7% |
| South Africa | 124 | 0.1% |
| Taipei | 39 | 0.0% |
| Singapore | 386 | 0.4% |
| Russia | 483 | 0.5% |
| Mexico | 622 | 0.7% |
| Malaysia | 140 | 0.2% |
| Other | 15,348 | 17.4% |
| Total | 88,446 | 100.0% |

Constructed using data from BIS Quarterly Review 2014, Table 11A International Debt Securities—All Issuers, bis.org/statistics/secstats.htm.

# IN THEIR OWN WORDS

## Merkel: Europe faces historic test in euro crisis

BERLIN—German Chancellor Angela Merkel called for tougher regulation aimed at stock and bond traders, along with a crackdown on government debt to contain the continent's financial crisis, warning that the future of the euro itself was at stake.

As she urged lawmakers to pass Germany's share of a new €750 billion ($1 trillion) eurozone rescue package, Merkel said that defending the shared European currency is "about no more and no less than the preservation of the European idea."

"That is our historic task; if the euro fails, then Europe fails," she told the lower house of parliament on Wednesday. "The euro is in danger; if we do not avert this danger, then the consequences for Europe are incalculable, and then the consequences beyond Europe are incalculable."

Merkel's warning follows Germany's decision Tuesday to ban so-called naked short-selling of eurozone government debt and shares of major financial companies, in an attempt to ward off steep market drops.

Naked short-selling involves traders selling shares or investments they don't hold, in hopes of buying them cheaper later; it's a way of betting a financial asset will fall in price, and profiting from the fall.

Germany's move roiled financial markets, in part because it suggested to traders that policymakers were grasping at straws to stem the crisis of confidence over the ability of European governments to pay off their heavy debt loads amid slow growth.

Fears that some governments may eventually fail to pay all they owe, or will have to cut back so severely that they sink their economies into prolonged recessions, have weighed on stocks and led to discussions that the 11-year-old eurozone will someday break up. The $1 trillion backstop is an attempt to calm those fears by removing the possibility of imminent default, though it does little to address the underlying debt issue.

Politicians have also roundly condemned "speculators" for selling off government bonds, which drives up government borrowing costs and makes it even harder to keep their finances under control. But many analysts say the real problem is simply too much debt.

Still, Europe is showing a newfound resolve to strengthen its regulatory grip. On Tuesday, European Union governments agreed to tighten rules for hedge funds—lightly regulated investment funds that cater to rich and institutional investors, and promise high returns from often complex trading strategies.

Citing the short-selling restriction, Merkel said Germany will act alone in areas that cause "no damage," and said the ban would remain until wider European rules are drawn up.

Germany, Europe's biggest economy, is to contribute at least €123 billion in loan guarantees to the new

---

Trading in international bonds is OTC and takes place in loosely connected individual markets. These individual markets are closely tied to the corresponding domestic bond markets. International bonds can be divided into two main types: foreign bonds and Eurobonds.

**Foreign Bonds**    Foreign bonds are issued by foreign borrowers in a particular country's domestic bond market. They are often nicknamed for the country of issuance. They are denominated in the country's domestic currency. For example, suppose a Swiss watch company issues U.S. dollar–denominated bonds in the United States. These foreign bonds would be called *Yankee bonds*. Like all foreign bonds issued in the United States, Yankee bonds are usually rated by a bond-rating agency such as Standard & Poor's Corporation. Many Yankee bonds are listed on the New York Stock Exchange.

In Canada, bonds issued by foreign companies are termed maple bonds or Canuck bonds. Many foreign bonds are registered. This makes them less attractive to investors having a disdain for tax authorities. For obvious reasons, these traders like the Eurobond market better than the foreign bond market. Registered bonds have an ownership name assigned to the bond's serial number. Most Eurobonds are bearer bonds. Ownership is established by possession of the bond. The transfer of ownership of a registered bond can take place only via legal transfer of the registered name. Transfer agents (for example, banks) are required.

rescue package. Parliament is expected to vote on Friday—just two weeks after approving a separate package for Greece, already unpopular at home.

In Paris, French Finance Minister Christine Lagarde said her country would provide loan guarantees of up to €111 billion, with legislation going to parliament on May 31.

Merkel stressed that aid decisions will need unanimous approval from all involved and that, where credit is from other governments instead of a common European pot of money, "we decide ourselves on every use of the funds."

The head of Germany's central bank, the Bundesbank, called for speedy approval this week of the package to calm markets. Axel Weber told parliament's budget committee that access to rescue funds should only be possible if the financial stability of the whole eurozone is at stake.

While the root cause of the debt crisis was insufficiently competitive countries living above their means, Merkel said that markets poured oil on the fire.

"We are now seeing anew how, through a lack of limits and rules, purely profit-oriented behaviour on the financial markets can be destructive," Merkel added. "It is the task of politicians, parliaments, and governments to intervene, to regulate, in case of doubt to ban, in order to keep the risks controllable."

Merkel renewed a pledge to push for taxation of financial markets—either a financial transaction tax or another form of levy—in Europe and beyond. She also pushed for quick action to put ratings agencies under European supervision and increase transparency on derivatives markets.

The chancellor acknowledged that Berlin faced accusations of being "hesitant or slow" in agreeing to rescue packages for debt-laden European nations but was unapologetic about pushing for them to be made to tackle their budget deficits.

"Europe needs a new culture of stability," she said, with faster and more effective punishment for countries that habitually run excessive deficits.

Those could include withholding European Union structural funds and temporarily withdrawing voting rights from repeat offenders, she said—adding that it was important to draw up procedures for an "orderly state insolvency."

Above all, though, Merkel said that all EU members must speed up cutting their deficits.

"Only then can the rescue attempts be effective, because continuing to cover up the real causes of the crisis wouldn't help Europe," she said. "Germany advocates lasting stability in Europe—we're not going to spare anyone in Europe from that."

**Eurobonds**  Eurobonds are denominated in a particular currency and are issued simultaneously in the bond markets of several countries. The prefix *Euro* means that the bonds are issued outside the countries in whose currencies they are denominated.

Most issues of Eurobonds are arranged by underwriting. However, some Eurobonds are privately placed.[16] A public issue with underwriting is similar to the public debt sold in domestic bond markets. The borrower sells its bonds to a group of managing banks. Managing banks, in turn, sell the bonds to other banks. The other banks are divided into two groups: underwriters and sellers. The underwriters and sellers sell the bonds to dealers and fund investors. The managing banks also serve as underwriters and sellers. Underwriters usually sell Eurobonds on a firm-commitment basis. That is, they are committed to buy the bonds at a prenegotiated price and attempt to sell them at a higher price in the market. Eurobonds appear as straight bonds, floating-rate notes, convertible bonds, zero-coupon bonds, mortgage-backed bonds, and dual-currency bonds.[17]

---

[16] In general, the issue costs are lower in private placements than in public issues, and the yields are higher.

[17] There is a small but growing international equity market. International equities are stock issues underwritten and distributed to a mix of investors without regard to national borders. Our definition of international equity encompasses two basic types: those issues that have been internationally syndicated and distributed outside all national exchanges (termed *Euroequities*) and those that are issued by underwriters in domestic markets other than their own.

A Canadian firm makes an offering of $500 million of floating-rate notes. The notes are offered in London. They mature in 2020 and have semiannual interest of 0.5 percent above the six-month LIBOR. When the bonds are issued, the six-month LIBOR is 10 percent. Thus, in the first six months the Canadian firm will pay interest (at the annual rate) of 10% + 0.5% = 10.5%.

**CONCEPT QUESTIONS ?**
- What are the three ways firms can finance foreign projects?
- What sources of financing are available?

## 32.7  REPORTING FOREIGN OPERATIONS

When a Canadian company prepares consolidated financial statements, the firm translates the local currency accounts of foreign subsidiaries into the currency that is used for reporting purposes, usually the currency of the home country (that is, dollars). If exchange rates change during the accounting period, accounting gains or losses can occur.

Suppose a Canadian firm acquired a British company in 1982. At that time the exchange rate was £1 = $2. The British firm performed very well during the next few years (according to sterling measurements). During the same period, the value of the pound fell to $1.25. Did the corresponding increase in the value of the dollar make the Canadian company better off? Should the increase be reflected in the measurement of income?

These questions have been among the most controversial accounting questions in recent years. Two issues seem to arise:

1. What is the appropriate exchange rate to use for translating each balance-sheet account?

2. How should unrealized accounting gains and losses from foreign currency translation be handled?

One obvious and consistent approach is simply to report the loss on the parent company's income statement. During periods of volatile exchange rates, this kind of treatment can dramatically impact an international company's reported earnings per share (EPS). This is purely an accounting phenomenon, but, even so, such fluctuations are disliked by financial managers.

Canadian GAAP's compromise approach to translation gains and losses is based on rules set out in the Canadian Institute of Chartered Accountants (CICA) *Handbook*, section 1650. The rules divided a firm's foreign subsidiaries into two categories: integrated and self-sustaining. In contrast, IFRS does not distinguish between different types of foreign operations. However, the relationship between the entity and its foreign operation is a factor in determining the functional currency of the foreign operation, which is assessed separately from that of the parent. The financial statements of foreign operations are translated for the purpose of consolidation as follows: assets and liabilities are translated at the closing rate, revenues and expenses are translated at actual rates or appropriate averages, and equity components are translated at historical rates. If the functional currency of a foreign operation is hyperinflationary, then current purchasing power adjustments are made to its financial statements prior to translation. The financial statements are then translated at the closing rate at the end of the current period. When the reporting date of a foreign operation is prior to that of the entity, adjustments are made for significant movements in exchange rates up to the reporting date, for consolidation purposes. When an investment in a foreign operation is disposed of, exchange differences previously recognized directly in equity are transferred to profit or loss.

*CONCEPT*
*QUESTION*

• **What issues arise when reporting foreign operations?**

## 32.8   POLITICAL RISK

One final element of risk in international investing is **political risk**: changes in value that arise as a consequence of political actions. This is not a problem faced exclusively by international firms. For example, changes in Canadian tax laws and regulations may benefit some Canadian firms and hurt others, so political risk exists domestically as well as internationally.

Some countries have more political risk than others, however. When firms have operations in these riskier countries, the extra political risk may lead the firms to require higher returns on overseas investments to compensate for the possibility that funds may be blocked, critical operations interrupted, and contracts abrogated. In the most extreme case, the possibility of outright confiscation may be a concern in countries with relatively unstable political environments.

Political risk also depends on the nature of the business. Some businesses are less likely to be confiscated because they are not particularly valuable in the hands of a different owner. An assembly operation supplying subcomponents that only the parent company uses would not be an attractive takeover target, for example. Similarly, a manufacturing operation that requires the use of specialized components from the parent is of little value without the parent company's cooperation.

Natural resource developments, such as copper mining or oil drilling, are just the opposite. Once the operation is in place, much of the value is in the commodity. The political risk for such investments is much higher for this reason. Also, the issue of exploitation is more pronounced with such investments, again increasing the political risk.

Political risk can be hedged in several ways, particularly when confiscation or nationalization is a concern. The use of local financing, perhaps from the government of the foreign country in question, reduces the possible loss because the company can refuse to pay the debt in the event of unfavourable political activities. Based on our discussion in this section, structuring the operation in such a way that it requires significant parent company involvement to function is another way to reduce political risk.

# 32.9

# SUMMARY AND CONCLUSIONS

The international firm has a more complicated life than the purely domestic firm. Management must understand the connection between interest rates, foreign currency exchange rates, and inflation, and it must become aware of a large number of different financial market regulations and tax systems.

1. This chapter describes some fundamental theories of international finance:
   - The law of one price (LOP) and the purchasing power parity theorem (PPP).
   - The expectations theory of exchange rates.
   - The interest rate parity theorem.

2. The purchasing power parity (PPP) theorem states that $1 should have the same purchasing power in each country. This means that an apple costs the same whether you buy it in Toronto or in Tokyo. One version of the PPP theorem states that the change in exchange rates between the currencies of two countries is connected to the inflation rates in the countries' commodity prices.

3. The expectations theory of exchange rates states that the forward rate of exchange is equal to the expected spot rate.

4. The interest rate parity theorem states that the interest rate differential between two countries will be equal to the difference between the forward exchange rate and the spot exchange rate. This equality must prevail to prevent arbitrageurs from devising get-rich-quick strategies. The equality requires the rate of return on risk-free investments in Canada to be the same as that in other countries measured in Canadian dollars.

   Of course, in practice the PPP theorem and the interest rate parity theorem cannot work perfectly. Government regulations and taxes prevent this. However, there is much empirical work and intuition that suggests that these theories approximately describe international financial markets.

5. The chapter also describes some of the problems of international capital budgeting. The net present value (NPV) rule is still the appropriate way to choose projects, but the main problem is to choose the correct cost of capital. We argue that it should be equal to the rate that shareholders can expect to earn on a portfolio of domestic and foreign securities. This rate should be about the same as for a portfolio of domestic securities. However, two adjustments may be necessary:
   a. The cost of capital of an international firm may be *lower* than that of a domestic counterpart because of the benefits of international diversification.
   b. The cost of capital of an international firm may be *higher* because of the extra risks of international investment.

6. We briefly describe international financial markets. International firms may want to consider borrowing in the local financial market or in the Eurocurrency and Eurobond markets. The interest rates are likely to appear different in these markets. Thus, international firms must be careful to consider differences in taxes and government regulations.

**KEY TERMS**

American Depository
  Receipt (ADR)  911
American options  921
Cross rate  910
Currency swap  920
Eurobanks  926
Eurobonds  911
Eurocurrency  911
Eurodollars  926
European currency unit
  (euro)  910
Exchange rate  912

Export Development Canada
  (EDC)  911
Foreign bonds  911
Foreign exchange
  market  912
Forward exchange rate  914
Forward trades  914
Interest rate parity
  theorem  917
Law of one price (LOP)  915
London Interbank Offered
  Rate (LIBOR)  911

Political risk  931
Purchasing power parity
  (PPP)  916
Relative purchasing power
  parity (RPPP)  916
Spot exchange rate  914
Spot trades  914
Swap rate  914
Swaps  911
Triangular arbitrage  913

### Using Exchange Rates

32.1  Take a look back at Figure 32.1A to answer the following questions:

    *a.* If you have CDN$100, how many euros can you get?

    *b.* How much is one euro worth in Canadian dollars?

    *c.* If you have 5 million euros, how many Canadian dollars can you get?

    *d.* Which is worth more, an Australian dollar or a Singapore dollar?

    *e.* Which is worth more, a Mexican peso or a Russian rouble?

    *f.* How many Mexican pesos can you get for a euro? What do you call this rate?

    *g.* Per unit, what is the most valuable currency of those listed? The least valuable?

### Using the Cross Rate

32.2  Use the information in Figure 32.1B to answer the following questions:

    *a.* Which would you rather have, CDN$100 or £100? Why?

    *b.* Which would you rather have, 100 Swiss francs (SF) or £100? Why?

    *c.* What is the cross rate for Swiss francs in terms of British pounds? For British pounds in terms of Swiss francs?

### Forward Exchange Rates

32.3  Use the information in Figure 32.1A and 32.1C to answer the following questions:

    *a.* What is the six-month forward rate for the Japanese yen, in yen per Canadian dollar? Is the yen selling at a premium or a discount? Explain.

    *b.* What is the three-month forward rate for British pounds in Canadian dollars per pound? Is the dollar selling at a premium or a discount? Explain.

    *c.* What do you think will happen to the value of the dollar relative to the yen and the pound, based on the information in the figure? Explain.

### Using Spot and Forward Exchange Rates

32.4  Suppose the spot exchange rate for the U.S. dollar is CDN$1.18 and the six-month forward rate is CDN$1.13.

    *a.* Which is worth more, a U.S. dollar or a Canadian dollar?

    *b.* Assuming absolute PPP holds, what is the cost in the United States of an Elkhead beer if the price in Canada is CDN$2.19? Why might the beer actually sell at a different price in the United States?

    *c.* Is the U.S. dollar selling at a premium or a discount relative to the Canadian dollar?

    *d.* Which currency is expected to appreciate in value?

    *e.* Which country do you think has higher interest rates—the United States or Canada? Explain.

### Cross Rates and Arbitrage

32.5  Suppose the Japanese yen exchange rate is ¥85 = CDN$1, and the U.K. pound exchange rate is £1 = CDN$1.53.

    *a.* What is the cross rate in terms of yen per pound?

    *b.* Suppose the cross rate is ¥131.4 = £1. Is there an arbitrage opportunity here? If there is, explain how to take advantage of the mispricing.

### Interest Rate Parity

32.6  Use Figure 32.1A and 32.1C to answer the following questions. Suppose interest rate parity holds, and the current six-month risk-free rate in Canada is 1.9 percent. What must the six-month risk-free rate be in the United Kingdom? in Japan? in Germany?

### Interest Rates and Arbitrage

32.7  The treasurer of a major Canadian firm has CDN$30 million to invest for three months. The annual interest rate in Canada is 0.21 percent per month. The interest rate in the United Kingdom is 0.57 percent per month. The spot exchange rate is £0.64, and the three-month forward rate is £0.65. Ignoring transaction costs, in which country would the treasurer want to invest the company's funds? Why?

### Inflation and Exchange Rates

32.8   Suppose the current exchange rate for the Polish zloty is Z3.14. The expected
exchange rate in three years is Z3.23. What is the difference in the annual inflation
rates for Canada and Poland over this period? Assume that the anticipated rate is
constant for both countries. What relationship are you relying on in answering?

### Exchange Rate Risk

32.9   Suppose your company imports computer motherboards from Singapore. The
exchange rate is given in Figure 32.1A. You have just placed an order for 30,000
motherboards at a cost to you of 168.5 Singapore dollars each. You will pay for the
shipment when it arrives in 90 days. You can sell the motherboards for CDN$125
each. Calculate your profit if the exchange rate goes up or down by 10 percent over
the next 90 days. What is the break-even exchange rate? What percentage rise or fall
does this represent in terms of the Singapore dollar versus the Canadian dollar?

### Exchange Rates and Arbitrage

32.10  Suppose the spot and six-month forward rates on the Norwegian krone are Kr5.61
and Kr5.72, respectively. The annual risk-free rate in Canada is 3 percent, and the
annual risk-free rate in Norway is 5 percent.
  *a.* Is there an arbitrage opportunity here? If so, how would you exploit it?
  *b.* What must the six-month forward rate be to prevent arbitrage?

### Spot versus Forward Rates

32.11  Suppose the spot and three-month forward rates for the yen are ¥80.13 and ¥78.96,
respectively.
  *a.* Is the yen expected to get stronger or weaker?
  *b.* What would you estimate is the difference between the inflation rates of Canada and Japan?

### Expected Spot Rates

32.12  Suppose the spot exchange rate for the Hungarian forint is HUF209. The inflation
rate per year is 3.5 percent in Canada and 5.7 percent in Hungary. What do you
predict the exchange rate will be in one year? In two years? In five years? What
relationship are you using?

### Capital Budgeting

32.13  Lakonishok Equipment has an investment opportunity in Europe. The project
costs €19 million and is expected to produce cash flows of €3.6 million in year 1,
€4.1 million in year 2, and €5.1 million in year 3. The current spot exchange rate
is CDN$1.09/€, and the current risk-free rate in Canada is 3.1 percent, compared to
that in Europe of 2.9 percent. The appropriate discount rate for the project is estimated to be 10.5 percent, the Canadian cost of capital for the company. In addition,
the subsidiary can be sold at the end of three years for an estimated €12.7 million.
What is the NPV of the project?

32.14  You are evaluating the proposed expansion of an existing subsidiary located in
Switzerland. The cost of the expansion would be SF25 million. The cash flows
from the project would be SF7.2 million per year for the next five years. The dollar required return is 13 percent per year, and the current exchange rate is SF1.72/
CDN$. The going rate on Eurodollars is 8 percent per year. It is 7 percent per year
on Swiss francs.
  *a.* What do you project will happen to exchange rates over the next four years?
  *b.* Based on your answer in (a), convert the projected Swiss franc flows into Canadian dollar flows and calculate the NPV.
  *c.* What is the required return on Swiss franc flows? Based on your answer, calculate the NPV in Swiss francs and then convert to Canadian dollars.

### Translation Exposure

32.15 Atreides International has operations in Arrakis. The balance sheet for this division in Arrakeen solaris shows assets of 23,000 solaris, debt in the amount of 9,000 solaris, and equity of 14,000 solaris.

   a. If the current exchange ratio is 1.20 solaris per Canadian dollar, what does the balance sheet look like in dollars?

   b. Assume that one year from now the balance sheet in solaris is exactly the same as at the beginning of the year. If the exchange rate is 1.40 solaris per Canadian dollar, what does the balance sheet look like in dollars now?

   c. Rework (b) assuming the exchange rate is 1.12 solaris per Canadian dollar.

32.16 In Problem 32.15, assume the equity increases by 1,750 solaris due to retained earnings. If the exchange rate at the end of the year is 1.24 solaris per Canadian dollar, what does the balance sheet look like?

## MINICASE

## East Coast Yachts Goes International

Larissa Warren, the owner of East Coast Yachts, has been in discussions with a yacht dealer in Monaco about selling the company's yachts in Europe. Jarek Jachowicz, the dealer, wants to add East Coast Yachts to his current retail line. Jarek has told Larissa that he feels the retail sales will be approximately €8 million per month. All sales will be made in euros, and Jarek will retain 5 percent of the retail sales as commission, which will be paid in euros. Because the yachts will be customized to order, the first sales will take place in one month. Jarek will pay East Coast Yachts for the order 90 days after it is filled. This payment schedule will continue for the length of the contract between the two companies.

Larissa is confident the company can handle the extra volume with its existing facilities, but she is unsure about any potential financial risks of selling yachts in Europe. In her discussion with Jarek, she found that the current exchange rate is CDN$1.34/€. At this exchange rate, the company would spend 80 percent of the sales income on production costs. This number does not reflect the sales commission to be paid to Jarek.

Larissa has decided to ask Dan Ervin, the company's financial analyst, to prepare an analysis of the proposed international sales. Dan asks you, his assistant, to answer the following questions:

1. What are the pros and cons of the international sales plan? What additional risks will the company face?

2. What will happen to the company's profits if the dollar strengthens? What if the dollar weakens?

3. Ignoring taxes, what are East Coast Yacht's projected gains or losses from this proposed arrangement at the current exchange rate of CDN$1.34/€? What will happen to profits if the exchange rate changes to CDN$1.25/€? At what exchange rate will the company break even?

4. How can the company hedge its exchange rate risk? What are the implications for this approach?

5. Taking all factors into account, should the company pursue international sales further? Why or why not?

# GLOSSARY

**Accounts receivable financing** A secured short-term loan that involves either the assigning of receivables or the factoring of receivables. Under assignment, the lender has a lien on the receivables and recourse to the borrower. Factoring involves the sale of accounts receivable. Then the purchaser, called the factor, must collect on the receivables. 807

**Acquisition method** Accounting guidelines describing how assets, liabilities, non-controlling interest, and goodwill must be reported by the purchasing company on its consolidated financial statements. This method requires that the purchased net identifiable assets and liabilities be measured at their acquisition-date fair market value. 862

**Adjusted present value (APV)** Base-case net present value of a project's operating cash flows plus present value of any financing benefits. 533

**Agency costs** Costs of conflicts of interest among shareholders, bondholders, and managers. Agency costs are the costs of resolving these conflicts. They include the costs of providing managers with an incentive to maximize shareholder wealth and then monitoring their behaviour, and the cost of protecting bondholders from shareholders. Agency costs are borne by shareholders. 13, 500

**Aggregation** Process in corporate financial planning whereby the smaller investment proposals of each of the firm's operational units are added up and in effect treated as a big picture. 66

**Aging schedule** A compilation of accounts receivable by the age of account. 850

**Allocated cost** Expenses that are allocated across different projects when determining income. 225

**American Depository Receipt (ADR)** A security issued in the United States to represent shares of a foreign stock, enabling that stock to be traded in the United States. 911

**American options** Options contracts that may be exercised any time up to the expiration date. A European option may be exercised only on the expiration date. 670, 921

**Annual percentage rate** See Stated Annual Interest Rate. 117

**Annuity** A level stream of equal dollar payments that lasts for a fixed time. An example of an annuity is the coupon part of a bond with level annual payments. 124

**Annuity factor** The term used to calculate the present value of the stream of level payments for a fixed period. 125

**Asset-backed bond** A bond backed by a diverse pool of assets, such as accounts receivable collections, credit card debt, or mortgages. 636

**Asset beta** The beta of the assets of the firm. 382

**Asset requirements** A common element of a financial plan that describes projected capital spending and the proposed use of net working capital. 67

**Average accounting return (AAR)** The average project earnings after taxes and depreciation divided by the average book value of the investment during its life. 196

**Average collection period (ACP)** Average amount of time required to collect an account receivable. Also referred to as days sales outstanding. 849

**Average daily sales (ADS)** Annual sales divided by 365 days. 850

**Average (mean)** The average of the observations in a frequency distribution. 294

**Balance sheet** See Statement of Financial Position. 33

**Banker's acceptance** Agreement by a bank to pay a given sum of money at a future date. 807

**Basic IRR rule** Accept the project if the IRR is greater than the discount rate; reject the project if the IRR is less than the discount rate. 200

**Bearer bond** A bond issued without record of the owner's name. Whoever holds the bond (the bearer) is the owner. 621

**Best-efforts underwriting** An offering in which an underwriter agrees to distribute as much of the offering as possible and to return any unsold shares to the issuer. 596

**Beta** A measure of the sensitivity of a security's return to movements in an underlying factor. It is a measure of systematic risk. 335

**Beta coefficient** The response of the stock's return to a systematic risk. 353

**Book value of equity** Per-share accounting equity value of a firm. Total accounting equity divided by the number of outstanding shares.   449

**Bought deal** A deal in which one underwriter buys securities from an issuing firm and sells them directly to a small number of investors.   596

**Break-even analysis** Analysis of the level of sales at which a project would make zero profit.   266

**Bubble theory** Security prices sometimes move wildly above their true values.   433

**Call option** The right—but not the obligation—to buy a fixed number of shares of stock at a stated price within a specified time.   670

**Call premium** The price of a call option on common stock.   623

**Call protected** Describes a bond that is not allowed to be called, usually for a certain early period in the life of the bond.   623

**Canada plus call** An approach designed to replace the traditional call feature by making it unattractive for the issuer ever to call the bonds. Unlike the standard call, with the Canada plus call the exact amount of the call premium is not set at the time of issuance. Instead, the Canada plus call stipulates that in the event of a call, the issuer must provide a call premium that will compensate investors for the difference in interest between the original bond and new debt issued to replace it. This compensation cancels the borrower's benefit from calling the debt, and the result is that the call will not occur.   457, 623

**Capital asset pricing model (CAPM)** An equilibrium asset pricing theory that shows that equilibrium rates of expected return on all risky assets are a function of their covariance with the market portfolio.   339

**Capital budgeting** Planning and managing expenditures for long-lived assets.   3

**Capital gains** The positive change in the value of an asset. A negative capital gain is a capital loss.   31

**Capital market line** The efficient set of all assets, both risky and risk free, that provides the investor with the best possible opportunities.   333

**Capital markets** Financial markets for long-term debt and for equity shares.   20

**Capital rationing** The case where funds are limited to a fixed dollar amount and must be allocated among competing projects.   212

**Capital structure** The mix of the various debt and equity capital maintained by a firm. Also called financial structure. The composition of a corporation's securities used to finance its investment activities; the relative proportions of short-term debt, long-term debt, and shareholders' equity.   3

**Carrying costs** Costs that increase with increases in the level of investment in current assets.   798

**Cash budget** A forecast of cash receipts and disbursements expected by a firm in the coming year. It is a short-term financial planning tool.   803

**Cash cycle** In general, the time between cash disbursement and cash collection. In net working capital management, it can be thought of as the operating cycle less the accounts payable payment period.   794

**Cash discount** Discount given for a cash purchase. One reason a cash discount may be offered is to speed up the collection of receivables.   840

**Cash flow** Cash generated by the firm and paid to creditors and shareholders. It can be classified as (1) cash flow from operations, (2) cash flow from changes in fixed assets, and (3) cash flow from changes in net working capital.   39

**Cash flow from operations** Earnings before interest and depreciation minus taxes that measure the cash generated from operations, not counting capital spending or working capital requirements.   41

**Cash flow timeline** Line depicting the operating activities and cash flows for a firm over a particular period.   794

**Cash transaction** A transaction where exchange is immediate, as contrasted with a forward contract, which calls for future delivery of an asset at an agreed-upon price.   756

**Change in net working capital** Difference in net working capital from one period to another.   38

**Characteristic line** The line relating the expected return on a security to different returns on the market.   335

**Circular bid** One of two types of takeover bids; mailed directly to the target's shareholders. Ontario securities law requires that the bidder mail a notice of the proposed share purchase to shareholders. In the case of a circular bid, the response must be mailed to shareholders.   858

**Clean price** The quoted price of a bond minus its accrued interest.   150

**Clienteles** Groups of investors attracted to different payouts.   576

**Coattail** A provision that protects the non-voting shareholders of a company by giving them the right either to vote or to convert their shares into voting shares that can be tendered to the takeover bid.   453

**Collection policy** Procedures followed by a firm in attempting to collect accounts receivable.   837

**Commercial paper** Short-term, unsecured promissory notes issued by corporations with a high credit standing. Their maturity ranges up to 270 days.   807

**Common stock (common shares)** Equity claims held by the "residual owners" of the firm, who are the last to receive any distribution of earnings or assets.   448

**Compound interest** Interest that is earned both on the initial principal and on interest earned on the initial principal in previous periods. The interest earned in one period becomes in effect part of the principal in a following period.   108

**Compound value** Value of a sum after investing it over one or more periods. Also called future value.   105

**Compounding** Process of reinvesting each interest payment to earn more interest. Compounding is based on the idea that interest itself becomes principal and therefore also earns interest in subsequent periods.   107

**Concentration banking** The use of geographically dispersed collection centres to speed up the collection of accounts receivable.   826

**Consolidation** A merger in which an entirely new firm is created.   858

**Contingent claims** Claim whose value is directly dependent on, or is contingent on, the value of its underlying assets. For example, the debt and equity securities issued by a firm derive their value from the total value of the firm.   9

**Continuous compounding** Interest compounded continuously, every instant, rather than at fixed intervals.   119

**Contribution margin** Amount that each additional product, such as a jet engine, contributes to the after-tax profit of the whole project: (Sale price − Variable cost) $\times (1 - T_c)$, where $T_c$ is the corporate tax rate.   268

**Control block** An interest controlling 50 percent of outstanding votes plus one; thus it may decide the fate of the firm.   879

**Conversion premium** Difference between the conversion price and the current share price divided by the current share price.   740

**Conversion price** The amount of par value exchangeable for one share of common stock. This term really refers to the share price and means the dollar amount of the bond's par value that is exchangeable for one share of stock.   740

**Conversion ratio** The number of shares per $1,000 bond (or debenture) that a bondholder would receive if the bond were converted into shares of stock.   740

**Conversion value** What a convertible bond would be worth if it were immediately converted into the common stock at the current price.   741

**Convertible bond** A bond that may be converted into another form of security, typically common stock, at the option of the holder at a specified price for a specified period of time.   636, 739

**Corporation** Form of business organization that is created as a distinct "legal person" composed of one or more actual individuals or legal entities. Primary advantages of a corporation are limited liability, ease of ownership transfer, and perpetual succession.   11

**Correlation** A standardized statistical measure of the dependence of two random variables. It is defined as the covariance divided by the standard deviations of two variables.   312

**Cost of equity** The required return on the company's common stock in capital markets. It is also called the equityholders' required rate of return because it is what equityholders can expect to obtain in a capital market. It is a cost from a firm's perspective.   372

**Counterparty risk** The risk to each party of a contract that the other may not honour its contractual obligations. For most financial contracts, this is similar to default risk.   780

**Coupons** The stated interest on a debt instrument.   147

**Covariance** A statistical measure of the degree to which random variables move together.   312

**Covenant** A written agreement or promise usually under seal between two or more parties especially for the performance of a particular action.   807

**Covered-call strategy** An options strategy whereby an investor holds a long position in an asset and sells call options on that same asset in an attempt to generate increased income from the asset.   679

**Credit analysis** The process of determining whether a credit applicant meets the firm's standards and what amount of credit the applicant should receive.   837

**Credit instrument** Device by which a firm offers credit, such as an invoice, a promissory note, or a conditional sales contract. 842

**Credit period** Time allowed a credit purchaser to remit the full payment for credit purchases. 839

**Credit scoring** Determining the probability of default when granting customers credit. 849

**Cross rate** The exchange rate between two foreign currencies, neither of which is generally the Canadian dollar. 910

**Crown jewels** An anti-takeover tactic in which major assets—the crown jewels—are sold by a firm when faced with a takeover threat. 882

**Cumulative probability** The probability that a drawing from the standardized normal distribution will be below a particular value. 689

**Cumulative voting** A procedure whereby a shareholder may cast all of his or her votes for one member of the board of directors. 451

**Currency swap** Sometimes called an FX swap; a swap of obligations to pay cash flows in one currency for obligations to pay in another currency. 920

**Date of payment** Date that dividend cheques are mailed. 557

**Date of record** Date on which holders of record in a firm's stock ledger are designated as the recipients of either dividends or stock rights. 556

**Debenture** An unsecured bond, usually with maturity of 15 years or more. A debt obligation backed by the general credit of the issuing corporation. 622

**Debit card** A card used with point-of-sale systems to transfer funds directly from a customer's bank account to a retailer's. 825

**Debt displacement** The amount of borrowing that leasing displaces. Firms that do a lot of leasing will be forced to cut back on borrowing. 655

**Decision trees** Graphical representations of alternative sequential decisions and the possible outcomes of those decisions. 261

**Declaration date** Date on which the board of directors passes a resolution to pay a dividend of a specified amount to all qualified holders of record on a specified date. 556

**Deferred call** A provision that prohibits the company from calling the bond before a certain date. During this period the bond is said to be call protected. 623

**Deliverable instrument** The asset in a forward contract that will be delivered in the future at an agreed-upon price. 755

**Depreciation tax shield** The depreciation deduction multiplied by the tax rate. 237

**Direct lease** Lease under which a lessor buys equipment from a manufacturer and leases it to a lessee. 644

**Dirty price** The actual price paid for a bond, which includes accrued interest. 150

**Discount** Refers to a bond selling below its face value. 151

**Discounted payback period rule** An investment decision rule in which the cash flows are discounted at an interest rate and the payback rule is applied on these discounted cash flows. 196

**Discounting** Calculating the present value of a future amount. The process is the opposite of compounding. 112

**Diversifiable (unique) (unsystematic) risk** A risk that specifically affects a single asset or a small group of assets. 329

**Dividend capture** A strategy by which portfolio managers purchase high-grade preferred stock or blue chip common stock just prior to a dividend payment. They hold the stock only long enough to receive the dividend. 831

**Dividend payout ratio** Cash dividends divided by net income. 69

**Dividends** Payments made by a firm to its shareholders, either in cash or in stock. Also called the "income component" on the return of an investment in stock. 452

**Duration** The weighted average time of an asset's cash flows. The weights are determined by present value factors. 772

**Economic assumptions** Economic environment in which the firm expects to reside over the life of the financial plan. 67

**Economic order quantity (EOQ)** The reorder quantity that minimizes the total inventory cost. 29A-6

**Effective annual interest rate** The interest rate as if it were compounded once per time period rather than several times per period. 117

**Efficient market hypothesis (EMH)** The prices of securities fully reflect available information. Investors buying bonds and stocks in an efficient market should expect to obtain an equilibrium rate of return. Firms should expect to receive the "fair" value (present value) for the securities they sell. 415

**Efficient set** Graph representing a set of portfolios that maximize expected return at each level of portfolio risk. 322

**Equilibrium rate of interest** The interest rate that clears the market. Also called market-clearing interest rate. 86

**Equity beta** Systematic risk of a firm's stock decomposed into contributions of risk from assets and financial leverage. 382

**Erosion** Cash flow amount transferred to a new project from customers and sales of other products of the firm. 225

**Euro (European currency unit)** See European currency unit. 910

**Eurobanks** Banks that make loans and accept deposits in foreign currencies. 926

**Eurobonds** International bonds sold primarily in countries other than the country in whose currency the issue is denominated. 911

**Eurocurrency** Money deposited in a financial centre outside of the country whose currency is involved. 911

**Eurodollars** A dollar deposited in a bank outside Canada. 926

**European currency unit (euro)** The European currency unit (ECU) was devised in 1979 by the initial European Union member states and served as an artificial currency for internal accounting purposes. By 1999, the euro replaced the ECU at a ratio of 1:1, with physical circulation beginning in 2002, and is currently the official currency of the Eurozone. 910

**European options** Options contracts that may be exercised only on the expiration date, as opposed to American options, which may be exercised any time up to the expiration date. 670

**Exchange offers** Offers that allow shareholders to exchange debt with stock and vice versa, either increasing or decreasing firm leverage. 509

**Exchange rate** Price of one country's currency for another's. 912

**Ex-dividend date** Date four business days before the date of record for a security. An individual purchasing stock before its ex-dividend date will receive the current dividend. 556

**Exercising the option** The act of buying or selling the underlying asset via the option contract. 669

**Exotics** The complicated blends of derivatives, swaps, options, forwards, and futures that often produce surprising results for their buyers. 780

**Expiration date** Maturity date of an option. 669

**Export Development Canada (EDC)** Federal crown corporation that promotes Canadian exports by making loans to foreign purchasers. 911

**Ex-rights** Indicates that a stock is selling without a recently declared right or dividend. The ex-rights or ex-dividend date is generally four business days before the date of record. 608

**Face value** The value of a bond that appears on its face. Also referred to as par value or principal. 147

**Factor model** A model in which each stock's return is generated by common factors, called the systematic sources of risk. 355

**Factoring** Sale of a firm's accounts receivable to a financial institution known as a factor. 851

**Financial distress** Events preceding and including bankruptcy, such as violation of loan contracts. 896

**Financial intermediaries** Institutions that provide the market function of matching borrowers and lenders or traders. Financial institutions may be categorized as depository, contractual savings, and investment type. 85

**Financial lease** Long-term non-cancellable lease, generally requiring the lessee to pay all maintenance costs. 645

**Financial requirements** In the financial plan, financing arrangements that are necessary to meet the overall corporate objective. 67

**Firm-commitment underwriting** An underwriting in which an investment banking firm commits to buy the entire issue and assumes all financial responsibility for any unsold shares. 596

**Fixed costs** Costs that are fixed in total for a given period of time and for given volume levels. They do not depend on the amount of goods or services produced during the period. 264

**Float** The difference between bank cash and book cash. Float represents the net effect of cheques in the process of collection, or clearing. Positive float means the firm's bank cash is greater than its book cash until the cheques' presentation. Cheques written by the firm generate disbursement float, causing an immediate decrease in book cash but no change in bank cash. In neutral float position, bank cash equals book cash. Cheques written by the firm represent collection float, which increases book cash immediately but does not immediately change bank cash. The sum of disbursement float and collection float is net float.   820

**Floating-rate bonds (floaters)** Debt obligations with adjustable coupon payments.   635

**Flow to equity (FTE)** An alternative budgeting approach. A project's cash flow to equityholders (of the levered firm) is discounted at the cost of equity capital.   535

**Force conversion** If the conversion value of a convertible is greater than the call price, the call can be used to force conversion.   748

**Foreign bonds** International bonds issued by foreign borrowers in another nation's capital market and traditionally denominated in that nation's currency.   911

**Foreign exchange market** Market in which arrangements are made today for future exchange of major currencies; used to hedge against major swings in foreign exchange rates.   22, 912

**Forward contract** An arrangement calling for future delivery of an asset at an agreed-upon price.   755

**Forward exchange rate** A future day's exchange rate between two major currencies.   914

**Forward trades** Agreements to buy or sell based on exchange rates established today for settlement in the future. 914

**Free cash flow** Cash that the firm is free to distribute to creditors and shareholders because it is not needed for working capital or fixed asset investment.   41

**Frequency distribution** The organization of data to show how often certain values or ranges of values occur.   294

**Future value** Value of a sum after investing it over one or more periods. Also called compound value.   105

**Futures contract** A contract that obliges traders to purchase or sell an asset at an agreed-upon price on a specified future date. The long position is held by the trader who commits to purchase. The short position is held by the trader who commits to sell. Futures differ from forward contracts in their standardization, exchange trading, margin requirements, and daily settling (marking to market).   756

**General cash offer** A public issue of a security that is sold to all interested investors rather than only to existing shareholders.   595

**Going-private transaction** A transaction in which publicly owned stock in a firm is replaced with complete equity ownership by a private group. The shares are delisted from stock exchanges and can no longer be purchased in the open market.   860

**Golden parachute** Compensation paid to top-level management by a target firm if a takeover occurs.   882

**Goodwill** The excess of the purchase price over the sum of the fair market values of the individual assets acquired.   862

**Growing annuity** A finite number of growing annual cash flows.   130

**Growing perpetuity** A constant stream of cash flows without end that is expected to rise indefinitely. For example, cash flows to the landlord of an apartment building might be expected to rise a certain percentage each year.   122

**Hedging** Taking a position in two or more securities that are negatively correlated (taking opposite trading positions) to reduce risk.   754

**Holder-of-record date** The date on which holders of record in a firm's stock ledger are designated as the recipients of either dividends or stock rights. Also called date of record.   608

**Holding-period return** The rate of return over a given period.   152

**Homemade dividends** A strategy in which an individual investor can undo corporate dividend policy by reinvesting excess dividends or selling off shares of stock to receive a desired cash flow.   561

**Homogeneous expectations** Idea that all individuals have the same beliefs concerning future investments, profits, and dividends.   334

**Immunized** Immune to interest-rate risk.   775

**Income bonds** Bonds for which the payment of income is contingent on sufficient earnings. Income bonds are commonly used during the reorganization of a failed or failing business.   636

**Incremental cash flow** Difference between the firm's cash flow with and without a project.   224

**Incremental IRR**  Internal rate of return (IRR) on the incremental investment from choosing a larger project instead of a smaller project.   207

**Indenture**  Written agreement between the corporate debt issuer and the lender, setting forth maturity date, interest rate, and other terms.   619

**Independent project**  A project whose acceptance or rejection is independent of the acceptance or rejection of other projects.   201

**Information content effect**  The rise in the stock price following the dividend signal.   574

**Initial public offering (IPO)**  The original sale of a company's securities to the public. Also called an unseasoned new issue.   598

**Interest rate parity theorem**  The interest rate differential between two countries will be equal to the difference between the forward exchange rate and the spot exchange rate.   917

**Internal financing**  Net income plus depreciation minus dividends. Internal financing comes from internally generated cash flow.   461

**Internal rate of return (IRR)**  A discount rate at which the net present value of an investment is zero. The IRR is a method of evaluating capital expenditure proposals.   199

**International Financial Reporting Standards (IFRS)**  A set of international accounting standards stating how particular types of transactions and other events should be reported in financial statements. In 2011, publicly traded firms in Canada switched to IFRS. The objective is to make international comparisons as easy as possible.   35

**Intertemporal consumption**  An economic theory that explains individual preferences for consuming now or saving for later.   84

**Inventory loan**  A secured short-term loan to purchase inventory. The three basic forms are a blanket inventory lien, a trust receipt, and field warehouse financing.   807

**Invoice**  Bill written by a seller of goods or services and submitted to the purchaser.   839

**Junk bonds**  A speculative grade bond, rated Ba or lower by Moody's, or BB or lower by Standard & Poor's, or an unrated bond. Also called a high-yield or low-grade bond.   631

**Just-in-time (JIT) inventory**  System under which inventories are reordered frequently in order to minimize such inventories, thereby maximizing turnover.   29A-9

**Law of one price (LOP)**  A commodity will cost the same regardless of what currency is used to purchase it.   915

**Lease**  A contractual arrangement to grant the use of specific fixed assets for a specified time in exchange for payment, usually in the form of rent. An operating lease is generally a short-term cancellable arrangement, whereas a financial, or capital, lease is a long-term non-cancellable agreement.   643

**Lessee**  One who receives the use of assets under a lease.   643

**Lessor**  One who conveys the use of assets under a lease.   643

**Letter of credit**  A common arrangement in international finance, where the bank issuing the letter promises to make a loan if certain conditions are met.   806

**Leveraged buyout (LBO)**  Takeover of a company by using borrowed funds, usually by a group including some member of existing management.   860

**Leveraged lease**  Tax-oriented leasing arrangement that involves one or more third-party lenders.   645

**Liquidation**  Termination of the firm as a going concern. Liquidation involves selling the assets of the firm for salvage value. The proceeds, net of transaction costs, are distributed to creditors in order of established priority.   901

**Liquidity**  The ease and quickness of converting assets to cash. Also called marketability.   790

**Lockbox**  Post office box set up to intercept accounts receivable payments. Lockboxes are the most widely used device to speed up collection of cash.   824

**London Interbank Offered Rate (LIBOR)**  Rate the most creditworthy banks charge one another for large loans of Eurodollars overnight in the London market.   911

**Long hedge**  Protecting the future cost of a purchase by purchasing a futures contract to protect against changes in the price of an asset.   763

**Making delivery**  The seller's actually turning over to the buyer the asset agreed upon in a forward contract.   756

**Management buyout (MBO)**  One of many exit strategies in which the equity shares of a public company are purchased primarily by existing management.   860

**Marked to the market** The daily settlement of obligations on futures positions.   758

**Market model** A one-factor model for returns where the index that is used for the factor is an index of the returns on the whole market.   356

**Market portfolio** In concept, a value-weighted index of all securities. In practice, it is an index, such as the S&P 500, that describes the return of the entire value of the stock market, or at least the stocks that make up the index. A market portfolio represents the average investor's return.   335

**Marketed claims** Claims that can be bought and sold in financial markets, such as those of shareholders and bondholders.   508

**Materials requirements planning (MRP)** Computer-based systems for ordering and/or scheduling production of demand-dependent types of inventories.   29A-9

**Maturity date** The date on which the last payment on a bond is due.   146

**Merger** Combination of two or more companies.   857

**MM Proposition I** A proposition of Modigliani and Miller (MM) stating that a firm cannot change the total value of its outstanding securities by changing its capital structure proportions. Also called an irrelevance result.   470

**MM Proposition I under corporate taxes** A proposition of Modigliani and Miller (MM) stating that by raising the debt-to-equity ratio, a firm can lower its taxes and thereby increase its total value. Capital structure does matter.   484

**MM Proposition II** A proposition of Modigliani and Miller (MM) stating that the cost of equity is a linear function of the firm's debt-to-equity ratio.   473

**MM Proposition II (no taxes)** A proposition of Modigliani and Miller (MM) stating that the required return on equity is a linear function of the firm's debt-to-equity ratio.   475

**MM Proposition II under corporate taxes** A proposition of Modigliani and Miller (MM) stating that the cost of equity is a linear function of the firm's debt-to-equity ratio.   486

**Modified IRR (MIRR)** An internal rate of return (IRR) calculation method that changes cash flows such that only one IRR exists. Cash flows are adjusted so that the sign on the cash flows only changes once.   205

**Money markets** Financial markets for debt securities that pay off in the short term (usually less than one year).   20

**Monte Carlo simulation** A problem-solving technique used to approximate the probability of certain outcomes by running multiple trial runs, called simulations, using random variables.   270

**Mutually exclusive investments** Investment decisions in which the acceptance of a project precludes the acceptance of one or more alternative projects.   201

**Negative covenant** Part of the indenture or loan agreement that limits or prohibits actions that the company may take.   503, 622

**Net present value (NPV)** The present value of future cash flows minus the present value of the cost of the investment.   106

**Net present value rule** A rule stating that an investment is worth making if it has a positive net present value.   97

**Net working capital** Current assets minus current liabilities.   3

**Nominal cash flow** A cash flow expressed in nominal terms if the actual dollars to be received (or paid out) are given.   233

**Nominal interest rate** Interest rate unadjusted for inflation.   231

**Non-cash items** Expenses against revenue that do not directly affect cash flow, such as depreciation and deferred taxes.   37

**Non-marketed claims** Claims that cannot be easily bought and sold in the financial markets, such as those of the government and litigants in lawsuits.   508

**Normal distribution** Symmetric bell-shaped frequency distribution that can be defined by its mean and standard deviation.   298

**Operating cycle** The time interval between the arrival of inventory stock and the date when cash is collected from receivables.   794

**Operating lease** Type of lease in which the period of the contract is less than the life of the equipment and the lessor pays all maintenance and servicing costs.   644

**Operating leverage** The degree to which a company's costs of operation are fixed as opposed to variable. A firm with high operating costs, when compared to a firm with a low operating leverage, has relatively larger changes in earnings before interest and taxes (EBIT) with respect to a change in the sales revenue.   381

**Operating loan** The most common way to finance a temporary cash deficit. This is an agreement under which a firm is authorized to borrow up to a specified amount for a given period, usually one year (much like a credit card).   806

**Opportunity costs** Most valuable alternative that is given up. The rate of return used in net present value computation is an opportunity interest rate.   224

**Opportunity (feasible) set** The possible expected return; standard deviation pairs of all portfolios that can be constructed from a given set of assets.   321

**Option** A right—but not an obligation—to buy or sell underlying assets at a fixed price during a specified time period.   669

**Over the counter (OTC)** Trades made through an informal network of brokers and dealers who negotiate sales of securities (not a formal exchange).   781

**Oversubscription privilege** Allows shareholders to purchase unsubscribed shares in a rights offer at the subscription price.   609

**Partnership** Form of business organization in which two or more co-owners form a business. In a general partnership, each partner is liable for the debts of the partnership. Limited partnership permits some partners to have limited liability.   10

**Payback period rule** An investment decision rule that states that all investment projects with payback periods equal to or less than a particular cutoff period are accepted, and all of those that pay off in more than the particular cutoff period are rejected. The payback period is the number of years required for a firm to recover its initial investment required by a project from the cash flow it generates.   193

**Payout ratio** Proportion of net income paid out in cash dividends.   159

**Pecking order** Hierarchy of long-term financing strategies, in which using internally generated cash is at the top and issuing new equity is at the bottom.   462

**Perfectly competitive financial market** Market in which no trader has the power to change the price of goods or services. Perfect markets are characterized by the following conditions: (1) Trading is costless, and access to the financial markets is free. (2) Information about borrowing and lending opportunities is freely available. (3) There are many traders, and no single trader can have a significant impact on market prices.   89

**Perpetuity** A constant stream of cash flows without end. A British consol is an example.   121

**Pie model** A model of a firm's debt-to-equity ratio. It graphically depicts slices of "pie" that represent the value of the firm in the capital markets.   465

**Plug** A variable that handles financial slack in the financial plan.   65

**Poison pill** Strategy by a takeover target company to make a stock less appealing to a company that wishes to acquire it.   883

**Political risk** In investing, changes in value that arise as a consequence of political action.   931

**Portfolio** Combined holding of more than one stock, bond, real estate asset, or other asset by an investor.   315

**Positive covenant** Part of the indenture or loan agreement that specifies an action that the company must abide by.   503, 622

**Precautionary motive** A reason for holding cash that arises from wanting to keep a safety supply to act as a financial reserve.   819

**Pre-emptive right** The right to share proportionally in any new stock sold.   604

**Preferred shares** A type of stock whose holders are given certain priority over common shareholders in the payment of dividends. Usually the dividend rate is fixed at the time of issue. Preferred shareholders normally do not receive voting rights.   458

**Premium** The state of a bond selling above its face value.   151

**Prepackaged bankruptcy** A combination of private workout and legal bankruptcy. A private reorganization is prepackaged and then the firm files for formal bankruptcy.   906

**Present value (PV)** The value of a future cash stream discounted at the appropriate market interest rate.   105

**Present value factor** Factor used to calculate an estimate of the present value of an amount to be received in a future period.   112

**Private placements** Sales of bonds or other securities directly to a limited number of investors.   637

**Private workout** Financial restructuring agreement that does not involve formal, legal bankruptcy.   904

**Pro forma statements** Projected income statements, balance sheets, and sources-and-uses statements for future years.   67

**Profitability index (PI)** A method used to evaluate projects. It is the ratio of the present value of the future expected cash flows after initial investment to the amount of the initial investment.   211

**Prospectus** The legal document that must be given to every investor who contemplates purchasing registered securities in an offering. It gives the details of the company and the particular offering.   593

**Protective covenants** Parts of the indenture or loan agreement that limit certain actions a company takes during the term of the loan to protect the lender's interest.   503, 622

**Proxy** A grant of authority by the shareholder to transfer his or her voting rights to someone else.   451

**Proxy contest** An attempt to gain control of a firm by soliciting a sufficient number of stockholder votes to replace the existing management.   860

**Public issue** Sale of securities to the public.   619

**Purchasing power parity (PPP)** Idea that the exchange rate adjusts to keep purchasing power constant among currencies.   916

**Pure discount bond** A bond that pays no coupons and only pays back face value at maturity. Also referred to as bullets and zeros.   146

**Put–call parity** The case when the value of a call equals the value of buying the stock plus buying the put plus borrowing at the risk-free rate.   678

**Put option** The right to sell a specified number of shares of stock at a stated price on or before a specified time.   672

**Random walk** Theory that stock price changes from day to day are at random; the changes are independent of each other and have the same probability distribution.   418

**Real cash flow** A cash flow for which the current, or date 0, purchasing power of the cash flow is given.   233

**Real interest rate** Interest rate expressed in terms of real goods, that is, the nominal interest rate minus the expected inflation rate.   231

**Real options** Options, or choices, that a firm takes after a project is accepted.   275

**Red herring** First document released by an underwriter of a new issue to prospective investors.   593

**Refunding** The process of replacing outstanding bonds, typically to issue new securities at a lower interest rate than those replaced.   624

**Registered bond** Bond in which the issuing company keeps records of the ownership of each registered bond. The company will pay the interest and principal by cheque mailed directly to the address of the owner of record.   620

**Regular cash dividends** Cash payments by a firm to its shareholders, usually four times a year.   555

**Regular underwriting** The purchase of securities from the issuing company by an investment banker for resale to the public.   596

**Relative purchasing power parity (RPPP)** Idea that the rate of change in the price level of commodities in one country relative to the price level in another determines the rate of change of the exchange rate between the two countries' currencies.   916

**Reorganization** Financial restructuring of a failed firm. Both the firm's asset structure and its financial structure are changed to reflect their true value, and claims are settled.   901

**Retained earnings** Earnings not paid out as dividends.   449

**Retention ratio (plowback ratio)** Retained earnings divided by net income.   70

**Retractable (put) bond** A bond that allows the holder to force the issuer to buy the bond back at a stated price.   636

**Return on equity (ROE)** Net income after interest and taxes divided by average common shareholders' equity.   157

**Reverse split** A procedure whereby the number of outstanding common shares is reduced; for example, in a one-for-three reverse split, each investor exchanges three old shares for one new share.   584

**Rights offer** An offer that gives current shareholders the opportunity to maintain a proportionate interest in the company before the shares are offered to the public. Also called a rights offering.   595

**Risk averse** The state of an investor who will consider risky portfolios only if they provide compensation for risk via a risk premium.   329

**Risk premium** The excess return on the risky asset that is the difference between the expected return on risky assets and the return on risk-free assets.   295

**Sale and lease-back** An arrangement whereby a firm sells its existing assets to a financial company, which then leases them back to the firm. This is often done to generate cash.   645

**Sales forecast** A key input to the firm's financial planning process. External sales forecasts are based on historical experience, statistical analysis, and consideration of various macroeconomic factors; internal sales forecasts are obtained from internal sources.   66

**Sales-type lease** An arrangement whereby a firm leases its own equipment, such as IBM leasing its own computers, thereby competing with an independent leasing company.   644

**Same-day value** On concentrator accounts, the firm has immediate use of the funds even though it takes 24 hours for a cheque to clear in Canada.   826

**Seasoned equity offering (SEO)** A new public common share issue after the company's stock has been previously issued publicly. Also called a seasoned new issue.   595

**Scenario analysis** Analysis of the effect of different scenarios on the project, with each scenario involving a confluence of factors.   266

**Security market line (SML)** A straight line that shows the equilibrium relationship between systematic risk and expected rates of return for individual securities. According to the SML, the excess return on a risky asset is equal to the excess return on the market portfolio multiplied by the beta coefficient.   340

**Semistrong-form efficiency** Theory that the market is efficient with respect to all publicly available information.   419

**Seniority** The order of repayment. In the event of bankruptcy, senior debt must be repaid before subordinated debt receives any payment.   457

**Sensitivity analysis** Analysis of the effect on the project when there is some change in critical variables such as sales and costs.   263

**Separation principle** The principle that portfolio choice can be separated into two independent tasks: (1) determination of the optimal risky portfolio, which is a purely technical problem, and (2) the personal choice of the best mix of the risky portfolio and the risk-free asset.   333

**Separation theorem** The value of an investment to an individual does not depend on consumption preferences. All investors will want to accept or reject the same investment projects by using the net present value rule, regardless of personal preference.   99

**Serial correlation** The correlation between the current return on a security and the return on the same security over a later period.   422

**Set-of-contracts viewpoint** View of the corporation as a set of contracting relationships among individuals who have conflicting objectives, such as shareholders and managers. The corporation is a legal contrivance that serves as the nexus for the contracting relationships.   13

**Short hedge** Protection of the value of an asset held by selling a futures contract.   762

**Short-run operating activities** Events and decisions concerning the short-term finance of a firm, such as how much inventory to order and whether to offer cash terms or credit terms to customers.   794

**Shortage costs** Costs that fall with increases in the level of investment in current assets.   798

**Simple interest** Interest calculated by considering only the original principal amount.   108

**Sinking fund** An account managed by the bond trustee for the purpose of repaying the bonds.   623

**Socially responsible investing** Investing by screening and selecting securities based on social or environmental criteria.   16

**Sole proprietorship** A business owned by a single individual. The sole proprietorship pays no corporate income tax but has unlimited liability for business debts and obligations.   9

**Speculative motive** A reason for holding cash that arises from wanting to take advantage of temporary opportunities such as bargain purchases or attractive interest rates.   818

**Spot exchange rate** Exchange rate between two currencies for immediate delivery.   914

**Spot trades** Agreements today on the exchange rates, for settlement in two days.   914

**Spread (discount)** The gap between the interest rate a bank pays on deposits and the interest rate it charges on loans.   595

**Standard deviation** The positive square root of the variance. This is the standard statistical measure of the spread of a sample. 298

**Standardized normal distribution** A normal distribution with an expected value of zero and a standard deviation of one. 689

**Standby fee** Amount paid to an underwriter who agrees to purchase any stock that is not subscribed to the public investor in a rights offer. 609

**Standby underwriting** An agreement whereby an underwriter agrees to purchase any stock that is not purchased by the public investor. 609

**Stated annual interest rate** The interest rate expressed as a percentage per annum, by which interest payment is determined. 117

**Statement of comprehensive income** Financial report that summarizes a firm's performance over a specified time period. 36

**Statement of financial position** Statement showing a firm's accounting value on a particular date. It reflects the following equation: Assets = Liabilities + Shareholders' equity. Also called a balance sheet. 33

**Stock dividend** Payment of a dividend in the form of stock rather than cash. A stock dividend comes from treasury stock, increasing the number of shares outstanding, and reduces the value of each share. 582

**Stock exchange bid** One of two types of takeover bids; must be communicated through the facilities of the TSX or other exchanges. Ontario securities law requires that the bidder mail a notice of the proposed share purchase to shareholders. If the bid is made through a stock exchange, the response is through a press release. 858

**Stock split** The increase in the number of outstanding shares of stock while making no change in shareholders' equity. 583

**Straight voting** Voting in which a shareholder may cast all of his or her votes for each candidate for the board of directors. 451

**Strike or exercise price** Price at which the put option or call option can be exercised. Also called the exercise price. 669

**Stripped common shares** Shares that entitle shareholders to receive either all the dividends from one or a group of well-known companies or an instalment receipt that packages any capital gain in the form of a call option. 562

**Stripped real-return bond** A zero-coupon bond issued by the Government of Canada with inflation protection and principal indexed to inflation. 636

**Strong-form efficiency** Theory that the market is efficient with respect to all available information, public or private. 419

**Subordinated (debt)** Debt whose holders have a claim on the firm's assets only after senior debtholders' claims have been satisfied. 457

**Subscription price** Price that existing shareholders are allowed to pay for a share of stock in a rights offer. 605

**Sunk cost** A cost that has already occurred and cannot be removed. Because sunk costs are in the past, such costs should be ignored when deciding whether to accept or reject a project. 224

**Sustainable growth rate** The only growth rate possible with preset values for four variables: profit margin, payout ratio, debt-to-equity ratio, and asset utilization ratio, if the firm issues no new equity. 74

**Swap rate** The difference between the sale (purchase) price of an asset and the price to repurchase (resell) the asset in a swap. 914

**Swaps** Exchange between two securities or currencies. One type of swap involves the sale (or purchase) of a foreign currency with a simultaneous agreement to repurchase (or sell) it. 777, 911

**Syndicate (banking group)** A corporate loan made by a group (or syndicate) of banks and other institutional investors. A syndicated bank loan may be publicly traded. 595

**Synergy** When the value of a combined firm after a merger is greater than the sum of the values of the firms pre-merger. 225

**Systematic (market) risk** Any risk that affects a large number of assets, each to a greater or lesser degree. 329

**Taking delivery** Assumption of possession by the buyer from the seller of the asset agreed upon in a forward contract. 755

**Target cash balance** Optimal amount of cash for a firm to hold, considering the trade-off between the opportunity costs of holding too much cash and the trading costs of holding too little. 817

**Targeted repurchase** A procedure in the United States by which firms may repurchase shares from specific individual stockholders. 564

**Tender offer** Public offer to buy shares of a target firm.   858

**Term loans** Direct business loans of, typically, one to five years.   637

**Terms of the sale** Conditions under which a firm proposes to sell its goods and services for cash or credit.   837

**Total cash flow of the firm** Total cash inflow minus total cash outflow.   41

**Trade credit** Credit granted to other firms.   807

**Trading range** Spread between high and low stock prices over a period of time. The desire to maintain stock price within a trading range may motivate a stock split.   584

**Transaction motive** A reason for holding cash that arises from normal disbursement and collection activities of the firm.   819

**Triangular arbitrage** Striking offsetting deals among three markets simultaneously to obtain an arbitrage profit.   913

**Value additivity** In an efficient market, the value of the sum of two cash flows is the sum of the values of the individual cash flows.   192

**Value at risk (VaR)** A popular risk measurement tool used by banks, insurance companies, and other financial institutions. VaR represents the maximum possible loss in dollars for a given confidence level.   299

**Variable costs** A cost that varies directly with volume and is zero when production is zero.   264

**Variance** In a probability distribution, the expected value of the squared deviation from the expected return.   298

**Venture capital** Early-stage financing of young companies seeking to grow rapidly.   611

**Warrants** Securities that give the holder the right—but not the obligation—to buy shares of common stock directly from a company at a fixed price for a given time period.   733

**Weak-form efficiency** Theory that the market is efficient with respect to historical price information.   418

**Weighted average cost of capital (WACC)** The average cost of capital on the firm's existing projects and activities. The weighted average cost of capital for the firm is calculated by weighting the cost of each source of funds by its proportion of the total market value of the firm. It is calculated on a before- and after-tax basis.   385, 536

**White knight** A takeover defence in which management seems to be a friendly bidder.   882

**Yield to maturity** The discount rate that equates the present value of interest payments and redemption value with the present price of the bond.   151

**Zero-balance account** A chequing account in which a zero balance is maintained by transfers of funds from a master account in an amount only large enough to cover cheques presented.   827

**Zero-coupon bonds (zeros)** Bonds that make no coupon payments and thus are initially priced at a deep discount.   634

# INDEX

## A

abandonment option, 276–277
abnormal return (AR), 424–425
accounting
  efficient capital markets, 437–438
  leasing, 646–648
  reporting foreign operations,
    930–931
accounting statements
  financial statement analysis,
    49–60
  net working capital, 38
  pro forma statements, 67
  statement of cash flows, 39–41
  statement of comprehensive
    income, 36–38
  statement of financial position,
    33–35
accounts payable period, 795
accounts receivable financing, 807
accounts receivable period, 794
acquisition method, 862–863
acquisitions
  accounting for, 862–863
  agency theory, 886–888
  assets, of, 859
  consolidation, 858
  defensive tactics, 877–883
  diversification, 873–874
  earnings growth, 872–873
  mergers, 857–858, 859
  real productivity, 888
  shareholders, 870–872, 883–886
  stock, of, 858
  synergies of, 857, 863–868
  takeovers, 859–860
  taxes, 861–862, 867–868
  value of the firm after, 868–870
activity, 49
activity ratios, 50–52, 58–59
Adelphia, 33
Adherex Technologies, 735
Aditya Birla Group, 848
adjusted cost of disposal, 257
adjusted present value (APV)
    method
  capital budgeting, 537–540
  defined, 533
  example of, 541–543
  firm valuation under leverage,
    533–535

  formula, 533–535
Advantage Energy, 739
adverse selection, 397–398
Aecon Group Inc., 739
AFG Flameguard Ltd., 593
Ag Growth Intl., 739
agency costs
  capital structure, 510–513
  convertible bonds, 747
  equity, 510–513
  financial distress, 500–503
  high-dividend policy, factors,
    572–573
  set-of-contracts theory, 13
agency theory, 882, 886–888
AGF Management Ltd., 379
aggregation, 66
aging schedule, 850
Agrawal, Anup, 523
Agrium, 785
Agueci, Eda, 427
Air Canada, 99, 278–279, 643,
    645, 808, 899
Air Wisconsin, 542
Alamos Gold Inc., 735
Alcan Aluminum, 410, 861
Aldeavision Inc., 409
Algoma Central Corp., 739
Alimentation Couche-Tard, 14
Allen, Jeffrey, 879
allocated cost, 225
Altman, E.I., 499, 500, 638
Altus Group, 739, 862–863
Amaya Gaming Group Inc., 735
Amazon.com, 577
American Airlines, 436
American Depository Receipt
    (ADR), 911
American option, 670, 680–681,
    684, 921
Amoako-Adu, B., 452, 453
amortization, 37, 39fn
Anderson, Scott, 612
Anderson Energy, 739
Andrade, Gregor, 500
Ang, J., 663
angels, 613
annual percentage rate (APR),
    117, 118–119
annual report, 22
annuity

  in advance, 128
  defined, 124
  delayed, 127
  growing, 130–131
  infrequent, 128
  mortgages, 126
  present value of, 124–125
  present value of two, 129–130
annuity due, 128
annuity factor, 125
annuity in advance, 128
anonymous market, 85
AOL, 887
Apollo Capital Management, 611
Apollo Global Management LC,
    881
Apple, 818
arbitrage
  defined, 90
  international financing
    decisions, 927
  market efficiency, 416, 417–418,
    421, 429–430
  MM Proposition I, 472, 479
  triangular, 913–914, 915
arbitrage pricing theory (APT),
    362–364
arbitrage profit, 680
arithmetic average returns, 301,
    303
articles of incorporation, 11, 449,
    604, 880
Asia Pacific Resources, 409
Asquith, P., 573, 601
asset beta, 382–383
asset pricing
  arbitrage pricing theory (APT),
    362–364
  CAPM. See capital asset pricing
    model (CAPM)
  empirical models, 364–366
asset requirements, 67, 74
asset-backed bond, 636
assets, 2, 33
assets minus liabilities, 35fn
Aston Hill Oil & Gas Inc., 735
Aston Hill VIP Income Fund, 735
AT&T, 669, 699–700
Athabasca Oil Corporation, 604
Atlantis Casino, 500
auction market, 21

automatic dividend reinvestment plans (ADPs or DRIPs), 562
availability float, 821
average (mean) return, 294–297, 301–303
average accounting return (AAR), 196–198, 214
average collection period (ACP), 51, 59, 849–850
average daily sales (ADS), 850
average payment period, 53, 59
average returns, 294–297, 301–303

B
backdoor equity, 748
Baker, H.K., 580
balance sheet model of the firm, 2–3
Ballard Power Systems Inc., 409
bank cash, 820
bank loans, 638
Bank of America (BofA), 734
Bank of Montreal, 18, 319, 378, 379, 558
Bank of Nova Scotia, 18, 19, 337, 379, 670, 675, 676
BankBoston, 887
banker's acceptances, 807–808, 842
banking group, 595
bankruptcy. *See also* financial distress
  avoidance, 904
  consolidation of debt, 505
  direct costs, 499
  indirect costs, 500–503
  liquidation, 901–902
  prepackaged, 906
  private workout vs., 904–905
  protective covenants, 503–504
  reorganization, 901, 903–904
  risk vs. cost, 496–498
  tax effects and costs, 505–508
*Bankruptcy and Insolvency Act* (1993), 901, 905
Barclays, 597
Bar-Or, Yuval, 500
Barrick Gold Corporation, 1, 555, 676–677, 861
Bartram, Sohnke, M., 785
basic IRR rule, 200
basic principle of financial investment decision making, 90
Bausch & Lomb, 410
BCE, 461
bearer bond, 621

bearer deposit notes (BDNs), 832
bearer instrument, 84
Becher, David, 441
behavioural finance
  efficient market theory, 434–436
  high-dividend policy, 571–572
  market efficiency, 412, 428–430
Bell Canada Enterprises Inc., 319, 612
benchmarks, 366
Berkshire Hathaway, 584
best-efforts underwriting, 596
beta
  asset/equity betas, 382–383
  beta coefficient, 353, 356
  capital asset pricing model (CAPM), 353
  cost of debt, 384–385
  cost of equity, 373, 375–383
  defined, 337
  determinants of, 380–383
  estimation, 375–380
  example, 335–337
  expected return, 360–362
  factor model, 355–356
  financial leverage, 382–383
  firm beta vs. project beta, 383–391
  firm valuation under leverage, 545–548
  formula for, 337–338
  GDP beta, 354–355
  industry beta, 379–380
  inflation beta, 354–355
  interest rate beta, 354–355
  market model, 356
  operating leverage, 380–382
  return on portfolio, 357–358
  revenue cycles, 380
  stability, 378–379
  systematic risk, 353–356
beta coefficient, 353–356
bid–ask spread, 396
Billes family, 453
binomial model. *See* two-state option model
Biovail Corporation, 409
Birchcliff Energy Ltd., 734, 735
Black, Leon, 881
BlackBerry, 378, 711
Black-Scholes model
  executive stock options, 709–714
  option pricing formula, 684, 687–691, 697
  two-state option model vs., 724
  valuing a start-up, 715–718
  warrant pricing, 738–739

blanket inventory lien, 807
Bloomberg, 58
Blume's formula, 303
BMO Capital Markets, 597
board out, 880
Bombardier Inc., 56, 452, 542
bond covenants, 504
bond refunding
  callable bonds, 624–626
  costs, 628–629
  interest rate, 626
  interest rate risk, 626–627
  non-callable bonds, 624
  protective covenants, 626
  taxes, 626
  value and analysis, 627–628
bondholders, 3fn, 35fn
bonds. *See also* public issue of bonds
  asset-backed, 636
  bond ratings, 630–634
  bond refunding, 624–629
  call options as, 692–694, 695
  call provisions, 150, 623, 624–626
  callable, 624–626
  clean price, 150
  consols, 121, 150, 152
  convertible bond, 636, 739–749
  coupons, 147
  defined, 146
  dirty price, 150
  discount, 151
  Eurobonds, 911, 929
  face value, 147
  financial crisis 2008, 303–304
  floating-rate bonds, 635–636
  foreign bonds, 911, 927–930
  high yield, 631
  holding-period return, 152
  income bond, 636
  interest rate futures contracts, 763–766
  international bond markets, 911, 927–930
  investment grade, 631
  junk bonds, 631–632
  level-coupon bonds, 147–152
  long-term debt, 456
  maturity date, 146
  non-callable, 624
  options, as, 692–697
  premium, 151
  price and interest rates, 150–151, 183–185
  pure discount bond, 146–147, 152
  quotations, 149–150

registered bond, 620
retractable bond, 636
risk, 747
sinking fund, 456–457, 622–623
stripped real-return bond, 636
valuing, 146–150, 152
warrants, 739–740
yield to maturity, 151, 152
zero-coupon bonds, 147,
    634–635, 678
book cash, 820
book value, 35, 450
book value of equity, 449
BOP analysis, 263–266
Boralex, 739
bought deal, 592, 596
Brand Leaders Income Fund, 735
Brascan, 873
break-even analysis, 266–270
Briggs and Stratton Corp., 410
British Columbia Investment
    Management Corporation,
    451
brokerage costs, 798
brokerage fees, 396
Brown, Gregory W., 785
bubble theory, 433–434

C

call options. *See also* valuing
    options
  covered-call strategy, 679
  defined, 670
  firm as, 692–693
  put-call parity, 677–679
  stock/bonds as, 692–694, 695
  value at expiration, 670–671
  valuing, 681–683
  warrants vs., 733, 735–738
call premium, 623, 628
call price, 457
call protected, 623
call provision
  callable bonds, 624–626
  defined, 457
  public issue of bonds, 150, 623
callable bonds, 624–626
Campeau Corporation, 526–527,
    899
Canaccord Genuity Corp., 597
Canada Deposit Insurance
    Corporation (CDIC), 501,
    696, 697
Canada Life Financial, 882–883
Canada Mortgage and Housing
    Corp., 18

Canada Plus call, 457, 623, 629
Canada Savings Bonds (CSBs), 623
Canadian Accounting Standards
    Board, 710
Canadian Coalition for Good
    Governance, 451
Canadian Commercial Bank, 696
Canadian Derivatives Clearing
    Corporation (CDCC), 670
Canadian Imperial Bank of
    Commerce, 18, 379
Canadian Institute of Chartered
    Accountants, 229, 930
Canadian Pacific Ltd., 319
Canadian Securities
    Administrators (CSA), 593
Canadian Tire Corporation, 319,
    452, 453, 802, 878
Canadian Tire Dealers
    Association, 453, 881
Canadian Utilities, 337
Canlan Ice Sports Corp., 409
Canwest, 897, 899, 906–907
Canwest Global Communications
    Corporation, 496
capital, 83
capital asset pricing model
    (CAPM), 338–342
  arbitrage pricing theory (APT),
    362–364
  beta coefficient, 353
  expected return, individual
    security, 339–340
  expected return, stock market,
    338–339
  formula, 339–340
  international diversification,
    924–925
  portfolio, 341
  security market line (SML), 340,
    342
  single-factor model, 360, 361
capital budgeting
  approaches to, 537–540
  average accounting return
    (AAR), 196–198, 214
  break-even analysis, 266–270
  cost of debt, 384–385
  cost of equity, 373–375
  cost of preferred stock, 385
  decision to replace, 242–246
  decision trees, 261–263
  defined, 3
  discounted payback period
    rule, 196, 214
  economic value added (EVA),
    407–410

equivalent annual cost method,
    240–246
  incremental cash flows, 223–230
  inflation, 231–235
  internal rate of return (IRR),
    199–211, 214
  international, 922–925
  levered firm, 533–548
  Monte Carlo simulation, 270–274
  net present value (NPV),
    191–193, 214
  operating cash flow definitions,
    236–237
  payback period rule, 193–195,
    213–214
  practice of, 213–214
  profitability index, 211–213, 214
  real options, 272–276
  sensitivity analysis, 263–266
  tax shield approach, 237–240
  weighted average cost of capital
    (WACC), 385–391
capital cost allowance (CCA)
  asset purchases and sales,
    257–258
  break-even analysis, 269–270
  calculation, 255–256
  depreciation tax shield, 237,
    268–269
  financial record keeping, 229
  incremental cash flows, 229
  leasing, 648, 659–661
  operating cash flow, 237–240
  in practice, 256
  present value of tax shield
    formula, 259–260
capital expenditure, 3
capital gains, 31, 287
capital gains effect, 861–862
capital lease, 646
capital market line (CML), 333
capital markets, 20
capital rationing, 212
capital structure. *See also*
    corporate fiancé; corporate
    firm
  agency costs of equity, 510–513
  corporate finance, 3–4
  debt-equity ratio, growth and,
    516–518
  defined, 3
  establishing, 523–527
  financial distress costs, 486–503
  financial leverage, 468–481
  firm valuation under leverage,
    533–548
  firm value and shareholders'

interests, 466–467
MM Proposition I, 470–472, 476–479, 481
MM Proposition II, 473–479, 481
pecking-order theory, 513–516
personal taxes, 518–523
pie model, 465–466
signalling, 508–510
taxes, 481–489, 518–523
trade-off theory, 506
weights, 386
caps, 780
captive finance companies, 852
CargoJet, 739
CARP, 459
carrying costs, 797–799, 846
carrying value, 35, 450
carve-out, 879
cash, 823. *See also* cash flows; liquidity
   budgeting, 803–805
   cycle, 794
   cash flow timeline, 794, 795
   collection and disbursement, 820–828
   disbursements, 804–805, 826, 827, 829
   electronic data interchange (EDI), 823
   equivalents, 819
   financial statements, 791–792
   holding, 818–819
   liquidity management vs., 819–820
   management, 818–833
   operating cycles, 794–797
   statement, 792–793
cash budget, 803–805
cash coverage, 53, 59
cash cow, 159–162
cash cycle, 794–797
cash disbursements, 804–805, 826, 827, 829
cash discounts, 840–842
cash equivalents, 819
cash flow from operations, 39, 41
cash flow timeline, 794, 795
cash flows, 699–700. *See also* cash; operating cash flow; statement of cash flows
   accounting income vs., 223–224
   cash budgeting, 803–805
   changes in long-term assets, 40
   defined, 39
   discount rate, 233–235
   financial cash flow, 39–41
   financial manager, 5

financial markets, 5
free cash flows, 41
identification, 6
incremental cash flows, 223–230
inflation, 232–233
leasing, 649–650
management, 63
net income vs., 41
net present value (NPV), 193
net working capital, 39, 40
nominal vs. real, 233–235
NPV of a merger, 874–875, 876–877
operating cash flow definitions, 236–237
operations, from, 39, 41
payback period method, 193–195
risk, 7
shareholders, 40–41
short-term vs. long-term, 791
short vs. long-term financing, 790
statement of cash flows, 39–41
tax shield vs. total project approach, 240
timing, 6–7
total cash flow of the firm, 41
cash offer
   general cash offer, 595
   initial public offering (IPO), 598–599
   investments banks, 596–597
   overallotment option, 596
   pricing, 597, 598–599
   selling period, 596
   underpricing, 597, 599–601
   underwriting, 595–596
cash ratio, 50, 58
cash transaction, 756
cash-out, 798
Cavalluzzo Hayes Shilton McIntyre & Cornish, 711
CBS Corp., 713
CCA. *See* capital cost allowance (CCA)
Cdn Life Cos Split Corp., 735
Celestica, 56, 452
Cenovus Energy Inc., 879
Central Guaranty Trust, 696
CGI Group Inc., 378
change in net working capital, 38
Chapters Online, 805
characteristic line, 335
Charmin Paper Company, 865
chartered banks, 18–19. *See also* financial institutions

Cheung, J.K., 437
Chevron Corp., 713
Chicago Board of Trade (CBT), 756
Chicago Board Options Exchange (CBOE), 674
Chicago Mercantile Exchange (CME), 756
chief executive officer, 4, 16–17
Chrysler, 887, 888
CIBC, 597
CICA *Handbook*, 929
circular bid, 858
civil law, 17
claims, 1
classes of shares, 452–453
clean price, 150
Cleary, Sean, 328
clientele effect, 575–577
clienteles, 576
closed-end mortgage, 622
CME Group, 756
CNBC effect, 436
CNOOC Limited, 860, 861
coattail provision, 453
Coca-Cola Company, 410, 583, 713, 714, 760
Cogeco Inc., 410
Cognos Inc., 409
coinsurance effect, 871–872
collateral trust bonds, 621
collected bank cash, 820
collection, 849
collection float, 821
collection policy, 837
Coller, M., 398
Com Dev International Ltd., 711
commercial paper, 807, 808
commercial draft, 842
common law, 17
common shares. *See* common stock; securities
common stock, 58. *See also* securities
   authorized vs. issued shares, 449
   book value, 450
   classes of shares, 452–453
   convertible bonds/warrants vs., 744–745
   defined, 448
   dividends, 452. *See also* dividends
   dividends vs. capital gains, 152–153
   market value, 450
   NPV of a merger, 875–877
   options, as, 692–697
   present value, 152–156

replacement value, 450
retained earnings, 449
shareholders' rights, 450–451
stock repurchase, 562–567
stripped common shares, 562
valuation of, 152–167
Companhia Vale do Rio Doce, 861
*Companies' Creditors Arrangement Act* (CCAA), 899, 904
compensating balance, 806fn
comply-or-explain regime, 22
compound interest, 108
compound value, 105
compounding
　annual percentage rate (APR), 117, 118–119
　continuous, 119–121
　defined, 107
　example, 107–109, 111
　more than once per year, 116–118
　over many years, 118–119
　periods, 117–119
computer technology, 23–24
concentration banking, 826
conditional sales contract, 843
conglomerate acquisition, 859
Conrad, Jennifer, 785
conservatism, 429
consolidation, 858
consols, 121, 150, 152
constant-growth pattern, 153–155
Consumers Distributing, 899
contingent claims, 9
contingent value rights (CVR), 699–700
continuous compounding, 119–121
contribution margin, 268
control block, 879–880
control versus ownership, 14–17
conversion premium, 740
conversion price, 740
conversion ratio, 740
conversion value, 741–742
convertible bonds
　agency costs, 747
　backdoor equity, 748
　conversion policy, 748–749
　conversion premium, 740
　conversion price, 740
　conversion ratio, 740
　conversion value, 741–742
　defined, 636, 739
　matching cash flows, 746–747
　option value, 742–743

risk synergy, 747
straight bond value, 740–741
uses of, 746–748
convertible debt, 743–746
Coors, 710
Copp, David, 328
corporate charter, 880
corporate discount rate, 383
corporate finance. *See also* capital structure; corporate firm
　accounting statements, 33–41
　balance sheet model, 2–3
　capital structure, 3–4
　cash flows, 6–7
　corporate firm forms, 9–12
　corporate firm goals, 12–17
　corporate securities, 8–9
　efficient capital markets implications, 430–435
　financial institutions, 18–19
　financial manager, 4–5
　financial markets, 20–26
　financial planning, 65–77
　financial statement analysis, 49–60
　financing and value creation, 412–414
　governance, 16–17
　international, 910–931
　investment decision making, 97–99
　long-term financing, 448–462
　options, 669–699
　ownership vs. control, 14–17
　taxes, 31–32
corporate firm. *See also* capital structure; corporate finance
　financial institutions, 18–20
　forms of, 9–12
　goals, 12–17
　governance, 16–17
　ownership vs. control, 14–17
　valuing, 168–169
corporate forms, 9–12
corporate governance, 16–17
corporate insiders, 16–17
corporate long-term debt. *See* long-term debt
corporate taxation. *See also* capital cost allowance (CCA)
　acquisitions, 861–862, 867–868
　beta and the leveraged firm, 545–548
　bond refunding, 626
　capital gains, 31

capital structure under, 481
deferred taxes, 37
expected return, 485–486
financial distress costs, 505–508
financial leverage, 520–523
income trust, 461
investment tax credits, 32
leasing, 648, 651–652, 659–661
Miller model and firm value, 520–523
MM Proposition I, 481
MM Proposition I, corporate taxes, 483–485
MM Proposition II, 481
MM Proposition II, corporate taxes, 485–489
preferred shares, 459–460
present value of tax shield, 483
rates, 31
stock price, 487–488
synergy of acquisitions, 867–868
weighted average cost of capital (WACC), 386–388, 486–487
corporation, 11–12
correlation
　calculation, 312–315
　coefficients of, 314–315
　defined, 312
　efficient set, two assets, 320–323
　securities within a portfolio, 310, 312
　serial correlation, 422–423
correlation coefficient, 314–315
Cost of Borrowing Disclosure, 118
cost of capital. *See also* weighted average cost of capital (WACC)
　acquisition synergy, 868
　liquidity, 396–398
cost of equity
　beta determinants, 380–383
　beta estimation, 375–380
　defined, 372
　expected return, 373–375
　firm beta vs. project beta, 383–391
　security market line (SML)., 384–385
costs, 37–38. *See also* agency costs
counterparty, 920
counterparty risk, 780
coupon rate, 151
coupons, 147
court protection case, 906–907
covariance
　beta, 337
　beta calculation, 375–377
　calculation, 312–315

calculation, many assets, 325–327
  portfolio, 317–319
  securities within a portfolio,
    310, 312, 327–329
covenant, 457–458, 503–505, 622,
  807
Coventree Capital Inc., 833
covered-call strategy, 679
credit analysis, 837, 848–849
credit crisis. *See* financial crisis
  2007–2009
credit default swaps (CDSs), 754,
  779–780. *See also* derivatives
credit derivatives. *See* derivatives
credit instrument, 842–843
credit insurance, 848
credit management, 837–852
  collection policy, 837, 849–851
  credit analysis, 837, 848–849
  decision to grant credit,
    843–845, 847
  factoring, 851
  financing trade credit, 851–852
  optimal credit policy, 846–848
  terms of sale, 837, 838–843
  trade credit, 837–839
credit period, 839–840
credit scoring, 849
Creditel, 848
creditors, 3, 35fn, 455
Crocodile Gold Corp., 735
cross rate, 910–911
cross-listing, 22
crown jewels, 882
crown-related firms, 612
CTVglobemedia Inc., 35
cumulative abnormal returns
  (CARs), 424–425
cumulative dividends, 458
cumulative probability, 689
cumulative voting, 451
currency options, 921
currency swaps, 778–779, 920–921
current assets
  alternative financing strategies,
    800–802
  balance sheet model, 2
  defined, 2, 790
  short-term financing and,
    797–803
current liability
  defined, 3, 791
  quick ratio, 50
  short-term financing, 800–802
current ratio, 50, 58
current taxes, 37
cutoff rate, 383

**D**

D&B Canada, 848
Dabora, Emil, 431
Daimler-Benz, 887, 888
Dalradian Resources Inc., 735
data mining, 365
date of payment, 557
date of record, 556
dates convention, 124
days in inventory ratio, 51
De Jong, Abe, 566
dealer market, 21
Dean Witter, 887
DeAngelo, H., 452, 572, 578, 880
DeAngelo, L., 452, 572, 578
debenture, 456, 622
debit cards, 825
debt. *See also* capital structure;
  short-term financing
  balance sheet model, 3
  consolidation, 505
  contingent claims, 8–9
  debentures, 456, 622
  equity vs., 455, 456
  long-term debt, 618–638
  notes, 456
  preferred shares as, 459
  protective covenants, 503–505
  securities, 1
  short-term debt, 3, 618
  signalling, 508–510
  statement of financial position,
    34–35
  trade-off theory, 506
debt capacity, 53
debt displacement, 654–657
debt ratio, 52, 59
debt securities, 621–622
debt service, 35
debtholders, 3fn
debt-to-equity ratio, 52, 59, 74,
  516–518
decision to replace, 242–246
decision trees, 261–263
declaration date, 556
deed of trust, 619
deferred call, 623
deferred taxes, 37
delayed annuity, 127
deliverable instrument, 755
Delta Airlines, 436
Delta Gold Corp., 735
denomination, 147
depreciation, 37, 39fn
depreciation tax shield, 237,
  259–260, 268–269

derivatives. *See also* hedging;
  swap contracts
  credit derivatives, 754
  defined, 754
  financial crisis 2008, 755
  R. A. Jarrow on, 782–784
  risk and, 754–755
  use of, 781, 784–785
Derosiers, Stephanie, 601
Deshpande, S.D., 573
DesRosiers, Dennis, 454
DesRosiers Automotive
  Consultants, 454
Deutsch, Yuval, 711
Deutsche Börse, 21
differential-growth pattern,
  153–156
Dipchand, C.R., 663
direct lease, 644
dirty price, 150
disbursements. *See* cash
  disbursements
disclosure requirements, 594,
  598
discount, 151, 595
discount rate
  arbitrage pricing theory (APT),
    372
  capital asset pricing model
    (CAPM), 372
  cost of equity, 375
  dividend discount model,
    157–159
  firm valuation under leverage,
    543–545
  lease versus buying decision, 653
  risky project, 372
discounted payback period rule,
  196, 214
discounting
  defined, 112
  earnings vs. dividends, 162–163
  nominal vs. real rates, 233–235
diversifiable (unique,
  unsystematic) risk, 329
diversification
  international shareholder, 924
  portfolio, 358–360
  risk, 318–319, 327–329, 358–360
  risk averse, 329–330
diversification effect
  calculation, 318–319
  efficient set, two assets, 320, 322
  example, 327–329
  international diversification,
    323–324
divestiture, 877–879

dividend capture, 831
dividend discount model, 157–159
dividend growth model, 163–164
dividend payout ratio, 69–70, 74
dividend policy
  cash dividend method, 555,
    556–558
  clientele effect, 575–577
  current practice, 578–581
  firms with insufficient cash,
    567–568
  firms with sufficient cash,
    568–570
  high-dividend policy, factors,
    570–575
  influences on, 580–581
  investment policy, 563
  irrelevance of, illustration,
    558–563
  Miller and Modigliani, 560, 563
  personal taxation, 567–570
  pros and cons of payment, 580
  stock dividend/split, 555–556,
    582–585
  stock repurchase, 563–570
  summary, 581–582
dividend signalling, 574–575
dividend valuation model, 153fn,
  155, 374fn
dividend yield, 56–57, 59
dividend-growth patterns,
  153–156
dividends
  automatic dividend
    reinvestment plans (ADPs or
    DRIPs), 562
  capital gains vs., 152–153
  common stock, 452
  cumulative and non-
    cumulative, 458
  date of payment, 557
  date of record, 556
  declaration date, 556
  defined, 452
  discount model, 157–159
  dividend capture, 831
  dollar earnings, 287
  ex-dividend date, 556–558
  extra cash dividend, 555
  growth pattern, 153–156
  homemade dividends, 561–562
  interest vs., 455
  no-dividend firm, 163
  payout ratio, 69–70, 74
  percentage returns, 288–290
  signalling, 574–575
  types of, 555–556

yield, 56–57, 59
dollar earnings, 287–288
Dome Petroleum, 867
Dominion Bond Rating Service
  (DBRS), 630, 807
Domtar Corporation, 585
Domtar Inc., 410
Donaldson, G., 3–14, 73, 462
Drexel Burnham Lambert, 631, 632
Dun & Bradstreet Corp., 410
Dun & Bradstreet Industry Norms
  and Key Business Ratios, 58
Dunav Resources Ltd., 735
Dundee Precious Metals Inc., 735
Dupont Canada Inc., 409
DuPont system of financial
  control, 54, 55
duration, 772–774
duration hedging
  duration concept, 772–774
  hedging, 770–776
  liabilities to assets matching,
    774–775
  in practice, 776
  two bonds, different coupons
    case, 771–772
  zero-coupon bonds case,
    770–771
Dutch auction, 564
Dutta, Shantanu, 428, 453, 580,
  886

E

earnings before interest and
  taxes (EBIT)
  incremental cash flows, 229
  interest coverage, 52–53
  MM Proposition I, 470–472
  operating cash flow, 236
earnings per share, 470–472
earnings surprise, 431
Eaton's, 899
Ebbers, Bernie, 22
EBIT. See earnings before interest
  and taxes (EBIT)
EBITDA, 53
EBITDA margin, 54, 59
Eccels, Robert, 864
Eckbo, B. Espen, 16, 17
economic assumptions, 67
economic value added (EVA),
  407–410
economies of scale, 865–867
EDS, 879
effective annual interest rate
  (EAR), 117–119

efficient capital markets. See also
  efficient market hypothesis
  (EMH)
  accounting, 437–438
  arbitrage, 417–418, 429–430
  corporate finance implications,
    430–435
  defined, 412, 414
  description, 414–416
  market prices forecasting,
    441–442
  random walk, 418
  rationality and, 416–417, 428–429
  speculation, 439–441
  timing decision, 438–439
  types of efficiency, 418–421
  valuing common stocks, 167
efficient market, 89
efficient market hypothesis
  (EMH). See also efficient
  capital markets
  arbitrage, 417–418, 429–430
  behavioural finance vs., 412,
    428–430, 434–436
  defined, 414–416
  empirical challenges, 430–434
  Grossman-Stiglitz paradox, 421
  information sets, 420
  misconceptions about, 421–422
  rationality, 416–417, 428–429
  semistrong-form efficiency,
    419–421, 424–427
  strong-form efficiency, 419–421,
    427–428
  summary, 443
  weak-form efficiency, 418–419,
    422–423
efficient set
  capital market line (CML), 333
  defined, 322
  international diversification,
    323–324
  many assets, 324–325
  optimal portfolio, 332–334
  separation principle, 333–334
  two assets, 320–323
electronic collection system,
  824–825
electronic data interchange (EDI),
  823
Eli Lilly & Co., 410
embedded options, 709, 717–718
Embraer, 542
Enbridge Inc., 163, 336, 337, 448,
  449
Encana Corp., 611, 879
end-of-year convention, 124

Enron, 438
enterprise value, 56, 59
enterprise value multiple, 56, 59
equilibrium rate of interest, 86
equity. *See also* capital structure
  agency costs, 510–513
  contingent claims, 8–9
  debt vs., 455, 456
  securities, 1
  statement of financial position,
    34–35
equity beta, 382–383
equity capitalization, 35fn
equity kickers. *See* warrants
equity multiplier, 52, 59
equity securities, 9. *See also*
    public issue of securities
equity shares, 3. *See also*
    common shares; securities
equivalent annual cost method,
    240–246, 268–270
erosion, 225
Estey Commission, 438
euro, 910
Eurobanks, 927
Eurobonds, 911, 929
Eurocurrency, 911
Eurodollar, 926–927
Euronext, 21
European currency unit, 910
European Monetary System
    (EMS), 910
European option, 670
event studies, 424–425
Excelsior Energy, 604
excess return on the market
    portfolio, 295
exchange offers, 509
exchange rate
  forward exchange rate, 914
  international corporate finance,
    912–913
  risk, 913, 919–921
  spot exchange rate, 914
exchange rate risk, 913, 919–920
exchange traded funds (ETFs),
    330
exclusionary offer, 881
ex-dividend date, 556–558
executive compensation
  current trends, 710–711, 712
  dividends vs. repurchase, 566
  market efficiency, 442
  options, 709–714
  ownership vs. control, 15
  valuing, 712–714
executive stock options, 709–714

exercise price, 669, 681–683
exercising the option, 669
exotics, 780–781
expectations hypothesis, 185–186
expected return, 316
  beta, 360–362
  calculation, single security, 310
  calculation, two or more
    securities, 316
  capital asset pricing model
    (CAPM), 338–340
  characteristic line, 335
  corporate taxation, 485–486
  cost of capital, 396–398
  cost of equity, 373–375
  defined, 309
  efficient set, two assets, 320–323
  factor model, 355–356
  liquidity, 397
  market model, 356
  MM Proposition II, corporate
    taxes, 485–486
  parts of, 351–352
  portfolio, return on, 316,
    357–358
  securities, 309, 310–312
  security market line (SML).,
    360–362
  single-factor model, 360–362
expense preference, 13
expensive lunch story, 745–746
expiration date, 669, 681–683
Export Development Canada
    (EDC), 848, 911
ex-rights, 608–609
external funds needed (EFN), 71
Exxon Corp., 866

**F**

F N X Mining Co. Inc., 409
face value, 147, 456, 620
factor, 807
factor model, 355–360
factoring, 851
fair market value, 55–56
fair value method, 35
Fairfax Financial, 18, 379, 899
Falconbridge Limited, 861
Fama, E.F., 365, 371, 432, 578
feasible set, 321–322
*Federal Bankruptcy Reform Act*,
    904
Federated Department Stores
    case study, 526–527
FEDI, 823
field warehouse financing, 807

Fields, W.C., 760
Financial Accounting Standards
    Board (FASB), 437
financial crisis 2007–2009
  bankruptcy, 505
  bonds, 303–304
  credit default swaps (CDSs),
    779–780
  derivatives, 755, 782–784
  financial markets, 434
  hedge funds, 24–26
  short-term financing, 808
financial distress. *See also*
    bankruptcy
  bankruptcy liquidation, 901–902
  bankruptcy vs. private workout,
    904–905
  capital structures and costs of,
    486–503
  court protection, 906–907
  defined, 896
  handling procedures, 899–901
  insolvency, 896, 898
financial engineering, 23
financial gap, 461–462
financial institutions, 18–20
financial instruments, 1, 84, 86
financial intermediaries, 85
financial lease, 645, 649–650
financial leverage
  beta, 382–383
  corporate taxation, 520–523
  defined, 49, 52
  financial markets, 24–26
  firm valuation under leverage,
    468–473, 533–548
  firm value and shareholder
    returns, 468–489
  MM Proposition II, no taxes,
    473–479, 481
  MM Proposition I, no taxes,
    470–472, 476, 481
  ratios, 49, 52–53, 59
  ROA vs. ROE, 55
  securities, 8–9
financial manager, 4–5
financial market economy, 84
  anonymous market, 85
  basic principle, 90
  borrowing example, 92–93
  competition, 89–90
  corporate investment decision
    making, 97–99
  financial intermediaries, 85
  intertemporal consumption, 84,
    86–88
  investment decision

illustration, 94–97
lending example, 91–92
market clearing, 85–86
financial markets
  capital market, 20
  computer technology, 23–24
  financial crisis 2008, 24–26, 434
  financial engineering, 23
  financial leverage, 24–26
  foreign exchange market, 22–23
  globalization, 23
  listing, 21–22
  money markets, 20
  primary markets, 20
  secondary markets, 20, 21
  trends in, 23–26
*Financial Performance Indicators*, 58
financial performance ratios,
  49–50, 57, 60
financial planning, 67
  assumptions of, 66
  defined, 65–66
  elements of, 65
  model for, 66–67, 76–77
  percentage of sales method,
    67–72
  pro forma statements, 67
  sustainable growth, 72–76
*Financial Post Advisor*, 58
financial ratios. *See* financial
  statement analysis
financial requirements, 67
financial slack, 516
financial statement analysis
  activity ratios, 49, 50–52, 58–59
  benchmarks, 58
  financial leverage ratios, 49,
    52–53, 59
  financial performance ratios,
    49–50, 57, 60
  financial ratios, using, 57, 60
  market value ratios, 55–57, 59
  profitability ratios, 49, 53–55, 59
  short-term solvency ratios, 49,
    50, 58
  sustainable growth rate ratio,
    55, 59
financial statements. *See*
  accounting statements
financial structure. *See* capital
  structure
financing. *See also* long-term
  financing; short-term
  financing
  internal, 461–462
  international, options, 926–930
  investing vs., 202–204

value creation, 412–414
venture capital, 613
firm. *See* corporate firm
firm valuation under leverage.
  *See also* value of the firm
  adjusted present value method,
    533–535, 537–543
  beta, 545–548
  comparison of approaches,
    537–540
  discount rate estimation, 543–545
  flow to equity approach,
    535–536, 537–540
  weighted average cost of capital
    (WACC) method, 536–540
firm value. *See also* value of the
  firm
  amount of debt, 506
  MM Proposition I, 470–472,
    476–479, 481
  MM Proposition I, corporate
    taxes, 483–485
  MM Proposition II, 473–479, 481
  MM Proposition II, corporate
    taxes, 485–489
  selfish investment strategies,
    500–503
  taxes, 481–483
  valuation under leverage.
    *See* firm valuation under
    leverage
firm-commitment underwriting,
  596
first principle of investment
  decision making, 90
Fisher, T.C.G., 499
five C's of credit, 848–849
fixed assets, 2, 38
fixed costs, 37–38, 264
Flath, D., 662
Fleet Financial Group, 887
float, 820–823
floatation costs, 602
floater, 780
floating-rate bonds (floaters),
  635–636
floor-and-ceiling provisions, 635
floors, 780–781
flotation costs
  adjusted present value, 541–542
  bond refunding, 628
  defined, 602
  dividend policy, 578
  internal equity, 395–396
  net present value (NPV), 395
  public issue of securities, 602–604
  share issues, 568

weighted average cost of capital
  (WACC), 393–395
flow to equity (FTE), 535–536,
  537–540
flow-based insolvency, 898
force conversion, 748
Fording Canadian Coal Trust,
  861
foreign bonds, 911, 927–930
foreign exchange market, 22–23,
  912
foreign operations reporting,
  930–931
forward contracts
  defined, 755–756
  futures contracts and, 758
  interest rate futures contracts,
    764–765
  swaps vs., 777
forward discount, 919
forward exchange rate, 914
forward rate, 181–183
forward trades, 914
Franklin, Benjamin, 108
free cash flow, 41
free cash flow hypothesis,
  512–513, 887
free lunch story, 745–746
French, K.R., 365, 371, 432, 578
frequency distribution, 294
Froot, Kenneth, 431
funded debt, 456, 618. *See also*
  long-term debt
future value, 105, 107–111
futures contracts
  data example, 757
  defaults, 760–761
  defined, 756
  forward contracts and, 758
  hedging with, 763
  interest rate futures, 763–770
  interest rate futures contracts,
    765–766
  marked to the market, 758–760
  swaps vs., 777

## G

Galifi, Vincent, 454
Gandalf Technologies Inc., 899
Gap Inc., 423
Gaussian copula model, 783
GDP beta, 354–355
Géczy, C., 920
Gemini Energy Corp., 748
general cash offer, 595. *See also*
  cash offer

General Dynamics Corp., 713
General Motors, 500, 505, 900
general partnership, 10
Genuity Capital Markets, 454
geometric average returns, 301–303
geometric series, 121
George Weston Ltd., 14
Getty, 866
Giammarino, R., 697
Global Crossing, 438
Global Opportunities for Association (GOA), 911
GMP Securities, 427, 597, 604
going private transactions, 860, 881–882
golden parachutes, 882
Goldman Sachs and Co., 597
goodwill, 862–863
Gordon model, 155
Gottesman, A., 638
governance, 22
Government of Canada bonds pricing, 763–765, 766–769
Graham, John, 265, 274, 524, 526, 576
Grand & Toy, 410
Great-West Lifeco, 882–883
Green Shoe provision, 596
greenmail, 880
gross return on assets, 54, 59
Grossman–Stiglitz paradox, 421
growing annuity, 130–131
growing perpetuity, 122–124
growth fund, 366
growth rate, 157–159
growth stocks, 366, 432
Gudikunst, A.C., 663
Guide to Venture Capital, 613

H

Hall, Brian, 442
Harvey, C., 265, 274, 524, 526
Hatch, James, 290
Healy, P.M., 573, 888
hedge, 317
hedge funds, 24, 25
hedging. See also derivatives; swap contracts
  defined, 754
  derivatives and, 754–755
  duration hedging, 770–776
  exchange rate risk, 920–921
  forward contracts, 755–756
  futures contracts, 756–761
  futures vs. options, with, 763

interest rate futures contracts, 763–770
long hedge, 762–763
maturity hedging, 802
short hedge, 761–762
Hewlett-Packard Co., 713
Higgins, Robert C., 72, 74
high-dividend policy, factors
  agency costs, 572–573
  behavioural finance, 571–572
  current income desire, 570–571
  dividend signalling, 574–575
  information content effect, 573–574
high-yield bonds, 631
Hochschild Mining Plc, 881
hockey stick diagram, 671
holder-of-record date, 608
holding-period return, 152, 290–293
Hollinger, 33, 897
homemade dividends, 561–562
homemade leverage strategy, 471
homogeneous expectations, 334
Honeywell International Inc., 713
Hong, H., 437
Hong Kong Exchanges, 21
horizontal acquisition, 859
Hughes Aircraft, 866
human capital, 83
Hunt Brothers, 760, 761fn
hurdle rate, 383
hybrid firms, 612
hybrid securities, 455

I

Ibbotson, Roger, 290
IBM, 818, 823
Icefloe Technologies Inc., 899
Idiosyncratic risk, 353
IFRS accounting standards, 22
ImClone Systems, 427
immunized, 775
Imperial Oil Ltd., 319
Inco Limited, 861
income bond, 636
income trust, 12, 461
incremental cash flows
  allocated cost, 225
  analysis example, 228–231
  capital budgeting, 223–230
  capital cost allowance (CCA), 229
  cash flows, 223–224, 229
  defined, 224
  earnings before interest and taxes (EBIT), 229

example, 226–231
interest expense, 231
leasing, 649–650
Majestic Mulch and Compost example, 226–230
net present value (NPV), 372
net working capital, 230
opportunity cost, 224
side effects, 225
sunk cost, 224
incremental IRR, 207–208
indenture, 455, 457–458, 619, 626
independent project, 201
index participation (IP), 924
Indigo, 15
inflation
  cash flows, 232–233
  discounting rates, 233–235
  interest rates, 231–232
  risk, 635
inflation beta, 354–355
inflation risk, 635
information content effect, 573–574
infrequent annuity, 128
Ingersoll, J., 749
in-house processing float, 821
initial public offering (IPO)
  case study, 604
  cash offer, 598
  defined, 20, 592, 598
  oversubscribed, 599
  pricing, 597, 598–599
  underpricing, 597, 599–601
  venture capital financing, 613
insider trading, 427–428
insolvency, 896, 898
insurance companies, 19
intangible fixed assets, 2
interest. See also interest rates
  compound interest, 108
  dividends vs., 455
  expense, 231
interest coverage, 52, 59
interest rate beta, 354–355
interest rate futures contracts
  forward contracts pricing, 764–765
  futures contracts, 765–766
  Government of Canada bonds pricing, 763–765, 766–769
  long hedge, 769–770
  short hedge, 766–769
interest rate parity theorem, 917–919
interest rate risk, 188–189, 626–627
interest rate swaps, 777–778

interest rates
  annual percentage rate (APR), 117, 118–119
  bond price, 150–151
  bond refunding, 626
  defined, 84
  effective annual interest rate (EAR), 117–119
  financial market competition, 89–90
  inflation, 231–232
  interest rate parity theorem, 917–919
  intertemporal consumption, 84, 86–88
  principal repayment, 84
  risk, 188–189, 626–627
  spot rates, 179–189
  stated annual, 117
  term structure of, 179–189
  valuing call options, 683
intermediate-term debt, 618fn
internal financing, 461–462
internal rate of return (IRR)
  basic IRR rule, 200
  calculation, 200–201
  defined, 199
  incremental IRR, 207–208
  modified IRR, 205–206
  mutually exclusive projects, 202–204, 206–210
  net present value (NPV), 199, 204
  problems with, 201–204
  use of, 214
international bond markets, 927–930
International Business Machines, 65
international capital budgeting, 922–925
international corporate finance
  exchange rate, 912–913
  exchange rate risk, 919–921, 923–924, 925
  financing options, 926
  foreign exchange market, 912
  interest rate parity theorem, 917–919
  international bond markets, 927–930
  law of one price (LOP), 915–916
  long-term financing, 926–927
  political risk, 931
  purchasing power parity (PPP), 916–917
  reporting foreign operations, 930–931
  short-term financing, 926–927
  terminology, 910–911
  transaction types, 914–915
international diversification, 323–324
International Financial Futures and Options Exchange (LIFFE), 756
International Financial Reporting Standards (IFRS), 35, 36–37, 646
international financing decisions, 926–930
International Swaps and Derivatives Association (ISDA), 754
intertemporal consumption, 84, 86–88
inventory loan, 807
inventory period, 794
inventory turnover, 51–52, 59
inverse floater, 780
investment banks, 596–597
investment dealers, 19
investment decision making
  basic principle, 90
  borrowing example, 92–93
  corporate, 97–99
  illustrated, 94–97
  lending example, 91–92
investment grade bonds, 631
Investment Industry Regulatory Organization of Canada (IIROC), 593
investment tax credits, 32
Investors Group, 337, 379
invoice, 839
Irving Oil, 879
issue costs. See flotation costs
Ivanhoe Mines, 610

J

Jackson, David, 428
January effect, 432
Japan Exchange Group, 21
Jarrow, Robert A., 782–784
J.C. Penney Corp., 410
Jensen, M.C., 866, 867
Joe Fresh, 372
Jog, Vijay, 432, 453, 573, 886
John Hancock Financial Services Inc., 861
Johnson, J.P., 664
junk bonds, 631–632
Jupiter Resources Inc., 611

K

Kaplan, R.S., 437, 526–527
Kaplan, Steven, 500, 878
Keil, Thomas, 711
Keim, D.B., 432
Keynes, John Maynard, 430, 506, 818
k-factor model, 355
Kolasinski, Adam, 431
Korwar, A.N., 601
Kraus, A., 626, 627
Kryzanowski, Lawrence, 598
Kumar, Alok, 576

L

Laamanen, Tomi, 711
Lagarde, Christine, 929
Lake Shore Gold, 881
Lamont, Owen, 431
Lamoureux, Claude, 832
Lanes, Kersten, 864
Lascaris, Dimitri, 711
law of one price (LOP), 915–916
Lazrak, Skander, 598
Leap Wireless International Inc., 669, 699–700
LEAPS, 677
lease, 643
Lease, R.C., 452
lease versus buying decision. See also leasing
  100 percent, 663
  accounting income, 662
  example, 644
  incremental cash flows, 649–650
  net present value analysis, 652–654, 657
  optimal debt level, 652
  taxes, 650, 659–661
  transaction costs, 662
  uncertainty reduction, 661–662
leasing
  accounting, 646–648
  buying vs. See lease versus buying decision
  cash flows, 649–650
  debt displacement, 654–657
  financial lease, 645
  lease, 643
  lessee, 643
  lessor, 643
  lessor's perspective, 658–659
  manufacturer vs. third-party, 664
  net present value analysis, 652–654, 657

operating lease, 644–645
optimal debt level, 652, 655–656
reasons to lease, 659–663
risk-free cash flows, 651–652
sales-type leases, 644
taxes, 648
use of, vs. debt, 663
which assets, 664
ledger cash, 820
Lehman Brothers, 434, 499, 755, 779–780
lender, 455
Leon's Furniture Limited, 409
lessee, 643
lessor, 643
letter of credit, 806–807
level-coupon bonds
defined, 147
holding-period return, 152
interest rates and price, 150–151
quotations, 149–150
valuing, 147–148, 152
yield to maturity, 151
leverage, 380–383
leveraged buyouts (LBOs), 860, 881–882
leveraged lease, 645
Lewis, Craig M., 748
L'Her, Jean-Francois, 601
Li, K., 866
Li, Xu, 431
liabilities, 2, 33, 34–35
LIBOR, 777–778, 780, 911
Liebman, Jeffrey, 442
limited liability, 448
limited liability instrument, 671
limited partnership, 10
Linn, S.G., 880
Linter, John, 579
Lionsgate, 883
liquidation, 901–902
liquidity. *See also* cash; cash flows
cost of capital, 396–398
defined, 790
management, 819–820
statement of financial position, 34
liquidity-preference hypothesis, 186–187
listed companies, 21–22
listing, 21–22
Lo, J., 613
loan covenants, 504
loan guarantees, 696–697
Loblaw Companies Limited, 372, 860, 861
lockbox, 824, 825

London Interbank Offered Rate (LIBOR), 777–778, 780, 911
long hedge, 762–763
Long Manufacturing, 410
long-term debt. *See also* long-term financing
balance sheet model, 2
bonds. *See* public issue of bonds
defined, 3, 456, 618
direct placement vs. public issues, 637
equity vs. debt, 455, 456
indenture, 457–458
interest vs. dividends, 455
maturity date, 456
principal, 455, 456
repayment, 456–457
security, 457
seniority, 457
syndicated bank loans, 638
types of, 456
long-term equity anticipation securities (LEAPS), 677
long-term financial gap, 461–462
long-term financing. *See also* long-term debt
common stock, 448–454
income trust, 461
internal financing, 461–462
international corporate finance, 926–927
leasing, 643–664
long-term debt, 455–458
patterns of, 461–462
pecking order, 462
preferred shares, 458–460
short-term vs., 791
lower bound, 680
lower of cost or proceeds (LOCP) rule, 257
Lowe's, 878
low-grade bonds, 631
Lucent Technologies, 514
Lululemon, 146

**M**

Magna International, 14, 453, 454
Maier, J.B., 612
mail float, 821
Majestic Mulch and Compost example
incremental cash flows, 226–230
interest expense, 231
net working capital, 230
tax shield approach, 237–240

making delivery, 756
Malkiel, Burton, 436
Malmendier, Ulrike, 887
management buyouts (MBOs), 860
managerial goals, 13–14
Mandelker, G., 437
manufacturer lessors, 664
Manulife Financial, 146, 337, 861, 883
Marathon Oil, 873
marked to the market, 758–760
market clearing, 85–86
market for corporate control, 867
market impact costs, 396–397
market model, 356
market portfolio. *See also* portfolio
beta, 335–338
defined, 335
homogeneous expectations, 334
risk averse, 337–338
single-factor model, 361–362
market price, 55–56
market risk, 329, 353
market value, 35, 450
market value ratios, 55–57, 59
marketable certificates of deposit, 832
marketed claims, 508
market-to-book (M/B) ratio, 56–57, 59
Martel, J., 499
Masulis, R., 601
matrix approach, 317
maturity date, 146, 456, 618
maturity factoring, 851
maturity hedging, 802
May Jensen Shawa Solomon, 711
Maynes, Elizabeth, 453
McConnell, J.J., 452, 866, 879, 880
McKinsey & Co., 10
mean return, 294
Medco Health Solutions Inc., 713
medium-term financing, 926–927
Mendelson, H., 398
mergers, 699–700. *See also* takeovers
acquisitions, 857–858, 859
cost to shareholders, 870–872
defined, 857–858
diversification, 873–874
earnings growth, 872–873
net present value of, 874–877
real productivity, 888
mergers of equals (MOEs), 887
Merkel, Angela, 928, 929
Merrill Lynch, 167

Merton, Robert, 684
Mesa Petroleum, 866
Metals USA, 881
Metro Inc., 409
Michaely, R., 573, 879
Middlemiss, Jim, 711
Mikkelson, W.H., 452, 601
Milken, Michael, 631
milking the property, 502
Miller, Merton, 414, 470–472, 479, 480. *See also* MM Proposition II; MM Proposition II
  dividend policy, 560, 563
  high-dividend policy, factors, 570–571
  MM theory, 505–508
  Modigliani–Miller theory, 627
Miller model, 520–523
minimum variance portfolio, 320
Minton, B., 920
MIRR, 205–206
Mitchells, 500
Mittoo, Usha R., 601
MM Proposition I
  under corporate taxes, 483–485
  defined, 469–470
  example, 476
  interpretation, 479
  key assumptions, 472
  no taxes, 470–472, 481
MM Proposition II
  under corporate taxes, 485–489
  example, 476
  formula, 475
  interpretation, 479
  no taxes, 473–479, 481
MM theory. *See also* MM Proposition I; MM Proposition II
  tax effects and bankruptcy costs, 505–508
Mobil Corp., 866
mobile wallet, 825
modified internal rate of return (IRR), 205–206, 214
Modigliani, F., 470–472, 479. *See also* MM Proposition II; MM Proposition II
  dividend policy, 560, 563
  high-dividend policy, factors, 570–571
  MM theory, 505–508
  Modigliani–Miller theory, 627
Modigliani-Miller Propositions. *See* MM Proposition I; MM Proposition II

Modigliani–Miller theory, 627
Molson, 710
money markets, 20
Monsanto, 410
Monte Carlo simulation, 270–274
Moody's, 630
Morgan Stanley, 887
Morgan Stanley Canada Ltd., 604
Morris Publishing, 906
mortgage securities, 622
mortgages, 126
mortgage-trust indenture, 622
Motorolla, 823
Mouvement des caisses Desjardins, 18
Mullins, D., Jr., 573, 601
multifactor model, 371
Multi-Jurisdictional Disclosure System (MJDS), 594
Munk, Peter, 1
Muscarella, C.J., 162, 866
mutual funds, 330, 425–427
mutually exclusive investments
  defined, 201
  incremental IRR, 207–208
  investing vs. financing, 202–204
  profitability index (PI), 212
  scale problem, 206–208
  timing problem, 208–210

N

Nagarajan, Nandu, 523
naked short-selling, 928
Napier Environmental Technologies, 409
NASDAQ, 21
National Bank Financial Inc., 597
National Bank of Canada, 18, 379
near-cash, 819
negative covenant, 503, 622
net float, 821
net income, 41
net present value (NPV). *See also* capital budgeting
  algebraic formula, 116
  bond refunding, 629
  capital budgeting, 191–193, 214
  corporate investment decision making, 97–99
  decision trees, 261–263
  discount rate, 372
  economic value added (EVA) vs., 410
  flotation costs, 395
  formula, 106–107, 372
  incremental cash flows, 372

investment decision illustration, 94–97
  leasing, 652–654, 657
  mergers, 874–877
  real options, 275–279
  stock growth opportunities, 159–165
net present value of a growth opportunity (NPVGO) effect, 159–162
net present value rule, 97
net profit margin, 53, 59
net return on assets, 54, 59
net working capital
  balance sheet model, 2
  cash, 790–791
  cash flows vs., 39
  defined, 3, 38, 790
  incremental cash flows, 230
  statement of cash flows, 40
net worth, 35fn
Network Ten, 897, 899
New York Mercantile Exchange (NYM), 756
Nexen Inc., 860, 861
Nitani, Miwako, 428
nominal cash flow, 233
nominal interest rate, 231, 233–235
non-callable bonds, 624
non-cash items, 37
non-cumulative dividends, 458
non-marketed claims, 508
normal distribution, 298–299
Nortel, 514
Nortel Networks, 63, 438, 887, 899
Northland Bank, 438
Northland Bank of Canada, 696
Northwest Airlines, 542
notes, 456
NPV. *See* net present value (NPV)
NPVGO, 159–165
NYSE, 21

O

one-factor model. *See* single-factor model
O'Neill, Dan, 710
Onex, 612, 710
Ontario Municipal Employees' Retirement System, 17
Ontario Securities Commission (OSC), 20, 427, 453, 593, 878
Ontario Teachers' Merchant Bank, 612
Ontario Teachers' Pension Board, 451

Ontario Teachers' Pension Plan, 17
open account, 842
open-end mortgage, 622
open-market purchase, 564
operating cash flow, 39, 41. *See
        also* cash flows
    bottom-up approach, 236–237
    tax shield approach, 237–240,
        259–260
    top-down approach, 237
operating cycle, 794, 795
operating lease, 644–645
operating leverage, 380–382
operating loan, 806
Opler, Tim, 798
opportunity (feasible) set, 321–322
opportunity cost, 193, 224, 846
optimal portfolio, 332–334
option pricing formula
    Black-Scholes model, 684,
        687–691, 697
    two-state option model, 685–687
option to abandon, 276–277
option to expand, 275–276
option value, 742–743
options
    American/European, 670
    call options, 670–671, 677–679
    combinations, 677–679
    contingent value rights,
        699–700
    currency options, 921
    defined, 669
    executive stock options, 709–714
    exercising, 669
    expiration date, 669
    hedging with, 763
    investment in, vs. projects,
        697–699
    option pricing formula, 684–691
    pricing, 684–691, 697
    put option, 672–673, 677–679
    quotations, 674–677
    selling, 673–674
    stock and bonds as, 692–697
    strike/exercise price, 669
    valuing a start-up as, 715–718
    valuing options, 679–684
Oracle Corporation, 713
over the counter (OTC), 21, 781
overallotment option, 596
oversubscribed, 599
oversubscription privilege, 609
over-the-counter (OTC) market,
        21, 781
owner's equity, 35fn
ownership versus control, 14–17

P
Palepu, K.G., 573, 888
Palm Inc., 431
par value, 620
parametric approaches to asset
        pricing, 364–366
Partch, M.M., 601
partnership, 10, 11
Pason Systems Inc., 409
payable turnover, 53, 59
payback period rule, 193–195, 214
payout ratio, 55, 59, 159
pecking order, 462
pecking-order theory, 513–516, 524
pension funds, 19
percentage of sales method
    defined, 67–69
    statement of comprehensive
        income, 69–70
    statement of financial position,
        70–72
perfect market, 89
perfectly competitive financial
        market, 89
period costs, 38
perpetuity, 121–122
personal taxation
    capital structure, 518–520
    dividends vs. stock repurchase,
        567–570
    investment income, 30–31
    Miller model and firm value,
        520–523
    rates, 28–29
Peterson, P.P., 663
Petro-Canada, 861
Philips, Hager & North
        Investment Ltd. (PH&N), 860
Phillips, 866
Pickens, T. Boone, 866
pie model
    bond refunding, 627
    capital structure, 465–466
    defined, 507–508
Pinkowitz, Lee, 798
Placer Dome Inc., 861
plowback ratio, 70
plug, 67
point-of-sale systems, 825
poison pill, 17, 883
political risk, 931
Polygram N.V., 861
POP (Prompt Offering Prospectus)
        system, 592, 594–595
Porter, Michael, 865
portfolio

capital asset pricing model
        (CAPM), 341
    defined, 315
    diversification effect, 318–319,
        358–360
    efficient set, two assets, 320–
        323
    efficient set, many assets,
        325–327
    exchange traded funds (ETFs),
        330
    expected return, 315–316,
        357–358
    factor model, 356–360
    hedge, 317
    international diversification,
        323–324
    many assets, 319
    market portfolio, 334–338
    mutual funds, 330
    opportunity set, 321–322
    optimal, 332–334
    risk averse, 329–330
    risk-free borrowing and
        lending, 330–332
    standard deviation, 317–318,
        325–327
    style portfolios, 366
    variance, 317–319, 325–327
portfolio risk, 329, 358–360
positive covenant, 503, 622
Postmedia Network, 496
Potash Corporation of
        Saskatchewan Inc., 319
Power Financial, 18, 379
PrairieSky Royalty Ltd., 598
preauthorized payments, 825
precautionary motive, 819
pre-emptive right, 450, 604
preferred shares
    cumulative and non-cumulative
        dividends, 458
    debt, as, 459
    defined, 458
    stated value, 458
    taxes, 459–460
premium, 151, 917
prepackaged bankruptcy, 906
present value factor, 112
present value (PV)
    annuity, 124–125
    break-even analysis, 268–269
    common stock, 152–156
    consols, 150, 152
    discounting, 112–115
    formula, 105
    future value, 105

growing annuity, 130–131
level-coupon bonds, 147–149, 152
net present value (NPV), 97, 106
number of periods, 115–116
perpetuity, 121–122
pure discount bond, 147, 152
tax shield, 238–239, 259–260, 483
two annuities, 129–130
value of the firm, 131–132
price takers, 89
price-earnings (P/E) ratio, 56, 59, 165–167, 365–366
Priceline.com, 436
price-pressure effect, 831
price-taking assumption, 89
pricing, 597, 598–599
primary markets, 20, 592
principal (bond), 147, 455, 456
Principal Group, 696
principal repayment, 84
principal value, 620
private equity market, 611–614
private placement, 20, 592, 611, 637
private workout, 904–905
pro forma statements, 67
Procter & Gamble, 65, 713, 865
product costs, 38
production set-up costs, 798
profit margin, 53, 74
profitability, 49
profitability index (PI), 211–213, 214
profitability ratios, 49, 53–55, 59
Program for Export Market Development (PEMD), 911
promissory note, 842
Prompt Offering Prospectus (POP), 592, 594–595
prospectus, 593. *See also* Prompt Offering Prospectus (POP)
protective covenants, 503–504, 622, 626
protective put, 677
proxy, 451
proxy contest, 860
public issue of bonds. *See also* bonds
  bearer bond, 621
  bond ratings, 630–634
  bond refunding, 624–629
  call provision, 623
  Canada Plus call, 623, 629
  debenture, 622
  debt securities, 621–622
  defined, 619
  financial engineering and, 636–637

indenture, 619
  protective covenants, 622
  ratings, 630–634
  security, 621–622
  seniority, 622
  sinking fund, 622–623
  terms, 620–621
  types of, 634–637
public issue of securities
  announcements and firm value, 601–602
  cash offer, 595–601
  costs, 602–604
  procedure, 593–595
  Prompt Offering Prospectus (POP), 592, 594–595
  regulation of, 592–593
  rights offerings, 604–611
purchasing power parity (PPP), 916–917
pure discount bond, 146, 147, 152
Pure Technologies Ltd., 56
put bond, 636
put option
  combinations, 677–679
  defined, 672–673
  stock/bonds as, 692–695
  valuing, 683–684
put provisions, 635
put-call parity, 678

**Q**

Qiu, B., 866
quantitative easing, 26
Quebecor World Inc., 899
quick assets, 50
quick ratio, 50, 58

**R**

Ragolski, Richard J., 748
Rakita, Ian, 598
random walk, 418
Rappaport, A., 73
ratios. *See* financial statement analysis
Raviv, A., 712
RBC Capital Markets, 597
RBC Dominion Securities, 595
RBC Financial Group, 379, 635
real cash flow, 233
real interest rate, 231, 233–235
real options, 275–279
receivables turnover, 51, 58
red herring, 593
refunding, 624. *See also* bond refunding

registered bond, 620
regression, 377
regular cash dividend, 555, 556–558
regular underwriting, 596
relative purchasing power parity (RPPP), 916–917
reorganization, 901
replacement value, 450
representativeness, 429
Research In Motion, 167, 711
residual losses, 13
restrictive covenants, 457–458
restrictive short-term financial policy, 797
retained earnings, 55, 157–159, 449
retention ratio, 55, 59, 70, 157–159
retractable (put) bond, 636
return on assets (ROA), 54, 59, 407–408, 410
return on equity (ROE)
  defined, 54–55, 59
  dividend discount model, 157–158
  MM Proposition II, 473–479
returns
  abnormal return (AR), 424–425
  annual market index, 291
  average return, 294–297, 301–303
  capital asset pricing model (CAPM), 338–342
  cumulative abnormal, 424–425
  dollar earnings, 287–288
  financial crisis 2008, 303–304, 434
  frequency distribution, 294
  geometric average, 301–303
  holding period, 290–293
  international diversification, 323–324
  percentage, 288–290
  portfolio, 357
  risk statistics, 297–300
  risk-free, 295
  statistics, 294
Reuiters Group PLC, 861
Revco, 882
revenue enhancement, 864–865
reverse split, 584, 585–586
Rice, E.M., 880
Riding, A., 612, 613
rights offer, 595
rights, 605
rights offerings
  costs, 610
  defined, 605
  ex-rights, 608–609

holder-of-record date, 608
number of rights for share
    purchase, 606
pre-emptive right, 604
process, 605
shareholders, 610
subscription price, 605
underwriting, 609
value of a right, 606–608, 609
Rio Tinto Group, 861
risk
    acquisitions, 870–872
    beta, 335–338
    capital asset pricing model
        (CAPM), 338–342
    cash flows, 7
    convertible bonds/warrants, 747
    cost of capital, 396–398
    cost of equity, 373–375
    credit management, 843–845
    derivatives and, 754–755
    diversification, 318–319,
        327–330, 358–360
    exchange rate risk, 913,
        919–921
    interest rates, 188–189, 626–627
    international diversification,
        323–324, 919–920, 925
    market portfolio, 335–338
    market risk, 353
    MM Proposition II, 473–479
    political risk, 931
    portfolio risk, 329
    returns, 295, 297–300
    risk averse, 329–330, 337–338
    risk premium, 295
    risk-free borrowing and
        lending, 330–332
    selfish investment strategies,
        500–501
    standard deviation, 298–299
    statistics, 297–300
    systematic risk, 329, 352
    total risk, 329
    unsystematic risk, 329, 352–353
    value at risk (VaR), 299–300
risk averse, 329–330, 337–338
risk incentive, 500–501
risk neutrality, 497fn
risk premium, 295
risk-based models, 364–365
risk-free borrowing and lending,
    330–332, 651–652
risk-free rate, 373–375
risk-free return, 295
Ritter, J.R., 439, 598, 600
ROA. See return on assets

Roberts, G.S., 504, 638, 663
Robin Hood Multifoods, 410
Robinson, Chris, 453
ROE. See return on equity (ROE)
Rogers Communications Inc.,
    163, 452, 577
Roll, R., 437
Rona Inc., 878
RosettaNet, 823
Royal Bank of Canada, 14, 18, 56,
    459, 595, 860
Royal Dutch Petroleum, 430
Ruback, R.S., 866, 867, 888
Rubbermaid Inc., 410
rule of 72, 113

S

S&P/TSX 60, 319
S&P/TSX Composite, 377, 378
Saadi, S., 580
safety reserves, 798
sale and lease-back, 645
sales forecast, 66
sales-type leases, 644
Salomon Brothers, 882
Sam the Record Man, 899
same-day value, 826
Samuelson, P., 17
Sarbanes-Oxley Act, 22
Sarbox. See Sarbanes-Oxley Act
Sauriol, Lorraine, 601
Savanna Energy Services Corp., 711
scenario analysis, 266
Sceptre Investment Counsel Ltd.,
    409
Schneider, H.S., 664
Scholes, Myron, 684
Schrand, C., 920
Schwartz, E., 697
Schwartz, Gerald, 710
scorched earth strategy, 882
Scotiabank, 597
seasoned equity offering (SEO),
    595
secondary markets, 21, 169, 592
secured loans, 807–808
securities. See also common stock
    correlation, 310, 312–315
    covariance, 310, 312–315
    defined, 1
    expected return, 309, 310–312
    firm value, 8–9
    portfolio of, 315
    portfolio risk and return, 309,
        315–320
    private equity market, 611–614

public issue of securities, 592–614
    standard deviation, 309
    variance, 309
Securities Act, 593
Securities and Exchange
    Commission (SEC), 593
securitization, 636
security market line (SML), 340,
    342, 360–362, 375
SEDAR, 58
selfish investment strategies,
    500–503
semistrong-form efficiency,
    419–421, 424–427
seniority, 457, 622
sensitivity analysis, 263–266
separation principle, 333–334
separation theorems, 92–93, 99
serial correlation, 422–423
set-of-contracts viewpoint, 13
Seward, James K., 748
Shanghai SE, 21
Shanker, L., 663
shareholders
    acquisitions, 870–872, 883–886
    agency theory, 886–888
    cash flows, 40–41
    classes of shares, 452–453
    defined, 3, 448
    firm value and shareholders'
        interests, 466–467
    governance, 16–17
    international diversification, 924
    limited liability, 448
    ownership vs. control, 14–17
    rights, 450–451
    rights offerings, 610
    underinvestment incentive,
        501–503
shareholders' equity, 2, 33, 35, 35fn
Shaw, Wayne, 879
Shaw Communications, 452, 496,
    899
Shefrin, Hersh M., 571
shelf life, 51
Shell Transport, 430
Shen, R., 866
Shenzhen SE, 21
Shleifer, A., 416
Shoppers Drug Mart
    Corporation, 860, 861
Short Form Prospectus
    Distribution (SFPD) system,
    23
short hedge, 761–762, 766–769
shortage costs, 797–799
short-run operating activities, 794

short-term debt, 3, 618
short-term financing
  absence of, 808
  cash and operating cycles,
    794–797
  cash budgeting, 803–805
  current assets and short-term
    policy, 797–803
  defined, 790
  international corporate finance,
    926–927
  long-term vs., 791
  net working capital and,
    790–791
  risk and planning, 805
  short-term borrowing
    alternatives, 805–808
short-term hedges, 920–921
short-term operating activities,
  795
short-term securities, 829–831
short-term solvency ratios, 49, 50,
  58
sight draft, 842
signalling, 508–510
simple interest, 108
single-factor model
  capital asset pricing model
    (CAPM), 360, 361
  defined, 355–356
  expected return, 360–362
  market portfolio, 361–362
  portfolio, 356–358
sinking fund, 456–457, 459,
  622–623
Sino-Forest Corporation, 899
Sinquefield, Rex, 290
Siskinds, 711
Sisli-Ciamarra, E., 712
size effect, 432
Skinner, D., 578
small capitalization effect, 432
Smith, Adam, 510
Smith, B., 452, 453
Smith, C.W., 503, 664
SmithKline Beecham, 431
socially responsible investing, 16
Society for Worldwide
    Interbank Financial
    Telecommunications
    (SWIFT), 23
sole proprietorship, 9–10
Solnik, B.H., 924–925
Sony, 823, 879
SOX. See Sarbanes-Oxley Act
speculative motive, 818
spot exchange rate, 914

spot rates
  bond price estimation, 183–185
  exchange rate, 912–913, 917, 919
  expectations hypothesis, 185–186
  forward rate and, 185
  pricing Canada bond, 763–764
  term structure of interest rates,
    180–183
  yield to maturity, 179–180
spot trades, 914
spread (discount), 595
spreading overhead, 865
Sprint, 410
stakeholders, 15–17
Standard & Poor's Industry Surveys,
  58
Standard & Poor's (S&P), 630, 807
standard deviation. See also
    covariance
  calculation, many assets, 325–327
  calculation, single security, 312
  calculation, two or more
    securities, 317–318
  diversification effect, 318–319
  efficient set, two assets, 320–323
  many assets, 319
  optimal portfolio, 332–334
  risk, 298–299
standardized normal
    distribution, 689
standby fee, 609
standby underwriting, 609
standstill agreements, 880–881
start-ups, 715, 806
stated annual interest rate, 117
statement of cash flows
  cash flow from financing
    activities, 61
  cash flow from investing
    activities, 61
  cash flow from operations, 39,
    41, 61
  cash flow management, 62–63
  changes in long-term assets, 40
  defined, 39
  free cash flow, 41
  net working capital, 40
  shareholders, 40–41
  total cash flow of the firm, 41
statement of comprehensive
    income
  defined, 36
  IFRS, 36–37
  non-cash items, 37
  percentage of sales method,
    69–70
  time and costs, 37–38

statement of financial position
  debt vs. equity, 34–35
  defined, 33
  liquidity, 34
  percentage of sales method,
    70–72
  value vs. cost, 35
static trade-off theory, 506
Statman, Meir, 328, 571
Sterlite Gold Ltd., 409
Stewart, Martha, 427
stock. See common stock; securities
stock dividend, 555–556, 582–585
stock exchange bid, 858
stock market. See secondary
    markets
stock market reporting, 169
stock options, 512, 566. See also
    options
stock prices, 430–434, 487–488
stock repurchase, 563–567
  dividends vs., 565–570
  Dutch auction, 564
  open-market purchase, 564
  targeted repurchase, 564
  tender offer, 564
stock split, 556, 582–585
stock-based insolvency, 898
stockholders. See shareholders
stock-out, 798
straight bond value, 740–741
straight voting, 451
strike price, 669
stripped common shares, 562
stripped real-return bond, 636
Strömqvist, Maria, 24, 25
Stronach, Frank, 454
strong-form efficiency, 419–421,
  424–428
Stulz, René, 798, 924–925
style portfolios, 366
subordinated (debt), 457, 622
subscription price, 605
subsidized loan, 542–543
Suggitt, 638
Sun Life, 437, 883
Suncor Energy, 14, 56, 391–393,
  619, 861
sunk cost, 224
superfloater, 780
superinverse floater, 780
Superior Plus Corp., 807
supermajority amendment, 880
sustainable growth, 72–76
sustainable growth rate, 55, 59, 74
SUX Swiss Exchange, 21
swap contracts. See also

derivatives; hedging
credit default swaps (CDSs), 779–780
currency swaps, 778–779
defined, 777
exchange trading, 781
exotics, 780–781
interest rate swaps, 777–778
swap rate, 914
swaps, 777, 911. *See also* swap contracts
sweep accounts, 827
SWIFT, 23
syndicate (banking group), 20, 595
syndicated bank loan, 638
synergy, 225
  acquisitions and, 857, 863–868
  cost of capital, 868
  cost reductions, 865–867
  revenue enhancements, 864–865
  tax gains, 867–868
systematic (market) risk, 329
  beta, 353–356
  beta coefficient, 353, 356
  calculation, 353
  defined, 352–353
  factor model, 355–356
  market model, 356
  single-factor model, 355, 356–358
systematic variability, 873–874
Szewczyk, Samuel, 424

**T**

takeovers
  acquisitions vs., 859–860
  control block, 879–880
  crown jewels, 882
  defensive tactics, 877–883
  divestiture, 877–879
  exclusionary offer, 881
  going private/leveraged buyouts, 881–882
  golden parachutes, 882
  poison pill, 883
  standstill agreements, 880–881
  white knight, 882–883
taking delivery, 755
Talisman Energy, 337
tangible fixed assets, 2, 34
target cash balance, 817
targeted repurchase, 564
Tashjian, E., 906
Tata Steel, 848
Tate, G., 887

Tate, Geoffrey, 887
tax shield approach
  cash flows, 237–240, 259–260
  CCA formula, 238, 239
  depreciation, 237, 268–269
  leasing, 648, 659–661
  operating cash flow, 237–239
  present value, 238–239, 259–260, 483
  total project cash flows approach vs., 240
tax shield from debt, 483
tax subsidy, 455, 508, 518, 533
taxable income, 31
taxes. *See* corporate taxation; personal taxation
TD Securities, 597
TD-Canada Trust, 379
technology bubble, 433–434, 436
Teck Resources Ltd., 336, 337, 378
Telfer, Ian, 427
Telus, 169, 461
tender offer, 564–565, 858, 860
term loans, 637
term structure of interest rates
  application of, 187–188
  bond price estimation, 183–185
  expectations hypothesis, 185–186
  forward rate, 183–185
  graphing, 180–181
  liquidity-preference hypothesis, 186–187
  rate risk, 188–189
  spot rates, 179–180, 183–185
  theories of term structure, 181–183
  yield to maturity, 179–180
terms of sale, 838–843
  cash discount, 840–842
  credit instrument, 842–843
  credit period, 839–840
  defined, 837
Thaler, Richard, 431, 573
*The General Theory of Employment, Interest, and Money*, 818
The Seagram Company Ltd., 861
The Thomson Corp., 861
theoretical value of a right, 608
third-party lessors, 664
Thornton, John, 1
3Com, 431
Tian, Yisong, 612
Tim Hortons, 563, 598, 784
time value of money, 105
  algebraic formula, 116

annuity, 124–131
compounding, 107, 111
compounding periods, 116–121
defined, 104
future value, 105, 107–111
growing perpetuity, 122–124
multiperiod case, 107–116
net present value (NPV), 106–107
number of periods, 115–116
one-period case, 104–107
perpetuity, 121–122
present value and discounting, 112–115
present value (PV), 105–106
value of the firm, 131–132
Time Warner, 887
timing options, 277–278
TMX Group, 21
Tobin's Q, 450
top-down approach, 237
Toronto Blue Jays, 921
Toronto Stock Exchange (TSE), 21
Toronto-Dominion Bank, 18
Torstar, 899
total asset turnover, 51, 58
total cash flow of the firm, 41
total credit cost curve, 846
total risk, 329
Toyota, 926
Toys R us, 410
trade credit, 807
  defined, 837–838
  existence of, 838–839
  financing, 851–852
trade-off theory, 506
trading costs, 397–398, 781, 924
trading range, 584
transaction motive, 819
TransCanada Corporation, 223, 502
Treasury bills, 20, 292, 295
triangular arbitrage, 913–914, 915
Trican Well Service Ltd., 711
trust companies, 19
trust deed, 622
trust receipt, 807
Tsetsekos, George, 424
TVI Pacific Inc., 711
two-state option model
  Black-Scholes model vs., 724
  formula, 685–687
  many dates, 722–724
  shutdown/reopening decision, 724–729
  three-date example, 720–722

two-date example, 718–720
Tyco, 33, 62
Tyerman, David, 454

**U**

undepreciated capital cost (UCC),
    255
underinvestment incentive,
    501–502
underpricing, 597, 599–601
underwriting
  cash offer, 595–596
  investment banks, 596–597
  rights offerings, 609
  underwriters, 20
unfunded debt, 618
Uniform Securities Legislation,
    593
Unilever N.V., 431
Unilever PLC, 431
unique risk, 329
United Airlines, 436
Unocal, 866
unseasoned new issue, 595
unsecured borrowing, 805–807
unsystematic risk, 329
  calculation, 353
  defined, 352
  return on portfolio, 357–358
upper bound, 680
U.S. Food and Drug
    Administration (FDA), 427
U.S. Postal Service, 410
U.S. Securities and Exchange
    Commission (SEC), 427
USX Corporation, 437

**V**

value, 35, 49
value additivity, 192
value at risk (VaR), 299–300, 783
value creation and corporate
    financing, 412–414
value fund, 366
value of the firm. *See also* firm
    vale; firm valuation under
    leverage; valuing the levered
    firm
  acquisitions, after, 868–870
  capital structure, 466–467,
    533–548
  common stocks, 168–169
  dividend discount model,
    157–159
  financial leverage and, 468–472,
    483–485

Miller model, 520–523
present value (PV), 131–132
public issue of securities,
    601–602
value stocks, 432
valuing bonds
  consols, 150, 152
  level-coupon bonds, 147–149,
    152
  pure discount bond, 146–147,
    152
valuing common stock
  comparables approach, 165–167
  dividend discount model,
    157–159
  dividend growth model, 163–164
  dividend-growth patterns,
    153–156
  growth opportunities, 160–165
  NPVGO model, 163–165
  present value, 151–156
  stock market reporting, 169
  value of the firm, 168–169
valuing options
  Black–Scholes option pricing
    model, 687–691
  executive compensation,
    709–714
  factors determining call option
    value, 681–683
  factors determining put option
    value, 683–684
  put option, 683–684
  two-state option model
    examples, 685–687, 718–720
  upper bound, 680
valuing start-ups, 715–718
valuing the levered firm. *See
    also* firm valuation under
    leverage; value of the firm
  adjusted present value (APV)
    valuation, 533–535, 540,
    541–543
  flow to equity (FTE) valuation,
    535–536, 540
  method comparison, 537–540
  weighted average cost of capital
    (WACC) valuation, 536–537,
    540
Van Dijk, Ronald, 566
variable costs, 38, 264
variance. *See also* covariance
  beta calculation, 375–377
  calculation, 317
  calculation, many assets,
    325–327
  calculation, single security, 309,

311–312
  diversification effect, 318–319,
    327–329
  efficient set, two assets, 320
  number of securities and,
    327–329
  risk, 298
Veld, Chris, 566
venture capital
  defined, 611–612
  realities of, 614
  stages of financing, 613
  suppliers of, 612–613
vertical acquisition, 859
Viscione, J.A., 504
Vivendi S.A., 861
Volkswagen, 926

**W**

Wakeman, L.M., 664
Waksal, Sam, 427
Waldman, M., 664
Walker, Don, 454, 612
Walt Disney Co., 713, 879
Warner, J.B., 499, 503
Warner, Jerold, 441
warrants
  Black–Scholes model, 738–739
  call options vs., 733, 735–738
  conversion policy, 748–749
  convertible bonds, 739–749
  defined, 733
  example, 734
  pricing, 738–739
  reasons to issue, 743–746
  risk, 747
  uses of, 746–748
Waskal, Sam, 427
Watts, Ross, 441
weak-form efficiency, 418–419,
    422–423
Weber, Axel, 929
weighted average cost of capital
    (WACC)
  capital structure weights, 386
  defined, 385
  examples, 388–391
  firm valuation under leverage,
    536–540
  flotation costs, 393–396
  MM Proposition II, 473–475
  MM Proposition II, corporate
    taxes, 486–487
  Suncor Energy Inc. example,
    391–393
  taxes, 386–388

Weil, Gotshal & Manges, 499
Weisbach, Michael, 878
Weiss, L.A., 499
Westinghouse, 760
WestJet Airlines, 337
WestJet Airlines Ltd., 319
Wetzel, W.E., 613
what-if analysis, 263–266
Whirlpool, 410
White, Alan, 453
White, M.J., 499
White, Robert, 290
white knight, 882–883
Williamson, O., 13
Williamson, Rohan, 798
Wilson, Thomas, 864
winner's curse, 601

Womack, K., 573
World Bank, 777
WorldCom, 438
Wright, Charles, 711
Wright, Michael, 711
write-up effect, 862
Wruck, Karen, 441
Wulf, Julie, 887, 888

**X**

Xstrata plc, 861

**Y**

Yahoo, 167
yield to maturity, 151, 152, 179–189

Yohn, T., 398
YTM (bonds), 151, 152

**Z**

Zantout, Zaher, 424
Zechner, J., 697
zero-balance account, 827–828
zero-coupon bonds, 147, 634–635, 678
zero-growth pattern, 153–154
zeros, 634–635
Zhu, Peng Cheng, 453
Zyblock, M., 461

# Some Useful Formulas

**1   Present Value**

The discounted value of $T$ future cash flows

$$PV = \frac{C_1}{1+r} + \frac{C_2}{(1+r)^2} + \ldots + \frac{C_T}{(1+r)^T} = \sum_{t=1}^{T} \frac{C_t}{(1+r)^t}$$

**2   Net Present Value**

Present value minus initial costs

$$NPV = PV - \text{Cost}$$

$$C_0 = -\text{Cost}$$

$$NPV = C_0 + \sum_{t=1}^{T} \frac{C_t}{(1+r)^t}$$

**3   Perpetuity**

The value of $C$ received each year, forever

$$PV = \frac{C}{r}$$

**4   Annuity**

The value of $C$ received each year for $T$ years

$$PV = \frac{C}{r}\left[1 - 1/(1+r)^t\right]$$

**5   Growing Perpetuity**

The value of a perpetuity that grows at rate $g$, where the first payment is $C$

$$PV = \frac{C}{r-g}$$

**6   Growing Annuity**

The value of a $T$-period annuity that grows at the rate $g$, where the first payment is $C$

$$PV = C\left[\frac{1}{r-g} - \frac{1}{r-g} \times \left(\frac{1+g}{1+r}\right)^T\right]$$

**7   Measures of Risk for Individual Assets**

$$\text{Var}(R_A) = \sigma_A^2 = \text{Expected value of } (R_A - \bar{R}_A)^2$$

$$\text{SD}(R_A) = \sigma_A = \sqrt{\text{Var}(R_A)}$$

$$\text{Cov}(R_A, R_B) = \sigma_{AB} = \text{Expected value of } [(R_A - \bar{R})_A)(R_B - \bar{R}_B)]$$

$$\text{Corr}(R_A, R_B) = \sigma_{AB} = \text{Cov}(R_A R_B)/\sigma_A \sigma_B$$

**8   Expected Return on a Portfolio of Two Assets**

$$\bar{R}_P = X_A \bar{R}_A + X_B \bar{R}_B$$